2500
recipes

everyday to extraordinary

Andrew Schloss

with Ken Bookman

Robert
ROSE

We dedicate this book to our mothers.

To PEGGY SCHLOSS. Her dread of the kitchen forced her son to cook,
and her love of words urged him to write.

To THELMA BOOKMAN. She always knew that food and love were connected.

2500 Recipes
Text copyright © 2007 Andrew Schloss and Ken Bookman
Cover photograph copyright © 2007 Robert Rose Inc.
Cover and text design copyright © 2007 Robert Rose Inc.

For complete cataloguing information, see page 562.

Disclaimers
The recipes in this book have been carefully tested by our kitchen and our tasters. To the best of our knowledge, they are safe and nutritious for ordinary use and users. For those people with food or other allergies, or who have special food requirements or health issues, please read the suggested contents of each recipe carefully and determine whether or not they may create a problem for you. All recipes are used at the risk of the consumer.

We cannot be responsible for any hazards, loss or damage that may occur as a result of any recipe use.

For those with special needs, allergies, requirements or health problems, in the event of any doubt, please contact your medical adviser prior to the use of any recipe.

Editor: Sue Sumeraj
Recipe Editor: Jennifer MacKenzie
Proofreader: Sheila Wawanash
Indexer: Gillian Watts
Design and Production: Andrew Smith/PageWave Graphics Inc.
Cover Photography: Colin Erricson
Food Styling: Kate Bush
Prop Styling: Charlene Erricson

Cover image: Stir-Fried Pasta Primavera (page 167)

We acknowledge the financial support of the Government of Canada through the Book Publishing Industry Development Program (BPIDP) for our publishing activities.

Published by Robert Rose Inc.
120 Eglinton Avenue East, Suite 800, Toronto, Ontario, Canada M4P 1E2
Tel: (416) 322-6552 Fax: (416) 322-6936

Printed in Canada

1 2 3 4 5 6 7 8 9 TCP 15 14 13 12 11 10 09 08 07

Contents

Introduction 4
About These Recipes 5

Part 1: The Toolbox
Basic Techniques for Cooking Anything 8
Basic Preparations Every Cook Should Know 15

Part 2: Cooking Basics
CHAPTER 1 • MARINADES: *Infinite Variations on Basic Ingredients* 27
CHAPTER 2 • SEASONING: *Because Flavoring Is Easy* 36
CHAPTER 3 • SAUCES: *To Turn Anything into a Meal* 49
CHAPTER 4 • DRESSINGS: *To Help You Kick the Bottle* 58
CHAPTER 5 • MACHINES THAT MAKE COOKING EASIER 66

Part 3: Everyday Cooking
CHAPTER 6 • SNACKS AND LITTLE PLATES: *To Help Spoil Dinner (or Any Meal)* . . 77
CHAPTER 7 • SANDWICHES: *The Ultimate One-Dish Meal* 85
CHAPTER 8 • KID FOOD: *Taste-Tested by Discriminating Third-Graders* . . . 96
CHAPTER 9 • LEFTOVERS: *Homemade Convenience Ingredients* 106
CHAPTER 10 • COOKING ON A BUDGET: *Good Food Doesn't Have to Cost a Lot* . . 116
CHAPTER 11 • BURGERS AND DOGS: *For the Whole Family* 128
CHAPTER 12 • GRILLING: *For the Flavor of Fire* . . 137
CHAPTER 13 • FRYING-PAN CUISINE: *For Dinner Right Now* 147
CHAPTER 14 • STIR-FRYING: *Quick, Healthful and Infinitely Variable* 159
CHAPTER 15 • HEATLESS COOKING: *When It's Too Hot to Turn on the Stove* . . . 172
CHAPTER 16 • SALADS: *For Any Meal* 181
CHAPTER 17 • SOUPS: *For Starters, Suppers, and Snacks* 191
CHAPTER 18 • CHILI: *Easy, Filling and Sophisticated* 201
CHAPTER 19 • PIZZA: *No Need to Order Out* . . . 212
CHAPTER 20 • PASTA: *It's All in the Sauce* 224
CHAPTER 21 • CASSEROLES: *Comfort Food at Its Best* 235
CHAPTER 22 • GROUND MEAT: *The Old Standby Reinvigorated* 248
CHAPTER 23 • STEWS: *Chase Away the Chill* . . . 259
CHAPTER 24 • ROAST CHICKENS: *The Whole Bird* . . 271

CHAPTER 25 • CHICKEN PARTS: *White and Dark Meats Cooked to Perfection* 283
CHAPTER 26 • TURKEY: *The Other Bird* 295
CHAPTER 27 • FISH: *Cooking Your Favorites* . . . 307
CHAPTER 28 • UNDERSTANDING FISH: *The Lean and Fat of Cooking* 320
CHAPTER 29 • SHELLFISH: *Easy and Sophisticated* 331
CHAPTER 30 • MEATLESS DISHES: *For Devoted and Occasional Vegetarians* 344
CHAPTER 31 • GRAINS: *From Rice to Quinoa* . . 356
CHAPTER 32 • GREENS: *Spinach, Kale, Endives and Cabbages* 366
CHAPTER 33 • HARVEST VEGETABLES: *Broccoli, Cauliflower, Beans and Squash* . . 376
CHAPTER 34 • WINTER VEGETABLES: *Beets, Carrots, Parsnips and Potatoes* 386
CHAPTER 35 • SUMMER BOUNTY: *Corn, Zucchini, Tomatoes and Other Garden Excesses* 394
CHAPTER 36 • FALL FRUIT: *Apples, Pears and Tropical Treats* 404
CHAPTER 37 • SUMMER FRUIT: *Berries, Peaches and Plums* 414
CHAPTER 38 • BREAKFAST: *For Any Time of Day (or Night)* 424
CHAPTER 39 • COOKIES: *For Every Day, Every Way* 435
CHAPTER 40 • DESSERT SAUCES: *For Better Mental Health* 444
CHAPTER 41 • DRINKS: *Because Everyone Gets Thirsty* 452

Part 4: Cooking for Special Occasions
CHAPTER 42 • ENTERTAINING: *Recipes That Let You Go to Your Own Party* 463
CHAPTER 43 • ROASTS: *For Celebration or Just to Show Off* 475
CHAPTER 44 • ROMANTIC RECIPES: *Because Some Foods Are Meant for Seduction* . . 486
CHAPTER 45 • LOW-CALORIE RECIPES: *For Keeping Slim* 497
CHAPTER 46 • HEALTH FOOD: *For You and Your Planet* 510
CHAPTER 47 • CHOCOLATE RECIPES: *For Happiness* 522
CHAPTER 48 • HOMEMADE PIE: *A Natural Extravagance* 533
CHAPTER 49 • HOMEMADE MUFFINS: *To Warm the Hearth* 542
CHAPTER 50 • HOMEMADE GIFTS: *To Warm the Heart* 551

Acknowledgments 563
Index 564

Introduction

This is one cookbook you'll use constantly. It won't be like so many others on your cookbook shelf, those that make you feel you've gotten your money's worth if they add just a recipe or two to your occasional repertoire. Mark our words: a couple of years from now, this book will bear the scars — dog-eared pages, marginal notes, food stains — of a cookbook used often. That's because it's geared not for special occasions but for every day. Breakfast, lunch, dinner, snack time, bedtime. You'll find dozens of recipes that talk to you. We're confident that you'll talk back.

Give the book its first test right now. Flip at random to any page, and once you're there, place a finger randomly on any recipe. With so many recipes in this book, we're not going to guarantee that the one you're pointing to will appeal to you. But we *will* say that, if it doesn't, the one above it or below it probably will. And that's our point. If you're like most home cooks, you're probably stuck in a food rut that has you preparing the same 10 recipes over and over again, week after month after year.

Does anyone *need* 2,500 recipes to get through life? Of course not. The reason we've put together a book containing so many recipes is to show you how easy it can be to introduce variety into your meal planning. After all, the more ways there are to escape a rut, the more likely you'll be to escape it.

Here's a common scenario: You've just bought a pound of chicken breasts, several fish fillets, a couple of pounds of ground beef or a few baking potatoes. And you wonder what you might do with them tonight. All too often, the decision takes only a few seconds, and then you prepare dinner the same way you've prepared it for years. Will it be good? Maybe. Will it be inspiring? Probably not. Will it be boring? Almost certainly. Can we help? Absolutely.

Here's how. Say you've got a chicken that's waiting to be roasted for dinner. Stop. Turn to page 271, where you'll find a full chapter of recipes for roast chicken. Fifty recipes, to be exact, and just about every one will be different and more interesting than what you might prepare out of sheer habit. If some don't appeal to you, if others appeal but call for an ingredient you don't have, if a few involve extra time that you can't spare tonight, you'll *still* find a few dozen recipes that can get you out of a cooking rut. You'll end up with a dinner that will have you eagerly looking forward to your next roast chicken, and *that* chicken will be different from *this* chicken.

Or take some other part of your cooking repertoire. You've got a nice fire going in your grill. Could you make the same hot dogs and hamburgers you've made for years? Sure you could. But you don't have to. Instead, turn to page 128, where you'll find 50 recipes for burgers and hot dogs that are well within your reach.

What's the secret? Thought. Here's an exercise that will take almost no time but that can reward you for years to come. The next time you order pizza, ask yourself why you got the toppings you got. Here's a possible answer: "I like the way pepperoni works on a pizza. I like how the soft, melted cheese contrasts with the crispy pepperoni." That answer reveals more than just your favorite pizza topping. It also reveals your feelings about contrasts and textures, and that information can be used on many other foods. So do it — and put this book to work.

This book has a parent. The parent book, *Fifty Ways to Cook Most Everything: 2500 Creative Solutions to the Daily Dilemma of What to Cook,* was published way, way, way back in the early 1990s. The parent-child metaphor is not perfect, since we are both the parents and the kids. But it's pretty good in that, just as in real life, the parent magically gets wiser as the years go by. We've made a huge number of changes since *Fifty Ways* was published, but we also recognized that some things shouldn't change.

The most significant constant goes to the premise of both books: that everyone has cooking ruts to overcome, that a vast number of easy recipes is the best way to conquer them, and that those recipes have to be written with the kind of brevity that will fit a reader's life.

But the changes are significant too. We've updated almost every recipe, we've tinkered with just about every one, we've expelled a bunch, and we've added new ones. Nasturtium blossoms are gone. Canola oil is in. And while we still steer clear of the granulated cardboard ingredients we've come to abhor, we've recognized and used the many fine and convenient products that have come into the food markets.

Almost all of the recipes are still quick, and therein lies another of our secrets. When recipes use just a small number of ingredients, each of those ingredients has to work harder than normal. You'll see recipe after recipe that relies on what we call "power flavors" — oils, herbs, sun-dried tomatoes, olives. These ingredients are easy to obtain (you probably already have a lot of them) and easy to incorporate into your cooking. This book will show you how. You'll find common ingredients, but in unexpected places. And you'll understand that the central point of this book is not the 2,500 recipes we've given you. It's number 2,501, which we think you'll be inspired to create.

About These Recipes

You'll notice this heading in each chapter, just before the recipes begin. It's a good idea to read the brief explanation under that heading before proceeding with recipes from that chapter. You'll find information common to all the recipes in that chapter — on cooking techniques, ingredients, seasonings and so forth.

Recipes are roadmaps that chart a path toward the completion of a particular dish. As on any trip, there are different ways to proceed, and the route you choose depends on your experience. First-time travelers need detailed maps to mark each turn and warn of rocky terrain. More seasoned visitors know each curve by heart and need to refer to the map only occasionally, such as for unexpected detours or to chart new ground.

We recognize the same diversity of experience among the users of this book. Some will want everything explained, while others will find a recitation of fundamentals unnecessary. To help both groups of cooks, we have included two segments in the first section of this book, "The Toolbox." One is a compilation of culinary techniques, the other a collection of basic recipes. Placing these cooking basics in their own section has allowed us to streamline the recipes without eliminating information you may need. If you're familiar with the technique or preparation you see in a recipe, just ignore our reference to the elaboration. If you want more help, you'll find the advice you need on the designated page.

With regard to ingredients, although we often avoid prepackaged ingredients, we've written this book for the real world, where time is scarce but where a lot of good products have come to market. True, the real world sells some abominable commercial food products, but many food manufacturers have cleaned up their acts in recent years and now offer some first-rate convenience foods. Pastry made from scratch by an experienced baker will always produce a better result than store-bought pastry, but if you are not an experienced baker, certain prepared pastry products will give you far better results than you can expect to make by hand, and our fillings in those crusts will produce great pies. Your supermarket's freezer case carries a puff pastry so superb we'd be crazy to suggest you even think of duplicating it at home. And though no one can make a better roasted pepper than you, excellent commercial versions are available in jars. Good spice blends and exotic ingredients have become more numerous over the years. You know what the good products are. Don't hesitate to use them.

Following are a few words on some specific ingredients and ideas:

- **Read before you cook.** There aren't many rules that are sacrosanct, but this one is. Read the entire recipe before you do any preparation or cooking. If you need an ingredient, or if you need to learn a technique, it's better to know that before you start.

- **Taste before you serve.** Seasoning a dish is often a matter of personal taste. But in professional kitchens, just about everything — sauces, soups, side dishes, dressings — gets tasted before it is served. You should do the same. It's just good sense for the cook to know what something tastes like before others taste it.

- **Butter.** The salt content of butter varies from one brand to the next. Although this is not an issue in savory recipes, where you are likely to add more salt than would ever be in the butter, it is a problem in baking, where just a little bit of salt can throw off the flavor balance. So in baking, unsalted butter is essential; in savory recipes, use whatever you want.

- **Broth and stock.** Many of our recipes build on a flavorful broth. Restaurants pay a lot of attention to these, and the best home cooks do too, especially now that excellent commercial versions can be found. But the distinction between broth and stock has gotten blurred. Stock is made from bones and not much meat, and it's intentionally bland so that it can be used in a wide variety of restaurant preparations. Its main attraction is its great body, derived from the collagen surrounding the bones. Broth is made from meat and bones. It's the liquid part of soup and is much richer-tasting than stock. Soups can be made from stock by adding meat and vegetables. We call for broth in our recipes, but feel free to use packaged products labeled "broth" or "stock"; regardless of what the label says, they are all technically broth. Make sure to check whether the product is condensed; if it is, follow the directions on the label to dilute it before adding it to the recipe.

- **Where size matters.** Assume all produce items are medium-sized, unless we state otherwise, and use large eggs unless we state otherwise. Sometimes it doesn't matter, so we leave the choice to you. Sometimes it does matter, and we'll specify.

- **Where variety matters.** If the fat level (such as for milk or sour cream) or the color (such as for wine vinegar) or the lightness/darkness (such as for brown sugar) matters, we'll say so. If it doesn't matter, the choice is yours.

- **Allergies.** Food allergies, like any other allergies, can strike any individual, and they come in too many varieties to count. People who suffer such allergies need to be constantly vigilant, not just when they cook for themselves but also when they are guests in other people's homes or in restaurants. At home, allergies are another good reason to read a recipe before cooking from it.

Finally, with the possible exception of some baking recipes, remember that the vast majority of our recipes are very forgiving. They allow — and, indeed, we encourage — variation and experimentation.

PART 1

The Toolbox

Basic Techniques for Cooking Anything

Inventive cooks cook with techniques, not recipes, for they understand that once you know how to roast a chicken, making one that's maple-glazed and stuffed with apples and sauerkraut is pretty much the same as roasting a garlic-herb chicken stuffed with oysters and cornbread. In truth, a roast is a roast is a roast (which Gertrude Stein would have understood if she had cooked every once in a while), and the only thing that differentiates one from another is the choice of flavoring.

This segment describes basic cooking procedures. You may be familiar with many of them; others may be new to you. Some of the recipes in the book will refer to these procedures. If you're familiar with a technique, just continue with the recipe; if you need instructions or a refresher, they're here for you. This chapter is divided into two categories — cooking techniques and baking techniques.

Cooking Techniques

Blanching • This technique usually precedes additional cooking. Tomatoes, peaches and almonds are blanched to remove their skins. Green beans and broccoli are blanched to soften their tough fibers. Meats are blanched to rid them of color, and smoked pork is sometimes blanched to reduce its aroma. The process is almost always the same. Bring a large pot of water, salted or not, as you prefer, to a boil. Drop the ingredient in the boiling water in small enough batches that the water never loses its boil, and cook until the desired effect is achieved. For skinning, 30 seconds is sufficient. Softening tough fibers usually takes a few minutes or more. To stop the cooking, remove the ingredient and plunge it into ice water. Then dry it.

Braising • A two-step technique for tough or fibrous ingredients. First, the ingredient is browned, then it's simmered in liquid in a covered pot until tender. Sautéing is the most common method of browning braised dishes, but they could just as easily start by being grilled or broiled to brown the surface. Either way, there should be just enough liquid to come no more than halfway up the side of the food. If the ingredient is wet, like meat, it must be dredged in seasoned flour to absorb surface moisture before sautéing.

Breading • The simplest way to bread an ingredient is to moisten the food and cover it with crumbs, which gives a very light coating. Better coverage is achieved by first dredging the food in flour or starch to absorb any surface moisture that might steam during cooking and cause the breading to flake off. Then the dredged ingredient is coated with egg wash and rolled in bread crumbs. A thicker crust can be achieved by redipping in egg and bread crumbs. The breaded food should sit on a rack for at least 10 minutes to give the egg a chance to dry, thereby "gluing" the crumbs in place. To keep from breading your hands as well as the food, use one hand to handle only dry ingredients, the other to handle an ingredient after it's wet.

Browning • Browning colors a food but does not cook it through. To brown, heat a thin film of oil or clarified butter (see page 16) until smoking. Add the food, leaving space between each ingredient, and cook until browned. Proceed with the recipe. Browning can also be done under a broiler, on a grill or in the oven.

Cleaning Clams and Mussels • Make sure clams and mussels are alive by checking to see that they are tightly closed. If one is open, tap its shell sharply. It should close. If it doesn't, discard it. Wash clam shells well in cold water, using a scrub brush. Clean mussels by scrubbing their shells with a stiff brush to remove debris and barnacles. Pull off the "beard," a collection of silky filaments with which the mussel clings to rocks, by tugging on it sharply. Cook clams and mussels immediately.

Cutting a Chicken • *To section:* Using a sharp, thin-bladed boning knife, remove wings by cutting through the inside joint where the wing joins the body. When the knife hits bone, bend the wing toward the neck until the wing joint pops out, then cut through the joint. To remove legs, cut through the interior joint where the thigh meets the body. Push the leg toward the back of the chicken until the joint pops, then cut through the joint. To separate breast from back, cut through the carcass with a large knife, starting at the leg cavity and cutting up along the back, through the ribs, to the neck. When you get to the shoulder, bend back away from the breast, exposing the shoulder joints, and cut through them. *To bone breasts:* Place breast skin side down and press down with the heel of your hand directly on the center of the breastbone until you hear a pop. The center breastbone will lift out. Run your fingers between the meat and the ribs, lifting each side of the rib cage off in a section. Run a knife along the collarbone and wishbone, and remove. Turn breast over and pull off skin. Trim and, if desired, halve. *To section legs:* Slit meat inside the joint where drumstick meets thigh. Pull drumstick back, away from its natural angle, until joint pops. Cut through the joint and disengage.

Cutting Vegetables • *Julienne:* A julienne is a 2- by ⅛- by ⅛-inch (5 by 0.25 by 0.25 cm) strip. Square off the vegetable and cut it in 2-inch (5 cm) lengths. Cut the lengths into ⅛-inch (0.25 cm) thick slices. Stack up 3 slices and cut into ⅛-inch (0.25 cm) thick strips. *Dice:* These cubes are cut in much the same way as a julienne. Square off the vegetable and cut into slices as thick as you want the diced vegetable to be. Large dice are about ¾ inch (2 cm); medium dice, about ½ inch (1 cm); small dice, about ¼ inch (0.5 cm); fine dice, about ⅛ inch (0.25 cm). Stack up a few slices and cut strips of the same width. Line up several strips and cut into cubes by slicing across the strips in the same width. *Slices:* Hold the food perpendicular to the blade of the knife and cut thin pieces across or down the length of the food. *Diagonal slices:* Hold the food at a 45-degree angle to the blade of the knife and cut thin pieces diagonally across the length of the food. *Spiral cuts:* An Asian style usually associated with stir-fries. Cut the vegetable on a diagonal, then give it a quarter turn so that the cut surface is facing up. Cut another diagonal slice across the cut face. Turn another quarter turn and slice again. Pieces will be multi-faceted, like jewels.

Deep-Frying • Heat at least 2 inches (5 cm) of mild oil, such as canola, in a deep pan or a deep-fat fryer to 375°F (190°C). Submerge small pieces of food (no more than a few bites) in the hot oil, a few pieces at a time, and cook until they are brown and crisp; do not crowd the pan. Lift the fried food with tongs or a slotted spoon into a strainer set over a drip bowl to drain, or onto several layers of paper towels to absorb surface oil. Season and serve immediately.

Degreasing • This simple process is used whenever you serve the liquid in which meat was cooked. The most effective method is to chill the liquid until the fat on the surface congeals. It can then be easily lifted off. If there is no time for this, large amounts of liquid fat can be skimmed with a large spoon or ladle, either by dipping just under the fat and moving the spoon across the surface of the liquid, or by placing a ladle into the liquid so that its rim just breaks the surface of the fat. If you keep the ladle very still at that level, fat will flow off the surface of the liquid into the ladle. Small amounts of fat can be removed by blotting the surface quickly with a folded paper towel.

Doneness of Meat • *Roasts:* The temperature of a meat indicates how firm, dry and red it will be, so judging doneness with a meat thermometer is a snap — if we can agree on what rare, medium and well-done mean. Our preference for final temperature is as follows: For beef, 125°F (52°C) is extra-rare, 130°F (54°C) is rare, 135°F (57°C) is medium-rare, 140°F (60°C) is medium, 150°F (65°C) is medium-well and anything above 160°F (71°C) is well-done. The doneness for medium-rare lamb is 135°F (57°C), and the minimum doneness for pork is 155°F (68°C). Other resources may specify higher temperatures for doneness; you can adjust timing based on your own preferences. When the temperature of the meat registers 5°F (3°C) less than the final meat temperature you want, remove the pan from the oven and set it aside for 10 to 20 minutes, depending on the size of the roast. During this time, the temperature will rise the extra 5°F (3°C), and the roast will become much easier to slice. Poultry breast is done at 160°F (71°C), legs at 170°F (77°C); a good compromise is 165°F (74°C). *Steaks and chops:* Because a meat thermometer needs 2 inches (5 cm) of thickness to get a proper reading, it is not effective for determining the doneness of steaks and chops. Your finger is the better tool. Raw meat is soft enough to take the impression of a poking finger without any resistance, while well-done meat will spring back and not show a dent. Between those extremes, the cook's experience and the diner's preference must determine doneness. Here are guidelines: Blood-rare meat has a firm crust but an interior as soft as pudding. Rare meat gives slight resistance at the surface. Medium-rare meat is soft only in the very center. Medium meat springs back. Medium-well meat is firm. And well-done meat is almost hard enough to be considered a blunt instrument.

Dredging • When a recipe directs you to dredge in flour or starch, trim the food well and pat it dry. Toss in a bag with flour or starch, or roll in a deep plate of flour or starch. Once the food is completely coated, pat or shake it until all but a thin powdering of the flour or starch falls off. Dredging too heavily can cause sautéed meats to be mushy and the batter for deep-frying to roll off after dipping. Any leftover flour or starch should be discarded unless the recipe specifies to add it.

Finishing • This term refers to adding ingredients to a sauce of reduced liquid to make it smoother, richer, thicker or more flavorful. Typically, after the liquid is reduced, it is removed from the heat, then butter, cream, mustard, yogurt or any other finishing ingredient is swirled in.

Flambéing • This technique rids a dish of the off-flavors of liquors and wines by burning off some of the alcohol. It is often also seen as a way to add drama to food presentation. To flambé, heat the liquor, and carefully touch its fumes with a flame. They will instantly ignite and will continue flaming until the alcohol in the liquor has burned away. The flame can come from a lighter, match or gas burner. Be careful that there is nothing in the way of the flame, such as dish towels (or yourself), that can ignite, and do not attempt to make the flame overly large by using more liquor than is called for. To extinguish a flambé prematurely, suffocate it with the lid of the pan. To get the same flavor effects without a flame, simply boil the liquor until the smell of alcohol dissipates.

Forming Potstickers • Place a dumpling wrapper on a work surface and brush the wrapper with egg wash. Place 1 teaspoon (5 mL) of filling in the center of the wrapper and fold the wrapper in half over the filling. Carefully pinch the edges of the wrapper together so that no air is trapped in the center. Crimp the edges, if desired. Flatten the straight side of the dumpling and set on a tray on its flat side. Keep potstickers covered with a damp towel to prevent drying out before cooking.

Grilling, Broiling and Barbecuing • Grilling and broiling accomplish the same things from different directions. In broiling the heat comes from above, while in grilling it comes from below. Either way, the food must be tender and $\frac{1}{4}$ inch to 2 inches (0.5 to 5 cm) thick. It helps if grilled or broiled food has a moderately high fat content to keep it from drying out, but even lean foods can be grilled or broiled if they have been marinated or are basted during cooking. Place the food 2 to 4 inches (5 to 10 cm) from a high-heat source. Because the heat is constant, cooking is regulated by moving the food farther from or closer to the heat source. The thinner the ingredient or the rarer you want it, the closer to the heat source it should get so as to quickly brown the surface of the food, leaving the

interior less done. When you move the food away from the heat, the surface browns more slowly and the food has a chance to cook through before the surface chars. Do not confuse grilling with barbecuing. Barbecuing is a method of braising tough meats over an open fire. Either the fire must be quite low or the food must be placed far from the flame. While the food cooks, it is basted with sauce. In this way, tough fibers are softened in simmering liquid as the meat is infused with the flavors of the sauce. The result is an aromatic meat that literally falls from the bone. Barbecue should never be charred. If it is, the fire was too hot. Hot fires are for tender foods, such as fish fillets, high-quality steaks and chicken breasts. The meats to choose for barbecuing are tougher and more flavorful, such as ribs, stew meats and chicken legs.

Heating Cooking Oil • Oil for softening vegetables should be heated over high heat for less than 30 seconds. Oil for browning should be heated over high heat for at least 1 minute. Oil for sautéing should be heated until it smokes, about 2 minutes. Oil for deep-frying should be about 375°F (190°C). This temperature can be judged by using a deep-fry or candy thermometer, or by dropping a small bit of the frying food in the fat. If the oil is up to temperature but not too hot, the food will bubble immediately and brown in no less than 1 minute.

Killing a Lobster or Crab • Like most shellfish, lobsters and crabs must be alive close to the time they're cooked, so you should always buy them alive or precooked. The easiest way to kill and cook a lobster or crab is to plunge it into a large pot of boiling water and simmer for the time stated in the recipe. If you're preparing a recipe that calls for a sectioned lobster, the lobster must be cut apart before it is cooked. Place the lobster on its belly on a clean surface. Kill it by plunging a knife into the lobster's back, right behind the head. Cut the lobster in half lengthwise. Clean out the body, reserving the dark green roe and lighter green tomalley, if desired. Crack the claws by rapping them with the blunt edge of a heavy knife. The lobster is now ready for broiling. For stewing or making soup, continue sectioning. Remove the claws and tail sections by twisting them from the body. Cook immediately.

Marination and Maceration • Marination infuses food with external elements, while maceration extracts something already in a food. Marinades infuse foods with aromatics and moisture while softening tough fibers and modifying harsh flavors. All marinades are a balance of acid, salt, oil and seasonings. Each element performs a specific function: acid and salt break down fiber; oil adds moisture; seasonings improve flavor. A balanced marinade will open up the food's fiber to allow moisture and flavor to enter. To use a marinade, rub the food with the marinade, cover and refrigerate. Refrigeration time depends on the size and density of the food, the strength of the marinade and the desired effect. If a marinade turns cloudy, it means the food has started to dehydrate and the marination has gone on for too long. Remove the food immediately and use as soon as possible. Maceration is typically done with acid, as with seviche (in which fish is "cooked" with citrus juice), or with salt, as when curing a salmon or ham in a mixture of salt, spices and sugar. The food should be covered with the macerating agent and refrigerated until the desired degree of dehydration takes place.

Opening Clams and Oysters

Opening Clams and Oysters • Shells should be tightly closed and washed well in cold water with a scrub brush. Protect your hand with a dish towel or potholder. Place the hinged end of the clam or the rounded end of the oyster in the towel, nestled into the fleshy pad at the base of your thumb. *For clams:* Place the sharp edge of a clam knife in the crack between the shells. Use the first three fingers of the hand that holds the clam to direct the knife between the two shells while steadily pushing it in. Once the knife is inside the clam, run it around and against the interior of the top shell to cut the two muscles that hold the clam closed. *For oysters:* Dig the pointed end of an oyster knife or church key (combination bottle and can opener) into the hinge of the oyster and pry upwards. The hinge will pop. Run a knife around and across the flatter of the two oyster shells, cutting the muscle that holds the shells together. Let the liquor drip through a strainer into a bowl. The strainer will catch stray bits of shell or debris.

Poaching

Poaching • This technique cooks tender foods in liquid heated just below the stage where bubbles form. Bring the liquid to a simmer, add the food to be poached and regulate the heat to keep the liquid just below a simmer. Cook until the desired results are achieved, turning as necessary.

Preparing Soft-Shell Crabs

Preparing Soft-Shell Crabs • Soft-shell crabs must be cleaned and killed before they are cooked. Using scissors, cut crab across the face at an upward angle so that the eye sockets and scaly section of the lower mouth are removed. Lift up the flaps on either side of the top shell (carapace) and remove the gills underneath. Turn crab over and remove the apron from the underside. Pat dry.

Reducing

Reducing • This is a sauce-making term for when liquid is boiled away, causing flavors to intensify and a natural thickening to take place. To reduce a liquid, boil it vigorously, but watch it closely near the end to keep it from scorching, especially if you are reducing it by more than half. You may need to reduce the heat as the liquid gets thicker. Liquid reduced to one-sixteenth its original volume is called a glaze.

Roasting Bell Peppers

Roasting Bell Peppers • Place any number of bell peppers directly over the high flame of a gas burner or under a broiler until they char on one side. Give the pepper a quarter turn and char again. Continue until the pepper has blackened all over. Place in a loosely closed paper bag and let cool for 10 minutes, during which time the flesh inside will soften slightly. Peel by rubbing the skin with your fingers. To avoid washing away the pepper's flavorful oils, wash the skin off your fingers rather than washing the peppers. Pull out stem and discard seeds. Good-quality roasted red peppers are available in jars and in the deli section of some grocery stores.

Roasting Tomatoes

Roasting Tomatoes • Place any number of tomatoes directly over a high gas flame or under a broiler and cook until the skins blister and they char slightly; this will take only a few seconds. Turn the tomato with tongs until the skin has blistered on all sides. Let cool. Peel the skin by slipping it off with your fingers. The result is a subtle, pleasant smokiness.

Sautéing Meat

Sautéing Meat • In a skillet, heat a thin film of oil or clarified butter (see page 16) until it smokes. Add a thin slice of boneless meat, dredged in flour, and cook it just long enough to brown well on both sides. Avoid overcrowding the pan. The meat must be thin enough and tender enough to cook to doneness in that amount of time. If it is thicker, it should be grilled, broiled or pan-fried.

Seeding Tomatoes

Seeding Tomatoes • To remove the seeds from a tomato, cut it in half along its equator. Squeeze each half gently, and the seeds will slip out.

Simmering and Boiling

Simmering and Boiling • Simmering liquid barely bubbles. Foods to be simmered should be more than half covered with liquid and cooked in a covered or uncovered pot until tender. Boiling is more vigorous. Fibrous or starchy foods are submerged in a large amount of rapidly bubbling water and cooked until tender, then drained.

Soaking Dried Beans

Soaking Dried Beans • There are two easy ways to hydrate dried legumes. The traditional way is to let the beans sit overnight in water, using four times as much water as beans. A quicker way, using the same ratio of water to beans, is to bring the beans and water to a boil, boil for 1 to 2 minutes, remove from heat and let stand for 1 hour. Drain beans and cook in fresh water as directed in the recipe.

Steaming • Food is trapped in an enclosed steam-infused environment until it is cooked through. This can be a covered, perforated basket or a covered plate perched above a pot of boiling water, a parchment wrapper baking in an oven, a plastic wrap–covered bowl in a microwave oven or a tightly sealed pressure cooker. Although steam is hotter than boiling water by a few degrees, it will not cook food as quickly unless it is under pressure, as is the case in a pressure cooker or microwave.

Stewing • Stewing is exactly the same as braising and simmering, except that the food is always in bite-size pieces and the liquid should almost cover the ingredients.

Water Bath • This is typically used when dissipated rather than direct heat is preferred. To make a water bath, simply place the cooked food in its container in a larger pan of hot water, and heat in the oven or over a low flame. It might be necessary to replenish the water during cooking. Water baths filled with ice water can be used to cool hot foods.

Wrapping in Parchment • Cut a large heart shape out of parchment paper, big enough so that the food you are wrapping can sit comfortably on one side of the heart with a $1\frac{1}{2}$-inch (4 cm) border all around. Place the food, any seasoning and a small amount of sauce in the widest part of one side of the parchment heart and fold the other side over the top. Starting with the rounded end, begin to fold the parchment in small, crisp creases along its open edge, making sure each triangular fold overlaps the one before it so as to lock it in place. When you get to the pointed end of the heart, lock the "chain" of folds in place by twisting the point tightly.

Zesting Citrus Fruits • To remove the colorful skin — the zest — from a lemon, lime, orange or grapefruit, peel thin strips with a vegetable peeler. These strips can be finely chopped, minced or julienned. Or you can grate zest by rubbing the citrus fruit against the smallest teeth of a grater or by using a microplane. Your strips are too thick if the underside contains any of the white layer of pith underneath the zest.

Baking Techniques

Assembling a Pot Pie • Roll out pastry to $\frac{3}{16}$-inch (0.4 cm) thickness. Cut a circle from the pastry wide enough to overlap the edge of the baking dish by 1 inch (2.5 cm) all the way around, and cut a 1-inch (2.5 cm) wide strip long enough to wrap around the baking dish (it need not be in one piece). Dampen the edge of the baking dish with water, and place pastry strip along the rim, making sure the ends overlap. Press down to secure. Brush this pastry rim with egg wash (see page 20) and cover with the pastry circle. Press edge to seal well. Crimp edge. Cut a decorative opening in the center of the pastry to allow steam to escape.

Assembling Turnovers • To form turnover pastries, roll out 8 ounces (250 g) of puff pastry on a lightly floured board to a $12\frac{1}{2}$-inch (31 cm) square. With a sharp knife, trim $\frac{1}{4}$ inch (0.5 cm) from each side, leaving a 12-inch (30 cm) square of dough. Cut into quarters to make four 6-inch (15 cm) squares. Brush with egg wash (see page 20) and make a small mound of filling in the center of each square. Fold each square by bringing one corner to the opposite corner, forming a triangle with filling in the center. Gently push edges together to seal. With the dull side of a small knife, make vertical indentations in the sealed edges of the turnovers. Cut a few small slashes in the top to serve as steam vents. *For mini- turnovers:* Roll, shape and trim dough as for regular turnover pastry, but cut the 12-inch (30 cm) square of dough into sixteen 3-inch (7.5 cm) squares. Prepare, fold, seal, make indentations and cut steam vents as described above.

Blind-Baking, or Prebaking, Pastry Shells • Line chilled pastry shell(s) with foil and fill with pastry weights, uncooked rice or dried beans. Bake in a preheated 400°F (200°C) oven for 12 minutes. Remove foil and weights, and bake for 10 to 25 minutes more, depending on how much more baking the pastry will get once it is filled. Let cool on a rack.

Caramelizing Sugar • Sugar will dissolve in water when heated, but the higher the proportion of sugar to liquid, the hotter the mixture must get before the sugar dissolves. Eventually, the proportion of sugar will near 100 percent, at which point the liquefied sugar will become golden brown and very complex in aroma and flavor: it caramelizes. You can caramelize sugar either by mixing it with half as much water and boiling until it turns brown, or by heating the sugar in a heavy pot by itself. The wet method will take longer but needs little attention. With the dry method, caramelizing occurs more quickly, but the sugar can burn in the blink of an eye if it is not stirred frequently near the end of cooking.

Collars on Soufflé Dishes • To get a soufflé to rise high and straight, or when making a chilled or frozen soufflé, you must tie a collar around the soufflé dish to build up the sides. Prepare a sheet of parchment paper or foil 3 inches (7.5 cm) longer than the perimeter of the soufflé dish and 3 inches (7.5 cm) wider than the height of the dish. Wrap it around the outside of the dish so that its width extends up beyond the rim of the dish by about 3 inches (7.5 cm). Secure with string or staples. If using foil, you can mold it into place. Grease and dust the interior of the collar as directed in the recipe.

Forming a Pastry Shell • Roll out chilled pastry on a lightly floured board with a floured rolling pin to a 3/16-inch (0.4 cm) thick disk at least 4 inches (10 cm) wider than the pan it will line. Roll pastry loosely onto the pin, using a spatula to help lift the pastry if it should stick, and transfer to a pie pan. Line the pan with the pastry, making sure the pastry comes all the way down into the corners of the pan, and trim so that the edge of the pastry extends 1 inch (2.5 cm) beyond the rim of the pan. Fold this excess pastry under the pastry lining the pan. Crimp the edges to seal.

Forming a Tart Shell • Roll out pastry and line a tart pan with a removable bottom as described in Forming a Pastry Shell (above). To finish the edge, press the pastry into the ridges in the sides of the tart pan and roll a rolling pin over the top of the pan to cut off the pastry flush to the edge of the pan.

Forming Tartlet Shells • Roll out pastry between 2 sheets of waxed paper to 3/16-inch (0.4 cm) thickness. Refrigerate for 30 minutes. Remove from refrigerator and remove the top sheet of waxed paper. Cut into circles, each 4 to 5 inches (10 to 12.5 cm) in diameter. Using a small spatula, remove each pastry circle from the back sheet of waxed paper and place in a 2- to 3-inch (5 to 7.5 cm) tartlet pan. Crimp the edges. Cover and freeze for at least 30 minutes.

Forming a Two-Crust Pie • Roll out pastry and line a pie pan as described in Forming a Pastry Shell (above). Trim the edge of the pastry so that it barely extends over the edge of the pan. Fill with pie filling. Roll out another pastry disk in the same way. Roll pastry around the pin, and unroll over the top of the filling. Trim so that the edge of the top pastry extends 1 inch (2.5 cm) beyond the rim of the pan. Fold this excess pastry under the pastry lining the pan. Crimp the edges to seal.

Freezing Sherbets, Ices, Granités and Sorbets without an Ice Cream Maker • Prepare the mixture you plan to freeze and pour into a wide, shallow pan. Freeze until ice crystals start to form around the edge of the pan, about 30 to 60 minutes, depending on alcohol content. Stir the crystals into the liquid mixture. Freeze for 30 to 60 minutes more, and stir again. Continue to freeze for another 3 hours, stirring the mixture several times. When mixture holds a shape, it is ready to serve. If mixture should freeze solid, cut it into small pieces and process in a blender or food processor for a few seconds before serving.

Grinding Nuts • When a recipe calls for ground nuts, it means the nuts should be ground to a powder. This can be done easily and well in a food processor, but don't overdo it or the nuts' oils will be released and the powder will turn into nut butter. Grind no more than 2 cups (500 mL) at a time, and use the processor in 3-second pulses to get even results. For very oily nuts, such as pecans or cashews, add a small amount (1 tbsp/15 mL or less) of flour or bread crumbs to help absorb the oil. Chopped nuts, even when finely chopped, are still coarser than ground nuts.

Icing a Cake • Place the cake on a flat cake plate that has been lined with 4 strips of waxed paper to protect the outer edges of the plate. Brush away any crumbs. *Frosting:* Prepare the frosting. Dip a long icing spatula into the frosting. Lift up a large blob and spread it around the side of the cake, keeping the spatula parallel to the side. Continue until the entire side is covered and a small rim has built up at the top of the cake. Spread more frosting over the top in swirls, going all the way out to the perimeter. Wipe the spatula clean. Holding the spatula parallel to the side, turn the cake to smooth the side. Wipe the spatula clean after each stroke. Remove waxed paper strips by pulling each piece by its narrow end. *Glazing:* Prepare glaze. Pour two-thirds of it over the top of the cake. With an icing spatula, spread it evenly over the top, letting some run down the side. Smooth the side, being sure all surfaces are covered with a layer of glaze. Use the remaining glaze as needed. Remove waxed paper strips by pulling each piece by its narrow end.

Lining Baking Pans • To line a baking pan of any size, cut a piece of parchment paper or waxed paper to size by placing the pan on a sheet of the paper. Trace the perimeter of the bottom of the pan on the paper, and cut out with scissors. Lightly grease the interior of the pan and place the paper, penciled side down, over the bottom, smoothing out any bubbles or wrinkles.

Melting Chocolate • Melted chocolate scorches easily and will seize without warning if it comes in contact with the least bit of moisture. Techniques for melting it center on avoiding these pitfalls. Do not store chocolate in the refrigerator or freezer. This will cause beads of moisture to settle on the surface of the chocolate, which will make it seize when melted. All utensils must be perfectly dry. Chop or grate the chocolate into uniformly small pieces that will melt quickly before any of it has a chance to scorch. Place the chocolate in the top of a double boiler over simmering water or in a microwave oven, and heat until half melted. Remove from heat and stir until completely smooth. By finishing the melting away from the heat, the chocolate will be cool enough to use immediately in a recipe. Seized chocolate will become smooth if you add 1 tablespoon (15 mL) oil for every 8 ounces (250 g) of chocolate or 1 tablespoon (15 mL) liquid for each ounce.

Unpanning Cakes • The first trick to unpanning cakes is to make sure the cake pan is prepared properly in the first place (see Lining Baking Pans, page 13). Let the cake cool in the pan long enough that the pan is cool enough to handle but still slightly warm to the touch. Run a small, sharp knife around the edge of the cake to loosen the sides.

Cover the cake with waxed paper. Top with a rack or a large, flat plate, and invert. The cake will fall from the pan. Remove the pan and, if necessary, the paper, place a cooling rack over the cake, and invert again. Remove the top rack or plate and waxed paper. Let cool to room temperature.

Unpanning Cheesecakes • If the cake is very soft, as with a crustless cheesecake, follow the procedure described in Unpanning Cakes (left), but loosen the sides by holding the warm panned cake on its side and letting gravity pull the cake away from the upper side. Rotate pan a quarter turn and let it drop from that side. Keep turning until the sides of the cake have been loosened all the way around.

Unpanning Stubborn Cakes • If a cake doesn't come out of the pan using conventional methods, shake the inverted pan vigorously from side to side. This should release any vacuums that could be holding the cake in the pan. Vacuums frequently form around the edges of cake during cooling, especially if the cake is soft and moist. If it still won't come out, turn it right side up and bang the pan and its covering plate sharply on the countertop. This should break any sticky spots across the bottom of the cake. If it still won't come out, turn it right side up and loosen the sides again with a knife, but this time push the sides of the cake away from the sides of the pan with the flat side of the knife. Invert again. If it still won't come out, resign yourself to failure and get on with your life by slicing the cake right in the pan and lifting out the pieces with a flexible spatula.

Basic Preparations Every Cook Should Know

Cooking Basics

Clarified Butter 16
Garlic Butter 16
Herb Butter 16
Tomato Butter 16
Homemade Yogurt 16
Homemade Mayonnaise 16
Aïoli 17
Roux 17
Slurry 17
Béchamel Sauce (White Sauce) 17
Mornay Sauce (Cheese Sauce) 17
Chicken Gravy 17
Beef Gravy 18
Court Bouillon 18
Chicken Broth 18
Beef Broth 18
Vegetable Broth 19
Quick Fish Broth 19
Homemade Croutons 19
Soft- and Hard-Cooked Eggs 19
Roasted Eggplant 19
Refried Black, White or
Kidney Beans 20
Egg Pasta 20
Doctored Jarred Pasta Sauce 20
Pesto 20

Baking Basics

Egg Wash 20
Bread and Pizza Dough 20
Cream Cheese Pastry 20
Flaky Pastry 21
Sweet Pastry 21
Sweet or Flaky Pastry Shell 21
Crumb Crust 21
Pâtes à Choux
(Cream Puff and Éclair Pastry) 22
Génoise (Sponge Cake) 22
Pound Cake 22
Shortcake 22
Shortcake Biscuits 22
Cornbread 22
Toasted Nuts 23
Streusel or Crumb Topping 23
Nut Streusel Topping 23
Simple Syrup 23
Fruit Glaze 23
Chocolate Glaze 23
Quick Buttercream 23
French Buttercream 24
Chocolate Sour Cream Frosting 24
Pastry Cream 24
Lemon Curd 24
Crème Anglaise 24

Cooking Basics

You can purchase perfectly good ready-made pie crusts, pestos and broths, but when you want to make them yourself out of need or just for fun, this introductory chapter will provide you with the basic recipes required. Most of them are parts of other recipes, such as sauces, flavorings and doughs that are not intended to deliver a finished dish. They are neither creative nor elaborate, but with them in your repertoire, you'll have the building blocks you need to really get cooking. If you already have a favorite pastry recipe, or you come from a family famous for its cornbread, go ahead and use your own formulas instead of ours.

Clarified Butter

In a saucepan, melt ½ cup (125 mL) butter over medium heat until it separates. There should be foam on top, clear golden liquid in the middle and solids on the bottom. Skim off the foam and carefully pour the clear liquid (which is the clarified butter) into a heat-resistant container. Discard solid particles left in the pot. Cover and keep refrigerated. **Makes about 6 tbsp (90 mL).**

Garlic Butter

1 tbsp	olive oil	15 mL
4	cloves garlic, minced	4
¼ cup	butter, softened	50 mL

In a small skillet, heat oil over medium heat. Sauté garlic until aromatic, about 1 minute. Let cool, then beat into softened butter. Refrigerate until ready to use. **Makes about ⅓ cup (75 mL).**

Herb Butter

1 tsp	olive oil	5 mL
1	shallot, minced	1
1 tbsp	minced fresh Italian (flat-leaf) parsley	15 mL
2 tsp	chopped fresh chervil	10 mL
2 tsp	chopped fresh dill	10 mL
1 tsp	chopped fresh tarragon	5 mL
⅓ cup	butter, softened	75 mL

In a small skillet, heat oil over medium heat. Sauté shallot until tender. Add parsley, chervil, dill and tarragon; sauté until leaves are wilted, about 1 minute. Beat into softened butter and let cool. Refrigerate until ready to use. **Makes about ⅓ cup (75 mL).**

Tomato Butter

1 tsp	canola oil	5 mL
1	clove garlic, minced	1
2 tbsp	tomato paste	25 mL
1	fresh basil leaf, minced	1
½ cup	butter, softened	125 mL

In a small skillet, heat oil over medium heat. Sauté garlic until aromatic, about 1 minute. Stir in tomato paste and basil; let cool to room temperature. Beat into softened butter. Refrigerate until ready to use. **Makes about ⅔ cup (150 mL).**

Homemade Yogurt

4 cups	low-fat milk	1 L
½ cup	powdered milk	125 mL
¼ cup	plain yogurt	50 mL

In a saucepan, heat low-fat milk until bubbles form around the edges. Let cool until warm to the touch (about 100°F/38°C) and remove any skin from the surface. Stir in powdered milk and yogurt. Cover with plastic wrap and set in a location with a constant temperature of about 100°F (38°C), such as a closed oven with a pilot light or near a warm radiator or hot-water heater, for 4 to 6 hours. When done, yogurt will be thickened like custard. Refrigerate for several hours, and it will become thicker. **Makes 4 cups (1 L).**

Homemade Mayonnaise

Pinch	cayenne pepper	Pinch
	Salt and freshly ground white pepper to taste	
1 tbsp	boiling water	15 mL
2	large or extra-large egg yolks	2
2 tsp	Dijon mustard	10 mL
2 tbsp	freshly squeezed lemon juice	25 mL
1½ cups	bland vegetable oil (such as safflower, peanut, sunflower)	375 mL

In a bowl (or food processor), dissolve cayenne, salt and white pepper in boiling water. Add egg yolks and mustard; beat with a whisk (or process) until lightly thickened. Stir in lemon juice. Add oil in a slow, steady stream (with the motor running, through the feed tube, if using a food processor), mixing constantly, until thick and creamy. Adjust seasoning, if necessary. **Makes about 2 cups (500 mL).** *(If you are concerned about the food safety of raw eggs, you may wish to skip this recipe.)*

Aïoli

Follow preceding recipe, but replace the mustard with 2 cloves garlic, finely chopped, and replace the bland vegetable oil with a mixture of 1 cup (250 mL) mild vegetable oil (such as canola oil) and ½ cup (125 mL) extra-virgin olive oil. **Makes about 2 cups (500 mL).** *(If you are concerned about the food safety of raw eggs, you may wish to skip this recipe.)*

Roux

| 1 part | clarified butter (see page 16) | 1 part |
| 1 part | all-purpose flour | 1 part |

In a heavy saucepan, melt butter over medium-low heat. Add flour and cook, stirring constantly, until incorporated. The longer a roux cooks, the browner and more flavorful it becomes. A white roux, used for cream sauces, soufflés and croquettes, cooks for less than 2 minutes. A blond roux, used for chicken gravies and other light sauces, cooks for 3 to 6 minutes. A brown roux, used for beef gravy and many stews, cooks for 10 minutes or more. (Take care not to splash brown roux, which can get dangerously hot.)

Slurry

1 tbsp	cornstarch	15 mL
2 tbsp	water	25 mL
2 to 3 cups	boiling liquid	500 to 750 mL

Stir cornstarch and water until smooth. Stir again just before adding to boiling liquid in a saucepan, and cook to thicken liquid into a sauce.

Béchamel Sauce (White Sauce)

2 cups	milk	500 mL
¼ cup	chopped onion	50 mL
2 tbsp	finely chopped carrot	25 mL
2 tbsp	finely chopped celery	25 mL
1 tbsp	butter	15 mL
1 tbsp	all-purpose flour	15 mL
Pinch	ground nutmeg	Pinch
	Salt and freshly ground white pepper to taste	

In a small saucepan, over medium heat, heat milk until steam rises from its surface. Add onion, carrot and celery. Remove from heat and let stand for 10 minutes, then strain out solids. In another saucepan, melt butter over medium heat. Add flour and cook, stirring constantly, for 1 to 2 minutes, or until incorporated (do not let brown). Whisk in hot milk until all lumps are gone. Simmer for 10 minutes, stirring frequently with a wooden spoon. Season with nutmeg, salt and white pepper. **Makes about 2 cups (500 mL).** *(For a thick béchamel sauce, use 2 tbsp/25 mL each butter and flour. For an extra-thick béchamel sauce, to use as a base for soufflés and croquettes, use ¼ cup/50 mL each butter and flour.)*

Mornay Sauce (Cheese Sauce)

Prepare preceding recipe. Bring sauce to a boil, remove from heat and stir in ⅔ cup (150 mL) finely shredded cheese until melted. Use as a sauce for vegetables or fish, or as a base for soufflés. **Makes about 2½ cups (625 mL).** *(Warning: Do not boil any mixture that contains cheese. Additional heat will not make the cheese melt; rather, it will cause it to congeal and split.)*

Chicken Gravy

2 tbsp	chicken fat, skimmed from pan drippings	25 mL
1 tbsp	all-purpose flour	15 mL
2 cups	chicken broth and/or juices from a roasted chicken	500 mL
	Salt and freshly ground black pepper to taste	
¼ cup	light (5%) cream (optional)	50 mL

In a saucepan, heat chicken fat over medium heat. Add flour and cook, stirring constantly, for 3 to 4 minutes, or until lightly browned. Whisk in broth until all lumps are gone. Simmer for 10 minutes, stirring frequently with a wooden spoon. Season with salt and pepper. If you'd like a cream gravy, stir in cream. **Makes about 2 cups (500 mL).**

Beef Gravy

3 tbsp	beef fat, skimmed from pan drippings	45 mL
½ cup	chopped onion	125 mL
¼ cup	finely chopped carrot	50 mL
¼ cup	finely chopped celery	50 mL
4	canned tomatoes, drained and chopped	4
1 tbsp	tomato paste	15 mL
2 tbsp	all-purpose flour	25 mL
4 cups	beef broth and/or juices from a roast beef	1 L
2	sprigs fresh Italian (flat-leaf) parsley	2
1	bay leaf	1
½ tsp	dried thyme	2 mL
	Salt and freshly ground black pepper to taste	

In a saucepan, heat beef fat over medium heat. Sauté onion, carrot and celery until browned. Add tomatoes and tomato paste; sauté for 3 minutes. Add flour and cook, stirring constantly, until browned, about 10 minutes. Whisk in broth until all lumps are gone. Add parsley, bay leaf and thyme; simmer for at least 30 minutes, stirring occasionally with a wooden spoon. Season with salt and pepper. Strain out solids. **Makes about 3 cups (750 mL).**

Court Bouillon

2 cups	water	500 mL
2 cups	dry white wine	500 mL
½ cup	chopped onion	125 mL
¼ cup	chopped carrot	50 mL
¼ cup	chopped celery	50 mL
1	bay leaf	1
Pinch	dried thyme	Pinch
1 tbsp	chopped fresh Italian (flat-leaf) parsley	15 mL
4	whole black peppercorns	4
1	whole clove	1
1 tbsp	freshly squeezed lemon juice	15 mL

In a large saucepan, combine all ingredients; bring to a boil. Reduce heat and simmer for 15 minutes. Strain out solids. **Makes about 4 cups (1 L).** *Store in an airtight container in the refrigerator for up to 1 week or in the freezer for up to 3 months.*

Chicken Broth

5 lbs	uncooked chicken parts (backs, necks, gizzards, hearts and trimmings)	2.5 kg
2	large carrots, chopped	2
2	stalks celery, chopped	2
1	large onion, chopped	1
1 tbsp	whole black peppercorns	15 mL
2 tsp	salt	10 mL
2 tsp	dried thyme	10 mL
2 tsp	chopped fresh dill	10 mL
5	sprigs fresh Italian (flat-leaf) parsley	5
1	whole clove	1
1	bay leaf	1

Place chicken parts in a large soup pot, add enough cold water to cover (about 2½ gallons/10 L) and bring to a boil. Skim away any impurities that rise to the surface and reduce to a simmer. Add carrots, celery, onion, peppercorns, salt, thyme, dill, parsley, clove and bay leaf; simmer for 3 hours. Strain out solids and let cool. **Makes about 2 gallons (8 L).** *Store in airtight containers in the refrigerator for up to 5 days or in the freezer for up to 3 months. Use for soups, sauces and stews.*

Beef Broth

5 to 7 lbs	beef bones	2.5 to 3.5 kg
	Vegetable oil	
2	large carrots, chopped	2
2	stalks celery, chopped	2
1	large onion, chopped	1
2 tbsp	tomato paste	25 mL
1 tbsp	whole black peppercorns	15 mL
2 tsp	salt	10 mL
2 tsp	dried thyme	10 mL
5	sprigs fresh Italian (flat-leaf) parsley	5
1	whole clove	1
1	bay leaf	1

Preheat oven to 450°F (230°C). Rub bones with oil, place on a rimmed baking sheet so they don't touch, and roast, turning twice, for about 30 minutes, or until uniformly browned. Place browned bones in a large soup pot, and set aside baking sheet. Add enough water to cover bones (about 2½ gallons/10 L) and bring to a boil. Skim away any impurities that rise to the surface. Reduce heat and simmer for 1 hour. Meanwhile, toss the carrots, celery and onion in the fat remaining in the browning pan. Return to the oven and roast, turning twice, for about 30 minutes, or until vegetables are uniformly browned. Add to the pot, along with tomato paste, peppercorns, salt, thyme, parsley, clove and bay leaf; simmer for 6 hours. Strain out solids and let cool. **Makes about 2 gallons (8 L).** *Store in airtight containers in the refrigerator for up to 5 days or in the freezer for up to 3 months. Use for soups, sauces and stews.*

Vegetable Broth

2 tbsp	vegetable oil	25 mL
10	tomatoes, chopped	10
4	leeks, white parts only, chopped	4
2	large onions (unpeeled), chopped	2
1	head garlic, cloves separated but unpeeled	1
1	bunch celery, chopped	1
1 lb	mushrooms	500 g
1 lb	carrots, chopped	500 g
8 oz	parsnips, chopped	250 g
2 gallons	cold water	8 L
1/3 cup	chopped fresh Italian (flat-leaf) parsley	75 mL
1 tbsp	salt	15 mL
2 tsp	dried thyme	10 mL
1 tsp	ground turmeric	5 mL
12	whole black peppercorns	12
2	whole cloves	2
1	bay leaf	1

In a large soup pot, heat oil over medium heat. Add tomatoes, leeks, onions, garlic, celery, mushrooms, carrots and parsnips; cover and cook, stirring occasionally, until vegetables soften, about 10 minutes. Add water, parsley, salt, thyme, turmeric, peppercorns, cloves and bay leaf; bring to a boil. Skim away any impurities that rise to the surface. Reduce heat and simmer for 2 hours. Strain out solids and let cool. **Makes about 1.5 gallons (6 L).** *Store in airtight containers in the refrigerator for up to 3 days, or in the freezer for up to 3 months. Use for soups, sauces and stews.*

Quick Fish Broth

1 tbsp	vegetable oil	15 mL
3	stalks celery, finely chopped	3
2	carrots, chopped	2
1	onion, finely chopped	1
1	parsnip, chopped	1
3 cups	dry white wine	750 mL
4 cups	clam juice	1 L
3 cups	water	750 mL
2	sprigs fresh dill	2
2	sprigs fresh Italian (flat-leaf) parsley	2
	Coarsely grated zest and juice of 1 large lemon	
	Salt and freshly ground black pepper to taste	

In a large saucepan or Dutch oven, heat oil over medium heat. Add celery, carrots, onion and parsnip, stirring to coat with oil. Cover and cook until vegetables are aromatic, about 10 minutes. Add wine, increase heat to medium-high and boil for 5 minutes. Add clam juice, water, dill, parsley, lemon zest, lemon juice, salt and pepper; bring to a boil. Skim away any impurities that rise to the surface. Reduce heat and simmer for 20 minutes. Strain out solids and let cool. **Makes about 8 cups (2 L).** *Store in airtight containers in the refrigerator for up to 2 days, or in the freezer for up to 3 months. Use in any recipe calling for fish stock.*

Homemade Croutons

4 cups	stale bread (any kind), cut into 1/2-inch (1 cm) cubes	1 L
2	cloves garlic, minced	2
1/4 cup	olive oil	50 mL
2 tsp	paprika	10 mL
	Salt and freshly ground black pepper to taste	
3 tbsp	finely grated Parmesan cheese	45 mL

Preheat oven to 375°F (190°C). Toss bread cubes with garlic, oil, paprika, salt and pepper. Spread on a baking sheet and bake for 20 minutes, stirring every 5 minutes. Toss with Parmesan. **Makes 4 cups (1 L).**

Soft- and Hard-Cooked Eggs

Place any number of eggs in a saucepan large enough to hold them in a single layer, cover with water, and heat to a simmer. Simmer for 1 minute, then turn off the heat. Let stand for 2 to 4 minutes for soft-cooked eggs, or 15 to 20 minutes for hard-cooked. Cool hard-cooked eggs immediately by draining and running under cold water.

Roasted Eggplant

Preheat oven to 400°F (200°C). Poke a medium eggplant all over with a fork and place in the oven for 45 minutes, until soft. Let cool for 10 minutes. Cut off stem, halve lengthwise and scrape out flesh with a spoon. **Makes about 2 cups (500 mL).**

Refried Black, White or Kidney Beans

2 tsp	olive oil	10 mL
¼ cup	finely chopped onion	50 mL
1	clove garlic, minced	1
2½ cups	cooked or drained canned black, white or kidney beans	625 mL
1 cup	liquid from cooking beans, or water	250 mL

In a nonstick skillet, heat oil over medium-high heat. Sauté onion until tender. Add garlic and sauté for 30 seconds. Add beans and liquid; reduce heat and bring to a simmer. Simmer, mashing beans into a coarse paste with the back of a fork or wooden spoon, until mixture is fairly dry. Set aside and keep warm. **Makes about 2 cups (500 mL), serving 6 to 8.**

Egg Pasta

2	extra-large eggs	2
1⅓ cups	unbleached all-purpose flour	325 mL
¼ tsp	salt	1 mL

In a food processor, process eggs, flour and salt until a smooth, stiff dough forms in the center of the bowl. Cover and let stand for 10 minutes. Using a pasta machine or a rolling pin, roll out to desired thickness. Cut into desired shape. **Makes about 12 oz (375 g).**

Doctored Jarred Pasta Sauce

2 tbsp	olive oil	25 mL
1 cup	chopped onion	250 mL
3	cloves garlic, minced	3
2 tsp	dried basil	10 mL
½ tsp	hot pepper flakes	2 mL
¼ tsp	dried oregano	1 mL
1 cup	dry white wine	250 mL
1	jar (24 to 32 oz/750 g to 1 L) tomato pasta sauce	1

In a large saucepan, heat oil over medium-high heat. Sauté onion until tender. Stir in garlic, basil, hot pepper flakes and oregano. Add wine and boil until reduced by half. Add pasta sauce and simmer for 15 minutes. **Serves 6 to 8.**

Pesto

2 cups	packed basil leaves	500 mL
4	cloves garlic	4
¼ cup	pine nuts	50 mL
½ cup	extra-virgin olive oil	125 mL
⅓ cup	freshly grated imported Parmesan cheese	75 mL

In a food processor, purée basil, garlic and pine nuts. With the motor running, through the feed tube, add oil in a slow, steady stream until a smooth paste forms. Stir in Parmesan. Use immediately or cover and refrigerate for up to 4 days. **Makes about ¾ cup (175 mL).**

Baking Basics

Egg Wash

2 tbsp	water or milk	25 mL
1	whole egg, 2 yolks or 2 whites	1

Whisk water into egg. **Makes about ⅓ cup (75 mL).** Brush on breads to make a shiny crust or use to coat ingredients before breading.

Bread and Pizza Dough

1	package (¼ oz/7 g) dry yeast	1
1 cup	warm water (about 100°F/38°C), divided	250 mL
2½ cups	bread flour (approx.), divided	625 mL
1 tsp	salt	5 mL
	Olive oil	

Dissolve yeast in half the warm water. Stir in 1 cup (250 mL) of the bread flour, cover loosely with plastic wrap and let rise in a warm place for 20 minutes. Stir in the remaining water and salt. Place in a food processor, add the remaining flour and process until dough forms a ball in the center of the bowl. (You may need to add up to ¼ cup (50 mL) additional flour to form dough stiff enough to knead.) Place dough on a floured work surface and knead lightly. Place in a bowl brushed with olive oil and turn dough so that the oiled side is up. Cover lightly and let rise in a warm place until doubled in bulk, about 1 hour. Punch down, divide in half and form into loaves or pizza disks. **Makes 2 loaves, 2 large pizzas, or 1 of each.** *Use immediately or store, tightly wrapped, in the freezer for up to 1 month. Thaw and let rise before using.*

Cream Cheese Pastry

2¼ cups	all-purpose flour, plus more for dusting	550 mL
1 tsp	granulated sugar	5 mL
1 tsp	salt	5 mL
1 cup	unsalted butter, cut into small pieces	250 mL
1 cup	cream cheese, cut into small pieces	250 mL

In a bowl, combine flour, sugar and salt. Beat in

butter and cream cheese until smooth. Halve the dough, dust with flour and pat each half into a flat disk. Wrap in plastic wrap and refrigerate for 1 hour. On a floured work surface, using a floured rolling pin, roll out dough to between $\frac{1}{8}$- and $\frac{1}{4}$-inch (0.25 and 0.5 cm) thickness. Bake as directed in the recipe you are using. **Makes 2 crusts.** *Store, tightly wrapped, in the refrigerator for up to 2 days or in the freezer for up to 1 month. Use for savory pies, tarts, tartlets, etc.*

Flaky Pastry

1½ cups	all-purpose flour	375 mL
6 tbsp	cold unsalted butter, cut into small pieces	90 mL
2 tbsp	cold vegetable shortening, cut into small pieces	25 mL
¼ tsp	salt	1 mL
4 to 6 tbsp	water	60 to 90 mL

In a large bowl, using a pastry cutter, or in a food processor, blend flour, butter, shortening and salt until mixture resembles coarse meal. Add water, a bit at a time, until flour is moistened but dough is still rough and unformed. Turn onto a clean work surface and quickly form into a flat disk. Wrap in plastic wrap and refrigerate for 30 minutes. Roll out and bake as directed in the recipe you are using. **Makes 1 crust for a 9-inch (23 cm) pie.** *Store, tightly wrapped, in the refrigerator for up to 2 days or in the freezer for up to 1 month.*

Sweet Pastry

1½ cups	all-purpose flour	375 mL
6 tbsp	unsalted butter, cut into small pieces	90 mL
¼ cup	granulated sugar	50 mL
Pinch	salt	Pinch
1	extra-large egg	1
1 tsp	vanilla	5 mL

In a large bowl, using a pastry cutter, or in a food processor, blend flour, butter, sugar and salt until mixture resembles coarse meal. Beat in egg and vanilla until mixture is fully moistened. Turn onto a clean work surface and knead small handfuls of dough until smooth. Form into a flat disk, wrap in plastic wrap and refrigerate for 30 minutes. Roll out and bake as directed in the recipe you are using. **Makes 1 crust for a 9-inch (23 cm) pie.** *Store, tightly wrapped, in the refrigerator for up to 2 days or in the freezer for up to 1 month.*

Sweet or Flaky Pastry Shell

Prepare either of the two previous recipes. On a lightly floured board, using a floured rolling pin, roll out chilled pastry into a disk at least 12 inches (30 cm) in diameter. Roll pastry loosely around the pin and transfer to an 8-, 9- or 10-inch (20, 23 or 25 cm) tart or pie pan. Line pan with the pastry, crimp edges and poke holes in the bottom of the pastry with the tines of a fork. Freeze for 20 minutes. Line pastry with foil and weight with uncooked rice, dried beans or pastry weights. Bake in preheated 400°F (200°C) oven for 10 minutes. Remove foil and weights, reduce oven heat to 375°F (190°C) and bake until fully browned, about 30 minutes. (This is also known as a blind-baked pastry shell.) **Makes 1 shell.** *(For more detailed explanations of Forming a Pastry Shell, Forming a Tart Shell, Forming Tartlet Shells, Forming a Two-Crust Pie, and Blind-Baking, or Prebaking, Pastry Shells, see those entries in Basic Techniques for Cooking Anything, pages 12–13).*

Crumb Crust

3 cups	plain cookie crumbs (any type)	750 mL
¼ cup	unsalted butter, melted	50 mL
2 tbsp	confectioner's (icing) sugar	25 mL
1 tsp	ground cinnamon	5 mL

Preheat oven to 400°F (200°C). Combine all ingredients. Line the interior of a 9- to 10-inch (23 to 25 cm) pie pan by pressing in mixture in a firm, even layer. Line with foil and bake for 10 minutes. Remove foil and bake for 5 to 10 minutes, until lightly browned. Let cool. **Makes 1 crust.**

Pâtes à Choux (Cream Puff and Éclair Pastry)

1 cup	water	250 mL
½ cup	unsalted butter, cut into chunks	125 mL
Pinch	salt	Pinch
1 cup	all-purpose flour	250 mL
4 to 5	eggs	4 to 5

Preheat oven to 400°F (200°C). In a saucepan, bring water, butter and salt to a boil. Immediately add flour, beating vigorously until batter forms a ball in the center of the pan. Remove from heat and beat in eggs, one at a time, until mixture is smooth and glossy. Pipe through a pastry bag fitted with a wide tip, or spoon onto a baking sheet lined with parchment paper. Bake for 15 minutes, until browned and puffed. Reduce heat to 350°F (180°C) and bake for 15 minutes, until sides are firm. Reduce heat to 250°F (120°C), poke holes in pastry bottoms and bake for 30 minutes, until dried and crisp. **Makes 12 large éclairs or 24 cream puffs.**

Génoise (Sponge Cake)

6	extra-large eggs, separated	6
1 cup	granulated sugar	250 mL
1 tsp	vanilla	5 mL
¾ cup	twice-sifted all-purpose flour	175 mL
Pinch	salt	Pinch

Preheat oven to 350°F (180°C) and grease and flour a 9- or 10-inch (23 or 25 cm) round cake pan. In a large bowl, beat egg yolks and sugar until very light and fluffy. Stir in vanilla, then fold in flour just until combined. In a separate bowl, beat egg whites and salt until firm peaks form; fold into batter. Pour into prepared pan and bake for 20 to 25 minutes, or until edges pull away from sides and center is springy. Remove from pan to a rack and let cool. **Makes 1 cake.** *(You can also bake this batter on a greased and parchment-lined jellyroll pan for 15 minutes. Roll up in a damp towel to cool.)*

Pound Cake

3 cups	granulated sugar	750 mL
2 cups	unsalted butter, cut into small pieces	500 mL
1 tbsp	vanilla	15 mL
10	extra-large eggs	10
4 cups	sifted all-purpose flour	1 L
	Finely grated zest of 1 lemon (optional)	

Preheat oven to 350°F (180°C) and grease a 10-inch (4 L) tube pan or 10-inch (3 L) Bundt pan. In a large bowl, beat sugar and butter until light and fluffy. Stir in vanilla, then beat in eggs, one at a time. Stir in flour and lemon zest (if using) just until mixed. Bake for 1 hour and 45 minutes, until a tester inserted in the crust comes out clean. (If cake begins to brown too much, cover with foil.) Let cool in pan on a rack for 15 minutes, then remove from pan to rack and let cool completely. **Makes 1 large cake.**

Shortcake

4 cups	sifted all-purpose flour	1 L
½ cup	granulated sugar	125 mL
2 tbsp	baking powder	25 mL
2 tsp	baking soda	10 mL
½ tsp	salt	2 mL
1 cup	cold unsalted butter, cut into small pieces	250 mL
2	large eggs, lightly beaten	2
1 cup	cream (any type, minimum 10%)	250 mL
¼ cup	buttermilk	50 mL

Preheat oven to 375°F (190°C) and grease a 9-inch (23 cm) round cake pan. In a large bowl, sift together flour, sugar, baking powder, baking soda and salt. Cut in butter until mixture resembles coarse meal. In another bowl, combine eggs, cream and buttermilk. Mix enough of the liquid into the dry ingredients to form a soft, cohesive dough. With floured hands, pat into prepared pan and brush with the remaining liquid. Bake for 35 minutes, until lightly browned. Let cool in pan on a rack for 10 minutes, then remove from pan to rack and let cool completely. Using a long serrated knife, slice cake in half horizontally. (This cake cracks easily, so handle carefully; if it breaks, push it back together.) **Serves 8 to 10.**

Shortcake Biscuits

Prepare dough as in preceding recipe, but halve the quantity of each ingredient. Pat dough out on a floured work surface and, using a biscuit cutter, cut out eight to ten 3-inch (7.5 cm) circles. Brush tops with reserved egg mixture and a sprinkling of additional granulated sugar. Place on a baking sheet and bake at 450°F (230°C) for 20 minutes, until lightly browned. **Serves 8 to 10.**

Cornbread

1 cup	yellow cornmeal	250 mL
1 cup	all-purpose flour	250 mL
¼ cup	granulated sugar	50 mL
4 tsp	baking powder	20 mL
½ tsp	salt	2 mL

1/3 cup	vegetable oil, divided	75 mL
1/2 cup	chopped onion	125 mL
1/2 cup	finely diced red bell pepper	125 mL
1/2 cup	finely diced green bell pepper	125 mL
1	extra-large egg, beaten	1
1 cup	milk	250 mL

Preheat oven to 400°F (200°C) and grease and flour a 9- by 5-inch (2 L) loaf pan. In a large bowl, combine cornmeal, flour, sugar, baking powder and salt; set aside. In a skillet, heat 1 tbsp (15 mL) of the oil over medium heat. Sauté onion and red and green peppers until tender. Stir into dry ingredients, then stir in the remaining oil, egg and milk. Pour into prepared pan and bake for 25 minutes, until a tester inserted in the center comes out with just a crumb clinging to it. Let cool in pan on a rack for 10 minutes. **Serves 6.**

Toasted Nuts

In conventional oven: Bake whole nuts in a pie plate at 350°F (180°C) for 15 minutes (sliced or slivered nuts for 10 minutes), stirring twice. *On stovetop:* Heat a heavy iron skillet over high heat for 4 minutes. Remove from heat, add nuts and stir constantly for 1 to 3 minutes, until nuts color. *In microwave:* Place 1 cup (250 mL) whole nuts in a shallow glass pie plate and microwave on High for 5 minutes (sliced or slivered nuts for 4 minutes), stirring twice.

Streusel or Crumb Topping

3/4 cup	all-purpose flour	175 mL
1/3 cup	packed brown sugar	75 mL
1/4 cup	cold unsalted butter, cut into small pieces	50 mL

Combine flour and brown sugar. Cut in butter until mixture resembles coarse meal. **Makes about 1 1/4 cups (300 mL).**

Nut Streusel Topping

Follow preceding recipe, but decrease the flour to 1/4 cup (50 mL), and add 1 1/2 cups (375 mL) chopped nuts (any variety) with the flour. **Makes about 2 1/4 cups (550 mL).**

Simple Syrup

2/3 cup	granulated sugar	150 mL
2/3 cup	water	150 mL

In a saucepan, bring sugar and water to a boil over medium-high heat, without stirring. Boil for 1 minute. Let cool. **Makes about 1 cup (250 mL).** *Use as a base for desserts or for moistening cakes, or add to cocktails.*

Fruit Glaze

1 cup	apricot preserves, orange marmalade or red currant jelly	250 mL
2 tbsp	granulated sugar	25 mL
2 tbsp	liqueur (any variety)	25 mL

In a small saucepan, melt preserves, sugar and liqueur over medium heat. Simmer for 3 minutes, then strain. Use while warm to glaze tarts or pastries. **Makes enough to glaze two 9- or 10-inch (23 or 25 cm) tarts.**

Chocolate Glaze

6 tbsp	unsalted butter	90 mL
2 oz	semisweet chocolate, finely chopped	60 g
2 oz	unsweetened chocolate, finely chopped	60 g
1 tbsp	honey	15 mL

In a saucepan, melt butter over medium heat. Remove from heat and stir in semisweet chocolate, unsweetened chocolate and honey until smooth. Place over a bowl of ice water and stir until slightly thickened. To coat a cake, place cake on a rack over a drip pan, brush away any crumbs, and, using an icing spatula, spread glaze evenly over top, letting some run down the sides. Smooth sides, covering all surfaces with glaze. Transfer cake to a platter. **Makes enough to cover 2 tortes or 1 large cake.**

Quick Buttercream

2 cups	confectioner's (icing) sugar	500 mL
6 tbsp	unsalted butter, softened	90 mL
2 to 3 tbsp	milk, brewed coffee, freshly squeezed lemon juice or liqueur	25 to 45 mL
1 tsp	vanilla	5 mL
Pinch	salt	Pinch

Beat all ingredients until fluffy. **Makes enough to frost one 9-inch (23 cm) cake layer.**

French Buttercream

6	large or extra-large egg yolks	6
2/3 cup	granulated sugar	150 mL
1/3 cup	water	75 mL
1 1/2 cups	unsalted butter, softened	375 mL

Using the whisk attachment of an electric mixer, beat egg yolks until fluffy. In a heavy saucepan, bring sugar and water to a boil; boil for about 4 minutes, until mixture reaches 240°F (115°C) on a candy thermometer, or until it's thick enough to form a loose blob when a small amount is dropped in a glass of water. Slowly pour hot syrup into egg yolks while beating at high speed; continue beating until mixture cools to just a little warmer than room temperature. Beat in butter, 1 tbsp (15 mL) at a time, until fluffy. **Makes enough to frost 1 large cake.**

Chocolate Sour Cream Frosting

1/2 cup	sour cream, at room temperature	125 mL
1 cup	semisweet chocolate chips, melted (see page 14)	250 mL

Beat sour cream into melted chocolate. **Makes enough to frost one 9-inch (23 cm) cake layer.**

Pastry Cream

1 cup	milk (not fat-free)	250 mL
6 tbsp	granulated sugar, divided	90 mL
Pinch	salt	Pinch
3	egg yolks	3
2 tbsp	cornstarch	25 mL
1 tbsp	all-purpose flour	15 mL
1 tsp	vanilla	5 mL

In a small, heavy saucepan, heat milk, half the sugar and salt over medium heat until bubbles form at the edges. Meanwhile, in a stainless steel or enamel-coated saucepan, beat egg yolks and the remaining sugar until slightly thickened. Stir in cornstarch and flour until smooth. Stir in hot milk mixture in a slow, steady stream. Cook over medium heat, stirring constantly with a wooden spoon, until mixture comes to a boil. Beat lumps out with a whisk. Transfer to a bowl and stir in vanilla. Cover loosely with plastic wrap and refrigerate for about 1 hour, until chilled. **Makes about 1 1/2 cups (375 mL).** *Use as a filling for pastry.*

Lemon Curd

2	egg yolks	2
1 cup	granulated sugar, divided	250 mL
	Juice of 1 lemon	
1 1/2 cups	water	375 mL
2 tbsp	cornstarch	25 mL
1/4 cup	unsalted butter, softened	50 mL
1 tbsp	finely grated lemon zest	15 mL
1 tsp	vanilla	5 mL

Beat egg yolks, half the sugar and the lemon juice until pale and light in texture. In an enamel-coated saucepan, combine the remaining sugar, water and cornstarch; cook over medium heat, stirring frequently, until very thick. Beat in yolk mixture in a slow, steady stream. Reduce heat to low and cook, stirring constantly, for 3 minutes. Remove from heat and stir in butter, lemon zest and vanilla. Let cool completely. **Makes 2 cups (500 mL).** *Use as a filling for pastry.*

Crème Anglaise

1 cup	milk	250 mL
1 cup	cream (any type, minimum 10%)	250 mL
2/3 cup	granulated sugar, divided	150 mL
6	egg yolks	6
Pinch	salt	Pinch
1 tsp	vanilla	5 mL

In a heavy saucepan, heat milk, cream and half the sugar over medium heat until bubbles form at the edges. Meanwhile, in the top of a double boiler, beat egg yolks, the remaining sugar and salt until thick and pale. Slowly whisk in hot milk mixture. Place over simmering water and cook, stirring with a wooden spoon, until custard lightly coats spoon (or reaches 180°F/82°C). Immediately pour into a bowl and stir in vanilla. Serve warm or let cool. **Makes about 2 1/2 cups (625 mL).** *Use as a sauce with fresh fruit.*

PART 2

Cooking Basics

Chapter 1
Marinades
Infinite Variations on Basic Ingredients

Lemon Cilantro Marinade 28
Lemon Basil Marinade 28
Lemon Garlic Marinade 29
Lime Jalapeño Marinade 29
Lime Caper Marinade 29
Orange Walnut Marinade 29
Orange Tarragon Marinade 29
Spicy Citrus Marinade 29
Provençal Marinade 30
Jerk Marinade 30
Super-Spicy Jerk Marinade 30
Jerk Citrus Marinade 30
Ginger Soy Marinade 30
Sweet Sesame Marinade 30
Tangerine Teriyaki 30
Apricot Marinade 31
Sweet Tomato Marinade 31
Apple and Spice Marinade 31
All-American Barbecue Marinade 31
Sweet-and-Sour Barbecue Marinade . . . 31
Fruity Barbecue Marinade 31
Smoky Tomato Barbecue Marinade 31
Hot-and-Sour Barbecue Marinade 32
Southwest Barbecue Marinade 32
Hot, Hot, Hot Barbecue Paste 32

Wine Barbecue Marinade 32
Easy Red Wine Marinade 32
Easy White Wine Marinade 32
White Wine Fines Herbes Marinade 32
Garlic and Wine Marinade 33
Hearty Red Wine Marinade 33
Dill Mustard Marinade 33
Honey Mustard Marinade 33
Spicy Apple Butter Marinade 33
Orange Cranberry Marinade 33
Pickling Marinade 33
Asian Peanut Marinade 34
Chipotle Peanut Marinade 34
Curry Marinade 34
Mint and Anise Marinade 34
Red Curry Marinade 34
Tandoori Curry Marinade 34
Sweet Garlic Paste 34
Chili Marinade 35
Yogurt, Garlic and Mint Marinade 35
Coriander Marinade 35
Basic Dry Rub 35
Citrus Dry Rub 35
Moroccan Dry Rub 35
Charcuterie Dry Rub 35

Good cooks work with food and a thought. Fine ingredients are essential, but they bring us only so far. The right equipment is important, but it does not make a dish great. Skill with a skillet and a well-honed knife can overcome much that is lacking in a kitchen. But if the cook does not think, the food will not come to life.

We breathe life into our ingredients by storing them properly and by using a cooking technique that complements their natural qualities, but most importantly by choosing a flavor direction that brings them to the table newly born.

It is our vision that every cook has the potential to come up with hundreds of culinary creations, and it is our mission in this book to help those visions take form, so we can think of no better first chapter than one that puts the exponential power of marinades at your fingertips.

Let's talk about flavor. Roast chicken is just roast chicken until it becomes roast chicken with a curry glaze, or roast chicken stuffed with peaches and almonds, or roast chicken in bourbon beurre blanc, or cold roast chicken in chilied aspic, or chicken barded with wild mushrooms, or chicken roasted with woodruff and cranberries, or chicken salad with roasted garlic, or chicken flamed with mustard and brandy, or chicken and mussels cacciatore, or anything that complements the flavor of the meat and fulfills the cook's vision of what a mere chicken can become.

All marinades take one of four forms — oily, acidic, salty or sweet. But most are a combination of two or more of these forms. Marinades for fatty or tough meats tend to be salty or acidic. Fish marinades are typically acidic and oily. Marinades for vegetables should be oily, as should those used on grilled foods. Sweet marinades require strongly flavored ingredients. Chicken and beef, and vegetables such as carrot, onion and yam, all work well with sweet marinades.

About these recipes . . .

These marinades are grouped by the type of ingredient from which they are made. Once marinated, the main ingredient may be roasted, grilled, sautéed, broiled, steamed, fried or cooked in any other way you wish. Each recipe yields enough to marinate 4 servings of the main ingredient. Always marinate in the refrigerator to prevent spoilage, and time your marination according to the thickness and density of the ingredient. Most

fish, for example, will pick up the flavors of a marinade in an hour or less, while beef or pork steaks may need several hours or overnight. It is safe to store marinades in the refrigerator for up to 2 months.

Technically, there are only 50 recipes below, but in reality there are hundreds, for each recipe is followed by a parenthetical list of abbreviations that indicates the main ingredients for which that marinade would be well suited. Here is the key to those abbreviations:

B = Beef
C = Chicken
D = Duck
F = Fish
FR = Fruit
G = Game Meat
L = Lamb
P = Pork
S = Shellfish
T = Turkey
V = Veal
VG = Vegetable

Lemon Cilantro Marinade

4	cloves garlic, minced	4
1/3 cup	olive oil	75 mL
1 tsp	ground coriander	5 mL
	Salt and freshly ground black pepper to taste	
1 cup	dry white wine	250 mL
1/4 cup	chopped fresh cilantro	50 mL
	Grated zest and juice of 1 lemon	

Combine garlic, oil, coriander, salt and pepper; mix into a thin paste. Mix in wine, cilantro, lemon zest and lemon juice. **Makes about 1½ cups (375 mL).** (C, F, S, T, VG)

Lemon Basil Marinade

4	cloves garlic, minced	4
1/3 cup	olive oil	75 mL
1 tsp	ground fennel seeds	5 mL
	Salt and freshly ground black pepper to taste	
1 cup	dry white wine	250 mL
1/4 cup	chopped fresh basil	50 mL
	Grated zest and juice of 1 lemon	

Combine garlic, oil, fennel seeds, salt and pepper; mix into a thin paste. Mix in wine, basil, lemon zest and lemon juice. **Makes about 1½ cups (375 mL).** *(C, F, S, T, V, VG)*

Lemon Garlic Marinade

4	cloves garlic, minced	4
2	green onions, sliced	2
⅓ cup	olive oil	75 mL
	Salt and freshly ground black pepper to taste	
1 cup	dry white wine	250 mL
2 tbsp	chopped fresh Italian (flat-leaf) parsley	25 mL
	Grated zest and juice of 1 lemon	

Combine garlic, green onions, oil, salt and pepper; mix into a thin paste. Mix in wine, parsley, lemon zest and lemon juice. **Makes about 1½ cups (375 mL).** *(C, F, P, S, T, V, VG)*

Lime Jalapeño Marinade

4	cloves garlic, minced	4
1	jalapeño pepper, seeded and minced	1
⅓ cup	olive oil	75 mL
	Salt and freshly ground black pepper to taste	
1 cup	dry white wine	250 mL
¼ cup	chopped fresh cilantro	50 mL
	Grated zest and juice of 1 lime	

Combine garlic, jalapeño, oil, salt and pepper; mix into a thin paste. Mix in wine, cilantro, lime zest and lime juice. **Makes about 1½ cups (375 mL).** *(C, D, F, P, S, T, V, VG)*

Lime Caper Marinade

4	cloves garlic, minced	4
⅓ cup	extra-virgin olive oil	75 mL
1 tsp	chopped fresh chives	5 mL
Pinch	hot pepper flakes	Pinch
	Salt and freshly ground black pepper to taste	
1 cup	dry white wine	250 mL
¼ cup	drained whole capers	50 mL
	Grated zest and juice of 1 lime	

Combine garlic, oil, chives, hot pepper flakes, salt and black pepper; mix into a thin paste. Mix in wine, capers, lime zest and lime juice. **Makes about 1½ cups (375 mL).** *(C, D, F, P, S, T, V)*

Orange Walnut Marinade

4	cloves garlic, minced	4
⅓ cup	walnut oil	75 mL
1 tsp	dried basil	5 mL
1 tsp	ground fennel seeds	5 mL
½ tsp	hot pepper flakes	2 mL
	Salt and freshly ground black pepper to taste	
1 cup	dry white wine	250 mL
¼ cup	ground walnuts	50 mL
	Grated zest and juice of 1 orange	

Combine garlic, oil, basil, fennel seeds, hot pepper flakes, salt and black pepper; mix into a thin paste. Mix in wine, walnuts, orange zest and orange juice. **Makes about 1½ cups (375 mL).** *(B, C, D, F, FR, L, P, S, T, V)*

Orange Tarragon Marinade

2	shallots, minced	2
1	clove garlic, minced	1
⅓ cup	canola oil	75 mL
2 tsp	dried tarragon	10 mL
1 tsp	dried chervil	5 mL
	Salt and freshly ground black pepper to taste	
1 cup	dry white wine	250 mL
2 tbsp	chopped fresh Italian (flat-leaf) parsley	25 mL
	Grated zest and juice of 1 orange	

Combine shallots, garlic, oil, tarragon, chervil, salt and pepper; mix into a thin paste. Mix in wine, parsley, orange zest and orange juice. **Makes about 1⅔ cups (400 mL).** *(C, F, FR, S, T, V)*

Spicy Citrus Marinade

2	cloves garlic, minced	2
¼ cup	minced onion	50 mL
⅓ cup	olive oil	75 mL
1 tsp	dried dillweed	5 mL
1 tsp	hot pepper flakes	5 mL
	Salt and freshly ground black pepper to taste	
2 tbsp	chopped fresh Italian (flat-leaf) parsley	25 mL
	Grated zest and juice of 1 orange, 1 lemon and 1 lime	

Combine garlic, onion, oil, dill, hot pepper flakes, salt and black pepper; mix into a thin paste. Mix in parsley, citrus zests and citrus juices. **Makes about ¾ cup (175 mL).** *(C, D, F, S, T, VG)*

Provençal Marinade

3	cloves garlic, minced	3
2	drained canned anchovies, mashed	2
1 tsp	dried herbes de Provence	5 mL
Pinch	hot pepper flakes	Pinch
	Salt and freshly ground black pepper to taste	
½ cup	dry white wine	125 mL
½ cup	canned crushed tomato, with juice	125 mL
¼ cup	extra-virgin olive oil	50 mL
	Grated zest of ½ orange	

Combine garlic, anchovies, herbes de Provence, hot pepper flakes, salt and black pepper. Mix in wine, tomato and juice, oil and orange zest. **Makes about 1⅓ cups (325 mL).** (C, F, S, V, VG)

Jerk Marinade

1½ tsp	coriander seeds	7 mL
1½ tsp	cumin seeds	7 mL
½ tsp	whole black peppercorns	2 mL
¼ tsp	hot pepper flakes	1 mL
1	whole clove	1
¼ cup	chopped fresh Italian (flat-leaf) parsley	50 mL
1 tbsp	packed brown sugar (light or dark)	15 mL
1 tbsp	ground allspice	15 mL
3 tbsp	ketchup	45 mL
2 tbsp	soy sauce	25 mL
2 tbsp	vegetable oil	25 mL
1 tbsp	dark rum	15 mL
2 tsp	chopped gingerroot	10 mL
1 tsp	hot pepper sauce (such as Tabasco)	5 mL
½ tsp	salt	2 mL

In a dry skillet, over high heat, toast coriander seeds, cumin seeds, peppercorns, hot pepper flakes and clove, shaking pan constantly, until lightly colored and aromatic, about 1 minute. Grind well and strain out hulls. Mix into a paste with the remaining ingredients. **Makes about ¾ cup (175 mL).** (B, C, D, F, G, P, S, T, V)

Super-Spicy Jerk Marinade

Follow preceding recipe, but add 2 dried chili peppers to the spices for toasting, and increase the peppercorns to 1 tsp (5 mL). **Makes about ¾ cup (175 mL).** (B, C, D, F, G, P, S, T)

Jerk Citrus Marinade

Follow recipe for Jerk Marinade (left), but replace 2 tbsp (25 mL) of the ketchup with lime juice or grapefruit juice. **Makes about ¾ cup (175 mL).** (C, D, F, G, P, S, T, V)

Ginger Soy Marinade

¼ cup	soy sauce	50 mL
¼ cup	rice vinegar	50 mL
¼ cup	honey	50 mL
¼ cup	water	50 mL
1½ tbsp	grated gingerroot	22 mL
1 tbsp	canola oil	15 mL
1 tbsp	dry sherry	15 mL
1 tsp	sesame oil	5 mL
½ tsp	ground ginger	2 mL
¼ tsp	Chinese chili paste	1 mL

Combine all ingredients. **Makes about 1 cup (250 mL).** (C, F, P, S, T, VG)

Sweet Sesame Marinade

Follow preceding recipe, but replace the gingerroot with toasted sesame seeds. **Makes about 1 cup (250 mL).** (C, F, P, S, T, V, VG)

Tangerine Teriyaki

¼ cup	soy sauce	50 mL
¼ cup	honey	50 mL
¼ cup	water	50 mL
1 tbsp	grated tangerine zest	15 mL
3 tbsp	freshly squeezed tangerine juice	45 mL
1 tbsp	rice vinegar	15 mL
1 tbsp	peanut oil	15 mL
1 tbsp	dry sherry	15 mL
1½ tsp	grated gingerroot	7 mL
1 tsp	sesame oil	5 mL
½ tsp	ground ginger	2 mL
¼ tsp	Chinese chili paste	1 mL

Combine all ingredients. **Makes about 1 cup (250 mL).** (C, D, F, P, S, V)

Apricot Marinade

1 tbsp	vegetable oil	15 mL
¼ cup	finely chopped onion	50 mL
6	drops hot pepper sauce (such as Tabasco)	6
2	cloves garlic, minced	2
1 cup	apricot preserves	250 mL
3 tbsp	almond oil (or other nut oil)	45 mL
1½ tbsp	Worcestershire sauce	22 mL
	Salt and freshly ground black pepper to taste	
	Juice of 1 lemon	

In a small skillet, heat vegetable oil over medium heat. Sauté onion until tender; remove from heat. Add hot pepper sauce, garlic, apricot preserves, almond oil, Worcestershire sauce, salt, pepper and lemon juice. **Makes about 1½ cups (375 mL).** (C, D, L, P, S, T, V)

Sweet Tomato Marinade

Follow preceding recipe, but replace the almond oil with olive oil, replace the apricot preserves with ketchup, and add 1 tbsp (15 mL) honey. **Makes about 1½ cups (375 mL).** (B, C, L, P, T)

Apple and Spice Marinade

Follow recipe for Apricot Marinade (above), but replace the almond oil with walnut oil and the apricot preserves with apple butter. **Makes about 1½ cups (375 mL).** (B, C, D, G, L, P)

All-American Barbecue Marinade

1 cup	ketchup	250 mL
¼ cup	finely chopped onion	50 mL
1 tbsp	packed dark brown sugar	15 mL
2 tbsp	spicy brown mustard	25 mL
2 tbsp	cider vinegar	25 mL
1 tbsp	vegetable oil	15 mL
1 tbsp	light (fancy) molasses	15 mL
1 tbsp	Worcestershire sauce	15 mL
2 tsp	hot pepper sauce (such as Tabasco)	10 mL
	Salt and freshly ground black pepper to taste	

In a small saucepan, combine ketchup, onion, brown sugar, mustard, vinegar, oil, molasses, Worcestershire sauce and hot pepper sauce. Bring to a boil over medium heat, stirring often. Season with salt and pepper. Let cool completely. **Makes about 1½ cups (375 mL).** (B, C, P, V)

Sweet-and-Sour Barbecue Marinade

¼ cup	finely chopped onion	50 mL
¼ cup	packed light brown sugar	50 mL
¼ cup	ketchup	50 mL
¼ cup	cider vinegar	50 mL
¼ cup	orange marmalade	50 mL
1 tbsp	vegetable oil	15 mL
1 tbsp	steak sauce	15 mL
2 tsp	hot pepper sauce (such as Tabasco)	10 mL
	Salt and freshly ground black pepper to taste	

In a small saucepan, combine onion, brown sugar, ketchup, vinegar, marmalade, oil, steak sauce and hot pepper sauce. Bring to a boil over medium heat, stirring often. Season with salt and pepper. Let cool completely. **Makes about 1¼ cups (300 mL).** (B, C, L, P, S)

Fruity Barbecue Marinade

1 cup	apricot preserves	250 mL
¼ cup	finely chopped onion	50 mL
2 tbsp	cider vinegar	25 mL
2 tbsp	soy sauce	25 mL
1 tbsp	vegetable oil	15 mL
2 tsp	hot pepper sauce (such as Tabasco)	10 mL
	Salt and freshly ground black pepper to taste	

In a small saucepan, combine apricot preserves, onion, vinegar, soy sauce, oil and hot pepper sauce. Bring to a boil over medium heat, stirring often. Season with salt and pepper. Let cool completely. **Makes about 1⅓ cups (325 mL).** (B, C, L, P, S)

Smoky Tomato Barbecue Marinade

4	slices bacon, cooked crisp and crumbled	4
1	clove garlic, minced	1
¼ cup	finely chopped onion	50 mL
1 cup	ketchup	250 mL
¼ cup	honey	50 mL
2 tbsp	spicy brown mustard	25 mL
2 tbsp	cider vinegar	25 mL
2 tsp	hot pepper sauce (such as Tabasco)	10 mL
	Salt and freshly ground black pepper to taste	

In a small saucepan, combine bacon, garlic, onion, ketchup, honey, mustard, vinegar and hot pepper sauce. Bring to a boil over medium heat, stirring often. Season with salt and pepper. Let cool completely. **Makes about 1½ cups (375 mL).** (B, C, L, P, S, V)

Hot-and-Sour Barbecue Marinade

2	cloves garlic	2
1	red bell pepper, coarsely chopped	1
1	jalapeño pepper, seeded and coarsely chopped	1
½ cup	coarsely chopped onion	125 mL
⅔ cup	water	150 mL
¼ cup	cider vinegar	50 mL
2 tbsp	vegetable oil	25 mL
1 tbsp	honey	15 mL
Pinch	ground allspice	Pinch
	Salt and freshly ground black pepper to taste	

In a food processor, mince garlic, red pepper, jalapeño and onion. Transfer to a small saucepan and add water, vinegar, oil, honey and allspice; simmer, stirring often, for about 10 minutes, or until slightly thickened. Season with salt and pepper. Let cool completely. **Makes about 1¼ cups (300 mL).** *(B, C, F, P, S, V)*

Southwest Barbecue Marinade

Follow preceding recipe, but replace the allspice with 1 tsp (5 mL) ground cumin, and add 2 tbsp (25 mL) chopped fresh cilantro after cooking. **Makes about 1 cup (250 mL).** *(C, F, P, S, V)*

Hot, Hot, Hot Barbecue Paste

3	cloves garlic	3
2	jalapeño peppers, seeded and coarsely chopped	2
1	red bell pepper, coarsely chopped	1
½ cup	chopped onion	125 mL
2 to 4 tbsp	hot pepper flakes	25 to 50 mL
1 tbsp	granulated sugar	15 mL
2 tbsp	cider vinegar	25 mL
1 tbsp	vegetable oil	15 mL
½ tsp	ground cumin	2 mL
	Salt and freshly ground black pepper to taste	

In a food processor, mince garlic, jalapeños, red pepper and onion. Transfer to a small saucepan and add hot pepper flakes to taste, sugar, vinegar, oil and cumin; simmer, stirring often, for 10 minutes, or until slightly thickened. Season with salt and black pepper. Let cool completely. **Makes about 1 cup (250 mL).** *(B, C, D, F, P, S)*

Wine Barbecue Marinade

1	clove garlic, minced	1
½ cup	chopped onion	125 mL
¾ cup	dry red wine	175 mL
¼ cup	red wine vinegar	50 mL
¼ cup	ketchup	50 mL
1 tbsp	granulated sugar	15 mL
2 tbsp	Worcestershire sauce	25 mL
1 tbsp	steak sauce	15 mL
1 tsp	brown mustard	5 mL
½ tsp	dried thyme	2 mL
Pinch	ground allspice	Pinch
1	bay leaf	1
	Salt and freshly ground black pepper to taste	

In a small saucepan, combine all ingredients; bring to a boil over medium heat. Reduce heat and simmer, stirring often, for 5 minutes. Remove bay leaf. Let cool completely. **Makes about 1⅔ cups (400 mL).** *(B, C, D, G, P)*

Easy Red Wine Marinade

1	clove garlic, minced	1
1 cup	finely chopped onion	250 mL
1 cup	dry red wine	250 mL
3 tbsp	olive oil	45 mL
2 tbsp	steak sauce	25 mL
1 tsp	freshly ground black pepper	5 mL
	Salt to taste	

Combine all ingredients. **Makes about 1⅓ cups (325 mL).** *(B, C, D, G, P)*

Easy White Wine Marinade

Follow preceding recipe, but use dry white wine instead of red and soy sauce instead of steak sauce. **Makes about 1⅓ cups (325 mL).** *(C, F, P, S, T, V)*

White Wine Fines Herbes Marinade

1	large onion, finely chopped	1
1	clove garlic, minced	1
1 cup	dry white wine	250 mL
3 tbsp	extra-virgin olive oil	45 mL
1 tbsp	chopped fresh Italian (flat-leaf) parsley	15 mL
2 tsp	chopped fresh basil	10 mL
2 tsp	chopped fresh thyme	10 mL
1 tsp	chopped fresh tarragon	5 mL
1 tsp	freshly ground black pepper	5 mL
	Salt to taste	

Combine all ingredients. **Makes about 1¾ cups (425 mL).** *(B, C, F, P, S, T)*

Garlic and Wine Marinade

Follow preceding recipe, but increase garlic to 3 cloves, and omit the thyme and tarragon. **Makes about 1¾ cups (425 mL).** *(C, F, S, T, V, VG)*

Hearty Red Wine Marinade

12	juniper berries, crushed	12
10	whole black peppercorns, cracked	10
6	whole cloves	6
1	carrot, sliced	1
1	bay leaf	1
½ cup	thinly sliced onion	125 mL
3 cups	full-bodied red wine	750 mL
¼ cup	red wine vinegar	50 mL
2 tbsp	packed brown sugar	25 mL
2 tsp	chopped fresh Italian (flat-leaf) parsley	10 mL
¼ tsp	dried thyme	1 mL
¼ cup	cognac	50 mL
	Salt to taste	

In a small saucepan, combine juniper berries, peppercorns, cloves, carrot, bay leaf, onion, wine, vinegar, brown sugar, parsley and thyme; simmer for 10 minutes. In a small skillet, heat cognac over medium-high heat; carefully ignite it, then add it to the marinade. Season with salt and remove bay leaf. Let cool completely. **Makes about 3 cups (750 mL).** *(B, D, G, L, P)*

Dill Mustard Marinade

2	cloves garlic, minced	2
¼ cup	chopped fresh dill	50 mL
¼ cup	olive oil	50 mL
3 tbsp	Dijon mustard	45 mL
2 tbsp	white wine vinegar	25 mL
	Salt and freshly ground black pepper to taste	

Using a whisk, combine all ingredients until smooth. **Makes about 1 cup (250 mL).** *(C, F, S, T, V, VG)*

Honey Mustard Marinade

6 tbsp	spicy brown mustard	90 mL
3 tbsp	honey	45 mL
1 tbsp	Worcestershire sauce	15 mL
	Salt and freshly ground black pepper to taste	

Combine all ingredients. **Makes about ⅔ cup (150 mL).** *(C, D, L, P, T, V)*

Spicy Apple Butter Marinade

¼ cup	apple butter	50 mL
2 tbsp	honey	25 mL
2 tsp	vegetable oil	10 mL
1 tsp	spicy brown mustard	5 mL
	Salt and freshly ground black pepper to taste	

Combine all ingredients. **Makes about ½ cup (125 mL).** *(B, C, D, L, P)*

Orange Cranberry Marinade

¼ cup	orange marmalade	50 mL
¼ cup	whole-berry cranberry sauce	50 mL
1 tbsp	grated orange zest	15 mL
1 tbsp	honey	15 mL
1 tbsp	soy sauce	15 mL
1 tbsp	cider vinegar	15 mL
Dash	hot pepper sauce (such as Tabasco)	Dash

Combine all ingredients. **Makes about ¾ cup (175 mL).** *(C, D, P, T, V)*

Pickling Marinade

10	whole black peppercorns, cracked	10
10	whole coriander seeds, cracked	10
6	whole cloves	6
3	bay leaves	3
3	cloves garlic, minced	3
2	small dried chili peppers	2
1	slice bacon	1
1 cup	water	250 mL
½ cup	thinly sliced onion	125 mL
¼ cup	red wine vinegar	50 mL
2 tbsp	packed brown sugar	25 mL
1 tbsp	yellow mustard seeds	15 mL
1 tbsp	kosher salt	15 mL
1 tbsp	chopped fresh Italian (flat-leaf) parsley	15 mL

In a saucepan, combine all ingredients; bring to a boil over medium heat. Reduce heat and simmer for 10 minutes, or until slightly thickened. Let cool, then remove bay leaves, chili peppers and bacon. **Makes about 1⅓ cups (325 mL).** *(B, C, D, P, T)*

Asian Peanut Marinade

1 tbsp	peanut oil	15 mL
½ cup	chopped onion	125 mL
1	clove garlic, minced	1
2 tsp	grated gingerroot	10 mL
1 tsp	ground coriander	5 mL
½ tsp	hot pepper flakes	2 mL
⅓ cup	peanut butter (chunky or smooth)	75 mL
¼ cup	water	50 mL
1 tbsp	orange marmalade	15 mL
1 tbsp	soy sauce	15 mL
2 tsp	rice wine vinegar	10 mL

In a skillet, heat oil over medium heat. Sauté onion until tender. Add garlic, ginger, coriander and hot pepper flakes; sauté for 1 minute. Stir in peanut butter, water, marmalade, soy sauce and vinegar; cook, stirring, until peanut butter has melted. Let cool completely. **Makes about ¾ cup (175 mL).** *(C, F, P, S, T, V)*

Chipotle Peanut Marinade

2	canned chipotle peppers in adobo sauce	2
¾ cup	canned tomato purée or crushed tomatoes	175 mL
2 tbsp	Chinese chili paste with garlic	25 mL
2 tbsp	packed brown sugar	25 mL
2 tbsp	peanut butter (chunky or smooth)	25 mL
2 tbsp	cider vinegar	25 mL
1 tbsp	chopped fresh cilantro	15 mL

In a food processor, purée chipotles, tomato purée and chili paste. Add brown sugar, peanut butter, vinegar and cilantro; process until smooth. **Makes about 1 cup (250 mL).** *(B, C, L, P, T)*

Curry Marinade

2 tbsp	vegetable oil	25 mL
1 cup	chopped onion	250 mL
1½ tsp	finely chopped gingerroot	7 mL
1 tsp	yellow mustard seeds	5 mL
1	clove garlic, minced	1
2 tsp	curry powder	10 mL
1 tsp	ground coriander	5 mL
1 tsp	ground cumin	5 mL
Pinch	hot pepper flakes	Pinch
2 tbsp	chopped fresh cilantro	25 mL
2 tbsp	freshly squeezed lemon juice	25 mL
	Salt and freshly ground black pepper to taste	
½ cup	plain yogurt	125 mL

In a skillet, heat oil over medium-high heat. Sauté onion, ginger and mustard seeds until onion is tender and mustard seeds pop. Add garlic, curry powder, coriander, cumin and hot pepper flakes; cook, stirring frequently, for 2 minutes. Add cilantro, lemon juice, salt and black pepper; heat through, then let cool completely. Mix in yogurt. **Makes about 1⅓ cups (325 mL).** *(C, F, L, P, S, V, VG)*

Mint and Anise Marinade

Follow preceding recipe, but reduce the curry powder to 1 tsp (5 mL), replace the cumin with ground anise seeds, increase the hot pepper flakes to ¼ tsp (1 mL), replace the cilantro with mint, and omit the lemon juice. **Makes about 1½ cups (375 mL).** *(C, L, S, P, V)*

Red Curry Marinade

1	can (14 oz/398 mL) coconut milk	1
3 tbsp	Thai red curry paste	45 mL
2 tsp	Chinese chili paste with garlic	10 mL
1 tbsp	Thai fish sauce (*nam pla*)	15 mL
	Juice of 1 lemon	

In a small skillet, combine coconut milk, curry paste and chili paste; simmer for 2 minutes. Remove from heat and blend in fish sauce and lemon juice. Let cool completely. **Makes about 2 cups (500 mL).** *(C, F, P, S, T, V, VG)*

Tandoori Curry Marinade

2	cloves garlic, minced	2
½ cup	plain yogurt	125 mL
2 tbsp	minced gingerroot	25 mL
2 tsp	curry powder	10 mL
1 tsp	ground cumin	5 mL
1 tsp	ground cardamom	5 mL
1 tsp	paprika (sweet or hot)	5 mL
1 tsp	salt	5 mL
	Juice of 1 small lemon	

Combine all ingredients. **Makes about 1 cup (250 mL).** *(C, D, L, P, T, V, G)*

Sweet Garlic Paste

2	large heads garlic	2
2 tbsp	olive oil, divided	25 mL
Pinch	hot pepper flakes	Pinch
1 tbsp	honey	15 mL
1 tsp	wine vinegar	5 mL
	Salt and freshly ground black pepper to taste	

Cut the pointed ends from the garlic heads, exposing the tops of the cloves. Rub the exposed cloves of each head with 1 tsp (5 mL) of the oil. Wrap in foil and bake at 375°F (190°C) for 40 minutes, or until soft to the touch. Let cool slightly, gently squeeze cloves from their peels and mash with a small fork. In a small skillet, over medium heat, heat the remaining oil with the hot pepper flakes until bubbles form at edges of pepper; add to garlic. Stir in honey and vinegar. Season with salt and pepper. Let cool completely. **Makes about ½ cup (125 mL).** *(B, C, D, F, L, P, S, T, VG)*

Chili Marinade

1 tbsp	canola or vegetable oil	15 mL
2	chili peppers (canned or fresh), finely chopped	2
1	large onion, chopped	1
1	clove garlic, minced	1
3 to 4 tbsp	chili powder	45 to 60 mL
1 tbsp	ground cumin	15 mL
2 tsp	dried oregano	10 mL
1 tsp	ground coriander	5 mL
	Salt and freshly ground black pepper to taste	

In a skillet, heat oil over medium heat. Sauté chili peppers and onion until tender. Add garlic, chili powder to taste, cumin, oregano and coriander; sauté for 1 minute. Season with salt and pepper. Let cool completely. **Makes about 1 cup (250 mL).** *(C, F, P, S, T)*

Yogurt, Garlic and Mint Marinade

4	cloves garlic, minced	4
1 cup	plain yogurt	250 mL
¼ cup	extra-virgin olive oil	50 mL
2½ tbsp	dried mint	32 mL
2 tbsp	freshly squeezed lemon juice	25 mL
½ tsp	hot pepper sauce (such as Tabasco)	2 mL
	Salt and freshly ground black pepper to taste	

Combine all ingredients. **Makes about 1⅓ cups (325 mL).** *(C, F, L, S, T, VG)*

Coriander Marinade

Follow preceding recipe, but add 2 tsp (10 mL) ground coriander, and replace the mint with ⅓ cup (75 mL) chopped fresh cilantro. **Makes about 1½ cups (375 mL).** *(C, F, P, S, T)*

Basic Dry Rub

2 tsp	freshly ground black pepper	10 mL
2 tsp	garlic salt	10 mL
1 tsp	onion powder	5 mL
1 tsp	packed brown sugar	5 mL
½ tsp	cayenne pepper	2 mL

Combine all ingredients. Rub evenly onto meat, cover and refrigerate for 1 hour. **Makes about 2 tbsp (25 mL).** *(B, C, L, P, V)*

Citrus Dry Rub

Follow preceding recipe, and add 1 tbsp (15 mL) grated orange zest and 1 tbsp (15 mL) grated lemon zest. **Makes about ¼ cup (50 mL).** *(B, C, L, P, V)*

Moroccan Dry Rub

1 tbsp	grated lemon zest	15 mL
1 tbsp	granulated sugar	15 mL
2 tsp	freshly ground black pepper	10 mL
2 tsp	garlic salt	10 mL
1 tsp	onion powder	5 mL
1 tsp	ground cinnamon	5 mL
1 tsp	ground coriander	5 mL
1 tsp	ground ginger	5 mL
½ tsp	cayenne pepper	2 mL
½ tsp	dried thyme	2 mL

Combine all ingredients. Rub evenly onto meat, cover and refrigerate for 1 hour. **Makes about ¼ cup (50 mL).** *(B, C, L, P, V)*

Charcuterie Dry Rub

2 tsp	kosher salt	10 mL
1 tsp	freshly ground black pepper	5 mL
1 tsp	freshly ground white pepper	5 mL
½ tsp	ground nutmeg	2 mL
½ tsp	ground ginger	2 mL
½ tsp	ground allspice	2 mL

Combine all ingredients. Rub evenly onto meat, cover and refrigerate for 1 hour. **Makes about 2 tbsp (25 mL).** *(C, D, G, P, V)*

Chapter 2
Seasoning
Because Flavoring Is Easy

Lemon Anise Spinach 38

Star-Anise Duck 38

Salad of Garden Lettuces and Arugula . . 38

Chicken Breast Steamed with
Basil Leaves 38

Out-of-Fresh-Basil Pesto 38

Veal Shanks with Tomato and Bay 39

Black Mustard 39

Caraway Raisin Soda Bread 39

Cardamom Tea Cake 39

Cayenne Pepper Gingerbread 40

Chilled Garden Soup with Celery Seed . . 40

Grilled Chicken Breast with Buttermilk
and Chervil 40

Chili Pepper Chutney 40

Chicken with Ginger, Soy and Chives . . . 41

Poached Salmon with Lemon
and Chives 41

Lime and Coriander Roast Chicken 41

Cilantro Catfish Soup 41

Grilled Shrimp in Cumin Paste 42

Curried Cabbage Flowers 42

Dill Popovers 42

Dilly Cabbage 42

Fines Herbes Vinaigrette 42

Five-Spice Eggs 43

Blackened Beef Steaks with
Fennel Seed 43

Fennel and Orange Salad 43

Steamed Clams with Garam Masala 43

Ginger Apple Cobbler 44

Garlic and Ginger Lamb Chops 44

Trout Stuffed with Pickled Ginger
and Green Onions 44

Veal Scallops Sautéed with Herbes de
Provence 44

Roasted Garlic Horseradish Paste 44

Jalapeño Bloody Marys 45

Frittata with Ham, Walnuts and Marjoram . . 45

Green Pea Soup with Mint 45

Watermelon Spearmint Granita 45

Salmon with Molasses and Mustard 45

Mussels Oreganato 46

Sweet Pepper Seared Snapper 46

Parsley Pasta 46

Szechuan Pepper Popcorn 46

Veal Chops with Rosemary, Sage
and Aïoli 46

Sage Roast Pork with Sage Mayonnaise . . 47

Sicilian Mushrooms with Savory 47

Sorrel Beurre Blanc 47

Tamarind Eggplant with Peanuts 47

Cherry Tarragon Compote 48

Lime and Thyme Vinaigrette 48

Golden Turmeric Tomato Relish 48

Watercress and Grapefruit Salad 48

Zesty Salt Substitute 48

Most home cooks are chicken when it comes to seasoning. They confine themselves to two or three favorites and rely on salt and pepper to fill in the gaps. Set in their ways, they think of herbs and spices as exotic gourmet ingredients, meant for upscale restaurant kitchens rather than for everyday home cooking.

Nothing could be further from the truth. Herbs and spices are natural flavor enhancers, just waiting to take a plain poached fish, grilled chicken or roast veal and transform it — whether with white wine and tarragon, curry and orange, ginger and soy, or some other combination — with little more than a pinch of this and a dash of that.

Herbs are the soft parts of aromatic plants, such as leaves and blossoms, and they can be bought fresh or dried. Spices are the harder parts — the root, seed or pod — and they are always dried.

Once a seasoning is ground, its aroma and flavor begin to dissipate. So, given a choice between ground thyme and fresh thyme, for example, choose the fresh. It will have a shelf life of nearly 6 months, while the ground thyme will begin losing its oomph before you even lift the lid on the bottle. Whole seeds and other hard spices keep for up to a year.

Store dried seasonings in a cool, dark place, packed in small containers with tight-fitting lids. Because all the flavor in an herb or spice comes from its volatile oils, degeneration of the oils due to exposure to light, heat or air will cause the seasoning to lose power and, in time, turn rancid.

Never keep dried seasonings over a stove or near a sunny window.

When using whole dried herbs and spices, wait until just before you start cooking to crush or grind them. Leafy herbs can be crushed between your fingers, but seeds must be ground. You can use a mortar and pestle, but that requires considerable time and elbow grease. A better solution is a coffee mill (used exclusively for spices) or an electric spice grinder. These grinders, which are miniature food processors, will pulverize the hardest dried seeds in no time. However, they have no effect on dried barks and hard roots such as turmeric, cinnamon stick or dried gingerroot. If a recipe calls for these ground, you must buy them ground.

Because dried herbs are dehydrated, their flavors are concentrated, but so is the natural bitterness of the leaf. Fresh herbs are less bitter but do not have the same flavor intensity as dried herbs, especially when they are cooked for a long time. So, when using fresh herbs in place of dried herbs in a recipe, use triple the quantity called for and expect a slightly sweeter and more subtle result.

Cook fresh herbs for a short time, as you would other tender, leafy vegetables. When the leaf is wilted, the herb is cooked. Any additional heat will only dissipate the herb's flavor and destroy its color.

About these recipes . . .

The following recipes each highlight an individual herb or spice.

Lemon Anise Spinach

2 tbsp	butter	25 mL
½ cup	chopped onion	125 mL
1 tsp	ground anise seeds	5 mL
1 tsp	finely grated lemon zest	5 mL
1¼ lbs	baby spinach (about 12 cups/3 L)	625 g
	Salt and freshly ground black pepper to taste	

In a large skillet, melt butter over medium-high heat. Sauté onion until tender. Add anise seeds and lemon zest; sauté for 30 seconds. Add spinach; cook, stirring, until wilted. Season with salt and pepper. **Serves 4.**

Star-Anise Duck

8	dried black mushrooms or dried shiitake mushrooms	8
1 cup	hot water	250 mL
	Vegetable oil	
1	duck (about 4 lbs/2 kg), cut into pieces	1
6	whole star anise	6
3	cloves garlic, minced	3
1 tbsp	minced gingerroot	15 mL
½ tsp	hot pepper flakes	2 mL
1 cup	chicken broth	250 mL
¼ cup	dry sherry	50 mL
3 tbsp	soy sauce	45 mL
2 tbsp	granulated sugar	25 mL
8	green onions, sliced	8
2 tsp	cornstarch, dissolved in 1 tbsp (15 mL) water	10 mL
1 tsp	dark sesame oil	5 mL

Soak mushrooms in hot water until soft, about 10 minutes. Meanwhile, in a large skillet, heat ⅛ inch (3 mm) oil over medium-high heat. Cook duck until browned on all sides; remove duck to a plate and pour off all but 1 tbsp (15 mL) of the oil. Add star anise, garlic, ginger and hot pepper flakes to the pan; sauté for 1 minute. Add mushrooms and soaking liquid, broth, sherry, soy sauce and sugar. Return duck to skillet, along with any juices on the plate. Reduce heat, cover and simmer for 25 minutes, or until desired doneness. Skim off excess fat from liquid, then add green onions and cornstarch mixture; simmer, stirring, until thickened. Stir in sesame oil. **Serves 4.**

Salad of Garden Lettuces and Arugula

1 lb	baby greens, cleaned (about 8 cups/2 L)	500 g
1	bunch arugula (about 4 oz/125 g), cleaned	1
1	small red onion, thinly sliced	1
3 tbsp	raspberry vinegar	45 mL
2 tbsp	walnut oil	25 mL
2 tbsp	olive oil	25 mL
	Salt and freshly ground black pepper to taste	
12	unblanched almonds, sliced	12

In a large salad bowl, toss greens, arugula and onion. In a small bowl, whisk together vinegar, walnut oil, olive oil, salt and pepper. Pour over salad and toss to coat. Sprinkle with almonds. **Serves 4.**

Chicken Breast Steamed with Basil Leaves

4	boneless skinless chicken breasts	4
	Salt and freshly ground black pepper to taste	
	Fresh basil leaves	
1 tbsp	butter (optional)	15 mL

Pound chicken breasts between sheets of plastic wrap until very thin. Season one side of each piece with salt and pepper and cover with basil leaves. Roll up, with the basil leaves on the inside, and wrap in several layers of plastic wrap. Steam over boiling water for 10 minutes, or until firm. Unwrap and drain juices from each roll into a saucepan. Cook juices over medium-high heat until slightly thickened. Swirl in butter, if desired. Slice each roll and nap with sauce. **Serves 4.**

Out-of-Fresh-Basil Pesto

⅔ cup	olive oil	150 mL
2 tbsp	dried basil	25 mL
4	cloves garlic	4
9 to 10 oz	baby spinach (about 6 cups/1.5 L)	275 to 300 g
⅓ cup	pine nuts	75 mL
¾ cup	freshly grated Parmesan cheese	175 mL
	Salt and freshly ground black pepper to taste	

In a small saucepan, warm oil over medium heat. Remove from heat, add basil and let steep for 10 minutes. Meanwhile, in a food processor, finely chop garlic, spinach and pine nuts. With the motor running, slowly add oil mixture through feed tube and process to a smooth sauce. Stir in Parmesan, salt and pepper. **Makes about 2 cups (500 mL).** *Store in an airtight container in the refrigerator for up to 1 week. Use as a sauce for pasta, grilled meats, roasts or poached fish.*

Veal Shanks with Tomato and Bay

8	bay leaves	8
4	2-inch (5 cm) thick slices veal shank, dredged in all-purpose flour	4
2 tbsp	butter	25 mL
2 tbsp	olive oil	25 mL
⅔ cup	finely chopped onion	150 mL
⅓ cup	finely chopped celery	75 mL
2	cloves garlic, minced, divided	2
1½ cups	canned diced tomatoes, with juice	375 mL
½ cup	dry white wine	125 mL
1 tsp	dried basil	5 mL
½ tsp	dried thyme	2 mL
¼ tsp	dried oregano	1 mL
	Salt and freshly ground black pepper to taste	
1 tbsp	finely chopped fresh Italian (flat-leaf) parsley	15 mL

Preheat oven to 350°F (180°C). Using kitchen twine, tie 2 bay leaves around the outside of each veal shank. In a large, deep ovenproof skillet or Dutch oven, heat butter and olive oil over medium-high heat. Cook veal until browned on both sides. Halfway through the browning, add onion, celery and two-thirds of the garlic. When meat is browned, add tomatoes, wine, basil, thyme, oregano, salt and pepper; bring to a boil. Cover and bake for about 2 hours, until veal is fork-tender. Remove veal, untie strings and discard bay leaves. Skim fat from sauce and stir in parsley and the remaining garlic. Spoon sauce over meat. **Serves 4.**

Black Mustard

¼ cup	black mustard seeds	50 mL
3 tbsp	balsamic vinegar	45 mL
1 cup	brown mustard	250 mL
2 tbsp	dark (cooking) molasses	25 mL

Soak mustard seeds in balsamic vinegar for 1 hour. Mix in brown mustard and molasses. **Makes about 1¼ cups (300 mL).** *Store in an airtight container in the refrigerator. Serve with grilled meats.*

Caraway Raisin Soda Bread

2 cups	unbleached all-purpose flour	500 mL
½ cup	granulated sugar, divided	125 mL
2 tsp	baking powder	10 mL
1 tsp	baking soda	5 mL
¼ tsp	salt	1 mL
¼ cup	cold unsalted butter, cubed	50 mL
1 tbsp	caraway seeds	15 mL
1 cup	buttermilk	250 mL
½ cup	raisins	125 mL

Preheat oven to 375°F (190°C). In a large bowl, combine flour, half the sugar, the baking powder, baking soda and salt. Cut in butter until mixture is the size of small peas. Mix in caraway seeds. Mix in buttermilk and raisins until just moistened. Form dough into a ball and place on a dry baking sheet. Cut a cross in the top of dough and sprinkle with the remaining sugar. Bake for 30 to 35 minutes, or until brown. **Serves 6.**

Cardamom Tea Cake

1½ cups	sifted all-purpose flour	375 mL
1 tbsp	ground cardamom	15 mL
1 tsp	baking powder	5 mL
5	eggs, separated	5
Pinch	salt	Pinch
¾ cup	confectioner's (icing) sugar	175 mL
¾ cup	granulated sugar	175 mL
1 cup	unsalted butter, at room temperature	250 mL
1 tsp	vanilla	5 mL
	Finely grated zest of 1 large orange	

Preheat oven to 350°F (180°C) and grease a 9- by 5-inch (2 L) loaf pan. In a small bowl, combine flour, cardamom and baking powder; set aside. In another bowl, beat egg whites and salt until soft peaks form. Add confectioner's sugar and beat until stiff, glossy peaks form; set aside. In another bowl, beat egg yolks and granulated sugar until thick; set aside. In a large bowl, cream the butter until fluffy. Beat in vanilla, orange zest and half the flour mixture. Beat in yolk mixture and the remaining flour mixture. Fold in egg whites, making 2 additions. Spoon batter into prepared pan and bake for 70 minutes, or until a tester inserted in the center comes out almost clean. Let cool in pan on a wire rack for 10 minutes, then invert onto rack to cool completely. **Serves 10 to 12.**

Cayenne Pepper Gingerbread

2½ cups	sifted all-purpose flour	625 mL
2 tsp	baking soda	10 mL
1 tsp	ground cinnamon	5 mL
½ tsp	salt	2 mL
½ tsp	ground cloves	2 mL
½ tsp	dry mustard	2 mL
½ tsp	freshly ground black pepper	2 mL
Pinch	cayenne pepper	Pinch
½ cup	firmly packed dark brown sugar	125 mL
½ cup	unsalted butter, slightly softened	125 mL
2 tbsp	grated gingerroot	25 mL
2	large or extra-large eggs	2
1 cup	dark (cooking) molasses	250 mL
1 cup	hot brewed coffee	250 mL

Preheat oven to 375°F (190°C) and grease a 9-inch (2.5 L) square baking pan. In a bowl, combine flour, baking soda, cinnamon, salt, cloves, mustard, black pepper and cayenne. In a large bowl, beat brown sugar, butter and ginger until fluffy. Beat in eggs and molasses. Stir in flour mixture alternately with coffee, making 3 additions of flour and 2 of coffee. Spoon batter into prepared pan and bake for 40 to 45 minutes, or until a tester inserted in the center comes out with a few crumbs clinging to it. Let cool for at least 15 minutes before cutting into 9 squares.

Chilled Garden Soup with Celery Seed

2	large tomatoes, quartered	2
1	roasted red pepper (see page 11), quartered	1
1	clove garlic	1
¼	onion	¼
¼ cup	celery leaves	50 mL
3 tbsp	extra-virgin olive oil	45 mL
	Salt and freshly ground black pepper to taste	
6	ice cubes, divided	6
1 tbsp	crushed celery seeds	15 mL
1 tbsp	chopped fresh Italian (flat-leaf) parsley	15 mL

In a food processor, combine tomatoes, red pepper, garlic, onion, celery leaves, oil, salt, pepper and 3 of the ice cubes; process until finely chopped, but not completely smooth. Transfer to a serving bowl and stir in the remaining ice cubes, celery seeds and parsley. Continue stirring until ice melts. Serve immediately, or cover and refrigerate for up to 2 hours. **Serves 4.**

Grilled Chicken Breast with Buttermilk and Chervil

2	green onions, finely chopped	2
1 cup	buttermilk	250 mL
2 tbsp	chopped fresh chervil	25 mL
1 tbsp	finely grated orange zest	15 mL
1 tbsp	extra-virgin olive oil	15 mL
Pinch	cayenne pepper	Pinch
	Salt and freshly ground black pepper to taste	
4	boneless skinless chicken breasts, lightly pounded	4
	Additional extra-virgin olive oil	

In a shallow dish, combine green onions, buttermilk, chervil, orange zest, oil, cayenne, salt and black pepper. Add chicken and turn to coat. Cover and refrigerate for at least 2 hours or for up to 8 hours. Preheat barbecue grill to medium. Remove chicken from marinade and discard marinade. Grill chicken, turning once, for about 4 minutes per side, or until chicken is no longer pink inside. Drizzle with additional olive oil. **Serves 4.**

Chili Pepper Chutney

2 tbsp	canola oil	25 mL
1	onion, finely chopped	1
1	serrano or jalapeño pepper, seeded and finely chopped	1
2	cloves garlic, minced	2
2 tbsp	ancho chili powder	25 mL
1 tbsp	grated gingerroot	15 mL
1 tsp	ground coriander	5 mL
¼ tsp	ground cloves	1 mL
1	poblano pepper, roasted and cut into small dice	1
1	red bell pepper, roasted and cut into small dice	1
1	yellow bell pepper, roasted and cut into small dice	1
1	green bell pepper, roasted and cut into small dice	1
¼ cup	granulated sugar	50 mL
¼ cup	cider vinegar	50 mL
¼ cup	water	50 mL
¼ cup	chopped fresh cilantro	50 mL

In a large saucepan, heat oil over medium heat. Sauté onion and serrano pepper until tender. Add garlic, ancho chili powder, ginger, coriander and cloves; sauté for 1 minute. Stir in roasted poblano and bell peppers, sugar, vinegar and water; cover, reduce heat and simmer for 20 minutes, or until peppers are very soft. Remove lid and simmer until excess liquid has evaporated. Stir in cilantro. **Makes about 2 cups (500 mL).** *Store in the refrigerator for up to 2 weeks. Serve with poultry, pork, eggs or fish.*

Chicken with Ginger, Soy and Chives

4	boneless skinless chicken breasts, lightly pounded	4
	Salt and freshly ground black pepper to taste	
2 tbsp	vegetable oil	25 mL
1	small clove garlic, minced	1
1 tsp	chopped gingerroot	5 mL
⅓ cup	chicken broth	75 mL
1 tbsp	reduced-sodium soy sauce	15 mL
Pinch	granulated sugar	Pinch
1 tbsp	sliced chives	15 mL
1 tsp	dark sesame oil	5 mL
1 tsp	dry sherry	5 mL

Season chicken with salt and pepper. In a large skillet, heat oil over medium-high heat. Sauté chicken until browned on both sides. Add garlic and ginger; sauté for 1 minute. Combine broth, soy sauce and sugar; pour into pan. Reduce heat and simmer for 3 minutes, or until sauce has thickened lightly and chicken is no longer pink inside. Transfer chicken to a platter. Add chives, sesame oil and sherry to the sauce. Pour sauce over chicken. **Serves 4.**

Poached Salmon with Lemon and Chives

1 cup	dry white wine	250 mL
½ cup	water	125 mL
	Juice of 1 large lemon	
	Salt and freshly ground black pepper to taste	
4	pieces skinless salmon fillet (each about 5 oz/150 g)	4
⅓ cup	finely chopped chives	75 mL
12	chive blossoms (optional)	12
¼ to ⅓ cup	butter, cut into cubes	50 to 75 mL

In a large skillet, bring wine, water, lemon juice, salt and pepper to a boil over medium-high heat. Add salmon, reduce heat and simmer for 8 to 10 minutes, or until fish is opaque and flakes easily with a fork. Transfer salmon to a warm plate. Simmer liquid until reduced by two-thirds. Add chives and chive blossoms (if using), bring to a boil and boil for 1 minute. Remove from heat and swirl in butter, a few pieces at a time, until a smooth sauce forms. Pour sauce over fish. **Serves 4.**

Lime and Coriander Roast Chicken

3	cloves garlic, minced	3
3 tbsp	extra-virgin olive oil	45 mL
1 tbsp	ground coriander	15 mL
1 tsp	kosher salt	5 mL
½ tsp	freshly ground black pepper	2 mL
1	whole chicken (4 to 5 lbs/2 to 2.5 kg)	1
3	limes, halved, divided	3

Combine garlic, oil, coriander, salt and pepper. Rub chicken inside and out with the mixture and place breast side down on a rack in a roasting pan. Cover and refrigerate for at least 1 hour or overnight. Preheat oven to 425°F (220°C). Squeeze juice from 4 of the lime halves over the chicken and place the lime shells in the chicken cavity. Roast for 15 minutes, then shake the rack to make sure chicken isn't sticking. Roast for 30 minutes. Turn chicken breast side up and squeeze juice from the remaining lime halves over top. Roast for 15 to 20 minutes, or until skin is golden brown and a meat thermometer inserted in the thickest part of the thigh registers between 170°F and 175°F (77°C and 80°C). Let rest for 10 minutes before carving. **Serves 4.**

Cilantro Catfish Soup

3 lbs	skinless catfish fillets, cut into bite-size chunks	1.5 kg
¼ cup	freshly squeezed lemon juice	50 mL
	Salt and freshly ground black pepper to taste	
2	cloves garlic	2
1	onion, cut into chunks	1
1	jalapeño pepper, seeded	1
1	red bell pepper, coarsely chopped	1
2 tbsp	olive oil	25 mL
1 cup	canned crushed tomatoes	250 mL
4 cups	fish broth	1 L
6 tbsp	chopped fresh cilantro	90 mL
1	avocado, finely diced	1

Toss catfish in lemon juice, salt and pepper; set aside. In a food processor, process garlic, onion, jalapeño and red pepper until finely chopped. In a large saucepan, heat oil over medium heat. Sauté pepper mixture until tender. Add tomatoes and broth; bring to a boil. Add fish, reduce heat and simmer for 6 minutes, or until fish is opaque and flakes easily with a fork. Stir in cilantro and avocado. **Serves 4.**

Grilled Shrimp in Cumin Paste

1 tbsp	olive oil	15 mL
1 cup	chopped onion	250 mL
1	jalapeño pepper, seeded and minced	1
1	clove garlic, minced	1
1 tbsp	ground cumin	15 mL
1 tsp	ground coriander	5 mL
½ tsp	dried oregano	2 mL
2 tbsp	freshly squeezed lemon juice	25 mL
	Salt and freshly ground black pepper to taste	
1 lb	jumbo shrimp, peeled, deveined and butterflied	500 g

In a large skillet, heat oil over medium heat. Sauté onion and jalapeño until tender. Add garlic and sauté for 30 seconds. Add cumin, coriander and oregano; sauté for 1 minute. Add lemon juice and season with salt and pepper. Let cool. Place shrimp in a shallow dish and coat evenly with cumin paste. Cover and refrigerate for 1 hour. Preheat barbecue grill to high. Grill shrimp, turning once, for about 2 minutes per side, or until pink and opaque. **Serves 4.**

Curried Cabbage Flowers

1 tbsp	clarified butter (see page 16)	15 mL
1 tbsp	yellow mustard seeds	15 mL
1 cup	chopped onion	250 mL
1 tbsp	curry powder	15 mL
1½ tsp	ground cumin	7 mL
1 tsp	ground cardamom	5 mL
1 tsp	ground coriander	5 mL
2 cups	small cauliflower florets	500 mL
2 cups	small broccoli florets	500 mL
1 cup	water	250 mL
½ cup	plain yogurt	125 mL
	Salt and freshly ground black pepper to taste	

In a large saucepan, heat butter over medium heat. Toast mustard seeds, stirring, for 10 seconds. Add onion, curry powder, cumin, cardamom and coriander; sauté until onion is almost tender, about 3 minutes. Stir in cauliflower and broccoli. Add water, reduce heat and simmer until vegetables are tender and most of the liquid has evaporated, about 15 minutes. Stir in yogurt and season with salt and pepper. **Serves 4.**

Dill Popovers

1 cup	all-purpose flour	250 mL
Pinch	salt	Pinch
1 cup	milk	250 mL
1 tbsp	melted butter	15 mL
2	eggs	2
¼ cup	minced fresh dill	50 mL

Preheat oven to 450°F (230°C). Place a 12-cup non-stick muffin tin or a popover pan with 6 deep cups in the oven while you make the batter. In a large bowl, combine flour and salt. Beat in milk and butter just until blended. Beat in eggs, one at a time, and dill. Coat the hot tin with nonstick baking spray and divide batter evenly among the cups. Bake for 15 minutes. Reduce oven temperature to 375°F (190°C) and bake for 10 to 15 minutes, or until popovers are fully puffed, brown and crisp over the entire surface. **Serves 6.**

Dilly Cabbage

2 tbsp	vegetable oil	25 mL
1	onion, sliced	1
2 tsp	dried dillweed	10 mL
1 lb	sliced cabbage	500 g
	Salt and freshly ground black pepper to taste	

In a large skillet, heat oil over medium heat. Sauté onion and dill until onion is tender. Add cabbage and cook until shiny and tender, about 4 minutes. Season with salt and pepper. **Serves 4.**

Fines Herbes Vinaigrette

1	clove garlic, minced	1
⅔ cup	olive oil	150 mL
⅓ cup	red wine vinegar	75 mL
1 tbsp	minced fresh Italian (flat-leaf) parsley	15 mL
2 tsp	chopped fresh chervil	10 mL
2 tsp	chopped fresh dill	10 mL
1 tsp	chopped fresh tarragon	5 mL
½ tsp	salt	2 mL
	Freshly ground black pepper to taste	

Whisk together all ingredients. **Makes about 1 cup (250 mL).** *Store in the refrigerator for up to 2 weeks. Use as a salad dressing, or spoon over grilled meats.*

Five-Spice Eggs

6	eggs	6
2	black tea bags (or 2 tsp/10 mL loose black tea)	2
1/4 cup	soy sauce	50 mL
2 tsp	Chinese five-spice powder	10 mL
	Dipping Sauce for Potstickers (page 249)	

Place eggs in about 8 cups (2 L) of simmering water and simmer for 10 minutes. Let cool completely, then crack shells all over, without removing them, by tapping them with the back of a spoon or rolling them gently over a countertop. Cover with cold water and add tea bags, soy sauce and five-spice powder. Cover and simmer for 1 hour. Let cool, transfer eggs and liquid to an airtight container and refrigerate for at least 2 days or for up to 1 month. Shortly before serving, peel and cut eggs into quarters. Serve with dipping sauce. **Serves 6.**

Blackened Beef Steaks with Fennel Seed

2 tbsp	freshly ground black pepper	25 mL
2 tbsp	dried minced garlic	25 mL
2 tbsp	kosher salt	25 mL
2 tbsp	ground fennel seeds	25 mL
1 tbsp	onion powder	15 mL
1/2 tsp	dry mustard	2 mL
1/2 tsp	cayenne pepper	2 mL
4	T-bone or porterhouse steaks (each about 1 inch/2.5 cm thick)	4
	Vegetable oil	

Combine black pepper, garlic, salt, fennel seeds, onion powder, mustard and cayenne. Place steaks in a shallow dish and rub evenly with spice mixture. Cover and refrigerate for at least 1 hour or for up to 6 hours. Heat a large cast-iron skillet over high heat for about 10 minutes. Carefully brush hot pan with oil (it may flame up). Cook steaks, turning once, for 3 to 4 minutes per side for medium-rare, or to desired doneness. **Serves 4.**

Fennel and Orange Salad

2	navel oranges, peeled and sectioned	2
1	bulb fennel, thinly sliced	1
1/2 cup	walnut pieces	125 mL
1/3 cup	freshly squeezed orange juice	75 mL
2 tbsp	extra-virgin olive oil	25 mL
1 tbsp	freshly squeezed lemon juice	15 mL
1 tsp	ground fennel seeds	5 mL
Pinch	ground nutmeg	Pinch
Pinch	cayenne pepper	Pinch
	Salt and freshly ground black pepper to taste	

In a large salad bowl, toss together orange sections, fennel and walnuts. In a small bowl, whisk together orange juice, oil, lemon juice, fennel seeds, nutmeg, cayenne, salt and black pepper. Pour over salad and toss to coat. **Serves 4.**

Steamed Clams with Garam Masala

1 tbsp	canola oil	15 mL
1	onion, finely chopped	1
1	small clove garlic, minced	1
1 tbsp	garam masala	15 mL
2 tsp	finely chopped gingerroot	10 mL
1 tsp	ground coriander	5 mL
1 tsp	ground cumin	5 mL
Pinch	hot pepper flakes	Pinch
48	littleneck clams, scrubbed (see page 8)	48
1/4 cup	chopped fresh cilantro	50 mL
1 tbsp	freshly squeezed lemon juice	15 mL

In a large skillet, heat oil over medium heat. Sauté onion until tender. Add garlic, garam masala, ginger, coriander, cumin and hot pepper flakes; sauté until mixture is highly aromatic, about 2 minutes. Add clams, cover and cook for 5 to 8 minutes, or until clams open. Discard any that do not open. Transfer opened clams to a serving bowl. Add cilantro and lemon juice to the pan. Spoon sauce over clams. **Serves 4.**

Ginger Apple Cobbler

3 lbs	tart apples, peeled and sliced (about 8 medium)	1.5 kg
	Juice of 1 lemon	
1 cup	granulated sugar, divided	250 mL
3 tbsp	unsalted butter, divided	45 mL
2 tsp	ground ginger	10 mL
1 tbsp	cornstarch	15 mL
2 tbsp	brandy	25 mL
1 cup	raisins	250 mL
2 tbsp	finely chopped candied ginger	25 mL
1 tsp	vanilla	5 mL
28	gingersnaps (about 2¼ inches/5.5 cm), divided	28

Preheat oven to 400°F (200°C). Toss apple slices with lemon juice. In a large skillet, heat ¾ cup (175 mL) of the sugar, 2 tbsp (25 mL) of the butter and ground ginger over medium heat, stirring often, until combined. Add apple slices and cook, stirring occasionally, until apples begin to release their moisture. Combine cornstarch and brandy; add to apples, reduce heat and simmer until sauce thickens. Remove from heat and stir in raisins, candied ginger and vanilla. Line a 9-inch (2.5 L) baking pan with 16 of the gingersnaps and pack in apple mixture. Melt the remaining butter and crumble the remaining gingersnaps. Combine butter, gingersnaps and the remaining sugar; sprinkle over apple mixture. Bake for 30 minutes, or until apples are bubbling and topping is golden brown. **Serves 8.**

Garlic and Ginger Lamb Chops

2	cloves garlic, minced	2
¼ cup	finely chopped gingerroot	50 mL
2 tbsp	olive oil	25 mL
8	lamb rib or loin chops	8
	Salt and freshly ground black pepper to taste	

Combine garlic, ginger and oil. Place lamb chops in a shallow dish, season with salt and pepper and coat with garlic mixture. Cover and refrigerate for at least 1 hour or for up to 8 hours. Preheat barbecue grill or broiler to high. Grill or broil lamb, turning once, for 3 to 4 minutes per side for medium-rare, or until desired doneness. **Serves 4.**

Trout Stuffed with Pickled Ginger and Green Onions

6	green onions, thinly sliced	6
¼ cup	finely chopped drained pickled sushi ginger (2 oz/60 g)	50 mL
	Grated zest and juice of 1 lemon	
4	whole rainbow trout (preferably boned)	4
1 tsp	olive oil	5 mL

Preheat broiler. Combine green onions, ginger and lemon zest. Place trout on a rimmed baking sheet. Stuff one-quarter of the onion mixture into each fish cavity and close fish over stuffing. Pour lemon juice over fish and rub fish with oil. Broil, turning once, for 4 minutes per side, or until fish is opaque and flakes easily with a fork. **Serves 4.**

Veal Scallops Sautéed with Herbes de Provence

2 tbsp	olive oil	25 mL
8	veal cutlets (each about 2 oz/60 g), pounded to ¼ inch (0.5 cm) thick	8
	All-purpose flour seasoned with salt and freshly ground black pepper	
2	cloves garlic, minced	2
1	shallot, minced	1
2 tsp	dried herbes de Provence	10 mL
1 cup	dry white wine	250 mL
2 tbsp	white wine vinegar	25 mL
¼ cup	butter, softened	50 mL

In a large skillet, heat oil over medium-high heat. Meanwhile, dredge veal in seasoned flour. Sauté veal, in batches, until golden brown on both sides and barely cooked through. Transfer to a plate and keep warm. Add garlic, shallot and herbes de Provence to pan; sauté for 30 seconds. Add wine and vinegar; cook until sauce is reduced by three-quarters. Add any juices from veal and bring to a boil. Remove from heat and gradually swirl in butter to thicken juices. Pour sauce over veal. **Serves 4.**

Roasted Garlic Horseradish Paste

2	large heads garlic	2
2 tsp	olive oil, divided	10 mL
⅓ cup	prepared horseradish	75 mL
1 tsp	Dijon mustard	5 mL
	Salt to taste	

Cut the pointed ends from the garlic heads, exposing the tops of the cloves. Rub the exposed cloves of each head with oil. Wrap in foil and bake at 375°F (190°C) for 40 minutes, or until soft to the touch.

Let cool slightly, gently squeeze cloves from their peels and mash with a small fork. Mix in horseradish, mustard and salt. **Makes about ⅔ cup (150 mL)**. *Store in the refrigerator for up to 1 week. Serve with plain roasted meats or steaks.*

Jalapeño Bloody Marys

2 cups	vegetable juice (such as V8)	500 mL
½ cup	tequila	125 mL
4 tsp	freshly squeezed lime juice	20 mL
1 tbsp	Worcestershire sauce	15 mL
1	jalapeño pepper, seeded and minced	1
4	whole pickled jalapeño peppers	4
8	thin slices garlic	8

Whisk or shake together vegetable juice, tequila, lime juice, Worcestershire sauce and minced jalapeño. Pour into glasses filled with ice. Make a slit in each side of each whole jalapeño and insert 1 garlic slice in each slit. Drop 1 pepper in each drink. **Serves 4.**

Frittata with Ham, Walnuts and Marjoram

8	eggs	8
2 tbsp	water	25 mL
¼ tsp	hot pepper sauce (such as Tabasco)	1 mL
2 tbsp	extra-virgin olive oil	25 mL
1 cup	diced baked ham	250 mL
½ cup	walnut halves	125 mL
1 tsp	dried marjoram	5 mL
	Salt and freshly ground black pepper to taste	
1	clove garlic, minced	1
1 tbsp	grated orange zest	15 mL
1 tsp	chopped fresh marjoram	5 mL

Beat eggs with water and hot pepper sauce; set aside. Preheat broiler. In a large ovenproof skillet, heat oil over medium heat. Sauté ham, walnuts and dried marjoram until walnuts are lightly toasted. Season with salt and pepper. Add garlic, orange zest and fresh marjoram. Add egg mixture and cook, without stirring, until eggs are set in the center. Broil for 2 to 3 minutes, or until frittata is puffed and brown. **Serves 4.**

Green Pea Soup with Mint

1 tbsp	butter	15 mL
1 cup	chopped onion	250 mL
6 cups	chicken broth	1.5 L
4 cups	frozen peas	1 L
1 tbsp	dried mint	15 mL
1 tbsp	granulated sugar	15 mL
	Salt and freshly ground black pepper to taste	
1 cup	light or table (18%) cream	250 mL
	Fresh mint leaves, for garnish	

In a large saucepan, melt butter over medium heat. Sauté onion until tender. Add broth, peas, dried mint, sugar, salt and pepper. Reduce heat and simmer for 20 minutes, or until peas are very tender. Working in batches, transfer to a blender and purée until smooth. Return to saucepan, stir in cream and season with salt and pepper. Heat through. Serve hot or cold, garnished with fresh mint. **Serves 6.**

Watermelon Spearmint Granita

½ cup	granulated sugar	125 mL
⅓ cup	water	75 mL
3 tbsp	dried spearmint	45 mL
8 cups	cubed seeded watermelon pulp	2 L
¼ cup	chopped fresh spearmint	50 mL
3 tbsp	freshly squeezed lemon juice	45 mL
Pinch	salt	Pinch

In a small saucepan, bring sugar, water and dried spearmint to a boil; boil for 3 minutes. Strain, reserve syrup and let cool. In a blender, working in batches, purée watermelon pulp and cooled syrup. Stir in fresh spearmint, lemon juice and salt. Pour into a shallow freezer-safe pan and freeze until solid. Cut into cubes and process in a food processor until finely chopped. Serve immediately or transfer to an airtight container and freeze for up to 2 hours. **Serves 6.**

Salmon with Molasses and Mustard

2 tbsp	brown mustard	25 mL
1 tsp	freshly squeezed lemon juice	5 mL
1 tsp	light (fancy) or dark (cooking) molasses	5 mL
4	salmon steaks (¾ inch/1.5 cm thick)	4
¾ cup	seasoned dry bread crumbs	175 mL
	Olive oil	

Combine mustard, lemon juice and molasses. Brush over salmon, then dredge salmon in bread crumbs and set on a rack for 10 minutes. In a large skillet, heat ⅛ inch (3 mm) oil over medium heat. Cook salmon, turning once, for 4 to 5 minutes per side, or until coating is browned and fish flakes easily with a fork. **Serves 4.**

Mussels Oreganato

¼ cup	olive oil	50 mL
2	cloves garlic, minced	2
1 cup	canned diced tomatoes, with juice	250 mL
1 tbsp	chopped fresh Italian (flat-leaf) parsley	15 mL
1 tsp	dried oregano	5 mL
Pinch	hot pepper flakes	Pinch
2 lbs	mussels, scrubbed	1 kg

In a large, heavy saucepan, heat oil over medium-high heat. Sauté garlic until aromatic, about 30 seconds. Add tomatoes, parsley, oregano and hot pepper flakes; reduce heat and simmer for 10 minutes. Add mussels, cover and simmer for 3 to 4 minutes, or until mussels open. Discard any that do not open. **Serves 4.** *Serve with crusty bread.*

Sweet Pepper Seared Snapper

2 tbsp	canola oil	25 mL
1	small onion, finely chopped	1
2	cloves garlic, minced	2
2 tbsp	Hungarian paprika	25 mL
1 tbsp	chili powder	15 mL
½ tsp	salt	2 mL
2	whole red snappers (each about 1½ lbs/750 g)	2
2	red bell peppers, cut into small dice	2
¾ cup	water	175 mL
1 tbsp	red wine vinegar	15 mL
1 tbsp	freshly squeezed lime juice	15 mL
1 tsp	granulated sugar	5 mL
	Salt and freshly ground black pepper to taste	
1 tbsp	butter	15 mL

Preheat barbecue grill to medium-high. In a large skillet, heat oil over medium heat. Sauté onion until tender. Add garlic, paprika, chili powder and salt; sauté for 30 seconds. Remove from heat. Make several slashes in the sides of each fish and rub with all but 1 tbsp (15 mL) of the onion mixture. Cook the remaining onion mixture, red peppers, water, vinegar, lime juice and sugar until reduced by about two-thirds. Transfer to a food processor and purée until smooth. Return to skillet, season with salt and pepper and heat through. Remove from heat and swirl in butter. Grill fish, turning once, for 3 to 4 minutes per side, or until fish is opaque and flakes easily with a fork. Serve with sauce. **Serves 4.**

Parsley Pasta

4 cups	boiling water	1 L
1	bunch fresh Italian (flat-leaf) parsley leaves (about 2 oz/60 g)	1
1	clove garlic	1
1	egg	1
Pinch	salt	Pinch
1 to 1¼ cups	all-purpose flour, divided	250 to 300 mL

Pour boiling water over parsley. Immediately drain, let cool and squeeze dry. In a food processor, purée parsley, garlic, egg and salt. Add 1 cup (250 mL) of flour and process until a smooth dough forms. Add up to ¼ cup (50 mL) additional flour, 1 tbsp (15 mL) at a time, until dough becomes stiff enough to form a ball in the center of the work bowl. Let dough rest for 10 minutes. Roll out with a rolling pin or pasta machine and cut into any shape pasta. Cook in boiling water until al dente (tender to the bite). **Serves 4.** *Serve with your choice of sauce, or with grated cheese and extra-virgin olive oil.*

Szechuan Pepper Popcorn

1 tsp	finely grated lemon zest	5 mL
1 tsp	salt	5 mL
½ tsp	ground coriander	2 mL
¼ tsp	freshly ground black pepper	1 mL
¼ tsp	freshly ground Szechuan peppercorns	1 mL
¼ tsp	ground ginger	1 mL
3 tbsp	vegetable oil	45 mL
¾ cup	popping corn	175 mL
1	clove garlic, minced	1

Combine lemon zest, salt, coriander, black pepper, Szechuan pepper and ginger; set aside. In a large, heavy pot, heat oil over high heat until it smokes. Add a few kernels of popping corn and heat until they pop. Add the remaining popping corn. Cover and shake gently until corn starts to pop. Shake vigorously until popping subsides. Remove from heat. Toss with spice mixture and garlic. **Serves 6.**

Veal Chops with Rosemary, Sage and Aïoli

½ cup	all-purpose flour	125 mL
2 tsp	dried rosemary	10 mL
2 tsp	dried sage	10 mL
	Salt and freshly ground black pepper to taste	
4	veal rib chops (each about 8 oz/250 g)	4
2 tbsp	Garlic Butter (see page 16)	25 mL
2 tbsp	olive oil	25 mL
1	clove garlic, minced	1

½ cup	mayonnaise	125 mL
2 tsp	freshly squeezed lemon juice	10 mL

Season flour with rosemary, sage, salt and pepper. Dust veal with seasoned flour. In a large skillet, heat garlic butter and olive oil over medium-high heat. Cook veal, in batches if necessary, until browned on both sides. Return veal to pan; reduce heat to medium, cover and cook, turning veal twice, for about 10 minutes for medium or until desired doneness. Meanwhile, make an aïoli by combining garlic, mayonnaise, lemon juice, salt and pepper. Serve veal with aïoli. **Serves 4.**

Sage Roast Pork with Sage Mayonnaise

2 lbs	boneless pork loin	1 kg
1 tbsp	olive oil	15 mL
	Salt and freshly ground black pepper to taste	
12	fresh sage leaves	12
1 cup	mayonnaise	250 mL
2 tbsp	freshly squeezed orange juice	25 mL
1 tsp	dried sage	5 mL
1 tsp	red or white wine vinegar	5 mL

Preheat oven to 375°F (190°C). Place pork in a roasting pan and rub with olive oil, salt and pepper. Lay sage leaves over the surface of the pork. Roast for 1 hour, or until a meat thermometer inserted in the thickest part of the pork registers 155°F (68°C) for medium, or until desired doneness. Let rest for 10 minutes before slicing. Meanwhile, combine mayonnaise, orange juice, dried sage, vinegar and 1 tbsp (15 mL) of pan drippings. Serve sliced pork with mayonnaise mixture. **Serves 4.**

Sicilian Mushrooms with Savory

2 tbsp	olive oil	25 mL
1	leek (white and light green parts only), finely chopped	1
1 cup	chopped onion	250 mL
2	cloves garlic, minced	2
2	stalks celery, sliced	2
½	bell pepper (any color), cut into medium dice	½
1 lb	mushrooms	500 g
2 tsp	dried savory	10 mL
1 tsp	dried thyme	5 mL
1 tsp	dried basil	5 mL
½ tsp	dried rosemary	2 mL
½ tsp	dried sage	2 mL
1 cup	drained canned diced tomatoes	250 mL
½ cup	chicken broth	125 mL
1 tbsp	red wine vinegar	15 mL

1 tbsp	tomato paste	15 mL
	Salt and freshly ground black pepper to taste	

In a large, heavy saucepan, heat oil over medium-high heat. Sauté leek and onion until tender. Add garlic, celery, bell pepper and mushrooms; sauté for 2 minutes. Add savory, thyme, basil, rosemary and sage; sauté for 3 minutes. Add tomatoes, broth, vinegar and tomato paste; reduce heat and simmer for 15 minutes, or until vegetables are tender. Season with salt and pepper. **Serves 4.**

Sorrel Beurre Blanc

½ cup	dry white wine	125 mL
2 tbsp	white wine vinegar	25 mL
1 tbsp	minced shallot	15 mL
¼ tsp	dried tarragon	1 mL
1 cup	whole sorrel leaves	250 mL
¼ cup	butter, cubed	50 mL

In a small skillet, combine wine, vinegar, shallot and tarragon. Cook over high heat until reduced by about half. Add sorrel leaves and cook for 30 seconds, or until wilted. Reduce heat to low and swirl in butter one piece at a time. **Makes about ¾ cup (175 mL).** *Serve over fish, shellfish, chicken or veal.*

Tamarind Eggplant with Peanuts

1 tbsp	olive oil	15 mL
1	large onion, chopped	1
2	cloves garlic, minced	2
1 tbsp	curry powder	15 mL
1 tsp	ground cumin	5 mL
1 tsp	chili powder	5 mL
1	large eggplant, peeled and diced	1
1 cup	boiling water (approx.), divided	250 mL
¼ cup	small Indian yellow split peas	50 mL
¼ cup	ketchup	50 mL
2 tsp	hot pepper sauce (such as Tabasco)	10 mL
¼ tsp	ground saffron	1 mL
1 tbsp	tamarind paste	15 mL
½ cup	roasted peanuts	125 mL

In a large skillet, heat oil over medium-high heat. Sauté onion and garlic until tender. Add curry powder, cumin and chili powder; sauté for 1 minute, until aromatic. Add eggplant, ¾ cup (175 mL) of the water, peas, ketchup, hot pepper sauce and saffron; reduce heat and simmer for 15 to 20 minutes, or until vegetables are tender, adding more water if necessary to keep the mixture from scorching. Dissolve tamarind paste in 2 tbsp (25 mL) water; add to skillet and simmer for 3 minutes. Add peanuts just before serving. **Serves 4.**

Cherry Tarragon Compote

1	small stick cinnamon	1
1	whole clove	1
1 lb	stemmed pitted cherries	500 g
¼ cup	granulated sugar	50 mL
¼ cup	brandy	50 mL
Pinch	salt	Pinch
	Grated zest of ½ lime	
	Juice of 2 limes	
1 tbsp	chopped fresh tarragon	15 mL

In a large saucepan, combine cinnamon, clove, cherries, sugar, brandy, salt and lime juice. Cook over medium-high heat for 5 minutes. Remove from heat and toss in lime zest and tarragon. Let cool. **Makes about 3 cups (750 mL)**. *Serve with cookies or over ice cream.*

Lime and Thyme Vinaigrette

1	clove garlic, minced	1
⅓ cup	extra-virgin olive oil	75 mL
2 tsp	dried thyme	10 mL
	Juice of 2 limes	
	Salt and freshly ground black pepper to taste	

Whisk together all ingredients. **Makes about ¾ cup (175 mL)**. *Store in the refrigerator for up to 2 weeks. Use as a dressing for a green salad.*

Golden Turmeric Tomato Relish

2	tomatoes, seeded and chopped	2
¼	small red onion, thinly sliced	¼
¼ cup	chopped fresh mint	50 mL
2 tbsp	plain yogurt	25 mL
2 tsp	ground turmeric	10 mL
1 tsp	granulated sugar	5 mL
1 tsp	chili powder	5 mL
	Juice of ½ lemon	

Toss together all ingredients. **Makes about 2 cups (500 mL)**. *Store in the refrigerator for up to 4 days. Serve with grilled meat or fish.*

Watercress and Grapefruit Salad

4	green onions, thinly sliced	4
2	grapefruit, peeled, trimmed of membrane and sectioned	2
4 cups	watercress leaves	1 L
⅓ cup	chopped pistachios	75 mL
3 tbsp	freshly squeezed lemon juice	45 mL
2 tbsp	canola oil	25 mL
1 tbsp	dark sesame oil	15 mL
Pinch	cayenne pepper	Pinch
	Salt and freshly ground black pepper to taste	

Toss together green onions, grapefruit sections, watercress and pistachios. In a small bowl, whisk together lemon juice, canola oil, sesame oil, cayenne, salt and black pepper. Pour over salad and toss to coat. **Serves 4.**

Zesty Salt Substitute

1 tbsp	finely grated lemon zest	15 mL
2 tsp	finely grated orange zest	10 mL
2 tsp	finely grated lime zest	10 mL
1 tsp	freshly ground black pepper	5 mL
1 tsp	freshly ground Szechuan peppercorns	5 mL
1 tsp	ground coriander	5 mL
¼ tsp	ground ginger	1 mL

Combine all ingredients. **Makes about ¼ cup (50 mL)**. *Store in the refrigerator for up to 1 week. Use as a seasoning for grilled meat, poultry or seafood.*

Chapter 3
Sauces
To Turn Anything into a Meal

Wine and Mushroom Sauce 50
Lemon Walnut Sauce 50
Sauce Véronique 50
Yogurt and Herb Sauce 51
Watercress and Cream Sauce 51
Sorrel and Crème Fraîche 51
Beurre Blanc 51
Herbed Beurre Blanc 51
Sage Glaze 51
Spicy Hoisin Sauce 51
Barbecue Pan Sauce 51
Worcestershire and Mustard Sauce 52
Confetti of Prosciutto, Peas
and Rosemary 52
Ginger, Soy and Sesame Sauce 52
Sweet-and-Sour Cider Sauce 52
Sherried Apricot Glaze 52
Crème Fraîche and Mustard Sauce 52
Onion, Brandy and Cream Sauce 52
Red Wine Pomegranate Sauce 52
Red Pepper Coulis 53
Warm Sun-Dried Tomato Vinaigrette ... 53
Sauce Provençal 53
Tomato, Chili and Mascarpone Sauce ... 53
Tomato, Olive and Parmesan Sauce 53
Peanut Sauce 53

Capers and Brown Butter Sauce 54
Beurre Rouge 54
Garlic Beurre Blanc 54
Scotch and Brown Sugar Sauce 54
Rosemary and Vermouth Sauce 54
Sherry and Balsamic Sauce 54
Bordelaise Sauce 54
Juniper Gin Sauce 55
Mushroom Ragoût 55
Oyster Sauce with Lime and Garlic 55
Curried Onion Sauce 55
White Wine Mushrooms 55
Julienned Peppers and Carrots 55
Garlic Vinaigrette 56
Basil and Garlic Sauce 56
Lemon Parsley Sauce 56
Anchovy Mayonnaise 56
Tapenade 56
Roasted Pepper Rouille 56
Roquefort Buttermilk Sauce 56
Tarragon Ranch Sauce 56
Tomato and Artichoke Salsa 56
Garlic Citrus Salsa 56
Spicy Avocado Sauce 57
Gazpacho Sauce 57

Why are so many people so shy about sauces? Is it fear of becoming mired in complicated technique? Or uneasiness at the prospect of unwanted calories and unfamiliar flavors? Why, in a country obsessed with convenience and culinary corner-cutting, do we ignore one of the simplest and least expensive ways to turn a basic ingredient into a meal?

For years, anxiety over sauce-making has held contemporary home cooking hostage. It has helped condemn us to a diet of excess salt as we struggle to eke out flavor without the natural complement of a sauce. It has created a false image of us as "plain eaters" when we are actually among the most adventurous eaters the world has known. And it stands in the way of our search for quick, healthful, convenient solutions to the nightly quandary of what to make for dinner.

We offer the following sauce recipes with hopes of changing that. None of them takes more than 10 minutes to prepare, all require little or no salt, and saturated fat is kept to a minimum. Most important, all of them provide fabulous flavor with minimum work.

About these recipes . . .

These sauces are arranged according to the foods they complement best. We note whether you would do well to serve a particular sauce with chicken, beef, veal, pork or fish. But these are only suggestions, and we encourage you to experiment with different combinations, trying sauces that appeal to you with different main ingredients, or substituting an herb here or a spice there as availability and taste suit you. As with the marinades in Chapter 1, these 50 sauces lead to hundreds of combinations.

Each of the following recipes is written for 4 portions of sautéed meat or fish. Before preparing the sauce, sauté the main ingredient, then transfer it to a warm platter. Pour off all but a thin film of fat from the pan and proceed with the sauce recipe. (The last group of recipes is for uncooked sauces, made separately from the main food.)

If you prefer to steam, poach or microwave your meat or fish, these recipes can still be used. Follow these procedures instead:

For poaching: Place the cooked food on a warm platter and reduce ½ cup (125 mL) of the poaching liquid over high heat by about two-thirds. Proceed with the sauce recipe of your choice, adding the reduced poaching liquid to the sauce along with the other liquids in the recipe.

For steaming or microwaving: Enclose the food in microwave-safe plastic wrap, which will hold in any juices weeping from the ingredients during cooking. When the food is done, remove from the steamer or microwave, snip a hole in the plastic and drain off the juices, adding them to the sauce along with the other liquids in the recipe.

These recipes make no mention of salt and pepper, which you should add to taste.

We suggest the following sauces for chicken, fish and veal.

Wine and Mushroom Sauce

2 tbsp	olive oil	25 mL
12	mushrooms, sliced	12
2 tbsp	minced onion	25 mL
2 cups	dry white wine	500 mL
¼ cup	sour cream, plain yogurt or crème fraîche	50 mL

Add oil, mushrooms and onion to the fat in the pan and sauté over medium heat until onion is lightly browned. Add wine and boil until reduced by half. Remove from heat and stir in sour cream. **Makes about 2 cups (500 mL).**

Lemon Walnut Sauce

¾ cup	chopped walnuts	175 mL
⅓ cup	walnut oil	75 mL
1	small clove garlic, minced	1
	Juice of ½ lemon	

Add walnuts to the fat in the pan and lightly toast over medium heat, stirring constantly. Remove from heat and stir in walnut oil, garlic and lemon juice. **Makes about 1 cup (250 mL).**

Sauce Véronique

1	small shallot, finely chopped	1
1 cup	dry white wine	250 mL
1 cup	chicken broth	250 mL
24	seedless grapes, halved	24
2 tbsp	butter	25 mL

Add shallot to the fat in the pan and sauté over medium heat until tender. Add wine and boil for 2 minutes. Add broth and boil until liquid is reduced by half. Reduce heat to low, add grape halves and butter, and heat through. **Makes about 2 cups (500 mL).**

Yogurt and Herb Sauce

2 tbsp	extra-virgin olive oil	25 mL
¼ cup	chopped leek (white and light green parts only)	50 mL
1	clove garlic, minced	1
1 cup	chicken, fish or vegetable broth	250 mL
⅓ cup	chopped fresh herbs	75 mL
1 cup	plain yogurt	250 mL

Add oil and leek to the fat in the pan and sauté over medium heat until leek is tender. Add garlic and sauté for 30 seconds. Add broth and herbs; boil until liquid is reduced by about three-quarters. Remove from heat and stir in yogurt. **Makes about 1½ cups (375 mL).**

Watercress and Cream Sauce

1 tbsp	minced onion	15 mL
½ cup	dry vermouth	125 mL
1 cup	whipping (35%) cream	250 mL
⅔ cup	watercress leaves	150 mL

Add onion to the fat in the pan and sauté over medium heat until tender. Increase heat to high, add vermouth, and boil until liquid is reduced by about two-thirds. Add cream and cook until thickened, about 1 minute. Stir in watercress and cook just until leaves wilt. **Makes about 1½ cups (375 mL).**

Sorrel and Crème Fraîche

Follow preceding recipe, but replace the whipping cream with crème fraîche and the watercress with coarsely chopped sorrel leaves. **Makes about 1½ cups (375 mL).**

Beurre Blanc

2	shallots, minced	2
1 cup	dry white wine	250 mL
¼ cup	white wine vinegar	50 mL
½ cup	butter, cut into 8 pieces	125 mL

Add shallots, wine and vinegar to the fat in the pan and boil over high heat until liquid is reduced by about three-quarters. Reduce heat to low and whisk in butter, one piece at a time. **Makes about ¾ cup (175 mL).**

Herbed Beurre Blanc

2	shallots, minced	2
1 cup	dry white wine	250 mL
¼ cup	white wine vinegar	50 mL
1 tbsp	dried tarragon, basil, chervil or dillweed	15 mL
½ cup	butter, cut into 8 pieces	125 mL
1 tbsp	minced fresh Italian (flat-leaf) parsley	15 mL

Add shallots, wine, vinegar and tarragon to the fat in the pan and boil over high heat until liquid is reduced by about three-quarters. Reduce heat to low and whisk in butter, one piece at a time. Stir in parsley. **Makes about ¾ cup (175 mL).**

The following sauces are well suited to chicken, pork and veal.

Sage Glaze

2 tbsp	butter	25 mL
10	fresh sage leaves	10
2 tbsp	finely chopped onion	25 mL
1½ cups	chicken broth	375 mL
Pinch	dried thyme	Pinch

Add butter to the fat in the pan and melt over medium heat. Sauté sage and onion until onion is lightly browned. Add broth and thyme; boil until sauce is slightly thickened. **Makes about 1 cup (250 mL).**

Spicy Hoisin Sauce

2	small cloves garlic, minced	2
2 tsp	minced gingerroot	10 mL
Pinch	hot pepper flakes	Pinch
⅔ cup	chicken broth	150 mL
¼ cup	hoisin sauce	50 mL

Add garlic, ginger and hot pepper flakes to the fat in the pan and sauté over medium-high heat until aromatic. Stir in broth and hoisin sauce; reduce heat and bring to a simmer. **Makes about 1 cup (250 mL).**

Barbecue Pan Sauce

2 tbsp	grated onion	25 mL
Pinch	granulated sugar	Pinch
½ cup	ketchup	125 mL
2 tbsp	cider vinegar	25 mL
2 tsp	spicy brown mustard	10 mL
2 tsp	Worcestershire sauce	10 mL
	Hot pepper sauce (such as Tabasco) to taste	

Add onion and sugar to the fat in the pan and sauté over medium heat until onion is lightly browned. Stir in ketchup, vinegar, mustard and Worcestershire sauce; bring to a boil. Season with hot pepper sauce. Return cooked meat to the pan and coat with sauce before serving. **Makes about 1 cup (250 mL).**

Worcestershire and Mustard Sauce

2 tbsp	finely chopped onion	25 mL
⅔ cup	chicken broth	150 mL
3 tbsp	Worcestershire sauce	45 mL
2 tbsp	brown mustard	25 mL

Add onion to the fat in the pan and sauté over medium heat until lightly browned. Add broth and Worcestershire sauce; boil for 1 minute. Stir in mustard; cook, stirring, until sauce is smooth and slightly thickened. **Makes about 1 cup (250 mL).**

Confetti of Prosciutto, Peas and Rosemary

2 tbsp	minced onion	25 mL
4 oz	prosciutto, cut in thin strips	125 g
1¼ cups	frozen peas, thawed	300 mL
1 tbsp	chopped fresh rosemary	15 mL
⅔ cup	cream (any type, minimum 10%)	150 mL

Add onion to the fat in the pan and sauté over medium-high heat until translucent Add prosciutto, peas and rosemary; sauté for 1 minute. Add cream and boil, stirring, until slightly thickened, about 1 minute. **Makes about 2 cups (500 mL).**

Ginger, Soy and Sesame Sauce

2 tbsp	dark sesame oil	25 mL
1	small clove garlic, minced	1
2 tsp	chopped gingerroot	10 mL
⅔ cup	chicken broth	150 mL
2 tbsp	reduced-sodium soy sauce	25 mL
Pinch	granulated sugar	Pinch

Add oil, garlic and ginger to the fat in the pan and sauté over medium-high heat until aromatic. Add broth, soy sauce and sugar; reduce heat and simmer for 1 minute. **Makes about 1 cup (250 mL).**

Sweet-and-Sour Cider Sauce

2 tbsp	finely chopped onion	25 mL
1¼ cups	apple cider	300 mL
1 tbsp	cider vinegar	15 mL
2 tsp	packed brown sugar	10 mL
2 tbsp	butter, cut into pieces	25 mL

Add onion to the fat in the pan and sauté over medium-high heat until lightly browned. Add cider, vinegar and brown sugar; reduce heat and simmer until slightly thickened. Whisk in butter, one piece at a time. **Makes about 1 cup (250 mL).**

Sherried Apricot Glaze

2 tbsp	butter	25 mL
¼ cup	minced onion	50 mL
2 tsp	grated gingerroot	10 mL
¼ cup	apricot preserves	50 mL
⅔ cup	dry sherry	150 mL
2 tbsp	freshly squeezed orange juice	25 mL

Add butter to the fat in the pan and melt over medium heat. Sauté onion and ginger until onion is translucent. Add preserves and cook, stirring, until melted. Stir in sherry and orange juice; carefully flambé (see page 10). **Makes about 1 cup (250 mL).**

Crème Fraîche and Mustard Sauce

2	shallots, chopped	2
⅔ cup	crème fraîche	150 mL
2 tbsp	Dijon mustard	25 mL

Add shallots to the fat in the pan and sauté over medium heat until tender; do not brown. Remove from heat and stir in crème fraîche and mustard. **Makes about ¾ cup (175 mL).**

Onion, Brandy and Cream Sauce

½ cup	brandy	125 mL
2 tbsp	minced onion	25 mL
2 cups	cream (any type, minimum 10%)	500 mL

Add brandy and onion to the fat in the pan; carefully flambé (see page 10). When flames subside, add cream and boil gently, stirring, until slightly thickened. **Makes about 1½ cups (375 mL).**

Red Wine Pomegranate Sauce

2 tbsp	finely chopped onion	25 mL
1 cup	light red wine (such as Beaujolais)	250 mL
1 cup	pomegranate juice (fresh or bottled)	250 mL
¼ cup	butter, cut into pieces	50 mL

Add onion to the fat in the pan and sauté over medium-high heat until translucent. Add wine and boil for 2 minutes. Add pomegranate juice (if using fresh, squeeze a halved pomegranate over a strainer to catch the seeds) and boil for 1 minute. Whisk in butter, one piece at a time. **Makes about 1½ cups (375 mL).**

The following sauces are excellent with chicken, fish, pork and veal.

Red Pepper Coulis

2	large red bell peppers, chopped	2
1	small onion, chopped	1
1	clove garlic, minced	1
½	jalapeño pepper, seeded and minced	½
½ cup	vegetable broth	125 mL
2 tbsp	freshly squeezed lemon juice	25 mL
1 tbsp	dark sesame oil	15 mL

Add all ingredients to the fat in the pan and bring to a boil over medium-high heat. Reduce heat, cover and simmer until red pepper is tender. Transfer to a food processor and purée until smooth. Strain through a fine-mesh sieve, discarding any solids. **Makes about 2 cups (500 mL).**

Warm Sun-Dried Tomato Vinaigrette

⅓ cup	extra-virgin olive oil, divided	75 mL
1	clove garlic, minced	1
Pinch	dried basil	Pinch
6	oil-packed sun-dried tomatoes, finely chopped	6
¼ cup	red wine vinegar	50 mL

Add 1 tbsp (15 mL) of the olive oil, garlic and basil to the fat in the pan and sauté over medium-high heat until garlic is fragrant. Stir in the remaining oil, sun-dried tomatoes and vinegar; heat through. **Makes about ¾ cup (175 mL).**

Sauce Provençal

¼ cup	extra-virgin olive oil	50 mL
¼ cup	minced onion	50 mL
2	cloves garlic, minced	2
1 tsp	dried herbes de Provence	5 mL
12	black olives, pitted and coarsely chopped	12
6	large plum (Roma) tomatoes, finely chopped	6
2 tbsp	chopped fresh basil	25 mL

Add oil, onion, garlic and herbes de Provence to the fat in the pan and sauté over medium-high heat until aromatic. Add olives, tomatoes and basil; heat through. **Makes about 2 cups (500 mL).**

Tomato, Chili and Mascarpone Sauce

2 tbsp	extra-virgin olive oil	25 mL
2	cloves garlic, minced	2
Pinch	hot pepper flakes (or to taste)	Pinch
3 cups	chopped tomatoes	750 mL
¼ cup	mascarpone cheese	50 mL

Add oil, garlic and hot pepper flakes to the fat in the pan and sauté over medium-high heat until aromatic. Add tomatoes, reduce heat and bring to a simmer. Stir in mascarpone. **Makes about 3 cups (750 mL).**

Tomato, Olive and Parmesan Sauce

2 tbsp	extra-virgin olive oil	25 mL
2	cloves garlic, minced	2
12	black olives, pitted and chopped	12
3 cups	chopped tomatoes	750 mL
2 tbsp	freshly grated Parmesan cheese	25 mL

Add oil and garlic to the fat in the pan and sauté over medium heat until aromatic. Add olives and tomatoes; reduce heat and bring to a simmer. Stir in Parmesan. **Makes about 3 cups (750 mL).**

Peanut Sauce

1	small onion, chopped	1
1	clove garlic, minced	1
2	green onions, sliced	2
1 tbsp	soy sauce	15 mL
2 tsp	finely chopped gingerroot	10 mL
1 tsp	Asian chili paste	5 mL
Pinch	ground cumin	Pinch
Pinch	ground coriander	Pinch
¼ cup	peanut butter (chunky or smooth)	50 mL
½ cup	buttermilk, plain yogurt, or chicken or vegetable broth	125 mL

Add onion and garlic to the fat in the pan and sauté over medium heat until tender. Add green onions, soy sauce, ginger, chili paste, cumin and coriander; sauté for 1 minute. Stir in peanut butter until melted. Add buttermilk and cook, stirring, until heated through; do not boil. **Makes about 1 cup (250 mL).**

The following recipes go well with beef, chicken, fish, pork and veal.

Capers and Brown Butter Sauce

½ cup	butter, divided	125 mL
2 tbsp	minced onion or shallot	25 mL
¼ cup	drained whole capers	50 mL
	Juice of 1 lemon	

Add half the butter to the fat in the pan and melt over medium heat. Sauté onion until browned. Add capers and the remaining butter; cook for 1 minute. Stir in lemon juice. (The sauce will darken.) **Makes about ¾ cup (175 mL).**

Beurre Rouge

1 cup	dry red wine	250 mL
¼ cup	red wine vinegar	50 mL
2 tbsp	minced onion	25 mL
1 tsp	tomato paste	5 mL
½ cup	butter, cut into 8 pieces	125 mL

Add wine, vinegar and onion to the fat in the pan and boil over medium-high heat until liquid is reduced by about three-quarters. Reduce heat to low and add tomato paste. Whisk in butter, one piece at a time, to form a smooth sauce. **Makes about ¾ cup (175 mL).**

Garlic Beurre Blanc

1	clove garlic, minced	1
½ cup	dry white wine	125 mL
2 tbsp	white wine vinegar	25 mL
¼ cup	butter, cut into 4 pieces	50 mL

Add garlic, wine and vinegar to the fat in the pan and boil over medium-high heat until liquid is reduced by about half. Reduce heat to low and whisk in butter, one piece at a time, to form a smooth sauce. **Makes about ½ cup (125 mL).**

Scotch and Brown Sugar Sauce

¼ cup	butter, divided	50 mL
¼ cup	chopped onion	50 mL
1 tbsp	packed dark brown sugar	15 mL
⅓ cup	Scotch whisky	75 mL
¾ cup	beef broth	175 mL

Add half the butter to the fat in the pan and melt over medium heat. Sauté onion until browned. Add brown sugar and cook for 1 minute. Deglaze pan with Scotch and carefully flambé (see page 10). When flames subside, stir in the remaining butter until melted. Add broth and boil until sauce is slightly thickened. **Makes about 1½ cups (375 mL).**

Rosemary and Vermouth Sauce

1 cup	dry vermouth	250 mL
¼ cup	white wine vinegar	50 mL
2 tbsp	minced onion	25 mL
1 tbsp	chopped fresh rosemary	15 mL
½ cup	butter, cut into 8 pieces	125 mL
1 tbsp	minced fresh Italian (flat-leaf) parsley	15 mL

Add vermouth, vinegar, onion and rosemary to the fat in the pan and cook over medium-high heat until liquid is reduced by about three-quarters. Reduce heat to low and whisk in butter, one piece at a time, to form a smooth sauce. Stir in parsley. **Makes about ¾ cup (175 mL).**

Sherry and Balsamic Sauce

1 cup	dry sherry	250 mL
¼ cup	balsamic vinegar	50 mL
2 tbsp	minced onion	25 mL
½ cup	butter, cut into 8 pieces	125 mL

Add sherry, vinegar and onion to the fat in the pan and cook over medium-high heat until liquid is reduced by about three-quarters. Reduce heat to low and whisk in butter, one piece at a time, to form a smooth sauce. **Makes about ¾ cup (175 mL).**

Bordelaise Sauce

¼ cup	minced onion	50 mL
¼ cup	finely chopped mushrooms	50 mL
1 tbsp	tomato paste	15 mL
Pinch	dried thyme	Pinch
1 cup	full-bodied red wine	250 mL
1 cup	beef broth	250 mL
2 tbsp	butter, cut into 4 pieces	25 mL

Add onion and mushrooms to the fat in the pan and sauté over medium-high heat until well browned. Add tomato paste and thyme; cook, stirring, for 1 minute. Add wine, increase heat to high and boil until liquid is reduced by half. Add broth and boil for 3 minutes. Reduce heat to medium and whisk in butter, one piece at a time, to form a smooth sauce. **Makes about 1½ cups (375 mL).**

Juniper Gin Sauce

4	juniper berries, crushed	4
1	small clove garlic, minced	1
1 tsp	whole green peppercorns	5 mL
½ cup	gin	125 mL
½ cup	whipping (35%) cream	125 mL

Add juniper berries, garlic and peppercorns to the fat in the pan and sauté over medium heat until aromatic. Add gin and carefully flambé (see page 10). When the flames subside, add cream, reduce heat and simmer, stirring, until sauce is thickened. **Makes about ¾ cup (175 mL).**

Mushroom Ragoût

¼ oz	dried wild mushrooms	7 g
¾ cup	warm water	175 mL
2 tbsp	butter	25 mL
4 oz	mushrooms, sliced	125 g
1	leek (white part only), thinly sliced	1
1	tomato, peeled, seeded and chopped	1
1 tbsp	chopped fresh Italian (flat-leaf) parsley	15 mL
Pinch	dried thyme	Pinch

Soak dried mushrooms in warm water for 15 minutes. Strain through cheesecloth or a coffee filter, reserving mushrooms and soaking liquid separately. Add butter to the fat in the pan and melt over medium heat. Sauté soaked and fresh mushrooms and leek until tender. Add mushroom soaking liquid, tomato, parsley and thyme; bring to a boil. Reduce heat and simmer for 3 minutes. **Makes about 2 cups (500 mL).**

Oyster Sauce with Lime and Garlic

1	large clove garlic, minced	1
1 cup	chicken broth	250 mL
½ cup	oyster sauce	125 mL
½ cup	dry sherry	125 mL
2 tsp	minced gingerroot	10 mL
	Juice of 2 large limes	
2 tsp	dark sesame oil	10 mL

In a bowl, combine garlic, broth, oyster sauce, sherry, ginger and lime juice. Add to the fat in the pan and bring to a boil over medium heat; boil for 3 minutes. Whisk in sesame oil. **Makes about 1½ cups (375 mL).**

Curried Onion Sauce

2 tbsp	vegetable oil	25 mL
1	large onion, finely chopped	1
1 tbsp	curry powder	15 mL
1 tsp	ground coriander	5 mL
Pinch	hot pepper flakes	Pinch
1 cup	low-fat plain yogurt	250 mL
2 tsp	orange marmalade	10 mL

Add oil and onion to the fat in the pan and sauté over medium-low heat until onion is tender. Add curry powder, coriander and hot pepper flakes; cook, stirring, for 1 minute. Reduce heat, stir in yogurt and cook until heated through; do not boil. Stir in marmalade. **Makes about 2 cups (500 mL).**

White Wine Mushrooms

¼ cup	olive oil	50 mL
4 oz	mushrooms, sliced	125 g
⅓ cup	dry white wine	75 mL
1 tbsp	finely chopped onion	15 mL
1 tbsp	freshly squeezed lemon juice	15 mL
1	bay leaf	1
Pinch	dried thyme	Pinch
Pinch	ground coriander	Pinch
2 tbsp	chopped fresh Italian (flat-leaf) parsley	25 mL

Add oil, mushrooms, wine, onion, lemon juice, bay leaf, thyme and coriander to the fat in the pan and bring to a boil over medium-high heat. Remove from heat and stir in parsley. Discard bay leaf. **Makes about 2 cups (500 mL).**

Julienned Peppers and Carrots

2 tbsp	extra-virgin olive oil	25 mL
2 tbsp	minced onion	25 mL
2	thin carrots, peeled and cut into thin strips	2
1	red bell pepper, cut into thin strips	1
½ cup	chicken broth	125 mL
	Juice of ½ lemon	
2 tbsp	chopped fresh Italian (flat-leaf) parsley	25 mL

Add oil and onion to the fat in the pan and sauté over medium heat until onion is tender but not browned. Add carrots and pepper; sauté for 2 minutes. Add broth and lemon juice; reduce heat and simmer until carrot is barely tender, about 2 minutes. Stir in parsley. **Makes about 1½ cups (375 mL).**

The following sauces for chicken, fish and veal are uncooked. They are made separately from the foods they accompany and can be made in advance and stored in the refrigerator for up to 5 days. If you're concerned about the food safety of uncooked eggs, you may want to avoid the first three recipes.

Garlic Vinaigrette

1	large clove garlic, minced	1
1	egg yolk	1
1 tbsp	Dijon mustard	15 mL
¼ cup	white wine vinegar	50 mL
½ cup	olive oil	125 mL

In a small bowl, combine garlic, egg yolk and mustard. Mix in vinegar. In a slow, steady stream, whisk in oil. **Makes about 1 cup (250 mL).**

Basil and Garlic Sauce

Follow preceding recipe, but add 3 tbsp (45 mL) chopped fresh basil with the garlic. **Makes about 1 cup (250 mL).**

Lemon Parsley Sauce

Follow recipe for Garlic Vinaigrette (above), but replace the garlic with 2 tsp (10 mL) finely grated lemon zest and replace the vinegar with lemon juice. Stir in 3 tbsp (45 mL) chopped fresh parsley at the end. **Makes about 1 cup (250 mL).**

Anchovy Mayonnaise

1	small clove garlic, minced	1
2 oz	canned anchovies, with oil, finely chopped	60 g
3 tbsp	mayonnaise	45 mL
2 tbsp	extra-virgin olive oil	25 mL
1 tbsp	freshly squeezed lemon juice	15 mL

Combine all ingredients. **Makes about ½ cup (125 mL).**

Tapenade

1	clove garlic, minced	1
⅓ cup	chopped pitted oil-cured black olives	75 mL
⅓ cup	extra-virgin olive oil	75 mL

Combine all ingredients. **Makes about ½ cup (125 mL).**

Roasted Pepper Rouille

1	large roasted red pepper (see page 11), minced	1
1	clove garlic, minced	1
¼ cup	finely chopped fresh basil	50 mL
¼ cup	extra-virgin olive oil	50 mL

Combine all ingredients. **Makes about ½ cup (125 mL).**

Roquefort Buttermilk Sauce

½ cup	Roquefort Dressing (see recipe, page 64)	125 mL
¼ cup	buttermilk	50 mL

In a small bowl, thin dressing with buttermilk. **Makes about ¾ cup (175 mL).**

Tarragon Ranch Sauce

½ cup	bottled ranch dressing	125 mL
3 tbsp	buttermilk	45 mL
1 tbsp	tarragon vinegar	15 mL

In a small bowl, thin dressing with buttermilk and vinegar. **Makes about ¾ cup (175 mL).**

Tomato and Artichoke Salsa

1	jar (6 oz/170 mL) marinated artichoke hearts	1
1	large tomato, finely chopped	1
1	clove garlic, minced	1

Drain artichoke hearts, reserving half the marinade (set the remaining marinade aside for another use, or discard). Chop artichoke hearts and combine with reserved marinade. Stir in tomato and garlic. **Makes about 1 cup (250 mL).**

Garlic Citrus Salsa

1	small clove garlic, minced	1
1 cup	chopped peeled orange, grapefruit, lemon, lime or tangerine	250 mL
1 tbsp	chopped red onion	15 mL
1 tsp	white wine vinegar	5 mL
Dash	hot pepper sauce (such as Tabasco)	Dash

Combine all ingredients. **Makes about 1 cup (250 mL).**

Spicy Avocado Sauce

1	avocado, mashed	1
1	clove garlic, minced	1
1	green onion, chopped	1
1½ tbsp	white wine vinegar	22 mL
1 tbsp	olive oil	15 mL
Dash	hot pepper sauce (such as Tabasco)	Dash

Combine all ingredients. **Makes about ¾ cup** (175 mL).

Gazpacho Sauce

2	plum (Roma) tomatoes, cut into chunks	2
1	small clove garlic, minced	1
¼	cucumber, peeled and cut into chunks	¼
¼	pickled jalapeño pepper	¼
1 tbsp	chopped onion	15 mL
2 tbsp	extra-virgin olive oil	25 mL
1 tbsp	red wine vinegar	15 mL

In a food processor, process tomatoes, garlic, cucumber, jalapeño and onion until finely chopped. Mix in oil and vinegar. **Makes about 1 cup (250 mL).**

Chapter 4
Dressings
To Help You Kick the Bottle

Oil and Vinegar Dressing 59

Hot Pepper Vinaigrette 60

Lemon and Olive Oil Dressing 60

Orange Walnut Dressing 60

Lime Vinaigrette 60

Creamy Avocado Dressing 60

Basic Wine Vinaigrette 60

Niçoise Vinaigrette 60

Garlic Herb Dressing 60

Creamy Italian Dressing 60

Balsamic–Olive Oil Vinaigrette 61

Sun-Dried Tomato Vinaigrette 61

Dijon Vinaigrette 61

Tarragon Mustard Vinaigrette 61

Creamy Rosemary Dressing 61

Creamy Orange-Fennel Dressing 61

Raspberry Vinaigrette 61

Sherry Vinaigrette 61

Classic Caesar Dressing 62

Tonnato Caesar Dressing 62

Warm Bacon Dressing 62

Real Russian Dressing 62

Clear Coleslaw Dressing 62

Sour Cream Coleslaw Dressing 62

Poppy Seed Dressing 62

Sesame Tofu Vinaigrette 62

Soy Ginger Dressing 63

Szechuan Ginger Dressing 63

Warm Tomato Vinaigrette 63

Sweet-and-Sour Creole Vinaigrette 63

Creamy Creole Dressing 63

Sweet Pepper Vinaigrette 63

Blue Cheese Dressing 63

Warm Blue Cheese Dressing 64

Roquefort Dressing 64

Spicy Ginger Vinaigrette 64

Garlic Ranch Dressing 64

Yogurt Dill Ranch Dressing 64

Basil Ranch Dressing 64

Green Goddess Ranch Dressing 64

Creamy Mayonnaise Dressing 64

Pesto Mayonnaise Dressing 64

Minted Yogurt Dressing 65

Yogurt Cilantro Dressing 65

Sweet Mustard Dressing 65

Apple Cider Dressing 65

Sweet Balsamic Dressing 65

Guacamole Vinaigrette 65

Salsa Vinaigrette 65

Pesto Vinaigrette 65

Salad dressing is easy — vinegar, oil and seasoning to taste. The measurements need not be exact, and the technique requires nothing more than a flick of the whisk. Why, then, is bottled dressing one of the most popular convenience foods in our culture? Why do we continue to pay so extravagantly for something that can be made at home for pennies in minutes?

For most of us, it's simply lack of practice. We aren't aware that many homemade salad dressings keep almost indefinitely in the refrigerator and can be replenished quickly when supplies run low. Nor do we know that hundreds of dressings stem from just three basic formulas; to know those formulas is to have the entire cuisine of salads at one's fingertips.

All salad dressings are a mixture of fat and acid. The simplest dressing is vinaigrette, usually made from oil and vinegar in a three-to-one or two-to-one proportion. Many popular salad dressings — including Italian dressing, white and red wine vinaigrettes, lemon and oil dressings, warm bacon dressings and sweet-and-sour salad dressings — are vinaigrettes. The only problem with vinaigrettes is that acid and fat do not readily blend together. Mix them rapidly and they'll appear to blend, but that's just an illusion; after they sit for a few minutes, the fat will come out of suspension and rise to the surface. That's why simple vinaigrettes must be shaken or whisked every time they're used.

To combat separation anxiety, cooks rely on culinary emulsifiers to stabilize the fragile suspension of oil and vinegar. Emulsified salad dressings are held together by an egg yolk, commercial mayonnaise or a fresh dairy product. Each of these products contains natural emulsifiers that, when beaten with a simple vinaigrette, help the shaky oil-and-vinegar suspension remain thick and creamy for a week or more. Emulsified salad dressings include creamy Italian vinaigrette, mayonnaise dressings, Russian dressing, ranch dressing and most blue cheese dressings.

In the third type of salad dressing, the oil and vinegar are held together by a purée, which can be anything from the tomato in a tomato vinaigrette to the tofu in a creamy Japanese dressing, the peanut butter in an Indonesian satay or the puréed basil and pine nuts in a pesto dressing.

Understand these three methods and any salad dressing is within your culinary grasp. The 50 recipes in this chapter include examples of each type. Use them as starting points for your own creations, if you wish, substituting an herb for the garlic in one, or walnut oil for olive oil in another. Once you know the basic techniques that are the root of all dressings, bottled products will be nothing more than a part of your past.

About these recipes . . .

Don't be confined by a lifelong habit of using dressings only with greens. Many dressings pair splendidly with grilled meats and fish, or work well as marinades. We've included suggestions with some of the more unusual dressings.

Extra-virgin olive oil is more flavorful than regular olive oil. We prefer it in salad dressings and other recipes where we want the flavor of olive oil to be pronounced. Replace it with pure olive oil if you want a milder flavor.

The dressings made without dairy products can be stored in an airtight container in the refrigerator for several weeks; those made with dairy products can be stored in the refrigerator for up to 1 week.

Many cooks, responding to the potential presence of salmonella bacteria in uncooked eggs, have stopped using salad dressings that call for raw egg yolks. We've included a few such recipes (Creamy Rosemary Dressing, Creamy Orange Fennel Dressing, Classic Caesar Dressing, Tonnato Caesar Dressing and Sweet Mustard Dressing) because we consider them classics. If you are concerned about the food safety of raw eggs, you may want to avoid these recipes or use pasteurized eggs.

Oil and Vinegar Dressing

1/3 cup	extra-virgin olive oil	75 mL
2 tbsp	red wine vinegar	25 mL
	Salt and freshly ground black pepper to taste	

Thoroughly whisk together all ingredients. **Makes about 1/2 cup (125 mL), enough for 4 servings of salad.**

Hot Pepper Vinaigrette

1	clove garlic, minced	1
1/3 cup	extra-virgin olive oil	75 mL
2 tbsp	red wine vinegar	25 mL
1/2 tsp	hot pepper flakes	2 mL
	Salt and freshly ground black pepper to taste	

Thoroughly whisk together all ingredients. Makes about 1/2 cup (125 mL), enough for 4 servings of salad.

Lemon and Olive Oil Dressing

1	clove garlic, minced	1
1/3 cup	extra-virgin olive oil	75 mL
	Juice of 2 lemons	
	Salt and freshly ground black pepper to taste	

Thoroughly whisk together all ingredients. Makes about 1/2 cup (125 mL), enough for 4 servings of salad.

Orange Walnut Dressing

1/3 cup	walnut oil	75 mL
Pinch	freshly grated nutmeg	Pinch
	Juice of 1 large orange	
	Juice of 1/2 lemon	

Thoroughly whisk together all ingredients. Makes about 1/2 cup (125 mL), enough for 4 servings of salad.

Lime Vinaigrette

1/3 cup	extra-virgin olive oil	75 mL
2 tbsp	red wine vinegar	25 mL
	Finely grated zest and juice of 1 large lime	
	Salt and freshly ground black pepper to taste	

Thoroughly whisk together all ingredients. Makes about 3/4 cup (175 mL), enough for 4 servings of salad.

Creamy Avocado Dressing

1	avocado, mashed	1
1	clove garlic, minced	1
1/3 cup	extra-virgin olive oil	75 mL
2 tbsp	red wine vinegar	25 mL
Dash	hot pepper sauce (such as Tabasco)	Dash
	Finely grated zest and juice of 1 large lime	
	Salt and freshly ground black pepper to taste	

Thoroughly whisk together all ingredients. Makes about 1 cup (250 mL), enough for 4 servings of salad. *Store in an airtight container in the refrigerator for up to 1 week.*

Basic Wine Vinaigrette

4	green onions, white parts only, minced	4
1/3 cup	white or red wine vinegar	75 mL
1/3 cup	canola oil	75 mL
1/3 cup	extra-virgin olive oil	75 mL
	Salt and freshly ground black pepper to taste	

Thoroughly whisk together all ingredients. Makes about 1 cup (250 mL), enough for 8 servings of salad.

Niçoise Vinaigrette

2	cloves garlic, minced	2
1/3 cup	white or red wine vinegar	75 mL
1/3 cup	canola oil	75 mL
1/3 cup	extra-virgin olive oil	75 mL
1/4 cup	finely chopped pitted black olives	50 mL
	Salt and freshly ground black pepper to taste	

Thoroughly whisk together all ingredients. Makes about 1 cup (250 mL), enough for 8 servings of salad.

Garlic Herb Dressing

2	large cloves garlic, minced	2
3/4 cup	extra-virgin olive oil	175 mL
1/4 cup	red wine vinegar	50 mL
1 tbsp	minced fresh Italian (flat-leaf) parsley	15 mL
2 tsp	chopped fresh green herb (such as basil, dill, oregano, chervil, tarragon)	10 mL
	Salt and freshly ground black pepper to taste	

Thoroughly whisk together all ingredients. Makes about 1 cup (250 mL), enough for 8 servings of salad.

Creamy Italian Dressing

2	large cloves garlic, minced	2
3/4 cup	extra-virgin olive oil	175 mL
1/4 cup	red wine vinegar	50 mL
2 tbsp	mayonnaise (not fat-free)	25 mL
1 tbsp	minced fresh Italian (flat-leaf) parsley	15 mL
1 tbsp	chopped fresh basil	15 mL

Salt and freshly ground black pepper
to taste

Thoroughly whisk together all ingredients. **Makes about 1 cup (250 mL), enough for 8 servings of salad.**

Balsamic–Olive Oil Vinaigrette

1	clove garlic, minced	1
½ cup	extra-virgin olive oil	125 mL
¼ cup	balsamic vinegar	50 mL
3 tbsp	freshly squeezed lemon juice	45 mL
Pinch	cayenne pepper	Pinch
	Salt and freshly ground black pepper to taste	

Thoroughly whisk together all ingredients. **Makes about ¾ cup (175 mL), enough for 6 servings of salad.**

Sun-Dried Tomato Vinaigrette

6	oil-packed sun-dried tomatoes, minced	6
2 tbsp	oil from sun-dried tomatoes	25 mL
1	clove garlic, minced	1
¼ cup	extra-virgin olive oil	50 mL
¼ cup	balsamic vinegar	50 mL
2 tbsp	freshly squeezed lemon juice	25 mL
Pinch	cayenne pepper	Pinch
	Salt and freshly ground black pepper to taste	

Thoroughly whisk together all ingredients. **Makes about ¾ cup (175 mL), enough for 4 servings of salad.**

Dijon Vinaigrette

1	clove garlic, minced	1
3 tbsp	red wine vinegar	45 mL
2 tbsp	Dijon mustard	25 mL
⅓ cup	canola oil	75 mL
⅓ cup	extra-virgin olive oil	75 mL
	Salt and freshly ground black pepper to taste	

Combine garlic, vinegar and mustard. Whisk in canola oil and olive oil in a slow, steady stream. Season with salt and pepper. **Makes about ¾ cup (175 mL), enough for 6 servings of salad.**

Tarragon Mustard Vinaigrette

Follow preceding recipe, but add 2 tsp (10 mL) dried tarragon or 2 tbsp (25 mL) chopped fresh tarragon. **Makes about ¾ cup (175 mL), enough for 6 servings of salad.**

Creamy Rosemary Dressing

2 tsp	fresh rosemary leaves	10 mL
1	small clove garlic, minced	1
1	egg yolk	1
1 tsp	Dijon mustard	5 mL
2 tbsp	red wine vinegar	25 mL
6 tbsp	peanut oil	90 mL
	Salt and freshly ground black pepper to taste	

In a small bowl, bruise rosemary with the back of a wooden spoon. Stir in garlic, egg yolk and mustard until lightly thickened. Stir in vinegar. Whisk in oil in a slow, steady stream. Season with salt and pepper. **Makes about ⅔ cup (150 mL), enough for 4 servings of salad.** *(If you are concerned about the food safety of raw eggs, you may wish to skip this recipe.)*

Creamy Orange-Fennel Dressing

Follow preceding recipe, but omit the rosemary, add ¼ cup (50 mL) minced fresh fennel bulb with the garlic, reduce the vinegar to 1 tbsp (15 mL), and add 3 tbsp (45 mL) freshly squeezed orange juice with the vinegar. **Makes about ¾ cup (175 mL), enough for 4 servings of salad.** *(If you are concerned about the food safety of raw eggs, you may wish to skip this recipe.)*

Raspberry Vinaigrette

½ cup	almond oil or walnut oil	125 mL
⅓ cup	raspberry vinegar	75 mL
Pinch	cayenne pepper	Pinch
	Salt to taste	
¼ cup	fresh or thawed unsweetened frozen raspberries, lightly crushed	50 mL

Combine oil, vinegar, cayenne and salt. Whisk in raspberries until thoroughly combined. **Makes about ¾ cup (175 mL), enough for 4 servings of salad.** *Use with delicate greens, chicken or fruit salad.*

Sherry Vinaigrette

2 tbsp	finely chopped raisins	25 mL
1 tbsp	dry sherry	15 mL
½ cup	almond oil or walnut oil	125 mL
¼ cup	sherry vinegar	50 mL
Pinch	cayenne pepper	Pinch
	Salt to taste	

In a small bowl, soak raisins in sherry for 5 minutes. Whisk in the remaining ingredients. **Makes about ¾ cup (175 mL), enough for 4 servings of salad.** *Use with delicate greens, chicken or fruit salad.*

Classic Caesar Dressing

2	drained canned anchovies, minced	2
1	egg yolk	1
1	clove garlic, minced	1
1 tsp	Dijon mustard	5 mL
1 tbsp	red wine vinegar	15 mL
2 tsp	Worcestershire sauce	10 mL
	Juice of ½ lemon	
6 tbsp	extra-virgin olive oil	90 mL
6 tbsp	canola oil	90 mL
	Salt and freshly ground black pepper to taste	

Whisk together anchovies, egg yolk, garlic and mustard until slightly thickened. Whisk in vinegar, Worcestershire sauce and lemon juice. Whisk in olive oil and canola oil in a slow, steady stream. Season with salt and pepper. **Makes about ¾ cup (175 mL), enough for 6 servings of salad.** *(If you are concerned about the food safety of raw eggs, you may wish to skip this recipe.)*

Tonnato Caesar Dressing

Follow preceding recipe, but add 2 oz (60 g) crumbled canned oil-packed tuna with the vinegar. **Makes about 1 cup (250 mL), enough for 6 servings of salad.** *(If you are concerned about the food safety of raw eggs, you may wish to skip this recipe.)*

Warm Bacon Dressing

3	slices bacon	3
1	large red onion, minced	1
1	large clove garlic, minced	1
½ cup	cider vinegar	125 mL
2 tbsp	granulated sugar	25 mL
1 tbsp	ketchup	15 mL
	Salt and freshly ground black pepper to taste	

In a deep skillet, cook bacon until crisp; crumble and set aside. Add onion to the fat in the pan and sauté over medium heat until tender. Stir in garlic, vinegar, sugar, ketchup, salt and pepper; heat through. **Makes about 1 cup (250 mL), enough for 4 servings of salad.** *Use hot, tossed with strong-tasting greens, such as escarole, chicory, endive or spinach. Garnish with crumbled bacon.*

Real Russian Dressing

¼ cup	mayonnaise	50 mL
¼ cup	sour cream	50 mL
3 tbsp	freshly squeezed lemon juice	45 mL
2 tbsp	tomato paste	25 mL

| 2 tbsp | red or black caviar | 25 mL |

Combine mayonnaise, sour cream, lemon juice and tomato paste. Fold in caviar. **Makes about 1 cup (250 mL), enough for 6 servings of salad.**

Clear Coleslaw Dressing

6 tbsp	canola oil	90 mL
6 tbsp	cider vinegar	90 mL
1 tbsp	granulated sugar	15 mL
2 tsp	caraway seeds	10 mL
1 tsp	kosher salt	5 mL

Thoroughly whisk together all ingredients. **Makes about ¾ cup (175 mL), enough for 4 servings of salad.**

Sour Cream Coleslaw Dressing

¼ cup	sour cream	50 mL
3 tbsp	mayonnaise	45 mL
3 tbsp	red wine vinegar	45 mL
2 tbsp	orange marmalade	25 mL
¾ tsp	salt	3 mL
¼ tsp	freshly ground black pepper	1 mL

Thoroughly whisk together all ingredients. **Makes about ¾ cup (175 mL), enough for 4 servings of salad.**

Poppy Seed Dressing

Follow either of the preceding two recipes, but use 2 tbsp (25 mL) poppy seeds instead of the caraway seeds in the Clear Coleslaw Dressing or add them to the Sour Cream Coleslaw Dressing. **Makes about ¾ cup (175 mL), enough for 4 servings of salad.**

Sesame Tofu Vinaigrette

1	small clove garlic	1
6 tbsp	canola oil	90 mL
¼ cup	cubed silken tofu	50 mL
3 tbsp	rice vinegar	45 mL
2 tbsp	dark sesame oil	25 mL
1 tsp	soy sauce	5 mL
¼ cup	toasted sesame seeds	50 mL

In a blender or food processor, purée garlic, canola oil, tofu, vinegar, sesame oil and soy sauce, thinning with a few drops of water, if necessary. Stir in sesame seeds. Serve with poached vegetable salads, Chinese cabbage coleslaw or fish and seafood salads. **Makes about 1 cup (250 mL), enough for 6 servings of salad.**

Soy Ginger Dressing

1	large clove garlic, minced	1
2 tbsp	grated gingerroot	25 mL
3/4 cup	dark sesame oil	175 mL
1/3 cup	rice vinegar	75 mL
2 tbsp	reduced-sodium soy sauce	25 mL
Pinch	cayenne pepper	Pinch
Pinch	granulated sugar	Pinch
	Salt to taste	

In a small bowl, mash garlic and ginger with the back of a spoon. Whisk in oil, vinegar, soy sauce, cayenne and sugar. Season with salt. **Makes about 1 cup (250 mL), enough for 6 servings of salad.**

Szechuan Ginger Dressing

Follow preceding recipe, but add 2 tsp (10 mL) crushed Szechuan peppercorns with the garlic. **Makes about 1 cup (250 mL), enough for 6 servings of salad.**

Warm Tomato Vinaigrette

1 cup	canned tomato purée or crushed tomatoes	250 mL
1/4 cup	extra-virgin olive oil	50 mL
2 tbsp	chopped fresh Italian (flat-leaf) parsley	25 mL
2 tbsp	red wine vinegar	25 mL
	Salt and freshly ground black pepper to taste	

Thoroughly whisk together all ingredients. Warm dressing over medium heat. Serve with chicken salad, seafood salad, spinach salad, pasta salad or potato salad. **Makes about 1 1/2 cups (375 mL), enough for 8 servings of salad.**

Sweet-and-Sour Creole Vinaigrette

1	clove garlic, minced	1
1/4 cup	ketchup	50 mL
1 tbsp	granulated sugar	15 mL
1 tbsp	spicy mustard	15 mL
1 tbsp	cider vinegar	15 mL
2 tsp	prepared horseradish	10 mL
1 cup	canola oil	250 mL
	Hot pepper sauce (such as Tabasco) to taste	
	Salt and freshly ground black pepper to taste	

Combine garlic, ketchup, sugar, mustard, vinegar and horseradish. Whisk in oil in a slow, steady stream until dressing is thickened. Season with hot pepper sauce, salt and pepper. Serve with hearty salad greens, such as endive, escarole or radicchio (it would also be good on hamburgers, ribs or broiled pork chops). **Makes about 1 1/2 cups (375 mL), enough for 8 servings of salad.**

Creamy Creole Dressing

1/2 cup	mayonnaise	125 mL
2 tbsp	white wine vinegar	25 mL
1 tsp	granulated sugar	5 mL
1 tsp	hot pepper sauce (such as Tabasco)	5 mL
	Juice of 1 lemon	
	Salt and freshly ground black pepper to taste	

Thoroughly whisk together all ingredients. **Makes about 3/4 cup (175 mL), enough for 4 servings of salad.**

Sweet Pepper Vinaigrette

2	roasted red bell peppers (see page 11), finely diced	2
2	cloves garlic, minced	2
3/4 cup	red wine vinegar	175 mL
1/4 cup	granulated sugar	50 mL
1/4 cup	olive oil	50 mL
	Salt and freshly ground black pepper to taste	

In a heavy saucepan, combine all ingredients and heat over medium heat, stirring, until sugar dissolves. Serve hot or cold with hearty salad greens, such as endive, escarole or radicchio, or with grilled chicken or pork. **Makes about 1 cup (250 mL), enough for 6 servings of salad.**

Blue Cheese Dressing

2	cloves garlic, minced	2
4 oz	crumbled blue cheese (about 1/2 cup/125 mL)	125 g
1/2 cup	sour cream	125 mL
1/4 cup	extra-virgin olive oil	50 mL
3 tbsp	red wine vinegar	45 mL
2 tbsp	milk	25 mL
	Salt and freshly ground black pepper to taste	

Thoroughly whisk together all ingredients. **Makes about 1 cup (250 mL), enough for 6 servings of salad.**

Warm Blue Cheese Dressing

¼ cup	extra-virgin olive oil	50 mL
2	cloves garlic, minced	2
⅔ cup	whipping (35%) cream	150 mL
3 tbsp	red wine vinegar	45 mL
4 oz	crumbled blue cheese (about ½ cup/125 mL)	125 g
	Salt and freshly ground black pepper to taste	

In a skillet, heat oil over medium heat. Sauté garlic until tender, about 30 seconds. Add whipping cream and vinegar; bring to a boil (the mixture will likely split). Remove from heat and stir in blue cheese until it melts and dressing is smooth. Season with salt and pepper. **Makes about 1 cup (250 mL), enough for 6 to 8 servings of salad.** *Serve over spinach salad.*

Roquefort Dressing

Follow either of the two preceding recipes, but reduce the vinegar to 2 tbsp (25 mL), add 2 tbsp (25 mL) freshly squeezed lemon juice with the vinegar and replace the blue cheese with Roquefort. **Makes about 1 cup (250 mL), enough for 6 to 8 servings of salad.**

Spicy Ginger Vinaigrette

1	clove garlic, minced	1
¼ cup	canola oil	50 mL
¼ cup	dark sesame oil	50 mL
2 tbsp	rice vinegar	25 mL
1 tbsp	finely grated gingerroot	15 mL
½ tsp	hot pepper flakes	2 mL
	Juice of 1 lemon	
	Salt and freshly ground black pepper to taste	

Thoroughly whisk together all ingredients. **Makes about ¾ cup (175 mL), enough for 4 servings of salad.**

Garlic Ranch Dressing

2	cloves garlic, minced	2
¼ cup	mayonnaise	50 mL
3 tbsp	buttermilk	45 mL
1 tsp	seasoning salt or salt-free seasoning blend	5 mL
1 tsp	cider vinegar	5 mL
½ tsp	onion powder	2 mL
	Freshly ground black pepper to taste	

Thoroughly whisk together all ingredients. **Makes about ½ cup (125 mL), enough for 4 servings of salad.**

Yogurt Dill Ranch Dressing

Follow preceding recipe, but replace the buttermilk with plain yogurt, and add 1 tsp (5 mL) dried dillweed or 1 tbsp (15 mL) chopped fresh dill. **Makes about ½ cup (125 mL), enough for 4 servings of salad.**

Basil Ranch Dressing

Follow recipe for Garlic Ranch Dressing (left), but add ¼ cup (50 mL) finely chopped fresh basil. **Makes about ⅔ cup (150 mL), enough for 4 servings of salad.**

Green Goddess Ranch Dressing

1	clove garlic, minced	1
1	drained canned anchovy, minced	1
¼ cup	mayonnaise	50 mL
3 tbsp	sour cream	45 mL
2 tbsp	minced fresh green herb (such as basil, tarragon or chervil)	25 mL
1 tbsp	minced fresh Italian (flat-leaf) parsley	15 mL
1 tsp	seasoning salt or salt-free seasoning blend	5 mL
1 tsp	cider vinegar	5 mL
½ tsp	onion powder	2 mL
	Freshly ground black pepper to taste	

Thoroughly whisk together all ingredients. **Makes about ⅔ cup (250 mL), enough for 4 servings of salad.**

Creamy Mayonnaise Dressing

3 oz	cream cheese, softened	90 g
⅓ cup	mayonnaise	75 mL
	Juice of ½ lemon	
Pinch	cayenne pepper	Pinch
	Salt and freshly ground black pepper to taste	

Whisk together cream cheese, mayonnaise and lemon juice until smooth. Season with cayenne, salt and black pepper. **Makes about ⅔ cup (150 mL), enough for 4 servings of salad.**

Pesto Mayonnaise Dressing

1	small clove garlic, minced	1
⅓ cup	finely chopped fresh basil	75 mL
⅓ cup	mayonnaise	75 mL
2 tbsp	freshly grated Parmesan cheese	25 mL
2 tbsp	extra-virgin olive oil	25 mL
Pinch	cayenne pepper	Pinch

Juice of ½ lemon
Salt and freshly ground black pepper
to taste

Thoroughly whisk together all ingredients. **Makes about ¾ cup (175 mL), enough for 4 servings of salad.**

Minted Yogurt Dressing

1	small clove garlic, minced	1
1 cup	plain yogurt	250 mL
1 tbsp	chopped fresh mint	15 mL
1 tbsp	extra-virgin olive oil	15 mL
	Juice of ½ lemon	
	Salt and freshly ground black pepper to taste	

Thoroughly whisk together all ingredients. **Makes about 1¼ cups (300 mL), enough for 4 servings of salad.**

Yogurt Cilantro Dressing

Follow preceding recipe, but omit the mint, and add ¼ cup (50 mL) chopped fresh cilantro. **Makes about 1¼ cups (300 mL), enough for 4 servings of salad.**

Sweet Mustard Dressing

1	egg yolk	1
1 tsp	brown mustard	5 mL
2 tbsp	cider vinegar	25 mL
1 tbsp	honey	15 mL
¾ cup	canola oil	175 mL
	Salt and freshly ground black pepper to taste	

Stir egg yolk and mustard until slightly thickened. Mix in vinegar and honey. Whisk in oil in a slow, steady stream. Season with salt and pepper. **Makes about 1 cup (250 mL), enough for 6 servings of salad.** *(If you are concerned about the food safety of raw eggs, you may wish to skip this recipe.)*

Apple Cider Dressing

½ cup	canola oil	125 mL
¼ cup	cider vinegar	50 mL
2 tbsp	minced onion	25 mL
2 tbsp	unsweetened apple juice	25 mL
2 tbsp	honey	25 mL
	Salt and freshly ground black pepper to taste	

Thoroughly whisk together all ingredients. **Makes about 1 cup (250 mL), enough for 6 servings of salad.**

Sweet Balsamic Dressing

1	clove garlic, minced	1
½ cup	extra-virgin olive oil	125 mL
2 tbsp	balsamic vinegar	25 mL
2 tbsp	red wine vinegar	25 mL
2 tbsp	unsweetened apple juice	25 mL
2 tbsp	honey	25 mL
	Salt and freshly ground black pepper to taste	

Thoroughly whisk together all ingredients. **Makes about 1 cup (250 mL), enough for 6 servings of salad.**

Guacamole Vinaigrette

1	avocado, mashed	1
1	clove garlic, minced	1
3 tbsp	white wine vinegar	45 mL
Pinch	cayenne pepper	Pinch
	Salt and freshly ground black pepper to taste	

Thoroughly whisk together all ingredients. **Makes about ⅔ cup (150 mL), enough for 4 servings of salad.** *Store in an airtight container for up to 1 week.*

Salsa Vinaigrette

2	pickled jalapeño peppers, seeded	2
2	tomatoes, quartered	2
1	clove garlic	1
¼ cup	extra-virgin olive oil	50 mL
2 tbsp	cider vinegar	25 mL

In a food processor, process all ingredients until vegetables are finely chopped. **Makes about ⅔ cup (150 mL), enough for 4 servings of salad.**

Pesto Vinaigrette

1	clove garlic	1
1 cup	basil leaves	250 mL
¼ cup	pine nuts	50 mL
2 tbsp	red wine vinegar	25 mL
⅓ cup	extra-virgin olive oil	75 mL
1 tbsp	freshly grated Parmesan cheese	15 mL
	Salt and freshly ground black pepper to taste	

In a food processor, purée garlic, basil and pine nuts. With the motor running, slowly add vinegar and oil through the feed tube; process until smooth. Season with Parmesan, salt and pepper. **Makes about ¾ cup (175 mL), enough for 4 servings of salad.**

Chapter 5
Machines That Make Cooking Easier

Microwave

Easy Homemade Applesauce 67

Steamed Asparagus 67

Crispy Bacon Strips 67

Baked Beets 68

Blanched Broccoli 68

Melted Butter — and Brown Butter 68

Blanched Cauliflower 68

Melted Chocolate 68

Toasted Coconut 68

Individual Fish Fillet 68

Individual Fish Steak 68

Whole Fish 68

Poached Fish 68

Toasted Nuts 68

Steamed New Potatoes 68

Stewed Prunes 69

Sweet Potatoes 69

Precooked Beans or Carrots 69

Slow Cooker

Slow-Cooked Chicken Broth 69

Slow-Cooked Beef Broth 69

Mushroom Pasta Sauce 69

Irish Oatmeal 70

Slow-Cooked Cinnamon Raisin
Bread Pudding 70

Braised Short Ribs 70

Spiced Fruit 70

Baked Beans 70

All-Day Lentil Soup 70

Duck Confit 71

Pulled Pork 71

Barbecued Beef 71

Pot Roast 71

Corned Beef and Cabbage 71

Pot au Feu 72

All-Day All-Beef Chili 72

Food Processor

Vichyssoise 72

Puréed Vegetable Soup 72

Gazpacho 73

Seafood Mousse 73

Chopped Liver 73

Pasta Dough 73

Pie Pastry 73

Quick Puff Pastry 74

Peanut Butter 74

Mayonnaise 74

Quick Sorbet 74

Ground Nuts 74

Seasoned Bread Crumbs 74

Shredded Cheese 74

Chopped Garlic 74

Chopped Onion 74

Occasionally, a piece of kitchen equipment redefines our very notions about the possibilities of what we can cook at home. Such was the case when affordable refrigeration turned every home kitchen into its own food distribution center, and when food processors debunked the pretensions of classic French cuisine for aspiring gourmets. Slow cookers have allowed generations of moms to prepare dinner in absentia, and microwaves have encouraged us to mark cooking times in seconds rather than hours.

We do not profess to be experts in every kitchen tool, nor are we proponents of switching from hand tools to machines across the board. (After all, chopping a single vegetable by hand sometimes makes a lot more sense than breaking out the food processor.) But at times we have found that microwaves, slow cookers and food processors not only make kitchen work less laborious, but actually do a better job than a similar hands-on technique.

Microwaves steam vegetables and fish more evenly and with less loss of water-soluble nutrients than a steamer basket set in a pot of water. Slow cookers require less liquid and simmer a stew more gently, yielding richer, falling-from-the-bone results than stews simmered on a stovetop. And no hand, no matter how skilled, can whip a mousse, purée a quenelle or grind a cup of toasted almonds to a fine powder more quickly or efficiently than a food processor.

About these recipes . . .

One of the insidious things about microwaves and microwave recipes is their inconsistency. Microwave ovens with different wattages cook the same food in a different amount of time — but, frequently, so do separate ovens of the same wattage or the same oven on different occasions. You can put 4 apples in a microwave to bake and have one melt into oblivion minutes before the others are ready. For that reason, we have given you a time range whenever our testing has produced varying results. Test for doneness at the lower end of the range, then proceed in two stages to the upper end of the range until the desired doneness is achieved.

Some experts warn of dangers from microwave cooking when the food is covered with plastic wrap. Their concern is that, as the plastic wrap heats, molecules can migrate into the food, making it dangerous to ingest. We believe that a couple of simple precautions neutralize that concern. First, use plastic wrap labeled "microwave-safe." This means the wrap won't break down during cooking. Second, keep the plastic wrap from making direct contact with the surface of the food. We believe that, if it's done right, the benefits of covering microwaved dishes with plastic — trapping steam to accelerate cooking time — make it a safe choice.

All the foods tested were microwaved on High, either uncovered or covered tightly with microwave-safe plastic wrap. When microwaving under a tight cover, steam will build up. Release this steam by carefully pricking the plastic before unwrapping.

Microwave

Easy Homemade Applesauce

8	McIntosh apples, peeled, and cut in 1-inch (2.5 cm) chunks	8
1/3 cup	granulated sugar (approx.)	75 mL
1 tbsp	freshly squeezed lemon juice	15 mL
1/2 tsp	ground cinnamon	2 mL

In an 8-cup (2 L) bowl, combine apple chunks, sugar, lemon juice and cinnamon. Cover tightly with microwave-safe plastic wrap and microwave on High for 6 to 8 minutes, or until apples are steaming and starting to soften. Remove wrap, stir and microwave on High for 6 to 8 minutes, or until apples are completely soft . Remove wrap, mash with a fork and stir in additional sugar, if desired, depending on your taste and the sweetness of the apples. **Makes about 3 cups (750 mL).**

Steamed Asparagus

Place 1 lb (500 g) trimmed thin asparagus stalks in a rectangular dish, layered up to 3 stalks deep. Add 2 tbsp (25 mL) water, cover with microwave-safe plastic and microwave on High for 3 to 4 minutes, or until tender-crisp. (Add another minute for medium-thick asparagus.) **Serves 4.**

Crispy Bacon Strips

Place 8 slices of bacon side by side in a single layer in a rectangular dish lined with 6 sheets of paper towel. Top with 2 more sheets of paper towel and microwave on High for 7 minutes, or until crispy.

Baked Beets

Place 1 lb (500 g) trimmed small beets in a shallow dish, cover with microwave-safe plastic wrap and microwave on High for 12 to 14 minutes, or until tender-crisp. For 1 lb (500 g) large beets (each weighing 4 oz/125 g or more), microwave on High for 15 to 18 minutes. Remove wrap, let cool slightly and peel off skins. **Serves 4.**

Blanched Broccoli

Separate 1 bunch of broccoli into stalks, peel the stems and place spoke-fashion on a 10-inch (25 cm) circular plate with the heads pointing toward the center. Place 1 to 2 tbsp (15 to 25 mL) water on the plate, cover with microwave-safe plastic wrap and microwave on High for 4 minutes, or until bright green and tender-crisp. **Serves 4.**

Melted Butter — and Brown Butter

Cut 1 or 2 sticks ($\frac{1}{2}$ or 1 cup/125 or 250 mL) refrigerated or frozen butter into small pats and place in a bowl at least 4 times the volume of the butter. Cover with waxed paper and microwave on High — 1 minute for 1 stick ($\frac{1}{2}$ cup/125 mL), 2 minutes for 2 sticks (1 cup/250 mL). If frozen, add 30 seconds. To make Brown Butter, double the cooking times.

Blanched Cauliflower

Break 1 small head of cauliflower into florets and place them in a single layer on a deep plate. Add 1 tbsp (15 mL) water, cover with microwave-safe plastic wrap and microwave on High for 4 to 5 minutes, or until tender, tossing halfway through. **Serves 4.**

Melted Chocolate

Break 2 to 4 oz (60 to 125 g) chocolate into $\frac{1}{2}$-oz (15 g) pieces. Place in a small bowl, cover with microwave-safe plastic wrap and make a vent in the wrap. Microwave on High for 2 minutes. Remove from microwave and stir until completely melted. (One ounce/30 g will melt in 1 minute; 8 oz/250 g will melt in 3 minutes, 15 seconds.)

Toasted Coconut

Spread 1 cup (250 mL) shredded unsweetened coconut over the bottom of a 10-inch (25 cm) plate. Microwave on High for 3 to 4 minutes, or until lightly toasted in spots, stirring twice.

Individual Fish Fillet

Season one 4-oz (125 g) boneless skinless fish fillet ($\frac{1}{2}$ to $\frac{3}{4}$ inch/1 to 2 cm thick) as desired or according to recipe. Place on a plate and wrap in microwave-safe plastic wrap. Microwave on High for 1 to 1$\frac{1}{2}$ minutes, or until fish is opaque and flakes easily with a fork. Let rest for 1 minute before unwrapping. **Serves 1.**

Individual Fish Steak

Season one 8-oz (250 g) bone-in fish steak (about $\frac{3}{4}$ inch/2 cm thick) as desired or according to recipe. Place on a plate and wrap in microwave-safe plastic wrap. Microwave on High for 2 to 2$\frac{1}{2}$ minutes, or until fish is opaque and flakes easily with a fork. Let rest for 1 minute before unwrapping. **Serves 1.**

Whole Fish

Slash the sides of a 2-lb (1 kg) fish and rub with desired seasonings. Place on a plate and wrap in microwave-safe plastic wrap. Microwave on High for 6 to 8 minutes, or until fish is opaque and flakes easily with a fork, flipping halfway through. Let rest for 1 minute before unwrapping. **Serves 4.**

Poached Fish

Place 1 lb (500 g) of fish fillets ($\frac{1}{2}$ to $\frac{3}{4}$ inch/1 to 2 cm thick) in a 1-inch (2.5 cm) deep dish large enough to hold them in a single layer. Pour in 2 cups (500 mL) liquid (sauce, broth, wine, juice) and cover with microwave-safe plastic wrap. Microwave on High for 2 minutes, or until fish is opaque and flakes easily with a fork. Let rest for 1 minute before removing the plastic wrap. **Serves 4.**

Toasted Nuts

Place 1 cup (250 mL) whole nuts in a 10-inch (25 cm) shallow glass pan and microwave on High for about 5 minutes, until lightly toasted and fragrant, stirring twice. Nuts with a high fat content, such as pine nuts, will toast more quickly than less oily nuts, such as almonds; watch carefully.

Steamed New Potatoes

Thoroughly wash 1 lb (500 g) new potatoes (each about 1 inch/2.5 cm) in diameter). With water still clinging to them, place them in a single layer in a large, deep dish. Dot with 1 tbsp (15 mL) butter and season to taste with salt. Cover with microwave-safe plastic wrap and microwave on High for 4 minutes. Shake and microwave on High for 4 minutes. Let rest for 1 minute before removing the plastic wrap. **Serves 4.**

Stewed Prunes

1 lb	pitted prunes	500 g
1/2 cup	water	125 mL
	Grated zest and juice of 1 lemon	
1/3 cup	freshly squeezed orange juice	75 mL
1/4 cup	honey	50 mL
1/4 tsp	ground cinnamon	1 mL
Pinch	ground cloves	Pinch

In a large bowl, combine prunes, water, lemon zest, lemon juice, orange juice and honey. Cover with microwave-safe plastic wrap and microwave on High for 3 minutes. Stir in cinnamon and cloves. **Serves 4.**

Sweet Potatoes

Wash and prick the skin of 2 large sweet potatoes. Place on a plate and microwave on High for 12 to 13 minutes, or until fork-tender, turning over halfway through. **Serves 4.**

Precooked Beans or Carrots

Place 1 lb (500 g) trimmed green beans or julienned carrots in a deep dish. Toss with 2 tbsp (25 mL) water, cover with microwave-safe plastic wrap and microwave on High for 7 minutes, or until tender-crisp. **Serves 4.**

Slow Cooker

Slow-Cooked Chicken Broth

3 lbs	chicken parts (backs, necks, gizzards, hearts and trimmings)	1.5 kg
16 cups	cold water	4 L
2	large carrots, chopped	2
2	stalks celery, chopped	2
1	large onion, chopped	1
1 tsp	salt	5 mL
1 tsp	whole black peppercorns	5 mL
1 tsp	poultry seasoning	5 mL
3	sprigs fresh Italian (flat-leaf) parsley	3
1	whole clove	1
1	bay leaf	1

Place chicken in a large slow cooker (minimum 6 quarts) and add water, carrots, celery, onion, salt, peppercorns, poultry seasoning, parsley, clove and bay leaf. Cover and cook on Low for 8 to 10 hours.

Strain out solids and let cool. **Makes about 16 cups (4 L).** *Store in the refrigerator for up to 5 days or in the freezer for up to 3 months. Use for soups, sauces and stews.*

Slow-Cooked Beef Broth

4 lbs	beef and/or veal bones	2 kg
2	large carrots, chopped	2
2	stalks celery, chopped	2
1	large onion, chopped	1
	Vegetable oil	
16 cups	cold water	4 L
1 tbsp	tomato paste	15 mL
1 tsp	salt	5 mL
1 tsp	whole black peppercorns	5 mL
1 tsp	dried thyme	5 mL
3	sprigs fresh Italian (flat-leaf) parsley	3
1	whole clove	1
1	bay leaf	1

Preheat oven to 450°F (230°C). Rub bones, carrots, celery and onion with oil, place on a rimmed baking sheet and roast, turning twice, until uniformly browned, about 30 minutes. Transfer to a large slow cooker (minimum 6 quarts) and add water, tomato paste, salt, peppercorns, thyme, parsley, clove and bay leaf. Cover and cook on Low for 10 to 12 hours. Strain out solids and let cool. **Makes about 16 cups (4 L).** *Store in the refrigerator for up to 5 days or in the freezer for up to 3 months. Use for soups, sauces and stews.*

Mushroom Pasta Sauce

1/4 cup	extra-virgin olive oil	50 mL
1	large onion, finely chopped	1
4	cloves garlic, minced	4
5	cans (each 28 oz/796 mL) crushed tomatoes	5
1/2 oz	dried mushrooms, chopped	14 g
1 cup	tomato paste	250 mL
1 tbsp	dried Italian seasoning	15 mL
	Salt and freshly ground black pepper to taste	

In a skillet, heat oil over medium-high heat. Sauté onion until tender, about 4 minutes. Add garlic and sauté for 30 seconds. Scrape into a large slow cooker (minimum 6 quarts) and add tomatoes, mushrooms, tomato paste, Italian seasoning, salt and pepper. Cover and cook on Low for 8 hours. **Makes about 16 cups (4 L).** *Use as a pasta sauce or with meat, poultry or seafood.*

Irish Oatmeal

4 cups	cold water	1 L
1¼ cups	steel-cut oats (such as McCann's)	300 mL
⅓ to ½ cup	packed light brown sugar	75 to 125 mL
½ tsp	kosher salt	2 mL
2 tbsp	butter (optional)	25 mL
½ cup	fruit-and-nut trail mix (optional) Warm milk or ice-cold buttermilk	125 mL

In a 3- to 4-quart slow cooker (preferably round), combine water, oats, brown sugar to taste and salt, stirring to evenly distribute oats. Cover and cook on Low for 4 to 5 hours, or until thick. Using a fork, stir to fluff the grain, then top with butter and trail mix, if desired. Serve with milk or buttermilk. **Serves 6.**

Slow-Cooked Cinnamon Raisin Bread Pudding

1	loaf (about 16 oz/500 g) sliced cinnamon raisin bread, cut in ½-inch (1 cm) pieces	1
1 cup	raisins	250 mL
8 cups	milk	2 L
1 cup	granulated sugar	250 mL
1 tsp	vanilla	5 mL
4	eggs	4

In a 5- to 6-quart slow cooker, toss bread and raisins. In a bowl, combine milk, sugar and vanilla, stirring until sugar dissolves. Beat in eggs until completely incorporated. Pour over bread and stir to moisten. Cover and cook on Low for 4 to 5 hours, or until set. (If your slow cooker has a Warming setting, you may keep the pudding warm for 2 to 3 hours; if it doesn't, the pudding will stay warm for up to an hour with the cooker turned off.) **Serves 8.**

Braised Short Ribs

4	beef short ribs (each about 7 oz/210 g) Salt and freshly ground black pepper to taste	4
1 tbsp	vegetable oil	15 mL
1 cup	chopped onion	250 mL
1 tsp	pumpkin pie spice	5 mL
¼ cup	packed dark brown sugar	50 mL
1 cup	beef broth	250 mL

Season ribs evenly with salt and pepper. In a large skillet, heat oil over high heat. Cook ribs until browned on all sides. Transfer to a 5- to 6-quart slow cooker. Add onion to the fat in the skillet,

reduce heat to medium-high and sauté until browned. Add pumpkin pie spice, brown sugar and broth, scraping up any brown bits clinging to the bottom of the pan. Pour into slow cooker. Cover and cook on Low for 6 to 8 hours, or until tender. **Serves 4.**

Spiced Fruit

8 oz	pitted prunes	250 g
8 oz	dried Calimyrna figs	250 g
8 oz	dried Turkish apricots	250 g
	Grated zest and juice of ½ lemon	
	Grated zest and juice of ½ orange	
1 cup	orange juice	250 mL
1 cup	water	250 mL
½ cup	honey	125 mL
1	whole clove	1
1	cinnamon stick (about 2 inches/5 cm)	1
½	vanilla bean	½

In a 3- to 4-quart slow cooker, combine all ingredients. Cover and cook on Low for 4 to 5 hours, or until fruit is very soft. **Makes about 6 cups (1.5 L).** *Store in an airtight container in the refrigerator for up to 2 weeks. If mixture becomes dry, add a small amount of water. Serve as is, with cookies or plain cake, or over ice cream.*

Baked Beans

1 lb	dried white beans (such as navy or Great Northern), soaked overnight	500 g
1	bottle (12 oz/341 mL) beer	1
4	slices bacon, finely chopped	4
1 cup	chopped onion	250 mL
1 cup	ketchup	250 mL
¼ cup	dark (cooking) molasses	50 mL
¼ cup	packed dark brown sugar	50 mL
1 tbsp	spicy brown mustard	15 mL
	Salt and freshly ground black pepper to taste	

In a 6-quart slow cooker, combine all ingredients. Cover and cook on Low for 10 to 12 hours, or until beans are tender. Stir before serving. **Serves 4.**

All-Day Lentil Soup

3	cloves garlic, minced	3
4 oz	smoked ham, diced	125 g
3 cups	chicken or beef broth	750 mL
2 cups	dried green or brown lentils	500 mL
2 cups	chopped onions	500 mL
2 cups	vegetable juice (such as V8)	500 mL
1 cup	chopped carrots	250 mL

1 tbsp	Worcestershire sauce	15 mL
1 tsp	dried rosemary	5 mL
	Salt and freshly ground black pepper to taste	
¼ cup	chopped fresh Italian (flat-leaf) parsley	50 mL

In a 6-quart slow cooker, combine garlic, ham, broth, lentils, onions, vegetable juice, carrots, Worcestershire sauce, rosemary, salt and pepper. Cover and cook on Low for 8 to 10 hours, or until lentils are tender. Stir in parsley. **Serves 4.**

Duck Confit

1	duck (about 5 lbs/2.5 kg), trimmed of fat and quartered	1
2 tbsp	quatre épices	25 mL
1 cup	extra-virgin olive oil	250 mL

Rub duck pieces with quatre épices. Place duck skin side down in a single layer on the bottom of a 5- to 6-quart slow cooker. Add oil, cover and cook on Low for 6 to 8 hours, until falling off the bone. To serve, remove duck from its liquid and spoon some of the juices over the top. (You may also refrigerate the duck in its juices for later use. Once chilled, the oil in the liquid will solidify, keeping the meat fresh for 4 to 6 weeks in the refrigerator.) **Serves 4.**

Pulled Pork

2 tbsp	chili powder	25 mL
2 tbsp	granulated sugar	25 mL
1 tsp	salt	5 mL
1 tsp	freshly ground black pepper	5 mL
2½ lb	boneless pork shoulder blade roast, cut into 4 slices	1.25 kg
¼ cup	cider vinegar	50 mL
1 tsp	hot pepper sauce (such as Tabasco)	5 mL
8	hamburger buns (optional)	8

Combine chili powder, sugar, salt and pepper; rub evenly over pork. Place in a 6-quart slow cooker and pour in vinegar and hot pepper sauce. Cover and cook on Low for 6 to 8 hours, or until pork is fork-tender. Shred pork with two forks and serve as is or on hamburger buns. **Serves 8.**

Barbecued Beef

1 tbsp	chili powder	15 mL
1 tbsp	granulated sugar	15 mL
1 tsp	salt	5 mL
1 tsp	freshly ground black pepper	5 mL
2½ lb	boneless beef chuck, blade or cross-rib roast, cut into 4 slices	1.25 kg

1	clove garlic, minced	1
½ cup	chopped onion	125 mL
2 cups	barbecue sauce	500 mL
8	hamburger buns (optional)	8

Combine chili powder, sugar, salt and pepper; rub evenly over beef. Place in a 6-quart slow cooker, scatter garlic and onion over beef and pour in barbecue sauce. Cover and cook on Low for 6 to 8 hours, or until beef is fork-tender. Shred beef with two forks and serve as is or on hamburger buns. **Serves 8.**

Pot Roast

2½ lb	boneless beef chuck, blade or cross-rib roast	1.25 kg
	Salt and freshly ground black pepper to taste	
1 tbsp	vegetable oil	15 mL
6	potatoes, peeled and cut into 1-inch (2.5 cm) chunks	6
3	large carrots, cut into chunks	3
2	stalks celery, cut into chunks	2
1	large onion, cut into chunks	1
½ cup	beef broth	125 mL
½ cup	vegetable juice (such as V8)	125 mL

Season beef evenly with salt and pepper. In a large skillet, heat oil over medium-high heat. Cook meat until browned on all sides. Transfer to a plate. Add potatoes, carrots, celery and onion to the fat in the skillet; sauté for 1 minute. Add broth and scrape up any brown bits clinging to the bottom of the pan. Pour into a 6-quart slow cooker. Add beef to slow cooker and pour in vegetable juice. Cover and cook on Low for about 6 hours, or until beef is tender. Slice beef and serve with vegetables. **Serves 6.**

Corned Beef and Cabbage

1	corned beef brisket (about 2½ lbs/1.25 kg)	1
2 lbs	small red or yellow round potatoes	1 kg
2	onions, quartered	2
1	head cabbage (about 2 lbs/1 kg), cored and cut into 8 wedges	1
1	bay leaf	1
¼ tsp	ground allspice	1 mL
	Freshly ground black pepper to taste	
1	bottle (12 oz/341 mL) beer	1

Place corned beef fat side down in a 6-quart slow cooker. Layer potatoes, onions and cabbage around meat. Add bay leaf, allspice and pepper, then pour in beer. Cover and cook on Low for about 8 hours, or until fork-tender. **Serves 6.**

Pot au Feu

4	beef short ribs (each about 7 oz/215 g)	4
1	small chicken (about 3 lbs/1.5 kg), quartered	1
	Salt and freshly ground black pepper to taste	
1	ham steak (about 8 oz/250 g), cut into quarters	1
1	turnip, peeled and cut into bite-size pieces	1
1	carrot, peeled and cut into bite-size pieces	1
1	parsnip, peeled and cut into bite-size pieces	1
1	onion, cut into bite-size pieces	1
1	stalk celery, cut into bite-size pieces	1
1 cup	dry white wine	250 mL
1 cup	chicken broth	250 mL
1	bay leaf	1
¼ cup	finely chopped fresh parsley	50 mL
2 tbsp	finely chopped fresh dill	25 mL
	Prepared mustard and/or horseradish (optional)	

Season beef ribs and chicken evenly with salt and pepper. Place in a large slow cooker (minimum 6 quarts) and nestle ham among the pieces. Add turnip, carrot, parsnip, onion, celery, wine, broth, bay leaf, parsley and dill. Cover and cook on Low for 8 hours. Discard bay leaf. Serve meat and vegetables moistened with some of the cooking liquid. Accompany with mustard and/or horseradish, if desired. **Serves 8.**

All-Day All-Beef Chili

3 lb	boneless beef round roast, cut into small chunks	1.5 kg
	Salt and freshly ground black pepper to taste	
1 tbsp	vegetable oil	15 mL
1	can (28 oz/796 mL) crushed tomatoes	1
1	can (4 oz/125 mL) diced green chili peppers, drained	1
1⅔ cup	beef broth	400 mL
1	stalk celery, finely chopped	1
1	red bell pepper, diced	1
1 cup	vegetable juice (such as V8)	250 mL
2 tbsp	chili powder	25 mL
1 tsp	ground cumin	5 mL
Pinch	cayenne pepper	Pinch
Pinch	dried oregano	Pinch

Season beef evenly with salt and pepper. In a large skillet, heat oil over medium-high heat. Sauté beef, in batches, until browned on all sides. Transfer to a 4- to 6-quart slow cooker and add the remaining ingredients. Cover and cook on Low for about 8 hours, or until beef is fork-tender. **Serves 4.**

Food Processor

Vichyssoise

3 tbsp	butter	45 mL
4	large leeks (white part only), chopped	4
2 lbs	russet potatoes, peeled and sliced	1 kg
6 cups	chicken broth	1.5 L
1 tsp	salt	5 mL
¼ tsp	freshly ground white pepper	1 mL
Pinch	ground nutmeg	Pinch
1 cup	light or table (18%) cream	250 mL
1 to 2 cups	milk (preferably whole)	250 to 500 mL
	Chopped fresh chives, for garnish	

In a heavy pot, melt butter over medium heat. Sauté leeks until softened. Add potatoes, broth, salt, pepper and nutmeg; reduce heat and simmer until potatoes are tender, about 20 minutes. Working in batches, transfer to a food processor and purée using 3-second pulses (do not over-process, or the soup will become gummy). Transfer to a serving bowl and stir in cream and 1 cup (250 mL) of the milk. Cover and refrigerate until chilled, about 2 hours. Thin as needed with additional milk to the consistency of unbeaten whipping cream. Serve chilled, garnished with chives. **Serves 4.**

Puréed Vegetable Soup

2 tbsp	butter	25 mL
1	onion, chopped	1
2½ lbs	fibrous vegetables (such as carrots, winter squash, sweet potatoes, parsnips, cauliflower, turnips, Jerusalem artichoke), cut into small chunks	1.25 kg
6 cups	chicken broth	1.5 L
1 tsp	dried herb (such as thyme, rosemary, oregano)	5 mL
Pinch	ground nutmeg	Pinch
	Salt and freshly ground black pepper to taste	

In a large pot, melt butter over medium heat. Sauté onion and vegetables until onion is translucent. Add broth, herb, nutmeg, salt and pepper; reduce heat and simmer for 20 to 30 minutes, or until vegetables are tender. With a slotted spoon, working in batches, transfer solids to a food processor and purée until almost smooth. Return to liquid in pot and season with salt and pepper. Reheat to steaming, if necessary. **Serves 8.**

Gazpacho

1	thick slice firm bread, cut into cubes	1
2	large tomatoes, cut into chunks	2
1	red bell pepper, cut into chunks	1
1	cucumber, peeled, seeded and cut into chunks	1
1	clove garlic	1
1/2	onion, cut into chunks	1/2
1	stalk celery, peeled and finely chopped	1
1/2	yellow bell pepper, diced	1/2
2 cups	vegetable juice (such as V8)	500 mL
2 tbsp	extra-virgin olive oil	25 mL
2 tsp	red wine vinegar	10 mL
1 tsp	hot pepper sauce (such as Tabasco)	5 mL
	Salt and freshly ground black pepper to taste	

In a food processor, chop bread into fine crumbs. Add tomatoes, red pepper, cucumber, garlic and onion; process until very finely chopped but not smooth. Transfer to a large bowl and stir in celery, yellow pepper, vegetable juice, oil, vinegar, hot pepper sauce, salt and pepper. Cover and refrigerate until chilled, about 2 hours. **Serves 6.**

Seafood Mousse

1 lb	shrimp or scallops	500 g
2	egg whites	2
Pinch	ground nutmeg	Pinch
2 cups	whipping (35%) cream	500 mL
	Sauce of your choice, such as Beurre Blanc (page 51) or Warm Tomato Vinaigrette (page 63) (optional)	
	Chopped lemon and/or caviar (optional)	

In a food processor, purée shrimp, egg whites and nutmeg. Transfer to a large bowl and set over ice until very cold. Preheat oven to 350°F (180°C). Beat in whipping cream, 1/4 cup (50 mL) at a time, until mixture is the consistency of softly beaten cream. Divide evenly among 6 well-buttered 5-oz (150 mL) ramekins and cover with buttered parchment paper. Place ramekins in a water bath (see page 12) and bake until set, about 25 minutes. Invert onto plates and blot up liquid. Serve with sauce or garnished with lemon and/or a spoonful of caviar (if you're feeling extravagant). **Serves 6.**

Chopped Liver

2	large onions, minced	2
1/3 cup	rendered chicken fat	75 mL
12 oz	chicken livers	375 g
Pinch	dried thyme	Pinch
2	hard-cooked eggs, chopped	2
	Salt and freshly ground black pepper	

In a dry skillet, cook onions, covered, over low heat until soft and dry. Add chicken fat and sauté onions until browned. Add chicken livers and thyme; sauté until firm. Transfer to a food processor and purée until smooth. Transfer to a bowl and stir in eggs. Season with salt and pepper. Cover and refrigerate until chilled, about 1 hour. **Serves 4.**

Pasta Dough

2	extra-large eggs	2
1/4 tsp	salt	1 mL
1 1/2 cups	all-purpose flour	375 mL

In the work bowl of a food processor, combine eggs and salt. Add flour and process, scraping the sides of the bowl as needed, until dough is very stiff. Remove dough, wrap tightly with plastic wrap and let rest for 10 minutes. Roll out with a pasta machine or a rolling pin. **Makes enough pasta to serve 2.**

Pie Pastry

1 1/2 cups	all-purpose flour	375 mL
1/4 tsp	salt	1 mL
1/2 cup	butter, chilled and cut into small pieces	125 mL
1/4 cup	ice water	50 mL

In a food processor, process flour and salt until combined. Scatter evenly with butter and pulse until mixture resembles coarse meal. Add half the water and pulse to distribute. Add the remaining water, a bit at a time, until dough begins to climb the walls of the work bowl but is still rough and unformed. Shape dough into a disk and wrap in plastic wrap. Refrigerate for at least 30 minutes or for up to 2 days before using in a recipe. **Makes one 9-inch (23 cm) crust.**

Quick Puff Pastry

2 cups	all-purpose flour	500 mL
½ tsp	salt	2 mL
1½ cups	butter, frozen and cut into small pieces	375 mL
½ cup	ice water	125 mL

In a food processor, process flour and salt until combined. Scatter evenly with butter and pulse until butter is the size of large peas. Add half the water and pulse to distribute. Add the remaining water, a bit at a time, until dough begins to climb the walls of the work bowl but is still rough and unformed. Place dough on a piece of plastic wrap and use the plastic to shape and wrap the dough into a rectangular brick. Refrigerate for 15 minutes. On a lightly floured work surface, roll out dough into a long rectangle. Fold into thirds as you would a letter and turn dough so that the open ends are at 6 and 12 o'clock. Roll out, fold into thirds and turn again. Repeat twice more. Wrap in plastic wrap and refrigerate for at least 1 hour or for up to 2 days before using in a recipe. **Makes about 1½ lbs (750 g).**

Peanut Butter

| 1 lb | salted dry-roasted peanuts | 500 g |
| 2 tsp | packed light brown sugar | 10 mL |

In a food processor, pulse peanuts and brown sugar until finely chopped, then process until smooth, about 3 minutes, stopping periodically to scrape the bowl. **Makes about 2 cups (500 mL).**

Mayonnaise

Pinch	cayenne pepper	Pinch
	Salt and freshly ground white pepper to taste	
1 tbsp	boiling water	15 mL
2	egg yolks	2
2 tsp	Dijon mustard	10 mL
2 tbsp	freshly squeezed lemon juice	25 mL
1½ cups	canola oil	375 mL

In a food processor, dissolve cayenne, salt and white pepper in boiling water. Add egg yolks and mustard; process until slightly thickened. Stir in lemon juice. With the motor running, slowly add oil through the feed tube and process until thick and creamy. Season with salt and pepper, if desired. **Makes about 2 cups (500 mL).** *Store in an airtight container in the refrigerator for up to 2 days. (If you are concerned about the food safety of raw eggs, you may wish to skip this recipe.)*

Quick Sorbet

| 1 | can (16 oz/500 g) fruit in heavy syrup (such as pears, apricots, peaches or lychees) | 1 |
| ½ tsp | sweet vinegar (such as raspberry, cider or aged balsamic) or vanilla | 2 mL |

Freeze the can of fruit until solid, at least overnight. No more than 2 hours before serving, run the frozen can under warm water to thaw the edges. Remove the top and bottom of the can, slide the contents into a large bowl and chop into coarse chunks. In a food processor, purée fruit chunks and vinegar until chopped finely enough to form a smooth ball. **Serves 4.** *Store in an airtight container in the freezer for up to 24 hours (if the mixture should freeze solid, purée it again to refresh it).*

Ground Nuts

In a food processor, pulse 8 oz (250 g) toasted shelled nuts until ground to a fine powder, scraping the bowl as needed to keep the mixture evenly ground. **Makes 2 cups (500 mL).**

Seasoned Bread Crumbs

Toast any number of bread slices until crisp. Cut toast into small pieces. Place in a food processor with a pinch each of dried Italian seasoning, salt and pepper per slice; pulse until coarsely ground. **Makes about ¼ cup (50 mL) per slice.**

Shredded Cheese

Use any amount of firm cheese, such as Cheddar, Monterey Jack or Swiss. Cut into logs that fit easily into the feed tube of a food processor. Using a grating disk, turn on the processor and insert cheese logs into the feed tube, one at a time, using the plastic pusher to push each log into the blade. (Do not place your fingers in the feed tube.) When the work bowl is three-quarters full, transfer the contents to a bowl and shred another batch.

Chopped Garlic

In a mini-chopper, pulse 2 to 6 cloves garlic until chopped to the desired size. (If chopping more than 6 cloves, use a food processor.)

Chopped Onion

Peel and quarter 1 onion. In a food processor, pulse onion until chopped to the desired size.

PART 3

Everyday Cooking

Chapter 6

Snacks and Little Plates
To Help Spoil Dinner (or Any Meal)

Vanilla Popcorn 78
Lemon Popcorn 78
Saffron Buttered Popcorn 78
Garlic and Parmesan Popcorn 78
Three-Pepper Popcorn 78
Popcorn with Basil and
Sun-Dried Tomatoes 78
Walnut Popcorn 79
Roasted Pepper Popcorn 79
Spicy Crab Popcorn 79
Bacon and Onion Popcorn 79
Hot Pepper Pecans 79
Chili Pumpkin Seeds 79
Sweet Curried Peanuts 80
Spicy Sweet Nuts 80
Healthy Snack Mix 80
Unhealthy Snack Mix 80
All-Almond Snack Mix 80
Shrimp Chips 80
Sesame Scallop Chips 80
Plantain Chips 80
Garlic Potato Chips 80
Spiced Brown Rice 80
Spanish Cauliflower 81
Lemon and Pepper Olives 81
Garlic Green Olives and Peppers 81

Curried Black Olives 81
Prosciutto and Pear 81
Eggplant Bruschetta 81
French Bread Pizza 81
Gorgonzola and Onion
French Bread Pizza 82
Marinated Salad French Bread Pizza 82
Provençal Mini-Pizzas 82
Walnut Garlic Baguette 82
Hot Pepper Oil 82
Sun-Dried Tomato Oil 82
Pine Nut and Garlic Butter 83
Cashew Date Butter 83
Chocolate Peanut Butter 83
Hot Pepper Peanut Butter 83
Molasses Mustard Dip 83
Spicy Cheese Dip 83
Microwave Chocolate Dip 83
Peanut Toffee Dip 83
Mustard Chutney Dip 84
Bagna Caôda 84
Warm Basil and Tomato Dip 84
Gorgonzola Mousse 84
Smoked Salmon Mousse 84
Cherry Fennel Compote 84
Prunes in Brandy 84

Quadequina was not a great warrior, nor was he a famed peacemaker like his brother Chief Massasoit, but he sure knew how to pack a snack. When the Pilgrims threw their big potluck bash in the fall of 1621, he didn't bring the sweet potato casserole or his mother's recipe for cornbread stuffing. Instead, he made American gastronomic history. He brought the popcorn.

Popcorn set the stage for the scores of great American snack foods to follow. Not only is it quick and easy to prepare, but it can be eaten almost anywhere by the handful. Like corn chips, pretzels and pizza, it lends itself to endless embellishment, and like dry roasted nuts and celery sticks, it is inherently healthy.

Snack food needn't be synonymous with junk. Though many of the recipes that follow hardly qualify as health food, all are made with wholesome ingredients and have been formulated with an eye toward eliminating excess fat, sugar and salt.

About these recipes . . .

In the name of Quadequina, we offer you the following 50 recipes for wonderful snacks. Most are fast and easy, and those that take a little time to prepare make up for it with elaborate results.

Several of these recipes are designed to be made ahead and stored — just right to have on hand for munching your way through the climax of a movie or the final inning, when a snack is essential but cooking is out of the question.

Vanilla Popcorn

¼ cup	corn or canola oil	50 mL
¾ cup	popping corn	175 mL
1	vanilla bean, split	1
1 tbsp	superfine sugar	15 mL
2 tbsp	melted butter	25 mL
	Salt to taste	

In a large, heavy pot, heat oil over high heat until it smokes. Add a few kernels of popping corn and heat until they pop. Add vanilla bean and the remaining popping corn. Cover and shake gently until corn starts to pop. Shake vigorously until popping subsides. Remove from heat. Remove vanilla bean and set aside; toss popcorn with sugar, butter and salt. Scrape seeds from vanilla bean and toss with popcorn; discard pod or reserve for another use. **Serves 6.**

Lemon Popcorn

Follow preceding recipe, but omit the vanilla bean and the sugar. Add the finely grated zest of 1 lemon and 2 tsp (10 mL) lemon juice to the melted butter and salt. **Serves 6.**

Saffron Buttered Popcorn

Follow recipe for Vanilla Popcorn (left), but instead of plain melted butter, use 3 tbsp (45 mL) melted butter heated with ¼ tsp (1 mL) finely chopped saffron threads for 1 minute. **Serves 6.**

Garlic and Parmesan Popcorn

¼ cup	olive oil	50 mL
¾ cup	popping corn	175 mL
2	cloves garlic, split	2
1	clove garlic, minced	1
¼ cup	freshly grated Parmesan cheese	50 mL
Pinch	cayenne pepper	Pinch
	Salt to taste	

In a large, heavy pot, heat oil over high heat until it smokes. Add a few kernels of popping corn and heat until they pop. Add split garlic and the remaining popping corn. Cover and shake gently until corn starts to pop. Shake vigorously until popping subsides. Remove from heat. Remove garlic cloves and toss popcorn with minced garlic, Parmesan, cayenne and salt. **Serves 4.**

Three-Pepper Popcorn

Follow preceding recipe, but omit the Parmesan, add 2 tsp (10 mL) coarsely ground black pepper, and add 3 to 4 tbsp (45 to 50 mL) hot pepper sauce (such as Frank's RedHot) mixed with 2 tbsp (25 mL) melted butter. **Serves 4.**

Popcorn with Basil and Sun-Dried Tomatoes

Follow recipe for Garlic and Parmesan Popcorn (above), but omit the minced garlic, replace the Parmesan with grated aged provolone, and add 6 finely chopped drained oil-packed sun-dried tomatoes, 1 tbsp (15 mL) oil from the tomatoes and 12 finely chopped basil leaves. **Serves 4.**

Walnut Popcorn

⅔ cup	walnut pieces	150 mL
¼ cup	olive oil	50 mL
¾ cup	popping corn	175 mL
	Garlic salt to taste	

In a food processor, grind walnut pieces until very finely chopped and oily. Set aside. In a large, heavy pot, heat oil over high heat until it smokes. Add a few kernels of popping corn and heat until they pop. Add the remaining popping corn. Cover and shake gently until corn starts to pop. Shake vigorously until popping subsides. Remove from heat and toss with reserved walnuts and garlic salt. **Serves 4.**

Roasted Pepper Popcorn

2 tbsp	olive oil	25 mL
2 tbsp	minced onion	25 mL
1	clove garlic, minced	1
1	roasted red bell pepper (see page 11), diced	1
3 tbsp	corn or canola oil	45 mL
¾ cup	popping corn	175 mL
	Salt and cayenne pepper to taste	

In a small skillet, heat olive oil over medium-high heat. Sauté onion until tender. Add garlic and roasted pepper; sauté until heated through. Remove from heat and set aside. In a large, heavy pot, heat corn oil over high heat until it smokes. Add a few kernels of popping corn and heat until they pop. Add the remaining popping corn. Cover and shake gently until corn starts to pop. Shake vigorously until popping subsides. Remove from heat and toss with reserved onion mixture, salt and cayenne. **Serves 6.**

Spicy Crab Popcorn

1 tbsp	olive oil	15 mL
4	green onions, thinly sliced	4
1	clove garlic, minced	1
4 oz	backfin (lump) crabmeat, shells picked out	125 g
3 tbsp	corn or canola oil	45 mL
¾ cup	popping corn	175 mL
	Salt and cayenne pepper to taste	

In a small skillet, heat olive oil over medium-high heat. Sauté green onions and garlic until tender. Add crabmeat and sauté until heated through. Remove from heat and set aside. In a large, heavy pot, heat corn oil over high heat until it smokes. Add a few kernels of popping corn and heat until they pop. Add the remaining popping corn. Cover and shake gently until corn starts to pop. Shake vigorously until popping subsides. Remove from heat and toss with reserved onion mixture, salt and cayenne. **Serves 6.**

Bacon and Onion Popcorn

6	slices bacon, cooked and crumbled, fat reserved	6
1	small onion, finely chopped	1
1 tbsp	corn or canola oil	15 mL
¾ cup	popping corn	175 mL
	Salt to taste	

In a skillet, heat 1 tbsp (15 mL) of the reserved bacon fat over medium heat. Sauté onion until tender. Remove from heat and set aside. In a large, heavy pot, heat oil and 2 tbsp (25 mL) of the bacon fat until fat smokes. Add a few kernels of popping corn and heat until they pop. Add the remaining popping corn. Cover and shake gently until corn starts to pop. Shake vigorously until popping subsides. Remove from heat and toss with crumbled bacon, reserved onion and salt. **Serves 6.**

Hot Pepper Pecans

2 tbsp	canola oil	25 mL
2 cups	pecan halves	500 mL
½ cup	granulated sugar	125 mL
1 to 2 tsp	kosher salt	5 to 10 mL
1 tsp	cayenne pepper	5 mL
¼ tsp	ground cinnamon	1 mL

In a large skillet, heat oil over medium-high heat. Lightly toast pecans, stirring constantly, for about 1 minute. Add sugar and cook, stirring constantly, until it caramelizes and coats the nuts. (Be careful: the sugar will get scorching hot!) Quickly spoon onto a baking sheet and spread into a thin layer with the back of a large spoon. Sprinkle evenly with salt to taste, cayenne and cinnamon. Let cool completely, then break into individual pecans.
Serves 8. *Store at room temperature in an airtight container for up to 2 days.*

Chili Pumpkin Seeds

Follow preceding recipe, but substitute pumpkin seeds for the pecans, omit the cinnamon, and add 1 tsp (5 mL) chili powder with the cayenne.
Serves 8. *Store at room temperature in an airtight container for up to 2 days.*

Sweet Curried Peanuts

Follow recipe for Hot Pepper Pecans (page 79), but substitute peanuts for the pecans, omit the cinnamon, and add ½ tsp (2 mL) curry powder with the cayenne. **Serves 8.** *Store at room temperature in an airtight container for up to 2 days.*

Spicy Sweet Nuts

Follow recipe for Hot Pepper Pecans (page 79), but substitute peanut oil for the canola oil, mixed nuts for the pecans, and curry powder for the cinnamon. **Serves 8.** *Store at room temperature in an airtight container for up to 2 days.*

Healthy Snack Mix

1 cup	whole almonds	250 mL
½ cup	roasted peanuts	125 mL
½ cup	golden raisins	125 mL
½ cup	dark raisins	125 mL
½ cup	toasted wheat germ	125 mL
¼ cup	toasted sesame seeds	50 mL
¼ cup	roasted sunflower seeds	50 mL

Combine all ingredients. **Serves 12.** *Store at room temperature in an airtight container for up to 2 days.*

Unhealthy Snack Mix

1 cup	salted roasted peanuts	250 mL
1 cup	pretzel sticks	250 mL
1 cup	raisins	250 mL
1 cup	semisweet chocolate chips	250 mL

Combine all ingredients. **Serves 8.** *Store at room temperature in an airtight container for up to 2 days.*

All-Almond Snack Mix

1 cup	whole almonds	250 mL
1 cup	whole smokehouse almonds	250 mL
1 cup	whole spiced almonds	250 mL

Combine all ingredients. **Serves 12.** *Store at room temperature in an airtight container for up to 2 days.*

Shrimp Chips

½ cup	cornstarch	125 mL
1 tsp	cayenne pepper	5 mL
20	large shrimp, peeled, deveined and butterflied	20
	Vegetable oil, for frying	
	Salt to taste	

Mix cornstarch and cayenne and thoroughly dredge shrimp in the mixture. Place each piece of shrimp between sheets of plastic wrap or waxed paper and pound gently until paper-thin. Lift carefully from paper and dredge again in the starch. Deep-fry (see page 9) in batches until crisp but still pale, about 1 minute. Remove and drain in a strainer set over a bowl. Let stand for 20 minutes. Just before serving, deep-fry again for a few seconds. Season with salt. **Serves 4.**

Sesame Scallop Chips

Follow preceding recipe, but use large whole sea scallops instead of shrimp, and add 2 tbsp (10 mL) ground sesame seeds to the cornstarch mixture. **Serves 4.**

Plantain Chips

2	large plantains	2
	Canola oil	
	Salt to taste	

Peel plantains by slitting along the ridges of the peel. Cut off stem end and remove peel in sections. Cut plantains into thin slices. Deep-fry (see page 9) in batches in 1 inch (2.5 cm) of oil until lightly browned. Remove and drain in a strainer set over a bowl. Season with salt. **Serves 4.**

Garlic Potato Chips

1 lb	russet potatoes, peeled and cut into ⅛-inch (3 mm) slices	500 g
	Vegetable oil	
	Garlic salt to taste	

Deep-fry (see page 9) potato slices, in batches, in 2 to 3 inches (5 to 7.5 inches) of oil heated to 325°F (160°C) until lightly browned. Remove with a slotted spoon to a strainer set over a bowl. Heat oil to 375°F (190°C) and deep-fry again in batches until crisp. Remove and drain in a strainer set over a bowl. Sprinkle with garlic salt. **Serves 4.**

Spiced Brown Rice

2 cups	cooked brown rice	500 mL
3 tbsp	dark sesame oil	45 mL
1 tbsp	chili powder	15 mL
¼ cup	sesame seeds	50 mL
1 tsp	ground coriander	5 mL

Toss rice in oil and chili powder. Set aside. In a large dry skillet, toast sesame seeds and coriander, stirring constantly, until seeds color lightly. Add rice and cook until grains are dry and separate. **Serves 4.**

Spanish Cauliflower

¼ cup	olive oil	50 mL
3	cloves garlic, minced	3
2 cups	small cauliflower florets, blanched	500 mL
2 tbsp	dry white wine	25 mL
1 tbsp	freshly squeezed lemon juice	15 mL
1 tsp	paprika	5 mL
	Salt and freshly ground black pepper to taste	

In a large skillet, heat oil over medium-high heat. Sauté garlic until browned, about 1 minute. Transfer to a large bowl and toss with cauliflower, wine, lemon juice, paprika, salt and pepper. Serve warm, or cover and refrigerate for up to 2 days. **Serves 4.**

Lemon and Pepper Olives

½ cup	olive oil	125 mL
2	cloves garlic, minced	2
1 tsp	kosher salt	5 mL
1 tsp	cracked black pepper	5 mL
2 cups	drained black olives	500 mL
1	lemon, thinly sliced	1

In a small saucepan, heat oil over medium heat. Sauté garlic, salt and pepper until garlic bubbles. Combine olives and lemon slices; toss with garlic mixture. **Serves 8 to 10.** *Store in an airtight container in the refrigerator for up to 2 weeks.*

Garlic Green Olives and Peppers

6	cloves garlic, minced	6
1	roasted red bell pepper (see page 11), diced	1
2 cups	green olives, with their brine	500 mL
1 tbsp	red or white wine vinegar	15 mL
Pinch	cayenne pepper	Pinch

Toss together all ingredients. **Serves 8 to 10.** *Store in an airtight container in the refrigerator for up to 2 weeks.*

Curried Black Olives

¼ cup	olive oil	50 mL
2 tbsp	finely chopped onion	25 mL
1 tbsp	curry powder	15 mL
1 tsp	ground coriander	5 mL
1 tsp	ground cumin	5 mL
2 tbsp	freshly squeezed orange juice	25 mL
1 tsp	cider vinegar	5 mL
2 cups	drained black olives	500 mL

In a small saucepan, heat oil over medium heat. Sauté onion until tender. Add curry powder, coriander and cumin; sauté for 30 seconds. Stir in orange juice and vinegar. Remove from heat and toss with olives. **Serves 8 to 10.** *Store in an airtight container in the refrigerator for up to 2 weeks.*

Prosciutto and Pear

2	large pears, peeled, cored and cut into 8 wedges	2
16	thin slices prosciutto (preferably imported)	16

Wrap each pear wedge in 1 slice of prosciutto. Serve immediately. **Serves 4.**

Eggplant Bruschetta

1	eggplant (1 to 1½ lbs/500 to 750 g), cut crosswise into 8 slices	1
⅓ cup	prepared Italian dressing	75 mL
8	basil leaves	8
8	oil-packed sun-dried tomatoes	8
1 cup	shredded fontina cheese	250 mL

Brush eggplant slices with Italian dressing; let stand for 15 minutes. Meanwhile, preheat broiler or barbecue grill to high. Broil or grill eggplant, turning once, for 3 minutes per side. Top each slice with 1 basil leaf, 1 sun-dried tomato and one-eighth of the cheese. Broil or grill until cheese melts, about 1 minute. **Serves 4.**

French Bread Pizza

2	large tomatoes, each cut in 4 slices	2
2	small loaves French bread (demi-baguettes), halved lengthwise	2
⅓ cup	prepared Italian dressing	75 mL
3 cups	shredded mozzarella cheese	750 mL
½ cup	freshly grated Parmesan cheese	125 mL

In a shallow dish, brush tomato slices with Italian dressing and let stand for 20 minutes. Meanwhile, preheat broiler. Brush excess dressing and juices from tomatoes over cut sides of bread. Place bread cut side up on a baking sheet and broil for about 1 minute, or until lightly toasted. Place tomato slices on bread and broil for 3 minutes. Top with mozzarella and Parmesan; broil until cheese melts, about 1 minute. **Serves 4.**

Gorgonzola and Onion French Bread Pizza

1 tbsp	butter	15 mL
2 tbsp	extra-virgin olive oil, divided	25 mL
3	onions, thinly sliced	3
1/4 tsp	hot pepper flakes	1 mL
	Kosher salt to taste	
2	small loaves French bread (demi-baguettes), halved lengthwise	2
24	black olives, pitted and coarsely chopped	24
4 oz	Gorgonzola cheese, crumbled	125 g

Preheat broiler. In a small skillet, heat butter and half the oil over medium heat. Sauté onions until lightly browned. Remove from heat and season with hot pepper flakes and salt; set aside. Brush cut sides of bread with remaining oil and place cut side up on a baking sheet. Broil for about 1 minute, or until lightly toasted. Spread onions on bread and broil for 3 minutes. Top with olives and Gorgonzola; broil until cheese melts, about 1 minute. **Serves 4.**

Marinated Salad French Bread Pizza

12	slices mozzarella cheese	12
8	oil-packed sun-dried tomatoes, julienned	8
2	cloves garlic, minced	2
1/2 cup	coarsely chopped basil leaves	125 mL
2 1/2 tbsp	extra-virgin olive oil	32 mL
1/4 tsp	hot pepper flakes	1 mL
	Salt and freshly ground black pepper to taste	
2	small loaves French bread (demi-baguettes), halved lengthwise	2

In a shallow dish, toss mozzarella with sun-dried tomatoes, garlic, basil, oil, hot pepper flakes, salt and pepper. Cover and refrigerate for at least 1 hour or for up to 1 day. Meanwhile, preheat broiler. Remove cheese from marinade. Brush cut sides of bread with liquid from the marinade and place cut side up on a baking sheet. Broil for about 1 minute, or until lightly toasted. Scatter solids from the marinade on bread and broil for 3 minutes. Top each with 3 slices of mozzarella and broil until cheese melts, about 1 minute. **Serves 4.**

Provençal Mini-Pizzas

1/3 cup	extra-virgin olive oil	75 mL
3	cloves garlic, minced	3
1 tsp	dried herbes de Provence	5 mL
1 cup	chopped fresh basil	250 mL
12	slices French bread, each 1/2 inch (1 cm) thick	12
12	slices mozzarella cheese	12
12	slices plum (Roma) tomato	12

Preheat oven to 450°F (230°C). Create a Provençal oil by heating olive oil with garlic and herbes de Provence until garlic bubbles, then adding the basil. Brush one side of each slice of bread with oil. Top each with 1 slice mozzarella, 1 slice tomato and a thin coating of Provençal oil. Place on a baking sheet and bake for 10 minutes, until cheese melts. Blot with a paper towel to absorb moisture. **Serves 4.**

Walnut Garlic Baguette

2	cloves garlic	2
1 cup	walnut pieces	250 mL
2 tbsp	extra-virgin olive oil	25 mL
1	loaf French bread	1

Preheat oven to 400°F (200°C). In a food processor, pulse garlic and nuts until ground. With the motor running, slowly add oil through the feed tube and process until mixture forms a paste. Cut bread into 1/2-inch (1 cm) thick diagonal slices, without cutting completely through. Spread some of the paste on one side of each bread slice. Wrap loaf tightly in foil and bake for 15 minutes. Serve warm. **Serves 4.**

Hot Pepper Oil

1 cup	extra-virgin olive oil	250 mL
6	whole dried chili peppers	6

In a saucepan, heat oil over medium heat. Cook chili peppers until they begin to bubble at the tips. Remove from heat and let stand overnight. **Makes about 1 cup (250 mL).** *Store in an airtight container in a cool, dark place for up to 3 months. Brush oil onto slices of crusty bread.*

Sun-Dried Tomato Oil

1 cup	extra-virgin olive oil	250 mL
1/2 cup	dry-packed sun-dried tomatoes, finely chopped	125 mL

In a saucepan, heat oil over medium heat. Add sun-dried tomatoes, remove from heat and let stand overnight. **Makes about 1 1/2 cups (375 mL).** *Store in an airtight container in a cool, dark place for up to 3 months. Brush oil onto slices of crusty bread, or toss with hot pasta and sprinkle with Parmesan.*

Pine Nut and Garlic Butter

1	clove garlic, minced	1
⅔ cup	pine nuts, toasted	150 mL
1½ tsp	extra-virgin olive oil	7 mL
	Salt to taste	

In a food processor, process garlic, pine nuts, oil and salt until nuts are finely chopped, then process for about 3 minutes, periodically scraping the sides of the bowl, until smooth. **Makes about ½ cup (125 mL).** *Store in an airtight container in the refrigerator for up to 1 month. Spread on warm French or Italian bread or on vegetables.*

Cashew Date Butter

10 oz	unsalted roasted cashews (about 2 cups/500 mL)	300 g
1 tbsp	canola oil	15 mL
2 tsp	packed light brown sugar	10 mL
Pinch	salt	Pinch
½ cup	finely chopped pitted dates	125 mL

In a food processor, pulse cashews, oil, brown sugar and salt until nuts are finely chopped, then process for about 3 minutes, periodically scraping the sides of the bowl, until smooth. Stir in dates. **Makes about 2 cups (500 mL).** *Store in an airtight container in the refrigerator for up to 1 month. Spread on bread or fruit slices.*

Chocolate Peanut Butter

10 oz	unsalted roasted peanuts (about 2½ cups/625 mL)	300 g
1 tsp	peanut oil	5 mL
Pinch	salt	Pinch
2 oz	semisweet chocolate, melted	60 g

In a food processor, pulse peanuts, oil and salt until nuts are finely chopped, then process for about 3 minutes, periodically scraping the sides of the bowl, until smooth. Add chocolate and process to blend. **Makes about 2 cups (500 mL).** *Store in an airtight container in the refrigerator for up to 1 month. Spread on bread or fruit slices.*

Hot Pepper Peanut Butter

1	small clove garlic, minced	1
½ cup	peanut butter (chunky or smooth)	125 mL
1 tbsp	hot pepper sauce (such as Tabasco)	15 mL
2 tsp	dark sesame oil	10 mL
1 tsp	hot pepper oil	5 mL
½ tsp	chili powder	2 mL
¼ tsp	ground coriander	1 mL

Combine all ingredients. **Makes about ½ cup (125 mL).** *Spread on crackers or use as a dip.*

Molasses Mustard Dip

⅓ cup	brown mustard	75 mL
2 tbsp	light (fancy) molasses	25 mL
1 tbsp	honey	15 mL

Combine all ingredients. **Makes about ½ cup (125 mL).** *Use as a dip with pretzel rods.*

Spicy Cheese Dip

½ cup	shredded Cheddar cheese	125 mL
2 tbsp	cream cheese, softened	25 mL
2 to 3 tbsp	hot pepper sauce (such as Frank's RedHot)	25 to 45 mL

In a microwave-safe bowl, mix Cheddar cheese and cream cheese. Microwave on High until melted, about 1 minute. Stir in hot pepper sauce to taste. **Makes about ¾ cup (175 mL).** *Serve warm as a dip with pretzel rods.*

Microwave Chocolate Dip

2 oz	unsweetened chocolate, chopped	60 g
6 tbsp	granulated sugar	90 mL
¼ cup	milk	50 mL
1 tbsp	vanilla	15 mL
1 tbsp	dark rum	15 mL

In a 4-cup (1 L) glass measure, combine chocolate, sugar, milk and vanilla. Cover with microwave-safe plastic wrap and microwave on High for 3 minutes, until chocolate is almost melted. Remove wrap and whisk until fully melted and smooth. Whisk in rum. **Makes about ¾ cup (175 mL).** *Use as a dip for banana chunks, orange sections or pretzels, or as a sauce for ice cream.*

Peanut Toffee Dip

2 tbsp	honey	25 mL
2 tsp	instant coffee granules	10 mL
¼ cup	boiling water	50 mL
6 tbsp	smooth peanut butter	90 mL
2 tbsp	butter	25 mL

Dissolve honey and instant coffee in boiling water. Whisk in peanut butter and butter. **Makes about ¾ cup (175 mL).** *Use as a dip for pretzels or as a sauce for ice cream.*

Mustard Chutney Dip

| ¼ cup | finely chopped mango chutney | 50 mL |
| ¼ cup | brown mustard | 50 mL |

Combine chutney and mustard. **Makes ½ cup (125 mL).** *Store in an airtight container in the refrigerator for up to 1 month. Use as a dip with pretzel rods or raw vegetables, or spread on ham slices, roll up and secure with a toothpick.*

Bagna Caôda

½ cup	extra-virgin olive oil	125 mL
2 tbsp	butter	25 mL
2	cloves garlic, minced	2
¼ cup	finely chopped drained canned anchovies	50 mL
	Salt and freshly ground black pepper to taste	

In a small saucepan, heat oil and butter over medium heat until butter foams. Sauté garlic until aromatic, about 1 minute. Add anchovies and sauté until very soft. Season with salt and pepper. **Makes about ¾ cup (175 mL).** *Serve warm as a dip with raw vegetables.*

Warm Basil and Tomato Dip

Follow preceding recipe, but replace the anchovies with ¼ cup (50 mL) chopped fresh basil and ¼ cup (50 mL) chopped tomato. **Makes about ¾ cup (175 mL).**

Gorgonzola Mousse

4 oz	Gorgonzola cheese, crumbled	125 g
2 tbsp	cream (any type, minimum 10%)	25 mL
1 tbsp	cream cheese, softened	15 mL
	Salt and freshly ground black pepper to taste	

Combine Gorgonzola, cream and cream cheese. Season with salt and pepper. **Makes about 1 cup (250 mL).** *Store in an airtight container in the refrigerator for up to 1 week. Serve surrounded by cherry tomatoes, celery sticks, carrot sticks and spinach leaves, or a selection of fruit.*

Smoked Salmon Mousse

6 oz	cream cheese, softened	175 g
2 oz	smoked salmon, finely chopped	60 g
2 tbsp	cream (any type, minimum 10%)	25 mL
1 tsp	chopped fresh dill	5 mL
	Salt and freshly ground black pepper to taste	

Combine cream cheese, salmon and cream. Season with dill, salt and pepper. **Makes about 1½ cups (375 mL).** *Store in an airtight container in the refrigerator for up to 1 week. Serve surrounded by cherry tomatoes, celery sticks, carrot sticks and spinach leaves.*

Cherry Fennel Compote

1 lb	cherries, stemmed and pitted	500 g
¼ cup	granulated sugar	50 mL
¼ cup	brandy	50 mL
1	small stick cinnamon (about 1½ inches/4 cm)	1
1	whole clove	1
¼ tsp	ground fennel seeds	1 mL
Pinch	salt	Pinch
	Finely grated zest of ½ lime	
	Juice of 2 limes	

In a saucepan, combine cherries, sugar, brandy, cinnamon, clove, fennel seeds, salt and lime juice. Simmer for 5 minutes. Remove from heat and toss with lime zest. Let cool. **Makes about 3 cups (750 mL).** *Store in an airtight container in the refrigerator for up to 6 months. Serve as is, with cookies, or over ice cream.*

Prunes in Brandy

1 lb	pitted prunes	500 g
⅓ cup	honey	75 mL
⅓ cup	water	75 mL
2	whole cloves	2
1	stick cinnamon (about 2 inches/5 cm)	1
½	vanilla bean, split	½
	Grated zest and juice of 1 lemon	
	Grated zest and juice of 1 orange	
½ cup	brandy	125 mL

In a saucepan, combine prunes, honey, water, cloves, cinnamon, vanilla bean, lemon zest, lemon juice, orange zest and orange juice. Simmer for 3 minutes. Remove from heat and stir in brandy. Let cool. **Makes about 2½ cups (625 mL).** *Store in an airtight container in the refrigerator for up to 6 months (add a bit of water if it thickens too much). Serve as is, with cookies, or over ice cream.*

Chapter 7
Sandwiches
The Ultimate One-Dish Meal

Ham, Apple and Mustard on Rye 86
Egg Salad and Olives on Toast 86
Spicy Anchovy Egg Salad Sandwiches ..87
Peanut Butter, Honey and
Raisin Sandwiches 87
Walnut Butter and Fig Sandwiches 87
Health Wraps 87
Corned Beef Deli Wraps 87
Ham and Cheese Wraps 87
Roast Beef on Rye with
Horseradish Sauce 87
Salami Muffaletta 88
Fennel Salmon Salad Sandwiches 88
Smoked Salmon Salad Sandwiches 88
Smoked Salmon, Feta and Tapenade
Sandwiches 88
Waldorf Salad on Rye 88
Shrimp Salad en Brioche 88
Dilled Tuna Sandwiches 88
Dill Tuna Melts 89
Smoked Turkey and Mozzarella Melts ...89
Meatloaf with Sauerkraut
and Mustard on Rye 89
Barbecued Meatloaf Sandwiches 89
Hot Dogs and Chilied Mustard 89
Hot Dogs Grilled with Bacon
and Honey Mustard 89
Chicken or Turkey Franks with
Avocado Salsa 90
Bratwurst with Mustard Applesauce 90
Chèvre and Sun-Dried Tomato
Open-Face Sandwiches 90
Grilled Cheese, Bacon and Tomato
Sandwiches 90

Grilled Chèvre and Smoked Salmon
on Bagels 90
Baked Brie Sandwiches 90
Crab Cake Sandwiches with
Creole Tartar Sauce 90
Shrimp Cake Sandwiches with
Lemon Yogurt Sauce 91
Filet Panier with Wine Butter Sauce 91
Italian Sausage with
Prosciutto and Capers 91
Fried Salmon Sandwiches with
Dill Tartar Sauce 91
Barbecued Pork Sandwiches 92
Barbecued Pork Sandwiches
with Sauerkraut 92
Barbecued Pork Sandwiches
with Coleslaw 92
Marinated Mozzarella, Olives
and Sun-Dried Tomatoes 92
Marinated Mozzarella Grinders 92
Gorgonzola Grinders 92
Three-Meat Deli Hoagies 93
Eggplant and Smoked Mozzarella
Grinders 93
Chèvre and Roasted Pepper
Mini-Sandwiches 93
Spinach Salad with Warm Bacon
Dressing in Baguettes 93
Caesar Salad Sandwiches 94
Grilled Lamb and Artichoke Pitas 94
Tuna and Guacamole Pitas 94
Middle Eastern Turkey Pitas 94
Chicken Chickpea Salad Pitas 95
Cold Crab and Avocado Tacos 95
Crab and Smoked Salmon Tea
Sandwiches 95

Few foods are more soulful than an honest sandwich. It's easy to prepare, effortless to serve and so common to our way of eating that we are apt to take it for granted. But there is more to building a great sandwich than just slapping a couple of things between two slices of bread.

The bread must never dominate. It certainly can give a sandwich textural interest, as when it's toasted for a BLT or dough-soft for a PBJ. Even a slow-risen, carefully crusted artisanal loaf, though magnificent on its own, must, in the case of a well-made sandwich, take a supportive role, barely more than a case for the filling.

Meat sandwiches need chewier breads — rye for roast beef and pastrami, hard rolls for submarines and steak sandwiches. More intricate and delicate club and tea sandwiches, those with three slices of bread, should get thinner bread that's toasted to prevent sogginess. If a sandwich will be served hot with a sauce, the bread must be sturdy and flexible. Rye bread, sourdough or rolls are common choices.

Rolls demand more filling because of their thickness, and a buttery roll like a croissant should be served warm with a warm filling. Large rolls, such as torpedo rolls, must sometimes be trimmed of some interior bread to make room for the filling.

Fillings need to be moist, yet not overly wet. For years, almost all sandwich bread was buttered, but for more flavor with less fat, mustard, horseradish, creamy vinaigrettes, herbed and spiced mayonnaises and yogurt-based sauces give you more bang for your calories.

More and more often, vegetables provide savory flavors and moisture for sandwiches. There are, of course, the ubiquitous tomato, the mandatory leaf of iceberg and the sloppy crunch of coleslaw, but think, too, of the peppery bite of watercress and arugula, the exotic touch of marinated artichoke or a garlic-laced eggplant purée. Cucumber marinated in vinaigrette, peppers preserved in oil or an onion salad can add spark to almost any meat sandwich, and a relish of pickled vegetables is great with grilled cheese or broiled meat.

There's an old construction trick, of which veteran sandwich makers are very fond, that adds flavor to a sandwich while reducing its cost. It takes advantage of the physical phenomenon that, no matter how delicious a sandwich's ingredients may be, their flavors will be lost if there is no space around them. Space is air, and air (besides being free) carries the aroma of food to the nose. Without aroma, our perception of flavor falls to a fraction of what it could be. Space is created in a sandwich by loosely folding flat ingredients, such as meat and cheese slices; by overlapping vegetables, such as tomato slices and lettuce leaves; and by fluffing shredded or finely chopped condiments.

About these recipes . . .

For all of the sandwiches that follow, we've assumed that you will season to taste with salt and pepper.

Ham, Apple and Mustard on Rye

3 tbsp	brown mustard	45 mL
1 tbsp	apple butter	15 mL
8	slices rye bread	8
12	thin slices baked ham	12
12	thin wedges cored apple	12

Combine mustard and apple butter; spread on each slice of bread. Arrange 3 slices of folded baked ham on each of 4 slices of the bread and top with 3 thin wedges of cored apple. Top with the remaining bread slices. **Serves 4.**

Egg Salad and Olives on Toast

8	hard-cooked eggs, chopped	8
¼ cup	diced pitted oil-cured black olives	50 mL
1 tbsp	finely chopped fresh Italian (flat-leaf) parsley	15 mL
1 tbsp	mayonnaise	15 mL
1 tbsp	extra-virgin olive oil	15 mL
1 tsp	freshly squeezed lemon juice	5 mL
½ tsp	brown mustard	2 mL
8	slices bread (any type), toasted	8
4	leaves Romaine lettuce	4

Combine eggs, olives, parsley, mayonnaise, oil, lemon juice and mustard. Use with the bread and romaine to make 4 sandwiches. **Serves 4.**

Spicy Anchovy Egg Salad Sandwiches

8	hard-cooked eggs, chopped	8
2 tbsp	minced drained canned anchovies, oil reserved	25 mL
1 tbsp	oil from anchovies	15 mL
1 tbsp	finely chopped fresh Italian (flat-leaf) parsley	15 mL
1 tbsp	mayonnaise	15 mL
1 tsp	freshly squeezed lemon juice	5 mL
½ tsp	brown mustard	2 mL
¼ tsp	hot pepper flakes	1 mL
8	slices bread (any type), toasted	8
4	leaves Romaine lettuce	4

Combine eggs, anchovies, oil, parsley, mayonnaise, lemon juice, mustard and hot pepper flakes. Use with the bread and romaine to make 4 sandwiches. Serves 4.

Peanut Butter, Honey and Raisin Sandwiches

8	slices raisin bread	8
½ cup	peanut butter	125 mL
½ cup	raisins	125 mL
¼ cup	honey	50 mL

Spread 4 slices of bread with peanut butter. Sprinkle each with a quarter of the raisins and drizzle with 1 tbsp (15 mL) honey. Top with the remaining bread. Serves 4.

Walnut Butter and Fig Sandwiches

1¼ cups	walnut pieces	300 mL
¼ tsp	light brown sugar	1 mL
Pinch	salt	Pinch
8	slices whole wheat bread	8
8	dried figs, sliced	8
3 tbsp	raspberry preserves	45 mL

In a food processor, process walnuts, brown sugar and salt until smooth and thick. Spread on 4 slices of bread and top each with a portion of the fig slices. Spread a portion of raspberry preserves on each of the remaining bread slices and make 4 sandwiches. Serves 4.

Health Wraps

1 cup	bulgur	250 mL
1½ cups	cold water	375 mL
¼ cup	olive oil	50 mL
3	green onions, finely chopped	3
1	clove garlic, minced	1
1	carrot, shredded	1
1	tomato, chopped	1
2 tbsp	finely chopped fresh mint	25 mL
	Juice of 1 lemon	
6	8-inch (20 cm) whole wheat flour tortillas	6
¾ cup	tahini	175 mL
⅔ cup	alfalfa sprouts	150 mL

Soak bulgur in water and oil for 30 minutes; drain off excess liquid. Mix in green onions, garlic, carrot, tomato, mint and lemon juice. In a hot, dry skillet, toast tortillas for 30 seconds per side. Spread warm tortillas with tahini and top each with a portion of the bulgur mixture. Top with alfalfa sprouts and roll up. Wrap in waxed paper or parchment, leaving one end open. Eat like pop-up Popsicles. Serves 6.

Corned Beef Deli Wraps

6	8-inch (20 cm) flour tortillas	6
½ cup	mayonnaise	125 mL
2 tbsp	ketchup	25 mL
8 oz	thinly sliced corned beef	250 g
1 cup	coleslaw	250 mL

In a hot, dry skillet, toast tortillas for 30 seconds per side. Combine mayonnaise and ketchup; spread over warm tortillas. Top each with a portion of corned beef and coleslaw. Roll up, wrap and eat as described in preceding recipe. Serves 6.

Ham and Cheese Wraps

6	8-inch (20 cm) flour tortillas	6
6 tbsp	brown mustard	90 mL
8 oz	baked ham, thinly sliced	250 g
5 oz	Swiss cheese, thinly sliced	150 g

In a hot, dry skillet, toast tortillas for 30 seconds per side. Spread each warm tortilla with 1 tbsp (15 mL) mustard. Top each with a portion of ham and cheese. Roll up, wrap and eat as described in Health Wraps (above). Serves 6.

Roast Beef on Rye with Horseradish Sauce

2 tbsp	prepared horseradish	25 mL
2 tbsp	mayonnaise	25 mL
1 tbsp	sour cream	15 mL
8	slices rye bread	8
8 oz	rare roast beef, thinly sliced	250 g

Combine horseradish, mayonnaise and sour cream; spread on each slice of bread. Loosely mound roast beef on 4 of the bread slices; top with the other 4 slices. Serves 4.

Salami Muffaletta

1	small clove garlic, minced	1
8 oz	Genoa salami, diced	250 g
5 oz	provolone cheese, diced	150 g
1/4 cup	chopped pitted oil-cured black olives	50 mL
1/4 cup	chopped tomato	50 mL
2 tbsp	chopped red onion	25 mL
1 tbsp	chopped fresh Italian (flat-leaf) parsley	15 mL
2 tbsp	extra-virgin olive oil	25 mL
1 tbsp	red wine vinegar	15 mL
4	kaiser rolls, split and hollowed out	4

Combine garlic, salami, provolone, olives, tomato, onion, parsley, oil and vinegar. Fill each roll with the mixture. **Serves 4.**

Fennel Salmon Salad Sandwiches

3 tbsp	mayonnaise	45 mL
2 tbsp	freshly squeezed lemon juice	25 mL
1 tbsp	sour cream	15 mL
8	slices black bread	8
1 tbsp	chopped fennel leaf	15 mL
1/2 cup	finely diced fennel bulb	125 mL
2	cans (each 6 oz/170 g) salmon, drained	2
4	leaves Romaine lettuce	4

Combine mayonnaise, lemon juice and sour cream; spread 1 tsp (5 mL) of this sauce on each slice of bread. In a large bowl, toss fennel leaf, diced fennel and salmon; combine with the remaining mayonnaise mixture. Build 4 sandwiches using the salmon salad and 1 lettuce leaf per sandwich. **Serves 4.**

Smoked Salmon Salad Sandwiches

3 tbsp	mayonnaise	45 mL
2 tbsp	freshly squeezed lemon juice	25 mL
1 tbsp	sour cream	15 mL
8	slices black bread	8
1	stalk celery, diced	1
1	can (6 oz/170 g) salmon, drained	1
4 oz	smoked salmon, chopped	125 g
1 tbsp	chopped fresh dill	15 mL
12	slices cucumber	12

Combine mayonnaise, lemon juice and sour cream; spread 1 tsp (5 mL) of this sauce on each slice of bread. In a large bowl, toss celery, salmon, smoked salmon and dill; combine with the remaining mayonnaise mixture. Build 4 sandwiches using the salmon salad and 3 slices of cucumber per sandwich. **Serves 4.**

Smoked Salmon, Feta and Tapenade Sandwiches

1/4 cup	tapenade (store-bought or see recipe, page 56)	50 mL
8	slices black bread (or 4 halved bagels)	8
8	spinach leaves	8
6 oz	smoked salmon, thinly sliced	175 g
2 oz	feta cheese, crumbled	60 g

Spread tapenade over bread and make 4 sandwiches from the spinach, smoked salmon and feta. **Serves 4.**

Waldorf Salad on Rye

1	large Granny Smith apple, grated	1
12 oz	baked ham, diced	375 g
2/3 cup	coarsely chopped walnuts	150 mL
1/3 cup	mayonnaise, divided	75 mL
1 tsp	cider vinegar	5 mL
8	slices rye bread	8
8	leaves lettuce	8

Combine apple, ham, walnuts, 3 tbsp (45 mL) of the mayonnaise and vinegar. Brush bread with the remaining mayonnaise. Top each of 4 slices with 1 lettuce leaf and mound with meat salad. Top with the remaining lettuce leaves and bread. **Serves 4.**

Shrimp Salad en Brioche

1	stalk celery, diced	1
12 oz	small shrimp, peeled, deveined and boiled	375 g
1/4 cup	chopped walnuts	50 mL
2 tbsp	mayonnaise	25 mL
1 tsp	freshly squeezed lemon juice	5 mL
1 tsp	Dijon mustard	5 mL
1/2 tsp	chopped fresh tarragon (or 1/4 tsp/1 mL dried)	2 mL
8	slices brioche-type bread (such as challah)	8
	Watercress sprigs	

Combine celery, shrimp, walnuts, mayonnaise, lemon juice, mustard and tarragon. Use to make 4 sandwiches with the brioche. Garnish each sandwich with watercress. **Serves 4.**

Dilled Tuna Sandwiches

1	cucumber, seeded and thinly sliced	1
1/2 tsp	salt	2 mL
2	cans (each 6 oz/170 g) tuna, drained	2
1/2 cup	ranch dressing (store-bought or see recipes, page 64), divided	125 mL
2 tbsp	chopped fresh dill	25 mL

1 tbsp	freshly squeezed lemon juice	15 mL
8	slices black bread	8
8	thin slices tomato	8

In a small bowl, toss cucumber and salt; let stand for 20 minutes, then squeeze out as much moisture as possible. Combine cucumber, tuna, $\frac{1}{3}$ cup (75 mL) of the dressing, dill and lemon juice. Spread the remaining dressing on each slice of bread and build 4 sandwiches using the tuna mixture and 2 slices of tomato per sandwich. **Serves 4.**

Dill Tuna Melts

Preheat broiler. Prepare cucumber-tuna salad as in preceding recipe. Spread each of 4 slices of black bread with 1 tsp (5 mL) of ranch dressing (store-bought or see recipes, page 64) and top each with tuna salad and 2 thin slices tomato. Lay $\frac{1}{2}$ oz (15 g) sliced dill havarti on top of each sandwich. Broil (or toast in a toaster oven) until cheese melts, about 2 minutes. **Serves 4.**

Smoked Turkey and Mozzarella Melts

2 tbsp	brown mustard	25 mL
4	slices rye bread, toasted	4
4 oz	smoked turkey breast, sliced	125 g
1	small onion, thinly sliced	1
1 tsp	corn oil	5 mL
4 oz	smoked mozzarella cheese, sliced	125 g

Preheat broiler. Spread mustard on each slice of bread and top each with a portion of turkey. In a small skillet, heat oil over medium heat. Sauté onion until lightly browned. Place onion over turkey and top each with a portion of the mozzarella. Broil (or toast in a toaster oven) for 2 to 3 minutes, or until cheese is bubbly. **Serves 4.**

Meatloaf with Sauerkraut and Mustard on Rye

3 tbsp	brown mustard	45 mL
8	slices rye bread	8
4	slices leftover meatloaf (such as Mom's Meatloaf, page 254)	4
$\frac{1}{2}$ cup	sauerkraut, drained	125 mL

Preheat oven to 375°F (190°C). Spread mustard on each slice of bread. Make 4 sandwiches, using 1 slice of meatloaf and a quarter of the sauerkraut for each. Wrap sandwiches in foil and warm in oven for 20 minutes. **Serves 4.**

Barbecued Meatloaf Sandwiches

4	slices leftover meatloaf (such as Mom's Meatloaf, page 254)	4
$\frac{1}{2}$ cup	barbecue sauce, divided	125 mL
4	kaiser rolls, split	4
$\frac{1}{2}$ cup	coleslaw	125 mL

Preheat oven to 400°F (200°C). Brush meatloaf slices with half of the sauce and warm in oven for 15 minutes (or microwave on High for $2\frac{1}{2}$ minutes). Warm rolls and brush with the remaining sauce. Place meatloaf slices on rolls and top each with one-quarter of the coleslaw. **Serves 4.**

Hot Dogs and Chilied Mustard

1 tsp	canola oil	5 mL
2 tbsp	chopped onion	25 mL
2 tbsp	chili powder	25 mL
1 tsp	ground cumin	5 mL
1 tsp	ground coriander	5 mL
2 tbsp	brown mustard	25 mL
4	hot dog rolls or small torpedo rolls, toasted	4
4	frankfurters or knockwurst, grilled, broiled or boiled	4

In a small skillet, heat oil over medium heat. Sauté onion until tender. Add chili powder, cumin and coriander; sauté for 30 seconds. Remove from heat and stir in mustard. Spread rolls with chilied mustard and serve frankfurters in rolls. **Serves 4.**

Hot Dogs Grilled with Bacon and Honey Mustard

8	frankfurters, split lengthwise	8
3 tbsp	honey mustard	45 mL
8	slices bacon	8
8	hot dog rolls, split and warmed	8
	Additional honey mustard	

Preheat broiler or barbecue grill. Spread frankfurters with honey mustard. Wrap 1 slice of bacon around each frank and secure the ends with toothpicks. Grill or broil franks, turning once, until bacon is crisp and franks are browned. Serve on rolls, with additional honey mustard on the side. **Serves 4.**

Chicken or Turkey Franks with Avocado Salsa

8	hot dog rolls, split	8
2 tbsp	olive oil	25 mL
8	chicken or turkey frankfurters, grilled, broiled or boiled	8
	Avocado Salsa (see recipe, page 177)	

Rub the interior of the rolls with oil and lightly toast. Place each frank in a roll and spoon Avocado Salsa on top. **Serves 4.**

Bratwurst with Mustard Applesauce

2 tsp	butter	10 mL
1/4 cup	minced onion	50 mL
1 tsp	light brown sugar	5 mL
1/2 cup	unsweetened applesauce	125 mL
3 tbsp	brown mustard, divided	45 mL
4	bratwurst, grilled, broiled or boiled	4
4	hot dog rolls, split	4

In a small skillet, melt butter over medium heat. Sauté onion until lightly browned. Add brown sugar and stir until melted. Stir in applesauce and 2 tbsp (30 mL) of the mustard. Brush the interior of the rolls with the remaining mustard. Place each bratwurst in a roll and top with mustard applesauce. **Serves 4.**

Chèvre and Sun-Dried Tomato Open-Face Sandwiches

16	slices French bread (baguette)	16
8	oil-packed sun-dried tomatoes, halved, plus their oil	8
16	basil leaves	16
16	thin slices chèvre	16

Preheat oven to 400°F (200°C). Place bread on a baking sheet and moisten each slice with oil from the sun-dried tomatoes. Place 1 basil leaf on each slice and top with a tomato half and 1 slice of chèvre. Bake for 4 to 5 minutes, or until cheese is plump, soft and lightly browned. **Serves 4.**

Grilled Cheese, Bacon and Tomato Sandwiches

8	slices bacon	8
6 oz	Muenster cheese, sliced	175 g
8	slices sourdough white bread	8
8	slices tomato	8

In a large skillet, cook bacon over medium heat until crisp. Drain on paper towels, reserving a thin film of fat in the pan. Divide cheese among 4 slices of bread and top each with 2 slices of tomato and 2 slices of bacon. Top with the remaining bread slices. In the fat remaining in the pan, brown sandwiches over medium heat, turning once, until golden on both sides. **Serves 4.**

Grilled Chèvre and Smoked Salmon on Bagels

7 oz	chèvre, divided	210 g
4	bagels, halved	4
4	paper-thin slices red onion	4
4	slices smoked salmon (each about 1 oz/30 g)	4

Preheat broiler. Divide 3 oz (90 g) of the chèvre among the 4 bottom halves of the bagels. Top each with 1 slice of onion and 1 slice of smoked salmon. Top with the remaining cheese. Broil 4 inches (10 cm) from a high flame for 3 to 4 minutes, or until cheese is plump, soft and lightly browned. Top with bagel tops and cut each sandwich in half. **Serves 4.**

Baked Brie Sandwiches

1	large loaf French bread (baguette), split lengthwise	1
8 oz	Brie, rind trimmed and cheese sliced	250 g

Preheat oven to 400°F (200°C). Fill baguette with Brie, wrap in foil and bake for 15 minutes. Cut into slices before serving. **Serves 4.**

Crab Cake Sandwiches with Creole Tartar Sauce

8 oz	backfin (lump) crabmeat, shells picked out	250 g
1/2 cup	fresh bread crumbs	125 mL
3 tbsp	mayonnaise	45 mL
2 tsp	chopped fresh Italian (flat-leaf) parsley	10 mL
2 tsp	freshly squeezed lemon juice	10 mL
1 tsp	Worcestershire sauce	5 mL
1/2 tsp	hot pepper sauce (such as Tabasco)	2 mL
1/2 tsp	dry mustard	2 mL
1/2 cup	seasoned dry bread crumbs	125 mL
	Vegetable oil	
4	hamburger buns, split	4
1/2 cup	Creole Tartar Sauce (see recipe, page 179)	125 mL
1/2 cup	shredded lettuce	125 mL

Combine crabmeat, fresh bread crumbs, mayonnaise, parsley, lemon juice, Worcestershire sauce, hot pepper sauce and mustard. Form into 4 patties, about ¾ inch (2 cm) thick, and coat with dry bread crumbs. Wrap in plastic wrap and refrigerate for 30 minutes. In a deep skillet, heat ¼ inch (0.5 cm) oil over medium-high heat. Cook crab cakes, turning once, for 3 to 4 minutes per side, or until golden brown. Meanwhile, spread buns with Creole Tartar Sauce. Serve crab cakes on buns, topped with lettuce. Serves 4.

Shrimp Cake Sandwiches with Lemon Yogurt Sauce

Follow preceding recipe, but substitute finely chopped cooked shrimp for the crab and replace the Creole Tartar sauce with a mixture of ½ cup (125 mL) plain yogurt, 1 small garlic clove, minced, and 1 tbsp (15 mL) freshly squeezed lemon juice. Serves 4.

Filet Panier with Wine Butter Sauce

4	filet mignon steaks (each about 4 oz/125 g) Salt and freshly ground black pepper to taste	4
3 tbsp	butter, divided	45 mL
2	shallots, finely chopped	2
½ cup	dry red wine	125 mL
4	small loaves French bread (demi-baguettes), halved lengthwise	4

Place a large iron skillet over high heat for 5 minutes. Season steaks with salt and pepper; cook to desired doneness. Remove steaks from pan and keep warm. Reduce heat to low, add 1 tbsp (15 mL) of the butter and sauté shallots until tender. Add wine and boil until reduced by half. Swirl in the remaining butter and simmer until sauce is slightly thickened. Slice steaks and arrange slices on half of each loaf. Pour sauce over meat and top with the other half. Cut in half and serve. Serves 4.

Italian Sausage with Prosciutto and Capers

1 lb	mild Italian sausage, cut into 4 pieces	500 g
2 tbsp	olive oil	25 mL
⅓ cup	drained capers, chopped	75 mL
2 tbsp	chopped fresh Italian (flat-leaf) parsley	25 mL
4	torpedo rolls, split lengthwise	4
4	thin slices prosciutto	4

Fill a skillet with ½ inch (1 cm) water. Add sausage, cover and bring to a boil over medium-high heat; boil for 4 minutes. Turn sausage and cook, uncovered, until water has evaporated and sausage is browned on the bottom. Flip and brown on the other side. Meanwhile, in a small skillet, heat oil over medium heat. Sauté capers for 30 seconds. Stir in parsley. Spread the interior of the rolls with caper mixture. Wrap each sausage piece in 1 slice of prosciutto and place in rolls. Serves 4.

Fried Salmon Sandwiches with Dill Tartar Sauce

1	egg	1
¼ cup	milk	50 mL
½ cup	cornmeal (yellow or white)	125 mL
¼ cup	all-purpose flour	50 mL
¼ tsp	salt	1 mL
Pinch	cayenne pepper	Pinch
4	pieces skinless salmon fillet (each about 4 oz/125 g)	4
1	hard-cooked egg, finely chopped	1
1	shallot, minced	1
6 tbsp	mayonnaise	90 mL
1½ tbsp	freshly squeezed lemon juice	22 mL
2 tsp	finely chopped fresh dill Olive oil	10 mL
4	kaiser rolls, split	4
2 cups	shredded lettuce	500 mL
4	slices tomato	4

In a wide, shallow dish, beat egg and milk. In another shallow dish, combine cornmeal, flour, salt and cayenne. Dip salmon in egg mixture, then in cornmeal mixture; place on a rack and let stand for 20 minutes. Discard any excess coating mixtures. Meanwhile, in a small bowl, make a tartar sauce by combining hard-cooked egg, shallot, mayonnaise, lemon juice and dill. In a large skillet, heat ⅛ inch (3 mm) oil over medium-high heat. Pan-fry salmon, turning once, until browned, about 2 minutes per side. Drain on paper towels. Spread the interior of the rolls with a thin coating of dill tartar sauce. Place 1 salmon fillet in each roll and top with lettuce, tomato and more sauce. Serves 4.

Barbecued Pork Sandwiches

2 lbs	boneless pork shoulder blade	1 kg
2	cloves garlic, minced	2
	Salt and freshly ground black pepper to taste	
2 cups	chicken broth	500 mL
1 cup	water	250 mL
½ cup	finely chopped onion	125 mL
½ cup	ketchup	125 mL
⅓ cup	cider vinegar	75 mL
¼ cup	packed dark brown sugar	50 mL
1 tbsp	brown mustard	15 mL
1 tbsp	Worcestershire sauce	15 mL
1 tbsp	hot pepper sauce (such as Frank's RedHot or Tabasco)	15 mL
8	hamburger buns, split	8

Preheat oven to 400°F (200°C). Rub pork with garlic, salt and pepper. Roast on a rack in a small roasting pan for 30 minutes. Meanwhile, combine broth, water, onion, ketchup, vinegar, brown sugar, mustard, Worcestershire sauce and hot pepper sauce. Remove rack from roasting pan, pour off fat and reduce oven temperature to 350°F (180°C). Return pork to the pan and pour in broth mixture. Roast for 1½ hours, or until pork is fork-tender. Thinly slice and break into small pieces. Toss with liquid remaining in pan and heap onto buns. **Serves 8.**

Barbecued Pork Sandwiches with Sauerkraut

Follow previous recipe, but top each sandwich with the following mixture: In a large skillet, cook 4 slices of bacon over medium heat until crisp. Remove bacon, crumble and set aside, leaving fat in pan. Add ½ cup (125 mL) finely chopped onion to the fat. Add 1 lb (500 g) sauerkraut, drained, and ¾ cup (175 mL) unsweetened apple juice; cook until all liquid has been absorbed. Add crumbled bacon. **Serves 8.**

Barbecued Pork Sandwiches with Coleslaw

Follow recipe for Barbecued Pork Sandwiches (above), then top each sandwich with ¼ cup (50 mL) Red Cabbage Slaw (page 187) or Sweet-and-Sour Coleslaw (page 187). **Serves 8.**

Marinated Mozzarella, Olives and Sun-Dried Tomatoes

1	clove garlic, minced	1
1 tbsp	red wine vinegar	15 mL
3 tbsp	olive oil	45 mL
1 tsp	minced fresh Italian (flat-leaf) parsley	5 mL
½ tsp	dried basil	2 mL
Pinch	salt	Pinch
	Freshly ground black pepper to taste	
8	oil-packed sun-dried tomatoes, chopped	8
8 oz	mozzarella cheese, diced	250 g
¼ cup	chopped pitted oil-cured black olives	50 mL
2	loaves French bread (baguettes), sliced	2

Whisk together garlic, vinegar, oil, parsley, basil, salt and pepper. Toss with sun-dried tomatoes, mozzarella and olives. Serve immediately, or cover and refrigerate for up to 1 day. Serve with baguette slices and have diners assemble their own open-face sandwiches. **Serves 4.**

Marinated Mozzarella Grinders

Preheat oven to 400°F (200°C). Follow preceding recipe, but pack the cheese mixture into 4 split torpedo rolls. Wrap sandwiches in foil and bake for 20 minutes. **Serves 4.**

Gorgonzola Grinders

2	cloves garlic, minced	2
½ cup	olive oil	125 mL
⅓ cup	red wine vinegar	75 mL
2 tbsp	chopped fresh basil	25 mL
2 tbsp	chopped fresh chives	25 mL
2 tbsp	chopped fresh Italian (flat-leaf) parsley	25 mL
½ tsp	hot pepper flakes	2 mL
	Freshly ground black pepper to taste	
4	torpedo rolls, split lengthwise	4
1 lb	Gorgonzola cheese, cubed	500 g

Preheat oven to 400°F (200°C). Combine garlic, oil, vinegar, basil, chives, parsley, hot pepper flakes and black pepper. Brush the interior of the rolls with a thin film of this dressing and pack with Gorgonzola. Pour the remaining dressing over the cheese. Wrap sandwiches in foil and bake for 10 minutes. **Serves 4.**

Three-Meat Deli Hoagies

¼ cup	olive oil	50 mL
2 tbsp	hot pepper oil (store-bought or see recipe, page 82), divided	25 mL
4	torpedo rolls, split lengthwise	4
4 oz	baked ham, sliced	125 g
4 oz	Genoa salami, sliced	125 g
4 oz	roast turkey breast, sliced	125 g
4 oz	aged provolone cheese, sliced	125 g
12	slices tomato	12
¾ cup	thinly sliced halved onion	175 mL
1 cup	shredded lettuce	250 mL
2 tbsp	red wine vinegar	25 mL

Combine olive oil and hot pepper oil. Brush the interior of the rolls with half the oil mixture. Layer each with a portion of ham, salami, turkey and provolone. Top each with tomato, onion and lettuce. Drizzle each with some of the remaining oil and a quarter of the vinegar. **Serves 4.**

Eggplant and Smoked Mozzarella Grinders

1	eggplant, sliced into thin rounds	1
	Olive oil, for coating eggplant	
2 tbsp	olive oil, divided	25 mL
¼ cup	chopped onion	50 mL
1	clove garlic, minced	1
12 oz	mushrooms, sliced	375 g
4	torpedo rolls, split lengthwise	4
4 tsp	freshly squeezed lemon juice	20 mL
6 oz	smoked mozzarella cheese, sliced	175 g
4	plum (Roma) tomatoes, chopped	4

Preheat broiler. Brush eggplant lightly with oil and broil, turning once, for 1 to 2 minutes per side, or until browned and tender. Remove eggplant and set oven temperature to 400°F (200°C). In a large skillet, heat half the oil over medium heat. Sauté onion until tender. Add garlic and sauté for 30 seconds. Add mushrooms and sauté until lightly browned. Brush the interior of the rolls with the remaining oil. Arrange eggplant slices down the length of each roll and drizzle each with 1 tsp (5 mL) lemon juice. Top with onion mixture, mozzarella and tomatoes. Wrap sandwiches in foil and bake for 15 minutes. **Serves 4.**

Chèvre and Roasted Pepper Mini-Sandwiches

8	small torpedo-shaped dinner rolls, split lengthwise	8
3 tbsp	Garlic Herb Dressing (see recipe, page 60)	45 mL
2 oz	chèvre, crumbled	60 g
¼ cup	diced roasted red bell pepper (see page 11)	50 mL

Preheat oven to 400°F (200°C). Brush the interior of the rolls with Garlic Herb Dressing. Pack each roll with chèvre and roasted pepper. Wrap sandwiches in foil and bake for 10 minutes. **Serves 4.**

Spinach Salad with Warm Bacon Dressing in Baguettes

10	slices bacon	10
1 cup	chopped onion	250 mL
2	cloves garlic, minced	2
½ cup	red wine vinegar	125 mL
1 tbsp	granulated sugar	15 mL
2 tbsp	extra-virgin olive oil	25 mL
	Salt and freshly ground black pepper to taste	
2	loaves French bread (baguettes), split lengthwise	2
12 oz	baby spinach (about 6 cups/1.5 L)	375 g

In a large skillet, cook bacon (in batches, if necessary) over medium heat until crisp. Remove bacon, crumble and set aside, leaving 3 tbsp (45 mL) fat in the pan. Add onion and garlic to the fat; sauté until tender. Add vinegar, sugar, oil, salt and pepper; heat through. Brush the interior of the baguettes with ¼ cup (50 mL) of this dressing. Toss spinach and reserved bacon with the remaining dressing. Mound salad into baguettes and cut into thirds. **Serves 6.**

Caesar Salad Sandwiches

6	drained canned anchovies	6
1	clove garlic, halved	1
1	extra-large egg yolk	1
⅓ cup	red wine vinegar	75 mL
2 tbsp	freshly squeezed lemon juice	25 mL
2 tsp	Dijon mustard	10 mL
Dash	Worcestershire sauce	Dash
½ cup	extra-virgin olive oil	125 mL
¼ cup	vegetable oil	50 mL
8	pitas, pockets opened by slicing off about ½ inch (1 cm) of one side, warmed	8
1	head romaine lettuce, leaves separated	1
1	head curly endive, torn into bite-size pieces	1
½	sweet onion, thinly sliced	½
1 cup	sliced mushrooms	250 mL
¼ cup	freshly grated Parmesan cheese	50 mL
16	thin slices tomato	16

In a food processor, purée anchovies, garlic, egg yolk, vinegar, lemon juice, mustard and Worcestershire sauce. With the motor running, add olive oil and vegetable oil through the feed tube in a slow, steady stream until mixture is smooth and thick. Spread pita interiors with half the dressing. Toss romaine, endive, onion, mushrooms, Parmesan and the remaining dressing. Heap into pitas and garnish with tomato. **Serves 8.** (*If you are concerned about the food safety of raw eggs, you may want to avoid this recipe.*)

Grilled Lamb and Artichoke Pitas

2 lbs	boneless leg of lamb, sliced	1 kg
2	cloves garlic, minced Salt and freshly ground black pepper to taste	2
6 oz	marinated artichoke hearts, drained and coarsely chopped	175 g
2	roasted red bell peppers (see page 11), diced	2
½	cucumber, peeled, seeded and diced	½
6 tbsp	plain yogurt	90 mL
¼ cup	chopped fresh mint	50 mL
4	pitas, pockets opened by slicing off about ½ inch (1 cm) of one side	4
3 tbsp	extra-virgin olive oil	45 mL

Preheat oven to 300°F (150°C) and preheat barbecue grill to high. Season lamb with garlic, salt and pepper; let rest for 15 minutes. Meanwhile, toss artichoke hearts, roasted pepper, cucumber, yogurt and mint; set aside. Brush pita interiors with oil and warm in oven. Grill lamb to desired doneness. Slice into strips and divide among pitas. Top each with reserved artichoke mixture. **Serves 4.**

Tuna and Guacamole Pitas

1	avocado (preferably Haas), puréed or mashed	1
1	small clove garlic, minced	1
1 tsp	freshly squeezed lemon juice	5 mL
¼ tsp	hot pepper sauce (such as Tabasco)	1 mL
4	pitas, pockets opened by slicing off about ½ inch (1 cm) of one side	4
1 tbsp	olive oil	15 mL
½	recipe Marinated Tuna and White Bean Salad (page 188), without romaine	½
¼ cup	finely chopped tomato	50 mL

Combine avocado, garlic, lemon juice and hot pepper sauce. Brush pita interiors with oil and fill with Spicy Tuna and avocado mixture. Top with tomato. **Serves 4.**

Middle Eastern Turkey Pitas

8 oz	shredded roast turkey breast	250 g
1	small clove garlic, minced	1
1 cup	plain yogurt	250 mL
1 tbsp	extra-virgin olive oil	15 mL
1 tbsp	chopped fresh mint	15 mL
	Juice of ½ lemon Salt and freshly ground black pepper to taste	
4	pitas, pockets opened by slicing off about ½ inch (1 cm) of one side	4
½	recipe Hummus Tahini (page 179)	½

Combine turkey, garlic, yogurt, oil, mint, lemon juice, salt and pepper. Brush pita interiors with Sesame Chickpea Spread and fill with turkey mixture. **Serves 4.**

Chicken Chickpea Salad Pitas

1	clove garlic, minced	1
1 cup	plain yogurt	250 mL
2 tbsp	extra-virgin olive oil	25 mL
1 tbsp	freshly squeezed lemon juice	15 mL
1 tsp	ground coriander	5 mL
½ tsp	ground cumin	2 mL
½ tsp	hot pepper sauce (such as Tabasco)	2 mL
1 cup	diced cooked chicken	250 mL
1 cup	cooked or canned chickpeas	250 mL
4	pitas, pockets opened by slicing off about ½ inch (1 cm) of one side	4
1 cup	shredded lettuce	250 mL

Combine garlic, yogurt, oil, lemon juice, coriander, cumin and hot pepper sauce; reserve 2 tbsp (25 mL) sauce. Toss chicken and chickpeas with the remaining sauce. Brush pita interiors with reserved sauce, fill with chicken mixture and top with lettuce. **Serves 4.**

Cold Crab and Avocado Tacos

1 lb	backfin (lump) crabmeat, shells picked out	500 g
2	green onions, thinly sliced	2
4 tsp	freshly squeezed lemon juice, divided	20 mL
½ tsp	hot pepper sauce (such as Tabasco), divided	2 mL
1	avocado (preferably Haas), peeled and pitted	1
1	small clove garlic, minced	1
8	taco shells, warmed	8
	Mild salsa (store-bought or see recipe, page 403)	

Gently toss crabmeat, green onions, 1 tbsp (15 mL) of the lemon juice and half the hot pepper sauce. In a food processor, purée avocado, garlic, the remaining lemon juice and the remaining hot pepper sauce. Layer crabmeat mixture and avocado mixture in taco shells and top with salsa. **Serves 4.**

Crab and Smoked Salmon Tea Sandwiches

6 oz	backfin (lump) crabmeat, shells picked out	175 g
3	green onions, finely chopped	3
3 tbsp	mayonnaise	45 mL
8	thin slices sandwich bread, 1 side buttered	8
4	thin slices sandwich bread, toasted and both sides buttered	4
2 oz	cream cheese, softened	60 g
1 oz	smoked salmon, chopped	30 g
1 tbsp	chopped fresh dill	15 mL

Combine crabmeat, green onions and mayonnaise; spoon on the buttered sides of 4 of the untoasted bread slices. Top with toasted slices. Combine cream cheese, smoked salmon and dill; spread on the exposed side of the toasted bread. Top with the remaining bread, buttered sides down. Cut off crusts and slice each sandwich into 3 fingers. **Serves 4.**

Chapter 8
Kid Food
Taste-Tested by Discriminating Third-Graders

Grilled Cheddar and Apple 98
Grilled Muenster with Pickles 98
Healthy Hoagie 98
Banana Sandwiches 98
Peanut Butter and Banana Sandwiches . . 98
Peanut Butter and Apple Raisin
Sandwiches 98
Roast Beef Pita Pocket 98
Vegetable "Dogs" 98
Vegetable Spread for Sandwiches 98
Turkey Tacos with Fresh Salsa 99
Chicken Fajitas 99
Make-Your-Own Pizza 99
Tuna Lettuce Pockets 99
Chicken and Grapes Lettuce Pockets . . . 99
Inside-Out Tacos 100
Inside-Out Lasagna 100
Cheesy Bread Pudding 100
Chicken and Noodle Salad
with Peanut Sauce 100
Sweet-and-Sour Apricot Chicken 100
Teriyaki London Broil 100
Japanese Grilled Shrimp 101
Pan-Fried Shrimp in Barbecue Sauce . . 101
Mild Macaroni and Cheese 101
Noodles and Cheese 101
Spaghetti with Fresh Tomato Sauce . . . 101
Turkey Meatball Chili 102

Surprise Cheeseburgers 102
Initial Burgers 102
Hamburger Hot Dogs 102
All-American Turkey Cheeseburgers . . . 102
Kiddie Nachos 102
Ham and Honey Mustard Roll-Ups 103
Banana French Toast 103
Cottage Cheese Pancakes 103
Chocolate Chip Pancakes 103
Double-Apple Applesauce 103
Peanut Butter Apple "Canapés" 103
Sweet Potato Chips 104
Sweet Chutney Mustard Dip 104
Apple Kugel 104
Julienned Vegetables with
Lemon Honey Dip 104
High-Protein Chocolate
Peanut Butter Shake 104
Watermelon Slush 104
Xylophone Milk 104
Yogurt Shake 105
Fig Squares 105
Fruit and Nut Bricks 105
Ice Cream Sandwich 105
Chocolate Ice Cream Cupcakes 105
Girl Scout Thin Mint Cookie
Ice Cream Log 105

Children are the most reactionary audience a cook is apt to face. Born with the ability to spot a speck of spinach from across the room, naturally cautious and unnaturally conservative, their lists of suspect foods can be encyclopedic. Eventually, even the most gastronomically committed parents acknowledge that preparing meals for grade-schoolers means simply deciding which side of the bread gets the peanut butter.

One mother we know was so determined to get her seven-year-old to eat vegetables that she decreed a special dinner routine. She would start at the beginning of the alphabet, and each dinner would include a vegetable beginning with that day's letter. After a week of vegetables, asparagus through eggplant — all cooked, in the tradition of the 1950s, for about 24 hours to be sure they were dead — she ended the experiment. Her son had made dinnertime very unpleasant and was further than ever from making his peace with vegetables.

There are better tactics. She might have tried expanding the child's palate slowly. Three methods, though not foolproof, work most of the time.

The first is to sneak a new or unpopular food in with an old favorite. Celery filled with peanut butter is a classic of this technique, but newer examples abound. Salsa and chips fill a kid's belly with vegetables that otherwise might never get there. Banana sandwiches mask the low-fat protein of cream cheese with slices of potassium-rich bananas. Bean sprouts add nutrition to a hoagie, and whole wheat flour is incognito when baked into a chocolate chip cookie.

The second method is to make the food so much fun that no child could resist it. Make tiny finger sandwiches and challenge children to see how many they can eat. Accompany vegetables with a tub of peanut butter or sweetened cream cheese for dipping. Give kids a pencil with their glass of milk and show them how by tapping on the glass they'll hear a different musical tone after every sip. The problem of unfinished milk vanishes with a song.

The third method is to slightly sweeten a new food when you introduce it. No one wants to load a child's diet with sugar, but the fact is that most children are attracted to sweetness beyond all other flavors, so a cheese dip sweetened with a bit of chutney is much more likely to convince a child that cheese dip is good stuff than one that's pungent with fresh herbs and Parmesan. Whole grains go down much easier in muffins or cookies than they do as side dishes, and yogurt becomes a treat when puréed with fruit and served as a shake.

To help you further, we've put together 50 kid-friendly recipes — for breakfast, lunch, dinner and anything in between. All of the recipes that we considered even slightly iffy from a kid's perspective have been tested on real children with real appetites and real food prejudices. The most suspect of the bunch underwent even more rigorous kid-testing: 50 third-graders, whose teachers allowed us to cater their lunch using a dozen of these recipes, were asked for their feedback.

Some of their critiques surprised us. A minted cucumber salad — sweetened enough that we were sure it would win over the kids — was nearly run out of town, so universally hated was it. (It wasn't run out of town, but it *was* run out of this chapter.) But lots of other vegetable combinations won their approval, as did a couple of unusual dishes, such as turkey meatballs and an Asian-style noodle dish.

Although no single recipe got universal applause from our young testers, nothing made it into this chapter without widespread support.

Don't stop here. There are many recipes in the other chapters that kids will enjoy. By the same token, you might find yourself sneaking a bite of one or two of the recipes in this chapter. They're not *only* for kids.

About these recipes . . .
The recipes in this chapter were designed for smaller appetites. If your child is a big eater, go ahead and increase the portion size.

Grilled Cheddar and Apple

	Butter	
8	slices bread	8
8	slices mild Cheddar cheese	8
16	thin slices apple	16

Preheat dry griddle or skillet on medium heat. Spread butter on one side of each slice of bread. Stack bread slices, buttered sides together, making 4 piles. Top each with 1 slice of cheese, then 4 apple slices, then another slice of cheese. Place top slice of bread (with the fillings) on preheated griddle, buttered-side down. Top with the remaining bread slices, buttered-side up. Cook, turning once, until bread is toasted on both sides and cheese has melted. **Serves 4.**

Grilled Muenster with Pickles

Follow preceding recipe, but replace the Cheddar cheese with sweet Muenster cheese and the apple slices with sweet pickle slices. **Serves 4.**

Healthy Hoagie

2	torpedo rolls, split	2
3 tbsp	olive oil, divided	45 mL
½ cup	bean sprouts, divided	125 mL
⅔ cup	tuna salad (use your own recipe)	150 mL
4	tomato slices, halved	4
2 tsp	freshly squeezed lemon juice	10 mL

Spread the interior of the rolls with half of the olive oil. Fill rolls with half of the bean sprouts and tuna salad. Top with tomato slices and the remaining sprouts. Drizzle with the remaining olive oil and lemon juice. Cut sandwiches in half and serve one half per person. **Serves 4.**

Banana Sandwiches

1 tbsp	honey	15 mL
4 oz	cream cheese, softened	125 g
4	slices raisin bread	4
1	banana, sliced	1

Whisk together honey and cream cheese; spread on one side of each slice of bread. Arrange banana slices in a single layer on 2 slices of bread and top with the other 2 slices. Halve and serve. **Serves 2.**

Peanut Butter and Banana Sandwiches

Follow preceding recipe, but replace the cream cheese with peanut butter. **Serves 2.**

Peanut Butter and Apple Raisin Sandwiches

½ cup	peanut butter	125 mL
4	slices raisin bread	4
¼ cup	raisins	50 mL
1	apple, thinly sliced	1

Spread peanut butter on one side of each slice of bread and sprinkle with raisins, lightly pressing them into the peanut butter. Arrange apple slices in a single layer on 2 slices of bread and top with the other 2 slices. Halve and serve. **Serves 2.**

Roast Beef Pita Pocket

2 tbsp	mayonnaise	25 mL
2 tsp	ketchup	10 mL
4	small pitas, pockets opened by slicing off about ½ inch (1 cm) of one side	4
8 oz	lean roast beef deli slices (about 16)	250 g
6 tbsp	coleslaw	90 mL

Combine mayonnaise and ketchup; spread inside pitas. Fill pitas with two alternating layers of roast beef and coleslaw. **Serves 4.**

Vegetable "Dogs"

2 tbsp	mayonnaise	25 mL
1 tsp	ketchup	5 mL
4	hot dog rolls, split	4
½ cup	alfalfa sprouts	125 mL
½ cup	shredded carrot	125 mL
½ cup	shredded mozzarella cheese	125 mL
1 tbsp	finely chopped tomato	15 mL
1 tbsp	finely chopped lettuce	15 mL
1 tbsp	finely chopped cucumber	15 mL

Combine mayonnaise and ketchup; spread inside rolls. Combine sprouts, carrot, mozzarella, tomato, lettuce, and cucumber; fill rolls with this mixture. **Serves 4.**

Vegetable Spread for Sandwiches

1	small carrot, peeled and diced	1
1	green onion, diced	1
1	clove garlic, minced	1
½	stalk celery, diced	½
2 tbsp	milk	25 mL
4 oz	cream cheese, softened	125 g
	Salt and freshly ground black pepper to taste	

In a small saucepan, bring carrot, green onion, garlic, celery and milk to a simmer over medium heat.

Let cool, stir in cream cheese and season with salt and pepper. **Makes about 1½ cups (375 mL).** *Use as a sandwich spread.*

Turkey Tacos with Fresh Salsa

2 tsp	vegetable oil	10 mL
1 lb	ground turkey	500 g
3 tbsp	finely chopped onion	45 mL
1 tbsp	chili powder	15 mL
3	tomatoes, finely chopped	3
2	green onions, white parts only, finely chopped	2
1	small clove garlic, minced	1
2 tbsp	finely chopped fresh Italian (flat-leaf) parsley	25 mL
	Salt and freshly ground black pepper to taste	
8	taco shells, warmed	8
2 cups	shredded lettuce	500 mL
1 cup	shredded Monterey Jack cheese	250 mL

In a skillet, heat oil over medium-high heat. Sauté turkey, onion and chili powder, breaking up turkey with a fork, until no pink remains. Make a mild salsa by combining tomatoes, green onions, garlic, parsley, salt and pepper. Fill warm taco shells with turkey mixture, lettuce, cheese and salsa. **Serves 4.**

Chicken Fajitas

1 tbsp	Worcestershire sauce	15 mL
1 tbsp	ketchup	15 mL
1 lb	chicken tenders or thin strips boneless skinless chicken breast	500 g
2 tsp	canola oil	10 mL
1	red bell pepper, cut into strips	1
1	green bell pepper, cut into strips	1
1	large onion, diced	1
8	flour tortillas, warmed	8
2 cups	chopped tomatoes	500 mL
1 cup	shredded mild Cheddar cheese	250 mL
¼ cup	sliced pitted black olives	50 mL
¼ cup	sour cream	50 mL

In a shallow dish, combine Worcestershire sauce and ketchup. Add chicken and toss to coat. Cover and refrigerate for 1 hour. In a skillet, heat oil over medium-high heat. Sauté red and green peppers and onion until tender. Transfer vegetables to a plate, add chicken mixture to the pan and sauté until no longer pink inside. Return vegetables to the pan and heat through. Serve chicken and vegetables on a platter with warm tortillas, tomatoes, cheese, olives and sour cream. Kids (and grownups) can assemble their own fajitas. **Serves 4.**

Make-Your-Own Pizza

1 lb	frozen bread dough, thawed and cut into 4 pieces	500 g
4 tsp	olive oil	20 mL

Toppings

1 cup	tomato pasta sauce	250 mL
1½ cups	shredded mozzarella cheese	375 mL
¼ cup	freshly grated Parmesan cheese	50 mL
4	mushrooms, sliced and sautéed	4
½	bell pepper (any color), diced	½
½ cup	blanched broccoli florets	125 mL
8 oz	ground meat, browned	125 g
8 oz	sausage or salami, cooked and chopped	125 g
8 oz	small shrimp, peeled and deveined	125 g

Preheat oven to 425°F (220°C), with rack placed in the lower third. Roll out each piece of dough into a 6-inch (15 cm) circle, rub with oil and place on a sheet of heavy foil. Top each with a portion of any 3 or 4 of the toppings. Slide foil onto oven rack and bake for 20 to 25 minutes, or until puffed and brown. Let cool for 5 minutes. **Serves 4.**

Tuna Lettuce Pockets

1	can (6 oz/170 g) tuna, drained and crumbled	1
1	carrot, finely shredded	1
2 tbsp	mayonnaise	25 mL
1½ tbsp	Italian dressing	22 mL
4	large leaves iceberg lettuce (or 8 small)	4

Combine tuna, carrot, mayonnaise and dressing. Cut the center ribs from the lettuce leaves, and place 2 to 3 tbsp (25 to 45 mL) of the tuna mixture in the center of each leaf. Fold leaf around filling to form an edible cup. Serve 1 or 2 pockets per person, depending on size of pockets. **Serves 4.**

Chicken and Grapes Lettuce Pockets

Follow preceding recipe, but replace the tuna mixture with the following mixture: Combine 1 stalk celery, sliced, 1 cup (250 mL) diced cooked chicken, ½ cup (125 mL) halved seedless grapes, ¼ cup (50 mL) chopped walnuts, 2 tbsp (25 mL) mayonnaise, 1 tsp (5 mL) yellow mustard and 1 tsp (5 mL) freshly squeezed lemon juice. **Serves 4.**

Inside-Out Tacos

2 tsp	canola oil	10 mL
1 lb	ground turkey	500 g
3 tbsp	finely chopped onion	45 mL
1 tbsp	chili powder	15 mL
6	large leaves iceberg lettuce (or 12 small)	6
¼ cup	shredded Monterey Jack cheese	50 mL
6 tbsp	crumbled taco shells	90 mL
2 tbsp	mild salsa	25 mL

In a skillet, heat oil over medium heat. Sauté turkey, onion and chili powder, breaking up turkey with a fork, until no pink remains. Divide mixture among lettuce leaves and form into cups as described in Tuna Lettuce Pockets (page 99). Top each with a portion of cheese, crumbled taco shells and salsa. **Serves 6.**

Inside-Out Lasagna

	Vegetable cooking spray	
1 tbsp	vegetable oil	15 mL
½ cup	chopped onion	125 mL
1	clove garlic, minced	1
1	jar (26 oz/780 mL) tomato pasta sauce	1
	Salt and freshly ground black pepper to taste	
2	eggs, beaten	2
8 oz	elbow macaroni, shells or ziti pasta, cooked	250 g
1 cup	shredded mozzarella cheese	250 mL
1 cup	ricotta cheese	250 mL

Preheat oven to 350°F (180°C) and spray a 13- by 9-inch (3 L) glass baking pan with cooking spray. In a skillet, heat oil over medium-high heat. Sauté onion and garlic until tender. Add pasta sauce, salt and pepper; reduce heat and simmer for 5 minutes. Meanwhile, combine eggs, pasta, mozzarella and ricotta; season with salt and pepper. Spread egg mixture in the bottom of prepared pan and top with sauce. Bake for 40 minutes, until bubbly. **Serves 4.**

Cheesy Bread Pudding

10	slices stale white or whole wheat bread, crusts trimmed	10
3 tbsp	butter	45 mL
1 cup	shredded Monterey Jack cheese	250 mL
3	eggs	3
2 cups	milk	500 mL

Grease a 6-cup (1.5 L) casserole dish. Spread bread with butter and layer with cheese in prepared dish.

Beat eggs and milk; pour over bread. Cover and refrigerate for at least 1 hour or for up to 8 hours. Preheat oven to 350°F (180°C). Bake for 45 minutes, until browned on the edges and set in the middle. **Serves 4.**

Chicken and Noodle Salad with Peanut Sauce

2	packages (each 3 oz/90 g) ramen noodles, flavor pack discarded	2
8 oz	boneless skinless chicken breast, cut into strips	250 g
1 tsp	cornstarch	5 mL
¼ tsp	dark sesame oil	1 mL
	Salt and freshly ground black pepper to taste	
2 tbsp	vegetable oil	25 mL
1	cucumber, seeded and julienned	1
1 cup	shredded carrot	250 mL
¾ cup	Peanut Sauce (see recipe, page 53)	175 mL

Cook noodles according to package directions; set aside. Combine chicken, cornstarch, sesame oil, salt and pepper. In a wok or large skillet, heat oil over medium-high heat. Stir-fry or sauté chicken until no longer pink inside. Toss with noodles, cucumber, carrot and peanut sauce. **Serves 4.**

Sweet-and-Sour Apricot Chicken

¾ cup	orange juice	175 mL
½ cup	apricot preserves	125 mL
1 tbsp	brown mustard	15 mL
1½ tsp	freshly squeezed lemon juice	7 mL
¼ tsp	ground ginger	1 mL
Pinch	ground cloves	Pinch
4 lbs	chicken pieces (bone-in)	2 kg

Preheat oven to 350°F (180°C). Combine orange juice, apricot preserves, mustard, lemon juice, ginger and cloves; brush chicken with about two-thirds of this mixture. Place in a single layer in a 13- by 9-inch (3 L) baking pan and bake for 1 hour, basting occasionally with the remaining sauce, until chicken is no longer pink inside and reaches an internal temperature of 170°F (77°C). **Serves 4.**

Teriyaki London Broil

1	clove garlic, minced	1
⅓ cup	soy sauce	75 mL
3 tbsp	packed light brown sugar	45 mL
2 tbsp	sesame oil	25 mL
1 tbsp	dry sherry	15 mL
¼ tsp	ground ginger	1 mL
2 lbs	London broil (flank steak)	1 kg

In a shallow dish, combine garlic, soy sauce, brown sugar, oil, sherry and ginger; add London broil and toss to coat. Cover and refrigerate for at least 2 hours or for up to 4 hours. Preheat broiler. Remove meat from marinade and discard marinade. Broil, turning once, for about 5 minutes per side for medium-rare, or until desired doneness. **Serves 4.**

Japanese Grilled Shrimp

1	clove garlic, minced	1
2 tbsp	soy sauce	25 mL
1 tbsp	freshly squeezed lemon juice	15 mL
1 tbsp	dry sherry	15 mL
1 tbsp	honey	15 mL
1 tsp	dark sesame oil	5 mL
¼ tsp	ground ginger	1 mL
1 lb	large shrimp, peeled and deveined	500 g

In a shallow dish, combine garlic, soy sauce, lemon juice, sherry, honey, oil and ginger; add shrimp and toss to coat. Cover and refrigerate for 30 minutes. Meanwhile, preheat broiler or barbecue grill to high. Broil or grill shrimp, turning once, for 2 minutes per side, until pink and opaque. **Serves 4.**

Pan-Fried Shrimp in Barbecue Sauce

1 tbsp	corn oil	15 mL
1 lb	jumbo shrimp, peeled, deveined and butterflied	500 g
1 tbsp	grated onion	15 mL
Pinch	granulated sugar	Pinch
¼ cup	ketchup	50 mL
1 tbsp	cider vinegar	15 mL
1 tsp	brown mustard	5 mL
1 tsp	Worcestershire sauce	5 mL
	Hot pepper sauce (such as Tabasco) to taste	

In a large skillet, heat oil over medium-high heat. Sauté shrimp for 2 to 3 minutes, or until pink and opaque; remove with a slotted spoon. Add onion and sugar to the pan and sauté until lightly browned. Add ketchup, vinegar, mustard and Worcestershire sauce; bring to a boil and season with hot pepper sauce. Return shrimp to pan and coat with sauce. **Serves 4.**

Mild Macaroni and Cheese

1	egg, beaten	1
2 cups	shredded mozzarella cheese	500 mL
1 cup	shredded sharp Cheddar cheese	250 mL
⅓ cup	milk	75 mL
½ tsp	brown mustard	2 mL
	Salt and freshly ground black pepper to taste	
8 oz	macaroni, cooked	250 g

Preheat oven to 350°F (180°C). In an 8-cup (2 L) casserole dish, combine egg, mozzarella, Cheddar, milk, mustard, salt and pepper. Add macaroni and toss to coat. Bake for 20 minutes, until browned and bubbly. **Serves 4.**

Noodles and Cheese

12 oz	pasta (any type), cooked	375 g
1 cup	small-curd cottage cheese	250 mL
2 tbsp	freshly grated Parmesan cheese	25 mL
1 tbsp	butter	15 mL
	Salt and freshly ground black pepper to taste	

In a large saucepan, combine all ingredients. Cook over medium heat, stirring, until heated through, about 4 minutes. **Serves 4.**

Spaghetti with Fresh Tomato Sauce

1 tbsp	extra-virgin olive oil	15 mL
¼ cup	chopped onion	50 mL
1	clove garlic, minced	1
1 tsp	dried basil	5 mL
3 cups	canned diced tomatoes, drained	750 mL
1½ cups	canned tomato purée or crushed tomatoes	375 mL
	Salt and freshly ground black pepper to taste	
1 lb	spaghetti	500 g
	Freshly grated Parmesan cheese	

In a large skillet, heat oil over medium heat. Sauté onion, garlic and basil until onion is translucent. Add tomatoes, tomato purée, salt and pepper; reduce heat and simmer for 15 to 20 minutes, or until slightly thickened. Meanwhile, cook spaghetti according to package directions. In a large serving bowl, toss spaghetti with sauce. Serve sprinkled with Parmesan. **Serves 4.**

Turkey Meatball Chili

1	slice white bread, crusts removed, cut into small cubes	1
2 tbsp	milk	25 mL
1	egg white, lightly beaten	1
1 lb	ground turkey	500 g
1 tbsp	ketchup	15 mL
1 tsp	brown mustard	5 mL
	Salt and freshly ground black pepper to taste	
2 tbsp	vegetable oil	25 mL
1	onion, finely chopped	1
2 tbsp	all-purpose flour	25 mL
2 tbsp	chili powder	25 mL
1 tbsp	ground cumin	15 mL
1 tsp	dried oregano	5 mL
2 cups	chicken broth	500 mL
1 cup	canned crushed tomatoes	250 mL
1	can (14 to 19 oz/398 to 540 mL) red kidney beans, drained and rinsed	1

Using your hands, combine bread and milk until bread is moistened. Mix in egg white, turkey, ketchup, mustard, salt and pepper until thoroughly combined. Form into 24 small meatballs. In a large skillet, heat oil over medium-high heat. Cook meatballs until evenly browned. When almost done, add onion and sauté until tender. Add flour, chili powder, cumin and oregano; sauté for 1 minute. Add broth and tomatoes; reduce heat and simmer for 10 minutes, until meatballs are cooked through. Add beans and heat through. **Serves 4.**

Surprise Cheeseburgers

1 lb	lean ground beef	500 g
3 tbsp	ice water	45 mL
	Salt and freshly ground black pepper to taste	
1/4 cup	shredded Cheddar cheese	50 mL
	Vegetable oil	
4	hamburger buns, split	4

Combine ground beef, ice water, salt and pepper; form into 8 thin patties, about 1/4 inch (0.5 cm) thick. Put one-quarter of the cheese in the center of each of 4 patties, top with another patty and mold into burgers, sealing the edges well. In a large skillet, heat a thin film of oil over medium-high heat. Cook burgers, turning once, until cooked through but still juicy in the center (see page 129). Serve on buns. **Serves 4.**

Initial Burgers

1	egg white, beaten	1
1 lb	lean ground beef	500 g
2 tbsp	ketchup	25 mL
1 tbsp	ice water	15 mL
	Salt and freshly ground black pepper to taste	
	Vegetable oil	

Combine egg white, ground beef, ketchup, ice water, salt and pepper. Divide into 4 portions and shape each into the first letter of a child's name. In a large skillet, heat a thin film of oil over medium-high heat. Cook burgers, turning once, until cooked through but still juicy in the center (see page 129). (Some letters, such as W, can be very fragile, so turn carefully.) **Serves 4.**

Hamburger Hot Dogs

Follow preceding recipe, but form the meat mixture into 4 sausage shapes. Cook as directed and serve in split hot dog rolls, with mustard, ketchup and relish. **Serves 4.**

All-American Turkey Cheeseburgers

1 lb	ground turkey	500 g
3 tbsp	seasoned dry bread crumbs	45 mL
2 tbsp	ketchup	25 mL
2 tbsp	grated onion	25 mL
2 tsp	steak sauce	10 mL
4	slices Muenster cheese	4

Combine turkey, bread crumbs, ketchup, onion and steak sauce. Form into 4 patties, about 1/4 inch (0.5 cm) thick. Preheat broiler or barbecue grill to high. Broil or grill patties, turning once, until cooked through but still juicy in the center (see page 129). Two minutes before burgers are done cooking, top each with 1 slice of cheese; cover and cook until cheese melts. **Serves 4.**

Kiddie Nachos

	Tortilla chips	
1/4 cup	shredded Cheddar or Monterey Jack cheese	50 mL
1/4 cup	mild salsa	50 mL

Place tortilla chips in a single layer on a microwave-safe plate and top with cheese. Microwave on High for 1 minute, until cheese has melted. Serve warm with salsa. **Serves 1.**

Ham and Honey Mustard Roll-Ups

1 tbsp	honey	15 mL
1 tbsp	brown mustard	15 mL
6 oz	baked ham deli slices	175 g
¼ cup	unsweetened applesauce	50 mL

Combine honey and mustard; spread over ham, then spread with applesauce. Roll each slice into a cigar shape. **Serves 4.**

Banana French Toast

4	large or extra-large eggs	4
2	very ripe bananas, puréed	2
¾ cup	milk	175 mL
2 tbsp	granulated sugar	25 mL
1 tsp	vanilla	5 mL
Pinch	salt	Pinch
8	thick slices bread (preferably day-old)	8
	Butter	
2 cups	fruit-flavored yogurt	500 mL

In a broad, shallow pan, whisk together eggs, banana purée, milk, sugar, vanilla and salt. Soak bread in egg mixture, turning once, until it has absorbed the liquid. Heat a large nonstick skillet over medium heat and lightly grease with butter. Add as many slices of bread as will fit in a single layer and brown on both sides, about 3 minutes on the first side, 1 to 2 minutes on the second. Remove to a warm platter and keep warm. Repeat with the remaining bread, lightly greasing pan as needed between batches. Serve with yogurt. **Serves 4.**

Cottage Cheese Pancakes

6	eggs, separated	6
Pinch	salt	Pinch
2 cups	drained cottage cheese	500 mL
6 tbsp	all-purpose flour	90 mL
¼ cup	granulated sugar	50 mL
½ tsp	vanilla	2 mL
	Butter	
	Fresh fruit of your choice	

In a bowl, beat egg whites and salt until soft peaks form; set aside. In a large bowl, beat egg yolks, cottage cheese, flour, sugar and vanilla. Fold in egg whites. Heat a griddle or large skillet over medium-high heat and grease with butter. Working in batches as necessary, pour in batter to make 2- to 3-inch (5 to 7.5 cm) pancakes. Cook, turning once, for 2 to 3 minutes per side, or until browned on both sides. Remove to a warm platter and keep warm. Repeat with remaining batter, greasing griddle as needed between batches. Serve immediately with fruit. **Makes 12 pancakes.**

Chocolate Chip Pancakes

1 cup	sifted unbleached flour	250 mL
1 cup	whole wheat flour	250 mL
2 tbsp	granulated sugar	25 mL
2 tsp	baking powder	10 mL
1 tsp	baking soda	5 mL
½ tsp	salt	2 mL
2	eggs, beaten	2
2 cups	buttermilk	500 mL
1 cup	semisweet chocolate chips	250 mL
3 tbsp	melted butter, divided	45 mL
	Syrup or fresh fruit (optional)	

Sift together unbleached flour, whole wheat flour, sugar, baking powder, baking soda and salt. Add eggs and buttermilk; mix until well combined. Stir in chocolate chips and 2 tbsp (25 mL) of the melted butter. Heat a griddle or large skillet over medium heat and grease with some of the remaining butter. For each pancake, pour in ¼ cup (50 mL) batter. Cook until tops are covered with bubbles. Flip and cook for 1 to 2 minutes, or until pancakes feel springy. Remove to a warm platter and keep warm. Repeat with remaining batter, greasing griddle as needed between batches. Serve alone, or with syrup or fresh fruit. **Makes 18 pancakes.**

Double-Apple Applesauce

6	McIntosh apples, cut into 1-inch (2.5 cm) chunks	6
½ cup	chopped dried apples	125 mL
2 tbsp	granulated sugar (approx.)	25 mL
	Juice of ½ lemon	

Combine all ingredients in a 12-cup (3 L) microwave-safe bowl and cover tightly with microwave-safe plastic wrap. Microwave on High for 6 minutes. Pierce plastic and uncover. Stir, recover and microwave on High for 3 minutes. Pierce plastic again and uncover. Press mixture through a food mill or a sieve. Add more sugar, if necessary, depending on the sweetness of the apples. **Makes about 3 cups (750 mL).** *Store in an airtight container in the refrigerator for up to 1 week.*

Peanut Butter Apple "Canapés"

3 tbsp	smooth peanut butter	45 mL
1	large apple, cut into 16 slices	1
16	raisins	16

Pipe peanut butter through a star-tipped pastry bag onto each apple slice. Top each rosette of peanut butter with 1 raisin. **Serves 4.**

Sweet Potato Chips

	Vegetable oil	
1 lb	sweet potatoes, peeled and cut into 1/8-inch (3 mm) slices	500 g
	Salt to taste	
	Sweet Chutney Mustard Dip (see recipe, below)	

Deep-fry (see page 9) potato slices, in batches, in at least 2 inches (5 cm) of oil heated to 350°F (180°C), until lightly browned and crisp. Remove and drain in a strainer set over a bowl. Sprinkle with salt and serve with dip. **Serves 4.**

Sweet Chutney Mustard Dip

3 tbsp	mayonnaise	45 mL
2 tbsp	Major Grey's chutney, chopped	25 mL
1 1/2 tbsp	yellow mustard	22 mL

Combine mayonnaise, chutney and mustard. **Makes about 1/3 cup (75 mL).** *Use as a dip with Sweet Potato Chips (above), chicken nuggets or fish sticks.*

Apple Kugel

1/4 cup	butter	50 mL
2	apples, peeled and sliced	2
1/2 cup	granulated sugar, divided	125 mL
1 lb	egg noodles, cooked	500 g
8 oz	cream cheese, softened	250 g
6	eggs, lightly beaten	6
3/4 cup	milk	175 mL
1/4 cup	cottage cheese	50 mL
1/4 cup	melted butter	50 mL
3 tbsp	sour cream	45 mL
Pinch	salt	Pinch

Preheat oven to 350°F (180°C) and butter a 13- by 9-inch (3 L) glass baking dish. In a large skillet, melt butter over medium heat. Sauté apple slices and half of the sugar until apples are tender. Combine noodles, cream cheese, eggs, milk, cottage cheese, melted butter, the remaining sugar, sour cream and salt. In prepared baking dish, alternate 3 layers of noodle mixture with 2 layers of apples. Bake for 1 hour, until browned and bubbling and a tester inserted in the center comes out almost clean. **Serves 4.**

Julienned Vegetables with Lemon Honey Dip

1 cup	plain yogurt	250 mL
1 1/2 tbsp	freshly squeezed lemon juice	22 mL
2 tsp	honey	10 mL
Pinch	salt	Pinch
2 cups	julienned vegetables (such as carrots, bell peppers, cucumbers, broccoli stems or celery)	500 mL

Combine yogurt, lemon juice, honey and salt; serve as a dip with vegetables. **Serves 4.**

High-Protein Chocolate Peanut Butter Shake

2 cups	ice-cold milk	500 mL
1 1/2 cups	vanilla-flavored yogurt	375 mL
1/2 cup	chocolate syrup	125 mL
1/4 cup	powdered nonfat milk	50 mL
1/4 cup	smooth peanut butter	50 mL

In a blender, blend all ingredients. Refrigerate until chilled. **Serves 4.**

Watermelon Slush

3/4 cup	granulated sugar	175 mL
3/4 cup	water	175 mL
4 cups	seeded watermelon chunks	1 L

In a saucepan, bring sugar and water to a boil over high heat, without stirring. Transfer to a shallow pan and let cool, then freeze until solid. Using a small knife, slice into cubes. Transfer to a food processor or blender and process until coarsely chopped. Add watermelon chunks and process until slushy. Serve in chilled glasses. **Serves 4.**

Xylophone Milk

1 tbsp	chocolate syrup	15 mL
	Milk	

Place chocolate syrup in a 6-oz (175 mL) drinking glass and freeze for 30 minutes. Remove from freezer and, using a small, thin watercolor paintbrush dipped in the chocolate syrup, paint a 2-inch (5 cm) horizontal line on the inside of the glass, one-quarter of the way up from the bottom. Paint another line halfway up and a third line three-quarters of the way up. Cover and store in freezer until needed. To serve, fill glass to the top line with milk. Have the child lightly tap the glass with the pencil and listen to the tone, then drink down to the first line and tap again, noticing how the tone changes. **Serves 1.** *(Multiply for as many servings as you wish.)*

Yogurt Shake

1 cup	fruit-flavored yogurt	250 mL
½ cup	milk	125 mL
½ tsp	vanilla	2 mL

In a blender or food processor, process all ingredients until well combined. **Serves 1.** *(Multiply for as many servings as you wish.)*

Fig Squares

½ cup	packed light brown sugar, divided	125 mL
6 tbsp	unsalted butter	90 mL
1	large egg white	1
7 tbsp	honey, divided	105 mL
1½ cups	all-purpose flour	375 mL
¾ cup	whole wheat flour	175 mL
1 tsp	baking powder	5 mL
¼ tsp	baking soda	1 mL
Pinch	salt	Pinch
3 cups	finely chopped stemmed dried figs	750 mL
¼ cup	water	50 mL
3 tbsp	freshly squeezed orange juice	45 mL
1 tbsp	freshly squeezed lemon juice	15 mL

Spray a 9-inch (2.5 L) square baking pan with baking spray. In a large bowl, cream half of the brown sugar and the butter. Beat in egg white and 5 tbsp (75 mL) of the honey. Mix in all-purpose flour, whole wheat flour, baking powder, baking soda and salt until a smooth dough forms. Divide dough in half. With floured hands, pat one half into prepared pan; freeze for 20 minutes. Form the other half into a disk, wrap in plastic wrap and refrigerate. Meanwhile, preheat oven to 350°F (180°C). Combine figs, the remaining brown sugar, water, orange juice, the remaining honey and lemon juice. Spread frozen dough base with fig mixture. Roll out remaining dough between sheets of waxed paper to a 9-inch (23 cm) square. Place on top of fig mixture and push down on edges. Bake for 25 minutes, until set. Let cool in pan on a rack for 10 minutes. Remove from pan and let cool completely on rack. Cut into 16 squares.

Fruit and Nut Bricks

6 tbsp	peanut butter (chunky or smooth)	90 mL
40	marshmallows	40
4 cups	crisp cereal (such as Kix, Rice Krispies or Chex)	1 L
1 cup	roasted peanuts	250 mL
1 cup	raisins	250 mL

Grease an 8-inch (2 L) square baking pan. In a large, heavy saucepan, melt peanut butter over medium heat. Add marshmallows, stirring continuously until melted. Stir in cereal, peanuts and raisins. Using the back of an oiled spoon, press mixture into prepared pan. Let cool for 20 minutes. Run a knife around the edge of the pan and unmold onto a clean surface. Using a serrated knife, cut into 4 strips, then cut each strip into 6 bricks. **Makes 24 bricks.**

Ice Cream Sandwich

1	large scoop vanilla ice cream, slightly softened	1
2	soft-baked chocolate chip cookies	2

Place ice cream on one of the cookies, then top with the other cookie and gently press together. Serve immediately or freeze for a few hours. **Serves 1.** *(Multiply for as many servings as you wish.)*

Chocolate Ice Cream Cupcakes

6	large chocolate cupcakes (from a bakery or homemade)	6
1 cup	chocolate chip ice cream, slightly softened	250 mL

Using a serrated knife, remove tops and hollow out the interiors of the cupcakes, leaving a ½-inch (1 cm) thick wall of cake all the way around. Fill interiors with ice cream, replace tops and freeze until ice cream is firm, at least 3 hours. **Serves 6.**

Girl Scout Thin Mint Cookie Ice Cream Log

8 cups	mint chocolate chip ice cream, slightly softened	2 L
35	Thin Mint Girl Scout (Girl Guide) Cookies	35

Place 1 tbsp (15 mL) ice cream in the center of 1 cookie. Top with another cookie and another 1 tbsp (15 mL) ice cream. Continue until you have 5 cookies and 4 layers of ice cream in a stack and place in the freezer. Make 5 more stacks. Coarsely chop the remaining cookies. Lay cookie stacks side by side on a baking sheet, forming a tight rectangle. Cover rectangle with the remaining ice cream to form a large log. Freeze until firm. Lightly press chopped cookies into top of log. Cover with plastic wrap and freeze for several hours. Remove 10 minutes before serving and slice. **Serves 4.**

Chapter 9
Leftovers
Homemade Convenience Ingredients

Lemon Yogurt Dressing 107

Garlic Yogurt Dressing 108

Yogurt Dessert Sauce 108

Eggless Caesar Dressing 108

Red Caesar Dressing 108

Spicy Tuna Sauce 108

Hot Pepper Peanut Vinaigrette 108

Tomato Vinaigrette 108

Scraping-the-Jar Russian Dressing 108

Homemade Steak Sauce 108

Anchovy Steak Sauce 109

Spicy Steak Sauce 109

Easy Tomato Sauce 109

Mediterranean Tomato Sauce 109

Capered Tomato Sauce 109

Chicken Glace 109

Meat Glace 109

Salt-Free Seasoning Mix 109

Celery-Top Seasoning Mix 109

Vegetable Top and Chicken
Carcass Soup 110

Turkey Carcass Split Pea Soup 110

Leftovers Chicken Noodle Soup 110

Leftovers Chicken Rice Soup 110

Lemon Chicken Soup 110

Leftovers Minestrone 110

Wilted Salad Gazpacho 110

Leftover Chicken Chili 111

Leftover Steak Chili 111

Chili Pasta Salad 111

Pepper Pasta Salad 111

Pasta, Bean and Tuna Salad 111

Chicken and Bean Salad 111

Rice and Bean Salad 112

Leftovers Tabbouleh 112

Leftover Fish Salad for Sandwiches 112

Barbecued Chicken or Pork Salad 112

Leftover Fried Chicken Coleslaw 112

Leftovers Escabèche 113

Meat and Potato Salad with
Blue Cheese Dressing 113

Cold Sliced Meats with Red and
Green Sauces 113

Stir-Fried Chicken with Apples
and Walnuts 113

Chicken and Gravy Frozen Dinner 114

Asian Fried Noodles 114

Fried Rice from Leftovers 114

Baked Potato Skins with
Yogurt Herb Sauce 114

A Little Chopped Liver 114

Onion Dip 115

Stale-Cookie Pie Crust 115

Chocolate Bread Pudding 115

White Chocolate Rice Pudding 115

It's a jungle in there. Rummage through the underbrush in the inner reaches of a refrigerator, and you'll find a miniature menagerie of lemon bits and onion fragments, a dab of tomato paste, a lonely anchovy or a solitary sardine. Perhaps a half-eaten yogurt is lurking, or a deserted celery stalk.

Beneath veils of plastic wrap and shields of foil hide the remnants of bygone recipes, destined for either disposal or resurrection. The choice is yours. We can all agree that wasting food is bad, but when we're confronted with a plateful of odds and ends and have no clue of how to turn them into something edible, disposal can seem like an attractive alternative.

Fortunately, options abound for combining the specks and spots of sundry ingredients into all-purpose preparations that can serve a useful role in day-to-day meal planning. A homemade salad dressing can use up half a yogurt or a wedge of lemon. A quick pasta sauce will finish off the last of the tomato paste, onion or celery. Vegetable soup clears out the refrigerator in a clean sweep when vegetable ends pile up, and with a leftover carcass or two and a few cups of vegetable tops, chicken soup is practically free of charge.

Leftovers are not only the mother of many distinguished culinary inventions, they are also the original convenience food. What could be better than a perfect roast ready to be wrapped in frozen puff pastry for an elegant return engagement? Or flavorful meat simmered with vegetables for a stew that takes 20 minutes to prepare instead of 2 hours? What cook would complain about a pasta salad that provides complete protein and savory flavors yet requires little more work than mixing vinaigrette with a can of tuna, a can of beans and last night's spaghetti?

Leftover egg whites can be the base for meringue cookies, macaroons or a quick cheese soufflé — the soufflé carries the added advantage of using up the block of Cheddar that has been quietly aging in the refrigerator door.

Sandwich spreads can be made by combining vegetable trimmings with bits of cheese, or sour cream and cottage cheese with green onions and cucumber, or by puréeing the liver from last night's roast chicken with some butter and browned onion. Use the giblets from that chicken to make a quick stock that can be reduced into a flavorful glaze for effortless professional-quality sauces. Embellished with mushrooms, capers, mustard or cream, glaze-based sauces turn ordinary grilled, roasted and poached meats into elegant entrées in seconds.

Create your own frozen dinners by arranging portions of leftover meats and vegetables on plastic plates, ready to be wrapped and frozen for another night, when they can be popped into the microwave to deliver a finished dinner in 5 minutes.

Once you get into the right frame of mind and begin transforming unused remainders into useful convenience foods, you won't be able to stop. What else can single-handedly clean out the refrigerator, cut back the food bill and dress up the table while wiping away the guilt of wasting good food?

About these recipes . . .

Because the contents of refrigerators differ from house to house and from day to day, the yield on each recipe is intended to be approximate. If you find yourself a little shy of tomato paste or wanting to get rid of more chicken broth than a recipe calls for, make the appropriate adjustments. All of these recipes are very forgiving.

We encourage you to adjust the ideas in this chapter to your needs. Chicken soup can mean turkey soup if a turkey carcass is what you have on hand. Steak sauce can be used on any roasted meat. A lemon half can be replaced with a lime half. The point here is not to follow recipes exactly but to use the ever-growing pile of leftovers in your refrigerator to your culinary advantage.

Remember, leftover food is not the same thing as spoiled food. If any of your leftovers show signs of spoilage — mold, off smells, a dried or cracked surface — discard them. A benefit of using leftovers in a timely way is that it keeps food from getting to that point.

Lemon Yogurt Dressing

1	clove garlic, minced	1
½ cup	low-fat plain yogurt	125 mL
½ tsp	chopped fresh Italian (flat-leaf) parsley	2 mL
	Grated zest and juice of ½ lemon	
	Salt and freshly ground black pepper to taste	

Thoroughly whisk together all ingredients. **Makes about ½ cup (125 mL).** Use as a salad dressing or sandwich spread.

Garlic Yogurt Dressing

1	clove garlic, minced	1
½ cup	low-fat plain yogurt	125 mL
¼ cup	extra-virgin olive oil	50 mL
	Salt and freshly ground black pepper to taste	

Thoroughly whisk together all ingredients. **Makes about ¾ cup (175 mL).** *Use as a salad dressing or sandwich spread.*

Yogurt Dessert Sauce

½ cup	low-fat fruit-flavored yogurt	125 mL
2 tbsp	milk	25 mL
1 tbsp	honey	15 mL
1 tbsp	orange liqueur	15 mL
¼ tsp	vanilla	1 mL
¼ tsp	freshly squeezed lemon juice	1 mL

Thoroughly whisk together all ingredients. **Makes about ¾ cup (175 mL).** *Serve with plain cakes or chopped fresh fruit.*

Eggless Caesar Dressing

2	drained canned anchovies, minced	2
1	clove garlic, minced	1
1 tbsp	Dijon mustard	15 mL
1 tbsp	red or white wine vinegar	15 mL
2 tsp	Worcestershire sauce	10 mL
1½ tsp	freshly squeezed lemon juice	7 mL
½ cup	extra-virgin olive oil	125 mL
½ cup	vegetable oil	125 mL
	Salt and freshly ground black pepper to taste	

Whisk together anchovies, garlic and mustard, then whisk in vinegar, Worcestershire sauce and lemon juice. Combine olive oil and vegetable oil; whisk into dressing in a slow, steady stream. Season with salt and pepper. **Makes about 1 cup (250 mL).**

Red Caesar Dressing

Follow preceding recipe, but reduce the mustard to 1 tsp (5 mL), and add 1 tbsp (15 mL) tomato paste. **Makes about 1 cup (250 mL).**

Spicy Tuna Sauce

Follow recipe for Eggless Caesar Dressing (above), but add 1 cup (250 mL) leftover tuna salad to the garlic mixture, reduce the Worcestershire sauce to 1 tsp (5 mL), and add ½ tsp (2 mL) hot pepper sauce (such as Tabasco). **Makes about 1½ cups (375 mL).**

Hot Pepper Peanut Vinaigrette

2	green onions, finely chopped	2
1	small clove garlic, minced	1
3 tbsp	rice vinegar	45 mL
2 tbsp	smooth peanut butter	25 mL
2 tbsp	vegetable oil	25 mL
1 tsp	finely chopped gingerroot	5 mL
1 tsp	soy sauce	5 mL
½ tsp	hot pepper sauce (such as Tabasco)	2 mL
Pinch	ground cumin	Pinch
Pinch	ground coriander	Pinch

Thoroughly whisk together all ingredients. **Makes about ½ cup (125 mL).** *Use as a salad dressing or as a sauce for grilled meats.*

Tomato Vinaigrette

1 tbsp	tomato paste	15 mL
2 tbsp	red wine vinegar	25 mL
¼ cup	extra-virgin olive oil	50 mL
1 tsp	chopped fresh Italian (flat-leaf) parsley	5 mL
	Salt and freshly ground black pepper to taste	

Thoroughly whisk together all ingredients. **Makes about ½ cup (125 mL).** *Use as a salad dressing or as a sauce for grilled meats.*

Scraping-the-Jar Russian Dressing

¼ cup	mayonnaise	50 mL
¼ cup	sour cream	50 mL
3 tbsp	freshly squeezed lemon juice	45 mL
1 tbsp	tomato paste	15 mL
Pinch	granulated sugar	Pinch

Thoroughly whisk together all ingredients. **Makes about ¾ cup (175 mL).**

Homemade Steak Sauce

¼ cup	butter, melted	50 mL
2 tbsp	Worcestershire sauce	25 mL
1 tbsp	tomato paste	15 mL
1 tbsp	brown mustard	15 mL

Thoroughly whisk together all ingredients. **Makes about ½ cup (125 mL).**

Anchovy Steak Sauce

Follow preceding recipe, but replace the tomato paste with anchovy paste or minced drained canned anchovies. **Makes about ½ cup (125 mL).**

Spicy Steak Sauce

Follow recipe for Homemade Steak Sauce (page 108), but add 1 tsp (5 mL) hot pepper sauce (such as Tabasco). **Makes about ½ cup (125 mL).**

Easy Tomato Sauce

2 tbsp	extra-virgin olive oil	25 mL
½	onion, chopped	½
½	red bell pepper, diced	½
1	clove garlic, minced	1
Pinch	hot pepper flakes	Pinch
1	can (14 oz/398 mL) crushed tomatoes, with juice	1
2 tbsp	tomato paste	25 mL
	Salt and freshly ground black pepper to taste	
1 tbsp	chopped fresh Italian (flat-leaf) parsley	15 mL

In a skillet, heat oil over medium heat. Sauté onion and red pepper until tender. Add garlic and hot pepper flakes; sauté for 30 seconds. Add tomatoes, with juice, and tomato paste; reduce heat and simmer for 5 minutes. Season with salt and black pepper. Stir in parsley and heat for 1 minute. **Makes about 3 cups (750 mL).**

Mediterranean Tomato Sauce

Follow preceding recipe, but double the garlic, and add ¼ cup (50 mL) chopped pitted black olives and 2 tsp (10 mL) chopped drained canned anchovies (or anchovy paste) with the red pepper. If desired, replace the parsley with basil. **Makes about 3 cups (750 mL).**

Capered Tomato Sauce

Follow recipe for Easy Tomato Sauce (above), but add 2 tbsp (25 mL) drained capers with the red pepper. **Makes about 3 cups (750 mL).**

Chicken Glace

4 cups	low-sodium chicken broth	1 L
	Chopped giblets (excluding the liver) from 1 chicken	
1 cup	dry white wine	250 mL
	Juice of ½ lemon	
½ tsp	chopped fresh thyme	2 mL
¼ tsp	cracked black pepper	1 mL
1	whole clove	1
1	sprig fresh Italian (flat-leaf) parsley	1
1	bay leaf	1

In a pot, bring all ingredients to a boil over medium-high heat. Skim away foam, reduce heat and simmer for 1 hour. Strain out solids and return liquid to the pot; simmer until reduced by two-thirds. Strain again. **Makes about 1½ cups (375 mL).** *Store in an airtight container in the refrigerator for up to 2 weeks. Use as chicken flavor base for soups, stews, sauces and gravies.*

Meat Glace

Follow preceding recipe, but replace the chicken broth with beef broth, replace the giblets with 1 lb (500 g) leftover roasted meat and bones, omit the lemon juice, and add 2 tsp (10 mL) tomato paste. **Makes about 1½ cups (375 mL).** *Store in an airtight container in the refrigerator for up to 2 weeks. Use as flavor base for soups, stews, sauces and gravies.*

Salt-Free Seasoning Mix

1	clove garlic, minced	1
2 tbsp	chopped fresh Italian (flat-leaf) parsley	25 mL
1 tsp	extra-virgin olive oil	5 mL
¼ tsp	coarsely ground black pepper	1 mL
	Grated zest and juice from ½ lemon	

Combine all ingredients. Rub over chicken, beef, veal or pork before roasting; sprinkle on baked fish; add to the poaching liquid for fish or chicken breasts; stir into stews, soups and stir-fries; or mix into eggs. **Makes about 2 tbsp (25 mL), enough for 6 to 8 portions of food.**

Celery-Top Seasoning Mix

Follow preceding recipe, but replace the parsley with chopped celery leaves, and add ½ tsp (2 mL) ground celery seeds. **Makes about 2 tbsp (25 mL), enough for 6 to 8 portions of food.**

Vegetable Top and Chicken Carcass Soup

3	cooked chicken carcasses	3
1 cup	dry white wine	250 mL
10 cups	water	2.5 L
4 cups	vegetable tops and trimmings (especially carrots, onions, celery), diced, unsightly parts discarded	1 L
1/2 cup	pearl barley	125 mL
3 tbsp	chopped fresh Italian (flat-leaf) parsley	45 mL
2 tbsp	chopped fresh dill	25 mL
1 tsp	dried thyme	5 mL
1	whole clove	1
	Salt and freshly ground black pepper to taste	
1	envelope (1/4 oz/7 g) unflavored gelatin, softened in 2 tbsp (25 mL) water	1

In a large stockpot, combine carcasses and wine; bring to a boil over medium heat. Boil for 3 minutes, then add water and return to a boil. Skim surface, reduce heat and simmer for 20 minutes. Add vegetable tops and trimmings, barley, parsley, dill, thyme, clove, salt, pepper and gelatin; simmer for 1 hour. Remove carcasses and let cool. Pick off any meat from the carcasses, add meat to the soup and heat through. Discard clove. **Serves 4.**

Turkey Carcass Split Pea Soup

Follow preceding recipe, but replace the chicken carcasses with 1 turkey carcass, omit the barley, and add 1/3 cup (75 mL) diced ham and 1 cup (250 mL) dried split peas with the vegetables. **Serves 4.**

Leftovers Chicken Noodle Soup

Follow recipe for Vegetable Top and Chicken Carcass Soup (above), but omit the barley, and add 3 cups (750 mL) cooked pasta with the meat from the carcasses. **Serves 4.**

Leftovers Chicken Rice Soup

Follow recipe for Vegetable Top and Chicken Carcass Soup (above), but omit the barley, and add 2 cups (500 mL) cooked rice with the meat from the carcasses. **Serves 4.**

Lemon Chicken Soup

Follow recipe for Vegetable Top and Chicken Carcass Soup (above), but omit the dill, and add 1 tbsp (15 mL) ground coriander, 1 tsp (5 mL) ground cumin, 1/2 tsp (2 mL) hot pepper flakes and 1 tbsp (15 mL) finely grated lemon zest with the parsley. Add the juice of 1 1/2 lemons and 1/3 cup (75 mL) chopped fresh cilantro with the meat from the carcasses. **Serves 4.**

Leftovers Minestrone

2 tbsp	extra-virgin olive oil	25 mL
1 cup	chopped onion	250 mL
2	cloves garlic, minced	2
2 to 3 cups	sliced vegetables (such as carrots, celery, zucchini, cauliflower, broccoli, green beans)	500 to 750 mL
1 tbsp	dried Italian seasoning	15 mL
1 tsp	dried thyme	5 mL
1/2 tsp	dried rosemary	2 mL
4	canned tomatoes, chopped	4
5 cups	chicken broth	1.25 L
1 tbsp	red wine vinegar	15 mL
1 tbsp	tomato paste	15 mL
	Salt and freshly ground black pepper to taste	
2 cups	cooked pasta in tomato sauce	500 mL
	Freshly grated Parmesan cheese	

In a large saucepan, heat oil over medium-high heat. Sauté onion until tender. Add garlic and sauté for 30 seconds. Add vegetables and sauté for 2 minutes. Add Italian seasoning, thyme and rosemary; sauté until vegetables are tender-crisp, about 3 minutes. Add tomatoes, broth, vinegar, tomato paste, salt and pepper; bring to a boil. Reduce heat and simmer for 10 minutes. Stir in pasta and heat through. Serve sprinkled with Parmesan. **Serves 8.**

Wilted Salad Gazpacho

1	small onion, chopped	1
1	clove garlic, minced	1
3 cups	vegetable juice (such as V8)	750 mL
2 cups	leftover dressed salad (preferably with vinaigrette dressing)	500 mL
1 to 2 tsp	hot pepper sauce (such as Tabasco)	5 to 10 mL
	Salt and freshly ground black pepper to taste	
1 cup	seasoned croutons	250 mL

In a blender or food processor, process onion, garlic, vegetable juice, salad, hot pepper sauce, salt and pepper until finely chopped. Transfer to a large bowl, cover and refrigerate until chilled. Serve in soup bowls, garnished with croutons. **Serves 4.**

Leftover Chicken Chili

2 tbsp	canola oil	25 mL
1	onion, finely chopped	1
1	clove garlic, minced	1
1	fresh hot chili pepper, seeded and chopped	1
1 tbsp	all-purpose flour	15 mL
1 tbsp	chili powder	15 mL
1 tsp	ground cumin	5 mL
¾ cup	chicken broth	175 mL
¼ cup	canned tomato purée or crushed tomatoes	50 mL
	Salt and freshly ground black pepper to taste	
3 cups	coarsely chopped cooked skinless chicken	750 mL

In a large skillet, heat oil over medium-high heat. Sauté onion until tender. Add garlic, chili pepper, flour, chili powder and cumin; sauté for 30 seconds. Add chicken broth, tomato purée, salt and pepper; bring to a boil. Add chicken, reduce heat and simmer until sauce is slightly thickened and chicken is hot. **Serves 4.**

Leftover Steak Chili

Follow preceding recipe, but omit the chicken stock, add ½ cup (125 mL) beef broth and 1 tbsp (15 mL) Worcestershire sauce with the tomato purée, and replace the chicken with chopped leftover steak or roasted beef. **Serves 4.**

Chili Pasta Salad

⅓ cup	canola oil	75 mL
3 tbsp	mayonnaise	45 mL
2 tbsp	chili powder	25 mL
2 tbsp	hot pepper sauce (such as Frank's RedHot or Tabasco)	25 mL
1 tbsp	ground cumin	15 mL
	Salt and freshly ground black pepper to taste	
3	green onions, chopped	3
1	can (19 oz/540 mL) red kidney beans, drained and rinsed	1
3 cups	cooked pasta (plain or with tomato sauce), cut into bite-size pieces	750 mL
1 cup	chopped cooked meat (such as beef, pork or chicken)	250 mL

Combine oil, mayonnaise, chili powder, hot pepper sauce, cumin, salt and pepper. Toss remaining ingredients in this dressing. **Serves 4.**

Pepper Pasta Salad

3 cups	cooked pasta, cut into bite-size pieces	750 mL
4	large roasted red bell peppers (see page 11), cut into strips	4
½	recipe Garlic Herb Dressing (page 60) or other vinaigrette	½

Toss together all ingredients. **Serves 4.**

Pasta, Bean and Tuna Salad

2 tbsp	extra-virgin olive oil	25 mL
2 tbsp	freshly squeezed lemon juice	25 mL
2 tbsp	white wine vinegar	25 mL
Pinch	hot pepper flakes	Pinch
	Salt and freshly ground black pepper to taste	
4	green onions, chopped	4
1	can (6 oz/175 g) tuna, drained and crumbled	1
1	can (19 oz/540 mL) white kidney beans, drained and rinsed	1
3 cups	cooked pasta	750 mL
2 tbsp	chopped fresh Italian (flat-leaf) parsley	25 mL

Whisk together oil, lemon juice, vinegar, hot pepper flakes, salt and black pepper. Toss remaining ingredients in this dressing. **Serves 4.**

Chicken and Bean Salad

⅓ cup	corn or peanut oil	75 mL
3 tbsp	mayonnaise	45 mL
2 tbsp	chili powder	25 mL
2 tbsp	hot pepper sauce (such as Frank's RedHot or Tabasco)	25 mL
1 tbsp	ground cumin	15 mL
	Salt and freshly ground black pepper to taste	
4	slices bacon, cooked crisp and crumbled	4
1	can (19 oz/540 mL) chickpeas, drained and rinsed	1
1	roasted red bell pepper (see page 11), sliced	1
1½ cups	diced cooked skinless chicken	375 mL
⅓ cup	thinly sliced green onions	75 mL
2 tbsp	chopped fresh Italian (flat-leaf) parsley	25 mL

Combine oil, mayonnaise, chili powder, hot pepper sauce, cumin, salt and pepper. Toss bacon, chickpeas, roasted pepper, chicken and green onions in this dressing. Just before serving, toss with parsley. **Serves 4.**

Rice and Bean Salad

2	roasted red bell peppers (see page 11), diced	2
1	small clove garlic, minced	1
2 cups	cold cooked rice	500 mL
2 cups	cooked or drained rinsed canned black beans	500 mL
1/3 cup	olive oil	75 mL
1/4 cup	red wine vinegar	50 mL
1/4 cup	chopped fresh Italian (flat-leaf) parsley	50 mL
	Juice of 1 lime	
	Salt and freshly ground black pepper to taste	

Toss together all ingredients. **Serves 4.**

Leftovers Tabbouleh

2 cups	bulgur	500 mL
2 1/2 cups	hot water	625 mL
1	clove garlic, minced	1
1/3 cup	extra-virgin olive oil	75 mL
3 tbsp	chopped fresh Italian (flat-leaf) parsley	45 mL
1 tbsp	dried mint	15 mL
1 tsp	hot pepper sauce (such as Tabasco)	5 mL
	Juice of 1 lemon	
	Salt and freshly ground black pepper to taste	
2 cups	diced vegetables (such as tomatoes, bell peppers, celery, cucumbers, fennel or mushrooms) and/or meat (such as cooked chicken)	500 mL

Soak bulgur in hot water for 30 minutes, until most of the water has been absorbed and bulgur is tender. Drain. Meanwhile, combine garlic, oil, parsley, mint, hot pepper sauce, lemon juice, salt and pepper. Toss soaked bulgur and vegetables and/or meat in this dressing. Cover and refrigerate until chilled. **Serves 4.**

Leftover Fish Salad for Sandwiches

2	stalks celery, chopped	2
2 cups	flaked cooked boneless skinless fish	500 mL
3 tbsp	mayonnaise	45 mL
2 tsp	freshly squeezed lemon juice	10 mL
	Salt and freshly ground black pepper to taste	

Toss together all ingredients. **Serves 4.**

Barbecued Chicken or Pork Salad

4	slices bacon	4
1/2	large onion, finely chopped	1/2
2	cloves garlic, minced	2
1/4 cup	cider vinegar	50 mL
2 tbsp	granulated sugar	25 mL
1 tbsp	Worcestershire sauce	15 mL
1/2 tsp	hot pepper sauce (such as Tabasco)	2 mL
	Salt and freshly ground black pepper to taste	
2	green onions, sliced	2
1	roasted red bell pepper (see page 11), diced	1
3 to 4 cups	diced boneless barbecued chicken or pork	750 mL to 1 L
4 oz	mushrooms, sliced	125 g

In a skillet, cook bacon over medium heat until crisp; remove and blot on paper towels. Increase heat to medium-high and sauté onion in the hot bacon fat until tender. Add garlic, vinegar, sugar, Worcestershire sauce, hot pepper sauce, salt and pepper; bring to a boil. Transfer to a serving bowl and toss with green onions, roasted pepper, meat and mushrooms. Crumble bacon over salad. **Serves 4.**

Leftover Fried Chicken Coleslaw

2 tsp	orange marmalade	10 mL
1 tsp	honey	5 mL
1 tbsp	mayonnaise	15 mL
1 1/2 tbsp	sour cream	22 mL
1 tbsp	red wine vinegar	15 mL
1 tbsp	hot pepper sauce (such as Frank's RedHot or Tabasco)	15 mL
2 tsp	ketchup	10 mL
	Salt and freshly ground black pepper to taste	
1 lb	fried chicken, with crust (about 3 pieces)	500 g
3	green onions, sliced	3
1	carrot, shredded	1
2 cups	shredded cabbage	500 mL

Combine marmalade and honey, then whisk in mayonnaise, sour cream, vinegar, hot pepper sauce, ketchup, salt and pepper. Remove bones from chicken pieces and cut chicken and crust into bite-size pieces; toss with green onions, carrot, cabbage and dressing. **Serves 4.**

Leftovers Escabèche

¼ cup	extra-virgin olive oil	50 mL
1	onion, sliced	1
2	cloves garlic, chopped	2
	Juice of 2 oranges, 2 lemons and 2 limes	
¼ cup	red wine vinegar	50 mL
1 tbsp	chopped fresh Italian (flat-leaf) parsley	15 mL
1 tsp	hot pepper sauce (such as Tabasco)	5 mL
	Salt to taste	
1½ lbs	grilled beef or chicken, cut into ½-inch (1 cm) thick slices	750 g

In a large skillet, heat oil over medium-high heat. Sauté onion until tender. Add garlic and sauté for 30 seconds. Stir in citrus juices, vinegar, parsley, hot pepper sauce and salt. In a serving bowl, toss together meat and sauce. Cover and refrigerate until chilled, or for up to 2 days. **Serves 4.**

Meat and Potato Salad with Blue Cheese Dressing

1	clove garlic, minced	1
3 cups	finely chopped roasted, grilled or sautéed meat	750 mL
2 oz	blue cheese, crumbled	60 g
¼ cup	sour cream	50 mL
3 tbsp	milk	45 mL
2 tbsp	extra-virgin olive oil	25 mL
1½ tbsp	red wine vinegar	22 mL
1½ lbs	red-skinned potatoes, cooked, peeled and cubed	750 g
2	stalks celery, sliced	2

Combine garlic, meat, blue cheese, sour cream, milk, oil and vinegar. Toss with potatoes and celery. **Serves 4.**

Cold Sliced Meats with Red and Green Sauces

Red Sauce

2	red bell peppers, chopped	2
1	fresh hot chili pepper, seeded and chopped	1
1	clove garlic, minced	1
¼ cup	chopped onion	50 mL
2 tbsp	extra-virgin olive oil	25 mL
2 tbsp	red wine vinegar	25 mL
	Juice of ½ lemon	
	Salt and freshly ground black pepper to taste	

Green Sauce

6	drained canned anchovies, finely chopped	6
1	clove garlic, minced	1
⅓ cup	extra-virgin olive oil	75 mL
¼ cup	finely chopped fresh Italian (flat-leaf) parsley	50 mL
4 tsp	red wine vinegar	20 mL
1 tsp	spicy brown mustard	5 mL
	Salt and freshly ground black pepper to taste	
4 to 6	portions cold sliced roast meat or poultry	4 to 6

For the red sauce: In a skillet, bring red peppers, chili pepper, garlic, onion, oil, vinegar and lemon juice to a boil over medium-high heat; reduce heat and simmer until peppers are soft. Season with salt and pepper. Keep warm.

For the green sauce: Combine all ingredients, cover and refrigerate until chilled.

Serve meat with either or both sauces. **Serves 4.**

Stir-Fried Chicken with Apples and Walnuts

1 tbsp	canola oil	15 mL
½ cup	walnut pieces	125 mL
¼ cup	chopped onion	50 mL
2	stalks celery, sliced	2
1	Granny Smith apple, diced	1
1	clove garlic, minced	1
3 cups	diced cooked skinless chicken	750 mL
2 tbsp	freshly squeezed lemon juice	25 mL
Pinch	hot pepper flakes	Pinch
	Salt and freshly ground black pepper to taste	

In a wok or a large skillet, heat oil over medium-high heat. Lightly toast walnuts, stirring constantly; using a slotted spoon, transfer walnuts to a plate. Add onion to the pan and stir-fry for 10 seconds. Add celery and apple; stir-fry until apple is barely tender. Stir in garlic, chicken, lemon juice and hot pepper flakes; heat, stirring, for 1 minutes. Add walnuts and season with salt and pepper. **Serves 4.**

Chicken and Gravy Frozen Dinner

1	portion cold roast chicken, sliced	1
¼ cup	cold chicken gravy	50 mL
¾ cup	cold leftover cooked vegetables (such as green beans, broccoli, peas, carrots)	75 mL
¾ cup	cold cooked rice or noodles	75 mL
2 tsp	melted butter	10 mL

Arrange chicken on a heavy-duty microwave-safe plastic dinner plate and cover with gravy. Place vegetables beside it. Toss rice with butter and place in remaining space on plate. Cover tightly with microwave-safe plastic wrap, then with foil. Freeze until solid and store in the freezer for up to 6 months. To serve, remove foil and microwave on High for 4 to 6 minutes, or until plastic swells. Carefully puncture plastic to let steam escape. **Serves 1.**

Asian Fried Noodles

3 tbsp	vegetable oil	45 mL
3	cloves garlic, finely chopped	3
½ tsp	hot pepper flakes	2 mL
2	eggs, beaten	2
4 cups	cooked spaghetti	1 L
1 cup	bean sprouts, divided	250 mL
½ cup	chopped cooked boneless meat, poultry or seafood	125 mL
1 tbsp	granulated sugar	15 mL
3 tbsp	soy sauce	45 mL
1½ tbsp	ketchup	22 mL
2	green onions, chopped	2
1	lime, sliced	1
2 tbsp	chopped peanuts	25 mL
2 tbsp	chopped fresh cilantro	25 mL

In a wok or a large skillet, heat oil over medium-high heat. Stir-fry garlic and hot pepper flakes for 10 seconds. Add eggs and spaghetti; stir-fry until eggs are set and spaghetti is crisp at the edges, about 2 minutes. Add ¾ cup (175 mL) of the bean sprouts and the meat; stir-fry for 1 minute. Stir in sugar, soy sauce and ketchup. Transfer to a serving platter and garnish with the remaining bean sprouts, green onions, lime slices, peanuts and cilantro. **Serves 4.**

Fried Rice from Leftovers

Follow preceding recipe, but omit the spaghetti, add 4 cups (1 L) cold cooked rice with the eggs, replace the peanuts with toasted sesame seeds, and omit the sugar and lime. **Serves 4.**

Baked Potato Skins with Yogurt Herb Sauce

4	shells from baked potatoes	4
	Garlic Yogurt Dressing (see recipe, page 108) or other creamy dressing	

Cut each potato shell into 6 pieces and deep-fry (see page 9) until crisp. Serve with Garlic Yogurt Dressing. **Serves 4.**

A Little Chopped Liver

1 cup	minced onion	250 mL
2 tbsp	butter	25 mL
3	chicken livers	3
Pinch	dried thyme	Pinch
	Salt and freshly ground black pepper to taste	
1 tsp	chopped fresh Italian (flat-leaf) parsley	5 mL
	Crackers	

In a nonstick skillet, over low heat, sauté onion until transparent. Add butter and sauté until onion is browned and very soft. Add chicken livers and thyme; sauté until livers are firm, about 4 minutes. Transfer livers to a cutting board and finely chop. In a bowl, combine chopped liver with the remaining contents of the skillet and season with salt and pepper. Stir in parsley. Cover and refrigerate until chilled. **Serves 1.** Serve as a spread with crackers.

Onion Dip

2 tsp	canola oil	10 mL
1 cup	finely chopped onion	250 mL
⅓ cup	mayonnaise	75 mL
⅓ cup	yogurt or sour cream	75 mL
Dash	hot pepper sauce (such as Tabasco)	Dash
	Salt and freshly ground black pepper to taste	

In a small skillet, heat oil over medium-high heat. Sauté onion until browned and crisp; let cool slightly. In a bowl, combine onion, mayonnaise and yogurt. Season with hot pepper sauce, salt and pepper. **Makes about 1⅓ cups (325 mL).** *Serve with potato chips or crudités.*

Stale-Cookie Pie Crust

8 oz	stale plain cookies	250 g
3 tbsp	packed light brown sugar	45 mL
1 tsp	ground cinnamon	5 mL
3 tbsp	melted butter	45 mL

Preheat oven to 350°F (180°C). In a food processor or using a heavy-duty rolling pin, crush cookies into fine crumbs, making about 1 cup (250 mL). In a bowl, combine cookie crumbs, brown sugar and cinnamon; stir in butter until blended. Press into a 10-inch (25 cm) pie pan and bake for 10 minutes. Let cool slightly, then refrigerate until firm. Use for cream pies or ice cream pies.

Chocolate Bread Pudding

3 cups	diced stale bread	750 mL
2	large or extra-large eggs	2
1 cup	strong brewed coffee, at room temperature	250 mL
6 tbsp	butter	90 mL
1 tsp	ground cinnamon	5 mL
2 oz	unsweetened chocolate, melted	60 g
1 cup	granulated sugar	250 mL
¾ cup	evaporated milk	175 mL
½ cup	sweetened condensed milk	125 mL
2 tbsp	milk	25 mL
1 tsp	vanilla	5 mL

Preheat oven to 350°F (180°C) and grease a 9-inch (2.5 L) square baking dish. In a food processor, process bread, eggs, coffee, butter and cinnamon until smooth. Add chocolate, sugar, evaporated milk, condensed milk, milk and vanilla; process until smooth. Pour batter into prepared baking dish and set in a larger pan of hot water. Bake for 75 minutes, until set. Let cool for at least 30 minutes. Serve warm, or let cool completely. **Serves 6.**

White Chocolate Rice Pudding

¼ cup	honey	50 mL
1 cup	cooked rice	250 mL
¼ cup	dried currants	50 mL
2 tbsp	brandy	25 mL
5 oz	white chocolate, finely chopped	150 g
2 cups	unsweetened whipped cream	500 mL

In a saucepan, melt honey over medium heat. Stir in rice, currants and brandy; heat through. Stir in white chocolate until it melts. Transfer to a bowl and let cool completely. Fold in whipped cream. Cover and refrigerate until chilled. **Serves 4.**

Chapter 10
Cooking on a Budget
Good Food Doesn't Have to Cost a Lot

Lemon Lamb Soup with Oatmeal 117
Lamb and Mushroom Barley Soup 117
Spicy Black Bean Soup 117
Potato Fennel Soup 117
Sweet Potato and Bacon Soup 118
Easy Clam and White Bean Chowder . . 118
Corn, Black Bean and Roasted
Tomato Salad 118
Corn and Lentil Salad 118
Spicy Sausage Potato Salad 118
Sweet-and-Sour Hot Sausage
Potato Salad 118
Potato and Tuna Vinaigrette Salad 119
Garlicky Pasta Primavera 119
Pasta with Garlic and White Beans 119
Fettuccine with Ricotta and Spinach . . . 119
Tortellini with Grilled Vegetables 120
Tuna Macaroni and Cheese 120
Crusty Macaroni and Cheese 120
Bell Peppers Stuffed with
Macaroni and Cheese 120
Rolled-Up Lasagna 120
Stuffed Shells 121
Pungent Orange Turkey Meatballs 121
Sweet-and-Sour Turkey Meatballs 121
Cranberry Turkey Meatballs 121
Cranberry Turkey Burgers 121
Turkey Mushroom Sloppy Joes 122
Pan-Roasted Turkey Legs 122

Pan-Roasted Chicken Legs 122
Tuscan Chicken Legs 122
Chili-Baked Chicken Drumsticks 122
Mushroom Strudel 123
Tuna Strudel 123
Quesadilla Casserole 123
Potatoes Baked with Anchovies
and Tomatoes 123
Sautéed Potatoes with
Garden Vegetables 123
Potato and Spinach Curry 124
Triple-Cheese Potatoes au Gratin 124
Brown Rice with Three Cheeses 124
Brown Rice with Red Beans 124
Orzo with Peas and Rosemary 124
Mixed Grilled Vegetables
with Hummus 125
Sweet-and-Spicy Stuffed Red Cabbage . . 125
Sausage-Stuffed Cabbage 125
Cabbage Stuffed with
Orzo and Cheese 125
Eggplant Rollatini 126
Cheddar Corn Soufflé 126
Roasted Onion Frittata 126
Fried Potato Frittata 126
Bacon Breakfast Cookies 127
Whole-Grain Breakfast Cookies 127
Peanut Butter Raisin Bran
Breakfast Cookies 127

G ood food doesn't have to cost a lot. Frequently, the best food is also the cheapest. That's good to keep in mind, because sooner or later most people will hit a patch when saving money is essential. A job will vanish, a high-priced emergency will hit, a big check won't materialize — and money will have to be saved. This chapter can help.

Budget-priced chuck has more beefy flavor than top-of-the-line fillet. A main-course soup fills the belly with heart-warming goodness as it fills your larder with a week's worth of meals. Sausages or meatballs paired with braised vegetables make low-cost stews, and curry or chili powder transforms a simple pot of rice or beans into dinner. Too often, we elevate a food's status to match its price, as if the cost of caviar defines its sensual charm or the rarity of a truffle elevates the prestige of the cook who slices it.

The next few pages contain 50 recipes that will save a lot of dollars even as they provide a wealth of flavor and creativity. Find some good sales, and you can make these dishes even more economically.

Lemon Lamb Soup with Oatmeal

2 tbsp	olive oil	25 mL
8 oz	boneless lamb, cut into small pieces	250 g
2	carrots, peeled and sliced	2
2	stalks celery, sliced	2
1	onion, sliced	1
3	cloves garlic, minced	3
1 tsp	ground coriander	5 mL
Pinch	ground ginger	Pinch
Pinch	hot pepper flakes	Pinch
	Finely grated zest and juice of 1 lemon	
4 cups	beef broth	1 L
	Salt and freshly ground black pepper to taste	
⅓ cup	old-fashioned rolled oats	75 mL
¼ cup	chopped fresh Italian (flat-leaf) parsley	50 mL

In a large saucepan, heat oil over medium-high heat. Sauté lamb until browned on all sides. Add carrots, celery, and onion; sauté until tender. Stir in garlic, coriander, ginger, hot pepper flakes and lemon zest, then add broth and season with salt and pepper. Reduce heat and simmer for 30 minutes, until lamb is tender. Stir in oats in a slow stream and simmer for 15 minutes, until oats are tender but not mushy. Stir in lemon juice and parsley. Serves 4.

Lamb and Mushroom Barley Soup

Follow preceding recipe, but add 8 oz (250 g) mushrooms, sliced, with onion, omit the ginger and oats, add ½ tsp (2 mL) crumbled dried rosemary with the coriander, and add ½ cup (125 mL) pearl barley and 1 tbsp (15 mL) tomato paste with the broth. Serves 4.

Spicy Black Bean Soup

2	slices bacon, minced	2
2	cloves garlic, minced	2
2	fresh hot chili peppers, seeded and chopped	2
8 cups	chicken broth	2 L
2 cups	dried black beans, soaked (see page 11) and drained	500 mL
2	carrots, diced	2
2	stalks celery, diced	2
1	large onion, chopped	1
½ cup	finely diced red bell pepper	125 mL
	Finely grated zest and juice of 1 orange	

In a large pot, cook bacon over medium heat until crisp. Add garlic and chili peppers; sauté until tender. Add broth and beans; reduce heat and simmer for 1 hour. Add carrots, celery and onion; simmer for 30 minutes, until beans and vegetables are tender. Add red pepper, orange zest and orange juice; simmer for 5 minutes. Serves 6 to 8.

Potato Fennel Soup

3 tbsp	butter	45 mL
1	large onion, finely chopped	1
½	bulb fennel, diced	½
1½ lbs	potatoes, peeled and diced	750 g
1½ tsp	ground fennel seeds	7 mL
3 cups	chicken broth	750 mL
	Salt and freshly ground black pepper to taste	
1 cup	milk	250 mL
1 cup	half-and-half (10%) cream	250 mL
¼ cup	chopped chives	50 mL

In a large pot, melt butter over medium heat. Sauté onion and fennel until tender. Add potatoes and fennel seeds, tossing to coat with butter. Add broth, salt and pepper; cook until potatoes are soft. Working in batches, transfer to a food processor or blender and process until almost smooth. Return to pot and stir in milk, cream and chives; heat through. Do not boil. Serves 4.

Sweet Potato and Bacon Soup

4	slices bacon	4
1	large onion, finely chopped	1
2 lbs	sweet potatoes, peeled and diced (3 to 4)	1 kg
4 cups	chicken broth	1 L
	Salt and freshly ground black pepper to taste	
1 cup	milk	250 mL

In a large pot, cook bacon over medium heat until crisp; remove, blot on paper towels and crumble. Set aside. Add onion to the fat in the pan and sauté until transparent. Add sweet potatoes, tossing to coat with fat. Add broth, salt and pepper; cook until sweet potatoes are soft. Working in batches, transfer to a food processor and purée. Return to pot and stir in bacon. Thin with milk and heat through. Do not boil. **Serves 4.**

Easy Clam and White Bean Chowder

2	cans (10 oz/284 mL) condensed New England Clam Chowder	2
3 cups	milk	750 mL
2	cloves garlic, minced	2
1	can (14 to 19 oz/398 to 540 mL) cannellini beans, drained and rinsed	1
¼ cup	chopped fresh Italian (flat-leaf) parsley	50 mL
Pinch	hot pepper flakes	Pinch

In a large pot, bring chowder and milk to a simmer over medium heat. Do not boil. Add garlic, beans, parsley and hot pepper flakes; heat through. **Serves 4.**

Corn, Black Bean and Roasted Tomato Salad

1 cup	Lime Vinaigrette (see recipe, page 60)	250 mL
2	heads escarole and/or curly endive	2
2	large roasted tomatoes (see page 11), cored and diced	2
2 cups	cooked or canned corn kernels	500 mL
1 cup	drained rinsed canned black beans	250 mL

In a small saucepan, bring Lime Vinaigrette to a simmer. Pour over remaining ingredients and toss to coat. **Serves 4.**

Corn and Lentil Salad

4	green onions, white parts only, sliced	4
1	roasted red bell pepper (see page 11), diced	1
½	cucumber, diced	½
2 cups	cooked or canned corn kernels	500 mL
2 cups	cooked lentils	500 mL
1 cup	chunky salsa (mild or medium)	250 mL
2 tbsp	olive oil	25 mL
2 tbsp	freshly squeezed lime juice	25 mL
	Salt and freshly ground black pepper to taste	

Toss together all ingredients. **Serves 4.**

Spicy Sausage Potato Salad

2 lbs	small red-skinned potatoes, quartered	1 kg
8 oz	mild Italian sausage	250 g
8 oz	spicy Italian sausage	250 g
4	green onions, sliced	4
3	stalks celery, diced	3
1	red bell pepper, diced	1
½ cup	finely diced red onion	125 mL
1	clove garlic, minced	1
¼ cup	red wine vinegar	50 mL
¼ cup	sour cream	50 mL
2 tbsp	granulated sugar	25 mL
2 tbsp	extra-virgin olive oil	25 mL
1½ tsp	salt	7 mL
Pinch	hot pepper flakes	Pinch

In a large pot of lightly salted water, boil potatoes until tender; drain and keep warm. In a large skillet, cook mild and spicy sausages over medium-high heat until browned on all sides and no longer pink inside; cut into thin slices. Toss together potatoes, sausage, green onions, celery, red pepper and red onion. Whisk together remaining ingredients until smooth; toss with salad while potatoes are still warm. **Serves 4.**

Sweet-and-Sour Hot Sausage Potato Salad

1½ lbs	red-skinned potatoes, peeled and quartered	750 g
8 oz	spicy Italian sausage, sliced	250 g
⅓ cup	cider vinegar	75 mL
3 tbsp	granulated sugar	45 mL
2	stalks celery, diced	2
1	small onion, finely chopped	1
2 tbsp	chopped fresh Italian (flat-leaf) parsley	25 mL
3 tbsp	mayonnaise	45 mL

1 tbsp	ketchup	15 mL
1 tsp	salt	5 mL
	Freshly ground black pepper to taste	

In a large pot of lightly salted water, boil potatoes until tender; drain and keep warm. In a small skillet, cook sausage over medium-high heat until browned on all sides and no longer pink inside. Add vinegar and sugar; heat, stirring, until sugar dissolves. Transfer to a large salad bowl and toss with potatoes and the remaining ingredients. **Serves 4.**

Potato and Tuna Vinaigrette Salad

1½ lbs	small red-skinned potatoes, quartered	750 g
2	cloves garlic, minced	2
½ cup	dry white wine	125 mL
¼ tsp	hot pepper flakes	1 mL
1	can (6 oz/170 g) water-packed tuna, drained and crumbled	1
¼ cup	olive oil	50 mL
2 tbsp	chopped fresh dill	25 mL
2 tbsp	chopped pitted olives	25 mL
3 tbsp	red wine vinegar	45 mL
1 tbsp	chopped fresh Italian (flat-leaf) parsley	15 mL

In a large pot of lightly salted water, boil potatoes until tender; drain and keep warm. In a small saucepan, bring garlic, wine and hot pepper flakes to a boil; boil until reduced by three-quarters. Stir in tuna, oil, dill, olives and vinegar. Transfer to a serving bowl and toss with potatoes and parsley. **Serves 4.**

Garlicky Pasta Primavera

1	roasted red bell pepper (see page 11), diced	1
1 cup	baby carrots	250 mL
1 cup	broccoli florets	250 mL
¼ cup	water	50 mL
1 tbsp	olive oil	15 mL
1	small onion, chopped	1
8	mushrooms, sliced	8
3	cloves garlic, minced	3
½ cup	frozen baby peas, thawed	125 mL
12 oz	pasta, cooked	375 g
2 tbsp	freshly grated Parmesan cheese	25 mL
2 tbsp	chopped fresh Italian (flat-leaf) parsley	25 mL
	Salt and freshly ground black pepper to taste	

In a microwave-safe bowl, combine roasted pepper, carrots, broccoli and water. Cover with microwave-safe plastic wrap and microwave on High for 3 minutes, until vegetables are tender. Drain and set aside. In a large skillet, heat oil over medium heat. Sauté onion until tender. Add mushrooms and garlic; sauté until mushrooms are wilted, about 2 minutes. Add cooked vegetables and heat through. Transfer to a serving bowl and toss with pasta, cheese, parsley, salt and pepper. **Serves 4.**

Pasta with Garlic and White Beans

¼ cup	olive oil	50 mL
2 tbsp	onion, minced	25 mL
2	cloves garlic, minced	2
1 tsp	dried basil	5 mL
1½ cups	drained rinsed canned white beans	375 mL
¼ tsp	hot pepper flakes	1 mL
	Salt and freshly ground black pepper to taste	
12 oz	pasta, cooked, one ladleful of cooking water reserved	375 g
¼ cup	freshly grated Parmesan cheese	50 mL
1 tbsp	chopped fresh Italian (flat-leaf) parsley	15 mL

In a large skillet, heat oil over medium heat. Sauté onion, garlic and basil for 30 seconds. Add beans, hot pepper flakes, salt, black pepper and pasta water; bring to a boil. Transfer to a serving bowl and toss with pasta, cheese and parsley. **Serves 4.**

Fettuccine with Ricotta and Spinach

3 tbsp	olive oil	45 mL
¼ cup	minced onion	50 mL
1	clove garlic, minced	1
1	package (10 oz/300 g) frozen chopped spinach, thawed and squeezed dry	1
Pinch	hot pepper flakes	Pinch
	Salt and freshly ground black pepper to taste	
1 cup	ricotta cheese	250 mL
1 lb	fettuccine, cooked	500 g

In a large skillet, heat oil over medium heat. Sauté onion, garlic, spinach and hot pepper flakes until mixture is dry. Season with salt and black pepper. Transfer to a serving bowl and stir in ricotta. Add fettuccine and toss to coat. **Serves 4.**

Tortellini with Grilled Vegetables

1	small zucchini, sliced lengthwise	1
1	small yellow summer squash, sliced lengthwise	1
1	tomato, sliced	1
½	small eggplant, sliced	½
	Olive oil	
	Salt and freshly ground black pepper to taste	
12 oz	cheese tortellini, cooked	375 g
¼ cup	finely chopped fresh basil	50 mL
2 tbsp	freshly grated Parmesan cheese	25 mL
Pinch	hot pepper flakes	Pinch

Preheat barbecue grill to medium-high. Brush zucchini, squash, tomato and eggplant with oil; season with salt and black pepper. Grill until lightly browned and tender. Dice the grilled vegetables. Toss together grilled vegetables, 3 tbsp (45 mL) of olive oil, tortellini, basil, cheese, hot pepper flakes and additional salt and black pepper. **Serves 4.**

Tuna Macaroni and Cheese

1	egg, beaten	1
8 oz	macaroni, cooked	250 g
⅓ cup	milk (preferably whole)	75 mL
2 tbsp	butter, melted	25 mL
1 tsp	brown mustard	5 mL
Pinch	cayenne pepper	Pinch
1	can (6 oz/170 g) tuna, drained and crumbled	1
2 cups	shredded Cheddar cheese, divided	500 mL
	Salt and freshly ground black pepper to taste	

Preheat oven to 350°F (180°C). In a 6-cup (1.5 L) casserole dish, toss together egg, macaroni, milk, butter, mustard and cayenne. Stir in tuna, half the cheese, salt and black pepper. Bake for 10 minutes. Stir in remaining cheese and bake for 10 minutes, until heated through. **Serves 4.**

Crusty Macaroni and Cheese

8 oz	macaroni, cooked and cooled	250 g
2 cups	shredded sharp Cheddar cheese	500 mL
1 cup	Béchamel Sauce (see recipe, page 17)	250 mL
1 tsp	yellow mustard	5 mL
Pinch	cayenne pepper	Pinch
	Salt and freshly ground black pepper to taste	
¼ cup	freshly grated Parmesan cheese	50 mL
2 tbsp	dry bread crumbs	25 mL
1 tbsp	butter	15 mL

Preheat oven to 375°F (190°C). In a 6-cup (1.5 L) casserole dish, combine macaroni, cheese, Béchamel Sauce, mustard, cayenne, salt and black pepper. Combine Parmesan and bread crumbs; sprinkle on top. Dot with butter and bake for 30 minutes, until heated through and topping is browned. **Serves 4.**

Bell Peppers Stuffed with Macaroni and Cheese

2 tbsp	olive oil	25 mL
3 tbsp	finely chopped onion	45 mL
3	cloves garlic, minced	3
3 cups	cooked macaroni	750 mL
1 tbsp	chopped fresh dill	15 mL
1 tbsp	chopped fresh Italian (flat-leaf) parsley	15 mL
Pinch	cayenne pepper	Pinch
	Salt and freshly ground black pepper to taste	
4 oz	Cheddar cheese, cut into small cubes	125 g
4	large bell peppers (any color), stems, cores and seeds removed	4
½ cup	chicken broth	125 mL

Preheat oven to 350°F (180°C). In a large skillet, heat oil over medium-high heat. Sauté onion until tender. Stir in garlic, macaroni, dill, parsley, cayenne, salt and black pepper. Place a few cheese cubes in each bell pepper, then fill each pepper halfway with macaroni mixture. Add a few more cheese cubes, more pasta, the remaining cheese and the remaining pasta. Set in a casserole dish small enough to hold peppers upright and pour broth over top. Cover with foil and bake for 45 minutes. Uncover and bake for 15 minutes, until peppers are tender and stuffing is hot. **Serves 4.**

Rolled-Up Lasagna

1	medium or large egg	1
2 cups	drained ricotta cheese	500 mL
¼ cup	freshly grated Parmesan cheese	50 mL
	Salt and freshly ground black pepper to taste	
8	lasagna noodles, cooked	8
2 cups	meat and tomato pasta sauce	500 mL

Preheat oven to 350°F (180°C) and grease an 8-cup (2 L) baking dish. Combine egg, ricotta, Parmesan, salt and pepper; spread over each cooked noodle. Roll up each noodle as you would a sleeping bag. Place rolled noodles, on end, side by side in prepared baking dish and pour pasta sauce over top. Cover and bake for 50 minutes, until filling is hot and set. **Serves 4.**

Stuffed Shells

Follow preceding recipe, but omit the lasagna noodles and fill 12 cooked jumbo pasta shells with cheese mixture. **Serves 4.**

Pungent Orange Turkey Meatballs

1	egg	1
1 lb	ground turkey	500 g
2 tbsp	seasoned dry bread crumbs	25 mL
2 tbsp	minced onion	25 mL
2	cloves garlic, minced	2
1 tbsp	ketchup	15 mL
1 tsp	brown mustard	5 mL
	Salt and freshly ground black pepper to taste	
1 tbsp	canola oil	15 mL
2 cups	chicken broth	500 mL
1/3 cup	orange juice	75 mL
1 tbsp	rice wine vinegar	15 mL
1 tbsp	honey	15 mL
2 tsp	soy sauce	10 mL
Pinch	ground ginger	Pinch
Pinch	cayenne pepper	Pinch

Using your hands, combine egg, turkey, bread crumbs, onion, garlic, ketchup, mustard, salt and pepper. Form into 24 meatballs. In a large skillet, heat oil over medium-high heat. Cook meatballs until browned on all sides. Add broth, reduce heat and simmer until meatballs are firm and no longer pink inside. Remove meatballs to a plate and keep warm. Add remaining ingredients to pan and simmer until slightly thickened, about 5 minutes. Return meatballs to pan and toss to coat. **Serves 4.**

Sweet-and-Sour Turkey Meatballs

1	egg, beaten	1
1 lb	ground turkey	500 g
1/3 cup	minced onion, divided	75 mL
2	cloves garlic, minced, divided	2
2 tbsp	Italian seasoned dry bread crumbs	25 mL
1 tbsp	ketchup	15 mL
1 tsp	spicy brown mustard	5 mL
2 tbsp	vegetable oil	25 mL
2 tsp	finely chopped gingerroot	10 mL
2 cups	chicken broth	500 mL
3 tbsp	packed light brown sugar	45 mL
3 tbsp	cider vinegar	45 mL
1 tbsp	soy sauce	15 mL
Pinch	cayenne pepper	Pinch
2 tsp	cornstarch, dissolved in 1 tbsp (15 mL) water	10 mL

Using your hands, combine egg, turkey, half the onion, half the garlic, bread crumbs, ketchup and mustard. Form into 24 meatballs. In a large skillet, heat oil over medium-high heat. Cook meatballs until browned on all sides. Add remaining onion, remaining garlic and ginger; cook for 1 minute. Add broth, brown sugar, vinegar, soy sauce and cayenne; reduce heat and simmer until liquid is reduced by half and meatballs are firm and no longer pink inside. Add cornstarch mixture (stirring first, if necessary) and simmer, stirring, until slightly thickened. **Serves 4.**

Cranberry Turkey Meatballs

Follow preceding recipe, but omit the ketchup, soy sauce and cayenne, and add 2 tbsp (25 mL) whole-berry cranberry sauce with the mustard and 1/4 cup (50 mL) whole-berry cranberry sauce with the vinegar. **Serves 4.**

Cranberry Turkey Burgers

1	egg	1
1 lb	ground turkey	500 g
2 tbsp	minced onion	25 mL
2	cloves garlic, minced	2
2 tbsp	seasoned dry bread crumbs	25 mL
1 tbsp	ketchup	15 mL
1 tsp	brown mustard	5 mL
	Salt and freshly ground black pepper to taste	
1 tbsp	canola oil	15 mL
1 cup	chicken broth	250 mL
Pinch	ground ginger	Pinch
Pinch	cayenne pepper	Pinch
1/3 cup	whole-berry cranberry sauce	75 mL
2 tsp	soy sauce	10 mL

Using your hands, combine egg, turkey, onion, garlic, bread crumbs, ketchup, mustard, salt and black pepper. Form into 4 burgers. In a large skillet, heat oil over medium-high heat. Cook burgers until browned on both sides. Add broth, ginger and cayenne; reduce heat and simmer until broth is reduced by three-quarters. Flip burgers and add cranberry sauce and soy sauce; simmer for 2 minutes, until sauce thickens slightly and burgers are cooked through but still juicy in the center (see page 129). **Serves 4.**

Turkey Mushroom Sloppy Joes

3 tbsp	canola oil	45 mL
1	onion, chopped	1
1	stalk celery, diced	1
1½ cups	sliced mushrooms	375 mL
½ cup	diced green bell pepper	125 mL
1 lb	ground turkey	500 g
¼ cup	beef broth	50 mL
3 tbsp	ketchup	45 mL
1 tsp	hot pepper sauce (such as Tabasco)	5 mL
4	hamburger buns, split and toasted	4

In a large skillet, heat oil over medium-high heat. Sauté onion, celery, mushrooms and green pepper until lightly browned and tender. Add turkey and cook, breaking up with a fork, until no longer pink. Add broth, ketchup and hot pepper sauce; reduce heat and simmer for 1 minute. Serve on buns. Serves 4.

Pan-Roasted Turkey Legs

2	small turkey legs, sectioned into thighs and drumsticks	2
	Kosher salt and coarsely ground black pepper to taste	
2 tbsp	olive oil	25 mL
1	head garlic, broken into cloves and peeled	1
4	sprigs fresh rosemary	4

Season turkey with salt and pepper. In a large, heavy skillet (preferably cast iron), heat oil over medium-high heat. Cook turkey, skin side down, until browned, about 5 minutes. Turn and brown on the other side, about 3 minutes. Scatter garlic cloves around turkey and place a sprig of rosemary on each piece. Reduce heat to medium-low, cover and cook until juices run clear when turkey is pierced and turkey reaches an internal temperature of 170°F (77°C), about 30 minutes. Serves 4.

Pan-Roasted Chicken Legs

Follow preceding recipe, but substitute 4 chicken legs for the turkey legs and reduce final cooking time to about 20 minutes. Serves 4.

Tuscan Chicken Legs

3 tbsp	olive oil	45 mL
4	chicken legs, sectioned into thighs and drumsticks	4
2	carrots, cut into large chunks	2
2	cloves garlic, minced	2
1	onion, cut into large chunks	1
1	stalk celery, cut into large chunks	1
2 oz	ham, cut into chunks	60 g
½ cup	dry red wine	125 mL
Pinch	ground nutmeg	Pinch
	Salt and freshly ground black pepper to taste	

In a large skillet, heat oil over medium-high heat. Cook chicken until browned on both sides. Scatter carrots, garlic, onion, celery and ham around chicken. Reduce heat to medium, cover and cook until vegetables are browned, about 10 minutes. Add wine, nutmeg, salt and pepper, scraping the bottom of the pan so that wine flows around the chicken and vegetables. Reduce heat and simmer until juices run clear when chicken is pierced and chicken reaches an internal temperature of 170°F (77°C), about 20 minutes. Serves 4.

Chili-Baked Chicken Drumsticks

1 tbsp	chili powder	15 mL
1 tbsp	hot paprika	15 mL
1 tsp	ground cumin	5 mL
½ tsp	dried oregano	2 mL
½ tsp	salt	2 mL
¼ tsp	freshly ground black pepper	1 mL
¼ cup	boiling water	50 mL
1	egg, beaten	1
1 tbsp	ketchup	15 mL
1 tsp	hot pepper sauce (such as Tabasco)	5 mL
2 lbs	chicken drumsticks	1 kg
1 cup	dry bread crumbs or corn flakes cereal crumbs	250 mL

In a large bowl, combine chili powder, paprika, cumin, oregano, salt and pepper. Add boiling water, then let cool. Stir in egg, ketchup and hot pepper sauce. Add drumsticks, turning to coat evenly. Cover and refrigerate for 1 to 2 hours. Preheat oven to 350°F (180°C). Remove chicken from marinade, discarding marinade, and coat chicken with bread crumbs. Discard any excess crumbs. Place chicken pieces on a baking sheet and bake until juices run clear when chicken is pierced and chicken reaches an internal temperature of 170°F (77°C), about 50 minutes. Serves 4.

Mushroom Strudel

2 tbsp	butter	25 mL
1	large onion, chopped	1
2	cloves garlic, minced	2
1½ lbs	mushrooms, finely chopped	750 g
1 tsp	dried thyme	5 mL
Pinch	dried sage	Pinch
	Salt and freshly ground black pepper to taste	
½ cup	dry white wine	125 mL
8	sheets phyllo dough, thawed	8
2 tbsp	melted butter	25 mL
	Tomato pasta sauce, heated	

In a large skillet, melt butter over medium heat. Sauté onion until tender. Add garlic and sauté for 30 seconds. Add mushrooms, thyme, sage, salt and pepper; sauté for 5 minutes. Add wine, reduce heat and simmer until most of the wine has evaporated. Remove from heat and let cool. Preheat oven to 400°F (200°C). Brush 4 phyllo sheets with melted butter, then stack them. Place half the mushroom mixture in a line parallel to a short edge and roll dough around filling (it should look like a large cigar). Repeat with the remaining phyllo and filling. Place both rolls on a baking sheet and brush with melted butter. Bake for 35 minutes, until phyllo is browned and filling is hot. Cut each strudel in half and serve with pasta sauce. **Serves 4.**

Tuna Strudel

Follow preceding recipe, but reduce the mushrooms to 8 oz (250 g), replace the thyme with dried dillweed, and replace the sage with dried tarragon. After wine has evaporated, stir in 1 can (6 oz/170 g) water-packed tuna, drained and crumbled. The pasta sauce is optional. **Serves 4.**

Quesadilla Casserole

	Nonstick cooking spray	
6	corn tortillas, cut into wedges	6
2	jars (each 16 oz/500 mL) salsa verde (mild or medium)	2
1	can (14 to 19 oz/398 to 540 mL) white beans, drained and rinsed	1
1 cup	sour cream, thinned slightly with milk	250 mL
1½ cups	shredded Monterey Jack cheese	375 mL

Preheat oven to 375°F (190°C) and spray a baking sheet with nonstick cooking spray. Place tortilla wedges on the pan in a single layer and spray with cooking spray. Bake for about 10 minutes, or until slightly toasted and warm. Place one-quarter of the salsa in a 12-cup (3 L) casserole dish. Top with one-third of the tortilla wedges, arranged in an even layer. Place half the beans on top, then another quarter of the salsa, one-third of the sour cream and one-third of the cheese. Repeat the layers, finishing with the remaining tortilla wedges, sour cream, salsa and cheese. Bake, uncovered, for about 20 minutes, or until browned and bubbly. **Serves 4.**

Potatoes Baked with Anchovies and Tomatoes

2 lbs	red-skinned or white potatoes, peeled	1 kg
2 tbsp	olive oil	25 mL
1	can (14 oz/398 mL) diced tomatoes, drained	1
1	clove garlic, minced	1
2 tbsp	chopped drained canned anchovies	25 mL
¼ cup	freshly grated Parmesan cheese	50 mL

In a large pot of lightly salted water, boil potatoes until tender; drain and slice. Preheat oven to 350°F (180°C). In a large skillet, heat oil over medium-high heat. Sauté tomatoes and garlic until aromatic. Stir in anchovies. Layer potatoes and tomato mixture in an 8-cup (2 L) casserole dish and sprinkle with cheese. Bake for 40 minutes, until hot and bubbling. **Serves 4.**

Sautéed Potatoes with Garden Vegetables

3 tbsp	olive oil	45 mL
2 lbs	baking potatoes, thinly sliced	1 kg
¼ cup	diced zucchini	50 mL
¼ cup	diced yellow summer squash	50 mL
¼ cup	sliced mushrooms	50 mL
¼ cup	diced red bell pepper	50 mL
¼ cup	diced carrot	50 mL
Pinch	ground nutmeg	Pinch
	Salt and freshly ground black pepper to taste	
1	clove garlic, minced	1
1 tbsp	chopped fresh Italian (flat-leaf) parsley	15 mL

In a large skillet, heat oil over medium-high heat. Blot potato slices to absorb surface moisture and sauté, tossing occasionally, until browned and tender. Add zucchini, squash, mushrooms, red pepper, carrot, nutmeg, salt and pepper; sauté until vegetables are tender. Toss with garlic and parsley. **Serves 4.**

Potato and Spinach Curry

2 tbsp	olive oil	25 mL
2	large onions, chopped	2
1½ lbs	baking potatoes, peeled and cut into ½-inch (1 cm) cubes	750 g
1	can (19 oz/540 mL) chickpeas, drained and rinsed	1
1	jar (16 oz/500 mL) curry sauce	1
1 cup	salsa	250 mL
	Salt and freshly ground black pepper to taste	
7 oz	baby spinach (about 4½ cups/1.125 L)	210 g
1 tbsp	chopped fresh cilantro	15 mL

In a large skillet, heat oil over medium-high heat. Sauté onions until softened. Add potatoes and sauté until onion and potatoes are evenly browned. Add chickpeas, curry sauce and salsa; reduce heat and simmer for 10 minutes. Season with salt and pepper. Add spinach and cook just until it wilts, about 2 minutes. Stir in cilantro. **Serves 4.**

Triple-Cheese Potatoes au Gratin

1 tbsp	butter	15 mL
½ cup	shredded mozzarella cheese	125 mL
½ cup	shredded Swiss cheese	125 mL
¼ cup	freshly grated Parmesan cheese	50 mL
1¼ lbs	baking potatoes, peeled and sliced	625 g
	Salt and freshly ground black pepper to taste	
1	small onion, sliced	1
1 cup	milk	250 mL

Preheat oven to 400°F (200°C) and grease an 8-inch (2 L) square baking pan with 1 tsp (5 mL) of the butter. Combine mozzarella, Swiss and Parmesan. Place one-third of the potato slices in the pan, season with salt and pepper, and top with half the onion and one-third of the cheese mixture. Make a second layer with half the remaining potatoes, salt, pepper, the remaining onion and half the remaining cheese mixture. Finish with a layer of the remaining potatoes and the remaining cheese. Pour in milk and dot with the remaining butter. Cover with foil and bake for 40 minutes. Uncover and bake for 15 minutes, until potatoes are tender and top is browned. **Serves 4.**

Brown Rice with Three Cheeses

Follow preceding recipe, but use Brown Rice Pilaf (page 359) instead of the potatoes and onion. **Serves 4.**

Brown Rice with Red Beans

2 tbsp	butter	25 mL
⅓ cup	finely diced bell pepper (any color)	75 mL
½ cup	finely chopped onion	125 mL
1 cup	long-grain brown rice, washed thoroughly and drained	250 mL
3 cups	water or vegetable broth	750 mL
	Salt to taste	
1 cup	cooked or drained rinsed canned red kidney beans	250 mL
1 cup	salsa (medium or hot)	250 mL
1 to 2 tbsp	chopped fresh cilantro	15 to 25 mL

In a large saucepan, melt butter over medium heat. Sauté bell pepper and onion until almost tender. Add rice, tossing to coat with butter. Add water and salt; reduce heat, cover and simmer for 45 minutes. Stir in beans, salsa and cilantro to taste; heat through. **Serves 4.**

Orzo with Peas and Rosemary

2 tbsp	butter	25 mL
¾ cup	chopped onion	175 mL
1	clove garlic, minced	1
2 tsp	chopped fresh rosemary	10 mL
1½ cups	orzo	375 mL
3 cups	hot chicken broth	750 mL
	Salt and freshly ground black pepper to taste	
2 cups	frozen peas, thawed	500 mL
1 tbsp	finely chopped fresh Italian (flat-leaf) parsley	15 mL

In a large saucepan, melt butter over medium heat. Sauté onion until tender. Add garlic and rosemary; sauté until aromatic, about 1 minute. Add orzo, tossing to coat with butter. Add broth, salt and pepper; reduce heat and simmer for 8 minutes. Stir in peas and simmer for 4 to 5 minutes, or until all the broth has been absorbed and peas and orzo are tender. Sprinkle with parsley. **Serves 4.**

Mixed Grilled Vegetables with Hummus

12	large mushrooms, stems trimmed	12
1	large red bell pepper, cut into 6 spears	1
1	large yellow bell pepper, cut into 6 spears	1
1	zucchini, cut into large chunks	1
1	yellow summer squash, cut into large chunks	1
1	large sweet onion, cut into wedges	1
1	large tomato, sliced	1
1 cup	Oil and Vinegar Dressing (see recipe, page 59) or other vinaigrette	250 mL
1¼ cups	drained rinsed canned chickpeas	300 mL
1	clove garlic	1
3 tbsp	extra-virgin olive oil	45 mL
1 tbsp	tahini	15 mL
	Juice of ½ lemon	
	Salt and hot pepper sauce (such as Tabasco) to taste	
1 tbsp	toasted sesame seeds	15 mL

In a large bowl, toss vegetables with dressing; cover and refrigerate for 1 hour. Preheat broiler or barbecue grill to high. In a food processor, make hummus by puréeing chickpeas, garlic, oil, tahini, lemon juice, salt and pepper until smooth; set aside. Broil or grill marinated vegetables, turning once, until browned and tender on both sides. (Onion needs about 6 minutes per side; peppers, zucchini, squash and mushrooms, 3 to 4 minutes per side; tomatoes, 2 minutes per side.) Garnish with sesame seeds and serve with hummus. **Serves 4.**

Sweet-and-Spicy Stuffed Red Cabbage

1 tbsp	canola oil	15 mL
1	Granny Smith apple, peeled and diced	1
1	stalk celery, diced	1
½	small onion, finely chopped	½
2	cloves garlic, minced	2
1 tbsp	chopped fresh Italian (flat-leaf) parsley	15 mL
½ tsp	dried thyme	2 mL
	Salt and freshly ground black pepper to taste	
2 cups	cooked long-grain rice	500 mL
12	large red cabbage leaves, blanched (see page 8)	12
1 cup	chicken broth	250 mL
¾ cup	spicy barbecue sauce	175 mL
½ cup	unsweetened apple juice	125 mL

Preheat oven to 350°F (180°C). In a large skillet, heat oil over medium-high heat. Sauté apple, celery and onion until barely tender. Add garlic, parsley, thyme, salt and pepper. Stir in rice. Divide filling among cabbage leaves, fold leaves loosely around filling and secure ends with toothpicks. Place snugly in a 12-cup (3 L) casserole dish. In a saucepan, combine broth, barbecue sauce, apple juice and additional salt and pepper; bring to a boil. Pour over cabbage. Cover and bake for 1 hour, until hot and bubbling. **Serves 4.**

Sausage-Stuffed Cabbage

Follow preceding recipe, but use green cabbage leaves instead of red, and add 8 oz (250 g) crumbled sausage with the onion, cooking until no longer pink. **Serves 4.**

Cabbage Stuffed with Orzo and Cheese

2 tbsp	olive oil	25 mL
3 tbsp	finely chopped onion	45 mL
3	cloves garlic, minced	3
1 tbsp	chopped fresh dill	15 mL
1 tbsp	chopped fresh Italian (flat-leaf) parsley	15 mL
	Salt and freshly ground black pepper to taste	
1½ cups	cooked orzo	375 mL
3 tbsp	ricotta cheese	45 mL
3 tbsp	freshly grated Parmesan cheese	45 mL
8	large cabbage leaves, blanched (see page 8)	8
½ cup	dry white wine	125 mL
½ cup	water	125 mL
	Juice of ½ lemon	

Preheat oven to 350°F (180°C). In a large skillet, heat oil over medium-high heat. Sauté onion until tender. Add garlic, dill, parsley, salt and pepper. Stir in orzo, ricotta and Parmesan. Divide filling among cabbage leaves, fold leaves loosely around filling and secure ends with toothpicks. Place snugly in a 12-cup (3 L) casserole dish. Pour in wine, water and lemon juice. Cover and bake for 1 hour, until hot and bubbling. **Serves 4.**

Eggplant Rollatini

1	large eggplant, peeled and cut lengthwise into 16 thin slices	1
2 tbsp	olive oil	25 mL
	Cheese filling from Rolled-Up Lasagna (see recipe, page 120)	500 mL
2 cups	tomato pasta sauce	

Preheat broiler. Brush eggplant slices with oil and broil until tender. Set oven temperature to 350°F (180°C) and brush a 13- by 9-inch (3 L) baking dish with olive oil. Place 2 eggplant slices so that they are overlapping slightly lengthwise. Place ¼ cup (50 mL) of cheese filling in the center of the eggplant slices and roll up eggplant like a sleeping bag. Repeat with remaining eggplant and filling. Place rolls side by side in prepared baking dish and pour in pasta sauce. Cover and bake for 40 minutes, until filling is hot and set. **Serves 4.**

Cheddar Corn Soufflé

1 tbsp	butter, divided	15 mL
1 cup	cornmeal, divided	250 mL
1	large onion, chopped	1
1	stalk celery, diced	1
½ cup	diced bell pepper (any color)	125 mL
1	clove garlic, minced	1
1½ cups	hot milk	375 mL
⅔ cup	shredded sharp Cheddar cheese	150 mL
Pinch	cayenne pepper	Pinch
	Salt and freshly ground black pepper to taste	
6	large or extra-large eggs, separated	6
Pinch	cream of tartar	Pinch

Preheat oven to 450°F (230°C). Grease an 8-cup (2 L) soufflé dish with 1 tsp (5 mL) of the butter and coat with 1 tbsp (15 mL) of the cornmeal. In a skillet, melt the remaining butter over medium heat. Sauté onion, celery and bell pepper until tender. Add garlic and sauté for 30 seconds. Add the remaining cornmeal and hot milk; cook, stirring, until smooth and thick, about 10 minutes. Stir in cheese, cayenne, salt and black pepper. Remove from heat and beat in egg yolks, 1 at a time. Let cool for 5 minutes. Meanwhile, beat egg whites and cream of tartar until soft peaks form; fold into cheese mixture in 3 additions. Pour into prepared soufflé dish and bake for 20 minutes. Reduce oven temperature to 350°F (180°C) and bake for 20 minutes, until puffed, brown and barely jiggly in the center. Serve immediately. **Serves 6.**

Roasted Onion Frittata

1	large onion, thinly sliced	1
1	large head garlic, broken into cloves and peeled	1
1½ tbsp	olive oil, divided	22 mL
	Salt to taste	
8	large or extra-large eggs	8
Pinch	cayenne pepper	Pinch
	Freshly ground black pepper to taste	

Preheat oven to 400°F (200°C). Toss onion and garlic with one-third of the oil and salt. Scatter on a baking sheet and roast for 30 minutes, until browned and tender. Beat eggs, cayenne, additional salt and black pepper until frothy. In a 12-inch (30 cm) ovenproof skillet, heat the remaining oil over medium heat. Pour in eggs and cook, stirring gently, until set across the bottom. Scatter onion and garlic over top and bake until top is puffed and brown, about 5 minutes. **Serves 4.**

Fried Potato Frittata

¼ cup	canola oil	50 mL
2	baking potatoes, thinly sliced	2
1	onion, sliced	1
	Salt and freshly ground black pepper to taste	
8	large or extra-large eggs	8
Pinch	cayenne pepper	Pinch

Preheat broiler. In a 12-inch (30 cm) ovenproof skillet, heat oil over medium-high heat. Sauté potatoes and onion until browned and tender; season with salt and black pepper. Beat eggs, cayenne and additional salt and black pepper until frothy. Add to skillet, tossing lightly so that egg coats bottom of pan, and cook, without stirring, until egg sets across the bottom. Broil until top is puffed and brown, about 3 minutes. **Serves 4.**

Bacon Breakfast Cookies

4	slices bacon, cooked crisp and crumbled	4
4½ cups	quick-cooking rolled oats	1.125 L
1 cup	unsalted dry-roasted peanuts	250 mL
1 cup	raisins	250 mL
1 cup	packed light brown sugar	250 mL
1½ cups	chunky peanut butter	375 mL
½ cup	butter, softened	125 mL
3	large or extra-large eggs	3
1 tbsp	baking soda, dissolved in 2 tsp (10 mL) strong brewed coffee	15 mL

Preheat oven to 350°F (180°C). In a large bowl, combine bacon, oats, peanuts and raisins. In another bowl, cream brown sugar, peanut butter and butter until soft and fluffy. Beat in eggs, then stir in baking soda mixture. Pour over bacon mixture, stirring to moisten. Drop in ¼-cup (50 mL) mounds, 2½ inches (6 cm) apart, on ungreased baking sheets. Bake for 21 minutes. Let cool for 2 minutes on pans, then transfer to racks and let cool completely. **Makes 24 cookies.**

Whole-Grain Breakfast Cookies

Follow preceding recipe, but omit the bacon, reduce the oats to 2 cups (500 mL), and add 1 cup (250 mL) rye flakes, 1 cup (250 mL) bran flakes cereal and ½ cup (125 mL) toasted wheat germ with the oats. **Makes 24 cookies.**

Peanut Butter Raisin Bran Breakfast Cookies

Follow recipe for Bacon Breakfast Cookies (above), but omit the bacon, replace the oats with raisin bran cereal, and dissolve the baking soda in vanilla instead of coffee. **Makes 24 cookies.**

Chapter 11
Burgers and Dogs
For the Whole Family

Great Burgers 130
Deli-Style Burgers 130
Steakhouse Burgers 130
Peppercorn Burgers 130
Whole-Seed Mustard Burgers 130
Steak and Onion Burgers 130
Cajun Burgers 130
Apple and Sage Burgers 130
Mexican Burgers 131
Smoked Bacon Burgers 131
Super Smoky Burgers 131
Three-Cheese Burgers 131
Ham and Swiss Cheeseburgers 131
Blue Cheese Burgers 131
Blackened Cajun Burgers 131
Meatloaf Burgers 131
Sicilian Mint and Ricotta Burgers 132
Tastes-Like-Hamburger Turkey Burgers . . 132
Down-Home Turkey Burgers 132
Teriyaki Turkey Burgers 132
Middle Eastern Turkey Burgers 132
Chicken Burgers with
Mustard and Green Peppercorns 132
Cheesy Chicken Burgers 132
Chicken Burgers Laced with Brandy . . . 133
Herb Cheese Veal Burgers 133
Roasted Pepper Veal Burgers 133
Veal Oscar Burgers 133

Garlic Spinach Lamb Burgers 133
Minted Lamb Burgers 133
Hoisin Burgers 133
Wasabi Tuna Burgers 134
Provençal Tuna Burgers 134
Hot Dogs with Cumin Mustard 134
Hot Dogs with Relish Fresca 134
Hot Dogs with the Works 134
Piggy Dogs 134
Hot Dog Wraps 134
Barbecue-Style Dogs 134
Sweet-and-Sour Hot Dogs 135
Chili Cheese Dogs 135
Hot Dogs Grilled with
Bacon and Horseradish Mustard 135
Chicken Franks with Gazpacho Salsa . . . 135
Chicken Franks with
Tomato Artichoke Salsa 135
Turkey Franks with Tapenade Ketchup . . 135
Turkey Sausages with Pesto and Tomato . . 135
Turkey Sausages with
Gorgonzola Butter 135
Bratwurst with Apple Butter Mustard . . 136
Grilled Smoked Sausages
with Apple Sauerkraut 136
Knockwurst Simmered in Beer
with Sauerkraut 136
Chicken Sausages over Spinach 136

When you bite into a masterful burger, dripping juice and wafting steam, or feel the snap as a perfect hot dog cleaves between your teeth, you know that gastronomy has no higher aim. Gourmets may scoff at the ubiquitous burger and dog, and we readily admit that these two icons of American cuisine suffer more than their share of abuse at the hands of fast-food chains and thoughtless cooks, but when they're good, they are transcendent.

Here's how you can achieve perfection every time.

For burgers:
Get the right meat. Tough meat is tasty, and tender meat is bland. We are usually willing to sacrifice some flavor for tenderness, but when it comes to ground meat, especially beef, there is no need for compromise. Grinding meat breaks down its tough fibers, so all that's left is the flavor. In other words, choose a tough cut for the best-tasting burger. We prefer ground chuck.

Don't buy meat that's too lean. When meat is ground, most of its natural moisture is released, and the little that remains evaporates quickly during cooking. Without moisture, the perception of juiciness depends entirely on the meat's fat content. That's why ground beef with a fat content of less than 10% (labeled "super-lean" in the U.S. and "extra-lean" in Canada) will be dry; ground beef with a fat content of 10% to 15% (labeled "extra-lean" or "ground round" in the U.S. and "lean" in Canada) will taste lean and juicy; ground beef with a fat content of 15% to 20% (labeled "lean" or "ground chuck" in the U.S. and "medium" in Canada) will taste richer; and ground beef with a fat content of more than 20% (labeled "regular" in both countries) will have a fatty mouth feel. We buy 85% lean ground chuck, which has 15% fat.

Add water. You can increase the perception of juiciness by adding a little water (or another liquid) to your burger mixture. We use ice water to keep the meat chilled.

When forming a burger patty, don't pack the meat too tightly. The patty has been sufficiently molded when it can hold its shape. Beyond that point, beneficial returns diminish. If you compress the meat too much, any moisture coming from the meat fibers during cooking will have no place to go but out of the burger, yielding substantially dryer results. In addition, heat passes more slowly through denser patties, slowing down cooking time.

Chop up garnishing ingredients such as tomato, onion, pickle, cheese, bell peppers and black olives and mix them right in with the ground meat. That way, the flavor comes through in every bite.

Because bacteria may be present in ground meats and poultry, the USDA and Health Canada specify that burgers made from beef, veal or lamb must be cooked until they are no longer pink inside and reach an internal temperature of 160°F (71°C). The USDA specifies that those made from ground chicken or turkey must reach an internal temperature of 165°F (74°C), while Health Canada recommends cooking ground poultry to an internal temperature of 175°F (80°C). At these temperatures, your ground meat will certainly be safe — but it will also be very dry. We prefer to cook beef, veal and lamb burgers to an internal temperature of 150°F (65°C), ensuring that all parts of the burger are hotter than 140°F (60°C) but that there still is some juiciness in the center. We cook ground poultry to 165°F (74°C).

To read the internal temperature of a burger, insert an instant-read meat thermometer horizontally into patties, making sure it goes at least 1 inch (2.5 cm) in. A thermometer is particularly helpful when burgers incorporate red ingredients, such as ketchup, chili powder or steak sauce, which may make it difficult to check doneness visually.

For hot dogs:
Buy the best frankfurters you can afford. We prefer all-beef, with natural casings.

Franks are fully cooked already; all you have to do is heat them up, and it doesn't matter how you do it. Grilling or broiling gives you a bit of browning, but not necessarily a snappier skin. Because the skin of a frankfurter is pure protein, it will become firmer as it heats. Boiling water does the best job of setting up the skin uniformly.

Franks plump when they are heated through completely. That's because steam inside makes the meat expand. If the casing is firm, a little bit of meat will force its way through the tips. If the casing bursts, that's an indication that the frank is overcooked.

Splitting the skin with a knife before heating will speed up the cooking, but the plumping won't be as obvious.

The meat in the typical frankfurter is ground to a purée and heavily spiced with salt and coriander seed. The red color in some brands comes from the addition of sodium nitrate, a known carcinogen. It is added, in theory, to ensure that the frank can't contain botulinum bacteria; however, because botulinum can grow only under anaerobic conditions, and because plenty of air permeates a frankfurter, the use of nitrates in frankfurters is purely cosmetic. (In denser meats, such as large hams, it does serve a bacteriological purpose.) Nitrate-free frankfurters are readily available; they are brown or beige rather than red.

Any sausage the size of a frankfurter can replace a frankfurter in a recipe. Just be aware of differences in flavor — usually a matter of spicing and/or smoking — and texture, which varies depending on how finely the meat filling is ground. Knockwurst is nothing more than an oversized frankfurter; bratwurst is a pale, smooth sausage made from pork and veal; and Italian sausage is made from coarsely ground pork, usually flavored with herbs and garlic.

About these recipes . . .

You may notice that not all of our burgers and dogs are served on buns. Sometimes the amount of sauce or garnish makes bread unnecessary. Even when we don't call for a bun, use one if you prefer. It is assumed that you will season to taste with salt and pepper.

Great Burgers

1½ lbs	ground beef	750 g
¼ cup	ice water	50 mL
	Salt and freshly ground black pepper to taste	
4	hamburger buns, split	4

Using your hands, combine beef, ice water, salt and pepper. Form into 4 patties, 1 to 1½ inches (2.5 to 4 cm) thick (do not pack too tightly). Broil or grill over a high fire, turning once, for 5 to 6 minutes per side, or until cooked through but still juicy in the center (see page 129). For the last minute of cooking, place buns on the grill to lightly toast the interior surfaces. Serve burgers on buns. Serves 4.

Deli-Style Burgers

Follow preceding recipe, but use kaiser rolls instead of hamburger buns. Combine 3 tbsp (45 mL) mayonnaise, 2 tsp (10 mL) ketchup and 1 tsp (5 mL) pickle relish; spread over the interior of the rolls. Place a lettuce leaf on one side of each roll and a tomato slice on the other. Place burgers on lettuce leaves and top with ½ cup (125 mL) coleslaw. **Serves 4.**

Steakhouse Burgers

Follow recipe for Great Burgers (left), but decrease the water to 2 tbsp (25 mL), and add 2 tbsp (25 mL) steak sauce with the water. **Serves 4.**

Peppercorn Burgers

Follow recipe for Great Burgers (left), but rub the surface of the patties with a mixture of 1 tsp (5 mL) each black, dried green and Szechuan peppercorns before cooking. **Serves 4.**

Whole-Seed Mustard Burgers

Follow recipe for Great Burgers (left), but add 1 clove garlic, minced, and 1 tbsp (15 mL) Dijon mustard to the ground beef. Rub the surface of the patties with ⅓ cup (75 mL) whole mustard seeds before cooking. **Serves 4.**

Steak and Onion Burger

Follow recipe for Great Burgers (left), but sauté ¼ cup (50 mL) finely chopped onion in 1 tsp (5 mL) vegetable oil until browned; let cool. Add onion, 2 tbsp (25 mL) steak sauce and 1 tsp (5 mL) brown mustard to the ground beef, and decrease the ice water to 2 tbsp (25 mL). **Serves 4.**

Cajun Burgers

Follow recipe for Great Burgers (left), but add 1 tbsp (15 mL) Cajun seasoning and 1 tsp (5 mL) tomato paste to the ground beef. **Serves 4.**

Apple and Sage Burgers

Follow recipe for Great Burgers (left), but sauté ½ cup (125 mL) finely diced peeled apple, ¼ cup (50 mL) finely chopped onion, 1 clove garlic, minced, ½ tsp (2 mL) dried sage and ¼ tsp (1 mL) dried thyme in 2 tsp (10 mL) vegetable oil until onion is softened; let cool. Add mixture to the ground beef. **Serves 4.**

Mexican Burgers

Follow recipe for Great Burgers (page 130), but omit the ice water, and add ½ cup (125 mL) spicy salsa, 1 tbsp (15 mL) chopped fresh cilantro, 1 tbsp (15 mL) chili powder and 1 tsp (5 mL) ground cumin to the ground beef. Top burgers with additional salsa and shredded lettuce. **Serves 4.**

Smoked Bacon Burgers

Follow recipe for Great Burgers (page 130), but wrap each patty with 1 slice of bacon, securing ends with toothpicks, before grilling. Grill 4 inches (10 cm) from a charcoal fire strewn with ½ cup (125 mL) hardwood chips that have been soaked in water for 30 minutes. **Serves 4.**

Super Smoky Burgers

Follow previous recipe, but add ¼ cup (50 mL) shredded smoked cheese (such as smoked mozzarella, Gouda or Cheddar) to the ground beef. **Serves 4.**

Three-Cheese Burgers

Follow recipe for Great Burgers (page 130), but omit the ice water, and add ⅓ cup (75 mL) ricotta cheese and ¼ cup (50 mL) freshly grated Parmesan cheese to the ground beef. Two minutes before burgers are done cooking, top each with 1 thin slice of provolone cheese; cover and cook until cheese melts. **Serves 4.**

Ham and Swiss Cheeseburgers

Follow recipe for Great Burgers (page 130), but sauté 8 oz (250 g) ham, finely diced, 2 tbsp (25 mL) finely chopped onion and a pinch of ground nutmeg in 1 tbsp (15 mL) vegetable oil until onion is lightly browned; let cool. Add mixture to the ground beef. Two minutes before burgers are done cooking, top each with 1 thin slice of Swiss cheese; cover and cook until cheese melts. **Serves 4.**

Blue Cheese Burgers

Follow recipe for Great Burgers (page 130), but omit the ice water, and add 3 tbsp (45 mL) blue cheese dressing and 2 oz (60 g) crumbled blue cheese to the ground beef. **Serves 4.**

Blackened Cajun Burgers

1½ lbs	ground beef	750 g
¼ cup	ice water	50 mL
2 tbsp	ground fennel seeds	25 mL
2 tbsp	garlic powder	25 mL
2 tbsp	salt	25 mL
2 tbsp	freshly ground white pepper	25 mL
2 tbsp	freshly ground black pepper	25 mL
2½ tsp	dry mustard	12 mL
2½ tsp	cayenne pepper	12 mL
4	hamburger buns, split	4
¼ cup	water	50 mL
3 tbsp	Worcestershire sauce	45 mL

Using your hands, combine beef and ice water. Form into 4 patties, 1 to 1½ inches (2.5 to 4 cm) thick (do not pack too tightly). Combine all spices and rub the surface of the patties with this mixture. In a large, white-hot iron skillet, cook burgers, turning once, for 5 to 6 minutes per side, or until cooked through but still juicy in the center (see page 129). Remove pan from heat and transfer burgers to buns. Add water and Worcestershire sauce to pan and scrape up any brown bits from the bottom. Pour liquid over burgers. **Serves 4.**

Meatloaf Burgers

1	slice bread, crust removed, bread crumbled	1
¼ cup	milk	50 mL
1	extra-large egg, beaten	1
12 oz	ground veal	375 g
12 oz	ground beef	375 g
1 tbsp	finely chopped onion	15 mL
1 tbsp	ketchup	15 mL
2 tsp	Worcestershire sauce	10 mL
1 tsp	mustard	5 mL

In a bowl, soak bread in milk until milk is absorbed. Add the remaining ingredients and mix with your hands until blended. Form into patties, cook and serve as described in Great Burgers (page 130). **Serves 4.**

Sicilian Mint and Ricotta Burgers

1	egg, beaten	1
1 lb	ground beef	500 g
¼ cup	ricotta cheese	50 mL
3 tbsp	seasoned dry bread crumbs	45 mL
3 tbsp	minced onion	45 mL
1	clove garlic, minced	1
2 tbsp	minced fresh mint	25 mL

Using your hands, combine all ingredients. Form into patties, cook and serve as described in Great Burgers (page 130). **Serves 4.**

Tastes-Like-Hamburger Turkey Burgers

1 lb	ground turkey	500 g
3 tbsp	Italian seasoned dry bread crumbs	45 mL
2 tbsp	grated onion	25 mL
2 tbsp	ketchup	25 mL
2 tsp	steak sauce	10 mL
4	hamburger buns, split	4

Using your hands, combine all ingredients. Form into 4 patties, 1 to 1½ inches (2.5 to 4 cm) thick (do not pack too tightly). Broil or grill over a medium-high fire, turning once, for 5 to 6 minutes per side, or until no longer pink inside. For the last minute of cooking, place buns on the grill to lightly toast the interior surfaces. Serve burgers on buns. **Serves 4.**

Down-Home Turkey Burgers

Follow previous recipe, but replace the ketchup with apple butter, omit the steak sauce, and add ½ tsp (2 mL) poultry seasoning. **Serves 4.**

Teriyaki Turkey Burgers

Follow recipe for Tastes-Like-Hamburger Turkey Burgers (above), but omit the ketchup and steak sauce, and add 1 tbsp (15 mL) each grated ginger-root, hoisin sauce and honey, and 2 tsp (10 mL) soy sauce. **Serves 4.**

Middle Eastern Turkey Burgers

1 lb	ground turkey	500 g
2 tbsp	grated onion	25 mL
1	small clove garlic, minced	1
2 tbsp	hummus	25 mL
4	kaiser rolls or hamburger buns, split	4
¼ cup	Cucumber Yogurt Sauce (see recipe, page 144)	50 mL

Using your hands, combine turkey, onion, garlic and hummus. Form into patties and cook as described in Great Burgers (page 130). For the last minute of cooking, place rolls on the grill to lightly toast the interior surfaces. Serve burgers on rolls, topped with Cucumber Yogurt Sauce. **Serves 4.**

Chicken Burgers with Mustard and Green Peppercorns

1	slice bread, crust removed, bread crumbled	1
¼ cup	milk	50 mL
1	egg, beaten	1
1½ lbs	ground chicken	750 g
2 tbsp	grated onion	25 mL
1 tbsp	Dijon mustard	15 mL
2 tsp	whole green peppercorns	10 mL

In a bowl, soak bread in milk until milk is absorbed. Add the remaining ingredients and mix with your hands until blended. Form into patties, cook and serve as described in Great Burgers (page 130). **Serves 4.**

Cheesy Chicken Burgers

1	egg, beaten	1
1½ lbs	ground chicken	750 g
2 tbsp	minced onion	25 mL
2	cloves garlic, minced	2
¼ cup	shredded fontina cheese	50 mL
2 tbsp	freshly grated Parmesan cheese	25 mL
2 tbsp	ricotta cheese	25 mL
2 tbsp	seasoned dry bread crumbs	25 mL
1 tbsp	chopped fresh Italian (flat-leaf) parsley	15 mL
1 tbsp	ketchup	15 mL
1 tsp	chopped fresh basil	5 mL

Using your hands, combine all ingredients. Form into patties, cook and serve as described in Great Burgers (page 130). **Serves 4.**

Chicken Burgers Laced with Brandy

1	egg, beaten	1
1½ lbs	ground chicken	750 g
2 tbsp	fresh bread crumbs	25 mL
2 tbsp	chopped shallot	25 mL
1 tbsp	chopped fresh tarragon	15 mL
2 tsp	brandy	10 mL
1 tsp	Dijon mustard	5 mL
Pinch	ground nutmeg	Pinch

Using your hands, combine all ingredients. Form into patties, cook and serve as described in Great Burgers (page 130). **Serves 4.**

Herb Cheese Veal Burgers

¼ cup	herbed cream cheese	50 mL
3	drained canned anchovies, finely chopped	3
1	small clove garlic, minced	1
1½ lbs	ground veal	750 g
⅓ cup	chopped fresh basil	75 mL
¼ cup	freshly grated Parmesan cheese	50 mL
2 tbsp	ice water	25 mL

Divide cheese into 4 nuggets and freeze until solid. Using your hands, combine the remaining ingredients. Form mixture into 4 patties, each molded around a frozen cheese nugget. Cook and serve as described in Great Burgers (page 130). **Serves 4.**

Roasted Pepper Veal Burgers

Follow preceding recipe, but omit the cream cheese nuggets, and add ⅓ cup (75 mL) chopped roasted red bell pepper (see page 11) with the ground veal. **Serves 4.**

Veal Oscar Burgers

Follow recipe for Great Burgers (page 130), but replace the ground beef with ground veal and add ⅓ cup (75 mL) chopped cooked asparagus. Combine ¼ cup (50 mL) mayonnaise and 1 tsp (5 mL) lemon juice. After burgers are cooked, top with mayonnaise mixture and 4 oz (125 g) backfin (lump) crabmeat, shells picked out. **Serves 4.**

Garlic Spinach Lamb Burgers

1	package (10 oz/300 g) frozen chopped spinach, thawed and squeezed dry	1
1	egg, beaten	1
1	clove garlic, minced	1
1½ lbs	ground lamb	750 g
2 tbsp	plain yogurt	25 mL
2 tsp	chopped fresh Italian (flat-leaf) parsley	10 mL

Using your hands, combine all ingredients. Form into patties and cook as described in Great Burgers (page 130). **Serves 4.**

Minted Lamb Burgers

Follow preceding recipe, but omit the spinach and egg, and add 2 tbsp (25 mL) finely chopped mint leaves to the ground lamb. **Serves 4.**

Hoisin Burgers

8 oz	ground turkey	250 g
8 oz	lean ground beef	250 g
3 tbsp	hoisin sauce	45 mL
¼ tsp	ground ginger	1 mL
	Salt and freshly ground black pepper to taste	
¼ cup	teriyaki sauce	50 mL
1 tsp	hot pepper sauce (such as Tabasco)	5 mL
4	hamburger buns, split	4
¼ cup	bean sprouts	50 mL
4	slices tomato	4

Using your hands, combine turkey, beef, hoisin, ginger, salt and pepper. Form into 4 patties, 1 to 1½ inches (2.5 to 4 cm) thick. Combine teriyaki sauce and hot pepper sauce. Grill or pan-fry patties over medium-high heat, turning once, for 5 to 6 minutes per side, or until no longer pink inside. Brush with teriyaki mixture and cook for 1 minute; turn burgers, brush with teriyaki mixture and cook for 1 minute. Serve on buns, topped with bean sprouts and tomato slices. **Serves 4.**

Wasabi Tuna Burgers

3	green onions, finely chopped	3
1½ lbs	tuna steak, trimmed and finely chopped	750 g
1 tsp	prepared wasabi	5 mL
1 tsp	soy sauce	5 mL
1 tbsp	dark sesame oil	15 mL

Combine green onions, tuna, wasabi and soy sauce. Form into 4 patties, 1 to 1½ inches (2.5 to 4 cm) thick, and coat with oil. Broil or grill over a high fire, turning once, until browned on the outside but still rare on the inside, about 2 minutes per side, or until desired doneness. **Serves 4.**

Provençal Tuna Burgers

1½ lbs	tuna steak, trimmed and finely chopped	750 g
¼ cup	finely chopped red onion	50 mL
1 tbsp	tomato paste	15 mL
1 tsp	dried herbes de Provence	5 mL
1 tbsp	extra-virgin olive oil	15 mL

Combine tuna, onion, tomato paste and herbes de Provence. Form into patties, 1 to 1½ inches (2.5 to 4 cm) thick, and coat with oil. Broil or grill over a high fire, turning once, until browned on the outside but still rare on the inside, about 2 minutes per side, or until desired doneness. **Serves 4.**

Hot Dogs with Cumin Mustard

1 tsp	canola oil	5 mL
2 tbsp	minced onion	25 mL
1	clove garlic, minced	1
2 tsp	toasted ground cumin	10 mL
2 tbsp	brown mustard	25 mL
4	frankfurters or knockwurst	4
4	hot dog rolls or small torpedo rolls, split and toasted	4

In a small skillet, heat oil over medium heat. Sauté onion until tender. Add garlic and cumin; sauté for 30 seconds. Remove from heat and stir in mustard. Grill, broil or boil franks until plump and steaming. Place in rolls and spread with cumin mustard. **Serves 4.**

Hot Dogs with Relish Fresca

4	frankfurters or knockwurst	4
¼ cup	sweet pickle relish	50 mL
¼ cup	finely chopped tomato	50 mL
4	hot dog rolls or small torpedo rolls, split and toasted	4

Grill, broil or boil franks until plump and steaming. Meanwhile, combine relish and tomato. Place franks in rolls and spread with relish mixture. **Serves 4.**

Hot Dogs with the Works

4	frankfurters or knockwurst	4
2 tbsp	finely shredded Cheddar cheese	25 mL
1 tbsp	sweet pickle relish	15 mL
1 tbsp	ketchup	15 mL
1 tbsp	spicy brown mustard	15 mL
4	hot dog rolls or small torpedo rolls, split and toasted	4

Grill, broil or boil franks until plump and steaming. Meanwhile, combine cheese, relish, ketchup and mustard. Place franks in rolls and spread with cheese mixture. **Serves 4.**

Piggy Dogs

Follow preceding recipe, but wrap each frank with 1 slice of bacon, securing ends with toothpicks. Grill or broil until bacon is crisp and franks are plump. **Serves 4.**

Hot Dog Wraps

Follow recipe for Hot Dogs with the Works (above), but instead of the rolls, use 6-inch (15 cm) flour tortillas, warmed according to package directions. Spread cheese mixture on warm tortillas. Wrap franks in tortillas. **Serves 4.**

Barbecue-Style Dogs

1 tsp	vegetable oil	5 mL
4	frankfurters or knockwurst	4
⅓ cup	barbecue sauce	75 mL
4	hot dog rolls or small torpedo rolls, split and toasted	4
1 tbsp	spicy brown mustard	15 mL

In a large nonstick skillet, heat oil over medium-high heat. Cook franks until browned on all sides. Add barbecue sauce and roll franks to coat with sauce. Spread the interior of the rolls with mustard and place franks in rolls. Spoon any remaining sauce over top. **Serves 4.**

Sweet-and-Sour Hot Dogs

Follow preceding recipe, but replace the barbecue sauce with store-bought sweet-and-sour sauce or Sweet-and-Sour Cider Sauce (page 52). **Serves 4.**

Chili Cheese Dogs

4	frankfurters or knockwurst	4
½ cup	prepared chili (store-bought or see recipe, page 203)	125 mL
¼ cup	shredded Cheddar cheese	50 mL
4	hot dog rolls or small torpedo rolls, split and toasted	4

Grill, broil or boil franks until plump and steaming. Meanwhile, in a saucepan, heat chili. Stir in cheese and keep warm. Place franks in rolls and top with chili mixture. **Serves 4.**

Hot Dogs Grilled with Bacon and Horseradish Mustard

3 tbsp	Dijon mustard	45 mL
1 tbsp	prepared horseradish	15 mL
8	frankfurters or knockwurst, split	8
8	slices bacon	8
8	hot dog rolls, split and warmed	8
	Additional Dijon mustard	

Combine mustard and horseradish; spread over franks. Wrap each frank with 1 slice of bacon, securing ends with toothpicks. Grill or broil until bacon is crisp and franks are browned. Serve in rolls, with additional mustard on the side. **Serves 8.**

Chicken Franks with Gazpacho Salsa

8	chicken or turkey frankfurters	8
8	hot dog rolls, split	8
2 tbsp	olive oil	25 mL
	Gazpacho Salsa (see recipe, page 177)	

Grill, broil or boil franks until plump and steaming. Meanwhile, brush the interior of the rolls with oil and lightly toast. Place franks in rolls and top with salsa. **Serves 8.**

Chicken Franks with Tomato Artichoke Salsa

Follow preceding recipe, but add 1 clove garlic, minced, to the oil, and replace the Gazpacho Salsa with Tomato and Artichoke Salsa (page 56). **Serves 8.**

Turkey Franks with Tapenade Ketchup

4	turkey frankfurters	4
3 tbsp	ketchup	45 mL
1 tbsp	black olive tapenade (store-bought or see recipe, page 56)	15 mL
4	torpedo rolls, split	4
1 tbsp	extra-virgin olive oil	15 mL

Grill, broil or boil the franks until plump and steaming. Meanwhile, combine ketchup and tapenade. Brush the interior of the rolls with oil and lightly toast. Place franks in rolls and spread with tapenade ketchup. **Serves 4.**

Turkey Sausages with Pesto and Tomato

4	turkey sausages	4
1 tbsp	extra-virgin olive oil	15 mL
4	torpedo rolls, split	4
¼ cup	basil pesto (store-bought or see recipe, page 178), divided	50 mL
1	large tomato, finely chopped	1

Coat sausages with oil and grill or broil until browned, plump and steaming. Meanwhile, brush the interior of the rolls with half the pesto and lightly toast. Combine the remaining pesto and tomato. Place sausages in rolls and top with pesto mixture. **Serves 4.**

Turkey Sausages with Gorgonzola Butter

4	turkey sausages	4
2 tbsp	extra-virgin olive oil, divided	25 mL
1	small clove garlic, minced	1
4	torpedo rolls, split	4
¼ cup	crumbled Gorgonzola cheese	50 mL
1 tbsp	butter	15 mL

Coat sausages with half the oil and grill or broil until browned, plump, and steaming. Meanwhile, combine the remaining oil and garlic. Brush the interior of the rolls with garlic oil and lightly toast. Mash together Gorgonzola and butter. Place sausages in rolls and spread with Gorgonzola butter. **Serves 4.**

Bratwurst with Apple Butter Mustard

4	bratwurst	4
1	small clove garlic, minced	1
3 tbsp	brown mustard, divided	45 mL
2 tbsp	apple butter	25 mL
4	hot dog rolls, split	4

Grill, broil or boil bratwurst until plump and steaming. Meanwhile, combine garlic, 2 tbsp (25 mL) of the mustard and apple butter. Brush the interior of the rolls with the remaining mustard. Place bratwurst in rolls and top with apple butter mustard. **Serves 4.**

Grilled Smoked Sausages with Apple Sauerkraut

2 tbsp	vegetable oil	25 mL
1	Granny Smith apple, peeled and diced	1
1/3 cup	finely chopped onion	75 mL
2 lbs	sauerkraut, washed and drained	1 kg
2 tbsp	packed light brown sugar	25 mL
8	smoked sausage links	8

In a skillet, heat oil over medium heat. Sauté apple and onion until tender. Add sauerkraut and sugar; heat through. Meanwhile, grill or broil sausage until browned and plump. Top sausage with warm apple sauerkraut. **Serves 8.**

Knockwurst Simmered in Beer with Sauerkraut

2	slices bacon, chopped	2
1	onion, sliced	1
2 lbs	sauerkraut, rinsed and drained	1 kg
2 cups	dark beer	500 mL
2 tsp	packed light brown sugar	10 mL
8	knockwurst	8

In a large skillet, cook bacon over medium heat until almost crisp. Add onion, sauerkraut, beer and brown sugar; bring to a boil. Add knockwurst; cover, reduce heat and simmer for about 15 minutes, or until knockwurst is plump and most of the beer has been absorbed. **Serves 8.**

Chicken Sausages over Spinach

1/4 cup	extra-virgin olive oil, divided	50 mL
4	chicken sausages	4
1/2 cup	chopped red onion	125 mL
2	cloves garlic, minced	2
1/4 cup	red wine vinegar	50 mL
1 tbsp	granulated sugar	15 mL
	Salt and freshly ground black pepper to taste	
10 oz	fresh spinach (about 6 cups/1.5 L)	300 g

In a large skillet, heat 1 tbsp (15 mL) of the oil over medium-high heat. Cook sausages until browned on all sides and no longer pink inside; drain on paper towels. Add onion to the oil in the pan and sauté until tender. Stir in garlic and remove from heat. Stir in the remaining oil, vinegar, sugar, salt and pepper. In a bowl, toss spinach with dressing. Serve sausages on a mound of spinach. **Serves 4.**

Chapter 12
Grilling
For the Flavor of Fire

Whole Fish Grilled in Foil
with Vegetables 138

Grilled Salmon Steak
with Lemon and Olive Oil 138

Grilled Salmon Potato Salad 138

Grilled Salmon with Avocado Salsa 139

Mesquite-Grilled Swordfish 139

Grilled Trout with Bacon and Dill 139

Grilled Tuna Salad 139

Grilled Chilied Shrimp 139

Grilled Rosemary Shrimp 140

Grilled Tea-Steamed Clams
and Mussels 140

Scallops Grilled with
Horseradish and Prosciutto 140

Grilled Scallop Kebabs
in Hazelnut Garlic Glaze 140

Grilled Curried Scallops 140

Middle Eastern Grilled Soft-Shell Crabs . . 140

Barbecued Soft-Shell Crabs 141

Chili Grilled Lobster 141

Grilled Turkey Genovese 141

Barbecued Chicken 141

Barbecued Chicken Sandwich 141

Leftover Barbecued Chicken Salad 141

Grilled Chicken Basted with Sage Butter . . 142

Grilled Ranch-Style Chicken Legs 142

Chilled Grilled Creamy Garlic
Chicken Breasts 142

Grilled Chicken Breasts with Pesto 142

Grilled Chicken Breasts
with Roquefort Dressing 142

Grilled Chicken Breasts
with Tomato-Dill Vinaigrette 142

Grilled Chicken Salad 142

Grilled Asian Chicken Salad 143

Grilled Chicken Livers
with Worcestershire Marinade 143

Asian Chicken Paillards 143

Marinated Veal Paillards 143

Mustard-Grilled Veal Chops 143

Veal Chops Stuffed
with Fontina and Sun-Dried Tomato . . . 143

Grilled Veal with Peanut Sauce 144

Grilled Liver with Onions 144

Grilled Steak with Caramelized Garlic . . 144

Grilled Honey-Mustard Pork Chops . . . 144

Grilled Lamb Chops
with Cucumber Yogurt Sauce 144

Grilled Lamb Steak Provençal 144

Lamb and Leek Kebabs 145

Grilled Corn 145

Mushroom Kebabs 145

Grilled Potato Chips 145

Grilled Ratatouille 145

Grilled Maple-Glazed
Breakfast Sausages 145

Grilled Honey Corn Cakes 146

Grilled Pound Cake
with Honey Butter 146

Spiked Bananas Grilled
with Vanilla and Candied Ginger 146

Grilled Brandied Peaches 146

Chocolate Liquor Fondue on a Grill . . . 146

We North Americans are fanatical about grilling, leaving the technology of our kitchens for the primitive facilities of cooking outdoors at the first sign of fair weather. Without ovens to preheat or burners to adjust, we return to our pioneer roots, facing flare-ups and dying embers for the glory of meal preparation over an open fire.

One of the oddest facets of our ardor for grilling is that it's the only form of home cooking considered macho. Not only are most men eager to cook outdoors, they often consider themselves experts in the field, jealously harboring recipes for sauces and techniques to make their grilled foods better than the next guy's. Such culinary one-upmanship has given birth to countless barbecue sauces and grilling tricks, but very few usable recipes.

We've got 50, including some innovative ideas for grilling fish, shellfish, chicken, steaks, chops and sausages. We've even got a few for grilled salads, breakfast breads and desserts. (See Chapter 11, on burgers and hot dogs, for some novel ideas for those favorites.) All the recipes are fast, requiring less than 20 minutes' actual cooking time. Although some call for several hours of marination, this can be done the day before or overnight.

About these recipes . . .

Unfortunately, timing directions for grilled foods can be only approximate. Because many grills do not have a thermostat, exact temperatures are impossible to control. Fires can flare up or die away without warning, so it is imperative to keep a close watch and check the food regularly. It is more important that food be cooked through and properly browned than that it sit over the heat for some prescribed time.

Unless otherwise stated, all items should be grilled 4 to 6 inches (10 to 15 cm) from a high fire. Do not allow the fire to flame uncontrolled. Although some scorching is unavoidable when cooking over an open fire, it's never desirable (unless you're executing a blackening technique). To ensure an even brownness, turn food frequently and move it away from flare-ups when they occur. It helps to keep a spray bottle of water by the grill to douse any flames immediately.

Grilling and broiling are two names for the same technique, so go ahead and adapt any of these grilling recipes for your broiler.

All recipes that call for boneless skinless chicken breasts refer to breast halves.

Whole Fish Grilled in Foil with Vegetables

1	large tomato, cut into 12 thin slices	1
1	navel orange, peeled and sliced	1
1	small chili pepper, minced	1
½	red onion, thinly sliced	½
1	whole lean fish (1½ to 2 lbs/750 g to 1 kg), scaled and gutted	1
	Salt and freshly ground black pepper to taste	
1 tbsp	freshly squeezed lemon juice	15 mL

Place tomatoes, orange, chili pepper and onion on a large sheet of greased foil. Place fish on top and season fish inside and out with salt and pepper. Sprinkle with lemon juice and wrap foil around fish. Grill over a medium fire for 12 to 15 minutes, or until fish is opaque and flakes easily with a fork. **Serves 4.**

Grilled Salmon Steak with Lemon and Olive Oil

¼ cup	extra-virgin olive oil	50 mL
	Juice of ½ lemon	
	Salt and freshly ground black pepper to taste	
4	salmon steaks (1 inch/2.5 cm thick)	4

In a shallow dish, whisk together oil, lemon juice, salt and pepper. Add salmon and turn to coat. Cover and refrigerate for 1 hour, turning halfway through. Remove salmon from marinade and discard marinade. Grill salmon, turning once, for 4 minutes per side, or until fish is opaque and flakes easily with a fork. **Serves 4.**

Grilled Salmon Potato Salad

6 tbsp	mayonnaise	90 mL
2 tbsp	chopped fresh herbs (such as flat-leaf parsley or dill)	25 mL
1 tbsp	red wine vinegar	15 mL
	Salt and freshly ground black pepper to taste	
2	russet potatoes, cut into 1-inch (2.5 cm) thick slices	2
2 tbsp	vegetable oil	25 mL
4	salmon steaks (1 inch/2.5 cm thick)	4
	Olive oil	
	Lettuce (optional)	

Combine mayonnaise, herbs, vinegar, salt and pepper; set aside. Brush potato slices with vegetable oil and grill, turning once, for 4 to 5 minutes per side, or until browned and cooked through. Meanwhile, rub salmon with olive oil. After potatoes have grilled for 2 minutes, add salmon to the grill and cook, turning once, for 3 to 4 minutes per side, or until fish is opaque and flakes easily with a fork. Flake salmon into small pieces, trimming away skin and bones. Cut potato slices into quarters. In a bowl, toss fish and potatoes with reserved mayonnaise mixture. Serve on a bed of lettuce or as a sandwich filling. **Serves 4.**

Grilled Salmon with Avocado Salsa

2	green onions, finely chopped	2
1	large avocado, diced	1
1	large tomato, chopped	1
1	clove garlic, minced	1
1/3 cup	freshly squeezed lemon juice, divided	75 mL
2 tsp	chopped fresh Italian (flat-leaf) parsley	10 mL
	Salt and hot pepper flakes to taste	
4	salmon steaks (1 inch/2.5 cm thick)	4
1 tbsp	olive oil	15 mL
	Freshly ground black pepper to taste	

Make salsa by combining green onions, avocado, tomato, garlic, 3 tbsp (45 mL) of the lemon juice, parsley, salt and hot pepper flakes. Cover and refrigerate while grilling salmon. Rub salmon with the remaining lemon juice, oil, additional salt and black pepper. Grill, turning once, for 4 to 5 minutes per side, or until fish is opaque and flakes easily with a fork. Serve with dollops of salsa. **Serves 4.**

Mesquite-Grilled Swordfish

4	cloves garlic, minced	4
1	bay leaf, crumbled	1
Pinch	dried oregano	Pinch
1/3 cup	olive oil	75 mL
4	swordfish steaks (about 1 inch/2.5 cm thick)	4
	Juice of 1 large lemon	
	Salt and freshly ground black pepper to taste	

Soak 4 or 5 chunks of mesquite in enough water to cover for at least 30 minutes. Meanwhile, in a small saucepan, heat garlic, bay leaf, oregano and oil over medium-low heat until oil is warm. Pour into a dish large enough to hold swordfish in a single layer and add lemon juice, salt and pepper. Let cool. Add swordfish and turn to coat. Cover and refrigerate for 30 minutes. Prepare grill by heating a bed of charcoal briquettes until they are white with ash. Place mesquite on the hot coals, and heat until wood starts to smoke vigorously. Remove swordfish from marinade, shake to remove excess marinade, and discard marinade. Grill swordfish, covered, turning once, for 4 to 5 minutes per side, or until fish is opaque and flakes easily with a fork. **Serves 4.**

Grilled Trout with Bacon and Dill

4	whole brook trout (each about 8 oz/250 g), scaled and bones removed	4
	Salt and freshly ground black pepper to taste	
4	sprigs fresh dill	4
4	slices bacon	4

Season trout inside and out with salt and pepper. Place 1 sprig of dill in the cavity of each fish, and wrap 1 slice of bacon around the outside. Grill, turning once, for 4 to 5 minutes per side, or until bacon is cooked and trout is opaque and flakes easily with a fork. **Serves 4.**

Grilled Tuna Salad

4	tuna steaks (1 inch/2.5 cm thick)	4
	Olive oil	
	Salt and freshly ground black pepper to taste	
2	green onions, thinly sliced	2
2	stalks celery, chopped	2
1 tbsp	chopped fresh Italian (flat-leaf) parsley	15 mL
6 tbsp	mayonnaise	90 mL
	Juice of 1/2 lemon	
	Lettuce (optional)	

Rub tuna with a thin film of oil and season with salt and pepper. Grill, turning once, for 3 to 4 minutes per side, or until tuna is opaque. Flake tuna into small pieces, trimming away any skin. Combine tuna, green onions, celery, parsley, mayonnaise and lemon juice. Serve on a bed of lettuce or as a sandwich filling. **Serves 4.**

Grilled Chilied Shrimp

1/4 cup	olive oil	50 mL
1 tbsp	Chinese chili paste with garlic	15 mL
1 tsp	soy sauce	5 mL
1 lb	jumbo shrimp, peeled and deveined	500 g

In a shallow dish, whisk together oil, chili paste and soy sauce. Add shrimp and turn to coat. Cover and refrigerate for 1 hour. Remove shrimp from marinade and discard marinade. Grill shrimp over a medium-high fire, turning once, for about 2 minutes per side, or until shrimp are pink and opaque. **Serves 4.**

Grilled Rosemary Shrimp

2	cloves garlic, minced	2
¼ cup	olive oil	50 mL
1 tbsp	crushed fresh rosemary	15 mL
	Salt and freshly ground black pepper to taste	
1 lb	jumbo shrimp, peeled and deveined	500 g
6	branches fresh rosemary	6

In a shallow dish, whisk together garlic, oil, crushed rosemary, salt and pepper. Add shrimp and turn to coat. Cover and refrigerate for 1 hour. Place rosemary branches on the hot coals of a charcoal fire. Remove shrimp from marinade and discard marinade. Grill shrimp, covered, turning once, for about 2 minutes per side, or until shrimp are pink and opaque. **Serves 4.**

Grilled Tea-Steamed Clams and Mussels

½ cup	loose black tea leaves	125 mL
1 cup	boiling water	250 mL
24	clams, scrubbed (see page 8)	24
24	mussels, scrubbed (see page 8)	24

Steep tea leaves in boiling water for 10 minutes. Place clams in a disposable aluminum roasting pan. Drain tea leaves and place on the hot coals of a charcoal fire. Place the pan of clams in the center of the grill, cover grill and cook for 2 minutes. Add mussels to the roasting pan, cover grill and cook for 3 to 5 minutes, until all shells have opened. (Discard any that do not open.) **Serves 4.**

Scallops Grilled with Horseradish and Prosciutto

1	clove garlic, minced	1
3 tbsp	canola oil	45 mL
2 tbsp	prepared horseradish	25 mL
	Juice of ½ lemon	
	Salt and freshly ground black pepper to taste	
1 lb	sea scallops, trimmed of hard side muscles	500 g
4 oz	prosciutto, thinly sliced and cut into ½-inch (1 cm) wide strips	125 g

In a nonmetallic bowl, whisk together garlic, oil, horseradish, lemon juice, salt and pepper. Add scallops and turn to coat. Cover and refrigerate for 30 minutes. Soak toothpicks and wooden skewers (if using) in water for at least 30 minutes. Remove scallops from marinade and discard marinade. Wrap each scallop with 1 strip of prosciutto and secure with a toothpick (or thread onto skewers, 3 scallops per skewer). Grill, turning often, for about 8 minutes, or until browned and almost firm in the center. **Serves 4.**

Grilled Scallop Kebabs in Hazelnut Garlic Glaze

Follow preceding recipe but, for the marinade, combine 1 clove garlic, minced, 3 tbsp (45 mL) mayonnaise, 1 tbsp (15 mL) finely ground toasted hazelnuts, 1 tbsp (15 mL) freshly squeezed lemon juice, and salt and pepper to taste. Garnish finished dish with 1 tbsp (15 mL) finely chopped toasted hazelnuts. **Serves 4.**

Grilled Curried Scallops

3 tbsp	canola oil	45 mL
2 tbsp	minced onion	25 mL
1 tbsp	curry powder	15 mL
1 tsp	ground coriander	5 mL
2 tsp	orange marmalade	10 mL
Pinch	cayenne pepper	Pinch
	Salt to taste	
1 lb	sea scallops, trimmed of hard side muscles	500 g

In a small saucepan, heat oil over medium-low heat. Sauté onion, curry powder and coriander until onion is tender. Stir in marmalade, cayenne and salt. Transfer to a bowl, let cool and toss with scallops. Cover and refrigerate for 1 hour. Remove scallops from marinade and discard marinade. Grill scallops, turning often, for about 8 minutes, or until browned and almost firm in the center. **Serves 4.**

Middle Eastern Grilled Soft-Shell Crabs

1 cup	plain yogurt	250 mL
2	cloves garlic, minced	2
¼ cup	minced onion	50 mL
3 tbsp	chopped fresh mint	45 mL
1 tbsp	chopped fresh Italian (flat-leaf) parsley	15 mL
	Juice of ½ lemon	
8	live soft-shell crabs, prepared (see page 11)	8

In a large bowl, combine yogurt, garlic, onion, mint, parsley and lemon juice. Add crabs, making sure they are completely covered with marinade. Cover and refrigerate for 30 minutes. Remove crabs from marinade and discard marinade. Grill crabs, turning once, for 3 to 4 minutes per side, or until crab is opaque. **Serves 4.**

Barbecued Soft-Shell Crabs

Follow preceding recipe but, for the marinade, sauté 1 small onion, chopped, and 1 clove garlic, minced, in 1 tbsp (15 mL) corn oil until softened. Transfer to a large bowl and stir in ½ cup (125 mL) ketchup, 2 tbsp (25 mL) cider vinegar, 1 tsp (5 mL) brown mustard, 1 tsp (5 mL) Worcestershire sauce, 1 tsp (5 mL) hot pepper sauce (such as Tabasco) and the juice of ½ lemon. **Serves 4.**

Chili Grilled Lobster

4	small live lobsters	4
3 tbsp	olive oil	45 mL
¼ cup	Chinese chili paste	50 mL
2 tbsp	Thai fish sauce (*nam pla*)	25 mL
1 tbsp	soy sauce	15 mL
1 tbsp	finely grated gingerroot	15 mL

Kill lobsters by splitting them in half lengthwise with a large, sharp knife, starting at the head and working toward the tail. Scrape out the tomalley from the carapace. Rub exposed meat with 2 tbsp (25 mL) of the oil. Place shell side down on grill and cook for 4 minutes. Turn and grill for 4 minutes, or until meat is opaque and shells are bright red. Meanwhile, whisk together chili paste, fish sauce, soy sauce, the remaining oil and ginger. Serve lobster with sauce on the side for dipping. **Serves 4.**

Grilled Turkey Genovese

2 oz	canned anchovies, with their oil	60 g
1	small clove garlic, minced	1
¼ cup	mayonnaise	50 mL
2 tbsp	olive oil	25 mL
	Freshly ground black pepper to taste	
4	turkey cutlets (each about 5 oz/150 g)	4

In a food processor, purée anchovies and the oil clinging to them. Stir in garlic, mayonnaise, oil and pepper. Rub each turkey cutlet with 1 tbsp (15 mL) of this sauce. Grill turkey, turning once, for 2 to 3 minutes per side, or until no longer pink inside. Serve with the remaining sauce. **Serves 4.**

Barbecued Chicken

¾ cup	ketchup	175 mL
¼ cup	grated onion	50 mL
2 tbsp	cider vinegar	25 mL
1 tbsp	brown mustard	15 mL
1 tbsp	Worcestershire sauce	15 mL
1 tbsp	dark (cooking) molasses	15 mL
1 tbsp	hot pepper sauce (such as Tabasco)	15 mL
3 lbs	chicken pieces	1.5 kg

In a small saucepan, combine ketchup, onion, vinegar, mustard, Worcestershire sauce, molasses and hot pepper sauce; bring to a simmer. Let cool. Place chicken in a shallow dish and brush with half the sauce, coating evenly. Reserve remaining sauce. Cover chicken and refrigerate for 1 hour. Remove chicken from sauce; wipe off excess sauce and discard. Grill chicken over a medium fire, turning frequently and basting with reserved sauce after the last two turns, until browned and juices run clear when chicken is pierced — about 20 minutes for drumsticks, thighs or wings, 30 minutes for breasts. **Serves 4.**

Barbecued Chicken Sandwich

Follow preceding recipe, but use 4 boneless skinless chicken breasts. Grill breasts for 4 to 5 minutes per side, or until no longer pink inside. Serve hot on 4 kaiser rolls, with coleslaw if desired. **Serves 4.**

Leftover Barbecued Chicken Salad

2	slices bacon, finely chopped	2
½	small onion, minced	½
1	clove garlic, chopped	1
1 tbsp	granulated sugar	15 mL
3 tbsp	cider vinegar	45 mL
2 tsp	Worcestershire sauce	10 mL
¼ tsp	hot pepper sauce (such as Tabasco)	1 mL
	Salt and freshly ground black pepper to taste	
1	roasted red bell pepper (see page 11), diced	1
1	green onion, chopped	1
½	head romaine lettuce, torn into bite-size pieces	½
1 to 1½ lbs	leftover barbecued chicken meat (3 to 4 cups/750 mL to 1 L)	500 to 750 g
2 oz	mushrooms, sliced	60 g

In a skillet, cook bacon over medium heat until crisp. Add onion and sauté until tender. Add garlic and sauté for 10 seconds. Stir in sugar, vinegar, Worcestershire sauce, hot pepper sauce, salt and pepper. Transfer to a serving bowl and toss with roasted pepper, green onion, romaine, chicken and mushrooms. **Serves 4.**

Grilled Chicken Basted with Sage Butter

½ cup	chicken broth	125 mL
2 tbsp	dried sage	25 mL
½ cup	salted butter, cut into small pieces	125 mL
	Freshly ground black pepper to taste	
3 lbs	chicken pieces	1.5 kg

In a small saucepan, bring broth and sage to a boil over medium-high heat; boil until reduced by about three-quarters. Reduce heat to low and swirl in butter, a few pieces at a time, until a smooth sauce forms. Season with pepper. Brush chicken with sage butter, coating evenly. Grill over a medium-high fire, turning frequently and basting with sage butter after each turn, until browned and juices run clear when chicken is pierced — about 20 minutes for drumsticks, thighs or wings, 30 minutes for breasts. **Serves 4.**

Grilled Ranch-Style Chicken Legs

8	chicken legs	8
1 cup	ranch dressing, divided	250 mL

Place chicken in a shallow dish and brush with half the dressing, coating evenly. Cover and refrigerate for 1 hour. Remove chicken from marinade and discard marinade. Grill chicken over medium-high heat, turning frequently and basting with the remaining dressing after each turn, for 20 to 25 minutes, or until juices run clear when chicken is pierced. **Serves 4.**

Chilled Grilled Creamy Garlic Chicken Breasts

2 tbsp	mayonnaise	25 mL
	Salt and freshly ground black pepper to taste	
4	boneless skinless chicken breasts	4
¼ cup	Garlic Ranch Dressing (see recipe, page 64)	50 mL

Combine mayonnaise, salt and pepper; rub over chicken. Grill over a medium-high fire, turning once, for 4 to 5 minutes per side, or until no longer pink inside. While still warm, toss with dressing. Cover and refrigerate until chilled. **Serves 4.**

Grilled Chicken Breasts with Pesto

4	bone-in chicken breasts	4
½ cup	pesto (store-bought or see recipe, page 178)	125 mL
2 tsp	olive oil	10 mL

Make a pocket in the center of each chicken breast. Place 2 tsp (10 mL) pesto inside each breast and rub with ½ tsp (2 mL) olive oil. Grill over a medium-high fire, turning once, for 8 to 10 minutes per side, or until no longer pink inside. Serve dolloped with the remaining pesto. **Serves 4.**

Grilled Chicken Breasts with Roquefort Dressing

4	boneless skinless chicken breasts	4
½ cup	Roquefort cheese dressing (store-bought or see recipe, page 64)	125 mL
2 tbsp	buttermilk	25 mL

Pound chicken to ⅜-inch (0.75 cm) thickness. Grill, turning once, for 3 to 4 minutes per side, or until no longer pink inside. Thin dressing with buttermilk and serve with chicken. **Serves 4.**

Grilled Chicken Breasts with Tomato-Dill Vinaigrette

2	large tomatoes, seeded and finely chopped	2
1	clove garlic, minced	1
½	red onion, finely chopped	½
¼ cup	chopped fresh dill	50 mL
¼ cup	olive oil, divided	50 mL
3 tbsp	red wine vinegar	45 mL
	Salt and freshly ground black pepper to taste	
4	boneless skinless chicken breasts	4

Combine tomatoes, garlic, onion, dill, half the oil, vinegar, salt and pepper; set aside. Pound chicken to ⅜-inch (0.75 cm) thickness and coat with the remaining oil. Grill over a medium-high fire, turning once, for 3 to 4 minutes per side or until no longer pink inside. Serve with vinaigrette. **Serves 4.**

Grilled Chicken Salad

4	boneless skinless chicken breasts	4
¼ cup	olive oil, divided	50 mL
	Salt and freshly ground black pepper to taste	
2 tbsp	red wine vinegar	25 mL
¼ cup	chopped red onion	50 mL
2 tbsp	drained capers	25 mL
	Lettuce	

Rub chicken with 2 tsp (10 mL) of the oil and season with salt and pepper. Grill over a medium-high fire, turning once, for 4 to 5 minutes per side, or until no longer pink inside. Cut into chunks. In a serving bowl, whisk together the remaining oil and vinegar. Add chicken, onion and capers; toss to coat. Serve over lettuce. **Serves 4.**

Grilled Asian Chicken Salad

4	boneless skinless chicken breasts	4
1/4 cup	canola oil, divided	50 mL
	Salt and freshly ground black pepper to taste	
1	clove garlic, minced	1
1 tbsp	finely grated gingerroot	15 mL
2 tbsp	reduced-sodium soy sauce	25 mL
2 tbsp	rice vinegar	25 mL
1 tbsp	dark sesame oil	15 mL
Pinch	cayenne pepper	Pinch
2	green onions, chopped	2
1	tangerine or clementine, peeled and broken into segments	1
1 tbsp	toasted sesame seeds	15 mL
	Lettuce	

Rub chicken with half the canola oil and season with salt and black pepper. Grill over a medium-high fire, turning once, for 4 to 5 minutes per side, or until no longer pink inside. Cut into chunks. In a serving bowl, whisk together the remaining canola oil, garlic, ginger, soy sauce, vinegar, sesame oil, cayenne and additional salt and black pepper. Add chicken, green onions, tangerine and sesame seeds; toss to coat. Serve over lettuce. **Serves 4.**

Grilled Chicken Livers with Worcestershire Marinade

1/4 cup	Worcestershire sauce	50 mL
1 tbsp	dark (cooking) molasses	15 mL
1 tbsp	spicy brown mustard	15 mL
1 lb	chicken livers, trimmed	500 g

Combine Worcestershire sauce, molasses and mustard. Set half aside. Place chicken livers in a shallow dish and brush with half the marinade, coating evenly. Cover livers and refrigerate for 20 minutes. Remove livers from marinade and discard marinade. Thread livers onto skewers, 3 to 4 livers per skewer, and grill over a medium-high fire, turning frequently and basting with the reserved marinade after each turn, for 2 to 3 minutes per side, or until firm. **Serves 4.**

Asian Chicken Paillards

4	boneless skinless chicken breasts	4
1/3 cup	Soy Ginger Dressing (see recipe, page 63)	75 mL

Rub each chicken breast with 1 tsp (5 mL) dressing and pound between sheets of plastic wrap to 1/8-inch (3 mm) thickness. Remove from plastic and cook on an oiled grill grate set as close as possible to a red-hot charcoal fire, turning once, for 30 to 60 seconds per side, or until no longer pink inside. Serve drizzled with the remaining dressing. **Serves 4.**

Marinated Veal Paillards

Follow preceding recipe, but substitute 4 veal scallops (each about 6 oz/175 g), for the chicken, and use Classic Caesar Dressing (page 62) instead of Soy Ginger Dressing. **Serves 4.**

Mustard-Grilled Veal Chops

1	clove garlic, minced	1
3 tbsp	whole-grain Dijon mustard	45 mL
1 tbsp	olive oil	15 mL
	Salt and freshly ground black pepper to taste	
4	veal chops (1 inch/2.5 cm thick)	4

In a shallow dish, whisk together garlic, mustard, oil, salt and pepper. Add veal chops and turn to coat. Grill over a medium-high fire, turning once, for 4 to 5 minutes per side, or until browned and resilient to the touch. **Serves 4.**

Veal Chops Stuffed with Fontina and Sun-Dried Tomato

4	veal chops (1 inch/2.5 cm thick)	4
4	sun-dried tomatoes, packed in olive oil	4
4	thin strips fontina cheese	4
	Additional oil from tomatoes	

Cut a small pocket in the side of each veal chop and stuff each chop with 1 sun-dried tomato and a strip of cheese. Rub exterior of chops with oil from the tomatoes. Grill over a medium-high fire, turning once, for 4 to 5 minutes per side, or until browned and resilient to the touch. **Serves 4.**

Grilled Veal with Peanut Sauce

8	veal scallops (each about 3 oz/90 g)	8
1 tbsp	sesame oil	15 mL
¾ cup	Peanut Sauce (see recipe, page 53), made with yogurt	175 mL

Pound veal scallops to ¼-inch (0.5 cm) thickness and brush with oil. Grill, turning once, for 2 to 3 minutes per side, or until cooked through. Serve topped with Peanut Sauce. **Serves 4.**

Grilled Liver with Onions

2 tbsp	butter	25 mL
2 tbsp	olive oil	25 mL
1	large onion, thinly sliced	1
12 oz	calf's liver, cut into ⅜-inch (0.75 cm) thick slices	375 g
	Salt and freshly ground black pepper to taste	

In a skillet, heat butter and oil over medium-low heat. Sauté onion until golden brown; set aside. Brush liver slices with fat from the pan and season with salt and pepper. Grill over a medium-high fire, turning once, for 2 to 3 minutes per side, or until browned and barely firm in the center. Serve with onions. **Serves 4.**

Grilled Steak with Caramelized Garlic

½ cup	butter	125 mL
2	heads garlic, broken into cloves and peeled	2
1 tbsp	granulated sugar	15 mL
1 tbsp	brandy	15 mL
	Salt to taste	
4	boneless sirloin strip steaks (each about 8 oz/250 g)	4
	Freshly ground black pepper to taste	
2 tsp	minced garlic	10 mL

In a small skillet, melt butter over medium-low heat. Sauté garlic cloves until golden brown. Stir in sugar and cook, stirring often, until mixture darkens slightly. Add brandy and salt; set aside. Season steaks with minced garlic, salt and pepper. Grill, turning once, to desired doneness. Serve topped with caramelized garlic. **Serves 4.**

Grilled Honey-Mustard Pork Chops

8	thin boneless pork chops	8
	Salt and freshly ground black pepper to taste	
3 tbsp	spicy brown mustard	45 mL
3 tbsp	honey	45 mL

Season pork with salt and pepper. Combine mustard and honey; brush onto pork chops, coating evenly. Grill over a medium-high fire, turning once, for 2 to 3 minutes per side, or until just a hint of pink remains in pork. **Serves 4.**

Grilled Lamb Chops with Cucumber Yogurt Sauce

Cucumber Yogurt Sauce

1	large cucumber, peeled, halved, seeded and thinly sliced	1
1 tsp	kosher salt	5 mL
1 cup	low-fat plain yogurt	250 mL
1 tbsp	chopped fresh mint	15 mL
2 tbsp	extra-virgin olive oil, divided	25 mL
	Juice of ½ lemon	
	Salt and freshly ground black pepper to taste	
8	lamb rib or loin chops (about 1 inch/2.5 cm thick)	8
Pinch	ground coriander	Pinch

Prepare the Cucumber Yogurt Sauce: Toss cucumber slices with kosher salt; let stand for 15 minutes. Rinse well and squeeze dry. Combine cucumber, yogurt, mint, half the oil, lemon juice, salt and pepper; set aside. Rub lamb with the remaining oil and season with coriander. Grill, turning once, for 3 to 4 minutes per side for medium-rare, or until desired doneness. Serve with Cucumber Yogurt Sauce. **Serves 4.**

Grilled Lamb Steak Provençal

2	cloves garlic, chopped	2
1	onion, minced	1
½ cup	finely diced drained canned tomatoes	125 mL
⅓ cup	extra-virgin olive oil	75 mL
1 tbsp	dried herbes de Provence	15 mL
8	boneless lamb leg slices (½ inch/1 cm thick)	8
	Salt and freshly ground black pepper to taste	

Combine garlic, onion, tomatoes, oil and herbes de Provence. Place lamb in a shallow dish, season with salt and pepper, and pour in half the marinade, turning lamb to coat. Reserve remaining marinade. Cover lamb and refrigerate for 1 to 2 hours. Remove lamb from marinade and discard marinade. Grill over a medium-high fire, turning frequently and basting with reserved marinade after each turn, for 4 to 5 minutes per side for medium-rare, or until desired doneness. **Serves 4.**

Lamb and Leek Kebabs

2	cloves garlic, minced	2
1	bay leaf, crumbled	1
¼ cup	chopped fresh basil	50 mL
3 tbsp	extra-virgin olive oil	45 mL
2 tbsp	red wine vinegar	25 mL
1 tbsp	tomato paste	15 mL
	Salt and freshly ground black pepper to taste	
1½ lbs	boneless leg of lamb, trimmed and cut into 1-inch (2.5 cm) cubes	750 g
4	leeks, white parts only, cut into 2-inch (5 cm) segments	4

Combine garlic, bay leaf, basil, oil, vinegar, tomato paste, salt and pepper. In a large bowl, toss lamb with half the marinade. Reserve remaining marinade. Cover lamb and refrigerate for 3 to 5 hours. Thread 3 pieces of lamb alternately with 2 pieces of leek onto each of four 12-inch (30 cm) skewers. Grill over a medium fire, turning every 5 minutes and basting with reserved marinade after each turn, for 12 to 15 minutes, or until browned and lamb is desired doneness. **Serves 4.**

Grilled Corn

8	ears corn (unhusked)	8
	Butter	
	Salt and freshly ground black pepper to taste	

Grill corn over a medium-high fire in a covered grill, turning every 3 to 4 minutes, for 15 minutes, or until husks are charred and kernels are tender. Let cool for 2 minutes, then remove husks and silks. Serve with butter, salt and pepper. **Serves 4.**

Mushroom Kebabs

2	cloves garlic, minced	2
¼ cup	extra-virgin olive oil	50 mL
2 tbsp	chopped chives	25 mL
1 tsp	dried thyme	5 mL
Pinch	hot pepper flakes	Pinch
	Juice of 1 lemon	
	Salt to taste	
16	large mushrooms, stem ends trimmed	16

In a bowl, whisk together garlic, oil, chives, thyme, hot pepper flakes, lemon juice and salt. Add mushrooms, cover and refrigerate for 1 hour. Thread mushrooms onto skewers, 3 to 4 per skewer, leaving at least ¼ inch (0.5 cm) between each. Grill over a medium fire, turning every 3 minutes and basting with marinade after each turn, for 9 minutes, or until uniformly browned. **Serves 4.**

Grilled Potato Chips

1½ lbs	russet potatoes, sliced paper-thin	750 g
	Vegetable oil	
	Salt	

Dip potato slices in oil and grill over a medium-high fire, turning once, for 3 to 4 minutes per side, or until brown and crispy. Dust with salt. **Serves 4.**

Grilled Ratatouille

12	large mushroom caps	12
2	leeks, white parts only, cut into 2-inch (5 cm) segments	2
2	large tomatoes, thickly sliced	2
1	large zucchini, cut into 1-inch (2.5 cm) thick slices	1
1	eggplant, peeled and cut into 3- by ½-inch (7.5 by 1 cm) batons	1
1	red onion, thickly sliced	1
½ cup	olive oil	125 mL
	Salt and freshly ground black pepper to taste	
	Garlic Vinaigrette (see recipe, page 56)	

Toss mushroom caps, leeks, tomatoes, zucchini, eggplant and onion in olive oil until well coated; season with salt and pepper. Grill vegetables over a medium-high fire, turning each several times while it cooks, until browned and tender: cook leeks for 8 to 10 minutes; mushrooms, onion and eggplant for 5 to 7 minutes; zucchini and tomatoes for 3 to 4 minutes. Arrange vegetables on a large platter and serve with Garlic Vinaigrette. **Serves 4.**

Grilled Maple-Glazed Breakfast Sausages

12	breakfast sausages	12
¼ cup	pure maple syrup	50 mL

Grill sausages over a medium-high fire, turning every 2 minutes, for 8 minutes, or until browned on all sides. Brush each sausage with 1 tsp (5 mL) maple syrup, cover grill and cook for 1 minute, until sausages are no longer pink inside. **Serves 4.**

Grilled Honey Corn Cakes

¼ cup	butter, softened	50 mL
2 tsp	honey	10 mL
8	corn toaster cakes (or 8 slices cornbread)	8

Combine butter and honey; brush on each side of toaster cakes. Grill over a medium fire, turning once, for 1 minute per side, or until lightly browned. Serve warm with the remaining honey-butter on the side. **Serves 4.**

Grilled Pound Cake with Honey Butter

½ cup	unsalted butter, softened	125 mL
¼ cup	honey	50 mL
8	slices pound cake	8
6 tbsp	melted unsalted butter	90 mL
	Fresh fruit	

Combine softened butter and honey; set aside. Brush cake with melted butter and grill over a medium fire, turning once, for about 90 seconds per side, or until lightly browned. Serve with honey-butter and fresh fruit. **Serves 4.**

Spiked Bananas Grilled with Vanilla and Candied Ginger

4	bananas, peeled	4
1	vanilla bean, cut into 4 pieces	1
4 tsp	chopped candied ginger	20 mL
¼ cup	orange-flavored liqueur	50 mL
4 tsp	butter	20 mL
4 tsp	honey	20 mL
	Ice cream	

Place each banana on an 8-inch (20 cm) square piece of foil. Place a piece of vanilla bean and 1 tsp (5 mL) ginger next to each banana. Drizzle each with 1 tbsp (15 mL) liqueur, 1 tsp (5 mL) butter and 1 tsp (5 mL) honey. Wrap each piece of foil around its contents and seal tightly. Grill over a medium fire for 5 minutes. Serve over ice cream. **Serves 4.**

Grilled Brandied Peaches

Follow preceding recipe, but replace each banana with 1 peach, quartered, peeled and pitted, and substitute brandy for the liqueur. **Serves 4.**

Chocolate Liquor Fondue on a Grill

½ cup	cream (any type, minimum 10%)	125 mL
1 tbsp	instant coffee granules	15 mL
8 oz	semisweet chocolate, finely chopped	250 g
¼ cup	rum or brandy	50 mL
	Fruit pieces, pound cake fingers or butter cookies	

In a small saucepan, bring cream and coffee to a boil over a low charcoal fire. Move pot to the edge of the fire and whisk in chocolate, then stir in rum. Keep warm by the side of the fire while guests dip fruit, cake or cookies into the pot using long skewers or fondue forks. **Serves 4.**

Chapter 13
Frying-Pan Cuisine
For Dinner Right Now

Seafood Provençal 148
Skillet Bouillabaisse 149
Shrimp with Vodka, Tomatoes
and Cream 149
Cajun Shrimp 149
Poached Chicken Breasts
with Warm Tomato Vinaigrette 149
Salmon Provençal 149
Chicken with Sausage and Clams 150
Chicken and Shrimp
in Garlic Black Bean Sauce 150
Chipotle Turkey 150
Thai Turkey Salad 150
Stir-Fried Thai Shrimp 150
Sautéed Turkey with Apple Glaze 151
Orange Hoisin Turkey 151
Stir-Fried Chicken with Cashews 151
Chicken with Lemon and Capers 151
Lemon Mushroom Turkey 151
Lime Cilantro Black Bean Chicken 151
Deviled Chicken Breasts 152
Garlic Hazelnut Chicken 152
Stuffing-Crusted Chicken Breasts
with Sage Butter 152
Chicken with Lime Avocado Relish 152
Chicken with Sun-Dried Tomato
Rouille 152
Sage and Rosemary Chicken Breast
Meunière 153
Sesame Chicken Breasts 153
Marinated Chicken Paillards 153

Chicken Paillards with Artichoke Pesto . . 153
"Grilled" Chicken Anchoiade 153
"Grilled" Chicken Breasts
with Herbed Blue Cheese Dressing 154
Pan-Barbecued Chicken Breasts 154
Pan-Barbecued Chicken Sandwiches . . 154
Pan-Seared Chicken Breasts
with Tomato Dill Salsa 154
Three-Olive Chicken 154
Chicken Braised with Cider 154
Chicken Braised with Spicy
Peanut Sauce 155
Chicken Braised with Red Wine
and Mushrooms 155
Thai Chicken 155
Chicken Chicharrones 156
Mahogany Chicken 156
Quick Chicken Chili 156
Garlic Chicken Sausage
over Spinach 156
Chipotle Cherry Pork 156
Spicy Peachy Chicken 157
Pork Chops with Bourbon Reduction . . 157
Pork Tacos 157
Vegetarian Tacos 157
Ground Chicken Fajitas 157
Pork Chops with Caramelized Onions . . 157
Veal with Melted Leeks 158
Sautéed Veal with Chardonnay
and Basil 158
Veal Marsala 158

If we could have only one cooking vessel in which to make everything we ate for the rest of our lives, the choice would be easy: a frying pan. It would have to be large enough to hold food for the whole family, heavy enough to distribute heat evenly without scorching, and deep enough to hold a sauce without spilling over. But that's about it. In it, we would make pancakes, sausage, ham and eggs, grilled cheese sandwiches, tacos, quesadillas, chilies, stir-fries and chicken every which way, whether fried, roasted, poached or sautéed.

A good skillet is a busy cook's best friend, not just for its versatility, but for its speed and ease. It is the pan of choice for browning meat and making a sauce right in the pan, a method that allows you to get dinner on the table, in most cases, in less than 15 minutes, dirtying only a single pan in the process.

Although you could get by with just one good frying pan in your collection, we suggest two: a 10- or 12-inch (25 or 30 cm) nonstick skillet for making eggs and sautéing delicate ingredients, and a large cast-iron skillet with a tight-fitting lid for cooking everything else. The good thing about iron is that it can go from stove to oven, and it's so heavy that you are guaranteed even cooking. The downside is also its weight — it's so heavy that you might not be able to lift it once it's full of food. If that's a potential problem, a heavy-gauge anodized aluminum pan would be a fine alternative.

For the most part, stay away from pure stainless steel for skillets. The metal does not transfer heat well, and it is so expensive that pure stainless steel cookware is usually made so thin that the pans scorch before the food browns. Pans made from other metals and lined with stainless steel perform better. They are easy to clean, they don't react with acidic foods the way aluminum does, and because they are really copper and/or aluminum pans coated with stainless steel, they are good at transferring heat. The only downside is that they can be frightfully expensive.

In the world of frying pans, size matters. You might think an 8-inch (20 cm) skillet will do, and if you are cooking for one or two, that's true. But for four portions of anything, you'll need at least 10 inches (25 cm) of cooking surface, and preferably 12 inches (30 cm). When you brown ingredients in a skillet, it's important to have ample space between each piece of food. As an ingredient heats, it releases its juices, which run into the pan

and form steam. If the liquid gets trapped between pieces of food, it will not evaporate, and as long as there is moisture sitting around your ingredients, they will not brown. Once everything is browned, it is fine to add broth or another flavorful liquid to finish the cooking and create a sauce.

About these recipes . . .

The 50 recipes that follow cover everything from fish to fowl to meat. Most include an easy pan sauce, and all but a few can be made in less than 20 minutes.

. . . .

Seafood Provençal

1 lb	large shrimp, peeled and deveined	500 g
1 lb	sea scallops, trimmed of hard side muscles	500 g
	Salt and freshly ground black pepper to taste	
¼ cup	extra-virgin olive oil, divided	50 mL
8 oz	backfin (lump) crabmeat, shells picked out	250 g
1	red bell pepper, chopped	1
½ cup	chopped onion	125 mL
2	cloves garlic, minced	2
1 tsp	dried basil	5 mL
1 tsp	dried herbes de Provence	5 mL
1 cup	dry white wine	250 mL
1 cup	canned diced tomatoes	250 mL
	Finely grated zest and juice of ½ lemon	
2 tbsp	chopped fresh Italian (flat-leaf) parsley	25 mL

Season shrimp and scallops with salt and pepper. In a large skillet, heat half the oil over medium-high heat. Sauté shrimp and scallops, in batches if necessary, until firm and opaque, about 3 minutes. Add crab and heat through. Transfer seafood to a plate. Add the remaining oil to the pan and sauté red pepper and onion until tender. Add garlic, basil and herbes de Provence; sauté for 30 seconds. Add wine and boil until reduced by half. Add tomatoes, lemon zest and lemon juice; reduce heat and simmer for 5 minutes. Return seafood to the pan and stir in parsley. Season with additional salt and pepper. **Serves 4.**

Skillet Bouillabaisse

Follow preceding recipe, but replace the herbes de Provence with ground anise seeds, and the lemon zest and juice with orange zest and juice. **Serves 4.**

Shrimp with Vodka, Tomatoes and Cream

2 tbsp	extra-virgin olive oil	25 mL
1½ lbs	extra-large shrimp, peeled and deveined	750 g
2	cloves garlic, minced	2
Pinch	hot pepper flakes	Pinch
12	plum (Roma) tomatoes, peeled, seeded and chopped	12
	Salt and freshly ground black pepper to taste	
½ cup	whipping (35%) cream	125 mL
¼ cup	vodka	50 mL
	Cooked rice or pasta (optional)	

In a large skillet, heat oil over medium-high heat. Add shrimp, in batches if necessary, and sauté until pink and opaque, about 2 minutes; transfer to a plate. Add garlic and hot pepper flakes to the pan and sauté for 10 seconds. Add tomatoes, salt and black pepper; sauté until tomatoes release their liquid, about 3 minutes. Add cream and vodka; reduce heat and simmer until cream thickens. Return shrimp to pan and coat with sauce. Serve with hot rice or pasta, if desired. **Serves 4.**

Cajun Shrimp

2 tbsp	extra-virgin olive oil	25 mL
1½ lbs	extra-large shrimp, peeled and deveined	750 g
	Salt and freshly ground black pepper to taste	
2	cloves garlic, minced	2
2 cups	whipping (35%) cream	500 mL
3 to 4 tbsp	hot pepper sauce (such as Tabasco)	45 to 50 mL
2 tbsp	chopped fresh Italian (flat-leaf) parsley	25 mL
	Cooked rice or pasta (optional)	

In a large skillet, heat oil over medium-high heat. Sauté shrimp, salt and pepper, in batches if necessary, until shrimp is pink and opaque, about 2 minutes. Transfer shrimp to a plate. Add garlic and cream to the pan, reduce heat and simmer for 1 minute. Add hot pepper sauce and simmer until cream thickens. Return shrimp to the pan and coat with sauce. Stir in parsley. Serve with hot rice or pasta, if desired. **Serves 4.**

Poached Chicken Breasts with Warm Tomato Vinaigrette

4	boneless skinless chicken breasts	4
	Salt and freshly ground black pepper to taste	
1 cup	chicken broth	250 mL
1	clove garlic, minced	1
1 cup	canned tomato purée or crushed tomatoes	250 mL
¼ cup	extra-virgin olive oil	50 mL
2 tbsp	red wine vinegar	25 mL
2 tbsp	chopped fresh Italian (flat-leaf) parsley	25 mL

Season chicken with salt and pepper. In a skillet, bring chicken broth and garlic to a simmer over medium heat. Add chicken, cover and simmer until chicken is no longer pink inside. Transfer chicken to a warm platter and keep warm. Increase heat and boil broth until reduced to a glaze. Add tomato purée and heat through. Remove from heat and stir in oil, vinegar and parsley. Pour sauce over chicken. **Serves 4.**

Salmon Provençal

Follow preceding recipe, but substitute four 5-oz (150 g) pieces salmon fillet for the chicken, substitute dry white wine for the chicken broth, and add 1 tsp (5 mL) dried herbes de Provence with the wine; cook until fish flakes easily with a fork. **Serves 4.**

Chicken with Sausage and Clams

1 lb	boneless skinless chicken thighs	500 g
	Salt and freshly ground black pepper to taste	
3 tbsp	extra-virgin olive oil	45 mL
12 oz	chorizo (or other spicy sausage), sliced	375 g
1	red bell pepper, chopped	1
½ cup	chopped onion	125 mL
3	cloves garlic, minced	3
1 tsp	dried basil	5 mL
½ tsp	dried oregano	2 mL
1 cup	chicken broth	250 mL
1	can (about 10 oz/284 g) chopped clams, with liquid	1
1 cup	drained canned diced tomatoes	250 mL
2 tbsp	chopped fresh Italian (flat-leaf) parsley	25 mL

Season chicken with salt and pepper. In a large skillet, heat oil over medium-high heat. Sauté chicken until browned on all sides. Add chorizo and sauté until juices run clear when chicken is pierced. Add red pepper and onion; sauté until tender. Add garlic, basil and oregano; sauté for 30 seconds. Add broth and clams, with liquid, and boil until reduced by half. Add tomatoes and simmer for 5 minutes. Stir in parsley and season with salt and pepper. **Serves 4.**

Chicken and Shrimp in Garlic Black Bean Sauce

⅓ cup	cornstarch	75 mL
1 tsp	ground ginger	5 mL
	Salt and freshly ground black pepper to taste	
12 oz	boneless skinless chicken breasts, cut into bite-size pieces	275 g
3 tbsp	vegetable oil	45 mL
24	large shrimp, peeled and deveined	24
1	stalk celery, sliced	1
¼ cup	finely chopped onion	50 mL
2	cloves garlic, minced	2
1 cup	chicken broth	250 mL
1 tbsp	Chinese garlic black bean sauce	15 mL
2	green onions, sliced	2

In a large, sealable plastic bag, combine cornstarch, ginger, salt and pepper. Add chicken, seal bag and toss to coat. Remove chicken and pat off excess cornstarch. In a large skillet, heat oil over medium-high heat. Sauté chicken until browned on all sides and no longer pink inside; transfer to a plate. Add shrimp to cornstarch mixture, seal bag and toss to coat. Remove shrimp and pat off excess cornstarch, reserving cornstarch mixture. Add shrimp to pan and sauté until pink and opaque; transfer to a plate. Add celery and onion to the pan and sauté until lightly browned. Add garlic, broth and black bean sauce; bring to a boil. Dissolve the reserved cornstarch mixture in 2 tbsp (25 mL) water. Return chicken and shrimp to the pan with dissolved cornstarch and cook, stirring, for at least 3 minutes, or until sauce is slightly thickened. Serve sprinkled with green onions. **Serves 4.**

Chipotle Turkey

Follow preceding recipe, but replace the ginger with ground cumin and the chicken and shrimp with 2 lbs (1 kg) boneless skinless turkey breast, cut into bite-size pieces; cook in batches. Omit the black bean sauce and add ½ cup (125 mL) chipotle salsa with the broth. Replace the green onions with 2 tbsp (25 mL) chopped fresh cilantro. **Serves 4.**

Thai Turkey Salad

2 tbsp	vegetable oil	25 mL
¼ cup	finely chopped onion	50 mL
1 lb	ground turkey	500 g
3 tbsp	granulated sugar	45 mL
2 tsp	ground coriander	10 mL
1½ tsp	finely chopped garlic	7 mL
¼ tsp	hot pepper flakes	1 mL
	Salt and freshly ground black pepper to taste	
½ cup	coarsely chopped roasted peanuts	125 mL
2 tbsp	freshly squeezed lime juice	25 mL
1 tbsp	Thai fish sauce (*nam pla*)	15 mL
1 tsp	dark sesame oil	5 mL
1 cup	bean sprouts	250 mL

In a large skillet, heat oil over medium-high heat. Sauté onion until slightly softened. Add turkey, sugar, coriander, garlic, hot pepper flakes, salt and black pepper; sauté, breaking up turkey with a fork, until turkey is no longer pink. Stir in peanuts, lime juice, fish sauce and sesame oil. Mound on a plate and scatter bean sprouts on top. **Serves 4.**

Stir-Fried Thai Shrimp

Follow preceding recipe, but replace the turkey with 1 lb (500 g) small shrimp, peeled and deveined. **Serves 4.**

Sautéed Turkey with Apple Glaze

4	turkey breast cutlets	4
	(each about 6 oz/175 g)	
	Salt and freshly ground black pepper	
	to taste	
1 tbsp	vegetable oil	15 mL
¼ cup	finely chopped onion	50 mL
½ tsp	dried sage	2 mL
1 cup	unsweetened apple juice	250 mL
2 tbsp	cider vinegar	25 mL
1 tsp	packed dark brown sugar	5 mL
2 tbsp	butter, cut into small pieces	25 mL

Season turkey with salt and pepper. In a large skillet, heat oil over medium-high heat. Cook turkey until browned on both sides and no longer pink inside; transfer to a warm platter and keep warm. Reduce heat to medium and add onion and sage to pan; sauté until onion is browned. Add apple juice, vinegar and brown sugar; increase heat and boil until liquid is reduced by about three-quarters. Remove from heat and stir in butter. Pour sauce over turkey. **Serves 4.**

Orange Hoisin Turkey

4	turkey breast cutlets	4
	(each about 6 oz/175 g)	
	Salt and freshly ground black pepper	
	to taste	
1 tbsp	vegetable oil	15 mL
¼ cup	finely chopped onion	50 mL
2	cloves garlic, minced	2
1 cup	orange juice	250 mL
2 tbsp	hoisin sauce	25 mL
2 tsp	orange marmalade	10 mL
2	green onions, sliced	2

Season turkey with salt and pepper. In a large skillet, heat oil over medium-high heat. Cook turkey until browned on both sides and no longer pink inside; transfer to a warm platter and keep warm. Reduce heat to medium and add onion and garlic to pan; sauté until onion is browned. Add orange juice, hoisin sauce and marmalade; increase heat and boil until liquid is reduced to a glaze. Remove from heat and stir in green onions. Pour sauce over turkey. **Serves 4.**

Stir-Fried Chicken with Cashews

Follow preceding recipe, but replace the turkey with 1½ lbs (750 g) boneless skinless chicken breasts, cut into bite-size chunks. Omit the orange juice, hoisin sauce and marmalade, and add ⅓ cup (75 mL) oyster sauce, 2 tbsp (25 mL) soy sauce and the juice of 1 lemon after onion is browned. Add 1 cup (250 mL) toasted whole cashews with the green onions. **Serves 4.**

Chicken with Lemon and Capers

4	boneless skinless chicken breasts	4
	Salt and freshly ground black pepper	
	to taste	
1 tbsp	extra-virgin olive oil	15 mL
⅓ cup	finely chopped onion	75 mL
1	clove garlic, minced	1
1½ cups	chicken broth	375 mL
2 tbsp	drained small capers	25 mL
	Finely grated zest and juice of 1 lemon	
2 tbsp	chopped fresh Italian (flat-leaf) parsley	25 mL
2 tbsp	butter, cut into small pieces	25 mL

Season chicken with salt and pepper. In a large skillet, heat oil over medium-high heat. Cook chicken until browned on both sides and no longer pink inside; transfer to a warm platter and keep warm. Reduce heat to medium and add onion to pan; sauté until tender. Add garlic and sauté for 30 seconds. Add broth, increase heat and boil until liquid is reduced by about two-thirds. Stir in capers, lemon zest and lemon juice; boil for 1 minute. Stir in parsley and any juices that have collected around the chicken. Remove from heat and stir in butter. Pour sauce over chicken. **Serves 4.**

Lemon Mushroom Turkey

Follow preceding recipe, but replace the chicken with four 6-oz (175 g) turkey breast cutlets, and add 8 mushrooms, sliced, with the onion. Omit the capers. **Serves 4.**

Lime Cilantro Black Bean Chicken

Follow recipe for Chicken with Lemon and Capers (above), but omit the capers, add 1 cup (250 mL) drained rinsed canned black beans after liquid is reduced, substitute lime zest and juice for the lemon zest and juice, and substitute chopped fresh cilantro for the parsley. **Serves 4.**

Deviled Chicken Breasts

1 cup	dry bread crumbs	250 mL
Pinch	cayenne pepper	Pinch
	Salt and freshly ground black pepper to taste	
4	boneless skinless chicken breasts	4
2 tbsp	spicy brown mustard	25 mL
2 tbsp	vegetable oil	25 mL
2 tbsp	butter	25 mL
1 tbsp	hot pepper sauce (such as Frank's RedHot)	15 mL
1 tbsp	freshly squeezed lemon juice	15 mL

Season bread crumbs with cayenne, salt and black pepper. Brush chicken with mustard and dredge in bread crumbs, coating evenly. Let stand on a rack for at least 10 minutes, but no more than 30 minutes. In a large skillet, heat oil over medium-high heat. Cook chicken until browned on both sides. Reduce heat to medium and cook, turning once or twice, until chicken is no longer pink inside. Transfer chicken to a warm platter and keep warm. Remove pan from heat and stir in butter, hot pepper sauce and lemon juice. Drizzle sauce over chicken. **Serves 4.**

Garlic Hazelnut Chicken

Follow preceding recipe, but substitute finely ground hazelnuts for the bread crumbs, add 2 cloves garlic, finely chopped, about 1 minute before chicken is done cooking, and omit the hot pepper sauce. **Serves 4.**

Stuffing-Crusted Chicken Breasts with Sage Butter

4	boneless skinless chicken breasts	4
	Salt and freshly ground black pepper to taste	
2 tbsp	mayonnaise	25 mL
1 cup	crushed packaged dry stuffing mix	250 mL
2 tbsp	vegetable oil	25 mL
1/4 cup	chicken broth	50 mL
2 tsp	dried sage	10 mL
2 tbsp	butter, cut into small pieces	25 mL

Season chicken with salt and pepper, brush with mayonnaise and dredge in stuffing mix, coating evenly. Let stand on a rack for at least 10 minutes, but no more than 30 minutes. In a large skillet, heat oil over medium-high heat. Cook chicken until browned on both sides. Reduce heat to medium and cook, turning once or twice, until chicken is no longer pink inside. Transfer chicken to a warm plat-ter and keep warm. Add broth and sage to the pan and boil until reduced to a glaze. Remove from heat and stir in butter. Drizzle sauce over chicken. **Serves 4.**

Chicken with Lime Avocado Relish

2	green onions, finely chopped	2
1	large avocado, finely diced	1
1	large tomato, chopped	1
1	clove garlic, minced	1
3 tbsp	freshly squeezed lime juice, divided	45 mL
2 tsp	chopped fresh Italian (flat-leaf) parsley	10 mL
	Salt, freshly ground black pepper and hot pepper flakes to taste	
4	boneless skinless chicken breasts	4
2 tbsp	extra-virgin olive oil	25 mL

Combine green onions, avocado, tomato, garlic, 1 tbsp (15 mL) of the lime juice, parsley, salt, black pepper and hot pepper flakes; set aside. Season chicken with salt and black pepper. Heat oil in a large skillet over medium-high heat. Cook chicken until browned on both sides and no longer pink inside. Add the remaining lime juice and turn chicken to glaze with drippings. Serve topped with relish. **Serves 4.**

Chicken with Sun-Dried Tomato Rouille

10	oil-packed sun-dried tomatoes	10
1/3 cup	oil from the sun-dried tomatoes	75 mL
2	cloves garlic, halved	2
1 cup	fresh basil leaves	250 mL
1/4 cup	extra-virgin olive oil, divided	50 mL
3 tbsp	aged balsamic vinegar, divided	45 mL
4	boneless skinless chicken breasts	4

In a food processor, purée sun-dried tomatoes, tomato oil, garlic and basil to a smooth paste. With the motor running, slowly add 2 tbsp (25 mL) of the olive oil and 1 tbsp (15 mL) of the balsamic vinegar and process until blended; set aside. Season chicken with salt and pepper. In a large skillet, heat the remaining olive oil over medium-high heat. Cook chicken until browned on both sides and no longer pink inside. Add the remaining vinegar and turn chicken to glaze with drippings. Serve topped with rouille. **Serves 4.**

Sage and Rosemary Chicken Breast Meunière

½ cup	dry bread crumbs	125 mL
2 tbsp	all-purpose flour	25 mL
1 tbsp	dried sage	15 mL
1 tbsp	dried rosemary, crumbled	15 mL
	Salt and freshly ground black pepper to taste	
4	boneless skinless chicken breasts	4
2 tbsp	extra-virgin olive oil	25 mL
1	clove garlic, minced	1
2 tbsp	butter	25 mL
1 tbsp	chopped fresh rosemary and/or sage	15 mL

Combine bread crumbs, flour, sage, rosemary, salt and pepper. Lightly pound chicken to an even thickness and dredge in crumb mixture, coating evenly. In a large nonstick skillet, heat oil over medium-high heat. Cook chicken until browned on both sides. Reduce heat to medium and cook, turning once or twice, until chicken is no longer pink inside. Transfer chicken to a warm platter and keep warm. Add garlic, butter and rosemary to the pan and cook until butter is foamy. Pour sauce over chicken. **Serves 4.**

Sesame Chicken Breasts

1 cup	sesame seeds	250 mL
2 tbsp	all-purpose flour	25 mL
Pinch	cayenne pepper	Pinch
	Salt and freshly ground black pepper to taste	
4	boneless skinless chicken breasts	4
2 tbsp	vegetable oil	25 mL
1	clove garlic, minced	1
2 tbsp	soy sauce	25 mL
1 tbsp	dark sesame oil	15 mL
2	green onions, sliced	2

Combine sesame seeds, flour, cayenne, salt and black pepper. Pound chicken breasts to an even thickness and dredge in seed mixture, coating evenly. In a large, nonstick skillet, heat vegetable oil over medium-high heat. Cook chicken until browned on both sides. Reduce heat to medium and cook, turning once or twice, until chicken is no longer pink inside. Transfer chicken to a warm platter and keep warm. Add garlic, soy sauce and sesame oil to the pan; bring to a boil. Pour sauce over chicken and sprinkle with green onions. **Serves 4.**

Marinated Chicken Paillards

4	boneless skinless chicken breasts	4
	Salt and freshly ground black pepper to taste	
1 cup	Italian dressing, divided	250 mL
1 tbsp	olive oil	15 mL

Pound chicken breasts to ⅛-inch (3 mm) thickness and rub with salt and pepper. Place in a shallow dish with ¾ cup (175 mL) of the dressing and turn to coat. Cover and refrigerate for 1 hour. Heat a large, heavy skillet over high heat until extremely hot, about 5 minutes. Remove chicken from marinade, wipe off any excess and discard marinade. Pour a thin film of oil into the skillet. When it smokes, add 1 piece of chicken and cook, turning once, for 30 seconds per side, until no longer pink inside. Transfer to a warm platter and keep warm. Repeat with remaining chicken, adding oil as needed. Drizzle each piece of chicken with 1 tbsp (15 mL) of the remaining dressing. **Serves 4.**

Chicken Paillards with Artichoke Pesto

Follow preceding recipe, but stir 4 marinated artichoke hearts, finely chopped, into the last ¼ cup (50 mL) Italian dressing before drizzling it over chicken. **Serves 4.**

"Grilled" Chicken Anchoiade

4	canned anchovies, with their oil, mashed to a paste	4
1	clove garlic, minced	1
¼ cup	mayonnaise	50 mL
¼ cup	extra-virgin olive oil, divided	50 mL
	Salt and freshly ground black pepper to taste	
4	boneless skinless chicken breasts	4

Combine anchovies, garlic, mayonnaise, 2 tbsp (25 mL) of the oil and pepper; set aside. Season chicken with salt and pepper, then brush with 1 tbsp (15 mL) of the oil, coating evenly. Pound chicken between sheets of plastic wrap to ¼-inch (0.5 cm) thickness. Heat a ridged cast-iron skillet over high heat until very hot. Brush skillet with the remaining oil. Cook chicken until browned on both sides and no longer pink inside. Serve with anchovy mayonnaise. **Serves 4.**

"Grilled" Chicken Breasts with Herbed Blue Cheese Dressing

Follow preceding recipe, but replace the anchovy mayonnaise with a mixture of ¾ cup (175 mL) blue cheese dressing and ¼ cup (50 mL) Italian dressing. Serves 4.

Pan-Barbecued Chicken Breasts

¾ cup	ketchup	175 mL
¼ cup	finely grated onion	50 mL
2 tbsp	cider vinegar	25 mL
1 tbsp	spicy brown mustard	15 mL
1 tbsp	Worcestershire sauce	15 mL
1 tbsp	dark (cooking) molasses	15 mL
Pinch	cayenne pepper	Pinch
4	boneless skinless chicken breasts	4
	Salt and freshly ground black pepper to taste	
2 tbsp	vegetable oil, divided	25 mL

Combine ketchup, onion, vinegar, mustard, Worcestershire sauce, molasses and cayenne; set aside. Season chicken with salt and black pepper, then brush with half the oil, coating evenly. Pound between sheets of plastic wrap to ¼-inch (0.5 cm) thickness. Heat a ridged cast-iron skillet over high heat until very hot. Brush skillet with the remaining oil. Cook chicken until browned on the bottom; turn and brush the cooked side with barbecue sauce. Cook until no longer pink inside. Serve chicken with the remaining sauce. **Serves 4.**

Pan-Barbecued Chicken Sandwiches

Follow preceding recipe, but serve chicken on 4 kaiser rolls with ¼ cup (50 mL) coleslaw on each sandwich. **Serves 4.**

Pan-Seared Chicken Breasts with Tomato Dill Salsa

2	large tomatoes, seeded and finely chopped	2
1	clove garlic, minced	1
½	red onion, finely chopped	½
¼ cup	chopped fresh dill	50 mL
3 tbsp	extra-virgin olive oil, divided	45 mL
	Salt and freshly ground black pepper to taste	
4	boneless skinless chicken breasts	4
	Juice of 1 lemon	

Combine tomatoes, garlic, onion, dill, 1 tbsp (15 mL) of the oil, salt and pepper; set aside. Season chicken with salt and pepper. In a large skillet, heat the remaining oil over medium-high heat. Cook chicken until browned on both sides and no longer pink inside. Squeeze lemon juice over chicken and turn to glaze with drippings. Serve topped with salsa. **Serves 4.**

Three-Olive Chicken

Follow preceding recipe, but replace the salsa with the following mixture: 1 small onion, finely chopped, ¼ cup (50 mL) chopped pitted green olives, ¼ cup (50 mL) chopped pitted ripe black olives, 2 tbsp (25 mL) brine from either of the olives, 2 tbsp (25 mL) finely chopped fresh parsley, 2 tbsp (25 mL) extra-virgin olive oil, and salt and pepper to taste. **Serves 4.**

Chicken Braised with Cider

2 lbs	boneless skinless chicken thighs	1 kg
	Salt and freshly ground black pepper to taste	
2 tbsp	vegetable oil	25 mL
1	onion, coarsely chopped	1
1	stalk celery, chopped	1
1	carrot, sliced	1
2	large tart apples, peeled and cut into wedges	2
1 tsp	dried rosemary	5 mL
1 tsp	dried sage	5 mL
1 tsp	dried thyme	5 mL
3 cups	unsweetened apple cider	750 mL

Season chicken with salt and pepper. In a large skillet, heat oil over medium-high heat. Cook chicken until browned on both sides. Add onion, celery and carrot; sauté until lightly browned. Stir in apples, rosemary, sage and thyme. Add cider, reduce heat and simmer until vegetables are tender, juices run clear when chicken is pierced and cider has thickened into a delicate sauce, about 20 minutes. **Serves 4 to 6.**

Chicken Braised with Spicy Peanut Sauce

2 lbs	boneless skinless chicken thighs	1 kg
	Salt and freshly ground black pepper to taste	
2 tbsp	vegetable oil	25 mL
1	onion, coarsely chopped	1
1	clove garlic, minced	1
1 tbsp	soy sauce	15 mL
2 tsp	finely chopped gingerroot	10 mL
1 tsp	ground coriander	5 mL
Pinch	hot pepper flakes	Pinch
2 cups	chicken broth	500 mL
¼ cup	smooth peanut butter	50 mL
2	green onions, sliced	2

Season chicken with salt and black pepper. In a large skillet, heat oil over medium-high heat. Cook chicken until browned on both sides. Add onion and sauté until lightly browned. Stir in garlic, soy sauce, ginger, coriander and hot pepper flakes. Add broth, reduce heat and simmer until juices run clear when chicken is pierced and broth has slightly thickened, about 20 minutes. Transfer chicken to a warm platter and keep warm. Add peanut butter to the pan and stir until melted. Pour sauce over chicken and sprinkle with green onions. **Serves 4 to 6.**

Chicken Braised with Red Wine and Mushrooms

½ cup	all-purpose flour	125 mL
2 tsp	dried thyme	10 mL
	Salt and freshly ground black pepper to taste	
1½ lbs	boneless skinless chicken thighs	750 g
2 tbsp	vegetable oil	25 mL
1	onion, finely chopped	1
8 oz	mushrooms, sliced	250 g
1 cup	dry red wine	250 mL
¼ cup	brandy	50 mL
1 cup	beef broth	250 mL
½ cup	tomato sauce	125 mL
2 tbsp	chopped fresh Italian (flat-leaf) parsley	25 mL

In a large, sealable plastic bag, combine flour, thyme, salt and pepper. Add chicken, seal and toss to coat. Remove chicken, pat off excess flour and discard flour mixture. In a large skillet, heat oil over medium-high heat. Cook chicken until browned on both sides; transfer to a plate. Add onion and mushrooms to the pan and sauté until lightly browned. Add wine and brandy; boil until reduced by half. Add broth and tomato sauce; reduce heat and bring to a simmer. Return chicken to pan, cover and simmer until juices run clear when chicken is pierced, about 20 minutes. Stir in parsley. **Serves 4.**

Thai Chicken

½ cup	all-purpose flour	125 mL
2 tsp	chopped chives	10 mL
	Salt and freshly ground black pepper to taste	
1½ lbs	boneless skinless chicken thighs	750 g
2 tbsp	vegetable oil	25 mL
1	onion, finely chopped	1
2	cloves garlic, minced	2
1 cup	beef broth	250 mL
2 cups	Peanut Sauce (see recipe, page 53) or store-bought peanut sauce	500 mL
2 tbsp	chopped fresh cilantro	25 mL

In a large, sealable plastic bag, combine flour, chives, salt and pepper. Add chicken, seal and toss to coat. Remove chicken, pat off excess flour and discard flour mixture. In a large skillet, heat oil over medium-high heat. Cook chicken until browned on both sides; transfer to a plate. Add onion to the pan and sauté until lightly browned. Add garlic and sauté for 30 seconds. Add broth and boil until reduced by half. Add peanut sauce, reduce heat and bring to a simmer. Return chicken to pan, cover and simmer until juices run clear when chicken is pierced, about 20 minutes. Stir in cilantro. **Serves 4.**

Chicken Chicharrones

½ cup	all-purpose flour	125 mL
1 tsp	ground cumin	5 mL
	Salt and freshly ground black pepper to taste	
1½ lbs	chicken thighs, skin and bones removed	750 g
2 tbsp	vegetable oil	25 mL
1 cup	chicken broth	250 mL
¼ cup	dark rum	50 mL
¼ cup	soy sauce	50 mL
¼ cup	freshly squeezed lime juice	50 mL
1 tbsp	chopped fresh cilantro	15 mL
1 to 2 tsp	hot pepper sauce (such as Tabasco)	5 to 10 mL
1	lime, cut into 8 wedges	1

In a large, sealable plastic bag, combine flour, cumin, salt and pepper. Add chicken, seal and toss to coat. Remove chicken, pat off excess flour and discard flour mixture. In a large skillet, heat oil over medium-high heat. Cook chicken until browned on both sides. Add broth, rum, soy sauce and lime juice; reduce heat and simmer until juices run clear when chicken is pierced and liquid is reduced to a glaze that coats the chicken. (Reduce heat as necessary near the end of cooking to prevent glaze from burning.) Stir in cilantro and hot pepper sauce to taste. Serve with lime wedges. **Serves 4.**

Mahogany Chicken

Follow preceding recipe, but substitute garlic powder for the cumin, sake for the rum, and 2 tbsp (25 mL) each honey and cider vinegar for the lime juice. Omit lime wedges. **Serves 4.**

Quick Chicken Chili

1 lb	boneless skinless chicken breasts, cut into bite-size chunks	500 g
½ cup	all-purpose flour	125 mL
2 tbsp	vegetable oil	25 mL
1	onion, finely chopped	1
1	clove garlic, minced	1
1 tbsp	chili powder	15 mL
1 tsp	ground cumin	5 mL
¾ cup	chicken broth	175 mL
¼ cup	canned crushed tomatoes	50 mL
	Salt and freshly ground black pepper to taste	

Dredge chicken in flour, coating evenly. Discard excess flour. In a large skillet, heat oil over medium-high heat. Sauté chicken until browned on all sides.

Add onion and sauté until onion is tender and chicken is no longer pink inside. Add garlic, chili powder and cumin; sauté for 30 seconds. Add broth, tomatoes, salt and pepper; reduce heat and simmer until sauce is slightly thickened, about 10 minutes. **Serves 4.**

Garlic Chicken Sausage over Spinach

2 tbsp	extra-virgin olive oil, divided	25 mL
4	chicken sausages	4
½ cup	chopped red onion	125 mL
2	cloves garlic, minced	2
¼ cup	red wine vinegar	50 mL
1 tbsp	granulated sugar	15 mL
	Salt and freshly ground black pepper to taste	
10 oz	fresh spinach leaves (about 6 cups/1.5 L)	300 g

In a large skillet, heat oil over medium-high heat. Cook sausages until browned on all sides and no longer pink inside; transfer to a plate and blot with paper towels. Add onion to the pan and sauté until tender. Stir in garlic and remove from heat. Stir in vinegar, sugar, salt and pepper. Transfer to a large bowl and toss with spinach. Serve sausages on a mound of dressed spinach. **Serves 4.**

Chipotle Cherry Pork

4	thinly cut boneless pork loin chops	4
	Salt and freshly ground black pepper to taste	
1 tbsp	extra-virgin olive oil	15 mL
⅓ cup	finely chopped onion	75 mL
2	cloves garlic, minced	2
2 cups	chicken broth	500 mL
½	canned chipotle pepper in adobo sauce, finely chopped	½
2 tbsp	chopped fresh cilantro or parsley	25 mL
2 tbsp	cherry preserves	25 mL
2 tbsp	butter, cut into small pieces	25 mL

Season pork with salt and pepper. In a large skillet, heat oil over medium-high heat. Cook pork, in batches if necessary, until browned on both sides and just a hint of pink remains inside. Transfer to a warm platter and keep warm. Reduce heat to medium and add onion to pan; sauté until tender. Add garlic and sauté for 30 seconds. Add broth and chipotle; increase heat and boil until liquid is reduced by about three-quarters. Stir in cilantro, cherry preserves and any juices that have collected around the pork; boil for 1 minute. Remove from heat and stir in butter. Pour sauce over pork. Serves 4.

Spicy Peachy Chicken

Follow preceding recipe, but replace the pork with 4 boneless skinless chicken breasts, pounded to an even thickness; omit the chipotle, and add a pinch of ground dried habanero chili with the broth; and substitute peach preserves for the cherry preserves. Serves 4.

Pork Chops with Bourbon Reduction

4	thinly cut boneless pork loin chops	4
	Salt and freshly ground black pepper to taste	
1 tbsp	vegetable oil	15 mL
¼ cup	finely chopped onion	50 mL
½ tsp	dried thyme	2 mL
½ cup	bourbon	125 mL
¼ cup	butter, cut into small pieces	50 mL
2 tbsp	chopped fresh parsley	25 mL

Season pork with salt and pepper. In a large skillet, heat oil over medium-high heat. Cook pork, in batches if necessary, until browned on both sides and just a hint of pink remains inside. Transfer to a warm platter and keep warm. Reduce heat to medium and add onion and thyme to pan; sauté until onion is tender. Add bourbon, increase heat and boil until liquid is reduced by about half. Remove from heat and stir in butter, one piece at a time, and parsley. Pour sauce over pork. Serves 4.

Pork Tacos

1 tbsp	olive oil	15 mL
1	large onion, chopped	1
1	jalapeño pepper, seeded and minced	1
1	clove garlic, minced	1
1 lb	ground pork	500 g
1 tbsp	chili powder	15 mL
2 tbsp	chopped fresh cilantro	25 mL
8	taco shells or corn tortillas, warmed according to package directions	8
1	roasted red bell pepper (see page 11), cut into strips	1
1 cup	crumbled queso fresco or farmer's cheese	250 mL
1 cup	salsa verde or Mild Green Salsa (see recipe, page 403)	250 mL

In a large skillet, heat oil over medium-high heat. Sauté onion, jalapeño and garlic until onion is almost tender. Add pork and sauté, breaking up with a fork, until starting to brown. Add chili powder and sauté until pork is no longer pink. Stir in cilantro. Divide meat mixture among taco shells and top with roasted pepper, cheese and salsa. Serves 4.

Vegetarian Tacos

Follow preceding recipe, but replace the pork with ground Quorn, soy ground meat substitute or vegetarian ground meat replacement (available frozen or in the produce department). Sauté until just heated through. Serves 4.

Ground Chicken Fajitas

Follow recipe for Pork Tacos (left), but substitute ground chicken for the pork, add the juice of 1 lime with the cilantro, and replace the cheese with guacamole or diced avocado. Serves 4.

Pork Chops with Caramelized Onions

¼ cup	all-purpose flour	50 mL
	Salt and freshly ground black pepper to taste	
4	thick pork chops (each about 7 oz/210 g)	4
2 tbsp	olive oil	25 mL
3	large onions, halved and thinly sliced	3
4	cloves garlic, minced	4
¼ cup	butter, cut into small pieces	50 mL
1 tsp	dried thyme	5 mL

Season flour with salt and pepper. Dredge pork chops in flour, coating evenly. Discard excess flour mixture. In a large skillet, heat oil over medium-high heat. Cook pork until browned on both sides; transfer to a plate. Add onion to the pan and sauté until tender. Stir in garlic, butter and thyme. Reduce heat to medium-low and place pork on the onions; cover tightly and cook for 15 minutes, stirring the onions once or twice, until just a hint of pink remains in pork, and onions are deep brown and meltingly soft. Serve chops smothered in onions. Serves 4.

Veal with Melted Leeks

Follow preceding recipe, but replace the pork chops with veal chops, browning in batches, and replace the onions with the white parts of 6 large leeks. Serves 4.

Sautéed Veal with Chardonnay and Basil

8	veal scallops (each about 3 oz/90 g), pounded paper-thin	8
	Salt and freshly ground black pepper to taste	
1 tbsp	extra-virgin olive oil, divided	15 mL
¼ cup	finely chopped onion	50 mL
1	clove garlic, minced	1
1	tomato, seeded and finely chopped	1
1 cup	chardonnay	250 mL
2 tbsp	white wine vinegar	25 mL
2 tbsp	chopped fresh basil	25 mL
¼ cup	butter, cut into 6 pieces	50 mL

Season veal with salt and pepper. In a large skillet, heat a thin layer of oil over high heat. Add veal scallops, in batches, and brown on both sides. Transfer to a warm platter and keep warm. Repeat with the remaining oil and veal. Reduce heat to medium and add onion to pan; sauté until softened. Add garlic and sauté for 30 seconds. Add tomato, chardonnay and vinegar; increase heat to medium-high and boil until liquid is reduced by about three-quarters. Stir in basil and any juices that have collected around the veal. Remove from heat and stir in butter, one piece at a time. Pour sauce over veal. Serves 4.

Veal Marsala

8	veal scallops (each about 3 oz/90 g), pounded paper-thin	8
	Salt and freshly ground black pepper to taste	
1 tbsp	extra-virgin olive oil	15 mL
8	mushrooms, sliced	8
⅓ cup	finely chopped onion	75 mL
2	cloves garlic, minced	2
2	tomatoes, seeded and finely chopped	2
1 cup	Marsala	250 mL
2 tbsp	chopped fresh Italian (flat-leaf) parsley	25 mL
2 tbsp	unsalted butter, cut into small pieces	25 mL

Season veal with salt and pepper. In a large skillet, heat a thin layer of oil over high heat. Add veal scallops, in batches, and brown on both sides. Transfer to a warm platter and keep warm. Repeat with the remaining oil and veal. Reduce heat to medium and add mushrooms and onion to pan; sauté until tender. Add garlic and sauté for 30 seconds. Add tomatoes and Marsala; increase heat and boil until liquid is reduced by about half. Stir in parsley and any juices that have collected around the veal. Remove from heat and stir in butter. Pour sauce over veal. Serves 4.

Chapter 14
Stir-Frying
Quick, Healthful and Infinitely Variable

Stir-Fried Fish and Vegetables 161

Ginger Sesame Salmon 161

Mussels in Red Clam Sauce 161

Stir-Fried Scallops with Garlic 162

Scallops with Oyster
and Shiitake Mushrooms 162

Herbed Shrimp 162

Sweet-and-Sour Spicy Shrimp 162

Crab with Salsa 163

Turkey with Garlic Black Beans 163

Chicken with Rosemary and Sage 163

Orange Chicken with Apricots 163

Chicken with Glazed Red Pepper 163

Creamy, Corny Chicken Stir-Fry 164

Stir-Fried Caramel Chicken 164

Sweet Anise Chicken 164

Spicy Anise Lamb 164

Beef and Mushrooms 164

Stir-Fried Beef Barbecue 165

Orange Beef 165

Veal with Olives 165

Veal with Hot and Sweet Peppers 165

Sweet-and-Sour Lemon Pork 165

Spicy Peanut Pork 166

Peanut Chicken 166

Spicy Peanut Shrimp 166

Stir-Fried Curry Mixture 166

Stir-Fried Curried Vegetables 166

Curried Lamb with Eggplant 166

Red Curry Chicken 166

Stir-Fried Pasta Primavera 167

Spaghetti with Stir-Fried Meat Sauce . . 167

Thai Fried Noodles 167

Shrimp Thai Noodles 167

High-Protein Vegetarian
Stir-Fried Noodles 167

Stir-Fried Pork and Shrimp
with Noodles 168

Stir-Fried Garlic Chicken
with Noodles 168

Stir-Fried Beans 168

Stir-Fried Broccoli
with Hoisin Almonds 168

Stir-Fried Carrots with Mint
and Red Pepper 168

Corn with Ham and Sweet Peppers 169

Italian Stir-Fried Green Beans 169

Stir-Fried Garlic Green Beans 169

Stir-Fried Herbed Mushrooms 169

Stir-Fried Wild Mushrooms
with Hazelnuts 169

Soy-Glazed Potatoes 169

Stir-Fried Apple Shortcake 170

Stir-Fried Banana Split 170

Rum Raisin Bananas 170

Stir-Fried Poached Pears 170

Peaches Stir-Fried with Framboise 171

Sweet Fried Rice 171

Stir-frying has long been a prisoner of the flavors of exotic Asian ingredients. True, it's an Asian technique, one that has produced many of our most memorable meals. But why does such a versatile cooking method have to be confined to ginger and soy sauce? Why not a stir-fry of steak spiced like a Texas barbecue? How about a bouillabaisse stir-fried in a wok? Why not a shortcake topped with a stir-fry of apples in butter, sugar and cinnamon?

Stir-frying is nothing more than sautéing or braising in a wok, and it can be applied to any dish in Western cuisine that typically uses these techniques. The biggest difference is that stir-frying intensifies the heat and thus cooks the food faster.

The design and construction of a wok permit the cook to control the intense heat without burning the food. A wok is a wide metal pan with sloping sides and a rounded bottom. This design concentrates heat in the swollen belly of the pan, where food can be quickly browned and moved along the sides to finish cooking more slowly.

If the food requires longer cooking, with moist heat, liquid can be added to the wok to create a steaming environment that softens tough fibers at the same time that it flavors food and creates a base for a sauce.

Woks can be made from any metal. Traditional Chinese woks are cast iron, are very heavy and take a long time to heat up. But once they're hot, they retain heat well. Today, most woks are made of carbon steel, a lighter metal that heats through quickly and cools down in minutes. The biggest drawbacks of carbon steel are that it discolors with use and rusts if not dried thoroughly and rubbed with oil after each washing.

Traditional woks with a rounded base will not sit securely on a burner, which is why they once all came with a metal ring in which they rested. To use a wok with a ring on a gas burner, place the ring narrow side up to help concentrate the heat near the center of the wok. To use one on an electric burner, place the ring wide side up so the wok can rest closer to the less intense heat source. These days, most manufacturers make flat-bottomed woks that can be used interchangeably on gas or electric burners. Nonstick woks are also available, but we don't recommend them. The nonstick coating will inhibit the wok's ability to brown ingredients, thus defeating one of its greatest attributes.

It is often said that a wok is not an essential kitchen tool. Indeed, if you do not have a wok and do not wish to buy one, any stir-fried recipe can be made in a large, heavy skillet. But the skillet will not cook food as quickly or as evenly.

Because stir-frying is such a quick method of cooking, all ingredients must be prepared and ready to go before the wok is heated. Vegetables must be chopped, sliced or diced. Meat must be trimmed and sliced. Sauce ingredients should be measured and mixed, and spices should be laid out on a plate.

When you're ready to start cooking, place the dry wok over the specified heat until it is smoking hot and the air above the center of the wok seems to shiver with heat waves, then add a tablespoon or two (15 to 25 mL) of oil to the wok and heat until smoking. If desired, you can flavor the oil with hot pepper, garlic or ginger — just place the whole spice in the oil and press it to release its oils. Stir-fry just long enough for the spice to begin to brown — often as little as 10 seconds. Then remove it with a slotted spoon and proceed with the recipe.

Tender, high-moisture vegetables, such as spinach, cabbage and zucchini, need only be wilted in the hot oil. The high heat helps to seal moisture in the vegetables and, so long as they are stirred continuously, they will not overcook or burn. By reducing the heat and covering the wok, firmer vegetables, such as broccoli or carrots, can be steamed to soften their fiber and extract some of their moisture.

Meat, on the other hand, should sit undisturbed in the hot oil for a moment or two to brown properly. When meat and vegetables are cooked together, the meat goes in first; after it is browned, it is either pushed to the sides of the wok or removed with a slotted spoon to a side plate. Then the vegetables are cooked, the meat goes back in, and the complete dish is sauced and seasoned.

Fibrous vegetables and tougher cuts of meat are partially cooked in the oil and then finished in stock, wine or a sauce mixture. In these cases, the heat is kept fairly high so that the sauce reduces and thickens at the same time that the meat and vegetables finish cooking. Sometimes, however, high-fiber foods require longer, slower cooking. In these cases, the heat is lowered after the liquid is added so that it simmers gently while the ingredients become tender.

The recipes in this chapter span a wide variety of flavors and techniques applicable to stir-frying. Yet they only skim the surface. Use them and adapt them to your taste, schedule and imagination.

About these recipes . . .

These 50 recipes are written for preparation in a wok. A skillet can be used, but the cooking won't be as quick, so be prepared to adjust cooking times as needed. To ensure even browning, it's important not to crowd the wok. Depending on the size of your wok, you may need to do the initial browning in batches. If so, return earlier batches after all the browning is finished. The water-cornstarch mixture that's added to many of the recipes is called a slurry, and it's used as a thickener late in the recipe. It should be thoroughly stirred just before it's added. Salt and pepper should be adjusted to taste before serving.

Stir-Fried Fish and Vegetables

1½ lbs	skinless flounder fillet, cut into 1-inch (2.5 cm) strips	750 g
	All-purpose flour seasoned with salt and pepper	
½ cup	vegetable oil	125 mL
1	clove garlic, minced	1
¼ cup	thinly sliced carrot	50 mL
¼ cup	thinly sliced cucumber	50 mL
¼ cup	thinly sliced water chestnuts	50 mL
2 tbsp	rice wine vinegar	25 mL
1 tbsp	dry sherry	15 mL
1 tsp	granulated sugar	5 mL

Dredge flounder in seasoned flour; discard excess flour. In a wok, heat oil over medium-high heat until smoking. Stir-fry flounder, a few pieces at a time, until fish is golden brown and flakes easily with a fork. Remove to a strainer set over a bowl. Repeat with the remaining fish. Discard all but a thin film of oil. Add garlic, carrots, cucumber and water chestnuts to the wok and stir-fry for 30 seconds. Add vinegar, sherry and sugar; heat through. Arrange fish on a platter and ladle vegetables and sauce over fish. **Serves 4.**

Ginger Sesame Salmon

3 tbsp	ground sesame seeds	45 mL
3 tbsp	cornstarch	45 mL
½ tsp	ground ginger	2 mL
1½ lbs	boneless skinless salmon fillet, cut into 1-inch (2.5 cm) strips	750 g
½ cup	vegetable oil	125 mL
3	cloves garlic, minced	3
1 tbsp	finely chopped gingerroot	15 mL
16	snow peas, stemmed	16
½ cup	bean sprouts	125 mL
2 tbsp	reduced-sodium soy sauce	25 mL
2 tbsp	freshly squeezed lemon juice	25 mL
2 tbsp	dry sherry	25 mL
2 tsp	granulated sugar	10 mL
¼ cup	toasted sesame seeds	50 mL

Combine ground sesame seeds, cornstarch and ginger; dredge salmon in the mixture. In a wok, heat oil over medium-high heat until smoking. Stir-fry salmon, a few pieces at a time, until fish is golden brown and flakes easily with a fork. Remove to a strainer set over a bowl. Repeat with the remaining salmon. Discard all but a thin film of oil. Add garlic and ginger to the wok and stir-fry for 10 seconds. Add snow peas and bean sprouts; stir-fry for 30 seconds. Add soy sauce, lemon juice, sherry and sugar; reduce heat and simmer until slightly thickened. Arrange salmon on a platter and ladle vegetables and sauce over fish. Sprinkle with toasted sesame seeds. **Serves 4.**

Mussels in Red Clam Sauce

1 tbsp	extra-virgin olive oil	15 mL
1 cup	chopped onion	250 mL
2	cloves garlic, minced	2
1	can (10 oz/284 g) chopped clams, drained	1
1½ cups	canned crushed tomatoes	375 mL
¼ cup	tomato paste	50 mL
Pinch	hot pepper flakes	Pinch
	Salt and freshly ground black pepper to taste	
48	fresh mussels, scrubbed (see page 8)	48
2 tbsp	chopped fresh Italian (flat-leaf) parsley	25 mL
1 tbsp	freshly squeezed lemon juice	15 mL

In a wok, heat oil over medium-high heat until smoking. Stir-fry onion and garlic for 30 seconds. Add clams and tomatoes; reduce heat and simmer for 3 minutes. Stir in tomato paste, hot pepper flakes, salt and black pepper. Stir in mussels, cover and steam for 3 minutes, until mussels open (discard any that don't). Transfer to a serving bowl and toss with parsley and lemon juice. **Serves 4.**

Stir-Fried Scallops with Garlic

1½ lbs	sea scallops, trimmed of hard side muscles	750 g
	Salt and freshly ground black pepper to taste	
2 tbsp	olive oil	25 mL
1	large onion, chopped	1
5	cloves garlic, minced	5
1 cup	dry white wine	250 mL
1 tbsp	chopped fresh Italian (flat-leaf) parsley	15 mL
1 tsp	freshly squeezed lemon juice	5 mL

Season scallops with salt and pepper. In a wok, heat oil over medium-high heat until smoking. Stir-fry scallops until firm and lightly browned on both sides; remove to a plate. Add onion and garlic to the wok and stir-fry for 1 minute. Add wine and boil until reduced to a glaze. Return scallops to the wok and add parsley and lemon juice; stir to coat scallops with glaze. **Serves 4.**

Scallops with Oyster and Shiitake Mushrooms

2 tbsp	vegetable oil	25 mL
1 lb	sea scallops, trimmed of hard side muscles	500 g
3	cloves garlic, minced	3
4 oz	oyster mushrooms, hard stems trimmed	125 g
4 oz	shiitake mushrooms, hard stems trimmed, halved	125 g
1 tbsp	minced gingerroot	15 mL
¼ cup	chicken broth	50 mL
1 tbsp	soy sauce	15 mL
1 tbsp	dry sherry	15 mL
1 tbsp	freshly squeezed lemon juice	15 mL
2 tsp	cornstarch, dissolved in 4 tsp (20 mL) water	10 mL

In a wok, heat oil over high heat until smoking. Stir-fry scallops until firm and lightly browned on both sides; remove to a plate. Add garlic, oyster mushrooms, shiitake mushrooms and ginger to the wok and stir-fry until mushrooms lose their raw look. Add broth, soy sauce, sherry and lemon juice; bring to a boil. Stir cornstarch mixture and add to wok; reduce heat and simmer until sauce is slightly thickened. Return scallops to wok and stir to coat with sauce. **Serves 4.**

Herbed Shrimp

2 tbsp	olive oil	25 mL
1	large onion, chopped	1
3	cloves garlic, minced	3
2 tbsp	dry vermouth	25 mL
1½ lbs	jumbo shrimp, peeled and deveined	750 g
¼ cup	clam juice	50 mL
1 tbsp	chopped fresh Italian (flat-leaf) parsley	15 mL
1 tbsp	chopped fresh dill	15 mL
1 tsp	chopped fresh tarragon	5 mL
1 tsp	freshly squeezed lemon juice	5 mL
	Salt and freshly ground black pepper to taste	

In a wok, heat oil over medium-high heat until smoking. Stir-fry onion and garlic for 10 seconds. Add vermouth and stir-fry for 15 seconds. Add shrimp and stir-fry for 1 minute. Add clam juice, parsley, dill and tarragon; stir-fry for 1 minute, or until shrimp are pink and opaque. Sprinkle with lemon juice and season with salt and pepper. **Serves 4.**

Sweet-and-Sour Spicy Shrimp

¼ cup	cider vinegar	50 mL
2 tbsp	soy sauce	25 mL
2 tbsp	dry sherry	25 mL
2 tsp	dark sesame oil	10 mL
1½ lbs	jumbo shrimp, peeled and deveined	750 g
⅓ cup	cornstarch, divided	75 mL
2 tbsp	vegetable oil	25 mL
3	cloves garlic, minced	3
1 tbsp	chopped gingerroot	15 mL
½ cup	chicken broth	125 mL
¼ cup	granulated sugar	50 mL
2 tbsp	ketchup	25 mL

In a large bowl, combine vinegar, soy sauce, sherry and sesame oil. Add shrimp and toss to coat. Cover and refrigerate for 30 minutes. Remove shrimp from marinade with a slotted spoon and dissolve 1 tbsp (15 mL) of the cornstarch in the marinade. Dredge shrimp in the remaining cornstarch. In a wok, heat vegetable oil over medium-high heat until smoking. Stir-fry shrimp until brown and firm; remove to a plate. Add garlic and ginger to the wok and stir-fry for 10 seconds. Add broth, sugar and ketchup; bring to a boil. Stir marinade and add to wok; boil, stirring constantly until sauce is slightly thickened. Return shrimp to the wok and stir to coat with sauce. **Serves 4.**

Crab with Salsa

2 tbsp	olive oil	25 mL
1 lb	backfin (lump) crabmeat, shells picked out	500 g
3	cloves garlic, minced	3
1	avocado, diced	1
1 cup	spicy salsa	250 mL
1 tbsp	freshly squeezed lemon juice	15 mL
	Corn chips	

In a wok, heat oil over medium-high heat until smoking. Stir-fry crabmeat and garlic until lightly browned. Transfer to a serving bowl and toss with avocado, salsa and lemon juice. Serve with corn chips. **Serves 4.**

Turkey with Garlic Black Beans

1 lb	boneless skinless turkey breast, cut into bite-size pieces	500 g
1 tbsp	cornstarch	15 mL
3 tbsp	vegetable oil	45 mL
1 cup	chopped onion	250 mL
½ cup	sliced celery	125 mL
½ cup	sliced carrot	125 mL
1	clove garlic, minced	1
Pinch	hot pepper flakes	Pinch
¾ cup	chicken broth	175 mL
1 tbsp	Chinese garlic black bean sauce	15 mL
2 tsp	cornstarch, dissolved in ¼ cup (50 mL) chicken broth	10 mL
2	green onions, sliced	2
1 tbsp	dry sherry	15 mL

Dredge turkey in cornstarch. In a wok, heat oil over medium-high heat until smoking. Stir-fry turkey until browned on all sides; remove to a plate. Add onion, celery, carrot, garlic and hot pepper flakes to the wok and stir-fry for 1 minute. Return turkey to the wok and add broth and black bean sauce; bring to a boil. Stir cornstarch mixture and add to wok; reduce heat and simmer until sauce is slightly thickened and turkey is no longer pink inside. Stir in green onions and sherry. **Serves 4.**

Chicken with Rosemary and Sage

Follow preceding recipe, but substitute chicken breast for the turkey breast, omit the black bean sauce, and add 1 tbsp (15 mL) each chopped fresh rosemary and chopped fresh sage with the broth. **Serves 4.**

Orange Chicken with Apricots

2 tbsp	soy sauce	25 mL
2 tbsp	dry sherry	25 mL
2 tsp	dark sesame oil	10 mL
	Finely grated zest and juice of ½ orange	
1½ lbs	boneless skinless chicken breasts, cut into bite-size pieces	750 g
⅓ cup	cornstarch, divided	75 mL
2 tbsp	vegetable oil	25 mL
3	cloves garlic, minced	3
1 tbsp	chopped gingerroot	15 mL
½ cup	chicken broth	125 mL
¼ cup	diced dried apricots	50 mL
1 tbsp	granulated sugar	15 mL

In a large bowl, combine soy sauce, sherry, sesame oil and orange juice. Add chicken and toss to coat. Cover and refrigerate for 30 minutes. Remove chicken from marinade and dissolve 1 tbsp (15 mL) of the cornstarch in the marinade. Dredge chicken in the remaining cornstarch. In a wok, heat vegetable oil over medium-high heat until smoking. Stir-fry chicken until browned on all sides and no longer pink inside; remove to a plate. Add garlic, ginger and orange zest to the wok and stir-fry for 10 seconds. Add broth, apricots and sugar; bring to a boil. Stir marinade and add to wok; boil, stirring constantly, for at least 3 minutes, or until sauce is slightly thickened. Return chicken to the wok and stir to coat with sauce. **Serves 4.**

Chicken with Glazed Red Pepper

1 lb	boneless skinless chicken breasts, cut into bite-size pieces	500 g
1 tbsp	cornstarch	15 mL
3 tbsp	vegetable oil	45 mL
1	small onion, finely chopped	1
1	clove garlic, minced	1
Pinch	hot pepper flakes	Pinch
2	roasted red bell peppers (page 11), cut into strips	2
3 tbsp	cider vinegar	45 mL
2 tbsp	granulated sugar	25 mL
1 tsp	Worcestershire sauce	5 mL

Dredge chicken in cornstarch. In a wok, heat oil over medium-high heat until smoking. Stir-fry chicken until brown on all sides and no longer pink inside; remove to a plate. Add onion, garlic and hot pepper flakes to the wok and stir-fry for 1 minute. Add roasted peppers and stir-fry for 1 minute. Add vinegar, sugar and Worcestershire sauce; stir-fry until sugar begins to color, about 1 minute. Return chicken to the wok and stir to coat with sauce. **Serves 4.**

Creamy, Corny Chicken Stir-Fry

Follow preceding recipe, but use only 1 roasted pepper, and add one 17-oz (510 mL) can cream-style corn with the Worcestershire sauce. Omit the vinegar and sugar. **Serves 4.**

Stir-Fried Caramel Chicken

1 lb	boneless skinless chicken breasts, cut into bite-size pieces	500 g
1 tbsp	cornstarch	15 mL
3 tbsp	vegetable oil	45 mL
1	large onion, finely chopped	1
1	carrot, julienned	1
1	clove garlic, minced	1
¼ cup	granulated sugar	50 mL
3 tbsp	cider vinegar	45 mL
1 tsp	Worcestershire sauce	5 mL

Dredge chicken in cornstarch. In a wok, heat oil over medium-high heat until smoking. Stir-fry chicken until browned on all sides and no longer pink inside; remove to a plate. Add onion and carrot to the wok and stir-fry for 1 minute. Add garlic and stir-fry for 1 minute. Add sugar, vinegar and Worcestershire sauce; stir-fry until sugar begins to color, about 1 minute. Return chicken to the wok and stir to coat with sauce. **Serves 4.**

Sweet Anise Chicken

2 tbsp	vegetable oil	25 mL
1½ lbs	boneless skinless chicken thighs, cut into bite-size pieces	750 g
3	cloves garlic, minced	3
8 oz	shiitake mushrooms, stems trimmed, sliced	250 g
1 cup	sliced fennel bulb	250 mL
1 tbsp	minced gingerroot	15 mL
1 tsp	ground anise seeds	5 mL
Pinch	hot pepper flakes	Pinch
¾ cup	chicken broth	175 mL
¼ cup	dry sherry	50 mL
2 tbsp	granulated sugar	25 mL
2 tbsp	soy sauce	25 mL
2 tsp	cornstarch, dissolved in ¼ cup (50 mL) chicken broth	10 mL
1 tsp	dark sesame oil	5 mL

In a wok, heat vegetable oil over medium-high heat until smoking. Stir-fry chicken until lightly browned on all sides. Add garlic, mushrooms, fennel, ginger, anise seeds and hot pepper flakes; stir-fry for 1 minute. Add broth, sherry, sugar and soy sauce; reduce heat and simmer for 4 to 5 minutes, or until juices run clear when chicken is pierced. Stir cornstarch mixture and add to wok; simmer until sauce is slightly thickened. Stir in sesame oil. **Serves 4.**

Spicy Anise Lamb

Follow preceding recipe, but replace the chicken with very thin slices of lean boneless leg of lamb, and replace the sesame oil with hot pepper oil. **Serves 4.**

Beef and Mushrooms

12	dried mushrooms (any type)	12
½ cup	warm beef broth	125 mL
2 tbsp	soy sauce	25 mL
1 tbsp	dry sherry	15 mL
2 tsp	cornstarch	10 mL
1½ lbs	beef flank steak or boneless sirloin, trimmed and thinly sliced Kosher salt and freshly ground black pepper to taste	750 g
2 tbsp	vegetable oil	25 mL
1	thick slice gingerroot	1
1	clove garlic	1
1	dried chili pepper	1
3	green onions, thinly sliced	3
1	clove garlic, minced	1

Soak mushrooms in broth for about 20 minutes, until softened. Slice mushrooms and return to broth. Add soy sauce, sherry and cornstarch; set aside. Season beef with salt and pepper. In a wok, heat oil over medium-high heat until smoking. Stir-fry ginger, garlic clove and chili pepper until garlic browns; remove with a slotted spoon and discard. Add beef to the wok and stir-fry until lightly browned on all sides. Add reserved mushroom mixture, reduce heat and simmer until slightly thickened. Stir in green onions and minced garlic. **Serves 4.**

Stir-Fried Beef Barbecue

1 tbsp	vegetable oil	15 mL
1½ lbs	beef flank steak or top round, trimmed and thinly sliced	750 g
Pinch	hot pepper flakes	Pinch
⅓ cup	grated onion	75 mL
1	clove garlic, minced	1
1 tbsp	grated gingerroot	15 mL
¼ cup	ketchup	50 mL
2 tbsp	cider vinegar	25 mL
1 tbsp	Worcestershire sauce	15 mL
1 tsp	packed dark brown sugar	5 mL
	Juice of 1 lime	

In a wok, heat oil over medium-high heat until smoking. Stir-fry beef and hot pepper flakes until meat is browned on all sides; remove to a plate. Add onion, garlic and ginger to the wok and stir-fry for 1 minute. Add ketchup, vinegar, Worcestershire sauce and brown sugar; stir-fry until slightly thickened. Return beef to the pan and stir to coat with sauce. Drizzle with lime juice. **Serves 4.**

Orange Beef

Follow preceding recipe, but omit the ketchup and vinegar, and add 1 cup (250 mL) orange juice, mixed with 1 tsp (5 mL) cornstarch, with the Worcestershire sauce. Omit the lime juice. **Serves 4.**

Veal with Olives

1½ lbs	boneless leg of veal, cut into strips	750 g
3	cloves garlic, minced, divided	3
	Salt and freshly ground black pepper to taste	
2 tbsp	olive oil	25 mL
1	small onion, finely chopped	1
4	plum (Roma) tomatoes, peeled, seeded and chopped	4
3 tbsp	pitted oil-cured black olives	45 mL
2 tbsp	chopped fresh basil	25 mL
2 tsp	chopped fresh Italian (flat-leaf) parsley	10 mL

Toss veal with one-third of the garlic, salt and pepper. In a wok, heat oil over medium-high heat until smoking. Stir-fry veal until lightly browned on all sides; remove to a plate. Add onion and the remaining garlic to the wok and stir-fry for 1 minute. Add tomatoes, olives and basil; reduce heat and bring to a simmer. Return veal to the wok and heat through. Sprinkle with parsley. **Serves 4.**

Veal with Hot and Sweet Peppers

Follow preceding recipe, but omit the olives, and add 1 tbsp (15 mL) finely diced seeded hot chili pepper and 1 roasted red bell pepper (see page 11), diced, with the tomatoes. **Serves 4.**

Sweet-and-Sour Lemon Pork

	Grated zest of 1 lemon	
6 tbsp	freshly squeezed lemon juice	90 mL
2 tbsp	soy sauce	25 mL
2 tbsp	dry sherry	25 mL
4 tsp	dark sesame oil	20 mL
1½ lbs	boneless pork loin, cut into bite-size pieces	750 g
⅓ cup	cornstarch, divided	75 mL
2 tbsp	vegetable oil	25 mL
3	cloves garlic, minced	3
1 tbsp	chopped gingerroot	15 mL
½ cup	chicken broth	125 mL
¼ cup	granulated sugar	50 mL

In a large bowl, combine lemon juice, soy sauce, sherry and sesame oil. Add pork and toss to coat. Cover and refrigerate for 30 minutes. Remove pork from marinade and dissolve 1 tbsp (15 mL) of the cornstarch in the marinade. Dredge pork in the remaining cornstarch. In a wok, heat vegetable oil over medium-high heat until smoking. Stir-fry pork until just a hint of pink remains inside; remove to a plate. Add garlic, ginger and lemon zest to the wok and stir-fry for 10 seconds. Add broth and sugar; bring to a boil. Stir marinade and add to wok; boil, stirring constantly, for at least 3 minutes, or until sauce is slightly thickened. Return pork to the wok and stir to coat with sauce. **Serves 4.**

Spicy Peanut Pork

2 tsp	peanut oil	10 mL
1 lb	boneless pork loin, trimmed and cut into thin strips	500 g
½	small onion, finely chopped	½
½ cup	diced red bell pepper	125 mL
2 tsp	grated gingerroot	10 mL
½ tsp	ground cumin	2 mL
½ tsp	ground coriander	2 mL
½ cup	chicken broth	125 mL
2 tsp	soy sauce	10 mL
1 tsp	Chinese chili paste with garlic	5 mL
1	clove garlic, minced	1
¼ cup	peanut butter (chunky or smooth)	50 mL
1 tbsp	dry sherry	15 mL
2	green onions, thinly sliced	2
½ cup	roasted peanuts	125 mL

In a wok, heat oil over medium-high heat until smoking. Stir-fry pork until lightly browned on all sides. Add onion, red pepper, ginger, cumin and coriander; stir-fry until onion is tender. Add broth, soy sauce and chili paste; cover, reduce heat and simmer for 2 to 3 minutes, or until just a hint of pink remains in pork. Stir in garlic, peanut butter and sherry until peanut butter melts. Sprinkle with green onions and peanuts. **Serves 4.**

Peanut Chicken

Follow preceding recipe, but replace the pork with boneless skinless chicken, cut into bite-size chunks. Simmer until chicken is no longer pink inside. **Serves 4.**

Spicy Peanut Shrimp

Follow recipe for Spicy Peanut Pork (above), but replace the pork with 1½ lbs (750 g) large shrimp, peeled and deveined. Do not cover after the broth is added, and simmer for only 1 minute, until shrimp are pink and opaque. Omit the sherry, and add the juice of ½ lemon with the peanut butter. **Serves 4.**

This seasoning mixture is used in the three recipes that follow.

Stir-Fried Curry Mixture

1 tbsp	vegetable oil, divided	15 mL
1 cup	finely chopped onion	250 mL
1	clove garlic, minced	1
2 tsp	finely chopped gingerroot	10 mL
2 tsp	curry powder	10 mL
1 tsp	ground coriander	5 mL
1 tsp	ground cumin	5 mL
Pinch	hot pepper flakes	Pinch
¼ cup	chopped fresh cilantro	50 mL
1 tbsp	freshly squeezed lemon juice	15 mL

In a wok, heat oil over medium-high heat until smoking. Stir-fry onion, garlic, ginger, curry powder, coriander, cumin and hot pepper flakes until onion is tender. Transfer to a bowl and stir in cilantro and lemon juice. **Makes about ½ cup (125 mL).** *Use as directed in the three recipes that follow.*

Stir-Fried Curried Vegetables

1 tbsp	vegetable oil	15 mL
1 tsp	yellow mustard seeds	5 mL
1 cup	broccoli florets	250 mL
1 cup	cauliflower florets	250 mL
1 cup	sliced green beans	250 mL
½ cup	sliced carrot	125 mL
½ cup	water	125 mL
1	recipe Stir-Fried Curry Mixture (left)	1

In a wok, heat oil over medium-high heat until smoking. Stir-fry mustard seeds until they start to pop. Add broccoli, cauliflower, green beans and carrots; stir-fry until vegetables are brightly colored. Add water, cover and steam for 3 minutes, until vegetables are tender-crisp. Stir in curry mixture. **Serves 4.**

Curried Lamb with Eggplant

1 tbsp	vegetable oil	15 mL
1 tsp	yellow mustard seeds	5 mL
1 lb	boneless leg of lamb, thinly sliced	500 g
2 cups	cubed eggplant	500 mL
1 cup	chopped tomato	250 mL
½ cup	chicken broth	125 mL
1	recipe Stir-Fried Curry Mixture (left)	1

In a wok, heat oil over medium-high heat until smoking. Stir-fry mustard seeds until they start to pop. Add lamb and stir-fry until lightly browned; remove to a plate. Add eggplant to the wok and stir-fry until browned on all sides. Add tomato and stir-fry until eggplant is tender. Return lamb to the wok and add broth and curry mixture; stir to coat lamb and vegetables with sauce, and heat through. **Serves 4.**

Red Curry Chicken

1 tbsp	vegetable oil	15 mL
1 tsp	yellow mustard seeds	5 mL
1½ lbs	boneless skinless chicken breast, diced	750 g

1 to 2 tbsp	Thai red curry paste	15 to 25 mL
½ cup	coconut milk	125 mL
1	recipe Stir-Fried Curry Mixture (page 166)	1

In a wok, heat oil over medium-high heat until smoking. Stir-fry mustard seeds until they start to pop. Add chicken and curry paste to taste; stir-fry until chicken is browned on all sides. Add coconut milk and curry mixture; cover, reduce heat and simmer for 3 minutes, or until chicken is no longer pink inside. **Serves 4.**

Stir-Fried Pasta Primavera

2 tbsp	extra-virgin olive oil	25 mL
1	large onion, chopped	1
1	large clove garlic, minced	1
4 oz	green beans, ends snapped, cut into 2-inch (5 cm) lengths	125 g
1 cup	small cauliflower or broccoli florets	250 mL
½ cup	diced red bell pepper	125 mL
½ cup	diced carrot	125 mL
12 oz	asparagus, trimmed and cut into 2-inch (5 cm) lengths	375 g
1 cup	vegetable broth	250 mL
1 tbsp	dried Italian seasoning	15 mL
10 oz	pasta, cooked	300 g
	Salt and freshly ground black pepper to taste	
1 cup	cream (any type, minimum 10%)	250 mL
⅓ cup	freshly grated Parmesan cheese	75 mL

In a wok, heat oil over medium-high heat until smoking. Stir-fry onion for 30 seconds. Add garlic, green beans, cauliflower, red pepper and carrot; stir-fry for 3 minutes. Add asparagus, broth and Italian seasoning; stir-fry until most of the broth has evaporated. Add pasta, salt and pepper; stir-fry for 1 minute. Add cream, reduce heat and simmer until pasta is coated with sauce. Stir in Parmesan. **Serves 4.**

Spaghetti with Stir-Fried Meat Sauce

1 tbsp	extra-virgin olive oil	15 mL
1	large onion, chopped	1
2	cloves garlic, minced	2
1 lb	ground beef	500 g
3 cups	chopped drained canned tomatoes	750 mL
¼ cup	tomato paste	50 mL
Pinch	hot pepper flakes	Pinch
	Salt and freshly ground black pepper to taste	
12 oz	spaghetti, cooked	375 g
1 tbsp	chopped fresh Italian (flat-leaf) parsley	15 mL

In a wok, heat oil over medium-high heat until smoking. Stir-fry onion and garlic for 30 seconds. Add ground beef and stir-fry, breaking beef up with a fork, until no longer pink. Add tomatoes, reduce heat and simmer for 3 minutes. Stir in tomato paste, hot pepper flakes, salt and black pepper. Add spaghetti and parsley; stir to coat with sauce, and heat through. **Serves 4.**

Thai Fried Noodles

12 oz	rice vermicelli	375 g
3 tbsp	canola oil	45 mL
3	cloves garlic, minced	3
½ tsp	hot pepper flakes	2 mL
1 tbsp	granulated sugar	15 mL
3 tbsp	Thai fish sauce (*nam pla*)	45 mL
1½ tbsp	ketchup	22 mL
2	eggs, beaten	2
1 cup	bean sprouts, divided	250 mL
2	green onions, sliced	2
2 tbsp	chopped peanuts	25 mL
2 tbsp	chopped fresh cilantro	25 mL
1	lime, sliced	1

Soak vermicelli in hot water for 15 minutes; drain and set aside. In a wok, heat oil over medium-high heat until smoking. Stir-fry garlic and hot pepper flakes for 10 seconds. Add sugar, fish sauce and ketchup; stir-fry until sugar dissolves. Add vermicelli and eggs; stir-fry for 1 minute. Add ¾ cup (175 mL) of the bean sprouts and stir-fry for 2 minutes. Transfer to a serving platter, sprinkle with the remaining bean sprouts, green onions, peanuts and cilantro, and garnish with lime slices. **Serves 4.**

Shrimp Thai Noodles

Follow preceding recipe, but add 8 oz (250 g) small shrimp, peeled and deveined, with the garlic. Stir-fry until shrimp are pink and opaque before proceeding. **Serves 4.**

High-Protein Vegetarian Stir-Fried Noodles

Follow recipe for Thai Fried Noodles (above), but stir-fry 1 cake of tofu, diced, and 3 oz (90 g) snow peas, trimmed, with the garlic for 1 minute; remove tofu and snow peas to a plate. Return to the wok for the final minute of cooking. **Serves 4.**

Stir-Fried Pork and Shrimp with Noodles

1 tbsp	vegetable oil	15 mL
3	cloves garlic, minced	3
1 tbsp	minced gingerroot	15 mL
8 oz	boneless pork loin, cut into thin strips	250 g
8 oz	medium shrimp, peeled and deveined	250 g
½ cup	thinly sliced carrot	125 mL
½ cup	drained canned sliced bamboo shoots	125 mL
½ cup	chicken broth	125 mL
8 oz	egg noodles, cooked	250 g
1 tbsp	granulated sugar	15 mL
2 tbsp	soy sauce	25 mL
1 tbsp	oyster sauce	15 mL
1 tsp	dark sesame oil	5 mL

In a wok, heat vegetable oil over medium-high heat until smoking. Stir-fry garlic and ginger for 10 seconds. Add pork and shrimp; stir-fry until pork is lightly browned and shrimp is starting to turn pink. Stir in carrot and bamboo shoots. Add broth, reduce heat and simmer for 3 minutes. Add noodles, sugar, soy sauce and oyster sauce; stir to coat noodles with sauce, and heat through. Drizzle with sesame oil. **Serves 4.**

Stir-Fried Garlic Chicken with Noodles

Follow preceding recipe, but replace the pork and shrimp with 1 lb (500 g) boneless skinless chicken, cut into bite-size pieces; stir-fry until no longer pink inside. Add an extra 1 tsp (5 mL) minced garlic with the sesame oil. **Serves 4.**

Stir-Fried Beans

2 tbsp	canola oil	25 mL
3	dried chili peppers	3
2	large onions, chopped	2
1	clove garlic, minced	1
4 cups	canned red kidney, white or black beans, drained and rinsed	1 L
1 tsp	ground cumin	5 mL
1 tsp	ground coriander	5 mL
¼ tsp	dried oregano	1 mL
2 tbsp	chopped fresh cilantro or Italian (flat-leaf) parsley	25 mL

In a wok, heat oil over medium-high heat until smoking. Stir-fry chili peppers until bubbling; remove with a slotted spoon and discard. Add onions to the wok and stir-fry until lightly browned. Add garlic, beans, cumin, coriander and oregano; stir-fry for 3 minutes, until heated through. Stir in cilantro. **Serves 4.**

Stir-Fried Broccoli with Hoisin Almonds

3 tbsp	canola oil, divided	45 mL
1	clove garlic	1
½	small onion, chopped	½
4 cups	broccoli florets	1 L
Pinch	hot pepper flakes	Pinch
⅓ cup	water	75 mL
⅓ cup	sliced almonds	75 mL
3 tbsp	granulated sugar	45 mL
1 tbsp	hoisin sauce	15 mL

In a wok, heat 2 tbsp (25 mL) of the oil over medium-high heat until smoking. Stir-fry garlic clove until browned, about 30 seconds; remove with a slotted spoon and discard. Add onion to the wok and stir-fry until tender. Add broccoli and hot pepper flakes; stir-fry for 1 minute. Add water; cover, reduce heat and simmer until broccoli is bright green and water has evaporated, about 4 minutes. Remove contents of the wok to a large bowl. Wipe out wok, add the remaining oil and heat over medium-high heat until smoking. Toast almonds until lightly colored. Add sugar and hoisin sauce; stir-fry until almonds are well glazed. Add to broccoli mixture and toss to coat. **Serves 4.**

Stir-Fried Carrots with Mint and Red Pepper

2 tbsp	olive oil	25 mL
1 lb	carrots, thinly sliced	500 g
½ cup	chopped onion	125 mL
1 tsp	minced gingerroot	5 mL
⅓ cup	brewed mint tea	75 mL
¼ cup	diced red bell pepper	50 mL
1	small clove garlic, minced	1
2 tbsp	finely chopped fresh mint	25 mL
1 tsp	freshly squeezed lemon juice	5 mL

In a wok, heat oil over medium-high heat until smoking. Stir-fry carrots, onion and ginger for 1 minute. Add tea and red pepper; cover and cook until carrots are tender, about 4 minutes. Uncover and boil off excess liquid. Stir in garlic, mint and lemon juice. **Serves 4.**

Corn with Ham and Sweet Peppers

1 tbsp	canola oil	15 mL
¼ cup	chopped onion	50 mL
1	small clove garlic, minced	1
1	red bell pepper, diced	1
4 oz	smoked ham, diced	125 g
4 cups	canned or frozen corn kernels	1 L
Pinch	ground nutmeg	Pinch
1 tbsp	chopped fresh Italian (flat-leaf) parsley	15 mL

In a wok, heat oil over medium-high heat until smoking. Stir-fry onion and garlic for 30 seconds. Add red pepper, ham, corn and nutmeg; stir-fry until corn is browned around the edges. Stir in parsley. **Serves 4.**

Italian Stir-Fried Green Beans

1 tbsp	extra-virgin olive oil	15 mL
1 lb	thin green beans, ends snapped off	500 g
1	clove garlic, minced	1
⅓ cup	water	75 mL
2 tbsp	toasted pine nuts	25 mL

In a wok, heat oil over medium-high heat until smoking. Stir-fry beans and garlic until beans are bright green. Add water, cover and steam for 3 minutes, until beans are tender-crisp. Stir in pine nuts. **Serves 4.**

Stir-Fried Garlic Green Beans

Follow preceding recipe, but double the garlic and omit the pine nuts. **Serves 4.**

Stir-Fried Herbed Mushrooms

1 tbsp	olive oil	15 mL
2 tbsp	chopped onion	25 mL
1 lb	small mushrooms, trimmed	500 g
1	clove garlic, minced	1
½ cup	chicken broth	125 mL
¼ cup	chopped fresh herbs (such as flat-leaf parsley, thyme, rosemary, basil)	50 mL
1 tsp	cornstarch, dissolved in 2 tsp (10 mL) water	5 mL
1 tsp	butter	5 mL
	Salt and freshly ground black pepper to taste	

In a wok, heat oil over high heat until smoking. Stir-fry onion for 30 seconds. Add mushrooms and stir-fry until they lose their raw look. Add garlic, broth and herbs; cover and cook for 2 minutes. Stir cornstarch mixture and add to wok; reduce heat and simmer until sauce is slightly thickened. Remove from heat and stir in butter, salt and pepper. **Serves 4.**

Stir-Fried Wild Mushrooms with Hazelnuts

2 tbsp	peanut oil	25 mL
2 tbsp	minced shallots	25 mL
1 lb	wild or exotic mushrooms (any type), trimmed and thickly sliced	500 g
1 cup	strong beef broth	250 mL
1 tbsp	soy sauce	15 mL
2 tsp	cornstarch, dissolved in 4 tsp (20 mL) water	10 mL
3	green onions, finely sliced	3
1	small clove garlic, minced	1
¼ cup	coarsely chopped hazelnuts	50 mL

In a wok, heat oil over medium-high heat until smoking. Stir-fry shallots for 10 seconds. Add mushrooms and stir-fry until they lose their raw look. Add broth and soy sauce; cover and cook for 2 minutes. Lift mushrooms onto sides of wok. Stir cornstarch mixture and add to wok, along with green onions and garlic; reduce heat and simmer until sauce is slightly thickened. Stir in mushrooms and hazelnuts. **Serves 4.**

Soy-Glazed Potatoes

1 lb	small red-skinned potatoes	500 g
2 tbsp	peanut oil	25 mL
1	onion, coarsely chopped	1
1	clove garlic, minced	1
¼ cup	reduced-sodium soy sauce	50 mL

Cook potatoes in boiling water until barely tender, about 20 minutes. Drain well and pat dry. In a wok, heat oil over medium-high heat until smoking. Stir-fry potatoes and onion until potatoes are browned on all sides. Add garlic and soy sauce; stir to coat potatoes with sauce. **Serves 4.**

Stir-Fried Apple Shortcake

6 tbsp	unsalted butter	90 mL
4	large tart apples, peeled and sliced	4
1 tbsp	freshly squeezed lemon juice	15 mL
1/3 cup	granulated sugar	75 mL
2 tsp	cornstarch	10 mL
2 tsp	water	10 mL
1 tsp	vanilla	5 mL
8	Shortcake Biscuits (see recipe, page 22), split	8

In a wok, melt butter over medium-high heat. Stir-fry apples and lemon juice until apples are barely tender. Add sugar and stir-fry until sugar dissolves, then boil for 3 minutes. Meanwhile, dissolve cornstarch in water and vanilla; stir, add to wok and stir-fry until sauce is slightly thickened. Pour over Shortcake Biscuits. **Serves 4.**

Stir-Fried Banana Split

2 tbsp	butter	25 mL
4	bananas, sliced into rounds	4
3 tbsp	packed light brown sugar	45 mL
2 tbsp	dark rum	25 mL
4	scoops vanilla ice cream	4
	Wet Bourbon Pecans (see recipe, page 450)	

In a wok, melt butter over medium heat. Stir-fry bananas for 1 minute. Add brown sugar and stir to coat bananas. Add rum and stir-fry until sugar dissolves, about 1 minute. Serve over ice cream; top with Wet Bourbon Pecans (which can be made in the wok). **Serves 4.**

Rum Raisin Bananas

Follow preceding recipe. After cooking, stir in 1/4 cup (50 mL) raisins that have been plumped in 1/4 cup (50 mL) dark rum. Serve over ice cream or slices of plain cake. **Serves 4.**

Stir-Fried Poached Pears

1/4 cup	honey	50 mL
1/4 cup	white wine	50 mL
1/4 cup	water	50 mL
	Finely grated zest and juice of 1/2 lemon and 1/2 orange	
1/4 cup	butter	50 mL
4	pears, peeled and sliced	4
2 tsp	cornstarch	10 mL
2 tbsp	orange-flavored liqueur	25 mL
1 tsp	vanilla	5 mL

Dissolve honey in wine, water and citrus juices; stir in citrus zests and set aside. In a wok, melt butter over medium-high heat. Stir-fry pears for 1 minute. Add honey mixture to wok, reduce heat and simmer, tossing gently, until pears are tender, about 3 minutes; with a slotted spoon, remove pears to a large bowl. Meanwhile, dissolve cornstarch in liqueur and vanilla; stir, add to wok and simmer until sauce is slightly thickened. Pour over pears. Serve warm. **Serves 4.**

Peaches Stir-Fried with Framboise

6 tbsp	butter	90 mL
4	large freestone peaches, peeled and sliced	4
¼ cup	granulated sugar	50 mL
1 tsp	raspberry vinegar	5 mL
2 tsp	cornstarch	10 mL
2 tbsp	framboise (raspberry liqueur) Ice cream or pound cake	25 mL

In a wok, melt butter over medium heat. Stir-fry peaches for 2 minutes. Add sugar and vinegar; stir-fry until sugar dissolves and liquid is boiling; boil for 2 minutes. Meanwhile, dissolve cornstarch in framboise; stir, add to wok and stir-fry until sauce is slightly thickened. Serve over ice cream or cake. **Serves 4.**

Sweet Fried Rice

1¼ cups	water	300 mL
2 tsp	vanilla, divided	10 mL
1 cup	diced mixed dried fruit	250 mL
¼ cup	butter, divided	50 mL
¼ cup	thinly sliced onion	50 mL
⅓ cup	granulated sugar, divided	75 mL
1 tsp	ground cinnamon, divided	5 mL
3 cups	cooked rice	750 mL
Pinch	salt	Pinch
½ cup	slivered almonds, toasted	125 mL
Pinch	ground cloves	Pinch

Combine water and half the vanilla. Add dried fruit and soak for 40 minutes. In a wok, melt half the butter over medium heat. Stir-fry onion until lightly browned. Add all but 1 tbsp (15 mL) of the sugar and stir-fry until sugar is dissolved and lightly caramelized. Add fruit mixture and half the cinnamon; stir-fry for 3 minutes. Remove contents of the wok to a bowl. Add the remaining butter and heat over medium-high heat. Stir-fry rice, the remaining sugar, the remaining vanilla and salt, pushing rice against the sides of the wok, until the mixture becomes sticky and brown in spots. Toss rice with fruit mixture. Spoon onto a serving platter and sprinkle with almonds. Combine the remaining cinnamon and cloves; sprinkle over rice mixture. **Serves 4.**

Chapter 15
Heatless Cooking
When It's Too Hot to Turn on the Stove

Four-Color Fish Seviche 173

Mexican Seviche 173

Green Seviche 173

Honey-Cured Gravlax 174

Fennel-Cured Bluefish 174

Brandied Summer Fruit 174

Three-Endive Slaw 174

Three-Can Salad 174

Chilled Tomato and Roasted
Pepper Soup 174

White Gazpacho 175

Honeydew Mint Soup 175

Gingered Mango Soup 175

Mango Orange Soup with Plums
and Blueberries 175

Sesame Tuna Sashimi 175

Carpaccio 175

Carpaccio Jalapeño 176

Carpaccio Tonnato 176

Cold Sage Sauce 176

Fennel Grapefruit Sauce 176

Tarragon Raspberry Sauce 176

Rich Red Tomato Salsa 176

Spicy Green Tomato Salsa 176

Confetti Salsa 177

Jalapeño Salsa 177

Gazpacho Salsa 177

Artichoke Salsa 177

Tomato Dill Salsa 177

Roasted Pepper Salsa 177

Avocado Salsa 177

Cucumber Mint Salsa 177

Ginger Lychee Salsa 178

Fresh Basil Pesto 178

Spicy Basil Pesto 178

Spinach Pesto 178

Mint Pesto 178

Oregano Walnut Pesto 178

Anchovy Olive Pesto 178

Hummus Tahini 179

Avocado Coulis 179

Green Herb Oil 179

Creole Tartar Sauce 179

Prosciutto and Summer Fruit Salad 179

Peaches Stuffed with
Smoked Salmon Mousse 179

Peaches Stuffed with Ham Mousse 179

Vegetable-Stuffed Deviled Eggs 180

Smoked Trout and Horseradish
Deviled Eggs 180

Cherries in Orange Honey
over Melon 180

Kiwi and Honeydew in
Margarita Glaze 180

Espresso Granita 180

Bourbon-Spiked Peach
and Praline "Bombe" 180

The survival of many a cook has rested as much on knowing when to turn a stove off as on knowing when to turn it on.

Take summer, for example. The only trick to cooking during summer's swelter lies in figuring out how *not* to do it. For most of us, this is no mean feat. After using up our quota of dinner reservations and tuna salad, it's the rare cook who doesn't yearn for inspiration.

How about 50 inspirations? This chapter includes recipes for appetizers, entrées, salads, soups, sauces and desserts — and you don't have to use a range, oven or grill to make any of them. Many are stand-alone dishes, but we've also included a number of sauces that can accompany cold leftover meat or fish. You can, of course, elect to reheat the meat; either way, these sauces are great for dressing up a steak or recycling a roast, and you'll never be accused of serving up leftovers.

We often think of marination as a way to flavor ingredients that are being cooked conventionally, but in this chapter we offer several dishes that are "cooked" without ever being exposed to heat. The cooking is done by soaking the ingredient, usually fish or shellfish, in acid or salt until its flesh becomes firm and its color changes from translucent to opaque. When you consider that these are the same changes that occur when a fish is heated, you can see that the fish prepared in the seviche and gravlax recipes below are every bit as cooked by exposure to acid and salt as if they had come out of the oven.

Many of these recipes are exciting, and all yield beautiful results that will delight any cook who can't stand the heat but can't get out of the kitchen.

About these recipes . . .

The following recipes can all be prepared without turning on the stove. Some are complete dishes unto themselves, while others complement cold leftovers.

Four-Color Fish Seviche

1 cup	freshly squeezed lemon juice	250 mL
12 oz	boneless skinless flounder fillet, thinly sliced	375 g
4 oz	smoked salmon, chopped	125 g
2	green onions, thinly sliced	2
1 tbsp	finely chopped red onion	15 mL
	Lettuce leaves, for serving	

Place lemon juice in a shallow dish. Add flounder and turn to coat. Cover and refrigerate for 1½ hours; drain and discard marinade. Add smoked salmon, green onions and red onion to flounder. Serve on lettuce leaves. **Serves 4.**

Mexican Seviche

½ cup	freshly squeezed lemon juice	125 mL
½ cup	freshly squeezed lime juice	125 mL
2 tbsp	cider vinegar	25 mL
1 lb	sea scallops, trimmed of hard side muscles and thinly sliced	500 g
2	green onions, thinly sliced	2
1	avocado, diced	1
1	canned chipotle or fresh jalapeño pepper, minced	1
1	tomato, diced	1
2 tbsp	chopped fresh cilantro	25 mL

In a large bowl, combine lemon juice, lime juice and vinegar. Add scallops and toss to coat. Cover and refrigerate for 2 hours; drain and discard marinade. Add green onions, avocado, chipotle, tomato and cilantro to scallops. **Serves 4.**

Green Seviche

½ cup	freshly squeezed lemon juice	125 mL
½ cup	freshly squeezed lime juice	125 mL
¼ cup	freshly squeezed orange juice	50 mL
1 lb	sea scallops, trimmed of hard side muscles and thinly sliced	500 g
⅓ cup	chopped fresh herbs (such as flat-leaf parsley, dill, tarragon, savory)	75 mL
1 tbsp	extra-virgin olive oil	15 mL

In a large bowl, combine lemon juice, lime juice and orange juice. Add scallops and toss to coat. Cover and refrigerate for 2 hours; drain and discard marinade. Add herbs and oil to scallops and toss to coat. **Serves 4.**

Honey-Cured Gravlax

⅓ cup	honey	75 mL
	Juice of ½ lemon	
2 lb	boneless salmon fillet (with skin)	1 kg
1 cup	kosher salt	250 mL
¼ cup	granulated sugar	50 mL
½ tsp	freshly ground white pepper	2 mL

In a shallow dish, combine honey and lemon juice. Add salmon and turn to coat. Cover and refrigerate for 2 hours. Combine salt, sugar and pepper; spread one-third of this mixture over the bottom of a clean glass dish large enough to hold the salmon. Lift salmon from marinade, place on salt mixture and pour remaining salt mixture over salmon, mounding it at the thickest part of the fish. Discard marinade. Cover dish with plastic wrap, weight with a dish and refrigerate for 48 hours. Lift salmon from salt mixture and rinse thoroughly. Discard salt mixture. Thinly slice salmon at an angle. Serve as you would lox or smoked salmon. **Serves 8.**

Fennel-Cured Bluefish

1 cup	kosher salt	250 mL
¼ cup	granulated sugar	50 mL
1 tbsp	ground fennel seeds	15 mL
½ tsp	freshly ground black pepper	2 mL
2 lb	bluefish fillet (with skin), pin bones removed	1 kg
	Rye bread	
	Sour cream, red onion slices and prepared horseradish	

Combine salt, sugar, fennel seeds and pepper; spread one-third of this mixture over the bottom of a glass dish large enough to hold the fish. Place fish on salt mixture and cover fish with remaining salt mixture. Cover with plastic wrap, weight with a dish and refrigerate for 36 hours. Lift fish from salt mixture and rinse thoroughly. Discard salt mixture. Slice and serve on rye bread with sour cream, red onion and horseradish. **Serves 8.**

Brandied Summer Fruit

¼ cup	brandy	50 mL
1 tbsp	honey	15 mL
1 tsp	raspberry vinegar	5 mL
8	large strawberries, hulled and halved	8
3	apricots, quartered	3
3	figs, quartered	3
1	peach, sliced	1
1	kiwi, peeled and thinly sliced	1
8 oz	sweet cherries, pitted and halved	250 g
1 cup	fresh blueberries	250 mL

In a large bowl, combine brandy, honey and Berry Vinegar. Add fruit and toss to coat. Cover and refrigerate for at least 2 hours or for up to 1 day. **Serves 4.** *(Note: You may substitute a similar amount of any ripe fruit for the fruit in the recipe.)*

Three-Endive Slaw

1	head curly endive, stemmed and broken into small pieces	1
1	head radicchio, shredded	1
1	head Belgian endive, julienned	1
3 tbsp	sesame seeds	45 mL
3 tbsp	walnut oil	45 mL
2 tbsp	white wine vinegar	25 mL
4 tsp	honey	20 mL
1 tbsp	sesame oil	15 mL
1 tbsp	soy sauce	15 mL

Combine curly endive, radicchio, Belgian endive and sesame seeds. Whisk together the remaining ingredients; pour over endive mixture and toss to coat. **Serves 4.**

Three-Can Salad

3	dill pickles, chopped	3
1	can (16 oz/454 mL) small potatoes, drained and quartered	1
1	can (16 oz/454 mL) beets, drained and quartered	1
1	jar (12 oz/360 g) pickled herring, drained and quartered	1
2 cups	walnut pieces	500 mL
½ cup	mayonnaise	125 mL
½ cup	sour cream	125 mL

Toss together all ingredients. Cover and refrigerate for about 1 hour, until chilled. **Serves 4.**

Chilled Tomato and Roasted Pepper Soup

2	large tomatoes, peeled (see "blanching," page 8) and quartered	2
2	roasted red bell peppers (see page 11), quartered	2
1	clove garlic	1
½	small onion, quartered	½
3 tbsp	olive oil	45 mL
6	ice cubes	6
	Chopped fresh Italian (flat-leaf) parsley	

In a food processor, process tomatoes, peppers, garlic, onion, oil and 3 of the ice cubes until finely chopped. Add 3 more ice cubes. When the ice has melted, stir and serve garnished with parsley. **Serves 4.**

White Gazpacho

3	green onions, white parts only, coarsely chopped	3
2	cucumbers, peeled, seeded and coarsely chopped	2
2	stalks celery, coarsely chopped	2
1	clove garlic	1
2 cups	chilled chicken broth	500 mL
1 cup	plain yogurt	250 mL
2 tbsp	white wine vinegar	25 mL
Dash	hot pepper sauce (such as Tabasco)	Dash
1 tbsp	chopped fresh dill	15 mL
2 tsp	finely grated lemon zest	10 mL

In a food processor, purée green onions, cucumbers, celery and garlic. Transfer to a bowl and stir in broth, yogurt, vinegar and hot pepper sauce. Cover and refrigerate for about 1 hour, until chilled. Serve in chilled bowls, garnished with dill and lemon zest. **Serves** 4.

Honeydew Mint Soup

8	fresh mint leaves	8
2	medium honeydew melons, seeded, peeled and coarsely chopped	2
1 tbsp	granulated sugar	15 mL
1/4 tsp	ground nutmeg	1 mL
Pinch	salt	Pinch
	Juice of 1 1/2 lemons	

In a food processor, purée all ingredients. Transfer to a bowl, cover and refrigerate for about 1 hour, until chilled. **Serves** 4.

Gingered Mango Soup

2	large mangoes, peeled, pitted and coarsely chopped	2
1 cup	orange juice	250 mL
1/2 cup	dry white wine	125 mL
4 tsp	honey	20 mL
2 tsp	minced gingerroot	10 mL
4 tsp	chopped candied ginger	20 mL

In a food processor, purée mangoes, orange juice, wine, honey and gingerroot. Transfer to a bowl, cover and refrigerate for about 1 hour, until chilled. Serve as a dessert soup, garnished with candied ginger. **Serves** 4.

Mango Orange Soup with Plums and Blueberries

Follow preceding recipe, but omit the gingerroot and candied ginger. Before chilling, garnish with 1 cup (250 mL) blueberries and 2 red plums, pitted and diced. **Serves** 4.

Sesame Tuna Sashimi

8 oz	sushi-quality tuna fillet (about 1 inch/2.5 cm thick), trimmed	250 g
4 tsp	soy sauce	20 mL
1/2 tsp	prepared wasabi	2 mL
1/2 cup	toasted sesame seeds	125 mL
1	lemon, thinly sliced	1
2	sheets toasted nori, julienned	2

Cut tuna into 16 thin slices. Combine soy sauce and wasabi; brush onto tuna. Roll tuna in sesame seeds and arrange on a platter garnished with lemon slices. Sprinkle with nori. **Serves** 4.

Carpaccio

6	cornichon pickles	6
3	drained canned anchovies	3
1	large clove garlic	1
1	small shallot, peeled	1
3 tbsp	chopped fresh Italian (flat-leaf) parsley	45 mL
1 tbsp	drained capers	15 mL
1/3 cup	extra-virgin olive oil	75 mL
1 tbsp	Dijon mustard	15 mL
1 tbsp	red wine vinegar	15 mL
8 oz	beef tenderloin, trimmed and sliced paper-thin	250 g
	Kosher salt and freshly ground black pepper	

In a food processor, process cornichons, anchovies, garlic, shallot, parsley and capers until finely chopped. With the motor running, slowly add oil, mustard and vinegar through the feed tube and process until thick. Arrange beef slices on a serving platter, overlapping slightly, and season with salt and pepper. Pour half the sauce over the beef and serve the rest on the side. **Serves** 4.

Carpaccio Jalapeño

2 to 3	jalapeño peppers, seeded and minced	2 to 3
1	clove garlic, minced	1
1/4 cup	minced onion	50 mL
1/4 cup	minced fresh cilantro	50 mL
3 tbsp	canola oil	45 mL
8 oz	beef tenderloin, trimmed and sliced paper-thin	250 g
	Kosher salt and freshly ground black pepper	

Combine jalapeños to taste, garlic, onion, cilantro and oil. Arrange beef slices on a serving platter, overlapping slightly, and season with salt and pepper. Spoon sauce over beef. **Serves 4.**

Carpaccio Tonnato

2	green onions, finely chopped	2
1	clove garlic, minced	1
1 tbsp	finely grated gingerroot	15 mL
2 tbsp	extra-virgin olive oil	25 mL
1 tbsp	freshly squeezed lemon juice	15 mL
1/4 tsp	hot pepper flakes	1 mL
1/4 tsp	ground coriander	1 mL
6 oz	sushi-quality tuna fillet, cut into 1/2-inch (1 cm) thick slices	175 g

Combine green onions, garlic, gingerroot, oil, lemon juice, hot pepper flakes and coriander. Dip tuna slices into sauce, then pound gently between sheets of waxed paper until paper-thin. Arrange on a platter, overlapping slightly, and top with remaining sauce. **Serves 4.**

Cold Sage Sauce

2	egg yolks	2
2 tsp	brown mustard	10 mL
1 tsp	balsamic vinegar	5 mL
	Juice of 1/2 orange	
1 cup	canola oil	250 mL
1 tbsp	minced fresh sage	15 mL
Pinch	cayenne pepper, dissolved in 1 tbsp (15 mL) boiling water	Pinch
	Salt and freshly ground white pepper to taste	

Whisk egg yolks and mustard until slightly thickened, then whisk in vinegar and orange juice. Whisk in oil in a slow, steady stream. Add sage, cayenne mixture, salt and white pepper. **Makes about 1 1/4 cups (300 mL).** *Serve with leftover roasts, especially pork, veal and poultry. (If you are concerned about the food safety of raw eggs, replace the egg yolks and oil with 1 1/2 cups/375 mL mayonnaise.)*

Fennel Grapefruit Sauce

2	egg yolks	2
2 tsp	brown mustard	10 mL
3 tbsp	freshly squeezed grapefruit juice	45 mL
1 tsp	freshly squeezed lemon juice	5 mL
1 cup	canola oil	250 mL
1 tsp	ground fennel seeds	5 mL
Pinch	cayenne pepper, dissolved in 1 tbsp (15 mL) boiling water	Pinch
	Salt and freshly ground white pepper to taste	

Whisk egg yolks and mustard until lightly thickened, then whisk in grapefruit and lemon juices. Whisk in oil in a slow, steady stream. Add fennel seeds, cayenne mixture, salt and white pepper. **Makes about 1 1/4 cups (300 mL).** *Serve with poached fish or in tuna salad. (If you are concerned about the food safety of raw eggs, replace the egg yolks and oil with 1 1/2 cups/375 mL mayonnaise.)*

Tarragon Raspberry Sauce

1	recipe Raspberry Vinaigrette (page 61)	1
1 tsp	dried tarragon (or 1 tbsp/15 mL chopped fresh)	5 mL

Prepare Raspberry Vinaigrette and add tarragon. **Makes about 1 cup (250 mL).** *Serve with grilled meats, poultry or fish.*

Rich Red Tomato Salsa

3	large tomatoes, quartered	3
2	jalapeño peppers, halved and seeded	2
1	small onion, quartered	1
1/4 cup	coarsely chopped fresh cilantro	50 mL
2 tbsp	finely chopped fresh Italian (flat-leaf) parsley	25 mL
2 tbsp	olive oil	25 mL
	Salt and freshly ground black pepper to taste	

In a food processor, chop tomatoes, jalapeños and onion to desired texture. Transfer to a bowl and stir in cilantro, parsley, oil, salt and pepper. **Makes about 4 cups (1 L).** *Store in an airtight container in the refrigerator for up to 2 days. Serve with chips or grilled meats.*

Spicy Green Tomato Salsa

Follow preceding recipe, but substitute green tomatoes for red, and omit the oil. **Makes about 4 cups (1 L).** *Store in an airtight container in the refrigerator for up to 2 days.*

Confetti Salsa

Follow recipe for Rich Red Tomato Salsa (page 176), but omit the onion, and add 4 to 5 green onions, chopped, and ½ cup (125 mL) diced yellow bell pepper with the cilantro. **Makes about 4 cups (1 L).** *Store in an airtight container in the refrigerator for up to 2 days. Use as a dip or as a sauce for plain meats.*

Jalapeño Salsa

6 or 7	pickled jalapeño peppers, drained, halved and seeded	6 or 7
2	large tomatoes, quartered	2
1	large clove garlic	1
⅓ cup	water	75 mL

In a food processor, process all ingredients until finely chopped. **Makes about 2½ cups (625 mL).** *Store in an airtight container in the refrigerator for up to 2 days. Use as a dip or as a sauce for chicken, fish or pork.*

Gazpacho Salsa

2	large tomatoes, quartered	2
1	small clove garlic	1
¼	small cucumber, peeled and cut into chunks	¼
¼	jalapeño pepper, halved and seeded	¼
1 tbsp	chopped onion	15 mL
2 tbsp	extra-virgin olive oil	25 mL
1 tbsp	red wine vinegar	15 mL

In a food processor, process all ingredients until finely chopped. **Makes about 3 cups (750 mL).** *Store in an airtight container in the refrigerator for up to 2 days. Serve with grilled or poached fish or with shellfish.*

Artichoke Salsa

1	jar (6 oz/170 mL) marinated artichoke hearts, drained	1
1	small clove garlic	1
⅓ cup	pine nuts	75 mL
	Juice of ½ large lemon	

In a food processor, process all ingredients until finely chopped. **Makes about 1½ cups (375 mL).** *Serve with grilled steaks, lamb, fish or chicken.*

Tomato Dill Salsa

2	large tomatoes, seeded and quartered	2
1	clove garlic	1
½	red onion, halved	½
¼ cup	chopped fresh dill	50 mL
3 tbsp	red wine vinegar	45 mL
2 tbsp	extra-virgin olive oil	25 mL

In a food processor, process all ingredients until finely chopped. **Makes about 2¼ cups (550 mL).** *Store in an airtight container in the refrigerator for up to 2 days. Serve with fish, chicken, veal, pork or shellfish.*

Roasted Pepper Salsa

2	large roasted red bell peppers (see page 11), finely chopped	2
1	small clove garlic, minced	1
1 tbsp	extra-virgin olive oil	15 mL
¼ tsp	hot pepper flakes	1 mL
	Juice of ½ lemon	

Combine all ingredients. **Makes about 3 cups (750 mL).** *Store in an airtight container in the refrigerator for up to 2 days. Serve with roasted or grilled meats, poultry or seafood.*

Avocado Salsa

2	green onions, finely chopped	2
1	large avocado, finely diced	1
1	large tomato, chopped	1
1	clove garlic, minced	1
3 tbsp	freshly squeezed lemon juice	45 mL
1 tbsp	extra-virgin olive oil	15 mL
2 tsp	chopped fresh Italian (flat-leaf) parsley	10 mL
	Hot pepper flakes to taste	

Combine all ingredients. **Makes about 3 cups (750 mL).** *Store in an airtight container in the refrigerator for up to 2 days. Serve with grilled meats, fish or seafood.*

Cucumber Mint Salsa

2	large cucumbers, peeled, seeded and cut into chunks	2
2	green onions, coarsely chopped	2
1	clove garlic	1
¼ cup	packed fresh mint leaves	50 mL
¼ cup	water	50 mL
3 tbsp	plain yogurt	45 mL
1 tbsp	extra-virgin olive oil	15 mL
1 tsp	white wine vinegar	5 mL

In a food processor, process all ingredients until finely chopped. **Makes about 3 cups (750 mL).** *Store in an airtight container in the refrigerator for up to 2 days. Serve with fish, chicken or veal.*

Ginger Lychee Salsa

24	lychees (canned or fresh), peeled and pitted	24
1	clove garlic	1
1 tbsp	chopped fresh cilantro	15 mL
2 tbsp	water (approx.)	25 mL
1 tsp	grated fresh gingerroot	5 mL
2 tsp	dark sesame oil	10 mL
1 tsp	freshly squeezed lemon juice	5 mL
½ tsp	soy sauce	2 mL

In a food processor, process all ingredients until finely chopped (add up to 1 tbsp/15 mL more water, if desired, to thin). **Makes about 1¾ cups (425 mL).** *Serve with grilled or poached fish or chicken.*

Fresh Basil Pesto

1	clove garlic	1
2 tbsp	pine nuts	25 mL
⅔ cup	firmly packed basil leaves	150 mL
⅓ cup	extra-virgin olive oil	75 mL
3 tbsp	freshly grated Parmesan cheese	45 mL
	Salt and freshly ground black pepper to taste	

In a food processor, process garlic and pine nuts until finely chopped. Add basil and process until finely chopped. With the motor running, slowly add oil through the feed tube. Transfer to a bowl and stir in Parmesan, salt and pepper. **Makes about ⅔ cup (150 mL).** *Store in an airtight container in the refrigerator for up to 1 week. Use in any recipe that calls for pesto.*

Spicy Basil Pesto

Follow preceding recipe, but add ¼ tsp (1 mL) hot pepper flakes and freshly ground black pepper to taste with the pine nuts. **Makes about ⅔ cup (150 mL).** *Store in an airtight container in the refrigerator for up to 1 week.*

Spinach Pesto

1	clove garlic	1
2 tbsp	pine nuts	25 mL
10 oz	fresh baby spinach (about 6 cups/1.5 L)	300 g
1 tbsp	basil oil or dried basil	15 mL
⅓ cup	extra-virgin olive oil	75 mL
3 tbsp	freshly grated Parmesan cheese	45 mL
	Salt and freshly ground black pepper to taste	

In a food processor, process garlic and pine nuts until finely chopped. Add spinach and basil oil;

process until finely chopped. With the motor running, slowly add oil through the feed tube. Transfer to a bowl and stir in Parmesan, salt and pepper. **Makes about 1½ cups (375 mL).** *Store in an airtight container in the refrigerator for up to 1 week. Use as a pasta sauce.*

Mint Pesto

1	clove garlic	1
2 cups	packed fresh mint leaves	500 mL
2 tbsp	sliced almonds (with skins)	25 mL
1 tbsp	freshly squeezed lemon juice	15 mL
	Salt and freshly ground black pepper to taste	
½ cup	olive oil	125 mL

In a food processor, process garlic, mint, almonds, lemon juice, salt and pepper until finely chopped. With the motor running, slowly add oil through the feed tube. **Makes about 1 cup (250 mL).** *Store in an airtight container in the refrigerator for up to 1 week. Serve with grilled fish or chicken.*

Oregano Walnut Pesto

2	cloves garlic	2
½ cup	packed fresh oregano leaves	125 mL
½ cup	packed fresh basil leaves	125 mL
¼ cup	walnuts	50 mL
¼ cup	extra-virgin olive oil	50 mL
¼ cup	walnut oil	50 mL
¼ cup	freshly grated Parmesan cheese	50 mL
	Salt and freshly ground black pepper to taste	

In a food processor, process garlic, oregano, basil and walnuts until finely chopped. With the motor running, slowly add olive oil and walnut oil through the feed tube. Transfer to a bowl and stir in Parmesan, salt and pepper. **Makes about 1¼ cups (300 mL).** *Store in an airtight container in the refrigerator for up to 1 week. Serve with steak or other grilled meats, or use as a pasta sauce.*

Anchovy Olive Pesto

8	drained canned anchovies, minced	8
2	cloves garlic, minced	2
⅔ cup	finely chopped pitted oil-cured black olives	150 mL
⅔ cup	extra-virgin olive oil	150 mL

Combine all ingredients. **Makes about 1 cup (250 mL).** *Store in an airtight container in the refrigerator for up to 1 week. Use as a bruschetta topping, or toss with pasta.*

Hummus Tahini

1	clove garlic	1
1 cup	drained rinsed canned chickpeas	250 mL
2 tbsp	dark sesame oil	25 mL
2 tbsp	olive oil	25 mL
1 tbsp	tahini	15 mL
½ tsp	hot pepper sauce (such as Tabasco)	2 mL
	Salt and freshly ground black pepper to taste	

In a food processor, purée all ingredients. **Makes about 1 cup (250 mL)**. *Store in an airtight container in the refrigerator for up to 1 week. Use as a dip or sandwich spread.*

Avocado Coulis

2	avocados, quartered	2
1	clove garlic	1
1 tsp	hot pepper sauce (such as Tabasco)	5 mL
	Juice of ½ lime	

In a food processor, purée all ingredients. **Makes about 1¼ cups (300 mL)**. *Use as a dip or sandwich spread, or serve with grilled fish.*

Green Herb Oil

1	small clove garlic, minced	1
¼ cup	olive oil	50 mL
¼ cup	peanut oil	50 mL
2 tbsp	minced fresh rosemary	25 mL
2 tbsp	minced fresh thyme	25 mL
2 tbsp	minced chives	25 mL
2 tbsp	minced fresh Italian (flat-leaf) parsley	25 mL
2 tbsp	minced fresh tarragon	25 mL

Combine all ingredients. **Makes about ¾ cup (175 mL)**. *Store in an airtight container in the refrigerator for up to 2 weeks. Serve with vegetables, fish or shellfish. (It's especially good with corn on the cob.)*

Creole Tartar Sauce

1	small clove garlic, minced	1
1 cup	mayonnaise	250 mL
½ cup	grated apple	125 mL
3 tbsp	sweet pickle relish	45 mL
2 tbsp	finely chopped onion	25 mL
1 tbsp	freshly squeezed lemon juice	15 mL
1 to 2 tsp	hot pepper sauce (such as Tabasco)	5 to 10 mL
1 tsp	cider vinegar	5 mL

Combine all ingredients, adding hot pepper sauce to taste. **Makes about 1½ cups (375 mL)**. *Store in an airtight container in the refrigerator for up to 1 week. Serve with seafood, fried fish or chicken breasts.*

Prosciutto and Summer Fruit Salad

4	apricots (or 2 peaches), pitted and coarsely chopped	4
3	fresh figs, stemmed and coarsely chopped	3
½	honeydew melon, seeded, peeled and diced	½
1 cup	fresh raspberries	250 mL
½ cup	halved grapes	125 mL
2 tbsp	chopped fresh mint	25 mL
8 oz	imported prosciutto, thinly sliced	250 g

Toss together apricots, figs, honeydew, raspberries, grapes and mint. Serve with prosciutto. **Serves 4.** *(Note: You may substitute a similar amount of any ripe summer fruit for the fruit in the recipe.)*

Peaches Stuffed with Smoked Salmon Mousse

1	small clove garlic, minced	1
8 oz	cream cheese, softened	250 g
6 oz	smoked salmon, finely chopped	175 g
1 tbsp	minced fresh dill	15 mL
3 tbsp	sour cream	45 mL
Pinch	ground nutmeg	Pinch
	Grated zest and juice of ½ lemon	
4	large freestone peaches	4
	Additional lemon juice	
4	dill fronds	4

Combine garlic, cream cheese, salmon, minced dill, sour cream, nutmeg, lemon zest and lemon juice. Slice tops off peaches and reserve them for "lids." Using a melon baller, remove pit and a small amount of flesh from peaches and cut a thin slice from the bottoms so they sit upright. Rub cut surfaces with lemon juice. Fill peaches with mousse and place "lids" on top. Garnish each with a dill frond. **Serves 4.**

Peaches Stuffed with Ham Mousse

Follow preceding recipe, but replace the salmon with baked ham, and replace the dill with parsley. **Serves 4.**

Vegetable-Stuffed Deviled Eggs

4	hard-cooked eggs, chilled, peeled and halved lengthwise	4
1	small clove garlic, minced	1
2 tbsp	mayonnaise	25 mL
1 tsp	spicy brown mustard	5 mL
1 cup	finely diced garden vegetables (such as carrots, green onions, onions, celery, cucumber, zucchini, radishes)	250 mL
	Salt and freshly ground black pepper to taste	

Mash egg yolks with garlic, mayonnaise and mustard. Stir in vegetables, and season with salt and pepper. Mound into the hollow of each egg white half. **Serves 4.**

Smoked Trout and Horseradish Deviled Eggs

Follow preceding recipe, but add 1 tbsp (15 mL) prepared horseradish with the mustard, and replace the vegetables with crumbled boneless skinless smoked trout. **Serves 4.**

Cherries in Orange Honey over Melon

½ cup	orange juice	125 mL
1 tbsp	honey	15 mL
1 tsp	brandy	5 mL
2 cups	sweet dark cherries, pitted	500 mL
1	honeydew melon or cantaloupe, seeded, peeled and sliced into wedges	1

In a large bowl, whisk together orange juice, honey and brandy. Add cherries and toss to coat. Serve over melon wedges. **Serves 4.**

Kiwi and Honeydew in Margarita Glaze

¼ cup	tequila	50 mL
3 tbsp	confectioner's (icing) sugar	45 mL
3 tbsp	freshly squeezed lime juice	45 mL
2 tbsp	orange-flavored liqueur	25 mL
½ tsp	kosher salt	2 mL
4	kiwis, peeled and quartered	4
1	honeydew melon, seeded, peeled and thinly sliced	1

In a large bowl, whisk together tequila, sugar, lime juice, liqueur and salt. Add kiwis and toss to coat. Serve over melon slices. **Serves 4.**

Espresso Granita

3 cups	brewed espresso or strong coffee	750 mL
½ cup	light corn syrup	125 mL
	Curls of lemon rind	

In a shallow pan, combine espresso and corn syrup. Freeze until ice crystals begin to form. Remove from freezer and stir. Continue freezing and stirring every half-hour for about 3 hours, until mixture is a firm slush. (If it should freeze solid, break into small pieces and crush in a food processor.) Serve in 4 chilled coffee cups or 8 chilled espresso cups, garnished with lemon rind. **Serves 4 to 8.**

Bourbon-Spiked Peach and Praline "Bombe"

1	carton (½ gallon/2 L) peach-flavored ice cream	1
1 cup	chopped pecans	250 mL
¼ cup	bourbon	50 mL
1 tbsp	light (fancy) molasses	15 mL
½ cup	whipping (35%) cream, whipped firm	125 mL
1	recipe Brandied Peaches (page 448)	1

Remove the center of the block of ice cream, leaving 1 inch (2.5 cm) across the bottom and sides of the carton. Return carton to freezer. Mash pecans, bourbon and molasses into ice cream. Fold in whipped cream. Pour into the hollowed-out center of the ice cream carton. Cover tightly and freeze for several hours, until center is firm, or overnight. To serve, rip carton away from ice cream and invert onto a serving plate. Slice and serve with Brandied Peaches. **Serves 8.**

Chapter 16
Salads
For Any Meal

Basic Green Salad 182

Tossed Winter Greens with Warm Bacon Dressing 182

Iceberg Lettuce with Three Tomatoes . . 182

Classic Caesar Salad 182

Mushroom Caesar Salad 183

Creole Beet Salad 183

Gingered Carrot Salad 183

Creamy Cucumber Salad 183

Warm Jerusalem Artichoke Salad 183

Orange and Celery Salad 183

Tri-Colored Peppers with Herbs . . . 183

Peppers with Basil and Walnuts 183

Roasted Peppers with Black Olives and Anchovies 183

Spinach Salad with Roasted Peppers and Feta 184

Spinach Salad with Blue Cheese Dressing 184

Grilled Summer Squash Salad 184

Composed Salad of Grilled Vegetables 184

Steamed Vegetable Salad with Lemon Dill Dressing 184

German-Style Potato Salad 184

Sweet-and-Sour Smoked Turkey Potato Salad 185

Waldorf Potato Salad 185

Potato Vinaigrette with Mussels and Olives 185

Sour Cream and Caviar Potato Salad . . 185

Seafood Potato Salad 185

Russian Herring Potato Salad 185

Bulgur Tortellini Salad 186

Middle Eastern Bulgur Orzo Salad 186

Mixed Herb Tabbouleh 186

Grilled Lamb and Tabbouleh Salad 186

Grilled Scallops and Shrimp Tabbouleh 187

Creole Coleslaw 187

Red Cabbage Slaw 187

White Cabbage Slaw 187

Sweet-and-Sour Coleslaw 187

Bacon and Fruit Slaw 187

Crab and Corn Slaw 187

Summer Salmon Salad 187

Dilled Salmon Salad 188

Pungent Tomato Salmon Salad 188

Asparagus-Orange Salmon Salad 188

Grilled Salmon Salad with Rosemary Vinaigrette 188

Marinated Tuna and White Bean Salad 188

Crab, Orange and Black Bean Salad . . . 188

Smoked Fish Salad with Belgian Endive 188

Grilled Fish Salad with Garden Greens 189

Grilled Chicken Breasts with Bitter Greens and Pine Nuts 189

Soy Ginger Chicken Salad 189

Southwest Garbanzo Turkey Salad 189

Smoked Turkey and Bitter Greens 190

Poached Winter Fruit Salad with Raspberry Vinaigrette 190

Salads have gotten a raw deal. Thrown together without thought, bathed in bottled dressing and written off as roughage by the meat-and-potato mainstream, salads too often fail to get serious culinary attention. Even as salads expanded from side dish to full entrée, they still couldn't escape the powerful stereotype of lettuce leaves tossed with a tomato.

We have to wonder why. Good lettuce, good tomato and good dressing make a splendid salad. But a salad can be so much more: olives, roasted peppers and anchovies bathed in olive oil and garlic; grilled chicken breast on a mound of winter greens, peppered with bacon bits; poached scallops tossed in a tangle of pasta and a pesto vinaigrette; or grapefruit sections nestled into the crooks of shrimp and cloaked with guacamole.

Salads can be hot, cold, tepid or frozen. They can be made from any combination of meat, poultry, seafood, vegetables, pasta, grains, beans and fruit. They can be raw, poached, roasted, grilled or barbecued. There are marinated salads, tossed salads, composed salads and molded salads. Salads can start a lunch, finish a dinner or provide a respite between courses.

What all salads have in common is strong, bright, sparkling flavor. True to their name (from the Latin root *sal*, meaning salt), salads have always been dishes that excite the palate. With a jolt of spice and a tart spark of acid, a salad perks the appetite and enlivens the other flavors in a meal. Whether a salad is seasoned with lemon, vinegar, wine, garlic or chili peppers, the reward is always the same: a bounty of flavor — often with a minimum of calories and fat.

The 50 recipes in this chapter deliver salad ideas far in excess of their number, for they will spark a myriad of possibilities in your culinary imagination.

About these recipes . . .

The recipes assume that you will clean and dry all greens, and season each salad with salt and pepper to taste. They are written for whole-head fresh lettuces. If you want to substitute prewashed bagged lettuce, the equivalent is roughly 1 bag = 1 medium head lettuce, washed and trimmed. Many of these recipes call for one of the homemade dressings in Chapter 4.

Basic Green Salad

6	leaves romaine lettuce, torn into bite-size pieces	6
½	head Boston lettuce, torn into bite-size pieces	½
½	head green- or red-leaf lettuce, torn into bite-size pieces	½
¼ cup	salad dressing (any type)	50 mL
¼ cup	croutons	50 mL

Toss together all ingredients. **Serves 4.**

Tossed Winter Greens with Warm Bacon Dressing

2	heads escarole, curly endive or chicory, torn into bite-size pieces	2
2	hard-cooked eggs, finely chopped	2
1	red onion, thinly sliced	1
4 oz	mushrooms, sliced	125 g
1	recipe Warm Bacon Dressing (page 62), bacon reserved and crumbled	1

Combine escarole, eggs, onions and mushrooms. Add dressing and toss to coat. Garnish with crumbled bacon and serve immediately. **Serves 4.**

Iceberg Lettuce with Three Tomatoes

1	small head iceberg lettuce, cored and quartered	1
1	recipe Warm Tomato Vinaigrette (page 63)	1
1	large tomato, cut into 12 wedges	1
½	recipe Real Russian Dressing (page 62)	½

Place each lettuce quarter on a salad plate in a pool of Warm Tomato Vinaigrette. Arrange 3 tomato wedges to one side of the lettuce. Top with Real Russian Dressing. **Serves 4.**

Classic Caesar Salad

1	head romaine lettuce, torn into bite-sized pieces	1
1	recipe Classic Caesar Dressing (page 62)	1
2 cups	croutons (preferably homemade, see recipe, page 19)	500 mL
¼ cup	freshly grated Parmesan cheese	50 mL

Toss romaine with dressing until thoroughly coated. Add croutons and Parmesan, and toss gently. **Serves 4.**

Mushroom Caesar Salad

Follow preceding recipe, but add 8 mushrooms, sliced, with the romaine. **Serves 4.**

Creole Beet Salad

1½ lbs	small beets	750 g
8 cups	boiling water	2 L
1 lb	carrots, diced	500 g
1	Granny Smith apple, peeled and diced	1
¼ cup	minced green onion	50 mL
1	recipe Sweet-and-Sour Creole Vinaigrette (page 63)	1

Add beets to boiling water; reduce heat and simmer until tender, about 30 minutes, adding carrots 4 minutes before beets are done. Drain well. Peel and dice beets, and toss beets and carrots with apple, green onion and dressing. **Serves 4.**

Gingered Carrot Salad

1 lb	carrots, shredded	500 g
½ cup	Spicy Ginger Vinaigrette (see recipe, page 64)	50 mL
2 tbsp	chopped chives	25 mL

Toss carrots with dressing. Cover and refrigerate for about 30 minutes, until chilled. Garnish with chives. **Serves 4 to 6.**

Creamy Cucumber Salad

1	large cucumber, peeled, halved, seeded and thinly sliced	1
1 tsp	kosher salt	5 mL
1	recipe Minted Yogurt Dressing (page 65)	1

Toss cucumber slices with salt; let stand for 15 minutes. Rinse thoroughly and drain well. Toss with dressing. **Serves 4.**

Warm Jerusalem Artichoke Salad

4 cups	water	1 L
½ tsp	salt	2 mL
	Juice of 2 lemons, divided	
2 lbs	Jerusalem artichokes, peeled and trimmed of hard ends	1 kg
3 tbsp	olive oil	45 mL
2	cloves garlic, minced	2
2 cups	julienned peeled celery root	500 mL
1 cup	diced fennel	250 mL
2 tbsp	sour cream	25 mL

In a large saucepan, bring water, salt and half the lemon juice to a boil. Add Jerusalem artichokes, reduce heat and simmer until barely tender and still crisp near the center, about 5 minutes. Refresh under cold water, slice into bite-size pieces and toss with the remaining lemon juice; set aside. In a large skillet, heat oil over medium heat. Sauté garlic for 30 seconds. Add Jerusalem artichokes (reserving lemon juice), celery root and fennel. Sauté for 2 to 3 minutes, or until vegetables are heated through. Remove from heat and stir in sour cream and the reserved lemon juice. **Serves 4.**

Orange and Celery Salad

4	stalks celery, sliced	4
2	navel oranges, segmented and cut into small pieces	2
1	recipe Orange Walnut Dressing (page 60)	1
⅓ cup	walnut pieces (preferably toasted)	75 mL

Toss together all ingredients. **Serves 4.**

Tri-Colored Peppers with Herbs

6	large roasted bell peppers (2 red, 2 green, 2 yellow; see page 11), sliced into strips	6
½	recipe Garlic Herb Dressing (page 60)	½

Toss peppers with dressing. **Serves 4.**

Peppers with Basil and Walnuts

Follow preceding recipe, but use only red or yellow peppers, add ¼ cup (50 mL) chopped fresh basil to the dressing, and garnish with ⅓ cup (75 mL) chopped walnuts. **Serves 4.**

Roasted Peppers with Black Olives and Anchovies

24	oil-cured black olives, pitted	24
6	drained canned anchovies, julienned	6
4	large roasted bell peppers (any color; see page 11), sliced into strips	4
1	clove garlic, minced	1
½	red onion, finely chopped	½
¼ cup	extra-virgin olive oil	50 mL
3 tbsp	red wine vinegar	45 mL

Toss together all ingredients. **Serves 4 to 6.**

Spinach Salad with Roasted Peppers and Feta

4	large roasted bell peppers (any color; see page 11), sliced into strips	4
1	clove garlic, minced	1
½	red onion, finely chopped	½
8 oz	feta cheese, crumbled	250 g
2 oz	Genoa salami, julienned	60 g
¼ cup	extra-virgin olive oil	50 mL
3 tbsp	red wine vinegar	45 mL
12 oz	spinach (about 8 cups/2 L), stemmed	375 g

Combine roasted peppers, garlic, onion, feta, salami, oil and vinegar. Add spinach and toss to coat. **Serves 4 to 6.**

Spinach Salad with Blue Cheese Dressing

1	red onion, diced	1
9 oz	baby spinach (about 6 cups/1.5 L)	275 g
1	recipe Blue Cheese Dressing (page 63)	1
¾ cup	chopped walnuts	175 mL

Toss together all ingredients. **Serves 4.**

Grilled Summer Squash Salad

2	small zucchini, sliced lengthwise	2
2	small yellow summer squash, sliced lengthwise	2
1	recipe Balsamic–Olive Oil Vinaigrette (page 61)	1

Toss zucchini and squash with dressing; let stand for 20 minutes. Meanwhile, preheat barbecue grill to high. Remove vegetables from dressing, reserving dressing. Grill vegetables for 2 minutes per side, until browned on both sides. Toss with enough reserved dressing to moisten. **Serves 4.**

Composed Salad of Grilled Vegetables

12	large mushrooms, stems trimmed	12
4	leeks, white parts only, halved lengthwise	4
3	ears corn, husked and cut into thirds	3
2	large beefsteak tomatoes, thickly sliced	2
1	sweet potato, cut into ½-inch (1 cm) thick slices	1
1	eggplant, peeled and cut into 3-inch (7.5 cm) batons	1
1	large zucchini, cut into 1-inch (2.5 cm) thick slices	1
	Olive oil	
1	recipe Dijon Vinaigrette (page 61)	1

Preheat barbecue grill to high. Coat all vegetables with oil. Grill vegetables, turning each several times while it cooks, until tender and lightly browned: cook leeks and sweet potatoes for 8 to 10 minutes; mushrooms, eggplant and corn for 5 to 7 minutes; zucchini and tomatoes for 3 to 4 minutes. Arrange vegetables on large platter and drizzle with dressing. Serve warm. **Serves 4.**

Steamed Vegetable Salad with Lemon Dill Dressing

2 tsp	chopped fresh dill	10 mL
1	recipe Lemon and Olive Oil Dressing (page 60)	1
8	baby carrots	8
½	bunch broccoli, broken into florets	½
¼	head cauliflower, broken in florets	¼
8	small mushrooms	8
6	cherry tomatoes	6
	Salt and freshly ground black pepper to taste	

Add dill to dressing and set aside. Select a platter large enough to hold vegetables in a single layer. Arrange carrots, broccoli and cauliflower close to the rim, mushrooms and tomatoes toward the center. Sprinkle with salt and pepper. Cover with microwave-safe plastic wrap and microwave on High for 4 to 5 minutes, or until carrots are just tender. Uncover and pour any juices into the dressing. Whisk dressing until smooth and thick, then pour over vegetables. Serve warm. **Serves 4.**

German-Style Potato Salad

1½ lbs	red-skinned potatoes, peeled	750 g
3	slices bacon	3
1	large red onion, minced	1
1	large clove garlic, minced	1
½ cup	cider vinegar	125 mL
2 tbsp	granulated sugar	25 mL
1 tbsp	mayonnaise	15 mL
	Salt and freshly ground black pepper to taste	
2	stalks celery, sliced	2

In a large pot, cook potatoes in boiling salted water until tender; drain, cut into large dice and keep warm. Meanwhile, in a deep skillet, cook bacon until crisp; crumble and set aside. Add onion to the fat in the pan and sauté over medium heat until tender. Stir in garlic, vinegar, sugar, mayonnaise, salt and pepper; heat through. Toss with potatoes and celery. Garnish with crumbled bacon. **Serves 4.**

Sweet-and-Sour Smoked Turkey Potato Salad

1½ lbs	red-skinned potatoes, peeled	750 g
⅓ cup	cider vinegar	75 mL
3 tbsp	granulated sugar	45 mL
1	small onion, finely chopped	1
3 tbsp	mayonnaise	45 mL
1 tbsp	ketchup	15 mL
1 tsp	salt	5 mL
	Freshly ground black pepper to taste	
2	stalks celery, diced	2
12 oz	smoked turkey breast, diced	375 g

In a large pot, cook potatoes in boiling salted water until tender; drain, cut into large dice and keep warm. In a small saucepan, heat vinegar and sugar until sugar dissolves. Pour into a large salad bowl and stir in onion, mayonnaise, ketchup, salt and pepper. Add potatoes, celery and turkey and toss to coat. **Serves 4.**

Waldorf Potato Salad

Follow preceding recipe, but replace the ketchup with sour cream or yogurt, omit the turkey, and add 8 oz (250 g) cooked ham, diced, and 2 Granny Smith apples, diced, with the celery. **Serves 4.**

Potato Vinaigrette with Mussels and Olives

1½ lbs	red-skinned potatoes, peeled	750 g
2	cloves garlic, minced, divided	2
½ cup	dry white wine	125 mL
¼ tsp	hot pepper flakes	1 mL
24	mussels, scrubbed (see page 8)	24
20	oil-cured black olives, pitted and halved	20
¼ cup	olive oil	50 mL
2 tbsp	chopped fresh dill	25 mL
3 tbsp	red wine vinegar	45 mL

In a large pot, cook potatoes in boiling salted water until tender; drain, cut into large dice and keep warm. In a large saucepan, bring half the garlic, the wine and hot pepper flakes to a boil. Add mussels, reduce heat and simmer for about 3 minutes, or until they open (discard any that don't). Remove mussels, reserving ¼ cup (50 mL) cooking liquid. Remove mussels from their shells. Combine reserved liquid, mussels, the remaining garlic, olives, oil, dill and vinegar. Add potatoes and toss to coat. **Serves 4.**

Sour Cream and Caviar Potato Salad

1½ lbs	red-skinned potatoes, peeled	750 g
6 tbsp	sour cream	90 mL
¼ cup	canola oil	50 mL
2 tbsp	red wine vinegar	25 mL
2 oz	salmon caviar	60 g
2 tbsp	thinly sliced chives	25 mL
	Salt and freshly ground black pepper to taste	

In a large pot, cook potatoes in boiling salted water until tender; drain and cut into large dice. Combine sour cream, oil and vinegar. Stir in caviar, chives, salt and pepper. Add potatoes and toss to coat. Cover and refrigerate for about 30 minutes, until chilled. **Serves 4.**

Seafood Potato Salad

1½ lbs	red-skinned potatoes	750 g
6 tbsp	sour cream	90 mL
¼ cup	canola oil	50 mL
2 tbsp	freshly squeezed lemon juice	25 mL
1 tbsp	red wine vinegar	15 mL
2 oz	salmon caviar	60 g
2 tbsp	thinly sliced chives	25 mL
1 tbsp	chopped fresh dill	15 mL
	Salt and freshly ground black pepper to taste	
8 oz	small shrimp, peeled, deveined and cooked	250 g
8 oz	backfin (lump) crabmeat, shells picked out	250 g

In a large pot, cook potatoes in boiling salted water until tender; drain and cut into bite-sized pieces. Combine sour cream, oil, lemon juice and vinegar. Stir in caviar, chives, dill, salt and pepper. Add potatoes, shrimp and crabmeat; toss to coat. Cover and refrigerate for about 30 minutes, until chilled. **Serves 4.**

Russian Herring Potato Salad

3 lbs	small red-skinned potatoes	1.5 kg
1	jar (16 oz/454 g) pickled herring, drained and cubed	1
1	small red onion, finely chopped	1
1	recipe Real Russian Dressing (page 62)	1

In a large pot, cook potatoes in boiling salted water until tender; drain and quarter. Toss with herring, onion and dressing. **Serves 4.**

Bulgur Tortellini Salad

2 cups	bulgur	500 mL
2½ cups	hot water	625 mL
1 lb	cheese or meat tortellini	500 g
1	clove garlic, minced	1
1½ cups	plain yogurt (not fat-free)	375 mL
¼ cup	chopped fresh basil	50 mL
¼ cup	freshly grated Parmesan cheese	50 mL
2 tbsp	extra-virgin olive oil	25 mL
	Juice of 1 lemon	
	Salt and freshly ground black pepper to taste	

Soak bulgur in water for 30 minutes; drain off any excess water. Meanwhile, cook tortellini according to package directions. Drain and let cool. Combine the remaining ingredients. Add bulgur, tortellini, and dressing; toss to coat. Cover and refrigerate for about 30 minutes, until chilled. **Serves 6 to 8.**

Middle Eastern Bulgur Orzo Salad

2 cups	bulgur	500 mL
2½ cups	hot water	625 mL
8 oz	orzo	250 g
1	clove garlic, minced	1
1½ cups	plain yogurt	375 mL
¼ cup	chopped fresh mint	50 mL
¼ cup	chopped fresh Italian (flat-leaf) parsley	50 mL
2 tbsp	extra-virgin olive oil	25 mL
	Juice of 1 lemon	
	Salt and freshly ground black pepper to taste	
2	tomatoes, seeded and diced	2
1	cucumber, peeled, seeded and diced	1

Soak bulgur in water for 30 minutes; drain off any excess water. Meanwhile, cook orzo according to package directions. Drain and let cool. Combine, garlic, yogurt, mint, parsley, oil, lemon juice, salt and pepper. Add bulgur, orzo, tomatoes and cucumber; toss to coat. Cover and refrigerate for about 30 minutes, until chilled. **Serves 6 to 8.**

Mixed Herb Tabbouleh

2 cups	bulgur	500 mL
2½ cups	hot water	625 mL
1	clove garlic, minced	1
⅓ cup	olive oil	75 mL
¼ cup	chopped fresh Italian (flat-leaf) parsley	50 mL
¼ cup	chopped fresh mint	50 mL
¼ cup	chopped fresh cilantro	50 mL
Pinch	hot pepper flakes	Pinch
	Juice of 1 lemon	
	Salt and freshly ground black pepper to taste	
2	large tomatoes, seeded and chopped	2
1	large cucumber, peeled, seeded and diced	1
3 tbsp	thinly sliced green onions	45 mL

Soak bulgur in water for 30 minutes; drain off any excess water. Combine garlic, oil, parsley, mint, cilantro, hot pepper flakes, lemon juice, salt and black pepper. Add bulgur, tomatoes, cucumber and green onions; toss to coat. **Serves 4.**

Grilled Lamb and Tabbouleh Salad

2	cloves garlic, minced	2
½ cup	chopped fresh Italian (flat-leaf) parsley	125 mL
½ cup	olive oil	125 mL
¼ cup	chopped fresh mint	50 mL
Pinch	hot pepper flakes	Pinch
	Juice of 2 lemons	
	Salt and freshly ground black pepper to taste	
1 cup	plain yogurt (not fat-free)	250 mL
1 lb	boneless leg of lamb, cut into steaks	500 g
2 cups	bulgur	500 mL
2½ cups	hot water	625 mL
2	large tomatoes, seeded and chopped	2
1	large cucumber, peeled, seeded and diced	1
3 tbsp	thinly sliced green onions	45 mL

Combine garlic, parsley, oil, mint, hot pepper flakes, lemon juice, salt and black pepper. Stir half of this dressing into yogurt. Place lamb in a shallow dish and coat with half the yogurt mixture. Cover and refrigerate for 30 minutes. Meanwhile, soak bulgur in water for 30 minutes; drain off any excess water. Preheat barbecue grill to high. Toss bulgur, tomatoes, cucumber and green onions with the remaining dressing; set aside. Remove lamb from marinade and discard marinade. Grill lamb to desired doneness, then cut into slices. Arrange lamb slices on a bed of tabbouleh and drizzle with remaining yogurt mixture. **Serves 4.**

Grilled Scallops and Shrimp Tabbouleh

Follow preceding recipe, but replace the lamb with 8 oz (250 g) large scallops, trimmed of hard side muscles, and 8 oz (250 g) large shrimp, peeled and deveined. Grill until firm and opaque. **Serves 4.**

Creole Coleslaw

1	recipe Sour Cream Coleslaw Dressing (page 62)	1
3 tbsp	hot pepper sauce (such as Frank's RedHot)	45 mL
2 tbsp	ketchup	25 mL
2	large Granny Smith apples, coarsely grated	2
1	bunch green onions, thinly sliced	1
2 lbs	cabbage (any type), cored and shredded (about 7 cups/1.75 L)	1 kg

Combine dressing, hot pepper sauce and ketchup. Add apples, green onions and cabbage; toss to coat. Refrigerate for at least 1 hour, until chilled, or overnight. **Serves 4.**

Red Cabbage Slaw

2	carrots, coarsely grated	2
2	stalks celery, diced	2
1	small head red cabbage, cored and shredded	1
1	Granny Smith apple, peeled and diced	1
1	recipe Clear Coleslaw Dressing (page 62)	1

Toss together all ingredients. **Serves 8.**

White Cabbage Slaw

2	carrots, coarsely grated	2
2	stalks celery, diced	2
1	small head white cabbage, cored and shredded	1
1	recipe Sour Cream Coleslaw Dressing (page 62)	1

Toss together all ingredients. **Serves 8.**

Sweet-and-Sour Coleslaw

8	slices bacon	8
1	large red onion, minced	1
1	large clove garlic, minced	1
½ cup	cider vinegar	125 mL
2 tbsp	granulated sugar	25 mL
2 tbsp	sour cream	25 mL
	Salt and freshly ground black pepper to taste	
1	small head savoy cabbage, cored and shredded	1
1	carrot, coarsely grated	1
1	roasted red bell pepper (see page 11), diced	1
1	large stalk celery, diced	1

In a deep skillet, cook bacon until crisp; crumble and set aside. Add onion to the fat in the pan and sauté over medium heat until tender. Add garlic and sauté for 30 seconds. Transfer to a large bowl and stir in vinegar, sugar, sour cream, salt and pepper. Add cabbage, carrot, roasted pepper, celery and crumbled bacon; toss to coat. **Serves 4.**

Bacon and Fruit Slaw

Follow preceding recipe, but omit the carrot and roasted pepper, and add 2 Granny Smith apples, peeled and diced, and 1 cup (250 mL) crushed pineapple with the cabbage. **Serves 4.**

Crab and Corn Slaw

4	ears white corn, cooked and kernels removed	4
2	stalks celery, diced	2
1	roasted red bell pepper (see page 11), diced	1
1	small avocado, diced	1
½	cucumber, peeled, seeded and diced	½
1 lb	backfin (lump) crabmeat, shells picked out	500 g
¼ cup	chopped chives	50 mL
1	recipe Creamy Creole Dressing (page 63)	1

Toss together all ingredients. **Serves 6.**

Summer Salmon Salad

1 cup	water	250 mL
1 cup	dry white wine	250 mL
1½ lbs	boneless skinless salmon fillet	750 g
⅓ cup	Lemon and Olive Oil Dressing (see recipe, page 60)	75 mL
¼ cup	toasted pine nuts	50 mL
2 tbsp	chopped fresh Italian (flat-leaf) parsley	25 mL
Pinch	cayenne pepper	Pinch

In a large skillet, bring water and wine to a boil. Add salmon, reduce heat to low, cover and poach until salmon flakes easily with a fork. Transfer salmon to a plate, discarding poaching liquid, and let cool to room temperature. Flake salmon into small pieces and toss with dressing, pine nuts, parsley and cayenne. **Serves 4.**

Dilled Salmon Salad

Follow preceding recipe, but replace the parsley with chopped fresh dill, and omit the pine nuts. **Serves 4.**

Pungent Tomato Salmon Salad

Follow recipe for Summer Salmon Salad (page 187), but replace the dressing with Sun-Dried Tomato Vinaigrette (page 61), replace the parsley with chopped fresh basil, and add 6 drained oil-packed sun-dried tomatoes, finely chopped, with the dressing. **Serves 4.**

Asparagus-Orange Salmon Salad

4	salmon steaks (½ inch/1 cm thick)	4
	Sesame oil	
24	spears asparagus, poached and kept warm	24
1	recipe Sesame Tofu Vinaigrette (page 62)	1
12	orange slices	12
	Toasted sesame seeds	

Preheat barbecue grill to high. Rub each salmon steak with oil. Grill, turning once, for 2 minutes per side, or until salmon flakes easily with a fork. Let cool slightly, then remove skin and bones. Place each steak on a warm plate with 6 asparagus spears. Drizzle with dressing and garnish each plate with 3 orange slices and toasted sesame seeds. **Serves 4.**

Grilled Salmon Salad with Rosemary Vinaigrette

2	large russet potatoes, cut into ½-inch (1 cm) thick slices	2
1½ lbs	boneless skinless salmon fillet	750 g
2 tbsp	olive oil	25 mL
2	tomatoes, sliced and rubbed with vegetable oil	2
1 lb	green beans, trimmed and blanched	500 g
1	recipe Creamy Rosemary Dressing (page 61)	1
	Rosemary sprigs	

Preheat barbecue grill to medium. Coat potatoes and salmon with oil. Grill, turning once, for 6 to 7 minutes per side, or until potatoes are tender and brown, and salmon flakes easily with a fork. Grill tomatoes, turning once, for 2 minutes per side. Cut salmon into 4 pieces and arrange on a platter. Bank salmon with potatoes, tomatoes and green beans. Drizzle with dressing and garnish with rosemary sprigs. **Serves 4.**

Marinated Tuna and White Bean Salad

¼ cup	red wine vinegar	50 mL
2 tbsp	extra-virgin olive oil	25 mL
Pinch	hot pepper flakes	Pinch
	Salt and freshly ground black pepper to taste	
1	small red onion, finely chopped	1
1	clove garlic, minced	1
1½ cups	flaked tuna (freshly cooked or drained canned)	375 mL
1½ cups	canned white beans, drained and rinsed	375 mL
½ cup	thinly sliced green onions	125 mL
12	oil-cured black olives, pitted and chopped	12
	Romaine lettuce leaves	

Combine vinegar, oil, hot pepper flakes, salt and black pepper. Add onion, garlic, tuna, beans and green onions; toss to coat. Garnish with olives. Cover and refrigerate for at least 30 minutes, until chilled, or for up to 1 day. Serve over romaine. **Serves 4.**

Crab, Orange and Black Bean Salad

Follow preceding recipe, but reduce the vinegar to 2 tbsp (25 mL); add 2 tbsp (25 mL) freshly squeezed orange juice with the vinegar; replace the tuna with backfin (lump) crabmeat, shells picked out; and replace the white beans with black beans. Add 2 tbsp (25 mL) finely grated orange zest to the dressing, if desired. **Serves 4.**

Smoked Fish Salad with Belgian Endive

1 lb	smoked fish (any variety), skin and bones removed	500 g
1	recipe Creamy Mayonnaise Dressing (page 64)	1
⅓ cup	thinly sliced celery	75 mL
2 tbsp	chopped chives	25 mL
3	heads Belgian endive, cored and broken into leaves	3
1	cucumber, peeled and sliced	1
1	red bell pepper, cut into strips	1
4	lemon slices	4

Flake fish and toss with dressing, celery and chives. Serve in the center of a large platter, surrounded by endive, cucumber and red pepper. Garnish with lemon slices. **Serves 4.**

Grilled Fish Salad with Garden Greens

1 lb	boneless fish fillet (any variety)	500 g
2 tbsp	olive oil	25 mL
1 tbsp	freshly squeezed lemon juice	15 mL
	Salt and freshly ground black pepper to taste	
4	green onions, thinly sliced	4
1	small head lettuce (any type), torn into small pieces	1
1	head radicchio (or 1 bunch arugula), torn into small pieces	1
¼ cup	chopped fresh Italian (flat-leaf) parsley	50 mL
½	recipe Balsamic–Olive Oil Vinaigrette (page 61)	½
8	sprigs watercress	8
4	lemon wedges	4
4	lime wedges	4

Preheat broiler or barbecue grill to high. Rub fish with oil, lemon juice, salt and pepper. Broil or grill, turning once, for 8 minutes per inch (2.5 cm) of thickness. Toss green onions, lettuce, radicchio and parsley with most of the dressing. Arrange salad to one side of each of 4 dinner plates. Place fish on the other side, overlapping salad by an inch or two (2.5 to 5 cm). Moisten fish with the remaining dressing. Garnish each plate with 2 watercress sprigs, 1 lemon wedge and 1 lime wedge. **Serves 4.**

Grilled Chicken Breasts with Bitter Greens and Pine Nuts

Follow preceding recipe, but replace the fish with 2 boneless skinless chicken breasts. Broil or grill, turning once, for 3 to 4 minutes per side, or until no longer pink inside. Replace the lettuce and radicchio with a combination of escarole, endive, radicchio and/or arugula, and garnish each salad with 1 tbsp (15 mL) toasted pine nuts. **Serves 4.**

Soy Ginger Chicken Salad

2	carrots, halved crosswise, then cut lengthwise into 3 strips	2
2	boneless skinless chicken breasts	2
1	recipe Soy Ginger Dressing (page 63), divided	1
2 cups	shredded savoy cabbage	500 mL
2 cups	julienned jicama (about 8 oz/250 g)	500 mL
1 cup	bean sprouts	250 mL
16	snow peas or sugar snap peas, trimmed	16
1	large navel orange, sectioned	1
4	red radishes, thinly sliced	4

Preheat barbecue grill to medium. Brush carrots and chicken with one-quarter of the dressing. Grill, turning once, for 4 to 5 minutes per side, or until surfaces of carrots and chicken are seared and chicken is no longer pink inside. Toss cabbage, jicama and bean sprouts with ¼ cup (50 mL) of the dressing. Mound cabbage mixture on a large serving platter. Slice chicken and fan slices over cabbage mixture. Decorate with carrots, peas, orange sections and radishes. Drizzle with the remaining dressing. **Serves 4.**

Southwest Garbanzo Turkey Salad

⅓ cup	canola oil	75 mL
2 tbsp	chili powder	25 mL
1 tbsp	ground cumin	15 mL
3 tbsp	mayonnaise	45 mL
2 tbsp	hot pepper sauce (such as Frank's RedHot)	25 mL
	Salt and freshly ground black pepper to taste	
1	roasted red bell pepper (see page 11), sliced	1
1½ cups	drained rinsed canned chickpeas (garbanzo beans)	375 mL
8 oz	smoked turkey breast, cut into bite-size pieces	250 g
⅓ cup	thinly sliced green onions	75 mL
1	avocado, diced	1
2 tbsp	chopped fresh cilantro	25 mL

Combine oil, chili powder, cumin, mayonnaise, hot pepper sauce, salt and pepper. Add roasted pepper, chickpeas, turkey and green onions; toss to coat. Just before serving, toss in avocado and cilantro. **Serves 6.**

Smoked Turkey and Bitter Greens

12	mushrooms, sliced	12
1	head escarole, torn into bite-size pieces	1
1	head curly endive, torn into bite-size pieces	1
6 oz	baby spinach (about 4 cups/1 L)	175 g
2/3 cup	finely chopped red onion	150 mL
1 lb	smoked turkey breast, cut into 12 thin slices	500 g
	Vegetable oil	
1	recipe Sweet Pepper Vinaigrette (page 63)	1

Toss together mushrooms, escarole, endive, spinach and onion; set aside. Heat an iron skillet over high heat for 4 minutes. Brush turkey lightly with oil and, in batches, brown for 30 seconds per side. Remove turkey to a plate. Add dressing to the skillet and bring to a boil. Pour over mushroom mixture and toss to coat (greens will soften slightly from heat of the dressing). Divide greens among 4 plates and top each with 3 slices of turkey. Serve immediately. **Serves 4.**

Poached Winter Fruit Salad with Raspberry Vinaigrette

1½ cups	white wine	375 mL
½ cup	granulated sugar	125 mL
½ cup	water	125 mL
1	stick cinnamon	1
1	whole clove	1
1	slice gingerroot	1
Pinch	salt	Pinch
1	underripe pear, sliced	1
1	Golden Delicious apple, sliced	1
1 cup	seedless red grapes	250 mL
2	tangerines, sectioned	2
1	recipe Raspberry Vinaigrette (page 61)	1

In a large saucepan, over medium-low heat, bring wine, sugar, water, cinnamon, clove, ginger and salt to a simmer. Add pear and simmer for 3 minutes; remove with a slotted spoon to a warm platter. Add apple to the poaching liquid and simmer for 2 minutes; remove with a slotted spoon to the platter. Add grapes to the poaching liquid and simmer for 1 minute; remove with a slotted spoon to the platter. Add tangerines to the poaching liquid and simmer for 30 seconds; remove with a slotted spoon to the platter. Whisk 2 tbsp (25 mL) of the poaching liquid into Raspberry Vinaigrette until smooth. Discard remaining liquid or reserve for another use. Pour dressing over poached fruit. Serve warm. **Serves 4.**

Chapter 17
Soups
For Starters, Suppers and Snacks

Chicken Soup with Three Rices 192
Curried Chicken Soup 192
Chicken Noodle Soup 192
Chicken Barley Soup 192
Chicken Soup with Tortellini 192
Chicken Matzo Ball Soup 193
Cream of Mushroom Soup 193
Mushroom Chowder 193
Lamb and Mushroom Soup 194
Mushroom Barley Soup 194
Wild Mushroom Bisque 194
Classic Minestrone 194
Minestrone with Beans 194
Cream of Chestnut Soup 194
Butternut Squash Soup
with Ginger Cream 195
Potato Cheese Soup 195
Potato Leek Soup 195
Potato Fennel Vichyssoise 195
Garlic Potato Soup 195
Sweet Potato Vichyssoise 195
Pumpkin Leek Soup 196
Caraway Potato Soup 196
Potato Watercress Soup 196
Apple Pumpkin Bisque 196
Apple Broccoli Bisque 196

Roasted Red Pepper Chowder 196
Curried Cucumber Soup 196
Lime Bisque 197
Avgolemono 197
Lemon Chicken Soup with Orzo 197
Lemon Chickpea Soup 197
Tomato Tarragon Consommé 197
Tomato Basil Consommé 197
New England Clam Chowder 198
Manhattan Clam Chowder 198
Italian Clam Soup 198
Mussel Marinara Soup 198
Salmon Bisque 198
Shrimp Bisque 198
Crab Bisque 198
Black Bean Soup
with Orange and Cilantro 199
Garden Split Pea Soup 199
African Peanut Soup 199
Spicy Red Bean Peanut Soup 199
Miso Soup 199
Miso Soup with Scallops 199
Miso Soup with Vegetables 199
Hot-and-Sour Soup 200
Hot-and-Sour Shrimp Soup 200
Hot-and-Sour Soup with Crab 200

Soup isn't much. A celery stalk, a carrot top, an onion and a meaty bone are about all you need. And lots of water, of course. A pinch of salt and a bit of herb to bring the flavor out. Perhaps a potato, chopped into chunks or sculpted into tiny balls, scattered through the broth like a string of pearls come unstrung. Maybe a bisque of lobster or crab, finished with a dram of cream, a bit of sweet butter and a snippet of chive.

No, soup isn't much. Just sustenance for us all.

Most good cooks make good soup. It is a challenge to them, and a delight to extract everything an ingredient has to give, until, from a pile of scraps, a meal emerges. Meat, vegetable, starch and beverage, neatly packed in one bowl.

Another challenge is to make soup quickly. Though perfectly wonderful soups are made with only trimmings and water, it saves time and energy to start with a broth, which is nothing more than a flavorful liquid. It can be the leftover cooking water from vegetables or stews, something concocted from last night's chicken carcass or a good-quality broth from a can. A good broth gives you speed. Because it holds most of the flavor of the soup, hours of simmering and long lists of ingredients become unnecessary. Homemade soups can be assembled in minutes and on the table a half-hour later.

To show you how easy it is, in this chapter we share 50 soup recipes, including chicken, mushroom, vegetable, bean and ethnic soups, chowders and bisques, and soups that can be served either hot or cold. All but a couple can be made in 30 minutes or less if you have your own broth on hand or use a good commercial broth.

About these recipes . . .

If you'd prefer to use homemade broth, we have included recipes for vegetable, fish, chicken and beef broths in Basic Preparations (pages 18–19), but there are so many high-quality, fully prepared canned broths available that we tested the recipes using prepared products. Salt and pepper should be adjusted to taste before serving.

Chicken Soup with Three Rices

1 tbsp	vegetable oil	15 mL
3	carrots, chopped	3
2	stalks celery, chopped	2
1	large onion, chopped	1
1	½-inch (1 cm) piece gingerroot	1
1	dried chili pepper	1
1	bay leaf	1
1 cup	white wine	250 mL
8 cups	chicken broth	2 L
	Salt and freshly ground black pepper to taste	
¼ cup	brown rice	50 mL
¼ cup	wild rice	50 mL
¼ cup	white rice	50 mL

In a large saucepan, heat oil over medium heat. Sauté carrots, celery and onion until onion is translucent. Add ginger, chili pepper, bay leaf and wine; boil for 1 minute. Add broth, salt and pepper; bring to a boil. Add brown rice and wild rice; reduce heat and simmer for 40 minutes. Add white rice and simmer for 12 to 15 minutes, or until rice is tender. (Note: you can use leftover cooked rice to eliminate the rice cooking time.) Discard bay leaf, ginger and chili pepper. **Serves 6 to 8.**

Curried Chicken Soup

Follow preceding recipe, but add 2 tsp (10 mL) curry powder with the ginger. **Serves 6 to 8.**

Chicken Noodle Soup

Follow recipe for Chicken Soup with Three Rices (above), but omit the rices. Decrease the initial simmering time to 20 minutes, then add 5 oz (150 g) broad egg noodles and simmer for 10 minutes, until tender. **Serves 6 to 8.**

Chicken Barley Soup

Follow recipe for Chicken Soup with Three Rices (above), but replace all three rices with 1½ cups (375 mL) pearl barley. Simmer for 50 to 55 minutes after adding barley. **Serves 6 to 8.**

Chicken Soup with Tortellini

1 tbsp	vegetable oil	15 mL
3	carrots, chopped	3
2	stalks celery, chopped	2
1	large onion, chopped	1
1 cup	dry white wine	250 mL
1 tsp	dried thyme	5 mL

1 tsp	dried basil	5 mL
½ tsp	dried rosemary	2 mL
½ tsp	dried oregano	2 mL
½ tsp	dried sage	2 mL
1	bay leaf	1
8 cups	chicken broth	2 L
1	can (14 oz/398 mL) diced tomatoes, drained	1
	Salt and freshly ground black pepper to taste	
8 oz	cheese or meat tortellini	250 g

In a large saucepan, heat oil over medium heat. Sauté carrots, celery and onion until onion is translucent. Add wine, thyme, basil, rosemary, oregano, sage and bay leaf; boil for 1 minute. Add broth, tomatoes, salt and pepper; bring to a boil and cook for 20 minutes. Add tortellini and cook for 10 minutes. Discard bay leaf. **Serves 6 to 8.**

Chicken Matzo Ball Soup

4	eggs	4
9 cups	chicken broth, divided	2.25 L
1 cup	matzo meal	200 mL
2 tbsp	rendered chicken fat or shortening, melted	25 mL
1 tbsp	finely chopped fresh Italian (flat-leaf) parsley	15 mL
Pinch	ground ginger	Pinch
1 tsp	salt	5 mL
1 tbsp	vegetable oil	15 mL
3	carrots, chopped	3
2	stalks celery, chopped	2
1	large onion, chopped	1
1	½-inch (1 cm) piece gingerroot	1
1	dried chili pepper	1
1	bay leaf	1
1 cup	dry white wine	250 mL
	Salt and freshly ground black pepper to taste	

Combine eggs, ½ cup (125 mL) of the broth, matzo meal, chicken fat, parsley, ginger and salt until uniformly moistened. Cover and refrigerate for 1 hour. Using wet hands, form balls of about 1½ inches (4 cm) in diameter, dropping them into a large pot of boiling salted water as they are made. Reduce heat, cover and simmer until matzo balls are puffed and light, about 30 minutes. Meanwhile, in a large saucepan, heat oil over medium heat. Sauté carrots, celery and onion until onion is translucent. Add ginger, chili pepper, bay leaf and wine; boil for 1 minute. Add the remaining broth, salt and pepper; reduce heat and simmer for 15 minutes. Discard ginger, chili pepper and bay leaf. Drain matzo balls, add to soup and heat through. **Serves 6 to 8.**

Cream of Mushroom Soup

2 tbsp	butter	25 mL
1	large onion, chopped	1
1	clove garlic, minced	1
1	carrot, diced	1
1	stalk celery, diced	1
8 oz	mushrooms, sliced	250 g
8 oz	mushrooms, minced	250 g
1 tbsp	all-purpose flour	15 mL
4 cups	chicken broth	1 L
	Salt and freshly ground white pepper to taste	
2 cups	cream (any type, minimum 10%)	500 mL
	Chopped chives	

In a large, heavy saucepan, melt butter over medium heat. Sauté onion, garlic, carrot and celery until barely tender. Increase heat to medium-high and add sliced mushrooms; sauté until mushrooms start to release their liquid. Add minced mushrooms and sauté until mushrooms start to brown. Add flour and sauté for 2 minutes. Add broth, salt and pepper; reduce heat and simmer until soup is fully flavored, about 20 minutes. Stir in cream and heat through. Garnish with chives. **Serves 6 to 8.**

Mushroom Chowder

1	slice bacon, finely chopped	1
2	carrots, diced	2
2	stalks celery, diced	2
2	large red-skinned or other boiling potatoes, peeled and diced	2
1	large onion, chopped	1
½	red bell pepper, diced	½
8 oz	smoked ham, diced	250 g
1 lb	mushrooms, sliced	500 g
1 tsp	dried thyme	5 mL
½ tsp	dried sage	2 mL
½ tsp	crumbled dried rosemary	2 mL
1	bay leaf	1
4 cups	chicken broth	1 L
	Salt and freshly ground black pepper to taste	
1 tbsp	cornstarch	15 mL
1 cup	milk (2% or whole)	250 mL

In a large saucepan, cook bacon over medium heat until crisp. Add carrots, celery, potatoes, onion, red pepper and ham; sauté until vegetables are barely tender. Add mushrooms, thyme, sage, rosemary and bay leaf; sauté until mushrooms start to release their liquid. Add broth, salt and pepper; reduce heat and simmer until vegetables are tender, about 20 minutes. Dissolve cornstarch in milk, stir into soup and bring to a boil. Discard bay leaf. **Serves 6 to 8.**

Lamb and Mushroom Soup

1 lb	lamb cubes for stew	500 g
	Salt and freshly ground black pepper to taste	
	Vegetable oil	
1	large onion, chopped	1
2	cloves garlic, minced	2
1 lb	mushrooms, sliced	500 g
1 tsp	ground coriander	5 mL
½ tsp	chopped fresh rosemary	2 mL
½ tsp	dried thyme	2 mL
2	carrots, sliced	2
1	stalk celery, sliced	1
1	bay leaf	1
8 cups	beef broth	2 L
2 tsp	tomato paste	10 mL
1 tbsp	chopped fresh Italian (flat-leaf) parsley	15 mL
	Juice of 1 lemon	

Generously season lamb with salt and pepper. In a large, heavy saucepan, heat a thin film of oil over medium-high heat. Sauté lamb until browned on all sides. Add onion and sauté until tender. Add garlic and mushrooms; sauté until mushrooms are lightly browned. Add coriander, rosemary, and thyme; sauté for 1 minute. Add carrots, celery, bay leaf, broth, tomato paste and additional salt and pepper; bring to a boil. Reduce heat and simmer for 1 hour, until lamb is fork-tender. Discard bay leaf and stir in parsley and lemon juice. **Serves 6 to 8.**

Mushroom Barley Soup

Follow preceding recipe, but omit the garlic, coriander and lemon juice, and add 1 cup (250 mL) pearl barley once the soup comes to a boil. **Serves 6 to 8.**

Wild Mushroom Bisque

¼ oz	dried wild or exotic mushrooms	7 g
1 cup	boiling water	250 mL
¼ cup	Madeira	50 mL
2 tbsp	butter	25 mL
1	onion, finely chopped	1
1 lb	mushrooms, minced	500 g
1 tsp	dried thyme	5 mL
½ tsp	crushed dried rosemary	2 mL
2 tbsp	all-purpose flour	25 mL
4 cups	chicken broth	1 L
	Salt and freshly ground black pepper to taste	
1 cup	cream (any type, minimum 10%)	250 mL

Soak dried mushrooms in boiling water and Madeira for 15 minutes. Drain mushrooms, reserving soaking liquid, and mince. Meanwhile, in a large, heavy saucepan, melt butter over medium heat. Sauté onion until tender. Add wild and fresh mushrooms, thyme and rosemary; sauté until fresh mushrooms start to release their liquid. Add flour and sauté until browned. Add broth, reserved mushroom soaking liquid, salt and pepper; reduce heat and simmer for 20 minutes. Stir in cream and heat through. **Serves 6 to 8.**

Classic Minestrone

2 tbsp	olive oil	25 mL
1	large onion, chopped	1
2	cloves garlic, minced	2
2	carrots, sliced	2
2	stalks celery, sliced	2
½	bell pepper (any color), diced	½
1 tsp	dried thyme	5 mL
1 tsp	dried basil	5 mL
½ tsp	dried rosemary	2 mL
½ tsp	dried oregano	2 mL
½ tsp	dried sage	2 mL
1	can (14 oz/398 mL) diced tomatoes, drained	1
6 cups	chicken broth	1.5 L
1 tbsp	red wine vinegar	15 mL
1 tbsp	tomato paste	15 mL
	Salt and freshly ground black pepper to taste	
	Freshly grated Parmesan cheese	

In a large saucepan, heat oil over medium heat. Sauté onion until tender. Add garlic, carrots, celery and bell pepper; sauté until barely tender. Add herbs and sauté for 30 seconds. Add tomatoes, broth, vinegar, tomato paste, salt and pepper; bring to a boil. Reduce heat and simmer until vegetables are tender, about 20 minutes. Serve sprinkled with Parmesan. **Serves 6 to 8.**

Minestrone with Beans

Follow preceding recipe, but add 1 cup (250 mL) drained rinsed canned chickpeas or cannellini beans with the broth. **Serves 6 to 8.**

Cream of Chestnut Soup

¼ cup	butter	50 mL
2	carrots, diced	2
2	stalks celery, diced	2
1	onion, finely chopped	1
1 cup	canned chestnut purée	250 mL

4 cups	chicken broth	1 L
Pinch	ground cloves	Pinch
	Salt and freshly ground white pepper to taste	
1 cup	cream (any type, minimum 10%)	250 mL
2 tbsp	chopped fresh Italian (flat-leaf) parsley	25 mL
2 tbsp	brandy	25 mL

In a large, heavy saucepan, melt butter over medium heat. Sauté carrots, celery and onion until tender. Whisk in chestnut purée and broth until smooth. Add cloves, salt and pepper; reduce heat and simmer, stirring often, for 10 minutes. Stir in cream, parsley and brandy; heat through. **Serves 4.**

Butternut Squash Soup with Ginger Cream

2 tbsp	butter	25 mL
2	leeks, white part only, chopped	2
1	parsnip, chopped	1
1½ cups	chopped carrots	375 mL
1½ tsp	grated gingerroot	7 mL
2 lbs	butternut squash, peeled, seeded and cut into chunks	1 kg
6 cups	chicken broth	1.5 L
1 tsp	dried thyme	5 mL
Pinch	ground nutmeg	Pinch
	Salt and freshly ground black pepper to taste	
1 cup	whipping (35%) cream	250 mL
1 tbsp	minced candied ginger	15 mL

In a large saucepan, melt butter over medium heat. Sauté leeks, parsnip, carrots and ginger until barely tender. Add squash, broth, thyme, nutmeg, salt and pepper; bring to a boil. Reduce heat and simmer until squash is tender, about 30 minutes. Working in batches, transfer solids to a food processor or blender and purée until almost smooth. Return to pan and heat through. In a bowl, beat cream to soft peaks and fold in candied ginger. Serve soup topped with spoonfuls of ginger cream. **Serves 8.**

Potato Cheese Soup

1 tbsp	vegetable oil	15 mL
1 tbsp	butter	15 mL
2	large onions, finely chopped	2
1½ lbs	red-skinned or other boiling potatoes, peeled and diced	750 g
4 cups	chicken broth	1 L
Pinch	dried thyme	Pinch
1 cup	cream (any type, minimum 10%)	250 mL
1 cup	milk	250 mL

	Salt and freshly ground white pepper to taste	
1 cup	shredded Cheddar cheese	250 mL
1 tbsp	cornstarch	15 mL

In a large, heavy saucepan, heat oil and butter over medium heat. Sauté onions until tender. Add potatoes, broth and thyme; reduce heat and simmer until potatoes are tender, about 20 minutes. Add cream, milk, salt and pepper; bring to a simmer. Toss shredded Cheddar with cornstarch and add gradually to soup, cooking just long enough to melt the cheese. Do not boil. **Serves 6 to 8.**

Potato Leek Soup

3 tbsp	butter	45 mL
4	large leeks, white part only, chopped	4
2 lbs	red-skinned or golden potatoes, peeled and sliced	1 kg
6 cups	chicken broth	1.5 L
1 tsp	salt	5 mL
¼ tsp	freshly ground white pepper	1 mL
	Ground nutmeg	
1 cup	light or table (18%) cream	250 mL
1 cup	whole milk	250 mL
	Chopped chives	
	Sour cream or buttermilk (if serving cold)	

In a large, heavy saucepan, melt butter over medium heat. Sauté leeks until tender. Add potatoes, broth, salt, pepper and nutmeg; reduce heat and simmer until potatoes are tender, about 20 minutes. Working in batches, transfer to a food processor or blender and purée (don't overprocess or potatoes will become gummy). Return to pan, stir in cream and milk, and heat through. Serve hot or cold, garnished with chopped chives. If serving cold, thin to desired consistency with sour cream or buttermilk. **Serves 6.**

Potato Fennel Vichyssoise

Follow preceding recipe, but use just 2 leeks, and add 1 chopped fennel bulb and 1 tsp (5 mL) ground fennel seeds with the leeks. Serve cold. **Serves 6.**

Garlic Potato Soup

Follow recipe for Potato Leek Soup (above), but replace 1 of the leeks with 1 head garlic, minced. **Serves 6.**

Sweet Potato Vichyssoise

Follow recipe for Potato Leek Soup (above), but replace the potatoes with sweet potatoes. Serve cold. **Serves 6.**

Pumpkin Leek Soup

Follow recipe for Potato Leek Soup (page 195), but replace the potatoes with one 16-oz (454 mL) can pumpkin purée (not pie filling). Reduce simmering time to 10 minutes. **Serves 6.**

Caraway Potato Soup

Follow recipe for Potato Leek Soup (page 195), but replace 2 of the leeks with 4 stalks celery, chopped, and add 1 tsp (5 mL) ground caraway seeds with the leeks. **Serves 6.**

Potato Watercress Soup

Follow recipe for Potato Leek Soup (page 195), but add leaves from 2 bunches watercress after the potatoes have been simmering for 10 minutes. **Serves 6.**

Apple Pumpkin Bisque

2 tbsp	butter	25 mL
1	small onion, finely chopped	1
2	large apples, peeled and finely chopped	2
1	cinnamon stick	1
1	small dried chili pepper	1
1 tbsp	finely chopped gingerroot	15 mL
4 cups	chicken broth	1 L
2 cups	canned pumpkin purée (not pie filling)	500 mL
2 tbsp	honey	25 mL
1 tsp	cider vinegar	5 mL
	Ground nutmeg	
	Salt and freshly ground white pepper to taste	
½ cup	sour cream	125 mL

In a large, heavy saucepan, melt butter over medium heat. Sauté onion until tender. Add apples, cinnamon stick, chili pepper and ginger; sauté until apple looks cooked. Add broth, pumpkin purée, honey, vinegar, nutmeg, salt and pepper; bring to a boil. Discard cinnamon stick and chili pepper. Serve hot or cold, stirring in sour cream just before serving. **Serves 6 to 8.**

Apple Broccoli Bisque

2 tbsp	butter	25 mL
1	small onion, finely chopped	1
2	large tart apples, peeled and finely chopped	2
1	bunch broccoli, chopped	1
4 cups	chicken broth	1 L
¼ cup	sour cream	50 mL
	Salt and freshly ground white pepper to taste	
	Milk (if serving cold)	

In a large saucepan, melt butter over medium heat. Sauté onion until tender. Add apples, broccoli and broth; cook until broccoli is soft, about 10 minutes. Working in batches, transfer to a food processor or blender and purée. Return to pan and stir in sour cream, salt and pepper; heat through. Serve hot or cold. If serving cold, thin to desired consistency with milk. **Serves 6 to 8.**

Roasted Red Pepper Chowder

2 tbsp	olive oil	25 mL
1	small onion, finely chopped	1
1	clove garlic, minced	1
1	stalk celery, diced	1
4	roasted red bell peppers (see page 11), diced	4
4 cups	chicken broth	1 L
1½ tsp	paprika	7 mL
1 tsp	curry powder	5 mL
Pinch	cayenne pepper	Pinch
	Salt and freshly ground black pepper to taste	
2 tbsp	freshly squeezed lime juice	25 mL
1 tbsp	sour cream	15 mL
	Canned jalapeño pepper, finely chopped	

In a large, heavy saucepan, heat oil over medium heat. Sauté onion, garlic and celery until tender. Add roasted peppers, broth, paprika, curry powder, cayenne, salt and pepper; bring to a boil. Reduce heat and simmer for 10 minutes. Stir in lime juice. Serve hot or cold, garnished with sour cream and jalapeño. **Serves 4.**

Curried Cucumber Soup

2 tbsp	butter	25 mL
1	small onion, chopped	1
2	cloves garlic, minced	2
4 cups	finely chopped seeded peeled cucumber	1 L
4 cups	chicken or vegetable broth	1 L
2 tsp	curry powder	10 mL
	Salt and freshly ground white pepper to taste	
½ cup	cream (any type, minimum 10%) or sour cream (plus a bit more if serving cold)	125 mL

In a large saucepan, melt butter over medium heat. Sauté onion and garlic until tender. Add cucumber, broth, curry powder, salt and pepper; reduce heat and simmer for 10 to 15 minutes, or until cucumber is tender. Working in batches, transfer to a food processor or blender and purée. Return to pan, stir in cream and heat through. Serve hot or cold. If serving cold, thin to desired consistency with additional cream. **Serves 6 to 8.**

Lime Bisque

8 cups	chicken broth	2 L
⅓ cup	long-grain white rice	75 mL
½ tsp	salt	2 mL
3	egg yolks	3
⅓ cup	freshly squeezed lime juice	75 mL
	Few drops of hot pepper sauce (such as Tabasco)	
	Lime slices	
	Chopped fresh cilantro	
	Additional chicken broth, chilled (if serving cold)	

In a large saucepan, bring broth to a boil. Add rice and salt; reduce heat and simmer for 12 to 15 minutes, or until rice is tender. Meanwhile, combine egg yolks, lime juice and hot pepper sauce. Slowly whisk 2 cups (500 mL) of the hot soup into egg mixture. Reduce heat so that soup barely simmers and slowly pour in egg mixture, stirring constantly. Increase heat to medium and cook, stirring, until soup thickens slightly (do not boil). Serve hot or cold, garnished with lime slices and cilantro. If serving cold, thin to desired consistency with chilled broth. **Serves 6 to 8.**

Avgolemono

8 cups	chicken broth	2 L
¾ cup	long-grain white rice	175 mL
	Salt and freshly ground black pepper to taste	
3	egg yolks	3
	Juice of 2 lemons	
	Chopped chives	
	Additional chicken broth, chilled (if serving cold)	

In a large saucepan, bring broth to a boil. Add rice, salt and pepper, reduce heat and simmer for 12 to 15 minutes, or until rice is tender. Meanwhile, combine egg yolks and lemon juice. Slowly whisk 2 cups (500 mL) of the hot soup into egg mixture. Reduce heat so that soup barely simmers and slowly pour in egg mixture, stirring constantly. Increase heat to medium and cook, stirring, until soup thickens slightly (do not boil). Serve hot or cold, garnished with chives. If served cold, thin to desired consistency with chilled broth. **Serves 6 to 8.**

Lemon Chicken Soup with Orzo

Follow preceding recipe, but substitute orzo or another pastina for the rice. **Serves 6 to 8.**

Lemon Chickpea Soup

Follow recipe for Avgolemono (left), but omit the rice, and add 1 cup (250 mL) drained rinsed canned chickpeas and 1 cup (250 mL) small pasta to the boiling broth. **Serves 6 to 8.**

Tomato Tarragon Consommé

1 tbsp	gelatin (one ¼ oz/7 g envelope)	15 mL
6 cups	chilled chicken broth, divided	1.5 L
6	whole black peppercorns	6
4	egg whites, beaten	4
1	stalk celery, finely chopped	1
1	bay leaf, crumbled	1
¼ cup	tomato paste	50 mL
3 tbsp	minced onion	45 mL
2 tsp	dried tarragon	10 mL
½ tsp	dried thyme	2 mL
	Salt to taste	
	Fresh tarragon leaves or sprigs	

Dissolve gelatin in ½ cup (125 mL) of the chilled chicken broth. Place the remaining broth in a large, heavy saucepan and stir in gelatin mixture. Whisk in peppercorns, egg whites, celery, bay leaf, tomato paste, onion, dried tarragon, thyme and salt until well blended and frothy. Cook over medium heat, stirring frequently, until soup becomes very cloudy. Stop stirring and wait for soup to boil. As soon as it does, a raft of egg white will form on the surface. Immediately reduce heat to a bare simmer and poke a hole near the edge of the raft; simmer for 15 minutes. Using a large slotted spoon, lift out the raft and discard. Strain soup through several layers of damp cheesecloth. Serve immediately, garnished with tarragon leaves, or chill and serve jellied, garnished with tarragon sprigs. **Serves 4.**

Tomato Basil Consommé

Follow preceding recipe, but omit the dried tarragon and thyme, and add 2 tbsp (25 mL) dried basil with the onion. Omit the fresh tarragon, and garnish soup with ½ cup (125 mL) finely chopped fresh basil. **Serves 4.**

New England Clam Chowder

24	littleneck clams, scrubbed (see page 8)	24
4 cups	boiling water	1 L
5 oz	salt pork, finely diced	150 g
1	large onion, diced	1
1 tbsp	all-purpose flour	15 mL
2	large red-skinned or other boiling potatoes, diced	2
	Salt and freshly ground black pepper to taste	
2 cups	cream (any type, minimum 10%)	500 mL
2 cups	milk (2% or whole)	500 mL
2 tbsp	butter	25 mL

Add clams to boiling water; reduce heat, cover and simmer for 5 minutes, until clams open (discard any that don't). Remove clams from their shells, chop and set aside. Strain cooking liquid through several layers of damp cheesecloth, adding any liquid that seeps from clams; set aside. In a large, heavy saucepan, over medium heat, sauté salt pork until fat is rendered. Remove cracklings of salt pork with a slotted spoon and blot on paper towels. Add onion to the fat remaining in the pan and sauté until tender. Add flour and sauté for 1 minute. Add clam cooking liquid and potatoes; increase heat to medium-high and cook until potatoes are barely tender. Add clams, cracklings, salt and pepper. In a separate saucepan, heat cream and milk, then stir into soup along with butter. **Serves 6 to 8.**

Manhattan Clam Chowder

Follow preceding recipe, but add 2 cups (500 mL) chopped canned tomatoes, with juices, 1 cup (250 mL) vegetable juice (such as V8), 1 bell pepper (any color), diced, 1 bay leaf, ¼ tsp (1 mL) each dried oregano and dried basil, and a dash of hot pepper sauce (such as Tabasco) as soon as potatoes are cooked. Simmer for 5 minutes. Omit cream, milk and butter. **Serves 6 to 8.**

Italian Clam Soup

¼ cup	olive oil	50 mL
2	cloves garlic, minced	2
1	can (14 oz/398 mL) diced tomatoes, with juices	1
2 tbsp	chopped fresh Italian (flat-leaf) parsley	25 mL
Pinch	hot pepper flakes	Pinch
24	littleneck clams, scrubbed (see page 8)	24
	Crusty bread	

In a large, heavy saucepan, heat oil over medium-high heat. Sauté garlic until aromatic. Add tomatoes, parsley and hot pepper flakes; reduce heat and simmer for 5 minutes. Add clams, cover and simmer for 5 minutes, until clams open (discard any that don't). Serve with crusty bread. **Serves 4.**

Mussel Marinara Soup

Follow preceding recipe, but replace the clams with 2 lbs (1 kg) mussels, scrubbed (see page 8). Simmer for 3 minutes, until mussels open (discard any that don't). **Serves 4.**

Salmon Bisque

2 tbsp	olive oil	25 mL
1	carrot, finely chopped	1
1	stalk celery, finely chopped	1
1	onion, chopped	1
2 cups	dry white wine	500 mL
1 lb	salmon steaks (with bones, skin removed), cut into small pieces	500 g
3 cups	fish broth	750 mL
⅓ cup	long-grain white rice	75 mL
1 tsp	dried dillweed	5 mL
Pinch	cayenne pepper	Pinch
	Salt and freshly ground black pepper to taste	
1 cup	light or table (18%) cream	250 mL
	Several sprigs of fresh dill or tarragon (optional)	

In a large, heavy saucepan, heat oil over medium-low heat. Sauté carrot, celery and onion until tender. Add wine and simmer for 2 minutes. Add salmon, broth, rice, dill, cayenne, salt and black pepper; simmer for 12 to 15 minutes, or until rice is tender. Working in batches, transfer to a food processor or blender and purée until completely smooth. Pass through a fine-mesh strainer, forcing the solids back into the pan as much as possible. Stir in cream and heat through. Garnish each bowl with a few sprigs of dill, if desired. **Serves 4.**

Shrimp Bisque

Follow preceding recipe, but replace the salmon with shrimp, peeled, deveined and chopped. **Serves 4.**

Crab Bisque

Follow recipe for Salmon Bisque (above), but replace the salmon with backfin (lump) crabmeat, shells picked out. **Serves 4.**

Black Bean Soup with Orange and Cilantro

2 tbsp	olive oil	25 mL
2	carrots, diced	2
1	large onion, chopped	1
2 oz	chorizo (or other spicy sausage), chopped	60 g
8 cups	chicken broth	2 L
3 cups	drained rinsed canned black beans	750 mL
1/2 cup	chopped fresh cilantro	125 mL
	Finely grated zest and juice of 1 orange	
	Salt and freshly ground black pepper to taste	

In a large saucepan, heat oil over medium heat. Sauté carrots, onion and chorizo until vegetables are tender. Add broth and beans; reduce heat and simmer for 15 minutes. Transfer half the soup to a food processor or blender and purée. Stir back into soup. Stir in cilantro, orange zest, orange juice, salt and pepper. **Serves 6 to 8.**

Garden Split Pea Soup

2 tbsp	butter	25 mL
1	large onion, diced	1
1	large cucumber, peeled, seeded and diced	1
1	head Boston lettuce, chopped	1
1/2 cup	coarsely chopped fresh Italian (flat-leaf) parsley	125 mL
2 oz	smoked ham, finely diced	60 g
8 cups	chicken broth	2 L
1 1/2 cups	split peas	375 mL
1 tsp	granulated sugar	5 mL
	Salt and freshly ground black pepper to taste	
1 cup	cream (any type, minimum 10%)	250 mL

In a large, heavy saucepan, melt butter over medium heat. Sauté onion, cucumber, lettuce and parsley until barely tender. Add ham, broth, peas, sugar, salt and pepper; reduce heat and simmer until peas are tender, about 45 minutes. Stir in cream and heat through. **Serves 6 to 8.**

African Peanut Soup

1 tbsp	peanut oil	15 mL
2	carrots, finely chopped	2
1	large onion, finely chopped	1
1	clove garlic, minced	1
1	small dried chili pepper	1
2 tsp	chopped gingerroot	10 mL
1 tsp	ground coriander	5 mL
1 tsp	ground cumin	5 mL
6 cups	chicken broth	1.5 L
1/4 cup	long-grain white rice	50 mL
	Salt to taste	
3/4 cup	smooth peanut butter	175 mL

In a large saucepan, heat oil over medium heat. Sauté carrots and onion until tender. Add garlic, chili pepper, ginger, coriander and cumin; sauté until aromatic. Add broth, rice and salt; reduce heat and simmer until vegetables and rice are tender, about 15 minutes. Whisk in peanut butter until smooth. Remove chili pepper. **Serves 6 to 8.**

Spicy Red Bean Peanut Soup

Follow preceding recipe, but omit the rice, and add 1 1/2 cups (375 mL) drained rinsed canned red kidney beans with the broth. **Serves 6 to 8.**

Miso Soup

2 tsp	vegetable oil	10 mL
8 oz	mushrooms, sliced	250 g
3	thin slices gingerroot	3
1/4 cup	soy miso	50 mL
1 cup	boiling water	250 mL
8 cups	vegetable broth	2 L
1 lb	firm tofu, cubed	500 g
Pinch	cayenne pepper	Pinch
3	green onions, thinly sliced	3

In a large, heavy saucepan, heat oil over medium-high heat. Sauté mushrooms until they start to release their liquid. Add ginger and sauté until aromatic. Dissolve miso in boiling water, then add to pan along with broth; bring to a boil. Add tofu and cayenne; reduce heat and simmer for 2 to 3 minutes, or until heated through. Remove ginger slices and stir in green onions. **Serves 6 to 8.**

Miso Soup with Scallops

Follow preceding recipe, but replace the tofu with scallops, trimmed of hard side muscles and thinly sliced. Simmer for 30 seconds, until scallops are firm and opaque. **Serves 6 to 8.**

Miso Soup with Vegetables

Follow recipe for Miso Soup (above), but add 1 thawed 10-oz (300 g) package frozen mixed vegetables with the mushrooms. **Serves 6 to 8.**

Hot-and-Sour Soup

2 tbsp	cornstarch	25 mL
½ cup	water	125 mL
¼ cup	rice vinegar	50 mL
2 tsp	sesame oil	10 mL
1 tsp	hot pepper sauce (such as Tabasco)	5 mL
½ tsp	hot pepper oil (store-bought or see recipe, page 82)	2 mL
4 cups	chicken or vegetable broth	1 L
1 tbsp	soy miso	15 mL
¼ cup	diced red bell pepper	50 mL
¼ cup	julienned carrot	50 mL
1 cup	drained canned straw mushrooms	250 mL
4 oz	firm tofu, cut into small cubes	125 g
2	green onions, thinly sliced	2

In a small bowl, dissolve cornstarch in water. Add vinegar, sesame oil, hot pepper sauce and hot pepper oil; set aside. In a large, heavy saucepan, bring broth to a boil over medium-high heat Soften miso with a bit of hot broth, then add to pan, stirring until miso dissolves. Add red pepper and carrot; reduce heat and simmer for 2 minutes. Add cornstarch mixture (stirring first, if necessary), straw mushrooms and tofu; simmer for 1 minute, until slightly thickened. Remove from heat and stir in green onions. **Serves 6 to 8.**

Hot-and-Sour Shrimp Soup

Follow preceding recipe, but omit the red pepper, and add 1 cup (250 mL) peeled and deveined baby shrimp with the tofu. Immediately after adding shrimp, stir in 1 beaten egg white and simmer for 30 seconds, until shrimp is pink and opaque. Serve immediately. **Serves 6 to 8.**

Hot-and-Sour Soup with Crab

Follow recipe for Hot and Sour Shrimp Soup (left), but replace the shrimp with 1 cup (250 mL) backfin (lump) crabmeat, shells picked out. **Serves 6 to 8.**

Chapter 18
Chili
Easy, Filling and Sophisticated

Basic Chili Mix (BCM) 202
Vegetarian Chili 202
Corn Chili 203
Garden Chili 203
Wild Mushroom Chili 203
All-Bean Vegan Chili 203
Quick Vegetable Chili 203
Ground Beef Chili 203
Ground Turkey Chili 203
Chunky Beef Chili 204
Venison Chili 204
Chili Inferno 204
Chili with Beer 204
Herbed Chili 204
Oven-Braised Chili 204
Cheesy Baked Chili 204
Cornbread Chili 204
Chili with Cornmeal Dumplings 204
Charbroiled Sirloin Chili 204
Roasted Pepper Chili 205
Veal Chili with Artichokes 205
All-Pork Chili 205
Three-Sausage Chili 206
Black-Eyed Pea Chili 206
Smoked Sausage Chili with Porter 206
Bourbon Chili 206

Honeyed Pork Chops in Chili Sauce . . . 206
Chilied Chicken Salad 206
Chilied Chicken Stew 207
Chorizo Chicken Chili 207
Sausage and Quail Chili 207
Curried Chicken Chili 207
Chocolate Chicken Chili 208
Turkey Mole Chili 208
Turkey and Avocado Chili 208
Grilled Salmon Chili 208
Chilied Scallop Kebabs 208
Grilled Tuna Chili on Black Beans 209
Chinese Shrimp Chili 209
Shrimp Chili with Black Beans 209
Shrimp Chili with Chickpeas 209
Chilied Scampi with Cannellini 209
Crab Chili 209
Smoked Turkey Chili 209
Chili Gumbo 210
Chilied Clams 210
Lamb Mole Chili 210
Duck Mole Chili 210
Lamb and Lentil Chili 211
Curried Lamb Chili 211
Rabbit Chili 211

Chili isn't simple. Yes, it's easy to prepare and as unpretentious as anything that can be ladled into a bowl, but the flavors in a great chili are exciting and complex. They might start with a slow burn of jalapeño, scorched with a crackle of cayenne and cooled by a balm of ancho. There are the scents of black pepper and the floral perfume of cumin and coriander, followed by a bittersweet hint of oregano. The sum is greater than any of its parts, and, once tasted, the raucous harmony that is chili forever demolishes any preconceptions about American food being bland.

There are countless "best" chili recipes — from county-fair prize-winners to treasured family formulas. Although most chilies still use ground beef and kidney beans, there are no rules, and the possibility of making chili from any meat-and-bean combination gives the dish spectacular versatility.

That's why this chapter exists. A handful of these chilies are probably pretty close to the concoctions you've enjoyed over the years, but many of them may surprise you at first glance. If so, just give them a moment's thought, and you'll realize that turkey chili is perfect with chickpeas, and lamb chili is complemented well by lentils. To broaden your chili horizons, there are seafood chilies, pork chilies, sausage chilies and chili sauces to serve over grilled meats.

Some chili aficionados have gone so far as to market their particular secret chili ingredients in premixed spice blends, thus creating well-known products that can be found on many a food shelf. We'll join their ranks with our own chili mix. It's more than a chili powder; our Basic Chili Mix precooks the spices with onions, peppers and garlic. Once that's made, it's quick work to finish many of these recipes — just brown the meat, add the liquid and simmer.

A common problem when making chili is finding the right pot to do it in. Those who regularly prepare chili usually own what they affectionately call a "chili pot" for that purpose. A standard saucepan is often not wide enough to brown the meat, and a skillet is not deep enough to simmer the chili once the liquid has been added, so most of us have to improvise. If you don't have a "chili pot" at your disposal, choose the deepest skillet or widest saucepot available; a small iron Dutch oven is ideal.

About these recipes . . .

Many of the 50 recipes in this chapter use the Basic Chili Mix (which we will call BCM), combined with a variety of meats and accompaniments. You can make this mixture ahead and freeze it to have on hand. Or you can incorporate it immediately into any of the recipes below. Start by making the BCM, then complete the recipe in the same pot.

Being that chili is such a popular party dish, you may want to make some of these recipes in large batches. Because all chilies are stews, and are therefore forgiving by nature, you can multiply any chili recipe without adjusting the proportion of seasonings or liquid. Be sure to increase the size of the pot accordingly. However, as in any cooking, it is advisable to spice lightly at first, then heighten the seasoning near the end to suit your taste.

Basic Chili Mix (BCM)

1 tbsp	vegetable oil	15 mL
2	canned or fresh hot chili peppers, finely chopped	2
1 cup	chopped onion	250 mL
1	clove garlic, minced	1
3 to 4 tbsp	chili powder	45 to 50 mL
1 tbsp	ground cumin	15 mL
2 tsp	dried oregano	10 mL
1 tbsp	all-purpose flour	15 mL

Heat oil over medium-high heat. Sauté chili peppers, onion and garlic until softened. Add chili powder to taste, cumin and oregano; sauté for 1 minute. Add flour and sauté until completely absorbed. Transfer to a bowl. **Makes about ½ cup (125 mL)**. *Recipe can be multiplied and frozen in single-recipe portions.*

Vegetarian Chili

2 tbsp	olive oil	25 mL
2	bell peppers (any color), cut into strips	2
2	carrots, sliced	2
2	stalks celery, sliced	2
2	cloves garlic, minced	2
1 cup	sliced mushrooms	250 mL
1	recipe BCM (above)	1
1 tbsp	ground coriander	15 mL
1 tsp	dried thyme	5 mL
2 cups	vegetable broth	500 mL
1 cup	canned crushed tomatoes	250 mL
1	zucchini, sliced	1

1	can (14 to 19 oz/398 to 540 mL)	1
	cannellini or white kidney beans,	
	drained and rinsed	
	Salt and freshly ground black pepper	
	to taste	
1	avocado, diced	1
¼ cup	chopped fresh cilantro	50 mL

In a large, deep skillet or Dutch oven, heat oil over medium-high heat. Sauté bell peppers, carrots, celery, garlic and mushrooms until tender. Add BCM, coriander and thyme; sauté for 1 minute. Add broth and tomatoes; reduce heat and simmer for 10 minutes. Add zucchini, beans, salt and pepper; simmer for 10 minutes, until zucchini is tender and flavors are blended. Serve garnished with avocado and cilantro. **Serves 6.**

Corn Chili

Follow preceding recipe, but omit the carrots, add 3 cups (750 mL) corn kernels with the zucchini, replace the cannellini beans with red kidney beans, and omit the avocado. **Serves 6.**

Garden Chili

Follow recipe for Vegetarian Chili (page 202), but omit the carrots, add 1 eggplant, diced, with the celery, replace the cannellini beans with black beans, and omit the avocado. **Serves 6.**

Wild Mushroom Chili

Follow recipe for Vegetarian Chili (page 202), but omit the carrots, add 1 lb (500 g) wild or exotic mushrooms, sliced, with the celery, replace the cannellini beans with lentils, and omit the avocado. **Serves 6.**

All-Bean Vegan Chili

2 cups	vegetable broth	500 mL
2 tbsp	tomato paste	25 mL
1	recipe BCM (page 202)	1
4 cups	drained rinsed canned beans (any type)	1 L
	Salt, freshly ground black pepper	
	and hot pepper sauce	
	(such as Tabasco) to taste	

In a large saucepan, bring broth, tomato paste and BCM to a boil. Stir in beans, salt, black pepper and hot pepper sauce; reduce heat and simmer for 10 minutes. **Serves 6.**

Quick Vegetable Chili

Follow preceding recipe, but reduce the beans to 2 cups (500 mL), and add 1 cup (250 mL) each sliced carrot, mushrooms and bell pepper with the beans. Increase simmering time to 20 minutes. **Serves 6.**

Ground Beef Chili

2 tbsp	vegetable oil	25 mL
3 lbs	ground beef	1.5 kg
1	recipe BCM (page 202)	1
1	green or red bell pepper, chopped	1
2 cups	tomato sauce	500 mL
1 cup	beef broth	250 mL
1 tsp	freshly ground black pepper	5 mL
1	can (14 to 19 oz/398 to 540 mL)	1
	red kidney beans, drained and rinsed	
	Salt and hot pepper sauce	
	(such as Tabasco) to taste	

In a wide, deep, heavy pot (such as a Dutch oven), heat oil over medium-high heat. Sauté beef, breaking it up with a fork, until no longer pink. Add BCM, bell pepper, tomato sauce, beef broth, and black pepper; reduce heat and simmer, partially covered, for 1 hour. Stir in beans, salt and hot pepper sauce; heat through. **Serves 6 to 8.**

Ground Turkey Chili

Follow preceding recipe, but replace the beef with ground turkey, add 1 tbsp (15 mL) ground coriander with the BCM, and add ¼ cup (50 mL) chopped fresh cilantro with the beans. **Serves 6 to 8.**

Chunky Beef Chili

3 lbs	beef cubes for stew	1.5 kg
¼ cup	all purpose-flour	50 mL
2 tbsp	vegetable oil	25 mL
1	recipe BCM (page 202)	1
1	green or red bell pepper, chopped	1
1	clove garlic, minced	1
2 tbsp	tomato paste	25 mL
3 cups	beef broth	750 mL
1 tsp	cider vinegar	5 mL
1	can (14 to 19 oz/398 to 540 mL) pinto beans, drained and rinsed (optional)	1
	Salt and freshly ground black pepper to taste	

Dredge beef in flour. In a wide, deep, heavy pot (such as a Dutch oven), heat oil over medium-high heat. Sauté beef, in batches, until browned on all sides. Return beef to pot and add BCM, bell pepper, garlic and tomato paste; sauté for 1 minute. Add broth and vinegar; reduce heat, cover and simmer for 2 hours, until beef is very tender. Stir in beans (if using), salt and pepper; heat through. **Serves 6 to 8.**

Venison Chili

Follow preceding recipe, but replace the oil with rendered fat from 3 slices of bacon (reserve the bacon for another use), replace the beef with venison, reduce the broth to 2 cups (500 mL) and add 1 cup (250 mL) dry red wine with the broth, and replace the cider vinegar with red wine vinegar. **Serves 6 to 8.**

Chili Inferno

Follow recipe for Chunky Beef Chili (above), but add 1 jalapeño pepper, minced, and 1 habanero pepper, minced, with the garlic. **Serves 6 to 8.**

Chili with Beer

Follow recipe for Chunky Beef Chili (above), but reduce the broth to 1½ cups (375 mL) and add 12 oz (341 mL) beer with the broth. **Serves 6 to 8.**

Herbed Chili

Follow recipe for Chunky Beef Chili (above), but add 1 tsp (5 mL) each dried thyme, dried rosemary and dried basil with the BCM, and add ¼ cup (50 mL) chopped fresh Italian (flat-leaf) parsley with the beans. **Serves 6 to 8.**

Oven-Braised Chili

Follow recipe for Chunky Beef Chili (left), but instead of simmering, bake, covered, for 3 hours in a 350°F (180°C) oven. **Serves 6 to 8.**

Cheesy Baked Chili

Follow recipe for Chunky Beef Chili (left), but instead of simmering, bake, covered, for 2¾ hours in a 350°F (180°C) oven. Sprinkle with 2 cups (500 mL) shredded Cheddar or Monterey Jack cheese and bake, uncovered, for 15 minutes. **Serves 6 to 8.**

Cornbread Chili

Follow recipe for Ground Beef Chili (page 203) or Chunky Beef Chili (left). After it is finished, pour into a large casserole dish, top with Cornbread batter (page 22) and bake in a 400°F (200°C) oven for 40 minutes, until cornbread is browned and crusty, and a tester inserted in the center of the topping comes out clean. **Serves 6 to 8.**

Chili with Cornmeal Dumplings

	Any chili recipe	
¾ cup	yellow cornmeal	175 mL
¾ cup	all-purpose flour	175 mL
2 tbsp	granulated sugar	25 mL
1 tbsp	baking powder	15 mL
Pinch	salt	Pinch
½ cup	milk	125 mL
¼ cup	finely chopped green onion	50 mL
2 tbsp	vegetable oil	25 mL

While chili is simmering, combine cornmeal, flour, sugar, baking powder and salt. Stir in milk, green onion and oil; let stand for 5 minutes. When chili is almost done cooking, drop small spoonfuls of cornmeal batter on top, leaving 1 inch (2.5 cm) or more between dumplings. Cover and simmer for 15 minutes, until dumplings are puffed and cooked through. **Serves 6 to 8.**

Charbroiled Sirloin Chili

3 lbs	beef sirloin steak (in one piece)	1.5 kg
1 tbsp	vegetable oil	15 mL
1	recipe BCM (page 202)	1
1	green bell pepper, chopped	1
1	clove garlic, minced	1
2 tbsp	tomato paste	25 mL
3 cups	beef broth	750 mL
1 tsp	cider vinegar	5 mL

	Salt and freshly ground black pepper to taste	
1	can (14 to 19 oz/398 to 540 mL) red kidney beans, drained and rinsed	1
1 to 3 tsp	hot pepper sauce (such as Tabasco)	5 to 15 mL

Grill beef over a high fire (preferably charcoal) until crusty and brown on both sides; cut into bite-size pieces. In a wide, deep, heavy pot (such as a Dutch oven), heat oil over medium-high heat. Sauté beef, BCM, bell pepper, garlic and tomato paste for 1 minute. Add broth, vinegar, salt and pepper; reduce heat, cover and simmer for 40 minutes, until beef is very tender. Stir in beans and hot pepper sauce to taste; heat through. **Serves 6 to 8.**

Roasted Pepper Chili

3 lbs	beef flank steak, sliced	1.5 kg
¼ cup	all-purpose flour	50 mL
2 tbsp	corn oil	25 mL
1	recipe BCM (page 202)	1
1	clove garlic, minced	1
2 tbsp	tomato paste	25 mL
3 cups	beef broth	750 mL
1 tsp	cider vinegar	5 mL
	Salt and freshly ground black pepper to taste	
3	roasted bell peppers (1 red, 1 green, 1 yellow; see page 11), cut into strips	3
1	can (14 to 19 oz/398 to 540 mL) cannellini or white kidney beans, drained and rinsed	1
1 to 3 tsp	hot pepper sauce (such as Tabasco)	5 to 15 mL

Dredge beef in flour. In a wide, deep, heavy pot (such as a Dutch oven), heat oil over medium-high heat. Sauté beef, in batches, until browned. Return beef to pot and add BCM, garlic and tomato paste; sauté for 1 minute. Add broth, vinegar, salt and pepper; reduce heat, cover and simmer for 1 hour. Add roasted peppers and simmer for 30 minutes, until beef is very tender. Stir in beans and hot pepper sauce to taste; heat through. **Serves 6 to 8.**

Veal Chili with Artichokes

3 lbs	veal cubes for stew	1.5 kg
¼ cup	all-purpose flour, seasoned with salt and pepper	50 mL
2 tbsp	olive oil	25 mL
1	recipe BCM (page 202)	1
2	cloves garlic, minced	2
1	bay leaf	1
1 tsp	dried basil	5 mL
1 tsp	dried thyme	5 mL
½ cup	dry white wine	125 mL
3 cups	chicken broth	750 mL
1	can (14 oz/398 mL) diced tomatoes, drained	1
1	can (14 to 19 oz/398 to 540 mL) chickpeas, drained and rinsed	1
1	can (8 oz/228 mL) quartered artichoke hearts, drained	1
1 tbsp	freshly squeezed lemon juice	15 mL

Dredge veal in seasoned flour. In a large, deep skillet or Dutch oven, heat oil over medium-high heat. Sauté veal, in batches, until browned on all sides. Return veal to pot and add BCM, garlic, bay leaf, basil and thyme; sauté for 1 minute. Add wine and boil for 1 minute. Add broth and tomatoes; reduce heat and simmer, partially covered, for 1 hour, or until veal is fork-tender. Add chickpeas and artichoke hearts; simmer for 10 minutes, until heated through. Stir in lemon juice and discard bay leaf. **Serves 6 to 8.**

All-Pork Chili

2 lbs	pork cubes for stew	1 kg
3 tbsp	all-purpose flour	45 mL
2 tbsp	vegetable oil	25 mL
1 lb	mild pork sausage (such as Italian or breakfast), chopped	500 g
1	recipe BCM (page 202)	1
1	green bell pepper, chopped	1
1	clove garlic, minced	1
2 tbsp	tomato paste	25 mL
1 tsp	dried sage	5 mL
3 cups	chicken broth	750 mL
1 tsp	cider vinegar	5 mL
1	can (14 to 19 oz/398 to 540 mL) light red kidney beans, drained and rinsed	1
	Salt and freshly ground black pepper to taste	

Dredge pork in flour. In a wide, deep, heavy pot (such as a Dutch oven), heat oil over medium-high heat. Sauté pork, in batches, until browned on all sides. Add sausage and sauté until starting to brown. Return pork to pot and add BCM, bell pepper, garlic, tomato paste and sage; sauté for 1 minute. Add broth and vinegar; reduce heat, cover and simmer for 1½ hours, until pork is very tender. Stir in beans, salt and pepper; heat through. **Serves 6 to 8.**

Three-Sausage Chili

Follow preceding recipe, but replace the pork cubes with 1 lb (500 g) garlic sausage and 1 lb (500 g) spicy Italian sausage, chopped. Reduce simmering time to 1 hour. **Serves 6 to 8.**

Black-Eyed Pea Chili

Follow recipe for All-Pork Chili (page 205), but substitute drained canned black-eyed peas for the kidney beans. **Serves 6 to 8.**

Smoked Sausage Chili with Porter

2 tbsp	vegetable oil	25 mL
3 lbs	smoked sausage (such as kielbasa), cut into chunks	1.5 kg
1	recipe BCM (page 202)	1
1	green bell pepper, chopped	1
1	clove garlic, minced	1
2 tbsp	tomato paste	25 mL
1	bottle (12 oz/341 mL) porter or dark beer	1
1 cup	beef broth	250 mL
1 tsp	dry mustard	5 mL
1 tsp	cider vinegar	5 mL
1	can (14 to 19 oz/398 to 540 mL) cannellini or white kidney beans, drained and rinsed	1
	Salt and freshly ground black pepper to taste	

In a wide, deep, heavy pot (such as a Dutch oven), heat oil over medium-high heat. Sauté sausage, in batches, until browned on all sides. Return sausage to pot and add BCM, bell pepper, garlic and tomato paste; sauté for 1 minute. Add porter, broth, mustard and vinegar; reduce heat, cover and simmer for 40 minutes. Stir in beans, salt and pepper; heat through. **Serves 6 to 8.**

Bourbon Chili

3 lbs	pork cubes for stew	1.5 kg
1/4 cup	all-purpose flour, seasoned with salt and pepper	50 mL
2 tbsp	corn oil	25 mL
1	recipe BCM (page 202)	1
2	cloves garlic, minced	2
1	bay leaf	1
1 tsp	dried sage	5 mL
1 tsp	dried rosemary	5 mL
1 tsp	dried thyme	5 mL
1/4 cup	bourbon	50 mL
3 cups	chicken broth	750 mL
5	plum (Roma) tomatoes, peeled and chopped	5
1	can (14 oz/398 mL) corn kernels, drained	1

Dredge pork in seasoned flour. In a wide, deep, heavy pot (such as a Dutch oven), heat oil over medium-high heat. Sauté pork, in batches, until browned on all sides. Return pork to pot and add BCM, garlic, bay leaf, sage, rosemary and thyme; sauté for 1 minute. Add bourbon and boil for 1 minute. Add broth and tomatoes; reduce heat and simmer, partially covered, for 1 hour, until pork is fork-tender. Add corn and simmer for 10 minutes, until heated through. Discard bay leaf. **Serves 6 to 8.**

Honeyed Pork Chops in Chili Sauce

6	pork shoulder chops	6
1/4 cup	all-purpose flour, seasoned with salt and pepper	50 mL
2 tbsp	vegetable oil	25 mL
1	recipe BCM (page 202)	1
2	cloves garlic, minced	2
1	bay leaf	1
1 tsp	ground coriander	5 mL
1 tsp	dried thyme	5 mL
1/2 cup	bourbon	125 mL
2 1/2 cups	chicken or vegetable broth	625 mL
2 tbsp	honey	25 mL
1	can (14 to 19 oz/398 to 540 mL) black-eyed peas, drained and rinsed	1
1 tsp	cider vinegar	5 mL

Dredge pork in seasoned flour. In a large, deep skillet or Dutch oven, heat oil over medium-high heat. Cook pork chops, in batches, until browned on both sides; remove to a plate. Add BCM, garlic, bay leaf, coriander and thyme to the fat in the pan and sauté for 1 minute. Add bourbon and boil for 1 minute. Add broth and honey; return pork to the pan. Reduce heat and simmer, partially covered, for 1 hour, until pork is fork-tender. Add peas and vinegar; simmer for 10 minutes, until heated through. Discard bay leaf. Serve chops on a bed of the black-eyed peas. **Serves 6.**

Chilied Chicken Salad

1/3 cup	vegetable oil	75 mL
2 tbsp	chili powder	25 mL
1 tbsp	ground cumin	15 mL
3 tbsp	mayonnaise	45 mL
2 tbsp	hot pepper sauce (such as Frank's RedHot)	25 mL
1 tbsp	cider vinegar	15 mL

1	can (14 to 19 oz/398 to 540 mL) red kidney beans, drained and rinsed	1
1	bunch green onions, thinly sliced	1
1	roasted red pepper (see page 11), diced	1
1	avocado, diced	1
2 lbs	cooked chicken, cut into bite-size pieces (about 6 cups/1.5 L)	1 kg
2 cups	canned or thawed frozen corn kernels	500 mL
2 tbsp	chopped fresh cilantro	25 mL

Combine oil, chili powder, cumin, mayonnaise, hot pepper sauce and vinegar. Add remaining ingredients and toss to coat. Cover and refrigerate for about 30 minutes, until chilled. **Serves 6 to 8.**

Chilied Chicken Stew

4 lbs	bone-in chicken pieces	2 kg
⅓ cup	all-purpose flour	75 mL
2 tbsp	vegetable oil	25 mL
1	recipe BCM (page 202)	1
2	cloves garlic, minced	2
2 tbsp	ground coriander	25 mL
1 tsp	ground ginger	5 mL
1 tsp	dried thyme	5 mL
	Juice of 1 lemon	
3 to 4 cups	chicken broth	750 mL to 1 L
2	carrots, sliced	2
2	red-skinned or other boiling potatoes, peeled and diced	2
1 cup	sliced mushrooms	250 mL
2 tbsp	chopped fresh Italian (flat-leaf) parsley	25 mL
	Salt and freshly ground black pepper to taste	

Dredge chicken in flour. In a large, deep skillet or Dutch oven, heat oil over medium-high heat. Sauté chicken, in batches, until browned on all sides. Return chicken to pot and add BCM, garlic, coriander, ginger and thyme; sauté for 1 minute. Add lemon juice and enough broth to come two-thirds of the way up the chicken; reduce heat and simmer, partially covered, for 30 minutes. Add carrots, potatoes and mushrooms; simmer, partially covered, for 30 minutes, until juices run clear when chicken is pierced and liquid is slightly thickened (add more broth as needed). Stir in parsley, salt and pepper. **Serves 6.**

Chorizo Chicken Chili

Follow preceding recipe, but add 1 lb (500 g) chorizo, sliced, after chicken is browned on one side. Replace the carrots, potatoes and mushrooms with 1 can (14 to 19 oz/398 to 540 mL) chickpeas, drained and rinsed. Replace the parsley with chopped fresh cilantro. **Serves 8.**

Sausage and Quail Chili

Follow preceding recipe, but replace the chicken with 8 quail, halved, and the chorizo with garlic sausage. After adding the chickpeas, reduce simmering time to 15 minutes. **Serves 8.**

Curried Chicken Chili

4 lbs	bone-in chicken pieces	2 kg
⅓ cup	all-purpose flour	75 mL
2 tbsp	vegetable oil	25 mL
½	recipe BCM (page 202)	½
2	cloves garlic, minced	2
2 tbsp	curry powder	25 mL
2 tbsp	ground coriander	25 mL
1 tsp	ground ginger	5 mL
1 tsp	dry mustard	5 mL
3 cups	chicken broth	750 mL
2	carrots, sliced	2
2	potatoes, diced	2
1 cup	dried lentils	250 mL
1 cup	sliced mushrooms	250 mL
	Juice of 1 lemon	

Dredge chicken in flour. In a large, deep skillet or Dutch oven, heat oil over medium-high heat. Sauté chicken, in batches, until browned on all sides. Return chicken to pot and add BCM, garlic, curry powder, coriander, ginger and mustard; sauté for 1 minute. Add broth, reduce heat and simmer, partially covered, for 30 minutes. Add carrots, potatoes, lentils and mushrooms; simmer, partially covered, for 30 minutes, until juice run clear when chicken is pierced and vegetables are tender. Stir in lemon juice. **Serves 6.**

Chocolate Chicken Chili

1 tbsp	vegetable oil, divided	15 mL
3	dried ancho or mulato chili peppers	3
2 cups	finely chopped onions	500 mL
2 lbs	boneless skinless chicken thighs, cut into bite-size chunks	1 kg
4	cloves garlic, minced	4
2 tsp	ground cumin	10 mL
1 tsp	dried oregano	5 mL
1 tsp	dried thyme	5 mL
½ tsp	ground cinnamon	2 mL
2 tbsp	all-purpose flour	25 mL
3 cups	chicken broth	500 mL
2	tomatoes, chopped	2
1 tbsp	tomato paste	15 mL
¼ cup	chopped fresh cilantro	50 mL
½ oz	bittersweet or unsweetened chocolate	15 g
	Cooked rice or beans	

In a large, deep skillet or Dutch oven, heat a thin film of oil over medium-high heat. Sauté chilies until browned on all sides. Let cool. Stem and seed chilies, break into small pieces and grind in a blender or spice grinder. Set aside. Return pot to medium-high heat and add the remaining oil. Sauté onion until lightly browned. Add chicken and sauté until lightly browned on all sides. Add garlic, cumin, oregano, thyme and cinnamon; sauté for 30 seconds. Add flour and sauté for 1 minute. Add broth and cook, stirring, until slightly thickened. Add tomatoes and tomato paste; reduce heat and simmer, partially covered, until juices run clear when chicken is pierced, about 15 minutes. Stir in cilantro and chocolate until chocolate is melted. Serve over rice or beans. **Serves 6.**

Turkey Mole Chili

Follow preceding recipe, but substitute boneless skinless turkey breast for the chicken. Simmer until no longer pink inside. **Serves 6.**

Turkey and Avocado Chili

2 lbs	boneless skinless turkey breast, cut into bite-size chunks	1 kg
3 tbsp	all-purpose flour	45 mL
2 tbsp	vegetable oil	25 mL
1	recipe BCM (page 202)	1
2	cloves garlic, minced	2
2 tbsp	ground coriander	25 mL
1 tsp	ground ginger	5 mL
1 tsp	dried thyme	5 mL
3 cups	chicken broth	750 mL
1	can (14 to 19 oz/398 to 540 mL) chickpeas, drained and rinsed	1
2 tbsp	chopped fresh cilantro	25 mL
	Juice of 1 lemon	
1	avocado, diced	1

Dredge turkey in flour. In a wide, deep, heavy pot (such as a Dutch oven), heat oil over medium-high heat. Sauté turkey until browned on all sides. Add BCM, garlic, coriander, ginger and thyme; sauté for 1 minute. Add broth, reduce heat and simmer, partially covered, for 40 minutes. Add chickpeas, cilantro and lemon juice; simmer, partially covered, for 10 minutes. Serve garnished with avocado. **Serves 6.**

Grilled Salmon Chili

1 tbsp	olive oil	15 mL
1	recipe BCM (page 202)	1
1 tbsp	ground coriander	15 mL
	Juice of 1 lemon	
	Salt and cayenne pepper to taste	
4	salmon steaks (each about 8 oz/250 g)	4
1 cup	bottled clam juice	250 mL
1	can (14 to 19 oz/398 to 540 mL) cannellini or white kidney beans, drained and rinsed	1
1 tbsp	chopped fresh cilantro or Italian (flat-leaf) parsley	15 mL

In a large, deep skillet, heat oil over medium-high heat. Remove from heat and stir in BCM, coriander, lemon juice, salt and cayenne. Let cool, then brush salmon with a thin film of this mixture. Cover and refrigerate salmon for 1 hour. Preheat broiler or barbecue grill to high. Add clam juice to mixture remaining in pan and simmer over medium-low heat for 3 minutes. Add beans and cilantro; heat through. Broil or grill salmon, turning once, for 8 minutes per inch (2.5 cm) of thickness, or until fish flakes easily with a fork. Serve each salmon steak on a bed of beans. **Serves 4.**

Chilied Scallop Kebabs

Follow preceding recipe, but replace the salmon with 1 lb (500 g) sea scallops, trimmed of hard side muscles. Thread scallops onto 4 skewers and grill, turning often, for about 8 minutes, or until browned and firm in the center. **Serves 4.**

Grilled Tuna Chili on Black Beans

Follow recipe for Grilled Salmon Chili (page 208), but add the grated zest of the lemon along with its juice, replace the salmon with tuna steaks, and replace the cannellini beans with black beans. Serves 4.

Chinese Shrimp Chili

1 cup	beef broth	250 mL
2½ tbsp	cornstarch, divided	32 mL
2 tbsp	soy sauce	25 mL
1 tbsp	Thai fish sauce (*nam pla*)	15 mL
2 tsp	Chinese chili paste	10 mL
2 tsp	tomato paste	10 mL
Pinch	granulated sugar	Pinch
	Juice of ½ lemon	
2 tbsp	chili powder	25 mL
1 lb	large shrimp, peeled and deveined	500 g
¼ cup	peanut oil	50 mL
2	green onions, chopped	2
2	cloves garlic, minced	2
1 tsp	minced gingerroot	5 mL
	Cooked rice or noodles	

Combine broth, 2 tsp (10 mL) of the cornstarch, soy sauce, fish sauce, chili paste, tomato paste, sugar and lemon juice; set aside. In a separate bowl, combine chili powder and the remaining cornstarch; add shrimp and toss to coat. In a wok or a large, deep skillet, heat oil over high heat. Stir-fry shrimp until pink and opaque. Add green onions, garlic and ginger; stir-fry for 1 minute. Add broth mixture and simmer until slightly thickened. Serve over rice or noodles. Serves 4.

Shrimp Chili with Black Beans

3 cups	drained rinsed canned black beans, divided	750 mL
2 tbsp	vegetable oil	25 mL
½ cup	finely chopped onion	125 mL
1	red bell pepper, diced	1
1	clove garlic, minced	1
1	recipe BCM (page 202)	1
1½ tsp	ground coriander	7 mL
1 lb	medium shrimp, peeled and deveined	500 g
1½ cups	bottled clam juice or Quick Fish Broth (see recipe, page 19)	375 mL
2 tbsp	chopped fresh dill	25 mL
	Salt and freshly ground black pepper to taste	
	Grated zest and juice of 1 lemon	

In a food processor, purée 1 cup (250 mL) of the beans. Set aside. In a wide, deep, heavy pot (such as a Dutch oven), heat oil over medium heat. Sauté onion, bell pepper and garlic until tender. Add BCM and coriander; sauté for 1 minute. Add shrimp and sauté until starting to turn pink. Add puréed beans and clam juice; bring to a boil. Add the remaining beans, reduce heat and simmer for 5 minutes. Stir in dill, salt, pepper, lemon zest and lemon juice. Serves 6.

Shrimp Chili with Chickpeas

Follow preceding recipe, but substitute chickpeas for the black beans. Serves 6.

Chilied Scampi with Cannellini

Follow recipe for Shrimp Chili with Black Beans (left), but substitute 1½ lbs (750 g) jumbo shrimp for the medium shrimp and cannellini or white kidney beans for the black beans. Serves 6.

Crab Chili

Follow recipe for Shrimp Chili with Black Beans (left), but substitute backfin (lump) crabmeat, shells picked out, for the shrimp, white beans for the black beans, and chopped fresh Italian (flat-leaf) parsley for the dill. Serves 6.

Smoked Turkey Chili

Follow recipe for Shrimp Chili with Black Beans (left), but substitute 2 lbs (1 kg) smoked turkey, diced, for the shrimp, light red kidney beans for the black beans, chicken broth for the clam juice, and chopped fresh Italian (flat-leaf) parsley for the dill. Serves 6.

Chili Gumbo

2 tbsp	vegetable oil	25 mL
1 cup	finely chopped onion	250 mL
1	red bell pepper, diced	1
1	stalk celery, diced	1
1	clove garlic, minced	1
½	recipe BCM (page 202)	½
2 tbsp	ground coriander	25 mL
1 lb	medium shrimp, peeled and deveined	500 g
1 lb	backfin (lump) crabmeat, shells picked out	500 g
2 cups	chicken broth	500 mL
2 cups	cooked or canned black-eyed peas	500 mL
½ tsp	filé powder	2 mL
	Salt and freshly ground black pepper to taste	
2 tbsp	chopped fresh Italian (flat-leaf) parsley	25 mL
	Grated zest and juice of 1 lemon	

In a wide, deep, heavy pot (such as a Dutch oven), heat oil over medium heat. Sauté onion, bell pepper, celery and garlic until tender. Add BCM and coriander; sauté for 1 minute. Add shrimp and crabmeat; sauté until shrimp are starting to turn pink. Add broth and bring to a boil. Add peas, filé powder, salt and pepper; reduce heat and simmer for 5 minutes. Stir in parsley, lemon zest and lemon juice. **Serves 6.**

Chilied Clams

1 cup	beef broth	250 mL
1 tbsp	chili powder	15 mL
2 tbsp	soy sauce	25 mL
1 tbsp	Thai fish sauce (nam pla)	15 mL
2 tsp	Chinese chili paste	10 mL
2 tsp	tomato paste	10 mL
1 tsp	cornstarch	5 mL
Pinch	granulated sugar	Pinch
	Juice of ½ lemon	
1 tbsp	vegetable oil	15 mL
24	littleneck clams, scrubbed (see page 8)	24
2	cloves garlic, minced	2
1 tsp	minced gingerroot	5 mL
1 tsp	dark sesame oil	5 mL
2	green onions, chopped	2

Combine broth, chili powder, soy sauce, fish sauce, chili paste, tomato paste, cornstarch, sugar and lemon juice; set aside. In a wok or a large, deep skillet, heat vegetable oil over high heat. Cook clams, garlic and ginger, covered, for about 4 minutes, or until clams open (discard any that don't). Using a slotted spoon, transfer clams to a serving bowl. Add broth mixture to the wok and cook, stirring, until slightly thickened. Pour over clams and toss to coat. Drizzle with sesame oil and garnish with green onions. **Serves 6.**

Lamb Mole Chili

3 lbs	lamb cubes for stew	1.5 kg
¼ cup	all-purpose flour	50 mL
2 tbsp	olive oil	25 mL
1	recipe BCM (page 202)	1
1 tbsp	ground coriander	15 mL
2 tsp	ground anise seeds	10 mL
2	tomatoes, chopped	2
1	clove garlic, minced	1
¼ cup	chopped fresh mint	50 mL
1 tbsp	tomato paste	15 mL
3 cups	beef broth	750 mL
	Salt and freshly ground black pepper to taste	
½ oz	bittersweet or unsweetened chocolate	15 g

Dredge lamb in flour. In a wide, deep, heavy pot (such as a Dutch oven), heat oil over medium-high heat. Sauté lamb, in batches, until browned on all sides. Return lamb to pot and add BCM, coriander and anise seeds; sauté for 1 minute. Add tomatoes, garlic, mint and tomato paste; sauté for 1 minute. Add broth, salt and pepper; reduce heat, cover and simmer for 1 hour, until lamb is very tender. Stir in chocolate until melted. **Serves 6 to 8.**

Duck Mole Chili

Follow preceding recipe, but replace the lamb with 4 lbs (2 kg) bone-in skinless duck pieces. Skim off any fat that collects on the surface of the chili. If desired, garnish with thin strips of duck skin, rendered until crisp. **Serves 6 to 8.**

Lamb and Lentil Chili

3 lbs	lamb cubes for stew	1.5 kg
¼ cup	all-purpose flour	50 mL
3 tbsp	olive oil	45 mL
1	recipe BCM (page 202)	1
1	clove garlic, minced	1
2 tbsp	dried mint	25 mL
1 tbsp	ground coriander	15 mL
Pinch	hot pepper flakes	Pinch
3 cups	chicken broth	750 mL
1 tbsp	orange juice	15 mL
	Salt and freshly ground black pepper to taste	
2 cups	dried brown or green lentils	1 L
2 tbsp	chopped fresh cilantro	25 mL

Dredge lamb in flour. In a large, deep skillet or Dutch oven, heat oil over medium-high heat. Sauté lamb, in batches, until browned on all sides. Add BCM, garlic, mint, coriander and hot pepper flakes; sauté for 30 seconds. Add broth, orange juice, salt and pepper; reduce heat, cover and simmer, stirring occasionally, for 1 hour, until lamb is fork-tender. Meanwhile, boil lentils in lightly salted water until tender, about 40 minutes, then toss with cilantro. Serve chili on a bed of lentils. **Serves 6 to 8.**

Curried Lamb Chili

Follow preceding recipe, but add 2 tbsp (25 mL) garam masala with the BCM. **Serves 6.**

Rabbit Chili

2	large rabbits, each cut into 6 pieces	2
⅓ cup	all-purpose flour	75 mL
2 tbsp	vegetable oil	25 mL
1	recipe BCM (page 202)	1
2	cloves garlic, minced	2
2 tbsp	ground coriander	25 mL
1 tsp	ground ginger	5 mL
1 tsp	dried thyme	5 mL
3 cups	chicken broth	750 mL
½ cup	dry white wine	125 mL
1	can (14 to 19 oz/398 to 540 mL) black-eyed peas, drained and rinsed	1
	Juice of 1 lemon	

Dredge rabbit in flour. In a large, deep skillet or Dutch oven, heat oil over medium-high heat. Sauté rabbit, in batches, until browned on all sides. Return rabbit to pot and add BCM, garlic, coriander, ginger and thyme; sauté for 1 minute. Add broth and wine; reduce heat and simmer, partially covered, for 30 minutes. Add peas and simmer, partially covered, for 15 minutes, until rabbit is tender and liquid is slightly thickened. Stir in lemon juice. **Serves 6.**

Chapter 19
Pizza
No Need to Order Out

Tomato and Cheese Pizza 213

Tomato and Basil Pizza 213

Tomato, Caper and Anchovy Pizza 213

Tomato and Three-Onion Pizza 213

Three-Tomato Pizza 213

Spicy Tomato and Mussel Pizza 214

Tomato, Basil and Chèvre Pizza 214

Tomato, Fennel and Olive Pizza 214

Tomato and Wild Mushroom Pizza 214

Smoky Tomato and Fontina Pizza 214

Spicy Tomato and Sausage
Meatball Pizza 215

Pepperoni and Meat Sauce Pizza 215

Bolognese and Mozzarella Pizza 215

Lamb and Feta Pizza 215

Naked Basil and Prosciutto Pizza 216

Artichoke and Mushroom Pizza 216

Crab, Tarragon and Chèvre Pizza 216

Tri-Color Roasted Pepper Pizza 216

Ricotta and Roasted Red Pepper Pizza . . 216

Roasted Pepper, Caper
and Anchovy Pizza 216

Roasted Pepper and Walnut Pizza 217

Pepper, Olive and Olive Oil Pizza 217

Roasted Eggplant and Feta Pizza 217

Garlic and Parmesan Pizza 217

Red, Black and Green Olive Pizza 218

Tuna, White Bean and Olive Pizza 218

Spinach, Olive and Feta Pizza 218

Duxelles and Parmesan Pizza 218

Sweet Sausage, Pine Nut
and Rosemary Pizza 218

Pancetta, Hazelnut and Garlic Pizza . . . 219

Three-Mushroom Pizza 219

Sausage and Mushroom Pizza 219

Clam and Leek Pizza 220

Brie and Scallop Pizza 220

Scallop and Herbed Cheese Pizza 220

Marinated Feta
and Artichoke Heart Pizza 220

Marinated Sun-Dried Tomato Pizza 220

Chicken and Olive Pizza 221

Sun-Dried Tomato and Tuna Pizza 221

Caramelized Onion
and Gorgonzola Pizza 221

Onion and Gruyère Pizza 221

Smoked Salmon and Onion Pizza 221

Smoked Turkey and Fontina Pizza 221

Prosciutto, Walnut and Feta Pizza 221

Red Onion and Herbed Cheese Pizza . . 222

Marinated Mozzarella Pizza 222

Hot Pepper, Bacon
and Gorgonzola Pizza 222

Dried Cherry, Tarragon
and Almond Dessert Pizza 223

Banana and Walnut Dessert Pizza 223

Sweet Ricotta Dessert Pizza 223

All who have sacrificed the roofs of their mouths to a scorching cap of mozzarella know the masochistic ecstasy of pizza fresh from the oven. Reasonable commercial versions abound, but with many arriving tepid and congealed via delivery truck, these disks of dyspepsia can be a far cry from the "real thing." Many of them suffer sensuously, and they're frequently packed with so much salt and saturated fat as to undermine the reputation of one of the most wholesome and natural Mediterranean mainstays.

Not only are pizzas self-contained, balanced meals, but they can be built in just minutes. The dough is the only part that takes much time, and with the availability of good-quality frozen bread doughs, even this chore can be dispensed with.

Beyond its ease, homemade pizza is just plain fun. Family members can build their own, and creative cooks can let their imaginations run wild. We let ours run wild to start you off with 50 pizza ideas, some of them quite novel — beginning with a simple tomato and cheese topping and ending with a trio of sweet dessert pizzas.

About these recipes . . .

The same simple method of assembly and construction applies to all the recipes. It requires no special equipment and guarantees a crisp, high-risen crust. If you have a favorite recipe for making your own dough, go ahead and use it, or use ours (page 20), but the basis for all of our recipes is 10 oz (300 g) of thawed, ready-to-bake frozen bread dough.

To build any pizza in this chapter, place an 18- by 16-inch (45 by 40 cm) piece of heavy aluminum foil on a work surface. Brush with oil and place the dough in the center. Flour your hands and spread dough into a rough 14-inch (35 cm) circle, making the circle as thin as you want but leaving a rim at least ½ inch (1 cm) high to contain the filling during baking. If the dough should tear while you're pushing it into place, pinch it with your fingers to seal it, or patch it with a small scrap of dough.

Arrange the filling on top, as described in the recipes, and slide the pizza, still on its foil backing, onto the middle rack of a preheated 450°F (230°C) oven. All the pizzas should bake for 20 to 25 minutes, or until dough is puffed and crisp. Remove, slice and serve. All recipes yield 8 small slices, enough for 2 to 3 portions.

Tomato and Cheese Pizza

	Prepared pizza dough (see "About these recipes," left)	
2 tbsp	extra-virgin olive oil, divided	25 mL
6	plum (Roma) tomatoes, peeled, seeded and coarsely puréed	6
1 cup	shredded mozzarella cheese	250 mL
2 tbsp	freshly grated Parmesan cheese	25 mL
½ tsp	dried oregano	2 mL
	Salt and freshly ground black pepper to taste	

Brush dough with half the oil, and spread tomatoes over dough. Sprinkle evenly with mozzarella, Parmesan, oregano, salt and pepper. Drizzle with the remaining oil. Bake as described in "About these recipes" (left). **Serves 2 to 3.**

Tomato and Basil Pizza

Follow preceding recipe, but scatter ¼ cup (50 mL) shredded fresh basil on the oiled dough before adding the tomatoes. Omit the oregano. **Serves 2 to 3.**

Tomato, Caper and Anchovy Pizza

Follow recipe for Tomato and Cheese Pizza (above), but top tomatoes with 2 tbsp (25 mL) drained capers and 6 drained canned anchovies, julienned, and drizzle with 2 tsp (10 mL) red wine vinegar. **Serves 2 to 3.**

Tomato and Three-Onion Pizza

Follow recipe for Tomato and Cheese Pizza (above), but first lightly brown 1 Spanish onion, thinly sliced, 1 red onion, thinly sliced, and 2 cloves garlic, minced, in 2 tbsp (25 mL) olive oil; scatter on top of cheese. Omit the oregano, and sprinkle with 2 tsp (10 mL) finely chopped fresh rosemary. **Serves 2 to 3.**

Three-Tomato Pizza

Follow recipe for Tomato and Cheese Pizza (above), but top the cheese with 3 plum (Roma) tomatoes, sliced, and 3 sun-dried tomatoes, coarsely chopped. Substitute basil for the oregano. **Serves 2 to 3.**

Spicy Tomato and Mussel Pizza

Follow recipe for Tomato and Cheese Pizza (page 213), but scatter 36 cooked and shelled mussels over the tomatoes. Omit the mozzarella and oregano, and sprinkle with 2 tbsp (25 mL) chopped fresh Italian (flat-leaf) parsley and a generous pinch of hot pepper flakes. **Serves 2 to 3.**

Tomato, Basil and Chèvre Pizza

	Prepared pizza dough (see "About these recipes," page 213)	
2 tbsp	olive oil, divided	25 mL
¼ cup	shredded fresh basil	50 mL
6	plum (Roma) tomatoes, peeled, seeded and coarsely puréed	6
6 oz	fresh chèvre (goat cheese), crumbled	175 g
2 tbsp	freshly grated Parmesan cheese	25 mL
¼ tsp	hot pepper flakes	1 mL
	Salt and freshly ground black pepper to taste	

Brush dough with half the oil, and scatter basil over dough. Spread tomatoes over basil, and scatter chèvre over tomatoes. Sprinkle evenly with Parmesan, hot pepper flakes, salt and black pepper, and drizzle with the remaining oil. Bake as described in "About these recipes" (page 213). **Serves 2 to 3.**

Tomato, Fennel and Olive Pizza

	Prepared pizza dough (see "About these recipes," page 213)	
2 tbsp	olive oil, divided	25 mL
6	plum (Roma) tomatoes, peeled, seeded and coarsely puréed	6
1 cup	diced fennel bulb	250 mL
1 cup	shredded mozzarella cheese	250 mL
1 cup	oil-cured black olives, pitted and coarsely chopped	250 mL
2 tbsp	freshly grated Parmesan cheese	25 mL
Pinch	dried oregano	Pinch
	Salt and freshly ground black pepper to taste	

Brush dough with half the oil. Spread tomatoes over dough, scatter fennel over tomato, sprinkle evenly with mozzarella, and scatter olives over the cheese. Sprinkle evenly with Parmesan, oregano, salt and pepper. Drizzle with the remaining oil. Bake as described in "About these recipes" (page 213). **Serves 2 to 3.**

Tomato and Wild Mushroom Pizza

1 tbsp	butter	15 mL
6	wild or exotic mushrooms (cèpes, morels or shiitakes), sliced	6
	Prepared pizza dough (see "About these recipes," page 213)	
2 tbsp	olive oil, divided	25 mL
6	plum (Roma) tomatoes, peeled, seeded and coarsely puréed	6
1 cup	shredded mozzarella cheese	250 mL
2 tbsp	freshly grated Parmesan cheese	25 mL
Pinch	dried thyme	Pinch
Pinch	dried oregano	Pinch
	Salt and freshly ground black pepper to taste	

In a small skillet, melt butter over medium-high heat. Sauté mushrooms until lightly browned. Brush dough with half the oil, spread tomatoes over dough, and scatter mushrooms over tomatoes. Sprinkle evenly with mozzarella, Parmesan, thyme, oregano, salt and pepper. Drizzle with the remaining oil. Bake as described in "About these recipes" (page 213). **Serves 2 to 3.**

Smoky Tomato and Fontina Pizza

6	plum (Roma) tomatoes	6
	Prepared pizza dough (see "About these recipes," page 213)	
2 tbsp	olive oil, divided	25 mL
6	drained canned anchovies, julienned	6
1 cup	shredded fontina cheese	250 mL
2 tbsp	drained capers	25 mL
2 tbsp	red wine vinegar	25 mL
2 tbsp	freshly grated Parmesan cheese	25 mL
Pinch	dried oregano	Pinch
	Salt and freshly ground black pepper to taste	

Place tomatoes directly over a gas flame on a stovetop, or over a gas grill, and turn so skins char evenly; let cool slightly, then remove skins by rubbing them with your fingers. In a food processor, coarsely purée tomatoes. Brush dough with half the oil and spread tomatoes over dough. Scatter with anchovies, fontina and capers, and drizzle with vinegar. Sprinkle evenly with Parmesan, oregano, salt and pepper. Drizzle with the remaining oil. Bake as described in "About these recipes" (page 213). **Serves 2 to 3.**

Spicy Tomato and Sausage Meatball Pizza

2	slices white bread, crusts removed, crumbled	2
1/3 cup	dry white wine	75 mL
1	egg white, beaten	1
1 lb	Italian sausage (bulk, or with casings removed)	500 g
2 tsp	dried mint	10 mL
2 tbsp	extra-virgin olive oil, divided	25 mL
	Prepared pizza dough (see "About these recipes," page 213)	
6	plum (Roma) tomatoes, peeled, seeded and coarsely puréed	6
1	jalapeño or serrano chili, seeded and finely chopped	1
1 cup	shredded Monterey Jack cheese	250 mL
Pinch	dried oregano	Pinch
	Salt and freshly ground black pepper to taste	

Soak bread in wine until completely moistened, then combine with egg white, sausage and mint. Form into 24 small meatballs. In a skillet, heat a thin film of oil over medium-high heat. Sauté meatballs until browned on all sides. Brush dough with half the remaining oil. Combine tomatoes and chili; spread over dough. Sprinkle evenly with cheese, oregano, salt and pepper. Scatter meatballs over top, and drizzle with the remaining oil. Bake as described in "About these recipes" (page 213). **Serves 2 to 3.**

Pepperoni and Meat Sauce Pizza

3 tbsp	olive oil, divided	45 mL
1 cup	chopped onion	250 mL
2	cloves garlic, minced	2
8 oz	lean ground beef	250 g
8 oz	ground veal	250 g
2 cups	canned crushed tomatoes	500 mL
1/4 cup	tomato paste	50 mL
1 tbsp	chopped fresh Italian (flat-leaf) parsley	15 mL
Pinch	hot pepper flakes	Pinch
	Salt and freshly ground black pepper to taste	
	Prepared pizza dough (see "About these recipes," page 213)	
4 oz	pepperoni, thinly sliced	125 g
1 cup	shredded provolone cheese	250 mL
2 tbsp	freshly grated Parmesan cheese	25 mL
Pinch	dried oregano	Pinch

In a large skillet, heat 1 tbsp (15 mL) of the oil over medium-high heat. Sauté onion and garlic until tender. Add beef and veal; sauté, breaking meat up with a fork, until no longer pink. Add tomatoes, tomato paste, parsley, hot pepper flakes, salt and black pepper; reduce heat and simmer for 20 minutes. Brush dough with 1 tbsp (15 mL) of the oil, and spread meat sauce over dough. Scatter with pepperoni, and sprinkle evenly with provolone, Parmesan, oregano and additional salt and pepper. Drizzle with the remaining oil. Bake as described in "About these recipes" (page 213). **Serves 2 to 3.**

Bolognese and Mozzarella Pizza

3 tbsp	olive oil, divided	45 mL
1 tbsp	butter	15 mL
2 tbsp	chopped onion	25 mL
2 tbsp	diced carrot	25 mL
2 tbsp	diced celery	25 mL
8 oz	lean ground beef	250 g
8 oz	ground veal	250 g
1/2 cup	milk (whole or 2%)	125 mL
2 cups	canned crushed tomatoes	500 mL
1/4 cup	tomato paste	50 mL
1/2 tsp	dried oregano	2 mL
	Salt and freshly ground black pepper to taste	
	Prepared pizza dough (see "About these recipes," page 213)	
1 cup	shredded mozzarella cheese	250 mL
2 tbsp	freshly grated Parmesan cheese	25 mL
1/4 cup	chopped fresh Italian (flat-leaf) parsley	50 mL

In a skillet, heat 1 tbsp (15 mL) of the oil and butter over medium heat. Sauté onion, carrot and celery until tender. Add beef and veal; sauté, breaking meat up with a fork, until no longer pink. Add milk and cook until liquid has evaporated. Add tomatoes, tomato paste and oregano; reduce heat and simmer gently for 20 minutes. Season with salt and pepper. Brush dough with 1 tbsp (15 mL) of the oil, and spread sauce over dough. Sprinkle evenly with mozzarella, Parmesan, parsley and additional salt and pepper. Drizzle with the remaining oil. Bake as described in "About these recipes" (page 213). **Serves 2 to 3.**

Lamb and Feta Pizza

Follow preceding recipe, but replace the ground beef with ground lamb, omit the mozzarella and Parmesan, and sprinkle with 6 oz (175 g) feta cheese, crumbled. **Serves 2 to 3.**

Naked Basil and Prosciutto Pizza

¼ cup	extra-virgin olive oil	50 mL
2	cloves garlic, minced	2
Pinch	hot pepper flakes	Pinch
	Prepared pizza dough (see "About these recipes," page 213)	
1 cup	chopped fresh basil	250 mL
½ cup	julienned prosciutto	125 mL
¼ cup	freshly grated Parmesan cheese	50 mL
	Salt and freshly ground black pepper to taste	

In a small skillet, heat oil over medium-low heat. Sauté garlic and hot pepper flakes until aromatic. Brush dough with oil mixture. Scatter basil and prosciutto over top and press lightly into dough. Sprinkle evenly with Parmesan, salt and pepper. Bake as described in "About these recipes" (page 213). **Serves 2 to 3.**

Artichoke and Mushroom Pizza

1 tbsp	extra-virgin olive oil	15 mL
1	clove garlic, minced	1
8	mushrooms, sliced	8
12 oz	marinated artichoke hearts, drained and coarsely chopped	375 mL
2 tbsp	chopped fresh Italian (flat-leaf) parsley	25 mL
	Salt and freshly ground black pepper to taste	
	Prepared pizza dough (see "About these recipes," page 213)	
2 tbsp	freshly grated Parmesan cheese	25 mL

In a large skillet, heat oil over medium-low heat. Sauté garlic until aromatic. Add mushrooms, and sauté until barely tender. Stir in artichoke hearts, parsley, salt and pepper; spread mixture over dough. Sprinkle evenly with Parmesan. Bake as described in "About these recipes" (page 213). **Serves 2 to 3.**

Crab, Tarragon and Chèvre Pizza

¼ cup	olive oil, divided	50 mL
2	shallots, finely chopped	2
1 lb	backfin (lump) crabmeat, shells picked out	500 g
1 tbsp	coarsely chopped fresh tarragon	15 mL
	Juice of 1 lemon	
	Salt and freshly ground black pepper to taste	
	Prepared pizza dough (see "About these recipes," page 213)	
4 oz	chèvre (goat cheese), crumbled	125 g

In a small skillet, heat half the oil over medium-low heat. Sauté shallots until tender. Add crab, tossing to coat with oil, and tarragon; sauté for 1 minute. Stir in lemon juice, salt and pepper. Spread mixture over dough, and scatter chèvre over crab mixture. Drizzle with the remaining oil. Bake as described in "About these recipes" (page 213). **Serves 2 to 3.**

Tri-Color Roasted Pepper Pizza

3	roasted bell peppers (1 red, 1 green, 1 yellow; see page 11), cut into strips	3
Pinch	hot pepper flakes	Pinch
	Salt and freshly ground black pepper to taste	
2 tbsp	olive oil, divided	25 mL
	Prepared pizza dough (see "About these recipes," page 213)	
1½ cups	shredded mozzarella cheese	375 mL
2 tbsp	freshly grated Parmesan cheese	25 mL
2 tbsp	finely chopped fresh Italian (flat-leaf) parsley	25 mL

Season roasted peppers with hot pepper flakes, salt, and black pepper, and toss with half the oil; spread over dough. Sprinkle evenly with mozzarella, Parmesan and parsley, and drizzle with the remaining oil. Bake as described in "About these recipes" (page 213). **Serves 2 to 3.**

Ricotta and Roasted Red Pepper Pizza

Follow preceding recipe, but use only 2 roasted red peppers, omit the mozzarella, and arrange 1 cup (250 mL) ricotta cheese in small mounds atop the pizza. **Serves 2 to 3.**

Roasted Pepper, Caper and Anchovy Pizza

3	roasted bell peppers (assorted colors; see page 11), cut into strips	3
	Salt and freshly ground black pepper to taste	
3 tbsp	olive oil	45 mL
1	clove garlic, minced	1
	Prepared pizza dough (see "About these recipes," page 213)	
6	drained canned anchovies, julienned	6
3 tbsp	drained capers	45 mL
1½ cups	shredded mozzarella cheese	375 mL
2 tbsp	freshly grated Parmesan cheese	25 mL
2 tbsp	finely chopped fresh parsley	25 mL

Season roasted peppers with salt and pepper. In a small skillet, heat oil over medium-low heat. Sauté garlic until aromatic. Brush dough with half the oil mixture, and scatter peppers, anchovies and capers over dough. Sprinkle evenly with mozzarella, Parmesan and parsley, and drizzle with the remaining oil mixture. Bake as described in "About these recipes" (page 213). **Serves 2 to 3.**

Roasted Pepper and Walnut Pizza

3	roasted bell peppers (assorted colors; see page 11), cut into strips	3
	Salt and freshly ground black pepper to taste	
2 tbsp	olive oil	25 mL
1	clove garlic, minced	1
	Prepared pizza dough (see "About these recipes," page 213)	
⅓ cup	walnut pieces	75 mL
1½ cups	shredded mozzarella cheese	375 mL
2 tbsp	freshly grated Parmesan cheese	25 mL
2 tbsp	finely chopped fresh Italian (flat-leaf) parsley	25 mL

Season roasted peppers with salt and pepper. In a small skillet, heat oil over medium-low heat. Sauté garlic until aromatic. Brush dough with half the oil mixture, and scatter peppers and walnuts over dough. Sprinkle evenly with mozzarella, Parmesan and parsley, and drizzle with the remaining oil mixture. Bake as described in "About these recipes" (page 213). **Serves 2 to 3.**

Pepper, Olive and Olive Oil Pizza

3	roasted bell peppers (assorted colors; see page 11), cut into strips	3
Pinch	hot pepper flakes	Pinch
	Salt and freshly ground black pepper to taste	
3 tbsp	extra-virgin olive oil, divided	45 mL
1	clove garlic, minced	1
	Prepared pizza dough (see "About these recipes," page 213)	
½ cup	oil-cured black olives, pitted and chopped	125 mL
1½ cups	shredded mozzarella cheese	375 mL
2 tbsp	freshly grated Parmesan cheese	25 mL
2 tbsp	finely chopped fresh Italian (flat-leaf) parsley	25 mL

Season roasted peppers with hot pepper flakes, salt and black pepper, and toss with 1 tbsp (15 mL) of the oil. In a small skillet, heat the remaining oil over medium-low heat. Sauté garlic until aromatic. Brush dough with half the oil mixture, and scatter peppers and olives over dough. Sprinkle evenly with mozzarella, Parmesan and parsley, and drizzle with the remaining oil mixture. Bake as described in "About these recipes" (page 213). **Serves 2 to 3.**

Roasted Eggplant and Feta Pizza

1	medium to large eggplant	1
3 tbsp	extra-virgin olive oil	45 mL
2	cloves garlic, minced	2
2 tbsp	freshly squeezed lemon juice	25 mL
1 tbsp	chopped fresh Italian (flat-leaf) parsley	15 mL
	Salt and freshly ground black pepper to taste	
	Prepared pizza dough (see "About these recipes," page 213)	
6 oz	feta cheese, crumbled	175 g

Roast eggplant by placing it over a high gas flame or under a broiler until its skin is uniformly blackened. Let cool, slice off stem, peel off skin with your fingers, and dice flesh. In a large skillet, heat oil over medium-high heat. Add garlic, eggplant, lemon juice, parsley, salt and pepper; bring to a simmer. Spread over dough and scatter feta over top. Bake as described in "About these recipes" (page 213). **Serves 2 to 3.**

Garlic and Parmesan Pizza

⅓ cup	extra-virgin olive oil	75 mL
2	cloves garlic, minced	2
½ tsp	hot pepper flakes	2 mL
	Prepared pizza dough (see "About these recipes," page 213)	
½ to ¾ cup	freshly grated Parmesan cheese	125 to 175 mL

In a small skillet, heat oil over medium-low heat. Sauté garlic and hot pepper flakes until aromatic. Brush dough with oil mixture, and sprinkle evenly with Parmesan to taste. Bake as described in "About these recipes" (page 213). **Serves 2 to 3.**

Red, Black and Green Olive Pizza

¼ cup	olive oil	50 mL
1	clove garlic, minced	1
	Prepared pizza dough (see "About these recipes," page 213)	
6	drained canned anchovies, chopped	6
½ cup	salt-cured Niçoise olives, pitted and chopped	125 mL
½ cup	oil-cured Niçoise olives, pitted and chopped	125 mL
½ cup	green Sicilian olives, pitted and chopped	125 mL
2 cups	shredded mozzarella	500 mL

In a small skillet, heat oil over medium-low heat. Sauté garlic until aromatic. Brush dough with half the oil mixture, and scatter anchovies and the three types of olives over dough. Sprinkle evenly with mozzarella, and drizzle with the remaining oil mixture. Bake as described in "About these recipes" (page 213). **Serves 2 to 3.**

Tuna, White Bean and Olive Pizza

¼ cup	extra-virgin olive oil	50 mL
1	clove garlic, minced	1
	Prepared pizza dough (see "About these recipes," page 213)	
1	can (6 oz/170 g) tuna, drained and crumbled	1
1 cup	canned white beans (such as Great Northern or cannellini), drained, rinsed and coarsely mashed	250 mL
½ cup	oil-cured Niçoise olives, pitted and chopped	125 mL
	Salt and freshly ground black pepper to taste	

In a small skillet, heat oil over medium-low heat. Sauté garlic until aromatic. Brush dough with half the oil mixture, and scatter tuna, beans and olives over dough. Season with salt and pepper, and drizzle with the remaining oil mixture. Bake as described in "About these recipes" (page 213). **Serves 2 to 3.**

Spinach, Olive and Feta Pizza

¼ cup	extra-virgin olive oil	50 mL
1	clove garlic, minced	1
	Prepared pizza dough (see "About these recipes," page 213)	
1	package (10 oz/300 g) frozen chopped spinach, thawed and thoroughly drained	1
1	pimento, julienned	1
6 oz	feta cheese, crumbled	175 g
½ cup	oil-cured Niçoise olives, pitted and chopped	125 mL
	Salt and freshly ground black pepper to taste	

In a small skillet, heat oil over medium-low heat. Sauté garlic until aromatic. Brush dough with half the oil mixture, and scatter spinach, pimento, feta and olives over dough. Season with salt and pepper, and drizzle with the remaining oil mixture. Bake as described in "About these recipes" (page 213). **Serves 2 to 3.**

Duxelles and Parmesan Pizza

⅓ cup	olive oil, divided	75 mL
1	onion, minced	1
3	cloves garlic, minced, divided	3
1 lb	mushrooms, diced	500 g
	Salt and freshly ground black pepper to taste	
½ cup	dry white wine	125 mL
1 tsp	tomato paste	5 mL
½ cup	chopped fresh Italian (flat-leaf) parsley	125 mL
	Prepared pizza dough (see "About these recipes," page 213)	
3 tbsp	freshly grated Parmesan cheese	45 mL

In a skillet, heat 3 tbsp (45 mL) of the oil over medium-high heat. Sauté onion and two-thirds of the garlic until tender. Add mushrooms, salt and pepper; sauté until mushrooms start to release their liquid. Add wine, increase heat and cook until liquid is almost completely absorbed. Stir in tomato paste and parsley; cook for 1 minute. Season with additional salt and pepper; remove from heat. In a small skillet, heat the remaining oil over low heat. Sauté the remaining garlic until aromatic. Brush dough with half the oil mixture, and top with mushroom mixture. Sprinkle evenly with Parmesan, and drizzle with the remaining oil mixture. Bake as described in "About these recipes" (page 213). **Serves 2 to 3.**

Sweet Sausage, Pine Nut and Rosemary Pizza

1 lb	sweet Italian sausage	500 g
2 tbsp	peanut oil	25 mL
1 tbsp	olive oil	15 mL
½ cup	pine nuts	125 mL
1	clove garlic, minced	1
1 tbsp	grated orange zest	15 mL
1 tsp	chopped fresh rosemary	5 mL
1 tsp	dried rosemary	5 mL

	Salt and freshly ground black pepper to taste	
	Prepared pizza dough (see "About these recipes," page 213)	
1 cup	shredded smoked mozzarella cheese	250 mL

Place sausage in a small, heavy skillet and add enough water to come halfway up the sausage. Cook over medium heat, turning every 5 minutes, until water has evaporated and sausage is lightly browned on top and bottom. Remove from skillet and chop coarsely; set aside. In the same skillet, heat peanut oil and olive oil over medium heat. Add pine nuts and sauté until they just begin to color. Add sausage, garlic, orange zest, fresh rosemary, dried rosemary, salt and pepper. Spread mixture over dough, and sprinkle evenly with mozzarella. Bake as described in "About these recipes" (page 213). **Serves 2 to 3.**

Pancetta, Hazelnut and Garlic Pizza

1 tbsp	olive oil	15 mL
1 cup	diced pancetta	250 mL
2	cloves garlic, finely julienned	2
½ cup	chopped skinned hazelnuts	125 mL
1	clove garlic, minced	1
1 tbsp	chopped fresh Italian (flat-leaf) parsley	15 mL
	Salt and freshly ground black pepper to taste	
	Prepared pizza dough (see "About these recipes," page 213)	
1½ cups	shredded mozzarella cheese	375 mL

In a small skillet, heat oil over medium heat. Sauté pancetta until crisp. Add julienned garlic and nuts; sauté until nuts are lightly toasted. Stir in minced garlic, parsley, salt and pepper. Brush dough with 2 tbsp (25 mL) fat from the pan. Sprinkle evenly with mozzarella, then top with pancetta mixture. Bake as described in "About these recipes" (page 213). **Serves 2 to 3.**

Three-Mushroom Pizza

2 tbsp	butter	25 mL
¼ cup	minced onion	50 mL
1	clove garlic, minced	1
¾ cup	diced mushrooms	175 mL
¾ cup	diced shiitake mushrooms	175 mL
¾ cup	diced wild or exotic mushrooms (any kind)	175 mL
¼ cup	dry white wine	50 mL
	Salt and freshly ground black pepper to taste	

	Prepared pizza dough (see "About these recipes," page 213)	
1 tbsp	olive oil	15 mL
½ cup	freshly grated Parmesan cheese	125 mL

In a large skillet, melt butter over medium heat. Sauté onion and garlic until tender. Add the three types of mushrooms and sauté until browned and liquid is evaporated. Add wine, bring to a boil and cook, stirring occasionally, until liquid is almost completely absorbed. Season with salt and pepper. Brush dough with oil, and top with mushroom mixture. Sprinkle evenly with Parmesan. Bake as described in "About these recipes" (page 213). **Serves 2 to 3.**

Sausage and Mushroom Pizza

1 lb	Italian sausage (bulk, or with casings removed)	500 g
¼ cup	finely chopped onion	50 mL
2	cloves garlic, minced	2
8	mushrooms, sliced	8
½ cup	dry white wine	125 mL
2 cups	tomato sauce	500 mL
	Prepared pizza dough (see "About these recipes," page 213)	
	Salt and freshly ground black pepper to taste	
¾ cup	shredded mozzarella cheese (optional)	175 mL

In a large skillet, over medium-high heat, sauté sausage, breaking it up with a fork, until it starts to brown. Add onion and garlic; sauté until sausage is lightly browned and onion is tender. Add mushrooms and sauté until softened. Add wine, bring to a boil and cook, stirring occasionally, until liquid is almost completely absorbed. Spread tomato sauce over dough, and top with sausage mixture. Season with salt and pepper, and sprinkle evenly with mozzarella (if using). Bake as described in "About these recipes" (page 213). **Serves 2 to 3.**

Clam and Leek Pizza

¼ cup	olive oil	50 mL
3	leeks (white and light green parts only), thinly sliced	3
1	small onion, finely chopped	1
4	cloves garlic, minced	4
2 cups	drained canned chopped clams	500 mL
¼ cup	chopped fresh Italian (flat-leaf) parsley	50 mL
	Salt and freshly ground black pepper to taste	
	Prepared pizza dough (see "About these recipes," page 213)	
2 tbsp	freshly grated Parmesan cheese	25 mL

In a large, heavy saucepan, heat oil over medium heat. Sauté leeks, onion and garlic until tender. Add clams, parsley, salt and pepper; heat through. Spread mixture over dough, and sprinkle evenly with Parmesan. Bake as described in "About these recipes" (page 213). **Serves 2 to 3.**

Brie and Scallop Pizza

¼ cup	olive oil	50 mL
1	small onion, finely chopped	1
4	cloves garlic, minced	4
1 lb	sea scallops, trimmed of hard side muscles and halved horizontally	500 g
	Salt and freshly ground black pepper to taste	
	Prepared pizza dough (see "About these recipes," page 213)	
6 oz	Brie cheese, thinly sliced	175 g

In a large, heavy saucepan, heat oil over medium heat. Sauté onion and garlic until tender. Increase heat to high, add scallops and sauté for 1 minute. Remove scallops with a slotted spoon. Boil pan liquid, adding any liquid that collects around the scallops, until reduced by three-quarters. Season with salt and pepper. Toss scallops in reduced syrup and scatter over dough. Top with Brie. Bake as described in "About these recipes" (page 213). **Serves 2 to 3.**

Scallop and Herbed Cheese Pizza

Follow preceding recipe, but omit the Brie, and arrange 4 oz (125 g) herbed cream cheese, softened, in small mounds atop the pizza. **Serves 2 to 3.**

Marinated Feta and Artichoke Heart Pizza

1	jar (12 oz/340 mL) marinated artichoke hearts	1
4 oz	feta cheese, crumbled	125 g
	Prepared pizza dough (see "About these recipes," page 213)	
¼ cup	chopped fresh Italian (flat-leaf) parsley	50 mL
2 tbsp	freshly grated Romano cheese	25 mL
	Salt and freshly ground black pepper to taste	

Drain half the liquid from artichoke hearts. Cut hearts into quarters. Combine artichokes and remaining liquid with feta. Spread mixture over dough, and sprinkle evenly with parsley, Romano, salt and pepper. Bake as described in "About these recipes" (page 213). **Serves 2 to 3.**

Marinated Sun-Dried Tomato Pizza

12	oil-packed sun-dried tomatoes, drained and diced, oil reserved	12
2 tbsp	oil from the sun-dried tomatoes	25 mL
1	clove garlic, minced	1
Pinch	hot pepper flakes	Pinch
	Prepared pizza dough (see "About these recipes," page 213)	
¼ cup	freshly grated Parmesan cheese	50 mL
¼ cup	chopped fresh Italian (flat-leaf) parsley	50 mL

Combine sun-dried tomatoes and their oil, garlic, and hot pepper flakes. Spread mixture over dough, and sprinkle evenly with Parmesan and parsley. Bake as described in "About these recipes" (page 213). **Serves 2 to 3.**

Chicken and Olive Pizza

⅓ cup	olive oil, divided	75 mL
1 lb	boneless skinless chicken breasts, diced	500 g
1	red onion, thinly sliced	1
1	clove garlic, minced	1
¼ cup	dry white wine	50 mL
18	black olives, pitted	18
	Salt and freshly ground black pepper to taste	
	Prepared pizza dough (see "About these recipes," page 213)	
2 tbsp	freshly grated Parmesan cheese	25 mL
2 tbsp	chopped fresh Italian (flat-leaf) parsley	25 mL

In a large skillet, heat all but 1 tbsp (15 mL) of the oil over medium-high heat. Sauté chicken until it turns white. Add onion and garlic; sauté until tender. Add wine, bring to a boil and cook, stirring occasionally, until liquid has evaporated. Add olives, salt and pepper; cook for 1 minute. Scatter chicken mixture over dough, and sprinkle evenly with Parmesan and parsley. Drizzle with the remaining oil. Bake as described in "About these recipes" (page 213). **Serves 2 to 3.**

Sun-Dried Tomato and Tuna Pizza

7	oil-packed sun-dried tomatoes, drained and chopped	7
2	green onions, chopped	2
2	cloves garlic, minced	2
1	can (6 oz/170 g) oil-packed tuna, drained and oil reserved	1
	Salt and freshly ground black pepper to taste	
	Prepared pizza dough (see "About these recipes," page 213)	
1½ cups	shredded provolone cheese	375 mL

Combine sun-dried tomatoes, green onions, garlic, tuna, salt and pepper. Brush dough with half the oil from the tuna, and spread tomato mixture over dough. Sprinkle evenly with provolone, and drizzle with the remaining oil. Bake as described in "About these recipes" (page 213). **Serves 2 to 3.**

Caramelized Onion and Gorgonzola Pizza

2 tbsp	olive oil, divided	25 mL
1 tbsp	butter	15 mL
3	large yellow onions, thinly sliced	3
4 oz	Gorgonzola cheese, crumbled	125 g
	Prepared pizza dough (see "About these recipes," page 213)	
1 tbsp	chopped fresh Italian (flat-leaf) parsley	15 mL
	Salt and freshly ground black pepper to taste	

In a large skillet, heat half the oil and the butter over medium heat. Sauté onions until lightly browned. Scatter onions and Gorgonzola over dough, and sprinkle evenly with parsley, salt and pepper. Drizzle with the remaining oil. Bake as described in "About these recipes" (page 213). **Serves 2 to 3.**

Onion and Gruyère Pizza

Follow preceding recipe, but replace the olive oil with peanut oil, omit the Gorgonzola, and sprinkle with 1½ cups (375 mL) shredded Gruyère cheese. **Serves 2 to 3.**

Smoked Salmon and Onion Pizza

Follow recipe for Caramelized Onion and Gorgonzola Pizza (above), but omit the Gorgonzola, scatter 8 oz (250 g) smoked salmon, julienned, over the onions, and replace the parsley with dill. **Serves 2 to 3.**

Smoked Turkey and Fontina Pizza

Follow recipe for Caramelized Onion and Gorgonzola Pizza (above), but omit the Gorgonzola, and scatter 6 oz (175 g) smoked turkey breast, julienned, and 1½ cups (375 mL) diced fontina cheese over the onions. **Serves 2 to 3.**

Prosciutto, Walnut and Feta Pizza

Follow recipe for Caramelized Onion and Gorgonzola Pizza (above), but omit the Gorgonzola, and scatter 6 oz (175 g) prosciutto, julienned, 6 oz (175 g) feta cheese, crumbled, and ¾ cup (175 mL) chopped walnuts over the onions. **Serves 2 to 3.**

Red Onion and Herbed Cheese Pizza

2 tbsp	olive oil, divided	25 mL
1 tbsp	butter	15 mL
3	large red onions, thinly sliced	3
1 tsp	dried thyme	5 mL
1 tsp	dried tarragon	5 mL
1 tsp	dried chervil	5 mL
	Prepared pizza dough (see "About these recipes," page 213)	
1	clove garlic, minced	1
3 tbsp	chopped fresh Italian (flat-leaf) parsley, divided	45 mL
6 oz	garlic-and-herb cream cheese, softened	175 g
	Salt and freshly ground black pepper to taste	

In a large skillet, heat half the oil and the butter over medium heat. Sauté onions, thyme, tarragon and chervil until onions are lightly browned. Spread mixture over dough, sprinkle evenly with garlic and 2 tbsp (25 mL) of the parsley, and top with small mounds of cream cheese. Sprinkle evenly with the remaining parsley, salt and pepper, and drizzle with the remaining oil. Bake as described in "About these recipes" (page 213). **Serves 2 to 3.**

Marinated Mozzarella Pizza

4	cloves garlic, minced	4
¼ cup	chopped fresh Italian (flat-leaf) parsley	50 mL
¼ cup	chopped fresh basil	50 mL
1 tsp	hot pepper flakes	5 mL
1 tsp	salt	5 mL
	Freshly ground black pepper to taste	
	Olive oil	
1 lb	mozzarella cheese, sliced	500 g
	Prepared pizza dough (see "About these recipes," page 213)	

Combine garlic, parsley, basil, hot pepper flakes, salt, black pepper and enough olive oil to cover. Add mozzarella and toss to coat. Cover and refrigerate for at least 2 hours or for up to 2 days. Arrange cheese on dough, and drizzle with 2 tbsp (25 mL) of the marinade. Bake as described in "About these recipes" (page 213). **Serves 2 to 3.**

Hot Pepper, Bacon and Gorgonzola Pizza

4	slices bacon	4
2	hot chili peppers, seeded and julienned	2
1	large onion, thinly sliced	1
2	cloves garlic, minced	2
	Salt and freshly ground black pepper to taste	
	Prepared pizza dough (see "About these recipes," page 213)	
4 oz	Gorgonzola cheese, crumbled	125 g

In a large skillet, cook bacon over medium heat until browned but still soft. Remove with tongs, blot off excess fat and coarsely chop. Add chili peppers, onion and garlic to the fat remaining in the pan and sauté until tender. Season with salt and pepper, then spread mixture over dough. Scatter bacon and Gorgonzola over onion mixture. Bake as described in "About these recipes" (page 213). **Serves 2 to 3.**

Dried Cherry, Tarragon and Almond Dessert Pizza

1 cup	dried cherries	250 mL
1 tsp	dried tarragon	5 mL
	Prepared pizza dough (see "About these recipes," page 213)	
¼ cup	honey	50 mL
¼ cup	sliced almonds, toasted	50 mL

Soak cherries and tarragon in enough boiling water to cover for 10 minutes; drain and blot cherries dry. Scatter mixture over dough, drizzle with honey, and sprinkle evenly with almonds. Bake as described in "About these recipes" (page 213). **Serves 2 to 3.**

Banana and Walnut Dessert Pizza

¼ cup	honey	50 mL
1 tsp	vanilla	5 mL
	Prepared pizza dough (see "About these recipes," page 213)	
3	bananas, thinly sliced	3
½ cup	walnut pieces	125 mL
2 tbsp	packed light brown sugar	25 mL

Combine honey and vanilla; brush dough with the mixture. Scatter bananas and walnuts over dough, and sprinkle evenly with brown sugar. Bake as described in "About these recipes" (page 213). **Serves 2 to 3.**

Sweet Ricotta Dessert Pizza

8 oz	ricotta cheese	250 g
¼ cup	packed light brown sugar	50 mL
1 tsp	vanilla	5 mL
1	large or extra-large egg	1
	Prepared pizza dough (see "About these recipes," page 213)	

Combine cheese, brown sugar and vanilla, then beat in egg. Spread mixture over dough. Bake as described in "About these recipes" (page 213). **Serves 2 to 3.**

Chapter 20
Pasta
It's All in the Sauce

Quick Fresh Tomato Sauce 225

Spicy Tomato Sauce and Red Beans . . . 225

Spicy Tomato Vinaigrette 225

Marinated Sun-Dried Tomato Sauce . . . 225

Sun-Dried Tomato Rouille 225

Ginger Tomato Sauce 226

Three-Mushroom Sauce 226

Mushroom Persillade 226

Tomato, Basil and Chèvre Sauce 226

Ricotta and Roasted Red Pepper
Sauce 226

Feta and Artichoke Sauce 227

Artichoke and Mushroom Sauce 227

Three-Pepper Sauce 227

Roasted Pepper and Walnut Sauce 227

Roasted Pepper and Olive Sauce 227

Roasted Eggplant and Garlic Sauce . . . 227

Spicy Peanut Sauce 228

Reduced-Fat Pesto 228

Parsley Sauce 228

Tomato Sauce with Tequila
and Cream 228

Herb, Tomato and Cream Sauce 228

Hot Pepper and Cream Sauce 229

Wild Mushroom, Brandy
and Cream Sauce 229

Cheese and Cream Sauce 229

Quick Meat Sauce 229

Bolognese Sauce 229

Meatballs and Sauce 230

Sicilian Turkey Meatballs and Sauce . . . 230

Sausage Meatballs and Sauce 230

Sausage and Mushroom Sauce 230

Ham, Pine Nut and Rosemary Sauce . . . 231

Basil and Prosciutto Sauce 231

Pancetta, Hazelnut and Garlic Sauce . . . 231

Carbonara Sauce 231

Bacon, Egg and Cheese Sauce 231

Chicken and Olive Sauce 232

Crab, Tarragon and Shallot Sauce 232

Fast Clam Sauce 232

Mussels in White Sauce 232

Mussels in Red Sauce 232

Scallop and Herbed Cheese Sauce 233

Fennel, Shrimp and Orange Sauce 233

Shrimp, Cucumber and Dill Sauce 233

Smoked Salmon, Cucumber
and Dill Sauce 233

Smoked Salmon, Caviar
and Cream Sauce 233

Sauce Tonnato 234

Sun-Dried Tomato and Tuna Sauce 234

White Bean, Tuna and Olive Oil Sauce . . 234

Tapenade Sauce 234

Pepper and Anchovy Sauce 234

*P*aesani eat pasta daily, meal after meal — simmered in soup, cut into ribbons and wrapped into rings. From tortes to tortellini, it appears everywhere, in every conceivable form, but for the most part, pasta is a simple affair — boiled, drained and tossed with sauce.

One might expect the great pasta pot of inspiration to soon boil dry, but it never does. Ever. There is always something new to prepare with pasta, and most of the tried and true methods are so good that a repeat performance is never tiring.

To wake up your palate, here are 50 perfect sauces to make plain boiled pasta extraordinary. They range from a simple coat of parsley and cheese to an exotic mélange of caviar, shallots and smoked salmon. All are simple to prepare and quick. Most need less than 10 minutes and a few require no cooking at all. None calls for more than an hour of cooking.

About these recipes . . .

All of the sauces in this chapter are presented in sufficient quantity to accompany 12 oz (375 g) of pasta, which should be cooked until al dente in 4 to 6 quarts (4 to 6 L) of rapidly boiling salted water. The cooked pasta should be thoroughly drained before it is mixed with the sauce. Pasta is bland and dilutes the flavor of the sauce when you toss them together, so season your sauces assertively with salt and pepper.

Quick Fresh Tomato Sauce

2 tbsp	olive oil	25 mL
1	large onion, chopped	1
1	dried hot chili pepper	1
2	cloves garlic, minced	2
12	plum (Roma) tomatoes, peeled, seeded and coarsely chopped	12
1	roasted red bell pepper (see page 11), chopped	1
1 tbsp	tomato paste	15 mL
1/3 cup	chopped fresh herbs (such as basil, flat-leaf parsley, rosemary, oregano)	75 mL
	Salt and freshly ground black pepper to taste	
	Hot pasta (see "About these recipes," above)	

In a large, deep skillet, heat oil over medium-high heat. Sauté onion, chili pepper and garlic until onion is barely tender. Add tomatoes and roasted pepper; sauté until tomatoes start to release their liquid. Stir in tomato paste, herbs, salt and pepper;

heat for 1 minute. Discard chili pepper. Toss sauce with pasta. **Serves 4.**

Spicy Tomato Sauce and Red Beans

Follow preceding recipe, but use 2 chili peppers instead of 1, add 1 cup (250 mL) cooked red kidney beans with the tomatoes, and omit the fresh herbs. **Serves 4.**

Spicy Tomato Vinaigrette

4 cups	canned crushed tomatoes	1 L
1/4 cup	extra-virgin olive oil	50 mL
1 tbsp	red wine vinegar	15 mL
Pinch	hot pepper flakes	Pinch
	Salt and freshly ground black pepper to taste	
	Hot pasta (see "About these recipes," left)	

In a large, heavy saucepan, over medium-high heat, cook tomatoes, stirring frequently, until thick. Whisk in oil, vinegar, hot pepper flakes, salt and black pepper. Toss with pasta. **Serves 4.**

Marinated Sun-Dried Tomato Sauce

12	oil-packed sun-dried tomatoes, drained and diced, oil reserved	12
2 tbsp	oil from the sun-dried tomatoes	25 mL
1	clove garlic, minced	1
	Hot pasta (see "About these recipes," left)	
1/4 cup	freshly grated Parmesan cheese	50 mL
1 tbsp	chopped fresh Italian (flat-leaf) parsley	15 mL

Toss together sun-dried tomatoes, tomato oil and garlic. Add pasta, Parmesan and parsley; toss to coat. **Serves 4.**

Sun-Dried Tomato Rouille

10	oil-packed sun-dried tomatoes, drained, oil reserved	10
1/3 cup	oil from the sun-dried tomatoes	75 mL
1	bunch basil leaves, finely chopped (about 1 cup/250 mL)	1
1	clove garlic, minced	1
2 tbsp	freshly grated Parmesan cheese	25 mL
1 tbsp	extra-virgin olive oil	15 mL
	Salt and freshly ground black pepper to taste	
	Hot pasta (see "About these recipes," left)	

In a food processor, purée sun-dried tomatoes and tomato oil. Stir in basil, garlic, Parmesan, olive oil, salt and pepper. Toss with pasta. **Serves 4.**

Ginger Tomato Sauce

2 tbsp	vegetable oil	25 mL
1	large onion, chopped	1
2	cloves garlic, minced	2
1 tbsp	finely chopped gingerroot	15 mL
12	plum (Roma) tomatoes, peeled, seeded and coarsely chopped	12
1 tbsp	tomato paste	15 mL
1 tbsp	finely chopped fresh cilantro	15 mL
Pinch	granulated sugar	Pinch
	Salt and freshly ground black pepper to taste	
	Hot pasta (see "About these recipes," page 225)	

In a large, deep skillet, heat oil over medium-high heat. Sauté onion, garlic and ginger until onion is barely tender. Add tomatoes and cook until they start to release their liquid. Stir in tomato paste, cilantro, sugar, salt and pepper. Toss with pasta. **Serves 4.**

Three-Mushroom Sauce

2 tbsp	butter	25 mL
¼ cup	minced onion	50 mL
1	clove garlic, minced	1
¾ cup	diced mushrooms	175 mL
¾ cup	diced shiitake mushrooms	175 mL
¾ cup	diced wild or exotic mushrooms	175 mL
¼ cup	dry white wine	50 mL
1 cup	chopped seeded peeled plum (Roma) tomatoes	250 mL
	Salt and freshly ground black pepper to taste	
	Hot pasta (see "About these recipes," page 225)	
	Freshly grated Parmesan cheese	

In a large, deep skillet, melt butter over medium-low heat. Sauté onion and garlic until tender. Add the three types of mushrooms and sauté until tender. Add wine, increase heat to medium-high and bring to a boil. Add tomatoes and cook until they start to release their liquid. Season with salt and pepper. Toss with pasta and Parmesan. **Serves 4.**

Mushroom Persillade

3 tbsp	olive oil	45 mL
1	onion, minced	1
2	cloves garlic, minced	2
1 lb	mushrooms, diced	500 g
	Salt and freshly ground black pepper to taste	
1 cup	dry white wine	250 mL
½ cup	chopped fresh Italian (flat-leaf) parsley	125 mL
1 tsp	tomato paste	5 mL
	Hot pasta (see "About these recipes," page 225)	

In a large, deep skillet, heat oil over medium-high heat. Sauté onion and garlic until tender. Add mushrooms, salt and pepper; sauté until mushrooms start to release their liquid. Add wine, increase heat to high and boil until liquid is reduced by half. Stir in parsley and tomato paste; cook for 1 minute. Toss with pasta. **Serves 4.**

Tomato, Basil and Chèvre Sauce

1 tbsp	extra-virgin olive oil	15 mL
1	clove garlic, halved	1
8	plum (Roma) tomatoes, peeled, seeded and chopped	8
⅓ cup	dry white wine	75 mL
2 tbsp	chopped fresh basil	25 mL
Pinch	cayenne pepper	Pinch
	Salt and freshly ground black pepper to taste	
	Hot pasta (see "About these recipes," page 225)	
6 oz	crumbled fresh chèvre (goat cheese)	175 g

In a large skillet, heat oil over medium-high heat. Sauté garlic until aromatic. Add tomatoes and wine; boil for 3 minutes. Add basil, cayenne, salt and black pepper; cook for 20 seconds. Discard garlic. Toss sauce with pasta and chèvre. **Serves 4.**

Ricotta and Roasted Red Pepper Sauce

1 tbsp	extra-virgin olive oil	15 mL
2	roasted red bell peppers (see page 11), diced	2
Pinch	hot pepper flakes	Pinch
	Salt and freshly ground black pepper to taste	
	Hot pasta (see "About these recipes," page 225)	
1 tbsp	butter	15 mL
½ cup	ricotta cheese, at room temperature	125 mL
2 tbsp	freshly grated Parmesan cheese	25 mL
2 tbsp	finely chopped fresh Italian (flat-leaf) parsley	25 mL

In a skillet, heat oil over medium-high heat. Sauté bell peppers, hot pepper flakes, salt and black pepper until heated through. Toss with pasta, butter, ricotta, Parmesan and parsley. **Serves 4.**

Feta and Artichoke Sauce

1	jar (12 oz/340 mL) marinated artichoke hearts, with liquid	1
4 oz	feta cheese, crumbled	125 g
	Hot pasta (see "About these recipes," page 225)	
1/4 cup	chopped fresh Italian (flat-leaf) parsley	50 mL
2 tbsp	freshly grated Parmesan cheese	25 mL
	Salt and freshly ground black pepper to taste	

Combine artichoke hearts, with their liquid, and feta; let stand for 10 minutes. Toss with pasta, parsley, Parmesan, salt and pepper. **Serves 4.**

Artichoke and Mushroom Sauce

1	jar (12 oz/340 mL) marinated artichoke hearts	1
1 tbsp	extra-virgin olive oil	15 mL
1	clove garlic, minced	1
8	mushrooms, sliced	8
2 tbsp	chopped fresh Italian (flat-leaf) parsley	25 mL
	Salt and freshly ground black pepper to taste	
	Hot pasta (see "About these recipes," page 225)	

Drain half the liquid from artichoke hearts and coarsely chop hearts. In a large skillet, heat oil over medium heat. Sauté garlic until tender. Add mushrooms and sauté until slightly softened, about 5 minutes. Add artichoke hearts with remaining liquid, parsley, salt and pepper. Toss with pasta. **Serves 4.**

Three-Pepper Sauce

3 tbsp	olive oil	45 mL
3	roasted bell peppers (assorted colors; see page 11), diced	3
Pinch	hot pepper flakes	Pinch
	Hot pasta (see "About these recipes," page 225)	
1/4 cup	freshly grated Parmesan cheese	50 mL
1 tbsp	chopped fresh Italian (flat-leaf) parsley	15 mL
	Salt and freshly ground black pepper to taste	

In a large skillet, heat oil over medium-high heat. Sauté bell peppers and hot pepper flakes until fragrant. Toss with pasta, Parmesan, parsley, salt and black pepper. **Serves 4.**

Roasted Pepper and Walnut Sauce

2	large roasted red bell peppers (see page 11), diced	2
1	clove garlic, minced	1
1/4 cup	extra-virgin olive oil	50 mL
	Salt and freshly ground black pepper to taste	
	Hot pasta (see "About these recipes," page 225)	
1/4 cup	walnut pieces	50 mL
2 tbsp	freshly grated Parmesan cheese	25 mL

Combine bell peppers, garlic, oil, salt and pepper; let stand for 10 minutes. Toss with pasta, walnuts and Parmesan. **Serves 4.**

Roasted Pepper and Olive Sauce

2	large roasted bell peppers (any color; see page 11), diced	2
1	clove garlic, minced	1
1/4 cup	chopped pitted oil-cured black olives	50 mL
1/4 cup	extra-virgin olive oil	50 mL
	Salt and freshly ground black pepper to taste	
	Hot pasta (see "About these recipes," page 225)	
2 tbsp	freshly grated Parmesan cheese	25 mL

Combine bell peppers, garlic, olives, oil, salt and pepper; let stand for 10 minutes. Toss with pasta and Parmesan. **Serves 4.**

Roasted Eggplant and Garlic Sauce

1	eggplant	1
3 tbsp	extra-virgin olive oil	45 mL
2	cloves garlic, minced	2
1/4 cup	freshly squeezed lemon juice	50 mL
1 tbsp	chopped fresh Italian (flat-leaf) parsley	15 mL
	Salt and freshly ground black pepper to taste	
	Hot pasta (see "About these recipes," page 225)	

Roast eggplant by placing it over a high gas flame or under a broiler until its skin is uniformly blackened. Let cool, slice off stem, peel off skin with your fingers, and dice flesh. In a large skillet, heat oil over medium heat. Sauté eggplant and garlic until eggplant is very soft. Stir in lemon juice, parsley, salt and pepper. Toss with pasta. **Serves 4.**

Spicy Peanut Sauce

1 tbsp	canola oil	15 mL
½	onion, minced	½
1	clove garlic, minced	1
1 tbsp	soy sauce	15 mL
2 tsp	grated gingerroot	10 mL
1 tsp	Chinese chili paste	5 mL
½ tsp	ground cumin	2 mL
½ tsp	ground coriander	2 mL
¼ cup	smooth peanut butter	50 mL
1 cup	buttermilk (approx.)	250 mL
	Hot pasta (see "About these recipes," page 225)	
2	green onions, thinly sliced	2

In a nonstick skillet, heat oil over medium heat. Sauté onion until tender. Add garlic and sauté until aromatic. Add soy sauce, ginger, chili paste, cumin and coriander; sauté until aromatic. Stir in peanut butter until melted, then thin with buttermilk until sauce has the consistency of whipping (35%) cream. Toss with pasta and green onions. **Serves 4.**

Reduced-Fat Pesto

1	clove garlic, minced	1
2 cups	finely chopped fresh basil	500 mL
3 tbsp	extra-virgin olive oil	45 mL
2 tbsp	freshly grated Parmesan cheese	25 mL
	Salt and freshly ground black pepper to taste	
	Hot pasta (see "About these recipes," page 225)	

Combine garlic, basil, oil, Parmesan, salt and pepper. Toss with pasta. **Serves 4.**

Parsley Sauce

¼ cup	extra-virgin olive oil	50 mL
2	shallots, minced	2
1	clove garlic, minced	1
1 cup	chopped fresh Italian (flat-leaf) parsley	250 mL
	Salt and freshly ground black pepper to taste	
	Hot pasta (see "About these recipes," above)	
¼ cup	freshly grated Parmesan cheese	50 mL

In a skillet, heat oil over medium-low heat. Sauté shallots and garlic until tender. Remove from heat and stir in parsley, salt and pepper. Toss with pasta and Parmesan. **Serves 4.**

Tomato Sauce with Tequila and Cream

2 tbsp	olive oil	25 mL
2	cloves garlic, minced	2
12	large plum (Roma) tomatoes, peeled, seeded and chopped	12
½ tsp	hot pepper flakes	2 mL
½ cup	cream (any type, minimum 10%)	125 mL
2 tbsp	tequila	25 mL
	Salt and freshly ground black pepper to taste	
	Hot pasta (see "About these recipes," page 225)	

In a large skillet, heat oil over medium-high heat. Sauté garlic until aromatic. Add tomatoes and hot pepper flakes; sauté until tomatoes start to release their liquid. Add cream, reduce heat and simmer until sauce is slightly thickened, about 1 minute. Remove from heat and stir in tequila, salt and black pepper. Toss with pasta. **Serves 4.**

Herb, Tomato and Cream Sauce

2 tbsp	olive oil	25 mL
2 tbsp	minced onion	25 mL
½ cup	chopped fresh Italian (flat-leaf) parsley	125 mL
1 tbsp	finely grated lemon zest	15 mL
Pinch	dried basil	Pinch
Pinch	dried marjoram	Pinch
Pinch	dried thyme	Pinch
12	large plum (Roma) tomatoes, peeled, seeded and chopped	12
½ cup	light or table (18%) cream	125 mL
	Salt and freshly ground black pepper to taste	
	Hot pasta (see "About these recipes," page 225)	

In a large skillet, heat oil over medium heat. Sauté onion until tender. Add parsley, lemon zest, basil, marjoram and thyme; sauté for 1 minute. Add tomatoes and sauté until they start to release their liquid. Add cream, reduce heat and simmer until sauce is slightly thickened, about 1 minute. Season with salt and pepper. Toss with pasta. **Serves 4.**

Hot Pepper and Cream Sauce

2 cups	whipping (35%) cream	500 mL
¼ cup	hot pepper sauce (such as Tabasco), or to taste	50 mL
	Salt and freshly ground black pepper to taste	
	Hot pasta (see "About these recipes," page 225)	

In a saucepan, bring cream to a boil over medium-high heat; cook until reduced by one-third. Add hot pepper sauce and cook until slightly thickened. Remove from heat and stir in salt and pepper. Toss with pasta. **Serves 4.**

Wild Mushroom, Brandy and Cream Sauce

½ oz	dried wild or exotic mushrooms	15 g
½ cup	boiling water	125 mL
2 tbsp	butter	25 mL
2	shallots, minced	2
8 oz	mushrooms, diced	250 g
2 tbsp	brandy	25 mL
1 cup	whipping (35%) cream	250 mL
	Salt and freshly ground black pepper to taste	
	Hot pasta (see "About these recipes," page 225)	

Soak wild mushrooms in boiling water until softened, about 20 minutes. Drain mushrooms, reserving liquid. Coarsely chop mushrooms and strain soaking liquid through a damp coffee filter to remove sediment; set both aside. In a large skillet, melt butter over medium heat. Sauté shallots until tender. Add fresh mushrooms and sauté until browned. Add brandy and carefully flambé (see page 10). When flames subside, add wild mushrooms and soaking liquid; cook until liquid is reduced by half. Add cream and cook until slightly thickened. Season with salt and pepper. Toss with pasta. **Serves 4.**

Cheese and Cream Sauce

2 cups	whipping (35%) cream	500 mL
⅓ cup	freshly grated Parmesan cheese	75 mL
	Salt and freshly ground black pepper to taste	
	Hot pasta (see "About these recipes," page 225)	
	Chopped fresh Italian (flat-leaf) parsley (optional)	

In a saucepan, bring cream to a boil over medium-high heat; cook until reduced by one-third. Remove from heat and stir in Parmesan, salt and pepper. Toss with pasta. Garnish with parsley, if desired. **Serves 4.**

Quick Meat Sauce

1 tbsp	olive oil	15 mL
1	large onion, chopped	1
2	cloves garlic, minced	2
1 lb	lean ground beef	500 g
3 cups	canned crushed tomatoes	750 mL
¼ cup	tomato paste	50 mL
Pinch	hot pepper flakes	Pinch
	Salt and freshly ground black pepper to taste	
1 tbsp	chopped fresh Italian (flat-leaf) parsley	15 mL
	Hot pasta (see "About these recipes," page 225)	

In a large, deep skillet, heat oil over medium heat. Sauté onion and garlic until tender. Add beef and sauté, breaking it up with a fork, until no longer pink. Add tomatoes, tomato paste, hot pepper flakes, salt and black pepper; reduce heat and simmer for 10 minutes. Stir in parsley. Toss with pasta. **Serves 4.**

Bolognese Sauce

1 tbsp	olive oil	15 mL
1 tbsp	butter	15 mL
2 tbsp	chopped onion	25 mL
2 tbsp	diced carrot	25 mL
2 tbsp	diced celery	25 mL
1 lb	ground veal	500 g
½ cup	milk	125 mL
3 cups	canned crushed tomatoes	750 mL
¼ cup	tomato paste	50 mL
	Salt and freshly ground black pepper to taste	
	Hot pasta (see "About these recipes," page 225)	

In a large saucepan, heat oil and butter over medium heat. Sauté onion, carrot and celery until tender. Add veal and sauté, breaking it up with a fork, until no longer pink. Add milk and cook, stirring occasionally, until liquid has evaporated. Add tomatoes and tomato paste; reduce heat and simmer gently for 1 hour. Season with salt and pepper. Toss with pasta. **Serves 4.**

Meatballs and Sauce

2	slices firm white bread, crusts removed, crumbled	2
¼ cup	milk	50 mL
1	egg, beaten	1
1	clove garlic, minced	1
8 oz	lean ground beef	250 g
8 oz	ground pork	250 g
8 oz	ground veal	250 g
¼ cup	minced onion	50 mL
1 tbsp	chopped fresh Italian (flat-leaf) parsley	15 mL
1 tsp	dried mint	5 mL
1 tsp	dried basil	5 mL
	Salt and freshly ground black pepper to taste	
2 tbsp	vegetable oil (approx.)	25 mL
	Chicken or beef broth	
3 cups	tomato pasta sauce	750 mL
	Hot pasta (see "About these recipes," page 225)	

Soak bread in milk until milk is absorbed. With wet hands, mix in egg, garlic, beef, pork, veal, onion, parsley, mint, basil, salt and pepper. Form into 24 meatballs. In a large, deep skillet, heat oil over medium-high heat. Cook meatballs, in batches if necessary, until browned on all sides, adding more oil as needed. Drain fat from pan. Return meatballs to pan and add 1 inch (2.5 cm) of broth. Reduce heat and simmer until meatballs are no longer pink inside. Drain meatballs and return to skillet. Add pasta sauce and heat through. Toss with pasta. Serves 4.

Sicilian Turkey Meatballs and Sauce

1	egg, beaten	1
1 lb	ground turkey	500 g
½ cup	fresh bread crumbs	125 mL
¼ cup	ricotta cheese	50 mL
¼ cup	finely chopped onion	50 mL
1 tbsp	dried mint	15 mL
2 tbsp	Worcestershire sauce	25 mL
1 tbsp	ketchup	15 mL
	Salt and freshly ground black pepper to taste	
2 tbsp	vegetable oil (approx.)	25 mL
	Chicken broth	
3 cups	tomato pasta sauce	750 mL
	Hot pasta (see "About these recipes," page 225)	

With wet hands, combine egg, turkey, bread crumbs, ricotta, onion, mint, Worcestershire sauce, ketchup, salt and pepper. Form into 24 meatballs. In a large, deep skillet, heat oil over medium-high heat. Cook meatballs, in batches if necessary, until browned on all sides, adding more oil as needed. Drain fat from pan. Return meatballs to pan and add 1 inch (2.5 cm) of broth. Reduce heat and simmer until meatballs are no longer pink inside. Drain meatballs and return to skillet. Add pasta sauce and heat through. Toss with pasta. Serves 4.

Sausage Meatballs and Sauce

2	slices firm white bread, crusts removed, crumbled	2
¼ cup	dry white wine	50 mL
1	egg, beaten	1
1 lb	Italian sausage (bulk, or with casings removed)	500 g
2 tsp	dried mint	10 mL
2 tbsp	vegetable oil (approx.)	25 mL
3 cups	tomato pasta sauce	750 mL
	Hot pasta (see "About these recipes," page 225)	

Soak bread in wine until wine is absorbed. With wet hands, mix in egg, sausage and mint. Form into 24 meatballs. In a large, deep skillet, heat oil over medium-high heat. Cook meatballs, in batches if necessary, until browned on all sides, adding more oil as needed. Drain fat from pan. Return meatballs to pan and add 1 inch (2.5 cm) water. Reduce heat and simmer until meatballs are no longer pink inside. Drain meatballs and return to skillet. Add pasta sauce and heat through. Toss with pasta. Serves 4.

Sausage and Mushroom Sauce

1 tbsp	olive oil	15 mL
1 lb	Italian sausage (bulk, or with casings removed)	500 g
¼ cup	finely chopped onion	50 mL
2	cloves garlic, minced	2
8	mushrooms, sliced	8
½ cup	dry white wine	125 mL
3 cups	tomato pasta sauce	750 mL
	Salt and freshly ground black pepper to taste	
	Hot pasta (see "About these recipes," page 225)	

In a large, deep skillet, heat oil over medium-high heat. Sauté sausage, breaking up with a fork, until starting to brown. Add onion and garlic; sauté until sausage is lightly browned and onion is tender. Add mushrooms and sauté until softened. Add wine, bring to a boil and cook, stirring occasionally, until liquid is almost completely absorbed. Add pasta sauce, salt and pepper; bring to a boil. Toss with pasta. **Serves 4.**

Ham, Pine Nut and Rosemary Sauce

¼ cup	extra-virgin olive oil, divided	50 mL
½ cup	pine nuts	125 mL
1	clove garlic, minced	1
1 cup	diced smoked ham	250 mL
1 tbsp	grated orange zest	15 mL
1 tbsp	chopped fresh rosemary	15 mL
	Salt and freshly ground black pepper to taste	
	Hot pasta (see "About these recipes," page 225)	

In a skillet, heat half the oil over medium heat. Sauté pine nuts until toasted. Add garlic, ham, orange zest and rosemary; sauté until aromatic. Season with salt and pepper. Toss with pasta and the remaining oil. **Serves 4.**

Basil and Prosciutto Sauce

¼ cup	extra-virgin olive oil	50 mL
2	cloves garlic, minced	2
1 cup	chopped fresh basil	250 mL
½ cup	julienned prosciutto	125 mL
Pinch	hot pepper flakes	Pinch
	Salt and freshly ground black pepper to taste	
	Hot pasta (see "About these recipes," page 225)	
¼ cup	freshly grated Parmesan cheese	50 mL

In a small skillet, heat oil over medium-low heat. Sauté garlic until tender. Remove from heat and stir in basil, prosciutto, hot pepper flakes, salt and black pepper. Toss with pasta and Parmesan. **Serves 4.**

Pancetta, Hazelnut and Garlic Sauce

1 tsp	olive oil	5 mL
1 cup	diced pancetta	250 mL
1 cup	hot water	250 mL
½ cup	chopped skinned hazelnuts	125 mL
4	cloves garlic, finely julienned	4
1 tbsp	chopped fresh Italian (flat-leaf) parsley	15 mL
	Salt and freshly ground black pepper to taste	
	Hot pasta (see "About these recipes," page 225)	

In a saucepan, heat oil over medium-high heat. Sauté pancetta until some of the fat is rendered. Add water, ¼ cup (50 mL) at a time, stirring until evaporated before making the next addition. When complete, pancetta will be crispy and brown, and there will be several tablespoons of fat in the pot. Add nuts and sauté until lightly toasted. Add garlic and sauté until aromatic. Stir in parsley, salt and pepper. Toss with pasta. **Serves 4.**

Carbonara Sauce

2 tbsp	olive oil	25 mL
1	clove garlic, crushed with the side of a knife	1
8 oz	pancetta, diced	250 g
3	large or extra-large eggs	3
¾ cup	freshly grated Parmesan cheese	175 mL
	Hot pasta (see "About these recipes," page 225)	

In a skillet, heat oil over medium heat. Sauté garlic until golden brown; discard garlic. Add pancetta and sauté until edges are browned; remove from heat. In a large, warm bowl, beat eggs and Parmesan. Add pasta and pancetta; toss to coat. **Serves 4.** *(If you are concerned about the food safety of softly cooked egg yolks, skip this recipe.)*

Bacon, Egg and Cheese Sauce

Follow preceding recipe, but substitute bacon for the pancetta. **Serves 4.**

Chicken and Olive Sauce

¼ cup	extra-virgin olive oil, divided	50 mL
8 oz	boneless skinless chicken breasts, diced	250 g
¼ cup	minced onion	50 mL
1	clove garlic, minced	1
¾ cup	dry white wine	175 mL
18	black olives, pitted and halved	18
2 tsp	chopped fresh Italian (flat-leaf) parsley	10 mL
	Salt and freshly ground black pepper to taste	
	Hot pasta (see "About these recipes," page 225)	

In a large skillet, heat half the oil over medium-high heat. Sauté chicken and onion until chicken is no longer pink inside and onion is tender. Add garlic and sauté until aromatic. Add wine and boil for 1 minute. Add olives and cook for 1 minute. Stir in the remaining oil, parsley, salt and pepper. Toss with pasta. **Serves 4.**

Crab, Tarragon and Shallot Sauce

¼ cup	olive oil	50 mL
2	shallots, finely chopped	2
1 lb	backfin (lump) crabmeat, shells picked out	500 g
2 tbsp	coarsely chopped fresh Italian (flat-leaf) parsley	25 mL
1 tbsp	coarsely chopped fresh tarragon	15 mL
	Juice of 1 lemon	
	Salt and freshly ground black pepper to taste	
	Hot pasta (see "About these recipes," page 225)	

In a skillet, heat oil over medium-low heat. Sauté shallots until tender. Add crab, tossing to coat with oil, parsley and tarragon; sauté for 1 minute. Stir in lemon juice, salt and pepper. Toss with pasta. **Serves 4.**

Fast Clam Sauce

2 tbsp	olive oil	25 mL
1	onion, finely chopped	1
4	cloves garlic, minced	4
1 cup	dry white wine	250 mL
2 tsp	chopped fresh dill	10 mL
	Juice of 1 lemon	
24	littleneck clams, scrubbed (see page 8)	24
¼ cup	chopped fresh Italian (flat-leaf) parsley	50 mL
2 tbsp	butter	25 mL
	Hot pasta (see "About these recipes," page 225)	

In a large, heavy saucepan, heat oil over medium-high heat. Sauté onion until tender. Add garlic and sauté until aromatic. Add wine, dill and lemon juice; bring to a boil. Add clams; reduce heat, cover and simmer until clams open (discard any that don't). Remove clams from shells and return to sauce. Stir in parsley and butter. Toss with pasta. **Serves 4.**

Mussels in White Sauce

2 tbsp	olive oil	25 mL
1	onion, finely chopped	1
4	cloves garlic, minced	4
1 cup	dry white wine	250 mL
1 tsp	chopped fresh oregano	5 mL
	Juice of 1 lemon	
24	mussels, scrubbed (see page 8)	24
¼ cup	chopped fresh Italian (flat-leaf) parsley	50 mL
	Additional olive oil (optional)	
	Hot pasta (see "About these recipes," page 225)	

In a large, heavy saucepan, heat oil over medium-high heat. Sauté onion until tender. Add garlic and sauté until aromatic. Add wine, oregano and lemon juice; bring to a boil. Add mussels; reduce heat, cover and simmer until mussels open (discard any that don't). Stir in parsley and, if desired, additional olive oil. Toss with pasta. **Serves 4.**

Mussels in Red Sauce

6 tbsp	olive oil	90 mL
1	clove garlic, minced	1
1	can (14 oz/398 g) diced tomatoes, with juice	1
1 tbsp	chopped fresh Italian (flat-leaf) parsley	15 mL
Pinch	hot pepper flakes	Pinch
24	mussels, scrubbed (see page 8)	24
	Hot pasta (see "About these recipes," page 225)	

In a large, deep skillet, heat oil over medium heat. Sauté garlic until lightly browned. Add tomatoes and their liquid, parsley and hot pepper flakes; reduce heat and simmer for 10 minutes, until tomatoes are soft and sauce is slightly thickened. Add mussels, cover and simmer until mussels open (discard any that don't). Serve over pasta. **Serves 4.**

Scallop and Herbed Cheese Sauce

1 tbsp	canola oil	15 mL
1	large shallot, finely chopped	1
1 cup	dry white wine	250 mL
12 oz	bay scallops	375 g
1 tbsp	freshly squeezed lemon juice	15 mL
4 oz	herbed cream cheese	125 g
1 tbsp	freshly grated Parmesan cheese	15 mL
2 tsp	chopped fresh Italian (flat-leaf) parsley	10 mL
	Salt and freshly ground white pepper to taste	
	Hot pasta (see "About these recipes," page 225)	

In a medium skillet, heat oil over medium heat. Sauté shallot until tender. Add wine, increase heat and boil until reduced by half. Add scallops and lemon juice; cook until scallops are firm and opaque. Remove from heat and stir in cream cheese and Parmesan until smooth. Stir in parsley, salt and pepper. Toss with pasta. **Serves 4.**

Fennel, Shrimp and Orange Sauce

2 tbsp	olive oil	25 mL
1 cup	diced fennel bulb	250 mL
¼ cup	minced onion	50 mL
1	clove garlic, minced	1
1 tsp	ground fennel seeds	5 mL
	Finely grated zest and juice of 1 orange	
1 cup	dry white wine	250 mL
1 cup	diced tomato (canned or fresh)	250 mL
Pinch	crumbled saffron threads (optional)	Pinch
1 lb	medium shrimp, peeled and deveined	500 g
	Salt and freshly ground black pepper to taste	
	Hot pasta (see "About these recipes," page 225)	

In a large skillet, heat oil over medium heat. Sauté diced fennel and onion until tender. Add garlic, ground fennel and orange zest; sauté for 1 minute. Add orange juice, wine, tomato and saffron (if using); increase heat and boil until liquid is reduced by about three-quarters. Add shrimp and cook, stirring, until pink and opaque. Season with salt and pepper. Toss with pasta. **Serves 4.**

Shrimp, Cucumber and Dill Sauce

1	cucumber, peeled, seeded and diced	1
1 tsp	kosher salt	5 mL
¼ cup	butter	50 mL
1	bunch green onions, white parts only, finely chopped	1
1	clove garlic, minced	1
1 cup	dry white wine	250 mL
1 lb	medium shrimp, peeled and deveined	500 g
1 tbsp	chopped fresh dill	15 mL
1 cup	whipping (35%) cream	250 mL
	Salt and freshly ground black pepper to taste	
	Hot pasta (see "About these recipes," page 225)	

Sprinkle cucumber with salt and let stand for 10 minutes. Place cucumber in a kitchen towel and squeeze out as much water as possible. Rinse thoroughly, drain and set aside. In a large, deep skillet, melt butter over medium heat. Sauté green onions and garlic until tender. Add wine, increase heat to medium-high and boil until liquid is reduced by two-thirds. Add shrimp and dill; cook, stirring, until shrimp are pink and opaque. Add cream and cook until slightly thickened, about 1 minute. Stir in cucumber, salt and pepper. Toss with pasta. **Serves 4.**

Smoked Salmon, Cucumber and Dill Sauce

Follow preceding recipe, but omit the shrimp, use light or table (18%) cream, add dill with the cream, and add 4 oz (125 g) smoked salmon, julienned, with the cucumber. **Serves 4.**

Smoked Salmon, Caviar and Cream Sauce

¼ cup	butter	50 mL
2	shallots, minced	2
1 cup	dry white wine	250 mL
1 cup	cream (any type, minimum 10%)	250 mL
1 tbsp	chopped fresh dill	15 mL
4 oz	smoked salmon, julienned	125 g
2 tbsp	salmon caviar	25 mL
2 tbsp	chopped fresh Italian (flat-leaf) parsley	25 mL
	Salt and freshly ground black pepper to taste	
	Hot pasta (see "About these recipes," page 225)	
	Additional salmon caviar (optional)	

In a large skillet, melt butter over medium heat. Sauté shallots until barely tender. Add wine, increase heat to medium-high and boil until reduced by two-thirds. Add cream and dill; cook until slightly thickened. Add smoked salmon and caviar. Remove from heat and stir in parsley, salt and pepper. Toss with pasta. Garnish with additional caviar, if desired. **Serves 4.**

Sauce Tonnato

3 tbsp	extra-virgin olive oil	45 mL
1	clove garlic, minced	1
2	cans (each 6 oz/170 g) oil-packed tuna, crumbled, with oil	2
2 cups	tomato pasta sauce	500 mL
3 tbsp	freshly squeezed lemon juice	45 mL
	Salt and freshly ground black pepper to taste	
	Hot pasta (see "About these recipes," page 225)	

In a large skillet, heat oil over medium heat. Sauté garlic until aromatic. Stir in tuna, with oil, pasta sauce, lemon juice, salt and pepper. Toss with pasta. Serves 4.

Sun-Dried Tomato and Tuna Sauce

7	oil-packed sun-dried tomatoes, drained and chopped	7
2	green onions, sliced	2
2	cloves garlic, minced	2
1	can (6 oz/170 g) oil-packed tuna, crumbled, with oil	1
2 tbsp	extra-virgin olive oil	25 mL
2 tsp	freshly squeezed lemon juice	10 mL
	Salt and freshly ground black pepper to taste	
	Hot pasta (see "About these recipes," page 225)	

Combine sun-dried tomatoes, green onions, garlic, tuna, tuna oil, olive oil, lemon juice, salt and pepper. Toss with pasta. Serves 4.

White Bean, Tuna and Olive Oil Sauce

1/4 cup	extra-virgin olive oil	50 mL
1 tbsp	crumbled fresh rosemary	15 mL
1	large shallot, minced	1
1	clove garlic, minced	1
1	can (6 oz/170 g) oil-packed tuna, crumbled, with oil	1
1 cup	canned cannellini or white kidney beans, drained and rinsed	250 mL
2 tbsp	chopped fresh Italian (flat-leaf) parsley	25 mL
	Salt and freshly ground black pepper to taste	
	Hot pasta (see "About these recipes," page 225)	

In a large, deep skillet, heat oil over medium heat. Warm rosemary for 10 seconds. Add shallot and garlic; sauté until aromatic. Add tuna, with oil, and sauté for 1 minute. Add beans, parsley, salt and pepper; heat through. Toss with pasta. Serves 4.

Tapenade Sauce

2	drained canned anchovies	2
1	clove garlic, halved	1
1/3 cup	chopped pitted oil-cured black olives	75 mL
1/3 cup	extra-virgin olive oil	75 mL
	Freshly ground black pepper to taste	
	Hot pasta (see "About these recipes," page 225)	

In a food processor, finely chop anchovies, garlic and olives. With the motor running, slowly add oil through the feed tube and process until blended. Season with pepper. Toss with pasta. Serves 4.

Pepper and Anchovy Sauce

16	drained canned anchovies, slivered	16
4	roasted red bell peppers (see page 11), cut into strips	4
1	clove garlic, minced	1
1/4 cup	extra-virgin olive oil	50 mL
2 tbsp	drained small (nonpareil) capers	25 mL
Pinch	dried oregano	Pinch
	Salt and freshly ground black pepper to taste	
	Hot pasta (see "About these recipes," page 225)	

Combine anchovies, roasted peppers, garlic, oil, capers, oregano, salt and pepper; let stand for 10 minutes. Toss with pasta. Serves 4.

Chapter 21
Casseroles
Comfort Food at Its Best

Real Macaroni and Cheese 236
Real Mac and Cheese
for the Whole Family 236
Extra-Cheesy Extra-Crusty
Mac and Cheese 236
Traditional Tuna Noodle Casserole 237
Souper Tuna Noodle Casserole 237
Tuna Tortellini Casserole 237
Tuna, Fontina and Ham Casserole 237
Real Tuna Noodle Casserole 237
Tuna Noodle Casserole Duxelles 237
Tuna Casserole with
Just a Few Noodles 237
Tuna, Orzo and Feta Casserole 238
Spanakopita Casserole 238
Tuna Penne Primavera 238
Curried Tuna and Lentils 238
Baked Shells Stuffed with
Tuna and Cheese 239
Shrimp-Stuffed Shells Alfredo 239
Tuna and Shrimp Casserole with Herbed
Cheese 239
Paella Casserole 239
Salmon Casserole 240
Herbed Salmon Casserole 240
Salmon Casserole Studded
with Shrimp and Herbs 240
Crab Cake Casserole 240
Clam, Ham and Orzo Pie 241
Quick Cassoulet 241
Seafood Cassoulet 241
Gorgonzola and Prosciutto au Gratin . . 241

Pork, Apple and Sweet Potato
Shepherd's Pie 242
Chicken and Garlic Mash Shepherd's Pie . . 242
Chicken Baked with Black Beans
and Lime 242
Oven-Braised Chicken with Apples
and Red Cabbage 243
Chicken Braised with Sauerkraut
and Sausage 243
Chicken Couscous 243
Chicken and Leek Pot Pie
with Herb Biscuit Crust 243
Chicken and Fennel Pot Pie 244
Chicken Curry Baked with Lentils 244
Indian Lamb and Rice 244
Layered Veal, Turkey
and Prosciutto Loaf 244
Creamy Wild Mushroom Casserole 244
Wild Mushroom Risotto Casserole 245
Cheesy Greens Casserole 245
Baked Rabe Romano 245
Rabe Baked with Potatoes
and Feta Cheese 245
Baked Eggplant Moussaka 246
Tomato and Feta au Gratin 246
Baked Pasta e Fagioli 246
Roasted Pepper and Brown Rice
Casserole 246
Tuna and Rice Casserole 247
Southwest Bread Pudding 247
Mexican Torta 247
Provençal Ricotta Bread Pudding 247

In 2004, the competition to choose a design for the flip side of the Minnesota state quarter was in full swing. The following entry, author unknown, did not win:

> Several years ago when a tornado ripped through south-central Minnesota, even before officials could name an official disaster relief center, sixteen Minnesota women showed up spontaneously with tuna fish casseroles that they wanted to donate to the relief effort. It was their way of pulling together at a critical time. I think that incident represents the essence of what is good about Minnesota, which is why I think the state quarter should carry the image of a tuna fish casserole. The ubiquitous hot dish stands for our lack of pretension, our desire to share love through food, and our eagerness to pull together as a community through challenging moments.

Like hearty soups and chunky stews, casseroles feed a hungry hoard in a hurry. They make it as easy to cook for a party of 20 as for a family of 4, and by delivering protein, vegetable, starch and sauce in a single vessel, they make the very idea of side dishes obsolete.

There are countless casserole recipes, but they all take one of three forms:

• Creamy casseroles, epitomized by tuna noodle casserole, are built from a cooked protein (such as canned tuna), a thick sauce and cooked small pasta, typically macaroni. They were originally seen as a money-saving way to spruce up leftovers. But after the Second World War, when Campbell's Soup Co. started to promote its condensed creamy soups as sauces, creamy casseroles were transformed into easy, everyday main dishes.

• Sauceless casseroles are an older form. In these casseroles, meat and vegetables are cooked in a flavorful broth in a casserole dish. The form is defined more by the baking vessel than by what goes in it.

• Layered casseroles, devised as a way to assemble a meat pie without making a crust, are the oldest. The starch — usually rice or potatoes — is packed on the top or bottom of the casserole, surrounding a stewy filling. Shepherd's pie is the iconic layered casserole.

We've put together recipes for 50 casseroles — tuna and otherwise — to give you a wide selection of side dishes and one-dish entrées.

About these recipes . . .

Casseroles may be baked ahead and reheated, and, so long as they contain some liquid, can be frozen without ill effect. Cover them tightly, and you can refrigerate them for about 4 days or freeze them for up to 2 months. Almost any casserole can be assembled ahead of time and refrigerated before baking. If the elements of the casserole you are making are very hot, you might want to chill them before assembling. For safety's sake, it is important that a refrigerated casserole reach refrigerator temperature within 2 hours.

Allow refrigerated casseroles to sit at room temperature for 30 minutes before baking, and add 20 to 30 minutes to the baking time. Allow frozen casseroles to thaw first.

Real Macaroni and Cheese

1	egg	1
3 cups	shredded sharp Cheddar cheese, divided	750 mL
1/3 cup	milk	75 mL
1/2 tsp	brown mustard	2 mL
	Salt and freshly ground black pepper to taste	
8 oz	macaroni, cooked	250 g

Preheat oven to 350°F (180°C). In a 6- to 8-cup (1.5 to 2 L) casserole dish, combine egg, two-thirds of the cheese, milk, mustard, salt and pepper. Add macaroni and toss to coat. Bake for 20 minutes. Stir in the remaining cheese and bake for 10 minutes. **Serves 4 to 6.**

Real Mac and Cheese for the Whole Family

Follow preceding recipe, but substitute American cheese for the Cheddar. **Serves 4 to 6.**

Extra-Cheesy Extra-Crusty Mac and Cheese

Follow recipe for Real Macaroni and Cheese (above), but increase the Cheddar cheese to 4 cups (1 L). Combine 1/4 cup (50 mL) freshly grated Parmesan and 1/4 cup (50 mL) seasoned dry bread crumbs; scatter over top after stirring in the second batch of Cheddar. **Serves 4 to 6.**

Traditional Tuna Noodle Casserole

2 tbsp	butter, divided	25 mL
1½ cups	hot Béchamel Sauce (page 17)	375 mL
1½ cups	shredded sharp Cheddar cheese	375 mL
1 tsp	spicy brown mustard	5 mL
2	cans (6 oz/170 g each) water-packed tuna, drained and crumbled	2
8 oz	medium-wide egg noodles, cooked, hot	250 g
	Salt and freshly ground black pepper to taste	
¼ cup	freshly grated Parmesan cheese	50 mL
2 tbsp	dry bread crumbs	25 mL

Preheat oven to 400°F (200°C) and grease an 8- to 10-cup (2 to 2.5 L) casserole dish with half the butter. Combine Béchamel Sauce, Cheddar and mustard, stirring until cheese is partially melted. Stir in tuna, noodles, salt and pepper. Pack into prepared casserole and smooth top. Sprinkle with Parmesan and bread crumbs, and dot with the remaining butter. Bake for 20 minutes, until browned and bubbling. **Serves 6 to 8.**

Souper Tuna Noodle Casserole

Follow preceding recipe, but omit the Béchamel Sauce, add 1 can (10 oz/284 mL) condensed cream of mushroom soup, undiluted, and ½ cup (125 mL) milk with the Cheddar, and increase baking time by 10 minutes. **Serves 6 to 8.**

Tuna Tortellini Casserole

Follow recipe for Traditional Tuna Noodle Casserole (above) but substitute provolone cheese for the Cheddar, replace the mustard with finely chopped drained canned anchovies, omit the noodles, and add 1 lb (500 g) cheese tortellini with the tuna. **Serves 6 to 8.**

Tuna, Fontina and Ham Casserole

Follow recipe for Traditional Tuna Noodle Casserole (above), but substitute fontina cheese for the Cheddar, and add ½ cup (125 mL) diced ham with the tuna. **Serves 6 to 8.**

Real Tuna Noodle Casserole

Follow recipe for Traditional Tuna Noodle Casserole (above), but replace the canned tuna with 12 oz (375 g) tuna steaks, grilled and chopped into small pieces. **Serves 6 to 8.**

Tuna Noodle Casserole Duxelles

3 tbsp	butter, divided	45 mL
2 cups	minced mushrooms	500 mL
1	clove garlic, minced	1
1	can (10 oz/284 mL) condensed cream of mushroom soup, undiluted	1
1½ cups	shredded sharp Cheddar cheese	375 mL
1 tsp	spicy brown mustard	5 mL
2	cans (each 6 oz/170 mL) water-packed tuna, drained and crumbled	2
8 oz	medium-wide egg noodles, cooked, hot	250 g
	Salt and freshly ground black pepper to taste	
¼ cup	freshly grated Parmesan cheese	50 mL
2 tbsp	dry bread crumbs	25 mL

Preheat oven to 400°F (200°C) and grease a 12-cup (3 L) casserole dish with 1 tbsp (15 mL) of the butter. In a saucepan, heat 1 tbsp (15 mL) of the butter over medium heat. Sauté mushrooms and garlic until mushrooms are tender. Add soup and heat through. Remove from heat and stir in Cheddar and mustard until cheese is melted. Stir in tuna, noodles, salt and pepper. Pack into prepared casserole and smooth top. Sprinkle with Parmesan and bread crumbs, and dot with the remaining butter. Bake for 20 minutes, until browned and bubbling. **Serves 6 to 8.**

Tuna Casserole with Just a Few Noodles

1 tbsp	butter	15 mL
3	cans (each 6 oz/170 g) water-packed tuna, drained and crumbled	3
2	stalks celery, diced	2
1	extra-large egg, beaten	1
1 cup	cooked macaroni	250 mL
¾ cup	mayonnaise	175 mL
2 tbsp	chopped fresh Italian (flat-leaf) parsley	25 mL
1½ tbsp	freshly squeezed lemon juice	22 mL
1 tbsp	soy sauce	15 mL
2 tsp	Dijon mustard	10 mL
½ tsp	hot pepper sauce	2 mL

Preheat oven to 350°F (180°C) and grease a 6-cup (1.5 L) casserole dish with butter. Combine the remaining ingredients, then pack into prepared casserole and smooth top. Bake for 45 minutes, until bubbling. **Serves 4 to 6.**

Tuna, Orzo and Feta Casserole

2 tbsp	butter, divided	25 mL
1	clove garlic, minced	1
6 oz	feta cheese, crumbled	175 g
1½ cups	hot Béchamel Sauce (page 17) or one 10-oz (284 mL) can condensed cream of mushroom soup	375 mL
2 tbsp	chopped pitted black olives	25 mL
1 tsp	dried dillweed	5 mL
2	cans (each 6 oz/170 g) oil-packed tuna, drained and crumbled	2
8 oz	orzo, cooked, hot	250 g
	Salt and freshly ground black pepper to taste	
¼ cup	freshly grated Parmesan cheese	50 mL
2 tbsp	dry bread crumbs	25 mL

Preheat oven to 400°F (200°C) and grease an 8-cup (2 L) casserole dish with half the butter. Combine garlic, feta, Béchamel Sauce, olives and dill, stirring until cheese is partially melted. Stir in tuna, orzo, salt and pepper. Pack into prepared casserole and smooth top. Sprinkle with Parmesan and bread crumbs, and dot with the remaining butter. Bake for 20 minutes, until browned and bubbling. **Serves 4 to 6.**

Spanakopita Casserole

Follow preceding recipe, but replace the tuna with 10 oz (300 g) frozen chopped spinach, thawed and squeezed dry. **Serves 4 to 6.**

Tuna Penne Primavera

2 tbsp	olive oil	25 mL
⅓ cup	chopped onion	75 mL
1	clove garlic, minced	1
1½ cups	diced vegetables (such as zucchini, yellow squash, mushrooms, bell peppers, carrots, celery)	375 mL
½ cup	chopped seeded peeled tomato	125 mL
¼ cup	frozen peas	50 mL
¼ cup	small broccoli florets	50 mL
2	cans (each 6 oz/170 g) tuna, drained and crumbled	2
12 oz	penne pasta, cooked, hot	375 g
1 cup	cream (any type, minimum 10%)	250 mL
6 tbsp	freshly grated Parmesan cheese, divided	90 mL
	Salt and freshly ground black pepper to taste	

Preheat oven to 375°F (190°C). In a large, deep skillet, heat oil over medium-high heat. Sauté onion until tender. Add garlic, diced vegetables, tomato, peas and broccoli; sauté for 1 minute. Stir in tuna, penne, cream, ¼ cup (50 mL) of the Parmesan, salt and pepper. Pack into a 12-cup (3 L) casserole dish and smooth top. Sprinkle with the remaining Parmesan. Bake for 30 minutes, until browned and bubbling. **Serves 4 to 6.**

Curried Tuna and Lentils

¼ cup	olive oil, divided	50 mL
1	onion, chopped	1
4	cloves garlic, minced	4
1 tbsp	curry powder	15 mL
1 tsp	ground coriander	5 mL
1 tsp	ground cumin	5 mL
1 tsp	ground ginger	5 mL
1 tsp	dry mustard	5 mL
½ cup	drained canned diced tomatoes	125 mL
2 tbsp	chopped fresh Italian (flat-leaf) parsley	25 mL
2 tsp	chopped fresh dill	10 mL
4 cups	cooked or canned lentils	1 L
1 cup	plain yogurt (not non-fat)	250 mL
	Salt and freshly ground black pepper to taste	
1 lb	tuna steaks	500 g

Preheat broiler or grill to high, and preheat oven to 350°F (180°C). In a skillet, heat half the oil over medium heat. Sauté onion until tender. Add garlic, curry powder, coriander, cumin, ginger, and mustard; sauté until aromatic. Add tomatoes, parsley and dill; heat through. Stir in lentils, yogurt, salt and pepper; set aside. Season tuna with additional salt and pepper, and coat with 1 tbsp (15 mL) of the remaining oil. Broil or grill until browned on both sides but not cooked through; cut into bite-size chunks. Pack lentil mixture into an 8-cup (2 L) casserole alternately with tuna, making 3 layers of lentils and 2 of tuna. Smooth top and drizzle with the remaining oil. Bake for 1 hour, until browned and bubbling. **Serves 4 to 6.**

Baked Shells Stuffed with Tuna and Cheese

1 tbsp	butter	15 mL
2	cans (each 6 oz/170 g) water-packed tuna, drained and crumbled	2
1	clove garlic, minced	1
1 cup	hot Béchamel Sauce (page 17) or one 10-oz (284 mL) can condensed cream of mushroom soup	250 mL
2 cups	shredded mozzarella cheese, divided	500 mL
3 tbsp	freshly grated Parmesan cheese Salt and freshly ground black pepper to taste	45 mL
12	jumbo shell-shaped pasta, cooked	12
2 cups	tomato pasta sauce	500 mL

Preheat oven to 375°F (190°C) and grease a 13- by 9-inch (3 L) baking dish with butter. Combine tuna, garlic, Béchamel Sauce, half the mozzarella, Parmesan, salt and pepper. Fill pasta shells with this mixture and pack into prepared casserole, stuffed sides up. Pour tomato sauce over top, and sprinkle with the remaining mozzarella. Bake for 30 to 40 minutes, or until bubbling. **Serves 4 to 6.**

Shrimp-Stuffed Shells Alfredo

Follow preceding recipe, but substitute 1 lb (500 g) shrimp, peeled, deveined, cooked and finely chopped, for the tuna, and replace the pasta sauce with prepared Alfredo sauce. **Serves 4 to 6.**

Tuna and Shrimp Casserole with Herbed Cheese

2 tbsp	olive oil	25 mL
1/4 cup	finely chopped onion	50 mL
1	clove garlic, minced	1
2 tbsp	all-purpose flour	25 mL
1 1/2 cups	milk	375 mL
8 oz	small shrimp, peeled and deveined	250 g
8 oz	herbed cream cheese, softened	250 g
1	can (6 oz/170 g) oil-packed tuna, crumbled, with oil	1
8 oz	macaroni, cooked, hot	250 g
Pinch	cayenne pepper Salt and freshly ground black pepper to taste	Pinch
1/4 cup	freshly grated Parmesan cheese	50 mL
2 tbsp	Italian seasoned dry bread crumbs	25 mL
1 tbsp	butter	15 mL

Preheat oven to 400°F (200°C). In a large nonstick skillet, heat oil over medium-high heat. Sauté onion until tender. Add garlic and flour; sauté until aromatic. Whisk in milk until slightly thickened; reduce heat and simmer for 5 minutes. Add shrimp and simmer for 1 minute. Remove from heat and stir in cream cheese until melted. Stir in tuna, macaroni, cayenne, salt and black pepper. Pack into an 8-cup (2 L) casserole dish and smooth top. Sprinkle with Parmesan and bread crumbs, and dot with butter. Bake for 25 minutes, until browned and bubbling. **Serves 4 to 6.**

Paella Casserole

3 tbsp	extra-virgin olive oil, divided	45 mL
1/4 cup	finely chopped onion	50 mL
1/4 cup	finely chopped celery	50 mL
3	cloves garlic, minced	3
2	roasted bell peppers (see page 11), diced	2
2 tbsp	all-purpose flour	25 mL
1 1/2 cups	chicken broth	375 mL
8 oz	small shrimp, peeled and deveined	250 g
1	can (6 oz/170 g) oil-packed tuna, crumbled, with oil	1
3 cups	cooked white rice	750 mL
1/4 cup	chopped fresh Italian (flat-leaf) parsley	50 mL
Pinch	cayenne pepper Salt and freshly ground black pepper to taste	Pinch
1/4 cup	seasoned dry bread crumbs	50 mL

Preheat oven to 400°F (200°C). In a large nonstick saucepan, heat 2 tbsp (25 mL) of the oil over medium-high heat. Sauté onion and celery until tender. Add garlic and roasted pepper; sauté until aromatic. Add flour and sauté for 1 minute. Whisk in broth until slightly thickened; reduce heat and simmer for 5 minutes. Add shrimp and simmer for 1 minute. Stir in tuna, rice, parsley, cayenne, salt and black pepper. Pack into an 8-cup (2 L) casserole dish and smooth top. Sprinkle with bread crumbs and drizzle with the remaining olive oil. Bake for 25 minutes, until browned and bubbling. **Serves 4 to 6.**

Salmon Casserole

2	cans (each 6 oz/170 g) pink salmon, drained and crumbled	2
1	green onion, finely sliced	1
1	egg	1
¾ cup	Béchamel Sauce (page 17)	175 mL
2 tbsp	chopped fresh Italian (flat-leaf) parsley	25 mL
2 tbsp	mayonnaise	25 mL
1 tbsp	freshly squeezed lemon juice	15 mL
1 tsp	Worcestershire sauce	5 mL
Dash	hot pepper sauce (such as Tabasco)	Dash
8 oz	macaroni or other small pasta, cooked	250 g
2 cups	tomato pasta sauce	500 mL
¼ cup	seasoned dry bread crumbs	50 mL
2 tbsp	freshly grated Parmesan cheese	25 mL

Preheat oven to 350°F (180°C). Combine salmon, green onion, egg, Béchamel Sauce, parsley, mayonnaise, lemon juice, Worcestershire sauce and hot pepper sauce. In a separate bowl, combine macaroni and pasta sauce. Pack macaroni mixture into a 10-cup (2.5 L) casserole dish alternately with salmon mixture, making 3 layers of macaroni and 2 of salmon. Smooth top and sprinkle with bread crumbs and Parmesan cheese. Bake for 45 minutes, until browned and bubbling. **Serves 4 to 6.**

Herbed Salmon Casserole

2 tbsp	butter, divided	25 mL
1	clove garlic, minced	1
6 oz	herbed cream cheese, cubed	175 g
1½ cups	hot Béchamel Sauce (page 17) or one 10-oz (284 mL) can condensed cream of mushroom soup	375 mL
1 tsp	dried dillweed	5 mL
2	cans (each 6 oz/170 g) pink salmon, drained and crumbled	2
8 oz	small shell-shaped pasta, cooked, hot	250 g
	Salt and freshly ground black pepper to taste	
¼ cup	freshly grated Parmesan cheese	50 mL
2 tbsp	seasoned dry bread crumbs	25 mL

Preheat oven to 400°F (200°C) and grease a 10-cup (2.5 L) casserole dish with half the butter. Combine garlic, cream cheese, Béchamel Sauce and dill until cheese is melted. Stir in salmon, pasta, salt and pepper. Pack into prepared casserole and smooth top. Sprinkle with Parmesan and bread crumbs, and dot with the remaining butter. Bake for 20 minutes, until browned and bubbling. **Serves 4 to 6.**

Salmon Casserole Studded with Shrimp and Herbs

1 tbsp	butter	15 mL
3	cans (each 6 oz/170 g) salmon, drained and crumbled	3
2	stalks celery, diced	2
1	extra-large egg, beaten	1
4 oz	shrimp, peeled, deveined and chopped	125 g
1⅔ cups	fresh bread crumbs	400 mL
¾ cup	mayonnaise	175 mL
1½ tbsp	freshly squeezed lemon juice	22 mL
1 tbsp	chopped fresh Italian (flat-leaf) parsley	15 mL
1 tbsp	soy sauce	15 mL
2 tsp	chopped fresh tarragon	10 mL
2 tsp	chopped fresh dill	10 mL
2 tsp	Dijon mustard	10 mL
½ tsp	hot pepper sauce (such as Tabasco)	2 mL

Preheat oven to 350°F (180°C) and grease a 4-cup (1 L) casserole dish with butter. Combine the remaining ingredients, then pack into prepared casserole and smooth top. Bake for 45 minutes, until bubbling. **Serves 4 to 6.**

Crab Cake Casserole

1 tbsp	butter	15 mL
1	bell pepper (any color), diced	1
1	egg, beaten	1
1 lb	backfin (lump) crabmeat, shells picked out	500 g
2 cups	cooked orzo (or other miniature pasta)	500 mL
½ cup	mayonnaise	125 mL
1 tbsp	chopped fresh Italian (flat-leaf) parsley	15 mL
1 tbsp	chopped fresh dill	15 mL
1 tbsp	freshly squeezed lemon juice	15 mL
2 tsp	paprika	10 mL
1 tsp	dry mustard	5 mL
2 tsp	Worcestershire sauce	10 mL
1 tsp	hot pepper sauce (such as Tabasco)	5 mL

Preheat oven to 350°F (180°C) and grease a 4-cup (1 L) casserole dish with butter. Combine the remaining ingredients, then pack into prepared casserole and smooth top. Bake for 45 minutes, until bubbling. **Serves 4 to 6.**

Clam, Ham and Orzo Pie

1 cup	orzo, cooked, hot	250 mL
¼ cup	freshly grated Parmesan cheese	50 mL
	Salt and freshly ground black pepper to taste	
2 tbsp	olive oil, divided	25 mL
1	onion, chopped	1
1	clove garlic, minced	1
4 oz	ham, diced	125 g
½ tsp	dried thyme, crumbled	2 mL
Pinch	hot pepper flakes	Pinch
3	cans (each 10 oz/284 mL) minced clams, drained	3

Preheat oven to 375°F (190°C). Toss together orzo, Parmesan, salt and pepper; set aside. In a large saucepan, heat half the oil over medium heat. Sauté onion until tender. Add garlic, ham, thyme and hot pepper flakes; sauté for 1 minute. Add clams and additional salt and pepper; bring to a simmer. Pour into an 8-cup (2 L) casserole dish and spoon orzo mixture on top in an even layer. Drizzle with the remaining oil. Bake for 30 minutes, until bubbling. **Serves 4 to 6.**

Quick Cassoulet

4	slices bacon, coarsely chopped	4
1 lb	smoked sausage (such as kielbasa), sliced	500 g
1 cup	chopped onion	250 mL
4	cloves garlic, minced	4
1 tbsp	ground coriander	15 mL
1 tsp	ground cumin	5 mL
1 tsp	ground ginger	5 mL
1 tsp	dry mustard	5 mL
Pinch	ground cloves	Pinch
½ cup	dry white wine	125 mL
2	cans (each 14 to 19 oz/ 398 to 540 mL) Great Northern beans, drained and rinsed	2
2 tbsp	chopped fresh Italian (flat-leaf) parsley	25 mL
2 tsp	chopped fresh dill	10 mL
	Salt and freshly ground black pepper to taste	
½ cup	seasoned dry bread crumbs	125 mL

Preheat oven to 350°F (180°C). In a skillet, over medium heat, sauté bacon until crisp. Add sausage and onion; sauté until onion is tender and sausage is lightly browned. Add garlic, coriander, cumin, ginger, mustard and cloves; sauté until aromatic. Add wine, increase heat to high and boil until wine has evaporated. Stir in beans, parsley, dill, salt and pepper. Pack into a 10-cup (2.5 L) casserole dish and smooth top. Sprinkle with bread crumbs. Bake for 1 hour, until browned and bubbling. **Serves 4 to 6.**

Seafood Cassoulet

Follow preceding recipe, but reduce the sausage to 8 oz (250 g), and add either 2 cans (each 6 oz/170 g) oil-packed tuna, drained and crumbled, or 1 lb (500 g) shrimp, peeled, deveined, cooked and chopped, with the beans. **Serves 4 to 6.**

Gorgonzola and Prosciutto au Gratin

2 tbsp	butter, divided	25 mL
1	clove garlic, minced	1
6 oz	Gorgonzola cheese, crumbled	175 g
1½ cups	hot Béchamel Sauce (page 17) or one 10-oz (284 mL) can condensed cream of mushroom soup	375 mL
8 oz	penne pasta, cooked, hot	250 g
6 oz	imported prosciutto, finely chopped	175 g
	Salt and freshly ground black pepper to taste	
¼ cup	grated Romano cheese	50 mL
2 tbsp	dry bread crumbs	25 mL

Preheat oven to 400°F (200°C) and grease an 8-cup (2 L) casserole dish with half the butter. Combine garlic, Gorgonzola and Béchamel Sauce, stirring until cheese is partially melted. Stir in penne, prosciutto, salt and pepper. Pack into prepared casserole and smooth top. Sprinkle with Romano and bread crumbs, and dot with the remaining butter. Bake for 20 minutes, until browned and bubbling. **Serves 4 to 6.**

Pork, Apple and Sweet Potato Shepherd's Pie

4	large sweet potatoes, peeled and cut into chunks	4
1 cup	unsweetened applesauce	250 mL
2 tbsp	honey	25 mL
2 tbsp	butter	25 mL
	Salt and freshly ground black pepper to taste	
1½ lbs	boneless pork loin, cut into bite-size pieces	750 g
2 tbsp	vegetable oil	25 mL
2	stalks celery, sliced	2
1	onion, chopped	1
1	Granny Smith apple, peeled and cubed	1
½ cup	unsweetened apple juice	125 mL
½ cup	chicken broth	125 mL
2 tsp	chopped fresh thyme	10 mL
1 tsp	chopped fresh sage	5 mL

In a large pot of boiling lightly salted water, cook sweet potatoes until tender, about 15 minutes; drain. Return to pot and mash with applesauce, honey, butter, salt and pepper; set aside. Meanwhile, preheat oven to 400°F (200°C). Season pork with additional salt and pepper. In a large, deep skillet, heat oil over medium-high heat. Cook pork, in batches, until browned on all sides; remove to a plate. Add celery and onion to the fat in the pan and sauté until lightly browned. Return pork to the pan with apple, apple juice, broth, thyme, sage and additional salt and pepper; reduce heat and simmer for 5 to 8 minutes, or until liquid has reduced by about two-thirds. Transfer to a 12-cup (3 L) casserole dish, top with sweet potato mixture and smooth top. Bake for about 30 minutes, until browned on top. **Serves 6 to 8.**

Chicken and Garlic Mash Shepherd's Pie

4	large golden or red-skinned (boiling) potatoes, peeled and cut into chunks	4
5	cloves garlic, minced, divided	5
⅓ cup	sour cream	75 mL
2 tbsp	butter	25 mL
	Salt and freshly ground black pepper to taste	
1 tbsp	vegetable oil	15 mL
1	onion, chopped	1
1	stalk celery, diced	1
2 lbs	boneless skinless chicken thighs, cut into bite-size pieces	1 kg

2 tbsp	all-purpose flour	25 mL
2 cups	chicken broth	500 mL
½ cup	dry white wine	125 mL
2 tbsp	chopped fresh dill	25 mL
¼ tsp	dried sage	1 mL

In a large pot of boiling lightly salted water, cook potatoes until tender, about 15 minutes; drain. Return to pot and mash with three-quarters of the garlic, sour cream, butter, salt and pepper; set aside. Meanwhile, preheat oven to 400°F (200°C). In a large, deep skillet, heat oil over medium-high heat. Sauté onion and celery until tender. Add chicken and sauté until it turns white. Add flour and sauté until flour browns lightly. Stir in broth, wine, dill, sage and the remaining garlic; cook, stirring, until sauce is smooth and slightly thickened. Transfer to a 10-cup (2.5 L) casserole dish, top with potato mixture and smooth top. Bake for about 30 minutes, until browned on top. **Serves 6.**

Chicken Baked with Black Beans and Lime

1½ lbs	boneless skinless chicken thighs, cut into bite-size pieces	750 g
	Salt and freshly ground black pepper to taste	
2 tbsp	olive oil	25 mL
2	carrots, finely diced	2
1	onion, finely chopped	1
2	cloves garlic, minced	2
2 oz	chorizo or other spicy sausage, finely chopped	60 g
3 cups	drained rinsed canned black beans	750 mL
1 cup	chicken broth	250 mL
¼ cup	chopped fresh cilantro	50 mL
	Finely grated zest and juice of 4 limes	
2 cups	shredded Monterey Jack cheese	500 mL

Preheat oven to 375°F (190°C). Season chicken with salt and pepper. In a large skillet, heat oil over medium-high heat. Sauté carrots and onion until almost tender. Add chicken and sauté until browned on all sides. Stir in garlic, chorizo, beans and broth; bring to a boil. Stir in cilantro, lime zest and lime juice. Pack half the chicken mixture into a 10-cup (2.5 L) casserole dish and sprinkle with half the cheese. Repeat layers. Bake for 45 minutes, until bubbling. **Serves 4 to 6.**

Oven-Braised Chicken with Apples and Red Cabbage

2 lbs	boneless skinless chicken thighs, cut into bite-size pieces	1 kg
	Salt and freshly ground black pepper to taste	
3	slices bacon, coarsely chopped	3
½ cup	chopped onion	125 mL
2	large tart apples, peeled and diced	2
4 cups	tightly packed shredded red cabbage	1 L
1 tsp	chopped fresh rosemary	5 mL
½ tsp	dried thyme	2 mL
½ tsp	dried sage	2 mL
1 cup	coarsely crushed canned fried onions (such as Durkee)	250 mL

Preheat oven to 350°F (180°C). Season chicken with salt and pepper. In a large, deep skillet, over medium heat, cook bacon until the bottom of the pan is coated with fat but bacon is not yet crisp. Add onion and sauté until translucent. Add chicken and sauté until browned on all sides. Stir in apples, cabbage, rosemary, thyme and sage; sauté until cabbage wilts. Pack into a 10-cup (2.5 L) casserole dish and top with fried onions. Bake for 45 minutes, until browned and bubbling. **Serves 4 to 6.**

Chicken Braised with Sauerkraut and Sausage

Follow preceding recipe, but replace the bacon with 8 oz (250 g) mild Italian sausage, finely chopped, use only 1 apple, omit the cabbage, and add 1 lb (500 g) sauerkraut with the apple. **Serves 4 to 6.**

Chicken Couscous

2 lbs	boneless skinless chicken thighs, cut into bite-size pieces	1 kg
	Salt and freshly ground black pepper to taste	
2 tbsp	olive oil	25 mL
3	stalks celery, thickly sliced	3
2	carrots, thickly sliced	2
1	large onion, coarsely chopped	1
3	cloves garlic, minced	3
1 tbsp	ground coriander	15 mL
2 tsp	ground cumin	10 mL
1 tsp	ground turmeric	5 mL
½ tsp	ground cinnamon	2 mL
Pinch	hot pepper flakes	Pinch
1	large sweet potato, peeled and cut into bite-size chunks	1
4 cups	chicken broth	1 L
2	zucchini, thickly sliced	2
2 cups	couscous	500 mL
¼ cup	chopped fresh cilantro	50 mL

Preheat oven to 350°F (180°C). Season chicken with salt and black pepper. In a large, deep skillet, heat oil over medium-high heat. Sauté celery, carrots and onion until tender. Add chicken and sauté until browned on all sides. Stir in garlic, coriander, cumin, turmeric, cinnamon and hot pepper flakes; sauté until aromatic. Add sweet potato and broth; reduce heat, cover and simmer for 10 minutes. Remove from heat and stir in zucchini, couscous, cilantro and additional salt and black pepper. Transfer to a 10-cup (2.5 L) casserole dish, cover and bake for 45 minutes, until heated through. **Serves 4 to 6.**

Chicken and Leek Pot Pie with Herb Biscuit Crust

4	slices bacon	4
2 lbs	boneless skinless chicken thighs, cut into bite-size pieces	1 kg
¼ cup	all-purpose flour, seasoned with salt and pepper	50 mL
3	leeks, white part only, sliced	3
1	onion, sliced	1
1	stalk celery, sliced	1
1	clove garlic, minced	1
4 oz	mushrooms, sliced	125 g
½ cup	dry white wine	125 mL
½ cup	chicken broth	125 mL
1 tbsp	soy sauce	15 mL
1 tsp	dried rosemary, crumbled	5 mL
	Finely grated zest and juice of ½ lemon	
½	recipe Herb Biscuit dough (page 431), completed just to the point where the dough is mixed	½
	Buttermilk mixture left over from biscuit dough	

In a large, deep skillet, over medium-high heat, cook bacon until crisp; using tongs, remove to a plate, blot off fat and crumble. Dredge chicken in seasoned flour. Add to the fat remaining in the pan and sauté until browned on all sides. Add leeks, onion, celery, garlic and mushrooms; sauté for 3 minutes. Add wine, broth, soy sauce, rosemary, lemon zest and lemon juice; reduce heat and simmer for 15 minutes. Meanwhile, preheat oven to 400°F (200°C). Stir in bacon. Transfer to a 10-cup (2.5 L) casserole dish and top with biscuit dough. Brush with buttermilk mixture. Bake for 20 minutes, until biscuits are golden. **Serves 6.**

Chicken and Fennel Pot Pie

Follow preceding recipe, but omit the leeks, mushrooms and rosemary, add 1 cup (250 mL) thinly sliced fennel bulb, and add 1 tsp (5 mL) each ground fennel seeds and dried thyme with the soy sauce. **Serves 6.**

Chicken Curry Baked with Lentils

2 lbs	boneless skinless chicken thighs, cut into bite-size pieces	1 kg
	Salt and freshly ground black pepper to taste	
¼ cup	vegetable oil, divided	50 mL
2 tsp	black mustard seeds	10 mL
1½ cups	finely chopped onions	375 mL
2	cloves garlic, minced	2
1 tbsp	finely chopped gingerroot	15 mL
1 cup	dried lentils	250 mL
2 tsp	ground coriander	10 mL
2 tsp	curry powder	10 mL
Pinch	hot pepper flakes	Pinch
3 cups	chicken broth	750 mL
¾ cup	plain yogurt (not non-fat)	175 mL
2 tbsp	finely chopped fresh cilantro	25 mL

Preheat oven to 375°F (190°C). Season chicken with salt and pepper. In a large, deep skillet, heat half the oil over medium-high heat. Sauté chicken until browned on all sides; using a slotted spoon, remove to a plate. Add the remaining oil to the pan. Sauté mustard seeds until they turn gray. Add onions and sauté until translucent. Add garlic and ginger; sauté for 1 minute. Stir in lentils, coriander, curry powder and hot pepper flakes. Add broth and bring to a boil. Remove from heat and stir in chicken. Transfer to a 10-cup (2.5 L) casserole dish and bake for 45 minutes, until heated through. Meanwhile, combine yogurt and cilantro; serve with the casserole. **Serves 4 to 6.**

Indian Lamb and Rice

Follow preceding recipe, but substitute boneless leg of lamb for the chicken, 1½ cups (375 mL) long-grain white rice for the lentils, and beef broth for the chicken broth. Add 1 tbsp (15 mL) tomato paste with the broth. **Serves 6.**

Layered Veal, Turkey and Prosciutto Loaf

1 tbsp	butter	15 mL
1 cup	freshly grated Parmesan cheese, plus some for dusting	250 mL
12	large or extra-large eggs	12
1½ cups	ricotta cheese	375 mL
9	slices veal leg scaloppini (about 1 lb/500g)	9
8	slices smoked turkey breast	8
8	thin slices prosciutto	8

Preheat oven to 350°F (180°C) and grease the sides of a 9- by 5-inch (2 L) loaf pan with butter. Cover the bottom of the pan with waxed paper and dust lightly with Parmesan. In a food processor, process eggs, ricotta and Parmesan until smooth. Dip veal scallops in egg mixture, then place 1 veal scallop in the bottom of the pan. Top with 1 slice of turkey, then 1 slice of prosciutto. Repeat layers until all meat is used, ending with veal. Pour any additional egg mixture over top. Cover with foil, place loaf pan in a larger pan and pour in enough hot water to reach 1½ inches (4 cm) up the sides of the loaf pan. Bake for 2 hours. Let cool for 10 minutes, then invert onto a serving platter and slice. **Serves 8 to 10.**

Creamy Wild Mushroom Casserole

3 tbsp	butter, divided	45 mL
8 oz	shiitake mushrooms, sliced	250 g
8 oz	mushrooms, sliced	250 g
½ cup	finely chopped onion	125 mL
½ tsp	dried thyme	2 mL
1	clove garlic, minced	1
8 oz	fettuccini, broken and cooked, hot	250 g
1½ cups	hot Béchamel Sauce (page 17) or one 10-oz (284 mL) can condensed cream of mushroom soup	375 mL
1 cup	sour cream	250 mL
	Salt and freshly ground black pepper to taste	
¼ cup	freshly grated Parmesan cheese	50 mL
2 tbsp	dry bread crumbs	25 mL

Preheat oven to 400°F (200°C) and grease a 10-cup (2.5 L) casserole with 1 tbsp (15 mL) of the butter. In a large skillet, heat 1 tbsp (15 mL) of the butter over medium-high heat. Sauté both types of mushrooms, onion and thyme until vegetables are tender. Add garlic and sauté until aromatic. Stir in fettuccini, Béchamel Sauce, sour cream, salt and pepper. Pack into prepared casserole and smooth top. Sprinkle with Parmesan and bread crumbs, and dot with remaining butter. Bake for 20 minutes, until browned and bubbling. **Serves 6.**

Wild Mushroom Risotto Casserole

¼ cup	butter, divided	50 mL
1 cup	chopped onion	250 mL
1 lb	wild or exotic mushrooms (such as cremini or portobello), sliced	500 g
1 lb	mushrooms, sliced	500 g
1 tsp	dried rosemary, crumbled	5 mL
1 cup	Arborio rice	250 mL
3 cups	vegetable broth, divided	750 mL
1	can (14 oz/398 mL) diced tomatoes, drained	1
2 tbsp	chopped fresh Italian (flat-leaf) parsley	25 mL
	Salt and freshly ground black pepper to taste	
¼ cup	freshly grated Parmesan cheese	50 mL

Preheat oven to 375°F (190°C). In a large, deep skillet, melt half the butter over medium-high heat. Sauté onion until softened. Add both types of mushrooms and rosemary; sauté until mushrooms start to release their liquid. Add rice and stir to coat. Add half the broth and bring to a boil. Remove from heat and stir in the remaining broth, tomatoes, parsley, salt and pepper. Transfer to a 12-cup (3 L) casserole dish, cover and bake for 45 minutes, or until most of the liquid has been absorbed. Stir in Parmesan and the remaining butter. **Serves 4 to 6.**

Cheesy Greens Casserole

2 lbs	collard greens, kale or Swiss chard, trimmed	1 kg
3 tbsp	butter	45 mL
8 oz	mushrooms, sliced	250 g
1	clove garlic, minced	1
1	extra-large egg, beaten	1
½ cup	ricotta cheese	125 mL
6 tbsp	freshly grated Parmesan cheese, divided	90 mL
2 tbsp	seasoned dry bread crumbs	25 mL

Preheat oven to 375°F (190°C). In a large pot of boiling lightly salted water, cook greens until tender, about 3 minutes; drain and shake dry. In a large skillet, melt butter over medium-high heat. Sauté mushrooms and garlic until mushrooms start to release their liquid. Remove from heat and stir in cooked greens, egg, ricotta and ¼ cup (50 mL) of the Parmesan. Pack into a 4-cup (1 L) casserole dish and smooth top. Sprinkle with bread crumbs and the remaining Parmesan. Bake for 35 minutes, until browned and bubbling. **Serves 4.**

Baked Rabe Romano

Follow preceding recipe, but substitute broccoli rabe, cut into 2-inch (5 cm) lengths, for the greens, and Pecorino Romano cheese for the Parmesan. **Serves 4.**

Rabe Baked with Potatoes and Feta Cheese

1 lb	potatoes, peeled and cut into ½-inch (1 cm) dice	500 g
2 lbs	broccoli rabe, cut into 2-inch (5 cm) lengths	1 kg
2 tbsp	extra-virgin olive oil, divided	25 mL
4	cloves garlic, minced	4
1	egg, lightly beaten	1
8 oz	feta cheese, crumbled	250 g
½ cup	sour cream	125 mL
	Salt and freshly ground black pepper to taste	

In a large pot of boiling salted water, cook potatoes until barely tender, about 10 minutes. Add rabe and cook until bright green and barely tender, about 3 minutes; drain well. In a small skillet, heat half the oil over medium heat. Sauté garlic until aromatic. Remove from heat and stir in egg, feta, sour cream, salt and pepper. Fold in rabe and potatoes until well coated. Pack into an 8-cup (2 L) casserole dish and smooth top. Drizzle with the remaining oil. Bake for 35 minutes, until browned and bubbling. **Serves 4 to 6.**

Baked Eggplant Moussaka

1	large eggplant, cut into ½-inch (1 cm) thick rounds	1
1 tbsp	kosher salt	15 mL
1 cup	chunky marinara sauce	250 mL
¼ cup	water	50 mL
1 tbsp	chopped fresh dill	15 mL
Pinch	ground cinnamon	Pinch
1	can (10 oz/284 mL) condensed cream of mushroom soup, undiluted	1
1	extra-large egg	1
6 oz	feta cheese, crumbled	175 g
½ cup	milk (preferably whole)	125 mL
	Olive oil spray	
½ cup	couscous	125 mL
3 tbsp	freshly grated Parmesan cheese	45 mL

Sprinkle eggplant slices with salt and let stand for 1 hour. Meanwhile, preheat oven to 400°F (200°C). Sandwich eggplant between layers of paper towels and press to release liquid. Place eggplant slices in a single layer on a baking sheet and bake for 15 minutes. Meanwhile, in a small bowl, combine marinara sauce, water, dill and cinnamon. In a separate bowl, combine soup, egg, feta and milk. Spray an 8-cup (2 L) casserole dish with oil. Pour one-third of the marinara sauce mixture over the bottom, then layer one-third of the couscous, one-third of the eggplant and one-third of the soup mixture. Repeat layers twice more. Sprinkle with Parmesan. Bake for 35 minutes, until browned and bubbling. Serves 4.

Tomato and Feta au Gratin

2 tbsp	extra-virgin olive oil, divided	25 mL
1	onion, thinly sliced	1
¼ tsp	dried oregano	1 mL
⅛ tsp	cayenne pepper, divided	0.5 mL
	Salt and freshly ground black pepper to taste	
4	large firm tomatoes, ends removed and thinly sliced	4
3 tbsp	all-purpose flour	45 mL
½ cup	couscous	125 mL
6 oz	feta cheese, crumbled	175 g

Preheat oven to 375°F (190°C) and grease a 4-cup (1 L) casserole dish with half the oil. In a medium skillet, heat the remaining oil over medium-high heat. Sauté onion until tender. Stir in oregano, half the cayenne, salt and black pepper; set aside. Combine tomatoes, flour, the remaining cayenne and additional salt and black pepper. Sprinkle half the couscous over the bottom of prepared casserole, then layer with half the onions, half the tomatoes and half the cheese. Repeat layers. Bake for 45 minutes, until bubbling. Let cool for 10 minutes. Serves 4.

Baked Pasta e Fagioli

1	can (14 to 19 oz/398 to 540 mL) cannellini or white kidney beans, drained and rinsed	1
1 cup	chicken broth	250 mL
½ tsp	dried thyme	2 mL
2	cloves garlic, minced	2
1	egg, beaten	1
1	package (10 oz/300 g) frozen chopped spinach, thawed and squeezed dry	1
8 oz	small shell-shaped pasta, cooked, hot	250 g
3 cups	shredded mozzarella cheese, divided	750 mL
2 tbsp	freshly grated Parmesan cheese	25 mL
	Salt and freshly ground black pepper to taste	

Preheat oven to 350°F (180°C). In a large saucepan, over medium-high heat, cook beans, broth and thyme until broth is reduced by about half. Remove from heat and stir in garlic, egg, spinach, pasta, two-thirds of the mozzarella and Parmesan. Pack into a 10-cup (2.5 L) casserole dish and smooth top. Bake for 20 minutes. Stir in the remaining mozzarella and bake for 10 minutes. Season with salt and pepper. Serves 4 to 6.

Roasted Pepper and Brown Rice Casserole

3 tbsp	extra-virgin olive oil, divided	45 mL
¼ cup	finely chopped onion	50 mL
¼ cup	finely chopped celery	50 mL
2	roasted bell peppers (see page 11), diced	2
2	cloves garlic, minced	2
2 tbsp	all-purpose flour	25 mL
1½ cups	chicken broth	375 mL
3 cups	cooked brown rice	750 mL
2 cups	shredded sharp Cheddar cheese	500 mL
¼ cup	chopped fresh Italian (flat-leaf) parsley	50 mL
Pinch	cayenne pepper	Pinch
	Salt and freshly ground black pepper to taste	
¼ cup	freshly grated Parmesan cheese	50 mL

Preheat oven to 400°F (200°C). In a large nonstick skillet, heat 2 tbsp (25 mL) of the oil over medium-high heat. Sauté onion and celery until tender. Add roasted peppers and garlic; sauté until aromatic. Add flour and sauté for 1 minute. Whisk in broth until slightly thickened, about 5 minutes. Remove from heat and stir in rice, Cheddar, parsley, cayenne, salt and black pepper. Pack into a 10-cup (2.5 L) casserole dish and smooth top. Sprinkle with Parmesan and the remaining oil. Bake for 25 minutes, until browned and bubbling. **Serves 4 to 6.**

Tuna and Rice Casserole

Follow preceding recipe, but omit the roasted peppers, and replace the chicken broth with milk and the brown rice with white rice. Add 2 cans (each 6 oz/170 g) tuna, drained and crumbled, with the rice. **Serves 4 to 6.**

Southwest Bread Pudding

	Olive oil spray	
10	slices good-quality white bread	10
2	jars (each 16 oz/454 mL) salsa verde (green salsa)	2
1	can (14 to 19 oz/398 to 540 mL) pinto beans, drained and rinsed	1
1 cup	sour cream	250 mL
1½ cups	shredded Monterey Jack cheese	375 mL

Preheat oven to 350°F (180°C) and spray a baking sheet with oil. Place bread on pan in a single layer and spray with more oil. Bake for about 10 minutes, until slightly toasted and warm; cut into 1-inch (2.5 cm) cubes. Place one-quarter of the salsa in the bottom of a 12-cup (3 L) casserole dish, and top with one-third of the bread cubes, arranged in an even layer. Layer with half the beans, another quarter of the salsa, half the sour cream, and one-third of the cheese. Repeat layers, then finish with the remaining bread, remaining salsa, and remaining cheese. Bake for about 20 minutes, until browned and bubbling. **Serves 6.**

Mexican Torta

Follow preceding recipe, but replace the bread with 10 corn tortillas, cut into wedges, and replace the pinto beans with navy beans. **Serves 6.**

Provençal Ricotta Bread Pudding

	Vegetable cooking spray	
1 cup	freshly grated imported Parmesan cheese, divided	250 mL
½	loaf white or whole wheat bread, cut into 1-inch (2.5 cm) pieces	½
4	eggs	4
2	cloves garlic, minced	2
4 cups	ricotta cheese (preferably whole-milk)	1 L
3 tbsp	basil pesto	45 mL
1 tbsp	white wine vinegar	15 mL
½ tsp	salt	2 mL
½ tsp	freshly ground black pepper	2 mL
Pinch	cayenne pepper	Pinch

Preheat oven to 325°F (160°C), spray a 12-cup (3 L) rectangular casserole dish with cooking spray and dust with 3 tbsp (45 mL) of the Parmesan. Place bread pieces in casserole. Combine the remaining ingredients and pour on top of bread. Mix gently to moisten bread thoroughly. Bake for about 75 minutes, until a tester inserted in the center comes out with a bit of set batter clinging to it. Let cool for at least 30 minutes, then cut into squares. **Serves 6.**

Chapter 22
Ground Meat
The Old Standby Reinvigorated

Dipping Sauce for Potstickers 249
Potstickers 250
Veal and Pork Potstickers 250
Chicken Spinach Potstickers 250
Turkey Fennel Potstickers 250
Sweet Sesame Meatballs 250
Meatballs Wrapped in Bacon 250
Meatball Chili 251
Spicy Cocktail Meatballs 251
Sweet-and-Sour Sesame Meatballs 251
Bavarian Meatballs 252
Apple and Gorgonzola
Sausage Patties 252
Wild Mushroom Sausage Patties 252
Country Pâté 252
Herbed Chicken Pâté 253
Brandied Liver Mousse 253
Shepherd's Pie 254
Mom's Meatloaf 254
Reduced-Calorie Meatloaf 254
Apple Sage Meatloaf 254
Chilied Meatloaf with Chorizo 254
Meatloaf Cupcakes 254
Surprise Meatloaf 254
Wild Mushroom Meatloaf 255
Roasted Pepper and Basil Meatloaf . . . 255
Sausage Meatloaf 255

Meatloaf Dijonnaise 255
Mexican Meatloaf 255
Meat and Potatoes Meatloaf 255
Prosciutto and Cheese Meatloaf 255
Ham Meatloaf 255
Ham and Cheddar Meatloaf 255
Sweet-and-Sour Meatloaf 255
Meatloaf Baked in Bread 255
Lots-of-Olives Meatloaf 255
Meatloaf with Spinach and Ricotta 255
Meatloaf with Easy Tomato Sauce 256
Turkey Meatloaf 256
Turkey Meatloaf with Cranberries 256
Turkey Meatloaf with Mint and Ricotta . . 256
Spicy Turkey Meatloaf with Chickpeas . . 256
Apple and Bacon Turkey Loaf 256
Turkey Cornbread Meatloaf 256
Turkey Loaf with Ham,
Lemon and Pistachios 256
Fresh and Smoked Turkey Meatloaf . . . 256
Turkey Meatloaf with Bread Stuffing . . . 257
Fragrant Turkey Loaf with Pineapple . . . 257
Turkey and Walnut Meatloaf 257
Veal Loaf with Artichokes 257
Herbed Veal Loaf 257
Lasagna Meatloaf 258

Centuries before Hamburger Helper helped reset the parameters of quick cooking in America, the ancient Romans, Greeks and Phoenicians knew just how easy ground meat could be. Not only did it cook up faster than a whole mutton on a spit, but it could be effortlessly preserved and flavored just by mixing it with spices.

Today, we often forget the versatility of ground meat, resorting to it for easy, unimaginative meals — foods that everyone will eat but no one will relish. There's a better approach. We've put together 50 easy, tasty ground meat dishes, including meatballs, meatloaves, dumplings, sausages and pâtés. Burgers — lots of burgers — are in Chapter 11 (page 128).

If your local butchers give you an odd look when you ask for ground pork, veal, lamb or chicken, it's probably because they don't get much call for them. Just ask them to run the desired variety of stew meat through a grinder twice. (Of course, if you have a meat grinder at home, you can grind the stew meat yourself, which can save money and ensure freshness. Ground meat is quite perishable.)

Although a food processor can chop meat, the machine will not grind. If you're not careful, you'll end up with a flaccid, unpleasantly textured purée. Quick pulsing throughout the chopping will give the best results.

A few words about meatloaf: We love it, probably because we have a great recipe for it (actually several dozen great recipes). In truth, a good meatloaf is hard to find, simply because too many people ignore the simple truth that the sensual charm of any ground meat mixture is in the filler, not the meat. Once meat is ground, any moisture or textural quality it might have had is nearly gone. Baking it manages only to dry up what's left and turn it into the equivalent of edible gravel. Mix in an egg, and you can get the gravel to hold together, but the result is more masonry than dinner.

To make a meatloaf succulent, you must refurbish its structure and replenish its moisture from the inside out. That can be done either by adding liquid, along with a starch to absorb the moisture and hold it inside the loaf, or by adding fat. Usually, both are added, forming what's commonly called filler. Unfortunately, the word "filler" is sullied by nuances of adulteration and deception. But makers of sausage, pâté and meatloaf have known since ancient times that such adulteration is exactly what ground meat needs. With it, one adds flavor, moisture and consistency. Without it, all you've got is gastronomic gravel.

Liquid ingredients in a filler add flavor as well as moisture. Often they are condiments, such as ketchup, chutney, mustard or relish. But they can also be sauces (anything from béchamel to Worcestershire), cooked vegetables or cheeses.

The starchy ingredients that hold the moisture must be wet themselves. If they aren't, rather than contributing moisture to the meat, they will soak up other surrounding moisture in an effort to rehydrate themselves. Typically, bread soaked in milk, beer, wine or broth is used, but cooked potatoes, rice, cereal or pasta are other alternatives.

About these recipes . . .

None of the ideas or techniques we use to work with ground meat are difficult, but some of them might be new to you. The direction for caramelizing sugar in Sweet Sesame Meatballs (page 250) means just what it says. The method for forming potstickers is described in detail in "Basic Techniques for Cooking Anything" (page 8).

This recipe is used in the four potstickers recipes that follow.

Dipping Sauce for Potstickers

½ cup	chicken broth	125 mL
½ cup	water	125 mL
¼ cup	soy sauce	50 mL
1	clove garlic, minced	1
1	whole star anise	1
1 tsp	freshly ground Szechuan or white pepper	5 mL
1 tsp	dark sesame oil	5 mL
Pinch	granulated sugar	Pinch
1 tsp	cornstarch, dissolved in 2 tsp (10 mL) water	5 mL

In a small saucepan, bring broth, water, soy sauce, garlic, star anise, pepper, oil and sugar to a boil; boil for 3 minutes. Add cornstarch mixture (stirring, if necessary, just before adding) and boil for 1 minute, until slightly thickened. **Makes about 1 cup (250 mL).**

Potstickers

1	large green onion, white part only, finely chopped	1
1	clove garlic, minced	1
8 oz	ground pork	250 g
2 tbsp	chopped fresh Italian (flat-leaf) parsley	25 mL
1 tbsp	finely chopped gingerroot	15 mL
1½ tbsp	soy sauce	22 mL
1½ tsp	dark sesame oil	7 mL
40	Chinese dumpling wrappers	40
	Egg wash (1 egg beaten with 2 tbsp/25 mL water)	
3 tbsp	peanut oil	45 mL
1 cup	chicken broth	250 mL
	Dipping Sauce for Potstickers (see recipe, page 249)	

Using wet hands, combine green onion, garlic, pork, parsley, ginger, soy sauce and sesame oil. Fill the dumpling wrappers, forming 40 potstickers (see page 10), sealing the edges by brushing with egg wash. In a large skillet, heat peanut oil over medium-high heat. Brown the bottoms of the pot-stickers for about 3 minutes. Add broth, cover and steam for 5 minutes. Serve with dipping sauce. **Serves 8.**

Veal and Pork Potstickers

Follow preceding recipe, but reduce the pork to 4 oz (125 g), omit the parsley, and add 4 oz (125 g) ground veal and 2 tbsp (25 mL) each chopped fresh cilantro and chopped fresh mint with the pork. **Serves 8.**

Chicken Spinach Potstickers

Follow recipe for Potstickers (above), but replace the pork with 4 oz (125 g) ground veal and 4 oz (125 g) ground chicken, replace the parsley with chopped fresh cilantro, and add ¼ cup (50 mL) cooked and drained chopped spinach with the cilantro. **Serves 8.**

Turkey Fennel Potstickers

Follow recipe for Potstickers (above), but replace the green onion with ¼ cup (50 mL) finely chopped fennel bulb, replace the pork with ground turkey, and add ½ tsp (2 mL) ground fennel seeds with the ginger. **Serves 8.**

Sweet Sesame Meatballs

1	clove garlic, minced	1
1 lb	ground pork	500 g
3 tbsp	cornstarch	45 mL
2 tsp	ground ginger	10 mL
	Vegetable oil	
¼ cup	granulated sugar	50 mL
6 to 8 tbsp	toasted sesame seeds	90 to 120 mL

Using wet hands, combine garlic, pork, cornstarch and ginger. Form into 24 meatballs. In a large skillet, heat a thin film of oil over medium-high heat. Sauté meatballs until no longer pink inside; remove meatballs to a plate and discard oil. Add sugar to the pan and cook, without stirring, until melted and caramelized, about 1 minute. Return meatballs to pan and coat with syrup. Transfer to a serving platter and sprinkle with sesame seeds to taste. **Serves 6.**

Meatballs Wrapped in Bacon

1	egg, beaten	1
1	clove garlic, minced	1
1 lb	ground beef	500 g
3 tbsp	seasoned dry bread crumbs	45 mL
3 tbsp	minced onion	45 mL
1 tbsp	chopped fresh Italian (flat-leaf) parsley	15 mL
2 tbsp	water	25 mL
12	slices bacon, halved	12

Preheat oven to 375°F (190°C). Using wet hands, combine egg, garlic, beef, bread crumbs, onion, parsley and water. Form into 24 meatballs, wrap each with a half-slice of bacon and secure with a toothpick. Place on a rimmed baking sheet and bake until meatballs are no longer pink inside, about 30 minutes. **Serves 6.**

Meatball Chili

1	egg, beaten	1
1	clove garlic, minced	1
1 lb	ground beef	500 g
3 tbsp	seasoned dry bread crumbs	45 mL
3 tbsp	minced onion	45 mL
1 tbsp	chopped fresh Italian (flat-leaf) parsley	15 mL
2 tbsp	water	25 mL
2 tbsp	vegetable oil	25 mL
1	bell pepper (any color), chopped	1
½	recipe Basic Chili Mix (page 202)	½
2 cups	tomato sauce	500 mL
1 cup	beef broth	250 mL
1 tsp	freshly ground black pepper	5 mL
	Salt to taste	
2 cups	drained rinsed canned red kidney beans	500 mL

Using wet hands, combine egg, garlic, beef, bread crumbs, onion, parsley and water. Form into 24 meatballs. In a large skillet, heat oil over medium-high heat. Sauté meatballs until browned on all sides; remove to plate. Add bell pepper, Basic Chili Mix, tomato sauce, broth and pepper to the pan and bring to a boil. Return meatballs to the pan, reduce heat and simmer for 1 hour. Season with salt and additional pepper. Stir in beans and heat through. **Serves 6.**

Spicy Cocktail Meatballs

2	cloves garlic, minced	2
1	egg, beaten	1
½	jalapeño pepper, seeded and minced	½
1 lb	ground beef	500 g
2 tbsp	seasoned dry bread crumbs	25 mL
2 tbsp	minced onion	25 mL
1 tbsp	chili powder	15 mL
1 tbsp	ketchup	15 mL
1 tsp	brown mustard	5 mL
Pinch	cayenne pepper	Pinch
½ cup	cornmeal, seasoned to taste with salt and cayenne pepper	125 mL
2 tbsp	vegetable oil	25 mL
¼ cup	melted butter	50 mL
1 to 2 tbsp	hot pepper sauce (such as Frank's RedHot)	15 to 25 mL

Using wet hands, combine garlic, egg, jalapeño, beef, bread crumbs, onion, chili powder, ketchup, mustard and cayenne. Form into 24 meatballs and roll in cornmeal. In a large skillet, heat oil over medium-high heat. Sauté meatballs until no longer pink inside. Combine butter and hot pepper sauce to taste, and serve as a dipping sauce with meatballs. **Serves 6.**

Sweet-and-Sour Sesame Meatballs

2	cloves garlic, minced, divided	2
1 lb	ground pork	500 g
¼ cup	dark sesame oil	50 mL
3 tbsp	cornstarch	45 mL
2 tbsp	chopped gingerroot, divided	25 mL
4 tsp	soy sauce, divided	20 mL
2 tbsp	vegetable oil	25 mL
¼ cup	chopped onion	50 mL
2 cups	chicken broth	500 mL
3 tbsp	packed brown sugar	45 mL
3 tbsp	cider vinegar	45 mL
Pinch	cayenne pepper	Pinch
2 tsp	cornstarch, dissolved in 1 tbsp (15 mL) water	10 mL

Using wet hands, combine half the garlic, the pork, sesame oil, cornstarch, 1 tbsp (15 mL) of the ginger and 1 tsp (5 mL) of the soy sauce. Form into 24 meatballs. In a large skillet, heat vegetable oil over medium-high heat. Sauté meatballs until browned on all sides. Add the remaining garlic, the remaining ginger and onion; sauté for 1 minute. Add the remaining soy sauce, broth, brown sugar, vinegar and cayenne; reduce heat and simmer until liquid is reduced by half. Stir cornstarch mixture and add to pan; simmer until lightly thickened. **Serves 6.**

Bavarian Meatballs

4	slices bacon, minced	4
2	slices bread, crusts removed, crumbled	2
2	whole eggs, beaten	2
2	drained canned anchovies, minced	2
1 lb	ground pork	500 g
1½ cups	chopped onions	375 mL
1½ tsp	dried thyme, divided	7 mL
	Salt and freshly ground black pepper to taste	
4 cups	chicken broth	1 L
2 tbsp	all-purpose flour	25 mL
2 tbsp	butter	25 mL
2	egg yolks	2
2 tsp	white wine vinegar	10 mL
2 tsp	drained capers	10 mL

Using wet hands, combine bacon, bread, whole eggs, anchovies, pork, onions, one-third of the thyme, salt and pepper. Form into 24 meatballs. In a large pot, bring broth to a simmer over medium-low heat. Add meatballs and simmer for 20 to 25 minutes, or until no longer pink inside. Using a slotted spoon, remove meatballs to a plate. Reserve cooking liquid and wipe out pot. Increase heat to medium and add flour and butter to the pot; cook, stirring, until lightly browned, about 5 minutes. Stir in cooking liquid and simmer for 10 minutes. Meanwhile, in a small bowl, beat egg yolks, vinegar, capers and the remaining thyme. Add to the pot in a slow stream, stirring constantly, until a creamy consistency develops, 1 to 2 minutes. Return meatballs to the pot and heat through. **Serves 6.**

Apple and Gorgonzola Sausage Patties

1 tbsp	vegetable oil, divided	15 mL
1	tart apple, finely diced	1
2 tbsp	minced onion	25 mL
1	small clove garlic, minced	1
½ tsp	dried thyme	2 mL
½ tsp	dried sage	2 mL
½ tsp	ground ginger	2 mL
Pinch	ground nutmeg	Pinch
Pinch	ground cloves	Pinch
	Salt and freshly ground black pepper to taste	
1 lb	sausage (bulk, or with casings removed)	500 g
3 oz	Gorgonzola cheese, crumbled	90 g

In a nonstick skillet, heat 1 tsp (5 mL) of the oil over medium heat. Sauté apple and onion until tender. Add garlic, thyme, sage, ginger, nutmeg, cloves, salt and pepper; sauté until aromatic. Let cool, then mix in sausage and Gorgonzola. Form into 12 patties, about ½ inch (1 cm) thick. In a large skillet, heat the remaining oil over medium-high heat. Cook patties until browned on both sides. Reduce heat to medium and cook patties, turning once or twice, until no longer pink inside. **Serves 6.**

Wild Mushroom Sausage Patties

¼ cup	dried wild or exotic mushrooms	50 mL
⅓ cup	very hot water	75 mL
1 tbsp	vegetable oil, divided	15 mL
2 tbsp	minced onion	25 mL
1	small clove garlic, minced	1
½ tsp	dried thyme	2 mL
½ tsp	dried sage	2 mL
½ tsp	dried rosemary	2 mL
½ tsp	ground ginger	2 mL
Pinch	ground nutmeg	Pinch
Pinch	ground cloves	Pinch
1 lb	sausage (bulk, or with casings removed)	500 g

Soak dried mushrooms in hot water for 10 minutes, until softened. Meanwhile, in a nonstick skillet, heat 1 tsp (5 mL) of the oil over medium heat. Sauté onion until tender. Add garlic, thyme, sage, rosemary, ginger, nutmeg and cloves; sauté for 1 minute. Add mushroom soaking liquid, increase heat to high and boil until liquid is reduced by three-quarters. Meanwhile, chop mushrooms. Add to skillet and let cool. Combine mushroom mixture and sausage; form into 12 patties, about ½ inch (1 cm) thick. In a large skillet, heat the remaining oil over medium-high heat. Cook patties until browned on both sides. Reduce heat to medium and cook patties, turning once or twice, until no longer pink inside. **Serves 6.**

Country Pâté

1 lb	veal leg, coarsely chopped	500 g
1 lb	pork fatback, coarsely chopped	500 g
1 lb	chicken livers, trimmed of fat and gristle	500 g
8 oz	boneless pork shoulder blade (butt), coarsely chopped	250 g
8 oz	smoked ham, cut into small dice	250 g
¼ cup	brandy	50 mL
¼ cup	whipping (35%) cream	50 mL
2 tbsp	chopped onion	25 mL
2 tsp	freshly ground white pepper	10 mL
1 tsp	salt	5 mL
¼ tsp	ground cloves	1 mL
¼ tsp	ground ginger	1 mL
¼ tsp	ground nutmeg	1 mL
¼ tsp	dried rosemary	1 mL

| 8 | slices bacon, divided | 8 |
| | Mustard | |

Preheat oven to 375°F (190°C). Using a meat grinder, grind veal, fatback, chicken livers and pork to a coarse ground meat consistency (or pulse in a food processor, in batches if necessary, until minced). Combine with ham, brandy, cream, onion, pepper, salt, cloves, ginger, nutmeg and rosemary. Line a 9- by 5-inch (2 L) loaf pan with 6 slices of the bacon. Pack meat mixture into pan, being careful not to disturb the bacon. Level top, wrap bacon ends over top and fill in any bare spots with the remaining bacon. Cover with foil and place in a larger pan half-full of hot water. Bake for 1½ hours, until pâté reaches an internal temperature of 160°F (71°C). Carefully remove loaf pan from the water bath and place a 4-lb (2 kg) weight on top. Let cool to room temperature on a rack. Refrigerate, weighted, for at least 8 hours or overnight. Remove from pan, slice and serve with mustard. **Serves 10.** *(In its pan, covered with its fat, the pâté will keep for up to 1 week. Once it is removed from the pan and the fat is disturbed, it will keep for 3 to 4 days.)*

Herbed Chicken Pâté

2 lbs	boneless skinless chicken pieces	1 kg
1 lb	pork fatback, coarsely chopped	500 g
2	shallots, chopped	2
1	egg, beaten	1
8 oz	smoked turkey breast, finely diced	250 g
½ cup	Madeira	125 mL
¼ cup	chopped fresh Italian (flat-leaf) parsley	50 mL
¼ cup	cream (any type, minimum 10%)	50 mL
2 tbsp	chopped fresh tarragon	25 mL
1 tbsp	chopped fresh rosemary	15 mL
2 tsp	salt	10 mL
1 tsp	freshly ground white pepper	5 mL
¼ tsp	ground ginger	1 mL
8 oz	pancetta, thinly sliced, divided	250 g
	Herbed mayonnaise	

Preheat oven to 375°F (190°C). Using a meat grinder, grind chicken and fatback to a coarse ground meat consistency (or pulse in a food processor, in batches if necessary, until minced). Combine with shallots, egg, turkey, Madeira, parsley, cream, tarragon, rosemary, salt, pepper and ginger. Line a 9- by 5-inch (2 L) loaf pan with all but 1 oz (30 g) of the pancetta. Pack chicken mixture into pan, being careful not to disturb the pancetta. Level top and cover with the remaining pancetta.

Cover with foil and place in a larger pan half-full of hot water. Bake for 1½ hours, or until pâté reaches an internal temperature of 165°F (74°C). Carefully remove loaf pan from the water bath and place a 4-lb (2 kg) weight on top. Let cool to room temperature on a rack. Refrigerate, weighted, for at least 8 hours or overnight. Remove from pan, slice and serve with herbed mayonnaise. **Serves 10.** *(In its pan, covered with its fat, the pâté will keep for up to 1 week. Once it is removed from the pan and the fat is disturbed, it will keep for 3 to 4 days.)*

Brandied Liver Mousse

8 oz	pork fatback, coarsely chopped	250 g
6	drained canned anchovies, chopped	6
1 lb	chicken livers, trimmed of fat and gristle	500 g
5	eggs, beaten	5
1 cup	whipping (35%) cream	250 mL
¼ cup	brandy	50 mL
1½ tsp	salt	7 mL
½ tsp	freshly ground white pepper	2 mL
Pinch	ground allspice	Pinch
8	slices bacon	8
	Toast, mustard and pickles	

Preheat oven to 300°F (150°C). In a food processor, pulse fatback until minced. Add anchovies and chicken livers; process until completely smooth. Add eggs, cream, brandy, salt, pepper and allspice; process until completely incorporated. Line a 9- by 5-inch (2 L) loaf pan with bacon. Pour mousse mixture into pan, being careful not to disturb the bacon. Level top and wrap bacon ends over top. Cover with foil and place in a larger pan half-full of hot water. Bake for 2½ hours, or until mousse reaches an internal temperature of 165°F (74°C). Carefully remove loaf pan from the water bath. Refrigerate overnight. Remove from pan, slice and serve with toast, mustard and pickles. **Serves 10.** *(In its pan, covered with its fat, the mousse will keep for 3 to 4 days.)*

Shepherd's Pie

1 tbsp	olive oil	15 mL
1	large onion, chopped	1
1	clove garlic, minced	1
1 lb	ground lamb	500 g
4	oil-cured black olives, pitted and chopped	4
1 cup	canned crushed tomatoes	250 mL
½ tsp	dried oregano	2 mL
1	recipe Mashed Potatoes with Roasted Garlic (page 389)	1

Preheat oven to 375°F (190°C). In a large skillet, heat oil over medium-high heat. Sauté onion until tender. Add garlic and lamb; sauté, breaking lamb up with a fork, until no longer pink. Stir in olives, tomatoes and oregano; reduce heat and simmer for 10 minutes. Pack into an 8-cup (2 L) casserole and top with mashed potatoes. Bake for 40 minutes, until bubbling. **Serves 4 to 6.**

Mom's Meatloaf

2	slices bread (preferably rye), crusts removed, crumbled	2
½ cup	milk	125 mL
2	eggs, beaten	2
1	onion, minced	1
1 lb	ground beef	500 g
8 oz	ground veal	250 g
8 oz	ground pork	250 g
½ cup	ketchup	125 mL
1 tbsp	Worcestershire sauce	15 mL
2 tsp	spicy brown mustard	10 mL
	Salt and freshly ground black pepper to taste	

Preheat oven to 375°F (190°C). Using your hands, combine bread and milk until bread is very soft and most of the milk has been absorbed. Mix in the remaining ingredients. Form into a rough loaf and place on a rimmed baking sheet, in a 6-cup (1.5 L) casserole dish or in a 9- by 5-inch (2 L) loaf pan. Bake for 1 hour, or until firm to the touch and a thermometer inserted in the center registers 160°F (71°C). Let cool in pan for 10 minutes. Remove from pan and slice. **Serves 6.**

Reduced-Calorie Meatloaf

1 cup	fresh whole-grain bread crumbs	250 mL
1 cup	quick-cooking rolled oats	250 mL
1 cup	hot skim milk	250 mL
2	egg whites, beaten	2
1	onion, minced	1
2 lbs	extra-lean ground beef or ground turkey	1 kg
⅔ cup	ketchup	150 mL
1 tbsp	reduced-sodium soy sauce	15 mL
2 tsp	brown mustard	10 mL
	Salt and freshly ground black pepper to taste	

Preheat oven to 375°F (190°C). Using your hands, combine bread crumbs, oats and milk until most of the milk has been absorbed. Mix in the remaining ingredients. Form into a rough loaf and place on a rimmed baking sheet, in a 6-cup (1.5 L) casserole dish or in a 9- by 5-inch (2 L) loaf pan. Bake for 1 hour, or until firm to the touch and a thermometer inserted in the center registers 160°F (71°C). Let cool in pan for 10 minutes. Remove from pan and slice. **Serves 6.**

Apple Sage Meatloaf

Follow recipe for Mom's Meatloaf or Reduced-Calorie Meatloaf (left), but add 1 tart apple, peeled and diced, 1 tsp (5 mL) dried sage and ½ tsp (2 mL) dried thyme to the meat mixture. **Serves 6.**

Chilied Meatloaf with Chorizo

Follow recipe for Mom's Meatloaf (left), but add 12 oz (375 g) chorizo, chopped, and 2 tsp (10 mL) ground cumin to the meat mixture. **Serves 6.**

Meatloaf Cupcakes

Follow recipe for Mom's Meatloaf or Reduced-Calorie Meatloaf (left), but instead of forming meat mixture into a loaf, form it into 12 large meatballs and place them in a 12-cup muffin tin. Bake for 40 minutes. Remove from oven, mound 2 tbsp (25 mL) shredded Swiss cheese on each "cupcake" and broil until cheese melts, about 2 minutes. **Serves 6.**

Surprise Meatloaf

Follow recipe for Mom's Meatloaf or Reduced-Calorie Meatloaf (left), but form the loaf around 2 peeled hard-cooked eggs, ends removed, placed end to end down the center of the loaf. **Serves 6.**

Wild Mushroom Meatloaf

Follow recipe for Mom's Meatloaf or Reduced-Calorie Meatloaf (page 254), but first soak 1 oz (30 g) dried wild or exotic mushrooms in 1 cup (250 mL) hot water for 10 minutes. Replace the milk with mushroom soaking liquid. Finely chop mushrooms, discarding tough ends, and add to the meat mixture. **Serves 6.**

Roasted Pepper and Basil Meatloaf

Follow recipe for Mom's Meatloaf or Reduced-Calorie Meatloaf (page 254), but add 2 roasted bell peppers (see page 11), diced, and 1/2 cup (125 mL) chopped fresh basil to the meat mixture. **Serves 6.**

Sausage Meatloaf

Follow recipe for Mom's Meatloaf (page 254), but first grill 8 oz (250 g) link breakfast sausage until browned and firm. Form the loaf around sausages, placed end to end in 2 rows down the center of the loaf. **Serves 6.**

Meatloaf Dijonnaise

Follow recipe for Mom's Meatloaf or Reduced-Calorie Meatloaf (page 254), but add 2 tbsp (25 mL) Dijon mustard to the meat mixture. **Serves 6.**

Mexican Meatloaf

Follow recipe for Mom's Meatloaf or Reduced-Calorie Meatloaf (page 254), but add 2/3 cup (150 mL) hot salsa, 2/3 cup (150 mL) cooked or canned kidney beans and 1 tbsp (15 mL) chili powder to the meat mixture. **Serves 6.**

Meat and Potatoes Meatloaf

Follow recipe for Mom's Meatloaf or Reduced-Calorie Meatloaf (page 254), but crumble a 12-oz (375 g) baked potato, cooked and peeled, into the meat mixture. **Serves 6.**

Prosciutto and Cheese Meatloaf

Follow recipe for Mom's Meatloaf (page 254), but first cut 2 oz (60 g) mozzarella cheese into 2 long sticks and roll each in 1 slice prosciutto. Form the loaf around rolls, placed end to end down the center of the loaf. **Serves 6.**

Ham Meatloaf

Follow recipe for Mom's Meatloaf or Reduced-Calorie Meatloaf (page 254), but add 12 oz (375 g) cooked ham, chopped, to the meat mixture. **Serves 6.**

Ham and Cheddar Meatloaf

Follow recipe for Mom's Meatloaf or Reduced-Calorie Meatloaf (page 254), but add 8 oz (250 g) cooked ham, chopped, and 1 cup (250 mL) shredded Cheddar cheese to the meat mixture. **Serves 6.**

Sweet-and-Sour Meatloaf

Follow recipe for Mom's Meatloaf or Reduced-Calorie Meatloaf (page 254), but combine 1 tbsp (15 mL) cider vinegar, 1 tbsp (15 mL) honey and 1 tsp (5 mL) hoisin sauce; baste the surface of the loaf with this mixture before baking. **Serves 6.**

Meatloaf Baked in Bread

Follow recipe for Mom's Meatloaf or Reduced-Calorie Meatloaf (page 254), but cut off one end of a large loaf of French bread and hollow out the center. Stuff meat mixture into bread, wrap in foil and bake for 1 1/2 hours. **Serves 6.**

Lots-of-Olives Meatloaf

Follow recipe for Mom's Meatloaf or Reduced-Calorie Meatloaf (page 254), but add 20 black olives, pitted and chopped, and 20 Spanish olives, pitted and chopped, to the meat mixture. **Serves 6.**

Meatloaf with Spinach and Ricotta

Follow recipe for Mom's Meatloaf or Reduced-Calorie Meatloaf (page 254), but add 1 clove garlic, minced, 1/3 cup (75 mL) drained ricotta cheese and 1 cup (250 mL) cooked and drained chopped spinach to the meat mixture. **Serves 6.**

Meatloaf with Easy Tomato Sauce

1 tbsp	olive oil	15 mL
1 cup	chopped onion	250 mL
2	cloves garlic, minced	2
½ cup	dry red wine	125 mL
3 cups	chopped canned tomatoes	750 mL
¼ cup	tomato paste	50 mL
Pinch	hot pepper flakes	Pinch
	Salt and freshly ground black pepper to taste	
1 tbsp	chopped fresh Italian (flat-leaf) parsley	15 mL
1	recipe Mom's Meatloaf or Reduced-Calorie Meatloaf (page 254)	1

In a large skillet, heat oil over medium-high heat. Sauté onion and garlic until onion is softened. Add wine and boil until reduced by one-third. Add tomatoes and cook until they start to release their liquid. Add tomato paste, hot pepper flakes, salt and black pepper; reduce heat and simmer for 15 minutes. Stir in parsley and simmer for 1 minute. Serve meatloaf with sauce. **Serves 6.**

Turkey Meatloaf

2	slices bread, crusts removed, crumbled	2
½ cup	milk	125 mL
2	eggs, beaten	2
1	small onion, minced	1
1½ lbs	ground turkey	750 g
4 oz	ground veal	125 g
4 oz	breakfast sausage (bulk, or with casings removed)	125 g
¼ cup	ketchup	50 mL
2 tbsp	apple butter	25 mL
2 tbsp	soy sauce	25 mL
2 tsp	brown mustard	10 mL

Preheat oven to 375°F (190°C). Using your hands, combine bread and milk until bread is very soft and most of the milk has been absorbed. Mix in the remaining ingredients. Form into a rough loaf and place on a rimmed baking sheet, in a 6-cup (1.5 L) casserole dish or in a 9- by 5-inch (2 L) loaf pan. Bake for 1 hour, or until firm to the touch and a thermometer inserted in the center registers 165°F (74°C). Let cool in pan for 10 minutes. Remove from pan and slice. **Serves 6.**

Turkey Meatloaf with Cranberries

Follow preceding recipe, but omit the ketchup and apple butter, and add 1 cup (250 mL) whole-berry cranberry sauce to the meat mixture. **Serves 6.**

Turkey Meatloaf with Mint and Ricotta

Follow recipe for Turkey Meatloaf (left), but replace the ketchup with tomato sauce, omit the apple butter, and add ⅓ cup (75 mL) drained ricotta cheese and 2 tbsp (25 mL) dried mint to the meat mixture. **Serves 6.**

Spicy Turkey Meatloaf with Chickpeas

Follow recipe for Turkey Meatloaf (left) or Reduced-Calorie Meatloaf (page 254) made with ground turkey, but add ½ cup (125 mL) cooked or canned chickpeas, 1 tsp (5 mL) chili powder and 1 tsp (5 mL) hot pepper sauce (such as Tabasco) to the meat mixture. **Serves 6.**

Apple and Bacon Turkey Loaf

Follow recipe for Turkey Meatloaf (left), but add 1 tart apple, peeled and diced, to the meat mixture, and lay 4 slices of bacon on top of the meatloaf before baking. **Serves 6.**

Turkey Cornbread Meatloaf

Follow recipe for Turkey Meatloaf (left) or Reduced-Calorie Meatloaf (page 254) made with ground turkey, but substitute 1 cup (250 mL) crumbled cornbread for the bread. **Serves 6.**

Turkey Loaf with Ham, Lemon and Pistachios

Follow recipe for Turkey Meatloaf (left) or Reduced-Calorie Meatloaf (page 254) made with ground turkey, but add 1 cup (250 mL) diced cooked ham, ¼ cup (50 mL) chopped pistachios, 2 tbsp (25 mL) minced fresh Italian (flat-leaf) parsley and 1 tsp (5 mL) finely grated lemon zest to the meat mixture. **Serves 6.**

Fresh and Smoked Turkey Meatloaf

Follow recipe for Turkey Meatloaf (left) or Reduced-Calorie Meatloaf (page 254) made with ground turkey, but add 1 cup (250 mL) diced smoked turkey breast to the meat mixture. **Serves 6.**

Turkey Meatloaf with Bread Stuffing

Follow recipe for Turkey Meatloaf (page 256), but omit the bread and milk, and add 1 cup (250 mL) cooked bread stuffing to the meat mixture. **Serves 6.**

Fragrant Turkey Loaf with Pineapple

Follow recipe for Turkey Meatloaf (page 256), but replace the apple butter with mango chutney, and add $\frac{1}{3}$ cup (75 mL) chopped dried pineapple, 1 tsp (5 mL) ground coriander and $\frac{1}{4}$ tsp (1 mL) ground turmeric to the meat mixture. **Serves 6.**

Turkey and Walnut Meatloaf

Follow recipe for Turkey Meatloaf (page 256) or Reduced-Calorie Meatloaf (page 254) made with ground turkey, but add 1 cup (250 mL) toasted walnut pieces to the meat mixture. **Serves 6.**

Veal Loaf with Artichokes

2	slices white bread, crusts removed, crumbled	2
1	jar (6 oz/170 mL) marinated artichoke hearts, with liquid	1
2	eggs, beaten	2
1	clove garlic, minced	1
1½ lbs	ground veal	750 g
8 oz	ground pork	250 g
½ cup	finely chopped onion	125 mL
½ tsp	dried rosemary, crumbled	2 mL
¼ tsp	dried thyme	1 mL

Preheat oven to 375°F (190°C). Using your hands, combine bread and artichoke liquid until bread is very soft and most of the liquid has been absorbed. Mix in eggs, garlic, veal, pork, onion, rosemary and thyme. Mix in artichoke hearts. Form into a rough loaf and place on a rimmed baking sheet, in a 6-cup (1.5 L) casserole dish or in a 9- by 5-inch (2 L) loaf pan. Bake for 1 hour, or until firm to the touch and a thermometer inserted in the center registers 160°F (71°C). Let cool in pan for 10 minutes. Remove from pan and slice. **Serves 6.**

Herbed Veal Loaf

2	slices white bread, crusts removed, crumbled	2
½ cup	dry white wine	125 mL
1 tbsp	extra-virgin olive oil	15 mL
2	eggs, beaten	2
1½ lbs	ground veal	750 g
8 oz	veal sausage (bulk, or with casings removed)	250 g
½ cup	finely chopped onion	125 mL
½ tsp	dried tarragon	2 mL
½ tsp	dried rosemary, crumbled	2 mL
¼ tsp	dried thyme	1 mL

Preheat oven to 375°F (190°C). Using your hands, combine bread, wine and oil until bread is very soft and most of the liquid has been absorbed. Mix in the remaining ingredients. Form into a rough loaf and place on a rimmed baking sheet, in a 6-cup (1.5 L) casserole dish or in a 9- by 5-inch (2 L) loaf pan. Bake for 1 hour, or until firm to the touch and a thermometer inserted in the center registers 160°F (71°C). Let cool in pan for 10 minutes. Remove from pan and slice. **Serves 6.**

Lasagna Meatloaf

	Olive oil	
2	slices white bread, crusts removed, crumbled	2
½ cup	dry white wine	125 mL
3	eggs, beaten, divided	3
1	large onion, chopped	1
1	clove garlic, minced	1
1 lb	ground beef	500 g
4 oz	ground pork	125 g
¼ cup	tomato sauce	50 mL
½ tsp	dried thyme	2 mL
¼ tsp	dried oregano	1 mL
1 tsp	dried basil	5 mL
8 oz	ricotta cheese, drained	250 g
¼ cup	freshly grated Parmesan cheese	50 mL
8 oz	lasagna noodles, cooked and cooled	250 g
2½ cups	shredded mozzarella cheese, divided	625 mL
	Tomato pasta sauce	

Preheat oven to 350°F (180°C). Line an 11- by 7-inch (2 L) baking pan with foil, leaving a 2-inch (5 cm) overhang, and grease foil with olive oil. Using your hands, combine bread and wine until bread is very soft and most of the wine has been absorbed. Mix in two-thirds of the eggs, the onion, garlic, beef, pork, tomato sauce, thyme, oregano and basil. In a separate bowl, combine the remaining egg, ricotta and Parmesan. Line prepared pan with a layer of noodles, then layer with one-quarter of the meat mixture, one-quarter of the ricotta mixture, ½ cup (125 mL) of the mozzarella and another layer of noodles. Repeat layers 3 more times, finishing with noodles. Top with the remaining mozzarella. Cover with foil and bake for 75 minutes, until a thermometer inserted in the center registers 160°F (71°C). Let cool in pan for 10 minutes. Using foil, remove loaf, slide onto a platter and slice. Serve with tomato pasta sauce. **Serves 6 to 8.**

Chapter 23
Stews
Chase Away the Chill

Beef Stew 260

Beef Stew with Roasted Garlic 260

Beef and Vegetable Stew 260

Sweet-and-Sour Beef Stew 261

Beef and Wild Mushroom Stew 261

Beef Stew with Rosemary and Ham 261

Barbecued Beef Stew 261

Barbecued Pork Stewed with Sausage . . 261

Barbecued Chicken Stew 261

Boeuf Bourguignonne 262

Veal Bourguignonne 262

Coq au Vin 262

Beef Stew Provençal 262

Chicken Provençal 262

Mussels Provençal 262

Shrimp Provençal 263

Catfish Corn Stew 263

Piquant Monkfish Stew 263

Mexican Bouillabaisse 263

Civet of Chicken 264

Civet of Beef 264

Moroccan Turkey Stew 264

Spiced Veal and Squash Stew 264

Veal Stew in the Style of Osso Buco . . . 264

Turkey Stew Milano 265

Mediterranean Chicken Stew 265

Veal Stewed with Artichoke Hearts 265

Veal and Asparagus Stew 265

Veal Stewed with Chickpeas
and Avocado 265

Veal Shanks with Apples and Cream . . . 265

Veal Stew Normandy 266

Pork Stewed with Apples and Prunes . . 266

Blanquette of Veal 266

Turkey Blanquette 266

Lamb Stewed with Anise and Orange . . 266

Lamb Stewed with Peppers 267

Veal Stewed with Peppers 267

Lamb with Red Curry 267

Brown Curry Duck 267

Spring Lamb Stew 268

Lamb Stewed with Asparagus 268

Lamb Stew with Lots of Garlic 268

Veal and Garlic Sausage Stew 268

Fresh Ham Hocks with Leeks
and White Beans 269

Smoky Lamb Stew 269

Sausage and Bean Stew 269

Pork Stewed with Red Cabbage 269

Duck Stewed with Red Cabbage 269

Jamaican Jerk Pork Stew 270

Jerk Ribs 270

By measuring culinary ease with a stopwatch, we have forgotten that there are ways to cook, as old as fire itself, that require *some* time but little labor and even less attention. More time doesn't have to mean more work. Soups, casseroles, pot roasts and stews infuse food with goodness that only time can give, and all we have to do to reap their benefits is slow down the cooking.

Speeding from one activity to the next, we risk thinking about eating as we do fueling up the car — as one more necessity, rather than as one of life's greatest pleasures. And once that happens, the quality of what we eat is bound to take a back seat to the speed of its preparation. A hand-built homemade hamburger has to be pretty good to warrant the time and energy required to produce it, while its two-minute microwaved counterpart, trapped in a form-fitted disposable oven-to-table warming coffin, needs only fill the belly to meet quality standards.

By slowing down, we can actually make mealtimes easier. Stew simmers and spits lazily on the back burner while we play. It rests in a low oven while we rest in the next room. It steams gently in a fragrant broth while we run errands, finish up work or just relax.

The best part is that, while we're occupied elsewhere, ingredients are being transformed in ways that faster food can't match. Flavors are blending, blossoming and balancing, and all we have to do is slow down, sit back and serve up the rewards.

About these recipes . . .

The following 50 stew recipes all take time, but very little work. Most can be made ahead and reheated the next day. For seafood stews, you can make the broth ahead, but add the seafood just before serving. Frequently, they are even better after a day in the refrigerator. When a recipe calls for "cubes for stew," the amount indicated refers to boneless meat. The recipes should all be seasoned with salt and pepper to taste.

Lots of stews are scattered elsewhere in this book, especially in Chapters 18 and 25 (on chilies and chicken parts).

Beef Stew

3 lbs	beef cubes for stew	1.5 kg
¼ cup	all-purpose flour	50 mL
2 tbsp	vegetable oil	25 mL
2	large onions, chopped	2
1	clove garlic, minced	1
1 cup	dry red wine	250 mL
3 cups	beef broth	750 mL
2 tbsp	Worcestershire sauce	25 mL
1 tbsp	tomato paste	15 mL
1½ cups	canned diced tomatoes, drained	375 mL
4	carrots, cut into chunks	4
3	stalks celery, cut into 2-inch (5 cm) lengths	3
3	potatoes, peeled and cut into chunks	3

Dredge beef in flour. In a large saucepan or Dutch oven, heat oil over medium-high heat. Sauté beef, in batches if necessary, until browned on all sides; remove to a plate. Add onion and garlic to the pan and sauté until lightly browned. Add wine and boil for 3 minutes. Return beef to the pan and add broth, Worcestershire sauce, tomato paste and tomatoes; reduce heat, cover and simmer for 30 minutes. Add carrots, celery and potatoes; cover and simmer until tender, about 1 hour. **Serves 6.**

Beef Stew with Roasted Garlic

Follow preceding recipe, but use olive oil instead of vegetable oil. While stew cooks, roast 2 large heads garlic at 375°F (190°C) for 45 minutes, or until soft to the touch; let cool slightly. Cut pointed end off each head, slip cloves from their peels, and purée the roasted garlic with ⅓ cup (75 mL) prepared horseradish, 1 tsp (5 mL) Dijon mustard and salt to taste. When stew is done, remove solids with a slotted spoon and place on a serving platter. Bring liquid to a boil and whisk in garlic purée. Pour over meat and vegetables. **Serves 6.**

Beef and Vegetable Stew

Follow recipe for Beef Stew (above), but add 1 tsp (5 mL) dried rosemary, crumbled, ½ tsp (5 mL) dried thyme and ¼ tsp (1 mL) ground allspice with the onions, and replace the potatoes with 2 turnips, peeled and diced, and 2 sweet potatoes, peeled and cut into chunks. **Serves 6.**

Sweet-and-Sour Beef Stew

Follow recipe for Beef Stew (page 260), but replace the red wine with a mixture of $\frac{1}{4}$ cup (50 mL) cider vinegar and 3 tbsp (45 mL) packed dark brown sugar. **Serves 6.**

Beef and Wild Mushroom Stew

Follow recipe for Beef Stew (page 260), but before browning the beef, soak $\frac{1}{2}$ oz (15 g) dried wild or exotic mushrooms in enough warm water to cover for 15 minutes. Squeeze liquid from the mushrooms, rinse well and set aside. Strain soaking liquid through a coffee filter to remove sediment. Reduce the beef broth to $2\frac{1}{2}$ cups (625 mL), add mushroom soaking liquid with the beef broth, and replace the potatoes with the soaked mushrooms. **Serves 6.**

Beef Stew with Rosemary and Ham

3 lbs	beef cubes for stew	1.5 kg
$\frac{1}{4}$ cup	all-purpose flour	50 mL
2 tbsp	vegetable oil	25 mL
2	large onions, chopped	2
1	clove garlic, minced	1
4 oz	baked ham, chopped	125 g
1 tbsp	chopped fresh rosemary	15 mL
$\frac{1}{2}$ tsp	dried thyme	2 mL
1 cup	dry red wine	250 mL
3 cups	beef broth	750 mL
2 tbsp	Worcestershire sauce	25 mL
2 tbsp	tomato paste	25 mL
4	carrots, cut into chunks	4
3	stalks celery, cut into 2-inch (5 cm) lengths	3
3	potatoes, peeled and cut into chunks	3

Dredge beef in flour. In a large saucepan or Dutch oven, heat oil over medium-high heat. Sauté beef, in batches if necessary, until browned on all sides; remove to a plate. Add onion, garlic, ham, rosemary and thyme to the pan and sauté until vegetables and ham are lightly browned. Add wine and boil for 3 minutes. Return beef to the pan and add broth, Worcestershire sauce and tomato paste; reduce heat, cover and simmer for 30 minutes. Add carrots, celery and potatoes; cover and simmer until tender, about 1 hour. **Serves 6.**

Barbecued Beef Stew

3 lbs	beef cubes for stew	1.5 kg
$\frac{1}{4}$ cup	all-purpose flour	50 mL
$\frac{1}{4}$ cup	vegetable oil	50 mL
$1\frac{1}{2}$	large onions, chopped	$1\frac{1}{2}$
1	clove garlic, minced	1
$\frac{1}{3}$ cup	chopped celery	75 mL
1 cup	canned diced tomatoes, drained	250 mL
1 cup	beef broth	250 mL
1 cup	beer	250 mL
$\frac{2}{3}$ cup	ketchup	150 mL
1 tbsp	light (fancy) molasses	15 mL
1 tbsp	hot pepper sauce (such as Frank's RedHot)	15 mL
1 tbsp	Worcestershire sauce	15 mL
1 tsp	brown mustard	5 mL

Dredge beef in flour. In a large saucepan or Dutch oven, heat oil over medium-high heat. Sauté beef, in batches if necessary, until browned on all sides; remove to a plate. Add onions, garlic and celery to the pan and sauté until tender. Return beef to the pan and add tomatoes, broth, beer, ketchup, molasses, hot pepper sauce, Worcestershire sauce and mustard; reduce heat, cover and simmer until tender, about $1\frac{1}{2}$ hours. **Serves 6.**

Barbecued Pork Stewed with Sausage

Follow preceding recipe, but replace the beef with pork cubes for stew and replace the beef broth with chicken broth. Add 1 lb (500 g) smoked sausage, sliced, during the last 30 minutes of cooking. **Serves 6.**

Barbecued Chicken Stew

Follow recipe for Barbecued Beef Stew (above), but replace the beef with bone-in chicken pieces, replace the beef broth with chicken broth, and reduce the simmering time to 1 hour. **Serves 6.**

Boeuf Bourguignonne

3 lbs	beef cubes for stew	1.5 kg
¼ cup	all-purpose flour	50 mL
4	slices bacon, coarsely chopped	4
2	large onions, chopped	2
1	clove garlic, minced	1
¼ cup	diced carrot	50 mL
¼ cup	diced celery	50 mL
2 cups	dry red wine	500 mL
3 cups	beef broth	750 mL
1 tbsp	chopped fresh Italian (flat-leaf) parsley	15 mL
1 tbsp	Worcestershire sauce	15 mL
1	bay leaf	1
1 tsp	dried thyme	5 mL
4	carrots, cut into chunks	4
3	stalks celery, cut into 2-inch (5 cm) lengths	3
1 tbsp	butter	15 mL
8 oz	small mushrooms	250 g
	Cooked egg noodles (optional)	

Dredge beef in flour. In a large, heavy saucepan or Dutch oven, over medium-high heat, cook bacon until crisp; remove with a slotted spoon and set aside. Add beef to the fat in the pan, in batches if necessary, and sauté until browned on all sides; remove to a plate. Add onions, garlic, diced carrot and diced celery to the pan and sauté until lightly browned. Add wine and boil for 5 minutes. Return beef to the pan and add broth, parsley, Worcestershire sauce, bay leaf and thyme; reduce heat, cover and simmer for 45 minutes. Add carrot and celery chunks; cover and simmer until tender, about 45 minutes. Discard bay leaf. Meanwhile, in a skillet, melt butter over medium-high heat. Sauté mushrooms until golden brown. Add mushrooms and reserved bacon to the stew. Serve with noodles, if desired. **Serves 6.**

Veal Bourguignonne

Follow preceding recipe, but replace the beef with veal cubes for stew, use white wine instead of red, and replace the beef broth with chicken broth. **Serves 6.**

Coq au Vin

Follow recipe for Boeuf Bourguignonne (above), but replace the beef with 4 lbs (2 kg) bone-in chicken pieces, replace the beef broth with chicken broth, add the carrot and celery chunks with the broth, and reduce the overall simmering time to 1 hour. **Serves 6.**

Beef Stew Provençal

3 lbs	beef cubes for stew	1.5 kg
¼ cup	all-purpose flour	50 mL
3 tbsp	extra-virgin olive oil	45 mL
1	large onion, chopped	1
1	head garlic, broken into cloves and peeled	1
½ cup	chopped carrot	125 mL
½ cup	chopped celery	125 mL
3 cups	beef broth	750 mL
1 cup	dry red wine	250 mL
1 cup	canned crushed tomatoes	250 mL
2 tsp	dried herbes de Provence	10 mL
	Grated zest and juice of ½ orange	
1	can (14 oz/398 mL) artichoke hearts, drained and quartered	1
½ cup	pitted black olives	125 mL

Dredge beef in flour. In a large saucepan or Dutch oven, heat oil over medium-high heat. Sauté beef, in batches if necessary, until browned on all sides; remove to a plate. Add onion, garlic, carrot and celery to the pan and sauté until lightly browned. Return beef to the pan and add broth, wine, tomatoes, herbes de Provence, orange zest and orange juice; reduce heat, cover and simmer until tender, about 75 minutes. Add artichoke hearts and olives; cover and simmer for 15 minutes. **Serves 6.**

Chicken Provençal

Follow preceding recipe, but replace the beef with 4 lbs (2 kg) bone-in chicken pieces, replace the beef broth with chicken broth, use white wine instead of red, and reduce the initial simmering time to 45 minutes. **Serves 6.**

Mussels Provençal

3 tbsp	extra-virgin olive oil	45 mL
1	large onion, chopped	1
1	head garlic, separated into cloves and peeled	1
½ cup	chopped carrot	125 mL
½ cup	chopped celery	125 mL
1 cup	clam juice	250 mL
1 cup	drained canned crushed tomatoes	250 mL
½ cup	dry white wine	125 mL
2 tsp	dried herbes de Provence	10 mL
	Grated zest and juice of ½ orange	
48	mussels, scrubbed (see page 8)	48
	Hot cooked pasta (optional)	

In a large saucepan or Dutch oven, heat oil over medium-high heat. Sauté onion, garlic, carrot and celery until tender. Add clam juice, tomatoes, wine, herbes de Provence, orange zest and orange juice; reduce heat, cover and simmer for 10 minutes. Add mussels, cover and simmer until mussels open (discard any that don't). Serve over pasta, if desired. Serves 6.

Shrimp Provençal

Follow preceding recipe, but replace the mussels with 1 lb (500 g) large shrimp, peeled and deveined. After adding shrimp, increase heat, bring to a boil and remove from heat. Serves 6.

Catfish Corn Stew

4	slices bacon, finely chopped	4
3 lbs	skinless catfish fillets	1.5 kg
1 tbsp	hot paprika	15 mL
	Salt and freshly ground black pepper to taste	
2	cloves garlic, minced	2
1	large onion, diced	1
1	red bell pepper, diced	1
3 cups	corn kernels	750 mL
½ cup	finely diced fennel bulb	125 mL
3 cups	Quick Fish Broth (see recipe, page 19)	750 mL
2 tbsp	chopped fresh dill	25 mL
Pinch	hot pepper flakes	Pinch
½ cup	light or table (18%) cream	125 mL
1 tbsp	chopped fresh Italian (flat-leaf) parsley	15 mL

In a large, heavy saucepan or Dutch oven, over medium-high heat, cook bacon until crisp; remove with a slotted spoon and set aside. Season catfish with paprika, salt and black pepper. Add fish to the fat in the pan, in batches if necessary, and brown on both sides; remove to a plate and cut into large strips. Add garlic, onion, bell pepper, corn and fennel to the pan and sauté until tender. Add broth, dill and hot pepper flakes; reduce heat and simmer for 15 to 20 minutes, or until broth is slightly thickened. Return catfish to the pan and simmer until fish is opaque and flakes easily with a fork, about 5 minutes. Stir in cream and parsley. Serves 6.

Piquant Monkfish Stew

2	cloves garlic	2
2	jalapeño peppers, seeded	2
1	red bell pepper, quartered	1
1	onion, quartered	1
2 tbsp	olive oil	25 mL
3 cups	Quick Fish Broth (see recipe, page 19)	750 mL
1½ cups	canned crushed tomatillos	375 mL
1 cup	canned crushed tomatoes	250 mL
3 lbs	monkfish fillets, cut into bite-size chunks	1.5 kg
¼ cup	freshly squeezed lemon juice	50 mL
	Salt and freshly ground black pepper to taste	
1	avocado, diced	1
¼ cup	chopped fresh cilantro	50 mL

In a food processor, finely chop garlic, jalapeño, red pepper and onion. In a large saucepan or Dutch oven, heat oil over medium-high heat. Sauté garlic mixture until tender. Add stock, tomatillos and tomatoes; bring to a boil. (Recipe can be prepared to this point up to 2 days ahead. Reheat to a simmer before proceeding.) Coat monkfish with lemon juice, salt and pepper. Add to pan and simmer for 6 minutes, until barely firm to the touch (do not overcook, or fish will become tough). Stir in avocado and cilantro. Serves 6.

Mexican Bouillabaisse

Follow preceding recipe, but omit the monkfish, lemon juice, salt and pepper, and add 12 littleneck clams, scrubbed (see page 8), to the pan; simmer for 3 minutes. Add 16 mussels, scrubbed (see page 8), 12 oz (375 g) large shrimp, peeled and deveined, and 8 oz (250 g) sea scallops, trimmed of hard side muscles; simmer for 3 to 5 minutes, or until shrimp and scallops are firm and opaque and mussels and clams have opened (discard any that don't). Serves 6.

Civet of Chicken

4 lbs	bone-in chicken pieces	2 kg
⅓ cup	all-purpose flour	75 mL
2 tbsp	vegetable oil	25 mL
1	large onion, chopped	1
1	stalk celery, chopped	1
1	small carrot, chopped	1
4	juniper berries, crushed	4
1	clove garlic, minced	1
1 cup	hearty red wine	250 mL
1	bay leaf	1
1 tbsp	chopped fresh Italian (flat-leaf) parsley	15 mL
½ tsp	dried thyme	2 mL
Pinch	ground cloves	Pinch
2 cups	beef broth	500 mL
1 tbsp	tomato paste	15 mL
	Salt and freshly ground black pepper to taste	
3 tbsp	butter	45 mL
12	small mushrooms	12
½ oz	bittersweet or unsweetened chocolate, finely chopped	15 g

Dredge chicken in flour, reserving any excess flour. In a large, heavy saucepan or Dutch oven, heat oil over medium-high heat. Sauté chicken, in batches if necessary, until browned on all sides; remove to a plate. Add onion, celery and carrot to the pan and sauté until just tender. Add the reserved flour and sauté until browned. Add juniper berries, garlic, wine, bay leaf, parsley, thyme and cloves; boil for 2 minutes. Return chicken to the pan and add broth, tomato paste, salt and pepper; reduce heat, cover and simmer until tender, about 45 minutes. Meanwhile, in a skillet, melt butter over medium-high heat. Sauté mushrooms until golden brown. Add mushrooms and chocolate to the stew. Discard bay leaf. **Serves 6.**

Civet of Beef

Follow preceding recipe, but replace the chicken with 3 lbs (1.5 kg) beef cubes for stew, increase wine to 2 cups (500 mL), and increase simmering time to 1½ hours. **Serves 6.**

Moroccan Turkey Stew

¼ cup	butter	50 mL
3	large onions, chopped	3
1	head garlic, separated into cloves and peeled	1
3	skinless turkey legs, sectioned into legs and thighs	3
1	dried hot chili pepper	1
4 cups	chicken broth	1 L
1 tbsp	ground coriander	15 mL
2 tsp	ground cumin	10 mL
1 tsp	ground turmeric	5 mL
2	carrots, cut into chunks	2
2	stalks celery, cut into 2-inch (5 cm) lengths	2
2	small zucchini, cut into chunks	2
1	sweet potato, cut into chunks	1
½	acorn squash, peeled and cut into chunks	½
1½ cups	coarsely chopped peeled plum (Roma) tomatoes	375 mL
	Cooked couscous, orzo or other small pasta	

In a large, heavy saucepan or Dutch oven, melt butter over medium-high heat. Sauté onions and garlic until tender. Add turkey, chili pepper, broth, coriander, cumin and turmeric; reduce heat, cover and simmer for 45 minutes. Add carrots, celery, zucchini, sweet potato, squash and tomatoes; cover and simmer until tender, about 45 minutes. Serve over couscous. **Serves 6.**

Spiced Veal and Squash Stew

Follow preceding recipe, but replace the turkey with 3 lbs (1.5 kg) veal cubes for stew, dredged in ¼ cup (50 mL) all-purpose flour. **Serves 6.**

Veal Stew in the Style of Osso Buco

3 lbs	veal cubes for stew	1.5 kg
¼ cup	all-purpose flour	50 mL
2 tbsp	butter	25 mL
2 tbsp	olive oil	25 mL
⅔ cup	finely chopped onion	150 mL
⅓ cup	finely chopped carrot	75 mL
⅓ cup	finely chopped celery	75 mL
3	cloves garlic, minced	3
1½ cups	beef broth	375 mL
1 cup	canned diced tomatoes	250 mL
½ cup	dry white wine	125 mL
1	bay leaf	1
1 tsp	dried basil	5 mL
½ tsp	dried thyme	2 mL
	Finely grated zest of 1 lemon	
	Salt and freshly ground black pepper to taste	
2 tbsp	finely chopped fresh Italian (flat-leaf) parsley	25 mL

Preheat oven to 350°F (180°C). Dredge veal in flour. In a large ovenproof saucepan or Dutch oven, heat butter and oil over medium-high heat. Sauté veal, in batches if necessary, until browned on all sides; remove to a plate. Add onion, carrot and celery to the pan and sauté until lightly browned. Return veal to the pan and add garlic, broth, tomatoes, wine, bay leaf, basil, thyme, lemon zest, salt and pepper; bring to a boil. Cover and bake until tender, about 2 hours. Skim off fat and stir in parsley. Discard bay leaf. **Serves 6.**

Turkey Stew Milano

Follow preceding recipe, but replace the veal with 4 lbs (2 kg) skinless turkey legs, sectioned into legs and thighs. **Serves 6.**

Mediterranean Chicken Stew

Follow recipe for Veal Stew in the Style of Osso Buco (page 264), but replace the veal with 4 lbs (2 kg) bone-in chicken pieces. **Serves 6.**

Veal Stewed with Artichoke Hearts

3 lbs	veal cubes for stew	1.5 kg
¼ cup	all-purpose flour	50 mL
¼ cup	olive oil	50 mL
1	large onion, chopped	1
1	stalk celery, chopped	1
3	cloves garlic, minced	3
½ cup	dry white wine	125 mL
1 tbsp	grated lemon zest	15 mL
1	bay leaf	1
1 tsp	dried rosemary, crumbled	5 mL
1 tsp	ground thyme	5 mL
¼ tsp	ground ginger	1 mL
2 cups	chicken broth	500 mL
	Salt and freshly ground black pepper to taste	
1	can (14 oz/398 mL) artichoke hearts, drained and quartered	1
1 cup	canned diced tomatoes	250 mL
2 tbsp	chopped fresh Italian (flat-leaf) parsley	25 mL

Dredge veal in flour. In a large, heavy saucepan or Dutch oven, heat oil over medium-high heat. Sauté veal, in batches if necessary, until browned on all sides; remove to a plate. Add onion, celery and garlic to the pan and sauté until softened. Add wine, lemon zest, bay leaf, rosemary, thyme and ginger; boil for 3 minutes. Return veal to the pan and add broth, salt and pepper; reduce heat, cover and simmer until tender, about 45 minutes. Add artichoke hearts, tomatoes and parsley; cover and simmer for 30 minutes. Discard bay leaf. **Serves 6.**

Veal and Asparagus Stew

Follow preceding recipe, but replace the rosemary with dried chervil, and replace the artichoke hearts with 1 lb (500 g) asparagus, cut into 1-inch (2.5 cm) sections, adding them 5 minutes before the stew is done simmering. **Serves 6.**

Veal Stewed with Chickpeas and Avocado

Follow recipe for Veal Stewed with Artichoke Hearts (left), but add 1 tbsp (15 mL) chili powder with the bay leaf, omit the ginger, replace the artichoke hearts with one 14- to 19-oz (398 to 540 mL) can chickpeas, drained and rinsed, and garnish with 1 large avocado, diced. **Serves 6.**

Veal Shanks with Apples and Cream

4	slices veal shank (2 inches/5 cm thick)	4
¼ cup	all-purpose flour	50 mL
2 tbsp	vegetable oil	25 mL
2 tbsp	butter	25 mL
2	leeks, white part only, sliced	2
2	stalks celery, diced	2
2	cloves garlic, minced	2
¼ cup	applejack brandy	50 mL
1 cup	chicken broth	250 mL
½ cup	unsweetened apple cider	125 mL
1	bay leaf	1
2 tsp	dried rosemary, crumbled	10 mL
1 tsp	dried thyme	5 mL
2	Granny Smith apples, peeled and cut into chunks	2
½ cup	whipping (35%) cream	125 mL

Dredge veal in flour and tie a string around each equator. In a large, heavy saucepan or Dutch oven, heat oil over medium-high heat. Cook veal until browned on both sides; remove to a plate. Reduce heat to medium, add butter to pan and heat until melted. Add leeks, celery and garlic; sauté until tender. Add brandy and carefully flambé (see page 10). When flames subside, return veal to the pan and add broth, cider, bay leaf, rosemary and thyme; cover and simmer until tender, about 1½ hours. Add apples, cover and simmer for 30 minutes. Discard bay leaf and skim off fat. Stir in cream. Untie shanks before serving. **Serves 4.**

Veal Stew Normandy

Follow preceding recipe, but replace the veal shanks with 3 lbs (1.5 kg) veal cubes for stew, and reduce the initial simmering time to 1 hour. **Serves 6.**

Pork Stewed with Apples and Prunes

Follow recipe for Veal Shanks with Apples and Cream (page 265), but first soak 12 pitted prunes in 1 cup (250 mL) boiling water until plump; drain. Replace the veal with 3 lbs (1.5 kg) pork cubes for stew, add the soaked prunes with the broth, add the finely grated zest and juice of 1/2 lemon with the thyme, and omit the whipping cream. **Serves 6.**

Blanquette of Veal

1/4 cup	butter	50 mL
1	onion, diced	1
1	stalk celery, diced	1
1/4	parsnip, diced	1/4
1/4 cup	all-purpose flour	50 mL
4 cups	chicken broth	1 L
2 1/2 lbs	veal cubes for stew	1.25 kg
12	small boiling onions	12
3	carrots, sliced	3
12	small mushrooms	12
1 tbsp	freshly squeezed lemon juice	15 mL
1 cup	frozen peas, thawed	250 mL
1/2 cup	cream (any type, minimum 10%)	150 mL
	Salt and freshly ground white pepper	

In a large, heavy saucepan or Dutch oven, melt butter over medium heat. Sauté onion, celery and parsnip until tender. Add flour and sauté for 1 minute. Add broth, reduce heat and bring to a simmer. Add veal, cover and simmer until tender, about 1 hour. Add small onions and carrots; cover and simmer for 15 minutes. Toss mushrooms in lemon juice and add to the pan, along with peas; cover and simmer for 10 minutes. Stir in cream, salt and pepper. **Serves 6.**

Turkey Blanquette

Follow preceding recipe, but replace the veal with boneless skinless turkey breast, cut into bite-size pieces, and reduce the initial simmering time to 30 minutes. **Serves 6.**

Lamb Stewed with Anise and Orange

3 lbs	lamb cubes for stew	1.5 kg
1/4 cup	all-purpose flour	50 mL
3 tbsp	extra-virgin olive oil	45 mL
1	large onion, chopped	1
1	head garlic, separated into cloves and peeled	1
1 cup	chopped fennel bulb	250 mL
1/2 cup	chopped carrot	125 mL
3 cups	beef broth	750 mL
1 cup	canned crushed tomatoes	250 mL
1/2 cup	dry red wine	125 mL
2 tsp	dried herbes de Provence	10 mL
1 tsp	ground anise seeds	5 mL
	Grated zest and juice of 1 orange	
1/2 cup	pitted black olives	125 mL

Dredge lamb in flour. In a large saucepan or Dutch oven, heat oil over medium-high heat. Sauté lamb, in batches if necessary, until browned on all sides; remove to a plate. Add onion, garlic, fennel and carrot to the pan and sauté until lightly browned. Return lamb to the pan and add broth, tomatoes, wine, herbes de Provence, anise seeds, orange zest and orange juice; reduce heat, cover and simmer until tender, about 1 1/2 hours. Stir in olives. **Serves 6.**

Lamb Stewed with Peppers

3 lbs	lamb cubes for stew	1.5 kg
¼ cup	all-purpose flour	50 mL
¼ cup	olive oil	50 mL
3	bell peppers of different colors, cut into chunks	3
1	large onion, chopped	1
1	stalk celery, chopped	1
1	small carrot, chopped	1
1	clove garlic, minced	1
1 tbsp	sweet paprika	15 mL
1 tsp	ground cumin	5 mL
1 tsp	dried thyme	5 mL
¼ tsp	dried oregano	1 mL
¼ tsp	ground ginger	1 mL
2 cups	beef broth	500 mL
2 tbsp	tomato paste	25 mL
	Salt and freshly ground black pepper to taste	

Dredge lamb in flour. In a large, heavy saucepan or Dutch oven, heat oil over medium-high heat. Sauté lamb, in batches if necessary, until browned on all sides; remove to a plate. Add bell peppers, onion, celery and carrot to the pan and sauté until lightly browned. Add garlic, paprika, cumin, thyme, oregano and ginger; sauté for 3 minutes. Add broth and bring to a boil. Return lamb to the pan and add tomato paste, salt and pepper; reduce heat, cover and simmer until tender, about 1½ hours. Skim off fat. **Serves 6.**

Veal Stewed with Peppers

Follow preceding recipe, but replace the lamb with veal cubes for stew, replace the cumin with dried basil, omit the oregano and ginger, and add ½ tsp (2 mL) dried rosemary, crumbled, with the thyme. **Serves 6.**

Lamb with Red Curry

3 lbs	lamb cubes for stew	1.5 kg
⅓ cup	all-purpose flour	75 mL
3 tbsp	vegetable oil	45 mL
1	large carrot, diced	1
1	stalk celery, diced	1
1	onion, finely chopped	1
1½ tbsp	curry powder	22 mL
1 tsp	ground coriander	5 mL
1 tsp	ground cumin	5 mL
¼ tsp	hot pepper flakes	1 mL
4 cups	canned crushed tomatoes	1 L
2 cups	beef broth	500 mL
	Salt and freshly ground black pepper to taste	
2 tbsp	dried mint	25 mL

Dredge lamb in flour, reserving any excess flour. In a large, heavy saucepan or Dutch oven, heat oil over medium-high heat. Sauté lamb, in batches if necessary, until browned on all sides; remove to a plate. Add carrot, celery and onion to the pan and sauté until lightly browned. Add the reserved flour, curry powder, coriander, cumin and hot pepper flakes; sauté for 1 minute. Return lamb to the pan and add tomatoes, broth, salt and black pepper; reduce heat, cover and simmer for 45 minutes. Add mint and simmer until tender, about 30 minutes. **Serves 6.**

Brown Curry Duck

Follow preceding recipe, but replace the lamb with two 4-lb (2 kg) ducks, each cut into 8 pieces, skin and all visible fat removed. Do not dredge in flour. Replace the mint with 1 tbsp (15 mL) ground anise seeds. **Serves 6.**

Spring Lamb Stew

3 lbs	lamb cubes for stew	1.5 kg
¼ cup	all-purpose flour	50 mL
¼ cup	olive oil, divided	50 mL
3	cloves garlic, minced, divided	3
2	stalks celery, chopped	2
2	carrots, chopped	2
1	large onion, chopped	1
1 cup	dry white wine	250 mL
2 cups	beef broth	500 mL
1½ cups	chopped peeled tomatoes	375 mL
2	bay leaves	2
2 tbsp	chopped fresh Italian (flat-leaf) parsley	25 mL
2 tbsp	finely grated orange zest	25 mL
½ tsp	dried thyme	2 mL
½ tsp	dried basil	2 mL
	Salt and freshly ground black pepper to taste	
8 oz	new potatoes, halved	250 g
12	baby carrots	12
4 oz	small mushrooms	125 g
2	small zucchini, sliced	2

Dredge lamb in flour. In a large, heavy saucepan or Dutch oven, heat 3 tbsp (45 mL) of the oil over medium-high heat. Sauté lamb, in batches if necessary, until browned on all sides; remove to a plate. Add two-thirds of the garlic and the celery, chopped carrots, onion and wine to the pan and boil for 2 minutes. Return lamb to the pan and add broth, tomatoes, bay leaves, parsley, orange zest, thyme, basil, salt and pepper; reduce heat, cover and simmer for 1 hour. Add potatoes and baby carrots; cover and simmer until tender, about 20 minutes. Meanwhile, in a skillet, heat the remaining oil over medium-high heat. Sauté mushrooms until they begin to release their liquid. Add the remaining garlic and zucchini; sauté for 2 minutes. Add mushroom mixture to the stew and simmer for 10 minutes. Discard bay leaves. **Serves 6.**

Lamb Stewed with Asparagus

Follow preceding recipe, but omit the baby carrots, mushrooms and zucchini. While stew is simmering, cut 1 lb (500 g) asparagus into 2-inch (5 cm) lengths. In a skillet, heat 1 tbsp (15 mL) olive oil over medium-high heat. Sauté asparagus and the remaining minced garlic until asparagus is bright green. Stir into the stew and serve immediately. **Serves 6.**

Lamb Stew with Lots of Garlic

3 lbs	lamb cubes for stew	1.5 kg
¼ cup	all-purpose flour	50 mL
3 tbsp	olive oil	45 mL
1	onion, coarsely chopped	1
40	cloves garlic	40
1	small eggplant, peeled and finely chopped	1
2 cups	dry white wine	500 mL
2 cups	beef broth	500 mL
2 tbsp	tomato paste	25 mL
2	bay leaves	2
1 tbsp	dried herbes de Provence	15 mL
¼ tsp	ground allspice	1 mL
	Salt and freshly ground black pepper to taste	

Dredge lamb in flour. In a large, heavy saucepan or Dutch oven, heat oil over medium-high heat. Sauté lamb, in batches if necessary, until browned on all sides; remove to a plate. Add onion and garlic to the pan and sauté until lightly browned. Add eggplant and sauté until tender. Add wine and boil for 3 minutes. Return lamb to the pan and add broth, tomato paste, bay leaves, herbes de Provence, allspice, salt and pepper; reduce heat, cover and simmer until tender, about 1½ hours. Discard bay leaves. **Serves 6.**

Veal and Garlic Sausage Stew

Follow preceding recipe, but replace the lamb with 2 lbs (1 kg) veal cubes for stew, and add 1 lb (500 g) garlic sausage, sliced, with the onion and garlic. **Serves 6.**

Fresh Ham Hocks with Leeks and White Beans

8	slices ham hock (each 2 inches/5 cm thick)	8
¼ cup	all-purpose flour	50 mL
4	slices bacon, coarsely chopped	4
6	leeks, white part only, sliced	6
1 cup	diced celery	250 mL
½ cup	finely chopped carrot	125 mL
1 tsp	dried thyme	5 mL
½ tsp	dried sage	2 mL
1 cup	dry white wine	250 mL
1 cup	chicken broth	250 mL
	Salt and freshly ground black pepper to taste	
1	can (14 to 19 oz/398 to 540 mL) cannellini or white kidney beans, drained and rinsed	1

Preheat oven to 350°F (180°C). Dredge ham hocks in flour and tie string around the perimeters. In a large ovenproof saucepan or Dutch oven, over medium-high heat, cook bacon until crisp; remove with a slotted spoon and set aside. Add ham hocks to the fat in the pan and cook until browned on both sides; remove to a plate. Add leeks, celery, carrot, thyme and sage to the pan and sauté until tender. Add wine and boil for 2 minutes. Return ham hocks to the pan and add broth, salt and pepper; bring to a boil. Scatter reserved bacon over top. Cover and bake for 1 hour. Add beans and bake until tender, about 1 hour. Skim off fat. Untie hocks before serving. **Serves 8.**

Smoky Lamb Stew

Follow preceding recipe, but replace the ham hocks with 3 lbs (1.5 kg) lamb cubes for stew, omit the leeks, add 2 large onions, chopped, with the celery, and add 2 roasted red bell peppers (see page 11), diced, with the cooked bacon. **Serves 6.**

Sausage and Bean Stew

Follow recipe for Fresh Ham Hocks with Leeks and White Beans (left), but replace the ham hocks with 1 lb (500 g) sweet Italian sausage and 1 lb (500 g) spicy Italian sausage, cut into 2-inch (5 cm) lengths. Do not dredge in flour. After adding the beans, reduce baking time to 30 minutes. **Serves 6.**

Pork Stewed with Red Cabbage

3 lbs	pork cubes for stew	1.5 kg
¼ cup	all-purpose flour	50 mL
4	slices bacon, cut into small pieces	4
1	onion, chopped	1
1	stalk celery, chopped	1
1	small carrot, chopped	1
1	small red cabbage, sliced	1
1 tbsp	caraway seeds	15 mL
3 cups	beef broth	750 mL
3 tbsp	packed light brown sugar	45 mL
3 tbsp	red wine vinegar	45 mL
	Boiled potatoes, buttered	

Dredge pork in flour. In a large, heavy saucepan or Dutch oven, over medium-high heat, cook bacon until crisp; remove with a slotted spoon and set aside. Add pork to the fat in the pan, in batches if necessary, and sauté until browned on all sides; remove to a plate. Add onion, celery, carrot, cabbage and caraway seeds to the pan and sauté until cabbage is starting to wilt. Return pork to the pan and add broth, brown sugar and vinegar; reduce heat, cover and simmer until tender, about 1½ hours. Scatter reserved bacon over top. Serve with potatoes. **Serves 6.**

Duck Stewed with Red Cabbage

Follow preceding recipe, but replace the pork with two 4-lb (2 kg) ducks, each cut into 8 pieces, skin and all visible fat removed. Do not dredge in flour. Add 2 tbsp (25 mL) flour with the cabbage. **Serves 6.**

Jamaican Jerk Pork Stew

3 tbsp	jerk seasoning, divided	45 mL
3 lbs	pork cubes for stew	1.5 kg
2 tbsp	rum (light or dark)	25 mL
2 tbsp	vegetable oil	25 mL
1	large onion, finely chopped	1
2 tbsp	all-purpose flour	25 mL
1 tbsp	packed brown sugar	15 mL
3 cups	chicken broth	750 mL
3 tbsp	ketchup	45 mL
1 tbsp	soy sauce	15 mL
1 tsp	hot pepper sauce (such as Tabasco)	5 mL
	Salt and freshly ground black pepper to taste	
	Juice of ½ lemon	
	Cooked rice (optional)	

Rub 1 tbsp (15 mL) of the jerk seasoning into pork and toss with rum. Cover and refrigerate for 1 hour. In a large, heavy saucepan or Dutch oven, heat oil over medium-high heat. Sauté pork, in batches if necessary, until browned on all sides; remove to a plate. Add onion to the fat in the pan and sauté until lightly browned. Add the remaining jerk seasoning and flour; sauté until mixture is deep brown. Add brown sugar and sauté until melted. Add broth, ketchup, soy sauce, hot pepper sauce, salt and pepper; bring to a boil. Return pork to the pan, reduce heat, cover and simmer for 1½ hours. Skim off fat and stir in lemon juice. Serve over rice, if desired. **Serves 6.**

Jerk Ribs

Follow preceding recipe, but increase jerk seasoning to ¼ cup (50 mL), and replace the pork shoulder with 4 lbs (2 kg) beef short ribs or pork spareribs, cut into pieces. Rub ribs with half the jerk seasoning, and add the rest with the flour. **Serves 6.**

Chapter 24
Roast Chickens
The Whole Bird

Traditional Small Roast Chicken 272

Traditional Large Roast Chicken 272

Garlic Roast Chicken 273

Sage and Rosemary Roast Chicken 273

Horseradish and Garlic Roast Chicken . . 273

Roast Chicken with
Horseradish Mustard 273

Worcestershire Mustard Roast Chicken . . 273

Anchovy Mustard Roast Chicken 273

Tuscan Chicken 273

Pesto Roast Chicken 273

Roast Chicken with Capers and Lemon . . 273

Lemon Coriander Chicken 273

Bouillabaisse Roast Chicken 274

Enchilada Roast Chicken 274

Roast Chicken Cacciatore 274

Roast Chicken in Spicy Peanut Paste . . . 274

Honey Mustard Roast Chicken 275

Orange Chinese Roast Chicken 275

Apple Rosemary Roast Chicken 275

Tropical Sweet-and-Sour
Roast Chicken 275

Spicy Pineapple Lime Roast Chicken . . . 275

Mahogany Roast Chicken 276

Barbecued Roast Chicken 276

Roast Chicken with Molasses
and Vinegar 276

Hazelnut Lemon Roast Chicken 276

Lemon Cilantro Roast Chicken 276

Chicken Roasted
with White Clam Sauce 277

Roast Chicken Provençal 277

Lebanese Chicken 277

Roast Chicken with Orange Glaze 277

Ranch Roast Chicken 278

Roast Chicken with
Tarragon and Brandy 278

Roast Chicken with Fines Herbes 278

Brown Sugar Bourbon Roast Chicken . . 278

Roasted Garlic Roast Chicken 278

Red Curry Roast Chicken 278

Roast Tandoori-Style Chicken 279

Cranberry Orange Roast Chicken 279

Roast Chicken with
Apple Butter Glaze 279

Jerk Roast Chicken 279

Sesame Ginger Roast Chicken 279

Roast Chicken with Vanilla Sauce 280

Roast Chicken Chasseur 280

Roast Chicken Véronique 280

Roast Chicken with
Sherry Balsamic Glaze 280

Roast Chicken with
Wild Mushroom Stuffing 280

Roast Chicken with Bread,
Sage and Apple Stuffing 281

Roast Chicken with
Cranberry Cornbread Stuffing 281

Roast Chicken with
Clam and Cracker Stuffing 281

Roast Chicken with Dried Fruit Stuffing . . 282

There was a time when an unadorned roasted chicken, gilded with nothing more than its own bronzed skin, was culinary gold, but that was before industrial poultry-raising, which gave us perfected birds of gargantuan girth with all the taste appeal of chicken feed. If you are longing for some flavor from the same old chicken you've come to know and dread, try one of the following 50 recipes for glazed, sauced, seasoned and stuffed chickens.

The first two entries are basic recipes for roast chicken. The first is for fryer-size chickens, which weigh around 4 lbs (2 kg). The second is for the larger roaster size. There are a few details to our roasting method that you may find unusual. Here's why we recommend them.

Before roasting, we suggest lifting the skin from the breast and leg sections by sliding your fingers under it. That way, you can better season the meat underneath, which accomplishes several things. It puts the flavorings right on the meat, where they will do the most good. For diners who remove the skin before eating, it ensures that seasoning will not be stripped away with the skin. And it gives easily scorched ingredients, such as fresh herbs or minced garlic, protection from the drying heat of the oven.

In addition to seasonings, we add a bit of oil, both under and over the skin. Not only does this help flavor and moisten the meat, but it also ensures that the skin will crisp well during roasting.

We start chickens roasting breast side down at a high temperature (at least 400°F/200°C) to crisp the roast's underside and give the thick part of the thighs a head start in cooking. After half an hour or so, turn the oven down, turn the chicken over, and stuff, baste or sauce it.

You'll notice that the roasting times we recommend are a bit long by recent cookbook standards. Of course, the proper doneness of any meat is always a personal choice, but our choice is never again to carve into a chicken with a rosy pink breast and jiggling thighs. We suggest a doneness between 170°F and 175°F (77°C to 80°C), taken by an instant-read thermometer inserted in the thickest part of the thigh. At this temperature, the breast may be a bit dry (white poultry meat begins to lose moisture after 165°F/74°C), but the dark meat will be cooked through.

About these recipes . . .

The first two recipes below are for ordinary roast chickens — both the smaller chickens often sold as fryers, and the larger chickens, usually called roasters. Both can be roasted, and the 48 recipes that follow are all based on whichever chicken you want to use.

Traditional Small Roast Chicken

	Vegetable cooking spray	
2 tsp	salt	10 mL
1 tsp	freshly ground black pepper	5 mL
1	whole chicken (about 4 lbs/2 kg)	1
2 tbsp	olive oil, divided	25 mL

Preheat oven to 400°F (200°C). Place a rack in the roasting pan and spray the rack with cooking spray. Rinse chicken inside and out and pat dry. Trim off visible fat. Combine salt and pepper, and rub into the walls of the interior cavity of the chicken. Run your fingers under the skin of the breast and legs, separating it gently from the meat underneath. Rub half the oil over the meat under the skin and the rest over surface of the skin. Place chicken, breast side down, on the rack and roast for 30 minutes. Reduce oven temperature to 375°F (190°C) and turn chicken breast side up. Roast for 45 minutes, until skin is golden brown and a thermometer inserted into the thickest part of a thigh registers 170°F to 175°F (77°C to 80°C). Let rest for 10 minutes before carving. **Serves 4.**

Traditional Large Roast Chicken

	Vegetable cooking spray	
2 tsp	salt	10 mL
1 tsp	freshly ground black pepper	5 mL
1	whole chicken (5½ to 8 lbs/2.75 to 4 kg)	1
3 tbsp	olive oil, divided	45 mL

Preheat oven to 400°F (200°C). Place a rack in the roasting pan and spray the rack with cooking spray. Rinse chicken inside and out and pat dry. Trim off visible fat. Combine salt and pepper, and rub into the walls of the interior cavity of the chicken. Run your fingers under the skin of the breast and legs, separating it gently from the meat underneath. Rub half the oil over the meat under the skin and the rest over surface of the skin. Place chicken, breast side down, on the rack and roast for 45 minutes. Reduce oven temperature to 375°F (190°C) and turn chicken breast side up. Roast for 45 to 90 minutes (depending on size), or until skin is golden brown and a thermometer inserted into the thickest part of a thigh registers 170°F to 175°F (77°C to 80°C). Let rest for 10 minutes before carving. **Serves 6 to 8.**

Garlic Roast Chicken

Follow either of the two preceding recipes, but add 3 to 6 cloves garlic, minced (depending on the size of the chicken), to the oil.

Sage and Rosemary Roast Chicken

Follow either recipe for Traditional Roast Chicken (page 272), but add 1 to 2 cloves garlic, minced, and 1 to 2 tsp (5 to 10 mL) each dried sage and dried rosemary, crumbled, to the oil (quantities depending on the size of the chicken).

Horseradish and Garlic Roast Chicken

Follow either recipe for Traditional Roast Chicken (page 272), but add 3 cloves garlic, minced, and 1 tbsp (15 mL) prepared horseradish to the oil.

Roast Chicken with Horseradish Mustard

Follow either recipe for Traditional Roast Chicken (page 272), but first combine 1 clove garlic, minced, 2 tbsp (25 mL) brown mustard and 1 tbsp (15 mL) prepared horseradish. Rub this mixture under the skin in place of the oil.

Worcestershire Mustard Roast Chicken

Follow either recipe for Traditional Roast Chicken (page 272), but first combine 1½ tbsp (22 mL) Worcestershire sauce and 1 tbsp (15 mL) brown mustard. Rub this mixture under the skin in place of the oil.

Anchovy Mustard Roast Chicken

Follow either recipe for Traditional Roast Chicken (page 272), but first combine 1 tbsp (15 mL) anchovy paste and 1 tbsp (15 mL) Dijon mustard. Rub this mixture under the skin in place of the oil.

Tuscan Chicken

Use the ingredients from either recipe for Traditional Roast Chicken (page 272), but double the amount of oil, and add 3 cloves garlic, sliced, and 1 tbsp (15 mL) each chopped fresh rosemary and chopped fresh Italian (flat-leaf) parsley to the oil.

Pesto Roast Chicken

Use the ingredients from either recipe for Traditional Roast Chicken (page 272), and add:

1	clove garlic	1
⅓ cup	packed fresh basil leaves	75 mL
1 tbsp	walnuts	15 mL
3 tbsp	olive oil	45 mL
1 tbsp	freshly grated Parmesan cheese	15 mL
	Salt and freshly ground black pepper to taste	

Follow either recipe for Traditional Roast Chicken, but first use a food processor to purée garlic, basil and walnuts. With the motor running, through the feed tube, slowly add oil and process until blended. Stir in Parmesan, salt and pepper. Rub this mixture under the skin in place of the oil.

Roast Chicken with Capers and Lemon

Follow either recipe for Traditional Roast Chicken (page 272), but add 2 tbsp (25 mL) grated onion and 1 tbsp (15 mL) finely chopped drained capers to the oil used under the skin. During the last 30 minutes of roasting, baste chicken frequently with the juice of 1 lemon.

Lemon Coriander Chicken

Use the ingredients from either recipe for Traditional Roast Chicken (page 272), and add:

2	cloves garlic, minced	2
1 tbsp	finely chopped fresh cilantro	15 mL
1 tbsp	ground coriander	15 mL
1 tsp	freshly ground black pepper	5 mL
1 tsp	ground cumin	5 mL
Pinch	cayenne pepper	Pinch
	Salt to taste	
	Juice of 2 large lemons	

Follow either recipe for Traditional Roast Chicken, but first combine garlic, cilantro, coriander, black pepper, cumin, cayenne and salt. Rub this mixture under the skin in place of the oil. After oiling the skin of the chicken, squeeze lemon juice over top.

Bouillabaisse Roast Chicken

Use the ingredients from either recipe for Traditional Roast Chicken (page 272), and add:

1 tbsp	olive oil	15 mL
1/4 cup	chopped onion	50 mL
1	clove garlic, minced	1
2 tsp	grated orange zest	10 mL
1/2 tsp	ground fennel seeds	2 mL
1/2 tsp	dried thyme	2 mL
1 cup	crushed tomatoes	250 mL
1/2 cup	dry white wine	125 mL
1/2 cup	clam juice	125 mL
12	small clams, scrubbed (see page 8)	12
12	mussels, scrubbed (see page 8)	12

Follow either recipe for Traditional Roast Chicken. During the first half-hour of roasting, in a skillet, heat oil over medium-high heat. Sauté onion until tender. Add garlic, orange zest, fennel seeds and thyme; sauté for 30 seconds. Add tomatoes and wine; bring to a boil. Stir in clam juice. Pour over chicken when you turn it breast side up, then baste chicken with pan juices 2 to 3 times during roasting. Ten minutes before chicken is done roasting, add clams to the pan. Five minutes later, add the mussels; cook until shellfish open (discard any that don't).

Enchilada Roast Chicken

Use the ingredients from either recipe for Traditional Roast Chicken (page 272), and add:

1 tbsp	olive oil	15 mL
3 tbsp	minced onion	45 mL
2	jalapeño peppers, seeded and finely chopped	2
1	clove garlic, minced	1
1 cup	crushed tomatoes	250 mL
3/4 cup	chicken broth	175 mL
	Salt and freshly ground black pepper to taste	
1/2 cup	plain yogurt (not fat-free)	125 mL

Follow either recipe for Traditional Roast Chicken. During the first half-hour of roasting, in a skillet, heat oil over medium-high heat. Sauté onion, jalapeños and garlic until softened. Add tomatoes, broth, salt and pepper; reduce heat and simmer for 5 minutes. Remove from heat and stir in yogurt. Pour over chicken when you turn it breast side up, then baste chicken with pan juices 2 to 3 times during roasting.

Roast Chicken Cacciatore

Use the ingredients from either recipe for Traditional Roast Chicken (page 272), and add:

2 tbsp	olive oil	25 mL
3/4 cup	sliced mushrooms	175 mL
1/2 cup	chopped onion	125 mL
2	cloves garlic, minced	2
1/4 tsp	dried oregano	1 mL
Pinch	hot pepper flakes	Pinch
	Salt and freshly ground black pepper to taste	
1 cup	dry white wine	250 mL
1 cup	crushed tomatoes	250 mL

Follow either recipe for Traditional Roast Chicken. During the first half-hour of roasting, in a skillet, heat oil over medium-high heat. Sauté mushrooms and onion until tender. Add garlic, oregano, hot pepper flakes, salt and black pepper; sauté for 1 minute. Add wine and tomatoes; bring to a boil. Pour over chicken when you turn it breast side up, then baste chicken with pan juices 2 to 3 times during roasting.

Roast Chicken in Spicy Peanut Paste

Use the ingredients from either recipe for Traditional Roast Chicken (page 272), and add:

1 tbsp	peanut oil	15 mL
1/2 cup	chopped onion	125 mL
1	clove garlic, minced	1
2 tsp	grated gingerroot	10 mL
1 tsp	ground coriander	5 mL
1/2 tsp	hot pepper flakes	2 mL
1/4 tsp	ground cumin	1 mL
1/3 cup	smooth peanut butter	75 mL
1/3 cup	water	75 mL
1 tbsp	honey	15 mL
1 tbsp	soy sauce	15 mL
2 tsp	rice wine vinegar	10 mL

Follow either recipe for Traditional Roast Chicken. During the first half-hour of roasting, in a skillet, heat oil over medium-high heat. Sauté onion, garlic and ginger until tender. Add coriander, hot pepper flakes and cumin; sauté for 1 minute. Stir in peanut butter, water, honey, soy sauce and vinegar; heat through. After turning chicken breast side up, baste 2 to 3 times with this sauce.

Honey Mustard Roast Chicken

Follow either recipe for Traditional Roast Chicken (page 272). During the first half-hour of roasting, combine ½ cup (125 mL) brown mustard, ¼ cup (50 mL) honey and 1½ tbsp (22 mL) Worcestershire sauce. After turning chicken breast side up, baste every 20 minutes with this sauce.

Orange Chinese Roast Chicken

Use the ingredients from either recipe for Traditional Roast Chicken (page 272), and add:

¼ cup	soy sauce	50 mL
¼ cup	orange juice	50 mL
2 tbsp	honey	25 mL
2 tbsp	orange marmalade	25 mL
1 tbsp	rice wine vinegar	15 mL
1 tbsp	peanut oil	15 mL
1 tsp	dark sesame oil	5 mL
½ tsp	ground ginger	2 mL
¼ tsp	hot pepper sauce (such as Tabasco)	1 mL

Follow either recipe for Traditional Roast Chicken. During the first half-hour of roasting, combine soy sauce, orange juice, honey, marmalade, vinegar, peanut oil, sesame oil, ginger and hot pepper sauce. After turning chicken breast side up, baste 2 to 3 times with this sauce.

Apple Rosemary Roast Chicken

Use the ingredients from either recipe for Traditional Roast Chicken (page 272), and add:

2	cloves garlic, minced	2
1 tbsp	dried rosemary, crushed	15 mL
¼ cup	apple butter	50 mL
2 tbsp	honey	25 mL
2 tsp	vegetable oil	10 mL
1 tsp	brown mustard	5 mL

Follow either recipe for Traditional Roast Chicken, but add garlic and rosemary to the oil used under the skin. During the first half-hour of roasting, combine apple butter, honey, oil and mustard. During the last 40 to 60 minutes of roasting, baste chicken 2 to 3 times with this sauce.

Tropical Sweet-and-Sour Roast Chicken

Use the ingredients from either recipe for Traditional Roast Chicken (page 272), and add:

2	cloves garlic, minced	2
1 tbsp	finely chopped fresh cilantro	15 mL
¼ cup	frozen pineapple juice concentrate, thawed	50 mL
2 tbsp	honey	25 mL
2 tbsp	cider vinegar	25 mL
1 tbsp	soy sauce	15 mL
2 tsp	hot pepper sauce (such as Tabasco)	10 mL

Follow either recipe for Traditional Roast Chicken, but add garlic and cilantro to the oil used under the skin. During the first half-hour of roasting, combine pineapple juice concentrate, honey, vinegar, soy sauce and hot pepper sauce. During the last 40 to 60 minutes of roasting, baste chicken 2 to 3 times with this sauce.

Spicy Pineapple Lime Roast Chicken

Use the ingredients from either recipe for Traditional Roast Chicken (page 272), and add:

2	cloves garlic, minced	2
1 tsp	finely grated lime zest	5 mL
⅓ cup	frozen pineapple juice concentrate, thawed	75 mL
¼ cup	freshly squeezed lime juice	50 mL
1 tbsp	soy sauce	15 mL
	Hot pepper sauce (such as Tabasco) to taste	

Follow either recipe for Traditional Roast Chicken, but add garlic and lime zest to the oil used under the skin. During the first half-hour of roasting, combine pineapple juice concentrate, lime juice, soy sauce and hot pepper sauce. During the last 40 to 60 minutes of roasting, baste chicken 2 to 3 times with this sauce.

Mahogany Roast Chicken

Use the ingredients from either recipe for Traditional Roast Chicken (page 272), and add:

2 tbsp	peanut oil	25 mL
2	cloves garlic, minced	2
1	dried hot chili pepper	1
⅓ cup	soy sauce	75 mL
¼ cup	honey	50 mL
¼ cup	water	50 mL
¼ cup	dry sherry	50 mL
2 tbsp	dark (cooking) molasses	25 mL
1 tbsp	rice wine vinegar	15 mL
1 tbsp	freshly grated gingerroot	15 mL

Follow either recipe for Traditional Roast Chicken. During the first half-hour of roasting, in a small skillet, heat oil over medium-high heat. Add garlic, chili pepper, soy sauce, honey, water, sherry, molasses, vinegar and ginger; bring to a boil. During the last 40 to 60 minutes of roasting, baste chicken 4 to 6 times with this sauce.

Barbecued Roast Chicken

Use the ingredients from either recipe for Traditional Roast Chicken (page 272), and add:

1 cup	ketchup	250 mL
¼ cup	chopped onion	50 mL
2 tbsp	brown mustard	25 mL
2 tbsp	cider vinegar	25 mL
1 tbsp	granulated sugar	15 mL
1 tbsp	vegetable oil	15 mL
1 tbsp	light (fancy) molasses	15 mL
1 tbsp	Worcestershire sauce	15 mL
2 tsp	hot pepper sauce (such as Tabasco)	10 mL
	Salt and freshly ground black pepper to taste	

Follow either recipe for Traditional Roast Chicken. During the first half-hour of roasting, bring ketchup, onion, mustard, vinegar, sugar, oil, molasses, Worcestershire sauce and hot pepper sauce to a boil; season with salt and pepper. After turning chicken breast side up, baste 2 to 3 times with this sauce.

Roast Chicken with Molasses and Vinegar

Use the ingredients from either recipe for Traditional Roast Chicken (page 272), and add:

1	clove garlic, minced	1
½ cup	dark (cooking) molasses	125 mL
¼ cup	balsamic vinegar	50 mL
1 tbsp	Worcestershire sauce	15 mL

Follow either recipe for Traditional Roast Chicken. During the first half-hour of roasting, combine garlic, molasses, vinegar and Worcestershire sauce. During the last 40 to 60 minutes of roasting, baste chicken 2 to 3 times with this sauce.

Hazelnut Lemon Roast Chicken

Use the ingredients from either recipe for Traditional Roast Chicken (page 272), and add:

3	cloves garlic	3
⅔ cup	toasted hazelnuts	150 mL
¼ cup	packed fresh Italian (flat-leaf) parsley leaves	50 mL
½ tsp	dried sage	2 mL
	Salt and freshly ground black pepper to taste	
	Juice of 1 large lemon	

Follow either recipe for Traditional Roast Chicken, but first use a food processor to purée garlic, hazelnuts, parsley, sage, salt, and pepper. Using a thin, sharp knife, make deep pockets through the skin and meat of the breast, thigh and leg, and stuff 1 tsp (5 mL) of the hazelnut mixture into each pocket. Roast chicken as directed. Thirty minutes before it's done roasting, squeeze lemon juice over top.

Lemon Cilantro Roast Chicken

Use the ingredients from either recipe for Traditional Roast Chicken (page 272), and add:

2 tbsp	ground coriander, divided	25 mL
2	cloves garlic, minced	2
2 tbsp	chopped fresh cilantro, stems reserved	25 mL
1 tsp	ground cumin	5 mL
1 cup	dry white wine	250 mL
	Juice of 2 lemons, rinds reserved	

Follow either recipe for Traditional Roast Chicken, but combine half the coriander with the salt and pepper to be rubbed into the interior cavity. Add garlic, cilantro, the remaining coriander and cumin to the oil used under the skin. Pour wine and lemon juice over chicken, and stuff lemon rinds and cilantro stems in the cavity. After turning chicken breast side up, baste 2 to 3 times with pan juices.

Chicken Roasted with White Clam Sauce

Use the ingredients from either recipe for Traditional Roast Chicken (page 272), and add:

1	clove garlic, minced	1
1 to 2	cans (each 15 oz/426 mL) clams in white clam sauce	1 to 2

Follow either recipe for Traditional Roast Chicken, but add garlic to the oil used under the skin, and spoon clams (1 can for a small roast, 2 cans for a large) into the cavity. Pour the liquid from the clam sauce over chicken when you turn it breast side up, then baste chicken with pan juices 2 to 3 times during roasting.

Roast Chicken Provençal

Use the ingredients from either recipe for Traditional Roast Chicken (page 272), and add:

1 tbsp	extra-virgin olive oil	15 mL
½ cup	chopped onion	125 mL
2	cloves garlic, minced	2
1	bell pepper (any color), chopped	1
1 tsp	dried basil	5 mL
1 tsp	dried herbes de Provence	5 mL
1 cup	dry white wine	250 mL
1 cup	chopped plum (Roma) tomatoes	250 mL
1 tsp	grated lemon zest	5 mL
	Salt and freshly ground black pepper to taste	

Follow either recipe for Traditional Roast Chicken. During the first half-hour of roasting, in a skillet, heat oil over medium-high heat. Sauté onion, garlic, bell pepper, basil and herbes de Provence until vegetables are tender. Add wine to pan and boil for 2 minutes, scraping up brown bits from the bottom of the pan. Add tomatoes and lemon zest; bring to a boil. Season with salt and pepper. Pour over chicken when you turn it breast side up, then baste chicken with pan juices 2 to 3 times during roasting.

Lebanese Chicken

Use the ingredients from either recipe for Traditional Roast Chicken (page 272), and add:

2 tbsp	ground coriander, divided	25 mL
2	cloves garlic, minced	2
2 tbsp	dried mint	25 mL
1 tsp	ground cumin	5 mL
1 cup	plain yogurt (not fat-free)	250 mL
	Juice of 2 lemons, rinds reserved	
	Several sprigs fresh mint	

Follow either recipe for Traditional Roast Chicken, but combine half the coriander with the salt and pepper to be rubbed into the interior cavity. Add garlic, mint, the remaining coriander and cumin to the oil used under the skin. Combine yogurt and lemon juice, and pour over chicken. Stuff lemon rinds and mint sprigs in the cavity. After turning chicken breast side up, baste 2 to 3 times with pan juices.

Roast Chicken with Orange Glaze

Use the ingredients from either recipe for Traditional Roast Chicken (page 272), and add:

	Julienned zest and juice of 1 orange	
1 cup	water	250 mL
¼ cup	honey	50 mL
¼ cup	freshly squeezed lemon juice	50 mL
4	cloves garlic, halved	4
½	onion, cut into chunks	½
½ cup	chicken broth	125 mL
	Salt and freshly ground black pepper to taste	

Follow either recipe for Traditional Roast Chicken. During the first half-hour of roasting, bring orange juice, water, honey and lemon juice to a simmer. Add orange zest, garlic and onion; simmer until reduced to a syrupy sauce. Discard onion and garlic, and stir broth, salt and pepper into the syrup. During the last 40 minutes of roasting, baste chicken 4 times with this sauce.

Ranch Roast Chicken

Follow either recipe for Traditional Roast Chicken (page 272), but add 1 tsp (5 mL) minced garlic to the oil used under the skin. After turning chicken breast side up, baste 2 to 3 times with ranch dressing (not fat-free), using a total of 1½ cups (375 mL).

Roast Chicken with Tarragon and Brandy

Follow either recipe for Traditional Roast Chicken (page 272), but add 1 small clove garlic, minced, and 2 tbsp (25 mL) brandy to the oil used under the skin, and place 4 tarragon sprigs under the skin of the breast and legs. After turning chicken breast side up, baste 2 to 3 times with an additional ½ cup (125 mL) brandy.

Roast Chicken with Fines Herbes

Use the ingredients from either recipe for Traditional Roast Chicken (page 272), and add:

1	clove garlic, minced	1
¼ cup	grated onion	50 mL
1 tsp	chopped fresh Italian (flat-leaf) parsley	5 mL
1 tsp	chopped fresh basil	5 mL
1 tsp	dried thyme	5 mL
1 tsp	dried tarragon	5 mL
2 cups	dry white wine	500 mL

Follow either recipe for Traditional Roast Chicken, but add garlic, onion, parsley, basil, thyme and tarragon to the oil used under the skin. Pour wine over chicken when you turn it breast side up, then baste chicken with pan juices 2 to 3 times during roasting.

Brown Sugar Bourbon Roast Chicken

Use the ingredients from either recipe for Traditional Roast Chicken (page 272), and add:

1 tbsp	butter	15 mL
½ cup	finely chopped onion	125 mL
1	clove garlic, minced	1
½ cup	packed light brown sugar	125 mL
1 tbsp	minced gingerroot	15 mL
1 tsp	ground coriander	5 mL
	Salt and freshly ground black pepper to taste	
1 cup	bourbon	250 mL
½ cup	light (fancy) molasses	125 mL
¼ cup	red wine vinegar	50 mL
1 tbsp	Worcestershire sauce	15 mL

Follow either recipe for Traditional Roast Chicken. During the first half-hour of roasting, in a small skillet, melt butter over medium-high heat. Sauté onion until browned. Add garlic, brown sugar, ginger, coriander, salt and pepper; sauté for 1 minute. Add bourbon, molasses, vinegar and Worcestershire sauce; bring to a boil. During the last 45 to 60 minutes of roasting, baste chicken 3 to 4 times with this sauce.

Roasted Garlic Roast Chicken

Use the ingredients from either recipe for Traditional Roast Chicken (page 272), and add:

2	heads garlic	2
1 tbsp	granulated sugar	15 mL
2 tbsp	olive oil	25 mL
1 tsp	hot pepper oil (store-bought, or see recipe, page 82)	5 mL
1 tsp	cider vinegar	5 mL

Follow either recipe for Traditional Roast Chicken, but first wrap garlic in foil and roast at 400°F (200°C) until soft, about 40 minutes; let cool slightly. Cut the pointed ends off each head and slip cloves from their peels. Mash garlic with sugar, olive oil, hot pepper oil and vinegar. Rub this mixture under the skin in place of the oil.

Red Curry Roast Chicken

Use the ingredients from either recipe for Traditional Roast Chicken (page 272), and add:

½ cup	canned coconut milk	125 mL
3 tbsp	Thai red curry paste	45 mL
1 tbsp	Thai fish sauce (*nam pla*)	15 mL
2 tsp	Asian garlic chili paste	10 mL
	Juice of 1 lemon	

Follow either recipe for Traditional Roast Chicken, but first combine coconut milk, curry paste, fish sauce and chili paste. Rub this mixture under the skin in place of the oil. About 30 minutes before chicken is done roasting, squeeze lemon juice over top.

Roast Tandoori-Style Chicken

Use the ingredients from either recipe for Traditional Roast Chicken (page 272), and add:

2	cloves garlic, minced	2
¾ cup	freshly squeezed lemon juice (about 4 medium lemons), divided	175 mL
½ cup	plain yogurt (not fat-free)	125 mL
2 tbsp	minced gingerroot	25 mL
2 tsp	curry powder	10 mL
1 tsp	ground cumin	5 mL
1 tsp	ground cardamom	5 mL
1 tsp	paprika	5 mL
1 tsp	salt	5 mL

Follow either recipe for Traditional Roast Chicken, but first combine garlic, 3 tbsp (45 mL) of the lemon juice, yogurt, ginger, curry powder, cumin, cardamom, paprika and salt. Rub this mixture under the skin in place of the oil. After turning chicken breast side up, baste 2 to 3 times with some of the remaining lemon juice.

Cranberry Orange Roast Chicken

Use the ingredients from either recipe for Traditional Roast Chicken (page 272), and add:

¼ cup	orange marmalade	50 mL
3 tbsp	whole-berry cranberry sauce	45 mL
1 tbsp	minced orange zest	15 mL
1 tbsp	honey	15 mL
1 tbsp	soy sauce	15 mL
1 tbsp	cider vinegar	15 mL
Dash	hot pepper sauce (such as Tabasco)	Dash

Follow either recipe for Traditional Roast Chicken. During the first half-hour of roasting, combine marmalade, cranberry sauce, orange zest, honey, soy sauce, vinegar and hot pepper sauce. During the last 40 to 60 minutes of roasting, baste chicken 2 to 3 times with this sauce.

Roast Chicken with Apple Butter Glaze

Use the ingredients from either recipe for Traditional Roast Chicken (page 272), and add:

1 cup	unsweetened apple cider	250 mL
¼ cup	apple butter	50 mL
2 tbsp	honey	25 mL
2 tsp	vegetable oil	10 mL
1 tsp	brown mustard	5 mL

Follow either recipe for Traditional Roast Chicken. During the first half-hour of roasting, combine apple cider, apple butter, honey, vegetable oil and mustard. During the last 40 to 60 minutes of roasting, baste chicken 2 to 3 times with this sauce.

Jerk Roast Chicken

Use the ingredients from either recipe for Traditional Roast Chicken (page 272), but omit the olive oil and add:

2 tbsp	jerk seasoning	25 mL
1 tbsp	packed light brown sugar	15 mL
3 tbsp	ketchup	45 mL
2 tbsp	soy sauce	25 mL
1 tbsp	dark rum	15 mL
2 tsp	chopped gingerroot	10 mL
1 tsp	hot pepper sauce (such as Tabasco)	5 mL
2 tbsp	vegetable oil	25 mL
¼ cup	chopped fresh Italian (flat-leaf) parsley	50 mL

Follow either recipe for Traditional Roast Chicken, but first combine jerk seasoning, brown sugar, ketchup, soy sauce, rum, ginger and hot pepper sauce. In a small skillet, heat oil over medium heat. Sauté spice mixture until aromatic. Remove from heat, stir in parsley and let cool. Use this paste in place of the olive oil, rubbing half under the skin and the other half over the skin.

Sesame Ginger Roast Chicken

Follow either recipe for Traditional Roast Chicken (page 272), but replace the olive oil with dark sesame oil. Add 1 clove garlic, minced, and 1 tbsp (15 mL) finely chopped gingerroot to the oil rubbed under the skin, and add ¼ cup (50 mL) soy sauce to the oil rubbed over the skin.

Roast Chicken with Vanilla Sauce

Use the ingredients from either recipe for Traditional Roast Chicken (page 272), and add:

2 tbsp	walnut oil, divided	25 mL
2 tsp	vanilla, divided	10 mL
½ cup	finely chopped onion	125 mL
1	vanilla bean, split lengthwise, seeds scraped out	1
1 cup	chicken broth	250 mL
	Juice of 1 lime	

Follow either recipe for Traditional Roast Chicken, but first combine half the walnut oil and half the vanilla. Use this mixture in place of the olive oil, rubbing half under the skin and the other half over the skin. During the first half-hour of roasting, in a small skillet, heat the remaining walnut oil over medium heat. Sauté onion until tender. Add vanilla seeds, vanilla pod, broth and lime juice; bring to a boil. Stir in the remaining vanilla. After turning chicken breast side up, baste 2 to 3 times with this sauce.

Roast Chicken Chasseur

Use the ingredients from either recipe for Traditional Roast Chicken (page 272), and add:

3 tbsp	vegetable oil	45 mL
4 oz	wild or exotic mushrooms, sliced	125 g
4 oz	mushrooms, sliced	125 g
2 tbsp	finely chopped onion	25 mL
1	clove garlic, minced	1
¼ cup	brandy	50 mL
1 cup	chopped tomatoes	250 mL
½ cup	beef broth	125 mL
½ tsp	dried tarragon	2 mL
	Salt and freshly ground black pepper to taste	

Follow either recipe for Traditional Roast Chicken, but replace the olive oil with 2 tbsp (25 mL) of the vegetable oil. During the first half-hour of roasting, in a skillet, heat the remaining vegetable oil over medium-high heat. Sauté both types of mushrooms, onion and garlic until lightly browned. Add brandy and boil for 2 minutes, scraping up brown bits from the bottom of the pan. Add tomatoes, broth, tarragon, salt and pepper; reduce heat and simmer for 5 minutes. After turning chicken breast side up, baste 2 to 3 times with this sauce.

Roast Chicken Véronique

Use the ingredients from either recipe for Traditional Roast Chicken (page 272), and add:

1	small clove garlic, minced	1
½ tsp	dried tarragon	2 mL
1 cup	dry vermouth	250 mL
1 cup	chicken broth	250 mL
2 cups	halved seedless grapes	500 mL
2 tbsp	freshly squeezed lemon juice	25 mL
1 tsp	chopped fresh tarragon	5 mL
1 tbsp	butter	15 mL

Follow either recipe for Traditional Roast Chicken, but add garlic and dried tarragon to the oil used under the skin. Pour vermouth and broth over chicken when you turn it breast side up, then baste chicken with pan juices 2 to 4 times during roasting. Fifteen minutes before chicken is done roasting, add grapes, lemon juice and fresh tarragon to the pan. When chicken is done, transfer to a board. Skim fat from pan juices, bring to a boil and swirl in butter.

Roast Chicken with Sherry Balsamic Glaze

Follow either recipe for Traditional Roast Chicken (page 272). During the first half-hour of roasting, combine 1 cup (250 mL) chicken broth, ½ cup (125 mL) dry sherry and ¼ cup (50 mL) balsamic vinegar. Pour over chicken when you turn it breast side up, then baste chicken with pan juices 3 to 4 times during roasting.

Roast Chicken with Wild Mushroom Stuffing

Use the ingredients from either recipe for Traditional Roast Chicken (page 272), and add:

¼ cup	butter	50 mL
1	large onion, chopped	1
1 lb	wild or exotic mushrooms, quartered	500 g
½ tsp	dried thyme	2 mL
½ tsp	dried rosemary, crumbled	2 mL
½ tsp	dried sage	2 mL
½ tsp	dried savory	2 mL
1 cup	fresh bread crumbs	250 mL
½ cup	hot chicken broth	125 mL
1 tbsp	tomato paste	15 mL
¼ cup	chopped fresh Italian (flat-leaf) parsley	50 mL
	Salt and freshly ground black pepper to taste	

Follow either recipe for Traditional Roast Chicken. During the first half-hour of roasting, in a large skillet, melt butter over medium-high heat. Sauté onion until tender. Add mushrooms, thyme, rosemary, sage and savory; sauté until mushrooms start to release their liquid. Add bread crumbs and sauté for 1 minute. Add broth and tomato paste; reduce heat and simmer until thickened. Stir in parsley, salt and pepper. After turning chicken breast side up, use a large spoon to stuff the cavity with this mixture.

Roast Chicken with Bread, Sage and Apple Stuffing

Use the ingredients from either recipe for Traditional Roast Chicken (page 272), and add:

1/4 cup	butter	50 mL
2	stalks celery, diced	2
1	large onion, minced	1
1	Granny Smith apple, peeled and diced	1
1 tsp	dried sage	5 mL
1 tsp	dried chervil	5 mL
1/2 tsp	dried thyme	2 mL
Pinch	ground nutmeg	Pinch
4 cups	toasted bread cubes	1 L
1 cup	hot chicken broth	250 mL
	Salt and freshly ground black pepper to taste	

Follow either recipe for Traditional Roast Chicken. During the first half-hour of roasting, in a large skillet, melt butter over medium-high heat. Sauté celery and onion until tender. Add apple, sage, chervil, thyme and nutmeg; sauté for 1 minute. Stir in bread cubes, broth, salt and pepper until bread is evenly moistened. After turning chicken breast side up, use a large spoon to stuff the cavity with this mixture.

Roast Chicken with Cranberry Cornbread Stuffing

Use the ingredients from either recipe for Traditional Roast Chicken (page 272), and add:

3 cups	fresh cranberries	750 mL
1 1/4 cups	granulated sugar	300 mL
6	green onions, chopped	6
2	cloves garlic, minced	2
3 cups	crumbled cornbread	750 mL
	Finely chopped zest and juice of 1 large orange	
	Salt and cayenne pepper to taste	

Follow either recipe for Traditional Roast Chicken. During the first half-hour of roasting, cook cranberries and sugar until berries burst. In a large bowl, combine berry mixture, green onions, garlic, cornbread, orange zest, orange juice, salt and cayenne. After turning chicken breast side up, use a large spoon to stuff the cavity with this mixture.

Roast Chicken with Clam and Cracker Stuffing

Use the ingredients from either recipe for Traditional Roast Chicken (page 272), and add:

1/4 cup	butter	50 mL
2	stalks celery, diced	2
1	large onion, minced	1
1 tsp	dried dillweed	5 mL
1 tsp	dried chervil	5 mL
1/2 tsp	dried thyme	2 mL
Pinch	ground nutmeg	Pinch
	Juice of 1/2 lemon	
4 cups	crackers (such as Saltines), crumbled	1 L
2 cups	chopped drained canned clams	500 mL
1 cup	clam juice	250 mL
	Salt and freshly ground black pepper to taste	

Follow either recipe for Traditional Roast Chicken. During the first half-hour of roasting, in a large skillet, melt butter over medium-high heat. Sauté celery and onion until tender. Add dill, chervil, thyme, nutmeg and lemon juice; sauté for 1 minute. Stir in crackers, clams, clam juice, salt and pepper until bread is evenly moistened. After turning chicken breast side up, use a large spoon to stuff the cavity with this mixture.

Roast Chicken with Dried Fruit Stuffing

Use the ingredients from either recipe for Traditional Roast Chicken (page 272), and add:

2 tbsp	butter	25 mL
1	large onion, diced	1
1	clove garlic, minced	1
1½ cups	brown rice	375 mL
3 cups	boiling chicken broth	750 mL
8 oz	mixed dried fruit, chopped	250 g
	Salt and freshly ground black pepper to taste	

Follow either recipe for Traditional Roast Chicken, but first, in a large saucepan, melt butter over medium-high heat. Sauté onion and garlic until tender. Stir in rice until well coated with butter. Stir in broth, reduce heat, cover and simmer gently for 40 minutes, until broth is absorbed. Meanwhile, soak dried fruit in boiling water until softened. Drain. Remove rice from heat and stir in fruit, salt and pepper. After turning chicken breast side up, use a large spoon to stuff the cavity with this mixture.

Chapter 25
Chicken Parts
White and Dark Meats Cooked to Perfection

Old-Fashioned Chicken Salad 284
Yogurt Dill Chicken Salad 284
Warm Grilled Chicken Salad
on Wilted Lettuce 284
Chicken Breasts Sautéed in
Capers and Brown Butter 285
Sautéed Chicken Breasts
with Brandy Cream Reduction 285
Sautéed Chicken Breasts
with Apple Glaze 285
Chicken Baked in Foil with Clams 285
Poached Chicken Breasts
in Beurre Blanc 285
Chilled Grilled Marinated
Chicken Breasts 286
Grilled Chicken Breasts
with Artichoke Relish 286
Pesto-Glazed Broiled Chicken 286
Grilled Chicken Breasts with Tapenade . 286
Grilled Chicken Breasts
with Roasted Pepper Salsa 286
Broiled Honey Mustard Chicken 286
Sautéed Chicken Breasts
with Vermouth and Tarragon 287
Chicken Lemon Véronique 287
Lemon Mushroom Chicken 287
Pecan Chicken Breasts
with Mustard Sauce 287
Chicken Breasts with Vodka,
Tomatoes and Cream 287
Broiled Ranch-Style Chicken Breasts . . . 288
Chicken Breasts Stuffed
with Herbed Cheese 288
Tangy Fried Chicken Breasts 288
Mahogany Chicken Wings 288

Ginger Black Bean Chicken Wings 288
Smoky Spicy Honey Wings 288
Spicy Thai Wings 289
Super Hot Mustard Wings 289
Garlic and Ginger Chicken Legs 289
Chicken Cacciatore 289
Chicken Legs Braised with Garlic 290
Chicken Stewed
with Parsley Dumplings 290
Chicken and Sausage Gumbo 290
Moroccan Chicken Stew 291
Anise Chicken Braised in a Wok 291
Chicken Legs Braised
with Sauerkraut and Beer 291
Chicken Legs and Sausage
in Red Gravy 292
Boiled Chicken with Mushrooms
and Broad Noodles 292
Chicken Pot au Feu with Sausage 292
Southern Fried Chicken 292
Sweet-and-Sour Fried Chicken 293
Parmesan-Coated Chicken Legs 293
Italian Fried Chicken 293
Chicken Crusted with Corn Flakes 293
Baked Chicken Legs
with Balsamic Glaze 293
Garlic and Molasses Chicken Legs 293
Buffalo Drumsticks 293
Meaty Chicken Noodle Soup 294
Creamy Chicken Soup
with Lemon and Mint 294
Chunky Chicken Minestrone 294
Chicken and Corn Chowder 294

The chicken is an odd bird. Its puny wings have no chance of lifting its girth into flight. Its legs are those of a sumo wrestler, and its Mae West breast seems better suited to take to a sauce than the skies. Bred away from its ornithological roots, the chicken is now primarily a culinary animal, and anyone who cooks should be eternally grateful for it. For we would be hard-pressed to find another ingredient as versatile, as convenient or as easy to prepare — especially the breast portion, which can be grilled, poached, baked or broiled a different way every day of the year without risking the threat of repetition.

As the white meat lends itself to the broiler, grill and sauté pan, the leg sections shine when moisture comes into play. These are the parts for soup, stew and broth. They come to life when fried or stewed, they become the very essence of home cooking in braising, and they take on a natural elegance when stuffed and baked.

About these recipes . . .

Below you'll find enough ideas for chicken parts to get you through 50 chicken dinners. We leave the addition of salt and pepper to your preference — with a reminder that, although each diner's taste will guide seasoning at the table, you should always taste-test a bit of meat or sauce in the kitchen before serving.

The breast recipes call for boneless skinless chicken breast halves that have been trimmed of excess fat. Chicken legs mean drumstick and thigh with the skin still on, unless otherwise noted. Three pounds (1.5 kg) of chicken legs usually equals about 6 full legs. Wing recipes are written for sectioned wings with tips discarded.

Old-Fashioned Chicken Salad

6	boneless skinless chicken breasts	6
2	stalks celery, finely diced	2
1	carrot, shredded	1
½	cucumber, seeded and diced	½
⅔ cup	mayonnaise	150 mL
1 tbsp	minced fresh Italian (flat-leaf) parsley	15 mL
1 tbsp	cider vinegar	15 mL

In a large saucepan, bring lightly salted water to a simmer and poach chicken (see page 11) until no longer pink inside. Cut into chunks while still warm, and toss with the remaining ingredients.

Serve immediately, or cover and refrigerate until chilled, about 1 hour. **Serves 6.**

Yogurt Dill Chicken Salad

6	boneless skinless chicken breasts	6
1	cucumber, peeled, seeded and diced	1
1 cup	plain yogurt	250 mL
2 tbsp	chopped fresh dill	25 mL
1 tbsp	freshly squeezed lemon juice	15 mL

In a large saucepan, bring lightly salted water to a simmer and poach chicken (see page 11) until no longer pink inside. Cut into chunks while still warm, and toss with the remaining ingredients. Serve immediately or cover and refrigerate until chilled, about 1 hour. **Serves 6.**

Warm Grilled Chicken Salad on Wilted Lettuce

4	boneless skinless chicken breasts	4
	Salt and freshly ground black pepper to taste	
⅓ cup	extra-virgin olive oil, divided	75 mL
1	clove garlic, chopped	1
2 tbsp	granulated sugar	25 mL
2 tbsp	white wine vinegar	25 mL
1 tsp	salt	5 mL
1	head escarole, torn into bite-size pieces	1
⅓ cup	chopped pecans	75 mL
¼ cup	finely chopped red onion	50 mL

Preheat broiler or barbecue grill to high. Season chicken with salt and pepper, then coat with 1 tbsp (15 mL) of the oil. Broil or grill for 4 to 5 minutes per side, or until browned on both sides and no longer pink inside. Cut into thin slices and keep warm. In a small saucepan, over medium-low heat, bring garlic, sugar, the remaining oil, vinegar and the 1 tsp (5 mL) salt to a simmer. In a large salad bowl, toss together escarole, pecans and onions. Add chicken and dressing; toss to coat. **Serves 4.**

Chicken Breasts Sautéed in Capers and Brown Butter

4	boneless skinless chicken breasts	4
	Salt and freshly ground black pepper to taste	
1 tbsp	olive oil	15 mL
¼ cup	butter	50 mL
¼ cup	capers, with liquid	50 mL

Season chicken with salt and pepper. In a large skillet, heat oil over medium heat. Cook chicken until browned on both sides and no longer pink inside; remove to a warm platter. Add butter to the pan and cook until bubbly. Add capers and their liquid; cook until sauce is brown and slightly thickened. Pour sauce over chicken. **Serves 4.**

Sautéed Chicken Breasts with Brandy Cream Reduction

4	boneless skinless chicken breasts	4
	Salt and freshly ground white pepper to taste	
1 tbsp	canola oil	15 mL
2 tbsp	minced onion	25 mL
½ cup	brandy	125 mL
1½ cups	cream (any type, minimum 10%)	375 mL
	Freshly ground white pepper to taste	

Season chicken with salt and black pepper. In a large skillet, heat oil over medium heat. Cook chicken until browned on both sides. Add onion and sauté until tender. Add brandy, heat to boiling and carefully flambé (see page 10). When flames subside, add cream, reduce heat and simmer until slightly thickened. Season with white pepper and additional salt. **Serves 4.**

Sautéed Chicken Breasts with Apple Glaze

4	boneless skinless chicken breasts	4
	Salt and freshly ground black pepper to taste	
1 tbsp	canola oil	15 mL
1 tbsp	minced onion	15 mL
1 cup	unsweetened apple juice	250 mL
2 tbsp	cider vinegar	25 mL
1 tsp	packed light brown sugar	5 mL
2 tbsp	butter, cut into small pieces	25 mL

Season chicken with salt and pepper. In a large skillet, heat oil over medium-high heat. Cook chicken until browned on both sides. Add onion and sauté until tender. Add apple juice, vinegar and brown sugar; reduce heat and simmer until chicken is no longer pink inside and liquid is slightly thickened. Remove from heat and, using tongs, transfer chicken to a warm platter. Swirl butter into sauce. Pour sauce over chicken. **Serves 4.**

Chicken Baked in Foil with Clams

4	boneless skinless chicken breasts	4
1 tbsp	olive oil	15 mL
1 tbsp	freshly squeezed lemon juice	15 mL
4 tsp	chopped fresh dill	20 mL
	Salt and freshly ground black pepper to taste	
8	littleneck clams, scrubbed (see page 8)	8

Preheat oven to 400°F (200°C). Rub chicken with oil and lemon juice. Place each breast in the center of a piece of foil that measures about 18 inches (45 cm) on each side. Season each breast with 1 tsp (5 mL) of the dill, salt and pepper, and surround with 2 clams. Wrap foil around chicken and clams, seal edges and place seam side up on a baking sheet. Bake for 30 minutes, until you hear vigorous bubbling inside the packets. Chicken should no longer be pink inside and clams should open (discard any that don't). **Serves 4.**

Poached Chicken Breasts in Beurre Blanc

4	boneless skinless chicken breasts	4
	Salt and freshly ground black pepper to taste	
2 cups	dry white wine	500 mL
¼ cup	white wine vinegar	50 mL
2 tbsp	minced shallot	25 mL
½ cup	butter, cut into small pieces	125 mL

Season chicken with salt and pepper. In a large skillet, bring wine, vinegar and shallot to a simmer. Add chicken and poach (see page 11) until no longer pink inside; remove chicken to a warm platter. Increase heat to high and boil pan liquid until thickened to a glaze. Remove from heat and swirl in butter, a few pieces at a time, until sauce is creamy. Pour sauce over chicken. **Serves 4.**

Chilled Grilled Marinated Chicken Breasts

4	boneless skinless chicken breasts	4
	Salt and freshly ground black pepper to taste	
1 tbsp	olive oil	15 mL
2/3 cup	Italian dressing	150 mL
	Chilled greens	

Preheat broiler or barbecue grill to high. Season chicken with salt and pepper, then coat with oil. Broil or grill for 4 to 5 minutes per side, or until browned on both sides and no longer pink inside. While still warm, toss with dressing. Serve immediately or cover and refrigerate until chilled, about 1 hour. Serve on a bed of greens. **Serves 4.**

Grilled Chicken Breasts with Artichoke Relish

1	jar (6 oz/170 mL) marinated artichoke hearts, drained and finely chopped	1
	Juice of 1/2 large lemon	
1/3 cup	toasted pine nuts	75 mL
4	boneless skinless chicken breasts	4
	Salt and freshly ground black pepper to taste	

Preheat broiler or barbecue grill to high. Combine artichokes, lemon juice and pine nuts; set aside. Season chicken with salt and pepper, then pound to 1/4-inch (0.5 cm) thickness. Broil or grill until browned on both sides and no longer pink inside, about 3 minutes per side. Serve a spoonful of artichoke mixture on each chicken breast. **Serves 4.**

Pesto-Glazed Broiled Chicken

4	cloves garlic	4
2 cups	packed fresh basil leaves	500 mL
1/2 cup	pine nuts	125 mL
1/2 cup	extra-virgin olive oil (approx.)	125 mL
1/2 cup	freshly grated Parmesan cheese	125 mL
4	boneless skinless chicken breasts	4
	Salt and freshly ground black pepper to taste	

Preheat broiler or barbecue grill to high. In a food processor, purée garlic, basil and pine nuts. With the motor running, through the feed tube, slowly add enough oil to make a smooth paste. Stir in Parmesan and set aside. Season chicken with salt and pepper, then pound to 1/4-inch (0.5 cm) thickness. Broil or grill until browned on both sides and no longer pink inside, about 3 minutes per side. Serve a spoonful of pesto on each chicken breast. **Serves 4.**

Grilled Chicken Breasts with Tapenade

12	oil-cured black olives, pitted and finely chopped	12
1	clove garlic, minced	1
1/3 cup	extra-virgin olive oil	75 mL
	Salt and freshly ground black pepper to taste	
4	boneless skinless chicken breasts	4

Preheat broiler or barbecue grill to high. Combine olives, garlic, oil, salt and pepper; set aside. Season chicken with additional salt and pepper, then pound to 1/4-inch (0.5 cm) thickness. Broil or grill until browned on both sides and no longer pink inside, about 3 minutes per side. Serve a spoonful of tapenade on each chicken breast. **Serves 4.**

Grilled Chicken Breasts with Roasted Pepper Salsa

2	roasted bell peppers (see page 11), finely chopped	2
1	small clove garlic, minced	1
1/4 tsp	hot pepper flakes	1 mL
	Salt to taste	
4	boneless skinless chicken breasts	4
	Freshly ground black pepper to taste	

Preheat broiler or barbecue grill to high. Combine roasted peppers, garlic, hot pepper flakes and salt; set aside. Season chicken with additional salt and black pepper, then pound to 1/4-inch (0.5 cm) thickness. Broil or grill until browned on both sides and no longer pink inside, about 3 minutes per side. Serve a spoonful of salsa on each chicken breast. **Serves 4.**

Broiled Honey Mustard Chicken

4	boneless skinless chicken breasts	4
	Salt and freshly ground black pepper to taste	
2 tbsp	Dijon mustard	25 mL
2 tsp	honey	10 mL

Preheat broiler or barbecue grill to high. Season chicken with salt and pepper, then pound to 1/4-inch (0.5 cm) thickness. Combine mustard and honey, and brush one side of each breast with 1 tsp (5 mL) of the mixture. Broil or grill until browned on one side, about 3 minutes. Turn chicken and brush each piece with another 1 tsp (5 mL) of the mustard mixture; broil or grill for 2 minutes, until browned and no longer pink inside. **Serves 4.**

Sautéed Chicken Breasts with Vermouth and Tarragon

4	boneless skinless chicken breasts	4
	Salt and freshly ground black pepper to taste	
1 tbsp	olive oil	15 mL
1 cup	dry vermouth	250 mL
2 tbsp	minced onion	25 mL
2 tbsp	white wine vinegar	25 mL
1 tbsp	dried tarragon	15 mL
¼ cup	butter, cut into small pieces	50 mL

Season chicken with salt and pepper. In a large skillet, heat oil over medium-high heat. Cook chicken until browned on both sides. Add vermouth, onion, vinegar and tarragon; reduce heat and simmer until chicken is no longer pink inside. Using tongs, remove chicken to a warm platter. Increase heat to high and boil pan liquid until slightly thickened. Remove from heat and swirl in butter. Pour sauce over chicken. **Serves 4.**

Chicken Lemon Véronique

4	boneless skinless chicken breasts	4
	Salt and freshly ground black pepper to taste	
1 tbsp	canola oil	15 mL
1 cup	chicken broth	250 mL
	Juice of 1 lemon	
24	seedless grapes, halved	24
1 tbsp	butter	15 mL

Season chicken with salt and pepper. In a large skillet, heat oil over medium-high heat. Cook chicken until browned on both sides. Add broth, reduce heat and simmer until chicken is no longer pink inside. Using tongs, remove chicken to a warm platter. Increase heat to high and boil pan liquid until slightly thickened. Add lemon juice and boil for 30 seconds. Add grapes, remove from heat and swirl in butter. Pour sauce over chicken. **Serves 4.**

Lemon Mushroom Chicken

4	boneless skinless chicken breasts	4
	Salt and freshly ground black pepper to taste	
1 tbsp	olive oil	15 mL
2 cups	sliced mushrooms	500 mL
	Juice of 1 lemon	

Season chicken with salt and pepper. In a large skillet, heat oil over medium-high heat. Cook chicken until browned on both sides. Reduce heat to medium-low, add mushrooms and simmer until mushrooms are tender and chicken is no longer pink inside. Add lemon juice and simmer for 30 seconds. **Serves 4.**

Pecan Chicken Breasts with Mustard Sauce

4	boneless skinless chicken breasts	4
	Salt and freshly ground black pepper to taste	
¼ cup	melted butter	50 mL
3 tbsp	brown mustard, divided	45 mL
6 tbsp	ground pecans	90 mL
2 tbsp	peanut oil	25 mL
⅔ cup	sour cream (not fat-free)	150 mL

Season chicken with salt and pepper, then pound lightly to an even thickness. Combine butter and 2 tbsp (25 mL) of the mustard, dip chicken in the mixture, and press pecans into the chicken. Discard any excess butter mixture. In a large skillet, heat oil over medium heat. Cook chicken until browned on both sides and no longer pink inside; remove to a warm platter. Reduce heat to low, add sour cream and the remaining mustard to the pan and stir to form a sauce. Pour sauce over chicken. **Serves 4.**

Chicken Breasts with Vodka, Tomatoes and Cream

4	boneless skinless chicken breasts	4
	Salt and freshly ground black pepper to taste	
2 tbsp	olive oil	25 mL
2	cloves garlic, minced	2
12	plum (Roma) tomatoes, peeled, seeded and chopped	12
Pinch	hot pepper flakes	Pinch
½ cup	whipping (35%) cream	125 mL
¼ cup	vodka	50 mL
1 tbsp	chopped fresh Italian (flat-leaf) parsley	15 mL

Season chicken with salt and black pepper. In a large skillet, heat oil over medium-high heat. Cook chicken until browned on both sides. Add garlic and cook for 30 seconds. Add tomatoes and hot pepper flakes; reduce heat and simmer until chicken is no longer pink inside. Using tongs, remove chicken to a warm platter. Add cream, vodka and parsley to the pan; simmer just until cream thickens. Pour sauce over chicken. **Serves 4.**

Broiled Ranch-Style Chicken Breasts

4	boneless skinless chicken breasts	4
	Salt and freshly ground black pepper	
	to taste	
1 cup	ranch dressing	250 mL

Season chicken with salt and pepper, then pound to ¼-inch (0.5 cm) thickness. Place in a shallow dish and pour in dressing, turning to coat. Cover and refrigerate for 1 hour. Preheat broiler. Remove chicken from marinade and discard marinade. Broil chicken until browned on both sides and no longer pink inside, about 3 minutes per side. **Serves 4.**

Chicken Breasts Stuffed with Herbed Cheese

4	boneless skinless chicken breasts	4
	Salt and freshly ground black pepper	
	to taste	
	Olive oil	
½ cup	soft herb cheese (such as Boursin or Alouette)	125 mL
1	extra-large egg, beaten with 2 tbsp (25 mL) water	1
1 cup	all-purpose flour	250 mL
1 cup	seasoned dry bread crumbs	250 mL
	Vegetable oil	

Season chicken with salt and pepper, then brush lightly with oil. Place each piece between sheets of plastic wrap and pound to ⅛-inch (3 mm) thickness, thinner near the edges. Remove the top sheets of plastic, place 2 tbsp (25 mL) of the cheese in the center of each piece, and wrap chicken around cheese as if you were wrapping a package. Dip in egg mixture, dredge in flour, dip in egg again, and coat with bread crumbs. Discard any excess egg, flour and crumbs. Set chicken on a rack and let stand for 10 minutes. Deep-fry (see page 9) in 350°F (180°C) oil until golden brown and no longer pink inside. **Serves 4.**

Tangy Fried Chicken Breasts

4	boneless skinless chicken breasts	4
	Salt and freshly ground black pepper	
	to taste	
1	egg	1
1	clove garlic, minced	1
1 cup	plain yogurt (not fat-free)	250 mL
1 tbsp	hot pepper sauce	15 mL
1 cup	all-purpose flour, seasoned with salt and pepper	250 mL
	Vegetable oil	

Season chicken with salt and pepper. Combine egg, garlic, yogurt and hot pepper sauce, dip chicken in this mixture, then dredge in flour. Discard any excess egg mixture and flour. In a large skillet, heat 1 to 1½ inches (2.5 to 4 cm) oil over medium-high heat to about 350°F (180°C), just enough to make chicken sizzle vigorously on contact. Pan-fry chicken, turning once, for 5 to 8 minutes, or until browned on both sides and no longer pink inside. **Serves 4.**

Mahogany Chicken Wings

1 tbsp	canola oil	15 mL
2	cloves garlic, minced	2
1	dried hot chili pepper	1
1 tbsp	freshly grated gingerroot	15 mL
⅓ cup	soy sauce	75 mL
¼ cup	water	50 mL
¼ cup	dry sherry	50 mL
¼ cup	honey	50 mL
2 tbsp	dark (cooking) molasses	25 mL
1 tbsp	rice wine vinegar	15 mL
2 lbs	chicken wings, sectioned and tips discarded	1 kg
1 tbsp	dark sesame oil	15 mL

In a large skillet, heat canola oil over medium-high heat. Sauté garlic, chili pepper and ginger for 30 seconds. Add soy sauce, water, sherry, honey, molasses and vinegar; bring to a boil. Add wings, reduce heat, cover and simmer for 5 minutes. Uncover and simmer until liquid is reduced enough to glaze the wings and juices run clear when chicken is pierced. Toss gently near the end of cooking to prevent scorching. Stir in sesame oil. **Serves 4.**

Ginger Black Bean Chicken Wings

Follow preceding recipe, but omit the soy sauce, and add ¼ cup (50 mL) black bean sauce, 1 tbsp (15 mL) garlic chili paste and 1 tbsp (15 mL) hoisin sauce with the water. **Serves 4.**

Smoky Spicy Honey Wings

	Vegetable cooking spray	
1½ cups	chipotle salsa	375 mL
3 tbsp	honey	45 mL
2 lbs	chicken wings, sectioned and tips discarded	1 kg
2 tbsp	chopped fresh cilantro	25 mL

Preheat oven to 400°F (200°C). Cover a baking sheet with heavy-duty foil and spray foil with cooking spray. In a blender or food processor, combine salsa and honey. Toss chicken wings in salsa mixture and place on prepared pan in a single layer, with as much space between pieces as possible. Bake for 30 minutes. Turn and bake for 15 minutes, until browned on both sides and juices run clear when chicken is pierced. Remove from pan and toss with cilantro. **Serves 4.**

Spicy Thai Wings

	Vegetable cooking spray	
2 lbs	chicken wings, sectioned and tips discarded	1 kg
3 tbsp	hoisin sauce	45 mL
2 tbsp	cider vinegar	25 mL
1 tbsp	Thai hot sauce (such as Sriracha)	15 mL

Preheat oven to 400°F (200°C). Cover a baking sheet with heavy-duty foil and spray foil with cooking spray. Place chicken wings on foil in a single layer, with as much space between them as possible. Bake for 30 minutes. Turn and bake for 15 minutes, until golden brown and crisp and juices run clear when chicken is pierced. Meanwhile, combine hoisin sauce, vinegar and Thai hot sauce. Toss wings in sauce. **Serves 4.**

Super Hot Mustard Wings

	Vegetable cooking spray	
2 tbsp	spicy brown mustard	25 mL
2 tbsp	cider vinegar	25 mL
1 tbsp	Chinese chili paste	15 mL
2 lbs	chicken wings, sectioned and tips discarded	1 kg

Preheat oven to 400°F (200°C). Cover a baking sheet with heavy-duty foil and spray foil with cooking spray. Combine mustard, vinegar and chili paste, and toss chicken wings in this sauce. Place wings on prepared pan in a single layer, with as much space between them as possible. Bake for 30 minutes. Turn and bake for 15 minutes, until browned on both sides and juices run clear when chicken is pierced. **Serves 4.**

Garlic and Ginger Chicken Legs

2	large cloves garlic, minced	2
1 tbsp	grated gingerroot	15 mL
2 tsp	dark sesame oil	10 mL
	Salt and freshly ground black pepper to taste	
3 lbs	chicken legs, sectioned into thighs and drumsticks	1.5 kg

Preheat oven to 375°F (190°C) and line a baking sheet with heavy-duty foil. Combine garlic, ginger, oil, salt and pepper; rub over chicken. Place in a single layer on prepared pan, with as much space between them as possible, and bake for 45 minutes, until browned and juices run clear when chicken is pierced. **Serves 4.**

Chicken Cacciatore

3 lbs	chicken legs, sectioned into thighs and drumsticks	1.5 kg
1/4 cup	all-purpose flour, seasoned with salt and pepper	50 mL
3 tbsp	olive oil	45 mL
2 cups	sliced mushrooms	500 mL
1 cup	sliced onion	250 mL
2	cloves garlic, minced	2
1 cup	dry white wine	250 mL
1/4 tsp	dried oregano	1 mL
1/2 tsp	hot pepper flakes	2 mL
1 1/2 cups	diced tomatoes	375 mL
1 cup	chicken broth	250 mL
	Salt and freshly ground black pepper to taste	
2	drained canned anchovies, minced	2
1 tbsp	minced fresh Italian (flat-leaf) parsley	15 mL

Dredge chicken in flour. In a large skillet, heat oil over medium-high heat. Cook chicken, in batches if necessary, until browned on all sides; remove to a plate. Add mushrooms and onion to the fat in the pan and sauté until browned. Add garlic, wine, oregano and hot pepper flakes; cook until liquid is reduced by half. Return chicken to pan and add tomatoes, broth, salt and pepper; reduce heat and simmer for 35 minutes, until juices run clear when chicken is pierced. If liquid is too thin, increase heat and boil until slightly thickened. Stir in anchovies and parsley. **Serves 4.**

Chicken Legs Braised with Garlic

3 lbs	chicken legs, sectioned into thighs and drumsticks	1.5 kg
¼ cup	all-purpose flour, seasoned with salt and pepper	50 mL
3 tbsp	olive oil	45 mL
1	chopped onion	1
1	head garlic, separated into cloves, divided	1
2 cups	dry white wine	500 mL
2 cups	chicken broth	500 mL
2 tbsp	tomato paste	25 mL
1 tbsp	dried herbes de Provence	15 mL
2	bay leaves	2
	Salt and freshly ground black pepper to taste	
⅓ cup	hummus	75 mL

Dredge chicken in flour. In a large skillet, heat oil over medium-high heat. Cook chicken, in batches if necessary, until browned on both sides. When browning last batch of chicken, cook until browned on one side, then turn chicken and add onion and all but 6 cloves of the garlic; cook until chicken is browned on the other side. Mince the remaining garlic. Add half the minced garlic, the remaining chicken, wine, broth, tomato paste, herbes de Provence, bay leaves, salt and pepper; reduce heat and simmer for 40 minutes, until juices run clear when chicken is pierced. Discard bay leaves and stir in hummus and the remaining garlic. **Serves 4.**

Chicken Stewed with Parsley Dumplings

5 lbs	chicken legs, sectioned into thighs and drumsticks	2.5 kg
¼ cup	all-purpose flour, seasoned with salt and pepper	50 mL
	Canola oil	
4	stalks celery, sliced	4
4	carrots, sliced	4
1	onion, chopped	1
2	cloves garlic, minced	2
1	bay leaf	1
1 tsp	dried thyme	5 mL
½ tsp	dried rosemary, crumbled	2 mL
½ tsp	poultry seasoning	2 mL
5 cups	chicken broth	1.25 L
1 tbsp	freshly squeezed lemon juice	15 mL
1 cup	biscuit mix	250 mL
⅓ cup	milk	125 mL
¼ cup	chopped fresh Italian (flat-leaf) parsley	50 mL

Dredge chicken legs in flour. In a heavy soup pot, heat a thin film of oil over medium-high heat. Cook chicken, in batches, until browned on all sides; remove to a plate. Add celery, carrots, onion, garlic, bay leaf, thyme, rosemary and poultry seasoning to the fat in the pot and sauté until vegetables are tender. Return chicken to the pot and add broth and lemon juice; reduce heat and simmer for 45 minutes, until juices run clear when chicken is pierced. Discard bay leaf. Meanwhile, combine biscuit mix, milk and parsley. Drop in small amounts across the surface of the stew, cover and simmer for 10 minutes, without disturbing. **Serves 6.**

Chicken and Sausage Gumbo

2 tsp	salt	10 mL
2 tsp	garlic powder	10 mL
2 tsp	cayenne pepper	10 mL
5 lbs	chicken legs, sectioned into thighs and drumsticks	2.5 kg
¾ cup	vegetable oil, divided	175 mL
½ cup	all-purpose flour	125 mL
2	large onions, chopped	2
1	bell pepper (any color), chopped	1
1 cup	chopped celery	250 mL
2	cloves garlic, minced	2
12 cups	hot chicken broth	3 L
1 lb	smoked sausage (such as andouille), sliced	500 g
2 cups	sliced okra (fresh or thawed frozen)	500 mL
	Cooked rice	

Combine salt, garlic powder and cayenne pepper; rub over chicken. In a large, deep skillet or Dutch oven, heat ¼ cup (50 mL) of the vegetable oil over medium-high heat. Cook chicken, in batches if necessary, until browned on all sides; remove to a plate. Add the remaining oil and flour to the pan, reduce heat to low and cook, stirring frequently, for about 10 minutes, or until mixture is chocolate brown (be careful: the mixture can get dangerously hot). Add onions, bell pepper and celery; sauté for 1 minute. Add garlic and sauté for 10 seconds. Carefully stir in broth (it will splatter) and bring to a boil. Return chicken to pot and add sausage and okra; reduce heat and simmer for 45 minutes, until juices run clear when chicken is pierced. Serve over rice. **Serves 6 to 8.**

Moroccan Chicken Stew

2	large onions, chopped coarsely	2
2	cloves garlic, minced	2
2	carrots, thickly sliced	2
2	stalks celery, thickly sliced	2
2	sticks cinnamon, each 2 inches (5 cm) long	2
1	dried hot chili pepper	1
3 lbs	chicken legs, sectioned into thighs and drumsticks	1.5 kg
4 cups	chicken broth	1 L
¼ cup	chopped fresh cilantro	50 mL
¼ cup	chopped fresh Italian (flat-leaf) parsley	50 mL
¼ cup	butter	50 mL
1 tbsp	ground coriander	15 mL
1½ tsp	ground cumin	7 mL
1 tsp	ground ginger	5 mL
1 tsp	dried thyme	5 mL
1 tsp	ground turmeric	5 mL
1	bay leaf	1

In a large pot, bring all ingredients to a boil. Reduce heat and simmer for 1 hour, until chicken is tender. With a slotted spoon, remove chicken and vegetables to a plate. Increase heat and boil pan liquid until reduced by half. Discard cinnamon sticks, bay leaf and chili pepper. Return chicken and vegetables to the pot and heat through. **Serves 4.** *Serve over rice, if desired.*

Anise Chicken Braised in a Wok

¼ cup	canola oil	50 mL
3 lbs	chicken legs, sectioned into thighs and drumsticks	1.5 kg
3	slices gingerroot	3
2	dried hot chili peppers	2
2	whole star anise	2
1½ cups	water	375 mL
⅓ cup	soy sauce	75 mL
¼ cup	dry white wine	50 mL
2 tbsp	packed light brown sugar	25 mL
4	green onions, chopped	4
1 tbsp	cornstarch, dissolved in 2 tbsp (25 mL) water	15 mL
½ tsp	dark sesame oil	2 mL
	Cooked rice	

In a wok, heat canola oil over medium-high heat until smoking. Cook chicken, in batches, until browned on all sides; remove to a plate. Add ginger, chili peppers and star anise to the wok and stir-fry for 10 seconds. Return chicken to wok and add water, soy sauce, wine and brown sugar; reduce heat, cover and simmer for 20 minutes, until juices run clear when chicken is pierced. Add green onions and cornstarch mixture (stirring first, if necessary); simmer until sauce is slightly thickened. Discard ginger, chili peppers and star anise. Stir in sesame oil. Serve over rice. **Serves 4.**

Chicken Legs Braised with Sauerkraut and Beer

4	slices bacon	4
3 lbs	chicken legs, sectioned into thighs and drumsticks	1.5 kg
1	large onion, sliced	1
3	cloves garlic, chopped	3
2 lbs	sauerkraut, drained	1 kg
1	bottle (12 oz/341 mL) beer	1
8 oz	ham, diced	250 g
8	juniper berries	8
2	bay leaves	2
1 tsp	ground coriander	5 mL
Pinch	ground cloves	Pinch
12	small red-skinned potatoes, halved	12

In a large, deep skillet, over medium-high heat, cook bacon until crisp; remove to a plate, blot with paper towels and crumble. Add chicken, in batches if necessary, and onion to the fat in the pan and cook until chicken is browned on all sides; remove chicken to a plate. Add garlic, sauerkraut, beer, ham, juniper berries, bay leaves, coriander and cloves to the pan and stir to combine. Arrange chicken and potatoes on top, reduce heat, cover tightly and simmer for 1 hour, until juices run clear when chicken is pierced and potatoes are tender. Remove bay leaf and sprinkle with bacon. **Serves 4.**

Chicken Legs and Sausage in Red Gravy

1 lb	mild Italian sausages, cut into 2-inch (5 cm) lengths	500 g
1 tbsp	olive oil	15 mL
2 lbs	chicken legs, sectioned into thighs and drumsticks	1 kg
1	large onion, chopped	1
2	cloves garlic, minced	2
4 cups	canned diced tomatoes, drained	1 L
1 cup	chicken broth	250 mL
¼ cup	tomato paste	50 mL
Pinch	hot pepper flakes	Pinch
	Salt and freshly ground black pepper to taste	
1 tbsp	chopped fresh Italian (flat-leaf) parsley	15 mL
	Cooked pasta	

In a large skillet, over medium-high heat, sauté sausage until browned on all sides; remove sausage to a plate. Add oil to skillet and cook chicken until browned on all sides, adding onion and garlic at the end to soften. Return sausage to the pan and add tomatoes, broth, tomato paste, hot pepper flakes, salt and black pepper; reduce heat and simmer for 1 hour, until juices run clear when chicken is pierced. Stir in parsley and simmer for 1 minute. Serve over pasta. **Serves 4.**

Boiled Chicken with Mushrooms and Broad Noodles

12	whole black peppercorns	12
6	sprigs fresh Italian (flat-leaf) parsley	6
2	whole cloves	2
1	dried hot chili pepper	1
1	bay leaf	1
1 tsp	dried thyme	5 mL
2	carrots, halved	2
2	stalks celery, halved	2
1	onion, halved	1
4 lbs	chicken legs, sectioned into thighs and drumsticks	2 kg
6 cups	chicken broth	1.5 L
6 cups	water	1.5 L
1 tsp	salt	5 mL
	Juice of 1 lemon	
1½ lbs	small mushrooms	750 g
12 oz	broad egg noodles	375 g
	Prepared horseradish and brown mustard	

Tie peppercorns, parsley, cloves, chili pepper, bay leaf and thyme in a piece of cheesecloth. Place in a large pot with carrots, celery, onion, chicken, broth, water, salt and lemon juice; simmer for 1 hour, until juices run clear when chicken is pierced. Add mushrooms and noodles; simmer for 10 minutes. Serve chicken and mushrooms with horseradish and mustard, and serve broth and noodles as soup. **Serves 6.**

Chicken Pot au Feu with Sausage

Follow preceding recipe, but add 6 pieces smoked sausage (each about 4 oz/125 g) with the chicken, add 2 lbs (1 kg) red-skinned potatoes, halved, in the last half-hour of cooking, and add 2 cups (500 mL) cooked rice in place of the mushrooms and noodles. Serve chicken, sausage and potatoes with small pickles and brown mustard. Serve broth and rice as soup. **Serves 8.**

Southern Fried Chicken

1 cup	all-purpose flour	250 mL
1 tsp	ground cumin	5 mL
	Salt and freshly ground black pepper to taste	
2 lbs	chicken legs, sectioned into thighs and drumsticks	1 kg
	Vegetable oil	

In a large paper or plastic bag, combine flour, cumin, salt and pepper. Add chicken and shake to coat. Shake off excess flour and discard. In a large, deep skillet, heat 1 inch (2.5 cm) vegetable oil over medium heat to about 350°F (180°C), just enough to make chicken sizzle vigorously on contact. Add chicken, cover, and pan-fry until dark brown on one side, checking occasionally to make sure pieces don't burn. Uncover, turn chicken, and pan-fry until the other side is dark brown and juices run clear when chicken is pierced. Drain on a rack set over a drip pan. **Serves 4.**

Sweet-and-Sour Fried Chicken

Follow preceding recipe, but while chicken is frying, in a separate skillet, melt ¼ cup (50 mL) butter. Sauté 1 tbsp (15 mL) chopped onion until browned. Add ⅔ cup (150 mL) unsweetened apple juice, 2 tsp (10 mL) cider vinegar and 1 tsp (5 mL) packed light brown sugar; boil for 3 minutes. Use as a dipping sauce for the chicken. **Serves 4.**

Parmesan-Coated Chicken Legs

½ cup	finely grated Parmesan cheese	125 mL
1¼ cups	Italian seasoned dry bread crumbs, divided	300 mL
1 tbsp	ground fennel seeds	15 mL
	Freshly ground black pepper to taste	
2 lbs	chicken legs, sectioned into thighs and drumsticks	1 kg
2	eggs, beaten	2

In a large paper or plastic bag, combine Parmesan, 2 tbsp (25 mL) of the bread crumbs, fennel seeds and pepper. Add chicken and shake to coat. Shake off excess coating and dip chicken in eggs. Add the remaining bread crumbs to the remaining coating and dredge chicken well in this mixture. Set on a rack and let stand for 15 minutes. Discard any excess egg and crumb mixture. Pan-fry as directed in Southern Fried Chicken (page 292). **Serves 4.**

Italian Fried Chicken

Follow preceding recipe, but replace the beaten eggs with ¼ cup (50 mL) Italian salad dressing, beaten with 1 extra-large egg yolk. **Serves 4.**

Chicken Crusted with Corn Flakes

	Vegetable cooking spray	
3 lbs	chicken legs, sectioned into thighs and drumsticks	1.5 kg
	Salt and freshly ground black pepper to taste	
½ cup	mayonnaise	125 mL
2 cups	crushed corn flakes cereal	500 mL

Preheat oven to 375°F (190°C) and spray a baking sheet with cooking spray. Season chicken with salt and pepper, brush with mayonnaise and coat well with corn flakes. Place on prepared pan and bake for 1 hour, turning after 30 minutes, until juices run clear when chicken is pierced. **Serves 4.**

Baked Chicken Legs with Balsamic Glaze

3 tbsp	extra-virgin olive oil	45 mL
3 lbs	chicken legs, sectioned into thighs and drumsticks	1.5 kg
4	cloves garlic, chopped	4
6	whole black peppercorns	6
2 cups	beef broth	500 mL
⅓ cup	balsamic vinegar	75 mL

Preheat oven to 400°F (200°C). In a large skillet, heat oil over medium-high heat. Cook chicken, in batches if necessary, until browned on all sides. Transfer chicken to a large rectangular baking dish and bake for 10 minutes. Meanwhile, add garlic to the fat in the skillet and sauté for 30 seconds. Add peppercorns, broth and vinegar; boil until reduced by about two-thirds. Brush chicken with some of the glaze and bake for 50 minutes, basting every 10 minutes, until juices run clear when chicken is pierced. **Serves 4.**

Garlic and Molasses Chicken Legs

Follow preceding recipe, but decrease the broth to 1½ cups (375 mL), add ½ cup (125 mL) dark (cooking) molasses with the broth, and replace the balsamic vinegar with cider vinegar. **Serves 4.**

Buffalo Drumsticks

	Vegetable oil	
3 lbs	small chicken drumsticks	1.5 kg
½ cup	melted butter	125 mL
¼ to ⅓ cup	hot pepper sauce (such as Frank's RedHot)	50 to 75 mL

In a large, deep skillet, heat 1 inch (2.5 cm) oil over medium-high heat until the hot fat bubbles quickly when a wooden spoon is inserted (about 350°F/180°C). Pan-fry drumsticks, in batches if necessary, turning once, until crisp and brown and juices run clear when chicken is pierced, about 15 minutes. Drain on paper towels. Combine melted butter and hot pepper sauce to taste; dip chicken in sauce. **Serves 4.**

Meaty Chicken Noodle Soup

3 tbsp	vegetable oil	45 mL
2 lbs	boneless skinless chicken thighs, cut into bite-size pieces	1 kg
3	carrots, chopped	3
2	stalks celery, chopped	2
1	large onion, chopped	1
1	dried hot chili pepper	1
1	bay leaf	1
1 cup	dry white wine	250 mL
2 tsp	minced gingerroot	10 mL
8 cups	chicken broth	2 L
	Salt and freshly ground black pepper to taste	
5 oz	egg noodles	150 g

In a large pot, heat oil over medium-high heat. Sauté chicken, carrots, celery and onion until chicken turns white. Add chili pepper, bay leaf, wine and ginger; boil for 1 minute. Add broth, salt and pepper; bring to a boil. Reduce heat and simmer for 45 minutes, until chicken is tender. Add noodles and simmer for about 10 minutes, until tender. Discard chili pepper and bay leaf. **Serves 6.**

Creamy Chicken Soup with Lemon and Mint

1 tbsp	olive oil	15 mL
2 lbs	boneless skinless chicken thighs, cut into bite-size pieces	1 kg
8 cups	chicken broth	2 L
¾ cup	long-grain white rice	175 mL
3	egg yolks	3
¼ cup	chopped fresh mint	50 mL
	Juice of 2 lemons	

In a large pot, heat oil over medium heat. Sauté chicken until it turns white. Add broth and bring to a boil. Add rice, reduce heat and simmer for about 15 minutes, until rice and chicken are tender. Meanwhile, combine egg yolks, mint and lemon juice; slowly add a ladleful of soup, stirring constantly. Reduce heat to low and slowly pour egg mixture into hot soup, stirring constantly. Increase heat to medium and cook, stirring constantly, until slightly thickened. **Serves 4.**

Chunky Chicken Minestrone

2 tbsp	olive oil	25 mL
1 lb	boneless skinless chicken thighs, cut into bite-size pieces	500 g
2	large onions, chopped	2
2	cloves garlic, minced	2
12	mushrooms, sliced	12
2	carrots, sliced	2
2	stalks celery, sliced	2
½	bell pepper (any color), diced	½
1 tsp	each dried thyme, basil and savory	5 mL
½ tsp	each dried rosemary, oregano and sage	2 mL
5 cups	chicken broth	1.25 L
1½ cups	canned diced tomatoes, drained	375 mL
1 tbsp	red wine vinegar	15 mL
1 tbsp	tomato paste	15 mL
	Salt and freshly ground black pepper to taste	
1 cup	drained rinsed canned cannellini or white kidney beans	250 mL
	Freshly grated Parmesan cheese	

In a large pot, heat oil over medium heat. Sauté chicken until it turns white. Add onions and garlic; sauté until onion is tender. Add mushrooms, carrots, celery and bell pepper; sauté for 2 minutes. Add thyme, basil, savory, rosemary, oregano and sage; sauté for 3 minutes. Add broth, tomatoes, vinegar, tomato paste, salt and pepper; bring to a boil. Reduce heat and simmer for 30 minutes, until vegetables and chicken are tender. Stir in beans. Serve sprinkled with Parmesan. **Serves 8.**

Chicken and Corn Chowder

4	slices bacon	4
1 lb	boneless skinless chicken thighs, cut into bite-size pieces	500 g
2	stalks celery, diced	2
1	large onion, diced	1
1	clove garlic, minced	1
1	red bell pepper, diced	1
Pinch	hot pepper flakes	Pinch
6 cups	chicken broth	1.5 L
2 cups	corn kernels	500 mL
2 tbsp	chopped fresh dill	25 mL
1 tbsp	chopped fresh Italian (flat-leaf) parsley	15 mL
2 cups	milk (preferably whole)	500 mL

In a large pot, over medium-high heat, cook bacon until crisp; remove to a plate, blot off fat and crumble. Add chicken to the fat in the pot and sauté until browned on all sides. Add celery, onion, garlic, bell pepper and hot pepper flakes; sauté until onion is tender. Add broth, corn, dill and parsley; reduce heat and simmer for 40 minutes, until soup is full-bodied. Add milk and heat through. Do not boil. **Serves 4.**

Chapter 26
Turkey
The Other Bird

Turkey I
Traditional Roast Turkey 296
Turkey Noodle Soup 296
Turkey Salad Vinaigrette 297
Hot Turkey Sandwiches 297
Southern Fried Turkey 297

Turkey II
Maple-Glazed Turkey with
Smoked Turkey Stuffing 297
Smoked Turkey Meatloaf 298
Sweet-and-Sour Turkey Salad 298
Sliced Turkey Breast with Chutney 298
Stir-Fried Turkey and Cranberries 298

Turkey III
Orange-Glazed Turkey Breast with
Brown Rice–Dried Fruit Stuffing 298
Turkey Fried Rice 299
Cranberry Turkey Casserole 299
Creole Turkey Salad 299
Turkey Cranberry Turnovers 299

Turkey IV
Herbed Brandy Turkey
with Wild Mushroom Stuffing 300
Turkey Kiev with Herbed Cheese 300
Turkey Mushroom Ragoût 300
Turkey Chowder 300
Green Peppercorn Turkey Salad 301

Turkey V
Slow-Roasted Turkey 301
Turkey Nuggets 301
Classic Turkey Salad 301
Turkey Tabbouleh 301
Turkey Sloppy Joes 302

Turkey VI
Lemon-Honey Turkey with
Cornbread and Crab Stuffing 302

Turkey Sautéed with Capers 302
Buffalo Turkey 302
Lemon-Walnut Turkey Salad 302
Sliced Turkey with
Lemon-Mustard Vinaigrette 303

Turkey VII
Mustard-Glazed Smoked
Turkey Breast 303
Smoked Turkey Salad with
Roasted Pepper Vinaigrette 303
Grilled Turkey Ham 303
Melon Wrapped with Smoked Turkey . . 303
Turkey Benedict 303

Turkey VIII
Roasted Turkey Breast Studded
with Hazelnuts and Garlic 304
Sliced Turkey Breast
with Horseradish Sauce 304
Grilled Turkey Steaks
with Steak Sauce 304
Turkey Hazelnut Salad 304
Turkey Cutlets in Hazelnut Crumbs 304

Turkey IX
Apple Butter–Glazed Turkey
with Apple-Sage Stuffing 304
Leftover Turkey Soup 305
Apple Turkey Meatloaf 305
Baked Apples Stuffed with Turkey 305
Turkey Waldorf Salad 305

Turkey X
Spicy Soy-Ginger Roast Turkey 305
Stir-Fried Turkey with Ginger
and Cashews 306
Asian Turkey Salad 306
Sesame Turkey 306
Sliced Turkey with Soy Vinaigrette 306

Sometimes it seems as though we track our years one turkey at a time.

There was the year of our first Thanksgiving dinner, when emotions ran as raw as the turkey we nearly forgot to roast. Or the Thanksgiving we feasted like kings on a great browned gobbler, stuffed with peaches and brandy we had put up that July.

Each year, we assemble to appreciate a feast so fat that no appetite can survive it. Try as we might, the meal always wins, leaving a week's worth of leftovers in its wake. Thanksgiving dinner lingers in turkey parts, turkey soups and hot turkey sandwiches. It comes back to haunt us as a meatloaf, a stir-fry, a turkey noodle casserole. It returns weeks later in a turkey pot pie, a turkey sage croquette or a cranberry bread.

The Thanksgiving feast is the meal of memories that won't let you forget. So to help you build those memories and survive the inevitable déjà vu of leftovers, we offer 10 memorable roast turkeys, each followed by four leftovers worth remembering.

About these recipes . . .

A whole roasted turkey should be cooked to an internal temperature of 165°F (74°C). To get an accurate reading, insert the thermometer into the thickest part of the breast or thigh meat, being sure not to touch the bone.

By the way, don't ignore the first recipe, for Traditional Roast Turkey. Even if you make one of the other nine roasts, a number of subsequent recipes use this one — and its stuffing — as a starting point.

Turkey I
Traditional Roast Turkey

1	turkey (about 15 lbs/7.5 kg), including giblets	1
	Salt and freshly ground black pepper to taste	
¼ cup	butter, softened	50 mL
Apple-Sage Stuffing		
¼ cup	butter	50 mL
2	stalks celery, diced	2
1	large onion, minced	1
1	Granny Smith apple, diced	1
1 tsp	dried sage	5 mL
1 tsp	dried chervil	5 mL
1 tsp	dried thyme	5 mL
½ tsp	dried rosemary, crumbled	2 mL
Pinch	ground nutmeg	Pinch
4 cups	toasted bread cubes	1 L
1 cup	chicken broth	250 mL
	Salt and freshly ground black pepper to taste	

Preheat oven to 450°F (230°C). Chop giblets and set aside. Season turkey inside and out with salt and pepper. Place on a rack in a roasting pan. Carefully lift breast skin by slipping your fingers under it and disengaging it from the meat. Spread butter over the meat and reposition the skin. Roast for 30 minutes, then scatter giblets around turkey. Reduce heat to 350°F (180°C) and roast for 3 hours, until a thermometer inserted in the thigh registers 165°F (74°C). Baste occasionally with pan drippings during the last 2 hours. Remove from oven, strain giblets out of pan drippings and reserve. Let turkey rest for 20 minutes before carving. *Meanwhile, prepare the stuffing:* In a large skillet, melt butter over medium heat. Sauté celery and onion until tender. Add apple, sage, chervil, thyme, rosemary and nutmeg; sauté for 3 minutes. Add bread cubes, broth and giblets; mix to moisten. Season with salt and pepper. Just before serving, stir ½ cup (125 mL) turkey drippings into stuffing and reheat. Serve turkey with stuffing. **Serves 8 to 10, plus leftovers.**

Turkey Noodle Soup

1 tbsp	turkey fat skimmed from drippings or vegetable oil	15 mL
2	large onions, chopped	2
2	small stalks celery, chopped	2
2	carrots, chopped	2
3 cups	bite-size pieces roasted turkey	750 mL
3 tbsp	chopped fresh Italian (flat-leaf) parsley	45 mL
2 tbsp	chopped fresh dill	25 mL
1 tsp	dried thyme	5 mL
1 tsp	ground turmeric	5 mL
Pinch	ground cloves	Pinch
	Salt and freshly ground black pepper to taste	
12 cups	chicken or turkey broth	3 L
1 cup	broad egg noodles	250 mL

In a large soup pot, heat turkey fat over medium heat. Sauté onions, celery and carrots until tender. Add turkey, parsley, dill, thyme, turmeric, cloves, salt and pepper; sauté for 3 minutes. Add broth, reduce heat and simmer for 15 minutes. Add noodles and simmer for 15 minutes. **Serves 4 to 6.**

Turkey Salad Vinaigrette

2	green onions, finely chopped	2
1	clove garlic, minced	1
¼ cup	chopped fresh Italian (flat-leaf) parsley	50 mL
¼ cup	cider vinegar	50 mL
¼ cup	vegetable oil	50 mL
3 tbsp	orange juice	45 mL
2 tbsp	walnut oil or other nut oil	25 mL
Pinch	cayenne pepper	Pinch
	Salt and freshly ground black pepper to taste	
2	stalks celery, diced	2
4 cups	diced skinned roasted turkey	1 L
1 cup	cooked rice or diced potatoes	250 mL
½ cup	finely diced red onion	125 mL
½ cup	sliced mushrooms	125 mL

Combine green onions, garlic, parsley, vinegar, vegetable oil, orange juice, walnut oil, cayenne, salt and black pepper. Add the remaining ingredients and toss to coat. **Serves 4 to 6.**

Hot Turkey Sandwiches

2½ cups	mixture of chicken or turkey broth and drippings from roast turkey, divided	625 mL
3 tbsp	all-purpose flour	45 mL
1 cup	half-and-half (10%) cream	250 mL
	Salt and freshly ground black pepper to taste	
12	slices roasted turkey breast	12
	Toast or freshly baked biscuits	

Slowly beat ½ cup (125 mL) of the broth mixture into the flour until a smooth paste forms. In a large saucepan, bring the remaining broth mixture to a boil. Whisk in paste a bit at a time, reduce heat and simmer for 20 minutes. Stir in cream, salt and pepper. Add turkey and heat through. Serve over toast or biscuits. **Serves 4 to 6.**

Southern Fried Turkey

2	eggs	2
2 tbsp	honey	25 mL
	Salt and freshly ground black pepper to taste	
4	pieces roasted turkey	4
1 to 1½ cups	dry bread crumbs	250 to 375 mL

Combine eggs, honey, salt and pepper; dip turkey pieces in this mixture, then dredge in bread crumbs. Let rest for 10 minutes, then deep-fry (see page 9) until golden brown. **Serves 4.**

Turkey II

Maple-Glazed Turkey with Smoked Turkey Stuffing

1	turkey (about 15 lbs/7.5 kg), including giblets	1
	Salt and freshly ground black pepper to taste	
¼ cup	butter, softened	50 mL
Glaze		
½ cup	pure maple syrup	125 mL
1 tbsp	Worcestershire sauce	15 mL
1 tbsp	peanut oil	15 mL
Smoked Turkey Stuffing		
4	slices bacon, finely chopped	4
2	stalks celery, diced	2
1	large tart apple, peeled and diced	1
1 cup	minced onion	250 mL
1 tsp	dried sage	5 mL
1 tsp	dried thyme	5 mL
½ tsp	dried rosemary, crumbled	2 mL
Pinch	ground nutmeg	Pinch
4 cups	toasted bread cubes	1 L
2 cups	diced smoked turkey breast	500 mL
1 cup	chopped toasted walnuts	250 mL
1 cup	chicken or turkey broth	250 mL
	Salt and freshly ground black pepper to taste	

Follow recipe for Traditional Roast Turkey (page 296), using turkey, salt, pepper and butter. *Prepare the glaze:* Combine maple syrup, Worcestershire sauce and oil. During the last hour of roasting, brush turkey every 20 minutes with glaze. *Prepare the stuffing:* In a skillet, over medium heat, sauté bacon until cooked but not crisp. Add celery, apple, onion, sage, thyme, rosemary and nutmeg; sauté for 3 minutes. Add bread cubes, smoked turkey, walnuts, broth, salt, pepper and giblets (if using). Just before serving, stir ½ cup (125 mL) turkey drippings into stuffing and reheat. Serve turkey with stuffing. **Serves 8 to 10, plus leftovers.**

Smoked Turkey Meatloaf

2	eggs, beaten	2
1 lb	ground beef	500 g
8 oz	ground veal	250 g
8 oz	ground pork	250 g
2 cups	Smoked Turkey Stuffing (see recipe, page 297)	500 mL
¼ cup	finely chopped onion	50 mL
¼ cup	ketchup	50 mL
2 tbsp	Worcestershire sauce	25 mL
2 tsp	brown mustard	10 mL
	Salt and freshly ground black pepper to taste	
1 cup	bite-size pieces roasted turkey	250 mL

Preheat oven to 375°F (190°C). Using your hands, combine eggs, beef, veal, pork, stuffing, onion, ketchup, Worcestershire sauce, mustard, salt and pepper. Mix in turkey. Form into a rough loaf and place on a rimmed baking sheet. Bake for 1 hour, or until firm to the touch and a thermometer inserted in the center registers 165°F (74°C). Let cool in pan for 10 minutes. Remove from pan and slice. **Serves 4 to 6.**

Sweet-and-Sour Turkey Salad

½ cup	mayonnaise	125 mL
3 tbsp	pure maple syrup	45 mL
2 tbsp	sweet orange marmalade	25 mL
2 tbsp	cider vinegar	25 mL
1 tbsp	hot pepper sauce (such as Frank's)	15 mL
	Salt and freshly ground black pepper to taste	
2	stalks celery, diced	2
4 cups	diced skinned roasted turkey	1 L
1 cup	halved orange sections	250 mL
⅓ cup	finely diced red onion	75 mL

Combine mayonnaise, maple syrup, marmalade, vinegar, hot pepper sauce, salt and pepper. Add the remaining ingredients and toss to coat. **Serves 4 to 6.**

Sliced Turkey Breast with Chutney

4	slices turkey breast, at room temperature	4
½ cup	mango chutney or other fruit chutney	125 mL

Serve turkey slices with chutney. **Serves 4.**

Stir-Fried Turkey and Cranberries

½ cup	fresh cranberries	125 mL
¼ cup	granulated sugar	50 mL
¼ cup	orange juice	50 mL
1 tbsp	soy sauce	15 mL
1 tbsp	cornstarch	15 mL
1 tbsp	vegetable oil	15 mL
1	onion, diced	1
1	clove garlic, minced	1
1 tbsp	minced gingerroot	15 mL
3 cups	bite-size pieces skinned roasted turkey	750 mL
¼ cup	sliced green onion	50 mL

In a small saucepan, bring cranberries, sugar, orange juice and soy sauce to a boil; boil for 1 minute. Let cool, stir in cornstarch and set aside. In a wok or large skillet, heat oil over high heat. Stir-fry onion until tender. Add garlic and ginger; stir-fry for 10 seconds. Add turkey and stir-fry until lightly browned. Add reserved cranberry mixture and cook until thickened, about 1 minute. Stir in green onion. **Serves 4 to 6.**

Turkey III

Orange-Glazed Turkey Breast with Brown Rice–Dried Fruit Stuffing

1	turkey (about 15 lbs/7.5 kg), without giblets	1
	Salt and freshly ground black pepper to taste	
¼ cup	butter, softened	50 mL

Glaze

¼ cup	orange marmalade	50 mL
¼ cup	orange juice	50 mL
1 tbsp	Dijon mustard	15 mL
1 tsp	cider vinegar	5 mL
	Salt and freshly ground black pepper to taste	

Brown Rice–Dried Fruit Stuffing

2 tbsp	butter	25 mL
1	large onion, diced	1
1	clove garlic, minced	1
1½ cups	brown rice	375 mL
3 cups	hot chicken broth	750 mL
	Salt and freshly ground black pepper to taste	
1⅓ cups	chopped mixed dried fruit	425 mL

Follow recipe for Traditional Roast Turkey (page 296), using turkey, salt, pepper and butter. *Prepare the glaze:* In a small saucepan, heat marmalade, orange juice, mustard, vinegar, salt and pepper until smooth and liquid. During the last hour of roasting, brush turkey every 20 minutes with glaze. *Prepare the stuffing:* In a large saucepan, melt butter over medium heat. Sauté onion until tender. Add garlic and sauté for 30 seconds. Add brown rice and stir to coat with butter. Stir in broth, salt and pepper; reduce heat, cover and simmer for 30 minutes. Scatter fruit over rice, cover and simmer until broth is completely absorbed. Season with additional salt and pepper, and stir to mix fruit and rice. Just before serving, stir ½ cup (125 mL) turkey drippings into stuffing and reheat. Serve turkey with stuffing. **Serves 8 to 10, plus leftovers.**

Turkey Fried Rice

2 tbsp	vegetable oil	25 mL
1	large onion, chopped	1
2	cloves garlic, minced	2
2 cups	bite-size pieces skinned roasted turkey	500 mL
½ cup	diced celery	125 mL
½ cup	diced red bell pepper	125 mL
1 tsp	minced gingerroot	5 mL
Pinch	hot pepper flakes	Pinch
2 cups	Brown Rice–Dried Fruit Stuffing (see recipe, page 298)	500 mL
1 tbsp	soy sauce	15 mL
4	green onions, sliced	4
1 tsp	dark sesame oil	5 mL

In a wok or large skillet, heat vegetable oil over high heat. Stir-fry onion until lightly browned. Add garlic, turkey, celery, red pepper, ginger and hot pepper flakes; stir-fry for 1 minute. Add stuffing and soy sauce; stir-fry for 5 minutes, mashing rice against the side of the wok to help it brown and scraping and tossing as needed. Stir in green onions and sesame oil. **Serves 4 to 6.**

Cranberry Turkey Casserole

1 tbsp	vegetable oil	15 mL
1	onion, chopped	1
1	clove garlic, minced	1
1 cup	fresh cranberries	250 mL
⅓ cup	granulated sugar	75 mL
1 cup	chicken or turkey broth	250 mL
3 cups	bite-size pieces skinned roasted turkey	750 mL
3 cups	Brown Rice–Dried Fruit Stuffing (see recipe, page 298)	750 mL

Preheat oven to 350°F (180°C). In a large saucepan, heat oil over medium-high heat. Sauté onion until browned. Add garlic, cranberries and sugar; sauté until cranberries pop. Stir in broth, turkey and stuffing. Transfer to an 8-cup (2 L) casserole dish and bake for 45 minutes, until browned and bubbling. **Serves 4 to 6.**

Creole Turkey Salad

½ cup	mayonnaise	125 mL
¼ cup	unsweetened applesauce	50 mL
3 tbsp	ketchup	45 mL
1 tbsp	granulated sugar	15 mL
1 tbsp	hot pepper sauce (such as Frank's)	15 mL
1 tbsp	cider vinegar	15 mL
	Salt and freshly ground black pepper to taste	
2	stalks celery, thinly sliced	2
4 cups	diced skinned roasted turkey	1 L
⅓ cup	finely diced red onion	75 mL

Combine mayonnaise, applesauce, ketchup, sugar, hot pepper sauce, vinegar, salt and pepper. Add celery, turkey and onion; toss to coat. **Serves 4 to 6.**

Turkey Cranberry Turnovers

⅔ cup	fresh cranberries	150 mL
¼ cup	granulated sugar	50 mL
	Finely grated zest and juice of ½ orange	
1 tsp	butter	5 mL
3 tbsp	chopped onion	45 mL
1 cup	finely chopped skinned roasted turkey	250 mL
	Salt and freshly ground black pepper to taste	
1	box (15 oz/425 g) frozen puff pastry, thawed	1

Preheat oven to 400°F (200°C). In a small saucepan, over medium-high heat, sauté cranberries, sugar, orange zest and orange juice until berries pop. Mash lightly with a fork. Meanwhile, in a skillet, melt butter over medium heat. Sauté onion until tender. Stir in cranberry mixture, turkey, salt and pepper; let cool. Use the puff pastry sheets to form 8 turnovers (see page 12), using the turkey mixture as filling. Place on a baking sheet and bake for 20 to 25 minutes, or until browned and puffed. **Serves 8 as an appetizer.**

Turkey IV

Herbed Brandy Turkey with Wild Mushroom Stuffing

1	turkey (about 15 lbs/7.5 kg), without giblets	1
	Salt and freshly ground black pepper to taste	
¼ cup	packed fresh herb leaves (such as flat-leaf parsley, sage, rosemary, thyme)	50 mL
2 to 3 tbsp	brandy, divided	25 to 45 mL

Wild Mushroom Stuffing

¼ cup	butter	50 mL
2	large onions, chopped	2
2 lbs	wild or exotic mushrooms, quartered	1 kg
1 tsp	dried thyme	5 mL
1 tsp	dried rosemary, crumbled	5 mL
1 tsp	dried sage	5 mL
1 tsp	dried savory	5 mL
1 cup	fresh bread crumbs	250 mL
1½ cups	hot chicken broth	375 mL
3 tbsp	tomato paste	45 mL
¼ cup	chopped fresh Italian (flat-leaf) parsley	50 mL
	Salt and freshly ground black pepper to taste	

Preheat oven to 450°F (230°C). Season turkey inside and out with salt and pepper. Place on a rack in a roasting pan. Carefully lift breast and leg skin by slipping your fingers under it and disengaging it from the meat. Place herb leaves under the skin, spoon in 1 tbsp (15 mL) of the brandy and reposition the skin. Roast for 30 minutes. Reduce heat to 350°F (180°C) and roast for 3 hours, basting with brandy every 20 minutes, until a thermometer inserted in the thigh registers 165°F (74°C). Remove from oven and let rest for 20 minutes before carving. *Meanwhile, prepare the stuffing:* In a large skillet, melt butter over medium heat. Sauté onion until tender. Add mushrooms, thyme, rosemary, sage and savory; sauté until mushrooms start to release their liquid. Add bread crumbs and sauté for 1 minute. Add broth and tomato paste; reduce heat and simmer until thickened. Stir in parsley, salt and pepper. Just before serving, stir ½ cup (125 mL) turkey drippings into stuffing and reheat. Serve turkey with stuffing. **Serves 8 to 10, plus leftovers.**

Turkey Kiev with Herbed Cheese

24	thin slices roasted turkey breast	24
½ cup	herbed cream cheese, softened	125 mL
3	eggs	3
2 tbsp	milk	25 mL
	Dry seasoned bread crumbs	

For each Turkey Kiev, lay out 3 turkey slices so that they overlap slightly in a cloverleaf pattern; place 1 tbsp (15 mL) cream cheese in the center, wrap turkey around cheese and secure loose ends with toothpicks. Repeat until you have 8 bundles. In a large bowl, beat eggs and milk. Dip bundles in egg mixture, then dredge heavily in bread crumbs. Dip in egg mixture again and cover with more bread crumbs. Place on a baking sheet and freeze for 1 hour. Dip frozen bundles in egg mixture again, then in another coat of bread crumbs. Deep-fry (see page 9) until golden brown. Remove toothpicks and serve immediately. **Serves 4.**

Turkey Mushroom Ragoût

2 tbsp	olive oil	25 mL
1	small onion, chopped	1
1	clove garlic, minced	1
4 oz	mushrooms, quartered	125 g
3 cups	large chunks skinned roasted turkey	750 mL
2 cups	Wild Mushroom Stuffing (see recipe, left)	500 mL
½ cup	turkey drippings or turkey broth	125 mL
1 tbsp	chopped fresh Italian (flat-leaf) parsley	15 mL
1 tsp	fresh thyme	5 mL
	Salt and freshly ground black pepper to taste	

In a large skillet, heat oil over medium-high heat. Sauté onion until lightly browned. Add garlic and sauté for 30 seconds. Add mushrooms and turkey; sauté for 1 minute. Add stuffing and drippings; reduce heat and simmer for 5 minutes. Stir in parsley, thyme, salt and pepper. **Serves 4 to 6.**

Turkey Chowder

1	slice bacon, finely chopped	1
2	carrots, diced	2
2	stalks celery, diced	2
2	red-skinned or other boiling potatoes, peeled and diced	2
1	large onion, finely chopped	2
½	red bell pepper, diced	½
2 cups	sliced mushrooms	500 mL
2 cups	diced skinned roasted turkey	500 mL

1 tbsp	all-purpose flour	15 mL
1 tsp	dried thyme	5 mL
½ tsp	ground sage	2 mL
½ tsp	dried rosemary	2 mL
1	bay leaf	1
4 cups	chicken or turkey broth	1 L
	Salt and freshly ground black pepper to taste	

In a large, heavy saucepan, over medium heat, sauté bacon until cooked but not crisp. Add carrots, celery, potatoes, onion, red pepper and mushrooms; sauté until tender. Add turkey, flour, thyme, sage, rosemary and bay leaf; sauté until flour is lightly toasted. Add broth, salt and pepper; reduce heat and simmer for 20 minutes, until flavors are blended. Discard bay leaf. **Serves 6.**

Green Peppercorn Turkey Salad

1	clove garlic, minced	1
½ cup	mayonnaise	125 mL
¼ cup	red wine vinegar	50 mL
3 tbsp	drained canned green peppercorns	45 mL
	Salt and freshly ground black pepper to taste	
2	stalks celery, diced	2
1	small red bell pepper, diced	1
4 cups	diced skinned roasted turkey	1 L
¼ cup	finely chopped green onion	50 mL

Combine garlic, mayonnaise, vinegar, peppercorns, salt and black pepper. Add the remaining ingredients and toss to coat. **Serves 4 to 6.**

Turkey V

Slow-Roasted Turkey

| 1 | turkey (about 15 lbs/7.5 kg), without giblets | 1 |
| | Salt and freshly ground black pepper to taste | |

Preheat oven to 450°F (230°C). Season turkey inside and out with salt and pepper. Place on a rack in a roasting pan and roast for 1 hour. Reduce heat to 170°F (80°C), and roast for at least 14 hours (if your oven is well calibrated, the turkey will not overcook; the bird will be amazingly juicy and tender). Remove from oven and let rest for 20 minutes before carving. **Serves 8 to 10, plus leftovers.**

Turkey Nuggets

2	eggs	2
1 tbsp	milk	15 mL
4 cups	large chunks skinned roasted turkey	1 L
2 cups	dry seasoned bread crumbs	500 mL

In a small bowl, beat eggs and milk. Dip turkey in egg mixture, then dredge in bread crumbs. Deep-fry (see page 9) until golden brown. **Serves 4 to 6.**

Classic Turkey Salad

2	stalks celery, diced	2
1	carrot, shredded	1
½	cucumber, peeled, seeded and diced	½
3 cups	diced skinned roasted turkey	750 mL
⅔ cup	mayonnaise	150 mL
1 tbsp	minced fresh Italian (flat-leaf) parsley	15 mL
1 tbsp	cider vinegar	15 mL
	Salt and freshly ground black pepper to taste	

Toss together all ingredients. Cover and refrigerate for at least 1 hour, until chilled, or for up to 3 days. **Serves 4 to 6.**

Turkey Tabbouleh

1 cup	bulgur	250 mL
1½ cups	cold water	375 mL
3	green onions, sliced	3
1	large tart apple, peeled and diced	1
1	clove garlic, minced	1
1	stalk celery, diced	1
3 cups	diced skinned roasted turkey	750 mL
1 cup	finely chopped fresh Italian (flat-leaf) parsley	250 mL
1 cup	plain yogurt	250 mL
½ cup	chopped almonds	125 mL
6 tbsp	extra-virgin olive oil	90 mL
¼ cup	finely chopped red onion	50 mL
	Salt and freshly ground black pepper to taste	

Soak bulgur in cold water until liquid is absorbed. Stir in the remaining ingredients. Cover and refrigerate for about 1 hour, until chilled. **Serves 4 to 6.**

Turkey Sloppy Joes

2 tbsp	butter	25 mL
½ cup	chopped onion	125 mL
½ cup	diced celery	125 mL
½ cup	diced green bell pepper	125 mL
3 cups	finely chopped skinned roasted turkey	750 mL
¼ cup	pan drippings from the turkey or turkey gravy	50 mL
3 tbsp	ketchup	45 mL
1 tsp	hot pepper sauce (such as Tabasco)	5 mL
4	hamburger buns, toasted	4

In a large skillet, melt butter over medium-high heat. Sauté onion, celery and green pepper until lightly browned. Add turkey and sauté until lightly browned. Add drippings, ketchup and hot pepper sauce; reduce heat and simmer for 1 minute. Spoon onto buns. **Serves 4 to 6.**

Turkey VI

Lemon-Honey Turkey with Cornbread and Crab Stuffing

1	turkey (about 15 lbs/7.5 kg), without giblets	1
	Salt and freshly ground black pepper to taste	
¼ cup	butter, softened	50 mL

Glaze

½ cup	honey	125 mL
¼ cup	freshly squeezed lemon juice	50 mL
2 tbsp	olive oil	25 mL
	Salt and freshly ground black pepper to taste	

Cornbread and Crab Stuffing

6	green onions, chopped	6
2	cloves garlic, minced	2
1½ lbs	backfin (lump) crabmeat, shells picked out	750 g
4 cups	crumbled cornbread or corn muffins	1 L
1 cup	pan drippings from the turkey	250 mL
	Finely grated zest and juice of 1 large lemon	
	Salt and cayenne pepper to taste	

Follow recipe for Traditional Roast Turkey (page 296), using turkey, salt, pepper and butter. *Prepare the glaze:* Combine honey, lemon juice, oil, salt and pepper. During the last hour of roasting, brush turkey every 20 minutes with glaze. *Prepare the stuffing:* In a large, deep skillet, over medium heat, combine all ingredients and heat through. Serve turkey with stuffing. **Serves 8 to 10, plus leftovers.**

Turkey Sautéed with Capers

¼ cup	butter, divided	50 mL
4	slices roasted turkey breast, each ¼ inch (0.5 cm) thick	4
¼ cup	whole capers, with their liquid	50 mL
1 tbsp	finely chopped fresh Italian (flat-leaf) parsley	15 mL

In a large skillet, heat 1 tbsp (15 mL) of the butter over medium-high heat. Cook turkey, in batches if necessary, until browned on both sides; remove to a warm platter. Add the remaining butter to the pan and heat until foamy. Add capers and their liquid; cook until butter browns. Stir in parsley. Pour sauce over turkey. **Serves 4.**

Buffalo Turkey

4 cups	large chunks roasted turkey	1 L
	All-purpose flour	
¼ cup	butter	50 mL
¼ cup	hot pepper sauce (such as Frank's RedHot)	50 mL

Dust turkey with flour. In a small saucepan, melt butter over medium-low heat, then stir in hot pepper sauce; set aside. Deep-fry turkey (see page 9) for 1 minute. Toss with butter mixture. **Serves 4 to 6.**

Lemon-Walnut Turkey Salad

2	green onions, finely chopped	2
1	clove garlic, minced	1
¼ cup	chopped fresh Italian (flat-leaf) parsley	50 mL
¼ cup	freshly squeezed lemon juice	50 mL
¼ cup	canola oil	50 mL
2 tbsp	walnut oil	25 mL
1 tbsp	white wine vinegar	15 mL
Pinch	cayenne pepper	Pinch
	Salt and freshly ground black pepper to taste	
2	stalks celery, diced	2
4 cups	diced skinned roasted turkey	1 L
1 cup	chopped toasted walnuts	250 mL
2 tbsp	diced candied ginger	25 mL

Combine green onions, garlic, parsley, lemon juice, canola oil, walnut oil, vinegar, cayenne, salt and black pepper. Add the remaining ingredients and toss to coat. **Serves 4 to 6.**

Sliced Turkey with Lemon-Mustard Vinaigrette

1	egg yolk	1
1 tbsp	brown mustard	15 mL
¼ cup	freshly squeezed lemon juice	50 mL
⅓ cup	olive oil	75 mL
2 tbsp	canola oil	25 mL
	Salt and freshly ground black pepper to taste	
8	thin slices roasted turkey breast	8

Whisk together egg yolk and mustard, then whisk in lemon juice until well combined. Slowly whisk in olive oil and canola oil, then season with salt and pepper. Serve with turkey slices. **Serves 4.**

Turkey VII

Mustard-Glazed Smoked Turkey Breast

¼ cup	brown mustard	50 mL
1 tbsp	fresh thyme leaves, crushed	15 mL
1	boneless smoked turkey breast (about 4 lbs/2 kg)	1

Preheat oven to 350°F (180°C). Combine mustard and thyme; brush half of this mixture onto turkey. Roast for 1 hour, basting with mustard mixture every 15 minutes, until a thermometer inserted into the thickest part of the breast registers 160°F (71°C). Remove from oven and let rest for 10 minutes before carving. Cut into thin slices. **Serves 8 to 10, plus leftovers.**

Smoked Turkey Salad with Roasted Pepper Vinaigrette

2	roasted bell peppers (any color; see page 11), diced	2
2	cloves garlic, minced	2
¾ cup	cider vinegar	175 mL
½ cup	water	125 mL
¼ cup	granulated sugar	50 mL
	Salt and freshly ground black pepper to taste	
½ cup	olive oil	125 mL
12	slices roasted smoked turkey breast	12
12	mushrooms, sliced	12
1	head curly endive, torn into small pieces	1
8 oz	spinach, torn into small pieces (about 5 cups/1.25 L)	250 g
⅔ cup	finely diced red onion	150 mL

Preheat broiler or barbecue grill to high. In a small saucepan, bring roasted peppers, garlic, vinegar, water, sugar, salt and pepper to a boil; reduce heat and simmer for 3 minutes. Stir in oil, remove from heat and keep warm. Broil or grill turkey, turning once, for 1 to 2 minutes per side, or until browned on both sides. Combine mushrooms, endive, spinach and onion; toss with roasted pepper sauce. Arrange salad on plates and top with grilled turkey. Serve immediately. **Serves 4 to 6.**

Grilled Turkey Ham

4	thick slices roasted smoked turkey breast	4
2 tbsp	honey mustard	25 mL

Preheat broiler or barbecue grill to high. Brush turkey with mustard and broil or grill, turning once, for 2 minutes per side. **Serves 4.**

Melon Wrapped with Smoked Turkey

12	very thin slices roasted smoked turkey breast	12
1	ripe honeydew melon, seeded, peeled and cut into thin wedges	1

Cut each turkey slice into 6- by 2-inch (15 by 5 cm) strips (you should get about 2 per slice). Wrap each honeydew wedge with 1 turkey slice. **Serves 4 to 6 as an appetizer.**

Turkey Benedict

8 cups	water	2 L
¼ cup	vinegar	50 mL
8	eggs	8
¾ cup	mayonnaise	175 mL
1 tbsp	Dijon mustard	15 mL
4	English muffins, split and toasted	4
8	thin slices roasted smoked turkey breast	8

In a large nonstick skillet, bring water and vinegar to a boil; reduce heat to a slow simmer. Crack eggs into the water and poach just until whites are set, about 4 minutes. Meanwhile, combine mayonnaise and mustard. For each portion, place 1 muffin on a plate, split side up, spread each half with 1 tsp (5 mL) of the mayonnaise mixture and top with 1 slice turkey. Remove eggs with a slotted spoon or spatula and set briefly on several layers of paper towel to absorb excess water. Place 1 egg on each turkey slice. Top each egg with a small dollop of mayonnaise mixture. **Serves 4.**

Turkey VIII

Roasted Turkey Breast Studded with Hazelnuts and Garlic

3	cloves garlic	3
⅔ cup	toasted skinned hazelnuts	150 mL
¼ cup	packed fresh Italian (flat-leaf) parsley	50 mL
½ tsp	dried sage	2 mL
	Salt and freshly ground black pepper to taste	
1	bone-in turkey breast (6 to 7 lbs/3 to 3.5 kg)	1
	Olive oil	
	Lemon juice	

Preheat oven to 400°F (200°C). In a food processor, grind garlic, hazelnuts, parsley, sage, salt and pepper into a paste. Using a thin, sharp knife, make deep slits in the turkey breast; fill each slit with 2 tsp (10 mL) of the paste. Place on a rack in a roasting pan and brush the skin of the breast with equal parts olive oil and lemon juice. Roast for 2¼ hours, until a thermometer inserted in the thickest part of the breast registers 165°F (74°C). **Serves 6 to 8, plus leftovers.**

Sliced Turkey Breast with Horseradish Sauce

½ cup	mayonnaise	125 mL
3 tbsp	prepared horseradish	45 mL
1 tbsp	freshly squeezed lemon juice	15 mL
8	slices roasted turkey breast, at room temperature	8

Combine mayonnaise, horseradish and lemon juice. Serve over turkey slices. **Serves 4.**

Grilled Turkey Steaks with Steak Sauce

4	thick slices roasted turkey breast	4
6 tbsp	steak sauce	90 mL

Preheat broiler or barbecue grill to high. Brush turkey with steak sauce and broil or grill, turning once, for 1 to 2 minutes per side, or until browned on both sides. **Serves 4.**

Turkey Hazelnut Salad

1	green onion, finely chopped	1
1	clove garlic, minced	1
½ cup	hazelnut oil	125 mL
¼ cup	chopped fresh Italian (flat-leaf) parsley	50 mL
¼ cup	white wine vinegar	50 mL
2 tbsp	freshly squeezed lemon juice	25 mL
Pinch	cayenne pepper	Pinch
	Salt and freshly ground black pepper to taste	
4 cups	diced skinless roasted turkey breast	1 L
1 cup	halved orange sections	250 mL
½ cup	finely diced fennel bulb	125 mL
½ cup	toasted skinned hazelnuts	125 mL

Combine green onion, garlic, oil, parsley, vinegar, lemon juice, cayenne, salt and black pepper. Add the remaining ingredients and toss to coat. **Serves 4 to 6.**

Turkey Cutlets in Hazelnut Crumbs

1	clove garlic, minced	1
2 tbsp	mayonnaise	25 mL
4	thick slices roasted turkey breast	4
½ cup	ground skinned hazelnuts	125 mL
¼ cup	seasoned dry bread crumbs	50 mL
2 tbsp	butter	25 mL
2 tbsp	vegetable oil	25 mL

Combine garlic and mayonnaise; brush onto turkey. Combine hazelnuts and bread crumbs; dredge turkey in this mixture. In a nonstick skillet, heat butter and oil over medium-high heat. Cook turkey, in batches if necessary, until browned on both sides. **Serves 4.**

Turkey IX

Apple Butter–Glazed Turkey with Apple-Sage Stuffing

1	turkey (about 15 lbs/7.5 kg), including giblets	1
	Salt and freshly ground black pepper to taste	
¼ cup	butter, softened	50 mL
	Apple-Sage Stuffing (see recipe, page 296), apple and sage doubled	

Glaze

⅓ cup	apple butter	75 mL
2 tbsp	cider vinegar	25 mL
1 tbsp	light (fancy) molasses	15 mL
1 tsp	salt	5 mL

Follow recipe for Traditional Roast Turkey (page 296), using turkey, salt, pepper and butter. *Prepare the glaze:* Combine apple butter, vinegar, molasses and salt. During the last hour of roasting, brush turkey every 20 minutes with glaze. Serve turkey with stuffing. **Serves 8 to 10, plus leftovers.**

Leftover Turkey Soup

	Carcass and bones from 1 large roasted turkey	
1 cup	dry white wine	250 mL
10 cups	water	2.5 L
4 cups	chopped vegetables (such as carrots, celery, onions, mushrooms, parsnips, turnips, leeks)	1 L
½ cup	pearl barley	125 mL
3 tbsp	chopped fresh Italian (flat-leaf) parsley	45 mL
2 tbsp	chopped fresh dill	25 mL
1 tsp	dried thyme	5 mL
1	whole clove	1
½ tsp	ground turmeric	2 mL
	Salt and freshly ground black pepper to taste	
1	envelope (¼ oz/7 g) unflavored gelatin	1
	Skinned roasted turkey, cut into bite-size pieces (optional)	

In a large pot, bring carcass, bones and wine to a boil over medium-high heat; cook until wine loses its sharp smell of alcohol. Add water, bring to a boil and skim away any foam that rises to the surface. Reduce heat and simmer for 20 minutes. Add vegetables, barley, parsley, dill, thyme, clove, turmeric, salt and pepper; simmer for 1 hour. Remove from heat. Remove bones to a bowl; set aside. Let soup cool slightly. Discard clove. Mix gelatin with ½ cup (125 mL) of the broth until softened. Add to soup and heat until gelatin dissolves. Pick any edible bits of meat from the bones and return to soup. Add turkey pieces, if using, and season with additional salt and pepper. **Serves 4 to 6.**

Apple Turkey Meatloaf

Follow recipe for Smoked Turkey Meatloaf (page 298), but replace the Smoked Turkey Stuffing with Apple-Sage Stuffing (page 296), apple and sage doubled. **Serves 4 to 6.**

Baked Apples Stuffed with Turkey

1 cup	chopped skinned roasted turkey	250 mL
½ cup	Apple-Sage Stuffing (see recipe, page 296), crumbled	125 mL
4	large Rome or other baking apples	4
3 tbsp	melted butter	45 mL
1 tbsp	honey	15 mL

Preheat oven to 400°F (200°C). Combine turkey and stuffing. Using a melon baller, make a hollow in the interior of each apple big enough to hold about 3 tbsp (45 mL) of filling. Stuff each apple with turkey mixture. Place apples in a baking dish and brush with butter and honey. Bake for 1¼ hours, until tender. **Serves 4.**

Turkey Waldorf Salad

⅓ cup	mayonnaise	75 mL
1 tbsp	apple butter	15 mL
1 tsp	cider vinegar	5 mL
	Salt and freshly ground black pepper to taste	
2	stalks celery, diced	2
1	large apple, peeled and diced	1
3 cups	diced skinned roasted turkey	750 mL
½ cup	toasted walnut pieces	125 mL

Combine mayonnaise, apple butter, vinegar, salt and pepper. Add the remaining ingredients and toss to coat. **Serves 4 to 6.**

Turkey X

Spicy Soy-Ginger Roast Turkey

1	turkey (about 15 lbs/7.5 kg), without giblets	1
	Salt and freshly ground black pepper to taste	
¼ cup	butter, softened	50 mL
Glaze		
1	clove garlic, minced	1
3 tbsp	soy sauce	45 mL
2 tbsp	grated gingerroot	25 mL
1 tbsp	dark sesame oil	15 mL
2 tsp	granulated sugar	10 mL
1 tsp	hot chili paste	5 mL

Follow recipe for Traditional Roast Turkey (page 296), using turkey, salt, pepper and butter. *Prepare the glaze:* Combine garlic, soy sauce, ginger, oil, sugar and chili paste. During the last hour of roasting, brush turkey every 20 minutes with glaze. **Serves 8 to 10, plus leftovers.**

Stir-Fried Turkey with Ginger and Cashews

1/3 cup	Chinese oyster sauce	75 mL
2 tbsp	soy sauce	25 mL
	Juice of 1 lemon	
2 tbsp	cornstarch	25 mL
2 tbsp	canola oil	25 mL
4 cups	bite-size pieces skinned roasted turkey	1 L
2 tbsp	minced gingerroot	25 mL
1 cup	chicken broth	250 mL
2	green onions, sliced	2
1	clove garlic, minced	1
1 cup	whole cashews	250 mL

Combine oyster sauce, soy sauce and lemon juice, then stir in cornstarch until dissolved. In a wok or large skillet, heat oil over high heat. Stir-fry turkey and ginger until turkey is lightly browned. Add broth and bring to a boil. Add cornstarch mixture (stirring first, if necessary) and cook, stirring, until thickened. Stir in green onions, garlic and cashews. **Serves 4 to 6.**

Asian Turkey Salad

1	clove garlic, minced	1
3 tbsp	canola oil	45 mL
2 tbsp	rice vinegar	25 mL
1 tbsp	dark sesame oil	15 mL
1 tbsp	soy sauce	15 mL
1/2 tsp	hot pepper sauce (such as Tabasco)	2 mL
1/4 tsp	ground ginger	1 mL
2	green onions, thinly sliced	2
1/2	red bell pepper, diced	1/2
3 cups	diced skinned roasted turkey	750 mL
1/3 cup	snow peas, halved and blanched (see page 8)	75 mL
1/4 cup	toasted sesame seeds	50 mL

Whisk together garlic, canola oil, vinegar, sesame oil, soy sauce, hot pepper sauce and ginger. Add the remaining ingredients and toss to coat. Sprinkle with sesame seeds. **Serves 4 to 6.**

Sesame Turkey

1 cup	sesame seeds	250 mL
	Salt, freshly ground black pepper and cayenne pepper to taste	
4	thick slices roasted turkey breast	4
2 tsp	dark sesame oil	10 mL
2 tbsp	vegetable oil	25 mL
1	clove garlic, minced	1
2 tbsp	soy sauce	25 mL

Combine sesame seeds, salt, black pepper and cayenne. Brush turkey with sesame oil and dredge in seed mixture. In a large skillet, heat vegetable oil over high heat. Cook turkey, in batches if necessary, until browned on both sides; remove to a platter. Pour off excess oil, add garlic and soy sauce to the pan and sauté for 10 seconds. Drizzle over turkey. **Serves 4.**

Sliced Turkey with Soy Vinaigrette

2	green onions, finely chopped	2
1	clove garlic, minced	1
1/4 cup	chopped fresh cilantro	50 mL
1/4 cup	vegetable oil	50 mL
3 tbsp	rice vinegar	45 mL
2 tbsp	orange juice	25 mL
2 tbsp	soy sauce	25 mL
1 tbsp	sesame oil	15 mL
Pinch	ground ginger	Pinch
Pinch	cayenne pepper	Pinch
8	slices roasted turkey breast, at room temperature	8

Combine green onions, garlic, cilantro, vegetable oil, vinegar, orange juice, soy sauce, sesame oil, ginger and cayenne. Serve over turkey slices. **Serves 4.**

Chapter 27
Fish
Cooking Your Favorites

Black Bass on Cucumber "Noodles" . . . 308
Tea-Steamed Black Bass 308
Bluefish Baked with
Easy Mustard Sauce 309
Ranch-Style Bluefish 309
Barbecued Catfish 309
Pecan Catfish Fingers and
Sweet Potato Chips 309
Cod and Avocado Salad 310
Microwaved Mediterranean Cod 310
Flounder Poached in
Fresh Tomato Sauce 310
Fried Flounder in Buttermilk Batter 310
Fluke Paupiettes Stuffed
with Smoked Salmon Mousse 310
Fluke Fillets Andalouse 311
Curried Grouper Chowder 311
Sautéed Grouper Fillets
with Corn-Pepper Relish 311
Pan-Fried Mackerel
with Homemade Tartar Sauce 312
Baked Mahi Mahi with
Grapefruit Butter Sauce 312
Mahi Mahi Meunière
with Asian Peanut Sauce 312
Mexican Baked Monkfish 312
Provençal Monkfish Soup 313
Pike Mousse with Beurre Blanc 313
Grilled Pompano with Lime and Dill . . . 313
Pompano en Papillote
with Baby Shrimp and Chives 313
Whole Grilled Porgy 313
Sesame Porgy Fillets 314
Bourride of Orange Roughy 314

Sautéed Roughy in
Anise-Parmesan Crust 314
Poached Salmon with
Middle Eastern Cucumbers 314
Salmon Seviche 315
Dill-Cured Salmon (Gravlax) 315
Grilled Salmon with Refried Beans 315
Shad in Mustard Crumbs 315
Shad Stuffed with Roe 315
Brochettes of Shark,
Sturgeon and Salmon 316
Chilied Grilled Sturgeon Fillets 316
Pan-Fried Breaded Smelts
with Pickled Peppers 316
Smelt Tempura 316
Broiled Red Snapper
with Green Chili Cream Sauce 316
Whole Steamed Red Snapper 317
Escabèche of Sole 317
Sole Steamed with
Tangerine and Chives 317
Broiled Swordfish Steak with
Mignonette Sauce 317
Lemon Rosemary Swordfish Steak 317
Mediterranean Tilefish Stew 318
Tortellini, Tilefish and Pesto 318
Grilled Trout with Bacon and Tarragon . . 318
Pan-Fried Trout with Tapenade Relish . . 318
Grilled Tuna and Roasted Pepper Salad . . 318
Grilled Tuna Steak with
Warm Tomato Vinaigrette 319
Whiting Baked with Apples and Thyme . . 319
Whiting, Asparagus and
Pine Nut Salad 319

ish has a lot going for it. Its fat content — the bane of all other animal proteins — is blessed with health benefits. Its protein is easy to digest, it has little cholesterol, and it is naturally low in calories. It can be cooked in just about any way, its flavor is complemented by hundreds of seasonings, and it comes in more varieties than breakfast cereal.

But fish is not without its problems. Net trawling for tuna threatens to wipe out whole species of sea life that get trapped by accident. The rising level of mercury in many wild-caught fish has caused governments to issue warnings for children, pregnant women and the elderly about eating too much tuna, swordfish or mackerel. And the industrial farming of salmon has been shown to cause problems for local native species of the fish.

At this point, the positives outweigh the negatives, leaving us with the dilemma that most of us, raised on cans of tuna and digits of frozen fish sticks, don't know much about cooking the real thing. Even adventurous cooks can become timid when it comes to preparing fish, confining themselves to the few familiar fish they have cooked before.

To help broaden your horizons and lift you out of the same-old-salmon rut, we have assembled 50 recipes for the fish you are most likely to find at the fish counter in your local supermarket. Virtually all of the recipes are quite quickly prepared. Though each of these recipes is complete, none is definitive. Go ahead and alter a seasoning here or a sauce here. If a recipe appeals to you, but the exact fish listed is not available, just make sure to substitute a fish of similar size and fat content. To ensure consistent results, flat fish should be replaced only by other flat fish, freshwater fish by other freshwater fish, and so on.

Use this guide to help you make substitutions:

- **Lean round fish:** Black bass, catfish, cod, grouper, haddock, ocean perch, pike, pompano, porgy, roughy, scrod, sea trout, snapper, tilefish, whiting
- **Fatty round fish:** Bluefish, mackerel, salmon, shad, smelt, freshwater trout, tuna
- **Dense-muscled fish:** Mahi mahi, monkfish, shark, sturgeon, swordfish
- **Flatfish:** Flounder, fluke, halibut, sole, turbot

About these recipes . . .

Although all of the following recipes have been tested as written, cooking times will vary with the thickness of a particular piece of fish. Judge 8 minutes of cooking for every inch (2.5 cm) of thickness when grilling, sautéing, boiling, broiling or frying; 10 minutes per inch (2.5 cm) of thickness when steaming, baking or using dense-muscled fish.

When a recipe calls for whole fish, it should be cleaned and scaled, with the fins removed (your fish purveyor might do this for you). Fish fillets have their skin and pin bones unless the recipe states otherwise.

Salt and pepper should be adjusted to taste before serving.

Black Bass on Cucumber "Noodles"

2	large cucumbers, peeled and seeded	2
1 tsp	kosher salt	5 mL
½ cup	all-purpose flour	125 mL
1 tbsp	dried dillweed	15 mL
	Freshly ground black pepper to taste	
4	black bass fillets (each about 6 oz/175 g)	4
¼ cup	low-fat plain yogurt	50 mL
3 tbsp	olive oil, divided	45 mL
1	clove garlic, minced	1
1 tbsp	chopped fresh dill	15 mL
	Juice of 1 lemon	

Using a vegetable peeler, pare long strips from each cucumber. Toss strips with salt and let stand for 10 minutes; rinse well and shake dry. Arrange in a ring on a platter. Combine flour, dried dill, pepper and additional salt. Brush fish with yogurt, then dredge in the seasoned flour. Discard any excess yogurt and flour. In a large skillet, heat 2 tbsp (25 mL) of the oil over medium-high heat. Cook fish, in batches if necessary, for 2 to 3 minutes per side, or until fish is opaque and flakes easily with a fork. Place fish in the center of the cucumber "noodles." Add the remaining oil, garlic, fresh dill and lemon juice to the pan; bring to a boil. Pour sauce over fish and cucumbers. **Serves 4.**

Tea-Steamed Black Bass

1 tbsp	dark sesame oil	15 mL
1 tsp	soy sauce	5 mL
1	whole black bass (about 2 lbs/1 kg), with 4 slashes in each side	1
2	tea bags (preferably oolong)	2
4	lemon wedges	4

Combine oil and soy sauce; rub fish with the mixture. Place in a large bamboo steamer, cover and set aside. In a saucepan large enough to hold the steamer on its rim, bring about 2 cups (500 mL) water to a boil. Add tea bags to the water, set the steamer on the pot and steam fish for 10 to 12 minutes, or until fish is opaque and flakes easily with a fork. Transfer to a platter and serve garnished with lemon wedges. **Serves 4.**

Bluefish Baked with Easy Mustard Sauce

3 tbsp	butter	45 mL
2 tbsp	minced onion	25 mL
1	clove garlic, minced	1
½ cup	dry white wine	125 mL
1½ lbs	bluefish fillet	750 g
⅔ cup	sour cream or yogurt (not fat-free)	150 mL
3 tbsp	Dijon mustard	45 mL

Preheat oven to 375°F (190°C). In a large ovenproof skillet, melt butter over medium-high heat. Sauté onion until tender. Add garlic and sauté for 30 seconds. Add wine and boil until reduced by half. Nestle fish into the liquid. Bake for 12 to 15 minutes, until fish is opaque and flakes easily with a fork. Meanwhile, combine sour cream and mustard. When fish is done, use a heavy potholder to move the pan to a burner. Remove fish to a warm platter. Bring pan juices to a boil; remove from heat and stir in mustard mixture. Pour sauce over fish. **Serves 4.**

Ranch-Style Bluefish

	Olive oil	
1½ lbs	bluefish fillet	750 g
2 tbsp	chopped onion	25 mL
1	clove garlic, minced	1
⅔ cup	ranch dressing	150 mL
2 tbsp	freshly squeezed lemon juice	25 mL

In a large skillet, heat a thin film of oil over medium-high heat. Cook fish for 3 to 4 minutes per side, or until fish is opaque and flakes easily with a fork; remove fish to a warm platter. Add onion and garlic to the fat in the pan and sauté until browned. Remove from heat and stir in dressing and lemon juice. Pour sauce over fish. **Serves 4.**

Barbecued Catfish

1 tbsp	vegetable oil	15 mL
1	onion, minced	1
1	clove garlic, minced	1
½ cup	ketchup	125 mL
1 tbsp	granulated sugar	15 mL
2 tbsp	cider vinegar	25 mL
1 tsp	brown mustard	5 mL
1 tsp	Worcestershire sauce	5 mL
1 tsp	hot pepper sauce (such as Tabasco)	5 mL
	Juice of ½ lemon	
1½ lbs	catfish fillets (1 inch/2.5 cm thick)	750 g

In a large skillet, heat oil over medium-high heat. Sauté onion until lightly browned. Add garlic and sauté for 30 seconds; let cool. Stir in ketchup, sugar, vinegar, mustard, Worcestershire sauce, hot pepper sauce and lemon juice. Place fish in a shallow dish and coat with half the sauce. Cover and refrigerate for 1 hour. Meanwhile, preheat broiler or barbecue grill to medium-high. Remove fish from marinade and discard marinade. Broil or grill fish, basting frequently with the remaining sauce, for 4 to 5 minutes per side, or until fish is opaque and flakes easily with a fork. **Serves 4.**

Pecan Catfish Fingers and Sweet Potato Chips

2 tbsp	brown mustard	25 mL
2 tsp	honey	10 mL
⅔ cup	finely ground pecans	150 mL
⅓ cup	seasoned dry bread crumbs	75 mL
1½ lbs	skinless catfish fillets, cut into 2- by ½-inch (5 by 1 cm) "fingers"	750 g
	Canola oil	
3 cups	thinly sliced sweet potatoes	750 mL
	Orange wedges	

Combine mustard and honey. In a separate bowl, combine pecans and bread crumbs. Dip fish in honey mixture, then dredge in crumbs. Set fish on a rack and let stand for 10 minutes. Discard any excess honey mixture and crumbs. In a large skillet, heat ¼ inch (0.5 cm) oil over medium-high heat until very hot but not smoking. Sauté sweet potato slices, in batches if necessary, turning once, until crisp and brown; drain on paper towels. Add more oil if needed to reach ¼ inch (0.5 cm), and heat until very hot but not smoking. Fry fish, in batches if necessary, for about 2 minutes per side, until coating is crispy and fish flakes easily with a fork. Drain on paper towels. Serve fish with sweet potato chips and orange wedges. **Serves 4.**

Cod and Avocado Salad

1 lb	skinless cod fillet (1 inch/2.5 cm thick)	500 g
2	green onions, sliced	2
1	large avocado, diced	1
1	clove garlic, minced	1
3 tbsp	chopped fresh cilantro	45 mL
	Juice of 1 lemon	
	Cayenne pepper to taste	
	Lettuce, endive or radicchio	

Place cod fillet in an oiled steaming basket or rack, set in a pot over boiling water, cover and steam for about 10 minutes, or until fish is opaque and flakes easily with a fork; let cool. Flake fish into bite-size pieces and toss with green onions, avocado, garlic, cilantro, lemon juice and cayenne. Serve on a bed of lettuce. **Serves 4.**

Microwaved Mediterranean Cod

1½ lbs	cod fillet (1 inch/2.5 cm thick)	750 g
1 tbsp	extra-virgin olive oil	15 mL
1	clove garlic, minced	1
¼ cup	finely chopped basil	50 mL
	Finely grated zest and juice of 1 large orange	
2 tbsp	freshly squeezed lemon juice	25 mL

Rub fish and the interior of a 10-inch (25 cm) microwave-safe baking dish with oil. Rub fish with garlic, basil and orange zest, place in prepared dish and pour in orange juice and lemon juice. Cover with microwave-safe plastic wrap and microwave on High for 3 to 4 minutes, or until fish is opaque and flakes easily with a fork. Poke a hole in plastic wrap to release steam. Unwrap and serve immediately. **Serves 4.**

Flounder Poached in Fresh Tomato Sauce

2 tbsp	olive oil	25 mL
1	onion, chopped	1
1	clove garlic, minced	1
½ cup	dry white wine	125 mL
2 tsp	dried basil	10 mL
Pinch	dried marjoram	Pinch
3	tomatoes, peeled, seeded and chopped	3
4	pieces skinless flounder fillet (each about 6 oz/175 g)	4
	Juice of ½ lemon	

In a large skillet, heat oil over medium heat. Sauté onion until tender. Add garlic and sauté for 30 seconds. Add wine, basil and marjoram; reduce heat and simmer until most of the liquid has evaporated. Add tomatoes and simmer for 3 minutes. Nestle fish into sauce, cover and simmer for 2 minutes, until fish is opaque and flakes easily with a fork; remove fish to a warm platter. Add lemon juice to the sauce. Pour sauce over fish. **Serves 4.**

Fried Flounder in Buttermilk Batter

½ cup	all-purpose flour	125 mL
1 tsp	dried dillweed	5 mL
¼ tsp	baking soda	1 mL
	Salt and freshly ground black pepper to taste	
1	egg, separated	1
¾ cup	buttermilk	175 mL
2 tsp	finely chopped fresh dill	10 mL
¼ cup	cornstarch	50 mL
1½ lbs	skinless flounder fillet, cut into 2-inch (5 cm) pieces	750 g
	Vegetable oil	
	Lemon wedges	

Sift together flour, dried dill, baking soda, salt and pepper, then beat in egg yolk and buttermilk. In a separate bowl, beat egg white until firm; fold into batter. Combine fresh dill and cornstarch; dredge fish in the mixture, then dip in batter. Discard any excess dill mixture and batter. In a deep, heavy skillet, heat 1 inch (2.5 cm) oil over medium-high heat until very hot but not smoking. Fry fish, in batches if necessary, for 2 to 3 minutes, turning halfway through, until coating is golden and fish flakes easily with a fork. Add more oil and reheat as necessary between batches. Drain on paper towels and serve with lemon wedges. **Serves 4.**

Fluke Paupiettes Stuffed with Smoked Salmon Mousse

1	egg white	1
4 oz	lean white-meat fish fillet, cut into chunks	125 g
4 oz	smoked salmon, cut into chunks	125 g
¼ tsp	salt	1 mL
Pinch	freshly ground white pepper	Pinch
Pinch	cayenne pepper	Pinch
½ cup	whipping (35%) cream, chilled	125 mL
4	skinless fluke fillets (each about 4 oz/125 g)	4
½ cup	dry white wine	125 mL
	Juice of 1 lemon	
2	green onions, finely chopped	2
2 tsp	finely chopped fresh tarragon	10 mL
¼ cup	butter, cut into small pieces	50 mL

Preheat oven to 350°F (180°C). In a food processor, purée egg white, white-meat fish, smoked salmon, salt, white pepper and cayenne. With the motor running, through the feed tube, slowly add cream and process until incorporated. Place one-quarter of the mousse in the center of each fluke fillet, roll fillets around mousse and place seam side down in a greased baking dish. Pour in wine and lemon juice. Cover and bake for 20 minutes, until mousse is set. Remove fish and keep warm. In a small skillet, bring pan juices, green onions and tarragon to a boil over high heat; boil until reduced by two-thirds. Remove from heat and swirl in butter. Pour sauce over fish. **Serves 4.**

Fluke Fillets Andalouse

2 tbsp	olive oil	25 mL
1	onion, chopped	1
1	small carrot, diced	1
1 cup	diced red and green bell pepper	250 mL
1	clove garlic, minced	1
½ cup	dry white wine	125 mL
½ tsp	crumbled saffron threads	2 mL
3 cups	canned diced tomatoes, drained	750 mL
4	skinless fluke fillets (each 5 to 6 oz/150 to 175 g)	4
2 tbsp	chopped fresh Italian (flat-leaf) parsley Juice of ½ lemon	25 mL

In a large skillet, heat oil over medium heat. Sauté onion, carrot and bell pepper until tender. Add garlic and sauté for 30 seconds. Add wine and saffron; reduce heat and simmer until most of the liquid has evaporated. Add tomatoes and simmer for 5 minutes. Nestle fish into sauce, cover and simmer for 4 minutes, until fish is opaque and flakes easily with a fork; remove fish to a warm platter. Add parsley and lemon juice to the sauce. Pour sauce over fish. **Serves 4.**

Curried Grouper Chowder

2 tbsp	butter	25 mL
1	large onion, chopped	1
1	carrot, diced	1
1	small stalk celery, diced	1
1	clove garlic, minced	1
1 tbsp	curry powder	15 mL
1	tart apple, peeled and diced	1
4 cups	diced peeled red-skinned or other boiling potatoes	1 L
4 cups	chicken broth	1 L

1½ lbs	skinless grouper fillet, cut into ½-inch (1 cm) cubes	750 g
1 cup	low-fat plain yogurt	250 mL
¼ cup	toasted nuts (such as pine nuts or sliced almonds)	50 mL

In a large, heavy saucepan, melt butter over medium heat. Sauté onion, carrot and celery until tender. Add garlic and curry powder; sauté for 30 seconds. Add apple, potatoes and broth; reduce heat and simmer for 15 to 20 minutes, until potatoes are tender. Add fish and simmer for 5 minutes, until fish is opaque and flakes easily with a fork. Remove from heat and stir in yogurt. Serve sprinkled with nuts. **Serves 4.**

Sautéed Grouper Fillets with Corn-Pepper Relish

4 tsp	canola oil, divided	20 mL
1	small onion, chopped	1
1	carrot, finely diced	1
¼ cup	water	50 mL
¼ cup	cider vinegar	50 mL
2 tbsp	granulated sugar	25 mL
1 tsp	pickling spice	5 mL
Pinch	hot pepper flakes	Pinch
1	roasted red bell pepper (see page 11), diced	1
2 cups	canned or thawed frozen corn kernels	500 mL
1 cup	all-purpose flour, seasoned with salt and pepper	250 mL
8	pieces grouper fillet (each about 4 oz/125 g)	8

In a large skillet, heat 1 tsp (5 mL) of the oil over medium-high heat. Sauté onion until browned. Add carrot, water, vinegar, sugar, pickling spice and hot pepper flakes; reduce heat and simmer for 5 minutes. Transfer to a bowl and add roasted pepper and corn; set aside. Dredge fish in seasoned flour. Wipe out skillet and heat the remaining oil over medium-high heat. Cook fish, in batches if necessary, for 3 to 4 minutes per side, or until fish is browned on both sides and flakes easily with a fork. Serve with corn-pepper relish. **Serves 4.**

Pan-Fried Mackerel with Homemade Tartar Sauce

2 tbsp	vegetable oil	25 mL
1	onion, chopped	1
2	cloves garlic, minced	2
1 cup	finely diced peeled tart apple	250 mL
1 tbsp	freshly squeezed lemon juice	15 mL
1 cup	mayonnaise	250 mL
3 tbsp	sweet pickle relish	45 mL
2 tsp	hot pepper sauce (such as Tabasco)	10 mL
2	whole mackerel (each about 1½ lbs/750 g) Milk	2
¾ cup	seasoned dry bread crumbs Additional vegetable oil	175 mL

In a large skillet, heat oil over medium heat. Sauté onion, garlic and apple until tender. Remove from heat, stir in lemon juice and let cool. Stir in mayonnaise, relish and hot pepper sauce; set aside. Dip fish in milk, then coat with bread crumbs. Wipe out skillet and heat ½ inch (1 cm) oil over medium-high heat until very hot but not smoking. Fry fish for 4 to 5 minutes per side, or until fish is browned on both sides and flakes easily with a fork. Serve with tartar sauce. **Serves 4.**

Baked Mahi Mahi with Grapefruit Butter Sauce

1½ lbs	skinless mahi mahi fillet (3 inches/7.5 cm thick)	750 g
4	green onions, cut into thin strips Finely grated zest and juice of 1 grapefruit	4
3 tbsp	butter, cut into small pieces	45 mL

Preheat oven to 350°F (180°C). Arrange fish in a greased roasting pan. Sprinkle with green onions, grapefruit zest and grapefruit juice. Bake for 30 minutes, until fish is firm. Remove fish to a warm platter. Over high heat, boil pan juices until reduced by half (if you used a metal roasting pan, do it right in the pan; if you used glass, transfer to a skillet). Remove from heat and swirl in butter. Pour sauce over fish. **Serves 4.**

Mahi Mahi Meunière with Asian Peanut Sauce

1½ lbs	skinless mahi mahi fillet, cut into 1-inch (2.5 cm) pieces	750 g
1 cup	all-purpose flour, seasoned with salt and pepper	250 mL
2 tbsp	peanut oil	25 mL
1	small onion, chopped	1
2	green onions, thinly sliced	2
1	clove garlic, minced	1
2 tsp	freshly grated gingerroot	10 mL
2 tsp	soy sauce	10 mL
1 tsp	Chinese chili paste	5 mL
½ tsp	ground cumin	2 mL
½ tsp	ground coriander	2 mL
¼ cup	smooth peanut butter	50 mL
2 tbsp	plain yogurt	25 mL

Dredge fish in seasoned flour. In a large skillet, heat oil over medium-high heat. Sauté fish until browned and firm, about 5 minutes; remove to a warm platter. Add onion to the pan and sauté until lightly browned. Add green onions, garlic, ginger, soy sauce, chili paste, cumin and coriander; sauté for 1 minute. Stir in peanut butter and heat until melted. Return fish to the pan and add yogurt and any juices that collected on the plate; heat through (do not boil). **Serves 4.**

Mexican Baked Monkfish

1½ lbs	monkfish fillets Salt and freshly ground black pepper to taste	750 g
2 tbsp	olive oil	25 mL
1	onion, chopped	1
1	clove garlic, minced	1
1	jalapeño pepper, seeded and minced	1
1	red bell pepper, chopped	1
½ cup	canned crushed tomatoes Juice of ½ lemon	125 mL
1	avocado, thinly sliced	1

Preheat oven to 350°F (180°C). Rub fish with salt and pepper; place in a baking dish large enough to hold it snugly. In a large skillet, heat oil over medium-high heat. Sauté onion, garlic, jalapeño and red pepper until tender. Add tomatoes, reduce heat and simmer for 3 minutes. Pour over fish and sprinkle with lemon juice. Bake for 25 minutes, until fish is firm. Serve garnished with avocado. **Serves 4.**

Provençal Monkfish Soup

1 cup	dry white wine	250 mL
1 tsp	crumbled saffron threads	5 mL
	Finely grated zest and juice of 1 large orange	
2 tbsp	extra-virgin olive oil	25 mL
1	large onion, chopped	1
2	cloves garlic, minced	2
2	stalks celery, chopped	2
1 tsp	ground fennel seeds	5 mL
1 tsp	dried basil	5 mL
½ tsp	dried thyme	2 mL
1	bay leaf	1
4 cups	canned diced tomatoes, drained	1 L
3 cups	Quick Fish Broth (see recipe, page 19) or clam juice	750 mL
Pinch	hot pepper flakes	Pinch
1½ lbs	monkfish fillets, cut into 1-inch (2.5 cm) chunks	750 g
¼ cup	chopped fresh Italian (flat-leaf) parsley	50 mL

Combine wine, saffron, orange zest and orange juice; set aside. In a large saucepan, heat oil over medium heat. Sauté onion and garlic until tender. Add celery, fennel seeds, basil, thyme and bay leaf; sauté for 1 minute. Add wine mixture and bring to a boil. Add tomatoes, broth and hot pepper flakes; bring to a boil. Add fish, reduce heat and simmer for 10 minutes, until firm. Discard bay leaf and stir in parsley. **Serves 4.**

Pike Mousse with Beurre Blanc

2	egg whites	2
1 lb	skinless boneless pike fillets	500 g
	Ground nutmeg to taste	
2 cups	whipping (35%) cream, well chilled	500 mL
	Beurre Blanc (see recipe, page 51)	

Preheat oven to 350°F (180°C). In a food processor, purée egg whites, fish and nutmeg. Transfer to a bowl, set in a larger bowl filled with ice, and mix until very cold. Beat in cream, a little at a time, until mixture has consistency of softly beaten cream. Spoon mixture into 6 well-greased 5-oz (150 g) ramekins. Cover with buttered parchment paper and place in a water bath (see page 12). Bake for about 25 minutes, or until set. Invert onto plates. Blot up liquid and serve with Beurre Blanc. **Serves 6 as an appetizer.**

Grilled Pompano with Lime and Dill

4	whole pompano or butterfish (each about 1 lb/500 g)	4
3 tbsp	freshly squeezed lime juice	45 mL
2 tbsp	extra-virgin olive oil	25 mL
8	sprigs fresh dill	8

Preheat broiler or barbecue grill to high. Cut 3 slits on each side of each fish and rub with lime juice and oil. Place 2 sprigs dill in each cavity. Place fish on a well-oiled rack and broil or grill for 4 minutes per side, until fish is browned and crisp and flakes easily with a fork. **Serves 4.**

Pompano en Papillote with Baby Shrimp and Chives

4	pompano or butterfish (each about 1 lb/500 g)	4
32	small shrimp, peeled and deveined	32
½ cup	dry white wine	125 mL
¼ cup	snipped fresh chives	50 mL
4 tsp	butter	20 mL
8	lemon wedges	8

Preheat oven to 350°F (180°C). Place each fish on a large piece of heart-shaped parchment paper (see page 12) with one-quarter each of the shrimp, wine, chives and butter. Wrap as explained on page 12 and place on a baking sheet. Bake for 20 to 25 minutes, or until parchment is puffed and brown. Slit the parchment sacks and slide contents onto 4 dinner plates. Garnish each with 2 lemon wedges. **Serves 4.**

Whole Grilled Porgy

2	whole porgies (each about 2 lbs/1 kg)	2
¼ cup	olive oil	50 mL
1 tsp	dried basil	5 mL
	Finely grated zest and juice of 1 lemon	

Cut 3 slits in each side of each fish. Combine oil, basil, lemon zest and lemon juice; rub fish with half this mixture, cover and refrigerate for 1 hour. Reserve remaining marinade. Preheat broiler or barbecue grill to high. Remove fish from marinade and discard marinade. Place fish on an oiled rack and broil or grill for 8 minutes per side, until fish flakes easily with a fork. Transfer fish to plates and spoon reserved marinade over fish. **Serves 4.**

Sesame Porgy Fillets

1	egg white	1
1 tbsp	soy sauce	15 mL
1 cup	sesame seeds	250 mL
¼ cup	cornstarch	50 mL
Pinch	cayenne pepper	Pinch
8	skinless porgy fillets (each about 4 oz/125 g)	8
3 tbsp	vegetable oil	45 mL
	Juice of 1 lemon	
1 tbsp	dark sesame oil	15 mL
1	green onion, thinly sliced	1

Whisk together egg white and soy sauce. In a separate bowl, combine sesame seeds, cornstarch and cayenne. Brush fish with egg mixture, then dredge in sesame mixture. Discard any excess egg mixture and sesame mixture. In a large skillet, heat vegetable oil over medium-high heat. Cook fish, in batches if necessary, for 2 to 3 minutes per side, or until coating is browned and fish flakes easily with a fork. Squeeze lemon juice over top, drizzle with sesame oil and garnish with green onion. **Serves 4.**

Bourride of Orange Roughy

2 tbsp	olive oil	25 mL
1	large onion, chopped	1
1	carrot, chopped	1
4	cloves garlic, minced, divided	4
1½ cups	dry white wine	375 mL
1½ cups	Quick Fish Broth (see recipe, page 19) or 1 fish bouillon cube dissolved in boiling water	375 mL
2 tbsp	grated orange zest	25 mL
1 tsp	ground fennel seeds	5 mL
½ tsp	dried thyme	2 mL
1	bay leaf	1
2 lbs	skinless orange roughy fillets, cut into 1-inch (2.5 cm) wide strips	1 kg
6	slices garlic bread	6
⅓ cup	mayonnaise	75 mL

In a large saucepan, heat oil over medium-high heat. Sauté onion and carrot until tender. Add one-quarter of the garlic and sauté for 30 seconds. Add wine, broth, orange zest, fennel seeds, thyme and bay leaf; reduce heat and simmer for 10 minutes. Add fish and simmer for 5 minutes, until fish is opaque and flakes easily with a fork. Place 1 slice of garlic bread in each of 6 soup bowls and divide fish among the bowls. Whisk the remaining garlic and the mayonnaise into the broth and ladle over fish. **Serves 6.**

Sautéed Roughy in Anise-Parmesan Crust

1 cup	freshly grated Parmesan cheese	250 mL
1 tbsp	finely chopped fresh Italian (flat-leaf) parsley	15 mL
2 tsp	ground anise seeds	10 mL
1	extra-large egg	1
3 tbsp	water	45 mL
4	skinless orange roughy fillets (each about 6 oz/175 g)	4
1½ cups	dry bread crumbs	375 mL
	Olive oil	
	Lemon wedges	

Combine Parmesan, parsley and anise seeds. In a separate bowl, beat egg with water. Dredge fish in Parmesan mixture, shake off any excess, gently dip in egg mixture, then dip in bread crumbs until well coated. Set fish on a rack and let stand for 10 minutes (or cover and refrigerate for up to 12 hours). Discard any excess Parmesan mixture, egg mixture and bread crumbs. In a large skillet, heat a thin film of oil over medium heat. Cook fish for about 3 minutes per side, or until coating is crispy and fish flakes easily with a fork; drain on paper towels. Serve garnished with lemon wedges. **Serves 4.**

Poached Salmon with Middle Eastern Cucumbers

2	cucumbers, peeled, seeded and thinly sliced	2
1 tbsp	kosher salt	15 mL
2 cups	water	500 mL
1 cup	dry white wine	250 mL
1	thick slice onion	1
1	whole clove	1
1	bay leaf	1
4	pieces salmon fillet (each about 6 oz/175 g)	4
1	clove garlic, minced	1
2 tbsp	extra-virgin olive oil	25 mL
1 tbsp	freshly squeezed lemon juice	15 mL
1 tbsp	plain yogurt	15 mL

Toss cucumber slices with salt; set aside. In a large skillet, bring water, wine, onion, clove and bay leaf to a boil. Reduce heat, add salmon and simmer for 8 minutes, until fish is opaque and flakes easily with a fork. Remove fish to a platter and let cool, moistening occasionally with a bit of poaching liquid. Wrap cucumbers in a clean kitchen towel and squeeze out as much liquid as you can. Combine cucumber, garlic, oil, lemon juice and yogurt. Serve salmon with cucumber salad on the side. Serves 4.

Salmon Seviche

1 lb	boneless skinless salmon fillet, cut into thin slices	500 g
	Juice of 4 lemons, 2 limes and 1 orange	
½	avocado	½
1 tbsp	extra-virgin olive oil	15 mL
Pinch	hot pepper flakes	Pinch

Toss salmon and citrus juices in a glass bowl. Cover and refrigerate for 3 hours, until fish is opaque. Remove fish from marinade and discard marinade. Thinly slice avocado and toss with fish, oil and hot pepper flakes. Serves 4.

Dill-Cured Salmon (Gravlax)

1 cup	kosher salt	250 mL
½ cup	granulated sugar	125 mL
1 tsp	freshly ground white pepper	5 mL
12	sprigs fresh dill, divided	12
1	side of salmon (about 2 lbs/1 kg)	1

Combine salt, sugar and pepper; spread one-third of this mixture in a thin layer in a large, deep glass baking dish. Place half the dill in the dish. Place salmon, skin side down, on top of dill. Arrange the remaining dill over salmon and mound the remaining salt mixture on top, using more on the thicker parts. Cover with several layers of plastic wrap or waxed paper and weight with a full tin can atop a dish. Refrigerate for 36 to 48 hours, depending on thickness of fish — when it's ready, the salmon will appear to be cooked. Remove fish, discarding salt mixture. Rinse salmon, pat dry and slice thinly on an angle against the grain. Serve as you would lox. Serves 12.

Grilled Salmon with Refried Beans

⅓ cup	olive oil	75 mL
2 tbsp	chopped fresh basil	25 mL
	Juice of 1 lemon	
4	salmon steaks (each about 6 oz/175 g)	4
	Refried Black, White or Kidney Beans (see recipe, page 20)	

In a shallow dish, combine oil, basil and lemon juice. Add salmon and turn to coat. Cover and refrigerate for 1 hour. Preheat broiler or barbecue grill (preferably charcoal) to high. Remove salmon from marinade and discard marinade. Broil or grill salmon for 4 to 5 minutes per side, or until fish is

opaque and flakes easily with a fork. Serve with Spicy Black Beans. Serves 4.

Shad in Mustard Crumbs

1½ lbs	boneless shad fillets	750 g
6 tbsp	spicy brown mustard, divided	90 mL
1 cup	seasoned dry bread crumbs	250 mL
2 tbsp	olive oil	25 mL
	Lemon wedges	

Brush flesh side of the shad with half the mustard and coat with bread crumbs. Dab the remaining mustard over the breading and cover with more bread crumbs (surface may look bumpy). In a large skillet, heat oil over medium-high heat. Cook shad, breaded side down, for 3 to 4 minutes, until browned. Turn fish, being careful to not dislodge the breading, and cook for about 5 minutes, until fish flakes easily with a fork. Serve with lemon wedges. Serves 4.

Shad Stuffed with Roe

2 tbsp	olive oil	25 mL
1	set shad roe, divided into 2 sacs	1
2	boneless shad fillets (each about 12 oz/375 g)	2
2 tbsp	chopped fresh dill	25 mL
2 tbsp	freshly squeezed lemon juice	25 mL
	Herbed Beurre Blanc (see recipe, page 51), made with dillweed	

In a nonstick skillet, heat oil over medium-high heat. Poke sacs several times with a fork and cook until firm on the surface. Lay sacs end to end down the center of 1 shad fillet. Place the second fillet on top and tie in several places to secure. Place in a steamer basket and sprinkle with dill and lemon juice. Steam over boiling water for 10 to 15 minutes, or until fish is opaque and flakes easily with a fork. Using 2 wide spatulas, carefully remove to a serving platter. Cover with Herbed Beurre Blanc. Serves 4.

Brochettes of Shark, Sturgeon and Salmon

1	clove garlic, minced	1
¼ cup	olive oil	50 mL
2 tbsp	chopped fresh basil	25 mL
	Juice of 1 lemon	
8 oz	skinless salmon fillet, cut into 8 chunks	250 g
8 oz	skinless shark fillet, cut into 8 chunks	250 g
8 oz	sturgeon fillet, cut into 8 chunks	250 g
16	mushrooms	16
1	red bell pepper, cut into 16 pieces	1

In a shallow dish, combine garlic, oil, basil and lemon juice. Add salmon, shark and sturgeon, coating evenly. Cover and refrigerate for 1 hour. Preheat broiler or barbecue grill to high. Remove fish from marinade and discard marinade. Thread 1 piece of each fish variety, alternating with 2 mushrooms and 2 pieces of pepper, onto each of 8 skewers. Broil or grill for 10 to 12 minutes, turning often, or until fish is firm and opaque. **Serves 4.**

Chilied Grilled Sturgeon Fillets

1½ lbs	sturgeon fillet	750 g
	Salt and freshly ground black pepper to taste	
	Juice of 2 lemons	
⅓ cup	olive oil	75 mL
2	cloves garlic, minced	2
2 tbsp	chili powder	25 mL
1 tbsp	ground cumin	15 mL
Pinch	dried oregano	Pinch
	Lemon wedges	

Rub sturgeon with salt, pepper and lemon juice; place in a dish that will hold it snugly and set aside. In a small skillet, heat oil over medium-low heat. Sauté garlic, chili powder, cumin and oregano until aromatic; let cool. Pour over fish, cover and refrigerate for 1 hour. Preheat broiler or barbecue grill to high. Remove fish from marinade and discard marinade. Broil or grill fish for 6 minutes per side, until firm. Serve with lemon wedges. **Serves 4.**

Pan-Fried Breaded Smelts with Pickled Peppers

2 lbs	smelts (each 3 to 4 inches/ 7.5 to 10 cm long), heads removed	1 kg
1 cup	milk	250 mL
1½ cups	dry seasoned bread crumbs	375 mL
	Olive oil	
	Pickled peppers	

Dip smelts in milk and coat with bread crumbs. Discard any excess milk and bread crumbs. In a large skillet, heat ¼ inch (0.5 cm) oil over medium-high heat. Fry smelts, in batches if necessary, for about 3 minutes per side, or until coating is crispy and fish flakes easily with a fork; drain on paper towels. Serve with pickled peppers. **Serves 4.**

Smelt Tempura

1	extra-large egg, beaten	1
2 cups	sifted all-purpose flour	500 mL
2 cups	ice water	500 mL
2 lbs	smelts (each 3 to 4 inches/ 7.5 to 10 cm long), heads removed	1 kg
1 cup	cornstarch	250 mL
	Vegetable oil	
	Soy sauce	

Combine egg, flour and ice water until barely blended. Dredge smelts in cornstarch, then dip in batter. Discard any excess cornstarch and batter. Deep-fry smelts (see page 9), in batches if necessary, until pale brown, about 2 minutes; drain on paper towels. Serve with soy sauce for dipping. **Serves 4.**

Broiled Red Snapper with Green Chili Cream Sauce

4	poblano peppers, roasted, skinned, seeded and chopped	4
4	green onions, white part only, chopped	4
1	clove garlic, minced	1
1 cup	chicken broth	250 mL
2 cups	cream (any type, minimum 10%)	500 mL
¼ cup	chopped fresh cilantro	50 mL
1 tsp	freshly squeezed lime juice	5 mL
	Salt and freshly ground black pepper to taste	
4	red snapper fillets (each about 6 oz/175 g)	4
2 tbsp	olive oil	25 mL

Preheat broiler or barbecue grill to medium-high. In a saucepan, bring poblanos, green onions, garlic and broth to a boil; boil until reduced by half. Add cream and boil for 3 to 4 minutes, or until slightly thickened. Transfer to a food processor and purée. Stir in cilantro, lime juice, salt and pepper; set aside. Rub snapper with oil and additional salt and pepper. Broil or grill for 3 to 4 minutes per side, or until fish is browned on both sides and flakes easily with a fork. Serve fish with sauce on top. **Serves 4.**

Whole Steamed Red Snapper

1	whole red snapper (2 to 3 lbs/1 to 1.5 kg)	1
2 tsp	dark sesame oil	10 mL
2	cloves garlic, julienned	2
2	green onions, julienned	2
1	piece gingerroot (about 1 inch/2.5 cm), julienned	1
	Juice of 1 lime	

Cut 4 slits in each side of the snapper and rub with oil. Place on a heatproof platter and scatter with garlic, green onions and ginger. Cover with foil and place over a pan of simmering water just large enough to hold the platter on its rim. Cover platter and pan with more foil to trap steam, and steam for 20 minutes, until fish is opaque and flakes easily with a fork. Uncover and pour lime juice over fish. Serves 4.

Escabèche of Sole

1½ lbs	skinless sole fillets	750 g
1 cup	all-purpose flour	250 mL
6 tbsp	olive oil, divided	90 mL
1	onion, sliced	1
2	cloves garlic, smashed	2
1	dried hot chili pepper	1
1	bay leaf	1
¼ cup	red or white wine vinegar	50 mL
	Juice of 2 oranges, 2 lemons and 2 limes	
2 tbsp	chopped fresh Italian (flat-leaf) parsley	25 mL
2 tbsp	chopped fresh dill	25 mL

Lightly coat fish with flour. In a large skillet, heat ¼ cup (50 mL) of the oil over medium-high heat. Cook fish, in batches if necessary, until browned on both sides (it doesn't need to be cooked through); remove to a glass dish. Add the remaining oil, onion and garlic to the pan and sauté until onion is tender. Add chili pepper, bay leaf, vinegar and citrus juices; bring to a boil. Stir in parsley and dill. Pour over fish, cover and refrigerate for 3 to 4 hours, or until fish is firm and opaque. Serve cold, using marinade as a sauce. Serves 4.

Sole Steamed with Tangerine and Chives

4	skinless sole fillets (each 5 to 6 oz/150 to 175 g)	4
⅓ cup	chopped fresh chives	75 mL
¼ cup	freshly squeezed tangerine juice	50 mL
1 tbsp	walnut oil, or other flavorful oil	15 mL
1 tsp	freshly squeezed lemon juice	5 mL
Pinch	ground nutmeg	Pinch
4	whole chives	4
4	lime wedges	4

Arrange sole, dark side down, on a heatproof platter. Sprinkle with chopped chives, tangerine juice, oil, lemon juice and nutmeg. Cover with foil and place over a pan of simmering water just large enough to hold the platter on its rim. Cover platter and pan with more foil to trap steam, and steam for 8 to 10 minutes, or until fish is opaque and flakes easily with a fork. Uncover and garnish each fillet with 1 chive and 1 lime wedge. Serves 4.

Broiled Swordfish Steak with Mignonette Sauce

4	swordfish steaks (1 inch/2.5 cm thick)	4
3 tbsp	olive oil	45 mL
2	shallots, minced	2
⅓ cup	red wine vinegar	75 mL
1 tsp	hot pepper flakes	5 mL

Preheat broiler. Rub swordfish with oil and broil for 4 minutes per side, until fish is firm and opaque. Meanwhile, combine shallots, vinegar and hot pepper flakes. Serve fish splashed with sauce. Serves 4.

Lemon Rosemary Swordfish Steak

2	cloves garlic, minced	2
1	dried hot chili pepper	1
⅓ cup	extra-virgin olive oil	75 mL
1 tbsp	chopped fresh rosemary	15 mL
	Juice of 2 lemons	
4	swordfish steaks (1 inch/2.5 cm thick)	4

In a small skillet, over low heat, warm garlic, chili pepper, oil and rosemary. Stir in lemon juice. Place swordfish in a glass dish and pour in all but 2 tbsp (25 mL) of the garlic mixture. Cover and refrigerate for 1 hour. Preheat broiler or barbecue grill (preferably charcoal) to high. Remove fish from marinade and discard marinade. Broil or grill fish for 4 to 5 minutes per side, or until fish is firm and opaque. Serve drizzled with the remaining garlic mixture. Serves 4.

Mediterranean Tilefish Stew

3 tbsp	extra-virgin olive oil	45 mL
2	stalks celery, chopped	2
1	large onion, chopped	1
1 cup	diced peeled eggplant	250 mL
½ cup	quartered mushrooms	125 mL
2	cloves garlic, minced	2
1 tsp	ground fennel seeds	5 mL
1 tsp	dried basil	5 mL
½ tsp	dried oregano	2 mL
½ cup	dry white wine	125 mL
3 cups	Quick Fish Broth (see recipe, page 19) or clam juice	750 mL
1 cup	canned diced tomatoes, drained	250 mL
1 tsp	hot pepper flakes	5 mL
1½ lbs	tilefish fillet, cut into 2-inch (5 cm) chunks	750 g
¼ cup	chopped fresh Italian (flat-leaf) parsley	50 mL

In a large saucepan, heat oil over medium heat. Sauté celery, onion, eggplant and mushrooms until tender. Add garlic, fennel seeds, basil and oregano; sauté for 1 minute. Add wine and bring to a boil. Add broth, tomatoes and hot pepper flakes; bring to a boil. Add fish, reduce heat and simmer for 8 minutes, until fish is opaque and flakes easily with a fork. Stir in parsley. **Serves 4.**

Tortellini, Tilefish and Pesto

1	clove garlic	1
2 cups	packed fresh basil leaves	500 mL
¼ cup	extra-virgin olive oil	50 mL
1 lb	cheese or herb tortellini	500 g
1 lb	skinless tilefish fillet, cut into bite-size chunks	500 g
¼ cup	freshly grated Parmesan cheese	50 mL

In a food processor, process garlic and basil until finely chopped. With the motor running, through the feed tube, slowly add oil and process until blended; set aside. Bring a large pot of salted water to a boil. Add tortellini and cook according to package directions, adding tilefish 1 minute before tortellini is done. Drain and toss with pesto and Parmesan. **Serves 4.**

Grilled Trout with Bacon and Tarragon

4	whole brook trout (each about 8 oz/250 g)	4
	Juice of 1 lemon	
4	sprigs fresh tarragon	4
4	slices bacon	4
	Lemon wedges	

Preheat broiler or barbecue grill to high. Rub fish inside and out with lemon juice. Place 1 sprig tarragon in each cavity and wrap 1 slice of bacon around each fish. Broil or grill for 4 to 5 minutes per side, or until bacon is crisp and fish is opaque and flakes easily with a fork. Serve garnished with lemon wedges. **Serves 4.**

Pan-Fried Trout with Tapenade Relish

2	green onions, trimmed and finely sliced	2
1	clove garlic, minced	1
1 cup	finely chopped pitted oil-cured black olives	250 mL
¼ cup	extra-virgin olive oil	50 mL
4	whole brook trout (each about 8 oz/250 g)	4
½ cup	milk	125 mL
½ cup	seasoned dry bread crumbs	125 mL
	Olive oil	

Combine green onions, garlic, olives and olive oil; set aside. Dip fish in milk and coat with bread crumbs. Discard any excess milk and bread crumbs. In a large nonstick skillet, heat ¼ inch (0.5 cm) oil over medium-high heat until very hot but not smoking. Fry fish, in batches if necessary, for about 3 minutes per side, or until coating is crispy and fish flakes easily with a fork; drain on paper towels. Serve fish with olive sauce. **Serves 4.**

Grilled Tuna and Roasted Pepper Salad

2	tuna steaks (each about 8 oz/250 g)	2
3 tbsp	olive oil	45 mL
⅓ cup	mayonnaise	75 mL
1 tbsp	freshly squeezed lemon juice	15 mL
¼ tsp	ground celery seeds	1 mL
½	roasted bell pepper (see page 11), diced	½
½ cup	diced seeded peeled cucumber	125 mL

Preheat broiler or barbecue grill to medium-high. Rub tuna with oil, and broil or grill for 5 minutes per side, until fish is firm and opaque; let cool, then flake into small pieces. Combine mayonnaise, lemon juice and celery seeds. Add tuna, roasted pepper and cucumber; toss to coat. **Serves 4.**

Grilled Tuna Steak with Warm Tomato Vinaigrette

1 cup	canned crushed tomatoes	250 mL
2	green onions, chopped	2
3 tbsp	extra-virgin olive oil	45 mL
1 tbsp	red wine vinegar	15 mL
Pinch	hot pepper flakes	Pinch
2	tuna steaks (each about 8 oz/250 g)	2
	Additional olive oil	

Preheat broiler or barbecue grill to high. In a small, heavy saucepan, over medium-high heat, cook tomatoes until thickened, about 5 minutes. Remove from heat and stir in green onions, oil, vinegar and hot pepper flakes; keep warm. Rub tuna with oil, and broil or grill for 1 to 2 minutes per side, until browned but still rare. Slice tuna and pour sauce over top. **Serves 4.**

Whiting Baked with Apples and Thyme

1 tbsp	butter	15 mL
2	stalks celery, chopped	2
1	small onion, chopped	1
1	Granny Smith apple, peeled and diced	1
1	clove garlic, minced	1
2 tsp	chopped fresh thyme	10 mL
½ tsp	minced fresh sage	2 mL
	Juice of ½ lemon	
1½ lbs	whiting fillets	750 g

Preheat oven to 375°F (190°C) and grease a 13- by 9-inch (3 L) baking pan. In a large skillet, melt butter over medium heat. Sauté celery, onion and apple until tender. Add garlic, thyme and sage; sauté for 1 minute. Stir in lemon juice. Place fish in prepared pan and pour in celery mixture. Cover and bake for 20 minutes, until fish is opaque and flakes easily with a fork. **Serves 4.**

Whiting, Asparagus and Pine Nut Salad

1 lb	whiting fillets	500 g
8 oz	asparagus, cut into 1½-inch (4 cm) lengths	250 g
2	green onions, sliced	2
¼ cup	pine nuts, toasted	50 mL
¼ cup	extra-virgin olive oil	50 mL
1 tbsp	chopped fresh Italian (flat-leaf) parsley	15 mL
	Juice of 1 lemon	
	Cayenne pepper to taste	
	Bibb lettuce	

In a large, deep skillet, bring 2 inches (5 cm) of salted water to a simmer. Poach fish for about 8 minutes, or until fish is opaque and flakes easily with a fork; remove with a slotted spoon and let cool. Add asparagus to the water in the skillet and simmer until bright green, about 2 minutes; drain and let cool. Flake fish into small pieces, discarding any large pieces of skin. Toss with asparagus, green onions, pine nuts, oil, parsley, lemon juice and cayenne. Serve on beds of Bibb lettuce. **Serves 4.**

Chapter 28
Understanding Fish
The Lean and Fat of Cooking

Poached Fish with Beurre Blanc 321

Fish Poached in Vegetable Juice 322

Poached Fish with Tomato Mint Salsa . . 322

Poached Fish with Wine Hollandaise . . 322

Bourride 322

Chilled Poached Fish
with Citrus Vinaigrette 322

Chilled Poached Fish
with Creamy Cucumbers 323

Fried Fish in Ranch Buttermilk Batter . . 323

Fish Tempura 323

Old Bay Fried Fish 323

Buffalo "Fins" 323

Whole Fried Sesame Fish 324

Orange-Fennel Fillet 324

Fish in Balsamic Brown Butter
with Capers 324

Sautéed Fish in Lemon Butter 324

Sautéed Fish with Lime and Olives 324

Fish Sautéed in Hazelnut-Garlic Crust . . 324

Rosemary, Sage and Garlic Fillets 325

Fish Fillets Steamed
with Lime and Chives 325

Fish Steamed with Baby Shrimp
in Tarragon Vinaigrette 325

Fish Steamed with Vegetables 325

Steamed Paupiettes Rolled
with Fresh Herbs 325

Fish en Papillote with Leeks 326

Fish en Papillote with
Julienne of Garden Vegetables 326

Fish en Papillote
with Olives and Tomatoes 326

Fish en Papillote
with Melon and Capers 326

Fish en Papillote, Bouillabaisse-Style . . 326

Fish en Papillote with Pickled Ginger . . 327

Fish Grilled with Bacon
and Green Onions 327

Broiled Fish with Walnut Butter 327

Baked Fish in Mustard Glaze 327

Baked Fish with Horseradish
and Sour Cream 327

Whole Baked Fish 327

Fish Baked in a Glaze of Herb Oil 327

Sweet-and-Sour Cranberry Fish 328

Smoky Grilled Fish 328

Grilled Fish in Chili Paste 328

Grilled Fish in Garlic Herb Marinade . . . 328

Grilled Fish in Garlic Sage Marinade . . . 328

Grilled Fish Glazed with Vinaigrette . . . 329

Grilled Fish with Olive Oil
and Balsamic Vinegar 329

Barbecued Fish 329

Teriyaki Grilled Fish 329

Marinated Fish Kebabs 329

Broiled Fish with
Lemon Ranch Dressing 329

Fish Chili 330

Fish, Black Beans and Cilantro 330

All-Fish Bouillabaisse 330

Clam and Fish Stew with Lots of Basil . . 330

Fish Braised with Mussels and Orange . . 330

ow that the preceding chapter has given you a couple of recipes for every fish variety you are likely to find at the market, let's multiply your repertoire in one fell swoop by dividing the fish of the world into two broad categories — lean and oily.

After all, the main culinary differences among fish are reflected in their fat content, and that's why, for cooking purposes, fish are classified as either lean or oily. A lean fish has a fat content of less than 5 percent. This would include all flatfish, codfish, snapper, perch, whiting, catfish and drum. Oily fish can have fat percentages up to 45 percent. Salmon, shark, bluefish, tuna and mackerel are examples.

Typically, as fish fat content increases, so do flesh color, aroma and flavor. That's why high-fat fish tend to work best with dry cooking techniques, such as grilling and baking, where their natural oils keep the meat moist. And they are usually served with more strongly flavored sauces.

Lean fish are better suited to moist cooking methods. Poaching and steaming delicately soften the flesh of these fish while keeping the meat moist in a bath of warm liquid. After cooking, they are usually served with buttery or creamy sauces to lend needed richness.

There are exceptions, of course, among cooking techniques and among fish. For example, both lean and oily fish fry and sauté well, provided the fillet of lean fish is thin enough, and salmon (the most popular of all oily fish) is equally good whether grilled or poached.

The following 50 recipes are divided between those for lean fish and those for oily fish. The recipes do not specify one variety, but you can use the following partial list as a guide. Because new varieties of fish are always coming to market, and because the same fish can be known by different names in different seasons or parts of the country, it is possible that the fish you have in hand may not be listed. In that case, use the guidelines given before each list.

Lean fish have snow-white flesh and no perceptible aroma. They might have a round or flat body profile, but all flatfish are lean. This group includes black bass, sea bass, catfish, cod, flounder, fluke, grouper, halibut, St. Peter's fish, perch, pompano, porgy, rockfish, orange roughy, snapper, sunfish, tilefish, whiting and yellow perch.

Oily fish have round body profiles and tinted flesh that can be beige, gray or pink-to-salmon color, depending on variety. Although no fish should ever smell fishy, oily fish will have an aroma characteristic of their type. This group includes anchovy, bluefish, butterfish, carp, chub, mahi mahi, eel, herring, mackerel, sable, salmon, sardine, shad, shark, smelt, sturgeon, swordfish and tuna.

About these recipes . . .

The following recipes should be seasoned to taste with salt and pepper. The first recipes are for lean fish; the latter ones are for oily fish. The appropriate type of fish is indicated in each recipe. When a recipe calls for whole fish, it should be cleaned and scaled, with the fins removed (your fish purveyor might do this for you). Fish fillets have their skin and pin bones unless the recipe states otherwise.

Some of the recipes in this chapter call for court bouillon as an added liquid. Use the recipe on page 18.

• •

Poached Fish with Beurre Blanc

1½ lbs	fillet of lean fish	750 g
4 cups	Court Bouillon (see recipe, page 18) or equal parts salted water and white wine	1 L
2 tbsp	finely chopped shallot	25 mL
2 tbsp	white wine vinegar	25 mL
¼ cup	butter, cut into small pieces	50 mL

Poach fish in bouillon (see page 11) for about 8 minutes per inch (2.5 cm) of thickness, or until fish is opaque and flakes easily with a fork; remove with a slotted spatula to a warm platter. Pour off all but ½ cup (125 mL) of the bouillon. Add shallot, vinegar and any liquid that has collected under the fish; boil over high heat until reduced by one-third. Reduce heat to low and swirl in butter, one piece at a time. Pour sauce over fish. **Serves 4.**

Fish Poached in Vegetable Juice

1½ lbs	fillet of lean fish	750 g
1½ cups	vegetable juice (such as V8)	375 mL
2 tbsp	chopped fresh basil	25 mL
2 tbsp	extra-virgin olive oil	25 mL
2 tsp	freshly squeezed lemon juice	10 mL

Poach fish in vegetable juice (see page 11) for about 8 minutes per inch (2.5 cm) of thickness, or until fish is opaque and flakes easily with a fork; remove with a slotted spatula to a warm platter. Add basil to the liquid remaining in the pan and boil over medium-high heat until reduced by half. Whisk in oil and lemon juice. Pour sauce over fish. **Serves 4.**

Poached Fish with Tomato Mint Salsa

2	large tomatoes, finely chopped	2
2	green onions, thinly sliced	2
⅓ cup	finely chopped fresh mint	75 mL
¼ tsp	chili powder	1 mL
Pinch	granulated sugar	Pinch
	Juice of ½ lemon	
1½ lbs	fillet of lean fish	750 g
4 cups	Court Bouillon (see recipe, page 18) or equal parts salted water and white wine	1 L
1 tbsp	olive oil	15 mL

Combine tomatoes, green onions, mint, chili powder, sugar and lemon juice; cover and refrigerate for 30 minutes. Poach fish in bouillon (see page 11) for about 8 minutes per inch (2.5 cm) of thickness, or until fish is opaque and flakes easily with a fork; remove with a slotted spatula to a warm platter and discard poaching liquid. Drizzle fish with oil and top with salsa. **Serves 4.**

Poached Fish with Wine Hollandaise

1½ lbs	fillet of lean fish	750 g
4 cups	Court Bouillon (see recipe, page 18) or equal parts salted water and white wine	1 L
2	extra-large egg yolks, beaten	2
	Juice of ½ lemon	
⅓ cup	melted butter	75 mL

Poach fish in bouillon (see page 11) for about 8 minutes per inch (2.5 cm) of thickness, or until fish is opaque and flakes easily with a fork; remove with a slotted spatula to a warm platter. Pour off all but 2 cups (500 mL) of the bouillon and boil over high heat until reduced by three-quarters. Transfer to the top of a double boiler, place over simmering water and whisk in egg yolks and lemon juice until thick and fluffy. Remove from heat and stir in butter. Pour sauce over fish. **Serves 4.**

Bourride

4	slices garlic bread, toasted	4
2 tbsp	olive oil	25 mL
1	large onion, chopped	1
1	carrot, chopped	1
3	cloves garlic, minced, divided	3
2½ cups	Court Bouillon (see recipe, page 18) or equal parts salted water and white wine	625 mL
2 tbsp	julienned orange zest	25 mL
½ tsp	ground fennel seeds	2 mL
½ tsp	dried thyme	2 mL
2 lbs	fillet of lean fish, cut into 2-inch (5 cm) wide strips	1 kg / 250 mL
1 cup	mayonnaise, preferably homemade (see recipe, page 16)	

Place 1 slice of garlic toast in each of 4 large soup bowls, and set aside. In a large skillet, heat oil over medium heat. Sauté onion and carrot until tender. Add one-third of the garlic and sauté for 30 seconds. Add bouillon, orange zest, fennel seeds and thyme; reduce heat and simmer for 10 minutes. Strain out solids, return broth to skillet and heat to a simmer. Poach fish (see page 11) for about 2 minutes, or until fish is opaque and flakes easily with a fork. With a slotted spoon, distribute fish over toast. Combine mayonnaise and the remaining garlic; whisk into broth and simmer gently, stirring constantly, until slightly thickened (do not let boil). Ladle sauce over fish. **Serves 4.**

Chilled Poached Fish with Citrus Vinaigrette

1½ lbs	fillet of lean fish	750 g
4 cups	Court Bouillon (see recipe, page 18) or equal parts salted water and white wine	1 L

Citrus Vinaigrette

1	clove garlic, minced	1
⅓ cup	extra-virgin olive oil	75 mL
	Juice of 1 lemon and ½ orange	

Poach fish in bouillon (see page 11) for about 8 minutes per inch (2.5 cm) of thickness, or until fish is opaque and flakes easily with a fork. Transfer to a large bowl and let cool, then cover and refrigerate for about 1 hour, until chilled. Remove fish with a slotted spatula to a serving platter. *Prepare the vinaigrette:* Whisk together garlic, oil and citrus juices. Pour vinaigrette over fish. **Serves 4.**

Chilled Poached Fish with Creamy Cucumbers

Follow preceding recipe, but substitute the following sauce for the vinaigrette: Toss 1 cucumber, peeled, seeded and thinly sliced, with 1 tsp (5 mL) salt; set aside for 30 minutes. Rinse well, squeeze out liquid and toss with 1 clove garlic, minced, ¼ cup (50 mL) plain yogurt or sour cream, 1 tbsp (15 mL) chopped fresh dill and 1 tbsp (15 mL) lemon juice. **Serves 4.**

Fried Fish in Ranch Buttermilk Batter

½ cup	all-purpose flour	125 mL
¼ tsp	baking soda	1 mL
1	packet (1 oz/30 g) powdered ranch dressing mix, divided	1
1	egg, separated	1
¾ cup	buttermilk	175 mL
½ cup	cornstarch	125 mL
1½ lbs	skinless fillet of lean fish, cut into 2-inch (5 cm) sections	750 g
	Vegetable oil	
	Lemon wedges	

Sift together flour, baking soda and half the dressing mix; beat in the egg yolk and buttermilk. In a separate bowl, beat egg white until firm; fold into batter. In another bowl, combine cornstarch and the remaining dressing mix. Dredge fish in cornstarch mixture, shaking off excess, then dip in batter. Discard any excess cornstarch mixture and batter. Deep-fry fish (see page 9) in 2 to 3 inches (5 to 7.5 cm) of oil for 2 to 3 minutes, or until fish is golden brown and flakes easily with a fork. Drain on paper towels. Serve garnished with lemon wedges. **Serves 4.**

Fish Tempura

1	extra-large egg	1
2 cups	sifted all-purpose flour	500 mL
2 cups	ice water	500 mL
1½ lbs	skinless fillet of lean fish, cut into 2-inch (5 cm) sections	750 g
1 cup	cornstarch	250 mL
	Vegetable oil	
	Soy sauce	

Beat egg, flour and ice water until barely blended. Dredge fish in cornstarch, shaking off excess, then dip in batter. Discard any excess cornstarch and batter. Deep-fry fish (see page 9) in 2 to 3 inches (5 to 7.5 cm) of oil for 2 to 3 minutes, or until fish is golden brown and flakes easily with a fork. Drain on paper towels. Serve with soy sauce for dipping. **Serves 4.**

Old Bay Fried Fish

½ cup	all-purpose flour	125 mL
2 tbsp	Old Bay seasoning, divided	25 mL
1 cup	dry bread crumbs	250 mL
1½ lbs	skinless fillets of lean fish	750 g
1	egg, beaten with 1 tbsp (15 mL) water	1
	Vegetable oil	
	Lemon wedges	

Combine flour and half the Old Bay seasoning; set aside. In a separate bowl, combine bread crumbs and the remaining seasoning. Dust fish with flour mixture, shaking off excess. Dip in egg mixture, then dredge in bread crumb mixture until well coated. Set fish on a rack and let stand for 10 minutes. Discard any excess flour, egg and bread crumb mixtures. In a large skillet, heat 1 inch (2.5 cm) of oil over medium-high heat until very hot but not smoking. Fry fish for 2 to 3 minutes per side, or until fish is golden brown and flakes easily with a fork. Drain on paper towels. Serve garnished with lemon wedges. **Serves 4.**

Buffalo "Fins"

1½ lbs	skinless fillet of lean fish, cut into 3- by 2-inch (7.5 by 5 cm) fingers	750 g
½ cup	all-purpose flour, seasoned with salt and pepper	125 mL
	Vegetable oil	
¼ cup	melted butter	50 mL
1 to 2 tbsp	hot pepper sauce (such as Frank's RedHot)	15 to 25 mL
1 cup	blue cheese or ranch dressing	250 mL

Dust fish fingers with seasoned flour, shaking off excess. Deep-fry fish (see page 9) in 2 to 3 inches (5 to 7.5 cm) inches of oil for 2 to 3 minutes, or until fish is golden brown and flakes easily with a fork. Drain on paper towels. Combine melted butter and hot pepper sauce to taste, and dip fish in the mixture. Serve with dressing as a dip. **Serves 4.**

Whole Fried Sesame Fish

1	whole lean fish (1½ to 2 lbs/750 g to 1 kg)	1
¼ cup	cornstarch	50 mL
	Vegetable oil	
1 tbsp	dark sesame oil	15 mL
1 tbsp	freshly squeezed lemon juice	15 mL
2 tsp	soy sauce	10 mL
1 tsp	honey	5 mL
2 tbsp	toasted sesame seeds	25 mL

Score each side of the fish down to the bone at 1½-inch (4 cm) intervals, and liberally dust fish with cornstarch. In a wok, heat 3 to 4 inches (7.5 to 10 cm) of vegetable oil over medium-high heat to 375°F (190°C). Carefully lower fish, head first, into the wok. (Most of the head and tail will probably extend out of the oil.) Fry for 8 minutes, carefully ladling hot oil over the exposed parts of the fish to ensure even browning, or until fish is golden brown and flakes easily with a fork. Lift fish with a large, flat strainer to a platter. Combine sesame oil, lemon juice, soy sauce and honey; pour over fish. Sprinkle with sesame seeds. **Serves 2.**

Orange-Fennel Fillet

1 cup	freshly grated Parmesan cheese	250 mL
1 tbsp	minced orange zest	15 mL
2 tsp	ground fennel seeds	10 mL
1	egg, beaten	1
3 tbsp	water	45 mL
1½ cups	dry bread crumbs	375 mL
1½ lbs	skinless fillet of lean fish	750 g
	Olive oil	
	Orange wedges	

In a bowl, combine Parmesan, orange zest and fennel seeds. In a separate bowl, beat egg and water. Place bread crumbs in a third bowl. Dredge fish in Parmesan mixture, shaking off any loose coating. Dip in egg mixture, then dredge in bread crumbs until well coated. Set fish on a rack and let stand for 10 minutes. Discard any excess Parmesan mixture, egg mixture and bread crumbs. In a large skillet, heat a thin film of olive oil over medium-high heat. Cook fish for 2 to 3 minutes per side, or until fish is browned on both sides and flakes easily with a fork. Drain on paper towels. Serve garnished with orange wedges. **Serves 4.**

Fish in Balsamic Brown Butter with Capers

1½ lbs	skinless fillet of lean fish	750 g
¼ cup	all-purpose flour, seasoned with salt and pepper	50 mL
6 tbsp	butter, cut into small pieces, divided	90 mL
2 tbsp	drained capers	25 mL
1 tbsp	balsamic vinegar	15 mL

Dust fish with seasoned flour. In a large skillet, melt half the butter over medium-high heat. Cook fish for 2 to 3 minutes per side, or until fish is browned on both sides and flakes easily with a fork; remove with a slotted spatula to a warm platter. Add capers and vinegar to the butter remaining in the pan and bring to a boil. Remove from heat and swirl in the remaining butter, one piece at a time. Pour sauce over fish. **Serves 4.**

Sautéed Fish in Lemon Butter

Follow preceding recipe, but replace the capers and vinegar with 2 tbsp (25 mL) freshly squeezed lemon juice. **Serves 4.**

Sautéed Fish with Lime and Olives

1½ lbs	skinless fillet of lean fish	750 g
1 cup	all-purpose flour, seasoned with salt and pepper	250 mL
¼ cup	butter	50 mL
¼ cup	chopped pitted oil-cured black olives	50 mL
2 tbsp	chopped fresh Italian (flat-leaf) parsley	25 mL
	Juice of 1 lime	

Dust fish with seasoned flour. In a large skillet, melt butter over medium-high heat. Cook fish for 2 to 3 minutes per side, or until fish is browned on both sides and flakes easily with a fork; remove with a slotted spatula to a warm platter. Add olives, parsley and lime juice to the butter remaining in the pan and bring to a boil. Pour sauce over fish. **Serves 4.**

Fish Sautéed in Hazelnut-Garlic Crust

¼ cup	butter, divided	50 mL
3	cloves garlic, minced, divided	3
¼ cup	mayonnaise	50 mL
1½ lbs	skinless fillet of lean fish	750 g
½ cup	finely ground skinned hazelnuts	125 mL
2 tbsp	olive oil	25 mL
	Lemon wedges	

In a large skillet, melt half the butter over medium heat. Sauté half the garlic for 30 seconds. Mix garlic into mayonnaise. Brush fish with this mixture, then press hazelnuts into fish. Discard any extra mayonnaise mixture and hazelnuts. In the same skillet, heat the remaining butter, the remaining garlic and oil over medium-high heat. Cook fish for 2 to 3 minutes per side, or until fish is browned on both sides and flakes easily with a fork. Serve garnished with lemon wedges. **Serves 4.**

Rosemary, Sage and Garlic Fillets

½ cup	all-purpose flour	125 mL
2 tsp	dried rosemary, crumbled	10 mL
2 tsp	dried sage	10 mL
	Salt and freshly ground black pepper to taste	
1½ lbs	skinless fillets of lean fish	750 g
2 tbsp	butter	25 mL
2 tbsp	olive oil	25 m
1	clove garlic, minced	1
	Lemon wedges	

Combine flour, rosemary, sage, salt and pepper, and dust fish with this mixture. In a large skillet, heat butter and oil over medium-high heat. Cook garlic and fish for 2 to 3 minutes per side, or until fish is browned on both sides and flakes easily with a fork. Serve garnished with lemon wedges. **Serves 4.**

Fish Fillets Steamed with Lime and Chives

4	fillets of lean fish (each about 6 oz/175 g)	4
	Juice of 1 large lime	
3 tbsp	chopped chives	45 mL
2 tsp	butter	10 mL
1	lime, cut into wedges	1

Arrange fish in a single layer on a heatproof platter. Squeeze lime juice over fish, scatter with chives and dot with butter. Cover with foil and place over a pan of simmering water just large enough to hold the platter on its rim. Cover platter and pan with more foil to trap steam, and steam for about 8 minutes, or until fish is opaque and flakes easily with a fork. Serve garnished with lime wedges. **Serves 4.**

Fish Steamed with Baby Shrimp in Tarragon Vinaigrette

4	fillets of lean fish (each about 6 oz/175 g)	4
	Olive oil	
4 oz	baby shrimp, peeled and deveined	125 g
1 tsp	chopped fresh tarragon	5 mL
½	recipe Tarragon Mustard Vinaigrette (page 61), made with fresh tarragon	½

Arrange fish in a single layer on a heatproof platter. Drizzle with oil and scatter with shrimp and tarragon. Cover with foil and place over a pan of simmering water just large enough to hold the platter on its rim. Cover platter and pan with more foil to trap steam, and steam for about 8 minutes, or until fish is opaque and flakes easily with a fork. Pour vinaigrette over fish. **Serves 4.**

Fish Steamed with Vegetables

1	whole lean fish (1½ to 2 lbs/750 g to 1 kg)	1
	Butter	
2 tsp	freshly squeezed lemon juice	10 mL
2 cups	julienned vegetables (any combination of carrots, bell pepper, green beans, leeks, celery, fennel, tomato)	500 mL
	Salt and freshly ground black pepper to taste	

Place fish on a heatproof platter. Dot with about 1 tsp (5 mL) of butter and sprinkle with lemon juice. Surround fish with vegetables, dotted with additional butter, and season with salt and pepper. Cover with foil and place over a pan of simmering water just large enough to hold the plate on its rim. Cover platter and pan with more foil to trap steam, and steam for about 8 minutes, or until vegetables are tender and fish is opaque and flakes easily with a fork. **Serves 2.**

Steamed Paupiettes Rolled with Fresh Herbs

4	skinless fillets of lean fish (each about 8 oz/250 g), halved lengthwise	4
	Salt and freshly ground black pepper to taste	
8	sprigs of fresh herb (such as dill, mint, flat-leaf parsley, tarragon)	8
4	lemon wedges	4

Season fillet halves with salt and pepper, and top each with a sprig of herb. Roll up fish, secure each with a toothpick and place spiral side up (with the edge of the fillet showing) in a steamer basket. Steam over boiling water for 4 to 5 minutes, or until fish is opaque and flakes easily with a fork. Serve garnished with lemon wedges. **Serves 4.**

Fish en Papillote with Leeks

4	pieces fillet of lean fish (each about 6 oz/175 g)	4
2	cloves garlic, minced	2
¾ cup	julienned leeks (white and light green parts only)	175 mL
4 tsp	chopped Italian (flat-leaf) parsley	20 mL
4 tsp	butter	20 mL
	Salt and freshly ground black pepper to taste	
8	lemon wedges	8

Preheat oven to 350°F (180°C). Place each fillet on a large piece of heart-shaped parchment paper (see page 12) with one-quarter of the garlic, leeks, parsley, butter, salt and pepper. Wrap as explained on page 12 and place on a baking sheet. Bake for 12 to 15 minutes, or until parchment is puffed and browned. Fish should be opaque and flake easily with a fork. Slit the parchment packets and slide contents onto each of 4 dinner plates. Garnish each with 2 lemon wedges. **Serves 4.**

Fish en Papillote with Julienne of Garden Vegetables

Follow preceding recipe, but use only 1 tbsp (15 mL) leek in each packet, and add 1 tbsp (15 mL) julienned carrot and 1 tbsp (15 mL) julienned celery to each. **Serves 4.**

Fish en Papillote with Olives and Tomatoes

4	pieces fillet of lean fish (each about 6 oz/175 g)	4
2	cloves garlic, minced	2
1 cup	chopped tomato	250 mL
½ cup	chopped pitted black olives	125 mL
¼ cup	chopped onion	50 mL
4 tsp	chopped fresh Italian (flat-leaf) parsley	20 mL
4 tsp	olive oil	20 mL
	Salt and freshly ground black pepper to taste	

Preheat oven to 350°F (180°C). Place each fillet on a large piece of heart-shaped parchment paper (see page 12) with one-quarter of the garlic, tomato, olives, onion, parsley, oil, salt and pepper. Wrap as explained on page 12 and place on a baking sheet. Bake for 12 to 15 minutes, or until parchment is puffed and browned. Fish should be opaque and flake easily with a fork. Slit the parchment packets and slide contents onto each of 4 dinner plates. **Serves 4.**

Fish en Papillote with Melon and Capers

4	pieces fillet of lean fish (each about 6 oz/175 g)	4
2 cups	diced honeydew melon	500 mL
4 tsp	freshly squeezed lemon juice	20 mL
4 tsp	butter	20 mL
2 tsp	drained capers	10 mL
4	lime wedges	4

Preheat oven to 350°F (180°C). Place each fillet on a large piece of heart-shaped parchment paper (see page 12) with one-quarter of the honeydew, lemon juice, butter and capers. Wrap as explained on page 12 and place on a baking sheet. Bake for 12 to 15 minutes, or until parchment is puffed and browned. Fish should be opaque and flake easily with a fork. Slit the parchment packets and slide contents onto each of 4 dinner plates. Garnish with lime wedges. **Serves 4.**

Fish en Papillote, Bouillabaisse-Style

1 tbsp	olive oil	15 mL
¼ cup	diced fennel bulb	50 mL
2 tbsp	finely chopped onion	25 mL
1	clove garlic, minced	1
	Finely grated zest and juice of ½ orange	
2	tomatoes, chopped	2
1 tbsp	chopped fresh basil	15 mL
Pinch	crumbled saffron threads	Pinch
4	pieces fillet of lean fish (each about 6 oz/175 g)	4

Preheat oven to 350°F (180°C). In a large skillet, heat oil over medium-high heat. Sauté fennel, onion, garlic and orange zest until softened. Add tomatoes, basil, saffron and orange juice; simmer for 1 minute. Place each fillet on a large piece of heart-shaped parchment paper (see page 12) and top with one-quarter of the sauce. Wrap as explained on page 12 and place on a baking sheet. Bake for 12 to 15 minutes, or until parchment is puffed and browned. Fish should be opaque and flake easily with a fork. Slit the parchment packets and slide contents onto each of 4 dinner plates. **Serves 4.** *Serve with crusty bread.*

Fish en Papillote with Pickled Ginger

4	pieces fillet of lean fish (each about 6 oz/175 g)	4
2 tsp	dark sesame oil	10 mL
12	whole chives	12
2	cloves garlic, slivered	2
¼ cup	julienned drained pickled ginger	50 mL
¼ cup	lemon juice	50 mL
4 tsp	reduced-sodium soy sauce	20 mL

Preheat oven to 350°F (180°C). Rub fish with oil. Place each fillet on a large piece of heart-shaped parchment paper (see page 12) with one-quarter of the chives, garlic, ginger, lemon juice and soy sauce. Wrap as explained on page 12 and place on a baking sheet. Bake for 12 to 15 minutes, or until parchment is puffed and browned. Fish should be opaque and flake easily with a fork. Slit the parchment packets and slide contents onto each of 4 dinner plates. **Serves 4.**

Fish Grilled with Bacon and Green Onions

4	fillets of lean fish (about ¾ inch/2 cm thick)	4
	Juice of 1 lemon	
4	green onions, julienned	4
4	slices bacon	4
4	lemon wedges	4

Preheat broiler or barbecue grill to high. Rub fish with lemon juice. Place 1 green onion on each fillet and wrap 1 strip bacon around each to hold onion in place. Broil or grill for 3 to 4 minutes per side, or until bacon is crisp and fish is opaque and flakes easily with a fork. Serve garnished with lemon wedges. **Serves 4.**

Broiled Fish with Walnut Butter

1½ lbs	fillet of lean fish	750 g
3 tbsp	walnut oil, divided	45 mL
½ cup	walnut pieces	125 mL
1 tbsp	butter	15 mL
1 tbsp	freshly squeezed lime juice	15 mL

Preheat broiler to high. Brush fish with 2 tbsp (25 mL) of the oil and broil for 4 to 5 minutes, or until fish is opaque and flakes easily with a fork. Meanwhile, in a skillet, heat the remaining oil over medium heat. Toast walnut pieces until browned. Stir in butter and lime juice. Serve fish drizzled with sauce. **Serves 4.**

Baked Fish in Mustard Glaze

1½ lbs	fillet of oily fish	750 g
3 tbsp	Dijon mustard	45 mL
⅔ cup	sour cream or plain yogurt	150 mL
1 tbsp	chopped fresh Italian (flat-leaf) parsley	15 mL

Preheat oven to 375°F (190°C) and grease a baking dish large enough to hold fish in a single layer. Bake fish for 15 to 20 minutes, or until fish is opaque and flakes easily with a fork. Meanwhile, combine mustard and sour cream. When fish is done, remove with a slotted spatula to a warm platter. Stir mustard mixture into the juices in the dish. Pour sauce over fish and garnish with parsley. **Serves 4.**

Baked Fish with Horseradish and Sour Cream

Follow preceding recipe, but replace the mustard with 2 tbsp (25 mL) prepared horseradish. **Serves 4.**

Whole Baked Fish

1	whole oily fish (about 3 lbs/1.5 kg)	1
1 tbsp	vegetable oil	15 mL
	Salt and freshly ground black pepper to taste	
	Juice of 1 lemon	
	Sauce (see choices below)	

Preheat oven to 375°F (190°C) and grease a baking dish. Cut 3 to 4 slits in each side of the fish and rub fish with oil, salt, pepper and lemon juice. Place in prepared baking dish and bake for 10 minutes per inch (2.5 cm) of thickness, until fish is opaque and flakes easily with a fork. Serve with one of the following sauces: Red Pepper Coulis (page 53), Warm Sun-Dried Tomato Vinaigrette (page 53), Sauce Provençal (page 53), Peanut Sauce (page 53), Mushroom Ragoût (page 55), Oyster Sauce with Lime and Garlic (page 55), White Wine Mushrooms (page 55) or Julienned Peppers and Carrots (page 55). **Serves 4.**

Fish Baked in a Glaze of Herb Oil

Bake a whole fish as described in preceding recipe, but omit the vegetable oil; instead, baste fish every 5 minutes during baking with ⅓ cup (75 mL) olive oil steeped with ¼ cup (50 mL) finely chopped fresh herbs (such as basil, parsley, dill). **Serves 4.**

Sweet-and-Sour Cranberry Fish

1	whole oily fish (2 to 3 lbs/1 to 1.5 kg)	1
3	cloves garlic, minced	3
2 tbsp	minced orange zest	25 mL
½ cup	freshly squeezed orange juice	125 mL
⅓ cup	granulated sugar	75 mL
¼ cup	cider vinegar	50 mL
1 tbsp	minced gingerroot	15 mL
1 tbsp	dry sherry	15 mL
1 tsp	Worcestershire sauce	5 mL
1 cup	fresh cranberries	250 mL

Bake fish as described in Whole Baked Fish (page 327) or fry as described in Whole Fried Sesame Fish (page 324). Meanwhile, in a saucepan, bring garlic, orange zest, orange juice, sugar, vinegar, ginger, sherry and Worcestershire sauce to a boil over medium-high heat. Add cranberries and simmer until they pop, about 4 minutes. Serve fish with sauce. **Serves 4.**

Smoky Grilled Fish

2	whole oily fish (each about 1½ lbs/750 g)	2
¼ cup	olive oil	50 mL
1 tsp	dried basil	5 mL
	Finely grated zest and juice of 1 lemon	

Cut 3 to 4 slits in each side of each fish. Combine oil, basil, lemon zest and lemon juice. Coat fish with half this mixture, cover tightly and refrigerate for 1 hour. Soak 1 cup (250 mL) hardwood chips in enough water to cover for 1 hour. Drain and scatter soaked chips over a hot charcoal fire or in a smoker box on a gas grill; cover grill until there is a lot of smoke. Remove fish from marinade and discard marinade. Oil the grill grate (or place fish in an oiled grill basket) and set fish directly over the fire. Cover grill and cook for 5 to 6 minutes per side, or until fish is browned on both sides and flakes easily with a fork. Serve drizzled with the remaining marinade. **Serves 4.**

Grilled Fish in Chili Paste

1½ lbs	steaks from oily fish (¾ inch/2 cm thick)	750 g
	Salt and freshly ground black pepper to taste	
	Juice of 2 lemons, divided	
⅓ cup	olive oil	75 mL
2	cloves garlic, minced	2
2 tbsp	chili powder	25 mL
1 tbsp	ground cumin	15 mL

| Pinch | dried oregano | Pinch |
| 4 | lemon wedges | 4 |

Rub fish with salt, pepper and half the lemon juice. Cover tightly and refrigerate for 30 minutes. Meanwhile, preheat broiler or barbecue grill to high. In a small skillet, heat oil over medium heat. Sauté garlic, chili powder, cumin and oregano until aromatic. Pour half this mixture over fish, turning to coat evenly. Combine the remaining oil mixture with the remaining lemon juice. Broil or grill fish, basting frequently with lemon mixture, for 5 to 6 minutes per side, or until fish is browned on both sides and flakes easily with a fork. Serve garnished with lemon wedges. **Serves 4.**

Grilled Fish in Garlic Herb Marinade

| 1½ lbs | steaks from oily fish (¾ inch/2 cm thick) | 750 g |
| 1 cup | Garlic Herb Dressing (see recipe, page 60), divided | 250 mL |

Coat fish with half the dressing, cover tightly and refrigerate for 1 hour. Preheat broiler or barbecue grill to high. Remove fish from marinade and discard marinade. Broil or grill fish, basting frequently with the remaining dressing, for 5 to 6 minutes per side, or until fish is browned on both sides and flakes easily with a fork. **Serves 4.**

Grilled Fish in Garlic Sage Marinade

2	large cloves garlic, minced	2
¾ cup	extra-virgin olive oil	175 mL
¼ cup	red wine vinegar	50 mL
1 tbsp	minced fresh Italian (flat-leaf) parsley	15 mL
2 tsp	chopped fresh sage	10 mL
	Salt and freshly ground black pepper to taste	
1½ lbs	steaks from oily fish (¾ inch/2 cm thick)	750 g

Thoroughly whisk together garlic, oil, vinegar, parsley, sage, salt and pepper. Coat fish with half the dressing, cover tightly and refrigerate for 1 hour. Preheat broiler or barbecue grill to high. Remove fish from marinade and discard marinade. Broil or grill fish, basting frequently with the remaining dressing, for 5 to 6 minutes per side, or until fish is browned on both sides and flakes easily with a fork. **Serves 4.**

Grilled Fish Glazed with Vinaigrette

Follow recipe for Grilled Fish in Garlic Herb Marinade (page 328), but replace the dressing with Basic Wine Vinaigrette (page 60). **Serves 4.**

Grilled Fish with Olive Oil and Balsamic Vinegar

Follow recipe for Grilled Fish in Garlic Herb Marinade (page 328), but replace the dressing with Balsamic–Olive Oil Vinaigrette (page 60). **Serves 4.**

Barbecued Fish

1 tbsp	corn oil	15 mL
1	small onion, chopped	1
1	clove garlic, minced	1
1/2 cup	ketchup	125 mL
2 tbsp	cider vinegar	25 mL
1 tsp	brown mustard	5 mL
1 tsp	Worcestershire sauce	5 mL
1 tsp	hot pepper sauce (such as Tabasco)	5 mL
	Juice of 1/2 lemon	
1 1/2 lbs	steaks from oily fish (3/4 inch/2 cm thick)	750 g

In a small skillet, heat oil over medium-high heat. Sauté onion and garlic until softened. Stir in ketchup, vinegar, mustard, Worcestershire sauce, hot pepper sauce and lemon juice. Coat fish with half this sauce, cover tightly and refrigerate for 1 hour. Preheat broiler or barbecue grill to high. Remove fish from marinade and discard marinade. Broil or grill fish, basting frequently with the remaining sauce, for 5 to 6 minutes per side, or until fish is browned on both sides and flakes easily with a fork. **Serves 4.**

Teriyaki Grilled Fish

1/4 cup	soy sauce	50 mL
2 tbsp	freshly squeezed lemon juice	25 mL
2 tbsp	dry sherry	25 mL
2 tbsp	honey	25 mL
2 tsp	dark sesame oil	10 mL
1 1/2 lbs	steaks from oily fish (3/4 inch/2 cm thick)	750 g

Combine soy sauce, lemon juice, sherry, honey and oil. Coat fish with half this sauce, cover tightly and refrigerate for 1 hour. Preheat broiler or barbecue grill to high. Remove fish from marinade and discard marinade. Broil or grill fish, basting frequently with the remaining sauce, for 5 to 6 minutes per side, or until fish is browned on both sides and flakes easily with a fork. **Serves 4.**

Marinated Fish Kebabs

1	clove garlic, minced	1
1/4 cup	extra-virgin olive oil	50 mL
2 tbsp	chopped fresh basil	25 mL
	Juice of 1 lemon	
	Salt and freshly ground black pepper to taste	
1 1/2 lbs	skinless fillet of oily fish, cut into 24 cubes	750 g
8	pieces (1 inch/2.5 cm) red bell pepper	8
8	small mushrooms	8

Combine garlic, oil, basil, lemon juice, salt and pepper. Rub fish with half this mixture, cover tightly and refrigerate for 1 hour. Preheat barbecue grill to high. Remove fish from marinade and discard marinade. Thread 3 pieces of fish, 1 piece of bell pepper and 1 mushroom onto each of 8 skewers. Grill, turning often and basting with the remaining marinade, for about 8 minutes, or until fish is browned on all sides and flakes easily with a fork. **Serves 4.**

Broiled Fish with Lemon Ranch Dressing

2/3 cup	ranch dressing	150 mL
2 tbsp	freshly squeezed lemon juice	25 mL
1 1/2 lbs	steaks or fillets from oily fish (3/4 inch/2 cm thick)	750 g

Combine dressing and lemon juice. Rub fish with half this mixture, cover tightly and refrigerate for 1 hour. Preheat broiler. Remove fish from marinade and discard marinade. Broil, basting frequently with the remaining dressing mixture, for 5 to 6 minutes per side, or until fish is browned on both sides and flakes easily with a fork. **Serves 4.**

Fish Chili

2 tbsp	vegetable oil	25 mL
1½ cups	finely chopped onions	375 mL
2	cloves garlic, minced	2
1	roasted bell pepper (see page 11), diced	1
2 tbsp	chili powder	25 mL
1½ tsp	ground cumin	7 mL
½ tsp	ground coriander	2 mL
½ tsp	hot pepper flakes	2 mL
2 cups	Quick Fish Broth (see recipe, page 19) or clam juice	500 mL
1½ lbs	skinless fillet of oily fish, cut into large chunks	750 g
3 cups	drained rinsed canned cannellini or white kidney beans	750 mL
2 tbsp	chopped fresh dill	25 mL
	Finely grated zest and juice of 1 lemon	

In a large saucepan, heat oil over medium-high heat. Sauté onions until lightly browned. Add garlic, roasted pepper, chili powder, cumin, coriander and hot pepper flakes; sauté for 1 minute. Add broth and bring to a boil. Add fish and beans; reduce heat and simmer for 5 minutes, until fish is opaque and flakes easily with a fork. Add dill, lemon zest and lemon juice; simmer for 1 minute. **Serves 4.**

Fish, Black Beans and Cilantro

Follow preceding recipe, but add 1 hot chili pepper (such as jalapeño), minced, with the onions, replace the cannellini beans with cooked black beans, replace the dill with ¼ cup (50 mL) chopped fresh cilantro, and replace the lemon zest and juice with lime zest and juice. **Serves 4.**

All-Fish Bouillabaisse

1 cup	dry white wine	250 mL
1 tsp	crumbled saffron threads	5 mL
	Finely grated zest and juice of 1 large orange	
2 tbsp	olive oil	25 mL
2	stalks celery, chopped	2
1	large onion, chopped	1
2	cloves garlic, minced	2
1 tsp	ground fennel seeds	5 mL
1 tsp	dried basil	5 mL
½ tsp	dried thyme	2 mL
3 cups	Quick Fish Broth (see recipe, page 19) or Court Bouillon (see recipe, page 18)	750 mL
2 cups	chopped seeded peeled tomatoes	500 mL
2 lbs	fillets of both lean and oily fish, cut into large chunks	1 kg
¼ cup	chopped fresh Italian (flat-leaf) parsley	50 mL

Combine wine, saffron, orange zest and orange juice; set aside. In a large saucepan, heat oil over medium heat. Sauté celery and onion until tender. Add garlic, fennel seeds, basil and thyme; sauté for 30 seconds. Add wine mixture and bring to a boil. Add broth and tomatoes; reduce heat and simmer for 10 minutes. Add fish and simmer for 5 minutes, until fish is opaque and flakes easily with a fork. Add parsley and simmer for 1 minute. **Serves 4.** *Serve with crusty bread.*

Clam and Fish Stew with Lots of Basil

3 tbsp	extra-virgin olive oil	45 mL
2	leeks, white parts only, thinly sliced	2
2	cloves garlic, minced	2
1 cup	dry white wine	250 mL
16	littleneck clams, scrubbed (see page 8)	16
2 cups	canned diced tomatoes, drained	2
1 cup	chopped fresh basil	250 mL
	Juice of ½ lemon	
1 lb	skinless fillet of oily fish, cut into large pieces	500 g

In a large skillet, heat oil over medium heat. Sauté leeks until tender. Add garlic and sauté for 30 seconds. Add wine and boil for 2 minutes. Add clams, tomatoes, basil and lemon juice; reduce heat and simmer for 5 minutes. Add fish and simmer for 5 minutes, until clams open (discard any that don't) and fish is opaque and flakes easily with a fork. **Serves 4.**

Fish Braised with Mussels and Orange

Follow preceding recipe, but replace the clams with mussels, omit the lemon juice, and add the finely grated zest and juice of 1 orange with the basil. **Serves 4.**

Chapter 29
Shellfish
Easy and Sophisticated

Scallop Seviche Skewered
with Avocado 332

Scallops Vinaigrette 333

Grilled Marinated Scallops 333

Scallops in Wine and Lemon Sauce 333

Scallops Escabèche 333

Scallops Poached with
Cider and Cream 333

Dill and Fennel Scallops 334

Tempura Scallops and Shrimp 334

Quick Shrimp Étouffée 334

Mustard Tarragon Shrimp Cocktail 334

Jalapeño Shrimp Cocktail 335

Deep-Fried Shrimp Cocktail 335

Shrimp and Guacamole Salad 335

Grilled Shrimp with Pesto 335

Grilled Barbecued Shrimp 336

Shrimp Poached in Tomato Vinaigrette . . 336

Shrimp with Herbs and Pasta 336

Fried Shrimp in Beer Batter 336

Clams in Tomato Vinaigrette 336

Clams Casino 336

Niçoise Clams 337

Clams with Capers and Lemon 337

Curried Clams 337

Ginger Soy Clams 337

Hoisin Clams 337

Spicy Black Bean Clams 338

Barbecued Steamed Clams 338

Tex-Mex Clams 338

Puerto Rican Clams 338

Mussels Niçoise 338

Portuguese Mussel Stew 338

Mussels Marseille 339

Oysters on the Half Shell with
Jalapeño Cocktail Sauce 339

Oysters Florentine 339

Oyster-Stuffed Mushroom Caps 339

Oyster Stew 340

Poached Oysters in Butter Sauce 340

Baked Creole Crabmeat 340

Fried Oysters with Tartar Sauce 340

Fried Oyster Sandwiches 340

Sautéed Soft-Shell Crabs
with Lime Mayonnaise 340

Grilled Soft-Shell Crabs 341

Soft-Shell Crab Sandwiches 341

Marinated Soft-Shell Crabs 341

Crab and Caviar Custard 341

Crab and Avocado Salad 341

Quick Crab Chowder 342

Italian Seafood Sandwiches 342

Squid Salad 343

Calamari with Potatoes and Tomatoes . . 343

It's miraculous that anyone ever thought to eat shellfish, since they are armored like medieval warriors and possess all the innate appeal of a sea-washed rock. Yet every time we feast on a lobster or imbibe the brackish essence of a newly opened oyster, we are grateful to that long-gone Neanderthal gourmet who had the vision and courage to taste the unknown.

Shellfish are easy and fast to prepare, and so naturally flavorful that they call for the barest embellishment on their way to the table. In fact, the surest way to ruin good shellfish is to fuss too much.

Fresh shellfish are best with just a dash of spice, a splash of acid and, most importantly, a minimum of heat. Bivalves (any shellfish with one hinge and two shells, such as mussels, clams, oysters and scallops) get tough and rubbery when heated too long, and crustaceans (shellfish with multiple hinges, such as shrimp, prawns, crayfish, lobsters and crabs), get tough and dry from overcooking. Only single-shelled mollusks (such as abalone, conch and snails) and cephalopods (such as squid and octopus) will tenderize during extended cooking. Steam bivalves just until their shells open, crustaceans until they are firm and opaque. Anything more is overkill.

Buy shellfish from a reputable and busy fish purveyor to ensure reasonable prices and fresh products. All shellfish should smell of fresh seawater. If they smell like fish, then something fishy is going on. Except for scallops, squid, octopus and single-shelled mollusks, all shellfish should be either alive or frozen at the time of purchase.

Live shellfish must be cooked while still alive. Live bivalves will be tightly closed, except for steaming clams, which will have a veil-like membrane across the opening between the shells, and live crustaceans will show considerable movement. Because these animals harbor large amounts of bacteria that will spread rapidly after they die, it is risky to eat any of them if their time of death is uncertain.

Simply plopping a shellfish in boiling liquid is the easiest way to kill and cook it. But for some preparations, it's important to open a bivalve's shell with a knife or to section a lobster before cooking it. These procedures require special techniques, which are described on pages 10 and 11. If you do not wish to go through the mess of doing it yourself, many fish markets will open or section shellfish to your specifications.

The most opulent of shellfish, the lobster, will not be found among the 50 recipes in this chapter. Its role as a special-occasion food convinced us to present it among our romantic foods (Chapter 44) and our grilled foods (Chapter 12).

About these recipes . . .

• To clean clams, simply scrub the shells under cold running water to remove any dirt, then soak them in a bowl of cold water, refreshing water once or twice, for about 30 minutes to purge any sand held inside the shells.
• To clean scallops, just peel the tough muscle from the side and discard; do not wash unless gritty.
• To clean shrimp, peel off the shells and make a slit along the back (the convex side); if there is a vein exposed, remove it with the tip of the knife.
• To clean squid, wash well under cold water, then remove and discard the clear, plastic-looking quill inside the sac.
• To pick shells out of crabmeat, heat it in a 350°F (180°C) oven for 5 minutes. During that time, any bits of shell will turn opaque and hard, after which they are easy to spot and remove.
• The methods for cleaning mussels and soft-shell crabs are more complex and are described on pages 8 and 11.

Scallop Seviche Skewered with Avocado

1	clove garlic, minced	1
1	jalapeño pepper, minced	1
⅔ cup	freshly squeezed lime juice, divided	150 mL
8 oz	bay scallops, trimmed of hard side muscles	250 g
1 tsp	extra-virgin olive oil	5 mL
	Salt and freshly ground black pepper to taste	
2	large avocados, diced	2

In a large bowl, combine garlic, jalapeño and ½ cup (125 mL) of the lime juice. Add scallops and toss to coat. Cover and refrigerate for 6 hours. Scallops should be firm and opaque. Remove from marinade and discard marinade. Toss scallops with oil, salt and pepper. Toss avocados in the remaining lime juice. Thread 6 scallops alternately with 3 pieces avocado onto each of 10 bamboo skewers.
Serves 10 as an hors d'oeuvre.

Scallops Vinaigrette

4 cups	Court Bouillon (see recipe, page 18) or equal parts dry white wine and water	1 L
1 lb	sea scallops, trimmed of hard side muscles	500 g
1	cucumber, peeled, seeded and diced	1
1 tbsp	minced fresh Italian (flat-leaf) parsley	15 mL

Vinaigrette

1	clove garlic, minced	1
1/4 cup	olive oil	50 mL
2 tbsp	red wine vinegar	25 mL
	Salt and freshly ground black pepper to taste	

In a large pot, bring bouillon to a boil. Add scallops, remove from heat, cover and let stand for 8 minutes, until scallops are firm and opaque. Remove scallops to a plate and let cool. Discard bouillon. In a serving bowl, combine garlic, oil, vinegar, salt and pepper. Add scallops, cucumber and parsley; toss to coat. **Serves 4.**

Grilled Marinated Scallops

Prepare vinaigrette from preceding recipe. Toss 1 lb (500 g) sea scallops, trimmed of hard side muscles, in half the dressing and let stand for 10 minutes. Meanwhile, preheat broiler or barbecue grill to high. Remove scallops from marinade and discard marinade. Broil or grill scallops on an oiled grill screen for 2 to 3 minutes per side, or until firm and opaque. Serve drizzled with the remaining dressing. **Serves 4.**

Scallops in Wine and Lemon Sauce

2 tbsp	extra-virgin olive oil	25 mL
4	cloves garlic, chopped	4
1	bunch green onions, white parts only, sliced	1
1/4 cup	dry white wine	50 mL
1 lb	sea scallops, trimmed of hard side muscles	500 g
Pinch	cayenne pepper	Pinch
	Salt and freshly ground black pepper to taste	
	Juice of 1 lemon	
1/4 cup	butter, cut into small pieces	50 mL

In a large skillet, heat oil over medium heat. Sauté garlic and green onions until barely tender. Add wine and bring to a boil. Add scallops and cook, stirring frequently, for 3 to 4 minutes, or until firm and opaque. Remove scallops with a slotted spoon to a warm platter. Add cayenne, salt, black pepper and lemon juice to the pan and boil until liquid is reduced by about half. Remove from heat and swirl in butter. Pour sauce over scallops. **Serves 4.**

Scallops Escabèche

1/3 cup	olive oil	75 mL
2	onions, thinly sliced	2
2	cloves garlic, minced	2
1 lb	sea scallops, trimmed of hard side muscles	500 g
1/2 tsp	ground ginger	2 mL
1/4 tsp	dried thyme	1 mL
2 tbsp	red wine vinegar	25 mL
	Juices of 1 lemon, 1 orange and 1 lime	
	Salt, cayenne pepper and freshly ground black pepper to taste	
2 tbsp	chopped fresh Italian (flat-leaf) parsley	25 mL

In a large skillet, heat oil over medium-high heat. Sauté onion and garlic until tender. Add scallops, ginger and thyme; sauté for about 3 minutes, or until scallops are firm and opaque. Add vinegar and citrus juices; bring to a boil. Season with salt, cayenne and black pepper. Let cool, then stir in parsley. **Serves 4.** *Store in an airtight container in the refrigerator for up to 4 days.*

Scallops Poached with Cider and Cream

1 cup	dry white wine	250 mL
1/2 cup	unsweetened apple cider	125 mL
1/4 cup	finely chopped onion	50 mL
1 lb	large sea scallops, trimmed of hard side muscles	500 g
2 tbsp	butter	25 mL
5 oz	mushrooms, sliced	150 g
1	Granny Smith apple, peeled and thinly sliced	1
2 tbsp	brandy	25 mL
1 cup	whipping (35%) cream	250 mL

In a saucepan, over medium heat, bring wine, cider and onion to a simmer. Add scallops and poach for about 3 minutes, or until firm and opaque. Remove scallops with a slotted spoon to a plate. Increase heat to medium-high and boil until liquid is reduced by about three-quarters; set aside. In a large skillet, melt butter over medium-high heat. Sauté mushrooms until browned. Add apple and sauté until browned. Add brandy and carefully flambé (see page 10). When flames subside, add poaching liquid and cream; reduce heat and simmer until slightly thickened, about 1 minute. Add scallops and heat through. **Serves 4.**

Dill and Fennel Scallops

1 cup	all-purpose flour	250 mL
1 tbsp	dried dillweed	15 mL
2 tsp	ground fennel seeds	10 mL
	Salt and freshly ground black pepper to taste	
1 lb	large sea scallops, trimmed of hard side muscles	500 g
¼ cup	olive oil	50 mL
1	clove garlic, halved	1
3	cloves garlic, minced	3
1 cup	mayonnaise	250 mL
1 tbsp	freshly squeezed lemon juice	15 mL

Combine flour, dill, fennel seeds, salt and pepper. Dredge scallops in this mixture, shaking off excess. Discard excess flour mixture. In a large skillet, heat oil over medium-high heat. Sauté halved garlic until browned; discard garlic. Add scallops to the oil in the pan and sauté until firm and browned on both sides. Remove with a slotted spoon to a warm platter. Combine minced garlic, mayonnaise and lemon juice. Stir in any liquid that has collected around scallops. Pour sauce over scallops. **Serves 4.**

Tempura Scallops and Shrimp

1	clove garlic, minced	1
1 tbsp	minced gingerroot	15 mL
2 tsp	soy sauce	10 mL
1 tsp	dark sesame oil	5 mL
8 oz	sea scallops, trimmed of hard side muscles and halved horizontally	250 g
8 oz	medium shrimp, peeled and deveined	250 g
2	egg yolks, beaten	2
2 cups	ice water	500 mL
2 cups	all-purpose flour	500 mL
½ cup	cornstarch	125 mL
	Vegetable oil	

In a large bowl, combine garlic, ginger, soy sauce and sesame oil. Add scallops and shrimp; toss to coat. Cover and refrigerate for 1 hour. Beat egg yolks and ice water, then stir in flour, leaving some lumps; do not overmix. Remove shellfish from marinade and discard marinade. Blot excess moisture from shellfish and toss with cornstarch, shaking off excess. Dip shellfish in batter. Discard any excess cornstarch and batter. Deep-fry shellfish (see page 9) for about 2 minutes, or until coating is lightly browned and crispy. Remove to a strainer set over a drip bowl and drain off excess oil. Keep warm in a 200°F (100°C) oven while frying the remaining shellfish. **Serves 4.**

Quick Shrimp Étouffée

¼ cup	vegetable oil	50 mL
¼ cup	all-purpose flour	50 mL
2	large onions, chopped	2
1	stalk celery, chopped	1
1	red bell pepper, diced	1
3	cloves garlic, minced	3
1 lb	large shrimp, peeled and deveined	500 g
1 cup	chicken broth	250 mL
1 cup	beef broth	250 mL
1	green onion, thinly sliced	15 mL
1 tbsp	chopped fresh Italian (flat-leaf) parsley	15 mL
3 cups	hot cooked rice	750 mL

In a large, deep cast-iron skillet, heat oil over low heat. Add flour and cook, stirring often, until dark chocolate brown, about 10 minutes (stir carefully; the roux will get very hot and can give you a nasty burn if you splash it). Add onion, celery and bell pepper, and cook until just starting to soften. Add garlic, shrimp, chicken broth and beef broth (again be careful; the mixture will probably splatter when the broth is added); simmer for 10 minutes, or until shrimp are pink and opaque. Garnish with green onion and parsley. Serve over rice. **Serves 4.**

Mustard Tarragon Shrimp Cocktail

4 cups	Court Bouillon (see recipe, page 18) or equal parts dry white wine and water	1 L
1 lb	jumbo shrimp, peeled and deveined	500 g
1	clove garlic, minced	1
3 tbsp	white wine vinegar	45 mL
2 tbsp	Dijon mustard	25 mL
1 tsp	dried tarragon	5 mL
½ cup	canola oil	125 mL
	Salt and freshly ground black pepper to taste	

In a large pot, bring bouillon to a boil. Add shrimp, remove from heat, cover and let stand for 8 minutes, until shrimp are pink and opaque. Remove shrimp to a serving bowl and let cool. Discard bouillon. In a small bowl, combine garlic, vinegar, mustard and tarragon. Whisk in oil in a slow, steady stream until sauce is thick. Season with salt and pepper. Add one-third of this sauce to the shrimp and toss to coat. Cover both bowls and refrigerate for about 1 hour, until chilled. Serve shrimp with the remaining sauce as a dip. **Serves 4.**

Jalapeño Shrimp Cocktail

4 cups	Court Bouillon (see recipe, page 18) or equal parts dry white wine and water	1 L
1 lb	jumbo shrimp, peeled and deveined	500 g
3 to 4	pickled jalapeño peppers, seeded	3 to 4
2	plum (Roma) tomatoes, cut into eighths	2
1	large clove garlic, halved	1
¼ cup	ketchup	50 mL
1 tbsp	freshly squeezed lemon juice	15 mL

In a large pot, bring bouillon to a boil. Add shrimp, remove from heat, cover and let stand for 8 minutes, until shrimp are pink and opaque. Remove shrimp to a plate and let cool. Discard bouillon. In a food processor, finely chop jalapeños to taste, tomatoes and garlic. Transfer to a serving bowl and mix in ketchup and lemon juice. Serve as a dip with the shrimp. **Serves 4.**

Deep-Fried Shrimp Cocktail

1	green onion, minced	1
3 tbsp	dry sherry	45 mL
2 tbsp	soy sauce, divided	25 mL
1 tsp	minced gingerroot	5 mL
Pinch	cayenne pepper	Pinch
	Salt and freshly ground black pepper to taste	
1 lb	jumbo shrimp, peeled, deveined and butterflied	500 g
2 tbsp	ketchup	25 mL
2 tbsp	honey	25 mL
2 tbsp	cider vinegar	25 mL
⅔ cup	cornstarch, divided	150 mL
½ cup	all-purpose flour	125 mL
1 tsp	baking powder	5 mL
½ cup	water	125 mL
	Vegetable oil	

In a large bowl, combine green onion, sherry, 1 tbsp (15 mL) of the soy sauce, ginger, cayenne, salt and black pepper. Add shrimp and toss to coat. Cover and refrigerate for 1 hour. Meanwhile, combine ketchup, honey, vinegar and the remaining soy sauce; set aside. Combine ½ cup (125 mL) of the cornstarch, flour and baking powder, then stir in water to make a thick batter. Remove shrimp from marinade and discard marinade. Pat shrimp dry, dust lightly with the remaining cornstarch and dip in batter. Discard any excess cornstarch and batter. Deep-fry shrimp (see page 9) for about 2 minutes, or until coating is browned and crispy. Remove shrimp to a strainer set over a drip bowl and drain off excess oil. Keep shrimp warm in a 200°F (100°C) oven while frying the remaining shrimp. Serve shrimp with ketchup mixture as a dip. **Serves 4.**

Shrimp and Guacamole Salad

4 cups	Court Bouillon (see recipe, page 18) or equal parts dry white wine and water	1 L
1 lb	medium shrimp, peeled and deveined	500 g
3	green onions, thinly sliced	3
4 tsp	freshly squeezed lemon juice, divided	20 mL
1	large avocado, coarsely chopped	1
1	clove garlic, minced	1
1 tbsp	grated onion	15 mL
¼ tsp	hot pepper sauce (such as Tabasco)	1 mL
1 tbsp	olive oil	15 mL
	Salt to taste	
	Romaine lettuce leaves	

In a large pot, bring bouillon to a boil. Add shrimp, remove from heat, cover and let stand for 4 minutes, until shrimp are pink and opaque. Remove shrimp to a serving bowl and toss with green onions and 1 tsp (5 mL) of the lemon juice. Discard bouillon. With a fork, mash avocado, garlic, onion, the remaining lemon juice, hot pepper sauce and oil. Season with salt. Add to shrimp and toss to coat. Serve on a bed of romaine. **Serves 4.**

Grilled Shrimp with Pesto

2 tbsp	extra-virgin olive oil	25 mL
1 tbsp	freshly squeezed lemon juice	15 mL
½ tsp	salt	2 mL
¼ tsp	hot pepper flakes	1 mL
1 lb	large shrimp (unpeeled)	500 g
	Fresh Basil Pesto (see recipe, page 178)	

In a large bowl, combine oil, lemon juice, salt and hot pepper flakes. Add shrimp and toss to coat. Cover and refrigerate for at least 4 hours or overnight. Preheat broiler or barbecue grill to high. Broil or grill shrimp on an oiled grill rack for 2 minutes per side, until pink and opaque. Let cool for 5 minutes. Serve shrimp with pesto as a dip. Diners will peel their own shrimp at the table. **Serves 4.**

Grilled Barbecued Shrimp

3	cloves garlic, minced	3
¼ cup	ketchup	50 mL
2 tbsp	minced onion	25 mL
1 tbsp	cider vinegar	15 mL
1 tsp	packed brown sugar	5 mL
1 tsp	brown mustard	5 mL
	Worcestershire sauce to taste	
	Hot pepper sauce (such as Tabasco), to taste	
1 lb	jumbo shrimp, peeled, deveined and butterflied	500 g

Preheat broiler or barbecue grill to high. Combine garlic, ketchup, onion, vinegar, brown sugar, mustard, Worcestershire sauce and hot pepper sauce. Toss shrimp with one-third of the sauce. Broil or grill on an oiled grill rack for 2 minutes per side, until pink and opaque. Serve with the remaining sauce as a dip. **Serves 4.**

Shrimp Poached in Tomato Vinaigrette

1	recipe Warm Tomato Vinaigrette (page 63)	1
1 lb	large shrimp, peeled and deveined	500 g
1 tbsp	chopped fresh dill	15 mL

In a large skillet, heat vinaigrette to a simmer. Add shrimp and dill; simmer for 2 to 3 minutes, until shrimp are pink and opaque. **Serves 4.** *Serve with crusty bread.*

Shrimp with Herbs and Pasta

1 lb	large shrimp, peeled and deveined	500 g
½ cup	all-purpose flour, seasoned with salt and pepper	125 mL
¼ cup	olive oil	50 mL
1 cup	chopped onion	250 mL
2	cloves garlic, minced	2
¾ cup	dry white wine	175 mL
1 cup	crushed tomatoes	250 mL
1 tbsp	chopped fresh Italian (flat-leaf) parsley	15 mL
1 tbsp	chopped fresh basil	15 mL
2 tbsp	butter, cut into small pieces	25 mL
12 oz	shell-shaped pasta, cooked	375 g

Dredge shrimp in seasoned flour, shaking off excess. Discard excess flour. In a large skillet, heat oil over medium-high heat. Sauté shrimp until lightly browned and firm; remove shrimp with a slotted spoon to a serving bowl. Add onion to the pan and sauté until tender. Add garlic and wine;

boil until wine is reduced by half. Add tomatoes and boil until liquid is reduced by half. Remove from heat and stir in parsley, basil and butter. Add sauce and pasta to shrimp and toss to coat. **Serves 4.**

Fried Shrimp in Beer Batter

2	eggs, separated	2
¾ cup	all-purpose flour	175 mL
¾ cup	beer	175 mL
2 tbsp	vegetable oil	25 mL
1 lb	large shrimp, peeled and deveined	500 g
¼ cup	cornstarch	50 mL
	Vegetable oil	
½ cup	ketchup	125 mL
¼ cup	prepared horseradish	50 mL
2 tbsp	mayonnaise	25 mL

Beat egg yolks, flour, beer and oil. In a separate bowl, beat egg whites to soft peaks; fold in to egg yolk mixture. Dredge shrimp in cornstarch, shaking off any excess, then dip in batter. Discard any excess cornstarch and batter. Deep-fry shrimp (see page 9) in oil for about 2 minutes, or until coating is golden brown and crispy. Remove to a strainer set over a drip bowl and drain off excess oil. Keep warm in a 200°F (100°C) oven while frying the remaining shrimp. Combine ketchup, horseradish and mayonnaise; serve with shrimp as a dip. **Serves 4.**

Clams in Tomato Vinaigrette

| 1 cup | Warm Tomato Vinaigrette (see recipe, page 63) | 250 mL |
| 36 | littleneck clams, scrubbed (see page 332) | 36 |

In a large, deep skillet, bring vinaigrette to a simmer. Add clams, cover and simmer for 5 to 7 minutes, or until clams open (discard any that don't). **Serves 4.** *Serve with pasta, rice or crusty bread.*

Clams Casino

1	clove garlic, minced	1
6 tbsp	butter, softened	90 mL
¼ cup	chopped green bell pepper	50 mL
¼ cup	chopped red bell pepper	50 mL
¼ cup	chopped green onion	50 mL
2 tbsp	chopped pitted green olives	25 mL
1 tbsp	chopped fresh Italian (flat-leaf) parsley	15 mL
	Salt and freshly ground black pepper to taste	
16	cherrystone clams, scrubbed (see page 332)	16
⅓ cup	dry bread crumbs	75 mL

Preheat oven to 400°F (200°C). Combine garlic, butter, green and red peppers, green onion, olives, parsley, salt and pepper. Open clams (see page 11) and place on half shells. Pack each half shell with garlic mixture and top with bread crumbs. Bake for 12 minutes, until bubbling. (If needed for color, brown briefly under a broiler.) **Serves 4.**

Niçoise Clams

1	clove garlic, minced	1
⅓ cup	butter, softened	75 mL
¼ cup	chopped green bell pepper	50 mL
¼ cup	chopped seeded tomato	50 mL
¼ cup	chopped green onion	50 mL
1 tbsp	chopped fresh basil	15 mL
1 tbsp	chopped pitted oil-cured black olives	15 mL
1 tbsp	extra-virgin olive oil	15 mL
	Salt and freshly ground black pepper to taste	
16	cherrystone clams, scrubbed (see page 332)	16
⅓ cup	dry bread crumbs	75 mL

Preheat oven to 400°F (200°C). Combine garlic, butter, green pepper, tomato, green onion, basil, olives, oil, salt and black pepper. Open clams (see page 11) and place on half shells. Pack each half shell with garlic mixture and top with bread crumbs. Bake for 12 minutes, until bubbling. (If needed for color, brown briefly under a broiler.) **Serves 4.**

Clams with Capers and Lemon

2 tbsp	butter, divided	25 mL
1 tbsp	minced onion	15 mL
2 tbsp	drained capers	25 mL
24	littleneck clams, scrubbed (see page 332)	24
1	green onion, finely sliced	1
2 tbsp	freshly squeezed lemon juice	25 mL

In a large skillet, melt half the butter over medium heat. Sauté onion until tender. Add capers and the remaining butter; sauté for 1 minute. Add clams, cover and cook for 5 to 8 minutes, or until clams open (discard any that don't). Remove clams with a slotted spoon to a warm serving bowl. Add green onion and lemon juice to liquid in pan. Pour sauce over clams. **Serves 4.**

Curried Clams

1 tbsp	vegetable oil	15 mL
¼ cup	chopped onion	50 mL
2 tsp	curry powder	10 mL
½ tsp	ground coriander	2 mL
Pinch	hot pepper flakes	Pinch
1 cup	canned coconut milk	250 mL
24	littleneck clams, scrubbed (see page 332)	24
½ cup	plain yogurt	125 mL

In a large skillet, heat oil over medium-low heat. Sauté onion until tender. Add curry powder, coriander and hot pepper flakes; sauté until aromatic. Increase heat to medium, add coconut milk and simmer for 1 minute. Add clams, cover and cook for 5 to 8 minutes, or until clams open (discard any that don't). Remove clams with a slotted spoon to a warm serving bowl. Add yogurt to pan, reduce heat and stir until well combined. Pour sauce over clams. **Serves 4.**

Ginger Soy Clams

1 tbsp	sesame oil	15 mL
½	small clove garlic, minced	½
1 tsp	chopped gingerroot	5 mL
Pinch	hot pepper flakes	Pinch
24	littleneck clams, scrubbed (see page 332)	24
¼ cup	dry sherry	50 mL
¼ cup	water	50 mL
1 tbsp	soy sauce	15 mL
Pinch	granulated sugar	Pinch

In a large skillet, heat oil over medium heat. Sauté garlic, ginger and hot pepper flakes until aromatic. Add clams, sherry, water, soy sauce and sugar; cover and cook for 5 to 8 minutes, or until clams open (discard any that don't). Remove clams with a slotted spoon to a warm serving bowl. Boil pan liquid for 1 minute. Pour sauce over clams. **Serves 4.**

Hoisin Clams

1 tbsp	canola oil	15 mL
½	small clove garlic, minced	½
1 tsp	minced gingerroot	5 mL
Pinch	hot pepper flakes	Pinch
¼ cup	chicken broth	50 mL
1½ tbsp	hoisin sauce	22 mL
24	littleneck clams, scrubbed (see page 332)	24

In a large skillet, heat oil over medium heat. Sauté garlic, ginger and hot pepper flakes until aromatic. Add broth and hoisin sauce; bring to a simmer. Add clams, cover and cook for 5 to 8 minutes, or until clams open (discard any that don't). Remove clams with a slotted spoon to a warm serving bowl. Boil pan liquid for 1 minute. Pour sauce over clams. **Serves 4.**

Spicy Black Bean Clams

Follow preceding recipe, but omit the hot pepper flakes and hoisin sauce, and add ¼ cup (50 mL) garlic black bean sauce and 1 tsp (5 mL) Asian chili paste with the broth. **Serves 4.**

Barbecued Steamed Clams

1 tbsp	vegetable oil	15 mL
1 tbsp	minced onion	15 mL
Pinch	granulated sugar	Pinch
¼ cup	ketchup	50 mL
1 tbsp	cider vinegar	15 mL
1 tsp	brown mustard	5 mL
1 tsp	Worcestershire sauce	5 mL
	Hot pepper sauce to taste	
24	littleneck clams, scrubbed (see page 332)	24

In a large skillet, heat oil over medium-high heat. Sauté onion and sugar until onion is browned. Add ketchup, vinegar, mustard and Worcestershire sauce; bring to a boil. Season with hot pepper sauce. Add clams, cover and cook for 5 to 8 minutes, or until clams open (discard any that don't). Remove clams with a slotted spoon to a warm serving bowl. Boil pan liquid for 1 minute. Pour sauce over clams. **Serves 4.**

Tex-Mex Clams

1 tbsp	canola oil	15 mL
2	jalapeño peppers, seeded and finely chopped	2
1	large onion, chopped	1
1	clove garlic, minced	1
2 tbsp	chili powder	25 mL
2 tsp	ground cumin	10 mL
1 tsp	ground coriander	5 mL
¼ cup	beer	50 mL
1 tbsp	tomato paste	15 mL
24	littleneck clams, scrubbed (see page 332)	24

In a large skillet, heat oil over medium heat. Sauté jalapeños and onion until tender. Add garlic, chili powder, cumin and coriander; sauté for 1 minute. Add beer and tomato paste; bring to a boil. Add clams, cover and cook for 5 to 8 minutes, or until clams open (discard any that don't). Remove clams with a slotted spoon to a warm serving bowl. Boil pan liquid for 1 minute. Pour sauce over clams. **Serves 4.**

Puerto Rican Clams

3 tbsp	olive oil	45 mL
2	bell peppers (any color), finely diced	2
1½ cups	finely chopped onions	375 mL
3	cloves garlic, minced	3
2 cups	canned diced tomatoes, with juice	500 mL
1 cup	finely diced ham	250 mL
	Salt and freshly ground black pepper to taste	
24	littleneck clams, scrubbed (see page 332)	24
2 tbsp	chopped fresh cilantro	25 mL

In a large skillet, heat oil over medium heat. Sauté peppers and onions until tender. Add garlic, and sauté for 30 seconds. Add tomatoes, with juice, ham, salt and pepper; simmer for 10 minutes. Add clams, cover and cook for 5 to 8 minutes, or until clams open (discard any that don't). Remove clams with a slotted spoon to a warm serving bowl. Boil pan liquid for 1 minute. Stir in cilantro. Pour sauce over clams. **Serves 4.**

Mussels Niçoise

2 tbsp	extra-virgin olive oil	25 mL
2 tbsp	minced onion	25 mL
3	cloves garlic, finely chopped	3
1 tsp	dried herbes de Provence	5 mL
½ cup	dry white wine	125 mL
12	oil-cured black olives, pitted	12
4	large plum (Roma) tomatoes, peeled and finely chopped	4
36	mussels, scrubbed (see page 8)	36
1 tbsp	chopped fresh basil	15 mL

In a large skillet, heat oil over medium heat. Sauté onion until tender. Add garlic and herbes de Provence; sauté for 30 seconds. Add wine and boil until reduced by about two-thirds. Add olives and tomatoes; bring to a boil. Add mussels, cover and cook for 3 to 5 minutes, or until mussels open (discard any that don't). Stir in basil. **Serves 4.**

Portuguese Mussel Stew

3 tbsp	extra-virgin olive oil	45 mL
2	large leeks, white parts only, sliced	2
2	cloves garlic, minced	2
1 cup	dry white wine	250 mL
1½ cups	canned diced tomatoes, drained	375 mL
	Juice of ½ lemon	
48	large mussels, scrubbed (see page 8)	48

| ½ cup | chopped fresh basil | 125 mL |
| 2 tbsp | freshly grated Parmesan cheese | 25 mL |

In a large skillet, heat oil over medium heat. Sauté leeks until tender. Add garlic and sauté for 30 seconds. Add wine and boil until reduced by half. Add tomatoes and lemon juice; bring to a boil. Add mussels, cover and cook for 3 to 5 minutes, or until mussels open (discard any that don't). Stir in basil and Parmesan. **Serves 4.**

Mussels Marseille

2 tbsp	extra-virgin olive oil	25 mL
1	large onion, finely chopped	1
1	red bell pepper, diced	1
2	cloves garlic, minced	2
1 tsp	dried basil	5 mL
¼ tsp	ground fennel seeds	1 mL
	Finely grated zest and juice of ½ orange	
	Salt and freshly ground black pepper to taste	
1	bay leaf	1
1 cup	diced canned tomatoes, with juice	250 mL
36	large mussels, scrubbed (see page 8)	36
2 tbsp	chopped fresh Italian (flat-leaf) parsley	25 mL

In a large skillet, heat oil over medium heat. Sauté onion and red pepper until tender. Add garlic, basil, fennel seeds, orange zest, salt and pepper; sauté for 1 minute. Add orange juice, bay leaf and tomatoes; simmer for 5 minutes. Add mussels, cover and cook for 3 to 5 minutes, or until mussels open (discard any that don't). Stir in parsley and discard bay leaf. **Serves 4.**

Oysters on the Half Shell with Jalapeño Cocktail Sauce

2	jalapeño peppers, seeded	2
2	tomatoes, cut into eighths	2
1	large clove garlic	1
⅓ cup	ketchup	75 mL
1 tbsp	freshly squeezed lemon juice	15 mL
24	oysters, scrubbed	24
	Thinly sliced lettuce or other greens	
6	lemon wedges	6

In a food processor, finely chop jalapeños, tomatoes and garlic. Stir in ketchup and lemon juice. Open oysters (see page 11) and place on half shells on a bed of lettuce. Top oysters with sauce and garnish with lemon wedges. **Serves 4.**

Oysters Florentine

	Kosher salt	
24	oysters, scrubbed (see page 11)	24
2 tbsp	butter	25 mL
1	leek, white part only, minced	1
2	packages (each 10 oz/300 g) frozen chopped spinach, thawed	2
½ cup	whipping (35%) cream	125 mL
2 tbsp	freshly grated Parmesan cheese	25 mL
Pinch	ground nutmeg	Pinch
	Salt and freshly ground black pepper to taste	
1½ cups	shredded Gruyère cheese, divided	375 mL

Preheat oven to 450°F (230°C) and line a broiler pan with a layer of kosher salt. Open oysters (see page 11) and place on half shells. In a large skillet, melt butter over medium heat. Sauté leek until tender. Add spinach and sauté until dry. Add cream and simmer until almost absorbed, about 3 minutes. Add Parmesan, nutmeg, salt and pepper. Pack each half shell with leek mixture and top with Gruyère. Bake for 10 minutes, until bubbling. (If needed for color, brown briefly under a broiler.) **Serves 4.**

Oyster-Stuffed Mushroom Caps

24	large mushrooms	24
2 tbsp	olive oil	25 mL
2	cloves garlic, minced	2
2 tbsp	chopped green onion	25 mL
¾ cup	dry bread crumbs	175 mL
3 tbsp	freshly grated Parmesan cheese	45 mL
24	shucked large oysters (see page 11), drained	24

Preheat oven to 400°F (200°C). Separate mushroom caps and stems, and chop stems. In a large skillet, heat oil over medium-high heat. Sauté mushroom caps until browned; remove with a slotted spoon to a plate. Add mushroom stems to the pan and sauté until browned. Add garlic and green onion; sauté for 30 seconds. Remove from heat and mix in bread crumbs and Parmesan; let cool. Place 1 oyster in each mushroom cap, then pack bread crumb mixture on top. Bake for 10 minutes, until oysters plump. (If needed for color, brown briefly under a broiler.) **Serves 4.**

Oyster Stew

24	shucked large oysters (see page 11), with their liquor	24
4 cups	milk	1 L
2 to 4 tbsp	butter, softened	25 to 50 mL
1 tbsp	paprika	15 mL
Pinch	cayenne pepper	Pinch
	Salt to taste	
	Oyster crackers	

In a large pot, over medium heat, heat oysters, oyster liquor and milk, stirring occasionally, until oysters plump and curl at the edges (do not boil). Stir in butter to taste, paprika, cayenne and salt until butter melts. Serve with oyster crackers. **Serves 4.**

Poached Oysters in Butter Sauce

8	slices French bread	8
1/3 cup	olive oil	75 mL
1	clove garlic, halved	1
1	large shallot, minced	1
1/4 cup	dry white wine	50 mL
2 tbsp	white wine vinegar	25 mL
24	shucked large oysters (see page 11), drained	24
1 tbsp	freshly squeezed lemon juice	15 mL
6 tbsp	butter, cut into pieces	90 mL

Brush both sides of bread with oil, rub with the cut side of the garlic, and toast. Place 2 slices on each of 4 plates. In a large skillet, over medium heat, bring shallot, wine and vinegar to a simmer. Add oysters and simmer until they plump and curl at the edges. Remove oysters with slotted spoon, place 3 oysters on each slice of toast and keep warm. Increase heat to high and boil pan liquid until reduced by about one-third. Reduce heat to low and stir in lemon juice and butter, one piece at a time. Pour sauce over oysters. **Serves 4.**

Baked Creole Crabmeat

4 tbsp	butter	50 mL
1 1/2 cups	chopped onions	375 mL
4	cloves garlic, minced	4
2 tbsp	chopped fresh Italian (flat-leaf) parsley	25 mL
1/2 tsp	dried thyme	2 mL
1/4 tsp	dried oregano	1 mL
Pinch	cayenne pepper	Pinch
	Salt and freshly ground black pepper to taste	
1 lb	backfin (lump) crabmeat, shells picked out	500 g

1/2 cup	freshly grated Parmesan cheese, divided	125 mL
1/4 cup	seasoned dry bread crumbs	50 mL

Preheat oven to 375°F (190°C). In a large skillet, melt butter over medium heat. Sauté onions until tender. Add garlic, parsley, thyme, oregano, cayenne, salt and black pepper; sauté for 1 minute. Add crabmeat and heat through. Stir in 1/3 cup (75 mL) of the Parmesan. Transfer to a 4-cup (1 L) casserole dish. Combine bread crumbs and the remaining Parmesan; sprinkle on top of crab mixture. Bake for 20 minutes, until browned and bubbly. **Serves 4.**

Fried Oysters with Tartar Sauce

1 cup	mayonnaise (not fat-free)	250 mL
1/4 cup	finely chopped dill pickle	50 mL
1 tbsp	freshly squeezed lemon juice	15 mL
1 tsp	hot pepper sauce (such as Tabasco)	5 mL
2	eggs, beaten	2
2 cups	seasoned dry bread crumbs	500 mL
24	shucked large oysters (see page 11), drained	24
1/2 cup	all-purpose flour	125 mL
	Vegetable oil	

Combine mayonnaise, pickle, lemon juice and hot pepper sauce; set aside. Place eggs and bread crumbs in separate bowls. Dust oysters with flour, shaking off excess. Dip in egg, then dredge in bread crumbs. Set on a rack and let stand for 5 minutes. Discard any excess flour, egg and bread crumbs. Deep-fry oysters (see page 9) for 2 to 3 minutes, until coating is browned and crispy. Serve with tartar sauce. **Serves 4.**

Fried Oyster Sandwiches

Follow preceding recipe, but serve 6 oysters on each of 4 large soft rolls spread with tartar sauce and topped with chopped lettuce and tomato. **Serves 4.**

Sautéed Soft-Shell Crabs with Lime Mayonnaise

1	clove garlic, minced	1
2 cups	mayonnaise	500 mL
3 tbsp	minced onion	45 mL
1/2 tsp	hot pepper sauce	2 mL
	Finely grated zest and juice of 1 lime	
	Juice of 1 additional lime	
8	live soft-shell crabs, prepared (see page 11)	8
3/4 cup	all-purpose flour, seasoned with salt and pepper	175 mL

2 cups	dry bread crumbs	500 mL
1/4 cup	clarified butter (see page 16)	50 mL
1/4 cup	spicy peanut oil	50 mL

Combine garlic, mayonnaise, onion, hot pepper sauce, lime zest and lime juice; set aside. Dredge crabs in seasoned flour, shaking off excess. Brush with 3/4 cup (175 mL) of the lime mayonnaise and dredge in bread crumbs. Set on a rack and let stand for 5 minutes. Discard any excess flour and bread crumbs. In a large skillet, heat butter and oil over medium-high heat. Sauté crabs, in batches, for 3 to 4 minutes per side, or until coating is browned and crispy. Serve with the remaining lime mayonnaise. **Serves 4.**

Grilled Soft-Shell Crabs

| 8 | live soft-shell crabs, prepared (see page 11) | 8 |
| 1 cup | Italian dressing | 250 mL |

Coat crabs with half the dressing, cover and refrigerate for 1 hour. Preheat broiler or barbecue grill to high. Remove crabs from marinade and discard marinade. Broil or grill crabs, basting frequently with the remaining dressing, for about 4 minutes per side, or until browned and crisp. **Serves 4.**

Soft-Shell Crab Sandwiches

Prepare 4 crabs according to either of the two preceding recipes. Serve each crab on a split kaiser roll spread with lime mayonnaise or Italian dressing and topped with 1 romaine lettuce leaf, 3 slices of cucumber and 1 large slice of tomato. **Serves 4.**

Marinated Soft-Shell Crabs

8	live soft-shell crabs, prepared (see page 11)	8
3/4 cup	all-purpose flour, seasoned with salt and pepper	175 mL
1/4 cup	olive oil	50 mL
4	cloves garlic, sliced	4
1	bunch green onions, white parts only, sliced	1
1/4 cup	dry white wine	50 mL
Pinch	cayenne pepper	Pinch
	Juice of 1 large lemon	
	Salt and freshly ground black pepper to taste	

Dredge crabs in seasoned flour. In a large skillet, heat oil over medium-high heat. Sauté crabs until browned on both sides. Add garlic, green onions and wine; bring to a boil. Remove from heat and stir in cayenne, lemon juice, salt and black pepper.

Transfer to a serving bowl and let cool. Cover and refrigerate for about 1 hour, until chilled. **Serves 4.**

Crab and Caviar Custard

4	large or extra-large whole eggs	4
2	large or extra-large egg yolks	2
Pinch	cayenne pepper	Pinch
Pinch	ground nutmeg	Pinch
	Salt and freshly ground white pepper to taste	
1 1/2 cups	milk	375 mL
1 cup	cream (any type, minimum 10%)	250 mL
8 oz	backfin (lump) crabmeat, shells picked out	250 g
2 oz	salmon caviar	60 g

Preheat oven to 350°F (180°C) and grease a 10-inch (25 cm) glass pie plate. Combine eggs, egg yolks, cayenne, nutmeg, salt and white pepper. In a saucepan, bring milk and cream to a simmer; stir gradually into egg mixture. Scatter crabmeat on bottom of prepared pie plate and pour egg mixture over top. Place in a larger pan of water and bake for 1 hour, until a tester inserted in the center comes out almost clean. Let cool on a rack for 30 minutes. Run a knife around the edge and invert onto a serving platter. Garnish top with caviar and cut into wedges. **Serves 4.**

Crab and Avocado Salad

1/2 cup	mayonnaise	125 mL
1/4 cup	chili sauce or ketchup	50 mL
2 tbsp	sour cream	25 mL
1 tbsp	minced onion	15 mL
1 tsp	hot pepper sauce (such as Tabasco)	5 mL
	Salt and freshly ground black pepper to taste	
1 lb	backfin (lump) crabmeat, shells picked out	500 g
2	avocados, halved lengthwise	2
4	lemon wedges	4

Combine mayonnaise, chili sauce, sour cream, onion, hot pepper sauce, salt and pepper. Stir in crabmeat. Cut a small slice from the rounded side of each avocado half to allow it to sit on a plate without wobbling. Using a small spoon, enlarge the cavity in each half and pack with crabmeat mixture. Serve garnished with lemon wedges. **Serves 4.**

Quick Crab Chowder

4	slices bacon, chopped	4
2	stalks celery, sliced	2
1	onion, finely chopped	1
½	red bell pepper, diced	½
8 oz	red-skinned or other boiling potatoes, peeled and diced	250 g
1	clove garlic, minced	1
2 cups	clam juice	500 mL
Pinch	ground nutmeg	Pinch
Pinch	cayenne pepper	Pinch
	Salt and freshly ground black pepper to taste	
1 lb	backfin (lump) crabmeat, shells picked out	500 g
3 cups	milk (not fat-free)	750 mL

In a large saucepan, over medium heat, cook bacon until crisp. Add celery, onion, red pepper and potatoes; sauté until onion is tender. Add garlic and sauté for 30 seconds. Add clam juice, nutmeg, cayenne, salt and black pepper; cook until potatoes are tender, about 15 minutes. Stir in crabmeat and milk; heat through. Do not boil. **Serves 4.**

Italian Seafood Sandwiches

1	dried hot chili pepper	1
6 tbsp	olive oil	90 mL
6 tbsp	red wine vinegar	90 mL
½ tsp	dried oregano	2 mL
½ tsp	dried dillweed	2 mL
½ tsp	dried thyme	2 mL
½ tsp	dried basil	2 mL
	Salt and freshly ground black pepper to taste	
8 oz	medium shrimp, peeled and deveined	250 g
8 oz	bay scallops, trimmed of hard side muscles	250 g
½	red onion, thinly sliced	½
8 oz	backfin (lump) crabmeat, shells picked out	250 g
¼ cup	chopped fresh Italian (flat-leaf) parsley	50 mL
4	torpedo rolls, split and warmed	4
2 cups	shredded romaine lettuce, divided	500 mL

In a large saucepan, bring chili pepper, oil, vinegar, oregano, dill, thyme, basil, salt and pepper to a boil. Add shrimp and return to a boil. Add scallops, remove from heat, cover and let stand for 5 minutes, until shellfish are firm and opaque. Stir in onion, crabmeat and parsley. Stuff each roll with one-quarter of the romaine and the seafood mixture. Moisten with some of the liquid left behind in the pan. **Serves 4.**

Squid Salad

1 lb	squid, cleaned (see page 332)	500 g
1	clove garlic, minced	1
1	green onion, thinly sliced	1
½ cup	olive oil	125 mL
¼ cup	freshly squeezed lemon juice	50 mL
1 tbsp	chopped fresh Italian (flat-leaf) parsley	15 mL
¼ tsp	dried oregano	1 mL
¼ tsp	hot pepper flakes	1 mL
	Salt and freshly ground black pepper to taste	
24	black olives, pitted and sliced	24
2	large tomatoes, diced	2
¼ cup	finely chopped red onion	50 mL
	Romaine lettuce leaves	
	Pita triangles	

Cut squid tentacles and sacs into ¼-inch (0.5 cm) slices. Simmer squid in salted water for 30 to 60 seconds, or until opaque; drain and let cool. Meanwhile, combine garlic, green onion, oil, lemon juice, parsley, oregano, hot pepper flakes, salt and black pepper. Add squid, olives, tomatoes and red onion; toss to coat. Cover and refrigerate for about 1 hour, until chilled. Serve on bed of romaine, accompanied by pita triangles. **Serves 4.**

Calamari with Potatoes and Tomatoes

2 lbs	squid, cleaned (see page 332)	1 kg
2 tbsp	olive oil	25 mL
1	large onion, chopped	1
½ cup	diced green bell pepper	125 mL
½ cup	diced red bell pepper	125 mL
1	clove garlic, minced	1
1 lb	red-skinned or other boiling potatoes, sliced	500 g
2 cups	canned diced tomatoes, drained	500 mL
¼ tsp	dried marjoram	1 mL
¼ tsp	dried oregano	1 mL
Large pinch	hot pepper flakes	Large pinch
	Salt and freshly ground black pepper to taste	
¼ cup	chopped fresh basil	50 mL

Slice squid sacs into 1-inch (2.5 cm) rings, and cut tentacles into 1-inch (2.5 cm) pieces. In a large skillet, heat oil over medium-high heat. Sauté onion, green pepper and red pepper until tender. Add garlic and sauté for 30 seconds. Add squid and sauté until opaque, about 1 minute. Stir in potatoes, tomatoes, marjoram, oregano, hot pepper flakes, salt and black pepper; reduce heat, cover and simmer until potatoes are tender, about 45 minutes. Stir in basil. **Serves 4.**

Chapter 30
Meatless Dishes
For Devoted and Occasional Vegetarians

Black Bean Tacos 345

Black Bean Falafel 346

Avocado Falafel 346

Eggplant Falafel 346

Pita Filled with Toasted Chickpeas,
Avocado and Eggplant "Caviar" 346

Chilied Corn Enchiladas 346

High-Protein Vegetarian Tostadas 347

Mixed Grilled Vegetables with
Black Bean Sauce 347

Mixed Grilled Vegetables with
Peanut Sauce 347

Mixed Grilled Vegetable Tostada 347

Pumpkin Bisque 348

Red Pepper Chowder Swirled with
Chili Cream 348

Chili and Corn Chowder 348

Middle Eastern Chickpea Soup 348

Spicy Chickpea Soup 348

Marinated Antipasto 349

Summer Antipasto 349

Fritto Misto (Fried Antipasto) 349

Brown Rice and Roasted Pepper Salad . . 349

Rice and Lentil Salad 349

Risotto e Fagioli 349

Squash Stuffed with Risotto 349

Winter Tempura 350

Carrot and Beet Latkes 350

Celery Parsnip Latkes 350

Sweet Potato, Carrot and
Apple Pancakes 350

Jerusalem Artichokes and
Mushrooms au Gratin 350

Stir-Fried Sesame Asparagus 351

Fried Rice with Vegetables 351

Spaghetti Squash with
Stir-Fried Vegetables 351

Spaghetti Squash with Artichoke
and Mushroom Sauce 351

Marinated Mozzarella Salad
in Tomatoes 351

Chilied Corn Salad Stuffed in
Roasted Peppers 352

Greek Marinated Mushrooms
in Artichokes 352

Caponata 352

Ratatouille 352

Marinated Lentil Salad 352

White and Black Bean Salad 353

Minted Curried Potatoes 353

Potatoes and Eggplant 353

Cheese Gnocchi with
Fresh Tomato Sauce 353

Herb Gnocchi with
Parmesan and Butter 353

Pizza Rustica 354

Peasant Pie 354

Fontina Fondue with
Garlic Roasted Potatoes 354

Cheddar Fondue with
Apples, Pickles and Toast 355

Leek and Chard Soufflé 355

Spinach and Feta Soufflé 355

Tarte Niçoise 355

Tarte Lyonnaise 355

Once upon a time, a balanced meal was meat, potatoes and a vegetable — in that order. But things have changed. Meat is no longer automatically the main course. Many people are looking to cut down on their consumption of animal fat, and one of the best ways to find alternatives is to look at cuisines that traditionally lack access to meat as their main protein source. Because meats are a luxury in all but a handful of cultures, we need only leave the Western world to find an array of inspired vegetarian dishes from which to choose.

From the chili-spiked beans and tortillas of Mexico to the fragrant vegetable curries of India, vegetarian cooking is rife with rich flavors that will enable you to erase meat from your diet without regret — whether you choose to do so for a single meal or for a lifetime. Grill marinated vegetables and serve them with high-protein Middle Eastern sauces made from eggplant, chickpeas and beans. Stuff cabbage with brown rice and vegetables. Serve a spaghetti squash as you would pasta primavera, in a sauce overrun with garden produce. Stir-fry vegetables, tofu and nuts. Assemble antipasto salads speckled with cheese, roasted peppers and fresh herbs. Prepare blini or latkes inundated with chopped vegetables and serve them with yogurt and chives. Make East African–inspired soups thick with peanuts, chili and grains. Try a vegetarian version of moussaka from Greece, vegetable tempura from Japan and South American stews laden with hearty winter vegetables and the perfume of cilantro.

These foods all have one thing in common: they combine complementing proteins, balancing the amino-acid deficiencies of one incomplete vegetable protein with the strengths of another. Most beans, for instance, are low in tryptophan and the essential sulfur-containing amino acids. But grains, such as rice or corn, supply these missing amino acids. A combination of beans and grains provides much more usable protein than either could supply alone.

The argument that beans and grains are high-calorie starches has long been used against them by weight-conscious as well as health-conscious diners. But look at the facts. A beef steak has more than three times as many calories as the same weight of cooked kidney beans. A pound (500 g) of fat packs twice the calories of a pound (500 g) of starch, and when you consider that a typical serving of meat weighs 6 to 8 ounces (175 to 250 g) and an average portion of beans or rice is closer to 5 ounces (150 g), the old "starch is fattening" argument loses most of its weight.

About these recipes . . .

The following recipes are filling, highly nutritious dishes that rely on flavorful oils and a combination of spices and vegetables to supply filling alternatives to meat with far fewer calories and saturated fat.

Black Bean Tacos

4	green onions, white part only, finely chopped	4
3	large tomatoes, finely chopped	3
2	jalapeño peppers, seeded and finely chopped	2
2 tbsp	finely chopped fresh Italian (flat-leaf) parsley	25 mL
2 tbsp	olive oil	25 mL
1 tbsp	grated orange zest Juice of 1 orange	15 mL
8	taco shells, warmed	8
1	avocado, diced	1
2 cups	shredded lettuce	500 mL
2 cups	refried black beans (store-bought or see recipe, page 20)	500 mL

Make a salsa by combining green onions, tomatoes, jalapeños, parsley, oil, orange zest and orange juice. Fill taco shells with layers of avocado, lettuce, refried beans and salsa. **Serves 4.**

Black Bean Falafel

2	cloves garlic, minced, divided	2
1 cup	drained rinsed canned black beans	250 g
1 cup	tahini, divided	250 mL
6 tbsp	freshly squeezed lemon juice, divided	90 mL
1/4 cup	olive oil, divided	50 mL
1/2 tsp	ground coriander	2 mL
1/2 tsp	ground cumin	2 mL
Pinch	dried oregano	Pinch
1/3 cup	whole wheat flour	75 mL
1/3 cup	sesame seeds	75 mL
	Salt and freshly ground black pepper to taste	
1	egg, beaten	1
	Vegetable oil	
1/2 cup	plain yogurt	125 mL
4	pitas, pockets opened by slicing off about 1/2 inch (1 cm) of one side	4
2	tomatoes, chopped	2
1 cup	shredded lettuce	250 mL
1/2 cup	diced cucumbers	125 mL
2 tbsp	chopped fresh Italian (flat-leaf) parsley	25 mL

In a food processor, purée half the garlic, beans, 1/3 cup (75 mL) of the tahini, half the lemon juice, 3 tbsp (45 mL) of the oil, and the coriander, cumin and oregano. Form into balls of about 2 tsp (10 mL) each. Combine flour, sesame seeds, salt and pepper. Dip black bean balls in egg, then dredge in flour mixture. Deep-fry black bean balls (see page 9) for about 3 minutes, until golden brown. Drain on paper towels. Combine the remaining garlic, tahini, lemon juice and oil with the yogurt. Spread the interior of the pitas with some of this sauce, then fill with black bean balls. Top with more sauce, tomatoes, lettuce, cucumbers and parsley. **Serves 4.**

Avocado Falafel

Follow preceding recipe, but replace the black beans with chickpeas, the lettuce with 1 avocado, diced, and the parsley with fresh mint. **Serves 4.**

Eggplant Falafel

Follow recipe for Black Bean Falafel (above), but first, in a large skillet, heat 1/4 cup (50 mL) olive oil over medium-high heat. Sauté 1 eggplant, diced, and 1/4 cup (50 mL) chopped onion until almost tender. Add 2 cloves garlic, minced, and 1 1/2 cups (375 mL) canned diced tomatoes, drained; reduce heat and simmer until mixture is soft, about 4 minutes. Season with 2 tsp (10 mL) dried mint, and salt and pepper to taste. Replace the black beans with chickpeas, and use the eggplant mixture in place of the tomatoes, lettuce and cucumbers. **Serves 4.**

Pita Filled with Toasted Chickpeas, Avocado and Eggplant "Caviar"

1	small eggplant	1
1	small clove garlic, minced	1
2 tbsp	mayonnaise	25 mL
1 tbsp	olive oil	15 mL
1 tbsp	freshly squeezed lemon juice	15 mL
	Salt and freshly ground black pepper to taste	
4	pitas, pockets opened by slicing off about 1/2 inch (1 cm) of one side	4
1	recipe Spiced Sesame Chickpeas (page 519)	1
1	avocado, diced	1
1	tomato, diced	1

Preheat oven to 400°F (200°C). Roast eggplant for 45 minutes, until fork-tender. Let cool, then halve lengthwise and scoop out flesh. In a food processor, purée eggplant, garlic, mayonnaise, oil, lemon juice, salt and pepper. Spread the interior of the pitas with half this mixture. Fill pitas with Spiced Sesame Chickpeas, the remaining eggplant mixture, avocado and tomato. **Serves 4.**

Chilied Corn Enchiladas

1 tbsp	vegetable oil	15 mL
1	large onion, chopped	1
1	clove garlic, minced	1
1	large roasted red bell pepper (see page 11), diced	1
1 cup	drained canned corn kernels	250 mL
1 tsp	chili powder	5 mL
1/2 tsp	ground cumin	2 mL
Pinch	hot pepper flakes	Pinch
	Salt and freshly ground black pepper to taste	
3/4 cup	refried black beans (store-bought or see recipe, page 20)	175 mL
4	large whole wheat tortillas, warmed	4
2 cups	Quick Fresh Tomato Sauce (see recipe, page 225)	500 mL
4 oz	farmer's cheese or queso fresco, crumbled	125 g

Preheat oven to 375°F (190°C). In a skillet, heat oil over medium-high heat. Sauté onion until tender. Add garlic, roasted pepper, corn, chili powder, cumin, hot pepper flakes, salt and black pepper; sauté for 5 minutes. Spread a portion of the refried beans on each tortilla. Spoon a line of chilied corn on top of the beans and roll up tortillas. Place seam side down in a 4-cup (1 L) baking dish, top with tomato sauce and sprinkle with cheese. Bake for 20 minutes, until cheese is melted and sauce is bubbly. **Serves 4.**

High-Protein Vegetarian Tostadas

2	tomatoes, chopped	2
1	large avocado, diced	1
1 tbsp	freshly squeezed lemon juice	15 mL
	Salt and hot pepper sauce (such as Tabasco) to taste	
	Corn oil	
8	soft corn tortillas	8
2 cups	refried black beans (store-bought or see recipe, page 20)	500 mL
2 cups	alfalfa sprouts	500 mL
1 cup	shredded Monterey Jack cheese	250 mL
1 tbsp	julienned red radish	15 mL

Combine tomatoes, avocado, lemon juice, salt and hot pepper sauce. In a large, heavy skillet, heat a thin film of oil over high heat until smoking. Toast tortillas, one at a time, for 1 minute per side, adding more oil as necessary. Place 2 tortillas on each of 4 plates and top each with refried beans, avocado mixture, alfalfa sprouts and cheese. Garnish with radish. **Serves 4.**

Mixed Grilled Vegetables with Black Bean Sauce

12	large mushrooms, stemmed	12
2	large bell peppers of different colors, each cut into 6 spears	2
2	zucchini, cut into large chunks	2
1	large onion, cut into wedges	1
1	large tomato, sliced	1
1 cup	Oil and Vinegar Dressing (see recipe, page 59)	250 mL
1	large clove garlic, halved	1
2 cups	drained rinsed canned black beans	500 mL
1/4 cup	olive oil	50 mL
1 tbsp	minced onion	15 mL
1 tsp	hot pepper sauce (such as Tabasco)	5 mL
	Salt to taste	
1/4 to 1/3 cup	orange juice	50 to 75 mL
1 tbsp	toasted sesame seeds	15 mL

Toss mushrooms, bell peppers, zucchini, onion wedges and tomato in dressing. Cover and refrigerate for 1 hour. Preheat broiler or barbecue grill to high. In a food processor, process garlic, beans, oil, minced onion, hot pepper sauce and salt until smooth. With the motor running, through the feed tube, slowly add just enough orange juice to make sauce the thickness of unbeaten whipping cream. Set aside. Broil or grill marinated vegetables, turning each several times while it cooks, until browned and tender: cook onion for about 12 minutes; mushrooms, peppers and zucchini for 6 to 8 minutes; tomato for 4 minutes. In a saucepan, over medium heat, cook black bean sauce until heated through. Serve vegetables drizzled with sauce and garnished with sesame seeds. **Serves 4.**

Mixed Grilled Vegetables with Peanut Sauce

Prepare grilled vegetables as in the preceding recipe, but replace the black bean sauce with a double recipe of Peanut Sauce (page 53). **Serves 4.**

Mixed Grilled Vegetable Tostada

Follow recipe for Mixed Grilled Vegetables with Black Bean Sauce (left). In addition, toast 4 soft tortillas, one at a time, in a thin film of corn oil in a skillet over medium-high heat. Spread each with 1/4 cup (50 mL) of the black bean sauce and mound with grilled vegetables. Top each with another 1/4 cup (50 mL) black bean sauce, 1/4 cup (50 mL) shredded Cheddar cheese, 1/4 cup (50 mL) diced avocado and 1 tbsp (15 mL) sour cream. **Serves 4.**

Pumpkin Bisque

2 tbsp	butter	25 mL
1	small onion, finely chopped	1
1	cinnamon stick (about 2 inches/5 cm)	1
1	dried hot chili pepper	1
2 tbsp	finely chopped gingerroot	25 mL
4 cups	vegetable broth	1 L
2 cups	canned pumpkin purée (not pie filling)	500 mL
2 tbsp	honey	25 mL
1 tsp	cider vinegar	5 mL
1/4 tsp	ground nutmeg	1 mL
	Salt and freshly ground black pepper to taste	
1/3 cup	sour cream	75 mL

In a large saucepan, melt butter over medium heat. Sauté onion until tender. Add cinnamon stick, chili pepper and ginger; sauté for 1 minute. Add broth, pumpkin purée, honey, vinegar, nutmeg, salt and pepper; bring to a boil. Reduce heat and simmer for 5 minutes. Discard cinnamon stick. Serve hot or cold, stirring in sour cream just before serving. **Serves 4.**

Red Pepper Chowder Swirled with Chili Cream

2 tbsp	olive oil	25 mL
1	small onion, finely chopped	1
1	stalk celery, diced	1
4	roasted red bell peppers (see page 11), diced	4
1	large clove garlic, minced	1
2 cups	drained canned corn kernels	500 mL
1 tsp	curry powder	5 mL
Pinch	cayenne pepper	Pinch
5 cups	vegetable broth	1.25 L
1 1/2 tsp	paprika	7 mL
	Salt and freshly ground black pepper to taste	
1/4 cup	finely chopped fresh Italian (flat-leaf) parsley	50 mL
2 tbsp	freshly squeezed lime juice	25 mL
1 cup	whipping (35%) cream	250 mL
3 tbsp	chopped canned green chili peppers	45 mL

In a large saucepan, heat oil over medium heat. Sauté onion and celery until tender. Add roasted peppers, garlic, corn, curry powder and cayenne; sauté for 30 seconds. Add broth, paprika, salt and black pepper; reduce heat and simmer for 20 minutes. Stir in parsley and lime juice. Meanwhile, in a saucepan, bring cream to a boil over medium heat; reduce heat and boil gently until reduced by half.

Transfer cream to a blender, add chili peppers and purée. Serve chowder swirled with chili cream. **Serves 4.**

Chili and Corn Chowder

Follow preceding recipe, but omit the curry powder, use only 1 roasted pepper, add 2 cups (500 mL) drained rinsed canned red kidney beans and 1 tbsp (15 mL) chili powder with the corn, and add 1/4 cup (50 mL) tomato paste with the broth. **Serves 4.**

Middle Eastern Chickpea Soup

1 tbsp	extra-virgin olive oil	15 mL
1	onion, finely chopped	1
4	cloves garlic, minced	4
1 tsp	ground coriander	5 mL
4 cups	vegetable broth	1 L
1 cup	macaroni	250 mL
1 1/2 cups	drained rinsed canned chickpeas	375 mL
1	extra-large egg yolk, beaten	1
1/4 cup	freshly squeezed lemon juice	50 mL
1/4 cup	finely chopped fresh Italian (flat-leaf) parsley	50 mL

In a large saucepan, heat oil over medium heat. Sauté onion until tender. Add garlic and coriander; sauté for 30 seconds. Add broth and bring to a boil. Add macaroni, reduce heat and simmer for 10 minutes. Add chickpeas and simmer for 5 minutes. Combine egg yolk and lemon juice; slowly whisk into soup and simmer, stirring constantly, until slightly thickened (do not boil). Stir in parsley. **Serves 4.**

Spicy Chickpea Soup

1 tbsp	extra-virgin olive oil	15 mL
1	onion, finely chopped	1
1	bell pepper (any color), diced	1
1	jalapeño pepper, seeded and finely chopped	1
4	cloves garlic, minced	4
1	large tomato, peeled and finely chopped	1
1 tsp	ground cumin	5 mL
1/4 tsp	dried oregano	1 mL
	Salt and freshly ground black pepper to taste	
4 cups	vegetable broth	1 L
1/2 cup	white rice	125 mL
1 1/2 cups	drained rinsed canned chickpeas	375 mL
1	extra-large egg yolk, beaten	1
1/4 cup	freshly squeezed lime juice	50 mL
1/4 cup	finely chopped fresh Italian (flat-leaf) parsley	50 mL

In a large saucepan, heat oil over medium heat. Sauté onion, bell pepper and jalapeño until tender. Add garlic, tomato, cumin, oregano, salt and pepper; sauté for 1 minute. Add broth and bring to a boil. Add rice, reduce heat and simmer for 10 minutes. Add chickpeas and simmer for 5 minutes. Combine egg yolk and lime juice; slowly whisk into soup and simmer, stirring constantly, until slightly thickened (do not boil). Stir in parsley. **Serves 4.**

Marinated Antipasto

Serve the following dishes, either at room temperature or warmed, with 1 loaf crusty bread, sliced, and 1 cup (250 mL) brine- or oil-cured black olives: Sicilian Artichokes (page 395), Grilled Mediterranean Eggplant (page 380), Mushrooms Boiled with Lots of Garlic (page 382) and Mélange of Roasted Peppers (page 379). **Serves 4.**

Summer Antipasto

Serve the following dishes, either chilled or at room temperature, on a bed of romaine lettuce, with 1 loaf crusty bread, sliced: Sicilian Artichokes (page 395), Marinated Tomato with Chèvre and Onion (page 399), Roasted Peppers with Black Olives and Anchovies (page 183), Grilled Summer Squash Salad (page 184) and Mixed Herb Tabbouleh (page 186). **Serves 4.**

Fritto Misto (Fried Antipasto)

Serve Sweet Potato Chips (page 104), Fried Kale (page 373) and Winter Tempura (page 350) with Anchovy Mayonnaise (page 56). **Serves 4.**

Brown Rice and Roasted Pepper Salad

5 cups	water	1.25 mL
1 tbsp	soy sauce	15 mL
2 cups	brown rice blend, rinsed thoroughly	500 mL
4	roasted bell peppers of assorted colors (see page 11), diced	4
1	small clove garlic, minced	1
1/3 cup	olive oil	75 mL
1/4 cup	red wine vinegar	50 mL
1/4 cup	chopped fresh Italian (flat-leaf) parsley	50 mL
	Juice of 1 lime	
	Salt and freshly ground black pepper to taste	

In a large saucepan, bring water and soy sauce to a boil. Add rice, cover tightly, reduce heat and sim-

mer for 45 minutes, until rice is tender and liquid is absorbed. Fluff with a fork. Toss with the remaining ingredients. Cover and refrigerate for about 1 hour, until chilled. **Serves 6 to 8.** *Store in an airtight container in the refrigerator for up to 4 days.*

Rice and Lentil Salad

Follow preceding recipe, but reduce the rice to 1 cup (250 mL) and add 1 cup (250 mL) soaked brown lentils (see page 11) with the rice. Add 1/4 cup (50 mL) chopped red onion and 1 tbsp (15 mL) dried mint with the peppers. **Serves 6 to 8.**

Risotto e Fagioli

2 tbsp	olive oil	25 mL
1/4 cup	finely chopped onion	50 mL
1 cup	Arborio rice	250 mL
1/2 cup	dry white wine	125 mL
4 1/2 cups	vegetable broth	1.125 L
1 cup	drained rinsed canned small white beans	250 mL
1/2 cup	toasted pumpkin seeds	125 mL
1/4 cup	freshly grated imported Parmesan cheese	50 mL
1 tbsp	dark sesame oil	15 mL

In a large saucepan, heat oil over medium heat. Sauté onion until tender. Add rice, stirring to coat with oil. Add wine and cook, stirring constantly with a wooden spoon, until wine is absorbed. Add broth, 1/2 cup (125 mL) at a time, stirring until each addition is absorbed before stirring in the next. When finished, rice should be al dente, with a creamy sauce developed throughout. Stir in beans, pumpkin seeds, Parmesan and sesame oil. **Serves 4.**

Squash Stuffed with Risotto

4	small acorn squash	4
1 tbsp	freshly squeezed lemon juice	15 mL
1 tbsp	soy sauce	15 mL
1/2	recipe Risotto e Fagioli (above)	1/2

Preheat oven to 400°F (200°C). Cut a thin slice from the pointed ends of the acorn squash so that they stand upright. Slice off stem ends and save as "lids." Hollow out interior cavities and discard seeds. Sprinkle the inside of each squash with lemon juice and soy sauce. Stuff squash with risotto and cover with "lids." Place in a 13- by 9-inch (3 L) baking pan, add 1/4 inch (0.5 cm) water and bake for 45 minutes, until squash are tender. **Serves 4.**

Winter Tempura

2	egg yolks, beaten	2
2 cups	ice water	500 mL
2 cups	sifted all-purpose flour	500 mL
2	carrots, julienned	2
2	leeks, white part only, thinly sliced	2
1	sweet potato, peeled and julienned	1
1	large red beet, peeled and julienned	1
½ cup	julienned fennel bulb	125 mL
8	sprigs fresh parsley	8
	Dipping Sauce for Potstickers (see recipe, page 249)	

Combine egg yolks and ice water, then stir in flour, leaving some small clumps. Dip carrots, leeks, sweet potato, beet and fennel in batter. Deep-fry vegetables (see page 9) for about 2 minutes, or until coating is browned and crispy. Remove vegetables to a strainer set over a drip bowl and drain off excess oil. Keep vegetables warm in a 200°F (100°C) oven while frying the remaining vegetables. Do the beets last, then deep-fry parsley for 10 seconds. Garnish vegetables with fried parsley and serve with dipping sauce. **Serves 4.**

Carrot and Beet Latkes

3	extra-large eggs, beaten	3
1¼ cups	coarsely shredded carrots	300 mL
1 cup	finely shredded peeled beets (about 8 oz/250 g)	250 mL
3 tbsp	finely chopped onion	45 mL
2 tbsp	all-purpose flour	25 mL
1 tsp	freshly squeezed lemon juice	5 mL
1 tsp	salt	5 mL
	Freshly ground black pepper to taste Vegetable oil	
¼ cup	sour cream	50 mL

Combine eggs, carrots, beets, onion, flour, lemon juice, salt and pepper. In a large, deep skillet, heat ¼ inch (0.5 cm) oil over medium-high heat. Add batter by spoonfuls, flattening mounds to form pancakes about 3 inches (7.5 cm) in diameter. Cook, turning once, for 4 to 5 minutes per side, until browned on both sides. Drain on paper towels and keep warm. Repeat with the remaining batter, adding oil to pan as necessary between batches. Serve with sour cream. **Serves 4.**

Celery Parsnip Latkes

Follow preceding recipe, but replace the carrots with parsnips, the beets with celery root, and the onion with leek (white part only). **Serves 4.**

Sweet Potato, Carrot and Apple Pancakes

3	extra-large eggs, beaten	3
½	tart apple, shredded	½
3 cups	shredded sweet potatoes (about 12 oz/375 g)	750 mL
⅔ cup	shredded carrot	150 mL
3 tbsp	finely chopped onion	45 mL
2 tbsp	all-purpose flour	25 mL
1 tsp	freshly squeezed lemon juice	5 mL
1 tsp	salt	5 mL
	Freshly ground black pepper to taste Vegetable oil	
¼ cup	sour cream	50 mL

Combine eggs, apple, sweet potatoes, carrot, onion, flour, lemon juice, salt and pepper. In a large, deep skillet, heat ¼ inch (0.5 cm) oil over medium-high heat. Add batter by spoonfuls, flattening mounds to form pancakes about 3 inches (7.5 cm) in diameter. Cook, turning once, for 4 to 5 minutes per side, until browned on both sides. Drain on paper towels and keep warm. Repeat with the remaining batter, adding oil to pan as necessary between batches. Serve with sour cream. **Serves 4.**

Jerusalem Artichokes and Mushrooms au Gratin

1 tbsp	butter	15 mL
2 tbsp	olive oil	25 mL
8 oz	mushrooms, sliced, divided	250 g
1 lb	Jerusalem artichokes, thinly sliced	500 g
2	large leeks, white part only, thinly sliced	2
	Salt and freshly ground black pepper to taste	
1 cup	shredded Swiss cheese, divided	250 mL
1 cup	mixed milk and half-and-half (10%) cream (in any proportion), divided	250 mL
2 tbsp	freshly grated Parmesan cheese, divided	25 mL

Preheat oven to 375°F (190°C) and grease a 10-inch (25 cm) shallow baking dish with the butter. In a large skillet, heat oil over medium-high heat. Sauté mushrooms until tender; set aside. Combine Jerusalem artichokes and leeks; place half this mixture in an even layer in prepared baking dish. Season with salt and pepper and top with half each of the mushrooms, Swiss cheese, milk mixture and Parmesan. Repeat layers in the same order. Bake for 1 hour, until Jerusalem artichokes are tender and top is browned and bubbling. **Serves 4.**

Stir-Fried Sesame Asparagus

1 tbsp	canola oil	15 mL
1	small onion, chopped	1
1	clove garlic, minced	1
2	large carrots, cut into 2-inch (5 cm) sticks	2
8 oz	mushrooms, sliced	250 g
1 tbsp	finely chopped gingerroot	15 mL
Pinch	hot pepper flakes	Pinch
1/4 cup	water	50 mL
2 tbsp	soy sauce	25 mL
1 lb	asparagus, trimmed and cut into 2-inch (5 cm) lengths	500 g
2	green onions, thinly sliced	2
1 cup	bean sprouts	250 mL
3 tbsp	toasted sesame seeds	45 mL
1 tbsp	freshly squeezed lime juice	15 mL
1 tsp	dark sesame oil	5 mL

In a wok or large skillet, heat oil over medium high-heat. Stir-fry onion and garlic for 10 seconds. Add carrots, mushrooms, ginger and hot pepper flakes; stir-fry for 1 minute. Add water and soy sauce; bring to a boil. Add asparagus, cover and cook for 3 minutes. Stir in green onions, bean sprouts, sesame seeds, lime juice and sesame oil. **Serves 4.**

Fried Rice with Vegetables

Follow preceding recipe, but add 2 extra-large eggs, beaten, with the onion and garlic, and stir-fry until eggs are set before adding the carrots. Add 3 cups (750 mL) cooked rice after mixture boils, scraping and stir-frying, before adding the asparagus. Serves 4.

Spaghetti Squash with Stir-Fried Vegetables

1	spaghetti squash (about 10 inches/25 cm long)	1
1/4 cup	canola oil	50 mL
3	cloves garlic, minced	3
	Salt and freshly ground black pepper to taste	
	Stir-Fried Sesame Asparagus (see recipe, above)	

Cut stem end off squash, halve lengthwise and scrape out the seeds. In a large pot of boiling water, boil squash until fork-tender, about 20 minutes. Drain and scrape out flesh with a fork. In a large skillet, heat oil over medium-high heat. Sauté squash, garlic, salt and pepper until heated through. Mound on a platter and top with Stir-Fried Sesame Asparagus. **Serves 4 to 6.**

Spaghetti Squash with Artichoke and Mushroom Sauce

1	spaghetti squash (about 10 inches/25 cm long)	1
1/4 cup	extra-virgin olive oil	50 mL
1	clove garlic, minced	1
	Salt and freshly ground black pepper to taste	
1/3 cup	freshly grated Parmesan cheese	75 mL
	Artichoke and Mushroom Sauce (see recipe, page 227)	

Cut stem end off squash, halve lengthwise and scrape out the seeds. In a large pot of boiling water, boil squash until fork-tender, about 20 minutes. Drain and scrape out flesh with a fork. In a large skillet, heat oil over medium-high heat. Sauté squash, garlic, salt and pepper until heated through. Stir in Parmesan. Mound on a platter and top with Artichoke and Mushroom Sauce. **Serves 4.**

Marinated Mozzarella Salad in Tomatoes

2	oil-packed sun-dried tomatoes, drained and minced	2
1	clove garlic, minced	1
1/4 cup	finely chopped fresh basil	50 mL
3 tbsp	extra-virgin olive oil	45 mL
1/4 tsp	hot pepper flakes	1 mL
4	large tomatoes	4
3 cups	shredded mozzarella cheese	750 mL
4	sprigs fresh basil	4

Combine sun-dried tomatoes, garlic, chopped basil, oil and hot pepper flakes. Cut stem ends off tomatoes, scrape out flesh with a small, serrated knife (or a spoon) and remove seeds. Chop tomato flesh and toss with sun-dried tomato mixture and mozzarella. Pack into tomatoes. Serve garnished with basil sprigs. **Serves 4.**

Chilied Corn Salad Stuffed in Roasted Peppers

6	large bell peppers (any color)	6
1	clove garlic, minced	1
3 tbsp	vegetable oil	45 mL
3 tbsp	mayonnaise	45 mL
2 tbsp	chili powder	25 mL
1 tbsp	ground cumin	15 mL
1 tbsp	hot pepper sauce (such as Frank's RedHot)	15 mL
	Salt and freshly ground black pepper to taste	
1	bunch green onions, white part only, sliced	1
1	can (14 to 19 oz/398 to 540 mL) red kidney beans, drained and rinsed	1
3 cups	drained canned corn kernels	750 mL
2 tbsp	chopped fresh cilantro	25 mL

Roast bell peppers (see page 11). (Make sure not to over-roast; the peppers need to be firm to hold their shape for stuffing.) Halve roasted peppers lengthwise and carefully scrape out seeds. Combine garlic, oil, mayonnaise, chili powder, cumin, hot pepper sauce, salt and pepper. Add green onion, beans and corn; toss to coat. Stir in cilantro. Fill pepper halves with corn mixture. **Serves 6.**

Greek Marinated Mushrooms in Artichokes

4	artichokes, trimmed of stems and leaf spines	4
1/4 cup	olive oil	50 mL
1 lb	mushrooms, sliced	500 g
1	clove garlic, minced	1
3	green onions, white part only, thinly sliced	3
	Salt and freshly ground black pepper to taste	
	Juice of 1 large lemon	

In a large pot of boiling salted water, boil artichokes until tender, about 30 minutes; drain and let cool. In a large skillet, heat oil over medium-high heat. Sauté mushrooms until tender. Add garlic and sauté for 30 seconds. Remove from heat and stir in green onions, salt, pepper and lemon juice. Scoop the choke from the center of each artichoke and fill cavities with mushroom mixture. Moisten artichoke leaves with some of the liquid left behind in the pan. **Serves 4.**

Caponata

6 tbsp	olive oil, divided	90 mL
1 lb	eggplant, peeled and diced	500 g
1	large stalk celery, diced	1
1	large onion, chopped	1
1	green bell pepper, diced	1
4	plum (Roma) tomatoes, chopped	4
1 tbsp	minced drained canned anchovies	15 mL
1 tsp	dried basil	5 mL
1/4 tsp	dried oregano	1 mL
1/4 cup	chopped pitted green olives	50 mL
2 tbsp	chopped fresh Italian (flat-leaf) parsley	25 mL
2 tbsp	red wine vinegar	25 mL
1 tbsp	drained capers	15 mL
	Salt and freshly ground black pepper to taste	

In a large skillet, heat 1/4 cup (50 mL) of the oil over medium-high heat. Sauté eggplant until browned on all sides. Add celery, onion and green pepper; sauté until tender. Add tomatoes, anchovies, basil and oregano; sauté until lightly thickened. Remove from heat and stir in olives, parsley, vinegar, the remaining oil, capers, salt and pepper. **Serves 4.** *Serve with crusty bread and sliced provolone cheese.*

Ratatouille

Follow preceding recipe, but replace the green olives with oil-cured black olives, replace the parsley with basil, and add 1 zucchini, sliced, and 1 yellow squash, sliced, with the tomatoes. **Serves 4.**

Marinated Lentil Salad

1/4 cup	extra-virgin olive oil, divided	50 mL
1	large onion, chopped	1
2	bay leaves	2
1	clove garlic, minced	1
8 cups	water	2 L
3 cups	dried brown lentils	750 mL
1/4 tsp	hot pepper flakes	1 mL
	Salt to taste	
3 tbsp	freshly squeezed lemon juice	45 mL
1/2 cup	Dijon Vinaigrette (see recipe, page 61)	125 mL
1/4 cup	chopped fresh Italian (flat-leaf) parsley	50 mL
	Freshly ground black pepper to taste	
12	oil-cured black olives, pitted	12
1	large tomato, cut into wedges	1

In a large skillet, heat half the oil over medium heat. Sauté onion until tender. Add bay leaves, garlic, water, lentils, hot pepper flakes and salt; simmer until lentils are tender, about 1 hour. Drain and stir in lemon juice and the remaining oil; let cool. Toss with vinaigrette, parsley, pepper and additional salt. Discard bay leaves. Cover and refrigerate for about 1 hour, until chilled. Serve garnished with olives and tomato wedges. **Serves 4.** *Store in an airtight container in the refrigerator for up to 4 days.*

White and Black Bean Salad

1	roasted red bell pepper (see page 11), diced	1
2 cups	drained rinsed canned black beans	500 mL
2 cups	drained rinsed canned white beans	500 mL
1/2 cup	Garlic Herb Dressing (see recipe, page 60)	125 mL
1/4 cup	chopped fresh Italian (flat-leaf) parsley	50 mL
1/4 cup	chopped red onion	50 mL
1	large tomato, cut into 8 wedges	1
1/2	lemon, cut into 4 wedges	1/2

Toss together roasted pepper, black beans, white beans, dressing, parsley and onion. Garnish with tomato and lemon. **Serves 4.**

Minted Curried Potatoes

1/4 cup	vegetable oil	50 mL
16	small red-skinned or other boiling potatoes, peeled	16
2 tsp	black mustard seeds	10 mL
1	large onion, finely chopped	1
1	clove garlic, minced	1
1/2 cup	yellow split peas	125 mL
1 tbsp	finely diced gingerroot	15 mL
2 tsp	ground coriander seeds	10 mL
2 tsp	curry powder	10 mL
1 tsp	ground anise seeds	5 mL
1/2 tsp	hot pepper flakes	2 mL
3 cups	water	750 mL
	Salt and freshly ground black pepper to taste	
2 tbsp	dried mint	25 mL
1/2 cup	plain yogurt	125 mL

In a large skillet, heat oil over medium-high heat. Sauté potatoes until browned on all sides. Add mustard seeds and sauté for 10 seconds. Add onion and sauté until tender. Add garlic, peas and ginger; sauté for 1 minute. Add coriander seeds, curry powder, anise seeds and hot pepper flakes; sauté for 1 minute. Add water, salt and pepper; cook for 30 minutes, until peas and potatoes are tender. Add mint, reduce heat and simmer for 5 minutes. Stir in yogurt. **Serves 4.**

Potatoes and Eggplant

Follow preceding recipe, but replace the split peas with 1 lb (500 g) eggplant, peeled and diced, and the mint with chopped fresh cilantro. **Serves 4.**

Cheese Gnocchi with Fresh Tomato Sauce

4 cups	milk	1 L
1 1/4 cups	semolina flour	300 mL
2	extra-large egg yolks	2
1 cup	freshly grated Parmesan cheese, divided	250 mL
1/4 cup	butter, cut into pieces	50 mL
2 tbsp	melted butter	25 mL
	Fresh Tomato Sauce (page 402), heated	

In a large saucepan, heat milk to a simmer. Whisk in flour and simmer, stirring constantly, until mixture becomes thick enough to pull away from the sides of the pan. Remove from heat and beat in egg yolks, 2/3 cup (150 mL) of the Parmesan and butter pieces. Moisten the bottom of a rimmed baking sheet and press milk mixture into a 1/2-inch (1 cm) thick layer. Refrigerate until firm. Preheat oven to 450°F (230°C). Using a 1 1/2-inch (4 cm) round cookie cutter, stamp out circles of dough and place in a buttered 8-cup (2 L) baking dish. Pour melted butter over top and sprinkle with the remaining Parmesan. Bake for 15 minutes, until browned. Top with tomato sauce. **Serves 4.**

Herb Gnocchi with Parmesan and Butter

Follow preceding recipe, but add 1 tbsp (15 mL) finely chopped fresh basil, 1 tbsp (15 mL) finely chopped fresh Italian (flat-leaf) parsley and 1 tsp (5 mL) chopped fresh oregano to the dough with the Parmesan. Omit the tomato sauce. **Serves 4.**

Pizza Rustica

2 tbsp	extra-virgin olive oil	25 mL
8 oz	fresh spinach, chopped in large pieces	250 g
1	clove garlic, minced	1
	Salt and freshly ground black pepper to taste	
3	extra-large eggs, beaten	3
¾ cup	ricotta cheese, drained	175 mL
½ cup	freshly grated Parmesan cheese	125 mL
2 tbsp	chopped onion	25 mL
1 tbsp	chopped fresh Italian (flat-leaf) parsley	15 mL
2	9-inch (23 cm) prepared pastry crusts (store-bought or see recipe, page 21)	2
8 oz	mozzarella cheese, sliced, divided	250 g
1	roasted bell pepper (see page 11), julienned, divided	1

In a large skillet, heat oil over medium-high heat. Add spinach and garlic, reduce heat to medium and cook, covered, until spinach wilts, about 1 minute. Uncover and sauté until dry. Season with salt and pepper; let cool. Meanwhile, preheat oven to 400°F (200°C). Combine spinach mixture, eggs, ricotta, Parmesan, onion and parsley. Line a 9-inch (23 cm) pie pan with 1 pastry crust. Cover with one-third of the mozzarella, half the spinach mixture, another third of the mozzarella and half the roasted pepper. Top with the remaining spinach mixture, mozzarella and roasted pepper. Top with the second pastry crust, crimp the edges and slit the top crust. Bake for 45 minutes, until pastry is browned and filling is bubbling. Let cool on a rack for 30 minutes. Serves 8.

Peasant Pie

3	large potatoes, peeled	3
3 tbsp	butter, divided	45 mL
1	onion, chopped	1
8 oz	mushrooms, sliced	250 g
4 cups	shredded green cabbage (preferably savoy)	1 L
2 tbsp	chopped fresh dill	25 mL
1 tbsp	chopped fresh Italian (flat-leaf) parsley	15 mL
1 tsp	dried basil	5 mL
½ tsp	ground fennel seeds	2 mL
	Salt and freshly ground black pepper to taste	
2	9-inch (23 cm) Cream Cheese Pastry crusts (see recipe, page 20)	2
4 oz	cream cheese, softened	125 g

In a large pot of salted water, boil potatoes until tender, about 30 minutes; drain, slice and set aside. In a large skillet, melt 2 tbsp (25 mL) of the butter over medium heat. Sauté onion, mushrooms, cabbage, dill, parsley, basil and fennel seeds until cabbage is tender and mixture is dry. Season with salt and pepper; let cool. Meanwhile, preheat oven to 400°F (200°C). Line a 9-inch (23 cm) pie pan with 1 pastry crust. Spread cream cheese over the bottom, and top with potatoes and onion mixture. Top with the second pastry crust, crimp the edges and slit the top crust. Bake for 45 minutes, until pastry is browned and filling is bubbling. Let cool on a rack for 30 minutes. Serves 8.

Fontina Fondue with Garlic Roasted Potatoes

2 lbs	russet potatoes, cut into chunks	1 kg
2 tbsp	olive oil	25 mL
1 tsp	garlic salt	5 mL
6 tbsp	water	90 mL
3 tbsp	cornstarch	45 mL
2 tsp	hot pepper sauce (such as Tabasco)	10 mL
1	clove garlic, halved	1
2 cups	dry white wine	500 mL
2 cups	shredded Gruyère cheese	500 mL
2 cups	shredded fontina cheese	500 mL
	Salt to taste	
Pinch	cayenne pepper	Pinch

Preheat oven to 400°F (200°C). Toss together potatoes, oil and garlic salt; place in a roasting pan. Roast for 45 minutes, until potatoes are browned and crisp. Meanwhile, combine water, cornstarch and hot pepper sauce; set aside. Rub the interior of a heavy saucepan with the cut side of the garlic. Add wine and bring to a simmer. Stir cornstarch mixture and add to pot. Bring to a boil, whisking until smooth. Remove from heat and stir in Gruyère and fontina, a handful at a time, until melted (return pot to low heat if the mixture cools and the cheeses stop melting). Season with salt and cayenne. Transfer to a fondue pot (or keep warm in the saucepan) and serve with potatoes and long forks for dipping. Serves 4.

Cheddar Fondue with Apples, Pickles and Toast

Prepare cheese sauce as in the preceding recipe, but replace the wine with beer, and replace the Gruyère and fontina with 4 cups (1 L) shredded sharp Cheddar cheese. Serve with 2 large tart apples, 1 dill pickle, and 1 loaf French bread, all cut into chunks. **Serves 4.**

Leek and Chard Soufflé

¼ cup	butter, divided	50 mL
½ cup	freshly grated Parmesan cheese, plus more for dusting	125 mL
¼ cup	all-purpose flour	50 mL
1¼ cups	hot milk (not fat-free)	300 mL
6	large or extra-large eggs, separated	6
	Salt and freshly ground black pepper to taste	
2 tbsp	olive oil	25 mL
1	large leek, white part only, finely chopped	1
1 lb	Swiss chard, trimmed of tough stems and coarsely chopped	500 g
1	clove garlic, minced	1

Preheat oven to 375°F (190°C). Grease an 8-cup (2 L) soufflé dish with 1 tbsp (15 mL) of the butter and dust with Parmesan. In a large saucepan, melt the remaining butter over medium heat. Stir in flour and cook, stirring, until cooked but not browned, about 2 minutes. Add milk in a slow stream, whisking constantly to remove lumps, and simmer until thick and smooth. Remove from heat and beat in egg yolks, one at a time. Season with salt and pepper; set aside. In a large skillet, heat oil over medium heat. Sauté leek until tender. Add Swiss chard, cover and cook until wilted, about 3 minutes. Add garlic and sauté until mixture is dry. Stir leek mixture and Parmesan into milk mixture. In a large bowl, beat egg whites and a pinch of salt until firm peaks form. Fold into milk mixture in 2 additions. Pour into prepared soufflé dish and bake for 35 to 40 minutes, or until puffed and brown. Serve immediately. **Serves 4.**

Spinach and Feta Soufflé

Follow preceding recipe, but replace the Swiss chard with fresh spinach, and replace the ½ cup (125 mL) Parmesan with 6 oz (175 g) feta cheese, crumbled. (You'll still need a little Parmesan for dusting the soufflé dish, or you can substitute dry bread crumbs.) **Serves 4.**

Tarte Niçoise

1	9-inch (23 cm) tart shell, blind-baked (see pages 12 and 13)	1
⅓ cup	freshly grated Parmesan cheese, divided	75 mL
½ cup	shredded Gruyère cheese	125 mL
1	recipe Ratatouille (page 352)	1
2	extra-large egg yolks, beaten	2
½ cup	milk (not fat-free)	125 mL
	Salt and cayenne pepper to taste	

Preheat oven to 350°F (180°C). Sprinkle the bottom of the tart shell with 1 tbsp (15 mL) of the Parmesan and the Gruyère. Top with Ratatouille. Combine egg yolks, the remaining Parmesan, milk, salt and cayenne until well blended; pour over Ratatouille. Bake for 40 to 45 minutes, until set. Let cool on a rack for 20 minutes. **Serves 6.**

Tarte Lyonnaise

Follow preceding recipe, but instead of the Ratatouille, use 3 large onions, thinly sliced and sautéed in vegetable oil over medium heat for about 15 minutes, or until golden brown and very tender. **Serves 6.**

Chapter 31
Grains
From Rice to Quinoa

Simple Rice Pilaf 357
Curried Rice Pilaf 357
Black Pepper Pilaf 358
Rice Pilaf with Walnuts 358
Low-Salt, Big-Flavor Rice Pilaf 358
Rice and Split Pea Pilaf 358
Sweet Curried Rice with Pistachios 358
Dirty Rice 358
Wild Rice Pilaf 359
Brown Rice Pilaf 359
Brown Rice with Wheat Berries 359
Brown Rice with Toasted Coconut 359
Brown Rice and Vegetable Pilaf 359
Confetti Brown Rice 359
Basmati Rice 360
Lemon or Lime Basmati Rice 360
Fragrant Basmati Rice 360
Risotto 360
Risotto Milanese 360
Spinach Risotto 360
Risotto with Mushrooms
and Chicken Livers 360
Risotto with Rosemary 360
Apple Brandy Raisin Risotto Pudding . . 361
Rice Pudding 361
Brown Rice Pudding 361

Stir-Fried Rice 361
Stir-Fried Rice with Spring Vegetables . . 361
Polenta 362
Fried Polenta with Tomato Sauce 362
Fontina Polenta 362
Polenta with Green Salsa 362
Buttermilk Spoon Bread with Garlic . . . 362
Mascarpone Spoon Bread 362
Quick Cheese Grits 362
Hominy with Peppers 362
Hominy Soufflé 362
Kasha with Onion and Dill 363
Kasha with Tortellini 363
Kasha with Wild Mushrooms 363
Kasha with Walnuts and Garlic 363
Millet Pilaf with Pistachios and Apricots . . 363
Barley Chicken Salad 363
Barley and Sausage Soup 364
Corn Chili Salad 364
Succotash Salad 364
Black Bean and Bulgur Salad with
Orange and Pepperoni 364
Tabbouleh with Lentils 365
Quinoa Tabbouleh 365
Quinoa Pilaf 365
Quinoa with Pecans 365

Grain is basic to every cuisine on earth. It's rice in Asia, millet in Africa, bulgur in the Middle East, semolina in Italy, masa in Mexico, barley in Scotland and a humble slice of wheat bread practically anywhere. Grain is basic to nutrition, yielding necessary fiber, protein and B vitamins with hardly a trace of fat, and it is basic to world agriculture, forming the great bulk of all edible crops.

Yet in America, whole grains are blatantly missing from our diets, and grain cookery remains a mystery. Though doctors and nutritionists chide us to eat more whole grains, few have much advice about how to do it.

The way to proceed is one step at a time — especially if your grain repertoire begins and ends with instant rice. If that's the case, longer-cooking rices, which give better nutrition and more flavor, would make a good second step. Most of the white rice you buy has already been parboiled (enriched or converted) to retain many of the nutrients of the whole grain. Long-grain white rice takes only 15 to 20 minutes to prepare — untended — and, so long as you don't stir it, there is little danger that it will get sticky. For more flavor with no more work, use chicken broth in place of water, or add soy sauce, onion or garlic to the liquid.

After that, try basmati or jasmine rice. These Asian rices have a redolent floral perfume that makes them flavorful even when cooked in water alone, and they need only 15 minutes to cook. Unlike other white rices, though, they need to be washed to remove surface starch that can produce off-flavors and cause stickiness. Wash rice in several changes of cold water until the water runs clear.

Making pilaf is another way to ensure that grains aren't stuck together. With pilafs, raw rice is tossed with melted butter or oil so that each grain gets a thin coating. The coating keeps one grain of rice from clinging to another as it softens, resulting in exceptionally fluffy, and separate, rice grains. Once you have mastered white rice pilaf, try the same technique with brown or wild rices. These take longer to cook but provide added nutrition and a rich nutty flavor that white rice can't match.

Next, move on to risotto, the exquisitely creamy rice concoction from Venice and Milan, and from there try less conventional grains, such as millet, bulgur, barley, cornmeal, buckwheat or sorghum.

If you are unfamiliar with quinoa (pronounced keen-WAH), you should really get acquainted. Quinoa is a small, round seed that resembles a tiny, pale lentil. It cooks in less than 15 minutes, during which time it doubles in size and sprouts a tiny curled thread. This appearance, along with its high protein content and delicate flavor, make it one of the most interesting ingredients at market. Be sure to rinse quinoa thoroughly; it is coated with a natural bitter alkaloid that must be removed by rinsing.

Grains can be kept in bulk indefinitely under refrigeration, or for several months tightly covered in a cool, dark cupboard. Avoid exposing grains to light, which can destroy some of their B vitamins, and keep them away from heat and humidity, which cause grains to ferment.

About these recipes . . .

Many of the recipes in this chapter are simmered in a covered saucepan, and it is important to ensure that the lid fits tightly so that the liquid absorbs into the grain, rather than evaporating. It is assumed that you will add salt and pepper to taste at the end of cooking.

Simple Rice Pilaf

1 tbsp	butter	15 mL
¼ cup	finely chopped onion	50 mL
1 cup	long-grain white rice	250 mL
2 cups	chicken broth	500 mL
	Salt and freshly ground black pepper to taste	

In a saucepan, melt butter over medium heat. Sauté onion until tender. Add rice, stirring to coat with butter. Add broth, salt and pepper, stirring briefly to moisten rice. Bring to a boil, reduce heat, cover and simmer for 15 to 20 minutes, or until liquid is absorbed and rice is tender. (Do not stir rice when checking for doneness.) Remove from heat and let stand, covered, for 5 minutes. Fluff with a fork.
Serves 4 to 6.

Curried Rice Pilaf

Follow preceding recipe, but add one 1-inch (2.5 cm) cinnamon stick, ½ tsp (2 mL) curry powder, ¼ tsp (1 mL) ground cumin, ¼ tsp (1 mL) freshly ground black pepper and a pinch of ground cloves with the onion. Discard cinnamon stick before fluffing rice.
Serves 4 to 6.

Black Pepper Pilaf

Follow recipe for Simple Rice Pilaf (page 357), but add 1 bay leaf and 2 tsp (10 mL) coarsely ground black pepper with the onion. Discard bay leaf before fluffing rice. Toss 1 tbsp (15 mL) freshly squeezed lemon juice with the rice while fluffing. Serves 4 to 6.

Rice Pilaf with Walnuts

Follow recipe for Simple Rice Pilaf (page 357), but while rice is cooking, toast $\frac{1}{3}$ cup (75 mL) chopped walnuts in 1 tbsp (15 mL) walnut oil. Toss with the rice while fluffing. Serves 4 to 6.

Low-Salt, Big-Flavor Rice Pilaf

1 tbsp	dark sesame oil, divided	15 mL
$\frac{1}{3}$ cup	chopped onion	75 mL
1	stalk celery, chopped	1
1	clove garlic, minced	1
Pinch	hot pepper flakes	Pinch
1 cup	long-grain white rice	250 mL
1	bay leaf	1
2 cups	reduced-sodium chicken broth	500 mL
$\frac{1}{4}$ cup	toasted sliced almonds	50 mL

In a saucepan, heat 2 tsp (10 mL) of the oil over low heat. Sauté onion, celery, garlic and hot pepper flakes until onion and celery are tender. Add rice, stirring to coat with oil. Add bay leaf and broth, stirring briefly to moisten rice. Cover and simmer for 15 to 20 minutes, or until liquid is absorbed and rice is tender. (Do not stir rice when checking for doneness.) Remove from heat and let stand, covered, for 5 minutes. Discard bay leaf. Fluff with a fork and toss with the remaining oil and almonds. Serves 4 to 6.

Rice and Split Pea Pilaf

3 cups	salted water	750 mL
$\frac{1}{2}$ cup	split peas	125 mL
1 tbsp	butter	15 mL
$\frac{1}{4}$ cup	finely chopped onion	50 mL
1 tsp	curry powder	5 mL
$\frac{1}{2}$ tsp	ground cumin	2 mL
$\frac{1}{2}$ tsp	coarsely ground black pepper	2 mL
1 cup	long-grain white rice	250 mL
4 cups	chicken or vegetable broth	1 L
	Salt to taste	

Bring water to a boil. Add peas and cook for 20 minutes, until barely tender; drain and set aside. In a large saucepan, melt butter over medium heat.

Sauté onion until tender. Add curry powder, cumin and pepper; sauté for 30 seconds. Add rice, stirring to coat with butter. Add peas, broth, salt and additional pepper, stirring briefly to moisten rice. Bring to a boil, reduce heat, cover and simmer for 15 to 20 minutes, or until liquid is absorbed and peas and rice are tender. (Do not stir rice when checking for doneness.) Remove from heat and let stand, covered, for 5 minutes. Fluff with a fork. Serves 4 to 6.

Sweet Curried Rice with Pistachios

1 tbsp	butter	15 mL
$\frac{1}{4}$ cup	finely chopped onion	50 mL
1	cinnamon stick (1 inch/2.5 cm)	1
$\frac{1}{2}$ tsp	curry powder	2 mL
$\frac{1}{4}$ tsp	ground cardamom	1 mL
Pinch	ground cloves	Pinch
1 cup	long-grain white rice	250 mL
2 cups	water	500 mL
	Salt and freshly ground black pepper to taste	
2 tbsp	peanut oil	25 mL
$\frac{1}{4}$ cup	chopped raisins	50 mL
$\frac{1}{4}$ cup	chopped pistachios	50 mL
2 tbsp	granulated sugar	25 mL

In a saucepan, melt butter over medium heat. Sauté onion until tender. Add cinnamon stick, curry powder, cardamom and cloves; sauté for 30 seconds. Add rice, stirring to coat with butter. Add water, salt and pepper, stirring briefly to moisten rice. Bring to a boil, reduce heat, cover and simmer for 15 to 20 minutes, or until liquid is absorbed and rice is tender. (Do not stir rice when checking for doneness.) Remove from heat and let stand, covered, for 5 minutes. Meanwhile, in a small skillet, heat oil over low heat. Sauté raisins and pistachios until raisins are plump and nuts are toasted; stir in sugar. Toss with rice while fluffing with a fork. Serves 4 to 6.

Dirty Rice

3 tbsp	canola oil	45 mL
8 oz	chicken giblets, finely chopped	250 g
8 oz	chicken livers, finely chopped	250 g
1	large onion, chopped	1
1	bell pepper (any color), finely diced	1
$\frac{1}{2}$ cup	chopped celery	125 mL
1 cup	long-grain white rice	250 mL
	Salt and freshly ground black pepper to taste	
$2\frac{1}{2}$ cups	hot chicken broth	625 mL

In a saucepan, heat oil over medium-high heat. Sauté giblets, livers, onion, bell pepper and celery until lightly browned. Add rice, salt and pepper, stirring to coat rice with oil. Add broth, stirring briefly to moisten rice. Bring to a boil, reduce heat, cover and simmer for 20 to 25 minutes, or until liquid is absorbed, giblets are cooked through and rice is tender. Remove from heat and let stand, covered, for 5 minutes. Fluff with a fork. **Serves 4 to 6.**

Wild Rice Pilaf

1 cup	wild rice	250 mL
2 tbsp	butter	25 mL
½ cup	finely chopped onion	125 mL
⅓ cup	finely diced mushrooms	75 mL
4 cups	beef broth	1 L
	Salt to taste	
1 tbsp	chopped fresh Italian (flat-leaf) parsley	15 mL

Wash rice in several changes of cold water, drain well and set aside. In a saucepan, melt butter over medium heat. Sauté onion and mushrooms until tender. Add rice, stirring to coat with butter. Add broth and salt, stirring briefly to moisten rice. Bring to a boil, reduce heat, cover and simmer for 45 to 60 minutes, or until rice grains burst. Remove from heat and let stand, covered, for 5 minutes. Fluff with a fork and stir in parsley. **Serves 4 to 6.**

Brown Rice Pilaf

1 cup	long-grain brown rice	250 mL
2 tbsp	butter	25 mL
½ cup	finely chopped onion	125 mL
⅓ cup	finely diced mushrooms	75 mL
3 cups	water or broth (chicken, vegetable or beef)	750 mL
	Salt to taste	
1 tbsp	chopped fresh Italian (flat-leaf) parsley	15 mL

Wash rice in several changes of cold water, drain well and set aside. In a saucepan, melt butter over medium heat. Sauté onion and mushrooms until tender. Add rice, stirring to coat with butter. Add water and salt, stirring briefly to moisten rice. Bring to a boil, reduce heat, cover and simmer for 40 to 45 minutes, or until liquid is absorbed and rice is tender. Remove from heat and let stand, covered, for 5 minutes. Fluff with a fork and stir in parsley. **Serves 4 to 6.**

Brown Rice with Wheat Berries

Follow preceding recipe, but reduce the rice to ¾ cup (175 mL), and add ¼ cup (50 mL) whole wheat berries with the rice. **Serves 4 to 6.**

Brown Rice with Toasted Coconut

Follow recipe for Brown Rice Pilaf (left), but omit the mushrooms, and add 1 cup (250 mL) unsweetened shredded coconut with the onions; sauté until onions and coconut are browned (watch coconut carefully to make sure it doesn't burn). Add 1 cup (250 mL) shredded carrot and 1 tbsp (15 mL) finely grated orange zest with the rice. **Serves 4 to 6.**

Brown Rice and Vegetable Pilaf

Follow recipe for Brown Rice Pilaf (left), but make this addition: Sauté 1 cup (250 mL) diced vegetables (such as zucchini, celery, eggplant, carrot, red bell pepper, corn, green beans, peas) in 2 tbsp (25 mL) butter until tender. Add to rice for the last 15 minutes of cooking, but do not stir in until fluffing. **Serves 4 to 6.**

Confetti Brown Rice

1 cup	long-grain brown rice	250 mL
3 cups	water	750 mL
¼ cup	minced onion	50 mL
1 tbsp	currants	15 mL
1½ tsp	soy sauce	7 mL
½ tsp	curry powder	2 mL
½ tsp	salt	2 mL
1 tbsp	vegetable oil	15 mL
2 tbsp	finely chopped green onion	25 mL
2 tbsp	finely chopped green bell pepper	25 mL
2 tbsp	finely chopped tomato	25 mL
2 tbsp	sliced toasted almonds	25 mL
1 tbsp	chopped fresh Italian (flat-leaf) parsley	15 mL

Wash rice in several changes of cold water; drain well. In a saucepan, bring rice, water, onion, currants, soy sauce, curry powder and salt to a boil. Reduce heat, cover and simmer for 40 to 45 minutes, or until liquid is absorbed and rice is tender. Remove from heat and let stand, covered, for 5 minutes. Meanwhile, in a small skillet, heat oil over medium heat. Sauté green onion, green pepper and tomato until tender. Fluff rice with a fork and toss with green onion mixture, almonds and parsley. **Serves 4 to 6.**

Basmati Rice

1 cup	basmati rice	250 mL
1¾ cups	water	425 mL
	Salt to taste	
2 tbsp	butter	25 mL

Wash rice in several changes of cold water until water runs clear. Bring water and salt to a boil. Stir in rice, reduce heat, cover and simmer for 15 minutes, until water is absorbed and rice is tender. Remove from heat and let stand, covered, for 5 minutes. Fluff with a fork and mix in butter. **Serves 4 to 6.**

Lemon or Lime Basmati Rice

Follow preceding recipe, but while cooked rice is standing, in small skillet melt 1 tbsp (15 mL) butter over medium-high heat. Toast ½ cup (125 mL) pine nuts and ½ tsp (2 mL) curry powder. Toss with the cooked rice, along with 2 tbsp (25 mL) freshly squeezed lemon or lime juice. **Serves 4 to 6.**

Fragrant Basmati Rice

1 cup	basmati rice	250 mL
1 tbsp	butter	15 mL
¼ cup	finely chopped onion	50 mL
1	cinnamon stick (1 inch/2.5 cm)	1
½ tsp	curry powder	2 mL
¼ tsp	ground cumin	1 mL
¼ tsp	freshly ground black pepper	1 mL
Pinch	ground cloves	Pinch
1¾ cups	chicken broth	425 mL
1 tsp	freshly squeezed lemon juice	5 mL
	Salt to taste	
2 tbsp	chopped fresh cilantro	25 mL

Wash rice in several changes of cold water until water runs clear; set aside. In a saucepan, melt butter over medium heat. Sauté onion until tender. Add cinnamon stick, curry powder, cumin, pepper and cloves; sauté for 30 seconds. Add rice, stirring to coat with butter. Add broth, lemon juice and salt, stirring briefly to moisten rice. Bring to a boil, reduce heat, cover and simmer for 15 to 20 minutes, or until liquid is absorbed and rice is tender. Remove from heat and let stand, covered, for 5 minutes. Fluff with a fork and stir in cilantro. **Serves 4 to 6.**

Risotto

2 tbsp	olive oil	25 mL
¼ cup	finely chopped onion	50 mL
1 cup	Arborio rice	250 mL
½ cup	dry white wine	125 mL
4½ cups	chicken broth	1.125 mL
¼ cup	freshly grated Parmesan cheese	50 mL
1 tbsp	butter	15 mL

In a large saucepan, heat oil over medium heat. Sauté onion until tender. Add rice, stirring to coat with oil. Add wine and cook, stirring constantly with a wooden spoon, until wine is absorbed. Add broth, ½ cup (125 mL) at a time, and cook, stirring occasionally, until each addition is absorbed before stirring in the next. When finished, rice should be al dente, with a creamy sauce developed throughout. Stir in Parmesan cheese and butter. Serve immediately. **Serves 4 to 6.**

Risotto Milanese

Follow preceding recipe, but soften 1 tsp (5 mL) saffron threads in the wine for 10 minutes before adding it. **Serves 4 to 6.**

Spinach Risotto

Follow recipe for Risotto (left), but first, in a large saucepan, heat 3 tbsp (45 mL) olive oil over medium heat. Sauté 1 package (10 oz/300 g) frozen chopped spinach and ¼ cup (50 mL) chopped onion until spinach is thawed and onion is tender, about 10 minutes. Add 1 clove garlic, minced, and sauté until mixture is almost dry; set aside. Add spinach mixture to rice with the last addition of broth. **Serves 4 to 6.**

Risotto with Mushrooms and Chicken Livers

Follow recipe for Risotto (left), but increase the onion to 1 cup (250 mL) and add 2 cloves garlic, minced, with the onion; sauté until browned. While rice is cooking, in a small saucepan, heat another 2 tbsp (25 mL) olive oil over medium-high heat. Sauté 1 lb (500 g) chicken livers, trimmed and quartered, and 4 oz (125 g) mushrooms, sliced. Toss liver mixture with rice when you add the Parmesan. **Serves 4 to 6.**

Risotto with Rosemary

Follow recipe for Risotto (left), but add 2 tsp (10 mL) dried rosemary, crumbled, and 1 tsp (5 mL) dried thyme with the onion. Add 1 small clove garlic, minced, with the Parmesan. **Serves 4 to 6.**

Apple Brandy Raisin Risotto Pudding

¼ cup	butter	50 mL
1	large tart apple, peeled and diced	1
1 cup	Arborio rice	250 mL
½ cup	brandy	125 mL
1 cup	unsweetened apple cider, divided	250 mL
1	cinnamon stick (1 inch/2.5 cm)	1
2 tbsp	granulated sugar	25 mL
1 tbsp	finely grated orange zest	15 mL
2½ cups	milk (not fat-free)	625 mL
2	large or extra-large egg yolks, beaten	2
½ cup	cream (any type, minimum 10%)	125 mL
1 tsp	vanilla	5 mL
½ cup	raisins	125 mL

In a large saucepan, melt butter over medium heat. Sauté apple until tender. Add rice, stirring to coat with butter. Add brandy and cook, stirring constantly with a wooden spoon, until brandy is absorbed. Add half the cider and cook, stirring constantly, until absorbed; repeat with the remaining cider. Stir in cinnamon stick, sugar and orange zest. Add milk, ½ cup (125 mL) at a time, and cook, stirring occasionally, until each addition is absorbed before stirring in the next. Combine egg yolks, cream and vanilla; add to rice, along with raisins, when the last addition of milk is almost absorbed. Remove from heat and stir until mixture is incorporated. Discard cinnamon stick. Serve warm. **Serves 4 to 6.**

Rice Pudding

4 cups	water	1 L
½ cup	medium-grain white rice	125 mL
4 cups	milk (not fat-free, and preferably whole)	1 L
1	vanilla bean	1
½ cup	raisins	125 mL
½ cup	granulated sugar	125 mL
2 tsp	finely grated orange zest	10 mL
3	extra-large egg yolks	3
½ cup	cream (any type, minimum 10%)	125 mL
1 tbsp	butter	15 mL

In a large saucepan, over medium-high heat, bring water and rice to a boil. Boil for 10 minutes; drain well. In the same saucepan, scald milk over medium-low heat just until bubbles form around the edge. Add rice and bring to a simmer. Add vanilla bean, raisins, sugar and orange zest; cover and simmer for 40 minutes, until rice is tender. Combine egg yolks and cream; add to rice and simmer, stirring frequently, for 15 minutes. Discard vanilla bean and stir in butter. Pour into individual dishes, cover and refrigerate for about 2 hours, or until firm. **Serves 4 to 6.**

Brown Rice Pudding

Follow preceding recipe, but replace the white rice with brown rice; parboil for 25 minutes instead of 10. **Serves 4 to 6.**

Stir-Fried Rice

2 tbsp	canola oil, divided	25 mL
1	stalk celery, diced	1
½	red bell pepper, diced	½
¼ cup	finely chopped onion	50 mL
1	extra-large egg, beaten	1
4 oz	shrimp, peeled, deveined and chopped	125 g
4 oz	ham, diced	125 g
3 cups	cooked rice	750 mL
2	green onions, chopped	2
1 cup	bean sprouts	250 mL
½ cup	shredded fresh spinach	125 mL

In a wok, heat half the oil over medium-high heat until smoking. Stir-fry celery, red pepper and onion until tender. Push vegetables up the sides of the wok, add remaining oil in the center, and stir-fry egg until set, chopping and turning to cut egg into shreds as it sets. Push egg into the vegetables. Add shrimp and ham to the center of the wok, and stir-fry for 1 minute. Add rice and mix everything together, pushing the mixture against the sides of the wok to help the rice brown and get crusty as it is stir-fried. When mixture is speckled with brown bits, stir in green onions, bean sprouts and spinach; heat through. **Serves 4 to 6.**

Stir-Fried Rice with Spring Vegetables

Follow preceding recipe, but replace the shrimp and ham with 8 oz (250 g) asparagus tips and 1 cup (250 mL) cooked peas, and replace the spinach with finely chopped tomato. **Serves 4 to 6.**

Polenta

5 cups	cold water	1.25 L
1 cup	stone-ground cornmeal	250 mL
1½ tsp	salt	7 mL
¼ cup	freshly grated Parmesan cheese	50 mL
3 tbsp	butter	45 mL
	Freshly ground black pepper to taste	

In a large, heavy saucepan, bring water, cornmeal and salt to a boil over medium heat, stirring constantly. Reduce heat and simmer for 20 minutes, stirring occasionally, until mixture is very thick and smooth and pulls away from the sides of the pan. Stir in Parmesan, butter and pepper. **Serves 4 to 6.**

Fried Polenta with Tomato Sauce

Follow preceding recipe. When polenta is finished, pour into a ½-inch (1 cm) thick layer on a rimmed baking sheet. Refrigerate until set, then cut into 2-inch (5 cm) squares or diamonds. In a large skillet, heat a thin film of olive oil over medium-high heat. Cook polenta squares, in batches, until browned on both sides, then blot with paper towels. Serve with Quick Fresh Tomato Sauce (page 225). **Serves 4 to 6.**

Fontina Polenta

Follow recipe for Polenta (above), but omit the Parmesan, and stir in 1¼ cups (300 mL) shredded fontina cheese with the butter. **Serves 4 to 6.**

Polenta with Green Salsa

Follow recipe for Polenta (above), but omit the Parmesan, and stir in 6 oz (175 g) queso fresca or farmer's cheese with the butter. Serve with Spicy Green Tomato Salsa (page 176). **Serves 4 to 6.**

Buttermilk Spoon Bread with Garlic

3	cloves garlic, minced	3
1½ cups	cold water	375 mL
1 cup	white cornmeal	250 mL
1	extra-large egg, beaten	1
1 cup	buttermilk	250 mL
½ cup	cream (any type, minimum 10%)	125 mL
1½ tbsp	butter, divided	22 mL
1 tsp	baking soda	5 mL
½ tsp	salt	2 mL

Preheat oven to 350°F (180°C) and place a 6-cup (1.5 L) soufflé dish in the oven. In a large saucepan, bring garlic, water and cornmeal to a boil over medium heat, stirring constantly. Reduce heat and simmer for 10 minutes, stirring occasionally.

Remove from heat and stir in egg, buttermilk, cream, 1 tbsp (15 mL) of the butter, baking soda and salt. Remove soufflé dish from oven, grease with the remaining butter and pour in batter. Bake for about 50 minutes, until puffed and brown. Serve immediately. **Serves 4 to 6.**

Mascarpone Spoon Bread

Follow preceding recipe, but replace the buttermilk with mascarpone cheese. **Serves 4 to 6.**

Quick Cheese Grits

3 cups	water	750 mL
	Salt to taste	
¾ cup	quick-cooking grits	175 mL
¾ cup	shredded Cheddar cheese	175 mL
1 tbsp	butter	15 mL
	Freshly ground black pepper to taste	

In a saucepan, bring water and salt to a simmer over medium heat. Add grits in a thin stream, stirring constantly, and simmer for 10 minutes, stirring occasionally, until thick and light. Stir in cheese, butter and pepper. **Serves 4 to 6.**

Hominy with Peppers

Follow preceding recipe, but omit the cheese and butter. While grits are simmering, in a skillet, melt ¼ cup (50 mL) butter over medium heat. Sauté 1 cup (250 mL) diced green bell pepper, ½ cup (125 mL) diced red bell pepper and ¼ onion, chopped, until tender. Stir in a dash of hot pepper sauce (such as Tabasco) and salt and freshly ground black pepper to taste. **Serves 4 to 6.**

Hominy Soufflé

¼ cup	butter, divided	50 mL
1 cup	quick-cooking grits, divided	250 mL
3 cups	water	750 mL
	Salt to taste	
3	green onions, sliced	3
1 cup	diced green bell pepper	250 mL
1 cup	diced baked ham	250 mL
½ cup	diced roasted red bell pepper (see page 11)	125 mL
3	eggs, separated	3
¾ cup	shredded Cheddar cheese	175 mL
Dash	hot-pepper sauce (such as Tabasco)	Dash
	Freshly ground black pepper to taste	

Preheat oven to 375°F (190°C). Grease a 6-cup (1.5 L) soufflé dish with 1 tbsp (15 mL) of the butter and dust with ¼ cup (50 mL) of the grits. In a saucepan, bring water and salt to a simmer over medium heat. Add the remaining grits in a thin stream, stirring constantly, and simmer for 10 minutes, stirring occasionally, until thick and light. Meanwhile, in a large skillet, melt the remaining butter over medium heat. Sauté green onions and green pepper until tender. Stir in ham and roasted pepper, then stir mixture into cooked grits. Beat in egg yolks, cheese, hot pepper sauce, pepper and additional salt. Beat egg whites to soft peaks, then fold into grits in 2 additions. Pour into prepared soufflé dish and bake for 30 minutes, until puffed and brown but still creamy in the center. Serve immediately. **Serves 4 to 6.**

Kasha with Onion and Dill

1	egg, beaten	1
1 cup	whole or coarsely cracked kasha	250 mL
2 tbsp	olive oil	25 mL
1/2 cup	chopped onion	125 mL
2 cups	chicken broth	500 mL
	Salt and freshly ground black pepper to taste	
1 tbsp	minced fresh dill	15 mL

In a small bowl, combine egg and kasha. Heat a large, heavy skillet over medium-high heat. Add kasha mixture and cook until grains separate; scrape back into the bowl. Wipe out skillet, add oil and heat over medium-high heat. Sauté onion until tender. Return kasha to the pan and add broth, salt and pepper; reduce heat, cover and simmer for 15 minutes, or until liquid is absorbed. Stir in dill. **Serves 4 to 6.**

Kasha with Tortellini

Follow preceding recipe, but replace the dill with parsley, and toss the cooked kasha with 2 cups (500 mL) cooked cheese or spinach tortellini. **Serves 6.**

Kasha with Wild Mushrooms

Follow recipe for Kasha with Onion and Dill (above), but first soak 1 oz (30 g) dried wild or exotic mushrooms in 1/2 cup (125 mL) boiling water for 30 minutes. Remove mushrooms and squeeze out excess water. Trim off stems and slice larger mushrooms. Strain soaking liquid through a coffee filter. Add mushrooms with the onion, and use the strained soaking liquid to replace a like amount of chicken broth. **Serves 6.**

Kasha with Walnuts and Garlic

Follow recipe for Kasha with Onion and Dill (left), but add 2 cloves garlic, minced, with the onion, and add 1/2 cup (125 mL) toasted walnut pieces with the dill. **Serves 6.**

Millet Pilaf with Pistachios and Apricots

3 tbsp	peanut oil	45 mL
1/4 cup	minced onion	50 mL
1/4 cup	diced dried apricots	50 mL
1 cup	millet	250 mL
3 cups	hot chicken broth	750 mL
	Salt and freshly ground black pepper to taste	
1/4 cup	toasted chopped pistachios	50 mL

In a heavy saucepan, heat oil over medium heat. Sauté onion and apricots until tender. Add millet and sauté until lightly toasted. Add broth, salt and pepper; bring to a simmer. Reduce heat, cover and simmer for 15 minutes, until liquid is absorbed and millet is tender. Fluff with a fork and stir in pistachios. **Serves 4 to 6.**

Barley Chicken Salad

6 cups	water	1.5 L
	Salt to taste	
1 cup	pearl barley	250 mL
2 lbs	boneless skinless chicken breasts	1 kg
3	stalks celery, diced	3
1 cup	chopped walnuts	250 mL
1 cup	mayonnaise	250 mL
2 tbsp	tarragon vinegar	25 mL
2 tsp	dried tarragon	10 mL
1 tsp	brown mustard	5 mL
	Freshly ground black pepper to taste	

In a large pot, bring water and 1/2 tsp (2 mL) salt to a boil. Add barley, reduce heat, cover and simmer for 20 minutes. Add chicken, cover and simmer for 20 minutes, until chicken is no longer pink inside and barley is tender. Drain, cut chicken into bite-size pieces and place in a serving bowl with barley, celery and walnuts. Whisk together mayonnaise, vinegar, tarragon, mustard, pepper and additional salt; pour over salad and toss to coat. **Serves 6 to 8.**

Barley and Sausage Soup

¼ cup	butter	50 mL
2	large onions, chopped	2
¼ cup	sliced mushrooms	50 mL
½ cup	pearl barley	125 mL
2	cloves garlic, minced	2
4 oz	smoked sausage, sliced	125 g
4 oz	smoked ham, diced	125 g
6 cups	chicken broth	1.5 L
1 cup	canned diced tomatoes, drained	250 mL
2 tbsp	chopped fresh dill	25 mL
2 tbsp	chopped fresh Italian (flat-leaf) parsley	25 mL
½ cup	sour cream	125 mL
	Salt and freshly ground black pepper to taste	

In a large saucepan, melt butter over medium heat. Sauté onion and mushrooms until browned. Add barley, stirring to coat with butter. Add garlic, sausage, ham, broth, tomatoes, dill and parsley; reduce heat, cover and simmer until barley is tender, about 40 minutes. Stir in sour cream, salt and pepper. **Serves 4 to 6.**

Corn Chili Salad

⅓ cup	canola oil	75 mL
2 tbsp	chili powder	25 mL
1 tbsp	ground cumin	15 mL
3 tbsp	mayonnaise	45 mL
2 tbsp	hot pepper sauce (such as Frank's RedHot)	25 mL
1	bunch green onions, thinly sliced	1
1	roasted red bell pepper (see page 11), diced	1
1	avocado, diced	1
1	can (14 to 19 oz/398 to 540 mL) red kidney beans, drained and rinsed	1
4 cups	drained canned corn kernels	1 L
2 tbsp	chopped fresh cilantro	25 mL

Whisk together oil, chili powder, cumin, mayonnaise and hot pepper sauce. Add the remaining ingredients and toss to coat. **Serves 4 to 6.**

Succotash Salad

6 tbsp	corn oil	90 mL
¼ cup	cider vinegar	50 mL
3 tbsp	light corn syrup	45 mL
2 tsp	brown mustard	10 mL
	Salt and freshly ground black pepper to taste	
2 cups	drained canned corn kernels	500 mL
2 cups	frozen lima beans, thawed	500 mL
2 cups	diced ham	500 mL
¼ cup	minced sweet pickles	50 mL

Whisk together oil, vinegar, corn syrup, mustard, salt and pepper. Add the remaining ingredients and toss to coat. **Serves 4 to 6.**

Black Bean and Bulgur Salad with Orange and Pepperoni

1 cup	bulgur	250 mL
1¼ cups	hot water	300 mL
	Finely grated zest and juice of 1 large orange	
⅓ cup	vegetable oil	75 mL
¼ cup	cider vinegar	50 mL
	Salt and freshly ground black pepper to taste	
2 cups	canned black beans, drained and rinsed	500 mL
½	onion, finely chopped	½
1	small chili pepper, minced	1
1	cucumber, peeled, seeded and diced	1
4 oz	pepperoni, finely diced	125 g

Soak bulgur in water until tender, about 15 minutes; drain. Whisk together orange zest, orange juice, oil, vinegar, salt and pepper. Add bulgur and the remaining ingredients; toss to coat. Cover and refrigerate for several hours to mingle flavors. **Serves 4 to 6.**

Tabbouleh with Lentils

1 cup	dried brown lentils	250 mL
5 cups	water, divided	1.25 mL
¾ cup	medium-grain bulgur, rinsed thoroughly	175 mL
½ tsp	salt	2 mL
Pinch	ground allspice	Pinch
3	green onions, finely chopped	3
2	cloves garlic, minced	2
1	cucumber, peeled, seeded and diced	1
1 cup	diced seeded tomato	250 mL
¼ cup	chopped fresh mint	50 mL
¼ cup	chopped fresh Italian (flat-leaf) parsley	50 mL
¼ cup	freshly squeezed lemon juice	50 mL
¼ cup	olive oil	50 mL
	Lettuce leaves	
	Lemon wedges	

Boil lentils in 4 cups (1 L) of the water for 40 minutes; drain. Combine bulgur and lentils in a large bowl. Bring the remaining water, salt and allspice to a boil; add to bulgur mixture and let stand until water is absorbed. Toss with green onions, garlic, cucumber, tomato, mint, parsley, lemon juice and olive oil. Serve on lettuce leaves, garnished with lemon wedges. **Serves 4 to 6.**

Quinoa Tabbouleh

2 cups	water	500 mL
1 cup	quinoa, rinsed in several changes of water	250 mL
¼ tsp	salt	1 mL
⅓ cup	extra-virgin olive oil	75 mL
3 tbsp	freshly squeezed lemon juice	45 mL
6	green onions, thinly sliced	6
2	tomatoes, seeded and chopped	2
1	cucumber, peeled, seeded and diced	1
1	clove garlic, minced	1
2 tbsp	chopped fresh mint	25 mL

In a saucepan, bring water, quinoa and salt to a simmer; cover and simmer for 12 to 14 minutes, or until water is absorbed and quinoa is tender. Spread out on a baking sheet and let cool. Toss quinoa with oil and lemon juice, separating clumps with your fingers. Toss with the remaining ingredients. **Serves 4 to 6.**

Quinoa Pilaf

1½ tbsp	canola oil	22 mL
2 tbsp	minced onion	25 mL
2 tbsp	diced celery	25 mL
2 tbsp	diced carrot	25 mL
1 cup	quinoa, rinsed in several changes of water	250 mL
2 cups	hot vegetable or chicken broth	500 mL
	Salt and freshly ground black pepper to taste	

In a heavy saucepan, heat oil over medium heat. Sauté onion, celery and carrot until tender. Add quinoa and cook, stirring, until grains separate. Add broth, salt and pepper; bring to a simmer. Reduce heat, cover and simmer for about 20 minutes, or until liquid is absorbed and quinoa is tender. Fluff with a fork. **Serves 4 to 6.**

Quinoa with Pecans

Follow preceding recipe, but omit the carrot. While quinoa is simmering, in a skillet, melt 2 tbsp (25 mL) butter over high heat. Toast ¼ cup (50 mL) chopped pecans. Stir into quinoa after fluffing. **Serves 4 to 6.**

Chapter 32
Greens
Spinach, Kale, Endives and Cabbages

Spinach Waldorf Salad 367

Warm Spinach Salad with
Chicken Livers 368

Watercress and Spinach Caesar Salad . . 368

Ruby Salad 368

Spinach Orzo Soup 368

Spinach and Wild Mushroom Soup 368

Garlic Spinach 369

Spinach with Mushrooms 369

Spinach with Lemon and Parsley 369

Spinach with Capers 369

Ricotta Creamed Spinach 369

Creamed Spinach with Herb Cheese . . 369

Spinach with Warm Bacon Dressing . . . 369

Spinach with Roasted Peppers
and Green Peppercorns 369

Cream of Spinach Soup 369

Spinach Pilaf 369

Spinach with Feta and Olives 370

Prosciutto and Fennel Spinach 370

Spiced Spinach 370

Spinach, Corn and Tomatoes 370

Creamed Spinach with
Wild Mushrooms 370

Stir-Fried Spinach with Pine Nuts 370

Spinach Strudel with
Tomato Vinaigrette 371

Stir-Fried Shrimp with Spinach 371

Stir-Fried Spinach with Hoisin Walnuts . . 371

Spinach Pasta 371

Spinach Timbales 372

Spinach and Blue Cheese Custard 372

Spinach Parmesan Soufflé 372

Broccoli Rabe Soufflé 372

Broccoli Rabe with Garlic and Olive Oil . . 372

Broccoli Rabe with Raisins
and Pine Nuts 372

Kale with Sausage and Apple 373

Fried Kale 373

Kale Smothered with
Bacon and Onions 373

Braised Belgian Endive 373

Braised Endive with Ham 373

Wilted Chicory 373

Sautéed Spring Greens 374

Sautéed Bitter Greens with
Sweet Pepper Vinaigrette 374

Gratin of Chard 374

Gratin of Spinach 374

Chard with Chorizo 374

Chilled Watercress Soup 374

Watercress Cream Sauce 375

Sweet Apple Sauerkraut 375

Caraway Sauerkraut 375

Brussels Sprouts Simmered in Milk 375

Brussels Sprouts Sautéed with
Bacon and Apples 375

Stir-Fried Brussels Sprouts 375

Spinach is a culinary litmus test, distinguishing Popeye from Brutus and an inspired cook from a kitchen hack every time it's served. Its name alone can make a contented youngster cringe and send otherwise mature adults running for cover. Yet its natural affinity for everything from garlic to ham hocks has made it, and other green leafy vegetables, among the most widely eaten, if underappreciated, side dishes on the North American table.

The challenge presented by almost all dark green leafy vegetables is how to deal with their bitterness. From the acrid aroma of simmering cabbage to the overtly bitter bite of broccoli rabe and chicory, whether you love or loathe these vegetables largely depends on your reaction to bitterness. Nature doesn't help. Our palates are built to reject bitter foods. Bitterness is often an indication of harmful alkaloids in food. We have come to accept low concentrations of some bitter flavors, such as quinine and caffeine, only by modifying them with the addition of sugar, fat, fruit or dairy products, or by balancing the bitterness with other strong flavors.

The same approach can make greens more palatable to diners who would otherwise reject them. Collard, mustard, chard and broccoli greens are typically counterbalanced with the subtle flavors of smoked meats or fruity olive oil, or with a pungent jolt of garlic. We serve sweet-and-sour cabbage, creamed spinach and Brussels sprouts with cheese sauce. We toss radicchio and escarole with creamy dressings and spicy vinaigrettes, and we shadow the sharpness of braised endive with lemon juice, white wine, shallots and chicken broth.

The bitterest of all greens are those in the chicory and endive families. Maturity, deeper green color and sunlight all increase bitterness. Many growers try to limit exposure to sunlight, sometimes exposing only the outer leaves to keep all but the outside of the endive from coloring, thereby cutting down on off-flavors.

In addition to buying paler specimens, you can also control bitterness during preparation. Soaking endive or chicory will increase bitterness, so wash these vegetables quickly and dry them well. Soon after they start cooking, the bitter components in the vegetables will be released. Eventually, this bitterness will dissipate, but in the interim it will be more pronounced. This means the most palatable ways to serve bitter greens are raw in salads; barely wilted in a flavorful mixture of herbs, acids and oil; or braised until fully softened. Don't try to stir-fry or serve these greens al dente unless a puckered palate is your idea of a good time.

About these recipes . . .

About half of the following 50 recipes are for spinach. The rest are for less common greens. We assume you will add salt and pepper to your taste, although we've added salt and pepper to many recipes that would suffer without them. Salads are intended as entrées.

The cooked spinach recipes are written for prewashed bagged fresh spinach, although an equal amount of thawed frozen spinach could be substituted. At one time, we would have used frozen spinach for convenience, but prewashed spinach not only tastes fresher, it is ready in far less time than it would take to thaw and cook a block of frozen spinach. In the recipes below, we use either 6-ounce (175 g) or 9-ounce (270 g) bags of spinach. The volume of a 6-ounce (175 g) bag of spinach is about 4 cups (1 L), which cooks down to about ⅔ cup (175 mL). The volume of a 9-ounce (270 g) bag is about 5½ cups (1.375 L), which cooks down to 1 cup (250 mL), or 2 portions, if nothing else is added.

Spinach Waldorf Salad

3 tbsp	cider vinegar	45 mL
1 tbsp	granulated sugar	15 mL
2	bags (each 6 oz/175 g) spinach, coarsely chopped	2
1	large tart apple, diced	1
1	stalk celery, sliced	1
8 oz	baked ham, diced	250 g
1 cup	walnut pieces	250 mL
¼ cup	diced red onion	50 mL
¼ cup	mayonnaise	50 mL
1 tbsp	sour cream	15 mL

Heat vinegar and sugar until sugar dissolves; let cool. In a serving bowl, combine spinach, apple, celery, ham, walnut pieces and onion. In a small bowl, combine mayonnaise and sour cream, then stir in vinegar mixture. Add to salad and toss to coat. **Serves 4 to 6.**

Warm Spinach Salad with Chicken Livers

8	large mushrooms, sliced	8
2	bags (each 9 oz/270 g) spinach, coarsely chopped	2
½	red onion, thinly sliced	½
3	slices bacon	3
1½ lbs	chicken livers, trimmed and cut into lobes	750 g
½ cup	olive oil	125 mL
⅓ cup	red wine vinegar	75 mL
2 tbsp	granulated sugar	25 mL
	Juice of ½ lemon	
	Salt and freshly ground black pepper to taste	
½ cup	plain yogurt	125 mL

Toss mushrooms, spinach and onion in a serving bowl. In a large skillet, over medium-high heat, cook bacon until crisp; drain on paper towels and crumble into salad. Add chicken livers to the fat in the pan and cook, turning once, until browned on both sides. Add oil, vinegar, sugar, lemon juice, salt and pepper; reduce heat and simmer for 2 to 3 minutes, until slightly reduced. Remove from heat and stir in yogurt. Pour over salad and toss to coat. **Serves 4 to 6.**

Watercress and Spinach Caesar Salad

4	drained canned anchovies	4
1	clove garlic	1
3 tbsp	red wine vinegar	45 mL
2 tsp	brown mustard	10 mL
6 tbsp	olive oil	90 mL
2	bags (each 6 oz/175 g) spinach, coarsely chopped	2
2	bunches watercress leaves, stemmed	2
1 cup	garlic-flavored croutons	250 mL
2 tbsp	freshly grated Parmesan cheese	25 mL

In a serving bowl, mash anchovies and garlic with the back of a fork. Whisk in vinegar and mustard, then slowly whisk in oil. Add spinach and watercress; toss to coat. Sprinkle with croutons and Parmesan. **Serves 4 to 6.**

Ruby Salad

1	small clove garlic, minced	1
½ cup	extra-virgin olive oil	125 mL
¼ cup	red wine vinegar	50 mL
½ tsp	salt	2 mL
	Freshly ground black pepper to taste	
8	red radishes, sliced	8
1	head romaine lettuce, leaves torn from ribs	1
1	head radicchio, leaves torn from ribs	1
1	bag (6 oz/175 g) spinach, coarsely chopped	1
1	small red onion, thinly sliced	1
½ cup	shelled pistachios	125 mL

In a serving bowl, whisk together garlic, oil, vinegar, salt and pepper. Add the remaining ingredients and toss to coat. **Serves 4 to 6.**

Spinach Orzo Soup

6 cups	rich chicken broth	1.5 L
	Salt and freshly ground black pepper to taste	
¾ cup	orzo	175 mL
3	egg yolks	3
2	bags (each 9 oz/270 g) spinach, coarsely chopped	2
1 tbsp	freshly squeezed lemon juice	15 mL

In a large pot, bring broth, salt and pepper to a boil. Add orzo, reduce heat and simmer for 10 minutes, until tender. Meanwhile, in a food processor, purée egg yolks and spinach. With the motor running, through the feed tube, slowly add a ladleful of soup and process until smooth Reduce heat so soup barely simmers and slowly pour in egg mixture, stirring constantly. Increase heat to medium and cook, stirring constantly, until soup is slightly thickened, about 1 minute. Stir in lemon juice. **Serves 4 to 6.**

Spinach and Wild Mushroom Soup

½ oz	dried wild or exotic mushrooms (any variety)	15 g
1 cup	boiling water	250 mL
2 tbsp	olive oil	25 mL
8 oz	mushrooms, sliced	250 g
¼ cup	chopped onion	50 mL
2 tbsp	all-purpose flour	25 mL
¼ tsp	dried thyme	1 mL
¼ tsp	dried rosemary	1 mL
2	bags (each 9 oz/270 g) spinach, coarsely chopped	2
3 cups	chicken broth	750 mL
½ cup	whipping (35%) cream	125 mL

Soak wild mushrooms in boiling water for 10 minutes; squeeze out excess liquid, reserving soaking liquid. Trim off stems and coarsely chop mushrooms. Strain soaking liquid. In a large saucepan, heat oil over medium-high heat. Sauté wild mushrooms, fresh mushrooms and onion until lightly browned. Add flour, thyme and rosemary; sauté for 3 minutes. Add soaking liquid, spinach and broth; reduce heat and simmer for about 15 minutes, or until soup is slightly thickened. Add cream and simmer for 1 to 2 minutes, or until heated through. Serves 4 to 6.

Garlic Spinach

2 tbsp	butter	25 mL
2 tbsp	minced onion	25 mL
1	clove garlic, minced	1
2	bags (each 9 oz/270 g) spinach, coarsely chopped	2
	Salt and freshly ground black pepper to taste	

In a large skillet, melt butter over medium-high heat. Sauté onion and garlic until browned. Add spinach, salt and pepper; sauté until spinach is wilted and dry, about 3 minutes. Serves 4 to 6.

Spinach with Mushrooms

Follow preceding recipe, but increase the butter to 3 tbsp (45 mL), omit the garlic, and add 4 oz (125 g) mushrooms, sliced, with the onion. Serves 4 to 6.

Spinach with Lemon and Parsley

Follow recipe for Garlic Spinach (above), but add 1 tbsp (15 mL) finely chopped fresh Italian (flat-leaf) parsley and 2 tsp (10 mL) finely grated lemon zest at the end of cooking. Serves 4 to 6.

Spinach with Capers

Follow recipe for Garlic Spinach (above), but add 1 tbsp (15 mL) drained small capers with the onion. Serves 4 to 6.

Ricotta Creamed Spinach

Follow recipe for Garlic Spinach (above), but add ¼ cup (50 mL) drained ricotta cheese and ½ tsp (2 mL) freshly squeezed lemon juice at the end of cooking. Serves 4 to 6.

Creamed Spinach with Herb Cheese

Follow recipe for Garlic Spinach (above), but add ¼ cup (50 mL) herbed cream cheese, softened, and 1 tsp (5 mL) sour cream at the end of cooking. Serves 4 to 6.

Spinach with Warm Bacon Dressing

Follow recipe for Garlic Spinach (left) but add ¼ cup (50 mL) Warm Bacon Dressing (page 62) at the end of cooking. Serves 4 to 6.

Spinach with Roasted Peppers and Green Peppercorns

Follow recipe for Garlic Spinach (left), but add 1 roasted red bell pepper (see page 11), diced, and 1 tsp (5 mL) whole green peppercorns with the onion. Serves 4 to 6.

Cream of Spinach Soup

Follow recipe for Garlic Spinach (left), but use a large saucepan instead of a skillet. Add 1 tbsp (15 mL) all-purpose flour when spinach is wilted and sauté for 1 minute. Add 3 cups (750 mL) chicken broth, reduce heat and simmer for 5 minutes. Transfer to a blender and purée. Return to saucepan, stir in 1 cup (250 mL) whipping (35%) cream and heat through. Serves 4 to 6.

Spinach Pilaf

1 tbsp	butter	15 mL
¼ cup	finely chopped onion	50 mL
1 cup	long-grain white rice	250 mL
2 cups	chicken broth	500 mL
	Salt and freshly ground black pepper to taste	
1	recipe Garlic Spinach (left)	1

In a medium saucepan, melt butter over medium heat. Sauté onion until tender. Add rice, stirring to coat with butter. Add broth, salt and pepper, stirring briefly to moisten rice. Bring to a boil, reduce heat, cover and simmer for 15 to 20 minutes, or until liquid is absorbed. (Do not stir rice when checking for doneness.) Remove from heat and let stand, covered, for 5 minutes. Fluff with a fork and toss with Garlic Spinach. Serves 6.

Spinach with Feta and Olives

2 tbsp	extra-virgin olive oil	25 mL
2 tbsp	minced onion	25 mL
1	clove garlic, minced	1
2	bags (each 9 oz/270 g) spinach, coarsely chopped	2
2 tbsp	chopped pitted oil-cured black olives	25 mL
1/3 cup	crumbled feta cheese	75 mL

In a large skillet, heat oil over medium-high heat. Sauté onion and garlic until tender. Add spinach and olives; sauté until spinach is wilted and dry, about 3 minutes. Stir in feta. **Serves 4 to 6.**

Prosciutto and Fennel Spinach

Follow preceding recipe, but add 1/2 tsp (2 mL) ground fennel seeds with the garlic, omit the olives and feta, and add 2 tbsp (25 mL) minced prosciutto with the spinach. **Serves 4 to 6.**

Spiced Spinach

2 tbsp	butter	25 mL
2 tbsp	minced onion	25 mL
1 tsp	ground coriander	5 mL
1 tsp	curry powder	5 mL
Pinch	freshly ground black pepper	Pinch
Pinch	cayenne pepper	Pinch
Pinch	ground nutmeg	Pinch
2	bags (each 9 oz/270 g) spinach, coarsely chopped	2
	Salt to taste	
1/3 cup	plain yogurt	75 mL

In a large skillet, melt butter over medium-high heat. Sauté onion, coriander, curry powder, black pepper, cayenne and nutmeg until onion is tender and spices are aromatic. Add spinach and salt; sauté until spinach is wilted and dry, about 3 minutes. Remove from heat and stir in yogurt. **Serves 4 to 6.**

Spinach, Corn and Tomatoes

2 tbsp	butter	25 mL
2 tbsp	finely chopped onion	25 mL
1/2	jalapeño pepper, seeded and minced	1/2
1 cup	drained canned corn kernels	250 mL
2	bags (each 9 oz/270 g) spinach, coarsely chopped	2
1	plum (Roma) tomato, seeded and chopped	1
	Salt and freshly ground black pepper to taste	

In a large skillet, melt butter over medium heat. Sauté onion, jalapeño and corn until tender. Add spinach and sauté until wilted and dry, about 3 minutes. Add tomato, salt and pepper; heat through. **Serves 4 to 6.**

Creamed Spinach with Wild Mushrooms

1/2 oz	dried wild or exotic mushrooms (any variety)	15 g
1/2 cup	boiling water	125 mL
2 tbsp	butter	25 mL
2 tbsp	finely chopped onion	25 mL
2	bags (each 9 oz/270 g) spinach, coarsely chopped	2
	Salt and freshly ground black pepper to taste	
1	egg yolk	1
1/4 cup	whipping (35%) cream	50 mL

Soak mushrooms in boiling water for 10 minutes; squeeze out excess liquid, reserving soaking liquid. Trim off stems and coarsely chop mushrooms. Strain soaking liquid. In a large skillet, melt butter over medium-high heat. Sauté mushrooms and onion until lightly browned. Add soaking liquid and cook until most of the liquid is absorbed. Add spinach, salt and pepper; sauté until spinach is wilted and dry, about 3 minutes. Beat together yolk and cream. Reduce heat to low, add egg mixture to pan and simmer for 1 to 2 minutes, or until sauce is creamy and thickened. **Serves 4 to 6.**

Stir-Fried Spinach with Pine Nuts

1 tbsp	peanut oil	15 mL
1/4 cup	pine nuts	50 mL
1/2	onion, chopped	1/2
1	small clove garlic, minced	1
2	bags (each 9 oz/270 g) spinach, coarsely chopped	2
	Salt and freshly ground black pepper to taste	

In a wok or large skillet, heat oil over medium-high heat. Stir-fry pine nuts until browned; remove with a slotted spoon. Add onion and garlic to the pan and stir-fry for 30 seconds. Add spinach, salt and pepper; stir-fry until spinach is wilted and dry, about 3 minutes. Toss with pine nuts. **Serves 4 to 6.**

Spinach Strudel with Tomato Vinaigrette

8	sheets phyllo dough	8
¼ cup	melted clarified butter (see page 16)	50 mL
1	recipe Stir-Fried Spinach with Pine Nuts (page 370)	1
	Warm Tomato Vinaigrette (see recipe, page 63)	

Preheat oven to 400°F (200°C) and butter a baking sheet. Place 1 sheet of phyllo dough on a clean work surface, brush with a thin film of melted butter and layer 3 more sheets, brushing each with butter. Spread half the prepared spinach mixture over the phyllo, roll up jelly-roll style and place seam side down on prepared baking sheet. Brush with more butter. Make another strudel the same way. Bake for 30 to 35 minutes, or until golden brown. Let cool for 10 minutes. Slice each strudel into 2 portions and serve each in a pool of Warm Tomato Vinaigrette. **Serves 4.**

Stir-Fried Shrimp with Spinach

2 tbsp	canola oil	25 mL
1 tbsp	minced gingerroot	15 mL
Pinch	hot pepper flakes	Pinch
6 oz	small shrimp, peeled and deveined	175 g
3	green onions, thinly sliced	3
2	bags (each 9 oz/270 g) spinach, coarsely chopped	2
2 tsp	Chinese oyster sauce	10 mL
1 tsp	soy sauce	5 mL
1 tsp	dark sesame oil	5 mL

In a wok or large skillet, heat oil over medium-high heat. Stir-fry ginger and hot pepper flakes for 10 seconds. Add shrimp and stir-fry until pink and opaque; remove with a slotted spoon. Add green onions and spinach to the pan and stir-fry until spinach is wilted and dry, about 3 minutes. Add oyster sauce and soy sauce, return shrimp to pan, toss to combine and heat through. Drizzle with sesame oil. **Serves 4.**

Stir-Fried Spinach with Hoisin Walnuts

3 tbsp	canola oil, divided	45 mL
1 cup	walnut pieces	250 mL
1	clove garlic, minced	1
1 tbsp	granulated sugar	15 mL
1 tbsp	hoisin sauce	15 mL
2	bags (each 9 oz/270 g) spinach, coarsely chopped	2
1 tsp	grated gingerroot	5 mL
2	green onions, sliced	2

In a wok or large skillet, heat 1 tbsp (15 mL) of the oil over medium-high heat until smoking. Stir-fry walnuts until toasted. Add garlic, sugar and hoisin sauce; sauté until sugar caramelizes and coats the nuts. Remove mixture to a plate. Wash out wok and heat the remaining oil over high heat. Add spinach and ginger; stir-fry until spinach is wilted and dry, about 3 minutes. Return walnut mixture to the pan, add green onions and toss to combine. **Serves 4 to 6.**

Spinach Pasta

3	extra-large eggs	3
5 oz	frozen chopped spinach, thawed and squeezed dry	150 g
½ tsp	salt	2 mL
2 cups	all-purpose flour	500 mL
1	clove garlic, minced	1
⅓ cup	freshly grated Parmesan cheese	75 mL
3 tbsp	extra-virgin olive oil	45 mL

In a food processor, purée eggs, spinach and salt. Add flour and pulse until a ball of dough forms. On a floured board, knead dough until very smooth and elastic; cover and let rest for 10 minutes. Using a pasta machine, or on a floured board, with a floured rolling pin, roll out to desired thickness, adding flour as necessary to keep dough from sticking. Cut into noodles. Cook in rapidly boiling salted water for 1 to 5 minutes, or until al dente (timing will depend on thickness). Drain and toss with garlic, Parmesan and oil. **Serves 4 to 6.**

Spinach Timbales

2 tbsp	butter	25 mL
¼ cup	finely chopped onion	50 mL
1	small clove garlic, minced	1
1	package (10 oz/300 g) frozen chopped spinach, thawed	1
Dash	ground nutmeg	Dash
	Salt and freshly ground black pepper to taste	
2	extra-large whole eggs	2
1	extra-large egg yolk	1
½ cup	cream (any type, minimum 10%)	125 mL
½ cup	milk (not fat-free)	125 mL
	Beurre Blanc (see recipe, page 51), Red Pepper Coulis (see recipe, page 53) or Warm Tomato Vinaigrette (see recipe, page 63)	

Preheat oven to 350°F (180°C) and butter four 5-oz (150 mL) ramekins. In a large skillet, melt butter over medium heat. Sauté onion and garlic until tender. Add spinach and sauté until wilted and dry. Season with nutmeg, salt and pepper; remove from heat. Combine eggs, egg yolk, cream and milk; stir into spinach. Pour into prepared ramekins and place ramekins in a shallow pan of warm water. Cover ramekins with parchment or waxed paper. Bake for 40 minutes, until firm to the touch but still a little wobbly in the center. Let cool for 5 minutes. Run a knife around the timbales to loosen, and invert onto a plate. Serve with your choice of Beurre Blanc, Red Pepper Coulis or Warm Tomato Vinaigrette. **Serves 4.**

Spinach and Blue Cheese Custard

Follow preceding recipe, but add 2 oz (60 g) blue cheese, crumbled, to the egg mixture, and use 5 ramekins. **Serves 5.**

Spinach Parmesan Soufflé

⅓ cup	butter, divided	75 mL
¾ cup	freshly grated imported Parmesan cheese, divided	175 mL
¼ cup	all-purpose flour	50 mL
1½ cups	hot milk (not fat-free)	375 mL
6	large or extra-large eggs, separated	6
1	recipe Garlic Spinach (page 369), finely chopped	1
	Salt and freshly ground black pepper to taste	

Preheat oven to 375°F (180°C). Grease an 8-cup (2 L) soufflé dish with 1 tbsp (15 mL) of the butter and dust with ¼ cup (50 mL) of the Parmesan. In a heavy saucepan, heat the remaining butter over medium heat. Sauté flour for 2 minutes. Slowly whisk in milk; reduce heat and simmer, whisking constantly, until sauce is smooth and thick. Remove from heat and let stand for 1 minute, then beat in egg yolks, one at a time. Stir in the remaining Parmesan, Garlic Spinach, salt and pepper. Beat egg whites with a pinch of salt until soft peaks form; fold into spinach mixture in 2 additions. Transfer to prepared soufflé dish and bake for 35 to 40 minutes, or until puffed and brown but still a little soft in the center. Serve immediately. **Serves 4 to 6.**

Broccoli Rabe Soufflé

Follow preceding recipe, but substitute Broccoli Rabe with Garlic and Olive Oil (below), finely chopped, for the Garlic Spinach. **Serves 4 to 6.**

Broccoli Rabe with Garlic and Olive Oil

2	bunches broccoli rabe	2
3 tbsp	extra-virgin olive oil	45 mL
3	cloves garlic, minced	3
Large pinch	hot pepper flakes	Large pinch
	Salt and freshly ground black pepper to taste	
	Additional extra-virgin olive oil (optional)	

Remove hard stem ends from rabe and cut rabe into 1-inch (2.5 cm) pieces. In a large pot of boiling salted water, boil rabe for 3 minutes, until tender; drain. In a large, deep skillet, heat oil over high heat. Add rabe, garlic, hot pepper flakes, salt and pepper; sauté until dry and fragrant, about 1 minute. Add more oil, if desired. **Serves 4 to 6.**

Broccoli Rabe with Raisins and Pine Nuts

2	bunches broccoli rabe	2
½ cup	raisins (golden or a mix of golden and dark)	125 mL
3 tbsp	extra-virgin olive oil	45 mL
3	cloves garlic, minced	3
½ cup	pine nuts	125 mL
	Kosher salt and coarsely ground black pepper to taste	

Remove hard stem ends from rabe and cut rabe into 1-inch (2.5 cm) pieces. In a large pot of boiling salted water, boil rabe for 2 minutes. Add raisins and boil for 1 minute, until rabe is tender; drain. In a large, deep skillet, heat oil over high heat. Add garlic and pine nuts; sauté until lightly browned. Add rabe, salt and pepper; sauté until heated through, about 1 minute. **Serves 4 to 6.**

Kale with Sausage and Apple

	Vegetable oil	
1	large tart apple, diced	1
8 oz	sweet Italian sausage, chopped	250 g
¼ cup	chopped onion	50 mL
1 cup	unsweetened apple juice	250 mL
1 lb	kale leaves, stemmed	500 g
2 tbsp	butter	25 mL
	Salt and freshly ground black pepper to taste	

In a large, deep skillet or Dutch oven, heat a thin film of oil over medium-high heat. Sauté apple, sausage and onion until lightly browned. Add apple juice and bring to a boil. Add kale, reduce heat, cover and simmer, stirring occasionally, until kale is tender and sausage is no longer pink inside, about 7 minutes. Stir in butter, salt and pepper. **Serves 4 to 6.**

Fried Kale

1 lb	perfect kale leaves, stemmed, with leaves kept whole	500 g
	Vegetable oil	
Dash	cider vinegar	Dash
	Salt and freshly ground black pepper to taste	

Wash and thoroughly dry kale. Deep-fry kale (see page 9), a few leaves at a time, for 15 to 30 seconds, or until bright green and crisp at the edges. Blot off excess oil and toss with vinegar, salt and pepper. **Serves 4 to 6.**

Kale Smothered with Bacon and Onions

4	slices bacon, finely chopped	4
2	onions, sliced	2
1 lb	kale leaves, stemmed	500 g
	Salt and freshly ground black pepper to taste	

In a large, deep skillet or Dutch oven, over medium heat, sauté bacon until the bottom of the pan is coated with fat but bacon is not yet crisp. Add onions, reduce heat to medium-low and sauté until golden brown, about 10 minutes. Add kale, cover and simmer, stirring occasionally, until tender, about 7 minutes. Season with salt and pepper. **Serves 4 to 6.**

Braised Belgian Endive

3 tbsp	olive oil	45 mL
4	fat heads Belgian endive, trimmed and halved lengthwise	4
½ cup	dry white wine	125 mL
½ cup	chicken broth	125 mL
	Salt and freshly ground black pepper to taste	
1 tbsp	freshly squeezed lemon juice	15 mL
2 tbsp	chopped fresh Italian (flat-leaf) parsley	25 mL

In a large skillet, heat oil over medium-high heat. Cook endive until browned on both sides. Add wine and boil for 1 to 2 minutes. Add broth, salt and pepper; reduce heat, cover and simmer for 20 minutes. Add lemon juice and simmer for 5 to 6 minutes, until endive is fork-tender. Sprinkle with parsley. **Serves 4.**

Braised Endive with Ham

Follow preceding recipe, but add ¼ cup (50 mL) chopped smoked ham with the endive. **Serves 4.**

Wilted Chicory

3	slices bacon, finely chopped	3
1	onion, chopped	1
2	cloves garlic, minced	2
Pinch	hot pepper flakes	Pinch
1	bunch chicory (about 1½ lbs/750 g), stemmed and torn into large pieces	1
8 oz	smoked ham, finely diced	250 g
½ cup	chicken broth	125 mL
2 tbsp	dry sherry	25 mL
1 tbsp	cider vinegar	15 mL
1 tbsp	brown mustard	15 mL
1 tbsp	honey	15 mL
	Salt and freshly ground black pepper to taste	

In a large skillet, over medium-high heat, sauté bacon until crisp. Add onion, garlic and hot pepper flakes; sauté until onion is tender. Add the remaining ingredients and cook, stirring occasionally, until chicory is wilted, about 5 minutes. **Serves 4 to 6.**

Sautéed Spring Greens

1	bunch Swiss chard, stemmed	1
2	bunches young dandelion greens, stemmed	2
	Salt and freshly ground black pepper to taste	
2 tbsp	olive oil	25 mL
1	small onion, finely chopped	1
1	clove garlic, minced	1
2 tbsp	drained capers	25 mL
	Juice of 1 lemon	

In a large pot of boiling salted water, boil chard and dandelion greens for 5 minutes; drain and season with salt and pepper. In a large skillet, heat oil over medium-high heat. Sauté onion until tender. Add greens and garlic; sauté for 1 to 2 minutes, or until heated through. Remove greens to a platter. Add capers and lemon juice to the pan, then pour over greens. **Serves 4 to 6.**

Sautéed Bitter Greens with Sweet Pepper Vinaigrette

1	head escarole, hard ribs trimmed	1
1	head curly endive, hard ribs trimmed	1
	Salt and freshly ground black pepper to taste	
2 tbsp	olive oil	25 mL
1	small onion, finely chopped	1
1	roasted red bell pepper (see page 11), diced	1
1/3 cup	finely diced smoked ham	75 mL
1	clove garlic, minced	1
1 tbsp	granulated sugar	15 mL
2 tbsp	red wine vinegar	25 mL

In a large pot of boiling salted water, boil escarole and curly endive for 5 minutes; drain and season with salt and pepper. In a large skillet, heat oil over medium-high heat. Sauté onion until tender. Add roasted pepper and ham; sauté for 1 minute. Add greens and garlic, sauté for 1 to 2 minutes, or until heated through. Remove greens to a platter. Add sugar and vinegar to the pan and stir until sugar dissolves, about 5 seconds; pour over greens. **Serves 4 to 6.**

Gratin of Chard

2 lbs	Swiss chard, stemmed	1 kg
3 tbsp	butter	45 mL
8 oz	mushrooms, sliced	250 g
1	clove garlic, minced	1
1	extra-large egg, beaten	1
1/2 cup	ricotta cheese	125 mL
1/3 cup	freshly grated Parmesan cheese, divided	75 mL
2 tbsp	seasoned dry bread crumbs	25 mL

Preheat oven to 375°F (190°C). In a large pot of boiling salted water, boil chard for 1 minute; drain, shake dry and place in a large bowl. In a large skillet, melt butter over medium-high heat. Sauté mushrooms until tender. Add garlic and sauté for 30 seconds. Add to chard and stir in egg, ricotta and 1/4 cup (50 mL) of the Parmesan. Mound into an 8-inch (2 L) baking dish. Combine bread crumbs and the remaining Parmesan; sprinkle over top. Bake for 35 to 40 minutes, or until browned and bubbling at the edges. **Serves 4 to 6.**

Gratin of Spinach

Follow preceding recipe, but substitute 1 1/2 lbs (750 g) spinach for the chard. **Serves 4 to 6.**

Chard with Chorizo

2 lbs	Swiss chard, stemmed and cut into 1-inch (2.5 cm) pieces	1 kg
	Salt and freshly ground black pepper to taste	
2 tbsp	olive oil	25 mL
1	small onion, finely chopped	1
4 oz	dry-cured chorizo sausage, finely chopped	125 g
1	clove garlic, minced	1

In a large pot of boiling salted water, boil chard for 1 minute; drain, season with salt and pepper, and set aside. In a large skillet, heat oil over medium-high heat. Sauté onion until tender. Add chard, chorizo and garlic; sauté until chard is bright green, about 2 minutes. Mound on a platter. **Serves 4 to 6.**

Chilled Watercress Soup

3 tbsp	butter	45 mL
1	small onion, finely chopped	1
1 tbsp	all-purpose flour	15 mL
4 cups	chicken broth	1 L
3	bunches watercress leaves (each about 4 oz/125 g), stemmed	3
Pinch	ground nutmeg	Pinch
	Salt and freshly ground black pepper to taste	
1 cup	sour cream or plain yogurt	250 mL

In a large saucepan, melt butter over medium heat. Sauté onion until tender. Add flour and sauté for 1 minute. Add broth and bring to a simmer. Add watercress, nutmeg, salt and pepper; simmer for

5 minutes. Transfer to a blender, add sour cream and purée. Cover and refrigerate for about 1 hour, until chilled. **Serves 4 to 6.**

Watercress Cream Sauce

1 tbsp	butter	15 mL
1	bunch watercress (about 4 oz/125 g), stemmed	1
1	shallot, finely chopped	1
1 cup	whipping (35%) cream	250 mL

In a large skillet, melt butter over medium heat. Sauté watercress and shallot until watercress is wilted, about 2 minutes. Add cream and simmer until slightly thickened, about 1 minute. **Makes about 1 cup (250 mL).** *Serve over poached fish, shellfish, eggs or grilled chicken breasts.*

Sweet Apple Sauerkraut

2 tsp	vegetable oil	10 mL
2	large tart apples, peeled and diced	2
1	small onion, chopped	1
1 lb	sauerkraut, thoroughly rinsed and drained	500 g
1 cup	unsweetened apple juice	250 mL
1 tbsp	packed light brown sugar	15 mL

In a large skillet, heat oil over medium-high heat. Sauté apples and onion until tender. Stir in sauerkraut, apple juice and brown sugar; reduce heat and simmer until liquid is absorbed. **Serves 4 to 6.**

Caraway Sauerkraut

2	slices bacon, finely chopped	2
1 lb	sauerkraut, thoroughly rinsed and drained	500 g
2 cups	dry white wine	500 mL
2 tsp	caraway seeds	10 mL
1 tsp	granulated sugar	5 mL

In a large skillet, over medium-high heat, sauté bacon until crisp. Add sauerkraut, wine, caraway seeds and sugar; reduce heat and simmer until liquid is absorbed, about 10 minutes. **Serves 4 to 6.**

Brussels Sprouts Simmered in Milk

2 cups	water	500 mL
2 cups	milk (not fat-free)	500 mL
2 cups	Brussels sprouts, trimmed	500 mL
2 tbsp	sour cream (not fat-free)	25 mL
	Salt and freshly ground black pepper to taste	

In a large saucepan, bring water and milk to a simmer. Meanwhile, cut a small X in the bottom of each Brussels sprout. Add sprouts to pan and simmer until tender, about 10 minutes. Drain and toss with sour cream, salt and pepper. **Serves 4 to 6.**

Brussels Sprouts Sautéed with Bacon and Apples

2	slices bacon, finely chopped	2
1	large tart apple, peeled and diced	1
1/4 cup	chopped onion	50 mL
1	recipe Brussels Sprouts Simmered in Milk (left), made without sour cream	1

In a large skillet, over medium-high heat, sauté bacon until crisp. Add apple and onion; sauté until tender. Add Brussels sprouts and heat through. **Serves 4 to 6.**

Stir-Fried Brussels Sprouts

1/4 cup	chicken broth	50 mL
1 tbsp	soy sauce	15 mL
2 tsp	hoisin sauce	10 mL
1 tsp	cornstarch	5 mL
2 tbsp	vegetable oil	25 mL
2 cups	Brussels sprouts, trimmed and halved	500 mL
1/2 cup	chopped onion	125 mL
2	cloves garlic, minced	2
2 tsp	minced gingerroot	10 mL
	Salt and freshly ground black pepper to taste	

Combine broth, soy sauce, hoisin sauce and cornstarch; set aside. In a wok or large skillet, heat oil over medium-high heat. Stir-fry Brussels sprouts and onion, covering pan between stirrings, for about 8 minutes, or until vegetables are browned and sprouts are almost tender. Add garlic, ginger, salt and pepper; stir-fry for 1 minute. Stir broth mixture, add to pan and stir-fry until vegetables are coated and sauce is slightly thickened, about 3 minutes. **Serves 4 to 6.**

Chapter 33
Harvest Vegetables
Broccoli, Cauliflower, Beans and Squash

Broccoli with Apples and Bacon 377
Broccoli with Cider and Rosemary 377
Broccoli with Walnuts 378
Cauliflower in Mustard Cream 378
Curried Cauliflower 378
Cauliflower with Capers 378
Stir-Fried Caramelized Cauliflower
and Cashews 378
Fennel Baked with Tomatoes
and Garlic 378
Garlic Green Beans 379
Green Beans with Pine Nuts 379
Green Beans with Thyme 379
Green Beans with Roasted Peppers . . . 379
Minted Peas 379
Peas with Brown Shallots 379
Stir-Fried Snow Peas with
Minced Shrimp 379
Pickled Peppers 379
Mélange of Roasted Peppers 379
Hash of Ham, Peppers and Peppercorns . . 380
Roasted Peppers with Anchovies 380
Grilled Mediterranean Eggplant 380
Eggplant with Garlic Jam 380
Sweet Potato Pancakes with Ham 380
Sweet Potato Apple Pancakes 380
Fall Garden Latkes 380
Mushroom Garden Latkes 381

Vegetable Burgers 381
Braised Lemon Celery 381
Indian Braised Vegetables 381
Mushrooms Boiled with Lots of Garlic . . 382
Marsala Mushrooms with Pancetta 382
Parsley Mushrooms 382
Mushrooms in Balsamic Glaze 382
Mushrooms in Tomato Broth 382
Pearl Onions Stewed with Olives 382
Tomato and Basil Potatoes 382
Refried Pumpkin 383
Acorn Squash with
Gingered Applesauce 383
Acorn Squash with Orange Molasses . . 383
Acorn Squash with Spiced Honey 383
Harvest Vegetable Stuffing 384
Wild Mushroom Stuffing 384
Harvest Rice Stuffing 384
Fall Orchard Stuffing 384
Harvest Quiche 384
Bacon, Peppers and Potatoes 384
Grilled Tomatillo and Rice Salad 384
Marinated Green Tomato
and White Bean Salad 385
Green Tomato Gazpacho 385
Tomato Sauce with Fennel
and Orange 385
Roasted Pepper and
Gorgonzola Grinder 385

There is nothing so gracious as a vegetable. Many vegetables, happy to move aside when meat or fish take center stage, never get their due. This is unfortunate, for vegetables comprise the most varied food source available to us, and nothing matches their innate versatility. Especially as side dishes, vegetables round out a meal nutritionally, reinforce or modify the style of an entrée and provide the principal source of color on a plate.

Their natural good looks and basic sweet flavor mean that most vegetables practically prepare themselves — as long as you choose the right way to cook them. And that choice depends on just two things: the vegetable's fiber content and its color. Hard, tough, high-fiber vegetables are cooked in liquid. Softer, moister vegetables are sautéed, baked or grilled. If you want to sauté or grill a tough vegetable, you must first soften its fiber, which can be done either by chopping it finely or by blanching it in boiling water.

Maintaining a vegetable's color requires a different technique for each pigment. Chlorophyll, the pigment in green vegetables, is destroyed by excessive heat or by exposure to acid, which means that green vegetables do not keep their color if they are marinated, cooked for a long time or cooked in an acidic liquid, such as wine or lemon juice. Cooking them in a covered pot will trap the vegetable's natural acids and cause the same problem.

Red-pigmented vegetables, on the other hand, have their color enhanced by exposure to acid but destroyed in an alkaline, or low-acid, environment. So when cooking red cabbage or red peppers, always add a bit of wine or lemon to the mixture, or keep the lid on the pot.

White vegetables discolor with long storage or overcooking, both of which allow oxygen to mix with the pigment and turn it gray or brown. That's why mushrooms and cauliflower are best cooked quickly, and why potatoes must be cooked as soon as they are peeled.

Orange vegetables, however, are almost impervious to culinary abuse. Nothing short of incineration will destroy their pigment.

About these recipes . . .

The following 50 side dishes offer ideas for hot and cold vegetables, stews, sautés, poached and boiled vegetables, and casseroles. It is assumed that you will add salt and pepper to taste to each recipe.

. . . .

Broccoli with Apples and Bacon

1	bunch broccoli, broken into florets, stalks trimmed, peeled and sliced	1
2	slices bacon	2
1/4 cup	chopped onion	50 mL
1	tart apple, peeled and diced	1
1 tsp	freshly squeezed lemon juice	5 mL

In a large pot of lightly salted boiling water, cook broccoli until bright green and barely tender, about 3 minutes; drain and run under cold water to stop cooking. Drain well. Meanwhile, in a skillet, over medium heat, cook bacon until crisp; remove to a plate, blot with paper towels, crumble and set aside. Add onion to the fat in the pan and sauté until tender. Add apple and sauté for 3 to 4 minutes, or until no longer raw but not yet soft. Add broccoli and toss until heated through. Stir in crumbled bacon and lemon juice. **Serves 4.**

. . . .

Broccoli with Cider and Rosemary

1/2 cup	unsweetened apple cider	125 mL
1	bunch broccoli, broken into florets, stalks trimmed, peeled and sliced	1
1 tbsp	canola oil	15 mL
1/4 cup	chopped onion	50 mL
1 tsp	chopped fresh rosemary	5 mL
1 tsp	freshly squeezed lemon juice	5 mL

In a small saucepan, over high heat, boil cider until reduced by about three-quarters. In a large pot of lightly salted boiling water, cook broccoli until bright green and barely tender, about 3 minutes; drain and run under cold water to stop cooking. In a large skillet, heat oil over medium-high heat. Sauté onion and rosemary until onion is translucent. Add broccoli and toss until heated through. Stir in reduced cider and lemon juice. **Serves 4.**

Broccoli with Walnuts

2 tbsp	walnut oil	25 mL
⅓ cup	chopped walnuts	75 mL
1	clove garlic, minced	1
1	bunch broccoli, broken into florets, stalks trimmed, peeled and sliced	1

In a small skillet, heat oil over medium-high heat. Sauté walnuts until toasted. Add garlic and sauté for 30 seconds; set aside. In a large pot of lightly salted boiling water, cook broccoli until bright green and barely tender, about 3 minutes; drain and run under cold water to stop cooking. Toss with walnut mixture. **Serves 4.**

Cauliflower in Mustard Cream

1	head cauliflower, broken into florets	1
1 tbsp	butter	15 mL
2 tbsp	minced onion	25 mL
1 cup	cream (any type, minimum 10%)	250 mL
1 tbsp	brown mustard	15 mL
	Salt and freshly ground white pepper to taste	

In a large pot of lightly salted boiling water, cook cauliflower until barely tender, about 3 minutes; drain and set aside. In a large skillet, melt butter over medium-high heat. Add onion and sauté until translucent. Add cream and mustard; cook until reduced by about half. Season with salt and pepper. Add cauliflower, toss to coat with sauce and heat through. **Serves 4.**

Curried Cauliflower

Follow preceding recipe, but increase the onion to ½ cup (125 mL), omit the mustard, and add 1 tbsp (15 mL) curry powder, 1½ tsp (7 mL) ground cumin and 1 tsp (5 mL) ground coriander with the cream. **Serves 4.**

Cauliflower with Capers

¼ cup	mayonnaise	50 mL
2 tsp	freshly squeezed lemon juice	10 mL
1 tsp	drained small capers	5 mL
Dash	hot pepper sauce (such as Tabasco)	Dash
1	head cauliflower, broken into florets	1

Combine mayonnaise, lemon juice, capers and hot pepper sauce. In a large pot of lightly salted boiling water, cook cauliflower until barely tender, about 3 minutes. Drain and toss with the mayonnaise mixture. **Serves 4.**

Stir-Fried Caramelized Cauliflower and Cashews

2 tbsp	peanut or canola oil	25 mL
1 cup	cashew pieces	250 mL
1	head cauliflower, broken into florets	1
1	clove garlic, minced	1
1 tsp	grated gingerroot	5 mL
1 tbsp	granulated sugar	15 mL
1 tbsp	hoisin sauce	15 mL
2	green onions, sliced	2

In a wok or large skillet, heat oil over medium-high heat. Stir-fry cashews until lightly toasted; remove with a slotted spoon to a plate. Add cauliflower and stir-fry until speckled with brown, about 4 minutes. Add garlic and ginger; stir-fry for 30 seconds. Add sugar and hoisin sauce; stir-fry until cauliflower is coated with sauce and sugar is caramelized. Toss with cashews and green onions. **Serves 4.**

Fennel Baked with Tomatoes and Garlic

2 tbsp	extra-virgin olive oil (plus some for oiling baking dish)	25 mL
½ cup	chopped onion	125 mL
2	bulbs fennel, trimmed and sliced	2
3	cloves garlic, minced, divided	3
2 cups	canned diced tomatoes, drained	500 mL
	Salt and freshly ground black pepper to taste	
¼ cup	dry bread crumbs	50 mL
¼ cup	freshly grated Parmesan cheese	50 mL
1 tsp	grated lemon zest	5 mL

Preheat oven to 375°F (190°C) and brush a 13- by 9-inch (3 L) baking dish with olive oil. In a large skillet, heat the 2 tbsp (25 mL) oil over medium-high heat. Sauté onion and fennel until onion is translucent. Add two-thirds of the garlic and sauté for 30 seconds. Add tomatoes, salt and pepper; heat through. Transfer to prepared baking dish. Combine the remaining garlic, bread crumbs, Parmesan and lemon zest; sprinkle on top of onion mixture. Bake for about 30 minutes, or until browned and bubbling around the edges. **Serves 4.**

Garlic Green Beans

1 lb	green beans, trimmed	500 g
1 tbsp	extra-virgin olive oil	15 mL
1	clove garlic, minced	1

In a large pot of lightly salted boiling water, cook beans until bright green and barely tender, about 3 minutes; drain well. Meanwhile, in a skillet, heat oil over medium-high heat. Sauté garlic until aromatic. Toss with beans. **Serves 4.**

Green Beans with Pine Nuts

Follow preceding recipe, but add 2 tbsp (25 mL) toasted pine nuts with the garlic. **Serves 4.**

Green Beans with Thyme

Follow recipe for Garlic Green Beans (above), but add 2 tsp (10 mL) chopped fresh thyme or ½ tsp (2 mL) dried thyme with the garlic. **Serves 4.**

Green Beans with Roasted Peppers

Follow recipe for Garlic Green Beans (above), but, after sautéing the garlic, add ¼ cup (50 mL) finely diced roasted red bell pepper (see page 11) to the skillet and heat through. Toss this mixture with the beans. **Serves 4.**

Minted Peas

2 tbsp	butter	25 mL
2 tbsp	minced onion	25 mL
1 lb	frozen peas, thawed	500 g
¼ cup	chopped fresh mint	50 mL
1 tsp	granulated sugar	5 mL

In a skillet, melt butter over medium heat. Sauté onion until translucent. Add peas, mint and sugar; sauté for 3 to 4 minutes, or until peas are heated through and tender. **Serves 4.**

Peas with Brown Shallots

2 tbsp	butter	25 mL
2 tbsp	chopped shallot	25 mL
Pinch	dried thyme	Pinch
1 lb	frozen peas, thawed	500 g

In a skillet, melt butter over medium-high heat. Sauté shallot and thyme until shallot is crisp and browned. Add peas and sauté for 3 to 4 minutes, or until heated through and tender. **Serves 4.**

Stir-Fried Snow Peas with Minced Shrimp

1 tbsp	peanut oil	15 mL
1	slice (½ inch/1 cm) gingerroot	1
2	green onions, sliced	2
10 oz	snow peas, stemmed	300 g
4 oz	shrimp, peeled, deveined and finely chopped	125 g
1	clove garlic, minced	1

In a wok or large skillet, heat oil over medium-high heat. Stir-fry ginger for 1 minute; remove ginger with a slotted spoon and discard. Add green onions, peas and shrimp to the wok and stir-fry for 1 minute, until peas turn bright green and shrimp is pink and opaque. Remove from heat and stir in garlic. **Serves 4.**

Pickled Peppers

1 tbsp	olive oil	15 mL
½ cup	chopped onion	125 mL
2	cloves garlic, minced	2
4	red and/or yellow bell peppers, cut into strips	4
½ cup	bottled Italian dressing or Garlic Herb Dressing (see recipe, page 60)	125 mL

In a skillet, heat oil over medium-high heat. Sauté onion and garlic until tender. Add peppers and sauté until barely tender. Add dressing, reduce heat and simmer for 2 minutes. **Serves 4.**

Mélange of Roasted Peppers

2 tbsp	extra-virgin olive oil	25 mL
2	roasted red bell peppers (see page 11), cut into strips	2
2	roasted yellow bell peppers (see page 11), cut into strips	2
2	roasted green bell peppers (see page 11), cut into strips	2
1	onion, thinly sliced	1
2	cloves garlic, minced	2
¼ cup	chopped fresh Italian (flat-leaf) parsley	50 mL
Pinch	hot pepper flakes	Pinch
	Juice of 1 lemon	

In a large skillet, heat oil over medium-high heat. Sauté red, yellow and green peppers, onion and garlic until heated through. Remove from heat and stir in parsley, hot pepper flakes and lemon juice. **Serves 4.**

Hash of Ham, Peppers and Peppercorns

1 tbsp	canola oil	15 mL
1	onion, chopped	1
2	bell peppers (any color), finely diced	2
8 oz	ham, finely diced	250 g
1 tbsp	chopped green peppercorns, with brine	15 mL

In a large skillet, heat oil over medium-high heat. Sauté onion until lightly browned. Add bell peppers, ham and peppercorns with their brine; sauté until peppers are tender. **Serves 4.**

Roasted Peppers with Anchovies

6	canned anchovies, drained and julienned, oil reserved	6
4	roasted bell peppers (any color; see page 11), cut into strips	4
1	clove garlic, minced	1
1 tbsp	oil from the anchovies	15 mL
1 tsp	red wine vinegar	5 mL
Pinch	hot pepper flakes	Pinch

Toss together all ingredients. **Serves 4.**

Grilled Mediterranean Eggplant

10	Asian eggplants, each cut into 4 lengthwise slices	10
2	firm tomatoes, sliced	2
3 tbsp	extra-virgin olive oil (plus some for brushing vegetables)	45 mL
2	cloves garlic, minced	2
2 tbsp	finely chopped basil	25 mL
2 tbsp	red wine vinegar	25 mL
2 tbsp	drained capers	25 mL
1 tbsp	chopped chives	15 mL
Pinch	hot pepper flakes	Pinch
	Juice of 1 lemon	

Preheat barbecue grill to high. Brush eggplant and tomato slices with oil. Grill vegetables, turning once, until browned and tender, about 2 minutes per side. Combine the remaining ingredients and drizzle over grilled vegetables. **Serves 6.**

Eggplant with Garlic Jam

¾ cup	dry white wine	175 mL
2 tsp	granulated sugar	10 mL
4	cloves garlic	4
1 tbsp	olive oil	15 mL
¼ cup	finely chopped onion	50 mL
1	eggplant, peeled and diced	1
2 cups	chicken broth	500 mL
¼ cup	finely chopped fresh Italian (flat-leaf) parsley	50 mL
	Salt and freshly ground black pepper to taste	

In a small saucepan, bring wine and sugar to a simmer. Add garlic and simmer until liquid turns amber. Transfer to a food processor or blender and purée until smooth; set aside. In a skillet, heat oil over medium-high heat. Sauté onion until lightly browned. Add eggplant and sauté for 1 minute. Add broth, parsley, salt and pepper; reduce heat and simmer until most of the liquid has evaporated and eggplant is very tender but not mushy. Gently stir in garlic mixture. **Serves 4.**

Sweet Potato Pancakes with Ham

3	eggs, beaten	3
1 lb	sweet potatoes, peeled and grated	500 g
⅓ cup	finely chopped ham	75 mL
3 tbsp	finely chopped onion	45 mL
2 tbsp	all-purpose flour	25 mL
1 tsp	salt	5 mL
	Freshly ground black pepper to taste	
	Vegetable oil	
	Applesauce (optional)	

Combine eggs, sweet potatoes, ham, onion, flour, salt and pepper. In a deep skillet, heat ¼ inch (0.5 cm) oil over medium-high heat until very hot but not smoking. Add potato mixture by heaping large spoonfuls, flattening the mounds into pancakes about 3 inches (7.5 cm) in diameter. Cook, turning once, for 4 to 5 minutes per side, or until browned on both sides. Drain on paper towels and keep warm. Repeat with the remaining potato mixture, adding and heating oil as necessary between batches. Serve with applesauce, if desired. **Serves 4.**

Sweet Potato Apple Pancakes

Follow preceding recipe, but increase the flour by 2 tsp (10 mL), omit the ham, and add 1 cup (250 mL) grated tart apple with the sweet potatoes. Serve with sour cream instead of applesauce. **Serves 4.**

Fall Garden Latkes

3	eggs, lightly beaten	3
¾ cup	grated peeled carrot	175 mL
¾ cup	grated peeled potato	175 mL
¾ cup	grated peeled apple	175 mL
¾ cup	grated peeled zucchini	175 mL
¼ cup	minced onion	50 mL
¼ cup	all-purpose flour	50 mL

1 tsp	salt	5 mL
½ tsp	freshly ground black pepper	2 mL
	Vegetable oil	
	Sour cream	

Combine eggs, carrot, potato, apple, zucchini, onion, flour, salt and pepper. In a deep skillet, heat ¼ inch (0.5 cm) oil over medium-high heat until very hot but not smoking. Add potato mixture by heaping large spoonfuls, flattening the mounds into pancakes about 3 inches (7.5 cm) in diameter. Cook, turning once, for 4 to 5 minutes per side, or until browned on both sides. Drain on paper towels and keep warm. Repeat with the remaining potato mixture, adding and heating oil as necessary between batches. Serve with sour cream. **Serves 4.**

Mushroom Garden Latkes

Follow preceding recipe, but omit the apple, and add ½ cup (125 mL) minced mushrooms with the zucchini. **Serves 4.**

Vegetable Burgers

2 tbsp	olive oil	25 mL
1	onion, minced	1
4 cups	minced mushrooms	1 L
1	carrot, finely shredded	1
2	cloves garlic, minced	2
1	roasted red bell pepper (see page 11), finely diced	1
	Salt and freshly ground black pepper to taste	
2	extra-large eggs, beaten	2
¾ cup	seasoned dry bread crumbs, divided	175 mL
Pinch	cayenne pepper	Pinch
6 tbsp	all-purpose flour	90 mL
	Vegetable oil	

In a large skillet, heat oil over medium-high heat. Sauté onion and mushrooms until browned and dry. Add carrot and sauté for 1 minute. Stir in garlic, roasted pepper, salt and pepper. Transfer to a bowl and mix in eggs, half the bread crumbs and cayenne until thoroughly blended. Cover and refrigerate for 1 hour. Combine the remaining bread crumbs and flour. Form vegetable mixture into patties, using ¼ cup (50 mL) for each patty, and dredge in flour mixture. In a large nonstick skillet, heat a thin film of oil over medium-high heat. Cook burgers until browned on both sides and hot in the center. **Serves 4.**

Braised Lemon Celery

2 tbsp	olive oil	25 mL
2	celery hearts, halved lengthwise	2
¼ cup	finely chopped onion	50 mL
1	clove garlic, minced	1
½ tsp	dried rosemary, crumbled	2 mL
2	plum (Roma) tomatoes, peeled, seeded and finely chopped	2
½ cup	chicken broth	125 mL
	Juice of ½ lemon	

In a large skillet, heat oil over medium-high heat. Sauté celery hearts until browned. Add onion, garlic and rosemary; sauté for 1 minute. Add tomatoes, broth and lemon juice; reduce heat, cover and simmer for 20 to 25 minutes, or until celery hearts are tender. **Serves 4.**

Indian Braised Vegetables

2 tbsp	vegetable oil, divided	25 mL
1	onion, finely chopped	1
½	clove garlic, minced	½
2 tsp	finely chopped gingerroot	10 mL
2 tsp	curry powder	10 mL
1 tsp	ground coriander	5 mL
1 tsp	ground cumin	5 mL
Pinch	hot pepper flakes	Pinch
¼ cup	chopped fresh cilantro	50 mL
1 tbsp	freshly squeezed lemon juice	15 mL
1 tsp	black mustard seeds	5 mL
1 cup	broccoli florets	250 mL
1 cup	cauliflower florets	250 mL
1 cup	sliced green beans	250 mL
½ cup	sliced carrots	125 mL
¼ cup	water	50 mL

In a large skillet, heat half the oil over medium heat. Sauté onion, garlic, ginger, curry powder, coriander, cumin and hot pepper flakes until onion is tender. Stir in cilantro and lemon juice; transfer to a bowl and set aside. (This paste can be stored indefinitely in the refrigerator.) Wipe out skillet and heat the remaining oil over medium-high heat. Toast mustard seeds until they turn gray. Add broccoli, cauliflower, beans and carrots; cover and cook, stirring frequently, until just tender, about 5 minutes. Add water, cover and cook for 3 minutes. Stir in reserved onion mixture. **Serves 4.**

Mushrooms Boiled with Lots of Garlic

1	head garlic, broken into cloves and peeled	1
2 tbsp	olive oil	25 mL
1 lb	small mushrooms	500 g
2 tbsp	chopped fresh Italian (flat-leaf) parsley	25 mL
½ tsp	dried thyme	2 mL
Pinch	hot pepper flakes	Pinch
1½ cups	chicken broth	375 mL

Cut any large garlic cloves into ½-inch (1 cm) pieces. In a skillet, heat oil over medium heat. Sauté garlic, mushrooms, parsley, thyme and hot pepper flakes until mushrooms start to release their liquid. Add broth and simmer for 12 minutes. Remove mushrooms and garlic with a slotted spoon to a plate. Reduce pan liquid by about three-quarters. Return mushrooms and garlic to the pan and heat through. **Serves 4.**

Marsala Mushrooms with Pancetta

2 oz	pancetta, finely chopped	60 g
2 tbsp	chopped onion	25 mL
1	clove garlic, minced	1
¼ tsp	dried rosemary, crumbled	1 mL
2 tsp	olive oil (if needed)	10 mL
1 lb	mushrooms, quartered	500 g
2 tbsp	Marsala	25 mL
1 tsp	freshly squeezed lemon juice	5 mL

In a skillet, over medium-high heat, cook pancetta until the bottom of the pan is coated with fat; remove with a slotted spoon to a plate. Add onion, garlic and rosemary to the fat in the pan and sauté until onion is tender, adding oil if there isn't enough fat. Add mushrooms and sauté until lightly browned. Add Marsala and lemon juice, scraping up any brown bits from the bottom of the pan. Sprinkle with pancetta. **Serves 4.**

Parsley Mushrooms

2 tbsp	olive oil	25 mL
2 tbsp	chopped onion	25 mL
1	clove garlic, minced	1
1 lb	mushrooms, sliced	500 g
¼ cup	chopped fresh Italian (flat-leaf) parsley	50 mL

In a skillet, heat oil over medium-high heat. Sauté onion and garlic until tender. Add mushrooms and sauté until lightly browned. Stir in parsley. **Serves 4.**

Mushrooms in Balsamic Glaze

Follow preceding recipe, but, after removing the mushrooms, add 1 tbsp (15 mL) balsamic vinegar to the pan and scrape up any brown bits from the bottom. Pour over mushrooms. **Serves 4.**

Mushrooms in Tomato Broth

2 tbsp	olive oil	25 mL
¼ cup	chopped onion	50 mL
1	stalk celery, chopped	1
1 lb	small mushrooms	500 g
1	bay leaf	1
½ tsp	dried basil	2 mL
¼ tsp	dried thyme	1 mL
3	tomatoes, chopped	3
½ cup	chicken broth	125 mL

In a skillet, heat oil over medium-high heat. Sauté onion and celery until tender. Add mushrooms, bay leaf, basil and thyme; sauté until mushrooms start to release their liquid. Add tomatoes and broth; reduce heat and simmer for 10 minutes. Discard bay leaf. Remove vegetables with a slotted spoon to a warm platter. Reduce pan liquid to a glaze. Pour over vegetables. **Serves 4.**

Pearl Onions Stewed with Olives

2 tbsp	olive oil	25 mL
2 cups	pearl onions, peeled	500 mL
12	oil-cured black olives, pitted and chopped	12
1	clove garlic, minced	1
¼ cup	finely diced red bell pepper	50 mL
½ cup	chicken broth	125 mL
2 tbsp	chopped fresh Italian (flat-leaf) parsley	25 mL

In a skillet, heat oil over medium-high heat. Sauté onions until browned. Add olives, garlic and red pepper; sauté for 1 minute. Add broth, reduce heat and simmer until onions are tender, about 25 minutes. Stir in parsley. **Serves 4.**

Tomato and Basil Potatoes

2 lbs	russet potatoes, peeled (about 4)	1 kg
2 tbsp	olive oil	25 mL
4	large tomatoes, peeled and chopped	4
1	clove garlic, minced	1
3 tbsp	chopped fresh basil	45 mL
¼ cup	freshly grated Parmesan cheese	50 mL

Preheat oven to 400°F (200°C). In a large pot of lightly salted boiling water, cook potatoes for 12 to 15 minutes, or until barely tender; drain and slice.

Meanwhile, in a large skillet, heat oil over medium heat. Sauté tomatoes and garlic for 5 minutes. Stir in basil. Spread half of the potatoes in an 8-cup (2 L) casserole and top with half of the tomato mixture; repeat layers. Top with Parmesan. Bake for 40 minutes, until bubbling. **Serves 4.**

Refried Pumpkin

2 tbsp	vegetable oil, divided	25 mL
3	garlic cloves	3
½ cup	fresh bread cubes	125 mL
⅓ cup	green pumpkin seeds	75 mL
1	jalapeño pepper, finely diced	1
⅓ cup	finely chopped onion	75 mL
½ tsp	ground cumin	2 mL
½ tsp	ground cinnamon	2 mL
2 tbsp	packed light brown sugar	25 mL
1 tbsp	red wine vinegar	15 mL
1	can (28 oz/796 mL) pumpkin purée (not pie filling)	1
	Salt and freshly ground black pepper to taste	

In a large skillet, heat half the oil over medium-high heat. Sauté garlic, bread cubes and pumpkin seeds until toasted. Add jalapeño, onion, cumin and cinnamon; sauté for 30 seconds. Transfer to a food processor, add brown sugar and vinegar, and process to a paste. Wipe out skillet and heat the remaining oil over medium-high heat. Add spice paste, pumpkin purée, salt and pepper; cook, stirring occasionally, until mixture bubbles vigorously and starts to brown at the edges. **Serves 4.**

Acorn Squash with Gingered Applesauce

2	acorn squash, halved at their equators, seeds and fibers removed	2
1 tbsp	minced gingerroot	15 mL
¼ cup	unsweetened applesauce	50 mL
2 tbsp	honey	25 mL
1 tsp	freshly squeezed lemon juice	5 mL
	Salt and freshly ground black pepper to taste	
1 tsp	butter	5 mL

Preheat oven to 350°F (180°C). Rub the interiors of the squash with ginger. Combine applesauce, honey, lemon juice, salt and pepper; brush squash with this mixture. Dot squash with butter, place cut side up in a baking dish and pour in a shallow layer of water. Bake for 45 minutes, until squash is fork-tender. **Serves 4.**

Acorn Squash with Orange Molasses

2	acorn squash, halved at their equators, seeds and fibers removed	2
1	clove garlic, minced	1
2 tbsp	light (fancy) molasses	25 mL
2 tbsp	honey	25 mL
1 tbsp	orange juice	15 mL
1 tsp	balsamic vinegar	5 mL
	Salt and freshly ground black pepper to taste	
1 tsp	butter	5 mL

Preheat oven to 350°F (180°C). Rub the interiors of the squash with garlic. Combine molasses, honey, orange juice, vinegar, salt and pepper; brush squash with this mixture. Dot squash with butter, place cut side up in a baking dish and pour in a shallow layer of water. Bake for 45 minutes, until squash is fork-tender. **Serves 4.**

Acorn Squash with Spiced Honey

2	acorn squash, halved at their equators, seeds and fibers removed	2
⅓ cup	honey	75 mL
1 tbsp	freshly squeezed lemon juice	15 mL
½ tsp	ground cinnamon	2 mL
½ tsp	ground ginger	2 mL
Pinch	cayenne pepper	Pinch
Pinch	ground allspice	Pinch
1 tsp	butter	5 mL

Preheat oven to 350°F (180°C). Combine honey, lemon juice, cinnamon, ginger, cayenne and allspice; brush squash with this mixture. Dot squash with butter, place cut side up in a baking dish and pour in a shallow layer of water. Bake for 45 minutes, until squash is fork-tender. **Serves 4.**

Harvest Vegetable Stuffing

2 tbsp	olive oil	25 mL
1	onion, finely chopped	1
1	stalk celery, sliced	1
1	clove garlic, minced	1
1 tbsp	poultry seasoning	15 mL
1 tsp	dried rosemary, crumbled	5 mL
4 cups	shredded vegetables (such as cabbage, zucchini, carrots or acorn squash)	1 L
2 cups	toasted bread cubes	500 mL
1/2 cup	chicken broth	125 mL
	Salt and freshly ground black pepper to taste	

In a large skillet, heat oil over medium-high heat. Sauté onion and celery until barely tender. Add garlic, poultry seasoning and rosemary; sauté for 30 seconds. Add vegetables and sauté until tender. Add bread cubes and broth; cook until mixture is hot and moist. Season with salt and pepper. **Makes enough to stuff 2 frying chickens; 1 roasting chicken, turkey or capon; 2 ducks; or 4 large fish.**

Wild Mushroom Stuffing

Follow preceding recipe, but add 2 cups (500 mL) sliced wild or exotic mushrooms with the vegetables.

Harvest Rice Stuffing

Follow recipe for Harvest Vegetable Stuffing (above), but substitute cooked rice for the bread cubes.

Fall Orchard Stuffing

1 tbsp	walnut oil	15 mL
1 tbsp	olive oil	15 mL
1	onion, finely chopped	1
1	clove garlic, minced	1
2 tsp	dried basil	10 mL
1 tsp	dried thyme	5 mL
1 tsp	dried rosemary, crumbled	5 mL
2 cups	shredded zucchini	500 mL
2 cups	chopped walnuts	500 mL
1 cup	toasted bread cubes	250 mL
1/2 cup	chicken broth	125 mL
Pinch	ground nutmeg	Pinch

In a large skillet, heat walnut oil and olive oil over medium-high heat. Sauté onion, garlic, basil, thyme and rosemary until onion is tender. Combine with the remaining ingredients. *Use as you would Harvest Vegetable Stuffing (above).*

Harvest Quiche

2 tbsp	olive oil	25 mL
1/2 cup	chopped onion	125 mL
1	clove garlic, minced	1
1 tsp	dried thyme	5 mL
3 cups	shredded zucchini	750 mL
2	eggs, beaten	2
1 cup	milk	250 mL
1 cup	shredded Swiss cheese	250 mL
1	prebaked 8-inch (20 cm) pastry shell (see recipe, page 21)	1

Preheat oven to 375°F (190°C). In a nonstick skillet, heat oil over medium-high heat. Sauté onion, garlic and thyme until onion is tender. Add zucchini and sauté for 2 minutes. Combine eggs, milk and cheese; stir in onion mixture. Pour into pastry shell, place on a baking sheet and bake for 45 minutes, until center is set. **Serves 4.**

Bacon, Peppers and Potatoes

4	slices bacon	4
2 lbs	russet potatoes, thinly sliced and blotted dry	1 kg
1/2 cup	thinly sliced onion	125 mL
2	cloves garlic, minced	2
1	roasted red bell pepper (see page 11), diced	1
1 tbsp	chopped fresh Italian (flat-leaf) parsley	15 mL
Pinch	ground nutmeg	Pinch
	Salt and freshly ground black pepper to taste	

In a large skillet, over medium heat, cook bacon until crisp; remove to a plate, blot with paper towels, crumble and set aside. Add potatoes and onion to the fat in the pan, increase heat to medium-high and sauté until potatoes are browned and tender, about 20 minutes. Stir in garlic, roasted pepper, parsley, nutmeg, salt and pepper. Sprinkle with crumbled bacon. **Serves 4.**

Grilled Tomatillo and Rice Salad

1/3 cup	extra-virgin olive oil	75 mL
1/4 cup	red wine vinegar	50 mL
1/4 cup	chopped fresh cilantro	50 mL
	Juice of 2 limes	
	Salt and freshly ground black pepper to taste	
8	tomatillos, husked	8
3 cups	warm cooked brown rice	750 mL

Preheat broiler or barbecue grill to high. Meanwhile, whisk together oil, vinegar, cilantro, lime juice, salt and pepper. Broil or grill tomatillos, turning every 20 seconds, until skins are evenly blistered; let cool and coarsely chop. Toss together tomatillos, brown rice and dressing. **Serves 4.**

Marinated Green Tomato and White Bean Salad

2	cloves garlic, minced	2
2	green onions, sliced	2
1	onion, minced	1
⅓ cup	extra-virgin olive oil	75 mL
¼ cup	red wine vinegar	50 mL
2 tbsp	minced fresh Italian (flat-leaf) parsley	25 mL
2 tbsp	chopped fresh basil	25 mL
2 tbsp	freshly squeezed lemon juice	25 mL
1 tsp	chopped hot chili pepper	5 mL
3	green (unripe) tomatoes, diced	3
1	can (14 to 19 oz/398 to 540 mL) cannellini or white kidney beans, drained and rinsed	1

In a serving bowl, whisk together garlic, green onions, onion, oil, vinegar, parsley, basil, lemon juice and chili pepper. Add green tomatoes and beans; toss to coat. Cover and refrigerate for about 1 hour, until chilled. **Serves 4.**

Green Tomato Gazpacho

6	ice cubes	6
2	large green (unripe) tomatoes, quartered	2
1	small onion, quartered	1
1	clove garlic	1
½	cucumber	½
3 tbsp	extra-virgin olive oil	45 mL
1 tbsp	white wine vinegar	15 mL
1 tsp	hot pepper sauce (such as Tabasco)	5 mL
	Salt and freshly ground black pepper to taste	

In a food processor, roughly chop ice cubes, green tomatoes, onion, garlic and cucumber. Add oil, vinegar, hot pepper sauce, salt and pepper; process until finely chopped. Cover and refrigerate for about 1 hour, until chilled. **Serves 4.**

Tomato Sauce with Fennel and Orange

2 tbsp	olive oil	25 mL
1	onion, chopped	1
1	clove garlic, minced	1
1 tbsp	finely grated orange zest	15 mL
½ tsp	ground fennel seeds	2 mL
½ tsp	ground turmeric	2 mL
1	can (14 to 19 oz/398 to 540 mL) crushed tomatoes	1
1	can (14 to 19 oz/398 to 540 mL) diced tomatoes, drained	1
Pinch	hot pepper flakes	Pinch
	Juice of 1 large orange	

In a large skillet, heat oil over medium heat. Sauté onion until tender. Add garlic, orange zest, fennel seeds and turmeric; sauté for 30 seconds. Add crushed tomatoes, diced tomatoes, hot pepper flakes and orange juice; reduce heat and simmer for 10 minutes. **Serves 4.** *Serve over shell-shaped pasta, fish, chicken, veal or rice.*

Roasted Pepper and Gorgonzola Grinder

4	long rolls, halved horizontally	4
¾ cup	oil and vinegar dressing, divided	175 mL
4 oz	Gorgonzola cheese, crumbled	125 g
2 cups	finely sliced romaine lettuce	500 mL
1⅓ cups	thinly sliced roasted bell peppers (see page 11)	325 mL

Preheat oven to 400°F (200°C). Remove a trough of bread from each half-roll and spoon 1 tbsp (15 mL) of the dressing along each trough. Fill troughs with equal amounts of Gorgonzola, romaine and roasted peppers. Top each sandwich with 1 tbsp (15 mL) dressing and wrap in foil. Bake for 15 minutes, until cheese melts and bread is warmed through. **Serves 4.**

Chapter 34
Winter Vegetables
Beets, Carrots, Parsnips and Potatoes

Honey-Baked Beets 387

Orange-Garlic Beets 388

Braised Fennel 388

Braised Orange Fennel 388

Mediterranean Braised Leeks 388

Roasted Onions and Olives 388

Cumin Carrots 388

Carrot and Red Pepper 388

Carrot, Parsnip and Chives 388

Creamed Parsnips 388

Potatoes au Gratin 389

Gorgonzola Gratin 389

Ham and Swiss Gratin 389

Potato and Celeriac Gratin 389

Potatoes au Gratin
with Caramelized Onions 389

Scalloped Potatoes with Feta 389

Scalloped Potatoes
with Onions and Anchovies 389

Potatoes Parmesan 389

Classic Mashed Potatoes 389

Mashed Potatoes with Roasted Garlic . . 389

Potato Celeriac Purée 390

Potato Fennel Purée 390

Sweet Potato and Apple Purée 390

Mashed Potatoes
with Yogurt and Herbs 390

Mashed Potatoes
with Ham and Cheese 390

Blue Cheese Mashed Potatoes 390

Sautéed Potatoes with Walnuts 390

Sautéed Potatoes with Garlic and Olives . . 390

Sautéed Potatoes,
Onions and Smoked Salmon 390

Roasted Potatoes with Turnips 390

Potato Chips 391

Spicy Potato Chips 391

Perfect Fries 391

Buffalo Fries 391

Parmesan Fries 391

Perfect Hash-Brown Potatoes 391

Peppered Hash Browns 391

Hash Browns and Cabbage 391

Chilied Hash Browns 391

Potato Pancakes 392

Potato Fennel Pancakes 392

Potato Leek Pancakes 392

Potato Garlic Galette 392

Potato Cheese Galette 392

Corned Beef and Potato Salad 392

Baked Potatoes with
Sour Cream Vinaigrette 392

Baked Potatoes with Mustard Sauce . . . 393

Baked Potatoes with Minted Yogurt . . . 393

Twice-Baked Cheddar
Jalapeño Potatoes 393

Twice-Baked Blue Cheese Potatoes . . . 393

During winter, when fields are stripped and the garden is plowed under, our choice of vegetables boils down to one thing: cook what you can get. In temperate climates, that generally means the roots, tubers and hearty greens that can stay in the ground well into the last days of harvest and then tolerate long storage with minimal loss of quality and nutrients.

Now that vegetables are grown globally, seasonal distinctions are more a matter of tradition than reality. You can get potatoes, sweet potatoes and cabbage all year round, but they never seem as attractive when the dazzling bounty of summer blinds us to their subtle pleasures. Eating what the earth provides on the earth's time schedule grounds us and, in large part, embodies the comfort of cooking and eating vegetables during winter.

More than half the recipes in this chapter are for potatoes. You'll also find delicious ways to prepare carrots, onions, parsnips and beets — vegetables that add color and flavor to cold-weather meals — but if you love potatoes as much as we do, you have arrived at comfort-food nirvana. Potatoes are cheap, plentiful and effortless to prepare, yet most of us never take advantage of their potential. Ignoring an international arsenal of potato recipes, we dig the rut of our cooking routines deeper by mindlessly repeating the same baked- and boiled-potato dishes year after year.

Potatoes are classified by starch and fiber content. Low-starch potatoes (sometimes referred to as waxy) are round and have thin skins that range in color from beige through yellow to red. They are usually sold by the color of their skins (for example, red-skinned potatoes or Yukon Gold potatoes), but regardless of their color, these potatoes are interchangeable in any recipe in which the potatoes are boiled. Baby round potatoes are called "new," and they are in season late in the spring into the summer, so you will find recipes for new potatoes in the Summer Bounty chapter (page 394).

Starchy potatoes are used for baking. They are known by several different names, including russet potatoes, baking potatoes and Idaho potatoes. Look for russets with thick, rough skin and a well-formed oblong shape.

Avoid any potato with soft spots, deep pits or bruises. Sprouting indicates age and is often accompanied by a softening of the potato. A green tinge to the skin comes from the alkaloid solanine, produced when a potato is exposed to light for extended periods. Solanine creates a bitter, unpleasant taste, and some people have allergic reactions to it, so always store potatoes away from light.

Never refrigerate potatoes or store them below 40°F (4°C). Store them at room temperature if you must, but they last longest when kept cool and dry. The best choice is a paper or burlap sack or a wooden box kept on a shelf in a cool cellar. At room temperature, some potatoes will sprout and shrivel in as little as a week; in the refrigerator, the starch breaks down into sugar, which destroys the texture and taste of the potato. Although it is possible to reverse this process by leaving the potato at cellar temperature for a week or more, the vegetable will never regain its original firmness.

About these recipes . . .

The following recipes assume that you will season to taste with salt and pepper, often especially important with potatoes. These ingredients are mentioned only in recipes where specific amounts are necessary or where their absence would be disastrous.

Honey-Baked Beets

4	beets, stems trimmed to within 2 inches (5 cm)	4
¼ cup	honey	50 mL
1 tsp	freshly squeezed lemon juice	5 mL
	Salt and freshly ground black pepper to taste	

Place beets in a deep microwave-safe dish, such as a pie plate, and add a small amount of water. Cover with microwave-safe plastic wrap and microwave on High for 15 to 18 minutes, or until tender, turning halfway through. Let cool for several minutes. Remove wrap, cut ends off beets, peel and quarter. Combine honey and lemon juice; add to beets and toss to coat. Season with salt and pepper. **Serves 4.**

Orange-Garlic Beets

4	beets, stems trimmed to within 2 inches (5 cm)	4
2 tbsp	butter	25 mL
1	clove garlic, minced	1
½ cup	orange juice	125 mL

Cook and prepare beets as in preceding recipe, then cut into thin wedges. In a large skillet, melt butter over medium heat. Sauté beets for 1 minute. Add garlic and orange juice; cook until liquid is reduced to a glaze, swirling pan to coat beets. **Serves 4.**

Braised Fennel

2 tbsp	olive oil	25 mL
1	large head fennel, trimmed of leaves and quartered lengthwise	1
¼ cup	finely chopped onion	50 mL
1	clove garlic, minced	1
½ tsp	dried rosemary, crumbled	2 mL
2	plum (Roma) tomatoes, peeled, seeded and finely chopped	2
⅔ cup	dry white wine	150 mL

In a large skillet, heat oil over medium-high heat. Sauté fennel until browned. Add onion, garlic and rosemary; sauté for 1 minute. Add tomatoes and wine; reduce heat, cover and simmer for 20 to 25 minutes, or until fennel is tender. **Serves 4.**

Braised Orange Fennel

Follow preceding recipe, but add the finely grated zest and juice of 1 orange with the tomatoes. Garnish with 1 tbsp (15 mL) chopped fresh Italian (flat-leaf) parsley. **Serves 4.**

Mediterranean Braised Leeks

Follow recipe for Braised Fennel (above), but replace the fennel with 4 leeks (white and light green parts only), halved. **Serves 4.**

Roasted Onions and Olives

4	large onions, cut into wedges	4
2 tbsp	extra-virgin olive oil	25 mL
	Salt and freshly ground black pepper to taste	
1	clove garlic, minced	1
⅓ cup	chopped pitted black olives	75 mL
2 tbsp	chopped fresh Italian (flat-leaf) parsley	25 mL

Preheat oven to 400°F (200°C). Toss onions with oil, salt and pepper; spread in an even layer on a large rimmed baking sheet. Roast until tender and browned, about 30 minutes. Toss with garlic, olives and parsley. **Serves 4.**

Cumin Carrots

1 cup	water	250 mL
3 tbsp	honey	45 mL
1 tbsp	freshly squeezed lemon juice	15 mL
1 lb	carrots, cut into diagonal slices (see page 9)	500 g
1 tbsp	butter	15 mL
½ tsp	ground cumin	2 mL
1 tbsp	chopped fresh Italian (flat-leaf) parsley	15 mL
	Salt and freshly ground black pepper to taste	

In a large saucepan, over high heat, bring water, honey and lemon juice to a boil. Add carrots and boil until tender, about 8 minutes; drain. In a skillet, melt butter over medium heat; sprinkle with cumin. Stir in carrots, parsley, salt and pepper. **Serves 4.**

Carrot and Red Pepper

1 tbsp	olive oil	15 mL
¼ cup	finely chopped onion	50 mL
1 cup	finely julienned carrot	250 mL
1 cup	finely julienned red bell pepper	250 mL
2 tbsp	vegetable or chicken broth, or water	25 mL
	Juice of ½ lemon	
1 tbsp	chopped fresh Italian (flat-leaf) parsley	15 mL
	Salt and freshly ground black pepper to taste	

In a skillet, heat oil over medium heat. Sauté onion for 30 seconds. Add carrot and red pepper; sauté for 2 minutes. Add broth and lemon juice; simmer for 2 minutes, until carrot is barely soft. Stir in parsley, salt and pepper. **Serves 4.**

Carrot, Parsnip and Chives

Follow preceding recipe, but replace the red pepper with parsnips, and replace the parsley with chopped fresh chives. **Serves 4.**

Creamed Parsnips

2 tbsp	butter	25 mL
1 tbsp	finely chopped onion	15 mL
1 lb	parsnips, peeled and chopped	500 g
½ cup	water (approx.)	125 mL
Pinch	ground nutmeg	Pinch
Pinch	cayenne pepper	Pinch

| 1 tbsp | sour cream or whipping (35%) cream | 15 mL |
| | (optional) | |

In a saucepan, melt butter over medium heat. Sauté onion until tender but not browned. Add parsnips and water; simmer until parsnips are tender, about 10 minutes (add more water if necessary). Drain well. Transfer to a food processor, add nutmeg and cayenne, and purée. Stir in sour cream, if desired. Serves 4.

Potatoes au Gratin

2 tsp	butter	10 mL
1 lb	russet potatoes, peeled and sliced	500 g
½ cup	sliced onion	125 mL
	Salt and freshly ground black pepper to taste	
½ cup	shredded Swiss cheese	125 mL
1 cup	milk and/or half-and-half (10%) cream	250 mL
2 tbsp	freshly grated Parmesan cheese	25 mL

Preheat oven to 375°F (190°C). Grease a shallow 8-inch (20 cm) baking dish with butter. Make a layer of half the potatoes and onion, then sprinkle with salt and pepper. Top with half the Swiss cheese, milk and Parmesan. Repeat with the remaining ingredients, in the same order. Bake for 1 hour, until potatoes are tender and top is bubbly and brown. Serves 4.

Gorgonzola Gratin

Follow preceding recipe, but add ½ clove garlic, minced, with the onion in each layer, replace the Swiss cheese with 2 oz (60 g) Gorgonzola, crumbled, and omit the Parmesan. Serves 4.

Ham and Swiss Gratin

Follow recipe for Potatoes au Gratin (above), but add 2 oz (60 g) baked ham, diced, with the potatoes in each layer. Serves 4.

Potato and Celeriac Gratin

Follow recipe for Potatoes au Gratin (above), but reduce the potatoes to 12 oz (375 g), add ¾ cup (175 mL) sliced peeled celery root (celeriac) with the potatoes in each layer, use cream (any type, minimum 10%) instead of milk, and omit the Parmesan. Serves 4.

Potatoes au Gratin with Caramelized Onions

Follow recipe for Potatoes au Gratin (left), but first, in a skillet, over low heat, cook 2 cups (500 mL) thinly sliced onion in 2 tbsp (25 mL) melted butter until deeply browned, about 15 minutes. Use instead of the ½ cup (125 mL) sliced onion. Serves 4.

Scalloped Potatoes with Feta

Follow recipe for Potatoes au Gratin (left), but replace the Swiss cheese with 2 oz (60 g) feta, crumbled, omit the Parmesan, and drizzle 1 tsp (5 mL) extra-virgin olive oil over each layer. Serves 4.

Scalloped Potatoes with Onions and Anchovies

Follow recipe for Potatoes au Gratin (left), but double the amount of onion and add 4 drained canned anchovies, chopped, with the onion in each layer. Serves 4.

Potatoes Parmesan

Follow recipe for Potatoes au Gratin (left), but add ½ clove garlic, minced, with the onion in each layer, and substitute additional freshly grated Parmesan cheese for the Swiss cheese. Serves 4.

Classic Mashed Potatoes

3 lbs	red-skinned, gold-skinned or other boiling potatoes, peeled and cut into large chunks	1.5 kg
1 cup	sour cream, half-and-half (10%) cream or plain yogurt	250 mL
2 tbsp	butter	25 mL
	Salt and freshly ground black pepper to taste	

In a large pot of salted water, boil potatoes until tender, about 15 minutes. Drain and return to saucepan. Add sour cream and, using a potato masher or the back of a fork, mash until light and fluffy. Stir in butter, salt and pepper. Reheat, if necessary. Serves 4.

Mashed Potatoes with Roasted Garlic

Follow preceding recipe, but add 2 tbsp (25 mL) Roasted Garlic Purée (see page 464) with the sour cream. Serves 4.

Potato Celeriac Purée

Follow recipe for Classic Mashed Potatoes (page 389), but replace 1 lb (500 g) of the potatoes with 1 lb (500 g) celery root (celeriac), peeled and diced. Serves 4.

Potato Fennel Purée

Follow recipe for Classic Mashed Potatoes (page 389), but replace 1 lb (500 g) of the potatoes with 1 lb (500 g) fennel bulbs, peeled and diced, and replace half the butter with 1 tbsp (15 mL) extra-virgin olive oil. Serves 4.

Sweet Potato and Apple Purée

Follow recipe for Classic Mashed Potatoes (page 389), but use sweet potatoes instead of boiling potatoes. While potatoes are boiling, in a skillet, melt 2 tbsp (25 mL) butter over medium heat. Sauté 1 tart apple, peeled and diced, and 1 clove garlic, minced, until tender. Transfer to a food processor and purée. Add with the sour cream, along with 1 tbsp (15 mL) packed light brown sugar. Serves 4.

Mashed Potatoes with Yogurt and Herbs

Follow recipe for Classic Mashed Potatoes (page 389), but use yogurt (not sour cream or half-and-half). Before adding butter to the potatoes, melt it in a skillet over medium heat, and sauté 3 tbsp (45 mL) of any combination of minced parsley, thyme, tarragon, chervil and basil for 1 minute. Serves 4.

Mashed Potatoes with Ham and Cheese

Follow recipe for Classic Mashed Potatoes (page 389), but add ½ cup (125 mL) shredded sharp Cheddar cheese and 2 oz (60 g) baked ham, finely diced, with the sour cream. Serves 4.

Blue Cheese Mashed Potatoes

Follow recipe for Classic Mashed Potatoes (page 389), but replace the sour cream with blue cheese dressing. Serves 4.

Sautéed Potatoes with Walnuts

3 tbsp	vegetable oil	45 mL
¼ cup	finely chopped onion	50 mL
2 lbs	russet potatoes, thinly sliced and blotted dry	1 kg
Pinch	ground ginger	Pinch
	Salt and freshly ground black pepper to taste	
½ cup	finely chopped toasted walnuts	125 mL

In a large nonstick skillet, heat oil over medium-high heat. Sauté onion until transparent. Add potatoes, ginger, salt and pepper; sauté until potatoes are browned and tender, about 20 minutes. Add walnuts for the last few minutes of cooking. Serves 4.

Sautéed Potatoes with Garlic and Olives

3 tbsp	vegetable oil	45 mL
2 lbs	russet potatoes, thinly sliced and blotted dry	1 kg
Pinch	ground nutmeg	Pinch
	Salt and freshly ground black pepper to taste	
2	cloves garlic, minced	2
¼ cup	chopped pitted oil-cured black olives	50 mL
1 tbsp	chopped fresh Italian (flat-leaf) parsley	15 mL

In a large nonstick skillet, heat oil over medium-high heat. Sauté potatoes, nutmeg, salt and pepper until potatoes are browned and tender, about 20 minutes. Stir in garlic, olives and parsley. Serves 4.

Sautéed Potatoes, Onions and Smoked Salmon

Follow preceding recipe, but add ½ cup (125 mL) thinly sliced onions with the potatoes, and replace the olives with 2 oz (60 g) smoked salmon, chopped. Serves 4.

Roasted Potatoes with Turnips

1¼ lbs	russet potatoes, cut into wedges	625 g
1 lb	turnips, peeled and cut into wedges	500 g
1 tbsp	melted butter	15 mL
	Salt and freshly ground black pepper to taste	

Preheat oven to 400°F (200°C). In a large pot of salted water, boil potatoes and turnips for 10 minutes; drain and pat dry. Place in a large roasting pan, toss with melted butter and sprinkle with salt and pepper. Roast for 30 to 40 minutes, turning 3 or 4 times, until tender and brown. **Serves 4.**

Potato Chips

2 lbs	russet potatoes	1 kg
4 cups	ice water, mixed with	1 L
	1 tbsp (15 mL) salt	
	Vegetable oil	
1 tsp	salt	5 mL

Slice potatoes paper-thin, adding immediately to salted ice water; drain and dry well. Deep-fry (see page 9) in 3 to 4 inches (7.5 to 10 cm) vegetable oil for about 3 minutes, or until golden and crisp. Drain on paper towels. Season with salt. **Serves 4.**

Spicy Potato Chips

Follow preceding recipe, but add $\frac{1}{4}$ tsp (1 mL) freshly ground black pepper and a pinch of cayenne pepper with the salt. **Serves 4.**

Perfect Fries

2 lbs	russet potatoes	1 kg
4 cups	ice water, mixed with	1 L
	1 tbsp (15 mL) salt	
	Vegetable oil	
1 tsp	salt	5 mL

Cut potatoes into $\frac{3}{4}$-inch (2 cm) thick rods, adding immediately to salted ice water; drain and dry well. Deep-fry (see page 9) in 3 to 4 inches (7.5 to 10 cm) vegetable oil heated to 300°F (150°C) for about 3 minutes, or until tender. Drain on paper towels and heat oil to 375°F (190°C). Deep-fry potatoes for 1 to 2 minutes, or until crisp and golden brown. Drain on paper towels. Season with salt. **Serves 4.**

Buffalo Fries

Follow preceding recipe, but omit the salt, and toss finished fries with a mixture of 2 tbsp (25 mL) melted butter and 2 tbsp (25 mL) hot pepper sauce (such as Frank's RedHot). **Serves 4.**

Parmesan Fries

Follow recipe for Perfect Fries (above), but add $\frac{1}{4}$ cup (50 mL) freshly grated Parmesan cheese with the salt. **Serves 4.**

Perfect Hash-Brown Potatoes

2 lbs	russet potatoes	1 kg
	Ice water	
1 tbsp	butter	15 mL
1 tbsp	vegetable oil	15 mL
1 cup	finely sliced onion	250 mL
	Salt and freshly ground black pepper to taste	

Grate potatoes directly into a bowl of ice water and swirl until water is cloudy. Lift grated potatoes from water with a slotted spoon and wring dry in a clean towel. In a large skillet, heat butter and oil over medium-high heat. Cook potatoes and onion until they begin to brown on the bottom, about 5 minutes. Coarsely chop with a spatula and turn pieces over; cook, chopping and turning every 3 to 5 minutes, until potatoes are uniformly tender and brown. Season with salt and pepper. **Serves 4.**

Peppered Hash Browns

Follow preceding recipe, but add 1 cup (250 mL) diced bell pepper (any color) with the onions, and add a pinch of hot pepper flakes halfway through cooking. **Serves 4.**

Hash Browns and Cabbage

Follow recipe for Perfect Hash-Brown Potatoes (above), but decrease the onion to $\frac{1}{2}$ cup (125 mL), and add 3 cups (750 mL) shredded cabbage with the onion. **Serves 4.**

Chilied Hash Browns

Follow recipe for Perfect Hash-Brown Potatoes (above), but halfway through cooking, sprinkle potatoes with 1 tbsp (15 mL) chili powder, 1 tbsp (15 mL) paprika, 1 tsp (5 mL) ground cumin and 1 tsp (5 mL) ground coriander. **Serves 4.**

Potato Pancakes

1 lb	russet potatoes	500 g
	Ice water	
3	large or extra-large eggs, beaten	3
3 tbsp	minced or grated onion	45 mL
2 tbsp	all-purpose flour	25 mL
1 tsp	salt	5 mL
	Freshly ground black pepper to taste	
	Vegetable oil	
	Sour cream	

Coarsely grate potatoes directly into a bowl of ice water and swirl until water is cloudy. Lift grated potatoes from water with a slotted spoon and wring dry in a clean towel. Combine potatoes, eggs, onion, flour, salt and pepper. In a deep skillet, heat ¼ inch (0.5 cm) oil over medium-high heat until very hot but not smoking. Add potato mixture by heaping large spoonfuls, flattening the mounds into pancakes about 3 inches (7.5 cm) in diameter. Cook, turning once, for 4 to 5 minutes per side, or until browned on both sides. Drain on paper towels and keep warm. Repeat with the remaining potato mixture, adding and heating oil as necessary between batches. Serve with sour cream. **Serves 4.**

Potato Fennel Pancakes

Follow preceding recipe, but add 1 cup (250 mL) finely chopped fennel bulb with the onion. **Serves 4.**

Potato Leek Pancakes

Follow recipe for Potato Pancakes (above), but omit the onion, and add 2 leeks (white and light green parts only), finely chopped, and 1 small clove garlic, minced, with the eggs. **Serves 4.**

Potato Garlic Galette

1 lb	russet potatoes	500 g
	Ice water	
¼ cup	butter, divided	50 mL
1	clove garlic, minced	1
	Salt and freshly ground black pepper to taste	

Coarsely grate potatoes directly into a bowl of ice water and swirl until water is cloudy. Lift grated potatoes from water with a slotted spoon and wring dry in a clean towel. In a large nonstick skillet, melt half the butter over medium-high heat until foamy. Add half the potatoes and press into an even layer. Sprinkle with garlic, salt and pepper. Add the remaining potatoes on top and pack into an even layer. Season again with salt and pepper. Cover and cook for about 15 minutes, or until potatoes are browned on the bottom. Flip onto a plate. Melt the remaining butter and slide the galette, brown side up, back into the pan. Cook for 10 minutes, until browned on the bottom. **Serves 4.**

Potato Cheese Galette

Follow preceding recipe, but add ¼ cup (50 mL) freshly grated Parmesan cheese with the garlic. After flipping galette, top with ⅓ cup (75 mL) shredded Gruyère or fontina cheese. Cover for the last 5 minutes of cooking. **Serves 4.**

Corned Beef and Potato Salad

1½ lbs	red-skinned or other boiling potatoes	750 g
¼ cup	cider vinegar	50 mL
2 tbsp	whole-grain mustard	25 mL
⅓ cup	canola oil	75 mL
	Salt and freshly ground black pepper to taste	
4 oz	shredded corned beef	125 g
3 tbsp	finely chopped onion	45 mL
2 tbsp	finely chopped fresh Italian (flat-leaf) parsley	25 mL

In a large pot of salted water, boil potatoes until tender, about 20 minutes; drain, peel and cut into bite-size pieces. Meanwhile, in a serving bowl, combine vinegar and mustard, then slowly whisk in oil until thick. Season with salt and pepper. Add potatoes, corned beef, onion and parsley; toss to coat. **Serves 4.**

Baked Potatoes with Sour Cream Vinaigrette

4	russet potatoes	4
2 tsp	vegetable oil	10 mL
⅓ cup	sour cream	75 mL
3 tbsp	Italian vinaigrette	45 mL

Preheat oven to 425°F (220°C). Rub potatoes with oil and poke each in several places with a fork. Place on an oven rack and bake until potatoes yield to a gentle push, about 45 minutes. Meanwhile, whisk together sour cream and dressing. Cut a cross through the skin of each potato and squeeze gently to lightly fluff the interior. Spoon 2 tbsp (25 mL) of the sauce over each potato. **Serves 4.**

Baked Potatoes with Mustard Sauce

Follow preceding recipe, but omit the dressing, and whisk 1 clove garlic, minced, and 2 tbsp (25 mL) Dijon mustard with the sour cream. **Serves 4.**

Baked Potatoes with Minted Yogurt

Prepare and bake potatoes as in Baked Potatoes with Sour Cream Vinaigrette (page 392), but omit the sour cream and dressing, and top potatoes with a mixture of 1 small clove garlic, minced, $\frac{1}{2}$ cup (125 mL) plain yogurt, 1 tbsp (15 mL) chopped fresh mint, 1 tbsp (15 mL) freshly squeezed lemon juice and 1 tbsp (15 mL) extra-virgin olive oil. **Serves 4.**

Twice-Baked Cheddar Jalapeño Potatoes

Prepare and bake potatoes as described in Baked Potatoes with Sour Cream Vinaigrette (page 392), but reduce the sour cream to $\frac{1}{4}$ cup (50 mL) and omit the dressing. Cut a 2-inch (5 cm) lengthwise slit along each baked potato, squeeze sides to force the slit open, and scoop out all but a thin shell of potato. Mix potato flesh with sour cream, 1 canned jalapeño pepper, minced, and $1\frac{1}{2}$ cups (375 mL) shredded Cheddar cheese. Refill potato shells with this mixture and return to oven for 10 minutes, until cheese is melted. **Serves 4.**

Twice-Baked Blue Cheese Potatoes

Prepare and bake potatoes as described in Baked Potatoes with Sour Cream Vinaigrette (page 392), but reduce the sour cream to $\frac{1}{4}$ cup (50 mL) and omit the dressing. Cut a 2-inch (5 cm) lengthwise slit along each baked potato, squeeze sides to force the slit open, and scoop out all but a thin shell of potato. Mix potato flesh with sour cream, 1 clove garlic, minced, and 4 oz (125 g) blue cheese, crumbled. Refill potato shells with this mixture and return to oven for 10 minutes, until cheese is melted. **Serves 4.**

Chapter 35
Summer Bounty
Corn, Zucchini, Tomatoes and Other Garden Excesses

Sicilian Artichokes 395
Artichoke with Tofu Dressing 395
Stir-Fried Asparagus with Cashews 395
Broiled Corn with Roasted Garlic Butter . . 396
Corn on the Cob with Paprika Butter . . 396
Chilied Corn with Peanut Sauce 396
Corn and Smoked Salmon 396
Crookneck Squash Parmesan 396
Zucchini Bread 396
Lemon Zucchini Muffins 397
Gingered Pecan Zucchini Bread 397
Zucchini Cornbread 397
Zucchini Soup 397
Chilled Curried Zucchini Soup 397
Lemon Zucchini Soup 397
Split Pea Zucchini Soup 397
Zucchini Minestrone 398
Zucchini Sautéed with Roasted Peppers . . 398
New Potatoes au Gratin with Bacon . . . 398
Roasted Balsamic Tomatoes 398
Parmesan-Crusted Baked Tomato 398
Rosemary-Grilled Tomato 399
Tomato with Black Pepper and Lime . . . 399
Quick Tomato Salad 399
Tomato Salad with
Mozzarella and Herbs 399
Marinated Tomato with
Chèvre and Onion 399

Tomato and Fried Spinach Salad 399
Tomato Tonnato 400
Spinach Salad with Tomato Vinaigrette . . 400
Cherry Tomato and
Caramelized Onion Salad 400
Red and Yellow Tomato Salad 400
Chili Salad 400
Tomato Slaw 400
Tomato and Crab Salad 401
Tomato Niçoise 401
Avocado, Tomato and Shrimp
with Chili Pepper Vinaigrette 401
Tomato with Pesto 401
Tomato Pesto Pasta Salad 401
Tomatoes Marinated in Olive Oil,
Garlic and Hot Pepper Flakes 401
Fresh Tomatoes and Pasta 402
Fresh Tomato Sauce 402
Fresh Tomato and Cream Sauce 402
Pasta with Tomatoes, Basil and Feta . . . 402
Tomato Sandwich 402
Mild Red Salsa 403
Mild Green Salsa 403
Cucumber Salad with Tomato Salsa . . . 403
Avocado and Tomato Salsa 403
Tomato and Corn Salsa 403
Tomato Raita 403

What cook could hope to compete with a newly picked tomato? When it's at its best, who could improve on its color, or its fragrance of sunshine and freshly tilled land? Who could contrive another flavor as intricately sweet and tart, or boast a new ingredient better able to turn a bowl of plain pasta or a stale crust of bread into a meal?

Smart cooks don't try, for they know that the best thing to do with perfectly ripe garden vegetables is as little as possible — and to do so whenever they can.

In temperate climates, vegetables are planted in spring, grow in summer and are harvested in the fall. Because summer is not harvest time, the vegetables associated with the season fall into two groups: those best picked when young and those with a relatively short growing season. New potatoes are just immature big potatoes, asparagus is the first shoot of a large plant, an artichoke is the flower bud of a large thistle, and sweet corn is picked while the kernels are still young and tender. Some short-season garden vegetables, such as tomatoes, cucumbers and summer squashes, are the very essence of summer.

About these recipes . . .

The following recipes offer ideas for hot and cold vegetables, salads, baked goods, soups and side dishes. Because there is a separate chapter for greens, you will not find recipes for spinach and lettuces here (although spinach is included in some of the recipes), but because the tomato is one of the few vegetables that is superior only in the summer, we have clustered almost all of our fresh tomato recipes here.

It is assumed that you will add salt and pepper to taste in each recipe. However, if the addition of salt or pepper is important to the success of the dish, it is included in the recipe.

Sicilian Artichokes

12	baby globe artichokes, trimmed of stems and thorns	12
6	whole black peppercorns	6
2	cloves garlic	2
1	bay leaf	1
¼ cup	red wine vinegar	50 mL
¼ cup	extra-virgin olive oil	50 mL
½ cup	chopped onion	125 mL
2	cloves garlic, minced	2
1 cup	canned diced tomatoes, drained	250 mL
¼ cup	chopped fresh Italian (flat-leaf) parsley	50 mL
	Juice of ½ lemon	

Heat 8 to 12 cups (2 to 3 L) of water to a rolling boil in a pot large enough to hold artichokes snugly. Add artichokes, peppercorns, garlic, bay leaf and vinegar, and boil for 20 to 30 minutes, or until stem ends can be easily pierced. Drain, quarter and pat dry. In a large skillet, heat oil over medium-high heat. Sauté onion until tender. Add minced garlic and sauté for 30 seconds. Add artichokes and sauté until lightly browned. Stir in tomato, parsley and lemon juice; heat through. **Serves 4.**

Artichoke with Tofu Dressing

4	large globe artichokes	4
1 tbsp	freshly squeezed lemon juice	15 mL
¼ cup	rice wine vinegar	50 mL
	Sesame Tofu Vinaigrette (see recipe, page 62)	

Heat 8 to 12 cups (2 to 3 L) of water to a rolling boil in a pot large enough to hold artichokes snugly. Meanwhile, trim artichokes of stems and thorns, and immediately rub cut surfaces with lemon juice. Add vinegar to the water, place artichokes stem end down in the water, and boil until stem ends can be easily pierced, about 40 minutes. Transfer to a colander, stem ends up, and drain well. Serve with Sesame Tofu Vinaigrette for dipping. **Serves 4.**

Stir-Fried Asparagus with Cashews

2 tbsp	canola oil	25 mL
1 lb	asparagus, trimmed and cut into 2-inch (5 cm) sections	500 g
⅓ cup	vegetable broth	75 mL
Pinch	hot pepper flakes	Pinch
1	clove garlic, minced	1
⅓ cup	oyster sauce	75 mL
1 tbsp	soy sauce	15 mL
	Juice of ½ lemon	
2	green onions, thinly sliced	2
1 cup	cashews	250 mL

In a large wok or heavy skillet, heat oil over medium-high heat until smoking. Stir-fry asparagus until bright green, about 1 minute. Add broth and hot pepper flakes, cover and steam for 3 minutes. Add garlic, oyster sauce, soy sauce and lemon juice; stir-fry until asparagus is glazed with sauce. Remove from heat and toss in green onions and cashews. **Serves 4.**

Broiled Corn with Roasted Garlic Butter

1	large head garlic	1
	Olive oil	
¼ cup	butter, softened	50 mL
4	ears corn, shucked	4

Preheat oven to 375°F (190°C). Cut the pointed ends from the garlic heads, exposing the tops of the cloves. Rub the exposed cloves of each head with oil. Wrap in foil and bake for 40 minutes, or until soft to the touch. Let cool slightly, gently squeeze cloves from their peels into the butter and mash with a small fork to combine. Preheat broiler or barbecue grill to high. Rub corn with a thin film of olive oil and broil or grill, turning three times, for a total of 8 minutes. Serve with garlic butter. **Serves 8.**

Corn on the Cob with Paprika Butter

4	ears corn (unshucked)	4
¼ cup	butter, softened	50 mL
2 tbsp	sweet paprika	25 mL
½ tsp	freshly squeezed lemon juice	2 mL
¼ tsp	freshly ground black pepper	1 mL
	Salt to taste	

Preheat barbecue grill to high. Grill corn, turning regularly, for about 15 minutes, or until husks are uniformly browned and corn is steamed inside (peek under the husk of 1 ear). Let cool for a few minutes, then remove husks and silk from each ear. Combine butter, paprika, lemon juice, pepper and salt; spread over corn at the table. **Serves 4.**

Chilied Corn with Peanut Sauce

1 tbsp	vegetable oil	15 mL
¼ cup	chopped onion	50 mL
1	clove garlic, minced	1
6	ears corn, kernels cut off (or 4 cups/1 L drained canned or thawed frozen corn kernels)	6
1	green onion, sliced	1
1 tbsp	chili powder	15 mL
1 tsp	soy sauce	5 mL
1 tsp	finely chopped gingerroot	5 mL
½ tsp	Chinese chili paste	2 mL
Pinch	ground cumin	Pinch
Pinch	ground coriander	Pinch
¼ cup	chicken or vegetable broth	50 mL
2 tbsp	smooth peanut butter	25 mL

In a large skillet, heat oil over medium heat. Sauté onion and garlic until transparent. Add corn, green onion, chili powder, soy sauce, ginger, chili paste, cumin and coriander; sauté for 4 to 5 minutes, or until corn is tender. Stir in broth and peanut butter until peanut butter is melted and liquid has thickened to a light sauce-like consistency. **Serves 4.**

Corn and Smoked Salmon

1 tbsp	olive oil	15 mL
1 tbsp	chopped shallot	15 mL
2 tsp	chopped fresh dill	10 mL
4 cups	cooked corn kernels	1 L
2 oz	smoked salmon, finely chopped	60 g

In a skillet, heat oil over medium heat. Sauté shallot and dill until shallot is tender. Add corn and heat through. Stir in smoked salmon. **Serves 4.**

Crookneck Squash Parmesan

2 tbsp	olive oil	25 mL
1	small red onion, thinly sliced	1
1	clove garlic, minced	1
4 cups	sliced yellow crookneck squash	1 L
¼ cup	freshly grated Parmesan cheese	50 mL
1 tbsp	chopped fresh Italian (flat-leaf) parsley	15 mL

In a large skillet, heat oil over medium heat. Sauté onion and garlic until tender. Add squash and sauté until tender, about 4 minutes; remove from heat. Toss with Parmesan and parsley. **Serves 4.**

Zucchini Bread

3 cups	all-purpose flour	750 mL
1 tsp	ground cinnamon	5 mL
1 tsp	baking powder	5 mL
½ tsp	salt	2 mL
¼ tsp	baking soda	1 mL
3	extra-large eggs	3
1 cup	granulated sugar	250 mL
1 cup	packed light brown sugar	250 mL
2 cups	canola oil	500 mL
2 tsp	vanilla	10 mL
2 cups	shredded zucchini	500 mL
1¾ cups	walnut pieces	425 mL

Preheat oven to 325°F (160°C) and grease and flour two 9- by 5-inch (2 L) loaf pans. Sift together flour, cinnamon, baking powder, salt and baking soda; set aside. Using an electric mixer, beat eggs, sugar and brown sugar until fluffy. Add oil and vanilla in a slow, steady stream, mixing constantly. Stir in flour mixture alternately with zucchini, making 3 additions of flour mixture and 2 of zucchini. Stir in nuts. Pour into prepared pans and bake for 75 minutes, or until a tester inserted in the center of a loaf comes out with a crumb clinging to it. Let cool in pans on a wire rack for 30 minutes. Remove from pans while warm. **Makes 2 loaves, or 24 slices.**

Lemon Zucchini Muffins

Follow preceding recipe, but prepare only half the batter, keeping the baking soda at $\frac{1}{4}$ tsp (1 mL) and adding the finely grated zest and juice of 1 large lemon with zucchini. Preheat oven to 350°F (180°C) and grease and flour a 12-cup muffin tin instead of the loaf pans. Bake for 30 minutes. **Makes 12 muffins.**

Gingered Pecan Zucchini Bread

Follow recipe for Zucchini Bread (page 396), but decrease the cinnamon to $\frac{1}{2}$ tsp (2 mL), add 2 tsp (10 mL) ground ginger with the cinnamon, replace the walnuts with pecans, and add $\frac{1}{4}$ cup (50 mL) minced candied ginger with the nuts. **Makes 2 loaves, or 24 slices.**

Zucchini Cornbread

1¼ cups	cornmeal	300 mL
¾ cup	all-purpose flour	175 mL
¼ cup	granulated sugar	50 mL
1 tsp	baking powder	5 mL
½ tsp	salt	2 mL
¼ tsp	baking soda	1 mL
2 tbsp	corn oil	25 mL
3 tbsp	finely chopped onion	45 mL
1 cup	shredded zucchini	250 mL
1	egg, beaten	1
1 cup	buttermilk	250 mL
	Vegetable cooking spray	

Preheat oven to 400°F (200°C) and place a 10-inch (25 cm) cast-iron skillet in the oven. Sift together cornmeal, flour, sugar, baking powder, salt and baking soda; set aside. In a small skillet, heat oil over medium heat. Sauté onion until tender. Add zucchini and heat through. Transfer to a bowl and stir in cornmeal mixture. Stir in egg and buttermilk until uniformly moist. Using a heavy potholder, remove skillet from oven and coat the interior with cooking spray. Pour in batter and bake for 25 minutes, until top is browned and a tester inserted in the center comes out with a crumb clinging to it. Remove from pan and let cool on a wire rack for 10 minutes. Cut into wedges. **Serves 8.**

Zucchini Soup

2 tbsp	butter	25 mL
1	onion, chopped	1
1	clove garlic, minced	1
4 cups	shredded zucchini	1 L
3 cups	chicken broth	750 mL
1 tsp	curry powder	5 mL
Pinch	cayenne pepper	Pinch
1 cup	cream (any type, minimum 10%)	250 mL

In a large saucepan, melt butter over medium heat. Sauté onion and garlic until translucent. Add zucchini, broth, curry powder and cayenne; simmer for 10 minutes. Stir in cream and heat through. **Serves 6.**

Chilled Curried Zucchini Soup

Follow preceding recipe, but double the curry powder, and add 1 tsp (5 mL) ground coriander with the curry powder. Replace the cream with plain yogurt, and do not heat once added. Chill before serving and garnish with chopped walnuts. **Serves 6.**

Lemon Zucchini Soup

Follow recipe for Zucchini Soup (above), but replace the cream with $\frac{1}{2}$ cup (125 mL) sour cream and 2 tbsp (25 mL) freshly squeezed lemon juice. **Serves 6.**

Split Pea Zucchini Soup

2 tbsp	canola oil	25 mL
1	onion, diced	1
2 cups	diced smoked ham	500 mL
5 cups	chicken broth	1.25 L
1 cup	green split peas, rinsed	250 mL
Pinch	hot pepper flakes	Pinch
3 cups	shredded zucchini	750 mL

In a large, heavy saucepan, heat oil over medium-high heat. Sauté onion and ham until onion is tender. Add broth, split peas and hot pepper flakes; simmer until peas are tender, about 45 minutes. Stir in zucchini and simmer for 5 minutes. **Serves 4.**

Zucchini Minestrone

2 tbsp	extra-virgin olive oil	25 mL
1 cup	chopped onion	250 mL
2	cloves garlic, minced	2
1	large leek, white part only, chopped	1
2	carrots, sliced	2
2	stalks celery, sliced	2
½	bell pepper (any color), diced	½
4 cups	shredded zucchini	1 L
1 tsp	dried thyme	5 mL
1 tsp	dried savory	5 mL
1 tsp	dried basil	5 mL
½ tsp	dried rosemary	2 mL
½ tsp	dried oregano	2 mL
½ tsp	dried sage	2 mL
5 cups	chicken broth	1.25 mL
2 cups	canned diced tomatoes, with juice	500 mL
1 tbsp	red wine vinegar	15 mL
1 tbsp	tomato paste	15 mL
	Freshly grated Parmesan cheese	

In a large saucepan, heat oil over medium-high heat. Sauté onion, garlic and leek until barely tender. Add carrots, celery, bell pepper and zucchini; sauté for 2 minutes. Add thyme, savory, basil, rosemary, oregano and sage; sauté for 5 minutes. Add broth, tomatoes, vinegar and tomato paste; bring to a boil. Reduce heat and simmer for 10 minutes. Serve sprinkled with Parmesan. **Serves 8.**

Zucchini Sautéed with Roasted Peppers

2 tbsp	extra-virgin olive oil	25 mL
1	onion, thinly sliced	1
1	clove garlic, minced	1
2	roasted red bell peppers (see page 11), diced	2
4 cups	shredded zucchini	1 L
1 tbsp	finely chopped fresh basil	15 mL

In a large, nonstick skillet, heat oil over medium-high heat. Sauté onion and garlic until barely tender. Add roasted peppers and sauté for 1 minute. Add zucchini and basil; sauté until zucchini is tender, about 5 minutes. **Serves 4.**

New Potatoes au Gratin with Bacon

1 tbsp	butter	15 mL
1½ lbs	new potatoes	750 g
½ cup	sliced onion	125 mL
	Salt and freshly ground black pepper to taste	
½ cup	shredded Cheddar cheese	125 mL
2 tbsp	freshly grated Parmesan cheese	25 mL
4	slices bacon, cooked crisp and crumbled	4
1 cup	milk and/or half-and-half (10%) cream	250 mL

Preheat oven to 375°F (190°C) and grease an 8-inch (2 L) baking dish with butter. In a large pot of lightly salted water, boil potatoes for about 10 minutes, until no longer hard but not fully tender. Let cool, peel and thickly slice. Toss potatoes and onion. Make an even layer of half the potato mixture in prepared baking dish and season with salt and pepper. Top with half each of the Cheddar, Parmesan, bacon and milk. Make another layer of the same ingredients in the same order. Bake for 1 hour, until potatoes are tender and top is brown and bubbly around the edges. **Serves 4.**

Roasted Balsamic Tomatoes

1½ lbs	tomatoes (4 to 5 medium), cut into large wedges	750 g
¼ cup	extra-virgin olive oil	50 mL
1 tsp	kosher salt	5 mL
½ tsp	freshly ground black pepper	2 mL
4 tsp	aged balsamic vinegar	20 mL

Preheat oven to 450°F (230°C). In a large roasting pan, toss tomatoes with oil, salt and pepper. Roast for about 8 minutes, or until juices start to run from the tomatoes but they are not yet fully softened. Drizzle with vinegar. **Serves 4.**

Parmesan-Crusted Baked Tomato

1 tbsp	olive oil, divided	15 mL
4	thick slices tomato	4
2 tbsp	dry bread crumbs	25 mL
2 tbsp	freshly grated Parmesan cheese	25 mL
¼ tsp	onion powder	1 mL
¼ tsp	garlic powder	1 mL
	Salt and freshly ground black pepper to taste	

Preheat oven to 425°F (220°C) and rub a rimmed baking sheet with 1 tsp (5 mL) of the oil. Place tomato slices on the pan and drizzle with 1 tsp (5 mL) of the oil. Combine bread crumbs, Parmesan, onion powder, garlic powder, salt and pepper. Place a thick layer of this mixture on top of each tomato and drizzle the remaining oil over top. Bake for 20 minutes, until golden brown. **Serves 4.**

Rosemary-Grilled Tomato

¼ cup	olive oil	50 mL
1 tbsp	dried rosemary	15 mL
4	thick tomato slices	4
	Salt and freshly ground black pepper to taste	
	Additional olive oil	
	Fresh rosemary leaves	

Preheat barbecue grill to high. Warm olive oil and dried rosemary for 2 minutes. Dip tomato slices in oil and grill for 2 minutes, seasoning tops with salt and pepper, and basting with additional oil halfway through. Turn and grill for 2 minutes, seasoning and basting the same way. Transfer to a serving platter and top with rosemary leaves. **Serves 4.**

Tomato with Black Pepper and Lime

2	large tomatoes, sliced	2
2 tbsp	extra-virgin olive oil	25 mL
	Juice of 1 lime	
	Kosher salt and freshly ground black pepper to taste	

Arrange tomato slices on a plate, drizzle with oil and lime juice, and sprinkle with salt and pepper. **Serves 4.**

Quick Tomato Salad

1	clove garlic, minced	1
½	onion, minced	½
⅓ cup	olive oil	75 mL
¼ cup	red wine vinegar	50 mL
1 tbsp	balsamic vinegar	15 mL
2 tbsp	minced fresh Italian (flat-leaf) parsley	25 mL
Pinch	hot pepper flakes	Pinch
	Salt and freshly ground black pepper to taste	
3	tomatoes, cut into wedges	3

In a serving bowl, whisk together garlic, onion, oil, wine vinegar, balsamic vinegar, parsley, hot pepper flakes, salt and pepper. Add tomatoes and toss to coat. Cover and refrigerate for 1 hour, until chilled. **Serves 4.**

Tomato Salad with Mozzarella and Herbs

2	cloves garlic, coarsely chopped	2
1	red onion, diced	1
½ cup	minced fresh herbs (such as basil, flat-leaf parsley, mint)	125 mL
½ cup	olive oil	125 mL
⅓ cup	red wine vinegar	75 mL
¼ tsp	hot pepper flakes	1 mL
	Salt and freshly ground black pepper to taste	
3	tomatoes, cut into wedges	3
8 oz	mozzarella cheese, cut into ½-inch (1 cm) cubes	250 g
	Crusty bread	

In a serving bowl, whisk together garlic, onion, herbs, oil, vinegar, hot pepper flakes, salt and black pepper. Add tomatoes and mozzarella; toss to coat. Cover and refrigerate for about 1 hour, until chilled. Serve with crusty bread. **Serves 4.**

Marinated Tomato with Chèvre and Onion

Follow preceding recipe, but use coarsely chopped fresh basil for the herbs, replace the red wine vinegar with 2 tbsp (25 mL) white wine vinegar, slice the tomatoes instead of cutting into wedges, and use 6 oz (175 g) fresh chèvre (goat cheese), sliced, instead of the mozzarella. **Serves 4.**

Tomato and Fried Spinach Salad

1	clove garlic, minced	1
½ cup	red wine vinegar	125 mL
½ tsp	hot pepper flakes	2 mL
	Salt to taste	
2	large tomatoes, diced	2
½	red onion, thinly sliced	½
1 cup	olive oil	250 mL
	Additional oil (any type)	
1 lb	spinach (about 10 cups/2.5 L), stemmed	500 g
	Toasted crusty bread	

In a serving bowl, whisk together garlic, vinegar, hot pepper flakes and salt. Add tomatoes and onion; toss to coat. In a large, heavy pot, combine olive oil and enough additional oil to make it 3 to 4 inches (7.5 to 10 cm) deep. Heat over medium-high heat until very hot but not smoking. Fry spinach, in three batches, for 30 seconds. Reheat oil between batches (the oil might splatter, so be careful). Drain on paper towels. Add spinach to salad and toss to coat. Serve over slices of crusty bread. **Serves 4.**

Tomato Tonnato

3	green onions, thinly sliced	3
1	clove garlic, minced	1
⅓ cup	olive oil	75 mL
¼ cup	freshly squeezed lemon juice	50 mL
2 tbsp	minced fresh dill	25 mL
	Salt and freshly ground black pepper to taste	
3	tomatoes, diced	3
1	can (6 oz/170 g) water-packed tuna, drained	1

In a serving bowl, whisk together green onions, garlic, oil, lemon juice, dill, salt and pepper. Add tomatoes and tuna; toss to coat. Cover and refrigerate for about 1 hour, until chilled. **Serves 4.**

Spinach Salad with Tomato Vinaigrette

1	clove garlic, minced	1
1	tomato, finely chopped	1
½	onion, minced	½
⅓ cup	olive oil	75 mL
¼ cup	red wine vinegar	50 mL
1 tbsp	balsamic vinegar	15 mL
2 tbsp	minced fresh Italian (flat-leaf) parsley	25 mL
Pinch	hot pepper flakes	Pinch
	Salt and freshly ground black pepper to taste	
1 lb	spinach (about 10 cups/2.5 L), stemmed	500 g
2 cups	garlic-flavored croutons	500 mL
2 tbsp	freshly grated Parmesan cheese	25 mL

In a serving bowl, whisk together garlic, tomato, onion, oil, wine vinegar, balsamic vinegar, parsley, hot pepper flakes, salt and black pepper. Add spinach and toss to coat. Sprinkle with croutons and Parmesan. **Serves 4.**

Cherry Tomato and Caramelized Onion Salad

1 tbsp	vegetable oil	15 mL
1	large onion, thinly sliced	1
1	clove garlic, minced	1
⅓ cup	olive oil	75 mL
¼ cup	red wine vinegar	50 mL
1 tbsp	balsamic vinegar	15 mL
2 tbsp	chopped fresh Italian (flat-leaf) parsley	25 mL
	Salt and freshly ground black pepper to taste	
2 cups	red cherry tomatoes, halved	500 mL
2 cups	yellow cherry tomatoes, halved	500 mL

In a skillet, heat oil over medium heat. Sauté onion until golden brown and very tender, about 10 minutes; set aside. In a serving bowl, whisk together garlic, oil, wine vinegar, balsamic vinegar, parsley, salt and pepper. Add onion and red and yellow cherry tomatoes; toss to coat. **Serves 4.**

Red and Yellow Tomato Salad

1	clove garlic, minced	1
½	onion, minced	½
⅓ cup	olive oil	75 mL
¼ cup	red wine vinegar	50 mL
2 tbsp	minced fresh parsley	25 mL
2 tbsp	coarsely chopped fresh herbs (such as basil, flat-leaf parsley, mint)	25 mL
1 tbsp	freshly squeezed lemon juice	15 mL
	Salt and freshly ground black pepper to taste	
1 cup	red cherry tomatoes, halved	250 mL
1 cup	yellow cherry tomatoes, halved	250 mL

In a serving bowl, whisk together garlic, onion, oil, vinegar, parsley, herbs, lemon juice, salt and pepper. Add tomatoes and toss to coat. Cover and refrigerate for 1 hour, until chilled. **Serves 4.**

Chili Salad

3	tomatoes, cut into thin wedges	3
¼	onion, minced	¼
1 cup	cooked or canned kidney beans	250 mL
¼ cup	chopped fresh cilantro	50 mL
¼ cup	corn oil	50 mL
2 tsp	chili powder	10 mL
1 tsp	ground cumin	5 mL
	Juice of 1 lime	
	Salt and freshly ground black pepper to taste	

Toss together all ingredients. **Serves 4.**

Tomato Slaw

1½ tsp	kosher salt, divided	7 mL
2	tomatoes, sliced	2
3 tbsp	mayonnaise	45 mL
1 tbsp	freshly squeezed lemon juice	15 mL
1 tsp	cider vinegar	5 mL
2 tsp	orange marmalade	10 mL
	Salt and freshly ground black pepper to taste	
4	green onions, thinly sliced	4
2	stalks celery, diced	2

Sprinkle ½ tsp (2 mL) of the salt on a large platter. Place tomato slices in a single layer on the salt and sprinkle the remaining salt on top. Let stand for 15 minutes. Wrap tomatoes in a clean towel and squeeze to remove most of the moisture. Cut into thin strips. In a serving bowl, whisk together mayonnaise, lemon juice, vinegar, marmalade, salt and pepper. Add tomatoes, green onions and celery; toss to coat. **Serves 4.**

Tomato and Crab Salad

½ cup	mayonnaise (not fat-free)	125 mL
2 tbsp	red wine vinegar	25 mL
1 tsp	hot pepper sauce (such as Tabasco)	5 mL
	Juice of 1 lemon	
	Salt and freshly ground black pepper to taste	
2	tomatoes, chopped	2
2	green onions, sliced	2
1	cucumber, peeled, seeded and diced	1
1	small avocado, diced	1
1 lb	backfin (lump) crabmeat, shells picked out	500 g
2 cups	cooked or canned corn kernels	500 mL

In a serving bowl, whisk together mayonnaise, vinegar, hot pepper sauce, lemon juice, salt and pepper. Add the remaining ingredients and toss to coat. **Serves 4.**

Tomato Niçoise

2	drained canned anchovies, minced	2
1	onion, sliced	1
1	clove garlic, minced	1
⅓ cup	olive oil	75 mL
⅓ cup	red wine vinegar	75 mL
¼ cup	chopped basil	50 mL
¼ cup	finely chopped fennel bulb	50 mL
	Salt and freshly ground black pepper to taste	
12	Niçoise olives	12
3	tomatoes, cut into wedges	3
1	can (6 oz/170 g) tuna, drained	1

In a serving bowl, whisk together anchovies, onion, garlic, oil, vinegar, basil, fennel, salt and pepper. Add olives, tomatoes and tuna; toss to coat. Cover and refrigerate for 1 hour, until chilled. **Serves 4.**

Avocado, Tomato and Shrimp with Chili Pepper Vinaigrette

6	large shrimp, cooked and peeled	6
4	thin tomato wedges	4
½	avocado, sliced	½
2 tbsp	oil and vinegar dressing	25 mL
Pinch	chili powder	Pinch
Pinch	hot pepper flakes	Pinch

Arrange shrimp, tomato wedges and avocado on a plate. Season dressing with chili powder and hot pepper flakes; spoon on top. **Serves 1.**

Tomato with Pesto

1	clove garlic	1
⅔ cup	firmly packed basil leaves	150 mL
2 tbsp	pine nuts	25 mL
6 tbsp	extra-virgin olive oil, divided	90 mL
2 to 3 tbsp	freshly grated Parmesan cheese	25 to 45 mL
	Salt and freshly ground black pepper to taste	
3	tomatoes, sliced ½ inch (1 cm) thick	3

In a blender or food processor, finely chop garlic, basil and pine nuts. With the motor running, slowly add 5 tbsp (75 mL) of the oil through the feed tube and process until smooth. Stir in Parmesan, salt and pepper. Drizzle tomatoes with the remaining oil and additional salt and pepper. Dollop each slice with 2 tsp (10 mL) of the pesto and serve the rest on the side. **Serves 4.**

Tomato Pesto Pasta Salad

Prepare pesto as in preceding recipe, but toss with 20 black olives, pitted and sliced, 4 green onions, thinly sliced, 2 tomatoes, diced, 12 oz (375 mL) pasta, cooked and cooled, and an additional 2 tbsp (25 mL) extra-virgin olive oil. **Serves 4.**

Tomatoes Marinated in Olive Oil, Garlic and Hot Pepper Flakes

2	cloves garlic, minced	2
½	onion, minced	½
½ cup	extra-virgin olive oil	125 mL
3 tbsp	chopped fresh Italian (flat-leaf) parsley	45 mL
¼ tsp	hot pepper flakes	1 mL
	Juice of ½ lemon	
	Salt and freshly ground black pepper to taste	
3	tomatoes, cut into wedges	3
	Freshly grated Parmesan cheese	

In a serving bowl, whisk together garlic, onion, oil, parsley, hot pepper flakes, lemon juice, salt and black pepper. Add tomatoes and toss to coat. Cover and refrigerate for 1 hour, until chilled. Serve sprinkled with Parmesan. **Serves 4.**

Fresh Tomatoes and Pasta

Follow preceding recipe, but omit the lemon juice, dice the tomato, and toss with 12 oz (375 g) pasta, cooked and hot, and ½ cup (125 mL) freshly grated Parmesan cheese. Do not chill. Serve with additional Parmesan. **Serves 4.**

Fresh Tomato Sauce

2 tbsp	olive oil	25 mL
1	large onion, chopped	1
2	cloves garlic, minced	2
1	dried hot chili pepper	1
5	tomatoes, coarsely chopped	5
⅓ cup	chopped fresh herbs of your choice	75 mL
1 tbsp	tomato paste	15 mL
	Salt and freshly ground black pepper to taste	

In a large skillet, heat oil over medium heat. Sauté onion, garlic and chili pepper until onion is just tender. Add tomatoes and sauté until they start to release their liquid. Add herbs, tomato paste, salt and pepper; heat for 1 minute. Discard chili pepper. **Makes about 2 cups (500 mL), enough for 4 servings of pasta.**

Fresh Tomato and Cream Sauce

2 tbsp	olive oil	25 mL
2 tbsp	minced onion	25 mL
1	clove garlic, minced	1
Pinch	hot pepper flakes	Pinch
4	tomatoes, chopped	4
½ cup	whipping (35%) cream	125 mL
1 tbsp	minced fresh Italian (flat-leaf) parsley	15 mL
	Salt and freshly ground black pepper to taste	

In a large skillet, heat oil over medium heat. Sauté onion, garlic and red pepper flakes until onion is just tender. Add tomatoes and sauté until they start to release their liquid. Add cream and parsley; simmer until sauce is slightly thickened, about 1 minute. Season with salt and black pepper. **Makes about 2 cups (500 mL), enough for 4 servings of pasta.**

Pasta with Tomatoes, Basil and Feta

1 tbsp	olive oil	15 mL
1	clove garlic, halved	1
3	tomatoes, chopped	3
⅓ cup	dry white wine	75 mL
2 tbsp	chopped fresh basil	25 mL
Pinch	cayenne pepper	Pinch
	Salt and freshly ground black pepper to taste	
12 oz	pasta, cooked, hot	375 g
6 oz	feta cheese, crumbled	175 g

In a skillet, heat oil over medium-low heat. Sauté garlic for 1 minute. Add tomatoes and wine, increase heat to high and boil for about 2 minutes. Add basil, cayenne, salt and black pepper; cook for 20 seconds. Discard garlic. Toss sauce with pasta and feta. **Serves 4.**

Tomato Sandwich

	Butter	
1	small loaf French bread (demi-baguette), halved horizontally	1
1	tomato, sliced	1
	Salt and freshly ground black pepper to taste	

Spread a thin layer of butter over the interior of the bread. Halve tomato slices and lay them overlapping down the length of one side of the bread. Sprinkle with salt and pepper, top with the other half of the bread and cut into 4 sections. **Serves 1 or 2.**

Mild Red Salsa

3	tomatoes, quartered	3
1	small onion, quartered	1
2 tbsp	chopped fresh cilantro	25 mL
2 tbsp	olive oil	25 mL
	Water	

In a food processor, coarsely chop tomatoes and onion. Stir in cilantro, oil and enough water to create a sauce-like consistency. **Makes about 2 cups (500 mL).** *Use as a dip or a sauce for plain meats.*

Mild Green Salsa

Follow preceding recipe, but replace the tomatoes with 8 tomatillos, peeled, and add 1 clove garlic with the onion. **Makes about 2 cups (500 mL).** *Use as a dip or a sauce for plain meats.*

Cucumber Salad with Tomato Salsa

2	cucumbers, thinly sliced	2
1 tbsp	salt	15 mL
½	recipe Mild Green Salsa or Mild Red Salsa (above)	½

Toss cucumber slices with salt and let stand for 15 minutes. Wring out liquid and rinse well. Toss with salsa. **Serves 4.**

Avocado and Tomato Salsa

1	large avocado, diced	1
1	jalapeño pepper, seeded and minced	1
1 tbsp	chopped fresh cilantro	15 mL
1	recipe Mild Red Tomato Salsa (above)	1

Combine all ingredients. **Makes about 3 cups (750 mL).** *Use as a dip or a condiment for grilled meat or seafood.*

Tomato and Corn Salsa

3	tomatoes, quartered	3
1	small onion	1
1	jalapeño pepper, seeded	1
½ cup	cooked or canned corn kernels	125 mL
1 tbsp	corn oil	15 mL
1 tsp	chili powder	5 mL

In a food processor, chop tomatoes, onion and jalapeño. Stir in corn, oil and chili powder. **Makes about 2½ cups (625 mL).** *Use as a dip or a condiment for grilled meat or seafood.*

Tomato Raita

2	tomatoes, seeded and chopped	2
¼	red onion, thinly sliced	¼
¼ cup	chopped fresh mint	50 mL
1 tbsp	plain yogurt	15 mL
2 tsp	chili powder	10 mL
1 tsp	granulated sugar	5 mL
	Juice of ½ lemon	

Toss together all ingredients. **Makes about 1½ cups (375 mL).** *Use as a condiment for grilled meat.*

Chapter 36
Fall Fruit
Apples, Pears and Tropical Treats

Smoked Turkey and Apple Tart 406
Ham and Apple Tart 406
Prosciutto Pear Galette 406
Apple and Sausage Pot Pie 406
Pear and Chicken Pot Pie 406
Broccoli and Apple Sauté 406
Sautéed Apples in Applejack 407
Apple Cheddar Cornbread 407
Pineapple Cornbread 407
Applesauce 407
Chunky Applesauce 407
Raisin Applesauce 407
Spiked Applesauce 407
Pear Applesauce 407
Cranberry Pear Sauce 407
Apple Butter 408
Mango Butter 408
Lemon-Glazed Baked Apples 408
Bourbon Pecan-Stuffed Baked Apples . . 408
Wet Walnut Baked Apples 409
Honey-Roasted Pears 409
Chinese Roasted Pears 409
Roasted Pineapple 409
Roasted Bananas 409
Spiced Poached Pears 409

Minted Pears 409
Ginger Poached Pears 409
Apple Charlotte 410
Apple Ginger Charlotte 410
Apple Turnovers 410
Apple Fennel Turnovers 410
Apple Cheddar Turnovers 410
Bartlett Turnovers 410
Pear and Roquefort Turnovers 410
Apple Crisp 411
Apple Hazelnut Crisp 411
Creamy Vanilla Pear Crisp 411
Tropical Crisp 411
Balsamic Pear Tarte Tatin 411
Pineapple Upside-Down Pie 411
Jewish Apple Cake 412
Lemon Apple Cake 412
Apple Walnut Cake 412
Cardamom Pear Cake 412
Apple Crumb Coffee Cake 412
Hungarian Apple Coffee Cake 413
Pear Ginger Coffee Cake 413
Mint Mango Soup 413
Grapefruit Cloud 413
Chili Mango Sorbet 413

There are apples and pears that beg to be baked and others destined for sauce. Some make perfect cake, balancing moisture and crumb with a spark of tartness and a floral scent, while others will swell into a pie, so opulently plump that a naive cook might be tempted to take the credit. But anyone who knows fall fruit knows that the praise belongs to nature, not to the baker.

No produce comes in as many varieties as fall orchard crops, and no variety tastes, smells, crunches or cooks exactly like another.

At one time, hundreds of apple varieties were sold in North American markets; now, the selection is usually fewer than a dozen. Red Delicious, Golden Delicious, Granny Smith, McIntosh, Fuji and Gala are the easiest to find, with Rome, Stayman, Braeburn, Empire, Ginger Gold and Honey Crisp occasionally thrown in to break the monotony. But venture out to farm stands or outlying orchards and you are likely to find a cornucopia of apple varieties, ranging from overlooked classics such as Gravensteins and Macouns to one-of-a-kind cultivated specialties.

Though specific varieties go hand in hand with certain preparations, such as McIntosh for applesauce or Romes for baking whole, the success of most apple preparations does not depend on varietals. Although a pie recipe written for a Rhode Island Greening apple will not be at its best when made with a delicate floral variety like Golden Delicious, anything tart, such as Granny Smiths, Northern Spies, Pippins or Gravensteins, will give good results.

There are far fewer commonly available varieties of pear. Anjou and Bartlett dominate the marketplace, but you will also find Bosc, Seckel, Comice and Forelle in most produce stands throughout the fall.

One of the most difficult things about pears is judging ripeness. Not only does each variety have its own criteria, but you must catch the pear at just the right moment. Take a bite too early and the fruit will be insipid and dry; wait too long and you run the risk of rot or the onslaught of grit in the flesh.

All pears have a tendency towards grittiness, caused by lignin, a woody component of plant tissue that congregates in the fiber of pears. As pears mature, these fibers become thicker, swelling with the last burst of ripening until they make the interior of a pear disintegrate into juice and sand. Because of this phenomenon, most pears are picked while still green. Thus separated from the source of enzymes that trigger the development of lignin, pears are more likely to remain smooth as they continue to soften off the tree.

Asian, Bosc and Seckel pears are eaten crisp, so they can usually be refrigerated at the time of purchase, but other pears will likely need to ripen for a while. Store them at an even, warm temperature — in a bowl or a loosely closed paper sack at room temperature works perfectly. But keep a vigilant eye: pears might take several days to ripen, but once they do, they fade quickly. Test them by gently pressing the neck end. They should barely yield. Refrigerate ripe pears immediately and plan to eat them within 24 hours. Pears are notorious for traveling from ripeness to rottenness in less than a day, so it's best to buy them in small quantities.

Choose ripe pears for eating fresh out of hand, tossing in a salad, or serving raw with prosciutto or cheese. But for baking and poaching, it is best to use underripe pears. Pear recipes almost always add a sweetener, an acid and some flavoring, so the subtle flavor of the pear becomes secondary. What is most important is a clean, crisp texture that's free of grittiness. If the pear is too ripe, it will fall apart during cooking; if it's very hard, it will need to be cooked longer.

Tropical fruits, such as mangoes, papayas, guavas, pineapples and bananas, are available year-round, but because local fruit is less available in North America during the cold months, we tend to view this season as the one for tropicals.

About these recipes . . .

In most of the following 50 recipes, we do not call for a specific variety of fruit; rather, we might call for a tart apple, or a firm or crisp pear. Unless otherwise stated, all sliced and diced fruit should first be peeled, cored and seeded.

Some advice before you start: when processing a large number of apples or pears, it's most efficient to do one step at a time. In other words, peel all the fruit, then core it all, then slice it all. While the peeled or cut fruit is waiting for the next step, store it in a container of cold water spiked with a little vinegar or lemon juice. This will keep it from discoloring without adversely affecting its flavor.

Though we provide cross-references to recipes for various pastries and toppings, many commercial products are of high enough quality that they would not compromise the finished dish. Feel free to use them.

A word about butter: our preference for unsalted butter is never stronger than with baking recipes, such as some you'll find below.

Finally, a reassuring word if you're a novice baker: pie crusts crack and cake edges crumble. Do not expect picture-perfect results anywhere this side of a picture.

Smoked Turkey and Apple Tart

1 tbsp	butter	15 mL
¼ cup	chopped onion	50 mL
½ cup	unsweetened apple cider or juice	125 mL
8 oz	smoked turkey breast, cut into thin strips	250 g
	Salt and freshly ground black pepper to taste	
1	round pastry for a 9-inch (23 cm) pie (store-bought or see recipe, page 21)	1
1 cup	shredded fontina cheese	250 mL
2	large tart apples, peeled and thinly sliced	2
3 tbsp	honey	45 mL
2 tbsp	brown mustard	25 mL

Preheat oven to 375°F (190°C). In a large skillet, melt butter over medium heat. Sauté onion until lightly browned. Add cider and boil until almost dry. Remove from heat and stir in smoked turkey, salt and pepper; let cool. Line a 9-inch (23 cm) pie pan with pastry. Cover crust with fontina and top with turkey mixture, then apples arranged in overlapping concentric circles. Bake for 40 minutes. Combine honey and mustard; brush over the surface of the tart. Bake for 20 minutes, until apples are tender, crust is browned and filling is bubbling around the edges. Let cool slightly before serving. **Serves 4.**

Ham and Apple Tart

Follow preceding recipe, but replace the turkey with baked ham, and add ½ tsp (2 mL) dried rosemary, crumbled, with the onion. **Serves 4.**

Prosciutto Pear Galette

Follow recipe for Smoked Turkey and Apple Tart (above), but replace the turkey with prosciutto, and replace the apples with crisp Bosc pears. Instead of the honey and mustard, combine 2 tbsp (25 mL) extra-virgin olive oil and 1 tbsp (15 mL) balsamic vinegar and brush over crust after the initial 40 minutes of baking. **Serves 4.**

Apple and Sausage Pot Pie

1 tbsp	vegetable oil	15 mL
1	onion, finely chopped	1
12 oz	mild Italian sausage, sliced	375 g
1	large tart apple (unpeeled), diced	1
½ tsp	dried thyme	2 mL
½ tsp	dried rosemary, crumbled	2 mL
1 tbsp	all-purpose flour	15 mL
⅔ cup	chicken broth	150 mL
1 cup	sauerkraut, drained and rinsed	250 mL
1	round pastry for a 9-inch (23 cm) pie (store-bought or see recipe, page 21)	1
1	egg yolk, beaten with 1 tbsp (15 mL) water	1

Preheat oven to 400°F (200°C). In a large skillet, heat oil over medium-high heat. Sauté onion and sausage until lightly browned. Add apple, thyme and rosemary; sauté until apple starts to soften. Stir in flour and sauté for 1 minute. Add broth, reduce heat and simmer until slightly thickened. Remove from heat and toss with sauerkraut. Place in an 8-cup (2 L) casserole dish and top with pastry as you would assemble a pot pie (see page 12). Brush top with egg wash. Bake for 30 minutes, until crust is browned and filling is bubbling around the edges. **Serves 4.**

Pear and Chicken Pot Pie

Follow preceding recipe, but substitute boneless skinless chicken pieces, cut into bite-size chunks, for the sausage, replace the apple with 2 large, crisp pears, and add ½ tsp (2 mL) dried sage with the rosemary. **Serves 4.**

Broccoli and Apple Sauté

1	bunch broccoli, broken into florets, stems peeled and thinly sliced	1
2 tbsp	butter	25 mL
1	large onion, coarsely chopped	1
2	cloves garlic, minced	2
1	tart apple, peeled and diced	1

In a large pot of boiling lightly salted water, boil broccoli until bright green and barely tender, about 3 minutes; drain well and blot dry. Meanwhile, in a large skillet, melt butter over medium heat. Sauté onion until tender. Add garlic and apples; sauté until apples are tender. Toss with broccoli. **Serves 4.**

Sautéed Apples in Applejack

2 tbsp	butter	25 mL
¼ cup	minced onion	50 mL
Pinch	ground nutmeg	Pinch
3	apples (any type), peeled and sliced	3
	Salt and freshly ground black pepper to taste	
¼ cup	applejack brandy	50 mL

In a large skillet, melt butter over medium heat. Sauté onion and nutmeg until onion is tender. Add apples, salt and pepper; sauté until apples are lightly browned. Add brandy, increase heat to medium-high and boil vigorously until apples are glazed. **Serves 4.** *Serve with pork roast or poultry.*

Apple Cheddar Cornbread

1¼ cups	yellow cornmeal	300 mL
¾ cup	all-purpose flour	175 mL
¼ cup	granulated sugar	50 mL
1 tbsp	baking powder	15 mL
½ tsp	salt	2 mL
2 tbsp	corn oil	25 mL
3 tbsp	finely chopped onion	45 mL
1	large apple (any type), peeled and cut into small dice	1
1	extra-large egg	1
1 cup	milk	250 mL
¾ cup	shredded sharp Cheddar cheese	175 mL
	Nonstick cooking spray	

Preheat oven to 425°F (220°C) and place a 10-inch (25 cm) cast-iron skillet in the oven. Sift together cornmeal, flour, sugar, baking powder and salt; set aside. In a small skillet, heat oil over medium-high heat. Sauté onion and apple until softened; let cool. Transfer to a bowl and stir in cornmeal mixture. Stir in egg, milk and cheese until uniformly moist, Using a heavy potholder, remove skillet from oven and coat the interior with cooking spray. Pour in batter and bake for 20 minutes, until top is browned and a tester inserted in the center comes out clean. Cut into wedges. **Serves 8 to 10.**

Pineapple Cornbread

Follow preceding recipe, but omit the apple and add 1½ cups (375 mL) drained canned pineapple tidbits and a pinch of hot pepper flakes with the onion. **Serves 8 to 10.**

Applesauce

3 lbs	McIntosh apples, peeled and coarsely chopped	1.5 kg
¼ cup	water	50 mL
1 to 4 tbsp	granulated sugar (depending on sweetness of apples)	15 to 50 mL
½ tsp	ground cinnamon	2 mL

In a large, heavy saucepan, combine apples, water and 1 tbsp (15 mL) of the sugar; cover and bring to a simmer over medium heat, stirring frequently. Simmer for 8 to 10 minutes, or until apples are tender. Using a potato masher, mash to desired consistency. Stir in cinnamon and sugar to taste. Serve warm or chilled. **Serves 4.**

Chunky Applesauce

Follow preceding recipe, but replace 1 lb (500 g) of the McIntosh apples with Granny Smith apples. Instead of using a potato masher, stir apples with a fork (most of the apples will turn into a smooth sauce, but some chunks will remain). **Serves 4.**

Raisin Applesauce

Follow preceding recipe, but add 1 cup (250 mL) golden raisins with the apples. **Serves 4.**

Spiked Applesauce

Follow recipe for Applesauce (above), but add 2 tbsp (25 mL) bourbon with the apples and 2 tbsp (25 mL) additional bourbon after cooking. **Serves 4.**

Pear Applesauce

Follow recipe for Applesauce (above), but reduce the apples to 1½ lbs (750 g), add 1½ lbs (750 g) pears with the apples, and replace the cinnamon with vanilla. **Serves 4.**

Cranberry Pear Sauce

Follow recipe for Applesauce (above), but replace the apples with pears, add ¼ cup (50 mL) dried cranberries with the pears, and replace the cinnamon with ground cardamom. **Serves 4.**

Apple Butter

2½ lbs	tart apples (about 5 large), peeled and cut into chunks	1.25 kg
½ cup	cider vinegar	125 mL
½ cup	unsweetened apple cider	125 mL
¾ cup	packed light brown sugar	175 mL
½ cup	granulated sugar	125 mL
2½ tbsp	freshly squeezed lemon juice	32 mL
1½ tsp	ground cinnamon	7 mL
Pinch	ground allspice	Pinch
Pinch	salt	Pinch
Pinch	freshly ground black pepper	Pinch

In a large, heavy saucepan, combine apples, vinegar and cider; cover and bring to a simmer over medium heat, stirring frequently. Simmer for 8 to 10 minutes, or until apples are tender. Transfer to a food processor and purée. Return to the pan and add brown sugar, granulated sugar, lemon juice, cinnamon, allspice, salt and pepper; simmer until very thick, stirring frequently near the end, about 40 minutes. Pack into jars and let cool. **Makes about 4 cups (1 L).** *Store in the refrigerator for up to 2 months.*

Mango Butter

3	large ripe mangoes, cut into chunks	3
½ cup	freshly squeezed lime juice	125 mL
½ cup	pineapple juice	125 mL
1 tbsp	chopped gingerroot	15 mL
½ cup	granulated sugar	125 mL
⅓ cup	honey	75 mL
Pinch	ground allspice	Pinch
Pinch	salt	Pinch
Pinch	cayenne pepper	Pinch

In a large, heavy saucepan, combine mango, lime juice, pineapple juice and ginger; cover and bring to a simmer over medium heat, stirring frequently. Simmer for about 8 minutes, or until mango is tender. Transfer to a food processor and purée. Return to the pan and add sugar, honey, allspice, salt and cayenne; simmer for 30 to 45 minutes, or until very thick, stirring frequently near the end. Pack into jars and let cool. **Makes about 4 cups (1 L).** *Store in the refrigerator for up to 2 months.*

Lemon-Glazed Baked Apples

¼ cup	freshly squeezed lemon juice	50 mL
¼ cup	honey	50 mL
2 tbsp	granulated sugar	25 mL
½ tsp	ground ginger	2 mL
½ cup	raisins	125 mL
1 tbsp	butter	15 mL
1 tsp	vanilla	5 mL
Pinch	salt	Pinch
4	Rome or other baking apples, cored without breaking through bottom	4

Preheat oven to 400°F (200°C). In a small saucepan, over medium heat, heat lemon juice, honey, sugar and ginger until sugar dissolves. Add raisins, butter, vanilla and salt; cook, stirring, until butter melts. Place apples in a baking dish just large enough to hold them snugly. Fill apples with raisin mixture and spoon glaze over top. Bake until tender, about 1 hour, basting with glaze from the bottom of the dish every 10 minutes. Let cool for 10 minutes before serving. **Serves 4.**

Bourbon Pecan-Stuffed Baked Apples

¼ cup	packed light brown sugar	50 mL
¼ cup	bourbon	50 mL
1 tbsp	cider vinegar	15 mL
Pinch	ground cloves	Pinch
½ cup	toasted pecan pieces	125 mL
1 tbsp	butter	15 mL
1 tsp	vanilla	5 mL
Pinch	salt	Pinch
4	Rome or other baking apples, cored without breaking through bottom	4

Preheat oven to 400°F (200°C). In a small saucepan, over medium heat, heat brown sugar, bourbon, vinegar and cloves until sugar dissolves. Add pecans, butter, vanilla and salt; cook, stirring, until butter melts. Place apples in a baking dish just large enough to hold them snugly. Fill apples with pecan mixture and spoon glaze over top. Bake until tender, about 1 hour, basting with glaze from the bottom of the dish every 10 minutes. Let cool for 10 minutes before serving. **Serves 4.**

Wet Walnut Baked Apples

Follow preceding recipe, but replace the pecans with walnuts, and replace the bourbon with unsweetened apple juice. **Serves 4.**

Honey-Roasted Pears

8	firm Bartlett pears	8
8	strips of lemon zest	8
	Juice of 1 lemon	
8	whole cloves	8
6 tbsp	honey	90 mL
¼ cup	butter	50 mL

Preheat oven to 400°F (200°C). Peel pears, leaving stems in place. Immediately coat cut surfaces with lemon juice. Using a coring knife or a small melon baller, dig out core from the bottom of each pear. Place 1 clove and 1 piece of lemon zest in the hollowed-out core of each pear and set pears in a baking dish just large enough to hold them snugly. In a small saucepan, heat honey and butter over medium heat until butter melts; spoon over pears. Wrap pear stems in foil. Roast until pears are browned and very tender, about 50 minutes, basting with juices from the bottom of the dish every 15 minutes. Remove foil before serving. **Serves 8.**

Chinese Roasted Pears

8	firm Bartlett pears	8
3 tbsp	rice vinegar	45 mL
8	whole star anise	8
6 tbsp	honey	90 mL
2 tbsp	dark sesame oil	25 mL
1 tbsp	soy sauce	15 mL

Preheat oven to 400°F (200°C). Peel pears, leaving stems in place. Immediately coat cut surfaces with rice vinegar. Using a coring knife or a small melon baller, dig out core from the bottom of each pear. Place 1 piece of star anise in the hollowed-out core of each pear and set pears in a baking dish just large enough to hold them snugly. In a small saucepan, heat honey, sesame oil and soy sauce over medium heat until honey melts; spoon over pears. Wrap pear stems in foil. Roast until pears are browned and very tender, about 50 minutes, basting with juices from the bottom of the dish every 15 minutes. Remove foil before serving. **Serves 8.**

Roasted Pineapple

½ cup	packed dark brown sugar	125 mL
¼ cup	dark rum	50 mL
1	large pineapple, peeled, cored and cut into 1-inch (2.5 cm) thick rings	1

Preheat oven to 400°F (200°C). In a small saucepan, over medium heat, stir brown sugar and rum until sugar dissolves. Coat pineapple with half the glaze and place on an oiled rack set in a roasting pan. Roast for 10 minutes. Turn, baste with the remaining glaze and roast for 10 minutes. **Serves 4.**

Roasted Bananas

Follow preceding recipe, but replace the pineapple with 4 bananas and cut the roasting time in half. **Serves 4.**

Spiced Poached Pears

2	whole cloves	2
1	stick cinnamon (2 inches/5 cm)	1
½	vanilla bean	½
½ cup	white wine	125 mL
⅓ cup	honey	75 mL
⅓ cup	water	75 mL
	Grated zest and juice of 1 lemon	
	Grated zest and juice of 1 orange	
4	firm pears, peeled and halved lengthwise	4

In a saucepan, over medium heat, bring cloves, cinnamon, vanilla bean, wine, honey, water, lemon zest, lemon juice, orange zest and orange juice to a simmer. Add pears, cover and poach until tender, about 10 minutes. Let cool in poaching liquid. **Serves 4.**

Minted Pears

Follow preceding recipe, but omit the cloves and cinnamon, add 3 mint teabags with the vanilla bean, and replace the orange zest and juice with the grated zest and juice of 1 lime. **Serves 4.**

Ginger Poached Pears

Follow recipe for Spiced Poached Pears (above), but omit the cloves, add a 1-inch (2.5 cm) piece of gingerroot, thinly sliced, with the cinnamon, and serve pears garnished with 3 tbsp (45 mL) finely chopped candied ginger. **Serves 4.**

Apple Charlotte

1¼ cups	butter, divided	300 mL
15	slices white bread, crusts trimmed	15
8	large tart apples, peeled and sliced	8
¼ cup	granulated sugar	50 mL
2 tbsp	freshly squeezed lemon juice	25 mL
1 tbsp	vanilla	15 mL

Preheat oven to 375°F (190°C). Melt 1 cup (250 mL) of the butter. Brush a 6-cup (1.5 L) soufflé dish or charlotte mold with a thin film of melted butter. Line the bottom with whole slices or cut pieces of bread and brush with melted butter. Line the sides of the mold with half-slices of bread, placed on end and overlapping slightly, brush with butter and trim flush with top of dish; set aside. In a large skillet, heat the remaining ¼ cup (50 mL) butter over medium heat. Sauté apples, sugar and lemon juice until apples are tender. Drain, stir in vanilla and pour into lined mold. Cut remaining bread to fit snugly over top, brushing both sides with butter. Bake for 45 minutes, until bread is browned. Let cool for 1 hour, then invert onto a serving platter and unmold. **Serves 8 to 10.**

If desired, serve warm with a dessert sauce (see Chapter 40).

Apple Ginger Charlotte

Follow preceding recipe, but add 1½ tsp (7 mL) ground ginger with the apples, and toss drained apples with 3 tbsp (45 mL) chopped candied ginger. Serve with Old-Fashioned Custard Sauce (page 447). **Serves 8 to 10.**

Apple Turnovers

1 tbsp	butter	15 mL
2	large tart apples, peeled and diced	2
¼ cup	granulated sugar	50 mL
2 tsp	cornstarch	10 mL
1 tbsp	freshly squeezed lemon juice	15 mL
1 tsp	vanilla	5 mL
8 oz	frozen puff pastry, thawed	250 g
1	egg yolk, beaten with 1 tbsp (15 mL) water	1

Preheat oven to 400°F (200°C). In a large saucepan, melt butter over medium heat. Sauté apples and sugar until apples are tender. Dissolve cornstarch in lemon juice and vanilla; stir into apples and let cool. If necessary, roll puff pastry out to a 12-inch (30 cm) square. Cut square into quarters. Divide apple mixture among pastry squares and assemble turnovers (see page 12). Place on a baking sheet and brush with egg wash. Bake for 20 to 25 minutes, or until fully puffed and brown. Let cool for 10 minutes before serving. **Serves 4.**

Apple Fennel Turnovers

Follow preceding recipe, but add ¼ cup finely chopped fennel bulb and 1 tsp (5 mL) ground fennel seeds with the apples, substitute 3 tbsp (45 mL) orange juice for the lemon juice, and omit the vanilla. **Serves 4.**

Apple Cheddar Turnovers

Follow recipe for Apple Turnovers (left), but add 1 cup (250 mL) shredded sharp Cheddar cheese to the cooled apple mixture. Use 12 oz (375 g) pastry and make 6 turnovers. **Serves 6.**

Bartlett Turnovers

Follow recipe for Apple Turnovers (left), but substitute 3 crisp Bartlett pears for the apples. **Serves 4.**

Pear and Roquefort Turnovers

1 tbsp	butter	15 mL
3	large crisp pears, peeled and diced	3
2 tbsp	granulated sugar	25 mL
¼ tsp	salt	1 mL
2 tsp	cornstarch	10 mL
1 tbsp	freshly squeezed lemon juice	15 mL
¼ cup	crumbled Roquefort cheese	50 mL
8 oz	frozen puff pastry, thawed	250 g
1	egg yolk, beaten with 1 tbsp (15 mL) water	1

Preheat oven to 400°F (200°C). In a large saucepan, melt butter over medium heat. Sauté pears, sugar and salt until pears are tender. Dissolve cornstarch in lemon juice; stir into pears and let cool. Mix in cheese. If necessary, roll out puff pastry to a 12-inch (30 cm) square. Cut square into quarters. Divide pear mixture among pastry squares and assemble turnovers (see page 12). Place on a baking sheet and brush with egg wash. Bake for 20 to 25 minutes, or until fully puffed and brown. Let cool for 10 minutes before serving. **Serves 4.**

Apple Crisp

⅓ cup	butter, chilled, divided	75 mL
1½ cups	chopped walnuts	375 mL
1 cup	packed light brown sugar, divided	250 mL
⅓ cup	all-purpose flour, divided	75 mL
3 lbs	tart apples, peeled and cut into chunks	1.5 kg
3 tbsp	cornstarch	45 mL
1 tsp	ground cinnamon	5 mL
¼ tsp	ground nutmeg	1 mL

Preheat oven to 375°F (190°C) and grease an 8-cup (2 L) shallow baking dish with 1 tbsp (15 mL) of the butter. Cut the remaining butter into small pieces. Combine nuts, half the brown sugar and ¼ cup (50 mL) of the flour. Mix butter into nut mixture until well dispersed and crumbly; set aside. Toss the remaining brown sugar and flour with apples, cornstarch, cinnamon and nutmeg. Pack into prepared baking dish and bake for 30 minutes. Top with nut mixture and bake for 30 minutes, until browned and bubbling. **Serves 8 to 10.**

Apple Hazelnut Crisp

Follow preceding recipe, but replace the walnuts with hazelnuts. **Serves 8 to 10.**

Creamy Vanilla Pear Crisp

Follow recipe for Apple Crisp (above), but replace the apples with firm pears, add 1 cup (250 mL) sour cream (not fat-free) and 1 tbsp (15 mL) vanilla with the pears, and omit the cinnamon. **Serves 8 to 10.**

Tropical Crisp

⅓ cup	butter, chilled, divided	75 mL
1½ cups	shredded sweetened coconut	375 mL
1 cup	granulated sugar, divided	250 mL
⅓ cup	all-purpose flour, divided	75 mL
2½ lbs	tropical fruit (such as mango or papaya), cut into chunks	1.25 kg
3 tbsp	cornstarch	45 mL
1 tsp	grated gingerroot	5 mL
1 tsp	vanilla	5 mL

Preheat oven to 375°F (190°C) and grease an 8-cup (2 L) shallow baking dish with 1 tbsp (15 mL) of the butter. Cut the remaining butter into small pieces. Combine coconut, half the sugar and ¼ cup (50 mL) of the flour. Mix butter into coconut mixture until well dispersed and crumbly; set aside. Toss the remaining sugar and flour with fruit, cornstarch, ginger and vanilla. Pack into prepared bak-ing dish and bake for 30 minutes. Top with coconut mixture and bake for 30 minutes, until browned and bubbling. **Serves 8 to 10.**

Balsamic Pear Tarte Tatin

4 oz	butter, cut into thin slices	125 g
1½ cups	granulated sugar	375 mL
9	large crisp pears, peeled and sliced lengthwise	9
2 tbsp	aged balsamic vinegar	25 mL
8 oz	frozen puff pastry, thawed	250 g

Preheat oven to 425°F (220°C). Lay butter slices across the bottom of a 10-inch (25 cm) ovenproof skillet (preferably nonstick). Sprinkle with sugar. Pack pear slices on top of sugar in a tight, even layer. Cook over medium heat until sugar is caramelized and pears are tender, about 30 minutes. Drizzle with vinegar, then remove from heat. If necessary, roll out puff pastry and cut into a 12-inch (30 cm) circle and place on top of skillet. Bake for 10 minutes. Reduce heat to 350°F (180°C) and bake until crust is crisp and brown, about 20 minutes. Let cool for 10 minutes, then invert onto a serving platter and unmold. **Serves 8 to 10.**

Pineapple Upside-Down Pie

Follow preceding recipe, but replace the pears with 1 pineapple, peeled, cored, cut into thin rings and quartered, omit the vinegar, and sprinkle cooked pineapple with 1 tbsp (15 mL) finely grated lime zest and 2 tbsp (25 mL) freshly squeezed lime juice. **Serves 8 to 10.**

Jewish Apple Cake

	Nonstick cooking spray	
6	large tart apples (unpeeled), cut into wedges	6
2 cups	granulated sugar, divided	500 mL
1 tbsp	ground cinnamon	15 mL
3 cups	all-purpose flour	750 mL
1 tbsp	baking powder	15 mL
½ tsp	salt	2 mL
4	large or extra-large eggs	4
½ cup	orange juice	125 mL
2 tsp	vanilla	10 mL
¾ cup	vegetable oil	175 mL

Preheat oven to 350°F (180°C) and spray a 10-inch (4 L) tube pan with cooking spray. Toss apples with ⅓ cup (75 mL) of the sugar and cinnamon; set aside. Sift together flour, baking powder and salt; set aside. In a large bowl, beat eggs and the remaining sugar until pale and thick. Mix in orange juice and vanilla, then beat in oil in a slow, steady stream until mixture is smooth and thick. Stir in flour mixture, just enough to incorporate. Spread one-third of the batter across the bottom of the pan and layer with one-third of the apple mixture. Repeat layers twice. Bake for 1 hour and 45 minutes, until a tester inserted in the center comes out barely moist. Let cool in pan on a rack for 1 hour, then invert onto a serving platter and unmold. **Serves 8 to 10.**

Lemon Apple Cake

Follow preceding recipe, but replace the orange juice with the finely grated zest and juice of 1 lemon. **Serves 8 to 10.**

Apple Walnut Cake

Follow recipe for Jewish Apple Cake (above), but instead of sugar and cinnamon, toss apples with Nut Streusel Topping (page 23), made with finely ground walnuts. **Serves 8 to 10.**

Cardamom Pear Cake

Follow recipe for Jewish Apple Cake (left), but replace the apples with large pears, replace the cinnamon with ground cardamom, and add ¼ cup (50 mL) finely chopped candied ginger to the batter with the flour mixture. **Serves 8 to 10.**

Apple Crumb Coffee Cake

	Nonstick cooking spray	
2 cups	sifted all-purpose flour	500 mL
¾ cup	granulated sugar	175 mL
¼ cup	packed light brown sugar	50 mL
2 tsp	baking powder	10 mL
1 tsp	baking soda	5 mL
1 tsp	ground cinnamon	5 mL
¼ tsp	ground nutmeg	1 mL
5 oz	cold butter, cut into small pieces	150 g
2	large tart apples, peeled and diced	2
½ cup	chopped walnuts	125 mL
1	extra-large egg, beaten	1
⅔ cup	buttermilk	150 mL
1 tsp	vanilla	5 mL

Preheat oven to 375°F (190°C) and spray a 9-inch (23 cm) round cake pan with cooking spray. In a large bowl, combine flour, sugar, brown sugar, baking powder, baking soda, cinnamon and nutmeg. Cut in butter until mixture resembles coarse meal. Toss ½ cup (125 mL) of this mixture with the apples and walnuts; set aside. Mix egg, buttermilk and vanilla into the remaining dry ingredients, just enough to incorporate. Turn half this batter into prepared pan, then top with half the apple mixture. Repeat layers. Bake for 45 minutes, until a tester inserted in the center comes out clean. Let cool in pan on a rack for 20 minutes, then remove from pan and serve warm. **Serves 8 to 10.**

Hungarian Apple Coffee Cake

Follow preceding recipe, but add ½ cup (125 mL) chopped raisins and 3 tbsp (45 mL) unsweetened cocoa powder, sifted, with the apples, and make 2 additions of apple mixture between 3 layers of batter. **Serves 8 to 10.**

Pear Ginger Coffee Cake

Follow the recipe for Apple Crumb Coffee Cake (page 412), but substitute ground ginger for the cinnamon, pears for the apples, and crushed gingersnaps for the walnuts. **Serves 8 to 10.**

Mint Mango Soup

2	large mangoes, quartered	2
1 cup	orange juice	250 mL
½ cup	white wine	125 mL
4 tsp	honey	20 mL
¼ cup	chopped fresh mint	50 mL

In a food processor, purée mangoes, orange juice, wine and honey. Stir in mint. Cover and refrigerate for 1 hour, until chilled. Serve as a dessert soup. **Serves 4.**

Grapefruit Cloud

1⅓ cups	granulated sugar	325 mL
1⅓ cups	water	325 mL
2 cups	unsweetened grapefruit juice	500 mL
¼ cup	freshly squeezed lemon juice	50 mL
4	egg whites	4
¼ tsp	salt	1 mL

In a saucepan, bring sugar and water to a boil; let cool. Stir in grapefruit juice and lemon juice. Beat egg whites and salt until frothy; stir into juice. Freeze in an ice cream maker according to manufacturer's directions. **Serves 4.** *Store in an airtight container in the freezer for up to 2 days. (If you are concerned about the food safety of raw eggs, you may wish to skip this recipe.)*

Chili Mango Sorbet

1	can (28 oz/796 mL) mango pieces in heavy syrup	1
½ tsp	rice wine vinegar	2 mL
¼ tsp	Thai hot sauce (such as Sriracha)	1 mL

Freeze the can of mango pieces until contents are solid, preferably overnight. Run under warm water to thaw edges, open can and dig out contents into a food processor. Add vinegar and hot sauce; pulse in batches until mixture is the smooth texture of sorbet. (Pulse as quickly as possible, and do not let melt.) **Serves 4.** *Store in an airtight container in the freezer for up to 1 day.*

Chapter 37
Summer Fruit
Berries, Peaches and Plums

Game Hens Braised with Blackberries . . 415

Blueberry Buttermilk Pancakes 416

Orange Raspberry Pancakes 416

Blueberry Sour Cream Corn Muffins . . . 416

Easy Blueberry Soup 416

Raspberry Soup 416

Honeydew Raspberry Soup 416

No-Heat Strawberry Wine Soup 416

Spiked Summer Fruit Salad 417

Strawberries in Grand Marnier 417

Blueberries with Rum and Lemon 417

Peaches in Peach Schnapps 417

Plums in Sambuca 417

Strawberries with
Warm Rhubarb Sauce 417

Summer Fruit with
Lime Crème Anglaise 417

Triple-Dipped Strawberries 418

Cherry Chocolate Fondue 418

Peaches Stuffed
with Minted Blueberries 418

Peaches Stuffed
with Chocolate Mousse 418

Raspberry Ricotta Mousse 418

Raspberry Lemon Laban 419

Plum and Blackberry Parfait 419

Easy Peach Melba 419

Low-Fat Peach Melba 419

Easy Tangy Strawberry Ice Cream 419

Caramel Peach Ice Cream 419

Deep-Dish Blueberry and
Raspberry Pot Pie 419

Sour Cream Peach Pot Pie 420

Strawberry Meringue Pie 420

Two-Crust Strawberry Pie 420

Strawberry Rhubarb Pie 420

Raspberry Nectarine Pie 420

Chocolate Strawberry Tartlets 420

Black-Bottom Raspberry Tart 420

Strawberry Cannoli Tart 420

Three-Berry Crisp 421

Strawberry Lime Crisp 421

Gingered Berry Crisp 421

Blueberry Shortcake Cobbler 421

Peach Blackberry Crunch 421

Plum Pudding Crisp 421

Strawberry Shortcake with
Whipped Crème Fraîche 422

Peaches and Cream Shortcake 422

Cherry Shortcake with
Ricotta Basil Filling 422

Warm Rhubarb and
Strawberry Shortcake 422

Quick Berry Compote 423

Strawberry Dessert Sauce 423

Sautéed Berry Syrup 423

Strawberry Lime Preserves 423

Summer Bounty Vinegar 423

Among the crown jewels of fruit, the berries, cherries, peaches and plums of summer are the most radiant. But the real attraction of summer fruit is more than surface-deep. It's in its lingering perfume and sweet-tart flavor. It's in the juice dripping down your chin and the memory of ripeness that glazes the palate and just won't quit.

Where fall fruit is often eaten crisp, tart and underripe, the fruit of summer is always best when caught at the fleeting moment of perfect ripeness. If you're lucky enough to catch that moment, the best thing you can do is to cook these fruits as little as possible.

They make miraculous sauces with just a glaze of sugar and a splash of juice. They are the filling for a shortcake or the jazz in a parfait as soon as they are sliced. And there is no more sophisticated dessert than a single, egg-size strawberry dipped in chocolate and consumed in its solitary perfection.

To dazzle any diner, ripe summer fruit needs little more than a dip in whipped cream, or a pastry shell and a lacquer of glaze. But when less than ripe, these fruits may need additional assistance. Hide the imperfection of underripe fruits under a pie crust or deep within a mouthful of muffin. Embellish their lack of sweetness with a balm of honey, or intensify their fruit flavor with a jolt of vinegar and a swirl of preserves.

If you want to know whether a fruit is ripe, smell it. Modern industrial farms may be able to grow gorgeous strawberries that look ripe and taste like sour water, but no one has ever been able to grow a specimen that smells like a strawberry without tasting like one. So when judging ripeness, always look with your nose instead of your eyes.

The 50 recipes in this chapter include savory entrées, pancakes, muffins, soups, mousses, parfaits, ice creams, pies, tarts, cobblers, shortcakes, simple, elegant dessert sauces and preserves.

About these recipes . . .

In the following recipes, it is assumed that you will add salt and pepper to taste for savory recipes and a dash of salt in sweet recipes.

Game Hens Braised with Blackberries

2	game hens, split lengthwise and backbones removed	2
	Salt and freshly ground black pepper to taste	
2 tbsp	vegetable oil	25 mL
2 tbsp	butter	25 mL
1	small onion, finely diced	1
¾ cup	chicken broth	175 mL
½ cup	dry white wine	125 mL
2 cups	blackberries	500 mL
2 tbsp	chopped fresh Italian (flat-leaf) parsley	25 mL
2 tbsp	balsamic vinegar	25 mL
1 tbsp	blackberry jam	15 mL

Season hens with salt and pepper. In a large skillet, heat oil and butter over medium-high heat. Cook hen halves, skin side down, for 4 to 5 minutes, or until golden brown. Turn hens, add onion, and sauté until onion is tender. Add broth and wine; reduce heat, cover and simmer, turning hens once or twice, until juices run clear when hens are pierced, about 20 minutes. Transfer hens to a warm platter. Increase heat and boil pan liquid until reduced by half. Add berries, parsley, vinegar and jam; swirl to combine and heat through. Pour sauce over hens. **Serves 4.**

Blueberry Buttermilk Pancakes

2 cups	unbleached all-purpose flour	500 mL
2 tbsp	granulated sugar	25 mL
2 tsp	baking powder	10 mL
1 tsp	baking soda	5 mL
Pinch	salt	Pinch
2	extra-large eggs, separated	2
2 cups	buttermilk	500 mL
¼ cup	unsalted butter, melted	50 mL
2 cups	blueberries	500 mL
	Sautéed Berry Syrup (see recipe, page 423)	

In a large bowl, sift together flour, sugar, baking powder, baking soda and salt. Stir in egg yolks, buttermilk and half the butter until smooth. In a separate bowl, beat egg whites to soft peaks; fold into batter. Fold in berries. In a large skillet or on a griddle, heat a thin film of the remaining butter over medium-high heat until foamy. For each pancake, pour in ¼ cup (50 mL) batter and cook until covered with bubbles. Flip and cook for 1 to 2 minutes, until pancakes feel springy. Transfer to a plate and keep warm. Repeat with the remaining batter, greasing pan with more butter for every batch. Serve with berry syrup. **Serves 4.**

Orange Raspberry Pancakes

Follow preceding recipe, but add 2 tbsp (25 mL) finely grated orange zest with the flour, and substitute raspberries for the blueberries. **Serves 4.**

Blueberry Sour Cream Corn Muffins

	Nonstick cooking spray	
1½ cups	white or yellow cornmeal	375 mL
¾ cup	all-purpose flour	175 mL
3 tbsp	granulated sugar	45 mL
1 tsp	baking powder	5 mL
½ tsp	baking soda	2 mL
2	extra-large eggs, separated	2
1½ cups	sour cream	375 mL
¼ cup	melted butter	50 mL
2 cups	blueberries	500 mL

Preheat oven to 400°F (200°C) and spray a 12-cup nonstick muffin tin with cooking spray. In a large bowl, combine cornmeal, flour, sugar, baking powder and baking soda. Stir in egg yolks, sour cream and butter. Fold in berries. In a separate bowl, beat egg whites to soft peaks; fold into batter. Spoon batter into prepared tin. Bake for 15 minutes, until puffed and browned and a tester inserted in the center of a muffin comes out with just a crumb clinging to it. Let cool in pan on a rack for 3 minutes, then remove from pan. **Makes 12 large muffins.**

Easy Blueberry Soup

1 cup	dry red wine	250 mL
2 cups	blueberries	500 mL
¼ cup	granulated sugar	50 mL
Pinch	salt	Pinch
1 cup	ice water	250 mL
1 cup	orange juice	250 mL
2 tbsp	freshly squeezed lemon juice	25 mL
¼ cup	sour cream (optional)	50 mL

In a saucepan, bring wine to a boil over medium-high heat; boil for 1 minute. Add berries, sugar and salt; return to a boil. Remove from heat and stir in ice water, orange juice and lemon juice. Cover and refrigerate for about 2 hours, until chilled. Serve dolloped with sour cream, if desired. **Serves 4.**

Raspberry Soup

Follow preceding recipe, but replace the red wine with white wine, replace the blueberries with raspberries, and replace the lemon juice with lime juice. **Serves 4.**

Honeydew Raspberry Soup

8	mint leaves	8
1	large honeydew melon, peeled, seeded and cut into chunks	1
1 cup	raspberries	250 mL
1 tbsp	granulated sugar	15 mL
Pinch	salt	Pinch

In a food processor, purée all ingredients. Cover and refrigerate for about 1 hour, until chilled. **Serves 4.**

No-Heat Strawberry Wine Soup

4 cups	strawberries, hulled and halved	1 L
1 cup	buttermilk	250 mL
½ cup	dry white wine	125 mL
¼ cup	confectioner's (icing) sugar	50 mL
Pinch	salt	Pinch

Reserve 4 strawberry halves for garnish. In a food processor, purée the remaining berries, buttermilk, wine, sugar and salt. Cover and refrigerate for about 1 hour, until chilled. Serve in chilled bowls, each garnished with a reserved strawberry half. **Serves 4.**

Spiked Summer Fruit Salad

3 tbsp	orange-flavored liqueur	45 mL
1 tbsp	honey	15 mL
1 tsp	red wine vinegar	5 mL
8	large strawberries, hulled and halved	8
3	apricots, quartered	3
2	red plums, sliced	2
1	peach, sliced	1
1 cup	halved cherries	250 mL
1 cup	blueberries	250 mL

In a serving bowl, combine liqueur, honey and vinegar. Add the remaining ingredients and toss to coat. Cover and refrigerate for about 1 hour, until chilled. **Serves 4.**

Strawberries in Grand Marnier

3 tbsp	Grand Marnier or other orange-flavored liqueur	45 mL
1 tsp	granulated sugar	5 mL
3 cups	strawberries, hulled and halved	750 mL
4	sprigs fresh mint	4

Combine liqueur and sugar. Add strawberries and toss to coat. Cover and refrigerate until flavors blend, about 20 minutes. Serve garnished with mint sprigs. **Serves 4.**

Blueberries with Rum and Lemon

¼ cup	light rum	50 mL
1 tbsp	granulated sugar	15 mL
	Finely grated zest and juice of ½ lemon	
3 cups	blueberries	750 mL

In a medium saucepan, bring rum, sugar, lemon zest and lemon juice to a boil. Stir in berries and cook briefly over medium-high heat, until berries are shiny. Transfer to a bowl, cover and refrigerate until flavors blend, about 20 minutes. Serve alone or over ice cream. **Serves 4.**

Peaches in Peach Schnapps

3 tbsp	peach schnapps	45 mL
1 tsp	granulated sugar	5 mL
¼ tsp	freshly squeezed lemon juice	1 mL
3	large peaches, peeled and sliced into wedges	3

Combine liqueur, sugar and lemon juice. Add peaches and toss to coat. Cover and refrigerate until flavors blend, about 20 minutes. **Serves 4.**

Plums in Sambuca

1 tbsp	sambuca or other anise-flavored liqueur	15 mL
1 tsp	honey	5 mL
¼ tsp	freshly squeezed lemon juice	1 mL
5	red plums, sliced into wedges	5
1 tsp	finely grated orange zest	5 mL

Combine liqueur, honey and lemon juice. Add plums and toss to coat. Cover and refrigerate until flavors blend, about 20 minutes. Serve sprinkled with orange zest. **Serves 4.**

Strawberries with Warm Rhubarb Sauce

2 lbs	rhubarb, thinly sliced (about 6 cups/1.5 L)	1 kg
½ cup	granulated sugar	125 mL
1 cup	strawberry preserves	250 mL
3 cups	strawberries, hulled and sliced	750 mL
¼ cup	sour cream (optional)	50 mL

In a saucepan, over medium heat, cook rhubarb and sugar until rhubarb is tender, about 10 minutes. Stir in preserves. Serve warm over sliced strawberries, garnished with sour cream, if desired. **Serves 4.**

Summer Fruit with Lime Crème Anglaise

2 cups	Crème Anglaise (see recipe, page 24)	500 mL
	Finely grated zest and juice of 1 lime	
4 cups	mixed berries, pitted cherries and/or sliced peaches or plums	1 L

Combine Crème Anglaise, lime zest and lime juice. Serve spooned over fruit. **Serves 4.**

Triple-Dipped Strawberries

8	large, perfect strawberries, with stems	8
2½ oz	white chocolate, melted (see page 14)	75 g
3 oz	semisweet chocolate, melted	90 g
2 to 3 tbsp	whipping (35%) cream, warm	25 to 45 mL

Dip strawberries in white chocolate, using the stems as handles and covering all but a ring at the top of each berry. Let excess chocolate run off. As they are coated, place berries on a baking sheet lined with waxed paper. Refrigerate until chocolate is firm, about 10 minutes. Grasp cooled berries by their stems and dip into semisweet chocolate, leaving a ring of white chocolate exposed near the top. Return berries to the baking sheet and refrigerate until chocolate is firm. Stir 2 tbsp (25 mL) of the whipping cream into the remaining semisweet chocolate, adding another 1 tbsp (15 mL) if the chocolate binds up. Dip the tips of the strawberries into the milk chocolate. Return berries to the baking sheet and refrigerate until chocolate is firm. **Serves 4.**

Cherry Chocolate Fondue

2 oz	unsweetened chocolate, finely chopped	60 g
½ cup	granulated sugar	125 mL
½ cup	milk (not fat-free)	125 mL
1 tbsp	kirsch or other cherry-flavored liqueur	15 mL
Dash	almond extract	Dash
4 cups	sweet cherries, on their stems	1 L

In a 4-cup (1 L) glass measure, combine chocolate, sugar and milk. Cover with microwave-safe plastic wrap and microwave on High for 3 minutes, until chocolate is half melted. Uncover and whisk until smooth. Whisk in kirsch and almond extract. Let cool for 5 minutes. Serve with cherries for dipping. **Serves 4.**

Peaches Stuffed with Minted Blueberries

2 cups	blueberries	500 mL
1 tbsp	granulated sugar	15 mL
1 tbsp	chopped fresh mint	15 mL
4	large freestone peaches	4
4	sprigs fresh mint	4

In a small saucepan, over medium heat, cook blueberries, sugar and chopped mint until berries are glossy, about 1 minute. Cover and refrigerate for about 1 hour, until chilled. Slice tops off peaches and reserve for "lids." Remove the pit and, using a small melon baller, hollow out the cavity of each peach. Cut a thin slice from the bottoms so they sit upright on a plate. Fill peaches with berries and place "lids" on top. Surround peaches with the remaining berries and crown each with 1 mint sprig. **Serves 4.**

Peaches Stuffed with Chocolate Mousse

2	large or extra-large eggs, separated	2
3 oz	semisweet chocolate, melted (see page 14)	90 g
¼ cup	whipping (35%) cream	50 mL
4	large freestone peaches	4
4	sprigs fresh mint	4

In a bowl, beat egg yolks and chocolate. In a separate bowl, beat egg whites to soft peaks; fold into yolk mixture in 2 additions. In another bowl, beat cream to soft peaks; fold into mousse. Cover and refrigerate for at least 1 hour or until ready to serve. Slice tops off peaches and reserve for "lids." Remove the pit and, using a small melon baller, hollow out the cavity of each peach. Cut a thin slice from the bottoms so they sit upright on a plate. Fill peaches with mousse and place "lids" on top. Garnish each with 1 mint sprig. **Serves 4.** *(If you are concerned about the food safety of raw eggs, you may wish to skip this recipe.)*

Raspberry Ricotta Mousse

1	container (15 oz/450 g) whole-milk ricotta cheese	1
2 cups	raspberries, divided	500 mL
1 cup	confectioner's (icing) sugar	250 mL
½ tsp	vanilla	2 mL
Pinch	salt	Pinch

Spoon ricotta into a strainer lined with a coffee filter and set over a bowl to catch the drips. Place in the refrigerator and drain for 1 to 2 hours, until excess liquid is drained off. In a food processor, purée ricotta, half the berries, sugar, vanilla and salt until smooth. Fold in the remaining berries. Spoon into 4 dessert cups or wine glasses, cover and refrigerate for about 1 hour, until chilled. **Serves 4.**

Raspberry Lemon Laban

3 cups	low-fat lemon-flavored yogurt	750 mL
3 cups	low-fat vanilla-flavored yogurt	750 mL
2 cups	raspberries	500 mL

Pour both yogurts into a cheesecloth-lined strainer. Tie the ends of the cheesecloth over the top, weight with a small plate and rest over a large bowl to catch the drips. Place in the refrigerator and drain for 6 hours. Unwrap and transfer to a bowl; fold in raspberries. Serve immediately or cover and refrigerate for up to 1 day. **Makes about 8 cups (2 L).** *Serve with cookies.*

Plum and Blackberry Parfait

5	red or black plums, cut into bite-size pieces	5
2 tbsp	granulated sugar, divided	25 mL
1 tsp	aged balsamic vinegar	5 mL
2 cups	blackberries, divided	500 mL
1 cup	plain yogurt or sour cream	250 mL
1 tbsp	honey	15 mL
½ tsp	vanilla	2 mL

Combine plums, half the sugar and vinegar; set it and 4 perfect berries aside. Toss the remaining berries with the remaining sugar; set aside. Combine yogurt, honey and vanilla. Form alternating layers of plums and blackberries in 4 parfait glasses, and top each with a portion of the yogurt. Decorate each with 1 reserved berry. **Serves 4.**

Easy Peach Melba

2	large peaches, peeled and halved	2
1 tbsp	granulated sugar	15 mL
½ tsp	vanilla	2 mL
Pinch	almond extract	Pinch
1 cup	raspberries	250 mL
1 tsp	honey	5 mL
1 tbsp	framboise or other raspberry-flavored liqueur (optional) Vanilla ice cream	15 mL

Toss peach halves with sugar, vanilla and almond extract until coated; let stand for 10 minutes. Mash raspberries with honey and framboise (if using) until saucy. Serve each peach half leaning against 1 scoop ice cream, drizzle some marinating liquid over each peach, and spoon the raspberry sauce in a wide band overlapping the peach and ice cream. **Serves 4.**

Low-Fat Peach Melba

Follow preceding recipe, but substitute Raspberry Lemon Laban (left) for the ice cream. **Serves 4.**

Easy Tangy Strawberry Ice Cream

1 cup	cream (any type, minimum 10%)	250 mL
¼ cup	cornstarch	50 mL
2 cups	milk (preferably whole)	500 mL
1 cup	granulated sugar	250 mL
4 cups	strawberries, hulled and puréed	1 L
2 cups	sour cream	500 mL
1 tsp	vanilla	5 mL

In a heavy saucepan, whisk together cream and cornstarch until smooth. Whisk in milk and sugar. Bring to a boil over medium heat and cook, stirring constantly, until thick; let cool to room temperature. Stir in strawberries, sour cream and vanilla. Transfer to an ice cream maker and freeze according to manufacturer's directions. **Makes about 8 cups (2 L).**

Caramel Peach Ice Cream

Follow preceding recipe, but replace the granulated sugar with packed light brown sugar, and replace the strawberries with 4 cups (1 L) sliced peeled peaches, puréed. **Makes about 8 cups (2 L).**

Deep-Dish Blueberry and Raspberry Pot Pie

4 cups	blueberries	1 L
2 cups	raspberries	500 mL
1 cup	granulated sugar	250 mL
¼ cup	all-purpose flour	50 mL
2 tbsp	freshly squeezed lemon juice	25 mL
2 tbsp	butter	25 mL
1	9-inch (23 cm) pie pastry round (store-bought or see recipe, page 21) Whipped cream or vanilla ice cream	1

Preheat oven to 375°F (190°C). Toss blueberries and raspberries with sugar, flour and lemon juice. Pour into a 9-inch (23 cm) deep-dish pie plate and dot with butter. Drape pastry over top and crimp edges to rim of pie plate. Bake for about 50 minutes, or until top is uniformly brown and fruit is bubbling. Let cool on a rack for 1 hour. Serve with whipped cream or ice cream. **Serves 6 to 8.**

Sour Cream Peach Pot Pie

Follow preceding recipe, but replace both berries with 3 lbs (1.5 kg) peaches, peeled and sliced, increase flour to ⅓ cup (125 mL), and add ½ cup (125 mL) sour cream (not fat-free) and 1 tsp (5 mL) vanilla to the fruit mixture. **Serves 6 to 8.**

Strawberry Meringue Pie

5	extra-large egg whites	5
½ tsp	white vinegar	2 mL
⅓ cup	granulated sugar	75 mL
6 cups	strawberries, hulled and sliced	1.5 L
1 cup	confectioner's (icing) sugar	250 mL
1	9-inch (23 cm) prebaked pie shell (see page 21)	1

Preheat oven to 300°F (150°C). Using a balloon whisk or an electric mixer, beat egg whites and vinegar until whites barely hold a shape. Add granulated sugar, 1 tbsp (15 mL) at a time, and beat until stiff, smooth and glossy; set aside. Toss strawberries with confectioner's sugar until uniformly coated; pack into pie shell. Mound meringue on top and smooth into a peak, making sure meringue overlaps the edges of the pie crust all around. Bake for 20 minutes, until meringue is golden brown. Let cool on a rack for 30 minutes, but serve within 1 hour. **Serves 6 to 8.**

Two-Crust Strawberry Pie

8 cups	strawberries, hulled and sliced	2 L
1¾ cups	confectioner's (icing) sugar	425 mL
¼ cup	cornstarch	50 mL
1 tbsp	freshly squeezed lemon juice	15 mL
Pinch	salt	Pinch
2	rounds pie pastry for a 9-inch (23 cm) pie (store-bought or see recipe, page 21)	2

Preheat oven to 375°F (190°C). Toss berries with sugar, cornstarch, lemon juice and salt. Assemble a two-crust pie (see page 13) and bake for about 50 minutes, or until pastry is lightly browned and filling is bubbling. Let cool on a rack for at least 30 minutes. **Serves 6 to 8.**

Strawberry Rhubarb Pie

Follow preceding recipe, but decrease the strawberries to 4 cups (1 L), and add 4 cups (1 L) rhubarb, cut into 1-inch (2.5 cm) pieces. **Serves 6 to 8.**

Raspberry Nectarine Pie

Follow recipe for Two-Crust Strawberry Pie (left), but substitute 2 cups (500 mL) raspberries and 4 cups (1 L) sliced peeled nectarines (about 6) for the strawberries. **Serves 6 to 8.**

Chocolate Strawberry Tartlets

1	round pie pastry for a 9-inch (23 cm) pie (store-bought or see recipe, page 21)	1
1 cup	strawberry preserves	250 mL
2 tbsp	orange-flavored liqueur	25 mL
½ cup	Chocolate Glaze (see recipe, page 23)	125 mL
4 cups	perfect strawberries, hulled	1 L

Prepare 8 prebaked tartlet shells (see page 13) from the pie pastry. In a small saucepan, melt strawberry preserves over medium-high heat, stirring often; strain out solids and stir liqueur into liquid. Dip berries, one at a time, in warm glaze. Spoon 1 tbsp (15 mL) Chocolate Glaze into each shell, then arrange berries in shells. Let cool for 10 minutes. **Serves 4.**

Black-Bottom Raspberry Tart

½ cup	red currant jelly	125 mL
1 tbsp	brandy	15 mL
1	8-inch (20 cm) prebaked tart shell (see page 21)	1
½ cup	Chocolate Glaze (see recipe, page 23)	125 mL
3 cups	perfect raspberries	750 mL

In a small saucepan, melt currant jelly over medium-high heat, stirring often. Stir in brandy and set aside. Spread Chocolate Glaze over bottom of tart shell. Arrange berries in closely packed concentric circles and brush with currant glaze. Refrigerate for about 1 hour, until glaze is set. **Serves 6 to 8.**

Strawberry Cannoli Tart

1 cup	ricotta cheese	250 mL
½ cup	red currant jelly	125 mL
1 tbsp	brandy	15 mL
¼ cup	pistachios, coarsely chopped	50 mL
¼ cup	raisins, chopped	50 mL
¼ cup	chopped candied lemon peel or citron	50 mL
3 tbsp	confectioner's (icing) sugar	45 mL
1	8-inch (20 cm) prebaked tart shell (see page 21)	1

| 4 cups | strawberries, hulled and halved lengthwise | 1 L |

Spoon ricotta into a strainer lined with a coffee filter and set over a bowl to catch the drips. Place in the refrigerator and drain for 1 to 2 hours, until excess liquid is drained off. In a small saucepan, melt currant jelly over medium-high heat, stirring often. Stir in brandy and set aside. Combine ricotta, pistachios, raisins, candied lemon peel and sugar; spread over bottom of tart shell. Arrange strawberries, cut side down, in closely packed concentric circles and brush with currant glaze. Refrigerate for about 1 hour, until glaze is set. **Serves 6 to 8.**

Three-Berry Crisp

⅓ cup	butter, chilled, divided	75 mL
1½ cups	chopped almonds	375 mL
½ cup	granulated sugar	125 mL
⅓ cup	all-purpose flour, divided	75 mL
2 cups	raspberries	500 mL
2 cups	strawberries, hulled and quartered	500 mL
2 cups	blueberries	500 mL
3 tbsp	confectioner's (icing) sugar	45 mL
2 tbsp	cornstarch	25 mL

Preheat oven to 375°F (190°C) and grease an 8-cup (2 L) shallow baking dish with 1 tbsp (15 mL) of the butter. Cut the remaining butter into small pieces. Combine almonds, granulated sugar and ¼ cup (50 mL) of the flour. Mix butter into nut mixture until well dispersed and crumbly; set aside. Toss raspberries, strawberries and blueberries with the remaining flour, confectioner's sugar and cornstarch. Pack into prepared baking dish and bake for 10 minutes. Top with nut mixture and bake for 30 minutes, until browned and bubbling. Serve warm. **Serves 6 to 8.**

Strawberry Lime Crisp

Follow preceding recipe, but substitute finely chopped hazelnuts for the almonds, use 6 cups (1.5 L) strawberries for the berries, and add the finely grated zest and juice of 1 lime when tossing the berries. **Serves 6 to 8.**

Gingered Berry Crisp

Follow recipe for Three-Berry Crisp (above), but substitute chopped pecans for the almonds, add 2 tbsp (25 mL) finely chopped candied ginger to the nut mixture, and add ½ tsp (2 mL) ground ginger when tossing the berries. **Serves 6 to 8.**

Blueberry Shortcake Cobbler

1 tbsp	butter, chilled	15 mL
6 cups	blueberries	1.5 L
3 tbsp	confectioner's (icing) sugar	45 mL
2 tbsp	cornstarch	25 mL
2 tbsp	all-purpose flour	25 mL
1	recipe Shortcake Biscuits (page 22)	1

Preheat oven to 375°F (190°C) and grease an 8-cup (2 L) shallow baking dish with butter. Toss berries with sugar, cornstarch and flour. Pack into prepared baking dish and bake for 10 minutes. Top with biscuits and bake for 30 minutes, until browned and bubbling. Serve warm. **Serves 6 to 8.**

Peach Blackberry Crunch

¼ cup	butter, chilled, divided	50 mL
¾ cup	chopped pecans	175 mL
½ cup	packed light brown sugar	125 mL
3 tbsp	all-purpose flour, divided	45 mL
¼ tsp	ground cinnamon	1 mL
2 lbs	peaches, peeled and cut into 8 wedges	1 kg
2 cups	blackberries or raspberries	500 mL
⅓ cup	granulated sugar	75 mL
2 tbsp	cornstarch	25 mL
1 tsp	vanilla	5 mL

Preheat oven to 375°F (190°C) and grease an 8-cup (2 L) shallow baking dish with 1 tbsp (15 mL) of the butter. Cut the remaining butter into small pieces. Combine pecans, brown sugar, 2 tbsp (25 mL) of the flour and cinnamon. Mix butter into nut mixture until well dispersed and crumbly; set aside. Toss peaches and blackberries with the remaining flour, granulated sugar, cornstarch and vanilla. Pack into prepared baking dish and bake for 10 minutes. Top with nut mixture and bake for 30 minutes, until browned and bubbling. Serve warm. **Serves 6 to 8.**

Plum Pudding Crisp

Follow preceding recipe, but add a pinch of allspice with the cinnamon, replace the peaches with unpeeled red plums, and replace the berries with 1½ cups (375 mL) chopped prunes and ½ cup (125 mL) golden raisins. **Serves 6 to 8.**

Strawberry Shortcake with Whipped Crème Fraîche

2 cups	crème fraîche	500 mL
½ cup	confectioner's (icing) sugar, divided	125 mL
1 cup	whipping (35%) cream	250 mL
4 cups	strawberries, hulled, divided	1 L
1	Shortcake (see recipe, page 22)	1

In a bowl, combine crème fraîche and 6 tbsp (90 mL) of the sugar. In a separate bowl, beat cream to soft peaks; fold into crème fraîche. Slice half the strawberries and toss with the remaining sugar. Using a serrated knife, carefully cut shortcake into two layers as specified on page 22. Place bottom layer on a serving plate and spread with a thin layer of crème fraîche mixture. Top with sliced berries and half the remaining crème fraîche mixture. Place top layer of shortcake on top, cover with the remaining crème fraîche mixture and decorate with the remaining whole strawberries. Refrigerate until ready to serve, but serve within 1 hour. **Serves 8.**

Peaches and Cream Shortcake

2 cups	whipping (35%) cream	500 mL
½ cup	confectioner's (icing) sugar, divided	125 mL
1 tsp	vanilla	5 mL
6	large peaches, peeled and thinly sliced	6
¼ tsp	almond extract	1 mL
1	Shortcake (see recipe, page 22)	1

Beat cream, half the sugar and the vanilla to soft peaks. Toss peaches with the remaining sugar and almond extract. Using a serrated knife, carefully cut shortcake into two layers as specified on page 22. Place bottom layer on a serving plate and spread with a thin layer of whipped cream. Top with peaches and half the remaining whipped cream. Place top layer of shortcake on top and cover with the remaining whipped cream. Refrigerate until ready to serve, but serve within 1 hour. **Serves 8.**

Cherry Shortcake with Ricotta Basil Filling

1 cup	whipping (35%) cream, divided	250 mL
½ cup	chopped fresh basil	125 mL
1	container (15 oz/450 g) ricotta cheese (preferably whole-milk)	1
¾ cup	confectioner's (icing) sugar, divided	175 mL
1 tsp	vanilla	5 mL
1½ lbs	cherries, halved	750 g
¼ tsp	almond extract	1 mL
1	Shortcake (see recipe, page 22)	1

In a small saucepan, bring half the cream to a simmer (do not boil). Transfer to a bowl and stir in basil. Cover and refrigerate for about 1 hour, until chilled. Strain out basil. Add the remaining cream and beat to soft peaks. In a separate bowl, combine ricotta, ½ cup (125 mL) of the confectioner's sugar and vanilla; fold into whipped cream. Toss cherries with the remaining sugar and almond extract. Using a serrated knife, carefully cut shortcake into two layers as specified on page 22. Place bottom layer on a serving plate and spread with a thin layer of ricotta cream. Top with cherries and half the remaining ricotta cream. Place top layer of shortcake on top and cover with the remaining ricotta cream. Refrigerate until ready to serve, but serve within 1 hour. **Serves 8.**

Warm Rhubarb and Strawberry Shortcake

2 lbs	rhubarb, thinly sliced (6 cups/1.5 L)	1 kg
1¼ cups	strawberry preserves	300 mL
½ cup	freshly squeezed orange juice	125 mL
1	Shortcake (see recipe, page 22), not sliced in half	1
2 cups	strawberries, hulled and sliced, divided	500 mL
	Vanilla ice cream (optional)	

In a heavy saucepan, over medium heat, cook rhubarb, preserves and orange juice until rhubarb is soft, about 8 minutes. Cut shortcake into 8 wedges and place 1 wedge on each of 8 plates. Top each with ¼ cup (50 mL) strawberries and ½ cup (125 mL) rhubarb mixture. Serve immediately, with scoops of ice cream, if desired. **Serves 8.**

Quick Berry Compote

4 cups	berries (any variety)	1 L
¼ cup	granulated sugar	50 mL
1 tbsp	freshly squeezed lime juice	15 mL
½ tsp	vanilla	2 mL

Combine all ingredients. Serve immediately or cover and refrigerate for up to 1 day. **Serves 4.** *Serve with cookies, or as a sauce for ice cream or plain cakes.*

Strawberry Dessert Sauce

2 tbsp	strawberry preserves	25 mL
2 tbsp	fruit brandy (any type)	25 mL
2 cups	strawberries, hulled and sliced	500 mL
Pinch	salt	Pinch

In a saucepan, melt strawberry preserves over medium heat, stirring often. Add brandy, strawberries and salt; cook until berries begin to weep. Let cool. **Makes about 1½ cups (375 mL).** *Serve over plain pound cake, fresh fruit or ice cream.*

Sautéed Berry Syrup

2 tbsp	butter	25 mL
3 cups	berries (any type)	750 mL
2 tbsp	granulated sugar	25 mL
2 tbsp	fruit brandy (any type) or dark rum	25 mL

In a large skillet, melt butter over medium heat. Cook berries and sugar until fruit is plump and glossy. Remove from heat and stir in brandy. **Makes about 3 cups (750 mL).** *Serve warm over plain cake, pancakes or ice cream.*

Strawberry Lime Preserves

4 cups	strawberries, hulled and halved	1 L
1½ cups	granulated sugar	375 mL
	Finely grated zest and juice of 2 limes	

In a large, heavy saucepan, combine strawberries, sugar and lime zest; let stand for 10 minutes. Cook over medium heat, stirring often, until slightly thickened, about 15 minutes. Stir in lime juice. Ladle into jars and seal airtight. **Makes about 2 cups (500 mL).** *Store in the refrigerator for up to 1 month.*

Summer Bounty Vinegar

2 cups	summer fruit (blueberries, raspberries, blackberries, chopped cherries, peaches or plums)	500 mL
2 cups	red wine vinegar	500 mL

In a large saucepan, bring fruit and vinegar to a boil. Remove from heat and let steep for 1 hour. Strain, pour into jars and seal airtight. **Makes about 2 cups (500 mL).** *Store in the refrigerator for up to 6 months.*

Chapter 38

Breakfast
For Any Time of Day (or Night)

Muesli Cereal 425

Five-Grain Cereal 425

Real Oatmeal 426

Sweet-and-Spicy Cornmeal Mush 426

Scrambled Eggs with Cheese 426

Stir-Fried Eggs with Shrimp 426

Stir-Fried Eggs and Ham 426

Poached Salmon and Eggs
with Lemon Butter Sauce 426

Poached Egg Tostadas 427

Eggs Steamed in Tomato Sauce 427

Potato Leek Frittata 427

Bacon Hash Browns 427

Onion and Garlic Hash Browns 427

Bourbon-Glazed Ham Steak
with Spiced Poached Pears 428

Grilled Chutney-Glazed Ham Steak 428

British Bacon 428

Homemade Breakfast Sausage 428

Grilled Tomatoes 428

Mushrooms Braised in Steak Sauce 428

Melon with Lime 428

Basic Buttermilk Pancakes 429

Yeasted Maple Walnut Pancakes 429

Buckwheat Pancakes
with Sour Cream and Caviar 429

Ricotta Cheese Pancakes 429

Sour Cream Walnut Waffles 430

Apple, Bacon and Cornmeal Waffles . . . 430

Real Good French Toast 430

Whole Wheat Buttermilk French Toast . 430

Honey-Dipped Corn Toast 430

Souffléd Cottage Cheese Sandwiches . . 431

Buttermilk Biscuits 431

Herb Biscuits 431

Whole Wheat Sour Cream Biscuits 431

Cheese-Filled Biscuits 431

Maple Sugar Biscuits 431

Bacon Biscuits 431

Poppy Seed Buttermilk Scones 432

Irish Soda Bread 432

Basic Popovers 432

Three-Cheese Popovers 432

Pecan Popovers 432

Maple Popovers 433

Corn Popovers 433

Easy Sour Cream Coffee Cake 433

Buttermilk Coffee Cake 433

Date Nut Coffee Cake 433

Sweet Almond Coffee Cake 434

Fruit and Honey Topping 434

Orange Butter 434

Pear Honey 434

Remember breakfast? No, not some skimpy continental affair, and not those instant meals where all you do is add water. Real breakfast. Sausages, hash browns and eggs; muffins, biscuits, popovers and cornbread; grilled ham, bacon and steak — all served up diner-style, with a bottle of ketchup, or down-home style, with plenty of gravy.

Breakfasts like these have fueled North Americans for generations. For most modern working people, such hearty country cooking is too time-consuming to prepare and too filling to eat regularly, but it's just the thing to warm body and soul on a frigid winter morning.

Country breakfasts are nostalgic. They connect us to the roots of North American food, to a time when "the good life" consisted of little more than working hard and eating well. Ham steaks an inch thick, crosshatched with scars from a hot coal fire, would be served with potatoes or grits, or maybe a pile of apple fritters and a cruet of maple syrup to help the ham along. There were overblown popovers rising halfway out of their tins, trout fried in bacon fat, mush with warm cream, farm cheese, buckwheat cakes and any style of egg you wanted, provided it was fried.

Preparing such robust fare is more complex than slipping an English muffin in the toaster oven, but it doesn't take nearly as much time as you might expect. Breakfast breads such as muffins, biscuits and popovers can be mixed up in minutes, especially if you sift the dry ingredients the night before. You can make a hearty breakfast by using leftover meat from the previous night's dinner; ham is a natural, but so is chicken meat mixed with gravy and served over biscuits. Or slice last night's steak, sauté it quickly in bacon fat and serve it with eggs for a quick and economical steak-and-eggs breakfast.

A sure way to countrify breakfast is to serve more than one course. Have a hot cereal before eggs, or serve hash brown potatoes as a side dish. Finish with a simple dessert such as baked apples or a fruit compote.

About these recipes . . .

Most people don't like cooking first thing in the morning, so a good many of these 50 recipes can be partially prepared the night before and finished quickly in the morning. Sift dry ingredients for baked goods and portion out cold cereals.

Chop vegetables and place them in an airtight container in the refrigerator. Bread for French toast is better if sliced the night before and left out to dry.

Muesli Cereal

2 cups	quick-cooking or old-fashioned rolled oats	500 mL
1 cup	slivered almonds	250 mL
½ cup	sesame seeds	125 mL
½ cup	flaked sweetened coconut	125 mL
½ cup	wheat germ	125 mL
1 cup	raisins	250 mL
Pinch	salt	Pinch

In a large, deep, cast-iron skillet, over medium-high heat, toast oatmeal, almonds, sesame seeds, coconut and wheat germ, stirring constantly, until small pieces begin to color lightly. Remove from heat and stir until cereal is uniformly lightly toasted. Stir in raisins and salt; let cool completely. **Makes 5½ cups (1.375 L), or about 8 servings.** *Store in an airtight container. Eat as is, or in a bowl with milk.*

Five-Grain Cereal

1 cup	quick-cooking or old-fashioned rolled oats	250 mL
1 cup	corn flakes cereal	250 mL
½ cup	rye flakes	125 mL
½ cup	wheat bran	125 mL
½ cup	rice bran	125 mL
½ cup	slivered almonds	125 mL
¼ cup	sesame seeds	50 mL
¼ cup	sunflower seeds	50 mL
2 cups	raisins	500 mL
2 tbsp	packed light brown sugar	25 mL
Pinch	salt	Pinch

In a large, deep, cast-iron skillet, over medium-high heat, toast oatmeal, corn flakes, rye flakes, wheat bran, rice bran, almonds, sesame seeds and sunflower seeds, stirring constantly, until small pieces begin to color lightly. Remove from heat and stir until cereal is uniformly lightly toasted. Stir in raisins, brown sugar and salt; let cool completely. **Makes 6½ cups (1.625 mL), or about 6 servings.** *Store in an airtight container. Eat as is, or in a bowl with milk.*

Real Oatmeal

4 cups	water	1 L
½ tsp	salt	2 mL
1 cup	Irish steel-cut oats	250 mL
2 tbsp	packed brown sugar	25 mL
2 tbsp	butter (optional)	25 mL
	Milk, cream or buttermilk	

In a heavy saucepan, bring water and salt to a boil over medium-high heat. Slowly add oats, stirring constantly; do not let water stop boiling. Cook briskly until water starts to cloud. Reduce heat to a bare simmer, partially cover pan, and simmer for 30 minutes, stirring briefly every 10 minutes. Stir in brown sugar and butter (if using). Serve with milk, cream or buttermilk. **Serves 4.**

Sweet-and-Spicy Cornmeal Mush

2 tbsp	butter	25 mL
¼ cup	diced onion	50 mL
¼ cup	diced red bell pepper	50 mL
1	apple, diced	1
4 cups	water	1 L
1 cup	yellow cornmeal	250 mL
½ cup	cold water	125 mL
1 tsp	salt	5 mL
1 to 2 tsp	hot pepper sauce (such as Tabasco)	5 to 10 mL
	Chilled cream and maple syrup	

In a heavy saucepan, melt butter over medium heat. Sauté onion, red pepper and apple until vegetables are tender. Add water and bring to a boil. Meanwhile, mix cornmeal, cold water and salt into a smooth paste; whisk into saucepan until completely distributed. Reduce heat and simmer, covered, stirring frequently, until thick, about 15 minutes. Stir in hot pepper sauce to taste. Serve with chilled cream and maple syrup. **Serves 4.**

Scrambled Eggs with Cheese

8	eggs	8
2 tbsp	milk	25 mL
½ tsp	hot pepper sauce (such as Tabasco)	2 mL
	Salt and freshly ground black pepper to taste	
2 tbsp	butter	25 mL
1 cup	shredded Cheddar cheese	250 mL

Beat eggs, milk, hot pepper sauce, salt and black pepper. In a large nonstick skillet, melt butter over medium-high heat until foamy. Pour in egg mixture and scrape with a spatula until mostly set but still quite wet, about 2 minutes. Remove from heat, sprinkle cheese over eggs and continue folding egg over itself until cheese melts, about 30 seconds. **Serves 4.**

Stir-Fried Eggs with Shrimp

6	large or extra-large eggs	6
1 tsp	hot pepper sauce (such as Tabasco)	5 mL
	Salt and freshly ground black pepper to taste	
2 tbsp	canola oil	25 mL
8 oz	baby shrimp, peeled and deveined	250 g
1	clove garlic, minced	1
3	green onions, sliced	3

Beat eggs, hot pepper sauce, salt and black pepper; set aside. In a wok or large skillet, heat oil over medium-high heat. Stir-fry shrimp and garlic until shrimp are pink and opaque, about 30 seconds. Add egg mixture and green onions; scrape eggs with a spatula until completely set. Serve immediately. **Serves 4.**

Stir-Fried Eggs and Ham

Follow preceding recipe, but replace the shrimp with diced smoked ham. **Serves 4.**

Poached Salmon and Eggs with Lemon Butter Sauce

2 cups	dry white wine	500 mL
2 cups	water	500 mL
¼ cup	white wine vinegar	50 mL
	Salt and freshly ground black pepper to taste	
4	pieces skinless salmon fillet (each about 4 oz/125 g)	4
2 tbsp	freshly squeezed lemon juice	25 mL
1 tbsp	minced shallot	15 mL
½ cup	softened butter, cut into small pieces	125 mL
8	eggs	8

In a large skillet, bring wine, water, vinegar, salt and pepper to a boil; boil for 5 minutes. Reduce heat to a simmer and poach salmon (see page 11) for 3 minutes. Remove salmon with a slotted spoon to a platter and keep warm. In a small skillet, boil 1 cup (250 mL) of the poaching liquid, lemon juice and shallot until reduced by about three-quarters. Whisk in butter, one piece at a time, until a creamy sauce forms; keep warm. Meanwhile, add eggs to remaining poaching liquid, heat to a mere simmer and poach until whites are set, about 4 minutes. Remove eggs with a slotted spoon and place 2 on each salmon fillet. Spoon sauce over eggs. **Serves 4.**

Poached Egg Tostadas

1	large avocado, peeled and pitted	1
1 tbsp	freshly squeezed lemon juice	15 mL
	Salt and hot pepper sauce (such as Tabasco) to taste	
4 cups	water	1 L
¼ cup	white wine vinegar	50 mL
8	eggs	8
8	corn tortillas, warmed	8
1	recipe Refried Black Beans (page 20), warm	1
1 cup	shredded romaine lettuce	250 mL
1 cup	chopped tomato	250 mL

Mash avocado, lemon juice, salt and hot pepper sauce; set aside. In a large skillet, bring water and vinegar to a simmer. Poach eggs (see page 11) until whites are set, about 4 minutes. Top each tortilla with a layer of refried beans, a handful of shredded romaine, 1 poached egg, a spoonful of avocado mixture and a spoonful of chopped tomato. Serves 4.

Eggs Steamed in Tomato Sauce

4 cups	canned crushed tomatoes	1 L
2 tbsp	extra-virgin olive oil	25 mL
1 tbsp	red wine vinegar	15 mL
	Salt and freshly ground black pepper to taste	
8	eggs	8

In a large skillet, over medium heat, cook tomatoes for 5 minutes. Add oil, vinegar, salt and pepper. Crack eggs into tomato mixture and season with additional salt and pepper; reduce heat, cover and simmer gently until whites are set, about 4 minutes. Serve eggs with sauce. Serves 4.

Potato Leek Frittata

1 tbsp	butter	15 mL
2 tbsp	olive oil, divided	25 mL
1	russet potato, peeled and thinly sliced	1
1	leek, white part only, thinly sliced	1
2	cloves garlic, minced	2
½ tsp	dried rosemary, crumbled	2 mL
	Salt and freshly ground black pepper to taste	
6	extra-large eggs	6
2 tbsp	water	25 mL

Preheat broiler. In a large ovenproof skillet, heat butter and half the oil over medium-high heat. Sauté potato until browned on both sides. Add leek and sauté until tender. Add garlic, rosemary, salt and pepper; sauté until aromatic. Reduce heat to medium and add the remaining oil, stirring so that it coats the bottom of the pan. Beat eggs, water and additional salt and pepper; pour into pan, lifting vegetables so that egg distributes evenly, and cook for 3 minutes. Broil for 2 to 3 minutes, or until browned and puffed. Cut into wedges. Serves 4.

Bacon Hash Browns

3	large russet potatoes	3
4	slices bacon	4
	Salt, freshly ground black pepper and cayenne pepper to taste	

Coarsely shred potatoes directly into a large bowl of ice water; let stand for 1 minute. Drain and wring dry in a clean towel. In a large, heavy skillet, over medium-high heat, cook bacon until crisp; remove to a plate, blot off fat and crumble. Pack potatoes into the fat remaining in the pan, and cook, undisturbed, until bottom is brown and crisp, about 4 minutes. Sprinkle with bacon, salt, black pepper and cayenne; using the edge of a spatula, chop into sections and flip. Cook, chopping and flipping, until potatoes are well browned and tender, about 10 minutes. Serves 4.

Onion and Garlic Hash Browns

Follow preceding recipe, but omit the bacon and cook potatoes in 3 tbsp (45 mL) olive oil instead of bacon fat. Add 1 large onion, finely sliced, with the potatoes, and add 2 cloves garlic, minced, for the last minute of cooking. Serves 4.

Bourbon-Glazed Ham Steak with Spiced Poached Pears

2 tbsp	butter	25 mL
1	slice (1 inch/2.5 cm thick) smoked ham (about 1½ lbs/750 g)	1
¼ cup	bourbon	50 mL
¼ cup	unsweetened apple cider	50 mL
Pinch	dried rosemary, crumbled	Pinch
	Freshly ground black pepper to taste	
	Spiced Poached Pears (see recipe, page 409)	
2 tbsp	packed light brown sugar	25 mL
¼ tsp	ground cinnamon	1 mL

In a large skillet, heat butter over medium heat. Cook ham, turning once, until lightly browned on both sides. Add bourbon, apple cider, rosemary and pepper; reduce heat, cover and simmer for 20 minutes, turning ham halfway through. Uncover, increase heat and boil any remaining liquid, turning ham frequently to coat evenly with glaze. Serve with Spiced Poached Pears dusted with a mixture of brown sugar and cinnamon. **Serves 4.**

Grilled Chutney-Glazed Ham Steak

2	slices (¼ inch/0.5 cm thick) smoked ham (each about 12 oz/375 g)	2
2 tbsp	mango chutney, puréed or finely chopped	25 mL
½ tsp	spicy brown mustard	2 mL

Preheat broiler or barbecue grill to high. Broil or grill ham, turning once, until seared on both sides. Combine chutney and mustard; brush over ham. **Serves 4.**

British Bacon

4	thick slices bacon	4
4	slices back bacon (Canadian bacon)	4

In a skillet, over medium-high heat, cook thick bacon until crisp; remove to a plate and blot off fat. Add back bacon to the fat remaining in the pan; cook until lightly browned on both sides. Serve both types of bacon together. **Serves 4.**

Homemade Breakfast Sausage

1 lb	ground pork	500 g
4 oz	pork fatback, finely chopped	125 g
¼ cup	minced onion	50 mL
1 tsp	dried sage	5 mL
1 tsp	salt	5 mL
½ tsp	freshly ground black pepper	2 mL
½ tsp	dried thyme	2 mL
Pinch	ground cloves	Pinch

Combine all ingredients, cover and refrigerate until flavors blend, about 6 hours. Form into 12 patties. In a large skillet, over medium heat, cook patties, turning once, until firm and browned on both sides and no longer pink inside. **Serves 4.**

Grilled Tomatoes

2	large tomatoes, cut into ⅜-inch (0.75 cm) thick slices	2
¼ cup	melted butter	50 mL
	Salt and freshly ground black pepper to taste	

Preheat broiler or barbecue grill to high. Brush tomatoes with melted butter and season with salt and pepper. Broil or grill for 2 minutes per side. **Serves 4.** *Serve with eggs or grilled breakfast meats.*

Mushrooms Braised in Steak Sauce

2 tbsp	butter	25 mL
12	large mushrooms, thickly sliced	12
2 tbsp	steak sauce	25 mL
1 tbsp	minced fresh Italian (flat-leaf) parsley	15 mL

In a large skillet, melt butter over medium-high heat. Sauté mushrooms until lightly browned. Add steak sauce, reduce heat and simmer for 1 minute. Stir in parsley. **Serves 4.** *Serve with eggs or grilled breakfast meats.*

Melon with Lime

1	honeydew melon, seeded and thinly sliced	1
1	lime, thinly sliced	1

Arrange honeydew slices in a spoke pattern on a large circular platter. Place 1 lime slice across each melon slice. **Serves 4.**

Basic Buttermilk Pancakes

2 cups	sifted all-purpose flour	500 mL
2 tbsp	granulated sugar	25 mL
2 tsp	baking powder	10 mL
1 tsp	baking soda	5 mL
½ tsp	salt	2 mL
2	large or extra-large eggs, beaten	2
2 cups	buttermilk	500 mL
2 tbsp	melted butter	25 mL
	Additional butter	
	Fruit and Honey Topping or Orange Butter (see recipes, page 434), or maple syrup	

In a large bowl, combine flour, sugar, baking powder, baking soda and salt. Stir in eggs and buttermilk until batter is smooth. Stir in melted butter. In a large skillet or on a griddle, melt a thin film of butter over medium heat until foamy. For each pancake, pour in ¼ cup (50 mL) batter and cook until covered with bubbles. Flip and cook for 1 to 2 minutes, or until pancakes feel springy. Transfer to a plate and keep warm. Repeat with the remaining batter, greasing pan with more butter for every batch. Serve with the topping of your choice. **Makes about 18 pancakes.**

Yeasted Maple Walnut Pancakes

1 tbsp	active dry yeast (1 envelope)	15 mL
1 cup	warm water	250 mL
3 cups	all-purpose flour	750 mL
1 cup	warm milk	250 mL
½ tsp	salt	2 mL
½ tsp	baking soda	2 mL
¼ cup	hot water	50 mL
¼ cup	pure maple syrup	50 mL
2 tbsp	melted butter	25 mL
1¼ cups	finely chopped walnuts	300 mL
	Additional butter	
	Fruit and Honey Topping or Orange Butter (see recipes, page 434), or maple syrup	

Dissolve yeast in warm water. Add flour, warm milk and salt; stir into a smooth batter. Cover loosely with plastic wrap and let stand at room temperature overnight. Dissolve baking soda in hot water. Stir in maple syrup and melted butter; add to batter. Stir in walnuts. Make pancakes as described in preceding recipe. Serve with the topping of your choice. **Makes about 12 pancakes.**

Buckwheat Pancakes with Sour Cream and Caviar

1 cup	unbleached all-purpose flour	250 mL
½ cup	buckwheat flour	125 mL
½ cup	whole wheat flour	125 mL
1 tbsp	granulated sugar	15 mL
2 tsp	baking powder	10 mL
1 tsp	baking soda	5 mL
½ tsp	salt	2 mL
2	extra-large eggs, separated	2
2 cups	buttermilk	500 mL
¼ cup	melted butter	50 mL
	Additional butter	
1 cup	sour cream	250 mL
6 tbsp	caviar	90 mL

In a large bowl, combine all-purpose flour, buckwheat flour, whole wheat flour, sugar, baking powder, baking soda and salt. In a separate bowl, beat egg yolks, buttermilk and melted butter; stir into flour mixture until batter is smooth. In a clean bowl, beat egg whites until soft peaks form; fold into batter. Make pancakes as described in Basic Buttermilk Pancakes (left). Serve topped with sour cream and caviar. **Makes about 18 pancakes.**

Ricotta Cheese Pancakes

6	eggs, separated	6
2 cups	ricotta cheese, drained	500 mL
6 tbsp	all-purpose flour	90 mL
¼ cup	granulated sugar	50 mL
½ tsp	vanilla	2 mL
Pinch	salt	Pinch
	Butter	
	Fruit	

In a large bowl, combine egg yolks, ricotta, flour, sugar and vanilla. In a separate bowl, beat egg whites and salt until soft peaks form; fold into batter. In a large skillet or on a griddle, melt a thin film of butter over medium-high heat until foamy. Spoon in batter to make pancakes 2 to 3 inches (5 to 7.5 cm) in diameter; cook for 2 to 3 minutes, or until browned. Flip and cook until browned on the other side. Transfer to a plate and keep warm. Repeat with the remaining batter, greasing pan with more butter for every batch. Serve immediately with fruit. **Makes about 12 pancakes.**

Sour Cream Walnut Waffles

1 cup	sifted cake flour	250 mL
2 tbsp	granulated sugar	25 mL
1¼ tsp	baking powder	6 mL
1 tsp	baking soda	5 mL
½ cup	finely ground walnuts	125 mL
3	extra-large eggs, separated	3
2 cups	sour cream (not fat-free)	500 mL
2 tbsp	walnut oil	25 mL
¼ tsp	salt	1 mL
	Butter	
	Sour cream and fruit, or maple syrup	

Preheat waffle iron. In a large bowl, sift together flour, sugar, baking powder and baking soda. Stir in walnuts. In a separate bowl, beat egg yolks, sour cream and oil; stir into flour mixture just until blended. In a clean bowl, beat egg whites and salt until soft peaks form; fold into batter. Grease waffle iron with butter and ladle on enough batter to fill three-quarters of the surface. Close iron and cook until waffle is brown and crisp on both sides. Transfer to a plate and keep warm. Repeat with the remaining batter, greasing iron with butter as necessary between batches. Serve with sour cream and fruit, or maple syrup. **Serves 4.**

Apple, Bacon and Cornmeal Waffles

4	slices bacon	4
1 cup	sifted cake flour	250 mL
1 tbsp	granulated sugar	15 mL
2 tsp	baking powder	10 mL
½ tsp	baking soda	2 mL
1 cup	yellow cornmeal	250 mL
2	eggs, separated	2
1 cup	milk	250 mL
1	large apple, coarsely shredded	1
¼ tsp	salt	1 mL
	Butter	
	Maple syrup	

In a large skillet, over medium heat, cook bacon until crisp; remove to a plate, blot off fat and crumble. Reserve ¼ cup (50 mL) of the fat. In a large bowl, sift together flour, sugar, baking powder and baking soda. Stir in cornmeal, then stir in reserved bacon fat until mixture is crumbly. In a separate bowl, beat egg yolks and milk; stir into flour mixture until batter is smooth. Stir in bacon and apple. In a clean bowl, beat egg whites and salt until soft peaks form; fold into batter. Make waffles as described in preceding recipe. Serve with maple syrup. **Serves 4.**

Real Good French Toast

4	large or extra-large eggs	4
1 cup	milk	250 mL
¼ cup	pure maple syrup	50 mL
1 tsp	vanilla	5 mL
Pinch	ground nutmeg	Pinch
Pinch	salt	Pinch
8	thick slices bakery-quality white bread	8
¼ cup	butter, divided	50 mL
	Warm Pear Purée (see recipe, page 449), Pear Honey (see recipe, page 434), Sautéed Fruit Salad (page 449) or maple syrup	

In a wide, shallow bowl, beat eggs, milk, maple syrup, vanilla, nutmeg and salt. Soak bread in this mixture, in batches if necessary, until all liquid is absorbed. In a large skillet, melt half the butter over medium heat. Add soaked bread, in batches, and cook, turning once, until browned on both sides. Transfer to a plate and keep warm. Repeat with the remaining soaked bread, melting the remaining butter between batches. Serve with the topping of your choice. **Serves 4.**

Whole Wheat Buttermilk French Toast

4	large or extra-large eggs	4
1 cup	buttermilk	250 mL
2 tbsp	granulated sugar	25 mL
1 tsp	vanilla	5 mL
Pinch	salt	Pinch
8	thick slices slightly stale whole wheat bread	8
¼ cup	butter, divided	50 mL
2 cups	fruit-flavored yogurt	500 mL

In a wide, shallow bowl, beat eggs, buttermilk, sugar, vanilla and salt. Soak bread in this mixture, in batches if necessary, until all liquid is absorbed. Cook soaked bread as described in preceding recipe. Serve with yogurt. **Serves 4.**

Honey-Dipped Corn Toast

2	large or extra-large eggs	2
1 cup	milk (not fat-free)	250 mL
3 tbsp	honey	45 mL
¼ tsp	salt	1 mL
6	drops hot pepper sauce (such as Tabasco)	6
6	corn cakes for the toaster	6

| 3 tbsp | butter | 45 mL |
| | Additional butter and honey | |

In a wide, shallow bowl, beat eggs, milk, honey, salt and hot pepper sauce. Soak corn cakes in this mixture, in batches if necessary, until all liquid is absorbed. In a large skillet, melt butter over medium-high heat. Using a spatula, transfer soaked corn cakes to the pan and cook, turning once, for 3 to 4 minutes per side, or until browned on both sides. Serve with butter and honey. **Serves 4.**

Souffléd Cottage Cheese Sandwiches

24	thin slices French bread	24
1 cup	cottage cheese, drained	250 mL
4	eggs, separated	4
3 tbsp	granulated sugar	45 mL
²⁄₃ cup	milk	150 mL
1 tsp	vanilla	5 mL
Pinch	ground nutmeg	Pinch
¼ tsp	salt	1 mL
4 to 6 tbsp	butter, divided	50 to 90 mL

Use bread and cottage cheese to make 12 mini sandwiches. In a large bowl, beat egg yolks and sugar until thick. Stir in milk, vanilla and nutmeg. In a separate bowl, beat egg whites and salt until soft peaks form; fold into yolk mixture. In a large skillet, melt 2 tbsp (25 mL) of the butter over medium heat. Dip half the sandwiches in batter, add to the pan and cook, turning once, until browned on both sides. Transfer to a plate and keep warm. Repeat with the remaining sandwiches, melting the remaining butter as needed between batches. **Serves 4.**

Buttermilk Biscuits

3 cups	all-purpose flour	750 mL
1 tbsp	granulated sugar	15 mL
4 tsp	baking powder	20 mL
1 tsp	salt	5 mL
1 tsp	baking soda	5 mL
¼ cup	cold butter	50 mL
¼ cup	cold vegetable shortening	50 mL
2	eggs	2
1½ cups	buttermilk	375 mL

Preheat oven to 400°F (200°C). In a large bowl, combine flour, sugar, baking powder, salt and baking soda. Cut in butter and shortening until mixture resembles coarse meal. In a separate bowl, beat eggs and buttermilk; stir all but ¼ cup (50 mL) into flour mixture, stirring just enough to moisten. On a floured board, with floured hands, pat dough to ½-inch (1 cm) thickness. Using a biscuit cutter, cut out 18 biscuits. Place close together on a baking sheet and brush tops with remaining egg mixture. Bake for 15 minutes, until puffed and brown. **Makes 18 biscuits.**

Herb Biscuits

Follow preceding recipe, but add 2 tbsp (25 mL) chopped fresh herbs with the flour. **Makes 18 biscuits.**

Whole Wheat Sour Cream Biscuits

Follow recipe for Buttermilk Biscuits (left), but replace half the all-purpose flour with whole wheat flour, add ½ cup (125 mL) raisins with the flour, and replace the buttermilk with 1 cup (250 mL) sour cream (not fat-free) and ½ cup (125 mL) milk. **Makes 18 biscuits.**

Cheese-Filled Biscuits

Prepare any of the previous biscuit doughs, but mix 1½ cups (375 mL) shredded Cheddar cheese into the dough. **Makes 18 biscuits.**

Maple Sugar Biscuits

Follow recipe for Buttermilk Biscuits (left), but replace ¼ cup (50 mL) of the buttermilk with pure maple syrup. **Makes 18 biscuits.**

Bacon Biscuits

6	slices bacon	6
3 cups	all-purpose flour	750 mL
2 tbsp	granulated sugar	25 mL
1½ tbsp	baking powder	22 mL
1 tsp	salt	5 mL
1 tsp	baking soda	5 mL
2 tbsp	chopped fresh chives	25 mL
¼ cup	cold vegetable shortening	50 mL
2	eggs	2
1 cup + 1 tbsp buttermilk		265 mL

Preheat oven to 400°F (200°C). In a large skillet, over medium heat, cook bacon until crisp; remove to a plate, blot off fat and crumble. Reserve ¼ cup (50 mL) of the fat. In a large bowl, sift together flour, sugar, baking powder, salt and baking soda. Stir in crumbled bacon and chives. Cut in shortening and reserved bacon fat with a fork until mixture resembles coarse meal. In a separate bowl, beat eggs and buttermilk; stir all but ¼ cup (50 mL) into flour mixture, stirring just until moistened. Prepare biscuits and bake as described in Buttermilk Biscuits (above). **Makes 18 biscuits.**

Poppy Seed Buttermilk Scones

1¾ cups	all-purpose flour	425 mL
1 tbsp	granulated sugar	15 mL
2 tsp	baking powder	10 mL
½ tsp	baking soda	2 mL
¼ tsp	salt	1 mL
⅓ cup	cold butter	75 mL
2	eggs	2
⅓ cup	buttermilk	75 mL
⅓ cup	poppy seed paste	75 mL

Preheat oven to 450°F (230°C). In a large bowl, combine flour, sugar, baking powder, baking soda and salt. Cut in butter until mixture resembles coarse meal. In a separate bowl, beat eggs and buttermilk; stir into flour mixture just until moistened. On a floured board, with floured hands, pat dough into a 6- by 8-inch (15 by 20 cm) rectangle. Cut in half across the long side. Spread poppy seed paste over one half, top with the other half and press together lightly. Cut into three 1-inch (2.5 cm) strips, and cut each strip into 8 triangles. Place on an ungreased baking sheet and bake for 15 minutes, until puffed and brown. Let cool in pan on a rack for 5 minutes. **Makes 24 scones.**

Irish Soda Bread

4 cups	all-purpose flour	1 L
1 tbsp	granulated sugar	15 mL
1 tsp	baking soda	5 mL
½ tsp	salt	2 mL
1½ to 2 cups	buttermilk	375 to 500 mL

Preheat oven to 425°F (220°C) and grease a baking sheet. In a large bowl, sift together flour, sugar, baking soda and salt. Stir in buttermilk, using just enough liquid to make a dough that can be gathered into a soft ball. On a floured board, with floured hands, pat dough into an 8-inch (20 cm) round loaf. Place on prepared baking sheet and cut a deep X in the center of the loaf. Brush with some of the remaining buttermilk. Bake until puffed and brown, about 30 minutes. Let cool in pan on a rack for 5 to 10 minutes. **Serves 8 to 10.**

Basic Popovers

1 cup	all-purpose flour	250 mL
Pinch	salt	Pinch
1 cup	milk (not non-fat)	250 mL
2 to 3 tbsp	melted butter, divided	25 to 45 mL
2	large or extra-large eggs	2
	Additional all-purpose flour	

Preheat oven to 450°F (230°C) and place a 12-cup nonstick muffin tin or a 6-cup deep popover pan in the oven. In a bowl, sift together flour and salt. In a separate bowl, combine milk and 1 tbsp (15 mL) of the butter; stir into flour mixture just until blended. Beat in eggs, one at a time. Grease hot tin with the remaining butter, sprinkle cups with additional flour and divide batter evenly among the cups. Bake for 15 minutes. Reduce heat to 375°F (190°C) and bake for 10 to 12 minutes, or until fully puffed, brown and crisp all over the surface. **Makes 6 or 12 popovers.**

Three-Cheese Popovers

Follow preceding recipe, but add a pinch each of cayenne pepper and garlic powder to the flour. When filling tin, pour a bit of batter in the bottom of each cup, distribute 3 tbsp (45 mL) freshly grated Parmesan cheese, 3 tbsp (45 mL) finely shredded sharp Cheddar cheese and 2 tbsp (25 mL) grated Romano cheese among the cups and divide the remaining batter among the cups. **Makes 6 or 12 popovers.**

Pecan Popovers

Follow recipe for Basic Popovers (above), but add ⅔ cup (150 mL) finely chopped pecans and 2 tbsp (25 mL) granulated sugar to the flour, and dust greased pan with additional sugar rather than with flour. **Makes 6 or 12 popovers.**

Maple Popovers

Follow recipe for Basic Popovers (page 432), but add 1 tbsp (15 mL) granulated sugar with the flour, add 3 tbsp (45 mL) maple syrup with the milk, and dust greased pan with additional sugar rather than with flour. Serve with additional syrup and unsalted butter. **Makes 6 or 12 popovers.**

Corn Popovers

¾ cup	all-purpose flour	175 mL
6 tbsp	yellow cornmeal	90 mL
¼ tsp	salt	1 mL
3	large or extra-large eggs, beaten	3
1¼ cups	milk (not non-fat)	300 mL
2 to 3 tbsp	melted butter, divided	25 to 45 mL
1 tbsp	honey	15 mL
	Additional cornmeal	
	Additional honey and butter	

Preheat oven to 450°F (230°C) and place a 12-cup nonstick muffin tin or a 6-cup deep popover pan in the oven. In a small bowl, combine flour, cornmeal and salt. In a large bowl, beat eggs, milk, 1 tbsp (15 mL) of the butter and honey. Whisk in flour mixture. Grease hot tin with the remaining butter, sprinkle cups with additional cornmeal and divide batter evenly among the cups. Bake as directed in Basic Popovers (page 432). Serve with honey and butter. **Makes 6 or 12 popovers.**

Easy Sour Cream Coffee Cake

2 cups	all-purpose flour	500 mL
1 tsp	baking powder	5 mL
1 cup	sour cream (not fat-free)	250 mL
1½ tsp	baking soda	7 mL
1 cup	granulated sugar	250 mL
½ cup	butter	125 mL
2	extra-large eggs	2
1 cup	raisins	250 mL
1 tsp	vanilla	5 mL
¼ cup	packed light brown sugar	50 mL
¼ cup	finely chopped walnuts	50 mL
½ tsp	ground cinnamon	2 mL

Preheat oven to 375°F (190°C) and grease and flour a 9-inch (23 cm) round cake pan. Sift together flour and baking powder; set aside. In a small bowl, combine sour cream and baking soda; set aside. In a large bowl, cream granulated sugar and butter until light and fluffy. Beat in eggs, one at a time. Stir in raisins and vanilla. Stir in flour mixture alternately with sour cream mixture, making 3 additions of flour and 2 of sour cream. Pour into prepared pan.

Combine brown sugar, walnuts and cinnamon; sprinkle over top. Bake for 45 minutes, until a tester inserted in the center comes out with just a crumb clinging to it. Let cool in pan on a rack for 10 to 20 minutes. **Serves 10.**

Buttermilk Coffee Cake

	Nonstick cooking spray	
2 cups	sifted all-purpose flour	500 mL
¾ cup	granulated sugar	175 mL
¼ cup	packed brown sugar	50 mL
2 tsp	baking powder	10 mL
1 tsp	baking soda	5 mL
1 tsp	ground cinnamon	5 mL
¼ tsp	ground nutmeg	1 mL
⅔ cup	butter, cut into small pieces	150 mL
1 cup	chopped pecans or walnuts, divided	250 mL
1	extra-large egg	1
⅔ cup	buttermilk	150 mL
1 tsp	vanilla	5 mL
½ cup	chopped raisins	125 mL

Preheat oven to 375°F (190°C) and spray a 9-inch (23 cm) baking pan with cooking spray. In a large bowl, combine flour, granulated sugar, brown sugar, baking powder, baking soda, cinnamon and nutmeg. Cut in butter until mixture resembles coarse meal. Make a crumb topping by combining ½ cup (125 mL) of the mixture with ¼ cup (50 mL) of the nuts; set aside. In a separate bowl, beat egg, buttermilk and vanilla; stir into the large bowl of dry ingredients. Stir in the remaining nuts and raisins. Pour into prepared pan and top with crumb topping. Bake for 40 to 45 minutes, or until a tester inserted in the center comes out with just a crumb clinging to it. Let cool in pan on a rack for 10 minutes. **Serves 8.**

Date Nut Coffee Cake

Follow preceding recipe, but add ¼ cup (50 mL) chopped dates to the crumb topping with the nuts, and replace the raisins with another ½ cup (125 mL) chopped dates. **Serves 8.**

Sweet Almond Coffee Cake

Follow recipe for Buttermilk Coffee Cake (page 433), but replace the pecans with almonds, add ¼ tsp (1 mL) almond extract with the vanilla, and replace the raisins with 2 oz (60 g) marzipan, cut into small pieces. Serves 8.

Fruit and Honey Topping

1 tbsp	butter	15 mL
1 tbsp	honey	15 mL
1 cup	strawberries, hulled and sliced	250 mL
2	bananas, sliced	2
24	seedless grapes	24
½ tsp	vanilla	2 mL

In a skillet, melt butter and honey over medium heat. Sauté strawberries, bananas and grapes until heated through. Stir in vanilla. **Makes about 3 cups (750 mL).** *Serve with pancakes, French toast or waffles.*

Orange Butter

½ cup	butter, beaten until light and fluffy	125 mL
¼ cup	sweet orange marmalade	50 mL
2 tsp	frozen orange juice concentrate	10 mL
1 tsp	freshly squeezed lemon juice	5 mL

Beat together butter, marmalade, orange juice concentrate and lemon juice. **Makes about ½ cup (125 mL).** *Use as a spread or a topping for pancakes, French toast or waffles.*

Pear Honey

2½ cups	finely chopped peeled pears (about 3 large)	625 mL
¾ cup	granulated sugar	175 mL
Pinch	freshly grated nutmeg	Pinch
Pinch	salt	Pinch
	Finely grated zest and juice of 1 lemon	

In a large saucepan, bring pears, sugar, nutmeg, salt and lemon juice to a boil. Reduce heat and simmer for 30 minutes, until pears are very soft. Add lemon zest, stirring to break up any large pieces; let cool. **Makes about 1½ cups (375 mL).** *Use as a spread or a topping for French toast, waffles or pancakes.*

Chapter 39
Cookies
For Every Day, Every Way

Chewy Chocolate Chip Cookies 436
White Chocolate Chunk Cookies 437
Chocolate Chunk Cookies 437
Chocolate Chocolate Chip Cookies . . . 437
Espresso Oatmeal Chocolate
Chip Cookies 437
Chocolate Pistachio Drops 437
Peanut Butter Jumbles 437
Candy Store Jumbles 437
Walnut Butter Jumbles 437
Oatmeal Jumbles 437
Chocolate Peanut Jumbles 438
Almond Macaroons 438
Pine Nut Macaroons 438
Hazelnut Macaroons 438
Chocolate Macaroons 438
Coconut Macaroons 438
Butter Cookies 438
Sugar Cookies 439
Spiced Cookies 439
Cardamom Currant Cookies 439
Sables 439
Chocolate Butter Cookies 439
Pinwheels 439
Hazelnut Crescents 439
Anise Almond Drops 439

Coconut Snowballs 439
Spiced Gumdrop Drops 439
Walnut Brown-Edge Wafers 440
Walnut Oat Lace Cookies 440
Ginger Lace Cookies 440
Honey Almond Tuiles 440
Shortbread 440
Almond Shortbread 440
Ginger Currant Shortbread 441
Walnut Chocolate Chip Shortbread . . . 441
Sweet Cream Cheese Pastry 441
Apricot Marzipan Drops 441
Apricot Schnecken 441
Chocolate Crescents 441
Eccles Cakes 441
Grand Marnier Almond Bars 442
Pecan Pie Bars 442
Chewy Gooey Lemon Pecan Bars 442
Dried Cherry Bars 442
Date Nut Bars 442
Peanut Butter Sandwich Squares 442
Chocolate Peanut Butter Squares 443
Raisin Squares 443
Wheat Germ Squares 443
Oaties 443
Butterscotch Oaties 443

The allure of cookies never ends. Cookies may not be grand, but from our first bite of zwieback to our last midnight nosh, all but the most Spartan of snackers are hopelessly hooked. What else can mend hurt feelings with less fuss or nourish a sweet-starved appetite with more aplomb?

Much to their detriment, cookies have increasingly become a prepackaged commodity. While no food benefits from commercial processing, the charm of most cookies all but disappears as their natural shelf life is unnaturally extended from several days to several months. There's not a prepackaged chocolate chip cookie that can hope to compete with a real tollhouse warm from the oven, nor a commercial butter cookie that's more than a hard shard of sugar when compared with a lacy tuile just peeled from its baking sheet.

The quality of most cookies is fleeting. If we don't make them ourselves, we must learn to accept less than the best. But with a few well-tested recipes and a basic understanding of cookie types, anyone armed with a mixing bowl and a preheated oven can create batch after batch of homemade perfection with negligible effort.

The following 50 cookie recipes include basic formulas, each followed by several variations. We found this arrangement expedient as a means of giving you maximum cookie recipes in minimum space, but it's also a way to help you understand the structure of various cookie types. Once you understand what makes one cookie chewy and another crisp, you'll be better able to judge which recipe best fits your image of cookie perfection — and you'll be better able to adjust when problems arise.

Soft cookies are large, thick and cakey. Like cakes, they have a high proportion of liquid to dry ingredients, considerable leavener and a moderate amount of fat and sugar. Many molasses cookies, hermits and some oatmeal cookies are of this type.

Chewy cookies are achieved by lowering the proportion of liquid and raising the amounts of egg and sugar in the recipe. Most of the drop cookies in this chapter follow this ratio.

Crisp cookies come from a dough practically devoid of liquid and leaveners but high in flour, butter and sugar. These would include shortbreads and cookies with a pastry base.

Textural changes also occur by altering the size of the cookie and the oven temperature. Large mounds of dough and moderate baking temperatures yield softer or chewier cookies, while flattening the dough or raising the temperature of the oven makes the same dough come out crisper.

About these recipes . . .

The following cookies are baked on ungreased baking sheets, with cookies placed 2 inches (5 cm) from one another, unless otherwise noted. When rolling cookie doughs, do so on a lightly floured board with a floured rolling pin. When you transfer rolled dough, formed cookies or baked cookies, do so with a wide spatula.

Because of the high sugar content of most cookies, they burn easily. For this reason, an oven's normal hot spots can prove disastrous in cookie baking. To help minimize the potential damage, it is advisable to rotate baking sheets from front to back and from top shelf to bottom midway through the baking time.

Remember that it is important to use unsalted butter in any baked goods.

Chewy Chocolate Chip Cookies

1 tsp	baking soda	5 mL
1 tsp	hot water	5 mL
1 tsp	vanilla	5 mL
1 cup	unsalted butter, softened	250 mL
¾ cup	granulated sugar	175 mL
¾ cup	firmly packed light brown sugar	175 mL
Pinch	salt	Pinch
2	extra-large eggs	2
2¼ cups	all-purpose flour, divided	550 mL
2 cups	semisweet chocolate chips	500 mL
1 cup	walnut pieces	250 mL

Preheat oven to 375°F (190°C). Dissolve baking soda in hot water and vanilla; set aside. In a large bowl, cream butter, granulated sugar, brown sugar and salt. Beat in eggs. Stir in 1¼ cups (320 mL) of the flour, then the baking soda mixture. Stir in the remaining flour, chocolate chips and walnut pieces. Drop in 2-tbsp (25 mL) mounds onto baking sheets. Bake for 11 minutes, until browned at the edges. Let cool on pans for 1 minute, then transfer to racks and let cool completely. **Makes about 24 cookies.**

White Chocolate Chunk Cookies

Follow preceding recipe, but increase the granulated sugar to 1½ cups (375 mL), omit the brown sugar, replace the chocolate chips with 8 oz (250 g) white chocolate, cut into chunks, and replace the walnut pieces with slivered almonds. **Makes about 24 cookies.**

Chocolate Chunk Cookies

Follow recipe for Chewy Chocolate Chip Cookies (page 436), but replace the chocolate chips with 8 oz (250 g) semisweet chocolate, cut into chunks. **Makes about 24 cookies.**

Chocolate Chocolate Chip Cookies

Follow recipe for Chewy Chocolate Chip Cookies (page 436), but decrease the flour to 2 cups (500 mL), and add ⅓ cup (75 mL) unsweetened cocoa powder, sifted, with the flour. **Makes about 24 cookies.**

Espresso Oatmeal Chocolate Chip Cookies

Follow recipe for Chewy Chocolate Chip Cookies (page 436), but dissolve 1 tbsp (15 mL) instant espresso granules with the baking soda, and add ½ cup (125 mL) quick-cooking rolled oats with the walnuts. **Makes about 24 cookies.**

Chocolate Pistachio Drops

⅓ cup	all-purpose flour	75 mL
1 tsp	baking powder	5 mL
¼ tsp	salt	1 mL
6 tbsp	unsalted butter, cut into large pieces	90 mL
8 oz	semisweet chocolate, cut into small pieces	250 g
2	extra-large eggs	2
¾ cup	granulated sugar	175 mL
1 tbsp	instant coffee granules	15 mL
1 tbsp	unsweetened cocoa powder, sifted	15 mL
2 tsp	vanilla	10 mL
1 cup	finely chopped pistachios	250 mL

Preheat oven to 325°F (160°C) and grease baking sheets. Sift together flour, baking powder and salt; set aside. In a large saucepan, melt butter over medium heat. Remove from heat and stir in chocolate until melted; let cool. In a large bowl, beat eggs, sugar, coffee granules, cocoa and vanilla until thick and fluffy. Stir in melted chocolate. Stir in flour mixture just until blended. Stir in pistachios. Drop

in 1½-tbsp (22 mL) mounds onto prepared baking sheets. Bake for about 15 minutes, or until set. Let cool on pans for 1 minute, then transfer to racks and let cool completely. **Makes 16 to 18 cookies.**

Peanut Butter Jumbles

1 tbsp	baking soda	15 mL
2 tsp	vanilla	10 mL
1 cup	granulated sugar	250 mL
1 cup	packed dark brown sugar	250 mL
1½ cups	chunky peanut butter	375 mL
½ cup	unsalted butter, softened	125 mL
Pinch	salt	Pinch
3	large or extra-large eggs	3
4½ cups	quick-cooking rolled oats	1.125 L
1½ cups	raisins	375 mL
1 cup	unsalted dry-roasted peanuts	250 mL

Preheat oven to 350°F (180°C). Dissolve baking soda in vanilla; set aside. In a large bowl, cream granulated sugar, brown sugar, peanut butter, butter and salt. Beat in eggs. Stir in baking soda mixture. Stir in oats, raisins and peanuts. Drop in ¼-cup (50 mL) mounds, 2½ inches (6 cm) apart, onto baking sheets. Bake for 18 minutes, until browned at the edges. Let cool on pans for 2 minutes, then transfer to racks and let cool completely. **Makes about 24 cookies.**

Candy Store Jumbles

Follow preceding recipe, but omit the raisins, and add 1 cup (250 mL) plain M&Ms and 1 cup (250 mL) peanut M&Ms with the oats. **Makes about 24 cookies.**

Walnut Butter Jumbles

Follow recipe for Peanut Butter Jumbles (above), but replace the peanut butter with Walnut Butter (page 561), omit the raisins, and add 1 cup (250 mL) semisweet chocolate chips and ½ cup (125 mL) chopped walnuts with the oats. **Makes about 24 cookies.**

Oatmeal Jumbles

Follow recipe for Peanut Butter Jumbles (above), but decrease the oats to 3½ cups (875 mL), add 1 cup (250 mL) wheat germ with the oats, decrease the raisins to 1 cup (250 mL), and add ½ cup (125 mL) toasted sunflower seeds with the raisins. **Makes about 24 cookies.**

Chocolate Peanut Jumbles

Follow the recipe for Peanut Butter Jumbles (page 437), but omit the raisins, and add 1 cup (250 mL) semisweet chocolate chips, 1 cup (250 mL) semisweet chocolate chunks and $\frac{1}{2}$ cup (125 mL) unsweetened cocoa powder, sifted, with the oats. **Makes about 24 cookies.**

Almond Macaroons

2 cups	finely ground almonds (see page 13)	500 mL
1$\frac{1}{4}$ cups	granulated sugar	300 mL
$\frac{1}{4}$ tsp	almond extract	1 mL
Pinch	salt	Pinch
2	large egg whites (approx.), beaten until frothy	2
12	whole blanched almonds	12
	Confectioner's (icing) sugar	

Preheat oven to 350°F (180°C). Combine ground almonds, granulated sugar, almond extract, salt and enough egg white to make a paste. Form into 12 prune-size balls, place on a baking sheet and top each with 1 whole almond. Bake for 20 minutes, until lightly browned. Let cool on pan for 1 minute, then transfer to a rack and let cool completely. Sprinkle with confectioner's sugar. **Makes 12 cookies.**

Pine Nut Macaroons

Follow preceding recipe, but replace the ground almonds with ground pine nuts, and top each cookie with 5 or 6 whole pine nuts instead of 1 almond. **Makes 12 cookies.**

Hazelnut Macaroons

2 cups	finely ground hazelnuts (see page 13)	500 mL
1 cup	granulated sugar	250 mL
2 tbsp	red currant jelly	25 mL
$\frac{1}{4}$ tsp	vanilla	1 mL
Pinch	salt	Pinch
2	egg whites (approx.), beaten	2
12	skinned hazelnuts	12
	Confectioner's (icing) sugar	

Preheat oven to 350°F (180°C). Combine ground hazelnuts, sugar, jelly, vanilla, salt and enough egg white to make a paste. Form into 12 prune-size balls, place on a baking sheet and top each with 1 hazelnut. Bake and finish as in Almond Macaroons (above). **Makes 12 cookies.**

Chocolate Macaroons

1$\frac{1}{2}$ cups	slivered or sliced almonds	375 mL
2 oz	unsweetened chocolate, broken into pieces	60 g
1$\frac{1}{4}$ cups	granulated sugar	300 mL
$\frac{1}{4}$ tsp	vanilla	1 mL
Pinch	salt	Pinch
2	egg whites (approx.)	2
12	whole blanched almonds	12
3 oz	semisweet chocolate, melted (see page 14)	90 g

Preheat oven to 350°F (180°C). In a food processor, finely grind slivered almonds and unsweetened chocolate. Stir in sugar, vanilla, salt and enough egg white to make a paste. Form into 12 prune-size balls, place on a baking sheet and top each with 1 whole almond. Bake for 20 minutes, until firm. Let cool on pan for 1 minute, then transfer to a rack and let cool completely. Dip tops in semisweet chocolate and let cool until chocolate is firm. **Makes 12 cookies.**

Coconut Macaroons

4 cups	shredded unsweetened coconut	1 L
1$\frac{3}{4}$ cups	granulated sugar, divided	425 mL
$\frac{1}{4}$ cup	finely grated orange zest	50 mL
$\frac{1}{4}$ tsp	salt	1 mL
5	large or extra-large egg whites	5

Preheat oven to 350°F (180°C) and grease baking sheets. In a large bowl, combine coconut, 1 cup (250 mL) of the sugar, orange zest and a pinch of salt; set aside. In another bowl, beat egg whites and another pinch of salt until foamy. Add the remaining sugar and beat until firm peaks form. Stir in coconut mixture. Drop by tablespoonfuls onto prepared baking sheets. Bake for 20 minutes, until browned. Immediately transfer to racks and let cool. **Makes about 36 cookies.**

Butter Cookies

1	egg, separated	1
1 cup	all-purpose flour	250 mL
$\frac{1}{2}$ cup	unsalted butter, softened	125 mL
6 tbsp	granulated sugar	90 mL
$\frac{1}{2}$ tsp	vanilla	2 mL
Pinch	salt	Pinch
36	whole blanched almonds	36

Beat egg yolk, flour, butter, sugar, vanilla and salt until a smooth dough forms. Form dough into 2 cylinders, each 1$\frac{1}{2}$ inches (4 cm) in diameter and 4$\frac{1}{2}$ inches (11 cm) long. Wrap in plastic wrap and refrigerate for at least 1 hour, until firm, or overnight. Preheat oven to 375°F (190°C) and grease baking sheets. Slice dough into $\frac{1}{4}$-inch (0.5 cm) thick rounds and place on prepared baking sheets. Brush with beaten egg white and top each cookie with 1 blanched almond. Bake for 13 minutes, until set and brown on the bottom. Transfer to racks and let cool. **Makes 36 cookies.**

Sugar Cookies

Follow preceding recipe, but sprinkle each cookie with a large pinch of granulated sugar instead of topping with an almond. **Makes 36 cookies.**

Spiced Cookies

Follow recipe for Butter Cookies (page 438), but first sift the flour with $\frac{1}{2}$ tsp (2 mL) each ground cinnamon and ground ginger, and a pinch each of ground cloves and dry mustard (yes, mustard). In place of an almond, sprinkle each cookie with a big pinch of cinnamon-sugar. **Makes 36 cookies.**

Cardamom Currant Cookies

Follow recipe for Butter Cookies (page 438), but first sift the flour with 1 tsp (5 mL) ground cardamom. Stir 1 cup (250 mL) dried currants into the dough and omit the almonds. **Makes 36 cookies.**

Sables

Follow recipe for Butter Cookies (page 438), but add $\frac{1}{4}$ cup (50 mL) finely ground almonds (see page 13) with the sugar, and replace half the vanilla with almond extract. **Makes 36 cookies.**

Chocolate Butter Cookies

Follow recipe for Butter Cookies (page 438), but stir 2 tbsp (25 mL) finely chopped bittersweet chocolate into the dough, and top with skinned hazelnuts instead of almonds. **Makes 36 cookies.**

Pinwheels

Prepare $\frac{1}{2}$ recipe each Butter Cookies (page 438) and Chocolate Butter Cookies (above), but instead of forming cylinders, roll out each dough between sheets of waxed paper into a 9- by 7-inch (23 by 18 cm) rectangle. Remove a sheet of waxed paper from each and flip one piece of dough onto the other, lining up edges as closely as possible. Remove top sheet of waxed paper and use the bottom sheet to help lift the pieces. Roll up dough jellyroll-style,

starting with a long side. Wrap in plastic wrap. Chill, slice and bake as described in Butter Cookies. Omit the nuts from both recipes. **Makes 36 cookies.**

Hazelnut Crescents

$\frac{2}{3}$ cup	granulated sugar	150 mL
1 cup	unsalted butter	250 mL
2 tsp	vanilla	10 mL
Pinch	salt	Pinch
$2\frac{1}{2}$ cups	all-purpose flour	625 mL
$\frac{1}{2}$ cup	finely ground toasted hazelnuts (see pages 68 and 13)	125 mL
	Confectioner's (icing) sugar	

Preheat oven to 350°F (180°C). In a large bowl, cream granulated sugar, butter, vanilla and salt. Stir in flour and hazelnuts, just enough to incorporate. Form scant tablespoonfuls (15 mL) of dough into elongated ovals and place on baking sheets, bending in the ends of each cookie to form a crescent. Bake for 19 minutes, until set and lightly toasted on the tips. Let cool on pans for 3 minutes, then dust with confectioner's sugar, transfer to racks and let cool completely. **Makes about 36 cookies.**

Anise Almond Drops

Follow preceding recipe, but replace half the vanilla with anise extract, and substitute almonds for the hazelnuts. Form into balls instead of crescents and bake for 22 to 24 minutes, or until set and lightly toasted on the tips. **Makes about 36 cookies.**

Coconut Snowballs

Follow recipe for Hazelnut Crescents (above), but replace the hazelnuts with shredded unsweetened coconut, and form the dough into balls instead of crescents. **Makes about 36 cookies.**

Spiced Gumdrop Drops

Follow recipe for Hazelnut Crescents (above), but first sift flour with $\frac{1}{4}$ tsp (1 mL) each ground cinnamon and ground ginger, and a pinch of ground cloves. Wrap each portion of dough around a small gumdrop and form into a rough ball. Bake for 22 to 24 minutes, or until set and lightly browned. **Makes about 36 cookies.**

Walnut Brown-Edge Wafers

1½ cups	finely ground walnuts (see page 13)	375 mL
¾ cup	granulated sugar	175 mL
6 tbsp	unsalted butter, softened	90 mL
3 tbsp	whipping (35%) cream	45 mL
1½ tbsp	all-purpose flour	22 mL
Pinch	salt	Pinch
1	egg, beaten	1

Preheat oven to 350°F (180°C) and grease baking sheets. In a large saucepan, over medium heat, cook walnuts, sugar, butter, cream, flour and salt, stirring often, until butter melts and ingredients are blended. Beat in egg. Drop by tablespoonfuls, 4 inches (10 cm) apart, on prepared baking sheets and spread into 3-inch (7.5 cm) circles with the back of a spoon. Bake for 9 minutes, until brown on the edges. Immediately transfer to racks and let cool. **Makes about 24 cookies.**

Walnut Oat Lace Cookies

¾ cup	granulated sugar	175 mL
½ cup	quick-cooking rolled oats	125 mL
½ cup	finely chopped walnuts	125 mL
2 tbsp	all-purpose flour	25 mL
Pinch	salt	Pinch
1	egg, beaten	1
½ cup	unsalted butter, melted	125 mL
½ tsp	almond extract	2 mL

Preheat oven to 350°F (180°C) and grease baking sheets. In a large bowl, combine sugar, oats, walnuts, flour and salt. Beat in egg, butter and almond extract to form a thin batter. Form cookies and bake as in preceding recipe. **Makes about 30 cookies.**

Ginger Lace Cookies

1 cup	quick-cooking rolled oats	250 mL
¾ cup	packed light brown sugar	175 mL
2 tbsp	all-purpose flour	25 mL
½ tsp	ground ginger	2 mL
Pinch	salt	Pinch
1	egg, beaten	1
½ cup	unsalted butter, melted	125 mL
½ tsp	vanilla	2 mL

Preheat oven to 350°F (180°C) and grease baking sheets. In a large bowl, combine oats, brown sugar, flour, ginger and salt. Beat in egg, butter and vanilla to form a thin batter. Form cookies and bake as in Walnut Brown-Edge Wafers (above). **Makes about 30 cookies.**

Honey Almond Tuiles

¼ cup	granulated sugar	50 mL
¼ cup	unsalted butter	50 mL
Pinch	salt	Pinch
2	egg whites	2
¾ cup	finely ground almonds (see page 13)	175 mL
¼ cup	all-purpose flour	50 mL
3 tbsp	honey	45 mL
2 tbsp	whipping (35%) cream	25 mL
	Sliced almonds	

Place rack in top third of oven, preheat oven to 350°F (180°C) and grease baking sheet. In a large bowl, cream sugar, butter and salt. Beat in egg whites, ground almonds, flour, honey and cream to form a thin batter. Drop by tablespoonfuls, 4 inches (10 cm) apart, on prepared baking sheet and spread into 3-inch (7.5 cm) circles with the back of a spoon. Sprinkle each cookie with 4 to 5 almond slices. Bake, in batches, for 6 minutes, until browned on the edges. Immediately remove with a wide spatula and drape cookies over a rolling pin; let cool. **Makes 12 to 16 cookies.**

Shortbread

2⅓ cups	cake flour	575 mL
½ cup	granulated sugar	125 mL
Pinch	salt	Pinch
1 cup	unsalted butter, cut into small pieces	250 mL
½ tsp	vanilla	2 mL

Preheat oven to 350°F (180°C). In a large bowl, combine flour, sugar and salt. Work in butter with your fingers until mixture resembles coarse meal. Add vanilla and work until a smooth dough forms. Pat into a ⅓-inch (0.75 cm) thick disk and cut out 2-inch (5 cm) circles. Reform scraps and cut out more cookies. Place cookies ½ inch (1 cm) apart on baking sheets. Bake for 17 to 20 minutes, or until browned at the edges. Transfer to racks and let cool. **Makes about 24 cookies.**

Almond Shortbread

Follow preceding recipe, but add ⅔ cup (150 mL) finely ground almonds (see page 13) with the flour, and replace half the vanilla with almond extract. **Makes about 24 cookies.**

Ginger Currant Shortbread

Follow recipe for Shortbread (page 440), but add 1 tsp (5 mL) ground ginger, ¼ tsp (1 mL) ground cinnamon and a pinch of allspice with the sugar, and stir 1 cup (250 mL) dried currants into the dough before forming cookies. **Makes about 24 cookies.**

Walnut Chocolate Chip Shortbread

Follow recipe for Shortbread (page 440), but add ⅔ cup (150 mL) finely ground walnuts (see page 13) with the flour, and stir 1 cup (250 mL) miniature semisweet chocolate chips into the dough before forming cookies. **Makes about 24 cookies.**

Use this pastry with the seven recipes that follow.

Sweet Cream Cheese Pastry

1 cup	all-purpose flour	250 mL
2 tbsp	granulated sugar	25 mL
½ cup	unsalted butter, cut into small pieces	125 mL
4 oz	cream cheese, softened	125 g
	Additional all-purpose flour	

In a bowl, combine flour and sugar. Work in butter with your fingers until mixture resembles coarse meal. Work in cream cheese until a smooth dough forms. Pat dough into a flat disk and dust with flour. Wrap in plastic wrap and refrigerate for at least 1 hour, until chilled, or overnight. On a floured work surface, with a floured rolling pin, roll out dough to between ⅛ and ¼ inch (0.25 and 0.5 cm) thick. Use as directed in the following recipes.

Apricot Marzipan Drops

1 oz	marzipan	30 g
12	extra-large dried apricots, each with a slit	12
1	recipe Sweet Cream Cheese Pastry (above)	1
¼ cup	confectioner's (icing) sugar	50 mL

Break marzipan into 12 nuggets and stuff each apricot with 1 nugget. Cut pastry into 12 circles, each 3½ inches (8.5 cm) in diameter, and wrap each apricot in a circle of dough, pinching seam to seal. Place seam side down on a baking sheet and refrigerate for 20 minutes. Meanwhile, preheat oven to 400°F (200°C). Bake for 30 minutes, until browned at the edges. Let cool on pan for 10 minutes, then dust with sugar, transfer to a rack and let cool completely. **Makes 12 cookies.**

Apricot Schnecken

1	recipe Sweet Cream Cheese Pastry (left)	1
1 tbsp	melted unsalted butter	15 mL
⅓ cup	apricot preserves, warmed	75 mL
½ cup	finely chopped dried apricots	125 mL
1	egg yolk, beaten with 1 tbsp (15 mL) water	1

Preheat oven to 350°F (180°C). Roll pastry out to a circle. Brush pastry with butter, then with apricot preserves. Sprinkle with dried apricots and cut into 16 wedges. Roll up each wedge, rolling from the wide edge to the point. Place point side down on baking sheets and brush with egg wash. Bake for 30 minutes, until browned. Transfer to racks and let cool. **Makes 16 cookies.**

Chocolate Crescents

Follow preceding recipe, but omit the preserves and dried apricots, and sprinkle the pastry with ⅓ cup (75 mL) finely chopped semisweet chocolate and ⅓ cup (75 mL) chopped walnuts. Place cookies on baking sheets point side up, and bend into a crescent shape. **Makes 16 cookies.**

Eccles Cakes

1 cup	dried currants	250 mL
3 tbsp	melted unsalted butter	45 mL
3 tbsp	granulated sugar	45 mL
2 tbsp	chopped candied orange peel or lemon peel	25 mL
Pinch	ground allspice	Pinch
Pinch	ground nutmeg	Pinch
2	recipes Sweet Cream Cheese Pastry (left)	2
1	egg yolk, beaten with 1 tbsp (15 mL) water	1
	Confectioner's (icing) sugar	

Preheat oven to 400°F (200°C). In a small bowl, combine currants, butter, granulated sugar, candied orange peel, allspice and nutmeg. Cut pastry into 24 circles, each 3½ inches (8.5 cm) in diameter, and place 1 tbsp (15 mL) filling in the center of each circle. Bring edges of pastry up around filling and twist to seal. Flip pastries, flatten lightly with a rolling pin and cut a small X in the top. Place on baking sheets and brush with egg wash. Bake for 13 to 14 minutes, or until lightly browned. Transfer to racks and let cool. Dust lightly with confectioner's sugar. **Makes 24 cookies.**

Grand Marnier Almond Bars

½	recipe Sweet Cream Cheese Pastry (page 441)	½
⅔ cup	coarsely chopped almonds	150 mL
⅔ cup	granulated sugar	150 mL
½ cup	cream (any type, minimum 10%)	125 mL
1 tbsp	Grand Marnier or other orange-flavored liqueur	15 mL
Pinch	salt	Pinch
Dash	almond extract	Dash
	Finely grated zest of 1 orange	

Preheat oven to 350°F (180°C) and line an 8-inch (2 L) square baking pan with foil. Press pastry into prepared pan, prick with a fork and bake for 15 minutes. Meanwhile, in a saucepan, bring almonds, sugar, cream, liqueur, salt and almond extract to a simmer; simmer for 10 minutes, then stir in orange zest. Spread almond mixture over pastry and bake for 30 minutes, until bubbly and lightly brown. Let cool in pan for 30 minutes. Invert onto a baking sheet, remove foil and invert onto a cutting board. Cut with serrated knife into 16 bars. Let cool completely on a rack.

Pecan Pie Bars

½	recipe Sweet Cream Cheese Pastry (page 441), made with packed light brown sugar instead of granulated sugar	½
1	extra-large egg	1
1 cup	pecan pieces	250 mL
6 tbsp	dark corn syrup	90 mL
2 tbsp	packed light brown sugar	25 mL
2 tbsp	all-purpose flour	25 mL
1 tbsp	bourbon	15 mL
½ tsp	vanilla	2 mL
Pinch	salt	Pinch

Preheat oven to 350°F (180°C) and line an 8-inch (2 L) square baking pan with foil. Press pastry into prepared pan, prick with a fork and bake for 15 minutes. Meanwhile, beat egg, pecan pieces, corn syrup, brown sugar, flour, bourbon, vanilla and salt. Spread mixture over pastry and bake for 30 minutes, until topping is set. Let cool in pan for 30 minutes, then invert onto a baking sheet, remove foil and invert onto a rack. Place in the freezer for 30 minutes, then cut with a serrated knife into 16 bars.

Chewy Gooey Lemon Pecan Bars

Follow preceding recipe, but when making the pastry add 1 tbsp (15 mL) finely grated lemon zest with the flour. Use light corn syrup instead of dark, and replace the bourbon with the juice of ½ lemon.

Dried Cherry Bars

	Nonstick cooking spray	
2 cups	unbleached all-purpose flour	500 mL
1 cup	unsalted butter, cut into pieces	250 mL
½ cup	granulated sugar	125 mL
Pinch	salt	Pinch

Topping

4	eggs, lightly beaten	4
2 cups	chopped skinned hazelnuts	500 mL
1½ cups	dried pitted cherries	375 mL
1 cup	packed brown sugar	250 mL
2 tbsp	all-purpose flour	25 mL

Preheat oven to 350°F (180°C). Line a 13- by 9-inch (3 L) baking pan with foil, and spray foil with cooking spray. Combine flour, butter, sugar and salt until a smooth dough forms. Press dough into baking pan and bake for 30 minutes. *Meanwhile, prepare the topping:* Combine eggs, hazelnuts, cherries, brown sugar and flour. Pour over crust and bake for 20 minutes, until topping is bubbling and brown on the edges. Let cool completely in pan, then remove from pan and peel off foil. Cut with a serrated knife into 24 bars.

Date Nut Bars

Follow preceding recipe, but replace the hazelnuts with walnuts, and the cherries with chopped pitted dates.

Peanut Butter Sandwich Squares

6 tbsp	unsalted butter	90 mL
¼ cup	packed light brown sugar	50 mL
1	egg white	1
6 tbsp	honey, divided	90 mL
1½ cups	all-purpose flour	375 mL
¾ cup	whole wheat flour	175 mL
1 tsp	baking powder	5 mL
¼ tsp	baking soda	1 mL
Pinch	salt	Pinch
	Nonstick cooking spray	
1 cup	chunky peanut butter	250 mL

In a large bowl, cream butter and brown sugar. Beat in egg white and 5 tbsp (75 mL) of the honey. Stir in all-purpose flour, whole wheat flour, baking powder, baking soda and salt until a smooth dough forms. With floured hands, press half the dough into prepared pan and place in the freezer for 20 minutes. Refrigerate the remaining dough. Preheat oven to 350°F (180°C). Line a 9-inch (2.5 L) square baking pan with foil, and spray foil with cooking spray. Combine peanut butter and the remaining honey. Remove dough from freezer and spread with peanut butter mixture. Roll out dough from refrigerator between sheets of waxed paper into a 9-inch (23 cm) square; place over peanut butter mixture and push down on edges. Bake for 25 minutes, until set and lightly browned. Let cool in pan for 10 minutes, then remove to a rack and let cool completely. Cut into 16 squares.

Chocolate Peanut Butter Squares

Follow preceding recipe, but use smooth peanut butter instead of chunky, and sprinkle 1 cup (250 mL) semisweet chocolate chips over the peanut butter before topping with rolled-out dough.

Raisin Squares

Follow recipe for Peanut Butter Sandwich Bars (page 442), but replace the peanut butter and honey mixture with the following filling: Simmer 1 cup (250 mL) raisins, ¾ cup (175 mL) water, 2 tbsp (25 mL) honey and 1½ tbsp (22 mL) freshly squeezed lemon juice until liquid is absorbed and raisins are softened. (Watch carefully: raisins may scorch near the end of the cooking time.) Let cool, then spread over dough from the freezer.

Wheat Germ Squares

	Nonstick cooking spray	
½ cup	powdered milk	125 mL
½ tsp	baking powder	2 mL
2	extra-large eggs, lightly beaten	2
1 cup	packed dark brown sugar	250 mL
1 cup	wheat germ	250 mL
½ cup	chopped walnuts	125 mL
½ cup	raisins	125 mL
¼ cup	vegetable oil	50 mL
2 tsp	vanilla	10 mL
Pinch	salt	Pinch

Preheat oven to 350°F (180°C) and spray an 8-inch (2 L) square baking pan with cooking spray. Sift together powdered milk and baking powder; set aside. In a large bowl, combine eggs, brown sugar, wheat germ, walnuts, raisins, oil, vanilla and salt. Stir in powdered milk mixture. Pour into prepared pan and smooth top. Bake for 35 minutes, until a tester inserted in the center comes out with just a crumb clinging to it. Let cool completely in pan, then remove to a rack and place in the freezer for 30 minutes. Cut into 16 squares.

Oaties

	Nonstick cooking spray	
2	large or extra-large eggs	2
1 cup	firmly packed light brown sugar	250 mL
½ cup	unsalted butter, melted	125 mL
1 tsp	baking powder	5 mL
2 cups	quick-cooking or old-fashioned rolled oats	500 mL
½ cup	chopped walnuts	125 mL
½ cup	chopped raisins	125 mL
1 tsp	vanilla	5 mL
Pinch	salt	Pinch

Preheat oven to 350°F (180°C). Line an 8-inch (2 L) square baking pan with foil, and spray foil with cooking spray. In a large bowl, beat eggs, brown sugar and butter. Sift in baking powder, then stir in oats, walnuts, raisins, vanilla and salt until thoroughly combined. Pour into prepared pan and smooth top. Bake for 45 minutes, until a tester inserted in the center comes out with just a crumb clinging to it. Let cool completely in pan, then remove to a rack, peel off foil and place in the freezer for 30 minutes. Cut into 16 squares.

Butterscotch Oaties

Follow preceding recipe, but replace the raisins with butterscotch chips.

Chapter 40
Dessert Sauces
For Better Mental Health

Hot Fudge Sauce 445
Milk Chocolate Sauce 445
Peanut Butter Chocolate Sauce 445
Chocolate Banana Sauce 445
Mocha Sauce 445
Chocolate Mint Sauce 445
Milk Chocolate Sauce with Almonds . . . 445
Quick Dark Chocolate Sauce 445
Bitter Chocolate Sauce 446
Peppered Chocolate Sauce 446
Chocolate Rum Sauce 446
Orange Chocolate Sauce 446
Black Forest Chocolate Sauce 446
Chocolate Raspberry Sauce 446
Praline Chocolate Caramel Sauce 446
White Chocolate Sauce 446
Raspberry White Chocolate Sauce 446
Old-Fashioned Custard Sauce 447
Coffee Custard Sauce 447
Chocolate Custard Sauce 447
Maple Custard Sauce 447
Praline Custard Sauce 447
Super-Rich Custard Sauce 447
Orange Custard Sauce 447
Creamy Caramel Sauce 447

Sour Cherry Coulis 447
Fresh Strawberry Sauce 448
Sugared Raspberries 448
Ginger Peach Sauce 448
Brandied Peaches 448
Warm Stir-Fried Grapes 448
Raspberries and Cream 448
Blueberry Orange Sauce 448
Warm Pear Purée 449
Sautéed Fruit Salad 449
Mango Coulis with Lime 449
Berry Concassé 449
Figs Preserved in Port 449
Melba Sauce 449
Suzette Sauce 450
Honey Walnut Sauce 450
Wet Bourbon Pecans 450
Honey Bourbon Sauce 450
Margarita Sauce 450
Butter Rum Raisin Sauce 450
Orange, Scotch and Espresso Sauce . . . 451
Maple Whipped Cream 451
Chocolate Chip Whipped Cream 451
Peanut Butter Cream 451
Candied Ginger Cream 451

W hen we rule the world, every city and town will have a Mental Health Food Store. It will be packed with hot fudge instead of ginseng tea. You'll find soft ice cream where the wheat germ used to be. For it's our unalterable belief that if you can't occasionally indulge in a few empty calories, then there's far too little happiness in staying fit.

With that in mind, we propose the following: one thing gooey, once a week, for everyone. And to get you through the first year of our regime, here are 50 dessert sauces. All are fast and easy, and are just the thing to top a scoop of ice cream, gild a fruit salad or crown a humble slice of cake as you eat your way to better mental health.

About these recipes . . .
All of the following recipes yield enough sauce to top 4 to 6 servings of dessert. We recommend that you use unsalted butter.

Hot Fudge Sauce

½ cup	whipping (35%) cream	125 mL
2 tbsp	butter	25 mL
⅓ cup	granulated sugar	75 mL
⅓ cup	packed dark brown sugar	75 mL
½ cup	unsweetened Dutch-process cocoa powder, sifted	125 mL
Pinch	salt	Pinch

In a small saucepan, heat cream and butter over medium heat until butter melts. Add granulated sugar and brown sugar; cook, stirring, until they dissolve. Whisk in cocoa and salt; cook, stirring, until smooth. Serve warm. **Makes about 1 cup (250 mL).**

Milk Chocolate Sauce

¾ cup	granulated sugar	175 mL
⅔ cup	sifted unsweetened cocoa powder	150 mL
1 cup	milk (not fat-free)	250 mL
¼ cup	whipping (35%) cream	50 mL
2 tbsp	butter	25 mL
1 tsp	vanilla	5 mL

In a heavy saucepan, combine sugar and cocoa. Slowly whisk in milk until smooth. Bring to a simmer over medium heat, stirring frequently. Add cream and simmer for 3 minutes. Add butter and simmer for 3 minutes. Stir in vanilla. Let cool. **Makes about 1½ cups (375 mL).**

Peanut Butter Chocolate Sauce
Follow preceding recipe, but replace the butter with ¼ cup (50 mL) smooth peanut butter. **Makes about 1½ cups (375 mL).**

Chocolate Banana Sauce
Follow recipe for Milk Chocolate Sauce (left), but first, in a food processor, purée 2 bananas. Add with the vanilla. **Makes about 1¾ cups (425 mL).**

Mocha Sauce
Follow recipe for Milk Chocolate Sauce (left), but add 1 tbsp (15 mL) instant coffee granules with the cream. **Makes about 1½ cups (375 mL).**

Chocolate Mint Sauce
Follow recipe for Milk Chocolate Sauce (left), but add a few drops of peppermint extract with the vanilla. **Makes about 1½ cups (375 mL).**

Milk Chocolate Sauce with Almonds

8 oz	milk chocolate bar with almonds, broken into pieces	250 g
¼ cup	boiling water	50 mL

In the top of a double boiler, melt chocolate over simmering water. Whisk in boiling water until smooth. Serve warm. **Makes about 1 cup (250 mL).**

Quick Dark Chocolate Sauce

¾ cup	sifted unsweetened cocoa powder	175 mL
⅔ cup	granulated sugar	150 mL
Pinch	salt	Pinch
1 cup	cold water	250 mL
1 tbsp	butter	15 mL

In a heavy saucepan, combine cocoa, sugar and salt. Slowly whisk in cold water until smooth. Bring to a simmer over medium heat and simmer, stirring frequently, for 2 minutes. Stir in butter and simmer for 2 minutes. Let cool. **Makes about 1½ cups (375 mL).**

Bitter Chocolate Sauce

¾ cup	sifted unsweetened cocoa powder	175 mL
½ cup	granulated sugar	125 mL
Pinch	salt	Pinch
¾ cup	cold water	175 mL
1 tbsp	butter	15 mL
1 tsp	instant coffee granules	5 mL

In a heavy saucepan, combine cocoa, sugar and salt. Slowly whisk in cold water until smooth. Bring to a simmer over medium heat and simmer, stirring frequently, for 2 minutes. Stir in butter and coffee; simmer for 2 minutes. Let cool. **Makes about 1¼ cups (300 mL).**

Peppered Chocolate Sauce

Follow preceding recipe, but add ½ tsp (2 mL) ground cinnamon, ¼ tsp (1 mL) freshly ground black pepper, ¼ tsp (1 mL) ground ginger and a pinch of ground cloves with the sugar, and omit the coffee. **Makes about 1¼ cups (300 mL).**

Chocolate Rum Sauce

¾ cup	sifted unsweetened cocoa powder	175 mL
¾ cup	packed light brown sugar	175 mL
Pinch	salt	Pinch
⅔ cup	cold water	150 mL
2 tbsp	dark rum	25 mL
1 tbsp	butter	15 mL

In a heavy saucepan, combine cocoa, brown sugar and salt. Slowly whisk in cold water until smooth. Bring to a simmer over medium heat and simmer, stirring frequently, for 2 minutes. Stir in rum and butter; simmer for 2 minutes. Let cool. **Makes about 1¼ cups (300 mL).**

Orange Chocolate Sauce

¾ cup	sifted unsweetened cocoa powder	175 mL
⅔ cup	granulated sugar	150 mL
Pinch	salt	Pinch
⅔ cup	cold water	150 mL
1 tbsp	orange marmalade	15 mL
1 tbsp	orange-flavored liqueur	15 mL
1 tbsp	butter	15 mL

In a heavy saucepan, combine cocoa, sugar and salt. Slowly whisk in cold water until smooth. Bring to a simmer over medium heat and simmer, stirring frequently, for 2 minutes. Stir in marmalade, liqueur and butter; simmer for 2 minutes. Let cool. **Makes about 1¼ cups (300 mL).**

Black Forest Chocolate Sauce

Follow preceding recipe, but omit the orange marmalade and orange-flavored liqueur, and add 2 tbsp (25 mL) sour cherry preserves and 1 tbsp (15 mL) Kirsch with the butter. **Makes about 1¼ cups (300 mL).**

Chocolate Raspberry Sauce

Follow recipe for Orange Chocolate Sauce (above), but omit the orange marmalade and orange-flavored liqueur, and add 2 tbsp (25 mL) seedless raspberry jam and 1 tbsp (15 mL) crème de cassis or framboise with the butter. **Makes about 1¼ cups (300 mL).**

Praline Chocolate Caramel Sauce

¾ cup	packed light brown sugar	175 mL
½ cup	sifted unsweetened cocoa powder	125 mL
Pinch	salt	Pinch
⅔ cup	cold milk (not fat-free)	150 mL
¼ cup	finely chopped toasted almonds	50 mL
2 tbsp	butter	25 mL
½ tsp	almond extract	2 mL

In a heavy saucepan, combine brown sugar, cocoa and salt. Slowly whisk in milk until smooth. Bring to a simmer over medium heat and simmer, stirring frequently, for 2 minutes. Stir in almonds, butter and almond extract; simmer for 2 minutes. Let cool. **Makes about 1½ cups (375 mL).**

White Chocolate Sauce

¼ cup	whipping (35%) cream	50 mL
¼ cup	milk	50 mL
5 oz	white chocolate, finely chopped	150 g

In a heavy stainless steel saucepan, bring cream and milk to a simmer. Remove from heat and whisk in white chocolate until melted. Serve warm. **Makes about 1 cup (250 mL).**

Raspberry White Chocolate Sauce

Follow preceding recipe, but once white chocolate is melted, stir in ½ cup (125 mL) fresh or frozen raspberries (thawed if frozen). Let cool. **Makes about 1½ cups (375 mL).**

Old-Fashioned Custard Sauce

2 cups	milk (not fat-free)	500 mL
½ cup	granulated sugar, divided	125 mL
5	large or extra-large egg yolks	5
Pinch	salt	Pinch
1 tsp	vanilla	5 mL

In a heavy saucepan, bring milk and half the sugar to a simmer over medium heat. Meanwhile, in the top of a double boiler, beat egg yolks, the remaining sugar and salt until thick and pale. Slowly whisk in the hot milk. Place over simmering water and cook, stirring with a heat-resistant rubber spatula, until the custard coats it lightly. Immediately pour into a container and stir in vanilla. Serve warm or let cool. **Makes about 2¾ cups (675 mL).**

Coffee Custard Sauce

Follow preceding recipe, but add 1 tbsp (15 mL) instant coffee granules with the vanilla. **Makes about 2¾ cups (675 mL).**

Chocolate Custard Sauce

Follow recipe for Old-Fashioned Custard Sauce (above), but whisk in 5 oz (150 g) semisweet chocolate, finely chopped, just before you add the vanilla. **Makes about 3 cups (750 mL).**

Maple Custard Sauce

Follow recipe for Old-Fashioned Custard Sauce (above), but decrease the sugar by half, omitting the half that is heated with the milk. Instead, heat ⅓ cup (75 mL) pure maple syrup with the milk. **Makes about 2¾ cups (675 mL).**

Praline Custard Sauce

Follow recipe for Old-Fashioned Custard Sauce (above), but decrease the sugar by half, omitting the half that is heated with the milk. Instead, heat ¼ cup (50 mL) packed light brown sugar with the milk. Add ½ cup (125 mL) chopped toasted pecans and ¼ tsp (1 mL) almond extract with the vanilla. **Makes about 2¾ cups (675 mL).**

Super-Rich Custard Sauce

Follow recipe for Old-Fashioned Custard Sauce (left), but replace half the milk with cream (any type, minimum 10%), and increase the egg yolks to 6. **Makes about 2¾ cups (675 mL).**

Orange Custard Sauce

Follow recipe for Old-Fashioned Custard Sauce (left), but replace half the milk with cream (any type, minimum 10%), increase the egg yolks to 6, and add 2 tbsp (25 mL) finely grated orange zest and 2 tbsp (25 mL) orange-flavored liqueur to the sauce as it cools. **Makes about 2¾ cups (675 mL).**

Creamy Caramel Sauce

1 cup	firmly packed brown sugar	250 mL
1 cup	cream (any type, minimum 10%)	250 mL
2 tbsp	butter	25 mL

In a heavy saucepan, bring brown sugar and cream to a simmer over medium heat; simmer for 2 minutes. Stir in butter and simmer for 2 minutes. Serve warm or let cool. **Makes about 1½ cups (375 mL).**

Sour Cherry Coulis

2 cups	pitted sour cherries	500 mL
2 cups	granulated sugar	500 mL
Pinch	salt	Pinch

In a heavy saucepan, over medium heat, cook cherries and sugar, stirring, until sugar dissolves and cherries release their juices. Increase heat and boil for 10 minutes. Transfer to a food processor, add salt, and purée. **Makes about 3 cups (750 mL).**

Fresh Strawberry Sauce

2 cups	strawberries, hulled and sliced	500 mL
1/4 cup	granulated sugar	50 mL
2 tbsp	fruit-flavored liqueur of your choice	25 mL

Toss strawberries with sugar until sugar dissolves. Stir in liqueur, cover and refrigerate for about 1 hour, until chilled. **Makes about 2 cups (500 mL).**

Sugared Raspberries

2 cups	raspberries	500 mL
1/4 cup	granulated sugar	50 mL
2 tbsp	framboise or other raspberry-flavored liqueur	25 mL
1 tsp	freshly squeezed lemon juice	5 mL

Toss berries with sugar until sugar dissolves. Stir in framboise and lemon juice, cover and refrigerate for about 1 hour, until chilled. **Makes about 2 cups (500 mL).**

Ginger Peach Sauce

4	peaches, peeled and diced	4
1/4 cup	granulated sugar	50 mL
2 tbsp	finely minced candied ginger	25 mL
1/2 cup	Madeira or sherry	125 mL

Toss peaches with sugar and candied ginger until sugar dissolves and peaches start to release their juices. Stir in Madeira, cover and refrigerate for about 1 hour, until chilled. **Makes about 3 cups (750 mL).**

Brandied Peaches

4	peaches, peeled and diced	4
1/4 cup	packed light brown sugar	50 mL
1/2 cup	brandy	125 mL

Toss diced peaches with brown sugar until sugar dissolves and peaches start to release their juices. Stir in brandy, cover and refrigerate for about 1 hour, until chilled. **Makes about 3 cups (750 mL).**

Warm Stir-Fried Grapes

1 tbsp	butter	15 mL
3 cups	mixed red and green seedless grapes	750 mL
2 tsp	granulated sugar	10 mL
3 tbsp	fruity white wine (such as Riesling)	45 mL
1 tsp	freshly squeezed lemon juice	5 mL
Pinch	salt	Pinch

In a large skillet, melt butter over medium heat. Stir-fry grapes and sugar until grapes become shiny. Remove grapes with a slotted spoon to a bowl. Add wine, lemon juice and salt to the pan and bring to a boil. Pour over grapes, stirring to coat. Serve immediately. **Makes about 3 cups (750 mL).**

Raspberries and Cream

2 cups	fresh or frozen raspberries (thawed if frozen)	500 mL
2 tbsp	granulated sugar	25 mL
1/4 cup	fruit-flavored liqueur of your choice	50 mL
1/4 cup	whipping (35%) cream	50 mL

Place berries and sugar in a bowl and mash berries with a fork. Stir in liqueur, cover and refrigerate for about 1 hour, until chilled. Stir in cream immediately before serving. **Makes about 2 cups (500 mL).**

Blueberry Orange Sauce

1/3 cup	orange juice	75 mL
3 tbsp	sweet orange marmalade	45 mL
1 tbsp	honey	15 mL
2 cups	blueberries	500 mL

In a heavy saucepan, bring orange juice, marmalade and honey to a boil over medium-high heat. Add berries and cook until they lose their silvery appearance and turn dark blue, about 2 minutes. Serve warm or let cool. **Makes about 2 cups (500 mL).**

Warm Pear Purée

1 cup	white wine	250 mL
1 cup	water	250 mL
2 tbsp	granulated sugar	25 mL
1½ lbs	pears, peeled and quartered (about 3)	750 g
2 tbsp	butter	25 mL

In a heavy saucepan, bring wine, water and sugar to a boil. Add pears, reduce heat and simmer for about 7 minutes, or until pears are tender. Remove pears with a slotted spoon to the work bowl of a food processor or blender. Increase heat and boil pan liquid until it is reduced by about three-quarters. Add to pears, along with butter, and purée. Serve warm. **Makes about 3 cups (750 mL).**

Sautéed Fruit Salad

1 tbsp	butter	15 mL
3 cups	chopped fresh fruit (cherries, berries, peaches, plums, bananas)	750 mL
2 tsp	granulated sugar	10 mL
2 tbsp	fruit-flavored liqueur of your choice	25 mL
½ tsp	vanilla	2 mL

In a large skillet, melt butter over medium heat. Sauté fruit and sugar until fruit becomes shiny and starts to release its liquid. Remove fruit with a slotted spoon to a bowl. Add liqueur and vanilla to the pan and stir to combine. Pour over fruit, stirring to coat. Serve immediately. **Makes about 3 cups (750 mL).**

Mango Coulis with Lime

2	large mangoes, peeled and diced	2
2 tsp	honey	10 mL
	Juice of 1½ limes	

In a food processor, purée all ingredients. Cover and refrigerate for about 1 hour, until chilled. **Makes about 2 cups (500 mL).**

Berry Concassé

2 cups	berries (any variety), coarsely chopped	500 mL
¼ cup	granulated sugar	50 mL
1 tbsp	freshly squeezed lemon juice	15 mL
½ tsp	vanilla	2 mL

Combine all ingredients. Cover and refrigerate for about 1 hour, until chilled. **Makes about 2 cups (500 mL).**

Figs Preserved in Port

5 oz	dried figs, stemmed	150 g
	Boiling water	
	Port wine	

Cover figs with boiling water and soak for 20 minutes, until plumped. Drain and pack in a jar large enough to fit them with just 1 inch (2.5 cm) of headroom. Fill jar with port, seal airtight and let stand for least 1 week before serving. **Makes about 2 cups (500 mL).** *Keeps for up to 6 months.*

Melba Sauce

2 cups	fresh or thawed frozen raspberries	500 mL
¼ cup	red currant jelly	50 mL

Purée berries and push through a fine-mesh sieve to strain out seeds. In a small saucepan, melt jelly over medium heat. Stir into raspberry purée, cover and refrigerate for about 1 hour, until chilled. **Makes about 2 cups (500 mL).**

Suzette Sauce

	Finely julienned zest and juice of 1 orange Juice of ½ lemon	
3 tbsp	granulated sugar	45 mL
2 tbsp	kirsch	25 mL
2 tbsp	rum	25 mL
2 tbsp	brandy	25 mL
2 tbsp	orange-flavored liqueur	25 mL
1 tbsp	butter	15 mL

In a saucepan, bring orange zest, orange juice, lemon juice and sugar to a simmer over medium heat; simmer for 10 minutes. Stir in kirsch, rum, brandy, liqueur and butter. Serve warm. **Makes about 1 cup (250 mL).**

Honey Walnut Sauce

3 tbsp	butter	45 mL
2 tsp	cornstarch	10 mL
⅔ cup	honey	150 mL
1 cup	walnut pieces	250 mL

In a heavy saucepan, melt butter over medium heat. Stir in cornstarch. Add honey and bring to a boil. Add walnut pieces and simmer for 2 minutes. Serve warm or let cool. **Makes about 1¼ cups (300 mL).**

Wet Bourbon Pecans

Follow preceding recipe, but replace the honey with ⅓ cup (75 mL) dark corn syrup and ⅓ cup (75 mL) bourbon, and replace the walnuts with pecan pieces. Simmer for 3 minutes after adding the pecans. **Makes about 1¼ cups (300 mL).**

Honey Bourbon Sauce

Whisk together equal parts bourbon and honey. Serve over coffee ice cream.

Margarita Sauce

½ cup	tequila	125 mL
2 tsp	frozen orange juice concentrate	10 mL
2 tbsp	granulated sugar	25 mL
	Juice of 2 limes	
½ tsp	salt	2 mL

In a small bowl, whisk tequila and orange juice concentrate until dissolved. Stir in sugar and lime juice until sugar dissolves. Stir in salt. Cover and refrigerate for about 1 hour, until chilled. **Makes about 1 cup (250 mL).**

Butter Rum Raisin Sauce

½ cup	granulated sugar	125 mL
1 tbsp	cornstarch	15 mL
1 cup	hot water	250 mL
¾ cup	raisins	175 mL
2 tbsp	butter, softened	25 mL
2 tbsp	whipping (35%) cream	25 mL
2 tbsp	dark rum	25 mL
1 tsp	vanilla	5 mL

In a heavy saucepan, combine sugar and cornstarch. Add hot water and stir to dissolve. Add raisins and cook over medium heat until sauce clears and thickens. Remove from heat and stir in butter, cream, rum and vanilla. Serve warm or cover and refrigerate for about 1 hour, until chilled. **Makes about 2 cups (500 mL).**

Orange, Scotch and Espresso Sauce

¼ cup	Scotch whisky	50 mL
1 tbsp	granulated sugar	15 mL
1 tsp	instant espresso powder	5 mL
	Finely grated zest and juice of 1 large orange	

In a jar, combine Scotch, sugar, espresso powder, orange zest and orange juice. Cover and shake well. **Makes about ½ cup (125 mL).**

Maple Whipped Cream

1 cup	whipping (35%) cream, chilled	250 mL
3 tbsp	pure maple syrup	45 mL
1 tbsp	confectioner's (icing) sugar	15 mL

In a chilled bowl, using chilled beaters, whip cream until it just holds a shape. Add syrup and sugar; beat until soft peaks form. Cover and refrigerate for about 1 hour, until chilled. **Makes about 2 cups (500 mL).**

Chocolate Chip Whipped Cream

1 cup	whipping (35%) cream, chilled	250 mL
1 tbsp	confectioner's (icing) sugar	15 mL
1 tsp	vanilla	5 mL
½ cup	miniature semisweet chocolate chips	125 mL

In a chilled bowl, using chilled beaters, whip cream until it just holds a shape. Add sugar and vanilla; beat until soft peaks form. Fold in chocolate chips. Cover and refrigerate for about 1 hour, until chilled. **Makes about 2¼ cups (550 mL).**

Peanut Butter Cream

½ cup	cream (any type, minimum 10%)	125 mL
¼ cup	packed light brown sugar	50 mL
½ cup	smooth peanut butter	125 mL
½ tsp	vanilla	2 mL

In a heavy saucepan, heat cream and brown sugar over medium heat until sugar dissolves. Whisk in peanut butter until smooth. Stir in vanilla. Serve warm or cover and refrigerate for about 1 hour, until chilled. **Makes about 1 cup (250 mL).**

Candied Ginger Cream

1 cup	whipping (35%) cream, chilled	250 mL
2 tbsp	confectioner's (icing) sugar	25 mL
1 tbsp	orange-flavored liqueur	15 mL
½ tsp	vanilla	2 mL
3 tbsp	finely chopped candied ginger	45 mL

In a chilled bowl, using chilled beaters, whip cream, sugar, liqueur and vanilla until soft peaks form. Fold in ginger. Cover and refrigerate for about 1 hour, until chilled. **Makes about 2 cups (500 mL).**

Chapter 41
Drinks
Because Everyone Gets Thirsty

Lemon-Lime Soft Drink 453
Gingered Ginger Ale 453
Gingered Apricot Ale 454
Sparkling Peach Melba 454
Raspberry Mint Seltzer 454
Citrus Seltzer 454
Grapefruit or Tangerine Seltzer 454
Grapefruitade 454
Lemon-Limeade 454
Spicy Lemonade 454
Honey Cranberry Cocktail 455
Double Orange Juice 455
Minted Apple Juice 455
Strawberry Lime Frappé 455
Cherry Raspberry Frappé 455
Fruit Cooler 455
True Brewed Iced Tea 455
Sun-Brewed Iced Tea 455
Minted Iced Tea 455
Double Iced Tea 455
Spiced Iced Tea 456
Mint Julep Iced Tea 456
Lemonade Iced Tea 456
Fruited Iced Tea Punch 456
Zesty Iced Tea 456

Iced Tea with Spicy Lemon Ice Cubes . . 456
Iced Mocha 457
Iced Espresso with Rum 457
Iced Spiked Cocoa 457
Banana Berry Kefir 457
Super-Protein Health Shake 457
Warm White Chocolate Egg Nog 457
Mulled Cider 457
Liquid Chocolate Bars 458
Cappuccino Cocoa 458
Hot Buttered Rum 458
Flaming Warm Spiced Wine 458
Modern-Day Mead 458
Café Brûlot Slush 458
Mint Julep Slush 458
Kahlúa and Cream Shake 459
Liquid Creamsicle 459
Sparkling Kir Punch 459
Berry Wine Punch 459
"Champagne" with Grapefruit Ice 459
Spicy Tomato Juice 459
Super Vegetable Juice Cocktail 460
Shrimp Bloody Marys 460
Gazpacho Cooler 460
Spicy Tomato Slush 460

Thirst hurts. It's more severe than hunger and worse than a burn. It thickens the tongue and stabs at the throat. It makes us see double and imagine swimming holes where there are none. It is one of the few pains that no one can ignore, for next to air we need nothing more than we need drink.

Fortunately for most of us, thirst is easy to beat. We live in a culture where thirst-quenching is big business. Sodas, juices, shakes, punches, coffees, teas, flavored waters, energy drinks and sport beverages compete for our dollars, but you can match any of them, and for a fraction of the cost, in your own kitchen.

Most drinks are simply flavored water, made either by mixing flavorful juices or liqueurs with still or sparkling waters and sweeteners, or by infusing flavors into water through steeping. The first method is how most punches and mixed drinks are made; the latter is how teas and coffees are prepared.

Juices can be mixed and sweetened, then thinned with water to become a drink, or they can be added when the beverage is served to flavor the drink more subtly. One of the most artful ways to do this is to freeze the juice into elegant, tasty ice cubes. Plop them into a glass of wine or iced tea, then sip and wait. As the beverage chills, it is infused with the flavor of the ice.

Steeping infuses a liquid with the flavors of aromatic leaves, beans or spices. The process is not difficult at all. In fact, if you know how to make a cup of tea, you have already become an expert at steeping.

Exotic iced teas, coffees and cocoa can be made by mixing herbs, spices, tea leaves, coffee beans, blossoms or citrus zests with boiling water. Allow the solids to steep in the water until it cools to room temperature. Strain it and ice it, and it's done. Always make iced steeped drinks on the strong side at first, because their flavor will be diluted once ice cubes are added.

For a cozy winter evening, nothing beats warm drinks. Flavored coffees, warm egg nogs and hot chocolates are all warm, nonalcoholic elixirs that instantly take the bite out of a winter night, but for a more potent brew, we've included spiked renditions of each and an aromatic warm spiced wine punch.

Though most of us have been forced to abandon the unlimited consumption of milkshakes (or replace them with calorie-deluding iced cappuccino shakes) as our waistlines have expanded, these high-calorie but nutritious drinks need not be dropped completely from our diets. We have included a few indulgent drinks made lower in calories by substituting yogurt, sorbet or crushed ice for ice cream and punched up in nutrition with the addition of powdered skim milk. For those obnoxious few who never need to watch their weight, there are some super-rich ice cream shakes as well.

About these recipes . . .

Although most beverages are best consumed immediately, any of these recipes (except the carbonated ones) could be stored in the refrigerator, tightly covered, for a day or two.

Lemon-Lime Soft Drink

¼ cup	freshly squeezed lemon juice	50 mL
¼ cup	freshly squeezed lime juice	50 mL
¾ cup	frozen apple juice concentrate	175 mL
4 cups	seltzer (soda water)	1 L

In a pitcher, combine lemon juice, lime juice and apple juice concentrate. Stir in seltzer, cover and chill. **Serves 4.**

Gingered Ginger Ale

1 cup	water, divided	250 mL
¼ cup	grated gingerroot	50 mL
2 tbsp	granulated sugar	25 mL
Pinch	cayenne pepper	Pinch
	Ice cubes	
1 cup	ginger ale	250 mL

In a small saucepan, boil half the water with the ginger, sugar and cayenne until most of the water has evaporated. Remove from heat and add the remaining water; let cool to room temperature, then strain, discarding solids. Cover and chill liquid. Divide among four 12-oz (375 mL) glasses filled with ice, pour in ginger ale and stir. **Serves 4.**

Gingered Apricot Ale

⅓ cup	water	75 mL
¼ cup	grated gingerroot	50 mL
2 tbsp	granulated sugar	25 mL
Pinch	cayenne pepper	Pinch
1 cup	apricot nectar	250 mL
	Ice cubes	
1 cup	ginger ale	250 mL

In a small saucepan, boil water, ginger, sugar and cayenne until most of the water has evaporated. Remove from heat and add apricot nectar; let cool to room temperature, then strain, discarding solids. Cover and chill liquid. Divide among four 12-oz (375 mL) glasses filled with ice, pour in ginger ale and stir. **Serves 4.**

Sparkling Peach Melba

2 cups	peach nectar	500 mL
1 cup	frozen raspberries, crushed and strained	250 mL
	Crushed ice	
	Seltzer (soda water)	

In a pitcher, combine peach nectar and berries; cover and chill. Divide among 4 glasses, each one-third filled with crushed ice. Fill each glass with seltzer and stir. **Serves 4.**

Raspberry Mint Seltzer

16	fresh raspberries	16
12	mint leaves	12
	Ice cubes	
	Seltzer (soda water)	
1	lime, cut into quarters	1

Alternate 4 berries and 3 mint leaves on each of 4 toothpicks or wooden skewers. Lightly bruise berries and mint with the back of a spoon. Fill four 12-oz (375 mL) glasses with ice and place 1 skewer in each glass. Fill with seltzer and squeeze 1 lime wedge into each glass. **Serves 4.**

Citrus Seltzer

4	lemon or lime wedges	4
	Ice cubes	
	Seltzer (soda water)	

Rub the rims of 4 tall glasses with the outside of a lemon or lime wedge. Place 1 wedge and 3 or 4 ice cubes in each glass, then fill glasses with seltzer. **Serves 4.**

Grapefruit or Tangerine Seltzer

8	strips grapefruit or tangerine peel	8
	Ice cubes	
	Seltzer (soda water)	
1	lime, cut into 4 wedges	1

Bruise the colored side of the citrus peel with the back of a spoon, then spear 2 strips on each of 4 toothpicks or wooden skewers. Fill four 12-oz (375 mL) glasses with ice and place 1 skewer in each glass. Fill with seltzer and squeeze 1 lime wedge into each glass. **Serves 4.**

Grapefruitade

3 cups	water	750 mL
½ cup	granulated sugar	125 mL
1 cup	freshly squeezed grapefruit juice	250 mL
1 tbsp	freshly squeezed lemon juice	15 mL
Pinch	salt	Pinch
	Ice cubes	

In a saucepan, heat water and sugar over medium heat until sugar has dissolved; let cool slightly. Pour into a pitcher, cover and chill. Add grapefruit juice, lemon juice and salt; cover and chill. Serve over ice. **Serves 4.**

Lemon-Limeade

4 cups	water	1 L
¾ cup	granulated sugar	175 mL
¼ cup	freshly squeezed lemon juice	50 mL
¼ cup	freshly squeezed lime juice	50 mL
Pinch	salt	Pinch
	Ice cubes	

In a saucepan, heat water and sugar over medium heat until sugar has dissolved; let cool slightly. Pour into a pitcher, cover and chill. Add lemon juice, lime juice and salt; cover and chill. Serve over ice. **Serves 4.**

Spicy Lemonade

Follow preceding recipe, but increase the lemon juice to ½ cup (125 mL), and omit the lime juice. Serve over Spicy Lemon Ice Cubes (page 456). **Serves 4.**

Honey Cranberry Cocktail

3 cups	cranberry juice cocktail	750 mL
1 cup	orange juice	250 mL
¼ cup	honey	50 mL
	Juice of ½ lime	

In a pitcher, combine all ingredients. Cover and chill, or serve over ice. **Serves 4.**

Double Orange Juice

3 cups	freshly squeezed orange juice	750 mL
1 cup	orange juice, frozen solid	250 mL

In a blender, purée juices until smooth. **Serves 4.**

Minted Apple Juice

4 cups	apple juice	1 L
3 tbsp	dried mint	45 mL

In a saucepan, bring apple juice to a boil. Add mint and let cool to room temperature, then strain. Pour into a pitcher, cover and chill. **Serves 4.**

Strawberry Lime Frappé

4 cups	strawberries, hulled	1 L
3 tbsp	granulated sugar	45 mL
	Juice of 1 large lime	
8	ice cubes	8

In a blender, purée all ingredients until smooth. **Serves 4.**

Cherry Raspberry Frappé

2 cups	cherry juice	500 mL
2 cups	raspberry sherbet	500 mL
1 tbsp	freshly squeezed lemon juice	15 mL
4	ice cubes	4

In a blender, purée all ingredients until smooth. **Serves 4.**

Fruit Cooler

2 cups	chopped fruit (any kind)	500 mL
¼ cup	grape juice	50 mL
6	ice cubes	6
2 cups	seltzer (soda water)	500 mL
	Ice cubes	
4	lemon or lime wedges	4

In a blender, purée fruit, juice and ice cubes until smooth. Pour into a pitcher and add seltzer. Serve in 4 tall glasses over ice. Squeeze 1 citrus wedge into each glass. **Serves 4.**

True Brewed Iced Tea

4½ cups	boiling water	1.125 L
6	teabags (or 3 tbsp/45 mL loose tea)	6
2	strips lemon zest (each 1 inch/2.5 cm long)	2
2 tbsp	granulated sugar	25 mL
1 tbsp	freshly squeezed lemon juice	15 mL
	Ice cubes	

Pour boiling water over teabags and lemon zest; let steep for 5 minutes. Strain into a pitcher and stir in sugar and lemon juice. Cover and chill. Serve over ice. **Serves 4.**

Sun-Brewed Iced Tea

6	teabags (or 3 tbsp/45 mL loose tea)	6
2	strips lemon zest (each 1 inch/2.5 cm long)	2
9 cups	water	2.25 L
3 tbsp	granulated sugar	45 mL
1 tbsp	freshly squeezed lemon juice	15 mL
	Ice cubes	

In a large clear jar, combine teabags, lemon zest, water and sugar. Cover and place in the sun for 4 hours. Strain into a pitcher and stir in lemon juice. Cover and chill. Serve over ice. **Serves 8.**

Minted Iced Tea

Follow either of the two preceding recipes, but use 2 herbal mint teabags in place of the lemon zest, replace the lemon juice with lime juice, and garnish glasses with mint sprigs. **Serves 4 or 8.**

Double Iced Tea

8 cups	boiling water	2 L
6	teabags (or 3 tbsp/45 mL loose tea)	6
2	strips lemon zest (each 1 inch/2.5 cm long)	2
2 tbsp	granulated sugar	25 mL
1 tbsp	freshly squeezed lemon juice	15 mL
1 tbsp	honey	15 mL

Pour boiling water over teabags and lemon zest; let steep for 5 minutes. Strain into a pitcher and stir in sugar. Cover and chill. Pour 2 cups (500 mL) of this tea into an ice cube tray and freeze solid. Add lemon juice and honey to the remaining tea. Cover and chill. Serve in glasses over the ice. **Serves 4.**

Spiced Iced Tea

½	orange	½
3	whole cloves	3
½	lemon	½
8	coriander seeds, crushed	8
6	thin slices gingerroot	6
2	orange-spice teabags (or 1 tbsp/15 mL loose tea)	2
2	regular teabags (or 1 tbsp/15 mL loose tea)	2
1	cinnamon stick (1½ inch/4 cm long)	1
4½ cups	boiling water	1.125 L
1 tbsp	honey	15 mL
	Ice cubes	

Stud orange half with cloves and place in a saucepan with lemon half, coriander seeds, ginger, teabags and cinnamon stick. Pour in boiling water and let steep for 5 minutes. Discard teabags and let steep for 5 minutes. Stir in honey. Strain into a pitcher, cover and chill. Serve over ice. **Serves 4.**

Mint Julep Iced Tea

5	mint teabags (or 2 tbsp/25 mL loose tea)	5
1	Chinese black tea teabag (or 2 tsp/10 mL loose tea)	1
4½ cups	boiling water	1.125 L
2 tbsp	granulated sugar	25 mL
8	sprigs fresh mint	8
	Ice cubes	
½ cup	bourbon	125 mL

Place teabags in a heatproof pitcher and pour in boiling water; let steep for 5 minutes. Discard teabags and stir in sugar. Cover and chill. Crush 2 mint sprigs in each of four 12-oz (375 mL) glasses. Fill glasses with ice and add 2 tbsp (25 mL) bourbon to each glass. Fill the rest of the way with tea. **Serves 4.**

Lemonade Iced Tea

4	lemon teabags (or 2 tbsp/25 mL loose tea)	4
2	regular teabags (or 1 tbsp/15 mL loose tea)	2
4½ cups	boiling water	1.125 L
1	can (12 oz/375 mL) frozen lemonade concentrate	1
1½ cups	water	375 mL
	Ice cubes	
	Lemon wedges	

Place teabags in a heatproof pitcher and pour in boiling water; let steep for 5 minutes. Discard teabags, cover and chill. Stir in lemonade concentrate and water. Serve over ice, garnished with lemon wedges. **Serves 4.**

Fruited Iced Tea Punch

4 cups	boiling water	1 L
5	fruit-tea teabags (raspberry, lemon, apple, orange, etc.) (or 2 tbsp/25 mL loose tea)	5
1	ginseng teabag (or 2 tsp/10 mL loose tea)	1
3 cups	grape juice	750 mL
	Ice cubes	

Place teabags in a heatproof pitcher and pour in boiling water; let steep for 5 minutes. Discard teabags, cover and chill. Stir in grape juice. Serve over ice. **Serves 4.**

Zesty Iced Tea

4	lemon or orange teabags (or 2 tbsp/25 mL loose tea)	4
2	regular teabags (or 1 tbsp/15 mL loose tea)	2
	Finely grated zest of 2 lemons	
	Finely grated zest of 2 oranges	
	Finely grated zest of 2 limes	
4½ cups	boiling water	1.125 L
2 tbsp	granulated sugar	25 mL
	Juice of ½ lemon	
	Ice cubes	

Place teabags and citrus zests in a heatproof pitcher and pour in boiling water; let steep for 5 minutes. Discard teabags and stir in sugar. Cover and chill. Stir in lemon juice. Serve over ice. **Serves 4.**

Iced Tea with Spicy Lemon Ice Cubes

2 cups	boiling water	500 mL
3	Lemon Zinger teabags	3
1 tsp	hot pepper flakes	5 mL
	Iced tea (from any recipe above)	

Pour boiling water over teabags and hot pepper flakes; let steep for 5 minutes. Strain, cover and chill. Pour into an ice cube tray and freeze until solid. Meanwhile, prepare iced tea. Serve over the ice cubes. **Serves 4.**

Iced Mocha

4 cups	cold brewed coffee	1 L
1 cup	milk or half-and-half (10%) cream	250 mL
½ cup	chocolate syrup	125 mL
¼ tsp	ground cinnamon	1 mL
	Ice cubes	

In a pitcher, combine coffee, milk, chocolate syrup and cinnamon. Serve over ice. **Serves 4.**

Iced Espresso with Rum

4 cups	brewed espresso	1 L
2 tbsp	granulated sugar	25 mL
	Finely grated zest of 1 orange	
	Ice cubes	
¼ cup	dark rum	50 g

In a saucepan, heat espresso, sugar and orange zest over medium heat until sugar has dissolved. Let cool, then strain. Fill each of four 12-oz (375 mL) glasses with ice. Add 1 tbsp (15 mL) rum to each glass and fill with espresso. **Serves 4.**

Iced Spiked Cocoa

¾ cup	boiling water	175 mL
6 tbsp	unsweetened cocoa powder, sifted	90 mL
6 tbsp	granulated sugar	90 mL
1½ tbsp	instant coffee granules	22 mL
1	cinnamon stick (1 inch/2.5 cm long)	1
1½ cups	cold milk	375 mL
¾ cup	brandy or cognac	175 mL
1½ tsp	vanilla	7 mL
1¼ cups	whipping (35%) cream	300 mL
	Ground cinnamon	

In a heatproof pitcher, combine boiling water, cocoa, sugar, coffee granules and cinnamon stick; let cool. Discard cinnamon stick, cover and chill. Stir in milk, brandy and vanilla. In a bowl, whip cream until soft peaks form; stir into cocoa. Serve sprinkled with ground cinnamon. **Serves 4.**

Banana Berry Kefir

2	bananas, sliced	2
1 cup	low-fat vanilla-flavored yogurt	250 mL
1 cup	low-fat raspberry-flavored yogurt	250 mL
1 cup	apple-raspberry juice	250 mL
1 tbsp	honey	15 mL

In a blender, purée all ingredients until smooth. Pour into a pitcher, cover and chill. **Serves 4.**

Super-Protein Health Shake

2	bananas, sliced	2
2 cups	low-fat milk	500 mL
1 cup	low-fat vanilla-flavored yogurt	250 mL
¼ cup	frozen orange juice concentrate	50 mL
¼ cup	skim milk powder	50 mL
2	egg whites	2
1 tbsp	granulated sugar	15 mL

In a blender, purée bananas, milk, yogurt, orange juice concentrate and milk powder until smooth. In a bowl, beat egg whites and sugar until soft peaks form; fold into fruit mixture. **Serves 4.** *(If you are concerned about the food safety of raw egg whites, you can replace them with ¼ cup/50 mL pasteurized liquid egg whites.)*

Warm White Chocolate Egg Nog

4 cups	milk	1 L
2	egg yolks, lightly beaten	2
4 oz	white chocolate, finely chopped	125 g
Pinch	ground nutmeg	Pinch

In a saucepan, heat milk over medium heat until bubbling around the edges. Stir very slowly into egg yolks. Return to the saucepan and cook over low heat, stirring constantly, for 3 minutes. Whisk in white chocolate and nutmeg. Serve warm. **Serves 4.**

Mulled Cider

12	dates, chopped	12
12	dried apricots, chopped	12
2	whole cloves	2
1	cinnamon stick (1½ inch/4 cm long)	1
1	piece gingerroot (1 inch/2.5 cm long)	1
8 cups	unsweetened apple cider	2 L
½ cup	raisins	125 mL
¼ cup	chopped dried apple	50 mL
Pinch	ground nutmeg	Pinch
	Finely grated zest and juice of 1 lemon	
	Cinnamon sticks, for garnish	

In a large saucepan, bring dates, apricots, cloves, cinnamon stick, ginger, apple cider, raisins, apple, nutmeg, lemon zest and lemon juice to a simmer over medium heat. Remove from heat and let stand for 15 minutes. Serve in mugs, each garnished with 1 cinnamon stick. **Serves 10.**

Liquid Chocolate Bars

3½ cups	milk (not fat-free)	875 mL
12 oz	semisweet chocolate, finely chopped	375 g
¼ cup	sweetened whipped cream	50 mL

In a large, heavy saucepan, bring milk to a simmer over medium heat. Remove from heat and stir in chocolate until melted. Pour into 4 mugs and top each with 1 tbsp (15 mL) whipped cream. **Serves 4.**

Cappuccino Cocoa

4 cups	milk (not fat-free)	1 L
¼ cup	Dutch-process cocoa powder	50 mL
¼ cup	granulated sugar	50 mL
3 tbsp	instant espresso powder	45 mL
1	cinnamon stick (1½ inch/4 cm long)	1
	Ground cinnamon	

In a saucepan, combine milk, cocoa, sugar, espresso powder and cinnamon stick; bring to a simmer over medium heat. Discard cinnamon stick, pour into cups and sprinkle with ground cinnamon. **Serves 4.**

Hot Buttered Rum

¼ cup	packed light brown sugar	50 mL
1 cup	boiling water	250 mL
1 cup	dark rum	250 mL
2 tbsp	butter, cut into small pieces	25 mL
1 tsp	vanilla	5 mL

Dissolve brown sugar in boiling water. Stir in rum, butter and vanilla until butter melts. **Serves 4.**

Flaming Warm Spiced Wine

1	bottle (750 mL) dry red wine	1
2	whole cloves	2
2	strips orange zest	2
2	strips lemon zest	2
1	cinnamon stick (1½ inch/4 cm long)	1
2 tbsp	granulated sugar	25 mL

In a large saucepan, heat all ingredients to a simmer over medium heat. Ignite carefully and let flames die out. **Serves 4.**

Modern-Day Mead

½ cup	water	125 mL
¼ cup	honey	50 mL
1 cup	brandy	250 mL

In a small saucepan, bring water and honey to a boil over medium heat; boil for 2 minutes. Stir in brandy. **Serves 4.**

Café Brûlot Slush

3 cups	water	750 mL
1½ cups	granulated sugar	375 mL
1	cinnamon stick (1½ inch/4 cm long)	1
½ cup	instant coffee granules	125 mL
Pinch	ground cloves	Pinch
	Finely grated zest of 1 large orange	
¼ cup	brandy	50 mL

In a saucepan, bring water and sugar to a boil. Remove from heat and add cinnamon stick, coffee granules, cloves and orange zest; let steep for 30 minutes. Strain into an 8-inch (2 L) square baking pan and freeze until solid. Cut into small cubes and place in a food processor. Add brandy and purée until slushy. **Serves 4.**

Mint Julep Slush

2 tbsp	dried mint	25 mL
1¾ cups	boiling water	425 mL
1 cup	cooled Simple Syrup (see recipe, page 23)	250 mL
1¼ cups	bourbon	300 mL
	Fresh mint sprigs	

Add dried mint to boiling water and let cool. Strain into an 8-inch (2 L) square baking pan, stir in Simple Syrup and freeze until solid. Cut into cubes and place in a food processor. Add bourbon and purée until slushy. Serve garnished with fresh mint sprigs. **Serves 4.**

Kahlúa and Cream Shake

2 cups	coffee ice cream, softened	500 mL
1 cup	milk	250 mL
½ cup	Kahlúa or other coffee-flavored liqueur	125 mL
½ tsp	vanilla	2 mL
½ cup	whipping (35%) cream	125 mL
2 tbsp	finely ground espresso beans (optional)	25 mL

In a pitcher, combine ice cream, milk, Kahlúa and vanilla. In a small bowl, whip cream until soft peaks form; fold into ice cream mixture. Pour into 4 chilled glasses and sprinkle with espresso, if desired. **Serves 4.**

Liquid Creamsicle

2 cups	vanilla ice cream, softened	500 mL
¾ cup	orange juice	175 mL
½ cup	orange-flavored liqueur (such as Triple Sec)	125 mL
½ cup	whipping (35%) cream	125 mL
2 tbsp	finely grated orange zest (optional)	25 mL

In a pitcher, combine ice cream, orange juice and liqueur. In a small bowl, whip cream until soft peaks form; fold into ice cream mixture. Pour into 4 chilled glasses and sprinkle with orange zest, if desired. **Serves 4.**

Sparkling Kir Punch

½ cup	crème de cassis	125 mL
¼ cup	cooled Simple Syrup (see recipe, page 23)	50 mL
	Juice of 1 lime	
1	bottle (750 mL) dry white wine (such as chardonnay)	1
2 cups	seltzer (soda water)	500 mL

In a pitcher, combine crème de cassis, Simple Syrup and lime juice. Stir in wine and seltzer, cover and chill. **Serves 4.**

Berry Wine Punch

1	bottle (750 mL) dry white wine (such as chardonnay)	1
1 cup	fresh raspberries	250 mL
1 cup	strawberries, hulled and halved	250 mL
⅓ cup	confectioner's (icing) sugar	75 mL
¼ cup	Madeira	50 mL

In a pitcher, combine all ingredients. **Serves 4.**

"Champagne" with Grapefruit Ice

1 cup	freshly squeezed grapefruit juice	250 mL
1 cup	cooled Simple Syrup (see recipe, page 23)	250 mL
Pinch	salt	Pinch
	Juice of ½ lemon	
1	bottle (750 mL) chilled inexpensive sparkling wine	1

Combine grapefruit juice, Simple Syrup, salt and lemon juice. Freeze until solid, stirring every hour. Scoop into balls and divide among 4 champagne glasses. Pour sparkling wine over top. **Serves 4.**

Spicy Tomato Juice

8 cups	chilled tomato juice or vegetable juice (such as V8)	2 L
1 tbsp	Worcestershire sauce	15 mL
	Spicy Lemon Ice Cubes (see recipe, page 456)	

Combine tomato juice and Worcestershire sauce. Pour over flavored ice cubes. **Serves 4.**

Super Vegetable Juice Cocktail

4 cups	vegetable juice (such as V8)	1 L
6	whole black peppercorns	6
2	Lemon Zinger teabags	2
1	dried chili pepper	1
1 tsp	Worcestershire sauce	5 mL

In a microwave-safe glass pitcher, combine all ingredients. Cover with microwave-safe plastic wrap and microwave on High for 4 minutes. Discard teabags and chili pepper, cover and chill. **Serves 6.**

Shrimp Bloody Marys

1½ cups	bottled clam juice	375 mL
10	whole black peppercorns	10
1 tsp	ground celery seeds	5 mL
8	large shrimp	8
5 cups	tomato juice	1.25 L
1 tbsp	finely chopped celery leaves	15 mL
1 tbsp	soy sauce	15 mL
1 tbsp	prepared horseradish	15 mL
2 tsp	finely chopped fresh dill	10 mL
2 tsp	hot pepper sauce (such as Tabasco)	10 mL
	Ice cubes	
4 oz	vodka (optional)	125 mL

In a saucepan, bring clam juice, peppercorns and celery seeds to a boil over medium heat. Add shrimp and return to a boil. Remove shrimp, cool under cold water and peel. Add shrimp peels to the pan and simmer for 5 minutes; let cool. Meanwhile, devein shrimp and set aside. Strain clam juice into a pitcher and stir in tomato juice, celery leaves, soy sauce, horseradish, dill and hot pepper sauce. Fill 4 tall chilled glasses with ice. Add 1 oz (30 g) vodka per glass, if desired, and pour in clam juice mixture. Set 2 shrimp on the rim of each glass, with their tails facing outward. **Serves 4.**

Gazpacho Cooler

3	ice cubes	3
2	tomatoes, cored and cut into chunks	2
1	stalk celery, sliced	1
1	small clove garlic	1
½	cucumber, peeled and cut into chunks	½
⅓	small hot chili pepper, seeded	⅓
¼	red bell pepper, cut into chunks	¼
⅓ cup	coarsely chopped onion	75 mL
2 tbsp	red wine vinegar	25 mL
⅔ cup	water	150 mL
	Salt and freshly ground black pepper to taste	

In a food processor or blender, in batches if necessary, process ice cubes, tomatoes, celery, garlic, cucumber, chili pepper, red pepper, onion and vinegar until pulpy. Pour into a pitcher and stir in water, salt and pepper. **Serves 4.**

Spicy Tomato Slush

3½ cups	spicy tomato juice or vegetable juice (such as V8), divided	875 mL
½ cup	cooled Simple Syrup (see recipe, page 23)	125 mL
	Juice of 1 lime	

Combine 3 cups (750 mL) of the tomato juice, Simple Syrup and lime juice. Freeze until solid. Cut into small cubes and place in a food processor or blender. Add the remaining tomato juice and purée until slushy. **Serves 4.**

PART 4

Cooking for Special Occasions

Chapter 42

Entertaining
Recipes That Let You Go to Your Own Party

Roasted Garlic Purée 464
Roasted Pepper Dip 464
Baba Ghanoush 465
Eggplant Rillettes 465
Vegetable Pâté Niçoise 465
Fennel Pâté 465
Garden Pâté 465
Quick Chopped Chicken Liver 466
Lemon Cheese 466
Garlic Cheese 466
Angel-of-Death Cheese 466
Marinated Mozzarella 466
Anise Tea Eggs 466
Marinated Roasted Peppers
and Olives 466
Marinated Garlic Mushrooms 466
Sausage-Stuffed Mushrooms 467
Spinach-Stuffed Mushroom Caps 467
Blue Cheese Grapes 467
Gingered Carrots with
Hot Pepper Vinaigrette 467
Roasted Pepper Tortellini Salad 467
Tyropites 468
Cheese Pockets 468
Niçoise Pizzas 468
Puff Pastry Mini Pizzas 468
Cheese Straws 468
Creole Crab Mini Turnovers 469

Liver and Bacon Mini Turnovers 469
Apple Mincemeat Mini Turnovers 469
Lemon Pear Mini Turnovers 469
Chicken Wellington 470
Spicy Molasses Chicken Wings 470
Garlic Black Bean Chicken Wings 470
Chicken Tandoori Brochettes 470
Turkey Kabobs Glazed
with Jalapeño Jelly 470
Charred Rare Beef with
Jalapeño Salsa 471
Charred Rare Lamb
with Roasted Garlic 471
Escabèche of Soft-Shell Crab 471
Balsamic Shrimp 471
Fried Herbed Shrimp 471
Pepper Peanut Shrimp 472
Lemon-Soy Smoked Shrimp 472
Shrimp with Smoked Salmon 472
Chilled Salmon Soufflé 472
Chilled Crab and Chive Soufflé 472
Spiked Smoked Salmon and
Gruyère Cheesecake 472
Blue Cheese Apple Cheesecake 473
Eight-Hour Brandy Cheesecake 473
Avocado Ice Cream 473
Chocolate Coronary 474
Crème Caramel 474

Almost everyone who loves to cook eventually gets pressured, either by external or inner forces, into showing off with a party. Although this can begin innocently enough as a way of sharing talents and good feelings with friends, it can easily become overwhelming. No one can pinpoint the exact moment at which an evening of gracious entertaining becomes a sentence of dinner with no parole, but it has happened to all of us. So we offer the following advice to help you avoid the pitfalls.

Start with a menu and a detailed cooking plan. Plan a combination of types of foods. Serve some items cold and others heated. Think about what can be cooked ahead and what ingredients will be hard to purchase or store well. Choose mainly tried and true dishes that are quick and easy, and if you want to make a grand impression, go for it once in the meal — and once only — rather than trying for fireworks at every course.

Don't try to do everything yourself. Unless you have a staff of four in your kitchen, you will probably need some outside help, even for a dinner party with as few as, say, a dozen people. Help can be as simple as having guests bring a dish or deciding that you will buy the dessert rather than prepare it yourself.

But if you insist on cooking everything from scratch with your own two hands, and you want to be able to attend the party as well, it is essential that you prepare as much of the food ahead of time as possible. Freeze whatever you can, and plan dishes that do not require last-minute fussing.

Hors d'oeuvres or appetizers wrapped in commercially prepared frozen puff pastry are infinitely elegant and keep for weeks in the freezer. Chilled soufflés and soups can be made a day ahead and are ready for service without so much as reheating. Pâtés keep for weeks and provide a score or more servings, and marinated salads offer brilliant colors and piquant flavors that only get better after a day in the refrigerator.

About these recipes . . .

The following 50 recipes are for hors d'oeuvres, appetizers and desserts that will be virtually ready to go long before the party begins, requiring no more than last-minute cooking or reheating. Many are written for a large number of servings and can be multiplied or divided to fit your guest count.

All of these foods can be refrigerated, and most can be frozen without ill effect, but to ensure good results, wrap them tightly in plastic wrap and then in foil. The food will freeze more rapidly if you're careful not to pack too many pieces together. For soft foods, freeze solid before wrapping to keep the food from becoming crushed.

You'll find these recipes a notch more elegant than most others in this book, making them suitable for parties or company dinners, but they are just as easy and no more time-consuming.

Roasted Garlic Purée

6	heads garlic	6
¼ cup	water	50 mL
2 tbsp	extra-virgin olive oil	25 mL
	Additional extra-virgin olive oil, as needed	
	Salt and freshly ground black pepper to taste	

Preheat oven to 375°F (190°C). Cut the pointed ends from the garlic heads, exposing the tops of the cloves. Place garlic heads and water in a baking dish large enough to hold garlic heads snugly. Drizzle with 2 tbsp (25 mL) oil and sprinkle with salt and pepper. Bake for 40 minutes. Let cool slightly, then gently squeeze cloves from their peels into the work bowl of a food processor or blender. Add pan juices and purée, adding oil as needed to make it a dip consistency. Season with salt and pepper. **Makes about 1½ cups (375 mL).** *Use as a dip for vegetables or poached shellfish, or as a bread spread.*

Roasted Pepper Dip

3	large roasted red peppers (see page 11), quartered	3
2 tbsp	mayonnaise	25 mL
1 tbsp	extra-virgin olive oil	15 mL
	Salt and freshly ground black pepper to taste	

In a food processor, chop peppers. Add mayonnaise, oil, salt and pepper; purée. **Makes about 2½ cups (625 mL).** *Store in an airtight container in the refrigerator for up to 4 days. Use as dip with vegetables or poached shellfish.*

Baba Ghanoush

2	eggplants	2
1	clove garlic, minced	1
2 tbsp	olive oil	25 mL
	Juice of ½ lemon	

Preheat oven to 400°F (200°C). Bake eggplants for 45 minutes, until skin blackens and they are very soft. Let cool for 10 minutes, then halve lengthwise and scoop out flesh into a bowl. Mash flesh with garlic, oil and lemon juice. **Makes about 3 cups (750 mL).** *Store in an airtight container in the refrigerator for up to 4 days. Use as dip with vegetables or bread.*

Eggplant Rillettes

Follow preceding recipe, but replace the oil with mayonnaise, add 6 drained canned anchovy fillets, minced, and 1 tbsp (15 mL) drained small capers with the mayonnaise, and double the amount of lemon juice. **Makes 3 cups (750 mL).** *Store in an airtight container in the refrigerator for up to 4 days. Serve as a dip or cracker spread.*

Vegetable Pâté Niçoise

	Vegetable cooking spray	
3 tbsp	extra-virgin olive oil	45 mL
½ cup	chopped onion	125 mL
2	cloves garlic, minced	2
1½	packages (each 10 oz/300 g) frozen chopped spinach, thawed	1½
2 tbsp	all-purpose flour	25 mL
1 cup	milk (not fat-free)	250 mL
10	large or extra-large egg yolks	10
½ cup	ricotta cheese (preferably whole-milk)	125 mL
½ cup	freshly grated Parmesan cheese	125 mL
½ tsp	brandy	2 mL
	Salt and freshly ground black pepper to taste	
1 cup	drained rinsed canned chickpeas	250 mL
1 cup	diced roasted red bell pepper (see page 11)	250 mL
1½ cups	chopped pitted black olives	375 mL
5	canned artichoke bottoms, drained	3
	Warm Tomato Vinaigrette (see recipe, page 63)	

Preheat oven to 375°F (190°C). Line a greased 9- by 5-inch (2 L) loaf pan with parchment paper and coat with cooking spray. In a large skillet, heat oil over medium-high heat. Sauté onion until tender. Add garlic and spinach; sauté until spinach is dry. Stir in flour, then milk; cook until thickened. Remove from heat and beat in egg yolks, ricotta, Parmesan, brandy, salt and pepper. In prepared pan, alternate 5 layers of spinach mixture with a layer each of chickpeas, roasted pepper, olives and artichoke bottoms. Top with greased parchment paper and foil, place in a water bath (see page 12) and bake for 1½ hours. Let cool in pan, then unmold. Cover and refrigerate for at least 2 hours, until chilled, or for up to 1 week. Serve in slices with Warm Tomato Vinaigrette. **Serves 12.**

Fennel Pâté

Follow preceding recipe, but substitute 1 fennel bulb (including leaves), finely chopped, for half the spinach, and add 1 tbsp (15 mL) dried herbes de Provence with the flour. **Serves 12.**

Garden Pâté

2 tbsp	butter	25 mL
1 cup	sliced mushrooms	250 mL
¼ cup	chopped onion	50 mL
1	package (10 oz/300 g) frozen chopped spinach, thawed	1
1 cup	blanched broccoli florets	250 mL
½ cup	seasoned dry bread crumbs	125 mL
½ cup	all-purpose flour	125 mL
½ cup	cottage cheese	125 mL
¼ cup	dry vermouth	50 mL
2 tsp	hot pepper sauce (such as Tabasco)	10 mL
	Salt and freshly ground black pepper to taste	
2 cups	diced carrots, boiled until tender	500 mL

Preheat oven to 375°F (190°C). In a large skillet, melt butter over medium-high heat. Sauté mushrooms and onion until tender. Add spinach and sauté until dry. Transfer to a food processor and add broccoli, bread crumbs, flour, cottage cheese, vermouth, hot pepper sauce, salt and pepper. Stir in carrots. Spoon into a loaf pan prepared as described in Vegetable Pâté Niçoise (left), and bake and chill as described in the same recipe. **Serves 8.**

Quick Chopped Chicken Liver

2	large onions, chopped	2
1/3 cup	rendered chicken fat	75 mL
1 lb	chicken livers, trimmed	500 g
Pinch	dried thyme	Pinch
2	hard-cooked eggs, chopped	2
	Salt and freshly ground black pepper to taste	
	Toasts (any type)	

In a nonstick skillet, cook onions, covered, over low heat, stirring occasionally, until very soft and lightly browned. Add chicken fat and sauté until onions are well browned. Add chicken livers and thyme; sauté until firm. Transfer to a food processor or meat grinder and grind until finely chopped but not puréed. Stir in eggs, salt and pepper. Cover and refrigerate for about 1 hour, until chilled. Serve with toasts. **Serves 6 to 8.**

Lemon Cheese

8 oz	farmer's cheese or cream cheese, softened	250 g
1 tbsp	minced lemon zest, bruised	15 mL
1 tbsp	freshly squeezed lemon juice	15 mL
1 tsp	granulated sugar	5 mL

Combine all ingredients and shape into a dome on a small plate. **Serves 4 to 6.** *Store in an airtight container in the refrigerator for up to 3 days. Serve with fresh bread or crackers.*

Garlic Cheese

Follow preceding recipe, but replace the lemon juice with 1 tsp (5 mL) wine vinegar, and add 3 cloves garlic, minced, and 1 tsp (5 mL) coarsely ground black pepper with the vinegar. **Serves 4 to 6.**

Angel-of-Death Cheese

Follow recipe for Lemon Cheese (above), but replace the lemon juice with 1 tsp (5 mL) red wine vinegar, and add 6 cloves garlic, minced, and 2 tsp (10 mL) dried sage. Sprinkle surface of cheese with 2 tbsp (25 mL) cracked black pepper. **Serves 4 to 6.**

Marinated Mozzarella

3	cloves garlic, minced	3
1/2 cup	extra-virgin olive oil	125 mL
1/4 cup	red wine vinegar	50 mL
2 tbsp	chopped fresh basil	25 mL
	Salt and freshly ground black pepper to taste	
1 lb	mozzarella cheese, sliced	500 g
	French bread	

Combine garlic, oil, vinegar, basil, salt and pepper. Add mozzarella and toss to coat. Cover and refrigerate for at least 1 hour, until chilled, or for up to 1 week. Serve with French bread. **Serves 8.**

Anise Tea Eggs

6	large or extra-large eggs	6
2	oolong teabags (or 1 tbsp/15 mL loose tea)	2
1/4 cup	soy sauce	50 mL
2 tbsp	anise seeds (or 4 whole star anise)	25 mL
	Dipping Sauce for Potstickers (see recipe, page 249)	

Place eggs and enough water to cover (about 8 cups/2 L) in a large saucepan. Bring to a simmer over medium heat and simmer for 10 minutes; drain and let cool completely. Crack shells all around, without removing them, by tapping them with the back of a spoon or rolling them gently over a countertop. Return to saucepan, cover with cold water, and add teabags, soy sauce and anise seeds. Cover and simmer for 1 hour; let cool. Transfer, with cooking liquid, to a large jar and store in the refrigerator for at least 2 days or for up to 1 week. Shortly before serving, peel and cut into quarters. Serve with dipping sauce. **Makes 24.**

Marinated Roasted Peppers and Olives

2	cloves garlic, minced	2
1/3 cup	olive oil	75 mL
2 tbsp	red wine vinegar	25 mL
1/2 tsp	hot pepper flakes	2 mL
	Salt and freshly ground black pepper to taste	
6	roasted bell peppers (see page 11), sliced	6
1 cup	oil-cured black olives	250 mL

Combine garlic, oil, vinegar, hot pepper flakes, salt and black pepper. Stir in roasted pepper slices and olives. Cover and refrigerate for at least 1 hour, until chilled, or for up to 4 days. **Serves 12.**

Marinated Garlic Mushrooms

1/3 cup	extra-virgin olive oil, divided	75 mL
2	cloves garlic, minced	2
1 lb	small mushrooms, cleaned	500 g
Pinch	cayenne pepper	Pinch
	Grated zest and juice of 1 lemon	

| | Salt and freshly ground black pepper to taste | |
| 2 tbsp | chopped fresh Italian (flat-leaf) parsley | 25 mL |

In a large skillet, heat all but 1 tbsp (15 mL) of the oil over medium-high heat. Sauté garlic and mushrooms until tender. Transfer to a bowl and toss with the remaining oil, cayenne, lemon zest, lemon juice, salt and black pepper. Cover and refrigerate for at least 1 hour, until chilled, or for up to 1 week. Toss with parsley. **Serves 8.**

Sausage-Stuffed Mushrooms

24	large mushrooms	24
2 tbsp	olive oil	25 mL
2	cloves garlic, minced	2
6 oz	sausage (bulk, or with casings removed)	175 g
2 tbsp	chopped green onion	25 mL
¾ cup	dry bread crumbs	175 mL
3 tbsp	freshly grated Parmesan cheese	45 mL

Preheat oven to 400°F (200°C). Separate mushroom caps and stems, and chop stems. In a large skillet, heat oil over medium-high heat. Sauté mushroom caps until browned; remove with a slotted spoon to a baking sheet. Add mushroom stems, garlic, sausage and green onion to the pan and sauté until mushrooms and sausage are browned. Remove from heat and stir in bread crumbs and Parmesan. Mound mixture into mushroom caps. Bake for 15 minutes, or until browned and bubbly. (Can be stored in an airtight container in the refrigerator for up to 3 days before baking. Add 5 minutes to the baking time.) **Serves 12.**

Spinach-Stuffed Mushroom Caps

Follow preceding recipe, but omit the sausage, and add 1 package (10 oz/300 g) frozen chopped spinach, thawed and squeezed dry, and ½ tsp (2 mL) Dijon mustard to the sautéed mushroom stems. After assembly, these can be frozen for several weeks. Thaw in the refrigerator before cooking. **Serves 12.**

Blue Cheese Grapes

6 oz	blue cheese	175 g
6 oz	cream cheese, softened	175 g
Dash	hot pepper sauce (such as Tabasco)	Dash
24	seedless grapes	24
1¾ cups	finely chopped toasted walnuts	425 mL

Combine blue cheese, cream cheese and hot pepper sauce. Mold cheese mixture around grapes, and roll grapes in walnuts. (Can be stored in the refrigerator

for 1 day before dredging in nuts. Roll in nuts no more than 4 hours before serving.) Arrange like a bunch of grapes on a serving tray. **Serves 12.**

Gingered Carrots with Hot Pepper Vinaigrette

2 lbs	carrots, spiral-cut (see page 9)	1 kg
1	clove garlic, minced	1
¼ cup	canola oil	50 mL
2 tbsp	dark sesame oil	25 mL
2 tbsp	red wine vinegar	25 mL
2 tsp	minced gingerroot	10 mL
1 tsp	hot pepper flakes	5 mL
	Juice of 1 lemon	
	Salt and freshly ground black pepper to taste	
2 tbsp	chopped fresh chives	25 mL

In a large pot of boiling salted water, cook carrots for 4 minutes, until barely tender; drain. Meanwhile, combine garlic, canola oil, sesame oil, vinegar, ginger, hot pepper flakes, lemon juice, salt and black pepper. Add carrots and toss to coat. Cover and refrigerate for at least 1 hour, until chilled, or for up to 1 week. Toss with chives. **Serves 12.**

Roasted Pepper Tortellini Salad

24	oil-cured black olives, pitted and quartered	24
4	roasted red bell peppers (see page 11), julienned	4
1	clove garlic, minced	1
½	red onion, chopped	½
2 cups	cheese tortellini, cooked	500 mL
¼ cup	extra-virgin olive oil	50 mL
3 tbsp	red wine vinegar	45 mL
	Salt and freshly ground black pepper to taste	
¼ cup	chopped fresh basil	50 mL

Combine olives, roasted peppers, garlic, onion, tortellini, oil, vinegar, salt and pepper. Cover and refrigerate for at least 1 hour, until chilled, or for up to 3 days. Toss with basil. **Serves 8.**

Tyropites

3 tbsp	extra-virgin olive oil	45 mL
½ cup	chopped onion	125 mL
3	cloves garlic, minced	3
1	package (10 oz/300 g) frozen chopped spinach, thawed	1
4 oz	feta cheese, crumbled	125 g
4 oz	cream cheese, softened	125 g
	Salt and freshly ground black pepper to taste	
8	sheets phyllo dough, each cut crosswise into 4 strips	8
	Clarified butter (see page 16), melted	

Preheat oven to 400°F (200°C). In a large skillet, heat oil over medium-high heat. Sauté onion and garlic until tender. Add spinach and sauté until dry. Remove from heat and stir in feta, cream cheese, salt and pepper; let cool. One at a time, brush phyllo strips with a thin film of clarified butter, place about 1 tbsp (15 mL) cheese mixture at the end of the strip, and fold into a triangle, as you would fold a flag. Brush with more clarified butter. Repeat until all ingredients have been used. Place on a baking sheet and bake until golden brown, about 15 minutes. (Can be stored in an airtight container in the refrigerator for up to 24 hours before baking, or in the freezer for up to 1 month. If refrigerated or thawed, add 5 minutes to the baking time; if frozen, add 8 to 10 minutes to the baking time.) **Makes 32.**

Cheese Pockets

Follow preceding recipe, but replace the spinach mixture with this cheese mixture: Combine 2 eggs, 1 small clove garlic, minced, 8 oz (250 g) farmer's cheese, 1 cup (250 mL) crumbled feta cheese, 2 tbsp (25 mL) chopped fresh dill, and salt and pepper to taste. **Makes 32.**

Niçoise Pizzas

2	cloves garlic, minced	2
1 cup	finely chopped pitted black olives	250 mL
1 tbsp	minced drained canned anchovies	15 mL
2 tsp	drained capers, finely chopped	10 mL
	Freshly ground black pepper to taste	
	Extra-virgin olive oil	
1	baguette, cut into 24 slices	1
24	slices plum (Roma) tomato	24
1 cup	shredded mozzarella cheese	250 mL

Preheat oven to 400°F (200°C). Combine garlic, olives, anchovies, capers and pepper. Add enough olive oil to make a smooth paste. (The paste can be stored in the refrigerator for up to 1 week.) Brush each baguette slice with a thin film of oil and bake for about 8 minutes, or until lightly toasted. (The toast can be stored at room temperature for up to 2 days.) Preheat broiler. Spread paste on toast and top each with 1 tomato slice and 2 tsp (10 mL) mozzarella. Broil until cheese melts. **Serves 12.**

Puff Pastry Mini Pizzas

8 oz	frozen puff pastry, thawed	250 g
⅓ cup	freshly grated Parmesan cheese	75 mL
1½ cups	tomato pasta sauce	375 mL
4 oz	mushrooms, sliced and sautéed	125 g
1	red or yellow bell pepper, finely diced	1
2 cups	shredded mozzarella cheese	500 mL
1 tbsp	olive oil	15 mL

If necessary, roll puff pastry out to a 12-inch (30 cm) square. Sprinkle with Parmesan, top with sauce, mushrooms, bell pepper and mozzarella, and drizzle with oil. Punch out 16 mini-pizzas with a 3-inch (7.5 cm) cutter and place on a baking sheet. Freeze until solid. (Can be wrapped well and stored in the freezer for up to 3 weeks.) Bake from frozen at 400°F (200°C) for 15 to 20 minutes, or until bubbly and crisp. **Makes 16.**

Cheese Straws

8 oz	frozen puff pastry, thawed	250 g
1	extra-large egg yolk, beaten with 1 tbsp (15 mL) water	1
1 cup	freshly grated Parmesan cheese	250 mL
½ cup	finely shredded Cheddar cheese	125 mL
1 tsp	cayenne pepper	5 mL
1 tsp	paprika	5 mL

If necessary, roll puff pastry out to a 12-inch (30 cm) square; brush both sides with egg wash. Combine Parmesan, Cheddar, cayenne and paprika; press mixture into both sides of pastry. Cut pastry in half, then cut into strips ½ inch (1 cm) wide and 6 inches (15 cm) long. Twist each strip 4 times and place on a dry baking sheet, pressing ends down to hold the twist in place. Cover and refrigerate for at least 1 hour or for up to 24 hours, or wrap well and freeze for up to 3 weeks (thaw in the refrigerator before baking). Preheat oven to 400°F (200°C). Bake for 15 minutes, until puffed and browned. **Makes 24.**

Creole Crab Mini Turnovers

¼ cup	whipping (35%) cream	50 mL
2 tsp	hot pepper sauce (such as Tabasco)	10 mL
1 tsp	cornstarch	5 mL
1 tbsp	butter	15 mL
1	green onion, minced	1
8 oz	backfin (lump) crabmeat, shells picked out	250 g
	Salt and freshly ground black pepper to taste	
8 oz	frozen puff pastry, thawed	250 g
1	egg yolk, beaten with 1 tbsp (15 mL) water	1

In a small bowl, combine cream, hot pepper sauce and cornstarch; set aside. In a skillet, melt butter over medium-high heat. Sauté green onion until tender. Add cream mixture and crabmeat; reduce heat and simmer until lightly thickened. Season with salt and pepper; let cool. Use crab mixture and puff pastry to assemble mini turnovers (see page 12). Cover and refrigerate for at least 1 hour or for up to 24 hours, or wrap well and freeze for up to 3 weeks (thaw in the refrigerator before baking). Preheat oven to 400°F (200°C). Brush turnovers with egg wash and bake for 10 minutes, until puffed and brown. **Makes 16.**

Liver and Bacon Mini Turnovers

2	slices bacon	2
2 tbsp	minced onion	25 mL
3	chicken livers, split and trimmed	3
2 tbsp	bourbon	25 mL
8 oz	frozen puff pastry, thawed	250 g
1	egg yolk, beaten with 1 tbsp (15 mL) water	1

In a skillet, over medium-high heat, cook bacon until crisp; remove to a plate, blot dry and crumble. Add onion to the fat in the pan and sauté until slightly browned. Add chicken livers and cook until browned on all sides. Add bourbon and boil until most of the liquid has evaporated. Remove and finely chop livers, then return livers and bacon to the pan; let cool. Use liver mixture and puff pastry to assemble mini turnovers (see page 12). Cover and refrigerate for at least 1 hour or for up to 24 hours, or wrap well and freeze for up to 3 weeks (thaw in the refrigerator before baking). Preheat oven to 400°F (200°C). Brush turnovers with egg wash and bake for 10 minutes, until puffed and brown. **Makes 16.**

Apple Mincemeat Mini Turnovers

1 tbsp	unsalted butter	15 mL
1	large apple, peeled and finely diced	1
½ cup	granulated sugar	125 mL
¾ cup	prepared mincemeat	175 mL
1 tbsp	freshly squeezed lemon juice	15 mL
1 tsp	vanilla	5 mL
8 oz	frozen puff pastry, thawed	250 g
1	egg yolk, beaten with 1 tbsp (15 mL) water	1

In a skillet, melt butter over medium heat. Sauté apple and sugar until apple is tender. Add mincemeat and sauté until mixture is dry. Stir in lemon juice and vanilla; let cool. Use apple mixture and puff pastry to assemble mini turnovers (see page 12). Cover and refrigerate for at least 1 hour or for up to 24 hours, or wrap well and freeze for up to 3 weeks (thaw in the refrigerator before baking). Preheat oven to 400°F (200°C). Brush turnovers with egg wash and bake for 20 to 25 minutes, until puffed and brown. **Makes 16.**

Lemon Pear Mini Turnovers

1½ tsp	cornstarch	7 mL
1 tbsp	water	15 mL
1½ tsp	vanilla	7 mL
2 tbsp	unsalted butter	25 mL
2	pears, peeled and diced	2
2 tbsp	granulated sugar	25 mL
	Finely grated zest and juice of ½ lemon	
8 oz	frozen puff pastry, thawed	250 g
1	egg yolk, beaten with 1 tbsp (15 mL) water	1

Dissolve cornstarch in water and vanilla; set aside. In a large skillet, melt butter over medium-high heat. Sauté pears, sugar, lemon zest and lemon juice until pears are tender. Stir cornstarch mixture and add to skillet; simmer until thickened, about 1 minute. Let cool completely. Use pear mixture and puff pastry to assemble mini turnovers (see page 12). Cover and refrigerate for at least 1 hour or for up to 24 hours, or wrap well and freeze for up to 3 weeks (thaw in the refrigerator before baking). Preheat oven to 400°F (200°C). Brush turnovers with egg wash and bake for 20 to 25 minutes, until puffed and brown. **Makes 16.**

Chicken Wellington

4	boneless skinless chicken breasts	4
	Salt and freshly ground black pepper to taste	
2 tbsp	olive oil	25 mL
8	fresh basil leaves	8
1	roasted red bell pepper (see page 11), quartered	1
4	slices prosciutto	4
1 lb	frozen puff pastry, thawed	500 g
1	egg yolk, beaten with 1 tbsp (15 mL) water	1

Season chicken with salt and pepper. In a large skillet, heat oil over high heat. Cook chicken until browned on both sides and no longer pink inside; let cool. Cut a pocket in each breast. Insert 2 basil leaves and ¼ roasted pepper in each pocket and wrap a slice of prosciutto around each breast. If necessary, roll puff pastry sheets out to 12-inch (30 cm) squares. Cut each sheet of pastry in half and wrap each breast in pastry, pinching seams to seal. Cover and refrigerate for at least 1 hour or for up to 24 hours, or wrap well and freeze for up to 3 weeks (thaw in the refrigerator before baking). Preheat oven to 400°F (200°C). Place packets seam side down on a dry baking sheet and brush with egg wash. Bake for 10 minutes. Reduce heat to 375°F (190°C) and bake for 10 minutes, until puffed and brown. **Serves 4.**

Spicy Molasses Chicken Wings

1 tbsp	canola oil	15 mL
2	cloves garlic, minced	2
1	dried chili pepper	1
1 tbsp	grated gingerroot	15 mL
⅓ cup	soy sauce	75 mL
⅓ cup	dark (cooking) molasses	75 mL
¼ cup	water	50 mL
¼ cup	dry sherry	50 mL
1 tbsp	rice vinegar	15 mL
2 lbs	chicken wings, sectioned and tips discarded	1 kg
1 tbsp	dark sesame oil	15 mL

In a large skillet, heat oil over medium-high heat. Sauté garlic, chili pepper and ginger for 30 seconds. Add soy sauce, molasses, water, sherry and vinegar; bring to a boil. Add wings, reduce heat, cover and simmer for 5 minutes. Uncover and simmer until liquid is reduced enough to glaze the wings. (Toss gently near the end of cooking to prevent scorching.) Stir in sesame oil. **Serves 8.**

Garlic Black Bean Chicken Wings

Follow preceding recipe, but use triple the amount of garlic, and replace the soy sauce with this mixture: ½ cup (125 mL) water, ¼ cup (50 mL) Chinese black bean sauce, 1 tbsp (15 mL) garlic chili paste and 1 tbsp (15 mL) hoisin sauce. **Serves 8.**

Chicken Tandoori Brochettes

1	recipe Tandoori Curry Marinade (see page 34)	1
2 lbs	boneless skinless chicken breasts, sliced into 1-inch (2.5 cm) wide strips	1 kg
1	recipe Asian Peanut Marinade (see page 34)	1

Place Tandoori Curry Marinade in a shallow dish. Add chicken strips and turn to coat. Cover and refrigerate overnight. Thread a soaked bamboo skewer lengthwise through each chicken strip and discard marinade. Grill immediately, or cover and refrigerate for up to 1 day. Preheat broiler or barbecue grill to high. Broil or grill for 2 to 3 minutes per side, or until no longer pink inside. Serve with Asian Peanut Marinade. **Serves 8.**

Turkey Kabobs Glazed with Jalapeño Jelly

1	clove garlic, minced	1
¼ cup	olive oil	50 mL
2 tbsp	cider vinegar	25 mL
1 tsp	hot pepper flakes	5 mL
2 lbs	boneless skinless turkey breast, sliced into 1-inch (2.5 cm) wide strips	1 kg
½ cup	melted jalapeño jelly	125 mL

In a shallow dish, combine garlic, oil, vinegar and hot pepper flakes. Add turkey "fingers" and toss to coat. Cover and refrigerate overnight. Thread a soaked bamboo skewer lengthwise through each turkey strip and discard marinade. Grill immediately, or cover and refrigerate for up to 1 day. Preheat broiler or barbecue grill to high. Brush turkey with jelly and broil or grill for 2 to 3 minutes per side, or until no longer pink inside. **Serves 8.**

Charred Rare Beef with Jalapeño Salsa

3 lbs	beef tenderloin, trimmed	1.5 kg
	Salt and freshly ground black pepper to taste	
	French bread	
	Jalapeño Salsa (see recipe, page 177)	

Heat a large iron skillet over high heat for 10 to 12 minutes. Rub beef with salt and pepper on all sides, then char on all sides in the hot pan. Do not lower heat, and do not overcook. Remove and let cool. (Can be stored in the refrigerator for up to 3 days.) Slice thin across the grain and serve on sliced French bread. Top each slice with 1 tsp (5 mL) Jalapeño Salsa. **Serves 15.**

Charred Rare Lamb with Roasted Garlic

Follow preceding recipe, but use boneless loin of lamb instead of beef, and use Roasted Garlic Purée (page 463) instead of salsa. **Serves 15.**

Escabèche of Soft-Shell Crab

8	live soft-shell crabs, prepared (see page 11)	8
1 cup	all-purpose flour, seasoned with salt and black pepper	250 mL
½ cup	olive oil, divided	125 mL
3 cups	thinly sliced onion	750 mL
2	cloves garlic, minced	2
2 tbsp	red wine vinegar	25 mL
	Juice of 1 lemon, 1 orange and 1 lime	
	Cayenne pepper to taste	
2 tbsp	chopped fresh Italian (flat-leaf) parsley	25 mL

Dredge crabs in seasoned flour, shaking off excess. In a large skillet, heat 3 tbsp (45 mL) of the oil over medium-high heat. Sauté crabs until browned on both sides; remove to a plate. Reduce heat to medium, add onion and sauté until tender. Add garlic, vinegar and citrus juices; bring to a boil. Season with cayenne and additional salt and black pepper. Return crabs to the liquid, remove from heat and let cool. Stir in parsley. **Serves 8.** *Store in an airtight container in the refrigerator for up to 4 days.*

Balsamic Shrimp

4	cloves garlic, sliced	4
1	bunch green onions, white parts only, sliced	1
¼ cup	dry white wine	50 mL
1 lb	medium shrimp, peeled and deveined	500 g
¼ cup	extra-virgin olive oil	50 mL
1 tbsp	balsamic vinegar	15 mL
Pinch	cayenne pepper	Pinch
	Salt and freshly ground black pepper to taste	

In a saucepan, bring garlic, green onions and wine to a boil. Add shrimp, tossing to distribute; remove from heat and let stand for 2 minutes, until shrimp are pink and opaque. Transfer to a bowl and stir in oil, vinegar, cayenne, salt and black pepper. Cover and refrigerate for at least 1 hour, until chilled, or for up to 3 days. **Serves 4 to 6.**

Fried Herbed Shrimp

1	small clove garlic, minced	1
½ tsp	freshly squeezed lemon juice	2 mL
3 tbsp	butter, softened	45 mL
1 tsp	chopped fresh Italian (flat-leaf) parsley	5 mL
Pinch	dried tarragon	Pinch
	Salt and freshly ground black pepper to taste	
20	jumbo shrimp, peeled, deveined and butterflied	20
2	eggs, beaten	2
2 cups	dry bread crumbs	500 mL
	Vegetable oil	

Combine garlic, lemon juice, butter, parsley, tarragon, salt and pepper. Spread interior of each shrimp with about ½ tsp (2 mL) of the mixture. Close shrimps, dip in egg and dredge in bread crumbs. Discard any excess egg and bread crumbs. Refrigerate shrimp for about 1 hour, until chilled, or wrap well and freeze for up to 1 month (thaw in the refrigerator before cooking). Deep-fry (page 9) for about 2 minutes, or until golden brown. **Makes 20.**

Pepper Peanut Shrimp

Follow preceding recipe, but replace the garlic mixture with the following mixture: Combine 1 clove garlic, minced, 3 tbsp (45 mL) peanut butter (smooth or chunky), 2 tsp (10 mL) finely chopped gingerroot, 1 tsp (5 mL) chili paste, 1/4 tsp (1 mL) ground cumin and 1/4 tsp (1 mL) ground coriander. **Makes 20.**

Lemon-Soy Smoked Shrimp

1	dried chili pepper	1
2 tbsp	soy sauce	25 mL
2 tbsp	cider vinegar	25 mL
	Finely grated zest and juice of 2 lemons	
2 lbs	extra-large shrimp	1 kg
1/2 cup	loose tea leaves (any type)	125 mL
1/2 cup	granulated sugar	125 mL
	Dipping Sauce for Potstickers (see recipe, page 249)	

In a shallow dish, combine chili pepper, soy sauce, vinegar, lemon zest and lemon juice. Add shrimp and toss to coat. Cover and refrigerate for at least 2 hours or overnight. Combine tea and sugar. Line a heavy wok, cast-iron skillet or Dutch oven with heavy-duty foil. Place tea mixture in bottom of pan and place a rack over top. Heat over high heat until tea smokes. Drain shrimp and discard marinade. Place shrimp on rack, cover pan tightly and smoke for about 10 minutes, or until shrimp are curled and firm. Serve immediately, or place in an airtight container and refrigerate for up to 2 days. Peel and serve with dipping sauce. **Serves 12.**

Shrimp with Smoked Salmon

2 cups	dry white wine	500 mL
2 cups	water	500 mL
1/2 tsp	salt	2 mL
6	whole black peppercorns	6
1	bay leaf	1
1	strip lemon zest	1
	Juice of 1/2 lemon	
24	jumbo shrimp, peeled and deveined	24
1	recipe Dijon Vinaigrette (see page 61)	1
2 tbsp	chopped fresh dill	25 mL
6 oz	smoked salmon, cut into 24 strips	175 g

In a large saucepan, bring wine, water, salt, peppercorns, bay leaf, lemon zest and lemon juice to a simmer. Add shrimp and simmer for about 2 minutes, or until firm and opaque; drain and shake off excess liquid. In a shallow dish, combine Dijon Vinaigrette and dill. Add shrimp and toss to coat.

Cover and refrigerate for at least 1 hour, until chilled, or for up to 2 days. No more than 24 hours before serving, wrap each shrimp with 1 strip of smoked salmon and secure with a toothpick. **Makes 24.**

Chilled Salmon Soufflé

2 lbs	skinless salmon fillet, cooked, cooled and flaked	1 kg
1 1/2 cups	mayonnaise	375 mL
2 tsp	Dijon mustard	10 mL
	Juice of 1 lemon, divided	
	Salt and freshly ground black pepper to taste	
1	envelope (1/4 oz/7 g) unflavored gelatin	1
1/3 cup	dry white wine	75 mL
1 cup	whipping (35%) cream	250 mL

In a large bowl, combine salmon, mayonnaise, mustard, half the lemon juice, salt and pepper; set aside. Soften gelatin in the remaining lemon juice. In a saucepan, bring wine to a boil. Add gelatin mixture and stir to dissolve. Stir into salmon mixture. In a separate bowl, whip cream to soft peaks; fold into salmon mixture. Attach a paper collar (see page 13) to a 4-cup (1 L) soufflé dish. Spoon salmon mixture into dish and smooth top. Cover loosely with plastic wrap and refrigerate for at least 4 hours, until firm, or for up to 24 hours. Remove collar before serving. **Serves 8.**

Chilled Crab and Chive Soufflé

Follow preceding recipe, but replace the salmon with 1 lb (500 g) white-fleshed fish fillet, cooked, cooled and flaked, and 1 lb (500 g) backfin (lump) crabmeat, shells picked out. Stir 1/4 cup (50 mL) chopped chives into the salmon mixture with the gelatin mixture. **Serves 8.**

Spiked Smoked Salmon and Gruyère Cheesecake

	Freshly grated Parmesan cheese, for dusting	
3 tbsp	olive oil	45 mL
1	onion, chopped	1
1	clove garlic, minced	1
1/3 cup	chopped fresh dill	75 mL
8 oz	smoked salmon, coarsely chopped	250 g
2 lbs	cream cheese, softened	1 kg
6	extra-large eggs	6
1 cup	shredded Gruyère cheese	250 mL
1/4 cup	freshly grated Parmesan cheese	50 mL
1/4 cup	Scotch or Irish whisky	50 mL

3 tbsp	red wine vinegar	45 mL
	Salt and freshly ground black pepper to taste	
	Sliced black bread	

Preheat oven to 200°F (100°C). Grease an 8-cup (2 L) soufflé dish and dust with Parmesan. In a large skillet, heat oil over medium-high heat. Sauté onion, garlic and dill until onion is tender. Remove from heat and stir in smoked salmon; set aside. In a large bowl, using an electric mixer, beat cream cheese until fluffy. Beat in eggs, Gruyère, Parmesan, whisky, vinegar, salt and pepper until smooth. Fold in salmon mixture. Pour into prepared soufflé dish. Bake for 8 hours, until set. Let cool in pan, then unmold. Cover and refrigerate for about 2 hours, until chilled. Serve with bread. **Serves 24.**

Blue Cheese Apple Cheesecake

	Freshly grated Parmesan cheese, for dusting	
8 oz	bacon	250 g
1	onion, chopped	1
1 cup	diced peeled apple	250 mL
1	clove garlic, minced	1
2 lbs	cream cheese, softened	1 kg
6	extra-large eggs	6
8 oz	blue cheese, crumbled	250 g
¼ cup	freshly grated Parmesan cheese	50 mL
¼ cup	Scotch or Irish whisky	50 mL
3 tbsp	red wine vinegar	45 mL
	Salt and freshly ground black pepper to taste	
	Sliced black bread	

Preheat oven to 200°F (100°C). Grease an 8-cup (2 L) soufflé dish and dust with Parmesan. In a large skillet, over medium-high heat, cook bacon until crisp; remove to a plate, blot dry and crumble. Remove all but 3 tbsp (45 mL) fat from the pan and reduce heat to medium. Add onion and apple to the fat in the pan and sauté until tender. Add garlic and sauté for 30 seconds. Remove from heat and stir in bacon; set aside. In a large bowl, using an electric mixer, beat cream cheese until fluffy. Beat in eggs, blue cheese, Parmesan, whisky, vinegar, salt and pepper until smooth. Fold in bacon mixture. Pour into prepared soufflé dish. Bake for 8 hours, until set. Let cool in pan, then unmold. Cover and refrigerate for about 2 hours, until chilled. Serve with bread. **Serves 24.**

Eight-Hour Brandy Cheesecake

1 tsp	unsalted butter	5 mL
⅓ cup	graham cracker crumbs or other plain cookie crumbs	75 mL
2 lbs	cream cheese, at room temperature	1 kg
1 cup	granulated sugar	250 mL
¼ cup	brandy	50 mL
2 tbsp	vanilla	25 mL
5	eggs	5

Preheat oven to 200°F (100°C). Grease an 8-cup (2 L) soufflé dish or 8-inch (20 cm) springform pan with the butter and dust with cracker crumbs. In a large bowl, using an electric mixer, beat cream cheese until fluffy. Beat in sugar, brandy and vanilla until very smooth. Beat in eggs, just long enough to incorporate. Pour into prepared soufflé dish and bake for 8 hours, until set. Let cool in pan, then unmold. Cover and refrigerate for about 2 hours, until chilled. **Serves 20.**

Avocado Ice Cream

3	avocados, peeled and coarsely chopped	3
	Juice of 1 lime	
2 cups	milk	500 mL
1 cup	granulated sugar	250 mL
1 cup	sour cream	250 mL
1 cup	cream (any type, minimum 10%)	250 mL
1 tsp	lemon extract	5 mL
¼ tsp	salt	1 mL
Pinch	cayenne pepper	Pinch

In a blender or food processor, purée avocados and lime juice until smooth; transfer to a bowl. In a saucepan, scald milk with sugar over medium-low heat just until bubbles form around the edge. Stir into avocado mixture, along with sour cream, cream, lemon extract, salt and cayenne; refrigerate until cold. Transfer to an ice cream maker and freeze according to manufacturer's directions. **Makes 6 cups (1.5 L).** *Store in an airtight container in the freezer for up to 3 days. Serve as a summer appetizer, palate cleanser or dessert.*

Chocolate Coronary

	Vegetable cooking spray	
1 cup	milk (not fat-free)	250 mL
1 lb	semisweet chocolate, finely chopped	500 g
1 tbsp	instant coffee granules	15 mL
2 tbsp	orange-flavored liqueur	25 mL
1 tbsp	vanilla	15 mL
8	extra-large egg yolks	8
1 cup	unsalted butter, softened	250 mL
	Whipped cream	

Preheat oven to 350°F (180°C). Spray a 9-inch (23 cm) springform pan with cooking spray, and line the bottom with parchment paper. In a saucepan, bring milk to a simmer over medium heat. Stir in chocolate and coffee granules; remove from heat and stir until chocolate melts. Stir in liqueur and vanilla. Beat in egg yolks and butter. Pour into prepared pan and bake for 23 minutes (it will not look done). Let cool in pan, then refrigerate until completely firm. Run a knife around the edge and remove pan. Serve with whipped cream. **Serves 24.** *Store in an airtight container in the refrigerator for up to 1 week.*

Crème Caramel

1½ cups	granulated sugar, divided	375 mL
4	eggs	4
4 cups	milk	1 L
2 tsp	vanilla	10 mL

Preheat oven to 350°F (180°C). Caramelize half the sugar (see page 12) and pour into a low, flat, oven-proof baking dish of at least a 6-cup (1.5 L) capacity. Tilt dish so caramel covers bottom in a sheet; set aside. Beat eggs with ¼ cup (50 mL) of the remaining sugar. In a saucepan, scald milk with the remaining sugar over medium-low heat just until bubbles form around the edge. Slowly stir into egg mixture, along with vanilla. Pour into baking dish, on top of caramel. Place in a water bath (see page 12) and bake for 1 to 1¼ hours, or until a knife inserted in the center comes out with just a bit of custard clinging to it. Let cool to room temperature in pan on a rack, then cover and refrigerate for 24 hours. Run a knife around the edge and invert onto a large platter, letting caramel fall around the custard. Cut into wedges. **Serves 12.**

Chapter 43
Roasts
For Celebration or Just to Show Off

Rib Roast of Beef with Garlic 477

Rib Roast with Roasted Potatoes
and Capers 477

Rib Roast with Yorkshire Pudding 477

Rib Roast with
Rosemary Red Wine Glaze 477

Rib Roast with Garlic Jus 477

Rib Roast with
Creamy Horseradish Sauce 477

Rib Roast with
Braised Wild Mushrooms 478

Roasted Whole Tenderloin of Beef 478

Roasted Beef Tenderloin with
Scotch Jus 478

Roasted Beef Tenderloin with
Wasabi Steak Sauce 478

Roasted Beef Tenderloin with
Caramelized Onions 478

Pesto-Crusted Tenderloin with
Roasted Pepper Rouille 478

Espresso-Rubbed Roast Tenderloin 478

Flank Steak Roasted with
Portobello Mushrooms 479

Flank Steak Stuffed with Wild Rice 479

Beef Sirloin Roast 479

Roast Sirloin with
Porter Barbecue Sauce 479

Roast Sirloin with Spicy Coffee Elixir . . . 480

Spicy Peanut Beef 480

Slow-Roasted Shoulder of Beef
with Chili Rub 480

Jerk Roasted Beef 480

Fragrant Slow-Cooked Beef 480

Sicilian Oven-Braised Top Round Beef . . 480

Greek Beef 481

Anise Braised Beef 481

Roasted Boneless Leg of Lamb 481

Roast Lamb Dijonnaise 481

Roast Lamb with Fresh Mint Sauce 481

Roast Lamb Provençal 481

Middle Eastern Roasted Lamb 482

Leg of Lamb Niçoise 482

Roasted Rack of Lamb 482

Roasted Rack of Lamb
with Mustard Crumbs 482

Roasted Rack of Lamb
with Wasabi Crumbs 482

Rack of Lamb with Roasted Garlic Jus . . 482

Honey-Baked Ham 482

Tropical Ham 482

Hot Pepper Ham 482

Herb-Crusted Roasted Pork Loin 482

Pistachio-Stuffed Pork Loin 483

Garlic Roasted Pork Loin 483

Roasted Pork Loin Stuffed
with Apples and Prunes 483

Stuffed Pork Loin Glazed
with Cider Syrup 483

Fresh Ham Braised with Cider 483

Pineapple Jerk Pork 484

Picnic Pork Roast 484

Lemon Coriander Pork 484

South Carolina–Style Pulled Pork 484

Rack of Pork with Roasted Pineapple . . 485

Roasted Fish Provençal 485

Andy's mother couldn't cook, but that never stopped her. Every Friday, she'd crank up the oven, throw in a roast and pray to the gods of desiccated protein for success. Most of the time, they spared her, but she still considered roasting a game of chance. We have a feeling she's not alone.

Granted, roasting is anything but an exact science, but the rules are simple, straightforward and pretty much the same regardless of what you're roasting. Your guiding principle should be one of benign neglect. A prime rib needs only a properly calibrated oven and the privilege of privacy to reach perfection. A loin of pork or a leg of lamb may benefit from a rub of rosemary and a little garlic, but aside from a sauce made from the drippings left in the pan, roasting meat calls for minimal interaction.

The first step is to remove the meat from the refrigerator about an hour before you're going to put it in the oven. Season it and place it fat side up on a rack set in a roasting pan. The rack can be metal or a bed of vegetables and/or bones, but some device is needed to raise the roast off the bottom of the pan so the meat doesn't sit in its own juices, and so hot air can circulate all around the roast. For the same reason, roasting pans must be low-sided. If the walls of the pan are too high, moisture coming from the meat will be held in the pan, and the meat will steam rather than roast.

To avoid steam, roasts should never be covered. Contrary to kitchen myth, a cover does not help keep meat moist. Rather, it traps steam, which cooks meat much more intensely than air, with the result that more juices are squeezed from the meat fibers and the roast is drier.

Once your roast is in the pan, place it in a hot oven and walk away. In general, if you want the roast to be rare or medium-rare, set the oven temperature above 400°F (200°C); for roasts that need to be cooked through, set it for around 350°F (180°C); and for tough meat that needs time to tenderize, roast at around 300°F or 325°F (150°C or 160°C).

The best way to take the temperature of a roast is to insert a meat thermometer into the thickest part of the meat, making sure it does not touch a bone, which would give you an inaccurate reading. Don't rely too heavily on charts that specify a number of minutes of cooking time per pound (or kilogram). Unless the chart specifies individual cuts, such guidelines are too general to be of specific use.

When the temperature of the meat registers 5°F (3°C) less than the final meat temperature you want (see table, below), remove the pan from the oven and set it aside for 10 to 20 minutes, depending on the size of the roast. During this time, the temperature will rise the extra 5°F (3°C), and the roast will become much easier to slice.

As meat cooks, its juices are forced out of the muscle fibers. Some of these juices flow to the surface, where they evaporate and form a rich savory crust, but most concentrate toward the cooler center of the roast. By the time a roast is finished cooking, its core is saturated with meat juices, like a wet sponge. If it is sliced right away, the juices will run out; if it is given a resting period, they will be reabsorbed by the drier sections of meat and will be less likely to be lost during slicing.

Meat Doneness Chart

Beef and Lamb

Extra-rare	125°F (52°C)
Rare	130°F (54°C)
Medium-rare	135°F (57°C)
Medium	140°F (60°C)
Medium-well	150°F (65°C)
Well done	160°F (71°C)

Pork

Medium	155°F (68°C)

About these recipes . . .

Unlike most of the recipes in this book, the following roasts are designed to feed a crowd. Most serve 6 to 8. The estimated roasting time given in each recipe is based on meat that has lost its chill by resting at room temperature for about an hour. For most recipes, the size of the roasting pan doesn't matter, as long as its sides are no higher than 2 inches and it provides ample space around the roast for good air circulation. The timing and oven temperatures given are for roasting in a conventional oven. If you want to use a convection oven, reduce the thermostat by 25°F (15°C) and the roasting time by about 25%. Either way, because roasting times can vary slightly depending on the size and configuration of the meat you are roasting, it's a good idea to start checking the internal temperature about 25 minutes before the meat is scheduled to be done so that you can gauge the exact timing more accurately.

Rib Roast of Beef with Garlic

6	cloves garlic, slivered	6
1	beef rib roast (4 to 5 lbs/2 to 2.5 kg)	1
2 tsp	kosher salt	10 mL
1 tsp	coarsely ground black pepper	5 mL

Preheat oven to 450°F (230°C). Slip garlic slivers between the meat and fat on the top of the roast, and between the meat and bones on the bottom. Season all over with salt and pepper. Place beef, fat side up, on a rack in a 14- by 10-inch (35 by 25 cm) metal roasting pan and roast for about 50 minutes, until a meat thermometer inserted in the center registers 125°F (52°C) for rare, or until desired doneness. Transfer to a carving board and let rest for 15 to 25 minutes before slicing. **Serves 6.**

Rib Roast with Roasted Potatoes and Capers

Follow preceding recipe, but surround beef with 2 lbs (1 kg) red-skinned or other boiling potatoes, halved, 1 onion, chopped, 2 cloves garlic, minced, and salt and freshly ground black pepper to taste. Toss halfway through roasting, and scatter 2 tbsp (25 mL) fresh capers over the potatoes about 15 minutes before they'll be done. **Serves 6.**

Rib Roast with Yorkshire Pudding

Follow recipe for Rib Roast of Beef with Garlic (above). While the meat roasts, beat 3 eggs, 1 cup (250 mL) all-purpose flour, 1 cup (250 mL) cold milk and ¼ tsp (1 mL) salt; cover and refrigerate. After transferring roast to a carving board, pour drippings into a gravy separator. Return 2 tbsp (25 mL) fat to the roasting pan (use the defatted drippings for juice, gravy or sauce). Pour the batter into the hot pan. Return pan to the oven and bake for 15 minutes. Reduce oven temperature to 375°F (190°C), turn the pan and cook for 10 minutes, until Yorkshire Pudding is puffed and brown. Cut into squares and serve with the roast. **Serves 6.**

Rib Roast with Rosemary Red Wine Glaze

Follow recipe for Rib Roast of Beef with Garlic (left). After transferring roast to a carving board, pour drippings into a gravy separator. Pour meat juices back into the roasting pan (leaving the fat). Add 1 sprig fresh rosemary and 2 cups (500 mL) dry red wine to the pan, place over medium-high heat and boil until reduced by half. Discard rosemary. Serve beef with sauce. **Serves 6.**

Rib Roast with Garlic Jus

Follow recipe for Rib Roast of Beef with Garlic (left). After transferring roast to a carving board, pour drippings into a gravy separator. Spoon 2 tbsp (25 mL) of the fat into a saucepan and heat over medium-high heat. Add 2 cloves garlic, minced, and sauté until aromatic, about 30 seconds. Add meat juices from the separator, leaving the remaining fat. Add 1 cup (250 mL) dry red wine and bring to a boil. Add 1 cup (250 mL) beef broth and boil until reduced by half. Stir in 1 tbsp (15 mL) chopped fresh Italian (flat-leaf) parsley and salt and freshly ground black pepper to taste. Serve beef with sauce. **Serves 6.**

Rib Roast with Creamy Horseradish Sauce

Follow recipe for Rib Roast of Beef with Garlic (left). After transferring roast to a carving board, pour drippings into a gravy separator. Pour meat juices into a small saucepan (leaving the fat) and boil until reduced by half. Meanwhile, combine 1 large clove garlic, minced, ¼ cup (50 mL) buttermilk, 2 tbsp (25 mL) spicy brown mustard and 1 tbsp (15 mL) prepared horseradish. Stir in reduced meat juices. Serve beef with sauce. **Serves 6.**

Rib Roast with Braised Wild Mushrooms

Use the ingredients from Rib Roast of Beef with Garlic (page 477), and add:

½ oz	dried wild or exotic mushrooms (any type)	15 g
1 cup	warm water	250 mL
1 cup	beef broth	250 mL
2 tbsp	butter	25 mL
1	onion, finely chopped	1
8 oz	fresh wild or exotic mushrooms (any type), sliced	250 g
8 oz	white mushrooms, sliced	250 g
1 tsp	coarsely chopped fresh rosemary	5 mL
2	plum (Roma) tomatoes, finely chopped	2
2 tbsp	chopped fresh Italian (flat-leaf) parsley	25 mL
	Salt and freshly ground black pepper to taste	

Follow recipe for Rib Roast of Beef with Garlic. While meat is roasting, soak dried mushrooms in warm water until tender, about 15 minutes. Remove mushrooms, cut large ones into chunks, and strain soaking liquid through a coffee filter. In a saucepan, combine soaking liquid and beef broth; boil until reduced by half. Meanwhile, in a large skillet, heat butter over medium-high heat. Sauté onion until tender. Add fresh mushrooms, soaked mushrooms and rosemary; sauté until mushrooms begin to release their moisture. Add reduced broth mixture, tomatoes, parsley, salt and pepper; simmer until mushrooms are cooked through, about 5 minutes. Serve beef with sauce. **Serves 6.**

Roasted Whole Tenderloin of Beef

1	whole beef tenderloin (3 to 4 lbs/1.5 to 2 kg), trimmed Kosher salt and coarsely ground black pepper to taste	1
2 tbsp	olive oil	25 mL
¾ cup	dry red wine	175 mL

Preheat oven to 450°F (230°C). Season beef with salt and pepper. Fold the pointed end under and tie in place to form a cylinder of uniform thickness. Rub the outside of the beef with oil. Place on a rack in a metal roasting pan and roast for 16 to 20 minutes, turning beef halfway through, until a meat thermometer inserted in the center registers 125°F (52°C) for rare, or until desired doneness. Transfer to a carving board and let rest for 5 to 10 minutes before slicing. Meanwhile, place roasting pan over medium heat until juices are bubbling. Add wine and boil for 1 minute, scraping up any brown bits from the bottom of the pan. Serve beef with red wine jus. **Serves 8.**

Roasted Beef Tenderloin with Scotch Jus

Follow preceding recipe. After transferring beef to carving board, set pan over medium-high heat and add 1½ cups (375 mL) beef broth and ½ cup (125 mL) Scotch whisky; boil until reduced by half. Stir in 2 tbsp (25 mL) chopped fresh Italian (flat-leaf) parsley and salt and freshly ground black pepper to taste. Serve beef with sauce. **Serves 8.**

Roasted Beef Tenderloin with Wasabi Steak Sauce

Follow recipe for Roasted Whole Tenderloin of Beef (left). While meat is roasting, whisk together 2 tbsp (25 mL) softened butter, 2 tbsp (25 mL) dark sesame oil, 1½ tbsp (22 mL) Worcestershire sauce, 1 tbsp (15 mL) prepared wasabi and 2 tsp (10 mL) ketchup until smooth. Serve beef with sauce. **Serves 8.**

Roasted Beef Tenderloin with Caramelized Onions

Follow recipe for Roasted Whole Tenderloin of Beef (left), but first toss 2 lbs (1 kg) large yellow onions, thinly sliced, 2 tbsp (25 mL) olive oil and plenty of salt and freshly ground black pepper on a rimmed baking sheet. Roast alongside the beef for 20 minutes, until browned on the edges. Stir in 2 tbsp (25 mL) balsamic vinegar, scraping up brown bits from the bottom of the pan. Serve with the beef. **Serves 8.**

Pesto-Crusted Tenderloin with Roasted Pepper Rouille

Follow recipe for Roasted Whole Tenderloin of Beef (left), but replace half the olive oil with 2 tbsp (25 mL) Fresh Basil Pesto (page 178). Serve beef with 1½ cups (375 mL) Roasted Pepper Rouille (page 56). **Serves 8.**

Espresso-Rubbed Roast Tenderloin

Follow recipe for Roasted Whole Tenderloin of Beef (left), but omit the salt and pepper, and season beef with this mixture: ¼ cup (50 mL) freshly ground espresso coffee beans, 1 tsp (5 mL) kosher salt, 1 tsp

(5 mL) finely grated orange zest and 1 tsp (5 mL) freshly ground black pepper. **Serves 8.**

Flank Steak Roasted with Portobello Mushrooms

1	beef flank steak (2 lbs/1 kg), trimmed	1
	Kosher salt and coarsely ground black pepper to taste	
6	cloves garlic, minced	6
⅓ cup	extra-virgin olive oil	75 mL
½ tsp	dried thyme	2 mL
4	portobello mushrooms, ends trimmed, sliced	4

Season steak with salt and pepper. Combine garlic and oil; rub 1 tbsp (15 mL) of the mixture over steak. Add thyme to the remaining garlic mixture and rub over mushrooms. Let stand for 1 hour. Preheat oven to 475°F (240°C). Place steak on a rack in a roasting pan and surround with mushrooms. Roast for 12 to 15 minutes, turning steak halfway through, until a meat thermometer inserted horizontally into the thicker end of the steak registers between 125°F and 130°F (52°C and 54°C) for rare, or until desired doneness. Let rest for 5 minutes before slicing against the grain at a slight angle. **Serves 6.**

Flank Steak Stuffed with Wild Rice

1	beef flank steak (2 lbs/1 kg), pocket cut into side	1
	Kosher salt and coarsely ground black pepper to taste	
3	cloves garlic, minced	3
3 tbsp	extra-virgin olive oil	45 mL
4 cups	water	1 L
⅓ cup	wild rice blend	75 mL
1	stalk celery, finely diced	1
½ cup	finely diced onion	125 mL
1	plum (Roma) tomato, finely diced	1
1 tsp	fresh rosemary leaves	5 mL
1 cup	dry red wine	250 mL

Season steak with salt and pepper. Combine garlic and oil; rub half of the mixture over steak. Let stand for 1 hour. Meanwhile, in a saucepan, bring water to a boil. Add rice, reduce heat to medium-low, cover and simmer until rice is tender (from 10 to 45 minutes, depending on the rice blend); drain off any remaining liquid. In a large skillet, heat the remaining garlic mixture over medium-high heat. Sauté celery and onion until tender. Add tomato and rosemary; sauté for 2 minutes. Stir into rice and season with salt and pepper; let cool.

Preheat oven to 475°F (240°C). Stuff the pocket in the beef with the rice mixture, and close the pocket with a skewer. Place beef on a rack in a roasting pan and roast for 12 to 15 minutes, until a meat thermometer inserted horizontally into a section of the steak that does not contain stuffing registers between 125°F and 130°F (52°C and 54°C) for rare, or until desired doneness. Transfer to a carving board and let rest for 5 minutes. Meanwhile, place roasting pan over medium-high heat. Add wine and boil until reduced by half, scraping up any brown bits from the bottom of the pan. Slice steak against the grain and serve with red wine jus. **Serves 6.**

Beef Sirloin Roast

2 tsp	packed dark brown sugar	10 mL
2 tsp	chili powder	10 mL
1 tsp	kosher salt	5 mL
1 tsp	sweet paprika	5 mL
½ tsp	ground chipotle chili pepper	2 mL
¼ tsp	ground cumin	1 mL
¼ tsp	freshly ground black pepper	1 mL
1	boneless beef sirloin roast (4 to 5 lbs/2 to 2.5 kg), surface fat trimmed to about ¼ inch (0.5 cm) thick	1

Combine brown sugar, chili powder, salt, paprika, chipotle, cumin and black pepper; rub spice mixture over beef. Let stand for 1 hour. Preheat oven to 375°F (190°C). Place beef, fat side up, on a rack in a large roasting pan and roast for about 1¼ hours, until a meat thermometer inserted in the thickest part registers 125°F (52°C) for rare, or until desired doneness. Transfer to a carving board and let rest for 10 to 15 minutes before slicing. **Serves 8.**

Roast Sirloin with Porter Barbecue Sauce

Follow preceding recipe, but double all the spices and reserve half the spice mixture. While beef is resting, skim most of the fat from the pan drippings. Place roasting pan over medium-high heat and add 1 bottle (12 oz/341 mL) porter (or other dark beer) and the remaining spice mixture; boil until reduced by half. Remove from heat and stir in 1 cup (250 mL) barbecue sauce. Serve beef with sauce. **Serves 8.**

Roast Sirloin with Spicy Coffee Elixir

Follow recipe for Beef Sirloin Roast (page 479), but double all the spices and reserve half the spice mixture. While beef is resting, skim most of the fat from the pan drippings. Place roasting pan over medium-high heat and add 1½ cups (375 mL) strong brewed coffee and the remaining spice mixture; boil until reduced by about two-thirds. Strain sauce and serve with beef. **Serves 8.**

Spicy Peanut Beef

Follow recipe for Beef Sirloin Roast (page 479), but replace the spice mixture with Asian Peanut Marinade (page 34). **Serves 8.**

Slow-Roasted Shoulder of Beef with Chili Rub

2 tbsp	packed dark brown sugar	25 mL
1 tbsp	hot paprika	15 mL
1 tbsp	chili powder	15 mL
1 tbsp	kosher salt	15 mL
1 tsp	freshly ground black pepper	5 mL
½ tsp	ground habanero chili pepper	2 mL
2 cups	beer (any type)	500 mL
1	boneless beef chuck roast (3 to 4 lbs/1.5 to 2 kg)	1
2 tsp	canola oil	10 mL

Combine brown sugar, paprika, chili powder, salt, black pepper and habanero. Place half the spice mixture and the beer in a large sealable plastic bag. Add beef, seal bag and toss to coat. Refrigerate for at least 6 hours or overnight. Preheat oven to 300°F (150°C). Remove beef from marinade, discarding marinade, and pat dry. Rub the remaining spice mixture over beef and coat with oil. Place beef on a rack in a roasting pan and roast for about 2½ hours, until a meat thermometer inserted in the thickest part registers 135°F (57°C) for medium, or until desired doneness. Transfer to a carving board and let rest for 10 minutes before slicing. **Serves 6 to 8.**

Jerk Roasted Beef

Follow preceding recipe, but replace the spice mixture with ⅓ cup (75 mL) jerk seasoning, and replace the beer with 1 cup (250 mL) each dark rum and water. **Serves 6 to 8.**

Fragrant Slow-Cooked Beef

3	cloves garlic, minced	3
½ cup	chopped fresh cilantro	125 mL
2 tbsp	ground toasted cumin	25 mL
2 tbsp	granulated sugar	25 mL
1 tbsp	minced gingerroot	15 mL
1 tbsp	kosher salt	15 mL
2 cups	water	500 mL
1	boneless beef chuck roast or top round (3 to 4 lbs/1.5 to 2 kg)	1
2 tsp	canola oil	10 mL

Combine garlic, cilantro, cumin, sugar, ginger and salt. Place half the spice mixture and the water in a large sealable plastic bag. Add beef, seal bag and toss to coat. Refrigerate for at least 6 hours or overnight. Preheat oven to 300°F (150°C). Remove beef from marinade, discarding marinade, and pat dry. Rub the remaining spice mixture over beef and coat with oil. Place beef on a rack in a roasting pan and roast for about 2½ hours, until a meat thermometer inserted in the thickest part registers 135°F (57°C) for medium, or until desired doneness. Transfer to a carving board and let rest for 10 minutes before slicing. **Serves 6 to 8.**

Sicilian Oven-Braised Top Round Beef

4	cloves garlic, minced	4
⅓ cup	extra-virgin olive oil, divided	75 mL
¼ cup	red wine vinegar	50 mL
2 tsp	kosher salt	10 mL
1 tsp	dried oregano	5 mL
1 tsp	freshly ground black pepper	5 mL
1	beef top round or rump roast (2 to 3 lbs/1 to 1.5 kg)	1
1 cup	dry red wine	250 mL
1 tbsp	tomato paste	15 mL
2	drained canned anchovies, mashed with a fork	2
½ cup	packed fresh basil leaves, torn into pieces	125 mL

Combine garlic, 2 tbsp (25 mL) of the oil, vinegar, salt, oregano and pepper. Rub half this mixture over beef, wrap tightly in plastic wrap and refrigerate for at least 6 hours or overnight. Add wine and tomato paste to the remaining garlic mixture; set aside. Preheat oven to 325°F (160°C). Remove beef from marinade, discarding marinade. Pat beef dry and rub with the remaining oil. Place on a rack in a roasting pan and roast for about 2 hours, basting with reserved wine mixture every 20 minutes and turning meat 3 or 4 times, until a meat thermometer inserted in the thickest part registers 135°F (57°C) for medium, or until desired doneness. Transfer to a carving board and let rest for 10 minutes. Meanwhile, place roasting pan over medium-high heat and bring pan juices to a boil. Stir in anchovies and basil. Slice beef against the grain and serve with sauce. **Serves 6 to 8.**

Greek Beef

Follow preceding recipe, but substitute freshly squeezed lemon juice for the vinegar, chopped kalamata olives for the anchovies, and Italian (flat-leaf) parsley for the basil. **Serves 6 to 8.**

Anise Braised Beef

4	cloves garlic, minced	4
¼ cup	peanut oil, divided	50 mL
¼ cup	balsamic vinegar	50 mL
2 tsp	kosher salt	10 mL
1 tsp	freshly ground black pepper	5 mL
½ tsp	ground cinnamon	2 mL
½ tsp	ground ginger	2 mL
1	beef top round or rump roast (2 to 3 lbs/1 to 1.5 kg)	1
1 cup	orange juice	250 mL
1 tbsp	dark (cooking) molasses	15 mL
6	whole star anise, broken into pieces	6
½ cup	packed fresh basil leaves, torn into pieces	125 mL

Combine garlic, half the oil, vinegar, salt, pepper, cinnamon and ginger. Rub half this mixture over beef, wrap tightly in plastic wrap and refrigerate for at least 6 hours or overnight. Add orange juice and molasses to the remaining garlic mixture; set aside. Preheat the oven to 325°F (160°C). Remove beef from marinade, discarding marinade. Pat beef dry and rub with the remaining oil. Place on a rack in a roasting pan, scatter star anise over top and roast for about 2 hours, basting with reserved orange juice mixture every 20 minutes and turning meat 3 or 4 times, until a meat thermometer inserted in the thickest part registers 135°F (57°C) for medium, or until desired doneness. Transfer to a carving board and let rest for 5 minutes. Meanwhile, place roasting pan over medium-high heat and bring pan juices to a boil. Strain into a serving bowl and stir in basil. Slice beef against the grain and serve with sauce. **Serves 6 to 8.**

Roasted Boneless Leg of Lamb

1	boneless leg of lamb (4 lbs/2 kg), rolled and tied	1
	Kosher salt and freshly ground black pepper to taste	
4	cloves garlic, minced	4
2 tbsp	olive oil	25 mL
1 tsp	chopped fresh rosemary	5 mL

Preheat oven to 475°F (240°C). Rub lamb with salt and pepper. Combine garlic, oil and rosemary; rub over lamb. Place lamb on a rack in a large roasting pan and roast for about 45 minutes, until a meat thermometer inserted in the thickest part registers 125°F (52°C) for rare, or until desired doneness. Transfer to a carving board, snip the strings and let rest for 15 minutes before slicing. **Serves 6.**

Roast Lamb Dijonnaise

Follow preceding recipe, but add 3 tbsp (45 mL) Dijon mustard to the garlic mixture. **Serves 6.**

Roast Lamb with Fresh Mint Sauce

Follow recipe for Roasted Boneless Leg of Lamb (above), but omit the rosemary. While lamb is resting, spoon fat from pan drippings and place pan over medium-high heat. Add 1 cup (250 mL) chopped fresh mint (about 1 bunch), ½ cup (125 mL) dry white wine, 1 tbsp (15 mL) granulated sugar and a big pinch of salt; bring to a boil. Serve lamb with sauce. **Serves 6.**

Roast Lamb Provençal

Follow recipe for Roasted Boneless Leg of Lamb (above), but replace the rosemary with dried herbes de Provence. While lamb is resting, spoon fat from pan drippings and place pan over medium-high heat. Add 2 cloves garlic, minced, 1½ cups (375 mL) dry red wine and 1 tsp (5 mL) dried herbes de Provence; boil until reduced by half, scraping up brown bits from the bottom of the pan. Strain sauce and serve with lamb. **Serves 6.**

Middle Eastern Roasted Lamb

Follow recipe for Roasted Boneless Leg of Lamb (page 481), but replace the rosemary with ground coriander. While lamb is resting, spoon fat from pan drippings and place pan over medium-high heat. Add 2 cloves garlic, minced, ½ cup (125 mL) dry white wine and ¼ cup (50 mL) chopped fresh mint; bring to a boil, scraping up brown bits from the bottom of the pan. Remove from heat and stir in 1 cup (250 mL) low-fat plain yogurt. Serve lamb with sauce. **Serves 6.**

Leg of Lamb Niçoise

Follow recipe for Roasted Boneless Leg of Lamb (page 481), but add 1 large red onion, sliced, to the roasting pan with the lamb. While lamb is resting, spoon fat from pan drippings and place pan over medium-high heat. Add 12 small oil-cured Niçoise olives, 1 cup (250 mL) orange juice and 2 tbsp (25 mL) chopped fresh mint; boil until reduced by half, scraping up brown bits from the bottom of the pan. Serve lamb with sauce. **Serves 6.**

Roasted Rack of Lamb

2	racks of lamb (each about 2 lbs/1 kg), chine bone removed	2
	Kosher salt and freshly ground black pepper to taste	
3	cloves garlic, minced	3
2 tbsp	olive oil	25 mL
1 tsp	chopped fresh rosemary	5 mL

Preheat oven to 475°F (240°C). Rub lamb with salt and pepper. Combine garlic, oil and rosemary; rub over the meaty parts of the lamb. Place fat side up on a rack in a large roasting pan and roast for about 20 minutes, until a meat thermometer inserted in the thickest part registers 125°F (52°C) for rare, or until desired doneness. Transfer to a carving board and let rest for 5 minutes before cutting into chops. (Note: The rack will be easier to separate into chops if you ask the butcher to crack the joint between each chop.) **Serves 6.**

Roasted Rack of Lamb with Mustard Crumbs

Follow preceding recipe, but add 1 tbsp (15 mL) whole-grain mustard to the garlic mixture, and pat 1 cup (250 mL) dry bread crumbs or cracker crumbs onto the portions coated with mustard. **Serves 6.**

Roasted Rack of Lamb with Wasabi Crumbs

Follow recipe for Roasted Rack of Lamb (left), but add 1 tbsp (15 mL) prepared wasabi to the garlic mixture, and pat 1 cup (250 mL) Japanese panko crumbs onto the portions coated with wasabi. **Serves 6.**

Rack of Lamb with Roasted Garlic Jus

Follow recipe for Roasted Rack of Lamb (left), but scatter the peeled cloves from 1 head of garlic around the lamb. While lamb is resting, mash garlic with the back of a fork into the pan juices. Place pan over medium-high heat and add 1 cup (250 mL) dry red wine; boil until reduced by half, scraping up brown bits from the bottom of the pan. Serve lamb with jus. **Serves 6.**

Honey-Baked Ham

1	clove garlic, minced	1
¼ cup	honey	50 mL
2 tbsp	spicy brown mustard	25 mL
Pinch	ground cloves	Pinch
3 lbs	boneless baked ham	1.5 kg

Preheat oven to 375°F (190°C). Combine garlic, honey, mustard and cloves; brush over ham. Place on a rack in a roasting pan and roast for 45 minutes, until a meat thermometer inserted in the thickest part registers 150°F (65°C). Transfer to a carving board and slice. **Serves 8.**

Tropical Ham

Follow preceding recipe, but substitute 1 tsp (5 mL) minced gingerroot for the garlic, and ½ cup (125 mL) pineapple dessert topping for the honey. **Serves 8.**

Hot Pepper Ham

Follow recipe for Honey Baked Ham (above), but omit the mustard and cloves, and add ¼ cup (50 mL) hot pepper sauce (such as Frank's RedHot) with the honey. **Serves 8.**

Herb-Crusted Roasted Pork Loin

2	cloves garlic, minced	2
¼ cup	finely chopped fresh Italian (flat-leaf) parsley	50 mL
2 tbsp	dried rosemary, crumbled	25 mL

1 tsp	kosher salt	5 mL
1 tsp	freshly ground black pepper	5 mL
1	boneless center-cut pork loin roast (3 to 4 lbs/1.5 to 2 kg)	1
2 tbsp	extra-virgin olive oil	25 mL
1 tbsp	freshly squeezed lemon juice	15 mL

Preheat oven to 375°F (190°C). Combine garlic, parsley, rosemary, salt and pepper. Rub pork with the oil and the spice mixture. Place on a rack in a roasting pan and roast for about 1 hour, or until a meat thermometer inserted in the center registers 150°F (65°C). Transfer to a carving board and let rest for 15 minutes before slicing. Meanwhile, spoon fat from pan drippings and stir in lemon juice. Drizzle juice over pork slices before serving. Serves 6 to 8.

Pistachio-Stuffed Pork Loin

Follow preceding recipe, but first form a pocket down the center of the roast by inserting a long, thin knife in the center of one end until the tip comes out the other. Enlarge the pocket to about 1 inch (2.5 cm) wide all the way through the roast. Combine 3 cloves garlic, minced, ½ cup (125 mL) coarsely chopped toasted pistachios, ⅓ cup (75 mL) chopped fresh Italian (flat-leaf) parsley, ¼ cup (50 mL) finely chopped golden raisins, 1 tbsp (15 mL) finely grated lemon zest, and salt and pepper to taste; stuff into the pocket. Serves 6 to 8.

Garlic Roasted Pork Loin

Follow recipe for Herb-Crusted Roasted Pork Loin (page 482), but substitute 2 tsp (10 mL) dried rubbed sage for the rosemary, and triple the amount of garlic. Serves 6 to 8.

Roasted Pork Loin Stuffed with Apples and Prunes

2 tbsp	butter	25 mL
1	small onion, finely chopped	1
1	large tart apple, peeled and cubed	1
2	cloves garlic, minced	2
1 tbsp	packed light brown sugar	15 mL
1 tsp	dried rosemary, crumbled	5 mL
1 tsp	dried thyme	5 mL
	Salt and freshly ground black pepper to taste	
12	pitted prunes, quartered	12
1	boneless center-cut pork loin roast (3 to 4 lbs/1.5 to 2 kg)	1
2 tbsp	extra-virgin olive oil	25 mL
1 tbsp	dried sage	15 mL

In a large skillet, melt butter over medium heat. Sauté onion and apple until tender. Add garlic, brown sugar, rosemary, thyme, salt and pepper; sauté for 1 minute. Stir in prunes; let cool. Preheat oven to 375°F (190°C). Form a pocket down the center of the pork roast by inserting a long, thin knife into the center of one end of the meat until the tip comes out the other end. Enlarge the pocket to about 1 inch (2.5 cm) wide all the way through the roast; stuff with the prune mixture. Rub the outside of the pork with oil, sage, and additional salt and pepper. Place on a rack in a roasting pan and roast for about 1 hour, or until a meat thermometer inserted in the center of the meat (but not into the stuffing) registers 150°F (65°C). Transfer to a carving board and let rest for 15 minutes before slicing. Serves 6 to 8.

Stuffed Pork Loin Glazed with Cider Syrup

Follow preceding recipe. While pork is resting, spoon fat from pan drippings, add 2 cups (500 mL) unsweetened apple cider and place pan over medium-high heat; boil until liquid is reduced by about three-quarters. Serve pork with syrup. Serves 6 to 8.

Fresh Ham Braised with Cider

1	clove garlic, minced	1
1 tbsp	dried rosemary	15 mL
2 tsp	salt	10 mL
1 tsp	freshly ground black pepper	5 mL
1 tsp	chili powder	5 mL
½ tsp	ground cinnamon	2 mL
4 to 5 lbs	boneless fresh ham	2 to 2.5 kg
2	stalks celery, chopped	2
2	apples, chopped	2
1	onion, chopped	1
2 cups	unsweetened apple cider	500 mL

Preheat oven to 375°F (190°C). Combine garlic, rosemary, salt, black pepper, chili powder and cinnamon; rub ham with spice mixture. Scatter celery, apples and onion across the bottom of a roasting pan. Place ham, fat side up, on vegetables and roast for 45 minutes. Pour cider over ham, reduce temperature to 325°F (160°C) and roast for 1 hour, basting several times with pan liquid, until a meat thermometer inserted in the center registers 150°F (65°C). Transfer to a carving board and let rest for 10 minutes before cutting into thin slices. Serve ham with pan drippings. Serves 8.

Pineapple Jerk Pork

Follow preceding recipe, but replace the spice mixture with 2 tbsp (25 mL) jerk seasoning, add 1 small pineapple, peeled and cut into chunks, to the vegetables in the pan, and substitute pineapple juice for the apple cider. Serves 8.

Picnic Pork Roast

1 tbsp	chili powder	15 mL
2 tsp	sweet paprika	10 mL
2 tsp	packed dark brown sugar	10 mL
1 tsp	kosher salt	5 mL
½ tsp	ground chipotle chili pepper	2 mL
¼ tsp	freshly ground black pepper	1 mL
¼ tsp	ground cumin	1 mL
1	boneless pork shoulder roast (picnic ham) (3 to 4 lbs/1.5 to 2 kg)	1
¾ cup	barbecue sauce	175 mL
½ cup	pure maple syrup	125 mL
1 tbsp	canola oil	15 mL

Combine chili powder, paprika, brown sugar, salt, chipotle, black pepper and cumin; rub over pork and let stand for 1 hour. Preheat oven to 325°F (160°C). Combine barbecue sauce and maple syrup; set aside. Rub oil over pork and place on a rack in a roasting pan. Roast for 2½ hours, basting with sauce mixture every 5 minutes during the last 30 minutes, until a thermometer inserted into the thickest part registers 160°F (71°C). Transfer pork to a carving board and let rest for 10 minutes before slicing. Serves 8.

Lemon Coriander Pork

Follow preceding recipe, but replace the spice mixture with 1 tbsp (15 mL) ground coriander and salt and pepper to taste, replace the barbecue sauce mixture with Lemon Cilantro Marinade (page 28), and replace the canola oil with extra-virgin olive oil. Serves 8.

South Carolina–Style Pulled Pork

1 tbsp	chili powder	15 mL
1 tbsp	kosher salt, divided	15 mL
2 tsp	sweet paprika	10 mL
2 tsp	packed dark brown sugar	10 mL
1 tsp	freshly ground black pepper, divided	5 mL
1	boneless pork shoulder roast (picnic ham) (4 to 5 lbs/2 to 2.5 kg)	1
2 tbsp	canola oil	25 mL
¾ cup	cider vinegar	175 mL
2 tbsp	granulated sugar	25 mL
2 tsp	hot pepper sauce (such as Tabasco)	10 mL
8	hamburger buns	8

Combine chili powder, 2 tsp (10 mL) of the salt, paprika, brown sugar and half the black pepper; rub over pork and let stand for 1 hour. Preheat oven to 325°F (160°C). Rub oil over pork and place on a rack in a roasting pan. Roast for 2½ to 3 hours, or until a meat thermometer inserted in the thickest part registers 160°F (71°C) and meat is ready to fall apart. Transfer to a carving board and let rest for 15 minutes. Meanwhile, in a small saucepan, combine vinegar and sugar; cook over medium heat until sugar dissolves. Stir in hot pepper sauce and the remaining salt and pepper. Cut pork into 1½-inch (4 cm) thick slices. Tear slices into shreds, discarding any large pockets of fat. Combine pork and sauce. Serve on buns. Serves 8.

Rack of Pork with Roasted Pineapple

2 tbsp	packed dark brown sugar, divided	25 mL
2 tbsp	spicy brown mustard	25 mL
2 tbsp	canola oil, divided	25 mL
1 tsp	kosher salt, divided	5 mL
1 tsp	dried rosemary, crumbled	5 mL
1/4 tsp	ground cinnamon	1 mL
1/4 tsp	freshly ground black pepper	1 mL
Pinch	ground allspice	Pinch
Pinch	hot pepper flakes, divided	Pinch
1	4-rib rack of pork (about 3 1/2 lbs/1.75 kg)	1
4	fresh pineapple slices, each 1/2 inch (1 cm) thick, peeled, cored and quartered	4

Combine 1 tbsp (15 mL) of the brown sugar, the mustard, 2 tsp (10 mL) of the oil, salt, rosemary, cinnamon, black pepper, allspice and half the hot pepper flakes; rub over the meaty parts of the pork and let stand for 30 minutes. Meanwhile, combine the remaining brown sugar, salt and hot pepper flakes; set aside. Preheat oven to 375°F (190°C). Place pork, fat side up, on a rack in a roasting pan and roast for 40 minutes. Coat pineapple with the remaining oil and sprinkle with reserved seasoning mixture; scatter around pork. Roast for about 20 minutes, or until a meat thermometer inserted in the center (without touching the bone) registers 150°F (65°C). Transfer to a carving board and let rest for 10 minutes. Return pineapple to the oven for 10 minutes, until lightly browned. Carve pork as you would a rib roast and serve with pineapple. **Serves 6.**

Roasted Fish Provençal

2 tbsp	extra-virgin olive oil	25 mL
1	onion, chopped	1
1/2 cup	diced fennel bulb	125 mL
2	cloves garlic, finely chopped	2
1/2 tsp	dried herbes de Provence	2 mL
1 1/2 cups	canned diced tomatoes, drained	375 mL
1/2 cup	orange juice	125 mL
	Kosher salt and freshly ground black pepper to taste	
2	whole fish, such as sea bass or red snapper (each about 2 lbs/1 kg), scales and fins removed	2
2	drained canned anchovies, finely chopped	2
1/4 cup	chopped fresh basil	50 mL

Preheat oven to 375°F (190°C). In a metal roasting pan, heat oil over medium-high heat. Sauté onion and fennel until lightly browned. Add garlic and herbes de Provence; sauté for 1 minute. Add tomatoes, orange juice, salt and pepper; bring to a boil. Rub fish with additional salt and pepper, place in roasting pan and spoon sauce on top. Roast for 20 to 30 minutes, or until fish is opaque and flakes easily with a fork; transfer fish to a serving platter. Stir anchovies and basil into sauce and pour over fish. **Serves 6 to 8.**

Chapter 44
Romantic Recipes
Because Some Foods Are Meant for Seduction

The Morning After or Before
Ultra-Rich Spiked French Toast 487
Souffléd French Toast 488
Buttermilk Biscuits with a Heart 488
Herbed Biscuits with a Secret 488
Croissants with Scallops in Beurre Blanc . . 488
Shrimp in Croissants 488

Foreplay
Cajun Oysters 488
Caviar Coeur à la Crème 489
Smoked Salmon Coeur à la Crème 489
Spicy Shiitake Mushrooms 489
French Fries with Tapenade 489
Garlic and Walnut Baguette 489
Spinach Artichoke Bread 489
Shrimp on a Stick with
Spicy Avocado Sauce 490
Roasted Anchovy Potatoes 490
Ragoût of Wild Mushrooms 490
Warm Orange Walnut Spinach Salad . . 490

The Main Course
Salmon en Papillote with Shrimp
and Asparagus 490
Lobster with Red Pepper Coulis 491
Lobster Bouillabaisse 491
Lobster with Avocado Lobster Salsa . . . 491
Poussin Roasted with
Garlic and Molasses 491

Eating in Bed
Oysters and Caviar 492

Crispy Cranberry Game Hens 492
Caramelized Szechuan Hen 492
Chicken Fingers with
Roasted Pepper Dip 492
Baked Brie with Croissants 492
Shrimp Marinated in Wine and Lemon . . 492
Steak Sandwich with Béarnaise 493

Sweet Seductions and Love Tokens
Melon Filled with Port 493
Honeydew Filled with Champagne 493
Brioches with Chocolate Butter 493
Cinnamon Rolls with
Spiced Brown Sugar Butter 493
Spiked Orange Saffron Honey 493
Hot Pepper Honey 493
Lemon Ginger Honey 494
Berries with Framboise Honey 494
Champagne Granita 494
Margarita Ice 494
Mimosa Sorbet 494
Soft Irish Ice Cream 494
Raspberry Chocolate Bombe 495
Espresso Anise Bombe 495
Coeur à la Crème Doux 495
Warm Pink Pear Purée 495
Sinful Chocolate Tartlets 495
Peaches in Chianti 495
Warm Peaches with Sesame Praline . . . 496
Grand Marnier White
Chocolate Truffles 496
Praline Lace Hearts 496

Anthropologists tell us that, early on in human evolution, men and women were brought together primarily for two physical necessities — eating and procreation. Food and love have remained intimately entwined ever since.

We are seduced by food, and we hunger for love. Our loved ones are "sweet" and "look good enough to eat," just as we "desire" our favorite flavors and find the most delicious dishes "lip-smacking." Whether it's a notorious aphrodisiac or a homebaked bread, beautiful, sensual food, thoughtfully prepared, is not just the fastest way to soften a lover's heart, it opens all the senses for pleasure.

But food does not seduce alone. Timing, setting, lighting and mood must all play their part if the full effect is to be irresistible. Candlelight, crisp linen and champagne flutes on a table set for two are always a good bet, provided they're unexpected, for the one element of romantic dining that can't be overestimated is the subtle surprise that is the essence of romance.

For example, winter can be the perfect time for a picnic — in bed. Set the bed with a cloth and dishes, or serve on large trays while you snuggle under a quilt. Then select foods that can be eaten without utensils: room-temperature hens that can be ripped apart by hand and dipped into warm cranberry glaze; raw oysters studded with pearls of caviar to slide from their half shells between awaiting lips; strawberries in a pool of warm chocolate that rise from their bath delicately dangling a droplet of sauce.

Or start off an entire day of romance with wedges of ripe peach dipped in sweetened framboise, or heart-shaped biscuits slathered with spiced brown sugar butter. Fill a melon with raspberries and champagne the night before to create a morning after that will never be forgotten, or stuff croissants with anything from chocolate butter to smoked salmon mousse.

Move on to an herb-infused savory rendition of a classic French coeur à la crème for midday, or greet your lover with a steak sandwich like no other, crowning a grilled filet with sautéed mushrooms and a cloak of béarnaise. Keep dinner light and passions keen with a simple poached fish, a seafood stew or a rare roast beef. Serve asparagus, artichoke or a fanciful salad. Dessert can be nothing more than a few pieces of per-fectly ripened fruit, or one of our more spectacular creations, such as Sinful Chocolate Tartlets or Grand Marnier White Chocolate Truffles. If they don't do the trick, nothing will. For beautiful food eaten with one you love is all the more memorable when you rise from the table with your hunger soothed and your appetite yearning for more.

About these recipes . . .

The following 50 recipes are grouped according to the time of day or the nature of the occasion when they might be presented, but go ahead and use them in your own way. Note that several recipes call for a coeur à la crème mold. These are heart-shaped ceramic molds with holes in their bottoms to permit drainage. They are available at gourmet stores. If you don't want to go to the expense of buying one, the cheese can be molded in a small strainer lined with damp cheesecloth, although the resulting "coeur" will not be heart-shaped.

The Morning After or Before

Ultra-Rich Spiked French Toast

2	extra-large egg yolks	2
1	whole extra-large egg	1
½ cup	milk	125 mL
¼ cup	cream (any type, minimum 10%)	50 mL
2 tbsp	granulated sugar	25 mL
2 tbsp	orange-flavored liqueur	25 mL
Pinch	ground nutmeg	Pinch
Pinch	salt	Pinch
4	thick slices challah or other rich, slightly sweet bread	4
2 tbsp	unsalted butter	25 mL

In a wide, shallow bowl, beat egg yolks, egg, milk, cream, sugar, liqueur, nutmeg and salt. Soak challah in batter, in batches if necessary, until all liquid is absorbed. In a large skillet or on a griddle, melt butter over medium heat. Add soaked bread and cook, turning once, until browned on both sides. **Serves 2.**

Souffléd French Toast

2	extra-large eggs, separated	2
¼ cup	cream (any type, minimum 10%)	50 mL
2 tbsp	granulated sugar	25 mL
2 tbsp	milk	25 mL
2 tbsp	brandy	25 mL
Pinch	ground nutmeg	Pinch
Pinch	salt	Pinch
4	thick slices challah or other rich, slightly sweet bread	4
2 tbsp	unsalted butter	25 mL

In a wide, shallow bowl, beat egg yolks, cream, sugar, milk, brandy and nutmeg. In a separate bowl, beat egg whites and salt until soft peaks form; fold into batter. Soak challah in batter, in batches if necessary, until all liquid is absorbed. In a large skillet or on a griddle, melt butter over medium heat. Add soaked bread and cook, turning once, until browned on both sides. **Serves 2.**

Buttermilk Biscuits with a Heart

1½ cups	all-purpose flour	375 mL
2 tbsp	granulated sugar	25 mL
1½ tsp	baking powder	7 mL
1 tsp	baking soda	5 mL
Pinch	salt	Pinch
6 tbsp	butter, cut into small pieces	90 mL
1	extra-large egg	1
⅓ cup	buttermilk	75 mL
1 tsp	vanilla	5 mL
4	strawberries, hulled	4

Preheat oven to 400°F (200°C). In a large bowl, sift together flour, sugar, baking powder, baking soda and salt. Cut in butter until mixture resembles coarse meal. In another bowl, beat egg, buttermilk and vanilla; reserve 3 tbsp (45 mL). Mix the remaining buttermilk mixture into dry ingredients until uniformly moistened. On a floured work surface, knead dough lightly for 30 seconds, then pat out to ¼-inch (0.5 cm) thickness. Cut into 8 biscuits using a 3-inch (7.5 cm) heart-shaped cutter. Brush with some of the reserved liquid, place a strawberry on 4 of the biscuits and cover with the remaining biscuits, easing dough over the berries to enclose them. Press lightly on edges to seal and brush with the remaining reserved egg mixture. Place on a dry baking sheet and bake for 20 minutes, until puffed and brown. **Serves 2.**

Herbed Biscuits with a Secret

Follow preceding recipe, but add 2 tbsp (25 mL) chopped fresh herbs (such as flat-leaf parsley, basil, tarragon) with the flour, and replace the strawberries with 4 frozen nuggets of herbed cream cheese. Serves 2.

Croissants with Scallops in Beurre Blanc

2	large croissants	2
⅓ cup	dry white wine	75 mL
12 oz	sea scallops, trimmed of hard side muscles	375 mL
¼ cup	white wine vinegar	50 mL
1 tbsp	finely chopped shallot	15 mL
1 tbsp	whipping (35%) cream	15 mL
6 tbsp	butter, cut into small pieces	90 mL
1 tbsp	chopped fresh Italian (flat-leaf) parsley	15 mL

Remove a thin slice from the top of each croissant and set aside. Hollow out the interiors and warm in a 350°F (180°C) oven for 10 minutes. Meanwhile, in a small skillet, heat wine over medium heat. Poach scallops for 2 minutes; remove with a slotted spoon to a bowl and keep warm. Add vinegar and shallot to the pan and boil until liquid is reduced by about three-quarters. Add cream and bring to a simmer. Reduce heat to low and swirl in butter, one piece at a time. Pour sauce over scallops and toss to coat. Stir in parsley. Fill croissants with scallops, pour sauce over all and lean croissant "lids" to the side. **Serves 2.**

Shrimp in Croissants

Follow preceding recipe, but replace the scallops with 12 jumbo shrimp, peeled, deveined and butterflied. **Serves 2.**

Foreplay

Cajun Oysters

2	large croissants	2
12	shucked large oysters (see page 11), with their liquor	12
1 cup	whipping (35%) cream	250 mL
2 to 3 tsp	hot pepper sauce (such as Tabasco)	10 to 15 mL
2 tsp	caviar, any type (optional)	10 mL

Remove a thin slice from the top of each croissant and hollow out the interiors; set aside. In a nonstick skillet, heat a thin film of oyster liquor over medium-high heat. Sauté oysters until they plump and curl at the edges; remove with a slotted spoon to a plate. Boil liquid until reduced to 3 tbsp (45 mL). Add cream and hot pepper sauce; cook until lightly thickened. Return oysters to the pan and heat through. Serve in croissants, topped with caviar, if desired. **Serves 2.**

Caviar Coeur à la Crème

4 oz	whole-milk ricotta cheese	125 g
1 oz	cream cheese, softened	30 g
Pinch	salt	Pinch
2	green onions, minced	2
1 oz	golden caviar	30 g
1 oz	salmon caviar	30 g
1 tsp	freshly squeezed lemon juice	5 mL
Pinch	cayenne pepper	Pinch
Pinch	ground nutmeg	Pinch
4	slices black bread	4

Line two 1/2-cup (125 mL) coeur à la crème molds (see page 487) with damp cheesecloth. In a bowl, combine ricotta, cream cheese and salt. Stir in green onions, golden caviar, salmon caviar, lemon juice, cayenne and nutmeg. Spoon into prepared molds, cover with plastic wrap, weight lightly and place in a pan in the refrigerator to drain overnight. Invert onto plates. Cut bread into small hearts with a cookie cutter, then toast; arrange around coeur à la crème. **Serves 2.**

Smoked Salmon Coeur à la Crème

Follow preceding recipe, but replace the green onions with 1 1/2 tsp (7 mL) chopped fresh chives, and replace both caviars with 2 oz (60 g) smoked salmon, finely chopped. **Serves 2.**

Spicy Shiitake Mushrooms

1/2	small clove garlic, minced	1/2
1 1/2 tbsp	hoisin sauce	22 mL
1 1/2 tsp	dark sesame oil	7 mL
1 tsp	minced gingerroot	5 mL
1 tsp	dry sherry	5 mL
Pinch	hot pepper flakes	Pinch
12	large shiitake mushrooms, stemmed	12
2	lemon wedges	2

Preheat broiler or barbecue grill to high. Combine garlic, hoisin sauce, sesame oil, ginger, sherry and hot pepper flakes. Add mushrooms and toss to coat; cover and refrigerate for 1 hour. Thread mushrooms onto long-handled skewers and broil or grill for 1 to 2 minutes per side, or until firm. Serve with lemon wedges. **Serves 2.**

French Fries with Tapenade

Prepare 1/2 recipe Perfect Fries (page 391) and serve with 1/2 recipe Tapenade (page 56). **Serves 2.**

Garlic and Walnut Baguette

1	clove garlic	1
1/2 cup	walnut pieces	125 mL
2 tbsp	olive oil	25 mL
Pinch	salt	Pinch
1	small loaf French bread (demi-baguette)	1

Preheat oven to 375°F (190°C). In a food processor, purée garlic, walnut pieces, oil and salt to a paste. Cut bread into 1/2-inch (1 cm) thick diagonal slices without cutting completely through. Spread paste on one side of each bread slice and wrap loaf tightly in foil. Bake for 15 minutes, until heated through. **Serves 2.**

Spinach Artichoke Bread

4 tsp	olive oil, divided	20 mL
1	leek, white part only, finely chopped	1
1	clove garlic, minced	1
5 oz	frozen chopped spinach, thawed and drained	150 g
Pinch	ground mace	Pinch
	Salt and freshly ground black pepper to taste	
2	marinated artichoke hearts, chopped	2
8 oz	white bread dough (homemade or frozen, thawed)	250 g
	Ice water	

Grease a baking sheet with half the oil. In a large skillet, heat the remaining oil over medium heat. Sauté leek and garlic until tender. Add spinach and sauté until almost dry. Season with mace, salt and pepper. Remove from heat and add artichoke hearts. Pat dough into an 8- by 6-inch (20 by 15 cm) rectangle. Spread artichoke mixture over dough and, starting with one long side, roll up jelly roll-style. Pinch ends closed and place seam side down on prepared baking sheet. Cover with a damp towel and let rise until doubled in bulk. Preheat oven to 400°F (200°C). Slash tops of loaf and brush with ice water. Bake for 35 to 40 minutes, until crisp and golden on top and bottom. Let cool on a rack for 15 minutes. Serve warm. **Serves 2.**

Shrimp on a Stick with Spicy Avocado Sauce

2 tbsp	olive oil	25 mL
1 tbsp	freshly squeezed lemon juice	15 mL
12	jumbo shrimp, peeled and deveined	12
	Spicy Avocado Sauce (page 57)	

In a shallow dish, combine oil and lemon juice. Add shrimp and toss to coat. Cover and refrigerate for 1 hour. Preheat broiler or barbecue grill to high. Remove shrimp from marinade and discard marinade. Place 2 shrimp on each of 6 long-handled skewers. Broil or grill for 1 to 2 minutes per side, until pink and opaque. Serve with Spicy Avocado Sauce as a dip. **Serves 2.**

Roasted Anchovy Potatoes

1	can (1½ oz/48 g) anchovies, with oil	1
2	large russet potatoes	2
1	small clove garlic, minced	1
2 tbsp	mayonnaise	25 mL
2 tbsp	olive oil	25 mL
	Freshly ground black pepper to taste	

Preheat oven to 400°F (200°C). Rub anchovy oil over potatoes, pierce with a fork and bake for 50 to 60 minutes, until tender. Meanwhile, mash anchovies and combine with garlic, mayonnaise, olive oil and pepper. Split potatoes and top with sauce. **Serves 2.**

Ragoût of Wild Mushrooms

½ oz	dried morels, chanterelles or other wild mushrooms	15 g
¾ cup	hot water	175 mL
2 tbsp	butter	25 mL
1	leek, white part only, sliced	1
2 oz	fresh shiitake mushrooms, stemmed	60 g
2 oz	fresh oyster mushrooms, stemmed	60 g
2 oz	white mushrooms, stemmed and sliced	60 g
1	plum (Roma) tomato, peeled, seeded and chopped	1
1½ tsp	chopped fresh Italian (flat-leaf) parsley	7 mL
1 tsp	freshly squeezed lemon juice	5 mL
½ tsp	chopped fresh rosemary	2 mL
	Salt and freshly ground black pepper to taste	

Soak dried mushrooms in hot water for 15 minutes, until hydrated. Remove mushrooms and set aside. Strain soaking liquid through a coffee filter into a small saucepan; bring to a boil over medium-high heat and boil until reduced by about three-quarters. Meanwhile, in a large skillet, melt butter over medium heat. Sauté leek, hydrated mushrooms and fresh shiitake, oyster and white mushrooms until tender. Add soaking liquid, tomato, parsley, lemon juice, rosemary, salt and pepper; simmer until slightly thickened, about 4 minutes. **Serves 2.**

Warm Orange Walnut Spinach Salad

3 tbsp	orange juice	45 mL
2 tbsp	walnut oil	25 mL
1 tbsp	white wine vinegar	15 mL
Dash	cayenne pepper	Dash
	Salt to taste	
1	bag (6 oz/175 g) baby spinach	1
1	navel orange, peeled and sectioned	1
1	stalk celery, thinly sliced	1
¼ cup	thinly sliced red onion	50 mL
¼ cup	walnut pieces	50 mL

In a serving bowl, combine orange juice, oil, vinegar, cayenne and salt. Add the remaining ingredients and toss to coat. **Serves 2.**

The Main Course

Salmon en Papillote with Shrimp and Asparagus

10 oz	salmon fillet, skin and pin bones removed, sliced into 6 thin pieces	300 g
8	baby shrimp, peeled and deveined	8
6	asparagus tips	6
1	fresh tarragon leaf	1
2 tbsp	dry white wine	25 mL
1 tsp	butter	5 mL
2	lemon wedges	2

Preheat oven to 350°F (180°C). Place salmon on a large piece of heart-shaped parchment paper (see page 12) with shrimp, asparagus tips, tarragon, wine and butter. Wrap as explained on page 12 and place on a rimmed baking sheet. Bake for 12 minutes, or until parchment is puffed and brown. Serve in parchment sack, slitting it open at the table and sliding contents onto a platter. Garnish with lemon wedges. **Serves 2.**

Lobster with Red Pepper Coulis

2	live lobsters	2
	(each 1 to 1½ lbs/500 to 750 g)	
2 tbsp	freshly squeezed lemon juice	25 mL
1 tbsp	olive oil	15 mL
	Salt and freshly ground black pepper	
	to taste	
	Red Pepper Coulis (page 53)	

Preheat broiler. Kill and clean lobsters as described on page 10; discard roe and tomalley. Place cut side down on a broiler pan and broil until shells turn bright red, about 5 minutes. Turn over and sprinkle meat with lemon juice, oil, salt and pepper. Broil until lightly browned and meat is firm, about 4 minutes. Serve with Red Pepper Coulis. **Serves 2.**

Lobster Bouillabaisse

8 cups	water	2 L
1	live lobster (about 1 lb/500 g)	1
6	littleneck clams, scrubbed	6
	(see page 8)	
8	large shrimp, peeled and deveined,	8
	shells reserved	
2 tbsp	extra-virgin olive oil	25 mL
1	large onion, chopped	1
1	clove garlic, chopped	1
¼ tsp	dried thyme	2 mL
¼ tsp	dried basil	2 mL
¼ tsp	ground fennel seeds	2 mL
2 cups	canned crushed tomatoes	500 mL
½ cup	dry white wine	125 mL
½ tsp	crumbled saffron threads	2 mL
8 oz	skinless fish fillet,	250 g
	cut into 2-inch (5 cm) strips	
2 tbsp	chopped fresh Italian (flat-leaf)	25 mL
	parsley	

In a large pot, bring water to a boil. Add lobster and cook until bright red, about 12 minutes. Remove and cut into 8 pieces; set aside. Add clams to the pot, reduce heat and simmer for about 5 minutes, or until they open (discard any that don't); remove to a plate. Add shrimp shells to the pot, increase heat and boil until liquid is reduced by three-quarters; strain and reserve. In the same pot, heat oil over medium heat. Sauté onion, garlic, thyme, basil and fennel seeds until onion is tender. Add reserved cooking liquid, tomatoes, wine and saffron; simmer for 5 minutes. (Can be made ahead to this point, covered and refrigerated for up to 2 days. Reheat before proceeding.) Add fish and simmer for 3 minutes. Add lobster, clams and shrimp; simmer for 2 minutes, until shrimp is pink and opaque. Stir in parsley. **Serves 2.**

Lobster with Avocado Lobster Salsa

2	live lobsters (each about 1½ lbs/750 g)	2
1	recipe Avocado Salsa (page 177)	1
1 tsp	hot pepper oil	5 mL
¼ cup	warm melted butter	50 mL
1 tbsp	freshly squeezed lemon juice	15 mL
1 tsp	minced hot chili pepper	5 mL

Preheat broiler or barbecue grill to high. In a large pot of boiling salted water, cook lobsters for 5 minutes; cool under cold water. Split in half horizontally and scoop out any roe from the central cavity. Remove and discard gills and green tomalley. Crumble roe into Avocado Salsa. Brush interior of each lobster with hot pepper oil. Broil or grill for 3 minutes on each side, or until meat is firm. Fill cavity with salsa. Combine butter, lemon juice and hot pepper. Serve with lobster as a dipping sauce. **Serves 2.**

Poussin Roasted with Garlic and Molasses

1	poussin or Cornish game hen	1
	(about 2 lbs/1 kg)	
	Salt and freshly ground black pepper	
	to taste	
2 tbsp	extra-virgin olive oil	25 mL
20	cloves garlic	20
3 tbsp	dark (cooking) molasses	45 mL
1 tbsp	cider vinegar	15 mL

Preheat oven to 400°F (200°C). Season poussin inside and out with salt and pepper. In a skillet, heat oil over medium heat. Sauté garlic until tender and lightly browned. Transfer garlic with a slotted spoon to the cavity of the poussin. Place poussin on a rack in a roasting pan and roast for 25 minutes. Add molasses and vinegar to the oil in the pan and brush poussin with some of the pan liquid. Roast for 20 to 25 minutes, basting twice with pan liquid, until a meat thermometer inserted in the thickest part of a thigh registers 165°F (74°C). Serve bird surrounded by roasted garlic cloves. **Serves 2.**

Eating in Bed

Oysters and Caviar

12	large oysters	12
12	thin lemon wedges	12
1½ tsp	caviar (any type)	7 mL
	Hot pepper sauce (such as Tabasco)	
	Cracked ice	

Open oysters (see page 11), and serve each with 1 thin lemon wedge, a pinch of caviar and 2 to 3 drops hot pepper sauce. Serve on a bed of cracked ice. **Serves 2.**

Crispy Cranberry Game Hens

1	game hen (about 2 lbs/1 kg), split in half lengthwise, backbone removed	1
	Salt and freshly ground black pepper to taste	
¼ cup	cranberry juice	50 mL
¼ cup	orange juice	50 mL
1 tbsp	raspberry vinegar	15 mL
1 tbsp	honey	15 mL
Pinch	cayenne pepper	Pinch

Season hen halves with salt and pepper. In a large sealable plastic bag, combine cranberry juice, orange juice, vinegar, honey, cayenne and additional salt. Add hen halves, seal and shake to coat. Refrigerate for 2 hours. Preheat broiler. Remove hen halves from marinade, reserving marinade. Broil hen halves for 10 minutes per side, or until juices run clear when thigh is pierced. Meanwhile, in a small saucepan, boil marinade until reduced by three-quarters. Baste hen halves with reduced marinade during the last 5 minutes of cooking. **Serves 2.**

Caramelized Szechuan Hen

Follow preceding recipe, but replace the cranberry marinade with Spicy Hoisin Sauce (page 51). **Serves 2.**

Chicken Fingers with Roasted Pepper Dip

12 oz	boneless skinless chicken breast, cut into fingers	375 g
½ cup	all-purpose flour, seasoned heavily with salt and cayenne pepper	125 mL
	Vegetable oil	
1	large roasted red bell pepper (see page 11), finely chopped	1
1	clove garlic, minced	1
¼ cup	finely chopped fresh basil	50 mL
2 tbsp	extra-virgin olive oil	25 mL
	Salt and cayenne pepper to taste	

Dredge chicken fingers in seasoned flour, shaking off excess. Deep-fry (see page 9) until golden brown, about 3 minutes. Combine roasted pepper, garlic, basil, oil, salt and cayenne. Serve with chicken fingers as a dipping sauce. **Serves 2.**

Baked Brie with Croissants

1	4½-inch (11 cm) round of Brie cheese	1
4	croissants	4

Preheat oven to 425°F (220°C). Place Brie in a baking dish and bake for 15 minutes. Place croissants in the oven for last 5 minutes of baking. Remove both from oven and slice off the top of the Brie. Serve cheese surrounded by croissants. **Serves 2.**

Shrimp Marinated in Wine and Lemon

12	jumbo shrimp, peeled and deveined	12
3	green onions, white parts only, sliced	3
2	cloves garlic, thinly sliced	2
2 tbsp	dry white wine	25 mL
1 tbsp	extra-virgin olive oil, divided	15 mL
2 tbsp	freshly squeezed lemon juice	25 mL
Pinch	cayenne pepper	Pinch
	Salt and freshly ground black pepper to taste	

In a small skillet, toss shrimp with green onions, garlic, wine and half the oil. Cook over medium-high heat until liquid begins to bubble and shrimp are pink and opaque. Remove from heat and stir in the remaining oil, lemon juice, cayenne, salt and black pepper. Transfer to a serving bowl, cover and refrigerate for about 1 hour, until chilled. Serve with toothpicks as finger food. **Serves 2.**

Steak Sandwich with Béarnaise

2	shallots, minced	2
¼ cup	dry white wine	50 mL
2½ tbsp	white wine vinegar	32 mL
½ tsp	dried tarragon	2 mL
1	extra-large egg yolk	1
6 tbsp	butter, cut into small pieces, divided	90 mL
6	large mushrooms, thinly sliced	6
8 oz	filet mignon, cut into 4 thin steaks	250 g
	Salt and freshly ground black pepper to taste	
2	4-inch (10 cm) French bread dinner rolls, halved	2
2	sprigs fresh tarragon	2

In a skillet, bring shallots, wine, vinegar and tarragon to a boil; boil until reduced by about two-thirds. Transfer to the top of a small double boiler, over simmering water, and whisk in egg yolk; cook, whisking, until fluffy and thick. Remove from heat and whisk in 4 tbsp (50 mL) of the butter in 2 additions; keep warm. In a large skillet, melt 1 tbsp (15 mL) of the butter over medium-high heat. Sauté mushrooms until tender; remove to a plate and keep warm. Season steaks with salt and pepper. In the same skillet, melt the remaining butter over medium-high heat. Cook steaks, turning once, until browned on both sides. Spoon mushrooms over bottom halves of rolls. Place 2 steaks, slightly overlapping, on top of mushrooms on each roll. Top with sauce and garnish each with 1 tarragon sprig. Crown with top halves of rolls. **Serves 2.**

Sweet Seduction and Love Tokens

Melon Filled with Port

1	small cantaloupe	1
¾ cup	red seedless grapes	175 mL
½ cup	ruby port	125 mL

Cut a plug from the stem end of the cantaloupe, leaving a hole large enough for a soup spoon. Remove plug, scrape away any seeds clinging to its underside and scoop out seeds from interior. Fill cavity with grapes and port; replace plug. Set melon in a bowl, with the plug facing up, and refrigerate for about 2 hours, until chilled. To serve, cut melon in half and serve each half filled with grapes and about 2 tbsp (25 mL) of the port. **Serves 2.**

Honeydew Filled with Champagne

Follow preceding recipe, but substitute 1 honeydew melon for the cantaloupe, 1 cup (250 mL) raspberries for the grapes, and ½ cup (125 mL) Champagne for the port. **Serves 2.**

Brioches with Chocolate Butter

¼ cup	unsalted butter, softened	50 mL
1 oz	semisweet chocolate, melted and cooled slightly	30 g
2	brioches or croissants	2

Beat butter until fluffy, then fold in chocolate. Pour into a ramekin and chill until firm. Warm brioches and serve with chocolate butter. **Serves 2.**

Cinnamon Rolls with Spiced Brown Sugar Butter

¼ cup	unsalted butter	50 mL
1 tbsp	packed brown sugar	15 mL
¼ tsp	ground cinnamon	1 mL
Pinch	ground allspice	Pinch
Pinch	ground ginger	Pinch
2	warm cinnamon rolls	2

Beat butter, brown sugar, cinnamon, allspice and ginger until fluffy. Spread on cinnamon rolls. **Serves 2.**

Spiked Orange Saffron Honey

10	threads saffron, crumbled	10
2 tbsp	warm orange-flavored liqueur	25 mL
½ cup	honey	125 mL

Combine saffron and liqueur, then stir in honey. **Makes about ⅔ cup (150 mL).** *Drizzle over fruit, or spread on bread or biscuits.*

Hot Pepper Honey

¼ cup	honey	50 mL
1 tbsp	hot pepper sauce (such as Frank's RedHot)	15 mL

Combine honey and hot pepper sauce. **Makes about ¼ cup (50 mL).** *Serve with corn muffins, corn cakes or warm biscuits.*

Lemon Ginger Honey

2 tbsp	minced candied ginger	25 mL
2 tbsp	honey	25 mL
1 tsp	freshly squeezed lemon juice	5 mL

Combine ginger, honey and lemon juice. **Makes about ¼ cup (50 mL).** *Serve on muffins, biscuits or buns.*

Berries with Framboise Honey

2 tbsp	honey	25 mL
1 tbsp	framboise or other raspberry-flavored liqueur	15 mL
2 cups	berries	500 mL

Combine honey and framboise. Serve as a dipping sauce with berries. **Serves 2.**

Champagne Granita

1¼ cups	water	300 mL
1 cup	granulated sugar	250 mL
2 tbsp	raspberry vinegar	25 mL
½ cup	Champagne (or sparkling wine)	125 mL
Pinch	salt	Pinch

In a saucepan, bring water, sugar and vinegar to a boil, without stirring. Let cool, then add Champagne and salt. Pour into a shallow pan and place in freezer for 1 hour. Stir the ice crystals forming at the edge of the pan into the more liquid portions. Freeze, stirring every 30 minutes, until the mixture is a firm slush, about 3 hours. Scrape into champagne flutes. **Serves 2.**

Margarita Ice

Follow preceding recipe, but replace the vinegar with freshly squeezed lime juice, and replace the Champagne with a mixture of ¼ cup (50 mL) water, 3 tbsp (45 mL) tequila and 1 tbsp (15 mL) orange-flavored liqueur. Serve in glasses with rims moistened and dipped in salt. **Serves 2.**

Mimosa Sorbet

1	egg white, beaten	1
1 cup	Simple Syrup (see recipe, page 23), chilled	250 mL
1 cup	orange juice	250 mL
½ cup	Champagne (or sparkling wine)	125 mL
½ cup	water	125 mL
1 tbsp	white wine vinegar	15 mL
1 tbsp	brandy	15 mL
	Juice of 1 lemon	

Combine all ingredients, cover and refrigerate until cold. Freeze in an ice cream maker according to manufacturer's directions. **Makes about 3 cups (750 mL).** *(If you are concerned about the food safety of the raw egg white, you can replace it with 2 tbsp/25 mL pasteurized liquid egg whites.)*

Soft Irish Ice Cream

1 cup	whole milk	250 mL
1 cup	granulated sugar, divided	250 mL
½ tsp	salt	2 mL
½	vanilla bean	½
3	egg yolks	3
1 cup	whipping (35%) cream	250 mL
3 tbsp	Irish whiskey	45 mL
	Ground cinnamon	

In a small saucepan, bring milk, half the sugar, salt and vanilla bean to a simmer over medium heat. Beat egg yolks with remaining sugar. Add milk mixture in a slow, steady stream, whisking constantly. Return to the saucepan and cook over low heat, stirring, until mixture coats a spoon (do not overcook). Let cool, then stir in cream and whiskey. Cover and refrigerate until cold. Freeze in an ice cream maker according to manufacturer's directions to the consistency of soft ice cream. Serve sprinkled with cinnamon. **Makes about 3 cups (750 mL).**

Raspberry Chocolate Bombe

4 cups	raspberry sherbet	1 L
2 oz	semisweet chocolate, shaved	60 g
2 cups	fresh raspberries	500 mL
2 cups	chocolate ice cream, softened	500 mL
	Chocolate sauce	

Press sherbet into a frozen 8-cup (2 L) metal bowl so it forms a shell ½ inch (1 cm) thick. Line with plastic wrap to hold in place and freeze until firm, about 1 hour. Remove plastic wrap and sprinkle chocolate shavings and raspberries over sherbet. Fill center with ice cream. Cover with plastic wrap and freeze overnight. To unmold, dip bowl in warm water for 10 seconds and invert onto a platter. Serve with chocolate sauce. **Serves 8.**

Espresso Anise Bombe

1 tbsp	instant espresso powder	15 mL
1½ tsp	warm milk	7 mL
1½ tbsp	coffee-flavored liqueur	22 mL
2 cups	coffee ice cream	500 mL
1 tbsp	anise-flavored liqueur (such as Pernod)	15 mL
¼ tsp	anise extract	1 mL
1½ cups	vanilla ice cream	375 mL

Dissolve espresso powder in warm milk. Stir in coffee-flavored liqueur. Beat espresso mixture into coffee ice cream and freeze. Beat anise-flavored liqueur and anise extract into vanilla ice cream and freeze. Follow preceding recipe, using the frozen coffee mixture for the outer shell and the frozen anise mixture for the center filling. Omit the chocolate shavings and raspberries. **Serves 8.**

Coeur à la Crème Doux

4 oz	ricotta cheese	125 g
1 oz	cream cheese, softened	30 g
1 tbsp	confectioner's (icing) sugar	15 mL
Pinch	salt	Pinch
½ cup	whipped cream	125 mL
1 tsp	honey	5 mL
1½ tsp	orange-flavored liqueur	7 mL
6	strawberries, halved	6

Line two ½-cup (125 mL) coeur à la crème molds (see page 487) with damp cheesecloth. Blend ricotta, cream cheese, confectioner's sugar and salt. Fold in whipped cream. Spoon into prepared molds, cover with plastic, weight lightly and place in a pan in the refrigerator to drain overnight. Invert onto plates. Combine honey and liqueur.

Add strawberries and toss to coat. Pour any excess honey mixture over coeur à la crème and top with berries. **Serves 2.**

Warm Pink Pear Purée

1	vanilla bean, split	1
1½ lbs	pears, peeled and coarsely chopped	750 g
1 cup	red wine	250 mL
¼ cup	granulated sugar	50 mL
1 tbsp	freshly squeezed lemon juice	15 mL
Pinch	salt	Pinch
2 tbsp	butter, softened	25 mL

In a heavy saucepan, combine vanilla bean, pears, wine, sugar, lemon juice and salt; bring to a simmer over medium heat. Simmer for 8 to 10 minutes, or until pears are tender. Remove pears with a slotted spoon to a food processor and purée. Simmer pan liquid until reduced by about three-quarters. Discard vanilla bean and add liquid to the purée. Whisk in butter. Serve warm. **Serves 2.**

Sinful Chocolate Tartlets

2 oz	semisweet chocolate, chopped	60 g
2 tbsp	granulated sugar	25 mL
⅓ cup	whipping (35%) cream	75 mL
4	prebaked 3-inch (7.5 cm) tartlet shells made from Sweet Pastry (see page 21)	4

Melt chocolate and sugar in the top of a double boiler over simmering water. In a small saucepan, scald cream over medium-low heat just until bubbles form around the edge. Slowly whisk cream into chocolate mixture and cook for 15 minutes, scraping sides occasionally with a rubber spatula. Remove from heat and chill over ice until cool to the touch. Pour into tartlet shells and refrigerate until set, about 2 hours. **Serves 2.**

Peaches in Chianti

2	perfectly ripe large peaches, peeled (see "blanching," page 8)	2
¾ cup	Chianti Classico	175 mL

Slice peaches into thin wedges. Place in a bowl and pour wine over top. Cover and refrigerate for 30 minutes. **Serves 2.**

Warm Peaches with Sesame Praline

1/3 cup	granulated sugar, divided	75 mL
1/2 cup	sesame seeds, toasted	50 mL
2 tbsp	unsalted butter	25 mL
2	peaches, peeled (see "blanching," page 8) and sliced	2
2 tbsp	white wine	25 mL
Dash	vanilla	Dash

In a small, heavy saucepan, melt all but 1 tbsp (15 mL) of the sugar until it turns amber, stirring frequently (be careful; sugar is scorching hot). Stir in sesame seeds. Pour mixture onto a baking sheet, spreading as thin as possible with the back of a spoon; let cool to room temperature. Break into pieces, place in a food processor and grind to a coarse powder; set aside. In a large skillet, melt butter over medium-high heat. Sauté peaches until they are glazed with butter, about 1 minute. Add wine and the remaining sugar; boil until liquid has evaporated and peaches look glossy. Add vanilla. Serve warm, topped with a generous sprinkling of praline powder. **Serves 2.**

Grand Marnier White Chocolate Truffles

1/2 cup	whipping (35%) cream	50 mL
1 tbsp	butter	15 mL
8 oz	white chocolate, finely chopped	250 g
1/4 cup	Grand Marnier or other orange-flavored liqueur	50 mL
4 oz	bittersweet chocolate, melted	125 g

In a small saucepan, heat cream and butter over low heat until butter is melted. Remove from heat and stir in white chocolate until melted. Transfer to a bowl and whisk in liqueur. Cover and refrigerate for 1 to 2 hours, until firm. Shape into rough balls that could fit in a soup spoon, place on a baking sheet lined with waxed paper and freeze until solid, about 10 minutes. Dip in bittersweet chocolate and return to baking sheet. Refrigerate until chocolate sets, about 1 hour. **Makes about 12 truffles.**

Praline Lace Hearts

6 tbsp	all-purpose flour	90 mL
1/4 tsp	baking powder	1 mL
1/2 cup	finely chopped pecans	125 mL
6 tbsp	granulated sugar	90 mL
1/3 cup	melted butter	70 mL
2 tbsp	milk	25 mL
2 tbsp	dark corn syrup	25 mL
1/4 tsp	almond extract	1 mL

Preheat oven to 350°F (180°C) and grease a baking sheet. Sift together flour and baking powder. Stir in pecans and sugar. Stir in butter, milk, corn syrup and almond extract. Using 2 tsp (10 mL) of this batter, form a V shape on prepared baking sheet, with each line of the V about 1 1/2 inches (4 cm) long. Make a total of 5 V's, placed about 3 inches (7.5 cm) apart. Bake for 10 to 12 minutes, rotating pan once during baking, until well browned around the edges. Let cool on pan for 2 minutes. Remove from pan with a wide spatula and let cool completely on a rack. **Serves 2.**

Chapter 45
Low-Calorie Recipes
For Keeping Slim

Middle Eastern Chicken Salad 498

Stir-Fried Chicken Chicory Salad 498

Chicken Steamed with
Roasted Pepper and Cilantro 499

Curried Tandoori-Style Chicken 499

Grilled Chicken with
Spicy Artichoke Relish 499

Stir-Fried Chicken in
Orange Black Bean Sauce 500

Grilled Chicken with
Red Pepper and Roasted Eggplant 500

Grilled Turkey Breast
with Tomato Basil Salsa 500

Spaghetti with Turkey Bolognese 500

Lemon Cilantro Turkey Breast 501

Roasted Turkey Breast with Mint 501

Fillets of Sole Steamed
with Lemon and Cilantro 501

Steamed Flounder
with Yogurt Dill Sauce 501

Dilled Salmon Salad 501

Flounder and Salmon
Steamed in Romaine 502

Snapper Steamed
with Green Peppercorns 502

Salmon Stewed with
Fennel and Mushrooms 502

Mexican Stewed Monkfish 502

Codfish and Cabbage 502

Gingered Black Bean Bluefish 503

Flounder with Arugula 503

Stir-Fry of Crab and Asparagus 503

Crab and Shrimp Stir-Fried
with Lime and Grapes 503

Middle Eastern Barbecued
Soft-Shell Crabs 504

Hard-Shell Crabs Cooked in Beer 504

Tea-Smoked Mussels and Clams 504

Mussels in Tomato over Orzo 504

Orange and Fennel Mussels 504

Clams Steamed in Tomato Broth 504

Curried Tandoori-Style Shrimp 505

Shrimp Stew with Mint Pesto 505

Stir-Fried Sesame Oysters 505

Shrimp and Oysters with Basil 505

Asparagus, Shrimp, Raspberry
and Grapefruit Salad 506

Sautéed Shrimp on
Cucumber "Noodles" 506

Seafood Pot au Feu 506

Artichoke Ratatouille 506

Tofu Braised with Wild Mushrooms 507

Asparagus Salad 507

Stir-Fried Sesame Vegetables 507

Grilled Rabbit 507

Venison in Mustard Crust 508

Veal Scallops with
Asparagus and Capers 508

Grilled Mustard-Glazed Veal Chops . . . 508

Veal au Poivre 508

Pork Medallions with
Mustard and Capers 508

Pork Braised in Apple Cider 509

Grilled Pork Medallions
with Mustard and Rosemary 509

Lamb Chops Braised
with Belgian Endive 509

Lamb with Lemon and Mint 509

From a culinary tradition steeped in calories, fat, salt and sugar, nothing short of a food revolution has occurred in the past few decades: we want less. All those things have become our kitchen enemies. So has time.

Today's home cooks judge recipes based on how complex they are and how many calories they contain. Those that call for pints of whipping cream and hours in the kitchen are inevitably left unused by busy, calorie-conscious cooks. Like unsung songs and unseen art, such untried recipes might as well not exist.

The following 50 recipes, which explore poultry, fish, shellfish, game meats, veal, pork and vegetables, were built with slimness in mind. They are as simple and streamlined as everything else in these pages, but in this chapter we pay special attention to calories. In most cases, we've done so by drastically cutting fat and sweeteners. Anyone can make food flavorful by using lots of butter and sugar. The trick to these recipes lies in our reliance on highly flavored ingredients — herbs, broths and purées — that have the added benefit of reducing the need for salt. And to help you keep tabs on everything going into your meals, we've minimized the use of processed food and prepackaged ingredients.

About these recipes . . .

Each of the following recipes contains less than 300 calories per serving, allowing you ample room for side dishes and a reasonable dessert while remaining well within the boundaries of most calorie-reduced or -restricted diets. But to stay within these calorie limits, you must follow ingredient quantities carefully. One tablespoon (15 mL) of oil means exactly that; another tablespoon (15 mL) would add 30 calories to one portion of a 4-serving dish. With regard to meat, "trimmed" means that all excess fat and skin should be removed. All recipes can be seasoned to taste with salt and pepper.

All chicken breasts are skinless, boneless and trimmed breast halves. When pounding chicken or turkey breasts (or other cuts that call for pounding), do so between two sheets of plastic wrap to ¼-inch (0.5 cm) thickness. Remove the wrap before proceeding with the recipe.

Middle Eastern Chicken Salad

1½ lbs	boneless skinless chicken breasts, cut into bite-size pieces	750 g
1	clove garlic, minced	1
1 cup	nonfat plain yogurt	250 mL
2 tbsp	chopped fresh Italian (flat-leaf) parsley	25 mL
2 tbsp	chopped fresh mint	25 mL
1 tbsp	freshly squeezed lemon juice	15 mL
2 tsp	extra-virgin olive oil	10 mL
Pinch	cayenne pepper	Pinch
	Salt and freshly ground black pepper to taste	
2	green onions, sliced	2
½	cucumber, peeled, seeded and diced	½

Bring a pot of lightly salted water to a boil. Stir in chicken, cover and remove from heat. Let stand for 5 minutes, until chicken is no longer pink inside; drain. In a serving bowl, combine garlic, yogurt, parsley, mint, lemon juice, oil, cayenne, salt and black pepper. Add chicken, green onions and cucumber; toss to coat. Cover and refrigerate for about 1 hour, until chilled. **Serves 4.**

Stir-Fried Chicken Chicory Salad

4	boneless skinless chicken breasts (each 6 oz/175 g), cut into bite-size pieces	4
	Kosher salt and freshly ground black pepper to taste	
1 tbsp	canola oil, divided	15 mL
1	red onion, coarsely chopped	1
2	cloves garlic, minced	2
4 oz	smoked turkey breast, diced	125 g
¼ cup	dry sherry	50 mL
Pinch	hot pepper flakes	Pinch
½ cup	fat-free chicken broth	125 mL
1 tbsp	cider vinegar	15 mL
1 tbsp	honey mustard	15 mL
1 tsp	soy sauce	5 mL
3 cups	shredded chicory, escarole, or curly endive	750 mL

Season chicken with salt and black pepper. In a heavy wok or large skillet, heat half the oil over medium-high heat. Stir-fry chicken until browned on all sides; remove to a plate. Add the remaining oil and onion to the pan and stir-fry until onion is translucent. Add garlic, turkey, sherry and hot pepper flakes; boil until reduced by half. Return chicken to pan and add broth; bring to a boil. Remove from heat and stir in vinegar, mustard and soy sauce. Toss with escarole and serve immediately. **Serves 4.**

Chicken Steamed with Roasted Pepper and Cilantro

2	cloves garlic, minced	2
2 tbsp	freshly squeezed lemon juice	25 mL
1 tbsp	extra-virgin olive oil	15 mL
½ tsp	ground coriander	2 mL
½ tsp	ground cumin	2 mL
Pinch	cayenne pepper	Pinch
4	boneless skinless chicken breasts (each 6 oz/175 g)	4
1	roasted red bell pepper (see page 11), cut into thin strips	1
¼ cup	chopped fresh cilantro	50 mL

In a shallow dish, combine garlic, lemon juice, oil, coriander, cumin and cayenne. Add chicken and turn to coat; cover and refrigerate for 1 hour. Remove chicken from marinade and discard marinade. Pound as directed in "About these recipes" (page 498). Roll each breast into a cigar shape around a portion of roasted pepper and cilantro; wrap each "cigar" in microwave-safe plastic wrap. Place in a steamer basket set in a pan of simmering water; cover and steam until firm, about 15 minutes. Snip one end of the plastic and pour any juices into a small saucepan; boil until slightly thickened. Slice chicken and pour juices on top. **Serves 4.**

Curried Tandoori-Style Chicken

2	large cloves garlic, minced	2
½ cup	nonfat plain yogurt	125 mL
2 tbsp	finely chopped gingerroot	25 mL
2 tsp	curry powder	10 mL
2 tsp	hot paprika	10 mL
1 tsp	ground cumin	5 mL
1 tsp	ground cardamom	5 mL
½ tsp	salt	2 mL
	Juice of 1 large lemon	
4	boneless skinless chicken breasts (each 6 oz/175 g)	4

In a shallow dish, combine garlic, yogurt, ginger, curry powder, paprika, cumin, cardamom and salt. Poke chicken all over with a fork, add to dish and turn to coat. Cover and refrigerate for 4 hours. Preheat broiler. Wipe excess yogurt mixture off chicken. Broil for 4 to 5 minutes per side, or until browned on both sides and no longer pink inside. **Serves 4.**

Grilled Chicken with Spicy Artichoke Relish

2	cloves garlic, minced	2
1	jar (6 oz/170 mL) marinated artichoke hearts, drained and finely chopped	1
1	jalapeño pepper, seeded and finely chopped	1
2 tbsp	freshly squeezed lemon juice	25 mL
1 tbsp	chopped fresh cilantro	15 mL
1 tbsp	chopped fresh Italian (flat-leaf) parsley	15 mL
4	boneless skinless chicken breasts (each 6 oz/175 g)	4
	Salt and freshly ground black pepper to taste	
1 tbsp	extra-virgin olive oil	15 mL

Preheat barbecue grill to high. Combine garlic, artichoke hearts, jalapeño, lemon juice, cilantro and parsley; set aside. Season chicken with salt and black pepper, then coat with oil. Pound as directed in "About these recipes" (page 498). Grill for 3 to 4 minutes per side, until browned on both sides and no longer pink inside. Serve topped with artichoke relish. **Serves 4.**

Stir-Fried Chicken in Orange Black Bean Sauce

1 tbsp	Chinese black bean sauce	15 mL
	Finely grated zest and juice of 1 orange	
1 lb	boneless skinless chicken breasts, cut into bite-size chunks	500 g
	Kosher salt and freshly ground black pepper to taste	
1 tbsp	cornstarch, dissolved in ¼ cup (50 mL) water	15 mL
1 tbsp	canola oil	15 mL
1	clove garlic, minced	1
1 tbsp	finely grated gingerroot	15 mL
Pinch	hot pepper flakes	Pinch
4 oz	somen noodles, cooked, hot	125 g
¼ tsp	dark sesame oil	1 mL
2	green onions, sliced	2

Combine black bean sauce, orange zest and orange juice; set aside. Season chicken with salt and black pepper, then toss with cornstarch mixture. In a heavy wok or large skillet, heat oil over medium-high heat. Remove chicken from cornstarch mixture, reserving liquid. Stir-fry chicken until no longer pink inside, about 4 minutes. Add garlic, ginger and hot pepper flakes; sauté for 30 seconds. Add black bean mixture and bring to a boil. Add reserved cornstarch mixture and cook until sauce thickens. Place noodles on a platter and spoon chicken on top. Drizzle with sesame oil and sprinkle with green onions. **Serves 4.**

Grilled Chicken with Red Pepper and Roasted Eggplant

2	cloves garlic, minced, divided	2
2 tbsp	extra-virgin olive oil, divided	25 mL
1 tsp	hot paprika	5 mL
	Salt and freshly ground black pepper to taste	
4	boneless skinless chicken breasts (each 6 oz/175 g)	4
8 oz	roasted eggplant (see page 19)	250 g
1½ tbsp	freshly squeezed lemon juice	22 mL
1	red bell pepper, diced	1
2 tbsp	minced fresh Italian (flat-leaf) parsley	25 mL
1 tbsp	finely chopped fresh chives	15 mL

Preheat barbecue grill to high. Combine half the garlic, 2 tsp (10 mL) of the oil, paprika, salt and black pepper; rub mixture over chicken. Pound as directed in "About these recipes" (page 498); set aside. In a food processor, purée the remaining garlic, 1 tbsp (15 mL) of the oil, eggplant and lemon juice; set aside and keep warm. In a small nonstick skillet, heat the remaining oil over medium heat. Sauté red pepper until tender. Remove from heat and stir in parsley and chives; set aside. Grill chicken for 3 to 4 minutes per side, until browned on both sides and no longer pink inside. Spoon eggplant sauce over top and sprinkle with pepper mixture. **Serves 4.**

Grilled Turkey Breast with Tomato Basil Salsa

½	clove garlic, minced	½
8 oz	tomatoes, finely chopped	250 g
⅓ cup	chopped fresh basil	75 mL
¼ cup	finely chopped red onion	50 mL
2 tsp	red wine vinegar	10 mL
	Salt and freshly ground black pepper to taste	
8	turkey breast cutlets (each 3 oz/90 g)	8
2 tsp	extra-virgin olive oil	10 mL

Preheat broiler or barbecue grill to high. Combine garlic, tomato, basil, onion, vinegar, salt and pepper; set aside. Season turkey with additional salt and pepper, then rub with oil. Pound as directed in "About these recipes" (page 498). Broil or grill for 1½ minutes per side, until browned on both sides and no longer pink inside. Serve with tomato basil salsa. **Serves 4.**

Spaghetti with Turkey Bolognese

1 tbsp	olive oil	15 mL
1	small carrot, finely diced	1
1	small stalk celery, finely diced	1
2 tbsp	finely chopped onion	25 mL
8 oz	lean ground turkey	250 g
½ cup	fat-free milk	125 mL
Pinch	ground nutmeg	Pinch
2 cups	canned crushed tomatoes	500 mL
1 tsp	dried basil	5 mL
1 tsp	tomato paste	5 mL
12 oz	spaghetti, cooked al dente, hot	375 g

In a large saucepan, heat oil over medium heat. Sauté carrot, celery and onion until tender. Add turkey and sauté, breaking up with a fork, until no longer pink. Add milk and nutmeg; cook until mixture is dry. Add tomatoes, basil and tomato paste; reduce heat and simmer gently for 1 hour. Serve tossed with spaghetti. **Serves 4.**

Lemon Cilantro Turkey Breast

3	cloves garlic, minced	3
1½ tbsp	extra-virgin olive oil, divided	22 mL
1 tbsp	ground coriander	15 mL
	Salt and freshly ground black pepper to taste	
	Finely grated zest and juice of 1 lemon	
1	bone-in turkey breast (6 lbs/3 kg)	1
1	bunch fresh cilantro, leaves and stems separated	1

Preheat oven to 375°F (190°C). Combine garlic, half the oil, coriander, salt, pepper and lemon zest. Loosen and lift skin from turkey and rub meat with garlic mixture. Lay cilantro leaves over meat, replace skin and rub with the remaining oil. Scatter cilantro stems in a roasting pan and place turkey, skin side up, on top. Roast for about 1 hour and 45 minutes, basting frequently with pan drippings, until a meat thermometer inserted in the thickest part registers 165°F (74°C). Transfer to a carving board and let rest for 15 minutes. Remove skin, drizzle lemon juice over top and slice. **Serves 12.**

Roasted Turkey Breast with Mint

1	bone-in turkey breast (6 lbs/3 kg)	1
	Salt and freshly ground black pepper to taste	
3	cloves garlic, minced	3
¼ cup	nonfat plain yogurt	50 mL
1 tbsp	extra-virgin olive oil, divided	15 mL
1 tbsp	freshly squeezed lemon juice	15 mL
1	bunch fresh mint, leaves and stems separated, leaves chopped	1

Preheat oven to 375°F (190°C). Loosen and lift skin from turkey and rub meat with salt and pepper. Combine garlic, yogurt, half the oil and lemon juice; rub over meat. Place mint leaves over meat, replace skin and rub with the remaining oil. Scatter mint stems in a roasting pan and place turkey, skin side up, on top. Roast for about 1 hour and 45 minutes, basting frequently with pan drippings, until a meat thermometer inserted in the thickest part registers 165°F (74°C). Transfer to a carving board and let rest for 15 minutes. Remove skin and slice. **Serves 12.**

Fillets of Sole Steamed with Lemon and Cilantro

4	skinless sole fillets	4
1 tsp	dark sesame oil	5 mL
	Juice of 1 lemon	
Pinch	ground nutmeg	Pinch
	Salt and freshly ground black pepper to taste	
2 tbsp	chopped fresh cilantro	25 mL
4	lemon wedges	4

Arrange fillets, dark side down, on a heatproof plate. Drizzle with oil and lemon juice, then season with nutmeg, salt and pepper. Sprinkle with cilantro and invert another plate on top or cover with foil. Place over a pot of simmering water just large enough to hold the plate on its rim, and steam for 8 minutes, until fish is opaque and flakes easily with a fork. Serve garnished with lemon wedges. **Serves 4.**

Steamed Flounder with Yogurt Dill Sauce

4	flounder fillets (each 4 oz/125 g)	4
1 tbsp	freshly squeezed lemon juice	15 mL
	Salt and freshly ground black pepper to taste	
1	shallot, minced	1
½ cup	nonfat plain yogurt	125 mL
2 tbsp	chopped fresh dill	25 mL

Season fillets with lemon juice, salt and pepper. Roll each fillet lengthwise into a tight roll and wrap each tightly in microwave-safe plastic wrap. Place in a steamer basket over simmering water and steam for 8 minutes, until fish is opaque and flakes easily with a fork. Snip one end from each package and pour juices into a small saucepan. Add shallot and boil for 1 minute. Stir in yogurt and dill. Remove fish from plastic wrap and pour sauce over top. **Serves 4.**

Dilled Salmon Salad

1¼ lbs	skinless salmon fillet	625 g
	Salt and freshly ground black pepper to taste	
3 cups	Court Bouillon (see recipe, page 18) or equal parts white wine and water	750 mL
2 tbsp	extra-virgin olive oil	25 mL
2 tbsp	red wine vinegar	25 mL
2 tbsp	finely chopped fresh dill	25 mL
1 tbsp	freshly squeezed lemon juice	15 mL

Season salmon with salt and pepper. In a large skillet, bring bouillon to a simmer over medium heat. Add salmon, cover and poach for 6 to 8 minutes, until salmon is opaque and flakes easily with a fork. Remove dark flesh from underside of salmon and flake fish into a serving bowl. Add oil, vinegar, dill and lemon juice; toss to coat. **Serves 4.**

Flounder and Salmon Steamed in Romaine

4	large romaine lettuce leaves, split lengthwise, ribs removed	4
4	skinless flounder fillets (each 3 oz/90 g), halved lengthwise	4
8 oz	skinless salmon fillet, cut into 8 slices	250 g
	Salt and freshly ground black pepper to taste	
⅓ cup	orange juice	75 mL
2 tbsp	walnut oil	25 mL

In a pot of boiling salted water, blanch romaine until wilted, about 10 seconds. Spread each leaf half out flat and top each with 1 piece of flounder, 1 slice salmon, salt and pepper. Roll up tightly, jelly-roll-style, and place seam side down in a steamer basket over simmering water. Steam until fish is opaque and flakes easily with a fork, about 10 minutes. Whisk together orange juice and oil; serve with steamed rolls. **Serves 4.**

Snapper Steamed with Green Peppercorns

1	clove garlic, minced	1
1 tbsp	extra-virgin olive oil	15 mL
1 tbsp	green peppercorns in brine, crushed	15 mL
½ tsp	soy sauce	2 mL
1	whole red snapper (2 lbs/1 kg), 4 slits cut into each side	1
2 tbsp	freshly squeezed lime juice	25 mL

Combine garlic, oil, peppercorns and soy sauce; rub over snapper. Place in a large bamboo steamer over simmering water and steam for 20 minutes, until fish is opaque and flakes easily with a fork. Transfer to a platter and drizzle with lime juice. **Serves 4.**

Salmon Stewed with Fennel and Mushrooms

4	pieces skinless salmon fillet (each 4 oz/125 g)	4
¼ cup	all-purpose flour, seasoned with salt and black pepper	50 mL
1 tbsp	olive oil	15 mL
½ cup	thinly sliced fennel bulb	125 mL
¼ cup	finely chopped onion	50 mL
8 oz	mushrooms, thinly sliced	250 g
1	clove garlic, minced	1
½ tsp	tomato paste	2 mL
1 cup	beef broth	250 mL
2 tbsp	freshly squeezed lemon juice	25 mL

Dredge salmon in seasoned flour, shaking off excess. In a large skillet, heat oil over medium-high heat. Cook salmon, turning once, until browned on both sides; remove to a platter. Add fennel and onion to the pan and sauté until tender. Add mushrooms and sauté until lightly browned. Stir in garlic and tomato paste. Add broth and lemon juice; bring to a simmer. Reduce heat to low, return salmon to the pan and simmer until fish flakes easily with a fork. Using a slotted spoon, remove solids to a platter. Boil liquid until slightly thickened; pour over fish. **Serves 4.**

Mexican Stewed Monkfish

1 lb	monkfish fillets, cut into 8 chunks	500 g
¼ cup	freshly squeezed lemon juice	50 mL
	Salt and freshly ground black pepper to taste	
2 tsp	extra-virgin olive oil, divided	10 mL
⅓ cup	chopped onion	75 mL
2	cloves garlic, minced	2
1	jalapeño pepper, seeded and finely chopped	1
1	red bell pepper, finely chopped	1
1 cup	canned diced tomatoes, drained	250 mL
½ cup	Quick Fish Broth (see recipe, page 19)	125 mL
6	canned whole tomatillos, drained	6
¼ cup	chopped fresh cilantro	50 mL

Rub monkfish with lemon juice, salt and black pepper; set aside. In a nonstick skillet, heat half the oil over medium heat. Sauté onion, garlic, jalapeño and bell pepper until tender. Add tomatoes and broth; bring to a simmer. Add fish, cover and simmer for 10 minutes, until firm. Meanwhile, in a blender or food processor, purée the remaining oil, tomatillos and cilantro until smooth. Using a slotted spoon, remove fish to a platter. Boil pan liquid until slightly thickened. Cover half the fish with the sauce from the pan, the other half with tomatillo mixture. **Serves 4.**

Codfish and Cabbage

1 lb	cod fillet	500 g
2 tbsp	freshly squeezed lemon juice	25 mL
	Salt and freshly ground black pepper to taste	
Pinch	ground nutmeg	Pinch
2 tbsp	butter, divided	25 mL
8 oz	celery root, peeled and thinly sliced	250 g
12 oz	red-skinned or other boiling potatoes, thinly sliced	375 g
1 lb	napa cabbage, thinly sliced	500 g

| 1½ cups | Quick Fish Broth (see recipe, page 19) | 375 mL |
| 1 tbsp | chopped fresh Italian (flat-leaf) parsley | 15 mL |

Preheat oven to 375°F (190°C). Sprinkle cod with lemon juice, salt, pepper and nutmeg; cover and refrigerate. Grease a 12-cup (3 L) casserole dish with 1 tsp (5 mL) of the butter. Build up alternating layers of celery root, potatoes and cabbage, seasoning each layer with salt and pepper and dabbing with a little butter. Pour broth over top and bake, covered, for 40 minutes. Uncover, place cod on top and bake for 20 minutes, until fish is opaque and flakes easily with a fork. Sprinkle with parsley. **Serves 4.**

Gingered Black Bean Bluefish

2 tbsp	finely chopped gingerroot	25 mL
1 tbsp	Chinese black bean sauce	15 mL
1 tbsp	hoisin sauce	15 mL
2 tsp	Chinese chili paste	10 mL
1½ lbs	bluefish fillet	750 g
4	lime or lemon wedges	4
1	green onion, sliced	1

Preheat oven to 350°F (180°C). Combine ginger, black bean sauce, hoisin sauce and chili paste; rub over fish. Place in a roasting pan and roast for 25 minutes, until fish is opaque and flakes easily with a fork. Serve garnished with lime wedges and green onion. **Serves 4.**

Flounder with Arugula

4	skinless flounder fillets, halved lengthwise	4
	Salt and freshly ground black pepper to taste	
2 cups	water	500 mL
1 cup	dry white wine	250 mL
¼ cup	finely chopped onion	50 mL
	Juice of ½ lemon	
1	roasted red bell pepper (see page 11), diced	1
½ cup	chopped arugula	125 mL
2 tbsp	butter	25 mL

Season flounder with salt and pepper. Roll up each piece jellyroll-style, starting at the thicker end, and secure with a toothpick. In a large saucepan, bring water, wine, onion and lemon juice to a boil. Place flounder rolls on end in the liquid, reduce heat, cover and simmer for 8 minutes, until fish is opaque and flakes easily with a fork. Using a slotted spoon, remove fish to a platter and keep warm. Boil pan liquid until reduced by about three-quarters.

Add roasted pepper and any liquid that has accumulated on the fish plate; boil for 2 minutes. Reduce heat to low and stir in arugula and butter. Pour over fish. **Serves 4.**

Stir-Fry of Crab and Asparagus

1 tbsp	olive oil	15 mL
8 oz	asparagus tips	250 g
2	cloves garlic, minced, divided	2
¼ cup	diced red bell pepper	50 mL
1 tbsp	finely chopped gingerroot	15 mL
Pinch	hot pepper flakes	Pinch
1 lb	backfin (lump) crabmeat, shells picked out	500 g
¼ cup	water	50 mL
2	green onions, thinly sliced	2
1 tbsp	freshly squeezed lemon juice	15 mL
1 tsp	soy sauce	5 mL
1 tsp	dark sesame oil	5 mL

In a wok or large skillet, heat oil over medium-high heat. Stir-fry asparagus tips until bright green; remove to a plate. Add half the garlic, red pepper, ginger and hot pepper flakes to the pan and stir-fry for 10 seconds. Return asparagus to the pan and add crabmeat and water; cover and steam for 2 to 3 minutes, until asparagus is tender. Stir in the remaining garlic, green onions, lemon juice, soy sauce and sesame oil. **Serves 4.**

Crab and Shrimp Stir-Fried with Lime and Grapes

1 tbsp	olive oil	15 mL
3	green onions, white part only, finely chopped	3
8 oz	large shrimp, peeled and deveined	250 g
24	red seedless grapes, halved	24
1 lb	backfin (lump) crabmeat, shells picked out	500 g
½ tsp	chopped fresh tarragon	2 mL
1 tbsp	dry sherry	15 mL
Pinch	cayenne pepper	Pinch
	Salt to taste	
	Juice of 1 lime	

In a wok or large skillet, heat oil over medium-high heat. Stir-fry green onions and shrimp until shrimp start to turn pink, about 30 seconds. Add grapes, crabmeat and tarragon; stir-fry for 1 minute, until shrimp are pink and opaque. Stir in sherry, cayenne, salt and lime juice. **Serves 4.**

Middle Eastern Barbecued Soft-Shell Crabs

24	fresh mint leaves, finely chopped	24
2	green onions, minced	2
2	cloves garlic, minced	2
1 cup	nonfat plain yogurt	250 mL
1 tbsp	chopped fresh Italian (flat-leaf) parsley	15 mL
	Juice of ½ lemon	
8	live soft-shell crabs, prepared (see page 11)	8

In a shallow dish, combine mint, green onions, garlic, yogurt, parsley and lemon juice. Add crabs and turn to coat. Cover and refrigerate for 1 hour. Preheat broiler or barbecue grill to high. Remove crabs from marinade and discard marinade. Broil or grill crabs for 3 to 4 minutes per side, or until brightly colored and firm. **Serves 4.**

Hard-Shell Crabs Cooked in Beer

1	bottle (12 oz/341 mL) beer (any type)	1
1 cup	water	250 mL
1 cup	clam juice	250 mL
¼ cup	Old Bay seasoning	50 mL
¼ cup	white vinegar	50 mL
1 tsp	salt	5 mL
¼ tsp	hot pepper flakes	1 mL
8 to 12	live large crabs (3 lbs/1.5 kg total), prepared (see page 10)	8 to 12

In a large pot, bring beer, water, clam juice, Old Bay seasoning, vinegar, salt and red pepper flakes to a boil. Add crabs, cover and shake the pot once. Reduce heat and simmer crabs for 10 to 12 minutes, or until brightly colored and firm. Turn off heat, uncover and let crabs cool in the liquid. **Serves 4.**

Tea-Smoked Mussels and Clams

½ cup	black tea leaves	125 mL
1 cup	boiling water	250 mL
24	littleneck clams, scrubbed (see page 8)	24
24	large mussels, scrubbed (see page 8)	24
4	lemon or lime wedges	4

Preheat barbecue grill (preferably charcoal) to high. Steep tea leaves in boiling water for 5 minutes, then drain and toss on the fire (if using a gas grill, place in a smoker box or in a foil pan on the grill). Place clams in a roasting pan and set pan directly over the fire. Cover grill tightly and smoke for 2 minutes. Add mussels to the pan, cover and smoke for 3 to 4 minutes, until clams and mussels open (discard any that don't). Serve garnished with lemon wedges. **Serves 4.**

Mussels in Tomato over Orzo

2 tbsp	extra-virgin olive oil	25 mL
3	cloves garlic, minced	3
1½ cups	canned diced tomatoes, drained	375 mL
Pinch	hot pepper flakes	Pinch
36	large mussels, scrubbed (see page 8)	36
½ cup	orzo, cooked, hot	125 mL

In a large saucepan, heat oil over medium-high heat. Sauté garlic for 30 seconds. Add tomatoes and hot pepper flakes; bring to a boil. Add mussels, reduce heat, cover and simmer for about 5 minutes, or until mussels open (discard any that don't). Divide orzo among 4 shallow soup bowls. Ladle mussels and broth over orzo. **Serves 4.**

Orange and Fennel Mussels

2	cloves garlic, minced	2
½ cup	chopped onion	125 mL
½ cup	dry white wine	125 mL
½ cup	orange juice	125 mL
½ cup	water	125 mL
⅓ cup	chopped fennel bulb	75 mL
2 tbsp	grated orange zest	25 mL
1 tbsp	chopped fresh basil	15 mL
2 tsp	ground fennel seeds	10 mL
48	large mussels, scrubbed (see page 8)	48

In a large saucepan, bring garlic, onion, wine, orange juice, water, fennel bulb, orange zest, basil and fennel seeds to a boil; boil for 10 minutes. Add mussels, reduce heat, cover and simmer for about 5 minutes, or until mussels open (discard any that don't). **Serves 4.**

Clams Steamed in Tomato Broth

1 tbsp	extra-virgin olive oil	15 mL
3	cloves garlic, coarsely chopped	3
½ cup	dry white wine	125 mL
Pinch	hot pepper flakes	Pinch
	Finely grated zest of 1 lemon	
1 cup	vegetable juice (such as V8)	250 mL
48	littleneck clams, scrubbed (see page 8)	48
¼ cup	finely chopped fresh Italian (flat-leaf) parsley	50 mL
12 oz	fettuccine, cooked, hot	375 g

In a large, deep skillet or Dutch oven with a tight-fitting lid, heat oil over medium-high heat. Sauté garlic until browned. Add wine, hot pepper flakes and lemon zest; bring to a boil. Add vegetable juice and bring to a boil. Add clams, cover and cook for about 5 minutes, or until clams open (discard any that don't). Stir in parsley and serve over fettuccine. **Serves 4.**

Curried Tandoori-Style Shrimp

1½ lbs	large shrimp, peeled and deveined	750 g
½ tsp	salt	2 mL
	Juice of 1 large lemon	
2	large cloves garlic, minced	2
2 tbsp	finely chopped gingerroot	25 mL
2 tsp	curry powder	10 mL
2 tsp	hot paprika	10 mL
1 tsp	ground cumin	5 mL
1 tsp	ground cardamom	5 mL
½ cup	nonfat plain yogurt	125 mL
4	lemon wedges	4

Toss shrimp with salt and lemon juice; cover and refrigerate for 15 minutes. Combine garlic, ginger, curry powder, paprika, cumin and cardamom; thoroughly rub into shrimp. Pour yogurt over top and rub into shrimp. Cover and refrigerate for 2 hours. Preheat broiler. Remove shrimp from marinade and discard marinade. Spread shrimp out on a broiler pan and broil for about 2 minutes per side, or until lightly browned and firm. Serve garnished with lemon wedges. **Serves 4.**

Shrimp Stew with Mint Pesto

3	cloves garlic, minced, divided	3
2 cups	packed fresh mint leaves, minced	500 mL
2 tbsp	nonfat plain yogurt	25 mL
4 tsp	olive oil, divided	20 mL
Pinch	cayenne pepper	Pinch
	Salt to taste	
2	leeks, white parts only, thinly sliced	2
2	large tomatoes, seeded and coarsely chopped	2
1 cup	dry white wine	250 mL
2 tbsp	freshly squeezed lemon juice	25 mL
1 lb	extra-large shrimp, peeled and deveined	500 g

Combine one-third of the garlic, mint, yogurt, half the oil, cayenne and salt into a paste; set aside. In a large skillet, heat the remaining oil over medium heat. Sauté leeks until tender. Add the remaining garlic and sauté for 10 seconds. Add tomatoes, wine and lemon juice; boil for 2 minutes. Add shrimp, reduce heat and simmer for 3 to 4 minutes, or until pink and opaque. Stir in mint pesto. **Serves 4.**

Stir-Fried Sesame Oysters

1 tsp	dark sesame oil	5 mL
1	clove garlic, minced	1
1	stalk celery, diced	1
½	jalapeño pepper, minced	½
2 cups	shucked large oysters (see page 11), with their liquor	500 mL
2 tbsp	Chinese oyster sauce	25 mL
1 tbsp	water	15 mL
1 tsp	cornstarch	5 mL
1 tbsp	sesame seeds	15 mL
2 cups	hot cooked rice	500 mL

In a heavy wok or large skillet, heat oil over medium-high heat. Stir-fry garlic, celery and jalapeño for 30 seconds. Add oysters and their liquor; stir-fry until oysters plump and curl at the edges, about 1 minute; remove oysters with a slotted spoon to a plate. Add oyster sauce, water and cornstarch to the wok and cook until liquid thickens. Return oysters to the wok and heat through. Sprinkle with sesame seeds and serve over rice. **Serves 4.**

Shrimp and Oysters with Basil

2 tbsp	extra-virgin olive oil, divided	25 mL
1	large onion, chopped	1
2	cloves garlic, minced	2
2	large tomatoes, peeled and chopped	2
1 cup	dry white wine	250 mL
2 tbsp	freshly squeezed lemon juice	25 mL
	Salt and freshly ground black pepper to taste	
8 oz	large shrimp, peeled and deveined	250 g
1 cup	chopped fresh basil	250 mL
1 cup	shucked oysters (see page 11), drained	250 mL

In a large saucepan, heat half the oil over medium heat. Sauté onion until tender. Add garlic and sauté for 30 seconds. Add tomatoes, wine, lemon juice, salt and pepper; bring to a boil. Add shrimp and basil; reduce heat and simmer for 2 minutes. Add oysters and simmer for 1 minute, until shrimp are pink and opaque and oysters plump and curl at the edges. Stir in the remaining oil. **Serves 4.**

Asparagus, Shrimp, Raspberry and Grapefruit Salad

6 oz	medium shrimp, peeled and deveined	175 g
8 oz	asparagus, trimmed	250 g
1	pink grapefruit, peeled, broken into sections, white pith removed	1
½ cup	fresh raspberries (preferably golden), slightly crushed	125 mL
2 tbsp	walnut oil	25 mL
1 tbsp	white wine vinegar	15 mL
	Salt and freshly ground black pepper to taste	

Bring a large saucepan of lightly salted water to a boil. Add shrimp, reduce heat and simmer until pink and opaque, about 1 minute. Remove with a slotted spoon to a plate and let cool. Add asparagus to the pan and boil until bright green, 1 to 3 minutes, depending on thickness. Drain asparagus and arrange with grapefruit sections and shrimp on 4 plates. Combine raspberries, oil, vinegar, salt and pepper; spoon over asparagus, shrimp and grapefruit. **Serves 4.**

Sautéed Shrimp on Cucumber "Noodles"

3	large cucumbers, peeled, halved lengthwise and seeded	3
1 tsp	kosher salt	5 mL
2 tbsp	extra-virgin olive oil	25 mL
2	cloves garlic, minced	2
1 lb	large shrimp, peeled and deveined	500 g
½ cup	dry white wine	125 mL
½ tsp	ground Szechuan peppercorns	2 mL
	Salt and freshly ground black pepper to taste	
⅓ cup	nonfat plain yogurt	75 mL
2 tbsp	chopped fresh dill	25 mL

With a vegetable peeler, cut long, thin ribbons from the cucumbers. Toss with salt and let stand for 10 minutes; rinse well and wring dry. Meanwhile, in a large skillet, heat oil over medium-high heat. Sauté garlic and shrimp until shrimp start to turn pink. Add wine, Szechuan peppercorns, salt and black pepper; reduce heat and simmer until shrimp are pink and opaque, about 1 minute. Remove shrimp with a slotted spoon to a plate. Boil pan juices until reduced by half. Remove from heat and stir in yogurt and dill until smooth. Toss shrimp in sauce and serve on a bed of cucumber "noodles." **Serves 4.**

Seafood Pot au Feu

1 tbsp	olive oil	15 mL
1	onion, chopped	1
3	cloves garlic, chopped	3
3 cups	dry white wine	750 mL
1½ cups	canned diced tomatoes, with juice	375 mL
1 cup	water	250 mL
1 tsp	dried dillweed	5 mL
½ tsp	dried thyme	2 mL
	Juice of 1 lemon	
	Salt and freshly ground black pepper to taste	
12	littleneck clams, scrubbed (see page 8)	12
24	mussels, scrubbed (see page 8)	24
12	large shrimp, peeled and deveined	12
8 oz	skinless lean fish fillet, cut into 4 pieces	250 g
2 tbsp	finely chopped fresh Italian (flat-leaf) parsley	25 mL

In a large saucepan, heat oil over medium heat. Sauté onion until tender. Add garlic and sauté for 30 seconds. Add wine, increase heat to high and boil for 5 minutes. Add tomatoes, with juice, water, dill, thyme, lemon juice, salt and pepper; reduce heat and simmer for 5 minutes. Add clams, cover and simmer for 3 minutes. Add mussels, cover and simmer for 3 minutes. Add shrimp and fish; simmer, uncovered, for 2 minutes, until fish is opaque and flakes easily with a fork, shrimp is pink and opaque, and clams and mussels open (discard any that don't). Stir in parsley. **Serves 4.**

Artichoke Ratatouille

2 tbsp	extra-virgin olive oil	25 mL
12	large mushrooms, sliced	12
1	onion, finely chopped	1
2	cloves garlic, minced	2
1	red bell pepper, diced	1
1 tsp	dried basil	5 mL
½ tsp	dried oregano	2 mL
	Finely grated zest of and juice of 1 lemon	
8	plum (Roma) tomatoes, finely chopped	8
6	large artichoke bottoms (fresh or frozen, thawed)	6
1	zucchini, cubed	1
1 tbsp	red wine vinegar	15 mL
½ cup	pitted small black olives	125 mL

In a large skillet, heat oil over medium-high heat. Sauté mushrooms and onion until tender. Add garlic, red pepper, basil, oregano and lemon zest; sauté for 3 minutes. Add lemon juice, tomatoes, artichoke bottoms, zucchini and vinegar; reduce heat and simmer for 10 minutes. Stir in olives. Serve hot or let cool to room temperature. **Serves 4.**

Tofu Braised with Wild Mushrooms

2 tbsp	olive oil, divided	25 mL
1 lb	extra-firm tofu	500 g
8 oz	wild or exotic mushrooms (any variety), thickly sliced	250 g
8 oz	white mushrooms, sliced	250 g
2	cloves garlic, minced	2
1 tbsp	soy sauce	15 mL
1 cup	beef broth	250 mL
3	green onions, finely sliced	3

In a large skillet, heat half the oil over medium-high heat. Cook tofu until browned on both sides; remove to a plate lined with paper towels. Drain tofu and cut into 1-inch (2.5 cm) cubes. Add the remaining oil to the pan and heat over medium-high heat. Sauté mushrooms until browned. Add garlic and sauté for 10 seconds. Add soy sauce and broth; bring to a boil. Return tofu to the pan, reduce heat and simmer until liquid is reduced by half. Stir in green onions. **Serves 4.**

Asparagus Salad

1	clove garlic, minced	1
1/4 cup	orange juice	50 mL
3 tbsp	walnut oil	45 mL
1 1/2 tbsp	red wine vinegar	22 mL
	Salt and freshly ground black pepper to taste	
12 oz	mixed hearty salad greens, preferably an endive mix	375 g
1 lb	asparagus, trimmed and blanched (see page 8)	500 g
1/4 cup	finely chopped toasted walnuts	50 mL

In a saucepan, bring garlic, orange juice, oil, vinegar, salt and pepper to a boil. Toss 3 tbsp (45 mL) of this dressing with the salad mix and mound on a serving platter. Top with asparagus and pour the remaining dressing on top. Sprinkle with walnuts and serve immediately. **Serves 4.**

Stir-Fried Sesame Vegetables

1 tbsp	canola oil	15 mL
2	stalks celery, julienned	2
1	small onion, chopped	1
8 oz	baby carrots	250 g
8 oz	mushrooms, halved	250 g
1	clove garlic, minced	1
2 tsp	finely chopped gingerroot	10 mL
Pinch	hot pepper flakes	Pinch
2/3 cup	vegetable broth	150 mL
2 tbsp	soy sauce	25 mL
1	yellow summer squash (zucchini), cut into cubes	1
12 oz	asparagus, trimmed	375 g
8 oz	snow peas, trimmed	250 g
2	green onions, thinly sliced	2
2 tbsp	toasted sesame seeds	25 mL
2 tsp	freshly squeezed lime juice	10 mL
1 tsp	dark sesame oil	5 mL

In a wok or large, deep skillet, heat oil over medium-high heat. Stir-fry celery, onion, carrots and mushrooms until tender. Add garlic, ginger and hot pepper flakes; stir-fry for 10 seconds. Add broth and soy sauce; reduce heat and bring to a simmer. Add squash and asparagus; cover and simmer for 2 to 3 minutes, or until asparagus is tender. Add snow peas and simmer for 1 minute. Remove from heat and stir in green onions, sesame seeds, lime juice and sesame oil. **Serves 4.**

Grilled Rabbit

1 1/2 lbs	rabbit pieces	750 g
1 cup	Easy Red Wine Marinade (see recipe, page 32)	250 mL
1/2 cup	chicken broth	125 mL
1 tbsp	olive oil	15 mL

Toss rabbit with Red Wine Marinade, cover and refrigerate for 8 hours or overnight. Preheat broiler or barbecue grill to high. Remove rabbit from marinade and strain marinade into a small saucepan. Add broth and boil until reduced by about three-quarters. Rub rabbit with oil, and broil or grill for 4 minutes per side. Brush rabbit with some of the reduced liquid and grill for 2 to 3 minutes per side, or until browned and firm to the touch. Serve drizzled with the remaining liquid. **Serves 4.**

Venison in Mustard Crust

1	clove garlic, minced	1
1 tsp	whole-grain Dijon mustard	5 mL
1 tsp	dry sherry	5 mL
1 lb	venison loin, trimmed and cut into 12 slices	500 g
2 tbsp	black or yellow mustard seeds	25 mL
4 tsp	olive oil	20 mL

Combine garlic, mustard and sherry; brush on venison. Sprinkle with mustard seeds. In a large non-stick skillet, heat oil over medium-high heat. Cook venison slices, turning once, for about 2 minutes per side, or until browned on both sides. **Serves 4.**

Veal Scallops with Asparagus and Capers

4	veal scallops (leg cutlets) (each 3 oz/90 g) Salt and freshly ground black pepper to taste	4
1 tbsp	olive oil, divided	15 mL
1/2 cup	chicken broth	125 mL
24	asparagus tips, blanched (see page 8)	24
2 tbsp	drained capers	25 mL
2 tbsp	freshly squeezed lemon juice	25 mL

Season veal with salt and pepper, then brush with 1 tsp (5 mL) of the oil. Pound as directed in "About these recipes" (page 498) to 1/8-inch (3 mm) thickness. In a large, heavy skillet, heat the remaining oil over medium-high heat until smoking. Sauté veal, in batches as necessary, for 1 minute per side; remove to a platter. Add broth to the pan and boil until reduced by half. Add asparagus tips and heat through; remove with a slotted spoon and place on and around the veal. Add capers and lemon juice to the pan; pour sauce over veal. **Serves 4.**

Grilled Mustard-Glazed Veal Chops

1	clove garlic, minced	1
1/3 cup	whole-grain Dijon mustard	75 mL
2 tbsp	bourbon	25 mL
1/4 tsp	freshly ground black pepper	1 mL
4	veal rib chops (each about 6 oz/175 g), well trimmed	4

Preheat broiler or barbecue grill to high. Combine garlic, mustard, bourbon and pepper; brush on veal. Broil or grill for 4 to 5 minutes per side, or until resilient to gentle pressure. **Serves 4.**

Veal au Poivre

1 1/2 lbs	lean boneless veal loin, trimmed and cut into 4 pieces	750 g
2 tsp	extra-virgin olive oil	10 mL
2 tbsp	freshly ground black pepper Salt to taste	25 mL

Preheat broiler or barbecue grill to high. Coat veal with oil and rub with pepper and salt. Broil or grill for 4 to 5 minutes per side, or until resilient to gentle pressure. **Serves 4.**

Pork Medallions with Mustard and Capers

12 oz	lean boneless center-cut pork loin, trimmed and cut into 1/4-inch (0.5 cm) slices Salt and freshly ground black pepper to taste Vegetable cooking spray	375 g
1	clove garlic, coarsely chopped	1
1 cup	apple juice	250 mL
2 tbsp	capers, with their liquid	25 mL
2 tbsp	spicy brown mustard	25 mL

Season pork with salt and pepper. Coat a large non-stick skillet with cooking spray and place over medium-high heat. Cook pork, turning once, until browned on both sides and just a hint of pink remains inside; remove to a plate. Add garlic, apple juice, capers, caper liquid and mustard to the pan and boil until liquid is slightly thickened. Return pork to the pan and heat through. **Serves 4.**

Pork Braised in Apple Cider

12 oz	lean boneless center-cut pork loin, trimmed	375 g
	Salt and freshly ground black pepper to taste	
	Vegetable cooking spray	
1	clove garlic, chopped	1
½ cup	chopped onion	125 mL
2 tsp	chopped fresh thyme	10 mL
1 cup	unsweetened apple cider	250 mL
½ cup	dry white wine	125 mL

Season pork with salt and pepper. Coat a nonstick skillet with cooking spray and place over medium-high heat. Cook pork until browned on all sides. Reduce heat to medium and scatter garlic, onion and thyme around pork. Cover and cook for 3 to 4 minutes, or until onion browns on the edges. Add cider and wine; simmer, covered, for 35 minutes. Remove pork to a plate. Boil pan liquid until slightly thickened. Slice pork against the grain and return to the pan; heat through. **Serves 4.**

Grilled Pork Medallions with Mustard and Rosemary

1 lb	lean boneless center-cut pork loin, trimmed and cut into 12 slices	500 g
1	clove garlic, halved	1
	Salt and freshly ground black pepper to taste	
¼ cup	spicy brown mustard	50 mL
1 tbsp	chopped fresh rosemary	15 mL
1 tbsp	chopped fresh Italian (flat-leaf) parsley	15 mL

Preheat broiler or barbecue grill to medium. Rub pork slices on both sides with the cut sides of garlic; season with salt and pepper. Combine mustard and rosemary; brush on pork. Broil or grill for about 3 minutes per side, or until browned on both sides and just a hint of pink remains inside. Serve sprinkled with parsley. **Serves 4.**

Lamb Chops Braised with Belgian Endive

4	lamb shoulder chops (each about 6 oz/175 g)	4
½ cup	all-purpose flour, seasoned with salt and black pepper	125 mL
1 tbsp	extra-virgin olive oil	15 mL
4	heads Belgian endive, trimmed and halved	4
2	cloves garlic, minced	2
¼ cup	dry white wine	50 mL
½ tsp	dried thyme	2 mL
½ cup	beef broth	125 mL
2 tbsp	chopped fresh Italian (flat-leaf) parsley	25 mL

Dredge lamb chops in seasoned flour, shaking off excess. In a large skillet, heat oil over medium-high heat. Cook chops, turning once, until browned on both sides; remove to a plate. Add endive to the pan and sear on both sides. Add garlic, wine and thyme; bring to a boil. Return chops to the pan and add broth; reduce heat, cover and simmer for 40 minutes. Remove chops and endive to a platter. Boil pan liquid until slightly thickened; skim off any fat. Pour liquid over meat and sprinkle with parsley. **Serves 4.**

Lamb with Lemon and Mint

2	cloves garlic, minced	2
¼ cup	freshly squeezed lemon juice	50 mL
1 tbsp	dried mint	15 mL
2 tsp	extra-virgin olive oil	10 mL
2 lbs	lean boneless leg of lamb, trimmed	1 kg

Combine garlic, lemon juice, mint and oil; rub over lamb and let stand for 1 hour. Preheat oven to 375°F (190°C). Place lamb on a rack in a roasting pan and roast for 1 hour, until a thermometer inserted in the thickest part registers 125°F (52°C) for rare, or until desired doneness. Transfer to a carving board and let rest for 10 minutes before slicing. **Serves 6.**

Chapter 46

Health Food
For You and Your Planet

Whole Wheat Vanilla Yogurt
French Toast 511

Buttermilk Bran Hotcakes 512

Whole Wheat Brown Rice Pancakes . . . 512

Wild Rice Pancakes
with Corn and Pepper Salsa 512

Protein-Packed Cornbread 512

Rabe and Peppers Baked in Bread 512

Spanakopita Bread 513

Broccoli Stem Crudités
with Warm Tofu Vinaigrette 513

Egg-Free Tofu Mayonnaise 513

Asian Tofu Dressing 513

Tofu Tuna Sandwich Spread 513

Apple Turnip Soup 513

Ginger Pumpkin Bisque 514

Smoky Lentil Soup 514

White Bean and Brown Rice Soup 514

Miso Soup with Dried Mushrooms 514

Miso Noodle Soup 514

Miso Soup with Brown Rice 515

Avocado Grapefruit Salad 515

Warm Buckwheat Pasta and
Sesame Salad 515

Chickpea and Red Onion Salad 515

Chickpea, Tomato and Onion Salad . . . 515

Chicken Cannellini Salad 515

Eggplant Chili 516

Grilled Chicken Breast
with Buttermilk and Herbs 516

Salmon Poached in Basil Tea
with Pine Nuts 516

Poached Salmon with Arugula 516

Stir-Fried Shrimp and Tofu in Yogurt . . . 517

Grilled Teriyaki Tofu 517

Grilled Tofu Steak with Pickled Ginger . . 517

Stir-Fried Asparagus
with Tofu and Almonds 517

Stir-Fried Broccoli and Apples 517

Eggplant and Feta au Gratin 518

Souffléd Sweet Potatoes 518

Garden Vegetable Whole-Grain
Tempura 518

Three-Bean Tempura 518

Vitamin A Tempura 518

Spiced Sesame Chickpeas 519

Brown Beans and Rice 519

Healthy Hoppin' John 519

Sesame Brown Rice Pilaf 519

Brown Rice Risotto
with Sage and Potatoes 520

Wild Rice Risotto 520

Stir-Fried Quinoa 520

Quinoa with Tofu and Mushrooms 520

Fresh Whole Wheat Wild Mushroom
Pasta 521

Whole Wheat Pasta
with Roasted Peppers 521

Whole Wheat Pasta Boiled
with Broccoli, Ricotta
and Roasted Peppers 521

Dried Fruit Roll 521

Tofu Rice Pudding 521

Like fast food, snack food and diet food, health food is a uniquely North American concept. Unlike the people of most other countries, who eat as well as they can for as long as they can so that they may experience as much happiness as they can, North Americans often seem compelled to compartmentalize their diets, eating one way in a rush, another to impress and still another for health.

The term "health food" has been used since the last quarter of the 1800s, when utopian communities practicing their own ideas of dietary perfection began springing up throughout the Midwest and Plains in the United States. They espoused eating less processed food, more whole grains and less meat. In the 1920s, the focus became more scientific, emphasizing vitamins and other nutritional supplements. But only in the late 1960s and early '70s was a complete retail industry built around health food, incorporating traditional American health food values with a drugstore-like inventory and lots of Asian and African herbs and enzymes.

In the decades that followed, healthy food became defined by what it *didn't* contain. Cholesterol-free, fat-free, sugar-free, gluten-free, low-salt, no-salt, no trans fats, no saturated fats, low-carbs and no-carbs traded market dominance as food fads flipped from one demonized nutrient to another.

At the turn of the millennium, the notion of health food broadened from foods that promise to enhance your physical well-being to those that lay claim to fixing the ecology of the planet. Organic, sustainable and locally grown ingredients promise to protect us, whether from feeding pesticides, growth hormones and modified DNA to our families, or from polluting our fields and water with chemical runoff. In the United States, organics has become big business, with major manufacturers producing organic versions of their most popular products. Organic tortilla chips, canned tomatoes and chicken noodle soup are fine, sometimes better than the originals, and they allow those of us who want to ingest less chemistry an alternative to traditionally processed foods, which is really what health food is all about — the notion that we may be able to improve ourselves and our quality of life by what we put in our mouths. Not a bad idea.

About these recipes . . .

The following 50 recipes take a broad overview of the health food field. All are designed with a reduction of fat, sugar, calories and cholesterol in mind. At times, we call for organic ingredients, but only where the organic choice (such as broth or tomatoes) is a tastier product than its traditional counterpart. Because cooking with organic or locally grown produce is no different from cooking with conventionally grown ingredients, we assume that you'll use organic items if you have them. Recipes that call for boneless skinless chicken breasts refer to breast halves. The recipes in this chapter include breakfasts, snacks, appetizers, soups, salads, entrées, side dishes and desserts.

Whole Wheat Vanilla Yogurt French Toast

4	large or extra-large eggs	4
1 cup	buttermilk	250 mL
1 cup	low-fat vanilla yogurt	250 mL
Pinch	salt	Pinch
2 tsp	butter	10 mL
8	thick slices whole wheat bread	8
2 cups	sliced fresh fruit	500 mL

In a wide, shallow bowl, beat eggs, buttermilk, yogurt and salt. Soak bread in this mixture, in batches if necessary, until all liquid is absorbed. In a large nonstick skillet, melt a thin film of butter over medium heat. Add soaked bread, in batches, and cook, turning once, until browned on both sides. Transfer to a plate and keep warm. Repeat with the remaining soaked bread, melting butter as necessary between batches. Serve with fresh fruit. **Serves 4.**

Buttermilk Bran Hotcakes

1 cup	100% Bran or All-Bran cereal (not flakes)	250 mL
1 cup	whole wheat flour	250 mL
2 tbsp	granulated raw sugar	25 mL
2 tsp	baking powder	10 mL
1 tsp	baking soda	5 mL
1/4 tsp	salt	1 mL
2	large or extra-large eggs, separated	2
2 cups	buttermilk	500 mL
2 tbsp	butter, melted	25 mL
2 tsp	vanilla	10 mL
	Vegetable cooking spray	
2 cups	warm applesauce	500 mL

In a large bowl, combine cereal, flour, sugar, baking powder, baking soda and salt. In a separate bowl, beat egg yolks, buttermilk, butter and vanilla; stir into dry ingredients. In a clean bowl, beat egg whites until soft peaks form; fold into batter. Place a griddle or large skillet over medium heat and spray with cooking spray. For each hotcake, pour in 1/4 cup (50 mL) batter and cook until covered with bubbles. Flip and cook for 1 to 2 minutes, or until hotcakes feel springy. Transfer to a plate and keep warm. Repeat with the remaining batter, spraying pan with cooking spray for every batch. Serve with applesauce. **Serves 4.**

Whole Wheat Brown Rice Pancakes

1 cup	whole wheat flour	250 mL
1 cup	unbleached all-purpose flour	250 mL
1 tbsp	granulated raw sugar	15 mL
2 tsp	baking powder	10 mL
1 tsp	baking soda	5 mL
1/2 tsp	salt	2 mL
2	large or extra-large eggs, separated	2
2 cups	buttermilk	500 mL
1/4 cup	melted butter	50 mL
2 cups	cooked brown rice	500 mL
	Vegetable cooking spray	
Pinch	ground cinnamon	Pinch
1 cup	sour cream	250 mL

In a large bowl, combine whole wheat flour, all-purpose flour, sugar, baking powder, baking soda, and salt. In a separate bowl, beat egg yolks, buttermilk and butter; stir into dry ingredients. Fold in rice. In a clean bowl, beat egg whites until soft peaks form; fold into batter. Cook pancakes as described in Buttermilk Bran Hotcakes (above). Sprinkle pancakes with cinnamon and serve with sour cream. **Serves 4.**

Wild Rice Pancakes with Corn and Pepper Salsa

Prepare batter as in preceding recipe, but replace the brown rice with wild rice. Serve pancakes with a mixture of 2 cups (500 mL) Confetti Salsa (page 177) and 1/2 cup (125 mL) canned or thawed frozen corn kernels. **Serves 4.**

Protein-Packed Cornbread

1 1/4 cups	stone-ground cornmeal	300 mL
1/2 cup	unbleached all-purpose flour	125 mL
1/4 cup	whole wheat flour	50 mL
1/4 cup	packed light brown sugar	50 mL
1 tbsp	baking powder	15 mL
1/2 tsp	salt	2 mL
1 cup	drained rinsed canned chickpeas	250 mL
3/4 cup	finely shredded sharp Cheddar cheese	175 mL
1	extra-large egg	1
1 cup	low-fat milk	250 mL
2 tbsp	corn oil, divided	25 mL

Preheat oven to 425°F (220°C) and place a 10-inch (25 cm) cast-iron skillet in the oven. In a large bowl, combine cornmeal, all-purpose flour, whole wheat flour, brown sugar, baking powder and salt. Stir in chickpeas and cheese. In a small bowl, beat egg, milk and half the oil; stir into dry ingredients. Brush hot skillet with the remaining oil and pour in batter. Bake for 20 to 25 minutes, or until puffed and brown and a tester inserted in the center comes out almost clean. **Serves 4.**

Rabe and Peppers Baked in Bread

2	bunches broccoli rabe, hard stems trimmed, cut into 1-inch (2.5 cm) sections	2
2 tbsp	extra-virgin olive oil	25 mL
2	cloves garlic, minced	2
1	roasted red bell pepper (see page 11), diced	1
Pinch	hot pepper flakes	Pinch
	Salt and freshly ground black pepper to taste	
1	round loaf crusty whole-grain bread (about 1 lb/500 g)	1
1 cup	shredded smoked cheese (such as smoked Cheddar)	250 mL

Preheat oven to 350°F (180°C). In a large pot of boiling lightly salted water, cook rabe until bright green and barely tender, about 2 minutes; drain well. In a large skillet, heat oil over high heat. Sauté garlic for

10 seconds. Add rabe, roasted pepper, hot pepper flakes, salt and black pepper; sauté until vegetables are glossy and heated through. Cut the top off the bread and hollow out the interior. Fill with rabe mixture, layered with cheese. Replace top of bread and place on a baking sheet. Bake for 30 minutes, until heated through. Cut into wedges. **Serves 4.**

Spanakopita Bread

1 tbsp	extra-virgin olive oil	15 mL
½ cup	chopped onion	125 mL
3	bags (each 9 oz/270 g) spinach, coarsely chopped	3
2	cloves garlic, minced	2
Pinch	hot pepper flakes	Pinch
	Salt and freshly ground black pepper to taste	
2 tbsp	freshly grated Parmesan cheese	25 mL
1	round loaf crusty whole-grain bread (about 1 lb/500 g)	1
4 oz	feta cheese, crumbled	125 g

Preheat oven to 350°F (180°C). In a large skillet, heat oil over medium-high heat. Sauté onion until tender. Add spinach, garlic, hot pepper flakes, salt and black pepper; sauté until spinach wilts and mixture is dry, about 3 minutes. Stir in Parmesan. Cut the top off the bread and hollow out the interior. Fill with spinach mixture, layered with cheese. Replace top of bread and place on a baking sheet. Bake for 30 minutes, until heated through. Cut into wedges. **Serves 4.**

Broccoli Stem Crudités with Warm Tofu Vinaigrette

8 oz	peeled broccoli stems, cut into 4-inch (10 cm) long strips	250 g
½	clove garlic	½
4 oz	silken tofu, drained	125 g
3 tbsp	dark sesame oil	45 mL
2 tbsp	rice wine vinegar	25 mL
1 tsp	soy sauce	5 mL
	Salt and freshly ground black pepper to taste	

Soak broccoli stems in ice water for 30 minutes. In a food processor, purée the remaining ingredients. Drain broccoli stems and serve with sauce. **Serves 4.**

Egg-Free Tofu Mayonnaise

8 oz	silken tofu, drained	250 g
2 tbsp	freshly squeezed lemon juice	25 mL
½ tsp	granulated sugar	2 mL
½ tsp	Dijon mustard	2 mL

	Salt and freshly ground white pepper to taste	
6 tbsp	canola oil	90 mL

In a food processor, purée tofu, lemon juice, sugar, mustard, salt and pepper. With the motor running, through the feed tube, add oil in a slow, steady stream and process until incorporated. **Makes about 1 cup (250 mL).**

Asian Tofu Dressing

½	clove garlic	½
4 oz	silken tofu, drained	125 g
2 tbsp	rice wine vinegar	25 mL
1 tsp	soy sauce	5 mL
	Salt and freshly ground white pepper to taste	
¼ cup	canola oil	50 mL
3 tbsp	dark sesame oil	45 mL

In a food processor, purée garlic, tofu, vinegar, soy sauce, salt and pepper. With the motor running, through the feed tube, add canola oil and sesame oil in a slow, steady stream and process until incorporated. **Makes about ¾ cup (175 mL).**

Tofu Tuna Sandwich Spread

Prepare either of the 2 preceding recipes. Toss with 2 cans (each 6 oz/170 g) water-packed tuna, drained and crumbled, 1 carrot, shredded, and 1 stalk celery, diced. **Serves 4.**

Apple Turnip Soup

1 tbsp	butter	15 mL
6	white turnips (small to medium), peeled and diced	6
2	large apples, peeled and finely chopped	2
½ cup	finely chopped onion	125 mL
4 cups	organic chicken or vegetable broth	1 L
	Salt and freshly ground white pepper to taste	
½ cup	whole milk	125 mL

In a large saucepan, melt butter over medium heat. Sauté turnips, apples and onion until tender. Add broth and simmer until vegetables are soft, about 10 minutes. Season with salt and pepper. Working in batches, transfer to a blender or food processor and purée. Return to saucepan, stir in milk and heat through (do not boil). **Serves 4.**

Ginger Pumpkin Bisque

2 tbsp	canola oil	25 mL
3	leeks, white parts only, finely chopped	3
1 tbsp	finely chopped gingerroot	15 mL
4 cups	organic vegetable broth	1 L
2½ cups	canned pumpkin purée (not pie filling)	625 mL
1 cup	milk	250 mL
2 tsp	granulated raw sugar	10 mL
Pinch	cayenne pepper	Pinch
Pinch	ground nutmeg	Pinch
	Salt and freshly ground white pepper to taste	
½ cup	sour cream, at room temperature	125 mL

In a large saucepan, heat oil over medium heat. Sauté leeks and ginger until tender. Add broth, pumpkin purée, milk, sugar, cayenne, nutmeg, salt and black pepper; simmer for 15 minutes, until flavors are blended. Strain, bring to a boil and stir in sour cream until smooth. **Serves 6.**

Smoky Lentil Soup

1 tbsp	canola oil	15 mL
1	carrot, diced	1
1	stalk celery, diced	1
½ cup	diced onion	125 mL
8 oz	dried brown or green lentils	250 g
6 cups	organic chicken or vegetable broth	1.5 L
1 cup	diced nitrate-free smoked turkey breast	250 mL
1	bay leaf	1
½ tsp	dried rosemary	2 mL
¼ tsp	dried thyme	1 mL
1	roasted red bell pepper (see page 11), diced	1
1 tbsp	tomato paste	15 mL

In a large saucepan, heat oil over medium heat. Sauté carrot, celery and onion until tender. Add lentils, broth, turkey, bay leaf, rosemary and thyme; simmer for 45 minutes, until lentils are tender. Discard bay leaf and stir in roasted pepper and tomato paste. **Serves 4.**

White Bean and Brown Rice Soup

2 tbsp	olive oil	25 mL
2	carrots, diced	2
½ cup	diced onion	125 mL
1	cinnamon stick (1½ inches/ 4 cm long)	1
1 cup	long- or medium-grain brown rice	250 mL
1 tsp	ground coriander	5 mL
1 tsp	dried thyme	5 mL
Pinch	hot pepper flakes	Pinch
8 cups	organic chicken or vegetable broth	2 L
	Salt and freshly ground black pepper to taste	
2 cups	drained rinsed canned white beans (such as cannellini or Great Northern)	500 mL
½ cup	chopped fresh cilantro Juice of 1 large lemon	125 mL

In a large saucepan, heat oil over medium heat. Sauté carrots and onion until tender. Add cinnamon stick, rice, coriander, thyme and hot pepper flakes, stirring to coat rice with oil. Add broth, salt and black pepper; simmer for 30 minutes. Add beans and simmer for 15 minutes, until rice is tender. Discard cinnamon stick and stir in cilantro and lemon juice. **Serves 4.**

Miso Soup with Dried Mushrooms

½ oz	dried Asian mushrooms (any variety)	15 g
2 cups	boiling water	500 mL
2 tbsp	red miso	25 mL
½ tsp	canola oil	2 mL
4 oz	white mushrooms, sliced	125 g
2	thin slices gingerroot	2
3 cups	organic vegetable broth	750 mL
3	green onions, thinly sliced	3
6 oz	firm tofu, cut into ½-inch (1 cm) dice	175 g

Soak dried mushrooms in boiling water until hydrated, about 15 minutes. Remove mushrooms, trim hard ends and coarsely chop. Strain soaking liquid through a coffee filter. Dissolve miso in soaking liquid; set aside. In a large saucepan, heat oil over medium-high heat. Sauté fresh mushrooms until tender. Add hydrated mushrooms, miso liquid, ginger and broth; reduce heat and simmer for 2 to 3 minutes, or until flavors are blended. Discard ginger and stir in green onions and tofu. **Serves 4.**

Miso Noodle Soup

2 oz	buckwheat or whole wheat noodles, in 2-inch (5 cm) lengths	60 g
3 tbsp	red miso	45 mL
1 cup	hot water	250 mL
1	strip kombu seaweed	1
3 cups	organic vegetable broth	750 mL
1 tsp	finely chopped gingerroot	5 mL
6 oz	firm tofu, cut into ½-inch (1 cm) dice	175 g
3	green onions, thinly sliced	3

In a large pot of boiling salted water, cook noodles until tender; drain and rinse with cold water and set aside. In a large saucepan, dissolve miso in hot water. Add seaweed, broth and ginger; simmer for 5 minutes. Discard seaweed and add noodles and tofu; simmer for 1 minute. Stir in green onions. **Serves 4.**

Miso Soup with Brown Rice

Follow preceding recipe, but substitute 1 cup (250 mL) cooked brown rice for the cooked noodles. **Serves 4.**

Avocado Grapefruit Salad

2	large pink grapefruit, peeled, white membrane removed	2
2	avocados, peeled, pitted and thinly sliced	2
1 tbsp	small fresh tarragon leaves	15 mL
	Salt to taste	

Carefully remove grapefruit sections by cutting on either side of the membranes that divide them. Place in a serving bowl and squeeze any remaining juice over top. Add avocados, tarragon and salt; toss to coat. **Serves 4.**

Warm Buckwheat Pasta and Sesame Salad

1 lb	Japanese buckwheat noodles (soba)	500 g
1 tbsp	dark sesame oil, divided	15 mL
1½	cloves garlic, minced	1½
6 tbsp	nonfat plain yogurt	90 mL
3 tbsp	rice wine vinegar	45 mL
3 tbsp	soy sauce	45 mL
4 tsp	finely chopped gingerroot	20 mL
1 tsp	granulated sugar	5 mL
Pinch	hot pepper flakes	Pinch
3	green onions, thinly sliced	3
1	cucumber, peeled, seeded and finely diced	1
½	small red onion, thinly sliced	½
¼ cup	toasted sesame seeds	50 mL

In a large pot of boiling salted water, boil noodles with 1 tsp (5 mL) of the oil until tender, about 8 minutes. Drain noodles, rinse and place in a bowl. Toss with remaining oil, garlic, yogurt, vinegar, soy sauce, ginger, sugar and hot pepper flakes. Add the remaining ingredients and toss lightly to coat. Serve warm. **Serves 4.**

Chickpea and Red Onion Salad

1	tomato (preferably organic), chopped	1
2 cups	drained rinsed canned chickpeas	500 mL
⅓ cup	chopped red onion	75 mL

3 tbsp	freshly squeezed lemon juice	45 mL
2 tbsp	extra-virgin olive oil	25 mL
2 tbsp	finely chopped fresh Italian (flat-leaf) parsley	25 mL
Pinch	hot pepper flakes	Pinch
	Salt and freshly ground black pepper to taste	

Toss together all ingredients, cover and refrigerate for about 1 hour, until chilled. **Serves 4.**

Chickpea, Tomato and Onion Salad

1	clove garlic, minced	1
1	tomato (preferably organic), chopped	1
2 cups	drained rinsed canned chickpeas	250 mL
⅓ cup	chopped onion	75 mL
3 tbsp	low-fat plain yogurt	45 mL
2 tbsp	finely chopped fresh Italian (flat-leaf) parsley	25 mL
2 tbsp	freshly squeezed lemon juice	25 mL
1 tbsp	extra-virgin olive oil	15 mL
Pinch	hot pepper flakes	Pinch
	Salt and freshly ground black pepper to taste	

Toss together all ingredients, cover and refrigerate for about 1 hour, until chilled. **Serves 4.**

Chicken Cannellini Salad

⅓ cup	buttermilk	75 mL
2 tbsp	reduced-fat mayonnaise	25 mL
1 tbsp	chili powder	15 mL
1 tbsp	ground cumin	15 mL
2 tbsp	hot pepper sauce (such as Frank's RedHot)	25 mL
	Salt and freshly ground black pepper to taste	
1	bunch green onions, thinly sliced	1
1	roasted red bell pepper (see page 11), diced	1
1 lb	leftover or freshly cooked chicken breast, diced	500 g
3 cups	drained rinsed canned cannellini or white kidney beans	750 mL
2 tbsp	chopped fresh Italian (flat-leaf) parsley	25 mL

Combine buttermilk, mayonnaise, chili powder, cumin, hot pepper sauce, salt and black pepper. Add the remaining ingredients and toss to coat. Cover and refrigerate for about 1 hour, until chilled. **Serves 4.**

Eggplant Chili

1	eggplant, peeled and diced	1
1 tsp	kosher salt	5 mL
1 tbsp	olive oil	15 mL
2	canned or fresh hot chili peppers, diced	2
1	large onion, chopped	250 mL
1	red bell pepper, diced	1
2	cloves garlic, minced	2
¼ cup	chili powder	50 mL
2 tbsp	cornmeal	25 mL
1 tbsp	ground cumin	15 mL
2 tsp	dried oregano	10 mL
3 cups	organic vegetable broth	750 mL
1 cup	canned diced tomatoes, drained	250 mL
1 tsp	cider vinegar	5 mL
	Salt and freshly ground black pepper to taste	
2 cups	drained rinsed canned cannellini or white kidney beans	500 mL

Toss eggplant with salt and let stand for 30 minutes; rinse and dry. In a large, deep skillet or Dutch oven, heat oil over medium-high heat. Sauté eggplant, chilies, onion and red pepper until onion starts to brown. Add garlic, chili powder, cornmeal, cumin and oregano; sauté for 1 minute. Add broth, tomatoes, vinegar, salt and pepper; reduce heat, cover and simmer for 30 minutes. Add beans and simmer for 10 to 20 minutes, or until flavors are blended and vegetables are tender. **Serves 4.**

Grilled Chicken Breast with Buttermilk and Herbs

2	green onions, thinly sliced	2
1 cup	buttermilk	250 mL
¼ cup	finely chopped celery	50 mL
1 tsp	hot pepper flakes	5 mL
1 tbsp	chopped fresh Italian (flat-leaf) parsley	15 mL
1 tbsp	chopped fresh herb of your choice	15 mL
1 tbsp	finely grated orange zest	15 mL
4	boneless skinless chicken breasts, pounded thin (see page 498)	4
	Salt and freshly ground black pepper to taste	

In a shallow dish, combine green onions, buttermilk, celery, hot pepper flakes, parsley, herb and orange zest. Season chicken with salt and black pepper, add to buttermilk mixture and turn to coat. Cover and refrigerate for 2 hours. Preheat broiler or barbecue grill to high. Remove chicken from marinade and discard marinade. Broil or grill chicken for 5 to 6 minutes per side, or until browned on both sides and no longer pink inside. **Serves 4.**

Salmon Poached in Basil Tea with Pine Nuts

1½ lbs	skinless salmon fillet (preferably wild-caught)	750 g
1½ cups	dry white wine	375 mL
1½ cups	water	375 mL
	Juice of 1 large lemon	
	Salt and freshly ground black pepper to taste	
¼ cup	chopped fresh basil	50 mL
8	thin lemon wedges	8
3 tbsp	toasted pine nuts	45 mL

Cut salmon on an angle into ½-inch (1 cm) thick slices. In a large skillet, bring wine, water, lemon juice, salt and pepper to a boil. Add salmon in a single layer, scatter basil over top, cover and remove from heat. Let stand for 2 minutes. Remove salmon with a slotted spatula to a platter. Serve garnished with lemon wedges and pine nuts. **Serves 4.**

Poached Salmon with Arugula

2 cups	water	500 mL
1 cup	dry white wine	250 mL
¼ cup	finely chopped onion	50 mL
	Juice of ½ lemon	
4	pieces skinless wild salmon fillet (each 5 oz/150 g)	4
1	roasted red bell pepper (see page 11), diced	1
½ cup	chopped arugula	125 mL
½ cup	low-fat plain yogurt	125 mL

In a large skillet, bring water, wine, onion and lemon juice to a boil. Reduce heat, add salmon in a single layer, cover and simmer for 6 to 8 minutes, or until fish is opaque and flakes easily with a fork. Remove fish with a slotted spatula to a warm platter. Boil poaching liquid until reduced to ⅓ cup (75 mL). Add roasted pepper and any liquid from the fish plate; return to a boil. Remove from heat and stir in arugula and yogurt. Pour sauce over fish. **Serves 4.**

Stir-Fried Shrimp and Tofu in Yogurt

1 lb	extra-firm tofu, cut into 1-inch (2.5 cm) cubes and patted dry	500 g
½ tsp	ground Szechwan peppercorns	2 mL
2 tbsp	canola oil	25 mL
2	cloves garlic, minced	2
1 lb	large shrimp, peeled and deveined	500 g
1 cup	dry white wine	250 mL
	Salt and freshly ground black pepper to taste	
½ cup	low-fat plain yogurt	125 mL
2 tbsp	chopped fresh dill	25 mL
	Hot cooked rice or pasta (optional)	

Toss tofu with Szechwan peppercorns. In a wok or large skillet, heat oil over high heat. Stir-fry tofu until browned on all sides; remove to a plate lined with paper towels to drain. Add garlic and shrimp to the wok and stir-fry until shrimp are pink and opaque, about 1 minute. Add wine, salt and pepper; bring to a boil. Remove shrimp to a plate. Boil pan liquid until reduced by two-thirds. Stir in yogurt and dill. Toss shrimp and tofu with sauce. Serve over rice or pasta, if desired. **Serves 4.**

Grilled Teriyaki Tofu

2	blocks extra-firm tofu (each 1 lb/500 g), halved horizontally	2
1	recipe Ginger Soy Marinade (page 30), divided	1
4 tsp	dark sesame oil	20 mL

Brush tofu with half the marinade and let stand for 30 minutes. Preheat broiler or barbecue grill to medium. Brush tofu with oil, then broil or grill until lightly browned, about 3 minutes per side, basting with the remaining marinade every 1 minute. **Serves 4.**

Grilled Tofu Steak with Pickled Ginger

Follow preceding recipe, but replace the marinade with ½ cup (125 mL) steak sauce and top each piece of grilled tofu with a small mound of finely sliced sushi ginger. **Serves 4.**

Stir-Fried Asparagus with Tofu and Almonds

⅓ cup	oyster sauce	75 mL
2 tbsp	soy sauce	25 mL
	Juice of ½ lemon	
2 tsp	cornstarch	10 mL
2 tbsp	canola oil	25 mL
1 lb	asparagus, trimmed and cut into 2-inch (5 cm) sections	500 g
8 oz	extra-firm tofu, cut into 1-inch (2.5 cm) dice	250 g
1 cup	organic vegetable broth	250 mL
Pinch	hot pepper flakes	Pinch
2	green onions, thinly sliced	2
1	clove garlic, minced	1
1 cup	toasted whole almonds	250 mL

Combine oyster sauce, soy sauce and lemon juice. Dissolve cornstarch in this mixture; set aside. In a wok or large skillet, heat oil over medium-high heat. Stir-fry asparagus until bright green. Add tofu, broth and hot pepper flakes; cover and cook for 3 minutes. Stir cornstarch mixture and add to wok; stir-fry until sauce thickens. Remove from heat and stir in green onions, garlic and almonds. **Serves 4.**

Stir-Fried Broccoli and Apples

3 tbsp	canola oil, divided	45 mL
1	clove garlic	1
½	small onion, chopped	½
1	large tart apple, peeled and thinly sliced	1
4 cups	broccoli florets	1 L
2 tsp	finely chopped gingerroot	10 mL
⅓ cup	water	75 mL
1	clove garlic, minced	1
1 tbsp	hoisin sauce	15 mL
1 tbsp	freshly squeezed lemon juice	15 mL

In a wok or large skillet, heat 2 tbsp (25 mL) of the oil over medium-high heat. Stir-fry garlic clove until browned. Discard garlic. Add onion to the wok and stir-fry until tender. Add apple, broccoli and ginger; stir-fry for 1 minute. Add water, reduce heat, cover and simmer until broccoli is bright green and water has evaporated, about 4 minutes. Stir in minced garlic, hoisin sauce and lemon juice. Serve immediately. **Serves 4.**

Eggplant and Feta au Gratin

1	large eggplant, cut into 18 slices	1
	Salt and freshly ground black pepper to taste	
6 tbsp	freshly grated Parmesan cheese, divided	90 mL
5 oz	feta cheese, crumbled, divided	150 g
8	fresh basil leaves, finely chopped, divided	8
1 cup	canned diced tomato, drained, divided	125 mL

Sprinkle eggplant with salt and pepper; let stand for 20 minutes, then blot surface with paper towels. Meanwhile, preheat broiler. Broil eggplant for 3 minutes. Turn and broil for 2 minutes. Set oven temperature to 375°F (190°C). Sprinkle 2 tbsp (25 mL) of the Parmesan on the bottom of a 9-inch (23 cm) pie plate. Top with 3 oz (90 g) of the feta and half the basil. Top with half the eggplant, half the tomato, another 2 tbsp (25 mL) of the Parmesan and the remaining basil. Cover with the remaining eggplant and tomato. Sprinkle with the remaining feta and Parmesan. Bake for 35 minutes, until browned and bubbling. **Serves 6.**

Souffléd Sweet Potatoes

	Vegetable cooking spray	
2	extra-large eggs, separated	2
1½ cups	mashed peeled cooked sweet potatoes	375 mL
¾ cup	low-fat plain yogurt	175 mL
1 tbsp	packed light brown sugar	15 mL
Pinch	ground nutmeg	Pinch
Pinch	ground cloves	Pinch
	Finely grated zest and juice of 1 orange	
	Salt and freshly ground white pepper to taste	

Preheat oven to 400°F (200°C) and coat a 6-cup (1.5 L) soufflé dish with cooking spray. In a large bowl, beat egg yolks, sweet potatoes, yogurt, brown sugar, nutmeg, cloves, orange zest, orange juice, salt and pepper. In a separate bowl, beat egg whites and a pinch of salt until soft peaks form; fold into sweet potato mixture. Transfer to prepared soufflé dish and bake for 35 minutes, until puffed and brown. Serve immediately. **Serves 4.**

Garden Vegetable Whole-Grain Tempura

2 cups	ice water	500 mL
2	egg yolks, beaten	2
2 cups	sifted whole wheat pastry flour	500 mL
2	carrots, julienned	2
½	bunch broccoli, broken into small florets	½
½	head cauliflower, broken into small florets	½
1	clove garlic, minced	1
¼ cup	soy sauce	50 mL
1 tsp	honey	5 mL

Stir ice water into egg yolks, then stir in flour (don't be too thorough; some small clumps should remain). Toss carrots, broccoli and cauliflower in batter. Deep-fry (see page 9) for about 2 minutes, or until coating is lightly browned and crispy; drain on paper towels. Keep warm in a 200°F (100°C) oven while frying the remaining vegetables. Combine garlic, soy sauce and honey; serve as a dipping sauce with tempura . **Serves 4.**

Three-Bean Tempura

Follow preceding recipe, but replace the vegetables with a mixture of 1 lb (500 g) firm tofu, diced, 1 cup (250 mL) bean sprouts and ½ cup (125 mL) chopped peanuts. To fry, drop small handfuls of the batter-coated bean mix into the hot oil. **Serves 4.**

Vitamin A Tempura

Follow recipe for Garden Vegetable Whole-Grain Tempura (above), but replace the cauliflower with 8 oz (250 g) sweet potato, peeled and diced. Before frying the vegetables, wash and dry 12 large perfect kale leaves, stemmed. Deep-fry leaves for 30 seconds, until bright green and crisp at the edges. Serve tempura on a bed of fried kale. **Serves 4.**

Spiced Sesame Chickpeas

2 tbsp	extra-virgin olive oil	25 mL
1	clove garlic, minced	1
2 tbsp	chili powder	25 mL
2 tsp	ground coriander	10 mL
2 cups	drained rinsed canned chickpeas	500 mL
¼ cup	toasted sesame seeds	50 mL
	Salt to taste	

In a skillet, heat oil over medium-high heat. Sauté garlic, chili powder and coriander for 30 seconds. Add chickpeas and sauté until chickpeas are lightly toasted. Stir in sesame seeds and salt. **Serves 4.**

Brown Beans and Rice

1 tbsp	olive oil	15 mL
1 cup	chopped onion	250 mL
1	canned or fresh jalapeño pepper, seeded and finely chopped	1
1	clove garlic, minced	1
2 cups	long-grain brown rice	250 mL
3 tbsp	chili powder	45 mL
1 tbsp	ground cumin	15 mL
2 tsp	ground coriander	10 mL
1 tsp	dried oregano	5 mL
5 cups	organic vegetable, chicken or beef broth	1.25 L
	Salt and freshly ground black pepper to taste	
2 cups	drained rinsed canned red kidney beans	500 mL
1 tbsp	chopped fresh cilantro	15 mL

In a large saucepan, heat oil over medium-high heat. Sauté onion until tender. Add jalapeño, garlic, rice, chili powder, cumin, coriander and oregano; sauté for 1 minute. Stir in broth, salt and black pepper; reduce heat, cover and simmer until liquid is absorbed and rice is tender, about 45 minutes. Add beans and cilantro, cover and remove from heat. Let rest for 5 minutes before fluffing with a fork to separate rice grains and distribute beans. **Serves 4.**

Healthy Hoppin' John

1 tbsp	canola oil	15 mL
2	stalks celery, diced	2
1	large onion, chopped	1
8 oz	dried black-eyed peas, soaked and drained (see page 11)	250 g
3 oz	nitrate-free smoked turkey breast, diced	90 g
7 cups	organic chicken broth	1.75 L
1	bay leaf	1
Pinch	cayenne pepper	Pinch
	Salt and freshly ground black pepper to taste	
1 cup	long-grain brown rice, rinsed	250 mL

In a large saucepan, heat oil over medium-high heat. Sauté celery and onion until tender. Add peas, turkey, broth, bay leaf, cayenne, salt and black pepper; boil for 30 minutes, until peas are barely tender. Add rice, reduce heat, cover and simmer until liquid is absorbed and rice and peas are tender, about 45 minutes. Let rest for 5 minutes, then fluff with a fork. **Serves 4.**

Sesame Brown Rice Pilaf

1 tsp	canola oil	5 mL
½ cup	chopped onion	125 mL
1	clove garlic, minced	1
1 cup	long-grain brown rice	250 mL
1 tsp	dark sesame oil	5 mL
2½ cups	boiling organic vegetable broth	625 mL
Pinch	hot pepper flakes	Pinch
	Salt and freshly ground black pepper to taste	
½ cup	toasted sesame seeds	125 mL
2 tsp	soy sauce	10 mL

In a large saucepan, heat oil over medium heat. Sauté onion until tender. Add garlic, rice and sesame oil; sauté for 30 seconds. Stir in broth, hot pepper flakes, salt and black pepper; cover and simmer until liquid is absorbed and rice is tender, about 40 minutes. Fluff with a fork and stir in sesame seeds and soy sauce. **Serves 4.**

Brown Rice Risotto with Sage and Potatoes

2 tsp	extra-virgin olive oil	10 ml
1	onion, chopped	1
2	cloves garlic, chopped	2
1½ cups	medium-grain brown rice	375 mL
1 tsp	dried sage	5 mL
½ tsp	dried rosemary, crumbled	2 mL
Pinch	ground allspice	Pinch
½ cup	dry white wine	125 mL
6 cups	organic chicken broth, divided	1.5 L
12 oz	red-skinned or other boiling potatoes, peeled and cut into ½-inch (1 cm) dice	375 g
2 tbsp	chopped fresh sage	25 mL
2 tbsp	freshly grated Parmesan cheese	25 mL
	Salt and freshly ground black pepper to taste	

In a large, heavy saucepan, heat oil over medium heat. Sauté onion until tender. Add garlic, rice, sage, rosemary and allspice; sauté for 1 minute. Add wine and cook, stirring constantly with a wooden spoon, until wine is absorbed. Add 1 cup (250 mL) of the broth and cook, stirring occasionally, until broth is absorbed. Stir in potatoes. Add the remaining broth, 1 cup (250 mL) at a time, and cook, stirring occasionally, until each addition is absorbed before stirring in the next. When finished, rice should be tender and saucy (the mixture should be quite wet). Remove from heat and stir in sage, Parmesan, salt and pepper. **Serves 4.**

Wild Rice Risotto

3 cups	water	750 mL
⅔ cup	wild rice	150 mL
2 tsp	extra-virgin olive oil	10 mL
1	onion, chopped	1
¼ cup	diced mushrooms	50 mL
2	cloves garlic, chopped	2
1 cup	Arborio rice	250 mL
½ cup	dry white wine	125 mL
5 cups	organic chicken broth	1.25 L
2 tbsp	finely chopped fresh Italian (flat-leaf) parsley	25 mL
2 tbsp	freshly grated Parmesan cheese	25 mL
	Salt and freshly ground black pepper to taste	

In a large saucepan, bring water to a boil. Add wild rice and boil for 20 minutes, until barely tender; drain. Meanwhile, in another large saucepan, heat oil over medium heat. Sauté onion and mushrooms until tender. Add garlic, Arborio rice and wild rice; sauté for 1 minute. Add wine and cook, stirring constantly with a wooden spoon, until wine is absorbed. Add broth, 1 cup (250 mL) at a time, and cook, stirring occasionally, until each addition is absorbed before stirring in the next. When finished, rice should be tender and saucy (the mixture should be quite wet). Remove from heat and stir in parsley, Parmesan, salt and pepper. **Serves 4.**

Stir-Fried Quinoa

2 cups	water	500 mL
¼ tsp	salt	1 mL
1 cup	quinoa, rinsed	250 mL
2 tbsp	canola oil, divided	25 mL
1	stalk celery, diced	1
½	red bell pepper, diced	½
¼ cup	finely chopped onion	50 mL
1	egg	1
12	large spinach leaves, stems trimmed, thinly sliced	12
2	green onions, thinly sliced	2
1 cup	bean sprouts	250 mL
¼ cup	roasted peanuts	50 mL
1 tsp	soy sauce	5 mL

In a saucepan, bring water and salt to a boil. Add quinoa, reduce heat, cover and simmer until water is absorbed and quinoa is tender, about 10 minutes; set aside. In a large wok, heat half the oil over medium-high heat. Stir-fry celery, red pepper and onion until lightly browned. Add quinoa and stir-fry until lightly toasted, about 3 minutes. Push quinoa and vegetables up the side of the wok and add the remaining oil to the center of the pan. Add egg and stir-fry until set. Toss with quinoa mixture. Add the remaining ingredients and toss to combine. **Serves 4.**

Quinoa with Tofu and Mushrooms

2 cups	water	500 mL
¼ tsp	salt	1 mL
1 cup	quinoa, rinsed	250 mL
2 tbsp	canola oil	25 mL
8 oz	small mushrooms, stem ends trimmed	250 g
2	cloves garlic, minced	2
12 oz	extra-firm tofu, cut into 1-inch (2.5 cm) cubes	375 g
1 cup	organic vegetable or chicken broth	250 mL
1 tbsp	soy sauce	15 mL
3	green onions, sliced	3
1 tsp	cornstarch, dissolved in 1 tbsp (15 mL) water	5 mL

In a saucepan, bring water and salt to a boil. Add quinoa, reduce heat, cover and simmer until water is absorbed and quinoa is tender, about 10 minutes; transfer to a serving bowl and keep warm. In a large wok, heat oil over medium-high heat. Stir-fry mushrooms until browned. Add garlic and stir-fry for 10 seconds. Add tofu, broth and soy sauce; reduce heat and simmer for 2 minutes. Add green onions and cornstarch mixture; stir-fry until lightly thickened. Pour over quinoa. **Serves 4.**

Fresh Whole Wheat Wild Mushroom Pasta

2 oz	dried wild mushrooms	60 g
¾ cup	whole wheat pastry flour	175 mL
½ cup	unbleached all-purpose flour	125 mL
¼ cup	bread flour	50 mL
2	extra-large eggs	2
1 tsp	olive oil	5 mL
½ tsp	salt	2 mL

In a mini-chopper, grind dried mushrooms to a powder. In the work bowl of a food processor, combine ground mushrooms, pastry flour, all-purpose flour and bread flour. Add eggs, oil and salt; process until mixture forms a ball of dough. Knead, let rest, roll, cut and cook dough as described in Egg Pasta (page 20). Serve tossed with the sauce of your choice. **Makes about 12 oz (375 g), enough to serve 4.**

Whole Wheat Pasta with Roasted Peppers

4	large roasted bell peppers (see page 11), cut into strips	4
2	cloves garlic, minced	2
½	small red onion, finely chopped	½
1 lb	whole wheat fettuccine, cooked, hot	500 g
2 tbsp	freshly grated Parmesan cheese	25 mL
1 tbsp	extra-virgin olive oil	15 mL
1 tbsp	red wine vinegar	15 mL
	Salt and freshly ground black pepper to taste	

Toss together all ingredients. **Serves 4.**

Whole Wheat Pasta Boiled with Broccoli, Ricotta and Roasted Peppers

12 oz	whole wheat pasta, any shape	375 g
1	bunch broccoli, broken into small florets, stalks trimmed, peeled and sliced	1
1	recipe Ricotta and Roasted Red Pepper Sauce (page 226)	1

In a large pot of boiling lightly salted water, cook pasta according to package directions. Add broccoli 4 minutes before pasta will be done. Drain and toss with sauce. **Serves 4.**

Dried Fruit Roll

2½ cups	assorted dried fruits (raisins, dates, apricots, apples, pineapple, etc.)	625 mL
1 tsp	ground cinnamon	5 mL
¼ tsp	ground ginger	1 mL
Pinch	ground allspice	Pinch
½ cup	walnut or pecan pieces	125 mL

In a food processor, finely chop or grind dried fruits, cinnamon, ginger and allspice. With wet hands, form mixture into a rough log. Roll log in nuts. Wrap in plastic wrap and refrigerate for 1 hour, until firm. Cut into slices. **Serves 4.**

Tofu Rice Pudding

2	egg whites	2
12 oz	silken tofu, drained	375 g
¾ cup	milk	175 mL
¼ cup	honey	50 mL
2 tsp	vanilla	10 mL
1 tsp	ground cinnamon	5 mL
Pinch	salt	Pinch
Pinch	ground nutmeg	Pinch
1 cup	cooked brown rice	250 mL
¼ cup	raisins	50 mL
1 tbsp	unsalted butter, melted	15 mL

In a blender or food processor, purée egg whites, tofu, milk, honey, vanilla, cinnamon, salt and nutmeg until smooth. Transfer to a saucepan and stir in rice, raisins and butter; cook over low heat, stirring frequently, for 10 minutes, until lightly thickened. Transfer to a bowl, cover and refrigerate for about 1 hour, until chilled. **Serves 4.**

Chapter 47
Chocolate Recipes
For Happiness

Real Hot Chocolate Spiked
with Scotch 523

Triple Chocolate Drops 523

Peanut Chocolate Drops 523

Chocolate Chocolate Chunk Cookies . . 524

Unbelievably Amazing Brownies 524

Date Nut Brownies 524

Very Nutty Brownies 524

White Chocolate Brownies 524

White Chocolate Brownies
with Chocolate-Dipped Almonds 525

Three-Layer Brownies 525

Chocolate Orange Liqueur Brownies . . 525

Chocolate Gingerbread 525

Chocolate Soufflé Cake 526

Mocha Torte 526

Devil's Food Layer Cake 526

Chocolate Black Pepper Pound Cake . . 526

Chocolate Brandy Pudding Cake 527

Black Forest Pudding Cake 527

Chocolate Glaze 527

Chocolate Almond Torte 527

Gâteau Bordeaux 528

French Chocolate Cake 528

Bitter Chocolate Torte 528

Chocolate Apricot Torte 528

MeMe's Chocolate Roll 528

Chocolate Peanut Pie 528

Chocolate Bourbon Pecan Pie 529

Chocolate Pâté 529

Best-Ever Chocolate Pudding 529

Chocolate Hazelnut Pudding 529

Chocolate Chocolate Chip Pudding . . . 529

White Chocolate Amaretto Pudding . . . 529

Chocolate Mousse with Dark Rum 530

Chocolate Mousse
with Chocolate Dumplings 530

Spiked Chocolate Mousse 530

Honey Brandy White
Chocolate Mousse 530

Fruit in Chocolate Cups 530

Peaches and White Chocolate
Mousse in Chocolate Cups 530

Triple Chocolate Parfait 531

White Chocolate Ice Cream 531

Chocolate Ice Cream
with Raspberry Swirl 531

Dipping Chocolate 531

Chocolate-Covered Prunes
with Marzipan "Pits" 531

Chocolate-Covered Almond Apricots . . 531

Chocolate Fruit Squares 532

Chocolate-Covered
Pretzel "Porcupines" 532

Chocolate Peanut Crunch Balls 532

Chocolate Peanut Grahams 532

Chocolate-Covered Potato Chips 532

Chocolate-Covered Chocolate
Chip Cookies 532

S'mores 532

Chocolate-Dipped Strawberries 532

To a true chocoholic, chocolate is a food set apart, a food for which the usual rules do not apply. An overabundance of sugar is cloying, and an overabundance of cayenne is painful, but too much chocolate? That's an oxymoron.

With that in mind, we've devoted a chapter to chocolate opulences, none of which is restrained or restricted by diet, budget or rational thought. These recipes range from homey puddings to elaborate tortes, and though some are impressive enough to serve on the most elegant occasions, not one is complicated or time-consuming to prepare.

So, if you swoon for chocolate chocolate cakes or chocolate chocolate-chip anything, loosen your belt a notch and try some of these desserts.

About these recipes . . .

Most of these recipes call for either semisweet or unsweetened chocolate. Substitutions of one for the other are possible but not recommended. Not only will it throw off the balance of sugar in the recipe, but it can also destroy the dessert's texture. Bitter chocolate not only has less sugar, but it has more chocolate per unit of weight than sweeter varieties. Using it in place of sweet chocolate can make a mousse implode or a cake come out like a chocolate flapjack.

Many cooks are a little scared of working with chocolate. Chocolate is an emulsion of water in fat and, like all emulsions, it is easily broken. A slight amount of moisture in melted chocolate will ruin its smoothness, causing the mixture to bind up like so much concrete. Ironically, you can relax the mess by adding a bit more warm liquid (up to 1 tbsp/15 mL) per ounce (30 g) of chocolate, or a bit more fat.

Melted chocolate will also seize if it gets cold. This makes sense when you realize that chocolate has a high proportion of fat, and that fat becomes firmer the colder it gets. If this should happen, warm the chocolate slightly and it will immediately relax.

To melt chocolate, chop it finely and place it in the top of a double boiler over barely simmering water. Stir until half melted, then remove from heat and stir until completely melted. Chocolate can also be melted in a bowl in the microwave. Heat up to 3 ounces (90 g) on High for 1 to 2 minutes. Remove and stir until melted. Never melt chocolate directly over a flame, unless it is protected by the addition of butter or a liquid. Alone, it will scorch easily.

Real Hot Chocolate Spiked with Scotch

12 oz	semisweet chocolate, chopped	375 g
3 cups	milk	750 mL
2 tbsp	Scotch whisky	25 mL
1 tbsp	instant coffee granules	15 mL
¼ cup	whipped cream (optional)	50 mL

In a saucepan, combine chocolate and milk. Cook over medium heat, stirring often, until chocolate melts. Stir in Scotch and coffee granules. Serve in mugs, each topped with 1 tbsp (15 mL) whipped cream, if desired. **Serves 4.**

Triple Chocolate Drops

⅓ cup	all-purpose flour	75 mL
1 tsp	baking powder	5 mL
¼ tsp	salt	1 mL
7 oz	semisweet chocolate, chopped	210 g
1 oz	unsweetened chocolate, chopped	30 g
6 tbsp	unsalted butter, cut into pieces	90 mL
2	extra-large eggs	2
¾ cup	granulated sugar	175 mL
1 tbsp	instant espresso powder	15 mL
2 tsp	vanilla	10 mL
1½ cups	semisweet chocolate chips	375 mL

Preheat oven to 325°F (160°C) and line baking sheets with parchment paper. Sift together flour, baking powder and salt; set aside. Melt semisweet chocolate, unsweetened chocolate and butter in the microwave (see "About these recipes," left) and let cool. In a large bowl, beat eggs, sugar, espresso powder and vanilla until thick and fluffy. Stir in chocolate mixture. Stir in flour mixture just until combined. Stir in chocolate chips. Drop batter in 1½-tbsp (22 mL) mounds, 2 inches (5 cm) apart, on prepared baking sheets. Bake until cookies are firm on top, about 15 minutes. Let cool on pans for 1 minute, then remove to racks to cool completely. Makes 16 to 18 large cookies.

Peanut Chocolate Drops

Follow preceding recipe, but replace the chocolate chips with 1 cup (250 mL) milk chocolate chunks and 1 cup (250 mL) unsalted roasted peanuts. Makes 16 to 18 large cookies.

Chocolate Chocolate Chunk Cookies

2¼ cups	all-purpose flour, divided	550 mL
½ cup	Dutch-process cocoa powder	125 mL
1 cup	unsalted butter, softened	250 mL
¾ cup	granulated sugar	175 mL
¾ cup	firmly packed brown sugar	175 mL
2	large or extra-large eggs	2
1 tsp	baking soda	5 mL
1 tsp	hot water	5 mL
1 tsp	vanilla	5 mL
8 oz	semisweet chocolate, cut into chunks	250 g
1 cup	walnut pieces	250 mL

Preheat oven to 375°F (190°C). Sift together flour and cocoa; set aside. In a large bowl, cream butter, granulated sugar and brown sugar until light and fluffy. Beat in eggs. Stir in half the flour mixture. Dissolve baking soda in water and vanilla; add to batter, followed by the remaining flour mixture. Stir in chocolate chunks and walnut pieces. Drop batter in 1 tbsp (15 mL) mounds, 2 inches (5 cm) apart, on ungreased baking sheets. Bake for 12 minutes, until tops are set but cookies are still soft in the center. Let cool on pans for 1 minute, then remove to racks to cool completely. **Makes about 36 cookies.**

Unbelievably Amazing Brownies

	Vegetable cooking spray	
8 oz	unsweetened chocolate, chopped	250 g
1 cup	unsalted butter	250 mL
5	extra-large eggs	5
2 cups	granulated sugar	500 mL
1½ cups	firmly packed light brown sugar	375 mL
2 tbsp	instant coffee granules	25 mL
1 tbsp	vanilla	15 mL
1½ cups	all-purpose flour	375 mL
2 cups	walnut pieces	500 mL

Preheat oven to 425°F (220°C) and spray a 13- by 9-inch (3 L) baking pan with cooking spray. Melt chocolate and butter together (see page 523); set aside. In a large bowl, beat eggs, sugars, coffee granules and vanilla until thick and fluffy. Stir in chocolate mixture. Stir in flour just until combined. Stir in walnuts. Pour into prepared pan and smooth top. Bake for 35 minutes, or until a tester inserted in the center comes out moist. Do not overbake. Let cool in pan on a rack. Unmold and refrigerate until firm. Cut into 24 squares.

Date Nut Brownies

Follow preceding recipe, but replace the walnuts with 1 cup (250 mL) pecan pieces and 1 cup (250 mL) chopped pitted dates.

Very Nutty Brownies

5 oz	unsweetened chocolate, chopped	150 g
⅔ cup	unsalted butter	150 mL
3 cups	walnut pieces	750 mL
1 cup	all-purpose flour	250 mL
4	large or extra-large eggs	4
2 cups	granulated sugar	500 mL
1 tbsp	instant coffee granules	15 mL
2 tsp	vanilla	10 mL

Preheat oven to 425°F (220°C) and grease and flour a 15- by 10-inch (38 by 25 cm) jellyroll pan. Melt chocolate and butter together (see page 523); set aside. Combine walnut pieces and flour; set aside. In a large bowl, beat eggs and sugar until light and fluffy. Stir in coffee granules and vanilla. Stir in reserved chocolate and nut mixtures. Pour into prepared pan and smooth top. Bake for 18 minutes, until top is crusty but center is still soft. Let cool in pan on a rack. Cut into 24 squares.

White Chocolate Brownies

	Vegetable cooking spray	
⅔ cup	unsalted butter	150 mL
	Finely grated zest of 1 orange	
8 oz	white chocolate, finely chopped	250 g
5	eggs	5
1½ cups	granulated sugar	375 mL
2 tbsp	orange-flavored liqueur	25 mL
1 tsp	vanilla	5 mL
1 cup	sifted all-purpose flour	250 mL

Preheat oven to 400°F (200°C). Line a 15- by 10-inch (38 by 25 cm) jellyroll pan with foil and spray with cooking spray. In a saucepan, melt butter with orange zest. Remove from heat and whisk in white chocolate until melted. In a large bowl, beat eggs, sugar, liqueur and vanilla until light and fluffy. Stir in chocolate mixture and flour. Pour into prepared pan and smooth top. Bake for 15 to 18 minutes, or until a tester comes out with just a crumb clinging to it. Invert onto a baking sheet, remove pan and foil and invert back into baking pan. Let cool completely on a rack. Cut into 24 squares.

White Chocolate Brownies with Chocolate-Dipped Almonds

Follow preceding recipe, but first melt ½ cup (125 mL) semisweet chocolate chips (see page 523). Pour over 1½ cups (375 mL) coarsely chopped almonds set in a pie plate and stir until well coated. Chill until chocolate is set, then break into pieces and set aside. Fold chocolate-covered almonds into batter after adding the flour.

Three-Layer Brownies

1¼ cups	all-purpose flour	300 mL
¼ cup	unsweetened cocoa powder, divided	50 mL
½ cup	unsalted butter, softened	125 mL
1 cup	packed light brown sugar, divided	250 mL
2	eggs	2
½ tsp	vanilla	2 mL
¼ tsp	salt	1 mL
2 cups	finely ground walnuts (see page 13)	500 mL
3 tbsp	strained raspberry preserves	45 mL
¾ cup	semisweet chocolate chips	175 mL
2 tbsp	honey	25 mL
2 tsp	dark rum	10 mL
2 tsp	strong brewed coffee	10 mL

Preheat oven to 375°F (190°C). Sift together flour and half the cocoa; set aside. In a large bowl, cream butter and ¼ cup (50 mL) of the brown sugar until smooth. Stir in flour mixture to form a firm dough. Press into a 9-inch (2.5 L) square baking pan and bake for 10 minutes. Meanwhile, beat eggs and the remaining brown sugar until thick. Add the remaining cocoa, vanilla and salt; beat for 2 minutes. Stir in walnuts. Spread raspberry preserves over baked dough and top with batter. Bake for 25 minutes, until just set. Let cool in pan on a rack. Melt chocolate chips with honey, rum and coffee (see page 523). Spread over cooled cake and let stand until set, about 30 minutes. Cut into 24 squares.

Chocolate Orange Liqueur Brownies

Follow preceding recipe, but add 2 tbsp (25 mL) finely grated orange zest to the batter, omit the rum and coffee, and add 4 tsp (20 mL) orange-flavored liqueur with the honey.

Chocolate Gingerbread

	Vegetable cooking spray	
2¼ cups	all-purpose flour	550 mL
2 tsp	ground ginger	10 mL
1½ tsp	baking soda	7 mL
1 tsp	ground cinnamon	5 mL
Pinch	ground cloves	Pinch
1 cup	hot strong brewed coffee	250 mL
1 cup	unsalted butter, softened	250 mL
4	extra-large eggs	4
1 cup	firmly packed dark brown sugar	250 mL
1 cup	dark corn syrup	250 mL
2 oz	unsweetened chocolate, melted (see page 523)	60 g
1 cup	cold whipping (35%) cream	250 mL
2 tbsp	honey	25 mL
1 tsp	vanilla	5 mL
2 tbsp	finely chopped candied ginger	25 mL

Preheat oven to 350°F (180°C). Spray a 13- by 9-inch (3 L) baking pan with cooking spray. Sift together flour, ground ginger, baking soda, cinnamon and cloves. In a large bowl, pour coffee over butter and stir until melted. Whisk in eggs, brown sugar and corn syrup until blended. Stir in flour mixture. Stir in melted chocolate until batter is smooth. Pour into prepared pan and smooth top. Bake for 50 minutes. Let cool in pan on a rack, then cut into 16 squares. Beat whipping cream, honey and vanilla to soft peaks. Serve gingerbread squares with a dollop of whipped cream, garnished with candied ginger. **Serves 16.**

Chocolate Soufflé Cake

	Vegetable cooking spray	
9 oz	semisweet chocolate, chopped	275 g
1 cup + 2 tbsp	unsalted butter	275 mL
6	extra-large eggs, separated	6
6 tbsp	cornstarch	90 mL
1/3 cup	granulated sugar	75 mL
2 tbsp	confectioner's (icing) sugar, plus more for dusting	25 mL
1 cup	cold whipping (35%) cream	250 mL

Preheat oven to 350°F (180°C) and spray a 9-inch (23 cm) springform pan with cooking spray. Melt chocolate and butter in the microwave (see page 523). Beat egg yolks and cornstarch; stir into melted chocolate mixture. In a separate bowl, beat egg whites until they just hold a shape. Add granulated sugar and beat until firm. Fold into chocolate mixture until completely incorporated. Pour into prepared pan and bake for 30 minutes, until a tester inserted in the center comes out with a wet crumb clinging to it. Let cool in pan on a rack for 10 minutes. Run a knife around the edge of the pan, then remove the sides. Invert onto a serving plate and remove bottom of pan. Let cool completely, then dust top with confectioner's sugar. Whip cream and the 2 tbsp (25 mL) confectioner's sugar until soft peaks form. Serve with cake. **Serves 12.**

Mocha Torte

Follow preceding recipe, but add 2 tbsp (25 mL) instant coffee granules with the egg yolks. Add 1 tsp (5 mL) instant coffee granules to the cream before whipping. **Serves 12.**

Devil's Food Layer Cake

	Vegetable cooking spray	
6 tbsp	unsweetened cocoa powder	90 mL
6 tbsp	water	90 mL
4 oz	semisweet chocolate, chopped	125 g
1 cup	unsalted butter	250 mL
1/2 cup	packed dark brown sugar	125 mL
6	eggs, separated	6
1 1/2 cups	all-purpose flour, divided	375 mL
2 1/4 cups	sour cream, divided	550 mL
2 tsp	baking soda, dissolved in 2 tsp (10 mL) hot water	10 mL
3 tbsp	granulated sugar	45 mL
3 cups	semisweet chocolate chips	750 mL
8 oz	milk chocolate, chopped	250 g
1 tsp	vanilla	5 mL

Preheat oven to 350°F (180°C) and spray three 8-inch (20 cm) round cake pans with cooking spray. In a small saucepan, whisk together cocoa and water; bring to a boil. Remove from heat and whisk in chopped semisweet chocolate until melted; set aside. In a large bowl, cream butter and brown sugar until light and fluffy. Beat in egg yolks. Stir in melted chocolate. Stir in half the flour, 1/4 cup (50 mL) of the sour cream and dissolved baking soda. Add the remaining flour and beat just until smooth. In a separate bowl, beat egg whites until soft peaks form. Add granulated sugar and beat until firm peaks form; fold into batter. Pour into prepared pans and bake for 25 minutes, until a tester inserted in the center of a cake comes out with just a crumb clinging to it. Let cool in pans on racks. Unmold and let cool completely on racks. Meanwhile, melt chocolate chips and milk chocolate (see page 523), then beat in the remaining sour cream and vanilla. Place one cake layer on a serving plate and spread frosting on top. Add another cake layer and spread with frosting. Top with the remaining cake layer and spread frosting over top and sides of cake. **Serves 12.**

Chocolate Black Pepper Pound Cake

	Vegetable cooking spray	
3 cups	all-purpose flour	750 mL
1 cup	unsweetened cocoa powder	250 mL
1 tbsp	baking powder	15 mL
1 tsp	freshly ground black pepper	5 mL
1/2 tsp	salt	2 mL
1/2 tsp	ground allspice	2 mL
3 cups	granulated sugar	750 mL
1 cup	unsalted butter, softened	250 mL
3	extra-large eggs	3
1 tsp	vanilla	5 mL
1 3/4 cup	milk	425 mL
6 tbsp	sour cream	90 mL
1/3 cup	semisweet chocolate chips, melted	75 mL

Preheat oven to 350°F (180°C) and spray a 10-inch (3 L) Bundt pan with cooking spray. Sift together flour, cocoa, baking powder, pepper, salt and allspice; set aside. In a large bowl, cream sugar and butter until light and fluffy. Beat in eggs, one at a time, and vanilla. Stir in flour mixture alternately with milk, making 3 additions of flour and 2 of milk. Pour into prepared pan and bake for about 70 minutes, or until a tester inserted into the crest of the cake comes out with a moist crumb clinging to it. Let cool in pan on a rack for 15 minutes. Unmold and let cool on rack for 30 minutes. Whisk together sour cream and melted chocolate chips; spoon over cake, allowing it to drip down the sides. **Serves 12.**

Chocolate Brandy Pudding Cake

1 cup	all-purpose flour	250 mL
1 cup	granulated sugar, divided	250 mL
½ cup	unsweetened cocoa powder, divided	125 mL
2 tsp	baking powder	10 mL
½ tsp	baking soda	2 mL
¼ tsp	salt	1 mL
Pinch	ground cinnamon	Pinch
¼ cup	milk (not fat-free)	50 mL
¼ cup	cream (any type, minimum 10%)	50 mL
¼ cup	unsalted butter, melted and cooled	50 mL
1 tsp	vanilla	5 mL
¾ cup	packed dark brown sugar	175 mL
1 cup	boiling water	250 mL
½ cup	brandy	125 mL
	Whipped cream (optional)	

Preheat oven to 350°F (180°C). In a large bowl, sift together flour, ¾ cup (175 mL) of the granulated sugar, half the cocoa, the baking powder, baking soda, salt and cinnamon. Stir in milk, cream, butter and vanilla. Pour into an 8-inch (2 L) square baking pan. Combine the remaining granulated sugar, the remaining cocoa and brown sugar; sprinkle on top. Combine boiling water and brandy; pour over top (do not stir). Bake for about 30 minutes, until top is set. Let cool in pan on a rack for at least 1 hour. Spoon cake and some of the sauce from the bottom of the pan onto plates and dollop with whipped cream, if desired. **Serves 8.**

Black Forest Pudding Cake

1 cup	all-purpose flour	250 mL
1 cup	granulated sugar, divided	250 mL
⅓ cup + 2 tbsp	Dutch-process cocoa powder, divided	100 mL
2 tsp	baking powder	10 mL
¾ cup	milk	175 mL
2 tbsp	melted unsalted butter	25 mL
1 tsp	vanilla	5 mL
½ tsp	almond extract	2 mL
1	can (16½ oz/470 g or 398 mL) pitted dark sweet cherries in syrup	1
½ cup	firmly packed dark brown sugar	125 mL
	Whipped cream	

Preheat oven to 350°F (180°C) and butter an 8-inch (2 L) square baking pan. In a large bowl, sift together flour, ⅔ cup (150 mL) of the granulated sugar, 2 tbsp (25 mL) of the cocoa and baking powder. Stir in

milk, butter, vanilla and almond extract. Pour into prepared pan. In a saucepan, combine the remaining granulated sugar, cherries, brown sugar and the remaining cocoa; bring to a boil, then ladle over batter (do not stir). Bake for about 30 minutes, until top is set. Let cool in pan on a rack for 30 minutes. Invert onto a deep-rimmed platter (sauce from the bottom of the pan will run over top). Let cool completely and serve with whipped cream. **Serves 8.**

Use this recipe for Chocolate Glaze with the five recipes that follow.

Chocolate Glaze

6 tbsp	unsalted butter	90 mL
1 tbsp	honey	15 mL
2 oz	semisweet chocolate, finely chopped	60 g
2 oz	unsweetened chocolate, finely chopped	60 g

In a small, heavy saucepan, heat butter and honey over medium heat. Add semisweet and unsweetened chocolate, remove from heat and stir until smooth. Place over a bowl of ice water and stir until slightly thickened. **Makes enough glaze for 2 tortes or 1 layer cake.** *To coat a cake, brush away any crumbs from the cake and place on a rack over a drip pan. Using an icing spatula, spread glaze evenly over top of cake, letting some run down the sides. Smooth sides, covering all surfaces with glaze, and transfer cake to a platter.*

Chocolate Almond Torte

	Vegetable cooking spray	
⅔ cup	granulated sugar	150 mL
½ cup	unsalted butter, softened	125 mL
3	extra-large eggs	3
2 cups	finely ground almonds (see page 13)	500 mL
4 oz	semisweet chocolate, melted (see page 523)	125 g
1	recipe Chocolate Glaze (above)	1

Preheat oven to 375°F (190°C). Spray an 8-inch (20 cm) round cake pan with cooking spray. Line bottom with parchment paper and spray with cooking spray. In a large bowl, cream sugar and butter until light and fluffy. Beat in eggs, one at a time, until light. Stir in almonds and chocolate. Pour into prepared pan and smooth top. Bake for 25 minutes, until set. Let cool in pan on a rack for 30 minutes. Unmold and let cool completely on rack. Top with Chocolate Glaze. **Serves 12.**

Gâteau Bordeaux

Follow preceding recipe, but first finely chop ½ cup (125 mL) raisins and toss with 3 tbsp (45 mL) cognac. Set aside until raisins have absorbed cognac. Use the raisins in place of one-third of the almonds. **Serves 12.**

French Chocolate Cake

	Vegetable cooking spray	
⅔ cup	granulated sugar	150 mL
¼ cup	unsalted butter, softened	50 mL
3	extra-large eggs	3
1½ cups	finely ground almonds (see page 13)	375 mL
4 oz	semisweet chocolate, melted (see page 523)	125 g
¼ cup	fine dry bread crumbs	50 mL
	Finely grated zest of 1 orange	
1	recipe Chocolate Glaze (page 527), made with Grand Marnier instead of honey	1

Preheat oven to 375°F (190°C). Spray an 8-inch (20 cm) round cake pan with cooking spray. Line bottom with parchment paper and spray with cooking spray. In a large bowl, cream sugar and butter until light and fluffy. Beat in eggs, one at a time, until light. Stir in almonds, chocolate, bread crumbs and orange zest. Pour into prepared pan and smooth top. Bake for 25 minutes. Let cool in pan on a rack for 30 minutes. Unmold and let cool completely on rack. Top with Chocolate Glaze. **Serves 12.**

Bitter Chocolate Torte

Follow preceding recipe, but replace the semisweet chocolate with 3 oz (90 g) unsweetened chocolate. **Serves 12.**

Chocolate Apricot Torte

Follow recipe for French Chocolate Cake (above), but first finely chop 12 dried apricots and soak in 3 tbsp (45 mL) orange-flavored liqueur. Replace the bread crumbs with the apricots. **Serves 12.**

MeMe's Chocolate Roll

1 tbsp	unsalted butter, divided	15 mL
2 tbsp	all-purpose flour	25 mL
8	extra-large eggs, separated	8
½ cup	granulated sugar	125 mL
½ cup	sifted unsweetened cocoa powder	125 mL
1 tsp	vanilla	5 mL
Pinch	salt	Pinch
1	jar (about 8 oz/228 mL) marshmallow crème (fluff)	1
3 cups	sweetened whipped cream	750 mL
1 oz	semisweet chocolate, shaved (optional)	30 g

Preheat oven to 375°F (190°C). Grease a 15- by 10-inch (4 L) jellyroll pan with half the butter. Line with parchment paper, coat parchment with the remaining butter and sprinkle with flour. In a large bowl, beat egg yolks until light in color. Stir in sugar, cocoa and vanilla. In a separate bowl, beat egg whites and salt until soft peaks form; fold into yolk mixture. Pour into prepared pan and smooth top. Bake for 10 minutes, until a tester inserted in the center comes out slightly moist. Cover cake with a damp lint-free kitchen towel and invert onto the towel. Remove pan and, starting at one short side, roll cake up in the towel. Place jar of marshmallow crème in a bowl of hot water until crème is softened. Unroll cake and spread crème over its surface. Using the towel to help lift the cake, roll it up jellyroll-style, starting from a short side. Wrap finished roll in the towel and refrigerate for several hours or overnight. Unwrap and place on a long platter. Ice with whipped cream and decorate with shaved chocolate, if desired. **Serves 8.**

Chocolate Peanut Pie

¼ cup	unsalted butter	50 mL
2 oz	semisweet chocolate, finely chopped	60 g
1	blind-baked deep-dish pastry shell (see pages 12 and 13)	1
3	eggs	3
¾ cup	packed light brown sugar	175 mL
¾ cup	dark corn syrup	175 mL
2 tbsp	smooth peanut butter	25 mL
1½ tbsp	all-purpose flour	22 mL
1 tsp	vanilla	5 mL
2 cups	roasted unsalted peanuts	500 mL

In a small, heavy saucepan, melt butter over medium heat. Add chocolate, remove from heat and stir until melted. Pour into pastry shell and refrigerate until set. Preheat oven to 350°F (180°C). Beat eggs, brown sugar, corn syrup, peanut butter, flour and vanilla until blended. Stir in peanuts. Pour into shell and bake for 1 hour, until set at the edges but center is still soft. Let cool on a rack for 2 to 3 hours, then cut into wedges. **Serves 8.**

Chocolate Bourbon Pecan Pie

Follow preceding recipe, but replace the peanut butter with melted butter, replace the peanuts with pecan halves, and add 2 tbsp (25 mL) bourbon to the filling. **Serves 8.**

Chocolate Pâté

	Vegetable cooking spray	
2 cups	all-purpose flour	500 mL
¼ cup	unsweetened cocoa powder	50 mL
1 tsp	baking soda	5 mL
1 tsp	ground cinnamon	5 mL
½ tsp	salt	2 mL
1 cup	granulated sugar	250 mL
½ cup	unsalted butter	125 mL
2	large or extra-large eggs	2
2 tsp	rum extract	10 mL
1 tsp	vanilla	5 mL
½ cup	milk (not fat-free)	125 mL
2 cups	raisins	500 mL
2 cups	semisweet chocolate chips	500 mL
⅓ cup	chopped candied ginger	75 mL

Preheat oven to 350°F (180°C) and spray a 9- by 5-inch (2 L) loaf pan with cooking spray. Sift together flour, cocoa, baking soda, cinnamon and salt. In a large bowl, cream sugar and butter until light and fluffy. Beat in eggs, one at a time, rum extract and vanilla. Stir in half the flour mixture, then the milk, then the remaining flour mixture, stirring just until incorporated. Stir in raisins, chocolate chips and candied ginger. Pour into prepared pan and bake for 1 hour and 40 minutes, until a tester inserted in the crest of the cake comes out with a moist crumb clinging to it. Let cool in pan on a rack for 15 minutes. Unmold and let cool completely on rack. Thinly slice with a serrated knife. **Serves 16.**

Best-Ever Chocolate Pudding

2 cups	milk (preferably whole)	500 mL
⅔ cup	granulated sugar, divided	150 mL
2 oz	unsweetened chocolate, finely chopped	60 g
2 oz	semisweet chocolate, finely chopped	60 g
2 tbsp	cornstarch	25 mL
2 tbsp	unsweetened cocoa powder	25 mL
Pinch	salt	Pinch
4	large or extra-large egg yolks	4
2 tbsp	unsalted butter	25 mL
1 tsp	vanilla	5 mL
	Whipped cream (optional)	

In a heavy saucepan, bring milk and ¼ cup (50 mL) of the sugar to a gentle boil over medium heat.

Remove from heat and stir in unsweetened and semisweet chocolates until melted. In a bowl, combine the remaining sugar, cornstarch, cocoa and salt. Beat in egg yolks until smooth. Slowly whisk in 1 cup (250 mL) of the chocolate mixture, then stir back into saucepan. Bring to a boil, stirring and scraping sides of the pan constantly. (If lumps form before it boils, remove from heat, whisk briskly to remove lumps and return to heat.) Whisk in butter and vanilla. Pour into 4 dessert dishes, cover with plastic wrap and refrigerate for about 2 hours, until chilled. Serve with whipped cream, if desired. **Serves 4.**

Chocolate Hazelnut Pudding

Follow preceding recipe, but replace the butter with hazelnut oil, and top each serving with 2 tbsp (25 mL) coarsely chopped toasted hazelnuts. **Serves 4.**

Chocolate Chocolate Chip Pudding

Follow recipe for Best-Ever Chocolate Pudding (left), but first freeze 1 cup (250 mL) semisweet chocolate chips on a baking sheet. After whisking in butter and vanilla, let pudding cool for 20 minutes, then stir in frozen chocolate chips. Pour pudding into 6 dessert dishes. **Serves 6.**

White Chocolate Amaretto Pudding

2 cups	milk (preferably whole)	500 mL
½ cup	granulated sugar, divided	125 mL
3 tbsp	cornstarch	45 mL
Pinch	salt	Pinch
4	large or extra-large egg yolks	4
½ tsp	almond extract	2 mL
6 oz	white chocolate, finely chopped	175 g
2 tbsp	amaretto or other almond-flavored liqueur	25 mL
1 tsp	vanilla	5 mL

In a saucepan, bring milk and half the sugar to a gentle boil over medium heat. In a bowl, combine the remaining sugar, cornstarch and salt. Beat in egg yolks and almond extract until smooth. Slowly whisk in 1 cup (250 mL) of the milk mixture, then stir back into saucepan. Bring to a boil, stirring and scraping sides of the pan constantly. (If lumps form before it boils, remove from heat, whisk briskly to remove lumps and return to heat.) Remove from heat and whisk in white chocolate until melted. Stir in amaretto and vanilla. Pour into 4 dessert dishes, cover with plastic wrap and refrigerate for about 1 hour, until chilled. **Serves 4.**

Chocolate Mousse with Dark Rum

3	extra-large egg yolks	3
2 tbsp	dark rum	25 mL
3 oz	semisweet chocolate, melted (see page 523)	90 g
2	extra-large egg whites	2
¼ cup	whipping (35%) cream	50 mL
	Whipped cream (optional)	

Beat egg yolks and rum into melted chocolate (the chocolate will bind up, but will then become smooth again). Beat egg whites until soft peaks form; fold into chocolate mixture in 2 additions. Whip cream until soft peaks form; fold into chocolate mixture. Spoon into 4 wine glasses, cover with plastic wrap and refrigerate for about 1 hour, until chilled. Top with whipped cream, if desired. **Serves 4.** *(If you are concerned about the food safety of raw eggs, you may wish to skip this recipe.)*

Chocolate Mousse with Chocolate Dumplings

Follow preceding recipe, but first melt 2 oz (60 g) semisweet chocolate (see page 523) and heat with ½ cup (125 mL) whipping (35%) cream in a double boiler over simmering water for 10 minutes. Pour into a bowl set over ice and let stand, stirring frequently, until firm. Using 2 spoons, form into ½-tsp (2 mL) dumplings. Layer 5 or 6 dumplings with mousse in each of 4 dessert dishes. Cover and chill. **Serves 4.**

Spiked Chocolate Mousse

3	extra-large eggs, separated	3
4 oz	semisweet chocolate, melted (see page 523)	125 g
1 to 2 tbsp	liquor (any type)	15 to 25 mL
	Whipped cream (optional)	

Beat egg yolks into melted chocolate, then thin with liquor until smooth. Beat egg whites until soft peaks form; fold into chocolate mixture. Pour into 4 dessert dishes, cover with plastic wrap and refrigerate for about 1 hour, until chilled. Top with whipped cream, if desired. **Serves 4.** *(If you are concerned about the food safety of raw eggs, you may wish to skip this recipe.)*

Honey Brandy White Chocolate Mousse

3 tbsp	honey	45 mL
1½ tbsp	brandy	22 mL
5 oz	white chocolate, finely chopped	150 g
2 cups	whipped cream	500 mL

In a small saucepan, heat honey and brandy over medium heat until honey melts. Remove from heat and whisk in white chocolate until melted. Let cool for 10 minutes, then fold in whipped cream. Spoon into 4 dessert dishes, cover with plastic wrap and refrigerate for 1 to 2 hours, until chilled. **Serves 4.**

Fruit in Chocolate Cups

4 oz	semisweet chocolate chips	125 g
1⅓ cups	fresh berries or chopped fruit	325 mL
¼ cup	whipped cream	50 mL
4 tsp	grated semisweet chocolate	20 mL

In the top of a double boiler, over barely simmering water, heat chocolate chips, stirring until half melted. Remove from heat and stir until smooth. Let cool for 5 minutes. Place 4 cupcake papers in a muffin tin and spoon a portion of the chocolate into each. Using the back of a spoon or a small spatula, spread chocolate up the sides of each cup, making an even layer without holes or thin spots. Refrigerate for at least 30 minutes, until chocolate hardens. Peel paper from the chocolate cups and refrigerate until ready to serve. Fill each cup with berries and top with whipped cream and grated chocolate. **Serves 4.**

Peaches and White Chocolate Mousse in Chocolate Cups

Prepare chocolate cups and Honey Brandy White Chocolate Mousse as in two previous recipes. Combine 1 cup (250 mL) diced peaches, 2 tsp (10 mL) orange-flavored liqueur and ½ tsp (2 mL) confectioner's (icing) sugar. Divide among chocolate cups and top with mousse. **Serves 4.**

Triple Chocolate Parfait

3 tbsp	light corn syrup	45 mL
1½ tbsp	brandy	22 mL
5 oz	white chocolate, finely chopped	150 g
1½ cups	whipping (35%) cream	375 mL
24	chocolate wafer cookies, crumbled	24
1¼ cups	semisweet chocolate chips	300 mL
6	large strawberries	6

In a saucepan, bring corn syrup and brandy to a boil. Remove from heat and stir in white chocolate until melted. Whip cream until soft peaks form; fold into the chocolate mixture. Cover and refrigerate for about 1 hour, until chilled. Make a ½-inch (1 cm) layer of cookie pieces in the bottom of 6 parfait glasses. Top each with a heaping tablespoon (15 mL) of chocolate chips and 1½ inches (4 cm) of mousse. Continue layering until you have three layers of each element, then cover with plastic wrap and refrigerate for 1 to 2 hours, until firm. Garnish each with 1 strawberry. **Serves 6.**

White Chocolate Ice Cream

5 oz	white chocolate, finely chopped	150 g
2 cups	whipping (35%) cream	500 mL
2 cups	milk	500 mL
1	whole clove	1
	Finely grated zest of 1 orange	
4	egg yolks	4
½ cup	granulated sugar	125 mL
1½ tbsp	vanilla	22 mL

Melt white chocolate with cream (see page 523); set aside. In a saucepan, scald milk with clove and orange zest over medium-low heat just until bubbles form around the edge. Beat egg yolks with sugar, then slowly whisk in scalded milk. Return to saucepan and cook over low heat, stirring constantly, until slightly thickened, about 10 minutes. Remove from heat and stir in chocolate mixture and vanilla. Cover and refrigerate for about 1 hour, until completely chilled. Discard clove. Transfer to an ice cream maker and freeze according to manufacturer's directions. **Serves 6.** *Store in an airtight container in the freezer for up to 2 days.*

Chocolate Ice Cream with Raspberry Swirl

Follow preceding recipe, but substitute semisweet chocolate for the white chocolate, and use an additional 2 tbsp (25 mL) granulated sugar. In a food processor, crush 10 oz (300 g) sweetened frozen raspberries with 2 tbsp (25 mL) raspberry- or orange-flavored liqueur. When ice cream is finished freezing, swirl in raspberries. **Serves 6.** *Store in an airtight container in the freezer for up to 2 days.*

The remaining recipes in this chapter use this dipping chocolate.

Dipping Chocolate

Semisweet chocolate, divided

Melt three-quarters of the chocolate (see page 523). Add the remaining chocolate, one-third at a time, stirring until each addition is completely melted before adding the next. Dip prepared centers (see recipes, below) in chocolate, one at a time; coat completely and lift out with a small fork. Shake off excess chocolate by lightly rapping fork on the edge of the bowl. Remove any drips by running fork across the edge of the bowl. Slide onto a baking sheet lined with parchment or waxed paper. Let cool until solid.

Chocolate-Covered Prunes with Marzipan "Pits"

1½ oz	almond paste, rolled into 18 small balls	45 g
18	extra-large pitted prunes	18
12 oz	Dipping Chocolate (see recipe, above)	375 g

Make a slit in the side of each prune and stuff 1 almond ball into each. Dip prunes in Dipping Chocolate. Let cool for 30 minutes to set chocolate. **Makes 18 candies.**

Chocolate-Covered Almond Apricots

Follow preceding recipe, but use extra-large dried apricots instead of prunes. After the 30 minutes cooling time, roll dipped apricots in 1½ cups (375 mL) finely ground almonds (see page 13), and refrigerate until chocolate is firm. **Makes 18 candies.**

Chocolate Fruit Squares

2½ cups	assorted dried fruit (raisins, dates, apricots, apples, pineapple, etc.)	625 mL
1 tsp	ground cinnamon	5 mL
¼ tsp	ground ginger	1 mL
Pinch	ground allspice	Pinch
⅓ cup	pistachios, skinned	75 mL
8 oz	Dipping Chocolate (see recipe, page 531)	250 g

In a food processor, finely chop or grind the dried fruit, cinnamon, ginger and allspice. Stir in pistachios. With wet hands, form mixture into a 4-inch (10 cm) square. Wrap in plastic wrap and freeze for 1 hour. Unwrap and, using a serrated knife, cut into 1-inch (2.5 cm) squares. Dip in Dipping Chocolate. **Makes 16 squares.**

Chocolate-Covered Pretzel "Porcupines"

8 oz	pretzel sticks, broken into bite-size pieces	250 g
4 oz	semisweet chocolate, melted and cooled	125 g
12 oz	Dipping Chocolate (see recipe, page 531)	375 g

Line a baking sheet with parchment paper. Stir pretzel pieces into cooled chocolate (they will be partially coated). Spoon in rounded tablespoonfuls (15 mL) onto prepared baking sheet. Refrigerate for 1 to 2 hours, until very firm. Dip in Dipping Chocolate. **Makes about 30 candies.**

Chocolate Peanut Crunch Balls

1 cup	crisp rice cereal (such as Rice Krispies)	250 mL
1 cup	chunky peanut butter	250 mL
½ cup	dark corn syrup	125 mL
8 oz	Dipping Chocolate (see recipe, page 531)	250 g

Thoroughly combine cereal, peanut butter and corn syrup. With wet hands, roll mixture between your palms to form 36 balls. Place on a baking sheet and freeze for 1 hour. Dip in Dipping Chocolate. **Makes 36 candies.**

Chocolate Peanut Grahams

Follow preceding recipe, but substitute crumbled graham crackers for the cereal. **Makes 36 candies.**

Chocolate-Covered Potato Chips

24 to 36	thick-sliced ridged potato chips	24 to 36
12 oz	Dipping Chocolate (see recipe, page 531)	375 g

Dip chips into Dipping Chocolate (how many you use will depend on the size of the potato chips).

Chocolate-Covered Chocolate Chip Cookies

12	chocolate chip cookies	12
8 oz	Dipping Chocolate (see recipe, page 531)	250 g

Dip cookies in Dipping Chocolate. **Makes 12 cookies.**

S'mores

24	marshmallows	24
8 oz	Dipping Chocolate (see recipe, page 531)	250 g
2 cups	graham cracker crumbs	500 mL

Line a baking sheet with parchment paper. Dip marshmallows in Dipping Chocolate and let set until chocolate is tacky, about 20 minutes. Roll in graham cracker crumbs, place on a prepared baking sheet and refrigerate until chocolate sets. **Makes 24 s'mores.**

Chocolate-Dipped Strawberries

2 cups	large perfect strawberries, patted dry	500 mL
8 oz	Dipping Chocolate (see recipe, page 531)	250 g

Line a baking sheet with parchment or waxed paper. Hold each strawberry by the stem and dip in Dipping Chocolate up to but without covering the stems. Set on prepared baking sheet and let cool until firm. **Makes about 12.**

Chapter 48
Homemade Pie
A Natural Extravagance

Pastry 534
Forming a Pastry Shell 534
Prebaking Pastry 534
Fruit Glaze 535
Classic Apple Pie 535
Apple Date Pie 535
Old World Boozy Apple Plum Pie 535
Old-Fashioned Apple Cheddar Pie 535
Apple Walnut Pie 535
Apple Pear Pie 535
Almond Pear Pie 535
Apple Caramel Peanut Pie 536
Candied Ginger Apple Pie 536
Praline Apple Pie Spiked with Bourbon . . 536
Apple Nectarine Pie 536
Apple Sour Cream Pie 536
Apple Butterscotch Custard Pie 536
Apple Lemon Custard Pie 536
Topless Apple Pie 536
Topless Lime Pear Pie 537
Topless Plum Pie 537
Open-Face Peach Pie 537
Tarte Tatin 537
Upside-Down Maple Apple Pie 537
Inverted Pear Tart 537
Honeyed Pear Upside-Down Pie 537
Peach Tatin 537
Smoky Apple Galette 537

Peach Pizza 538
Classic Peach Pie 538
Melba Tart 538
Almond Peach Pie 538
Praline Peach Pie 538
Hazelnut Cherry Pie 538
Anise Cherry Pie 538
Open-Face Cherry Pie 539
No-Fuss Fresh Berry Tart 539
Chocolate Raspberry Tart 539
Blueberry Ricotta Tart 539
Out-of-Season Blueberry Pie 539
Blueberry Rhubarb Pie 539
Raspberry Rhubarb Pie 539
Raspberry Blueberry Pie 539
Anytime Peach Pie 540
Fig Meringue Tart 540
Classic Pumpkin Pie 540
Pumpkin Chiffon Pie 540
Buttermilk Pumpkin Pie 540
Double Chocolate Pudding Pie 540
Chocolate Peanut Butter Pie 541
Completely Decadent Chocolate Tart . . 541
Grand Marnier Almond Tart 541
Chocolate Almond Pie 541
Perfect Pecan Pie 541

Who came up with the expression "easy as pie"? Mastering pastry crust takes as much practice as preparing for a marathon. Assembling the filling is a whole other step. Then there's lining the pan and crimping the crust, and baking time can easily exceed an hour. By the time a pie cools down enough to take the first bite, the better part of a day has passed.

No, pie isn't easy — unless you learn how to break it apart before you put it together. None of the individual elements that make up a pie are complex, but taken all at once, they can seem daunting. The trick is to take them a step at a time.

Prepare a batch of pastry and freeze it in individual packages, each large enough to make one pie. Or buy refrigerated or frozen pastry at your market. Yes, pastry made from scratch by practiced hands will always produce a better result than store-bought doughs, but several of the frozen and refrigerated pastry products we have found are quite good. Your supermarket freezer case carries a puff pastry so expertly made that it's ridiculous to even think of duplicating it at home.

Pie pans can be lined with pastry and frozen for weeks before you're planning to serve them. Or they can be prebaked before freezing. Either way, you'll have instant pie shells, waiting to be filled.

Mix up pie fillings anytime, then store them. Many cooked fillings can be refrigerated for weeks without ill effect. Come baking day, all that's left to do is assemble the pie and put it in the oven. With an arsenal of pie fixings on hand, there's no reason that everyone shouldn't find pies as easy as pie.

About these recipes . . .
We favor unsalted butter, and we especially urge you to follow that preference here, where the flavor balance can suffer if you don't.

Pastry

1½ cups	all-purpose flour	375 mL
¼ cup	cold unsalted butter	50 mL
¼ cup	cold vegetable shortening	50 mL
¼ tsp	salt	1 mL
4 to 6 tbsp	water	60 to 90 mL

In a large bowl, using your fingers, or in a food processor, combine flour, butter, shortening and salt until the mixture resembles coarse meal. Add water, a bit at a time, and pinch with your fingers or pulse the food processor until all the flour is moistened but the dough is still rough and unformed. Turn dough onto a clean work surface and quickly form into a flat disk. Wrap in plastic wrap and refrigerate for at least 30 minutes. **Makes enough dough for one 9-inch (23 cm) crust. For a 2-crust pie, double the recipe.**

Forming a Pastry Shell
Remove prepared pastry from the refrigerator and place on a lightly floured work surface. Roll out with a floured rolling pin to a disk at least 12 inches (30 cm) in diameter. Roll pastry loosely onto the pin, using a spatula or pastry scraper to help lift it from the board. Transfer to a 9-inch (23 cm) tart or pie pan by unrolling the pastry from the pin onto the pan. Ease the pastry evenly across the sides and bottom of the pan, making sure the pastry extends all the way into the edges of the pan.

If you're making a single-crust pie, trim the perimeter of the pastry to extend 1 inch (2.5 cm) over the edge of the pan. Fold this overhang under to make a thick pastry rim around the edge of the pan. Decorate the edge by pinching it between your fingers or pressing it with the tines of a fork.

If you're making a 2-crust pie, you'll need a double recipe of pastry. Trim the edge of the pastry shell so that it barely extends over the edge of the pan. Pour in the pie filling. Roll out the second pastry disk as described above, roll it up on the pin and unroll it over the filling. Trim so that the edge of the top pastry extends 1 inch (2.5 cm) beyond the rim of the pan. Fold this excess pastry under the pastry lining the pan. Crimp the edges to seal them.

To form a tart shell, line a tart pan with removable sides with pastry. Using a finger, press the pastry into the flutes in the sides of the pan. Roll a rolling pin over the top of the pan to cut off any excess pastry.

Prebaking Pastry (Only for Single-Crust Pies)
Preheat oven to 400°F (200°C). Freeze the pastry shell until firm, about 10 minutes. Line the chilled shell with foil and fill with pastry weights, uncooked rice or dried beans. Bake for 12 minutes. Remove foil and weights and bake for 10 minutes (half-baked) to 25 minutes (fully baked), depending on how much more baking the pastry will get once it is filled. Let cool on a rack.

Fruit Glaze

½ cup	apricot preserves, orange marmalade or red currant jelly	125 mL
1 tbsp	granulated sugar	15 mL
1 tbsp	liqueur (any variety)	15 mL

In a small saucepan, melt preserves, sugar and liqueur over medium heat. Simmer for 3 minutes, then strain. Use while warm. **Makes enough to glaze 1 tart.**

Classic Apple Pie

¼ cup	unsalted butter	50 mL
3 lbs	apples, peeled and sliced (about 9 cups/2.25 L)	1.5 kg
½ cup	granulated sugar	125 mL
¼ cup	packed light brown sugar	50 mL
1 tbsp	ground cinnamon	15 mL
1 tbsp	freshly squeezed lemon juice	15 mL
2 tbsp	cornstarch	25 mL
2 tsp	vanilla	10 mL
	Pastry for a 2-crust pie (see page 533)	

Preheat oven to 400°F (200°C). In a large skillet, melt butter over medium heat. Sauté apples, granulated sugar, brown sugar, cinnamon and lemon juice until apples are tender. Let cool, then stir in cornstarch and vanilla. Mound into pastry shell and seal with top pastry (see page 533). Bake for 50 minutes, until pastry is browned and filling is bubbling. Let cool before slicing. **Serves 8.**

Apple Date Pie

Follow preceding recipe, but add ¾ cup (175 mL) chopped dates with the apples. **Serves 8.**

Old World Boozy Apple Plum Pie

Follow recipe for Classic Apple Pie (above), but substitute 1 cup (250 mL) pitted prunes for 1 cup (250 mL) of the apples, and add 2 tbsp (25 mL) Scotch or Irish whisky with the vanilla. **Serves 8.**

Old-Fashioned Apple Cheddar Pie

Follow recipe for Classic Apple Pie (left), but add 1¼ cups (300 mL) diced Cheddar cheese to the apples after they have cooled. **Serves 8.**

Apple Walnut Pie

¼ cup	unsalted butter	50 mL
3 lbs	apples, peeled and thickly sliced (about 9 cups/2.25 L)	1.5 kg
⅔ cup	granulated sugar	150 mL
3 tbsp	freshly squeezed lemon juice	45 mL
1½ tsp	ground cinnamon, divided	7 mL
Pinch	ground cloves	Pinch
Pinch	ground nutmeg	Pinch
2 tbsp	cornstarch	25 mL
2 tbsp	rum	25 mL
2 tsp	vanilla	10 mL
1	pie pastry shell (see page 533)	1
1½ cups	chopped walnuts	375 mL
⅓ cup	packed brown sugar	75 mL
¼ cup	all-purpose flour	50 mL
¼ cup	melted unsalted butter	50 mL

Preheat oven to 400°F (200°C). In a large skillet, melt butter over medium heat. Sauté apples, sugar, lemon juice, 1 tsp (5 mL) of the cinnamon, cloves and nutmeg until apples are tender. Let cool, then stir in cornstarch, rum and vanilla. Mound into pastry shell. Combine walnuts, brown sugar, flour, melted butter and the remaining cinnamon; pack into an even layer over the filling. Bake for 50 to 60 minutes, or until pastry is browned and filling is bubbling. Let cool before slicing. **Serves 8.**

Apple Pear Pie

Follow preceding recipe, but replace half the apples with 1½ lbs (750 g) firm pears (about 3½ cups/ 875 mL). **Serves 8.**

Almond Pear Pie

Follow recipe for Apple Walnut Pie (above), but substitute 3 lbs (1.5 kg) firm pears (about 7cups/ 1.75 L) for the apples, replace half the vanilla with ½ tsp (2 mL) almond extract, omit the cinnamon from the filling, and replace the walnuts with chopped almonds (preferably not blanched). **Serves 8.**

Apple Caramel Peanut Pie

Follow recipe for Apple Walnut Pie (page 535), but toss 24 soft caramel candies into the filling, replace the walnuts with toasted peanuts, and add 8 coarsely chopped soft caramel candies to the topping. Serves 8.

Candied Ginger Apple Pie

Follow recipe for Apple Walnut Pie (page 535), but substitute ground ginger for the cinnamon, add ¼ cup (50 mL) finely chopped candied ginger to the filling, and replace the walnuts with chopped almonds. Serves 8.

Praline Apple Pie Spiked with Bourbon

Follow the recipe for Walnut Apple Pie (page 535), but substitute packed light brown sugar for the granulated sugar, bourbon for the lemon juice, and pecans for the walnuts. Serves 8.

Apple Nectarine Pie

¼ cup	unsalted butter	50 mL
2 lbs	apples, peeled and thickly sliced (about 6 cups/1.5 L)	1 kg
1 lb	firm nectarines, peeled and sliced (about 2½ cups/625 mL)	500 g
⅔ cup	granulated sugar	150 mL
3 tbsp	freshly squeezed lemon juice	45 mL
Pinch	ground cloves	Pinch
Pinch	ground nutmeg	Pinch
¼ cup	cornstarch	50 mL
2 tbsp	bourbon	25 mL
1 tsp	vanilla	5 mL
½ tsp	almond extract	2 mL
1	pie pastry shell (see page 534)	1
1¼ cups	all-purpose flour	300 mL
½ cup	packed brown sugar	125 mL
6 tbsp	melted unsalted butter	90 mL
½ tsp	ground cinnamon	2 mL

Preheat oven to 400°F (200°C). In a large skillet, melt butter over medium heat. Sauté apples, nectarines, granulated sugar, lemon juice, cloves and nutmeg until fruit is tender. Let cool, then stir in cornstarch, bourbon, vanilla and almond extract. Mound into pastry shell. Combine flour, brown sugar, melted butter and cinnamon; pack into an even layer over the filling. Bake for 50 to 60 minutes, or until pastry is browned and filling is bubbling. Let cool before slicing. Serves 8.

Apple Sour Cream Pie

2 tbsp	unsalted butter	25 mL
3 lbs	apples, peeled and sliced (about 9 cups/2.25 L)	1.5 kg
1 cup	granulated sugar, divided	250 mL
1 tbsp	freshly squeezed lemon juice	15 mL
1½ tsp	ground cinnamon, divided	7 mL
1	egg, beaten	1
¾ cup	sour cream	175 mL
½ cup	all-purpose flour, divided	125 mL
2 tsp	vanilla	10 mL
¼ tsp	salt	1 mL
Pinch	ground nutmeg	Pinch
1	pie pastry shell, half-baked (see page 534)	1
1½ cups	chopped walnuts	325 mL
⅓ cup	packed brown sugar	75 mL
¼ cup	melted unsalted butter	50 mL

Preheat oven to 375°F (190°C). In a large skillet, melt butter over medium heat. Sauté apples, half the sugar, lemon juice and 1 tsp (5 mL) of the cinnamon until apples are tender. Let cool and drain off most of the liquid. Stir in the remaining sugar, egg, sour cream, ⅓ cup (75 mL) of the flour, vanilla, salt and nutmeg. Mound in pastry shell. Combine the remaining flour and cinnamon with the walnuts, brown sugar and melted butter; pack into an even layer over the filling. Bake for about 1 hour, or until topping is browned and custard is set. Let cool before slicing. Serves 8.

Apple Butterscotch Custard Pie

Follow preceding recipe, but omit the granulated sugar, add ½ cup (125 mL) packed light brown sugar with the apples, and replace the sour cream with sweetened condensed milk. Serves 8.

Apple Lemon Custard Pie

Follow recipe for Apple Sour Cream Pie (above), but double the amount of lemon juice, and add 2 tbsp (25 mL) finely grated lemon zest with the sour cream. Serves 8.

Topless Apple Pie

4 lbs	apples, peeled and sliced (about 12 cups/3 L)	2 kg
½ cup	granulated sugar	125 mL
1 tsp	ground cinnamon	5 mL
Pinch	ground cloves	Pinch
Pinch	ground nutmeg	Pinch
1	pie pastry shell, untrimmed (see page 534)	1

| 2 tbsp | unsalted butter | 25 mL |
| 1/4 cup | packed light brown sugar | 50 mL |

Preheat oven to 375°F (190°C). Toss together apples, granulated sugar, cinnamon, cloves and nutmeg. Mound into pastry shell and flip the overhanging pastry up over the edge of the apples. Dot with butter and sprinkle with brown sugar. Bake for 50 to 55 minutes, or until pastry is browned and filling is bubbling. Let cool before slicing. **Serves 8.**

Topless Lime Pear Pie

Follow preceding recipe, but replace the apples with 4 lbs (2 kg) firm pears (about 9 cups/2.25 L), omit the cinnamon, and add 3 tbsp (45 mL) cornstarch, 1 tbsp (15 mL) finely grated lime zest and 1 tbsp (15 mL) freshly squeezed lime juice with the pears. **Serves 8.**

Topless Plum Pie

Follow recipe for Topless Apple Pie (page 536), but substitute 3½ lbs (1.5 kg) small Italian plums, quartered (about 8 cups/2 L), for the apples, and add 3 tbsp (45 mL) cornstarch with the granulated sugar. Bake at 400°F (200°C) for 45 to 50 minutes. **Serves 8.**

Open-Face Peach Pie

Follow recipe for Topless Apple Pie (page 536), but substitute 3½ lbs (1.5 kg) peaches, peeled and sliced (about 8 cups/2 L), for the apples, add 3 tbsp (45 mL) cornstarch with the granulated sugar, and omit the cinnamon and cloves. Bake at 400°F (200°C) for 45 to 50 minutes. **Serves 8.**

Tarte Tatin

½ cup	unsalted butter, cut into thin slices	125 mL
1½ cups	granulated sugar	375 mL
6	large tart apples, peeled and sliced	6
8 oz	frozen puff pastry, thawed	250 g

Lay butter slices in the bottom of a 10-inch (25 cm) ovenproof skillet (preferably nonstick), and sprinkle with sugar. Pack apple slices on top and cook over medium heat until sugar has caramelized and apples are tender, about 30 minutes. Preheat oven to 425°F (220°C). If necessary, roll out puff pastry and cut into a 12-inch (30 cm) circle. Place pastry over apples. Bake for 10 minutes, then reduce oven temperature to 350°F (180°C) and bake until pastry is crisp and brown, about 20 minutes. Let cool for 10 minutes. Invert a large serving platter over the pan and carefully (the pan and its contents will still be hot) flip so that the tart unmolds upside down onto the platter. Remove the skillet. If any apples stick to the bottom of the pan, remove with a small spatula and replace on tart. Serve warm. **Serves 8.**

Upside-Down Maple Apple Pie

Follow preceding recipe, but substitute ½ cup (125 mL) pure maple syrup and ¼ cup (50 mL) packed light brown sugar for half the granulated sugar. **Serves 8.**

Inverted Pear Tart

Follow recipe for Tarte Tatin (left), but replace the apples with 8 firm pears. **Serves 8.**

Honeyed Pear Upside-Down Pie

Follow recipe for Tarte Tatin (left), but substitute ½ cup (125 mL) honey and ¼ cup (50 mL) packed light brown sugar for half the granulated sugar, and replace the apples with 8 firm pears. **Serves 8.**

Peach Tatin

Follow recipe for Tarte Tatin (left), but replace the apples with 8 large peaches. **Serves 8.**

Smoky Apple Galette

1 tbsp	unsalted butter	15 mL
8 oz	baked ham, cut into thin strips	250 g
¼ cup	chopped onion	50 mL
½ tsp	dried thyme	2 mL
2 tbsp	unsweetened apple cider or apple juice	25 mL
	Salt and freshly ground black pepper to taste	
1 cup	shredded Cheddar cheese	250 mL
1	tart pastry shell (see page 534)	1
2	large Granny Smith apples, peeled and thinly sliced	2
3 tbsp	light (fancy) molasses	45 mL
2 tbsp	brown mustard	25 mL

Preheat oven to 375°F (190°C). In a large skillet, melt butter over medium-high heat. Sauté ham, onion and thyme until ham and onion are lightly browned. Add apple cider, salt and pepper, scraping up any brown bits from the bottom of the pan; let cool. Scatter cheese over bottom of tart shell, spoon in ham mixture and arrange apples on top in overlapping concentric circles. Bake for 40 minutes. Meanwhile, in a small skillet, melt molasses and mustard; brush over tart. Bake for 20 minutes, until pastry is browned and filling is bubbling. Let cool before slicing. **Serves 8.**

Peach Pizza

3 tbsp	cornstarch	45 mL
2 tbsp	orange juice	25 mL
1 tbsp	water	15 mL
2 tbsp	unsalted butter	25 mL
2 lbs	peaches (about 8 large), peeled (see "blanching," page 8) and sliced	1 kg
⅓ cup	granulated sugar	75 mL
1 tsp	freshly squeezed lemon juice	5 mL
Pinch	ground nutmeg	Pinch
1 tsp	vanilla	5 mL
1	recipe Pastry, unrolled (see page 534)	1

Preheat oven to 400°F (200°C). Dissolve cornstarch in orange juice and water. In a large skillet, melt butter over medium heat. Add peaches, sugar, lemon juice and nutmeg; bring to a simmer. Stir cornstarch mixture and add to skillet; simmer until thickened. Remove from heat and stir in vanilla. Roll out pastry to a rough circle about ¼ inch (0.5 cm) thick and place on a baking sheet. Turn up edges to make a shallow rim all around. Bake for 10 minutes, until lightly browned. Top with peach mixture and bake for 20 minutes. Let cool for 15 minutes before slicing. **Serves 8.**

Classic Peach Pie

Prepare a double batch of peaches from the previous recipe and a double batch of Pastry. Let cool, mound into a pastry shell and seal with top pastry (see page 534). Bake for 50 minutes. **Serves 8.**

Melba Tart

Prepare peaches from the recipe for Peach Pizza (above) and let cool. Toss with 2 cups (500 mL) raspberries, ½ cup (125 mL) confectioner's (icing) sugar and 1 tbsp (15 mL) additional cornstarch. Place in a half-baked tart pastry shell (see page 534) and bake at 375°F (190°C) for 45 minutes. **Serves 8.**

Almond Peach Pie

6 tbsp	cornstarch	90 mL
¼ cup	orange juice	50 mL
2 tbsp	water	25 mL
¼ cup	unsalted butter	50 mL
4 lbs	peaches (about 16 large), peeled (see "blanching," page 8) and sliced	2 kg
⅔ cup	granulated sugar	150 mL
2 tsp	freshly squeezed lemon juice	10 mL
1 tsp	ground nutmeg	5 mL
2 tsp	vanilla	10 mL
1	pie pastry shell (see page 534)	1
1½ cups	chopped almonds	375 mL
⅓ cup	packed light brown sugar	75 mL
¼ cup	all-purpose flour	50 mL
¼ cup	melted unsalted butter	50 mL
¼ tsp	ground ginger	1 mL

Preheat oven to 375°F (190°C). Dissolve cornstarch in orange juice and water. In a large skillet, melt butter over medium heat. Add peaches, sugar, lemon juice and nutmeg; bring to a simmer. Stir cornstarch mixture and add to skillet; simmer until thickened. Let cool, then stir in vanilla. Mound into a pastry shell. Combine almonds, brown sugar, flour, melted butter and ginger; pack into an even layer over the filling. Bake for 1 hour, until pastry is browned and filling is bubbling. Let cool before slicing. **Serves 8.**

Praline Peach Pie

Follow preceding recipe, but replace the almonds with pecans, and replace the ginger with cinnamon. **Serves 8.**

Hazelnut Cherry Pie

8 cups	pitted sour cherries, thawed and drained if frozen	2 L
2½ to 3 cups	granulated sugar (depending on sourness of fruit)	625 to 750 mL
6 tbsp	cornstarch	90 mL
1 tbsp	vanilla	15 mL
¼ tsp	almond extract	1 mL
1	pie pastry shell, half-baked (see page 534)	1
1½ cups	chopped skinned hazelnuts	375 mL
⅓ cup	packed light brown sugar	75 mL
¼ cup	all-purpose flour	50 mL
¼ cup	melted unsalted butter	50 mL
¼ tsp	ground cinnamon	1 mL

Preheat oven to 375°F (190°C). Toss together cherries, sugar, cornstarch, vanilla and almond extract. Mound into pastry shell. Combine hazelnuts, brown sugar, flour, butter and cinnamon; scatter over top. Bake for 1 hour, until pastry is browned and filling is bubbling. Let cool before slicing. **Serves 8.**

Anise Cherry Pie

Follow preceding recipe, but substitute ½ tsp (2 mL) anise extract for ½ tsp (2 mL) of the vanilla, almonds for the hazelnuts, and ground fennel seeds for the cinnamon. **Serves 8.**

Open-Face Cherry Pie

8 cups	pitted sour cherries, thawed and drained if frozen	2 L
2 cups	granulated sugar (or more to taste)	500 mL
6 tbsp	cornstarch	90 mL
Pinch	ground nutmeg	Pinch
1	pie pastry shell, untrimmed (see page 534)	1

Preheat oven to 400°F (200°C). Toss together cherries, sugar, cornstarch and nutmeg. Mound into pastry shell and flip overhanging pastry up over the edge of the cherries. Bake for about 1 hour, or until pastry is browned and filling is bubbling. Let cool before slicing. **Serves 8.**

No-Fuss Fresh Berry Tart

4 cups	berries	1 L
3 tbsp	Grand Marnier or other orange-flavored liqueur	45 mL
2 tbsp	granulated sugar	25 mL
1	pie pastry shell, fully baked (see page 534)	1
	Sweetened whipped cream	

Toss together berries, liqueur and sugar. Mound into pastry shell and serve with whipped cream. **Serves 8.**

Chocolate Raspberry Tart

1 cup	semisweet chocolate chips, melted	250 mL
1 cup	sour cream, divided	250 mL
1	tart pastry shell, fully baked (see page 534)	1
3 cups	raspberries	750 mL
½	recipe Fruit Glaze (page 535), made from red currant jelly	½

Beat together chocolate chips and ¼ cup (50 mL) of the sour cream; spread evenly over bottom of pastry shell. Spread with the remaining sour cream and top with berries in closely packed concentric circles. Brush berries with glaze. Refrigerate for about 30 minutes to set the glaze. **Serves 8.**

Blueberry Ricotta Tart

1½ cups	whole-milk ricotta cheese	375 mL
6 tbsp	granulated sugar	90 mL
2 tbsp	finely grated lemon zest	25 mL
1 tsp	freshly squeezed lemon juice	5 mL
1 cup	whipped cream	250 mL
2 tbsp	confectioner's (icing) sugar	25 mL
1	tart pastry shell, fully baked (see page 534)	1
3 cups	blueberries	750 mL
½	recipe Fruit Glaze (page 534), made from red currant jelly	½

Spoon ricotta into a strainer lined with a coffee filter, set over a bowl to catch the drips. Place in the refrigerator and drain for 1 to 2 hours, or until excess liquid is drained off. In a large bowl, combine ricotta, granulated sugar, lemon zest and lemon juice. In a separate bowl, combine whipped cream and confectioner's sugar; fold into ricotta mixture. Spread evenly over bottom of pastry shell and top with blueberries, closely packed in concentric circles. Brush berries with glaze. Refrigerate for about 30 minutes to set the glaze. **Serves 8.**

Out-of-Season Blueberry Pie

2 lbs	frozen blueberries (about 5⅓ cups/1.3 L), thawed and drained	1 kg
1¾ cups	confectioner's (icing) sugar	425 mL
¼ cup	cornstarch	50 mL
1 tbsp	freshly squeezed lemon juice	15 mL
½ tsp	ground cinnamon	2 mL
Pinch	salt	Pinch
	Pastry for a 2-crust pie (see page 534)	

Preheat oven to 400°F (200°C). Toss together berries, confectioner's sugar, cornstarch, lemon juice, cinnamon and salt. Mound into pastry shell and seal with top pastry (see page 534). Bake for 1 hour, until pastry is lightly browned and filling is bubbling. Let cool for 30 minutes before slicing. **Serves 8.**

Blueberry Rhubarb Pie

Follow preceding recipe, but replace half the blueberries with 1 lb (500 g) frozen rhubarb pieces (about 3 cups/750 mL), thawed, and increase the confectioner's (icing) sugar to 2 cups (500 mL). **Serves 8.**

Raspberry Rhubarb Pie

Follow recipe for Out-of-Season Blueberry Pie (above), but replace the blueberries with 1 lb (500 g) frozen rhubarb pieces (about 3 cups/750 mL), thawed, and 2 cups (500 mL) frozen raspberries, thawed. **Serves 8.**

Raspberry Blueberry Pie

Follow recipe for Out-of-Season Blueberry Pie (above), but replace half the blueberries with 1½ cups (500 mL) fresh or frozen raspberries (thawed if frozen). **Serves 8.**

Anytime Peach Pie

Follow recipe for Out-of-Season Blueberry Pie (page 539), but replace the blueberries with fresh or frozen sliced peaches (about 4½ cups/1.125 L), thawed. **Serves 8.**

Fig Meringue Tart

5	extra-large egg whites	5
1 tsp	balsamic vinegar	5 mL
⅓ cup	granulated sugar, divided	75 mL
3 cups	sliced fresh figs	750 mL
1	fully baked 9-inch tart shell (see page 534)	1

Preheat oven to 400°F (200°C). Beat egg whites and vinegar until whites barely hold a shape. Add sugar, 1 tbsp (15 mL) at a time, beating until meringue is stiff, smooth and glossy; set aside. Arrange fig slices in tart shell in a solid layer. Mound meringue on top of figs and smooth into a peak, making sure meringue overlaps the edges of the pie crust all around. Bake for 7 to 8 minutes, or until meringue is browned. Let cool for 30 to 60 minutes before slicing. **Serves 8.**

Classic Pumpkin Pie

3	eggs	3
1½ cups	canned pumpkin purée (not pie filling)	375 mL
1 cup	granulated sugar	250 mL
½ cup	milk	125 mL
1 tsp	ground cinnamon	5 mL
½ tsp	ground ginger	2 mL
¼ tsp	salt	1 mL
1	pie pastry shell, half-baked (see page 534)	1

Preheat oven to 375°F (190°C). Combine eggs, pumpkin pie filling, sugar, milk, cinnamon, ginger and salt. Pour into pastry shell and bake for about 1 hour, or until pastry is browned and filling is set. Let cool before slicing. **Serves 8.**

Pumpkin Chiffon Pie

3	eggs, separated	3
1½ cups	canned pumpkin purée (not pie filling)	375 mL
1 cup	granulated sugar	250 mL
½ cup	milk	125 mL
1 tsp	ground cinnamon	5 mL
½ tsp	ground ginger	2 mL
¼ tsp	salt	1 mL
1	pie pastry shell, half-baked (see page 534)	1

Preheat oven to 375°F (190°C). In a large bowl, combine egg yolks, pumpkin, sugar, milk, cinnamon and ginger. In a separate bowl, beat egg whites and salt until soft peaks form; fold into pumpkin mixture. Pour into pastry shell and bake for about 1 hour, or until pastry is browned and filling is set. Let cool before slicing. **Serves 8.**

Buttermilk Pumpkin Pie

Follow preceding recipe, but replace the granulated sugar with packed light brown sugar, and substitute ⅔ cup (150 mL) buttermilk for the milk. **Serves 8.**

Double Chocolate Pudding Pie

3 cups	hot chocolate pudding (store-bought or see recipe, page 529)	750 mL
4 oz	semisweet chocolate, finely chopped	125 g
1	pie pastry shell, fully baked (see page 534)	1
	Sweetened whipped cream	

Combine pudding and chocolate until chocolate is completely incorporated. Pour into pastry shell and refrigerate until set, about 2 hours. Serve with whipped cream. **Serves 8.**

Chocolate Peanut Butter Pie

Follow preceding recipe, but before filling pastry shell with hot pudding, cover the bottom of the shell with 2 cups (500 mL) peanut butter chips. **Serves 8.**

Completely Decadent Chocolate Tart

8 oz	semisweet chocolate, chopped	250 g
½ cup	granulated sugar	125 mL
2 cups	hot whipping (35%) cream	500 mL
1	tart pastry shell, fully baked (see page 534)	1
	Sweetened whipped cream (optional)	

In the top of a double boiler, over simmering water, melt chocolate and sugar. Slowly whisk in cream and cook for 15 minutes, scraping sides occasionally with rubber spatula. Remove from heat and chill over ice until cool to the touch. Pour into pastry shell and refrigerate until set, about 2 hours. Serve with whipped cream, if desired. **Serves 8.**

Grand Marnier Almond Tart

2 cups	chopped almonds	500 mL
1¾ cups	whipping (35%) cream	425 mL
1½ cups	granulated sugar	375 mL
2½ tbsp	Grand Marnier or other orange-flavored liqueur	32 mL
¼ tsp	almond extract	1 mL
Pinch	salt	Pinch
2 tbsp	finely grated orange zest	25 mL
1	tart pastry shell, half-baked (see page 534)	1

Preheat oven to 350°F (180°C). In a heavy saucepan, combine almonds, cream, sugar, liqueur, almond extract and salt; simmer over low heat, stirring occasionally, until sugar is completely dissolved, about 10 minutes. Stir in orange zest. Pour into pastry shell and bake for 50 minutes, until the top of the tart bubbles up and caramelizes slightly. Let cool in pan for 20 minutes, then remove sides of tart pan and let cool to room temperature. **Serves 10.**

Chocolate Almond Pie

2 oz	semisweet chocolate, finely chopped	60 g
¼ cup	unsalted butter	50 mL
1	pie pastry shell, half-baked (see page 534)	1
3	large or extra-large eggs	3
1 cup	packed light brown sugar	250 mL
2 tbsp	all-purpose flour	25 mL
2 cups	chopped toasted almonds	500 mL
1 cup	dark corn syrup	250 mL
2 tbsp	almond butter	25 mL
1 tsp	vanilla	5 mL

Preheat oven to 350°F (180°C). In a small saucepan, melt chocolate and butter over low heat. Pour into pastry shell and refrigerate until set. Meanwhile, beat eggs, sugar and flour until smooth, then stir in almonds, corn syrup, almond butter and vanilla. Pour over chocolate in pastry shell and bake for about 1 hour, or until pastry is browned and filling is set. Let cool for at least 3 hours before slicing. **Serves 8.**

Perfect Pecan Pie

3	extra-large eggs	3
1 cup	granulated sugar	250 mL
2 tbsp	all-purpose flour	25 mL
2 cups	pecan halves	500 mL
1 cup	corn syrup	250 mL
2 tbsp	strong brewed coffee	25 mL
1 tsp	vanilla	5 mL
1	pie pastry shell, half-baked (see page 534)	1

Preheat oven to 375°F (190°C). Beat eggs, sugar and flour until smooth. Stir in pecan halves, corn syrup, coffee and vanilla until blended. Pour into pastry shell and bake for 45 to 50 minutes, or until pastry is browned and filling is set. Let cool for at least 3 hours before slicing. **Serves 8.**

Chapter 49
Homemade Muffins
To Warm the Hearth

Orange Currant Muffins 543
Blueberry Muffins 543
Toasted Walnut Muffins 544
Apple Walnut Muffins 544
Jam-Filled Muffins 544
Ginger Peachy Muffins 544
Cinnamon Swirl Muffins 544
Raspberry Chocolate Chip Muffins 544
Date Nut Muffins 545
Brown Sugar Pecan Muffins 545
Sour Cream Banana Muffins 545
Banana Bran Muffins 545
Banana Oat Bran Raisin Muffins 545
Tropical Banana Muffins 545
Bran Muffins 545
Raisin Bran Muffins 545
Blueberry Bran Muffins 546
Nutty Bran Muffins 546
Honey Bran Muffins 546
Oat Bran and Fig Muffins 546
All–Oat Bran Muffins 546
Blueberry Corn Muffins 546
Cranberry Orange Corn Muffins 546
Pecan Peach Corn Muffins 546
Cheddar Corn Muffins 546

Garden Corn Muffins 547
Bacon and Apple Corn Muffins 547
Pepperoni Pepper Corn Muffins 547
Corn and Green Chili Muffins 547
Pecan Corn Muffins 547
Spicy White Cornsticks 548
Blue Cornsticks 548
Bacon Cornsticks 548
Carrot Muffins 548
Orange Carrot Muffins 548
Currant Carrot Muffins 548
Zucchini Walnut Muffins 548
Lemon-Lime Zucchini Muffins 548
Candied Ginger Zucchini Muffins 548
Zucchini Apple Muffins 549
Applesauce Walnut Muffins 549
Apple Oatmeal Spice Muffins 549
Banana Oatmeal Muffins 549
Yogurt Muffins 549
Lemon Yogurt Muffins 549
Apricot Cardamom Muffins 549
Walnut Fig Sinkers 549
Ricotta Rosemary Muffins 550
Herb Cheese Muffins 550
Ham and Cheese Muffins 550

Muffins. The word stirs an immediate response, bringing back a flood of memories. Phantoms of fragrances swirl as we remember the flavors — apple, walnut, buttermilk, blueberry, cornmeal, bran — that made the prospect of a warm muffin in the morning reason enough to wake up.

It's not surprising that homemade muffins are so much a part of our collective past, for American cookbooks are full of muffin recipes, both savory and sweet. But they've changed over the years. Originally leavened with yeast and baked on griddles like English muffins, today's muffins are more likely to be leavened with baking soda and baking powder and to have a high proportion of liquid to dry ingredients. The result is something closer to a miniature cake than to a bread. Load them up with fruit and nuts, and they're almost confections.

How a muffin's ingredients go together determines the type of muffin you'll end up with. Fats in the batter (such as butter or oil) produce a flaky, crumbly texture, while egg makes a muffin chewier. Although most muffin recipes call for both, one usually dominates. Muffins that start with beating sugar into butter and then adding egg will turn out cakier. Those in which sugar is beaten with egg, then melted butter is added, will be more elastic. If you're baking muffins with a chewy ingredient, such as dried fruit, a cake-like batter works best. But bran, which tends to make baked goods crumble, is better with an egg-based batter.

The only substantial differences between a muffin and a cake are that muffins aren't as sweet and aren't as big, so they have a drier interior, a crisper crust and a faster baking time. Most muffins will bake in 15 to 30 minutes, and that makes them one of the most convenient home-baked breakfast foods.

To facilitate early-morning preparation, measure ingredients the night before, sift the dry ingredients together and prepare the muffin tins. Come morning, just mix in the liquids, pop the tin in the oven and pull out another muffin memory.

About these recipes . . .
The following 50 recipes are written to yield 12 medium-size muffins. All of them use a 12-cup muffin tin where each cup has a capacity of 4 fluid ounces (125 mL). Prepare the pan by greasing the interior of each cup and the top surface of the tin (vegetable cooking spray works well), or place a paper or foil cupcake liner in each cup. It's best to use a nonstick tin if you're not using cupcake liners. Fill each cup about three-quarters full.

Muffins are done when fully risen, browned and pulling slightly away from the sides of the tin. A tester inserted in the middle of the largest muffin should come out with a moist crumb clinging to it. Let all muffins cool in the pan for 5 minutes, unless otherwise noted.

Use extra-large eggs in all of these recipes, unless otherwise noted, and use unsalted butter.

Three of the recipes call for cornstick pans. These heavy iron pans are traditional for making cornbreads and are available at most cookware stores. If you don't have one, cornsticks can also be baked in mini muffin pans.

Orange Currant Muffins

2 cups	all-purpose flour	500 mL
2 tsp	baking powder	10 mL
½ tsp	ground cardamom (optional)	2 mL
1 cup	dried currants	250 mL
¾ cup	granulated sugar	175 mL
½ cup	unsalted butter, softened	125 mL
1 tbsp	finely grated orange zest	15 mL
1 tsp	vanilla	5 mL
2	extra-large eggs	2
½ cup	milk (not fat-free)	125 mL

Preheat oven to 375°F (190°C) and prepare muffin tin (see above). Sift together flour, baking powder and cardamom, then stir in currants; set aside. In a large bowl, beat sugar and butter until light and fluffy. Stir in orange zest and vanilla. Beat in eggs, one at a time. Stir in half the flour mixture, then milk, then the remaining flour mixture. Spoon into prepared tin and bake for 25 minutes, until fully risen and browned. **Makes 12 muffins.**

Blueberry Muffins

Follow preceding recipe, but omit the currants and orange zest. Fold in 2 cups (500 mL) blueberries before spooning batter into tin. Bake for 30 minutes. **Makes 12 muffins.**

Toasted Walnut Muffins

Follow recipe for Orange Currant Muffins (page 543), but replace the cardamom with ground cinnamon, and replace the currants with chopped toasted walnuts. Increase the milk to ⅔ cup (150 mL). **Makes 12 muffins.**

Apple Walnut Muffins

Follow recipe for Orange Currant Muffins (page 543), but replace the cardamom with ground cinnamon, replace the currants with ½ cup (125 mL) chopped walnuts, and fold in 1 Granny Smith apple, peeled and diced, before spooning batter into tin. Before baking, sprinkle tops with a mixture of 1 tbsp (15 mL) granulated sugar and ¼ tsp (1 mL) ground cinnamon. Bake for 30 minutes. **Makes 12 muffins.**

Jam-Filled Muffins

Follow recipe for Orange Currant Muffins (page 543). When filling the tins, spoon 2 tbsp (25 mL) batter into each cup. Make an indentation in the batter with the back of a spoon and place 1 tsp (5 mL) jam, marmalade or preserves on top. Top with the remaining batter. **Makes 12 muffins.**

Ginger Peachy Muffins

2 cups	all-purpose flour	500 mL
2 tsp	baking powder	10 mL
1 tsp	ground ginger	5 mL
¾ cup	granulated sugar	175 mL
½ cup	unsalted butter, softened	125 mL
1 tbsp	finely grated lemon zest	15 mL
1 tsp	vanilla	5 mL
2	extra-large eggs	2
½ cup	milk (not fat-free)	125 mL
2	peaches, peeled and diced	2

Preheat oven to 375°F (190°C) and prepare muffin tin (see page 543). Sift together flour, baking powder and ginger; set aside. In a large bowl, beat sugar and butter until light and fluffy. Stir in lemon zest and vanilla. Beat in eggs, one at a time. Stir in half the flour mixture, then milk, then the remaining flour mixture. Fold in peaches. Spoon into prepared tin and bake for 30 minutes, until fully risen and browned. **Makes 12 muffins.**

Cinnamon Swirl Muffins

¼ cup	chopped pecans or walnuts	50 mL
¼ cup	packed dark brown sugar	50 mL
1 tsp	ground cinnamon, divided	5 mL
2 cups	all-purpose flour	500 mL
2 tsp	baking powder	10 mL
1 cup	chopped raisins	250 mL
¾ cup	granulated sugar	175 mL
½ cup	unsalted butter, softened	125 mL
1 tbsp	finely grated orange zest	15 mL
1 tsp	vanilla	5 mL
2	extra-large eggs	2
½ cup	milk (not fat-free)	125 mL

Preheat oven to 375°F (190°C) and prepare muffin tin (see page 543). Combine pecans, brown sugar and ½ tsp (2 mL) of the cinnamon; set aside. Sift together flour, baking powder and the remaining cinnamon, then stir in raisins; set aside. In a large bowl, beat granulated sugar and butter until light and fluffy. Stir in orange zest and vanilla. Beat in eggs, one at a time. Stir in half the flour mixture, then milk, then the remaining flour mixture. Spoon 2 tbsp (25 mL) batter into each prepared cup, top each with 2 tsp (10 mL) pecan mixture, then add the remaining batter. Bake for 25 minutes, until fully risen and browned. **Makes 12 muffins.**

Raspberry Chocolate Chip Muffins

2 cups	all-purpose flour	500 mL
2 tsp	baking powder	10 mL
1 cup	miniature semisweet chocolate chips	250 mL
¾ cup	granulated sugar	175 mL
½ cup	unsalted butter, softened	125 mL
1 tbsp	finely grated orange zest	15 mL
1 tsp	vanilla	5 mL
2	extra-large eggs	2
½ cup	milk (not fat-free)	125 mL
2 cups	raspberries	500 mL

Preheat oven to 375°F (190°C) and prepare muffin tin (see page 543). Sift together flour and baking powder, then stir in chocolate chips; set aside. In a large bowl, beat sugar and butter until light and fluffy. Stir in orange zest and vanilla. Beat in eggs, one at a time. Stir in half the flour mixture, then milk, then the remaining flour mixture. Fold in raspberries. Spoon into prepared tin and bake for 30 minutes, until fully risen and browned. Let cool for 10 minutes before unmolding. **Makes 12 muffins.**

Date Nut Muffins

2 cups	all-purpose flour	500 mL
2 tsp	baking powder	10 mL
¼ tsp	ground allspice	1 mL
1 cup	chopped pitted dates	250 mL
1 cup	chopped walnut pieces	250 mL
½ cup	unsalted butter, softened	125 mL
⅓ cup	granulated sugar	75 mL
⅓ cup	packed light brown sugar	75 mL
1 tbsp	finely grated orange zest	15 mL
1 tsp	vanilla	5 mL
2	extra-large eggs	2
½ cup	milk (not fat-free)	125 mL

Preheat oven to 375°F (190°C) and prepare muffin tin (see page 543). Sift together flour, baking powder and allspice, then stir in dates and walnuts; set aside. In a large bowl, beat butter and sugars until light and fluffy. Stir in orange zest and vanilla. Beat in eggs, one at a time. Stir in half the flour mixture, then milk, then the remaining flour mixture. Spoon into prepared tin and bake for 25 minutes, until fully risen and browned. Let cool for 10 minutes before unmolding. **Makes 12 muffins.**

Brown Sugar Pecan Muffins

Follow preceding recipe, but substitute cardamom for the allspice, use 2 cups (500 mL) pecan pieces instead of the dates and walnuts, and substitute lemon zest for orange zest. **Makes 12 muffins.**

Sour Cream Banana Muffins

2 cups	all-purpose flour	500 mL
¾ tsp	baking soda	4 mL
½ tsp	baking powder	2 mL
½ cup	chopped walnuts	125 mL
3	very ripe bananas	3
¼ cup	sour cream	50 mL
1 cup	granulated sugar	250 mL
½ cup	unsalted butter, softened	125 mL
1 tsp	vanilla	5 mL
2	extra-large eggs	2

Preheat oven to 350°F (180°C) and prepare muffin tin (see page 543). Sift together flour, baking soda and baking powder, then stir in walnuts; set aside. In a food processor, purée bananas and sour cream until smooth; set aside. In a large bowl, beat sugar and butter until light and fluffy. Stir in vanilla. Beat in eggs, one at a time. Stir in half the flour mixture, then the banana mixture, then the remaining flour mixture. Spoon into prepared tin and bake for 20 minutes, until fully risen and browned. **Makes 12 muffins.**

Banana Bran Muffins

Follow preceding recipe, but instead of the 2 cups (500 mL) flour, use a mixture of ¾ cup (175 mL) all-purpose flour and ¾ cup (175 mL) whole wheat flour. After sifting dry ingredients, stir in ½ cup (125 mL) bran cereal (such as 100% Bran or All-Bran). **Makes 12 muffins.**

Banana Oat Bran Raisin Muffins

Follow recipe for Sour Cream Banana Muffins (left), but instead of the 2 cups (500 mL) flour, use a mixture of ¾ cup (175 mL) all-purpose flour and ¾ cup (175 mL) whole wheat flour. After sifting dry ingredients, stir in ½ cup (125 mL) oat bran. Replace the walnuts with chopped raisins. **Makes 12 muffins.**

Tropical Banana Muffins

Follow recipe for Sour Cream Banana Muffins (left), but replace the walnuts with ½ cup (125 mL) chopped pitted dates and ½ cup (125 mL) shredded sweetened coconut. **Makes 12 muffins.**

Bran Muffins

1 cup	all-purpose flour	250 mL
2 tsp	baking powder	10 mL
2	extra-large eggs	2
2 tbsp	packed dark brown sugar	25 mL
2 tbsp	granulated sugar	25 mL
1 tsp	vanilla	5 mL
¼ cup	canola oil	50 mL
2 cups	bran cereal (such as 100% Bran or All-Bran)	500 mL
1 cup	milk (not fat-free)	250 mL

Preheat oven to 375°F (190°C) and prepare muffin tin (see page 543). Sift together flour and baking powder; set aside. In a large bowl, beat eggs, brown sugar, granulated sugar and vanilla until well combined. Beat in oil until smooth. Stir in half the bran cereal, then milk, then the remaining bran cereal. Let rest for 5 minutes, then stir in flour mixture. Spoon into prepared tin and bake for 25 minutes, until fully risen and browned. **Makes 12 muffins.**

Raisin Bran Muffins

Follow preceding recipe, but substitute raisin bran for the bran cereal, and add ½ cup (125 mL) raisins with the cereal. **Makes 12 muffins.**

Blueberry Bran Muffins

Follow recipe for Bran Muffins (page 545), but fold in 1½ cups (375 mL) blueberries and 1 tbsp (15 mL) finely grated lemon zest before spooning batter into tin. Makes 12 muffins.

Nutty Bran Muffins

Follow recipe for Bran Muffins (page 545), but add 1 cup (250 mL) chopped walnuts before spooning batter into tin. Makes 12 muffins.

Honey Bran Muffins

Follow recipe for Bran Muffins (page 545), but omit the brown sugar and granulated sugar, add ¼ cup (50 mL) honey with the eggs, replace the oil with melted butter, and replace the bran cereal with raisin bran. Makes 12 muffins.

Oat Bran and Fig Muffins

Follow recipe for Bran Muffins (page 545), but replace the bran cereal with oat bran cereal, and add 12 dried figs, diced, with the oat bran. Makes 12 muffins.

All–Oat Bran Muffins

2	extra-large eggs, separated	2
2½ cups	oat bran	625 mL
¾ cup	milk (not fat-free)	175 mL
½ cup	honey	125 mL
⅓ cup	raisins	75 mL
2 tbsp	canola oil	25 mL
1 tbsp	baking powder	15 mL
¼ tsp	salt	1 mL

Preheat oven to 400°F (200°C) and prepare muffin tin (see page 543). In a large bowl, beat egg yolks, oat bran, milk, honey, raisins, oil, baking powder and salt. In a separate bowl, beat egg whites until soft peaks form; fold into batter. Spoon into prepared tin and bake for 20 minutes, until fully risen and browned. Makes 12 muffins.

Blueberry Corn Muffins

1⅓ cups	yellow cornmeal	325 mL
⅔ cup	all-purpose flour	150 mL
2 tsp	baking powder	10 mL
½ tsp	salt	2 mL
2 cups	blueberries	500 mL
1	extra-large egg	1
¼ cup	granulated sugar	50 mL
1 cup	milk (not fat-free)	250 mL
3 tbsp	corn oil	45 mL

Preheat oven to 400°F (200°C) and prepare muffin tin (see page 543). Combine cornmeal, flour, baking powder and salt, then stir in blueberries; set aside. In a large bowl, beat egg and sugar until blended, then stir in milk and oil. Stir in cornmeal mixture until evenly moistened. Spoon into prepared tin and bake for 20 to 25 minutes, or until fully risen and browned. Let cool for 3 minutes before unmolding. Makes 12 muffins.

Cranberry Orange Corn Muffins

Follow preceding recipe, but replace the blueberries with mixture of 1 cup (250 mL) chopped fresh cranberries, ¼ cup (50 mL) granulated sugar and 2 tsp (10 mL) grated orange zest. Makes 12 muffins.

Pecan Peach Corn Muffins

Follow recipe for Blueberry Corn Muffins (above), but add ¼ tsp (1 mL) ground ginger with the salt, and replace the blueberries with 1 large peach, peeled and diced, and 1 cup (500 mL) chopped pecans. Makes 12 muffins.

Cheddar Corn Muffins

Follow recipe for Blueberry Corn Muffins (above), but add a pinch of cayenne pepper with the salt, replace the blueberries with 1 cup (500 mL) shredded sharp Cheddar cheese, and decrease the sugar to 1 tbsp (15 mL). Makes 12 muffins.

Garden Corn Muffins

1⅓ cups	yellow cornmeal	325 mL
⅔ cup	all-purpose flour	150 mL
2 tsp	baking powder	10 mL
½ tsp	salt	2 mL
¼ cup	corn oil	50 mL
½ cup	canned or frozen corn kernels (thawed if frozen), drained	125 mL
¼ cup	diced red bell pepper	50 mL
¼ cup	diced carrot	50 mL
¼ cup	diced onion	50 mL
¼ cup	diced celery	50 mL
1	extra-large egg	1
2 tbsp	granulated sugar	25 mL
1 cup	milk (not fat-free)	250 mL

Preheat oven to 400°F (200°C) and prepare muffin tin (see page 543). Combine cornmeal, flour, baking powder and salt; set aside. In a large skillet, heat oil over medium heat. Sauté corn, red pepper, carrot, onion and celery until tender; set aside. In a large bowl, beat egg and sugar until blended, then stir in corn mixture and milk. Stir in cornmeal mixture until evenly moistened. Spoon into prepared tin and bake for 20 to 25 minutes, until fully risen and browned. Let cool for 3 minutes before unmolding. Makes 12 muffins.

Bacon and Apple Corn Muffins

4	slices bacon	4
1	Granny Smith apple, peeled and diced	1
⅓ cup	chopped onion	75 mL
1⅓ cups	yellow cornmeal	325 mL
⅔ cup	all-purpose flour	150 mL
2 tsp	baking powder	10 mL
½ tsp	salt	2 mL
1	extra-large egg	1
2 tbsp	granulated sugar	25 mL
1 cup	milk (not fat-free)	250 mL

Preheat oven to 400°F (200°C) and prepare muffin tin (see page 543). In a large skillet, over medium heat, cook bacon until crisp; remove to a plate, blot dry and crumble. Add apple and onion to the fat remaining in the pan and cook until tender. Combine crumbled bacon, cornmeal, flour, baking powder and salt; set aside. In a large bowl, beat egg and sugar until blended, then stir in apple mixture and milk. Stir in cornmeal mixture until evenly moistened. Spoon batter into prepared tins and bake for 20 to 25 minutes, until fully risen and browned. Makes 12 muffins.

Pepperoni Pepper Corn Muffins

1 cup	yellow cornmeal	250 mL
1 cup	all-purpose flour	250 mL
¼ cup	granulated sugar	50 mL
4 tsp	baking powder	20 mL
½ tsp	salt	2 mL
¼ cup	corn oil	50 mL
¼ cup	finely chopped onion	50 mL
1	red bell pepper, diced	1
⅓ cup	chopped pepperoni	75 mL
¼ cup	chopped green onion	50 mL
1	extra-large egg, beaten	1
1 cup	milk (not fat-free)	250 mL

Preheat oven to 400°F (200°C) and prepare muffin tin (see page 543). Combine cornmeal, flour, sugar, baking powder and salt; set aside. In a skillet, heat oil over medium heat. Sauté onion and red pepper until tender. Stir in pepperoni and green onion. Stir into cornmeal mixture, then stir in egg and milk. Spoon into prepared tin and bake for 20 minutes, until fully risen and browned. Makes 12 muffins.

Corn and Green Chili Muffins

Follow preceding recipe, but replace the red pepper with 1 cup (250 mL) drained canned corn kernels and 2 tbsp (25 mL) finely chopped pickled jalapeño pepper. Omit the pepperoni. Makes 12 muffins.

Pecan Corn Muffins

1 cup	yellow cornmeal	250 mL
1 cup	all-purpose flour	250 mL
¼ cup	granulated sugar	50 mL
4 tsp	baking powder	20 mL
½ tsp	salt	2 mL
¼ cup	unsalted butter	50 mL
1 cup	finely chopped pecans	250 mL
3 tbsp	minced onion	45 mL
1	extra-large egg, beaten	1
1 cup	milk (not fat-free)	250 mL

Preheat oven to 400°F (200°C) and prepare muffin tin (see page 543). Combine cornmeal, flour, sugar, baking powder and salt; set aside. In a skillet, melt butter over medium-high heat. Sauté pecans and onion until lightly browned. Stir into cornmeal mixture, then stir in egg and milk. Spoon into prepared tin and bake for 20 minutes, until fully risen and browned. Makes 12 muffins.

Spicy White Cornsticks

3 tbsp	butter	45 mL
2 tbsp	minced onion	25 mL
¾ cup	white cornmeal	175 mL
¼ cup	all-purpose flour	50 mL
3 tbsp	granulated sugar	45 mL
1½ tsp	baking powder	7 mL
½ tsp	salt	2 mL
¼ tsp	cayenne pepper	1 mL
1	extra-large egg	1
1 cup	whipping (35%) cream	250 mL
1 tbsp	corn oil	15 mL

Preheat oven to 400°F (200°C) and place a 7-stick cast-iron cornstick pan in the oven. In a skillet, melt butter over medium heat. Sauté onion until tender; let cool. Combine cornmeal, flour, sugar, baking powder, salt and cayenne. Stir in onion, then egg, then cream. Grease hot cornstick pan with oil and spoon batter into pan. Bake for 15 minutes, until fully risen and browned. Unmold carefully. Makes 7 cornsticks.

Blue Cornsticks

Follow preceding recipe, but use blue cornmeal instead of white, and omit the cayenne pepper. Makes 7 cornsticks.

Bacon Cornsticks

Follow recipe for Spicy White Cornsticks (above), but first, in a skillet, over medium heat, cook 2 slices of bacon until crisp; blot dry and crumble. Use the bacon fat in place of the butter, use yellow cornmeal instead of white, and add the crumbled bacon to the dry ingredients. Makes 7 cornsticks.

Carrot Muffins

1 cup	all-purpose flour	250 mL
1 tsp	baking soda	5 mL
1 tsp	ground cinnamon	5 mL
½ tsp	salt	2 mL
2	extra-large eggs	2
¾ cup	granulated sugar	175 mL
1 tsp	vanilla	5 mL
¾ cup	canola oil	175 mL
3	carrots, shredded	3
½ cup	chopped walnuts	125 mL
	Confectioner's (icing) sugar (optional)	

Preheat oven to 375°F (190°C) and prepare muffin tin (see page 543). Sift together flour, baking soda, cinnamon and salt; set aside. In a large bowl, beat eggs, sugar and vanilla until very light and thick, then add oil in a slow stream. Stir in flour mixture, then fold in carrots and walnuts. Spoon into prepared tin and bake for 20 to 25 minutes, or until fully risen and browned. Let cool in pan for 10 minutes, then unmold and dust tops with confectioner's sugar. Makes 12 muffins.

Orange Carrot Muffins

Follow preceding recipe, but add 1 tbsp (15 mL) finely grated orange zest with the carrots, and replace the walnuts with pecans. Makes 12 muffins.

Currant Carrot Muffins

Follow recipe for Carrot Muffins (above), but use 2½ carrots, and add 1 cup (250 mL) dried currants with the carrots. Makes 12 muffins.

Zucchini Walnut Muffins

1½ cups	all-purpose flour	375 mL
½ tsp	salt	2 mL
½ tsp	ground cinnamon	2 mL
½ tsp	baking soda	2 mL
¼ tsp	baking powder	1 mL
2	large eggs	2
1 cup	granulated sugar	250 mL
1 tsp	vanilla	5 mL
½ cup	canola oil	125 mL
1 cup	shredded zucchini	250 mL
¾ cup	chopped walnuts	175 mL

Preheat oven to 350°F (180°C) and prepare muffin tin (see page 543). Sift together flour, salt, cinnamon, baking soda and baking powder; set aside. In a large bowl, beat eggs, sugar and vanilla until light and fluffy, then add oil in a slow stream. Stir in flour mixture, then fold in zucchini and walnuts. Spoon into prepared tin and bake for 27 minutes, until fully risen and browned. Makes 12 muffins.

Lemon-Lime Zucchini Muffins

Follow preceding recipe, but add 1 tbsp (15 mL) finely grated lime zest, 1 tbsp (15 mL) finely grated lemon zest and 1 tbsp (15 mL) freshly squeezed lemon juice to the batter after the oil. Makes 12 muffins.

Candied Ginger Zucchini Muffins

Follow recipe for Zucchini Walnut Muffins (above), but replace the cinnamon with ground ginger, and add 2 tbsp (25 mL) finely chopped candied ginger with the walnuts. Makes 12 muffins.

Zucchini Apple Muffins

Follow recipe for Zucchini Walnut Muffins (page 548), but replace ½ cup (125 mL) of the zucchini with ½ cup (125 mL) coarsely shredded tart apple. Makes 12 muffins.

Applesauce Walnut Muffins

1½ cups	all-purpose flour	375 mL
2 tsp	ground cinnamon	10 mL
1 tsp	baking powder	5 mL
1 tsp	baking soda	5 mL
½ tsp	salt	2 mL
¾ cup	quick-cooking or old-fashioned rolled oats	175 mL
⅔ cup	packed light brown sugar	150 mL
¼ cup	unsalted butter, softened	50 mL
1	extra-large egg	1
⅔ cup	applesauce (preferably chunky)	150 mL
⅔ cup	chopped walnuts	150 mL

Preheat oven to 350°F (180°C) and prepare muffin tin (see page 543). Sift together flour, cinnamon, baking powder, baking soda and salt, then stir in oats; set aside. In a large bowl, beat brown sugar and butter until light and fluffy. Beat in egg, then stir in applesauce. Stir in flour mixture until just incorporated, then fold in walnuts. Spoon into prepared tin and bake for 25 to 30 minutes, until fully risen and browned. Makes 12 muffins.

Apple Oatmeal Spice Muffins

Follow preceding recipe, but replace the brown sugar with ½ cup (125 mL) granulated sugar, and replace the applesauce with apple butter. Makes 12 muffins.

Banana Oatmeal Muffins

Follow recipe for Applesauce Walnut Muffins (above), but replace the brown sugar with ½ cup (125 mL) granulated sugar, and replace the applesauce with 2 very ripe bananas, mashed. Makes 12 muffins.

Yogurt Muffins

1½ cups	all-purpose flour	375 mL
1 tsp	baking powder	5 mL
½ tsp	baking soda	2 mL
Pinch	salt	Pinch
1 cup	granulated sugar	250 mL
½ cup	unsalted butter, softened	125 mL
2	extra-large eggs	2
1 cup	vanilla-flavored yogurt	250 mL
	Confectioner's (icing) sugar (optional)	

Preheat oven to 375°F (190°C) and prepare muffin tin (see page 543). Sift together flour, baking powder, baking soda and salt; set aside. In a large bowl, beat sugar and butter until light and fluffy. Beat in eggs, one at a time. Stir in half the flour mixture, then the yogurt, then the remaining flour mixture. Spoon into prepared tin and bake for 30 minutes, until fully risen and browned. Let cool in pan for 10 minutes, then unmold and dust tops with confectioner's sugar. Makes 12 muffins.

Lemon Yogurt Muffins

Follow preceding recipe, but replace the vanilla-flavored yogurt with a mixture of 1 cup (250 mL) lemon-flavored yogurt, 1 tbsp (15 mL) finely grated lemon zest and 2 tbsp (25 mL) freshly squeezed lemon juice. Makes 12 muffins.

Apricot Cardamom Muffins

Follow recipe for Yogurt Muffins (above), but add 1 tsp (5 mL) ground cardamom with the flour, and add 1 cup (250 mL) chopped dried apricots with the yogurt. Makes 12 muffins.

Walnut Fig Sinkers

½ cup	all-purpose flour	125 mL
½ tsp	baking powder	2 mL
¼ tsp	salt	1 mL
3 cups	quartered dried figs	750 mL
3 cups	walnut pieces	750 mL
2	extra-large eggs, separated	2
½ cup	granulated sugar	125 mL
2 tbsp	freshly squeezed lemon juice	25 mL

Preheat oven to 350°F (180°C) and line a 12-cup muffin tin with foil cupcake liners. Sift together flour, baking powder and salt. Toss figs and walnuts with 2 tbsp (25 mL) of the flour mixture; set both aside. In a large bowl, beat egg yolks and sugar until light and fluffy, then stir in lemon juice. Stir in flour mixture until smooth. In a separate bowl, beat egg whites until firm peaks form; fold into batter. Fold in fig mixture (there will be just enough batter to coat the fruit and nuts). Pack into prepared tin, mounding each muffin slightly. They will not rise. Bake for 35 minutes, until set in the center and browned. Let cool for at least 10 minutes before unmolding. Makes 12 muffins.

Ricotta Rosemary Muffins

¼ cup	unsalted butter	50 mL
½ cup	chopped onion	125 mL
¼ cup	diced celery	50 mL
¼ tsp	crumbled dried rosemary	1 mL
¼ tsp	dried sage	1 mL
	Salt and freshly ground black pepper to taste	
2 cups	all-purpose flour	500 mL
1 tbsp	baking powder	15 mL
1	extra-large egg	1
1 cup	ricotta cheese	250 mL
½ cup	milk (not fat-free)	125 mL

Preheat oven to 400°F (200°C) and prepare muffin tin (see page 543). In a skillet, melt butter over medium heat. Sauté onion, celery, rosemary, sage, salt and pepper until onion and celery are tender. In a large bowl, sift together flour and baking powder, then stir in onion mixture. In a separate bowl, beat egg, ricotta and milk; stir into flour mixture. Spoon into prepared tin and bake for 20 minutes, until fully risen and browned. **Makes 12 muffins.**

Herb Cheese Muffins

¼ cup	unsalted butter	50 mL
½ cup	chopped onion	125 mL
1	small clove garlic, minced	1
1 tbsp	chopped fresh chives	15 mL
1 tbsp	chopped fresh Italian (flat-leaf) parsley	15 mL
	Salt and freshly ground black pepper to taste	
2 cups	all-purpose flour	500 mL
1 tbsp	baking powder	15 mL
1	extra-large egg	1
¾ cup	milk (not fat-free)	175 mL
½ cup	herbed cream cheese, softened	125 mL

Preheat oven to 400°F (200°C) and prepare muffin tin (see page 543). In a skillet, melt butter over medium heat. Sauté onion, garlic, chives, parsley, salt and pepper until onion is tender. In a large bowl, sift together flour and baking powder, then stir in onion mixture. In a separate bowl, beat egg, milk and cream cheese; stir into flour mixture. Spoon into prepared muffin tin and bake for 20 minutes, until fully risen and browned. **Makes 12 muffins.**

Ham and Cheese Muffins

2 cups	all-purpose flour	500 mL
1 tbsp	baking powder	15 mL
½ tsp	salt	2 mL
¼ tsp	freshly ground black pepper	1 mL
Pinch	cayenne pepper	Pinch
1	extra-large egg	1
1 cup	milk (not fat-free)	250 mL
¼ cup	melted unsalted butter	50 mL
2 tbsp	brown mustard	25 mL
¾ cup	shredded sharp Cheddar cheese	175 mL
¾ cup	finely chopped smoked ham	175 mL

Preheat oven to 400°F (200°C) and prepare muffin tin (see page 543). In a large bowl, sift together flour, baking powder, salt, black pepper and cayenne. In a separate bowl, beat egg, milk, butter and mustard; stir into flour mixture. Stir in cheese and ham. Spoon into prepared tin and bake for 20 minutes, until fully risen and browned. **Makes 12 muffins.**

Chapter 50
Homemade Gifts
To Warm the Heart

Gingerbread Muffins 552
Hot Pepper Gingerbread Muffins 552
Gingerbread Men 553
Gingerbread Wreaths 553
Spiked Fruitcake Brownies 553
Bourbon Walnut Fig Bars 553
Sugar Plums 554
Pecan Shortbread 554
Praline Shortbread 554
Orange Liqueur Brownies 554
Kumquat Pound Cakes 554
Cardamom Apricot Pound Cakes 555
Whisky Pound Cakes 555
Walnut Cupcakes 555
Pistachio Tea Cake 555
Honey Rum Raisin Tea Cake 556
Two-Ton Bourbon Nut Cake 556
Almond Amaretto Cake 556
Pepper Cheddar Skillet Cornbread 556
Savarin 557
Orange Savarin 557
Baba au Rhum 557
Heavy-Duty Hazelnut Truffles 557
Meatless Mincemeat 557
Cider Syrup 558

Spicy Garlic Oil 558
Citrus Oil 558
Ginger Sesame Oil 558
Provençal Oil 558
Orange-Fennel Walnut Oil 558
Herb Vinegar 558
Fruit Vinegar 558
Pear Vinegar 558
Lemon Garlic Vinegar 558
Spicy Corn Relish 559
Curried Eggplant Chutney 559
Sweet Spiked Walnuts 559
Bourbon Pecans 559
Bitter Grapefruit Marmalade 559
Lemon Green Peppercorn Marmalade . . 559
Gingered Carrot Marmalade 560
Jalapeño Jelly 560
Caramel Pear Preserves 560
Marinated Herbed Mushrooms 560
Easy Honey Mustard 560
Green Peppercorn Mustard 560
Red Wine Whole-Grain Mustard 561
Raisin Chocolate Chip Peanut Butter . . 561
Pecan or Walnut Butter 561
Ginger Tahini 561

There is no greater pleasure for one who loves to cook than to share food with another who loves to eat. Yet at holiday time, many cooks overlook the treasure trove of gift ideas in their cooking repertoires. They run from store to store in search of the perfect gift when all they need to do is leaf through a few recipes and preheat the oven.

If a recipe makes something solid enough to travel and moist enough to resist going stale, it can easily be converted into a portion size and presentation perfect for gift giving. And who doesn't love to eat pound cakes sodden with booze and a ton of nuts, brownies damp enough to leave their mark on anything they touch, or homemade marmalade packed with pulp and bright-colored whiskers of rind?

Recipes for tea cakes, fruitcakes, nut cakes and pound cakes fit the mold perfectly. Try your favorite brownie or bar cookie wrapped in cellophane and tied up with ribbons, or bake cakes in easy-to-cut sheets, mini-loaf pans or muffin tins to yield enough individual portions to instantly satisfy the better part of your gift list.

Recipes for homemade jellies, preserves and pickles are alien to most modern cooks, but they are typically inexpensive, are technically easy, and yield enough to fill a home pantry with each batch. Most sweet preserves and sour relishes don't require tricky canning procedures, since their high sugar and acid contents make the possibility of bacterial contamination negligble.

Flavored vinegars, oils and mustards are unbelievably easy and inexpensive to make at home, often requiring little more than the ability to mix and heat a few ingredients for a few minutes. Flavor mustard with peppercorns, honey, brown sugar or wine; infuse vinegars with herbs or fruit; or scent oil with chili, garlic or nuts.

With the help of a food processor, homemade nut butters can be whipped up in a few minutes. Though peanut butter is the most popular, don't stop there. Make cashew butter spiked with ginger, or pecan butter sweetened with brown sugar and a jolt of bourbon. Stud walnut butter with morsels of figs, or turn peanut butter into a confection with a generous fistful of roasted peanuts, raisins and chocolate chips.

About these recipes . . .

The following 50 recipes will take care of your gift lists for years, with flavorful, heartwarming, belly-filling goodies. Many kitchen gifts can be made ahead, but use common sense on how long they will stay fresh. Flavored oils, vinegars, preserves and mustards will last for several weeks, as will some cakes that are soaked in liquor. But no one wants to eat a three-day-old muffin or a stale cookie.

Gingerbread Muffins

2 cups	all-purpose flour	500 mL
1 tbsp	ground ginger	15 mL
2 tsp	baking soda	10 mL
¼ tsp	dry mustard	1 mL
Pinch	salt	Pinch
2	extra-large eggs	2
½ cup	packed dark brown sugar	125 mL
¼ cup	granulated sugar	50 mL
¾ cup	light (fancy) molasses	175 mL
½ cup	vegetable oil	125 mL
¾ cup	boiling strong brewed coffee	175 mL
¾ cup	finely chopped walnuts	175 mL
½ cup	confectioner's (icing) sugar	125 mL

Preheat oven to 400°F (200°C) and line a 12-cup muffin tin with paper cupcake liners. Sift together flour, ginger, baking soda, mustard and salt; set aside. In a large bowl, beat eggs, brown sugar and granulated sugar until thick. Beat in molasses, then oil in a slow, steady stream. Add half the flour mixture, then coffee, then the remaining flour mixture. Pour into prepared tin and sprinkle tops with walnuts. Bake for 20 to 25 minutes, until fully risen and browned. Let cool completely, then dust with confectioner's sugar. Wrap individually. **Makes 12 muffins.**

Hot Pepper Gingerbread Muffins

Follow preceding recipe, but sift 1 tsp (5 mL) ground cinnamon, ½ tsp (2 mL) ground cloves, ½ tsp (2 mL) freshly ground black pepper, a pinch of freshly ground white pepper and a pinch of cayenne pepper with the flour. Stir in 3 tbsp (45 mL) grated gingerroot after sifting. Replace the walnuts with hazelnuts. **Makes 12 muffins.**

Gingerbread Men

⅔ cup	unsalted butter, cut into small pieces	150 mL
⅔ cup	granulated sugar	150 mL
⅔ cup	light (fancy) molasses	150 mL
2 tbsp	instant coffee granules	25 mL
1 tbsp	ground ginger	15 mL
1 tbsp	ground cinnamon	15 mL
1 tbsp	baking soda	15 mL
1	whole extra-large egg, beaten	1
5 cups	all-purpose flour	1.25 L
1	extra-large egg yolk, beaten with 1 tbsp (15 mL) water	1
	Dried and candied fruit for decoration (optional)	

Preheat oven to 325°F (160°C) and line 2 baking sheets with parchment paper. Place butter in a large bowl and set aside. In a large saucepan, bring sugar, molasses, coffee granules, ginger and cinnamon to a boil over medium heat. Immediately stir in baking soda and pour over butter, stirring until melted. Beat in egg and gradually stir in flour, kneading in the last cup (250 mL) until a smooth dough forms. On a floured work surface, roll out one-third of the dough to ¼-inch (0.5 cm) thickness. Cut with a gingerbread man cookie cutter and transfer to a baking sheet. Repeat with the remaining dough, rerolling scraps. Brush cookies with egg wash. Make eyes, noses, mouths, and buttons with scraps of dough or dried and candied fruit; brush again with egg wash. Bake for 20 to 25 minutes, until cookies are set. Let cool on pans on a rack, then tie a ribbon around the neck of each cookie. **Makes 12 large or 18 small gingerbread men.**

Gingerbread Wreaths

Follow preceding recipe, but cut each portion of rolled dough with a 3-inch (7.5 cm) leaf-shaped cookie cutter into 20 leaves. Brush each leaf with egg wash and arrange each group of 20 on a baking sheet lined with parchment paper, overlapping one another in a wreath shape. Form scraps of dough into clusters of berries and stems, attaching them to the wreaths for decoration. Brush again with egg wash before baking. When cool, tie ribbons around wreaths for hanging. **Makes 3 wreaths, each 6 portions.**

Spiked Fruitcake Brownies

1 cup	raisins	250 mL
1 cup	coarsely chopped pitted dates	250 mL
1 cup	chopped dried apricots	250 mL
1 cup	chopped candied fruit	250 mL
½ cup	brandy or dark rum, divided	125 mL
2 cups	coarsely chopped walnuts	500 mL
	Vegetable cooking spray	
1 cup	all-purpose flour	250 mL
1 tsp	ground cinnamon	5 mL
1 tsp	ground ginger	5 mL
Pinch	ground cloves	Pinch
	Finely chopped zest of 2 lemons	
4	extra-large eggs	4
1 cup	firmly packed dark brown sugar	250 mL
1 tsp	vanilla	5 mL
¼ tsp	salt	1 mL
1½ cups	confectioner's (icing) sugar	375 mL
2 tbsp	melted unsalted butter	25 mL

In a large bowl, toss together raisins, dates, apricots, candied fruit and half the brandy. Cover and let stand for 24 hours, then stir in walnuts. Preheat oven to 325°F (160°C) and spray a 15- by 10-inch (38 by 25 cm) rimmed baking sheet with cooking spray. Sift together flour, cinnamon, ginger, cloves and lemon zest. In a large bowl, beat eggs, brown sugar, vanilla and salt until thick and fluffy. Stir in flour mixture. Stir in raisin mixture, along with any brandy remaining in the bowl. Pour into prepared pan and smooth top. Bake for 35 minutes, until a tester inserted in the center comes out almost clean. Let cool in pan on a rack. Meanwhile, combine the remaining brandy, confectioner's sugar and butter; drizzle over cooled cake and let dry for 10 minutes. Cut into 32 brownies.

Bourbon Walnut Fig Bars

Follow preceding recipe, but replace the raisins, dates, apricots and candied fruit with 3 cups (750 mL) finely chopped dried figs, replace the brandy with bourbon, and increase the walnuts to 2 cups (500 mL). **Makes 32 bars.**

Sugar Plums

	Vegetable cooking spray	
1½ oz	almond paste	45 g
18	extra-large prunes, pitted, each with a small slit	18
1	recipe Flaky Pastry (page 21)	1
1	egg yolk, beaten with 1 tbsp (15 mL) water	1
½ cup	confectioner's (icing) sugar	125 mL

Preheat oven to 400°F (200°C) and spray a baking sheet with cooking spray. Form almond paste into 18 small balls, about the size of a cherry pit. Stuff each into a prune through the slit. On a floured work surface, roll out pastry to ⅛-inch (3 mm) thickness and punch out eighteen 4-inch (10 cm) circles. Brush each with egg wash. Place 1 prune in the center of each circle and wrap pastry around the prunes, using egg wash to help the seams stay together. Place seam side down on prepared baking sheet and bake for about 30 minutes, or until pastry is crisp and lightly browned. Let cool on pan on a rack for 10 minutes, then dust with confectioner's sugar. **Makes 18 cookies.**

Pecan Shortbread

1 cup	pecan pieces	250 mL
2 cups	all-purpose flour	500 mL
½ cup	granulated sugar	125 mL
⅓ cup	cornstarch	75 mL
1 cup	unsalted butter, chilled and cut into small pieces	250 mL
½ tsp	vanilla	2 mL

Preheat oven to 375°F (190°C). In a food processor, coarsely chop the pecans. Add flour, sugar and cornstarch; process to a fine meal. Add butter and vanilla; process until mixture climbs the sides of the work bowl. Turn out onto a floured work surface and knead until smooth and homogeneous. Keeping surface floured, roll out to ⅓-inch (0.75 cm) thickness and cut into 2-inch (5 cm) circles. Place about ½ inch (1 cm) apart on a baking sheet. Bake for 20 minutes, until bottoms are lightly browned and dough is set. Let cool on pan on a rack. **Makes 36 cookies.**

Praline Shortbread

Follow preceding recipe, but substitute light brown sugar for the granulated sugar. **Makes 36 cookies.**

Orange Liqueur Brownies

	Vegetable cooking spray	
5 oz	unsweetened chocolate, cut into small pieces	150 g
⅔ cup	unsalted butter	150 mL
1 tsp	orange extract	5 mL
4	eggs	4
2 cups	granulated sugar	500 mL
1 cup	sifted all-purpose flour	250 mL
2 tbsp	orange-flavored liqueur	25 mL
	Finely grated zest of 1 large orange	

Preheat oven to 400°F (200°C) and spray a 15- by 10-inch (38 by 25 cm) rimmed baking sheet with cooking spray. Melt chocolate and butter together (see page 523). Stir in orange extract and let cool until just warm. In a large bowl, beat eggs and sugar until thick. Beat in chocolate mixture, flour, liqueur and orange zest until smooth. Pour onto prepared pan and bake for 21 minutes, until top is set but cake is still moist in the center. Let cool in pan on a rack. Cut into 32 brownies.

Kumquat Pound Cakes

	Vegetable cooking spray	
36	kumquats	36
3 cups	granulated sugar	750 mL
2 cups	unsalted butter, softened	500 mL
1 tbsp	vanilla	15 mL
½ tsp	ground ginger	2 mL
¼ tsp	ground nutmeg	1 mL
10	eggs	10
4 cups	sifted all-purpose flour	1 L

Preheat oven to 350°F (180°C) and spray 10 mini loaf pans (each about 6 by 4 inches/15 by 10 cm) with cooking spray. Cut kumquats in half and squeeze out juice and seeds; discard. Mince rinds and flesh; set aside. In a large bowl, beat sugar, butter, vanilla, ginger and nutmeg until light and fluffy. Beat in eggs, 2 at a time, scraping to keep batter smooth. Stir in kumquats and flour. Pour into prepared pans and bake for 45 minutes, until a tester inserted in the center of a cake comes out with a crumb clinging to it. Let cool in pans on racks for 5 minutes. Remove from pans to racks and let cool completely. Wrap individually. **Makes 10 mini pound cakes.**

Cardamom Apricot Pound Cakes

Follow preceding recipe, but replace the kumquats with 36 dried apricots, chopped, and substitute 1 tsp (5 mL) ground cardamom for the nutmeg. Makes 10 mini pound cakes.

Whisky Pound Cakes

	Vegetable cooking spray	
3¼ cups	all-purpose flour	800 mL
2 tsp	baking powder	10 mL
½ cup	whisky (such as Scotch or Irish whisky)	125 mL
½ cup	buttermilk	125 mL
3 cups	packed light brown sugar	750 mL
1½ cups	unsalted butter, softened	375 mL
1 tbsp	vanilla	15 mL
½ tsp	grated nutmeg	2 mL
Pinch	ground cloves	Pinch
6	extra-large eggs	6

Preheat oven to 350°F (180°C) and spray 8 mini loaf pans (each about 6 by 4 inches/15 by 10 cm) with cooking spray. Sift together flour and baking powder; set aside. In a separate bowl, combine whisky and buttermilk. In a large bowl, beat brown sugar, butter, vanilla, nutmeg and cloves until light and fluffy. Beat in eggs, 2 at a time, scraping to keep batter smooth. Stir in flour mixture alternately with whisky mixture, making 3 additions of flour and 2 of whisky. Pour batter into prepared pans and bake for 45 minutes, until a tester inserted in the center of a cake comes out with a crumb clinging to it. Let cool in pans on racks for 5 minutes. Remove from pans to racks and let cool completely. Wrap individually. Makes 8 mini pound cakes.

Walnut Cupcakes

2 cups	all-purpose flour	500 mL
1 tsp	baking powder	5 mL
Pinch	salt	Pinch
¾ cup	finely chopped walnuts	175 mL
1½ cups	granulated sugar	375 mL
⅔ cup	unsalted butter, softened	150 mL
½ tsp	vanilla	2 mL
½ tsp	almond extract	2 mL
3	extra-large eggs	3
1 cup	milk (not fat-free)	250 mL
½ cup	coarsely chopped walnuts	125 mL
½ cup	confectioner's (icing) sugar	125 mL

Preheat oven to 350°F (180°C) and line a 12-cup muffin tin with paper cupcake liners. Sift together flour, baking powder and salt, then stir in finely chopped walnuts. In a large bowl, beat sugar, butter, vanilla and almond extract until light and fluffy. Beat in eggs, one at a time, beating until smooth. Stir in flour mixture alternately with the milk, making 3 additions of flour and 2 of milk. Pour into prepared tin and sprinkle with coarsely chopped walnuts. Bake for 25 minutes, until browned and fully risen. Let cool completely in tin on a rack, then dust with confectioner's sugar. Makes 12 large cupcakes.

Pistachio Tea Cake

	Vegetable cooking spray	
1⅓ cups	all-purpose flour	325 mL
1 tsp	baking powder	5 mL
1 cup	granulated sugar	250 mL
1 cup	unsalted butter, softened	250 mL
4 oz	almond paste	125 g
2 tsp	almond extract	10 mL
4	eggs	4
¾ cup	finely ground pistachios (see page 13)	175 mL
¼ cup	chopped pistachios	50 mL

Preheat oven to 350°F (180°C) and spray a 9- by 5-inch (2 L) loaf pan with cooking spray. Sift together the flour and baking powder; set aside. In a large bowl, beat sugar, butter, almond paste and almond extract until light and fluffy. Add eggs, one at a time, scraping to keep batter smooth. Stir in flour mixture until incorporated, then stir in ground pistachios. Pour into prepared pan and sprinkle top with chopped pistachios. Bake for about 70 minutes, or until cake is fully risen and a tester inserted into a crack in the top comes out clean. Let cool in pan on a rack for 10 minutes. Remove from pan to rack and let cool completely. Makes 1 cake that will serve 12.

Honey Rum Raisin Tea Cake

	Vegetable cooking spray	
1 cup	raisins	250 mL
	Finely grated zest of 2 oranges	
¾ cup	dark rum	175 mL
2 cups	all-purpose flour	500 mL
2 tsp	ground cinnamon	10 mL
1 tsp	ground ginger	5 mL
¾ tsp	baking powder	4 mL
¾ tsp	baking soda	4 mL
¼ tsp	salt	1 mL
3	eggs	3
¾ cup	packed dark brown sugar	175 mL
¾ cup	honey	175 mL
3 tbsp	melted unsalted butter	45 mL

Preheat oven to 350°F (180°C) and spray a 9- by 5-inch (2 L) loaf pan with cooking spray. Soak raisins and orange zest in rum for 30 minutes. Sift together flour, cinnamon, ginger, baking powder, baking soda and salt; set aside. In a large bowl, beat eggs and brown sugar until fluffy. Stir in honey and butter until well combined. Stir in half the flour mixture, then the raisin mixture, then the remaining flour mixture. Pour into prepared pan and bake for about 70 minutes, until cake is fully risen and a tester inserted into a crack in the top comes out clean. Let cool in pan on a rack for 10 minutes. Remove from pan to rack and let cool completely. **Makes 1 cake that will serve 12.**

Two-Ton Bourbon Nut Cake

	Vegetable cooking spray	
3½ cups	all-purpose flour	875 mL
1 tbsp	baking powder	15 mL
1 tsp	ground nutmeg	5 mL
1½ cups	bourbon, divided	375 mL
½ cup	milk	125 mL
1 tsp	vanilla	5 mL
2¼ cups	packed light brown sugar	550 mL
1½ cups	unsalted butter, softened	375 mL
6	extra-large eggs	6
7½ cups	pecan pieces (about 2 lbs/1 kg)	1.875 L
2⅔ cups	pecan halves (about 10 oz/300 g)	650 mL

Preheat oven to 350°F (180°C) and spray a 10-inch (4 L) tube pan with cooking spray. Sift together flour, baking powder and nutmeg; set aside. Combine ½ cup (125 mL) of the bourbon, milk and vanilla; set aside. In a large bowl, beat brown sugar and butter until light and fluffy. Beat in eggs, one at a time, scraping to keep batter smooth. Stir in flour mixture alternately with the milk mixture, making 3 additions of flour and 2 of milk. Stir in pecan pieces. Pour into prepared pan and arrange pecan halves in concentric circles over top. Bake for 1 hour. Cover with foil and bake for 45 minutes, until a tester inserted in the thickest part of the cake comes out clean. Let cool in pan on a rack for 20 minutes. Remove from pan and brush cake with the remaining bourbon until fully absorbed. Let cool completely on rack. **Makes 30 slices.**

Almond Amaretto Cake

Follow preceding recipe, but replace the bourbon with amaretto, halve the vanilla, add ½ tsp (2 mL) almond extract with the vanilla, replace the pecan pieces with 9 cups (2.25 L) sliced almonds (about 2 lbs/1 kg), and replace the pecan halves with 2 cups (500 mL) whole blanched almonds (about 10 oz/ 300 g). **Makes 30 slices.**

Pepper Cheddar Skillet Cornbread

¼ cup	corn oil, divided	50 mL
3	green onions, sliced	3
1	red bell pepper, diced	1
1 cup	yellow cornmeal	250 mL
1 cup	all-purpose flour	250 mL
¼ cup	granulated sugar	50 mL
4 tsp	baking powder	20 mL
½ tsp	salt	2 mL
1 cup	milk (not fat-free)	250 mL
1 cup	shredded Cheddar cheese	250 mL

Preheat oven to 425°F (220°C). Brush a 9-inch (23 cm) cast-iron skillet with a thin film of oil and place in oven. In another skillet, heat the remaining oil over medium heat. Sauté green onions and red pepper until tender; set aside. In a large bowl, combine cornmeal, flour, sugar, baking powder and salt, then stir in sautéed vegetables. Stir in milk until smooth. Fold in cheese. Pour into hot skillet and bake for 35 minutes, until browned and risen and a tester inserted in the center comes out clean. Let cool in pan on a rack for 5 minutes. **Serves 6 to 8.**

Savarin

	Vegetable cooking spray	
2 tsp	active dry yeast	10 mL
½ cup	whole milk, heated to about 100°F (37°C)	125 mL
2⅔ cups	all-purpose flour, divided	650 mL
2½ cups	granulated sugar, divided	625 mL
½ cup	unsalted butter, softened	125 mL
6	extra-large eggs	6
5 cups	water	1.25 L
½ cup	dark rum	125 mL
	Sweetened whipped cream (optional)	

Coat an 8-inch (2 L) nonstick Bundt pan with baking spray. Dissolve yeast in warm milk, then stir in ½ cup (125 mL) of the flour just until smooth; cover and let stand in a warm place for 30 minutes. In a large bowl, beat 2 tbsp (25 mL) of the flour, 3 tbsp (45 mL) of the sugar and butter until light and fluffy. Beat in eggs, one at a time, until smooth. Stir in the remaining flour and the yeast mixture until smooth. Pour into prepared pan, cover and let rise for 45 minutes, until doubled in size and bubbly. Meanwhile, preheat oven to 350°F (180°C). Bake cake for 40 minutes, until browned and fully risen. Meanwhile, in a saucepan, combine water and the remaining sugar; bring to a boil over medium-high heat and boil until reduced by about half. Stir in rum. Pour slowly over baked savarin until syrup is absorbed. Let cool in pan on a rack for 45 minutes. Remove from pan and let cool completely on a rack. Serve with whipped cream, if desired. **Makes 1 large cake that will serve 12.** *Store wrapped in plastic wrap in the refrigerator for up to 2 weeks.*

Orange Savarin

Follow preceding recipe, but add ¼ cup (50 mL) finely grated orange zest to the batter. Serve with candied orange peel or candied orange slices, along with the whipped cream. **Makes 1 large cake that will serve 12.** *Store wrapped in plastic in the refrigerator for up to 2 weeks.*

Baba au Rhum

Follow recipe for Savarin (above), but divide finished batter among 12 well-greased muffin cups and bake for 23 minutes. Remove from tin and place in a pan that will hold them in 1 layer before pouring syrup over them; turn in the syrup until all the syrup has been absorbed. **Makes 12 mini cakes.** *Store wrapped in plastic in the refrigerator for up to 2 weeks.*

Heavy-Duty Hazelnut Truffles

½ cup	whipping (35%) cream	125 mL
1 tbsp	unsalted butter	15 mL
8 oz	semisweet chocolate, finely chopped	250 g
3 tbsp	Frangelico or other nut-flavored liqueur	45 mL
2 tbsp	strong brewed coffee	25 mL
¼ cup	ground hazelnuts (see page 13), toasted	50 mL
2 tbsp	confectioner's (icing) sugar	25 mL

In a small saucepan, melt cream and butter over low heat. Add chocolate, and heat, stirring, until melted. Transfer to a bowl and whisk in liqueur and coffee; let cool completely. Meanwhile, combine hazelnuts and confectioner's sugar. Form chocolate mixture into 12 balls and roll in hazelnut mixture. Place in foil or paper candy cups, if desired. **Makes 12 truffles.**

Meatless Mincemeat

1 cup	unsweetened apple cider	250 mL
1 cup	dark (cooking) molasses	250 mL
½ cup	brandy	125 mL
¼ cup	unsalted butter	50 mL
15	unsalted soda crackers, crumbled	15
4 lbs	Granny Smith apples, peeled and finely chopped (about 12 cups/3 L)	2 kg
1 lb	raisins (3 cups/750 mL)	500 g
1 lb	dried currants (3¼ cups/800 mL)	500 g
4 oz	candied citron, chopped	125 g
4 oz	candied orange peel	125 g
4 oz	dried apricots	125 g
1 cup	granulated sugar	250 mL
1 tbsp	ground cinnamon	15 mL
1 tbsp	ground ginger	15 mL
1 tbsp	ground cloves	15 mL
1 tbsp	ground nutmeg	15 mL
1 tsp	salt	5 mL
½ tsp	freshly ground black pepper	2 mL
	Grated zest and juice of 1 lemon	

In a saucepan, heat cider, molasses, brandy and butter over medium heat until butter is melted. Pour into a large bowl, add the remaining ingredients and toss to coat. Cover and refrigerate for at least 24 hours. **Makes 12 cups (3 L).** *Store in decorative jars in the refrigerator for up to 1 month.*

Cider Syrup

| 5⅓ cups | unsweetened apple cider | 1.325 L |
| ⅓ cup | granulated sugar | 75 mL |

In a large, heavy saucepan, bring cider and sugar to a boil over medium-high heat; boil until reduced to 1 cup (250 mL), skimming away any foam that rises to the surface. Pour into a decorative jar and let cool. **Makes 1 cup (250 mL).** *Store in the refrigerator for up to 1 month.*

Spicy Garlic Oil

6	dried chili peppers	6
1	head garlic, cloves peeled	1
2 cups	corn oil, sesame oil or olive oil	500 mL

In a saucepan, heat chili peppers, garlic and oil over medium heat until garlic and peppers start to bubble at the tips, about 4 minutes. Let cool, then pour into a decorative bottle. **Makes 2 cups (500 mL).** *Store in the refrigerator for up to 1 week.*

Citrus Oil

2 cups	peanut oil	500 mL
	Strips of zest from 2 oranges	
	Strips of zest from 2 lemons	

In a saucepan, heat oil and citrus zests over medium heat until strips bubble at the ends, about 4 minutes. Let cool, then pour into a decorative bottle. **Makes 2 cups (500 mL).** *Store in the refrigerator for up to 1 month.*

Ginger Sesame Oil

| 2 cups | dark sesame oil | 500 mL |
| ⅓ cup | julienned gingerroot | 75 mL |

In a saucepan, heat oil and ginger over medium heat until ginger bubbles at the ends, about 4 minutes. Let cool, then pour into a decorative bottle. **Makes 2 cups (500 mL).** *Store in the refrigerator for up to 1 month.*

Provençal Oil

4	cloves garlic, sliced	4
2 cups	extra-virgin olive oil	500 mL
2 tbsp	dried herbes de Provence	25 mL

In a saucepan, heat garlic, oil and herbes de Provence over medium heat until bubbles form around garlic (do not let garlic brown). Let cool, then pour into a decorative bottle. **Makes 2 cups (500 mL).** *Store in the refrigerator for up to 1 week.*

Orange-Fennel Walnut Oil

2 cups	walnut oil	500 mL
¼ cup	finely chopped orange zest	50 mL
2 tbsp	fennel seeds	25 mL

In a saucepan, heat oil, orange zest and fennel seeds over medium heat until bubbles form around fennel seeds. Let cool, then pour into a decorative bottle. **Makes 2 cups (500 mL).** *Store in the refrigerator for up to 1 month.*

Herb Vinegar

| 1 cup | chopped fresh herbs (such as basil, tarragon, chervil, oregano, cilantro) | 250 mL |
| 2 cups | red or white wine vinegar | 500 mL |

In a saucepan, bring herbs and vinegar to a boil over medium heat. Let cool, then strain into a decorative jar. **Makes 2 cups (500 mL).**

Fruit Vinegar

| 2 cups | chopped citrus fruit, pears, peaches, plums, grapes and/or berries | 500 mL |
| 1½ cups | red or white wine vinegar | 375 mL |

In a saucepan, bring fruits and vinegar to a boil over medium heat. Let cool, then strain into a decorative jar. **Makes 2 cups (500 mL).**

Pear Vinegar

3	ripe pears, finely chopped	3
2 cups	white wine vinegar	500 mL
1	large perfect pear	1

In a saucepan, bring chopped pears and vinegar to a boil over medium heat. Let cool, then strain. Place whole pear in a wide-mouthed decorative jar and pour strained vinegar over top. **Makes 4 cups (1 L).**

Lemon Garlic Vinegar

1	head garlic, cloves peeled	1
¼ cup	finely chopped lemon zest	50 mL
1½ cups	white wine vinegar	375 mL
	Juice of 2 lemons	

In a saucepan, bring garlic, lemon zest and vinegar to a boil over medium heat. Let cool, then strain into a decorative jar. Stir in lemon juice. **Makes 2 cups (500 mL).**

Spicy Corn Relish

1 tsp	corn oil	5 mL
1	large onion, chopped	1
1	dried chili pepper	1
1	bay leaf	1
1 cup	water	250 mL
¾ cup	cider vinegar	175 mL
3 tbsp	granulated sugar	45 mL
1 tbsp	pickling spice	15 mL
⅓ cup	diced carrot	75 mL
2	roasted red bell peppers (see page 11), diced	2
4 cups	canned or frozen corn, thawed if frozen	1 L

In a large skillet, heat oil over medium-high heat. Sauté onion until browned. Add chili, bay leaf, water, vinegar, sugar and pickling spice; bring to a boil. Add carrot, reduce heat to medium and simmer for 5 minutes. Add roasted peppers and corn; heat through. Discard chili and bay leaf. **Makes 4 cups (1 L).**

Curried Eggplant Chutney

1 tbsp	olive oil	15 mL
1	large onion, chopped	1
1	clove garlic, minced	1
1 tbsp	curry powder	15 mL
1 tsp	ground cumin	5 mL
1 tsp	chili powder	5 mL
1	large eggplant, peeled and diced	1
1 cup	chopped canned tomatoes, drained	250 mL
2 tbsp	granulated sugar	25 mL
	Salt and freshly ground black pepper to taste	
¼ tsp	crumbled saffron threads, dissolved in ¼ cup (50 mL) vinegar	1 mL
½ cup	roasted peanuts	125 mL

In a skillet, heat oil over medium heat. Sauté onion and garlic until tender. Add curry powder, cumin and chili powder; sauté for 2 minutes. Stir in eggplant, tomatoes, sugar, salt and pepper. Stir in saffron mixture and simmer for 15 minutes, until vegetables are tender. Stir in peanuts. **Makes 3 cups (750 mL).**

Sweet Spiked Walnuts

2 cups	walnut pieces (about 10 oz/300 g)	500 mL
1 cup	strong brewed coffee	250 mL
1½ cups	granulated sugar	375 mL
¼ cup	Scotch whisky	50 mL
½ tsp	salt	2 mL
2 oz	liquid pectin	60 g

In a saucepan, bring walnuts and coffee to a simmer over medium heat; simmer for 3 minutes. Add sugar, Scotch and salt; bring to a boil, stirring constantly. Add pectin and boil for 2 minutes. Let cool and pour into decorative jars. **Makes 2 cups (500 mL).** *Store in the refrigerator for up to 1 month.*

Bourbon Pecans

Follow preceding recipe, but replace the walnuts with pecans, replace the Scotch with bourbon, and replace half the granulated sugar with packed light brown sugar. **Makes 2 cups (500 mL).** *Store in the refrigerator for up to 1 month.*

Bitter Grapefruit Marmalade

	Julienned zest of 3 large grapefruits	
	Juice of 6 large grapefruits (about 6 cups/1.5 L)	
3½ cups	granulated sugar	825 mL
1 tbsp	freshly squeezed lemon juice	15 mL
Pinch	salt	Pinch
9 oz	liquid pectin	255 mL

In a large pot of boiling water, boil grapefruit zest for 5 minutes. Drain and return to pot with grapefruit juice; bring to a simmer over medium heat and simmer for 5 minutes. Add sugar, lemon juice and salt; bring to a boil, stirring constantly, and boil for 5 minutes. Add pectin and boil for 1 minute. Pour into decorative jars and let cool. **Makes 6 cups (1.5 L).** *Store in the refrigerator for up to 1 month.*

Lemon Green Peppercorn Marmalade

	Julienned zest of 9 lemons	
5 cups	freshly squeezed lemon juice (20 to 30 lemons)	1.25 L
1 cup	water	250 mL
3½ cups	granulated sugar	825 mL
Pinch	salt	Pinch
9 oz	liquid pectin	255 mL
⅓ cup	drained canned green peppercorns	75 mL

In a large pot of boiling water, boil lemon zest for 5 minutes. Drain and return to pot with lemon juice and water; bring to a simmer over medium heat and simmer for 5 minutes. Add sugar and salt; bring to a boil, stirring constantly, and boil for 5 minutes. Add pectin and boil for 1 minute. Crush peppercorns with the back of a spoon and stir into marmalade. Pour into decorative jars and let cool. **Makes 6 cups (1.5 L).** *Store in the refrigerator for up to 1 month.*

Gingered Carrot Marmalade

1 lb	carrots	500 g
1	piece (1 inch/2.5 cm) gingerroot	1
1 cup	orange juice	250 mL
1 cup	cider vinegar or rice vinegar	250 mL
4 cups	granulated sugar	1 L
1 tsp	salt	5 mL
6 oz	liquid pectin	170 mL

In a food processor, finely chop carrots and ginger. Transfer to a saucepan and add orange juice and vinegar; bring to a simmer over medium-high heat and simmer for 10 minutes, skimming any foam that rises to the surface. Stir in sugar and salt; heat over high heat, stirring constantly, until mixture comes to a boil that can't be stirred down. Boil for 1 minute, then stir in pectin; boil for 1 minute. Pour into decorative jars and let cool. **Makes 4 to 5 cups (1 to 1.25 L).** *Store in the refrigerator for up to 1 month.*

Jalapeño Jelly

16	jalapeño peppers, seeded	16
1	large bell pepper (any color), quartered	1
1	large apple, quartered	1
1½ cups	cider vinegar	375 mL
4¼ cups	granulated sugar	1.05 L
¼ tsp	salt	1 mL
6 oz	liquid pectin	170 mL

In a food processor, finely chop jalapeños; remove one-quarter of the chopped jalapeños and set aside. Add bell pepper and apple to food processor and finely chop. Transfer to a saucepan and add vinegar; bring to a simmer over medium-high and simmer for 15 minutes. Strain liquid and discard pulp. Return liquid to saucepan and add sugar and salt; heat over high heat, stirring constantly, until mixture comes to a boil that can't be stirred down. Boil for 3 minutes, then stir in pectin and reserved jalapeños; boil for 1 minute. Pour into small decorative jars and let cool. **Makes 3½ cups (875 mL).** *Store in the refrigerator for up to 1 month.*

Caramel Pear Preserves

1 cup	water	250 mL
2 tbsp	white wine vinegar	25 mL
	Juice of 1 lemon	
5	large pears, diced (about 5 cups/1.25 L)	5
2 cups	granulated sugar	500 mL
2 cups	packed brown sugar	500 mL
¼ tsp	salt	1 mL
9 oz	liquid pectin	255 mL

In a heavy saucepan, bring water, vinegar and lemon juice to a simmer over medium-high heat. Add pears, cover and simmer for 10 to 15 minutes, or until tender. Add granulated sugar, brown sugar and salt; heat over high heat, stirring constantly, until mixture comes to a boil that can't be stirred down. Boil for 5 minutes, then stir in pectin; boil for 1 minute. Pour into decorative jars and let cool. **Makes 6 cups (1.5 L).** *Store in the refrigerator for up to 1 month.*

Marinated Herbed Mushrooms

4	green onions, finely sliced	4
1	bay leaf	1
1 lb	small mushrooms, trimmed	500 g
1½ cups	dry white wine	375 mL
⅔ cup	olive oil	150 mL
1½ tbsp	freshly squeezed lemon juice	22 mL
¼ tsp	dried thyme	1 mL
¼ tsp	ground coriander	1 mL
⅓ cup	chopped fresh Italian (flat-leaf) parsley	75 mL

In a large saucepan, combine green onions, bay leaf, mushrooms, wine, oil, lemon juice, thyme and coriander; bring to a simmer over medium heat and simmer for 5 minutes. Remove mushrooms to a bowl. Boil pan liquid until reduced by one-third. Return mushrooms to the pan, add parsley and return to a boil. Let cool, then pour into decorative jars. **Makes 3 cups (750 mL).** *Store in the refrigerator for up to 2 weeks.*

Easy Honey Mustard

2 cups	brown mustard	500 mL
1 cup	honey	250 mL

Whisk together mustard and honey until completely blended. **Makes 3 cups (750 mL).** *Store in small decorative jars in the refrigerator for up to 1 month.*

Green Peppercorn Mustard

3 tbsp	drained canned green peppercorns	45 mL
1 tsp	dried tarragon	5 mL
1 tsp	vinegar	5 mL
1 cup	Dijon mustard	250 mL

In a small saucepan, combine peppercorns, tarragon and vinegar, crushing peppercorns with the back of a spoon. Bring to a simmer, then stir into mustard. **Makes 1 cup (250 mL).** *Store in small decorative jars in the refrigerator for up to 1 month.*

Red Wine Whole-Grain Mustard

¼ cup	mustard seeds	50 mL
2 tbsp	dry red wine	25 mL
1 tsp	red wine vinegar	5 mL
1 cup	Dijon mustard	250 mL

In a small saucepan, combine mustard seeds, wine and vinegar; let soak overnight. Bring to a boil, then stir into mustard. **Makes about 1 cup (250 mL).** *Store in small decorative jars in the refrigerator for up to 1 month.*

Raisin Chocolate Chip Peanut Butter

2 cups	unsalted roasted peanuts	500 mL
Pinch	salt	Pinch
⅓ cup	semisweet chocolate chips	75 mL
⅓ cup	raisins	75 mL

In a food processor, process peanuts and salt until smooth, about 3 minutes, stopping periodically to scrape the bowl. Transfer to a bowl and stir in chocolate chips and raisins. **Makes 2 cups (500 mL).** *Store in decorative jars in the refrigerator for up to 1 month.*

Pecan or Walnut Butter

3½ cups	pecan or walnut pieces (about 1 lb/500 g)	875 mL
2 tsp	packed light brown sugar	10 mL
Pinch	salt	Pinch

In a food processor, finely chop nuts, brown sugar and salt, using a pulsing action. Process continuously until smooth, about 3 minutes, stopping periodically to scrape the bowl. **Makes 2 cups (500 mL).** *Store in decorative jars in the refrigerator for up to 1 month.*

Ginger Tahini

2 cups	sesame seeds	500 mL
¼ tsp	ground ginger	1 mL
Pinch	salt	Pinch
Pinch	ground nutmeg	Pinch
¼ cup	minced candied ginger	50 mL

In a skillet, over medium heat, toast sesame seeds, shaking pan constantly, for 3 to 4 minutes, or until they pop and color lightly. Transfer to a food processor and add ginger, salt and nutmeg; finely chop, using a pulsing action. Process continuously until smooth, about 3 minutes, periodically stopping to scrape the bowl. Stir in candied ginger. **Makes 2 cups (500 mL).** *Store in decorative jars in the refrigerator for up to 1 month.*

Library and Archives Canada Cataloguing in Publication

Schloss, Andrew
2500 recipes : everyday to extraordinary / Andrew Schloss ; with Ken Bookman.

Includes index
ISBN 978-0-7788-0171-9 (bound)
ISBN 978-0-7788-0162-7 (pbk.)

1. Cookery. I. Bookman, Ken. II. Title. III. Title: Two thousand
five hundred recipes.

TX833.5.S35 2007   641.5   C2007-902864-0

Acknowledgments

We'd like to thank the people who liked the first incarnation of this book enough to ensure that there'd be a second. Lisa Ekus, our literary agent, is an avid foodie who has spent a lot of time with *Fifty Ways to Cook Most Everything: 2500 Creative Solutions to the Daily Dilemma of What to Cook*. We're happy that her cooking efforts were rewarded, happier still that she helped steer us toward the book you're now holding, and even happier that that she has been such a good friend for so many years.

Several friends became avid fans of *Fifty Ways*, cooking hundreds of recipes with enthusiasm and good critiques. Georgette Jasen, Herb Kestenbaum, Toni Kestenbaum, Rick Nichols and Max Van Gilder were five of them, and we are grateful to them.

Lauren Zakheim is a talented young lady whose help in preparing our manuscript proved timely and invaluable.

Karen Shain Schloss and Ruth Adelman have probably grown accustomed to sharing homes where cookbooks take on a life of their own. We hope so, and we thank them for doing it again.

If you ever write a book, you want Bob Dees to publish it and Sue Sumeraj to edit it. We had a mission, and Bob took the time and effort to understand it thoroughly and to assemble the people whose work would help it shine through. Sue's diligence was breathtaking. A word of advice: If she's ever your editor, learn the phrase "Good catch" to convey your gratitude that she has once again saved you from a horrible mistake.

We were in good hands with Robert Rose Inc. Jennifer MacKenzie tested recipes and cast her keen eye over the text, making quite a few good catches herself. Thanks also to designers Andrew Smith and Joseph Gisini of PageWave Graphics; Marian Jarkovich, who helped with marketing; Sheila Wawanash, our proofreader; and Gillian Watts, who assembled the index.

Despite our substantial overhaul of *Fifty Ways*, some of the important contributions to that book were vital to this one as well. One of our most memorable experiences was the lunch we catered for a few dozen eight-year-old kids from Cheltenham Elementary School in Cheltenham, Pennsylvania, who gave credibility to Chapter 8, on foods that kids would like. That was in 1990. Some of those third-graders are probably parents themselves by now, but their likes and dislikes live on in these pages. And Chapter 45 was helped immensely by nutritionist Mona Sutnick.

But we reserve our biggest thanks for the many fans of these recipes. They first made their response known as they read a few installments in the Food section of *The Philadelphia Inquirer*, and they later voted with their wallets when they responded so favorably to *Fifty Ways*. We hope they'll be rewarded again with the recipes in these pages.

Andrew Schloss   Ken Bookman
Elkins Park, Pa.   Bala Cynwyd, Pa.

April 2007

Index

A

Acorn Squash with Gingered Applesauce, 383
Acorn Squash with Orange Molasses, 383
Acorn Squash with Spiced Honey, 383
African Peanut Soup, 199
Aïoli, 17
All-Almond Snack Mix, 80
All-American Barbecue Marinade, 31
All-American Turkey Cheeseburgers, 102
All-Bean Vegan Chili, 203
All-Day All-Beef Chili, 72
All-Day Lentil Soup, 70
All-Fish Bouillabaisse, 330
All-Pork Chili, 205
All–Oat Bran Muffins, 546
almonds
  cakes
    Almond Amaretto Cake, 556
    Chocolate Almond Torte, 527
    Gâteau Bordeaux, 528
    Sweet Almond Coffee Cake, 434
  Chocolate-Covered Almond Apricots, 531
  cookies and bars
    Almond Macaroons, 438
    Almond Shortbread, 440
    Anise Almond Drops, 439
    Grand Marnier Almond Bars, 442
    Honey Almond Tuiles, 440
  Dried Cherry, Tarragon and Almond Dessert Pizza, 223
  pies and tarts
    Almond Peach Pie, 538
    Almond Pear Pie, 535
    Chocolate Almond Pie, 541
    Grand Marnier Almond Tart, 541
  Snack Mix, All-Almond, 80
  Snack Mix, Healthy, 80
anchovies
  Anchovy Mayonnaise, 56
  Anchovy Olive Pesto, 178
  Anchovy Steak Sauce, 109
  Bagna Caôda, 84
  Pepper and Anchovy Sauce, 234
  Roasted Pepper, Caper and Anchovy Pizza, 216
  Tomato, Caper and Anchovy Pizza, 213
Angel-of-Death Cheese, 466
Anise Almond Drops, 439
Anise Braised Beef, 481
Anise Cherry Pie, 538
Anise Chicken Braised in a Wok, 291
Anise Tea Eggs, 466
antipasto, 349

Anytime Peach Pie, 540
appetizers, 464–73
apple cider and juice. See also apples
  Apple Cider Dressing, 65
  Cider Syrup, 558
  Lemon-Lime Soft Drink, 453
  Minted Apple Juice, 455
  Mulled Cider, 457
  Sweet-and-Sour Cider Sauce, 52
apples. See also apple cider and juice
  Apple and Spice Marinade, 31
  Apple Butter, 408
  applesauce
    Applesauce, 407
    Chunky Applesauce, 407
    Double-Apple Applesauce, 103
    Easy Homemade Applesauce, 67
    Pear Applesauce, 407
    Raisin Applesauce, 407
    Spiked Applesauce, 407
  baked apples
    Baked Apples Stuffed with Turkey, 305
    Bourbon Pecan-Stuffed Baked Apples, 408
    Lemon-Glazed Baked Apples, 408
    Wet Walnut Baked Apples, 409
  cakes
    Apple Crumb Coffee Cake, 412
    Apple Walnut Cake, 412
    Hungarian Apple Coffee Cake, 413
    Jewish Apple Cake, 412
    Lemon Apple Cake, 412
  Meatless Mincemeat, 557
  muffins and loaves
    Apple Cheddar Cornbread, 407
    Apple Oatmeal Spice Muffins, 549
    Apple Walnut Muffins, 544
    Applesauce Walnut Muffins, 549
    Bacon and Apple Corn Muffins, 547
    Zucchini Apple Muffins, 549
  pastries
    Apple Cheddar Turnovers, 410
    Apple Fennel Turnovers, 410
    Apple Mincemeat Mini Turnovers, 469
    Apple Turnovers, 410
  pies and tarts
    Apple Butterscotch Custard Pie, 536
    Apple Caramel Peanut Pie, 536
    Apple Date Pie, 535
    Apple Lemon Custard Pie, 536
    Apple Nectarine Pie, 536
    Apple Pear Pie, 535
    Apple Sour Cream Pie, 536
    Apple Walnut Pie, 535
    Candied Ginger Apple Pie, 536

apples
  pies and tarts (continued)
    Classic Apple Pie, 535
    Ham and Apple Tart, 406
    Old-Fashioned Apple Cheddar Pie, 534
    Old World Boozy Apple Plum Pie, 535
    Praline Apple Pie Spiked with Bourbon, 536
    Smoked Turkey and Apple Tart, 406
    Smoky Apple Galette, 537
    Tarte Tatin, 537
    Topless Apple Pie, 536
    Upside-Down Maple Apple Pie, 537
  puddings and other desserts
    Apple Brandy Raisin Risotto Pudding, 361
    Apple Charlotte, 410
    Apple Crisp, 411
    Apple Ginger Charlotte, 410
    Apple Hazelnut Crisp, 411
    Apple Kugel, 104
    Blue Cheese Apple Cheesecake, 473
    Ginger Apple Cobbler, 44
    Poached Winter Fruit Salad with Raspberry Vinaigrette, 190
    Sautéed Apples in Applejack, 407
    Stir-Fried Apple Shortcake, 170
  soups
    Apple Broccoli Bisque, 196
    Apple Pumpkin Bisque, 196
    Apple Turnip Soup, 513
  Spicy Apple Butter Marinade, 33
apricots
  Apricot Cardamom Muffins, 549
  Apricot Marinade, 31
  Apricot Marzipan Drops, 441
  Apricot Schnecken, 441
  Brandied Summer Fruit, 174
  Cardamom Apricot Pound Cakes, 555
  Chocolate Apricot Torte, 528
  Chocolate-Covered Almond Apricots, 531
  Fruit Glaze, 23, 535
  Fruity Barbecue Marinade, 31
  Prosciutto and Summer Fruit Salad, 179
  Sherried Apricot Glaze, 52
  Spiced Fruit, 70
  Spiked Fruitcake Brownies, 553
  Spiked Summer Fruit Salad, 417
artichokes. See also Jerusalem artichokes
  Artichoke and Mushroom Pizza, 216

artichokes (*continued*)
Artichoke and Mushroom Sauce, 227
Artichoke Ratatouille, 506
Artichoke Salsa, 177
Artichoke with Tofu Dressing, 395
Feta and Artichoke Sauce, 227
Greek Marinated Mushrooms in Artichokes, 352
Marinated Antipasto, 349
Marinated Feta and Artichoke Heart Pizza, 220
Sicilian Artichokes, 395
Spinach Artichoke Bread, 489
Tomato and Artichoke Salsa, 56
Vegetable Pâté Niçoise, 465
arugula. *See* greens
Asian Chicken Paillards, 143
Asian Fried Noodles, 114
Asian Peanut Marinade, 34
Asian Tofu Dressing, 513
Asian Turkey Salad, 306
asparagus
Asparagus, Shrimp, Raspberry and Grapefruit Salad, 506
Asparagus-Orange Salmon Salad, 188
Asparagus Salad, 507
Steamed Asparagus, 67
Stir-Fried Asparagus with Cashews, 395
Stir-Fried Asparagus with Tofu and Almonds, 517
Stir-Fried Sesame Asparagus, 351
Stir-Fried Sesame Vegetables, 507
Stir-Fry of Crab and Asparagus, 503
Summer Antipasto, 349
Whiting, Asparagus and Pine Nut Salad, 319
Avgolemono, 197
avocado
Avocado, Tomato and Shrimp with Chili Pepper Vinaigrette, 401
Avocado and Tomato Salsa, 403
Avocado Coulis, 179
Avocado Falafel, 346
Avocado Grapefruit Salad, 515
Avocado Ice Cream, 473
Avocado Salsa, 177
Crab and Avocado Salad, 341
Creamy Avocado Dressing, 60
Guacamole Vinaigrette, 65
Pita Filled with Toasted Chickpeas, Avocado and Eggplant "Caviar," 346
Scallop Seviche Skewered with Avocado, 332
Spicy Avocado Sauce, 57
Tuna and Guacamole Pitas, 94

B

Baba au Rhum, 557
Baba Ghanoush, 465

bacon
Apple, Bacon and Cornmeal Waffles, 430
Bacon, Egg and Cheese Sauce, 231
Bacon, Peppers and Potatoes, 384
Bacon and Apple Corn Muffins, 547
Bacon and Fruit Slaw, 187
Bacon and Onion Popcorn, 79
Bacon Biscuits, 431
Bacon Breakfast Cookies, 127
Bacon Cornsticks, 548
Bacon Hash Browns, 427
British Bacon, 428
Crispy Bacon Strips, 67
Grilled Cheese, Bacon and Tomato Sandwiches, 90
Hot Pepper, Bacon and Gorgonzola Pizza, 222
Smoked Bacon Burgers, 131
Warm Bacon Dressing, 62
Bagna Caôda, 84
Baked Apples Stuffed with Turkey, 305
Baked Beans, 70
Baked Beets, 68
Baked Brie Sandwiches, 90
Baked Brie with Croissants, 492
Baked Chicken Legs with Balsamic Glaze, 293
Baked Creole Crabmeat, 340
Baked Eggplant Moussaka, 246
Baked Fish in Mustard Glaze, 327
Baked Fish with Horseradish and Sour Cream, 327
Baked Mahi Mahi with Grapefruit Butter Sauce, 312
Baked Pasta e Fagioli, 246
Baked Potato Skins with Yogurt Herb Sauce, 114
Baked Potatoes with Minted Yogurt, 393
Baked Potatoes with Mustard Sauce, 393
Baked Potatoes with Sour Cream Vinaigrette, 392
Baked Rabe Romano, 245
Baked Shells Stuffed with Tuna and Cheese, 239
Balsamic Pear Tarte Tatin, 411
Balsamic Shrimp, 471
Balsamic–Olive Oil Vinaigrette, 61
bananas
Banana and Walnut Dessert Pizza, 223
Banana Berry Kefir, 457
Banana French Toast, 103
Banana Sandwiches, 98
Chocolate Banana Sauce, 445
Fruit and Honey Topping, 434
muffins
Banana Bran Muffins, 545
Banana Oat Bran Raisin Muffins, 545
Banana Oatmeal Muffins, 549
Sour Cream Banana Muffins, 545
Tropical Banana Muffins, 545

bananas (*continued*)
Peanut Butter and Banana Sandwiches, 98
Roasted Bananas, 409
Rum Raisin Bananas, 170
Spiked Bananas Grilled with Vanilla and Candied Ginger, 146
Stir-Fried Banana Split, 170
Super-Protein Health Shake, 457
Barbecue Pan Sauce, 51
Barbecue-Style Dogs, 134
Barbecued Beef, 71
Barbecued Beef Stew, 261
Barbecued Catfish, 309
Barbecued Chicken, 141
Barbecued Chicken or Pork Salad, 112
Barbecued Chicken Salad, Leftover, 141
Barbecued Chicken Sandwich, 141
Barbecued Chicken Stew, 261
Barbecued Fish, 329
Barbecued Meatloaf Sandwiches, 89
Barbecued Pork Sandwiches, 92
Barbecued Pork Sandwiches with Coleslaw, 92
Barbecued Pork Sandwiches with Sauerkraut, 92
Barbecued Pork Stewed with Sausage, 261
Barbecued Roast Chicken, 276
Barbecued Shrimp, Grilled, 336
Barbecued Soft-Shell Crabs, 141
Barbecued Steamed Clams, 338
Barley and Sausage Soup, 364
Barley Chicken Salad, 363
bars and squares, 105, 442–43, 524, 525, 532, 553. *See also* brownies
Bartlett Turnovers, 410
Basic Buttermilk Pancakes, 429
Basic Chili Mix (BCM), 202
Basic Dry Rub, 35
Basic Green Salad, 182
Basic Popovers, 432
Basic Wine Vinaigrette, 60
basil (fresh)
Basil and Garlic Sauce, 56
Basil and Prosciutto Sauce, 231
Basil Ranch Dressing, 64
Fresh Basil Pesto, 178
Lemon Basil Marinade, 28
Naked Basil and Prosciutto Pizza, 216
Pesto, 20
Pesto Mayonnaise Dressing, 64
Pesto Vinaigrette, 65
Reduced-Fat Pesto, 228
Spicy Basil Pesto, 178
Warm Basil and Tomato Dip, 84
Basmati Rice, 360
Bavarian Meatballs, 252
beans, dried, 11–12. *See also* beans, green
Baked Beans, 70
Baked Pasta e Fagioli, 246

beans, dried (*continued*)
Black Bean Tacos, 345
Brown Beans and Rice, 519
Brown Rice with Red Beans, 124
chilis
All-Bean Vegan Chili, 203
Fish, Black Beans and Cilantro, 330
Garden Chili, 203
Quick Vegetable Chili, 203
Vegetarian Chili, 202
High-Protein Vegetarian Tostadas, 347
Mexican Torta, 247
Mixed Grilled Vegetable Tostada, 347
Mixed Grilled Vegetables with Black Bean Sauce, 347
Pasta with Garlic and White Beans, 119
Quesadilla Casserole, 123
Quick Cassoulet, 241
Refried Black, White or Kidney Beans, 20
salads
Black Bean and Bulgur Salad with Orange and Pepperoni, 364
Black Bean Falafel, 346
Chicken Cannellini Salad, 515
Corn, Black Bean and Roasted Tomato Salad, 118
Crab, Orange and Black Bean Salad, 188
Marinated Green Tomato and White Bean Salad, 385
Marinated Tuna and White Bean Salad, 188
Pasta, Bean and Tuna Salad, 111
Rice and Bean Salad, 112
Succotash Salad, 364
White and Black Bean Salad, 353
soups
Black Bean Soup with Orange and Cilantro, 199
Chili and Corn Chowder, 348
Easy Clam and White Bean Chowder, 118
Minestrone with Beans, 194
Spicy Black Bean Soup, 117
Spicy Red Bean Peanut Soup, 199
White Bean and Brown Rice Soup, 514
Southwest Bread Pudding, 247
Spicy Tomato Sauce and Red Beans, 225
Stir-Fried Beans, 168
Tuna, White Bean and Olive Pizza, 218
White Bean, Tuna and Olive Oil Sauce, 234
beans, green
Garlic Green Beans, 379
Green Beans with Pine Nuts, 379
Green Beans with Roasted Peppers, 379

beans, green (*continued*)
Green Beans with Thyme, 379
Indian Braised Vegetables, 381
Italian Stir-Fried Green Beans, 169
Precooked Beans or Carrots, 69
Stir-Fried Curried Vegetables, 166
Stir-Fried Garlic Green Beans, 169
Béchamel Sauce (White Sauce), 17
beef
Beef Broth, 18
Beef Broth, Slow-Cooked, 69
burgers
Apple and Sage Burgers, 130
Blackened Cajun Burgers, 131
Blue Cheese Burgers, 131
Cajun Burgers, 130
Great Burgers, 130
Ham and Swiss Cheeseburgers, 131
Hamburger Hot Dogs, 102
Hoisin Burgers, 133
Initial Burgers, 102
Meatloaf Burgers, 131
Mexican Burgers, 131
Peppercorn Burgers, 130
Sicilian Mint and Ricotta Burgers, 132
Smoked Bacon Burgers, 131
Steak and Onion Burger, 130
Steakhouse Burgers, 130
Super Smoky Burgers, 131
Surprise Cheeseburgers, 102
Three-Cheese Burgers, 131
Whole-Seed Mustard Burgers, 130
chilis
All-Day All-Beef Chili, 72
Charbroiled Sirloin Chili, 204
Cheesy Baked Chili, 204
Chili Inferno, 204
Chili with Beer, 204
Chunky Beef Chili, 204
Cornbread Chili, 204
Ground Beef Chili, 203
Herbed Chili, 204
Leftover Steak Chili, 111
Meatball Chili, 251
Oven-Braised Chili, 204
Roasted Pepper Chili, 205
Corned Beef and Cabbage, 71
Corned Beef and Potato Salad, 392
Corned Beef Deli Wraps, 87
Leftovers Escabèche, 113
marinades for, 29–35
Meat Sauce, Quick, 229
meatballs
Meatballs and Sauce, 230
Meatballs Wrapped in Bacon, 250
Spicy Cocktail Meatballs, 251
meatloaf
Apple Sage Meatloaf, 254
Apple Turkey Meatloaf, 305
Chilied Meatloaf with Chorizo, 254
Ham and Cheddar Meatloaf, 255
Ham Meatloaf, 255

beef
meatloaf (*continued*)
Lasagna Meatloaf, 258
Lots-of-Olives Meatloaf, 255
Meat and Potatoes Meatloaf, 255
Meatloaf Baked in Bread, 255
Meatloaf Cupcakes, 254
Meatloaf Dijonnaise, 255
Meatloaf with Easy Tomato Sauce, 256
Meatloaf with Spinach and Ricotta, 255
Mexican Meatloaf, 255
Mom's Meatloaf, 254
Prosciutto and Cheese Meatloaf, 255
Reduced-Calorie Meatloaf, 254
Roasted Pepper and Basil Meatloaf, 255
Sausage Meatloaf, 255
Smoked Turkey Meatloaf, 298
Surprise Meatloaf, 254
Sweet-and-Sour Meatloaf, 255
Wild Mushroom Meatloaf, 255
ribs
Braised Short Ribs, 70
Jerk Ribs, 270
Pot au Feu, 72
roasts
Anise Braised Beef, 481
Barbecued Beef, 71
Beef Sirloin Roast, 479
Fragrant Slow-Cooked Beef, 480
Greek Beef, 481
Jerk Roasted Beef, 480
Pot Roast, 71
Rib Roast of Beef with Garlic, 477
Rib Roast with Braised Wild Mushrooms, 478
Rib Roast with Creamy Horseradish Sauce, 477
Rib Roast with Garlic Jus, 477
Rib Roast with Roasted Potatoes and Capers, 477
Rib Roast with Rosemary Red Wine Glaze, 477
Rib Roast with Yorkshire Pudding, 477
Roast Sirloin with Porter Barbecue Sauce, 479
Roast Sirloin with Spicy Coffee Elixir, 480
Slow-Roasted Shoulder of Beef with Chili Rub, 480
Spicy Peanut Beef, 480
sandwiches
Roast Beef on Rye with Horseradish Sauce, 87
Roast Beef Pita Pocket, 98
Steak Sandwich with Béarnaise, 493
sauces for, 54–55
Sicilian Oven-Braised Top Round Beef, 480

beef (*continued*)
Spaghetti with Stir-Fried Meat Sauce, 167
steaks
Blackened Beef Steaks with Fennel Seed, 43
Filet Panier with Wine Butter Sauce, 91
Flank Steak Roasted with Portobello Mushrooms, 479
Flank Steak Stuffed with Wild Rice, 479
Grilled Steak with Caramelized Garlic, 144
Teriyaki London Broil, 100
stews
Barbecued Beef Stew, 261
Beef and Vegetable Stew, 260
Beef and Wild Mushroom Stew, 261
Beef Stew, 260
Beef Stew Provençal, 262
Beef Stew with Roasted Garlic, 260
Beef Stew with Rosemary and Ham, 261
Boeuf Bourguignonne, 262
Civet of Beef, 264
Sweet-and-Sour Beef Stew, 261
stir-fries
Beef and Mushrooms, 164
Orange Beef, 165
Stir-Fried Beef Barbecue, 165
tenderloin
Carpaccio, 175
Carpaccio Jalapeño, 176
Charred Rare Beef with Jalapeño Salsa, 471
Espresso-Rubbed Roast Tenderloin, 478
Pesto-Crusted Tenderloin with Roasted Pepper Rouille, 478
Roasted Beef Tenderloin with Caramelized Onions, 478
Roasted Beef Tenderloin with Scotch Jus, 478
Roasted Beef Tenderloin with Wasabi Steak Sauce, 478
Roasted Whole Tenderloin of Beef, 478
beets
Baked Beets, 68
Carrot and Beet Latkes, 350
Creole Beet Salad, 183
Honey-Baked Beets, 387
Orange-Garlic Beets, 388
Three-Can Salad, 174
Winter Tempura, 350
Belgian endive. *See* endive, Belgian
Bell Peppers Stuffed with Macaroni and Cheese, 120
berries. *See also specific types of berries*
Berries with Framboise Honey, 494
Berry Concassé, 449
Berry Wine Punch, 459
Fruit in Chocolate Cups, 530

berries (*continued*)
No-Fuss Fresh Berry Tart, 539
Peach Blackberry Crunch, 421
Plum and Blackberry Parfait, 419
Quick Berry Compote, 423
Sautéed Berry Syrup, 423
Summer Bounty Vinegar, 423
Summer Fruit with Lime Crème Anglaise, 417
Best-Ever Chocolate Pudding, 529
Beurre Blanc, 51
Beurre Rouge, 54
biscuits, 22, 431, 488
Bitter Chocolate Sauce, 446
Bitter Chocolate Torte, 528
Bitter Grapefruit Marmalade, 559
Black Bean and Bulgur Salad with Orange and Pepperoni, 364
Black Bean Falafel, 346
Black Bean Soup with Orange and Cilantro, 199
Black Bean Tacos, 345
Black-Bottom Raspberry Tart, 420
Black-Eyed Pea Chili, 206
Black Forest Chocolate Sauce, 446
Black Forest Pudding Cake, 527
Black Mustard, 39
Black Pepper Pilaf, 358
Blackened Beef Steaks with Fennel Seed, 43
Blackened Cajun Burgers, 131
Blanched Broccoli, 68
Blanched Cauliflower, 68
blanching, 8
Blanquette of Veal, 266
Blue Cheese Apple Cheesecake, 473
Blue Cheese Burgers, 131
Blue Cheese Dressing, 63
Blue Cheese Grapes, 467
Blue Cheese Mashed Potatoes, 390
Blue Cornsticks, 548
blueberries
Blueberries with Rum and Lemon, 417
Blueberry Buttermilk Pancakes, 416
Blueberry Orange Sauce, 448
Brandied Summer Fruit, 174
crisps and cobblers
Blueberry Shortcake Cobbler, 421
Gingered Berry Crisp, 421
Three-Berry Crisp, 421
Easy Blueberry Soup, 416
muffins
Blueberry Bran Muffins, 546
Blueberry Corn Muffins, 546
Blueberry Muffins, 543
Blueberry Sour Cream Corn Muffins, 416
Peaches Stuffed with Minted Blueberries, 418
pies and tarts
Blueberry Rhubarb Pie, 539
Blueberry Ricotta Tart, 539
Deep-Dish Blueberry and Raspberry Pot Pie, 419

blueberries
pies and tarts (*continued*)
Out-of-Season Blueberry Pie, 539
Raspberry Blueberry Pie, 539
Spiked Summer Fruit Salad, 417
bluefish
Bluefish Baked with Easy Mustard Sauce, 309
Fennel-Cured Bluefish, 174
Gingered Black Bean Bluefish, 503
Ranch-Style Bluefish, 309
Boeuf Bourguignonne, 262
Boiled Chicken with Mushrooms and Broad Noodles, 292
boiling, 11
Bolognese and Mozzarella Pizza, 215
Bolognese Sauce, 229
Bordelaise Sauce, 54
Bouillabaisse Roast Chicken, 274
bourbon
Honey Bourbon Sauce, 450
Mint Julep Iced Tea, 456
Mint Julep Slush, 458
Bourbon Chili, 206
Bourbon-Glazed Ham Steak with Apple Fritters, 428
Bourbon Pecan-Stuffed Baked Apples, 408
Bourbon Pecans, 450, 559
Bourbon-Spiked Peach and Praline "Bombe," 180
Bourbon Walnut Fig Bars, 553
Bourride, 322
Bourride of Orange Roughy, 314
Braised Belgian Endive, 373
Braised Endive with Ham, 373
Braised Fennel, 388
Braised Lemon Celery, 381
Braised Orange Fennel, 388
Braised Short Ribs, 70
braising, 8
bran. *See also* oat bran
Banana Bran Muffins, 545
Blueberry Bran Muffins, 546
Bran Muffins, 545
Buttermilk Bran Hotcakes, 512
Honey Bran Muffins, 546
Nutty Bran Muffins, 546
Raisin Bran Muffins, 545
Brandied Liver Mousse, 253
Brandied Peaches, 448
Brandied Summer Fruit, 174
brandy
Café Brûlot Slush, 458
Iced Spiked Cocoa, 457
Modern-Day Mead, 458
bratwurst, 130
Bratwurst with Apple Butter Mustard, 136
Bratwurst with Mustard Applesauce, 90
Bread and Pizza Dough, 20
bread puddings, 70, 100, 115, 247
breading, 8

breads, 20, 489, 513. *See also* biscuits; muffins; popovers
  quick, 39, 396–97, 432
Brie and Scallop Pizza, 220
Brioches with Chocolate Butter, 493
British Bacon, 428
broccoli
  Apple Broccoli Bisque, 196
  Blanched Broccoli, 68
  Broccoli and Apple Sauté, 406
  Broccoli Stem Crudités with Warm Tofu Vinaigrette, 513
  Broccoli with Apples and Bacon, 377
  Broccoli with Cider and Rosemary, 377
  Broccoli with Walnuts, 378
  Curried Cabbage Flowers, 42
  Garden Pâté, 465
  Garden Vegetable Whole-Grain Tempura, 518
  Garlicky Pasta Primavera, 119
  Indian Braised Vegetables, 381
  Make-Your-Own Pizza, 99
  Steamed Vegetable Salad with Lemon Dill Dressing, 184
  Stir-Fried Broccoli and Apples, 517
  Stir-Fried Broccoli with Hoisin Almonds, 168
  Stir-Fried Curried Vegetables, 166
  Vitamin A Tempura, 518
  Whole Wheat Pasta Boiled with Broccoli, Ricotta and Roasted Peppers, 521
broccoli rabe (rapini)
  Baked Rabe Romano, 245
  Broccoli Rabe Soufflé, 372
  Broccoli Rabe with Garlic and Olive Oil, 372
  Broccoli Rabe with Raisins and Pine Nuts, 372
  Rabe and Peppers Baked in Bread, 512
  Rabe Baked with Potatoes and Feta Cheese, 245
Brochettes of Shark, Sturgeon and Salmon, 316
Broiled Corn with Roasted Garlic, 396
Broiled Fish with Lemon Ranch Dressing, 329
Broiled Fish with Walnut Butter, 327
Broiled Honey Mustard Chicken, 286
Broiled Ranch-Style Chicken Breasts, 288
Broiled Red Snapper with Green Chili Cream Sauce, 316
Broiled Swordfish Steak with Mignonette Sauce, 317
broiling, 10
broths, 6, 18–19, 69
Brown Beans and Rice, 519
Brown Butter, 68
Brown Curry Duck, 267
Brown Rice and Roasted Pepper Salad, 349

Brown Rice and Vegetable Pilaf, 359
Brown Rice Pilaf, 359
Brown Rice Pudding, 361
Brown Rice Risotto with Sage and Potatoes, 520
Brown Rice with Red Beans, 124
Brown Rice with Three Cheeses, 124
Brown Rice with Toasted Coconut, 359
Brown Rice with Wheat Berries, 359
Brown Rice–Dried Fruit Stuffing, 298
Brown Sugar Bourbon Roast Chicken, 278
Brown Sugar Pecan Muffins, 545
brownies, 524–25, 553, 554
browning, 8
Brussels Sprouts, Stir-Fried, 375
Brussels Sprouts Sautéed with Bacon and Apples, 375
Brussels Sprouts Simmered in Milk, 375
Buckwheat Pancakes with Sour Cream and Caviar, 429
Buffalo Drumsticks, 293
Buffalo "Fins," 323
Buffalo Fries, 391
Buffalo Turkey, 302
bulgur
  Black Bean and Bulgur Salad with Orange and Pepperoni, 364
  Bulgur Tortellini Salad, 186
  Grilled Lamb and Tabbouleh Salad, 186
  Grilled Scallops and Shrimp Tabbouleh, 187
  Health Wraps, 87
  Leftovers Tabbouleh, 112
  Middle Eastern Bulgur Orzo Salad, 186
  Mixed Herb Tabbouleh, 186
  Tabbouleh with Lentils, 365
  Turkey Tabbouleh, 301
burgers, 102, 121, 128–34
butter, 5, 68
  flavored, 16, 82–83, 561
Butter Cookies, 438
Butter Rum Raisin Sauce, 450
butterfish. *See* pompano
Buttermilk Biscuits, 431
Buttermilk Biscuits with a Heart, 488
Buttermilk Bran Hotcakes, 512
Buttermilk Coffee Cake, 433
Buttermilk Pumpkin Pie, 540
Buttermilk Spoon Bread with Garlic, 362
Butternut Squash Soup with Ginger Cream, 195
Butterscotch Oaties, 443

C

cabbage
  Bacon and Fruit Slaw, 187
  Cabbage Stuffed with Orzo and Cheese, 125

cabbage (*continued*)
  Codfish and Cabbage, 502
  Corned Beef and Cabbage, 71
  Creole Coleslaw, 187
  Dilly Cabbage, 42
  Hash Browns and Cabbage, 391
  Leftover Fried Chicken Coleslaw, 112
  Red Cabbage Slaw, 187
  Sausage-Stuffed Cabbage, 125
  Soy Ginger Chicken Salad, 189
  Sweet-and-Sour Coleslaw, 187
  Sweet-and-Spicy Stuffed Red Cabbage, 125
  White Cabbage Slaw, 187
Caesar Salad Sandwiches, 94
Café Brûlot Slush, 458
Cajun Burgers, 130
Cajun Oysters, 488
Cajun Shrimp, 149
cakes, 22, 39, 412–13, 433–34, 526–28, 554–57
  techniques for, 13, 14
Calamari with Potatoes and Tomatoes, 343
Candied Ginger Apple Pie, 536
Candied Ginger Cream, 451
Candied Ginger Zucchini Muffins, 548
candies. *See* confections
Candy Store Jumbles, 437
cantaloupe. *See* melon
Capered Tomato Sauce, 109
Capers and Brown Butter Sauce, 54
Caponata, 352
Cappuccino Cocoa, 458
Caramel Peach Ice Cream, 419
Caramel Pear Preserves, 560
Caramelized Onion and Gorgonzola Pizza, 221
Caramelized Szechuan Hen, 492
Caraway Potato Soup, 196
Caraway Raisin Soda Bread, 39
Caraway Sauerkraut, 375
Carbonara Sauce, 231
Cardamom Apricot Pound Cakes, 555
Cardamom Currant Cookies, 439
Cardamom Pear Cake, 412
Cardamom Tea Cake, 39
Carpaccio, 175
Carpaccio Jalapeño, 176
Carpaccio Tonnato, 176
carrots
  Carrot, Parsnip and Chives, 388
  Carrot and Beet Latkes, 350
  Carrot and Red Pepper, 388
  Cumin Carrots, 388
  Garden Pâté, 465
  Garden Vegetable Whole-Grain Tempura, 518
  Gingered Carrot Marmalade, 560
  Gingered Carrot Salad, 183
  Gingered Carrots with Hot Pepper Vinaigrette, 467
  Julienned Peppers and Carrots, 55

carrots (*continued*)
muffins
Carrot Muffins, 548
Currant Carrot Muffins, 548
Orange Carrot Muffins, 548
Precooked Beans or Carrots, 69
Stir-Fried Carrots with Mint and
Red Pepper, 168
Stir-Fried Sesame Vegetables, 507
Vegetable Broth, 19
Vitamin A Tempura, 518
Cashew Date Butter, 83
casseroles, 123, 235–47, 299
catfish
Barbecued Catfish, 309
Catfish Corn Stew, 263
Cilantro Catfish Soup, 41
Pecan Catfish Fingers and Sweet
Potato Chips, 309
cauliflower
Blanched Cauliflower, 68
Cauliflower in Mustard Cream,
378
Cauliflower with Capers, 378
Curried Cabbage Flowers, 42
Curried Cauliflower, 378
Garden Vegetable Whole-Grain
Tempura, 518
Indian Braised Vegetables, 381
Spanish Cauliflower, 81
Steamed Vegetable Salad with
Lemon Dill Dressing, 184
Stir-Fried Caramelized Cauliflower
and Cashews, 378
Stir-Fried Curried Vegetables, 166
Stir-Fried Pasta Primavera, 167
Caviar Coeur à la Crème, 489
Cayenne Pepper Gingerbread, 40
celery
Braised Lemon Celery, 381
Celery-Top Seasoning Mix, 109
Orange and Celery Salad, 183
Vegetable Broth, 19
celery root (celeriac)
Celery Parsnip Latkes, 350
Potato and Celeriac Gratin, 389
Potato Celeriac Purée, 390
cereals (breakfast), 70, 425–26
Champagne Granita, 494
"Champagne" with Grapefruit Ice,
459
Charbroiled Sirloin Chili, 204
Charcuterie Dry Rub, 35
chard
Chard with Chorizo, 374
Cheesy Greens Casserole, 245
Gratin of Chard, 374
Leek and Chard Soufflé, 355
Sautéed Spring Greens, 374
Charred Rare Beef with Jalapeño
Salsa, 471
Charred Rare Lamb with Roasted
Garlic, 471
Cheddar Corn Muffins, 546
Cheddar Corn Soufflé, 126

Cheddar Fondue with Apples, Pickles
and Toast, 355
cheese
Blue Cheese Grapes, 467
Cheddar Corn Soufflé, 126
Cheddar Fondue with Apples,
Pickles and Toast, 355
cheesecakes, 14
Blue Cheese Apple Cheesecake,
473
Eight-Hour Brandy Cheesecake,
473
Spiked Smoked Salmon and
Gruyère Cheesecake, 472
coeur à la crème
Caviar Coeur à la Crème, 489
Coeur à la Crème Doux, 495
Smoked Salmon Coeur à la
Crème, 489
Cottage Cheese Pancakes, 103
Cream Cheese Pastry, 20
dips and spreads
Angel-of-Death Cheese, 466
Baked Brie with Croissants, 492
Garlic Cheese, 466
Gorgonzola Mousse, 84
Lemon Cheese, 466
Spicy Cheese Dip, 83
Fontina Fondue with Garlic Roasted
Potatoes, 354
Harvest Quiche, 384
Hominy Soufflé, 362
Marinated Mozzarella, 466
Marinated Mozzarella, Olives and
Sun-Dried Tomatoes, 92
Marinated Mozzarella Salad in
Tomatoes, 351
muffins, breads and biscuits
Cheddar Corn Muffins, 546
Cheese-Filled Biscuits, 431
Ham and Cheese Muffins, 550
Herb Cheese Muffins, 550
Herbed Biscuits with a Secret, 488
Pepper Cheddar Skillet
Cornbread, 556
Ricotta Rosemary Muffins, 550
Three-Cheese Popovers, 432
pasta dishes
Baked Shells Stuffed with Tuna
and Cheese, 239
Cheese Gnocchi with Fresh
Tomato Sauce, 353
Crusty Macaroni and Cheese, 120
Extra-Cheesy Extra-Crusty Mac
and Cheese, 236
Fettuccine with Ricotta and
Spinach, 119
Gorgonzola and Prosciutto au
Gratin, 241
Mild Macaroni and Cheese, 101
Noodles and Cheese, 101
Real Mac and Cheese for the
Whole Family, 236
Real Macaroni and Cheese, 236
Stuffed Shells, 121

cheese (*continued*)
pastries
Cheese Pockets, 468
Cheese Straws, 468
Puff Pastry Mini Pizzas, 468
pizza
Brie and Scallop Pizza, 220
French Bread Pizza, 81
Gorgonzola and Onion French
Bread Pizza, 82
Make-Your-Own Pizza, 99
Marinated Feta and Artichoke
Heart Pizza, 220
Marinated Mozzarella Pizza, 222
Pizza Rustica, 354
Ricotta and Roasted Red Pepper
Pizza, 216
Sweet Ricotta Dessert Pizza, 223
puddings
Cheesy Bread Pudding, 100
Mascarpone Spoon Bread, 362
Mexican Torta, 247
Provençal Ricotta Bread Pudding,
247
Southwest Bread Pudding, 247
Ricotta Cheese Pancakes, 429
sandwiches
Baked Brie Sandwiches, 90
Chèvre and Roasted Pepper Mini-
Sandwiches, 93
Chèvre and Sun-Dried Tomato
Open-Face Sandwiches, 90
Gorgonzola Grinders, 92
Grilled Cheddar and Apple, 98
Grilled Cheese, Bacon and Tomato
Sandwiches, 90
Grilled Chèvre and Smoked
Salmon on Bagels, 90
Grilled Muenster with Pickles, 98
Marinated Mozzarella Grinders, 92
Souffléd Cottage Cheese
Sandwiches, 431
Vegetable Spread for Sandwiches,
98
sauces and dressings
Blue Cheese Dressing, 63
Carbonara Sauce, 231
Cheese and Cream Sauce, 229
Feta and Artichoke Sauce, 227
Mornay Sauce (Cheese Sauce), 17
Ricotta and Roasted Red Pepper
Sauce, 226
Roquefort Dressing, 64
Warm Blue Cheese Dressing, 64
Shredded Cheese, 74
Sweet Cream Cheese Pastry, 441
Cheesy Baked Chili, 204
Cheesy Chicken Burgers, 132
Cheesy Greens Casserole, 245
cherries
Black Forest Pudding Cake, 527
Brandied Summer Fruit, 174
Cherries in Orange Honey over
Melon, 180
Cherry Chocolate Fondue, 418

cherries (*continued*)
  Cherry Shortcake with Ricotta Basil
    Filling, 422
  Dried Cherry, Tarragon and
    Almond Dessert Pizza, 223
  Dried Cherry Bars, 442
  pies
    Anise Cherry Pie, 538
    Hazelnut Cherry Pie, 538
    Open-Face Cherry Pie, 539
  sauces and dressings
    Black Forest Chocolate Sauce, 446
    Cherry Fennel Compote, 84
    Cherry Tarragon Compote, 48
    Sour Cherry Coulis, 447
    Summer Bounty Vinegar, 423
    Spiked Summer Fruit Salad, 417
    Summer Fruit with Lime Crème
      Anglaise, 417
Cherry Tomato and Caramelized
  Onion Salad, 400
Chewy Chocolate Chip Cookies, 436
Chewy Gooey Lemon Pecan Bars, 442
chicken, 8–9, 28–35, 50–57. *See also*
  chicken, whole; chicken livers
Barbecued Chicken, 141
breasts, 9
  Asian Chicken Paillards, 143
  Broiled Honey Mustard Chicken,
    286
  Broiled Ranch-Style Chicken
    Breasts, 288
  Chicken and Shrimp in Garlic
    Black Bean Sauce, 150
  Chicken Baked in Foil with Clams,
    285
  Chicken Breast Steamed with Basil
    Leaves, 38
  Chicken Breasts Sautéed in Capers
    and Brown Butter, 285
  Chicken Breasts Stuffed with
    Herbed Cheese, 288
  Chicken Breasts with Vodka,
    Tomatoes and Cream, 287
  Chicken Fajitas, 99
  Chicken Fingers with Roasted
    Pepper Dip, 492
  Chicken Lemon Véronique, 287
  Chicken Paillards with Artichoke
    Pesto, 153
  Chicken Steamed with Roasted
    Pepper and Cilantro, 499
  Chicken Tandoori Brochettes,
    470
  Chicken Wellington, 470
  Chicken with Ginger, Soy and
    Chives, 41
  Chicken with Lemon and Capers,
    151
  Chicken with Lime Avocado
    Relish, 152
  Chicken with Sun-Dried Tomato
    Rouille, 152
  Chilled Grilled Creamy Garlic
    Chicken Breasts, 142

chicken
  breasts (*continued*)
    Chilled Grilled Marinated Chicken
      Breasts, 286
    Curried Tandoori-Style Chicken,
      499
    Deviled Chicken Breasts, 152
    Garlic Hazelnut Chicken, 152
    "Grilled" Chicken Anchoiade, 153
    Grilled Chicken Breast with
      Buttermilk and Chervil, 40
    Grilled Chicken Breast with
      Buttermilk and Herbs, 516
    Grilled Chicken Breasts with
      Artichoke Relish, 286
    Grilled Chicken Breasts with Bitter
      Greens and Pine Nuts, 189
    "Grilled" Chicken Breasts with
      Herbed Blue Cheese Dressing,
      154
    Grilled Chicken Breasts with
      Pesto, 142
    Grilled Chicken Breasts with
      Roasted Pepper Salsa, 286
    Grilled Chicken Breasts with
      Roquefort Dressing, 142
    Grilled Chicken Breasts with
      Tapenade, 286
    Grilled Chicken Breasts with
      Tomato-Dill Vinaigrette, 142
    Grilled Chicken with Red Pepper
      and Roasted Eggplant, 500
    Grilled Chicken with Spicy
      Artichoke Relish, 499
    Lemon Mushroom Chicken, 287
    Lime Cilantro Black Bean
      Chicken, 151
    Marinated Chicken Paillards, 153
    Pan-Barbecued Chicken Breasts,
      154
    Pan-Seared Chicken Breasts with
      Tomato Dill Salsa, 154
    Pecan Chicken Breasts with
      Mustard Sauce, 287
    Pesto-Glazed Broiled Chicken,
      286
    Poached Chicken Breasts in Beurre
      Blanc, 285
    Poached Chicken Breasts with
      Warm Tomato Vinaigrette, 149
    Sage and Rosemary Chicken
      Breast Meunière, 153
    Sautéed Chicken Breasts with
      Apple Glaze, 285
    Sautéed Chicken Breasts with
      Brandy Cream Reduction, 285
    Sautéed Chicken Breasts with
      Vermouth and Tarragon, 287
    Sesame Chicken Breasts, 153
    Spicy Peachy Chicken, 157
    Stuffing-Crusted Chicken Breasts
      with Sage Butter, 152
    Three-Olive Chicken, 154
  burgers
    Cheesy Chicken Burgers, 132

chicken
  burgers (*continued*)
    Chicken Burgers Laced with
      Brandy, 133
    Chicken Burgers with Mustard
      and Green Peppercorns, 132
  casseroles
    Chicken and Fennel Pot Pie, 244
    Chicken and Garlic Mash
      Shepherd's Pie, 242
    Chicken and Leek Pot Pie with
      Herb Biscuit Crust, 243
    Chicken Baked with Black Beans
      and Lime, 242
    Chicken Braised with Sauerkraut
      and Sausage, 243
    Chicken Couscous, 243
    Chicken Curry Baked with Lentils,
      244
    Oven-Braised Chicken with
      Apples and Red Cabbage, 243
    Pear and Chicken Pot Pie, 406
  Chicken and Olive Pizza, 221
  Chicken Spinach Potstickers, 250
  chilis
    Chocolate Chicken Chili, 208
    Chorizo Chicken Chili, 207
    Curried Chicken Chili, 207
    Leftover Chicken Chili, 111
    Quick Chicken Chili, 156
  frankfurters
    Chicken Franks with Gazpacho
      Salsa, 135
    Chicken Franks with Tomato
      Artichoke Salsa, 135
    Chicken or Turkey Franks with
      Avocado Salsa, 90
  fried chicken
    Italian Fried Chicken, 293
    Southern Fried Chicken, 292
    Sweet-and-Sour Fried Chicken,
      293
    Tangy Fried Chicken Breasts,
      288
  Grilled Chicken Basted with Sage,
    142
  Ground Chicken Fajitas, 157
  Herbed Chicken Pâté, 253
  leftovers
    Chicken and Gravy Frozen Dinner,
      114
    Leftover Barbecued Chicken Salad,
      141
    Leftover Fried Chicken Coleslaw,
      112
    Leftovers Escabèche, 113
  legs and thighs
    Anise Chicken Braised in a Wok,
      291
    Baked Chicken Legs with Balsamic
      Glaze, 293
    Boiled Chicken with Mushrooms
      and Broad Noodles, 292
    Buffalo Drumsticks, 293
    Chicken Braised with Cider, 154

chicken

legs and thighs (*continued*)

Chicken Braised with Red Wine and Mushrooms, 155

Chicken Braised with Spicy Peanut Sauce, 155

Chicken Cacciatore, 289

Chicken Chicharrones, 156

Chicken Crusted with Corn Flakes, 293

Chicken Legs and Sausage in Red Gravy, 292

Chicken Legs Braised with Garlic, 290

Chicken Legs Braised with Sauerkraut and Beer, 291

Chicken with Sausage and Clams, 150

Chili-Baked Chicken Drumsticks, 122

Garlic and Ginger Chicken Legs, 289

Garlic and Molasses Chicken Legs, 293

Grilled Ranch-Style Chicken Legs, 142

Mahogany Chicken, 156

Pan-Roasted Chicken Legs, 122

Parmesan-Coated Chicken Legs, 293

Thai Chicken, 155

Tuscan Chicken Legs, 122

salads

Barbecued Chicken or Pork Salad, 112

Barley Chicken Salad, 363

Chicken and Bean Salad, 111

Chicken and Noodle Salad with Peanut Sauce, 100

Chicken Cannellini Salad, 515

Chilied Chicken Salad, 206

Grilled Asian Chicken Salad, 143

Grilled Chicken Salad, 142

Middle Eastern Chicken Salad, 498

Old-Fashioned Chicken Salad, 284

Soy Ginger Chicken Salad, 189

Warm Grilled Chicken Salad on Wilted Lettuce, 284

Yogurt Dill Chicken Salad, 284

sandwiches

Barbecued Chicken Sandwich, 141

Chicken and Grapes Lettuce Pockets, 99

Chicken Chickpea Salad Pitas, 95

sauces and gravies

Chicken and Olive Sauce, 232

Chicken Glace, 109

Chicken Gravy, 17

soups and broths

Chicken and Corn Chowder, 294

Chicken Broth, 18

Chunky Chicken Minestrone, 294

Creamy Chicken Soup with Lemon and Mint, 294

Leftovers Chicken Noodle Soup, 110

chicken

soups and broths (*continued*)

Leftovers Chicken Rice Soup, 110

Lemon Chicken Soup, 110

Meaty Chicken Noodle Soup, 294

Slow-Cooked Chicken Broth, 69

Vegetable Top and Chicken Carcass Soup, 110

stews

Barbecued Chicken Stew, 261

Chicken and Sausage Gumbo, 290

Chicken Pot au Feu with Sausage, 292

Chicken Provençal, 262

Chicken Stewed with Parsley Dumplings, 290

Chilied Chicken Stew, 207

Civet of Chicken, 264

Coq au Vin, 262

Mediterranean Chicken Stew, 265

Moroccan Chicken Stew, 291

stir-fries

Chicken with Glazed Red Pepper, 163

Chicken with Rosemary and Sage, 163

Creamy, Corny Chicken Stir-Fry, 164

Orange Chicken with Apricots, 163

Peanut Chicken, 166

Red Curry Chicken, 166

Stir-Fried Caramel Chicken, 164

Stir-Fried Chicken Chicory Salad, 498

Stir-Fried Chicken in Orange Black Bean Sauce, 500

Stir-Fried Chicken with Apples and Walnuts, 113

Stir-Fried Chicken with Cashews, 151

Stir-Fried Garlic Chicken with Noodles, 168

Sweet Anise Chicken, 164

Sweet-and-Sour Apricot Chicken, 100

thighs (*see* legs and thighs)

wings

Garlic Black Bean Chicken Wings, 470

Ginger Black Bean Chicken Wings, 288

Mahogany Chicken Wings, 288

Smoky Spicy Honey Wings, 288

Spicy Molasses Chicken Wings, 470

Spicy Thai Wings, 289

Super Hot Mustard Wings, 289

chicken, whole

Anchovy Mustard Roast Chicken, 273

Apple Rosemary Roast Chicken, 275

Barbecued Roast Chicken, 276

Bouillabaisse Roast Chicken, 274

chicken, whole (*continued*)

Brown Sugar Bourbon Roast Chicken, 278

Chicken Roasted with White Clam Sauce, 277

Cranberry Orange Roast Chicken, 279

Enchilada Roast Chicken, 274

Garlic Roast Chicken, 273

Hazelnut Lemon Roast Chicken, 276

Honey Mustard Roast Chicken, 275

Horseradish and Garlic Roast Chicken, 273

Jerk Roast Chicken, 279

Lebanese Chicken, 277

Lemon Cilantro Roast Chicken, 276

Lemon Coriander Chicken, 273

Lime and Coriander Roast Chicken, 41

Mahogany Roast Chicken, 276

Orange Chinese Roast Chicken, 275

Pesto Roast Chicken, 273

Pot au Feu, 72

Poussin Roasted with Garlic and Molasses, 491

Ranch Roast Chicken, 278

Red Curry Roast Chicken, 278

Roast Chicken Cacciatore, 274

Roast Chicken Chasseur, 280

Roast Chicken in Spicy Peanut Paste, 274

Roast Chicken Provençal, 277

Roast Chicken Véronique, 280

Roast Chicken with Apple Butter Glaze, 279

Roast Chicken with Bread, Sage and Apple Stuffing, 281

Roast Chicken with Capers and Lemon, 273

Roast Chicken with Clam and Cracker Stuffing, 281

Roast Chicken with Cranberry Cornbread Stuffing, 281

Roast Chicken with Dried Fruit Stuffing, 282

Roast Chicken with Fines Herbes, 278

Roast Chicken with Horseradish Mustard, 273

Roast Chicken with Molasses and Vinegar, 276

Roast Chicken with Orange Glaze, 277

Roast Chicken with Sherry Balsamic Glaze, 280

Roast Chicken with Tarragon and Brandy, 278

Roast Chicken with Vanilla Sauce, 280

Roast Chicken with Wild Mushroom Stuffing, 280

Roast Tandoori-Style Chicken, 279

Roasted Garlic Roast Chicken, 278

chicken, whole (*continued*)
  Sage and Rosemary Roast Chicken, 273
  Sesame Ginger Roast Chicken, 279
  Spicy Pineapple Lime Roast Chicken, 275
  Traditional Large Roast Chicken, 272
  Traditional Small Roast Chicken, 272
  Tropical Sweet-and-Sour Roast Chicken, 275
  Tuscan Chicken, 273
  Worcestershire Mustard Roast Chicken, 273
Chicken Barley Soup, 192
chicken livers
  Brandied Liver Mousse, 253
  Chopped Liver, 73
  Country Pâté, 252
  Dirty Rice, 358
  Grilled Chicken Livers with Worcestershire Marinade, 143
  A Little Chopped Liver, 114
  Liver and Bacon Mini Turnovers, 469
  Quick Chopped Chicken Liver, 466
  Risotto with Mushrooms and Chicken Livers, 360
  Warm Spinach Salad with Chicken Livers, 368
Chicken Matzo Ball Soup, 193
Chicken Noodle Soup, 192
Chicken Soup with Three Rices, 192
Chicken Soup with Tortellini, 192
chickpeas
  Chicken Chickpea Salad Pitas, 95
  Hummus Tahini, 179
  Mixed Grilled Vegetables with Hummus, 125
  Pita Filled with Toasted Chickpeas, Avocado and Eggplant "Caviar," 346
  Protein-Packed Cornbread, 512
  salads
    Chicken and Bean Salad, 111
    Chickpea, Tomato and Onion Salad, 515
    Chickpea and Red Onion Salad, 515
    Southwest Garbanzo Turkey Salad, 189
  Shrimp Chili with Chickpeas, 209
  soups
    Lemon Chickpea Soup, 197
    Middle Eastern Chickpea Soup, 348
    Minestrone with Beans, 194
    Spicy Chickpea Soup, 348
  Spiced Sesame Chickpeas, 519
chicory. *See* greens
children's dishes, 96–105
chili, 201–211
  fish and seafood, 208–9, 210, 330
  meat, 72, 111, 203–6, 210, 211, 251

chili (*continued*)
  poultry, 102, 111, 156, 203, 207–8, 211
  vegetable, 202–3, 330
Chili and Corn Chowder, 348
Chili-Baked Chicken Drumsticks, 122
Chili Cheese Dogs, 135
Chili Grilled Lobster, 141
Chili Gumbo, 210
Chili Inferno, 204
Chili Mango Sorbet, 413
Chili Marinade, 35
Chili Pasta Salad, 111
Chili Pepper Chutney, 40
Chili Pumpkin Seeds, 79
Chili Salad, 400
Chili with Beer, 204
Chili with Cornmeal Dumplings, 204
Chilied Chicken Salad, 206
Chilied Chicken Stew, 207
Chilied Clams, 210
Chilied Corn and Peanut Sauce, 396
Chilied Corn Enchiladas, 346
Chilied Corn Salad Stuffed in Roasted Peppers, 352
Chilied Grilled Sturgeon Fillets, 316
Chilied Hash Browns, 391
Chilied Meatloaf with Chorizo, 254
Chilied Scallop Kebabs, 208
Chilied Scampi with Cannellini, 209
Chilled Crab and Chive Soufflé, 472
Chilled Curried Zucchini Soup, 397
Chilled Garden Soup with Celery, 40
Chilled Grilled Creamy Garlic Chicken Breasts, 142
Chilled Grilled Marinated Chicken Breasts, 286
Chilled Poached Fish with Citrus Vinaigrette, 322
Chilled Poached Fish with Creamy Cucumbers, 323
Chilled Salmon Soufflé, 472
Chilled Tomato and Roasted Pepper Soup, 174
Chilled Watercress Soup, 374
Chinese Roasted Pears, 409
Chinese Shrimp Chili, 209
Chipotle Cherry Pork, 156
Chipotle Peanut Marinade, 34
Chipotle Turkey, 150
chips, 80, 104, 145, 309, 391, 532
chocolate, 14. *See also* chocolate, white
  bars, squares and brownies
    Chocolate Fruit Squares, 532
    Chocolate Gingerbread, 525
    Chocolate Orange Liqueur Brownies, 525
    Chocolate Peanut Butter Squares, 443
    Date Nut Brownies, 524
    Orange Liqueur Brownies, 554
    Three-Layer Brownies, 525
    Unbelievably Amazing Brownies, 524

chocolate
  bars, squares and brownies (*continued*)
    Very Nutty Brownies, 524
  cakes and muffins
    Bitter Chocolate Torte, 528
    Black Forest Pudding Cake, 527
    Chocolate Almond Torte, 527
    Chocolate Apricot Torte, 528
    Chocolate Black Pepper Pound Cake, 526
    Chocolate Brandy Pudding Cake, 527
    Chocolate Soufflé Cake, 526
    Devil's Food Layer Cake, 526
    French Chocolate Cake, 528
    Gâteau Bordeaux, 528
    MeMe's Chocolate Roll, 528
    Mocha Torte, 526
    Raspberry Chocolate Chip Muffins, 544
  Cherry Chocolate Fondue, 418
  Chocolate Chip Pancakes, 103
  Chocolate Glaze, 23, 527
  Chocolate Ice Cream with Raspberry Swirl, 531
  Chocolate Liquor Fondue on a Grill, 146
  Chocolate Sour Cream Frosting, 24
  confections
    Chocolate-Covered Almond Apricots, 531
    Chocolate-Covered Potato Chips, 532
    Chocolate-Covered Pretzel "Porcupines," 532
    Chocolate-Covered Prunes with Marzipan "Pits," 531
    Chocolate Peanut Crunch Balls, 532
    Chocolate Peanut Grahams, 532
    Heavy-Duty Hazelnut Truffles, 557
  cookies
    Chewy Chocolate Chip Cookies, 436
    Chocolate Butter Cookies, 439
    Chocolate Chocolate Chip Cookies, 437
    Chocolate Chocolate Chunk Cookies, 524
    Chocolate Chunk Cookies, 437
    Chocolate-Covered Chocolate Chip Cookies, 532
    Chocolate Crescents, 441
    Chocolate Macaroons, 438
    Chocolate Peanut Jumbles, 438
    Chocolate Pistachio Drops, 437
    Espresso Oatmeal Chocolate Chip Cookies, 437
    Peanut Chocolate Drops, 523
    S'mores, 532
    Triple Chocolate Drops, 523
    Walnut Butter Jumbles, 437
    Walnut Chocolate Chip Shortbread, 441

chocolate (*continued*)
dips and spreads
Brioches with Chocolate Butter, 493
Chocolate Pâté, 529
Chocolate Peanut Butter, 83
Dipping Chocolate, 531
Microwave Chocolate Dip, 83
Raisin Chocolate Chip Peanut Butter, 561
drinks
Cappuccino Cocoa, 458
High-Protein Chocolate Peanut Butter Shake, 104
Iced Mocha, 457
Iced Spiked Cocoa, 457
Liquid Chocolate Bars, 458
Real Hot Chocolate Spiked with Scotch, 523
Xylophone Milk, 104
fruit desserts
Chocolate-Dipped Strawberries, 532
Fruit in Chocolate Cups, 530
Triple-Dipped Strawberries, 418
Melted Chocolate, 68
pies and tarts
Black-Bottom Raspberry Tart, 420
Chocolate Almond Pie, 541
Chocolate Bourbon Pecan Pie, 529
Chocolate Peanut Butter Pie, 541
Chocolate Peanut Pie, 528
Chocolate Raspberry Tart, 539
Chocolate Strawberry Tartlets, 420
Completely Decadent Chocolate Tart, 541
Double Chocolate Pudding Pie, 540
Sinful Chocolate Tartlets, 495
puddings and mousses
Best-Ever Chocolate Pudding, 529
Chocolate Bread Pudding, 115
Chocolate Chocolate Chip Pudding, 529
Chocolate Coronary, 474
Chocolate Hazelnut Pudding, 529
Chocolate Mousse with Chocolate Dumplings, 530
Chocolate Mousse with Dark Rum, 530
Peaches Stuffed with Chocolate Mousse, 418
Spiked Chocolate Mousse, 530
Triple Chocolate Parfait, 531
sauces and toppings
Bitter Chocolate Sauce, 446
Black Forest Chocolate Sauce, 446
Chocolate Banana Sauce, 445
Chocolate Chip Whipped Cream, 451
Chocolate Custard Sauce, 447
Chocolate Mint Sauce, 445
Chocolate Raspberry Sauce, 446
Chocolate Rum Sauce, 446
Hot Fudge Sauce, 445

chocolate
sauces and toppings (*continued*)
Milk Chocolate Sauce, 445
Milk Chocolate Sauce with Almonds, 445
Mocha Sauce, 445
Orange Chocolate Sauce, 446
Peanut Butter Chocolate Sauce, 445
Peppered Chocolate Sauce, 446
Praline Chocolate Caramel Sauce, 446
Quick Dark Chocolate Sauce, 445
savory dishes
Chocolate Chicken Chili, 208
Civet of Beef, 264
Civet of Chicken, 264
Duck Mole Chili, 210
Lamb Mole Chili, 210
Turkey Mole Chili, 208
Unhealthy Snack Mix, 80
chocolate, white
Grand Marnier White Chocolate Truffles, 496
Honey Brandy White Chocolate Mousse, 530
Peaches and White Chocolate Mousse in Chocolate Cups, 530
Raspberry White Chocolate Sauce, 446
Triple Chocolate Parfait, 531
Triple-Dipped Strawberries, 418
Warm White Chocolate Egg Nog, 457
White Chocolate Amaretto Pudding, 529
White Chocolate Brownies, 524
White Chocolate Brownies with Chocolate-Dipped Almonds, 525
White Chocolate Chunk Cookies, 437
White Chocolate Ice Cream, 531
White Chocolate Rice Pudding, 115
White Chocolate Sauce, 446
Chocolate Ice Cream Cupcakes, 105
Chopped Garlic, 74
Chopped Liver, 73
Chopped Onion, 74
Chunky Applesauce, 407
Chunky Beef Chili, 204
Chunky Chicken Minestrone, 294
chutneys, 40, 559. *See also* relishes
Cider Syrup, 558
cilantro (fresh)
Coriander Marinade, 35
Lemon Cilantro Marinade, 28
Yogurt Cilantro Dressing, 65
Cinnamon Rolls with Spiced Brown Sugar Butter, 493
Cinnamon Swirl Muffins, 544
Citrus Dry Rub, 35
Citrus Oil, 558
Citrus Seltzer, 454
Citrus Vinaigrette, 322
Civet of Beef, 264

Civet of Chicken, 264
clams, 8, 11, 332
Barbecued Steamed Clams, 338
Chilied Clams, 210
Clam, Ham and Orzo Pie, 241
Clam and Leek Pizza, 220
Clams Casino, 336
Clams in Tomato Vinaigrette, 336
Clams Steamed in Tomato Broth, 504
Clams with Capers and Lemon, 337
Curried Clams, 337
Fast Clam Sauce, 232
Ginger Soy Clams, 337
Grilled Tea-Steamed Clams and Mussels, 140
Hoisin Clams, 337
Niçoise Clams, 337
Puerto Rican Clams, 338
soups and stews
Clam and Fish Stew with Lots of Basil, 330
Italian Clam Soup, 198
Manhattan Clam Chowder, 198
Mexican Bouillabaisse, 263
New England Clam Chowder, 198
Seafood Pot au Feu, 506
Spicy Black Bean Clams, 338
Steamed Clams with Garam Masala, 43
Tea-Smoked Mussels and Clams, 504
Tex-Mex Clams, 338
Classic Apple Pie, 535
Classic Caesar Dressing, 62
Classic Caesar Salad, 182
Classic Mashed Potatoes, 389
Classic Minestrone, 194
Classic Peach Pie, 538
Classic Pumpkin Pie, 540
Classic Turkey Salad, 301
Clear Coleslaw Dressing, 62
cobblers, 44, 421
coconut
Coconut Macaroons, 438
Coconut Snowballs, 439
Toasted Coconut, 68
cod
Cod and Avocado Salad, 310
Codfish and Cabbage, 502
Microwaved Mediterranean Cod, 310
Coeur à la Crème Doux, 495
coffee
Café Brûlot Slush, 458
Cappuccino Cocoa, 458
Coffee Custard Sauce, 447
Espresso Anise Bombe, 495
Espresso Granita, 180
Iced Espresso with Rum, 457
Iced Mocha, 457
Mocha Sauce, 445
Mocha Torte, 526
Orange, Scotch and Espresso Sauce, 451

coffee cakes, 412–13, 433–34
Cold Crab and Avocado Tacos, 95
Cold Sage Sauce, 176
Cold Sliced Meats with Red and
   Green Sauces, 113
Completely Decadent Chocolate Tart,
   541
Composed Salad of Grilled
   Vegetables, 184
compotes, 48, 84, 423
confections, 496, 531–32, 557, 559
Confetti Brown Rice, 359
Confetti of Prosciutto, Peas and
   Rosemary, 52
Confetti Salsa, 177
cookies, 127, 435–43, 523–24, 553,
   554
Coq au Vin, 262
Coriander Marinade, 35
corn. *See also* cornmeal; popcorn
   Broiled Corn with Roasted Garlic,
     396
   Chilied Corn and Peanut Sauce, 396
   Chilied Corn Enchiladas, 346
   Corn and Green Chili Muffins, 547
   Corn and Smoked Salmon, 396
   Corn Chili, 203
   Corn on the Cob with Paprika
     Butter, 396
   Corn with Ham and Sweet Peppers,
     169
   Garden Corn Muffins, 547
   Grilled Corn, 145
   salads
     Chilied Corn Salad Stuffed in
       Roasted Peppers, 352
     Corn, Black Bean and Roasted
       Tomato Salad, 118
     Corn and Lentil Salad, 118
     Corn Chili Salad, 364
     Crab and Corn Slaw, 187
     Succotash Salad, 364
   soups and stews
     Catfish Corn Stew, 263
     Chicken and Corn Chowder, 294
     Chili and Corn Chowder, 348
     Spicy Corn Relish, 559
     Tomato and Corn Salsa, 403
Corn Cakes, Grilled Honey, 146
Corn Toast, Honey-Dipped, 430
Cornbread Chili, 204
Corned Beef and Cabbage, 71
Corned Beef and Potato Salad, 392
Corned Beef Deli Wraps, 87
cornmeal
   Apple, Bacon and Cornmeal
     Waffles, 430
   breads
     Apple Cheddar Cornbread, 407
     Bacon Cornsticks, 548
     Blue Cornsticks, 548
     Corn Popovers, 433
     Cornbread, 22
     Pepper Cheddar Skillet
       Cornbread, 556

cornmeal
  breads (*continued*)
    Pineapple Cornbread, 407
    Protein-Packed Cornbread, 512
    Spicy White Cornsticks, 548
    Zucchini Cornbread, 397
   Buttermilk Spoon Bread with
     Garlic, 362
   Cheddar Corn Soufflé, 126
   Mascarpone Spoon Bread, 362
   muffins
    Bacon and Apple Corn Muffins,
      547
    Blueberry Corn Muffins, 546
    Blueberry Sour Cream Corn
      Muffins, 416
    Cheddar Corn Muffins, 546
    Corn and Green Chili Muffins,
      547
    Cranberry Orange Corn Muffins,
      546
    Garden Corn Muffins, 547
    Pecan Corn Muffins, 547
    Pecan Peach Corn Muffins, 546
    Pepperoni Pepper Corn Muffins,
      547
   polenta
    Fontina Polenta, 362
    Fried Polenta with Tomato Sauce,
      362
    Polenta, 362
    Polenta with Green Salsa, 362
   Sweet-and-Spicy Cornmeal Mush, 426
Cottage Cheese Pancakes, 103
Country Pâté, 252
Court Bouillon, 18
crab, 332
  Baked Creole Crabmeat, 340
  Chilled Crab and Chive Soufflé, 472
  Crab, Tarragon and Chèvre Pizza,
    216
  Crab, Tarragon and Shallot Sauce,
    232
  Crab and Caviar Custard, 341
  Crab Cake Casserole, 240
  Crab Chili, 209
  Creole Crab Mini Turnovers, 469
  salads
    Crab, Orange and Black Bean
      Salad, 188
    Crab and Avocado Salad, 341
    Crab and Corn Slaw, 187
    Seafood Potato Salad, 185
    Tomato and Crab Salad, 401
  sandwiches
    Cold Crab and Avocado Tacos, 95
    Crab and Smoked Salmon Tea
      Sandwiches, 95
    Crab Cake Sandwiches with
      Creole Tartar Sauce, 90
    Italian Seafood Sandwiches, 342
    Soft-Shell Crab Sandwiches, 341
  Seafood Provençal, 148
  soups and stews
    Chili Gumbo, 210

crab
  soups and stews (*continued*)
    Crab Bisque, 198
    Hot-and-Sour Soup with Crab,
      200
    Quick Crab Chowder, 342
  Spicy Crab Popcorn, 79
  stir-fries
    Crab and Shrimp Stir-Fried with
      Lime and Grapes, 503
    Crab with Salsa, 163
    Stir-Fry of Crab and Asparagus,
      503
  whole, 10, 11
    Barbecued Soft-Shell Crabs, 141
    Escabèche of Soft-Shell Crab, 471
    Grilled Soft-Shell Crabs, 341
    Hard-Shell Crabs Cooked in Beer,
      504
    Marinated Soft-Shell Crabs, 341
    Middle Eastern Barbecued Soft-
      Shell Crabs, 504
    Middle Eastern Grilled Soft-Shell
      Crabs, 140
    Sautéed Soft-Shell Crabs with
      Lime Mayonnaise, 340
cranberries
  Cranberry Orange Corn Muffins,
    546
  Cranberry Pear Sauce, 407
  Orange Cranberry Marinade, 33
Cranberry Orange Roast Chicken, 279
Cranberry Turkey Burgers, 121
Cranberry Turkey Casserole, 299
Cranberry Turkey Meatballs, 121
cream, 195
Cream Cheese Pastry, 20
Cream of Chestnut Soup, 194
Cream of Mushroom Soup, 193
Cream of Spinach Soup, 369
Cream Puff and Éclair Pastry (Pâte à
   Choux), 22
Creamed Parsnips, 388
Creamed Spinach with Herb Cheese,
   369
Creamed Spinach with Wild
   Mushrooms, 370
Creamy, Corny Chicken Stir-Fry, 164
Creamy Avocado Dressing, 60
Creamy Caramel Sauce, 447
Creamy Chicken Soup with Lemon
   and Mint, 294
Creamy Creole Dressing, 63
Creamy Cucumber Salad, 183
Creamy Italian Dressing, 60
Creamy Mayonnaise Dressing, 64
Creamy Orange-Fennel Dressing, 61
Creamy Rosemary Dressing, 61
Creamy Vanilla Pear Crisp, 411
Creamy Wild Mushroom Casserole,
   244
Crème Anglaise, 24
Crème Caramel, 474
Crème Fraîche and Mustard Sauce, 52
Creole Beet Salad, 183

Creole Coleslaw, 187
Creole Crab Mini Turnovers, 469
Creole Tartar Sauce, 179
Creole Turkey Salad, 299
crisps, 411, 421
Crispy Bacon Strips, 67
Crispy Cranberry Game Hens, 492
Croissants with Scallops in Beurre
      Blanc, 488
Crookneck Squash Parmesan, 396
Croutons, Homemade, 19
Crumb Crust, 21
Crusty Macaroni and Cheese, 120
cucumber
   Creamy Cucumber Salad, 183
   Cucumber Salad with Tomato Salsa,
      403
   Gazpacho Cooler, 460
   sauces and salsas
      Cucumber Mint Salsa, 177
      Cucumber Yogurt Sauce, 144
      Gazpacho Salsa, 177
      Gazpacho Sauce, 57
      Shrimp, Cucumber and Dill Sauce,
         233
      Smoked Salmon, Cucumber and
         Dill Sauce, 233
   soups
      Curried Cucumber Soup, 196
      Gazpacho, 73
      Green Tomato Gazpacho, 385
      White Gazpacho, 175
Cumin Carrots, 388
currants and currant jelly
   Cardamom Currant Cookies, 439
   Currant Carrot Muffins, 548
   Eccles Cakes, 441
   Fruit Glaze, 23, 535
   Ginger Currant Shortbread, 441
   Meatless Mincemeat, 557
   Orange Currant Muffins, 543
Curried Black Olives, 81
Curried Cabbage Flowers, 42
Curried Cauliflower, 378
Curried Chicken Chili, 207
Curried Chicken Soup, 192
Curried Clams, 337
Curried Cucumber Soup, 196
Curried Eggplant Chutney, 559
Curried Grouper Chowder, 311
Curried Lamb Chili, 211
Curried Lamb with Eggplant, 166
Curried Onion Sauce, 55
Curried Rice Pilaf, 357
Curried Tandoori-Style Chicken,
      499
Curried Tandoori-Style Shrimp, 505
Curried Tuna and Lentils, 238
curries
   fish and seafood, 140, 238, 337,
      505
   meat, 166, 244, 267
   poultry, 166, 244, 267, 278, 499
   vegetable, 42, 124, 353, 378, 381
Curry Marinade, 34

D

dates
   Apple Date Pie, 535
   Cashew Date Butter, 83
   Date Nut Bars, 442
   Date Nut Brownies, 524
   Date Nut Coffee Cake, 433
   Date Nut Muffins, 545
   Spiked Fruitcake Brownies, 553
Deep-Dish Blueberry and Raspberry
      Pot Pie, 419
Deep-Fried Shrimp Cocktail, 335
deep-frying, 9
degreasing, 9
Deli-Style Burgers, 130
desserts, 104, 170–71, 180, 223, 473–74.
      See also specific types of desserts
Deviled Chicken Breasts, 152
Devil's Food Layer Cake, 526
dicing, 9
Dijon Vinaigrette, 61
Dill and Fennel Scallops, 334
Dill-Cured Salmon (Gravlax), 315
Dill Mustard Marinade, 33
Dill Popovers, 42
Dill Tuna Melts, 89
Dilled Salmon Salad, 501
Dilled Salmon Sandwiches, 188
Dilled Tuna Sandwiches, 88
Dilly Cabbage, 42
Dipping Chocolate, 531
dips, 83–84, 104, 115, 464
Dirty Rice, 358
Doctored Jarred Pasta Sauce, 20
Double-Apple Applesauce, 103
Double Chocolate Pudding Pie, 540
Double Iced Tea, 455
Double Orange Juice, 455
Down-Home Turkey Burgers, 132
dredging, 9–10
dressings, 59–65, 93, 107–8, 113, 513.
      See also marinades
   vinaigrettes, 42, 48, 53, 56, 60–65,
      108, 225
Dried Cherry, Tarragon and Almond
      Dessert Pizza, 223
Dried Cherry Bars, 442
Dried Fruit Roll, 521
drinks, 45, 104–5, 452–60, 523. See
      also specific types of beverages
duck
   Brown Curry Duck, 267
   Duck Confit, 71
   Duck Mole Chili, 210
   Duck Stewed with Red Cabbage, 269
   marinades for, 29–35
   Star-Anise Duck, 38
dumplings, 204, 250, 290
Duxelles and Parmesan Pizza, 218

E

Easy Blueberry Soup, 416
Easy Clam and White Bean Chowder, 118
Easy Homemade Applesauce, 67
Easy Honey Mustard, 560
Easy Peach Melba, 419
Easy Red Wine Marinade, 32
Easy Sour Cream Coffee Cake, 433
Easy Tangy Strawberry Ice Cream,
      419
Easy Tomato Sauce, 109
Easy White Wine Marinade, 32
Eccles Cakes, 441
Egg-Free Tofu Mayonnaise, 513
Eggless Caesar Dressing, 108
eggplant
   Baba Ghanoush, 465
   Baked Eggplant Moussaka, 246
   Caponata, 352
   Composed Salad of Grilled
      Vegetables, 184
   Curried Eggplant Chutney, 559
   Eggplant and Feta au Gratin, 518
   Eggplant Chili, 516
   Eggplant Rillettes, 465
   Eggplant Rollatini, 126
   Eggplant with Garlic Jam, 380
   Garden Chili, 203
   Grilled Mediterranean Eggplant,
      380
   Grilled Ratatouille, 145
   Marinated Antipasto, 349
   Potatoes and Eggplant, 353
   Ratatouille, 352
   Roasted Eggplant, 19
   Roasted Eggplant and Feta Pizza,
      217
   Roasted Eggplant and Garlic Sauce,
      227
   sandwiches
      Eggplant and Smoked Mozzarella
         Grinders, 93
      Eggplant Bruschetta, 81
      Eggplant Falafel, 346
      Pita Filled with Toasted Chickpeas,
         Avocado and Eggplant "Caviar,"
         346
   Tamarind Eggplant with Peanuts, 47
eggs
   Anise Tea Eggs, 466
   Custard, Crab and Caviar, 341
   Custard, Spinach and Blue Cheese,
      372
   custard sauces
      Chocolate Custard Sauce, 447
      Coffee Custard Sauce, 447
      Maple Custard Sauce, 447
      Old-Fashioned Custard Sauce, 447
      Orange Custard Sauce, 447
      Praline Custard Sauce, 447
      Super-Rich Custard Sauce, 447
   desserts
      Fig Meringue Tart, 540
      Grapefruit Cloud, 413
      Strawberry Meringue Pie, 420
   Deviled Eggs, Smoked Trout and
      Horseradish, 180
   Deviled Eggs, Vegetable-Stuffed, 180

eggs (continued)
Egg Pasta, 20
Egg Wash, 20
Eggs Steamed in Tomato Sauce, 427
Five-Spice Eggs, 43
frittatas and quiche
Fried Potato Frittata, 126
Frittata with Ham, Walnuts and
Marjoram, 45
Harvest Quiche, 384
Potato Leek Frittata, 427
Roasted Onion Frittata, 126
Poached Egg Tostadas, 427
Poached Salmon and Eggs with
Lemon Butter Sauce, 426
sandwiches
Egg Salad and Olives on Toast, 86
Souffléd Cottage Cheese
Sandwiches, 431
Spicy Anchovy Egg Salad
Sandwiches, 87
Scrambled Eggs with Cheese, 426
Soft- and Hard-Cooked Eggs, 19
Souffléd French Toast, 488
soufflés
Broccoli Rabe Soufflé, 372
Cheddar Corn Soufflé, 126
Hominy Soufflé, 362
Leek and Chard Soufflé, 355
Spinach and Feta Soufflé, 355
Spinach Parmesan Soufflé, 372
soups
Avgolemono, 197
Lemon Chicken Soup with Orzo,
197
Lemon Chickpea Soup, 197
Lime Bisque, 197
Tomato Basil Consommé, 197
Tomato Tarragon Consommé, 197
Stir-Fried Eggs and Ham, 426
Stir-Fried Eggs with Shrimp, 426
Turkey Benedict, 303
Eight-Hour Brandy Cheesecake, 473
Enchilada Roast Chicken, 274
endive, Belgian
Braised Belgian Endive, 373
Braised Endive with Ham, 373
Lamb Chops Braised with Belgian
Endive, 509
Smoked Fish Salad with Belgian
Endive, 188
Three-Endive Slaw, 174
endive, curly. See greens
Escabèche of Soft-Shell Crab, 471
Escabèche of Sole, 317
escarole. See greens
espresso. See coffee
Extra-Cheesy Extra-Crusty Mac and
Cheese, 236

F

Fall Garden Latkes, 380
Fall Orchard Stuffing, 384
Fast Clam Sauce, 232

fennel (bulb)
Apple Fennel Turnovers, 410
Braised Fennel, 388
Braised Orange Fennel, 388
Chicken and Fennel Pot Pie, 244
Creamy Orange-Fennel Dressing, 61
Fennel, Shrimp and Orange Sauce,
233
Fennel and Orange Salad, 43
Fennel Baked with Tomatoes and
Garlic, 378
Fennel Pâté, 465
Fennel Salmon Salad Sandwiches,
88
Orange and Fennel Mussels, 504
Potato Fennel Pancakes, 392
Potato Fennel Purée, 390
Potato Fennel Soup, 117
Potato Fennel Vichyssoise, 195
Tomato, Fennel and Olive Pizza, 214
Turkey Fennel Potstickers, 250
Winter Tempura, 350
Fennel-Cured Bluefish, 174
Fennel Grapefruit Sauce, 176
Feta and Artichoke Sauce, 227
Fettuccine with Ricotta and Spinach,
119
figs
Bourbon Walnut Fig Bars, 553
Brandied Summer Fruit, 174
Fig Meringue Tart, 540
Fig Squares, 105
Figs Preserved in Port, 449
Oat Bran and Fig Muffins, 546
Prosciutto and Summer Fruit Salad,
179
Spiced Fruit, 70
Walnut Butter and Fig Sandwiches, 87
Walnut Fig Sinkers, 549
Filet Panier with Wine Butter Sauce, 91
Fillets of Sole Steamed with Lemon
and Cilantro, 501
Fines Herbes Vinaigrette, 42
fish, 68, 308. See also specific types of
fish; seafood
Barbecued Fish, 329
Brochettes of Shark, Sturgeon and
Salmon, 316
Broiled Fish with Lemon Ranch
Dressing, 329
fillets
Baked Fish in Mustard Glaze, 327
Baked Fish with Horseradish and
Sour Cream, 327
Black Bass on Cucumber
"Noodles," 308
Broiled Fish with Walnut Butter,
327
Buffalo "Fins," 323
Chilled Poached Fish with Citrus
Vinaigrette, 322
Chilled Poached Fish with Creamy
Cucumbers, 323
Fish, Black Beans and Cilantro,
330

fish
fillets (continued)
Fish Braised with Mussels and
Orange, 330
Fish Chili, 330
Fish en Papillote, Bouillabaisse-
Style, 326
Fish en Papillote with Julienne of
Garden Vegetables, 326
Fish en Papillote with Leeks, 326
Fish en Papillote with Melon and
Capers, 326
Fish en Papillote with Olives and
Tomatoes, 326
Fish en Papillote with Pickled
Ginger, 327
Fish Fillets Steamed with Lime
and Chives, 325
Fish Grilled with Bacon and Green
Onions, 327
Fish in Balsamic Brown Butter
with Capers, 324
Fish Poached in Vegetable Juice,
322
Fish Sautéed in Hazelnut-Garlic
Crust, 324
Fish Steamed with Baby Shrimp in
Tarragon Vinaigrette, 325
Fish Tempura, 323
Fluke Paupiettes Stuffed with
Smoked Salmon Mousse, 310
Fried Fish, Old Bay, 323
Fried Fish in Ranch Buttermilk
Batter, 323
Grilled Fish Salad with Garden
Greens, 189
Individual Fish Fillet, 68
Marinated Fish Kebabs, 329
Orange-Fennel Fillet, 324
Poached Fish with Beurre Blanc,
321
Poached Fish with Tomato Mint
Salsa, 322
Poached Fish with Wine
Hollandaise, 322
Rosemary, Sage and Garlic Fillets,
325
Sautéed Fish in Lemon Butter, 324
Sautéed Fish with Lime and
Olives, 324
Steamed Paupiettes Rolled with
Fresh Herbs, 325
Grilled Fish Glazed with Vinaigrette,
329
Grilled Fish in Chili Paste, 328
Grilled Fish in Garlic Herb
Marinade, 328
Grilled Fish in Garlic Sage
Marinade, 328
Grilled Fish with Olive Oil and
Balsamic Vinegar, 329
Individual Fish Steak, 68
lean fish, 321–26
Leftover Fish Salad for Sandwiches,
112

fish (*continued*)
marinades for, 28–30, 32–35
oily fish, 321, 326–30
Pike Mousse with Beurre Blanc, 313
sauces for, 50–51, 53–57
Smoked Fish Salad with Belgian
    Endive, 188
soups and stews
    All-Fish Bouillabaisse, 330
    Bourride, 322
    Clam and Fish Stew with Lots of
      Basil, 330
    Lobster Bouillabaisse, 491
    Seafood Pot au Feu, 506
Teriyaki Grilled Fish, 329
whole fish
    Fish Baked in a Glaze of Herb Oil,
      327
    Fish Steamed with Vegetables, 325
    Roasted Fish Provençal, 485
    Smoky Grilled Fish, 328
    Snapper Steamed with Green
      Peppercorns, 502
    Sweet-and-Sour Cranberry Fish,
      328
    Tea-Steamed Black Bass, 308
    Whole Baked Fish, 327
    Whole Fish Grilled in Foil with
      Vegetables, 138
    Whole Fried Sesame Fish, 324
Five-Grain Cereal, 425
Five-Spice Eggs, 43
Flaky Pastry, 21
flambéing, 10
Flaming Warm Spiced Wine, 458
Flank Steak Roasted with Portobello
    Mushrooms, 479
Flank Steak Stuffed with Wild Rice,
    479
flounder
Flounder and Salmon Steamed in
    Romaine, 502
Flounder Poached in Fresh Tomato
    Sauce, 310
Flounder with Arugula, 503
Four-Color Fish Seviche, 173
Fried Flounder in Buttermilk Batter,
    310
Steamed Flounder with Yogurt Dill
    Sauce, 501
Stir-Fried Fish and Vegetables, 161
Fluke Fillets Andalouse, 311
Fluke Paupiettes Stuffed with Smoked
    Salmon Mousse, 310
Fontina Fondue with Garlic Roasted
    Potatoes, 354
Fontina Polenta, 362
food processors, 67, 72–74
Four-Color Fish Seviche, 173
Fragrant Basmati Rice, 360
Fragrant Slow-Cooked Beef, 480
Fragrant Turkey Loaf with Pineapple,
    257
frankfurters
Barbecue-Style Dogs, 134

frankfurters (*continued*)
Chicken Franks with Gazpacho
    Salsa, 135
Chicken Franks with Tomato
    Artichoke Salsa, 135
Chicken or Turkey Franks with
    Avocado Salsa, 90
Chili Cheese Dogs, 135
Hot Dogs and Chilied Mustard, 89
Hot Dogs Grilled with Bacon and
    Horseradish Mustard, 135
Hot Dogs with Bacon and Honey
    Mustard, 89
Hot Dogs with Cumin Mustard, 134
Hot Dogs with Relish Fresca, 134
Hot Dogs with the Works, 134
Piggy Dogs, 134
Sweet-and-Sour Hot Dogs, 135
Turkey Franks with Tapenade
    Ketchup, 135
French Bread Pizza, 81
French Buttercream, 24
French Chocolate Cake, 528
French Fries with Tapenade, 489
French toast, 103, 430–31, 487–88,
    511
Fresh and Smoked Turkey Meatloaf,
    256
Fresh Basil Pesto, 178
Fresh Ham Braised with Cider, 483
Fresh Ham Hocks with Leeks and
    White Beans, 269
Fresh Strawberry Sauce, 448
Fresh Tomato and Cream Sauce, 402
Fresh Tomato Sauce, 402
Fresh Tomatoes and Pasta, 402
Fresh Whole Wheat Wild Mushroom
    Pasta, 521
Fried Fish in Ranch Buttermilk
    Batter, 323
Fried Flounder in Buttermilk Batter,
    310
Fried Herbed Shrimp, 471
Fried Kale, 373
Fried Oyster Sandwiches, 340
Fried Oysters with Tartar Sauce, 340
Fried Polenta with Tomato Sauce, 362
Fried Potato Frittata, 126
Fried Rice from Leftovers, 114
Fried Rice with Vegetables, 351
Fried Salmon Sandwiches with Dill
    Tartar Sauce, 91
Fried Shrimp in Beer Batter, 336
Frittata with Ham, Walnuts and
    Marjoram, 45
Fritto Misto (Fried Antipasto), 349
frosting, 13, 23, 24
fruit and fruit juices, 12, 29. *See also
    specific types of fruit*; berries
Apple Nectarine Pie, 536
bars and squares
    Chocolate Fruit Squares, 532
    Fruit and Nut Bricks, 105
    Spiked Fruitcake Brownies, 553
Dried Fruit Roll, 521

fruit and fruit juices (*continued*)
drinks
    Cherry Raspberry Frappé, 455
    Fruit Cooler, 455
    Fruited Iced Tea Punch, 456
    Gingered Apricot Ale, 454
    Honey Cranberry Cocktail, 455
    Sparkling Peach Melba, 454
Fruit in Chocolate Cups, 530
Meatless Mincemeat, 557
Quick Sorbet, 74
Raspberry Nectarine Pie, 420
sauces and marinades
    Fruit and Honey Topping, 434
    Fruit Glaze, 23, 535
    Fruit Vinegar, 558
    Fruity Barbecue Marinade, 31
    Garlic Citrus Salsa, 56
    Ginger Lychee Salsa, 178
    Red Wine Pomegranate Sauce, 52
Sautéed Fruit Salad, 449
Tropical Crisp, 411
frying, 147–58. *See also* stir-frying

G

game. *See also* rabbit
Caramelized Szechuan Hen, 492
Crispy Cranberry Game Hens, 492
Game Hens Braised with
    Blackberries, 415
marinades for, 30–33, 35
Poussin Roasted with Garlic and
    Molasses, 491
Sausage and Quail Chili, 207
Venison Chili, 204
Venison in Mustard Crust, 508
Garden Chili, 203
Garden Corn Muffins, 547
Garden Pâté, 465
Garden Split Pea Soup, 199
Garden Vegetable Whole-Grain
    Tempura, 518
garlic
Chopped Garlic, 74
dips and spreads
    Angel-of-Death Cheese, 466
    Garlic Cheese, 466
    Roasted Garlic Purée, 464
dressings and marinades
    Aïoli, 17
    Garlic and Wine Marinade, 33
    Garlic Herb Dressing, 60
    Garlic Ranch Dressing, 64
    Garlic Vinaigrette, 56
    Garlic Yogurt Dressing, 108
    Lemon Garlic Marinade, 29
    Yogurt, Garlic and Mint Marinade,
      35
sauces and seasonings
    Basil and Garlic Sauce, 56
    Garlic Beurre Blanc, 53
    Garlic Butter, 16
    Garlic Citrus Salsa, 56
    Lemon Garlic Vinegar, 558

garlic
  sauces and seasoning (*continued*)
    Pesto, 20
      Provençal Oil, 558
      Roasted Garlic Horseradish Paste, 44
      Spicy Garlic Oil, 558
      Sweet Garlic Paste, 34
Garlic and Ginger Chicken Legs, 289
Garlic and Ginger Lamb Chops, 44
Garlic and Molasses Chicken Legs, 293
Garlic and Parmesan Pizza, 217
Garlic and Parmesan Popcorn, 78
Garlic and Walnut Baguette, 489
Garlic Black Bean Chicken Wings, 470
Garlic Chicken Sausage over Spinach, 156
Garlic Green Beans, 379
Garlic Green Olives and Peppers, 81
Garlic Hazelnut Chicken, 152
Garlic Potato Chips, 80
Garlic Potato Soup, 195
Garlic Roast Chicken, 273
Garlic Roasted Pork Loin, 483
Garlic Spinach, 369
Garlic Spinach Lamb Burgers, 133
Garlicky Pasta Primavera, 119
Gâteau Bordeaux, 528
Gazpacho, 73
Gazpacho Cooler, 460
Gazpacho Salsa, 177
Gazpacho Sauce, 57
Génoise (Sponge Cake), 22
German-Style Potato Salad, 184
ginger
  Cayenne Pepper Gingerbread, 40
  Chocolate Gingerbread, 525
  dressings and marinades
    Ginger Soy Marinade, 30
    Soy Ginger Dressing, 63
    Szechuan Ginger Dressing, 63
  Ginger Currant Shortbread, 441
  Ginger Lace Cookies, 440
  Gingerbread Men, 553
  Gingerbread Muffins, 552
  Gingerbread Wreaths, 553
  Gingered Apricot Ale, 454
  Gingered Ginger Ale, 453
  Hot Pepper Gingerbread Muffins, 552
  sauces and seasonings
    Candied Ginger Cream, 451
    Ginger, Soy and Sesame Sauce, 52
    Ginger Lychee Salsa, 178
    Ginger Peach Sauce, 448
    Ginger Sesame Oil, 558
    Ginger Tahini, 561
    Ginger Tomato Sauce, 226
    Lemon Ginger Honey, 494
Ginger Apple Cobbler, 44
Ginger Black Bean Chicken Wings, 288
Ginger Poached Pears, 409

Ginger Pumpkin Bisque, 514
Ginger Sesame Salmon, 161
Ginger Soy Clams, 337
Gingered Berry Crisp, 421
Gingered Black Bean Bluefish, 503
Gingered Carrot Marmalade, 560
Gingered Carrot Salad, 183
Gingered Carrots with Hot Pepper Vinaigrette, 467
Gingered Mango Soup, 175
Gingered Pecan Zucchini Bread, 397
Girl Scout Thin Mint Cookie Ice Cream Log, 105
glazes, 11, 13, 23
Golden Turmeric Tomato Relish, 48
Gorgonzola and Onion French Bread Pizza, 82
Gorgonzola and Prosciutto au Gratin, 241
Gorgonzola Gratin, 389
Gorgonzola Grinders, 92
Gorgonzola Mousse, 84
grains, 356–65. *See also specific grains*
Grand Marnier Almond Bars, 442
Grand Marnier Almond Tart, 541
Grand Marnier White Chocolate Truffles, 496
grapefruit and grapefruit juice
  Asparagus, Shrimp, Raspberry and Grapefruit Salad, 506
  Avocado Grapefruit Salad, 515
  Bitter Grapefruit Marmalade, 559
  "Champagne" with Grapefruit Ice, 459
  Grapefruit Cloud, 413
  Grapefruit or Tangerine Seltzer, 454
  Grapefruitade, 454
  Watercress and Grapefruit Salad, 48
grapes and grape juice
  Blue Cheese Grapes, 467
  Fruit and Honey Topping, 434
  Fruit Cooler, 455
  Fruited Iced Tea Punch, 456
  Poached Winter Fruit Salad with Raspberry Vinaigrette, 190
  Prosciutto and Summer Fruit Salad, 179
  Sauce Véronique, 50
  Warm Stir-Fried Grapes, 448
Gratin of Chard, 374
Gratin of Spinach, 374
Gravlax, Honey-Cured, 174
Gravlax (Dill-Cured Salmon), 315
gravy, 17–18
Great Burgers, 130
Greek Beef, 481
Greek Marinated Mushrooms in Artichokes, 352
Green Beans with Pine Nuts, 379
Green Beans with Roasted Peppers, 379
Green Beans with Thyme, 379
Green Goddess Ranch Dressing, 64
Green Herb Oil, 179
Green Pea Soup with Mint, 45

Green Peppercorn Mustard, 560
Green Peppercorn Turkey Salad, 301
Green Sauce, 113
Green Seviche, 173
Green Tomato Gazpacho, 385
greens. *See also specific greens*
  Caesar Salad Sandwiches, 94
  Cheesy Greens Casserole, 245
  Salad of Garden Lettuces and Arugula, 38
  Sautéed Bitter Greens with Sweet Pepper Vinaigrette, 374
  Sautéed Spring Greens, 374
  Three-Endive Slaw, 174
  Tossed Winter Greens with Warm Bacon Dressing, 182
  Wilted Chicory, 373
Grilled Asian Chicken Salad, 143
Grilled Barbecued Shrimp, 336
Grilled Brandied Peaches, 146
Grilled Cheddar and Apple, 98
Grilled Cheese, Bacon and Tomato Sandwiches, 90
Grilled Chèvre and Smoked Salmon on Bagels, 90
"Grilled" Chicken Anchoiade, 153
Grilled Chicken Basted with Sage, 142
Grilled Chicken Breast with Buttermilk and Chervil, 40
Grilled Chicken Breast with Buttermilk and Herbs, 516
Grilled Chicken Breasts with Artichoke Relish, 286
Grilled Chicken Breasts with Bitter Greens and Pine Nuts, 189
"Grilled" Chicken Breasts with Herbed Blue Cheese Dressing, 154
Grilled Chicken Breasts with Pesto, 142
Grilled Chicken Breasts with Roasted Pepper Salsa, 286
Grilled Chicken Breasts with Roquefort Dressing, 142
Grilled Chicken Breasts with Tapenade, 286
Grilled Chicken Breasts with Tomato-Dill Vinaigrette, 142
Grilled Chicken Livers with Worcestershire Marinade, 143
Grilled Chicken Salad, 142
Grilled Chicken with Red Pepper and Roasted Eggplant, 500
Grilled Chicken with Spicy Artichoke Relish, 499
Grilled Chilied Shrimp, 139
Grilled Chutney-Glazed Ham Steak, 428
Grilled Corn, 145
Grilled Curried Scallops, 140
Grilled Fish Glazed with Vinaigrette, 329
Grilled Fish in Chili Paste, 328
Grilled Fish in Garlic Herb Marinade, 328

Grilled Fish in Garlic Sage Marinade, 328

Grilled Fish Salad with Garden Greens, 189

Grilled Fish with Olive Oil and Balsamic Vinegar, 329

Grilled Honey Corn Cakes, 146

Grilled Honey-Mustard Pork Chops, 144

Grilled Lamb and Artichoke Pitas, 94

Grilled Lamb and Tabbouleh Salad, 186

Grilled Lamb Chops with Cucumber Yogurt Sauce, 144

Grilled Lamb Steak Provençal, 144

Grilled Liver with Onions, 144

Grilled Maple-Glazed Breakfast Sausages, 145

Grilled Marinated Scallops, 333

Grilled Mediterranean Eggplant, 380

Grilled Muenster with Pickles, 98

Grilled Mustard-Glazed Veal Chops, 508

Grilled Pompano with Lime and Dill, 313

Grilled Pork Medallions with Mustard and Rosemary, 509

Grilled Potato Chips, 145

Grilled Pound Cake with Honey Butter, 146

Grilled Rabbit, 507

Grilled Ranch-Style Chicken Legs, 142

Grilled Ratatouille, 145

Grilled Rosemary Shrimp, 140

Grilled Salmon Chili, 208

Grilled Salmon Potato Salad, 138

Grilled Salmon Salad with Rosemary Vinaigrette, 188

Grilled Salmon Steak with Lemon and Olive Oil, 138

Grilled Salmon with Avocado Salsa, 139

Grilled Salmon with Refried Beans, 315

Grilled Scallop Kebabs in Hazelnut Garlic Glaze, 140

Grilled Scallops and Shrimp Tabbouleh, 187

Grilled Shrimp in Cumin Paste, 42

Grilled Shrimp with Pesto, 335

Grilled Smoked Sausages with Apple Sauerkraut, 136

Grilled Soft-Shell Crabs, 341

Grilled Steak with Caramelized Garlic, 144

Grilled Summer Squash Salad, 184

Grilled Tea-Steamed Clams and Mussels, 140

Grilled Teriyaki Tofu, 517

Grilled Tofu Steak with Pickled Ginger, 517

Grilled Tomatillo and Rice Salad, 384

Grilled Tomatoes, 428

Grilled Trout with Bacon and Dill, 139

Grilled Trout with Bacon and Tarragon, 318

Grilled Tuna and Roasted Pepper Salad, 318

Grilled Tuna Chili on Black Beans, 209

Grilled Tuna Salad, 139

Grilled Tuna Steak with Warm Tomato Vinaigrette, 319

Grilled Turkey Breast with Tomato Basil Sauce, 500

Grilled Turkey Genovese, 141

Grilled Turkey Ham, 303

Grilled Turkey Steaks with Steak Sauce, 304

Grilled Veal with Peanut Sauce, 144

grilling, 10

grits
Hominy Soufflé, 362
Hominy with Peppers, 362
Quick Cheese Grits, 362

Ground Beef Chili, 203

Ground Chicken Fajitas, 157

Ground Nuts, 74

Ground Turkey Chili, 203

grouper
Curried Grouper Chowder, 311
Sautéed Grouper Fillets with Corn-Pepper Relish, 311

Guacamole Vinaigrette, 65

H

ham. *See also* pork, shoulder (picnic ham); prosciutto
Clam, Ham and Orzo Pie, 241
Country Pâté, 252
Fresh Ham Braised with Cider, 483
Fresh Ham Hocks with Leeks and White Beans, 269
Frittata with Ham, Walnuts and Marjoram, 45
Ham, Pine Nut and Rosemary Sauce, 231
Ham and Apple Tart, 406
Ham and Cheddar Meatloaf, 255
Ham and Cheese Muffins, 550
Ham and Swiss Cheeseburgers, 131
Ham and Swiss Gratin, 389
Ham Meatloaf, 255
ham steak
Bourbon-Glazed Ham Steak with Apple Fritters, 428
Grilled Chutney-Glazed Ham Steak, 428
Pot au Feu, 72
Hash of Ham, Peppers and Peppercorns, 380
Honey-Baked Ham, 482
Hot Pepper Ham, 482
sandwiches
Ham, Apple and Mustard on Rye, 86
Ham and Cheese Wraps, 87
Ham and Honey Mustard Roll-Ups, 103

ham
sandwiches (*continued*)
Three-Meat Deli Hoagies, 93
Tropical Ham, 482
Tuna, Fontina and Ham Casserole, 237

Hamburger Hot Dogs, 102

Hard-Shell Crabs Cooked in Beer, 504

Harvest Quiche, 384

Harvest Rice Stuffing, 384

Harvest Vegetable Stuffing, 384

Hash Browns and Cabbage, 391

Hash of Ham, Peppers and Peppercorns, 380

Hazelnut Lemon Roast Chicken, 276

hazelnuts
Apple Hazelnut Crisp, 411
Chocolate Hazelnut Pudding, 529
Hazelnut Cherry Pie, 538
Hazelnut Crescents, 439
Hazelnut Macaroons, 438
Heavy-Duty Hazelnut Truffles, 557
Pancetta, Hazelnut and Garlic Pizza, 219
Pancetta, Hazelnut and Garlic Sauce, 231

Health Wraps, 87

Healthy Hoagie, 98

Healthy Hoppin' John, 519

Healthy Snack Mix, 80

Hearty Red Wine Marinade, 33

Heavy-Duty Hazelnut Truffles, 557

Herb, Tomato and Cream Sauce, 228

Herb Biscuits, 431

Herb Butter, 16

Herb Cheese Muffins, 550

Herb Cheese Veal Burgers, 133

Herb-Crusted Roasted Pork Loin, 482

Herb Gnocchi with Parmesan and Butter, 353

Herb Vinegar, 558

Herbed Beurre Blanc, 51

Herbed Biscuits with a Secret, 488

Herbed Brandy Turkey with Wild Mushroom Stuffing, 300

Herbed Chicken Pâté, 253

Herbed Chili, 204

Herbed Salmon Casserole, 240

Herbed Shrimp, 162

Herbed Veal Loaf, 257

herbs. *See specific herbs*; seasonings

herring (pickled)
Russian Herring Potato Salad, 185
Three-Can Salad, 174

High-Protein Chocolate Peanut Butter Shake, 104

High-Protein Vegetarian Stir-Fried Noodles, 167

High-Protein Vegetarian Tostadas, 347

Hoisin Burgers, 133

Hoisin Clams, 337

Homemade Breakfast Sausage, 428

Homemade Croutons, 19

Homemade Mayonnaise, 16

Homemade Steak Sauce, 108
Homemade Yogurt, 16
hominy. *See* grits
honey
  Honey Cranberry Cocktail, 455
  Modern-Day Mead, 458
  sauces and marinades
    Honey Bourbon Sauce, 450
    Honey Mustard Marinade, 33
    Honey Walnut Sauce, 450
    Hot Pepper Honey, 493
    Lemon Ginger Honey, 494
    Spiked Orange Saffron Honey, 493
Honey Almond Tuiles, 440
Honey-Baked Beets, 387
Honey-Baked Ham, 482
Honey Bran Muffins, 546
Honey Brandy White Chocolate
    Mousse, 530
Honey-Cured Gravlax, 174
Honey-Dipped Corn Toast, 430
Honey Mustard, Easy, 560
Honey Mustard Roast Chicken, 275
Honey-Roasted Pears, 409
Honey Rum Raisin Tea Cake, 556
Honeydew Filled with Champagne, 493
Honeydew Mint Soup, 175
Honeydew Raspberry Soup, 416
Honeyed Pear Upside-Down Pie, 537
Honeyed Pork Chops in Chili Sauce,
    206
Horseradish and Garlic Roast
    Chicken, 273
Hot, Hot, Hot Barbecue Paste, 32
Hot-and-Sour Barbecue Marinade,
    32
Hot-and-Sour Shrimp Soup, 200
Hot-and-Sour Soup, 200
Hot-and-Sour Soup with Crab, 200
Hot Buttered Rum, 458
Hot Dog Wraps, 134
hot dogs, 89, 129–30, 134–36
Hot Dogs and Chilied Mustard, 89
Hot Dogs Grilled with Bacon and
    Horseradish Mustard, 135
Hot Dogs with Bacon and Honey
    Mustard, 89
Hot Dogs with Cumin Mustard, 134
Hot Dogs with Relish Fresca, 134
Hot Dogs with the Works, 134
Hot Fudge Sauce, 445
Hot Pepper, Bacon and Gorgonzola
    Pizza, 222
Hot Pepper and Cream Sauce, 229
Hot Pepper Gingerbread Muffins, 552
Hot Pepper Ham, 482
Hot Pepper Honey, 493
Hot Pepper Oil, 82
Hot Pepper Peanut Butter, 83
Hot Pepper Peanut Vinaigrette, 108
Hot Pepper Pecans, 79
Hot Pepper Vinaigrette, 60
Hot Turkey Sandwiches, 297
Hummus Tahini, 179
Hungarian Apple Coffee Cake, 413

I

ice cream and ices, 13
  ice cream, 419, 473, 494, 531
  ices, 45, 74, 413, 494
ice cream and ices (as ingredient)
  Bourbon-Spiked Peach and Praline
    "Bombe," 180
  Cherry Raspberry Frappé, 455
  Chocolate Ice Cream Cupcakes, 105
  Easy Peach Melba, 419
  Espresso Anise Bombe, 495
  Girl Scout Thin Mint Cookie Ice
    Cream Log, 105
  Ice Cream Sandwich, 105
  Kahlúa and Cream Shake, 459
  Liquid Creamsicle, 459
  Raspberry Chocolate Bombe, 495
  Stir-Fried Banana Split, 170
Iceberg Lettuce with Three Tomatoes,
    182
Iced Espresso with Rum, 457
Iced Mocha, 457
Iced Spiked Cocoa, 457
Iced Tea with Spicy Lemon Ice Cubes,
    456
icing, 13, 23
Indian Braised Vegetables, 381
Indian Lamb and Rice, 244
Individual Fish Fillet, 68
Individual Fish Steak, 68
Initial Burgers, 102
Inside-Out Lasagna, 100
Inside-Out Tacos, 100
Inverted Pear Tart, 537
Irish Oatmeal, 70
Irish Soda Bread, 432
Italian Clam Soup, 198
Italian Fried Chicken, 293
Italian Sausage with Prosciutto and
    Capers, 91
Italian Seafood Sandwiches, 342
Italian Stir-Fried Green Beans, 169

J

Jalapeño Bloody Marys, 45
Jalapeño Jelly, 560
Jalapeño Salsa, 177
Jalapeño Shrimp Cocktail, 335
Jam-Filled Muffins, 544
Jamaican Jerk Stew, 270
Japanese Grilled Shrimp, 101
Jerk Citrus Marinade, 30
Jerk Marinade, 30
Jerk Ribs, 270
Jerk Roast Chicken, 279
Jerk Roasted Beef, 480
Jerusalem artichokes
  Jerusalem Artichokes and
    Mushrooms au Gratin, 350
  Warm Jerusalem Artichoke Salad, 183
Jewish Apple Cake, 412
julienne, 9
Julienned Peppers and Carrots, 55

Julienned Vegetables with Lemon
    Honey Dip, 104
Juniper Gin Sauce, 55

K

Kahlúa and Cream Shake, 459
kale
  Cheesy Greens Casserole, 245
  Fried Kale, 373
  Fritto Misto (Fried Antipasto), 349
  Kale Smothered with Bacon and
    Onions, 373
  Kale with Sausage and Apple, 373
  Vitamin A Tempura, 518
Kasha with Onion and Dill, 363
Kasha with Tortellini, 363
Kasha with Walnuts and Garlic, 363
Kasha with Wild Mushrooms, 363
kebabs, 145, 470
  fish and seafood, 140, 208, 316, 329,
    332
Kiddie Nachos, 102
kids' food, 96–105
kiwis
  Brandied Summer Fruit, 174
  Kiwi and Honeydew in Margarita
    Glaze, 180
knockwurst, 130
  Barbecue-Style Dogs, 134
  Chili Cheese Dogs, 135
  Hot Dogs and Chilied Mustard, 89
  Hot Dogs Grilled with Bacon and
    Horseradish Mustard, 135
  Hot Dogs with Cumin Mustard,
    134
  Hot Dogs with Relish Fresca, 134
  Hot Dogs with the Works, 134
  Knockwurst Simmered in Beer with
    Sauerkraut, 136
  Piggy Dogs, 134
  Sweet-and-Sour Hot Dogs, 135
Kumquat Pound Cakes, 554

L

lamb
  boneless leg
    Curried Lamb with Eggplant, 166
    Grilled Lamb and Artichoke Pitas,
      94
    Grilled Lamb and Tabbouleh
      Salad, 186
    Grilled Lamb Steak Provençal, 144
    Indian Lamb and Rice, 244
    Lamb and Leek Kebabs, 145
    Lamb with Lemon and Mint, 509
    Leg of Lamb Niçoise, 482
    Middle Eastern Roasted Lamb, 482
    Roast Lamb Dijonnaise, 481
    Roast Lamb Provençal, 481
    Roast Lamb with Fresh Mint
      Sauce, 481
    Roasted Boneless Leg of Lamb, 481
    Spicy Anise Lamb, 164

lamb (*continued*)
 Charred Rare Lamb with Roasted Garlic, 471
 chilis
  Curried Lamb Chili, 211
  Lamb and Lentil Chili, 211
  Lamb Mole Chili, 210
 chops
  Garlic and Ginger Lamb Chops, 44
  Grilled Lamb Chops with Cucumber Yogurt Sauce, 144
  Lamb Chops Braised with Belgian Endive, 509
 Garlic Spinach Lamb Burgers, 133
 Lamb and Feta Pizza, 215
 marinades for, 29, 31, 33–34
 Minted Lamb Burgers, 133
 rack of lamb
  Rack of Lamb with Roasted Garlic Jus, 482
  Roasted Rack of Lamb, 482
  Roasted Rack of Lamb with Mustard Crumbs, 482
  Roasted Rack of Lamb with Wasabi Crumbs, 482
 Shepherd's Pie, 254
 soups
  Lamb and Mushroom Barley Soup, 117
  Lamb and Mushroom Soup, 194
  Lemon Lamb Soup with Oatmeal, 117
  Mushroom Barley Soup, 194
 stews
  Lamb Stewed with Anise and Orange, 266
  Lamb Stewed with Asparagus, 268
  Lamb Stewed with Peppers, 267
  Lamb with Red Curry, 267
  Smoky Lamb Stew, 269
  Spring Lamb Stew, 268
Lasagna Meatloaf, 258
latkes, 350, 380–81
Layered Veal, Turkey and Prosciutto Loaf, 244
Lebanese Chicken, 277
leeks
 Clam and Leek Pizza, 220
 Composed Salad of Grilled Vegetables, 184
 Lamb and Leek Kebabs, 145
 Leek and Chard Soufflé, 355
 Mediterranean Braised Leeks, 388
 Potato Leek Frittata, 427
 Potato Leek Pancakes, 392
 soups
  Potato Leek Soup, 195
  Pumpkin Leek Soup, 196
  Sweet Potato Vichyssoise, 195
  Vegetable Broth, 19
  Vichyssoise, 72
 Winter Tempura, 350
Leftover Barbecued Chicken Salad, 141
Leftover Chicken Chili, 111

Leftover Fish Salad for Sandwiches, 112
Leftover Fried Chicken Coleslaw, 112
Leftover Steak Chili, 111
Leftover Turkey Soup, 305
leftovers, 106–15
Leftovers Chicken Noodle Soup, 110
Leftovers Chicken Rice Soup, 110
Leftovers Escabèche, 113
Leftovers Minestrone, 110
Leftovers Tabbouleh, 112
Leftovers Turkey Soup, 305
Leg of Lamb Niçoise, 482
Lemon and Pepper Olives, 81
Lemon Anise Spinach, 38
Lemon Apple Cake, 412
Lemon Chicken Soup, 110
Lemon Chicken Soup with Orzo, 197
Lemon Chickpea Soup, 197
Lemon Cilantro Roast Chicken, 276
Lemon Cilantro Turkey Breast, 501
Lemon Coriander Chicken, 273
Lemon Coriander Pork, 484
Lemon-Glazed Baked Apples, 408
Lemon-Honey Turkey with Cornbread and Crab Stuffing, 302
Lemon Lamb Soup with Oatmeal, 117
Lemon Mushroom Chicken, 287
Lemon Mushroom Turkey, 151
Lemon or Lime Basmati Rice, 360
Lemon Pear Mini Turnovers, 469
Lemon Popcorn, 78
Lemon Rosemary Swordfish Steak, 317
Lemon-Soy Smoked Shrimp, 472
Lemon-Walnut Turkey Salad, 302
Lemon Zucchini Soup, 397
lemons and lemon juice
 Apple Lemon Custard Pie, 536
 Chewy Gooey Lemon Pecan Bars, 442
 dips and spreads
  Lemon Cheese, 466
  Lemon Curd, 24
  Lemon Ginger Honey, 494
  Lemon Green Peppercorn Marmalade, 559
 dressings and marinades
  Lemon and Olive Oil Dressing, 60
  Lemon Basil Marinade, 28
  Lemon Cilantro Marinade, 28
  Lemon Garlic Marinade, 29
  Lemon Yogurt Dressing, 107
  Spicy Citrus Marinade, 29
 drinks
  Lemon-Lime Soft Drink, 453
  Lemon-Limeade, 454
  Lemonade Iced Tea, 456
  Spicy Lemonade, 454
  Zesty Iced Tea, 456
 muffins and loaves
  Lemon-Lime Zucchini Muffins, 548

lemons and lemon juice
 muffins and loaves (*continued*)
  Lemon Yogurt Muffins, 549
  Lemon Zucchini Muffins, 397
 sauces and seasonings
  Citrus Oil, 558
  Lemon Garlic Vinegar, 558
  Lemon Parsley Sauce, 56
  Lemon Walnut Sauce, 50
lentils
 All-Day Lentil Soup, 70
 Corn and Lentil Salad, 118
 Marinated Lentil Salad, 352
 Smoky Lentil Soup, 514
 Tabbouleh with Lentils, 365
lettuce
 Basic Green Salad, 182
 Caesar Salad Sandwiches, 94
 Chicken and Grapes Lettuce Pockets, 99
 Classic Caesar Salad, 182
 Iceberg Lettuce with Three Tomatoes, 182
 Ruby Salad, 368
 Tuna Lettuce Pockets, 99
Lime and Coriander Roast Chicken, 41
Lime Cilantro Black Bean Chicken, 151
limes and lime juice
 dressings and marinades
  Lime and Thyme Vinaigrette, 48
  Lime Caper Marinade, 29
  Lime Jalapeño Marinade, 29
  Lime Vinaigrette, 60
  Spicy Citrus Marinade, 29
 drinks
  Lemon-Lime Soft Drink, 453
  Lemon-Limeade, 454
  Zesty Iced Tea, 456
 Lime Bisque, 197
 Margarita Sauce, 450
liqueurs
 Kahlúa and Cream Shake, 459
 Liquid Creamsicle, 459
 Sparkling Kir Punch, 459
 Suzette Sauce, 450
Liquid Chocolate Bars, 458
Liquid Creamsicle, 459
A Little Chopped Liver, 114
Liver and Bacon Mini Turnovers, 469
Liver with Onions, Grilled, 144
lobster, 10
 Chili Grilled Lobster, 141
 Lobster Bouillabaisse, 491
 Lobster with Avocado Lobster Salsa, 491
 Lobster with Red Pepper Coulis, 491
Lots-of-Olives Meatloaf, 255
Low-Fat Peach Melba, 419
Low-Salt, Big-Flavor Rice Pilaf, 358

M

macaroni. *See also* pasta
 Bell Peppers Stuffed with Macaroni and Cheese, 120

macaroni (*continued*)
Crusty Macaroni and Cheese, 120
Extra-Cheesy Extra-Crusty Mac and Cheese, 236
Inside-Out Lasagna, 100
Mild Macaroni and Cheese, 101
Real Mac and Cheese for the Whole Family, 236
Real Macaroni and Cheese, 236
Tuna and Shrimp Casserole with Herbed Cheese, 239
Tuna Casserole with Just a Few Noodles, 237
Tuna Macaroni and Cheese, 120
Tuna Noodle Casserole Duxelles, 237
maceration, 10, 11
Mackerel with Homemade Tartar Sauce, Pan-Fried, 312
Mahi Mahi Meunière with Asian Peanut Sauce, 312
Mahi Mahi with Grapefruit Butter Sauce, Baked, 312
Mahogany Chicken, 156
Mahogany Chicken Wings, 288
Mahogany Roast Chicken, 276
Make-Your-Own Pizza, 99
mango
Chili Mango Sorbet, 413
Gingered Mango Soup, 175
Mango Butter, 408
Mango Coulis with Lime, 449
Mango Orange Soup with Plums and Blueberries, 175
Mint Mango Soup, 413
Manhattan Clam Chowder, 198
Maple Custard Sauce, 447
Maple Whipped Cream, 451
Margarita Ice, 494
Margarita Sauce, 450
marinades, 10–11, 27–35. *See also* dressings
Marinated Antipasto, 349
Marinated Chicken Paillards, 153
Marinated Feta and Artichoke Heart Pizza, 220
Marinated Fish Kebabs, 329
Marinated Garlic Mushrooms, 466
Marinated Green Tomato and White Bean Salad, 385
Marinated Herbed Mushrooms, 560
Marinated Lentil Salad, 352
Marinated Mozzarella, 466
Marinated Mozzarella, Olives and Sun-Dried Tomatoes, 92
Marinated Mozzarella Grinders, 92
Marinated Mozzarella Pizza, 222
Marinated Mozzarella Salad in Tomatoes, 351
Marinated Roasted Peppers and Olives, 466
Marinated Salad French Bread Pizza, 82
Marinated Soft-Shell Crabs, 341
Marinated Sun-Dried Tomato Pizza, 220

Marinated Sun-Dried Tomato Sauce, 225
Marinated Tomato with Chèvre and Onion, 399
Marinated Tuna and White Bean Salad, 188
Marinated Veal Paillards, 143
marmalade, 559–60
Marsala Mushrooms with Pancetta, 382
marshmallow
Fruit and Nut Bricks, 105
MeMe's Chocolate Roll, 528
S'mores, 532
marzipan (almond paste)
Chocolate-Covered Almond Apricots, 531
Chocolate-Covered Prunes with Marzipan "Pits," 531
Pistachio Tea Cake, 555
Sugar Plums, 554
Mascarpone Spoon Bread, 362
Mashed Potatoes with Ham and Cheese, 390
Mashed Potatoes with Roasted Garlic, 389
Mashed Potatoes with Yogurt and Herbs, 390
Matzo Ball Soup, Chicken, 193
Mayonnaise, 74
mayonnaise, 16–17, 74, 513
Mead, Modern-Day, 458
meat, 9, 11. *See also specific types of meat*
Cold Sliced Meats with Red and Green Sauces, 113
Make-Your-Own Pizza, 99
Meat and Potato Salad with Blue Cheese Dressing, 113
Meat Glace, 109
Meat and Potatoes Meatloaf, 255
Meatball Chili, 251
meatballs, 102, 121, 230, 250–52
Meatballs and Sauce, 230
Meatballs Wrapped in Bacon, 250
Meatless Mincemeat, 557
meatloaf, 89, 254–58, 298, 305
Meatloaf Baked in Bread, 255
Meatloaf Burgers, 131
Meatloaf Cupcakes, 254
Meatloaf Dijonnaise, 255
Meatloaf with Easy Tomato Sauce, 256
Meatloaf with Sauerkraut and Mustard on Rye, 89
Meatloaf with Spinach and Ricotta, 255
Meaty Chicken Noodle Soup, 294
Mediterranean Braised Leeks, 388
Mediterranean Chicken Stew, 265
Mediterranean Tilefish Stew, 318
Mediterranean Tomato Sauce, 109
Mélange of Roasted Peppers, 379
Melba Sauce, 449
Melba Tart, 538

melon
Cherries in Orange Honey over Melon, 180
Honeydew Filled with Champagne, 493
Honeydew Mint Soup, 175
Honeydew Raspberry Soup, 416
Kiwi and Honeydew in Margarita Glaze, 180
Melon Filled with Port, 493
Melon with Lime, 428
Melon Wrapped with Smoked Turkey, 303
Prosciutto and Summer Fruit Salad, 179
Melted Chocolate, 68
MeMe's Chocolate Roll, 528
Mesquite-Grilled Swordfish, 139
Mexican Baked Monkfish, 312
Mexican Bouillabaisse, 263
Mexican Burgers, 131
Mexican Meatloaf, 255
Mexican Seviche, 173
Mexican Stewed Monkfish, 502
Mexican Torta, 247
Microwave Chocolate Dip, 83
microwave cooking, 50, 67–69, 83, 310
Microwaved Mediterranean Cod, 310
Middle Eastern Barbecued Soft-Shell Crabs, 504
Middle Eastern Bulgur Orzo Salad, 186
Middle Eastern Chicken Salad, 498
Middle Eastern Chickpea Soup, 348
Middle Eastern Grilled Soft-Shell Crabs, 140
Middle Eastern Roasted Lamb, 482
Middle Eastern Turkey Burgers, 132
Middle Eastern Turkey Pitas, 94
Mild Green Salsa, 403
Mild Macaroni and Cheese, 101
Mild Red Salsa, 403
milk
Crab and Caviar Custard, 341
Crème Caramel, 474
drinks
Cappuccino Cocoa, 458
High-Protein Chocolate Peanut Butter Shake, 104
Iced Mocha, 457
Iced Spiked Cocoa, 457
Kahlúa and Cream Shake, 459
Liquid Chocolate Bars, 458
Real Hot Chocolate Spiked with Scotch, 523
Super-Protein Health Shake, 457
Warm White Chocolate Egg Nog, 457
Xylophone Milk, 104
Homemade Yogurt, 16
puddings
Best-Ever Chocolate Pudding, 529
Brown Rice Pudding, 361
Chocolate Chocolate Chip Pudding, 529

milk
  puddings (continued)
    Chocolate Hazelnut Pudding, 529
    Rice Pudding, 361
    Slow-Cooked Cinnamon Raisin
      Bread Pudding, 70
    White Chocolate Amaretto
      Pudding, 529
  sauces
    Béchamel Sauce (White Sauce), 17
    Chocolate Custard Sauce, 447
    Coffee Custard Sauce, 447
    Crème Anglaise, 24
    Maple Custard Sauce, 447
    Milk Chocolate Sauce, 445
    Old-Fashioned Custard Sauce, 447
    Orange Custard Sauce, 447
    Praline Custard Sauce, 447
    Super-Rich Custard Sauce, 447
Milk Chocolate Sauce with Almonds,
  445
Millet Pilaf with Pistachios and
  Apricots, 363
Mimosa Sorbet, 494
Minestrone with Beans, 194
mint
  drinks
    Mint Julep Iced Tea, 456
    Mint Julep Slush, 458
    Minted Apple Juice, 455
    Minted Iced Tea, 455
    Raspberry Mint Seltzer, 454
  Mint and Anise Marinade, 34
  Mint Pesto, 178
  Minted Yogurt Dressing, 65
Mint Mango Soup, 413
Minted Curried Potatoes, 353
Minted Lamb Burgers, 133
Minted Pears, 409
Minted Peas, 379
Miso Noodle Soup, 514
Miso Soup, 199
Miso Soup with Brown Rice, 515
Miso Soup with Dried Mushrooms,
  514
Miso Soup with Scallops, 199
Miso Soup with Vegetables, 199
Mixed Grilled Vegetable Tostada, 347
Mixed Grilled Vegetables with Black
  Bean Sauce, 347
Mixed Grilled Vegetables with
  Hummus, 125
Mixed Grilled Vegetables with Peanut
  Sauce, 347
Mixed Herb Tabbouleh, 186
Mocha Sauce, 445
Mocha Torte, 526
Modern-Day Mead, 458
Molasses Mustard Dip, 83
Mom's Meatloaf, 254
monkfish
  Mexican Baked Monkfish, 312
  Mexican Stewed Monkfish, 502
  Piquant Monkfish Stew, 263
  Provençal Monkfish Soup, 313

Mornay Sauce (Cheese Sauce), 17
Moroccan Chicken Stew, 291
Moroccan Dry Rub, 35
Moroccan Turkey Stew, 264
Muesli Cereal, 425
muffins, 397, 416, 542–50, 552
Mulled Cider, 457
mushrooms
  Composed Salad of Grilled
    Vegetables, 184
  Creamy Wild Mushroom Casserole,
    244
  Fresh Whole Wheat Wild
    Mushroom Pasta, 521
  Greek Marinated Mushrooms in
    Artichokes, 352
  Grilled Ratatouille, 145
  Marinated Antipasto, 349
  Marinated Garlic Mushrooms, 466
  Marinated Herbed Mushrooms, 560
  Marsala Mushrooms with Pancetta,
    382
  Mushroom Caesar Salad, 183
  Mushroom Garden Latkes, 381
  Mushroom Kebabs, 145
  Mushroom Persillade, 226
  Mushroom Strudel, 123
  Mushrooms Boiled with Lots of
    Garlic, 382
  Mushrooms Braised in Steak Sauce,
    428
  Mushrooms in Balsamic Glaze, 382
  Oyster-Stuffed Mushroom Caps,
    339
  Parsley Mushrooms, 382
  pizza
    Artichoke and Mushroom Pizza,
      216
    Duxelles and Parmesan Pizza, 218
    Sausage and Mushroom Pizza, 219
    Three-Mushroom Pizza, 219
    Tomato and Wild Mushroom
      Pizza, 214
  Quick Vegetable Chili, 203
  sauces
    Artichoke and Mushroom Sauce,
      227
    Mushroom Pasta Sauce, 69
    Sausage and Mushroom Sauce,
      230
    Three-Mushroom Sauce, 226
    Wild Mushroom, Brandy and
      Cream Sauce, 229
    Wine and Mushroom Sauce, 50
  Sausage-Stuffed Mushrooms, 467
  Sicilian Mushrooms with Savory, 47
  soups and stews
    Cream of Mushroom Soup, 193
    Miso Soup with Dried
      Mushrooms, 514
    Mushroom Barley Soup, 194
    Mushroom Chowder, 193
    Mushroom Ragoût, 55
    Mushrooms in Tomato Broth,
      382

mushrooms
  soups and stews (continued)
    Ragoût of Wild Mushrooms, 490
    Spinach and Wild Mushroom
      Soup, 368
    Turkey Mushroom Ragoût, 300
    Vegetable Broth, 19
    Wild Mushroom Bisque, 194
  Spicy Shiitake Mushrooms, 489
  Spinach-Stuffed Mushroom Caps,
    467
  Stir-Fried Herbed Mushrooms, 169
  Stir-Fried Wild Mushrooms with
    Hazelnuts, 169
  Tofu Braised with Wild Mushrooms,
    507
  White Wine Mushrooms, 55
  Wild Mushroom Chili, 203
  Wild Mushroom Meatloaf, 255
  Wild Mushroom Risotto Casserole,
    245
  Wild Mushroom Sausage Patties,
    252
  Wild Mushroom Stuffing, 384
mussels, 8, 161
  Grilled Tea-Steamed Clams and
    Mussels, 140
  Mexican Bouillabaisse, 263
  Mussel Marinara Soup, 198
  Mussels in Red Clam Sauce, 161
  Mussels in Red Sauce, 232
  Mussels in Tomato over Orzo, 504
  Mussels in White Sauce, 232
  Mussels Marseille, 339
  Mussels Niçoise, 338
  Mussels Oreganato, 46
  Mussels Provençal, 262
  Orange and Fennel Mussels, 504
  Portuguese Mussel Stew, 338
  Seafood Pot au Feu, 506
  Spicy Tomato and Mussel Pizza,
    214
  Tea-Smoked Mussels and Clams,
    504
Mustard, Black, 39
Mustard Chutney Dip, 84
Mustard-Glazed Smoked Turkey,
  303
Mustard-Grilled Veal Chops, 143
Mustard Tarragon Shrimp Cocktail,
  334
mustards, 39, 560–61

N

nachos, 102
Naked Basil and Prosciutto Pizza, 216
New England Clam Chowder, 198
New Potatoes au Gratin with Bacon,
  398
Niçoise Clams, 337
Niçoise Pizzas, 468
Niçoise Vinaigrette, 60
No-Fuss Fresh Berry Tart, 539
No-Heat Strawberry Wine Soup, 416

noodles. *See also* pasta
  Apple Kugel, 104
  Chicken and Noodle Salad with
    Peanut Sauce, 100
  High-Protein Vegetarian Stir-Fried
    Noodles, 167
  Noodles and Cheese, 101
  Real Tuna Noodle Casserole, 237
  Shrimp Thai Noodles, 167
  Souper Tuna Noodle Casserole, 237
  Thai Fried Noodles, 167
  Traditional Tuna Noodle Casserole,
    237
  Warm Buckwheat Pasta and Sesame
    Salad, 515
nuts, 13. *See also specific types of nuts*
  Ground Nuts, 74
  Nut Streusel Topping, 23
  Spicy Sweet Nuts, 80
  Toasted Nuts, 23, 68
Nutty Bran Muffins, 546

O

oat bran
  All–Oat Bran Muffins, 546
  Banana Oat Bran Raisin Muffins,
    545
  Oat Bran and Fig Muffins, 546
oats
  cereals
    Five-Grain Cereal, 425
    Irish Oatmeal, 70
    Muesli Cereal, 425
    Real Oatmeal, 426
  cookies
    Bacon Breakfast Cookies, 127
    Butterscotch Oaties, 443
    Candy Store Jumbles, 437
    Chocolate Peanut Jumbles, 438
    Espresso Oatmeal Chocolate Chip
      Cookies, 437
    Ginger Lace Cookies, 440
    Oaties, 443
    Oatmeal Jumbles, 437
    Peanut Butter Jumbles, 437
    Walnut Butter Jumbles, 437
    Walnut Oat Lace Cookies, 440
    Whole-Grain Breakfast Cookies, 127
  muffins
    Apple Oatmeal Spice Muffins, 549
    Applesauce Walnut Muffins, 549
    Banana Oatmeal Muffins, 549
Oil and Vinegar Dressing, 59
oils, 10, 59, 82, 558
Old Bay Fried Fish, 323
Old-Fashioned Apple Cheddar Pie, 535
Old-Fashioned Chicken Salad, 284
Old-Fashioned Custard Sauce, 447
Old World Boozy Apple Plum Pie,
  535
olives
  Curried Black Olives, 81
  Garlic Green Olives and Peppers, 81

olives *(continued)*
  Lemon and Pepper Olives, 81
  Marinated Mozzarella, Olives and
    Sun-Dried Tomatoes, 92
  Marinated Roasted Peppers and
    Olives, 466
  Niçoise Vinaigrette, 60
  pizza
    Chicken and Olive Pizza, 221
    Niçoise Pizzas, 468
    Pepper, Olive and Olive Oil Pizza,
      217
    Red, Black and Green Olive Pizza,
      218
    Spinach, Olive and Feta Pizza, 218
    Tomato, Fennel and Olive Pizza,
      214
    Tuna, White Bean and Olive Pizza,
      218
  Roasted Onions and Olives, 388
  sauces
    Anchovy Olive Pesto, 178
    Chicken and Olive Sauce, 232
    Roasted Pepper and Olive Sauce,
      227
    Sauce Provençal, 53
    Tomato, Olive and Parmesan
      Sauce, 53
  Tapenade, 56
  Tapenade Sauce, 234
  Vegetable Pâté Niçoise, 465
onions
  Cherry Tomato and Caramelized
    Onion Salad, 400
  Chopped Onion, 74
  Curried Onion Sauce, 55
  Onion, Brandy and Cream Sauce, 52
  Onion Dip, 115
  Pearl Onions Stewed with Olives,
    382
  pizza
    Caramelized Onion and
      Gorgonzola Pizza, 221
    Gorgonzola and Onion French
      Bread Pizza, 82
    Onion and Gruyère Pizza, 221
    Red Onion and Herbed Cheese
      Pizza, 222
    Smoked Salmon and Onion Pizza,
      221
    Tomato and Three-Onion Pizza,
      213
  Roasted Onions and Olives, 388
Open-Face Cherry Pie, 539
Open-Face Peach Pie, 537
Orange and Fennel Mussels, 504
Orange Beef, 165
Orange Chicken with Apricots, 163
Orange Chinese Roast Chicken, 275
Orange-Fennel Fillet, 324
Orange-Garlic Beets, 388
Orange-Glazed Turkey Breast with
    Brown Rice–Dried Fruit Stuffing,
    298
Orange Hoisin Turkey, 151

orange roughy
  Bourride of Orange Roughy, 314
  Sautéed Roughy in Anise-Parmesan
    Crust, 314
oranges and orange juice
  dressings and marinades
    Orange Tarragon Marinade, 29
    Orange Walnut Dressing, 60
    Orange Walnut Marinade, 29
    Spicy Citrus Marinade, 29
  drinks
    Double Orange Juice, 455
    Liquid Creamsicle, 459
    Zesty Iced Tea, 456
  Gingered Carrot Marmalade, 560
  Mango Orange Soup with Plums
    and Blueberries, 175
  Mimosa Sorbet, 494
  Orange Carrot Muffins, 548
  Orange Currant Muffins, 543
  Orange Liqueur Brownies, 554
  Orange Raspberry Pancakes, 416
  Orange Savarin, 557
  salads
    Crab, Orange and Black Bean
      Salad, 188
    Fennel and Orange Salad, 43
    Orange and Celery Salad, 183
    Warm Orange Walnut Spinach
      Salad, 490
  sauces and seasonings
    Blueberry Orange Sauce, 448
    Citrus Oil, 558
    Orange, Scotch and Espresso
      Sauce, 450
    Orange Butter, 434
    Orange Custard Sauce, 447
    Orange-Fennel Walnut Oil, 558
Oregano Walnut Pesto, 178
Orzo with Peas and Rosemary, 124
Out-of-Fresh-Basil Pesto, 38
Out-of-Season Blueberry Pie, 539
Oven-Braised Chicken with Apples
    and Red Cabbage, 243
Oven-Braised Chili, 204
Oyster Sauce with Lime and Garlic, 55
oysters, 11
  Cajun Oysters, 488
  Fried Oyster Sandwiches, 340
  Fried Oysters with Tartar Sauce, 340
  Oyster Stew, 340
  Oyster-Stuffed Mushroom Caps, 339
  Oysters and Caviar, 492
  Oysters Florentine, 339
  Oysters on the Half Shell with
    Jalapeño Cocktail Sauce, 339
  Poached Oysters in Butter Sauce,
    340
  Shrimp and Oysters with Basil, 505
  Stir-Fried Sesame Oysters, 505

P

Paella Casserole, 239
Pan-Barbecued Chicken Breasts, 154

Pan-Barbecued Chicken Sandwiches, 154
Pan-Fried Breaded Smelts with Pickled Peppers, 316
Pan-Fried Mackerel with Homemade Tartar Sauce, 312
Pan-Fried Shrimp in Barbecue Sauce, 101
Pan-Fried Trout with Tapenade Relish, 318
Pan-Roasted Chicken Legs, 122
Pan-Roasted Turkey Legs, 122
Pan-Seared Chicken Breasts with Tomato Dill Salsa, 154
pancakes, 103, 350, 380, 392, 416, 429. *See also* latkes
pancetta
    Carbonara Sauce, 231
    Pancetta, Hazelnut and Garlic Pizza, 219
    Pancetta, Hazelnut and Garlic Sauce, 231
parchment (for cooking), 12, 13–14
Parmesan-Coated Chicken Legs, 293
Parmesan-Crusted Baked Tomato, 398
Parmesan Fries, 391
parsley (fresh)
    Lemon Parsley Sauce, 56
    Mushroom Persillade, 226
    Parsley Mushrooms, 382
    Parsley Pasta, 46
    Parsley Sauce, 228
parsnips
    Carrot, Parsnip and Chives, 388
    Celery Parsnip Latkes, 350
    Creamed Parsnips, 388
    Vegetable Broth, 19
pasta
    homemade, 20, 46, 73, 371, 521
    sauces for, 20, 69, 224–34
pasta dishes. *See also* macaroni; noodles
    Asian Fried Noodles, 114
    Baked Pasta e Fagioli, 246
    Baked Shells Stuffed with Tuna and Cheese, 239
    Fettuccine with Ricotta and Spinach, 119
    Fresh Tomatoes and Pasta, 402
    Garlicky Pasta Primavera, 119
    Lasagna, Inside-Out, 100
    Lasagna, Rolled-Up, 120
    Lasagna Meatloaf, 258
    Noodles and Cheese, 101
    Orzo with Peas and Rosemary, 124
    Pasta with Garlic and White Beans, 119
    Pasta with Tomatoes, Basil and Feta, 402
    salads
        Chili Pasta Salad, 111
        Middle Eastern Bulgur Orzo Salad, 186
        Pasta, Bean and Tuna Salad, 111

pasta dishes
    salads (*continued*)
        Pepper Pasta Salad, 111
        Tomato Pesto Pasta Salad, 401
    Spaghetti with Fresh Tomato Sauce, 101
    Spaghetti with Stir-Fried Meat Sauce, 167
    Spaghetti with Turkey Bolognese, 500
    Spanakopita Casserole, 238
    Stir-Fried Pasta Primavera, 167
    Whole Wheat Pasta Boiled with Broccoli, Ricotta and Roasted Peppers, 521
    Whole Wheat Pasta with Roasted Peppers, 521
Pasta Dough, 73
Pastry, 534
pastry. *See also* phyllo dough; puff pastry
    in pie shells, 12, 13, 21
    recipes for, 20–21, 73–74, 534
Pastry Cream, 24
Pâte à Choux (Cream Puff and Éclair Pastry), 22
pâtés, 252–53, 465
peaches
    Bourbon-Spiked Peach and Praline "Bombe," 180
    Brandied Peaches, 448
    Brandied Summer Fruit, 174
    Caramel Peach Ice Cream, 419
    Easy Peach Melba, 419
    Ginger Peach Sauce, 448
    Ginger Peachy Muffins, 544
    Grilled Brandied Peaches, 146
    Low-Fat Peach Melba, 419
    Peach Blackberry Crunch, 421
    Peach Pizza, 538
    Peaches and Cream Shortcake, 422
    Peaches and White Chocolate Mousse in Chocolate Cups, 530
    Peaches in Chianti, 495
    Peaches in Peach Schnapps, 417
    Peaches Stir-Fried with Framboise, 171
    Peaches Stuffed with Chocolate Mousse, 418
    Peaches Stuffed with Ham Mousse, 179
    Peaches Stuffed with Minted Blueberries, 418
    Peaches Stuffed with Smoked Salmon Mousse, 179
    Pecan Peach Corn Muffins, 546
    pies and tarts
        Almond Peach Pie, 538
        Anytime Peach Pie, 540
        Classic Peach Pie, 538
        Melba Tart, 538
        Open-Face Peach Pie, 537
        Peach Tatin, 537
        Praline Peach Pie, 538
        Sour Cream Peach Pot Pie, 420

peaches (*continued*)
    salads
        Prosciutto and Summer Fruit Salad, 179
        Spiked Summer Fruit Salad, 417
        Summer Fruit with Lime Crème Anglaise, 417
        Summer Bounty Vinegar, 423
        Warm Peaches with Sesame Praline, 496
Peanut Chicken, 166
peanuts and peanut butter
    African Peanut Soup, 199
    Apple Caramel Peanut Pie, 536
    bars and squares
        Chocolate Peanut Butter Squares, 443
        Fruit and Nut Bricks, 105
        Peanut Butter Sandwich Squares, 441
    Chocolate Peanut Butter Pie, 541
    Chocolate Peanut Crunch Balls, 532
    Chocolate Peanut Grahams, 532
    cookies
        Bacon Breakfast Cookies, 127
        Candy Store Jumbles, 437
        Chocolate Peanut Jumbles, 438
        Oatmeal Jumbles, 437
        Peanut Butter Jumbles, 437
        Peanut Butter Raisin Bran Breakfast Cookies, 127
        Peanut Chocolate Drops, 523
        Whole-Grain Breakfast Cookies, 127
    dips and spreads
        Chocolate Peanut Butter, 83
        Hot Pepper Peanut Butter, 83
        Peanut Butter, 74
        Peanut Toffee Dip, 83
        Raisin Chocolate Chip Peanut Butter, 561
    dressings and marinades
        Asian Peanut Marinade, 34
        Chipotle Peanut Marinade, 34
        Hot Pepper Peanut Vinaigrette, 108
    High-Protein Chocolate Peanut Butter Shake, 104
    sandwiches
        Peanut Butter, Honey and Raisin Sandwiches, 87
        Peanut Butter and Apple Raisin Sandwiches, 98
        Peanut Butter and Banana Sandwiches, 98
        Peanut Butter Apple "Canapés," 103
    sauces
        Peanut Butter Chocolate Sauce, 445
        Peanut Butter Cream, 451
        Peanut Sauce, 53
        Spicy Peanut Sauce, 228
    snacks
        Healthy Snack Mix, 80

peanuts and peanut butter
  snacks (*continued*)
      Sweet Curried Peanuts, 80
      Unhealthy Snack Mix, 80
Pear and Chicken Pot Pie, 406
Pearl Onions Stewed with Olives, 382
pears
  cakes
      Cardamom Pear Cake, 412
      Pear Ginger Coffee Cake, 413
      Prosciutto Pear Galette, 406
  Chinese Roasted Pears, 409
  Creamy Vanilla Pear Crisp, 411
  Ginger Poached Pears, 409
  Honey-Roasted Pears, 409
  Minted Pears, 409
  pastries
      Bartlett Turnovers, 410
      Lemon Pear Mini Turnovers, 469
      Pear and Roquefort Turnovers, 410
  Pear Applesauce, 407
  pies and tarts
      Almond Pear Pie, 535
      Apple Pear Pie, 535
      Balsamic Pear Tarte Tatin, 411
      Honeyed Pear Upside-Down Pie, 537
      Inverted Pear Tart, 537
      Topless Lime Pear Pie, 537
  Poached Winter Fruit Salad with Raspberry Vinaigrette, 190
  Prosciutto and Pear, 81
  sauces and seasonings
      Caramel Pear Preserves, 560
      Cranberry Pear Sauce, 407
      Pear Honey, 434
      Pear Vinegar, 558
  Spiced Poached Pears, 409
  Stir-Fried Poached Pears, 170
  Warm Pear Purée, 449
  Warm Pink Pear Purée, 495
peas, dried
  Black-Eyed Pea Chili, 206
  Chili Gumbo, 210
  Garden Split Pea Soup, 199
  Healthy Hoppin' John, 519
  Rice and Split Pea Pilaf, 358
  Split Pea Zucchini Soup, 397
  Turkey Carcass Split Pea Soup, 110
peas, fresh. *See also* snow peas
  Confetti of Prosciutto, Peas and Rosemary, 52
  Garlicky Pasta Primavera, 119
  Green Pea Soup with Mint, 45
  Minted Peas, 379
  Orzo with Peas and Rosemary, 124
  Peas with Brown Shallots, 379
  Stir-Fried Rice with Spring Vegetables, 361
Peasant Pie, 354
Pecan Catfish Fingers and Sweet Potato Chips, 309
Pecan Chicken Breasts with Mustard Sauce, 287

pecans
  bars and squares
      Chewy Gooey Lemon Pecan Bars, 442
      Date Nut Brownies, 524
      Pecan Pie Bars, 442
  cakes
      Buttermilk Coffee Cake, 433
      Date Nut Coffee Cake, 433
      Two-Ton Bourbon Nut Cake, 556
  cookies
      Pecan Shortbread, 554
      Praline Lace Hearts, 496
      Praline Shortbread, 554
  Hot Pepper Pecans, 79
  muffins and breads
      Brown Sugar Pecan Muffins, 545
      Cinnamon Swirl Muffins, 544
      Gingered Pecan Zucchini Bread, 397
      Pecan Corn Muffins, 547
      Pecan Peach Corn Muffins, 546
      Pecan Popovers, 432
  pies
      Chocolate Bourbon Pecan Pie, 529
      Perfect Pecan Pie, 541
      Praline Apple Pie Spiked with Bourbon, 536
      Praline Peach Pie, 538
  sauces
      Bourbon Pecans, 559
      Pecan or Walnut Butter, 561
      Praline Custard Sauce, 447
      Wet Bourbon Pecans, 450
Pepper Peanut Shrimp, 472
Peppercorn Burgers, 130
Peppered Chocolate Sauce, 446
Pepperoni and Meat Sauce Pizza, 215
Pepperoni Pepper Corn Muffins, 547
peppers, bell. *See also* peppers, roasted bell
  Bell Peppers Stuffed with Macaroni and Cheese, 120
  Carrot and Red Pepper, 388
  Chilied Corn Salad Stuffed in Roasted Peppers, 352
  Gazpacho, 73
  Hominy with Peppers, 362
  Julienned Peppers and Carrots, 55
  Mixed Grilled Vegetable Tostada, 347
  Mixed Grilled Vegetables with Black Bean Sauce, 347
  Mixed Grilled Vegetables with Hummus, 125
  Mixed Grilled Vegetables with Peanut Sauce, 347
  Pepper Cheddar Skillet Cornbread, 556
  Pickled Peppers, 379
  sauces and marinades
      Hot, Hot, Hot Barbecue Paste, 32
      Hot-and-Sour Barbecue Marinade, 32
      Red Pepper Coulis, 53

peppers, bell
  sauces and marinades (*continued*)
      Southwest Barbecue Marinade, 32
  Vegetarian Chili, 202
peppers, chili
  Basic Chili Mix (BCM), 202
  Chili Inferno, 204
  Chili Marinade, 35
  Chili Pepper Chutney, 40
  Chipotle Peanut Marinade, 34
  Hot Pepper, Bacon and Gorgonzola Pizza, 222
  jalapeños
      Carpaccio Jalapeño, 176
      Confetti Salsa, 177
      Hot, Hot, Hot Barbecue Paste, 32
      Hot-and-Sour Barbecue Marinade, 32
      Jalapeño Bloody Marys, 45
      Jalapeño Jelly, 560
      Jalapeño Salsa, 177
      Jalapeño Shrimp Cocktail, 335
      Lime Jalapeño Marinade, 29
      Salsa Vinaigrette, 65
      Southwest Barbecue Marinade, 32
peppers, roasted bell, 11
  appetizers
      Garlic Green Olives and Peppers, 81
      Marinated Antipasto, 349
      Marinated Roasted Peppers and Olives, 466
      Summer Antipasto, 348
  Chèvre and Roasted Pepper Mini-Sandwiches, 93
  Mélange of Roasted Peppers, 379
  Peppers with Basil and Walnuts, 183
  pizza
      Pepper, Olive and Olive Oil Pizza, 217
      Ricotta and Roasted Red Pepper Pizza, 216
      Roasted Pepper, Caper and Anchovy Pizza, 216
      Roasted Pepper and Walnut Pizza, 217
      Tri-Color Roasted Pepper Pizza, 216
  Roasted Pepper and Gorgonzola Grinder, 385
  Roasted Pepper Popcorn, 79
  Roasted Peppers with Anchovies, 380
  Roasted Peppers with Black Olives and Anchovies, 183
  salads
      Brown Rice and Roasted Pepper Salad, 349
      Pepper Pasta Salad, 111
      Rice and Bean Salad, 112
      Roasted Pepper Tortellini Salad, 467
  sauces, dips and dressings
      Pepper and Anchovy Sauce, 234
      Ricotta and Roasted Red Pepper Sauce, 226

peppers, roasted bell
sauces, dips and dressings (*continued*)
Roasted Pepper and Olive Sauce, 227
Roasted Pepper and Walnut Sauce, 227
Roasted Pepper Dip, 464
Roasted Pepper Rouille, 56
Roasted Pepper Salsa, 177
Sweet Pepper Vinaigrette, 63
Three-Pepper Sauce, 227
soups
Chilled Tomato and Roasted Pepper Soup, 174
Red Pepper Chowder Swirled with Chili Cream, 348
Roasted Red Pepper Chowder, 196
Tri-Colored Peppers with Herbs, 183
Whole Wheat Pasta with Roasted Peppers, 521
Perfect Fries, 391
Perfect Hash-Brown Potatoes, 391
Perfect Pecan Pie, 541
Pesto, 20
pesto, 20, 38, 178, 228
Pesto-Crusted Tenderloin with Roasted Pepper Rouille, 478
Pesto-Glazed Broiled Chicken, 286
Pesto Mayonnaise Dressing, 64
Pesto Roast Chicken, 273
Pesto Vinaigrette, 65
phyllo dough
Cheese Pockets, 468
Mushroom Strudel, 123
Spinach Strudel with Tomato Vinaigrette, 371
Tuna Strudel, 123
Tyropites, 468
Pickled Peppers, 379
Pickling Marinade, 33
Picnic Pork Roast, 484
Pie Pastry, 73
pies, 411, 419–20, 528–29, 533–41
pot pies, 12, 243–44, 406, 419–20
shells for, 12, 13, 21, 115
Piggy Dogs, 134
pine nuts
Ham, Pine Nut and Rosemary Sauce, 231
pesto
Fresh Basil Pesto, 178
Out-of-Fresh-Basil Pesto, 38
Pesto, 20
Spicy Basil Pesto, 178
Spinach Pesto, 178
Pesto Vinaigrette, 65
Pine Nut and Garlic Butter, 83
Pine Nut Macaroons, 438
pineapple
Bacon and Fruit Slaw, 187
Pineapple Cornbread, 407
Pineapple Upside-Down Pie, 411
Roasted Pineapple, 409

Pineapple Jerk Pork, 484
Pinwheels, 439
Piquant Monkfish Stew, 263
pistachios
Chocolate Fruit Squares, 532
Chocolate Pistachio Drops, 437
Pistachio Tea Cake, 555
Ruby Salad, 368
pitas (as ingredient)
Avocado Falafel, 346
Black Bean Falafel, 346
Caesar Salad Sandwiches, 94
Chicken Chickpea Salad Pitas, 95
Eggplant Falafel, 346
Grilled Lamb and Artichoke Pitas, 94
Middle Eastern Turkey Pitas, 94
Pita Filled with Toasted Chickpeas, Avocado and Eggplant "Caviar," 346
Roast Beef Pita Pocket, 98
Tuna and Guacamole Pitas, 94
Pizza Rustica, 354
pizzas, 81–82, 99, 212–23, 354, 468
dessert, 195, 538
dough for, 20
Plantain Chips, 80
plums. *See also* prunes
Plum and Blackberry Parfait, 419
Plum Pudding Crisp, 421
Plums in Sambuca, 417
Spiked Summer Fruit Salad, 417
Summer Bounty Vinegar, 423
Summer Fruit with Lime Crème Anglaise, 417
Topless Plum Pie, 537
Poached Chicken Breasts in Beurre Blanc, 285
Poached Chicken Breasts with Warm Tomato Vinaigrette, 149
Poached Egg Tostadas, 427
Poached Fish, 68
Poached Fish with Beurre Blanc, 321
Poached Fish with Tomato Mint Salsa, 322
Poached Fish with Wine Hollandaise, 322
Poached Oysters in Butter Sauce, 340
Poached Salmon and Eggs with Lemon Butter Sauce, 426
Poached Salmon with Arugula, 516
Poached Salmon with Lemon and Chives, 41
Poached Salmon with Middle Eastern Cucumbers, 314
Poached Winter Fruit Salad with Raspberry Vinaigrette, 190
poaching, 11, 50, 68
Polenta, 362
Polenta with Green Salsa, 362
pompano
Grilled Pompano with Lime and Dill, 313
Pompano en Papillote with Baby Shrimp and Chives, 313
popcorn, 46, 78–79

Popcorn with Basil and Sun-Dried Tomatoes, 78
popovers, 42, 432–33
Poppy Seed Buttermilk Scones, 432
Poppy Seed Dressing, 62
porgy
Sesame Porgy Fillets, 314
Whole Grilled Porgy, 313
pork. *See also* bacon; ham; sausage
boneless loin
Barbecued Chicken or Pork Salad, 112
Garlic Roasted Pork Loin, 483
Herb-Crusted Roasted Pork Loin, 482
Pistachio-Stuffed Pork Loin, 483
Pork, Apple and Sweet Potato Shepherd's Pie, 242
Pork Braised in Apple Cider, 509
Roasted Pork Loin Stuffed with Apples and Prunes, 483
Sage Roast Pork with Sage Mayonnaise, 47
Spicy Peanut Pork, 166
Stir-Fried Pork and Shrimp with Noodles, 168
Stuffed Pork Loin Glazed with Cider Syrup, 483
Sweet-and-Sour Lemon Pork, 165
chilis
All-Pork Chili, 205
Black-Eyed Pea Chili, 206
Bourbon Chili, 206
chops
Chipotle Cherry Pork, 156
Grilled Honey-Mustard Pork Chops, 144
Honeyed Pork Chops in Chili Sauce, 206
Pork Chops with Bourbon Reduction, 157
Pork Chops with Caramelized Onions, 157
Homemade Breakfast Sausage, 428
Jerk Ribs, 270
marinades for, 29–35
meatballs
Meatballs and Sauce, 230
Sweet-and-Sour Sesame Meatballs, 251
Sweet Sesame Meatballs, 250
meatloaf
Apple Sage Meatloaf, 254
Apple Turkey Meatloaf, 305
Chilied Meatloaf with Chorizo, 254
Ham and Cheddar Meatloaf, 255
Ham Meatloaf, 255
Lasagna Meatloaf, 258
Lots-of-Olives Meatloaf, 255
Meat and Potatoes Meatloaf, 255
Meatloaf Baked in Bread, 255
Meatloaf Cupcakes, 254
Meatloaf Dijonnaise, 255
Meatloaf with Easy Tomato Sauce, 256

pork

  meatloaf (*continued*)

    Meatloaf with Spinach and
      Ricotta, 255
    Mexican Meatloaf, 255
    Mom's Meatloaf, 254
    Prosciutto and Cheese Meatloaf, 255
    Sausage Meatloaf, 255
    Smoked Turkey Meatloaf, 298
    Surprise Meatloaf, 254
    Sweet-and-Sour Meatloaf, 255
    Veal Loaf with Artichokes, 257
    Wild Mushroom Meatloaf, 255
  Pork Medallions with Mustard and
    Rosemary, Grilled, 509
  Pork Medallions with Mustard and
    Capers, 508
  Pork Tacos, 157
  Potstickers, 250
  Rack of Pork with Roasted
    Pineapple, 485
  sauces for, 51–55
  shoulder (picnic ham)
    Barbecued Pork Sandwiches, 92
    Barbecued Pork Sandwiches with
      Coleslaw, 92
    Barbecued Pork Sandwiches with
      Sauerkraut, 92
    Lemon Coriander Pork, 484
    Picnic Pork Roast, 484
    Pulled Pork, 71
    South Carolina–Style Pulled Pork,
      484
  stews
    Barbecued Pork Stewed with
      Sausage, 261
    Jamaican Jerk Stew, 270
    Pork Stewed with Apples and
      Prunes, 266
    Pork Stewed with Red Cabbage, 269
  Veal and Pork Potstickers, 250
Port, Figs Preserved in, 449
Portuguese Mussel Stew, 338
Pot au Feu, 72
Pot Roast, 71
potatoes
  Bacon, Peppers and Potatoes, 384
  baked
    Baked Potato Skins with Yogurt
      Herb Sauce, 114
    Baked Potatoes with Minted
      Yogurt, 393
    Baked Potatoes with Mustard
      Sauce, 393
    Baked Potatoes with Sour Cream
      Vinaigrette, 392
    Potatoes Baked with Anchovies
      and Tomatoes, 123
    Twice-Baked Blue Cheese
      Potatoes, 393
    Twice-Baked Cheddar Jalapeño
      Potatoes, 393
  chips
    Garlic Potato Chips, 80
    Grilled Potato Chips, 145

potatoes

  chips (*continued*)

    Potato Chips, 391
    Spicy Potato Chips, 391
  Fried Potato Frittata, 126
  fries
    Buffalo Fries, 391
    French Fries with Tapenade, 489
    Parmesan Fries, 391
    Perfect Fries, 391
  gratins
    Gorgonzola Gratin, 389
    Ham and Swiss Gratin, 389
    New Potatoes au Gratin with
      Bacon, 398
    Potato and Celeriac Gratin, 389
    Potatoes au Gratin, 389
    Potatoes au Gratin with
      Caramelized Onions, 389
    Potatoes Parmesan, 389
    Triple-Cheese Potatoes au Gratin,
      124
  hash browns
    Bacon Hash Browns, 427
    Chilied Hash Browns, 391
    Hash Browns and Cabbage, 391
    Onion and Garlic Hash Browns,
      427
    Peppered Hash Browns, 391
    Perfect Hash-Brown Potatoes, 391
  mashed
    Blue Cheese Mashed Potatoes, 390
    Classic Mashed Potatoes, 389
    Mashed Potatoes with Ham and
      Cheese, 390
    Mashed Potatoes with Roasted
      Garlic, 389
    Mashed Potatoes with Yogurt and
      Herbs, 390
    Potato Celeriac Purée, 390
    Potato Fennel Purée, 390
  Minted Curried Potatoes, 353
  pancakes and galettes
    Fall Garden Latkes, 380
    Potato Cheese Galette, 392
    Potato Fennel Pancakes, 392
    Potato Garlic Galette, 392
    Potato Leek Pancakes, 392
    Potato Pancakes, 392
  Potato and Spinach Curry, 124
  Potato Leek Frittata, 427
  Potatoes and Eggplant, 353
  Roasted Anchovy Potatoes, 490
  Roasted Potatoes with Turnips, 390
  salads
    Corned Beef and Potato Salad, 392
    German-Style Potato Salad, 184
    Grilled Salmon Potato Salad, 138
    Meat and Potato Salad with Blue
      Cheese Dressing, 113
    Potato and Tuna Vinaigrette Salad,
      119
    Potato Vinaigrette with Mussels
      and Olives, 185
    Russian Herring Potato Salad, 185

potatoes

  salads (*continued*)

    Seafood Potato Salad, 185
    Sour Cream and Caviar Potato
      Salad, 185
    Spicy Sausage Potato Salad, 118
    Sweet-and-Sour Hot Sausage
      Potato Salad, 118
    Sweet-and-Sour Smoked Turkey
      Potato Salad, 185
    Three-Can Salad, 174
    Waldorf Potato Salad, 185
  Sautéed Potatoes, Onions and
    Smoked Salmon, 390
  Sautéed Potatoes with Garden
    Vegetables, 123
  Sautéed Potatoes with Garlic and
    Olives, 390
  Sautéed Potatoes with Walnuts, 390
  Scalloped Potatoes with Feta, 389
  Scalloped Potatoes with Onions and
    Anchovies, 389
  soups
    Caraway Potato Soup, 196
    Garlic Potato Soup, 195
    Potato Cheese Soup, 195
    Potato Fennel Soup, 117, 195
    Potato Fennel Vichyssoise, 195
    Potato Leek Soup, 195
    Potato Watercress Soup, 196
    Vichyssoise, 72
  Soy-Glazed Potatoes, 169
  Steamed New Potatoes, 68
  Tomato and Basil Potatoes, 382
Potstickers, 250
potstickers, 10, 250
poultry. *See also* chicken; duck; game;
    turkey
  Asian Fried Noodles, 114
  Cold Sliced Meats with Red and
    Green Sauces, 113
  Fried Rice from Leftovers, 114
Pound Cake, 22
Poussin Roasted with Garlic and
    Molasses, 491
Praline Apple Pie Spiked with
    Bourbon, 536
Praline Chocolate Caramel Sauce, 446
Praline Custard Sauce, 447
Praline Lace Hearts, 496
Praline Peach Pie, 538
Praline Shortbread, 554
Precooked Beans or Carrots, 69
prosciutto
  Basil and Prosciutto Sauce, 231
  Confetti of Prosciutto, Peas and
    Rosemary, 52
  Gorgonzola and Prosciutto au
    Gratin, 241
  Layered Veal, Turkey and Prosciutto
    Loaf, 244
  Naked Basil and Prosciutto Pizza, 216
  Prosciutto, Walnut and Feta Pizza,
    221
  Prosciutto and Cheese Meatloaf, 255

prosciutto (*continued*)
  Prosciutto and Fennel Spinach, 370
  Prosciutto and Pear, 81
  Prosciutto and Summer Fruit Salad,
    179
  Prosciutto Pear Galette, 406
Protein-Packed Cornbread, 512
Provençal Marinade, 30
Provençal Mini-Pizzas, 82
Provençal Monkfish Soup, 313
Provençal Oil, 558
Provençal Ricotta Bread Pudding, 247
Provençal Tuna Burgers, 134
prunes. *See also* plums
  Chocolate-Covered Prunes with
    Marzipan "Pits," 531
  Old World Boozy Apple Plum Pie,
    535
  Plum Pudding Crisp, 421
  Prunes in Brandy, 84
  Spiced Fruit, 70
  Stewed Prunes, 69
  Sugar Plums, 554
puddings, 361, 362. *See also* cobblers
  bread, 70, 100, 115, 247
  chocolate, 115, 474, 529
  fruit, 104, 361, 410–11
  rice, 115, 361, 521
  Yorkshire, 477
Puerto Rican Clams, 338
Puff Pastry, Quick, 74
puff pastry (as ingredient)
  Cheese Straws, 468
  Chicken Wellington, 470
  pies and tarts
    Balsamic Pear Tarte Tatin, 411
    Honeyed Pear Upside-Down Pie,
      537
    Inverted Pear Tart, 537
    Peach Tatin, 537
    Pineapple Upside-Down Pie, 411
    Tarte Tatin, 537
    Upside-Down Maple Apple Pie,
      537
  Puff Pastry Mini Pizzas, 468
  turnovers
    Apple Cheddar Turnovers, 410
    Apple Fennel Turnovers, 410
    Apple Mincemeat Mini Turnovers,
      469
    Apple Turnovers, 410
    Bartlett Turnovers, 410
    Creole Crab Mini Turnovers, 469
    Lemon Pear Mini Turnovers, 469
    Liver and Bacon Mini Turnovers,
      469
    Pear and Roquefort Turnovers,
      410
    Turkey Cranberry Turnovers, 299
Pulled Pork, 71
pumpkin
  Apple Pumpkin Bisque, 196
  Buttermilk Pumpkin Pie, 540
  Classic Pumpkin Pie, 540
  Ginger Pumpkin Bisque, 514

pumpkin (*continued*)
  Pumpkin Bisque, 348
  Pumpkin Chiffon Pie, 540
  Pumpkin Leek Soup, 196
  Refried Pumpkin, 383
Pumpkin Seeds, Chili, 79
Pungent Orange Turkey Meatballs,
  121
Pungent Tomato Salmon Salad, 188
Puréed Vegetable Soup, 72

Q

Quesadilla Casserole, 123
Quick Berry Compote, 423
quick breads, 39, 396–97, 432. *See also*
  biscuits; muffins; popovers
Quick Buttercream, 23
Quick Cassoulet, 241
Quick Cheese Grits, 362
Quick Chicken Chili, 156
Quick Chopped Chicken Liver, 466
Quick Crab Chowder, 342
Quick Dark Chocolate Sauce, 445
Quick Fish Broth, 19
Quick Fresh Tomato Sauce, 225
Quick Meat Sauce, 229
Quick Puff Pastry, 74
Quick Shrimp Étouffée, 334
Quick Sorbet, 74
Quick Tomato Salad, 399
Quick Vegetable Chili, 203
quinoa
  Quinoa Pilaf, 365
  Quinoa Tabbouleh, 365
  Quinoa with Pecans, 365
  Quinoa with Tofu and Mushrooms,
    520
  Stir-Fried Quinoa, 520

R

rabbit
  Grilled Rabbit, 507
  Rabbit Chili, 211
rabe (rapini). *See* broccoli rabe
Rack of Lamb with Roasted Garlic
  Jus, 482
Rack of Pork with Roasted Pineapple,
  485
radicchio
  Ruby Salad, 368
  Three-Endive Slaw, 174
Ragoût of Wild Mushrooms, 490
raisins
  Apple Brandy Raisin Risotto
    Pudding, 361
  Banana Oat Bran Raisin Muffins, 545
  bars and squares
    Fruit and Nut Bricks, 105
    Raisin Squares, 443
    Spiked Fruitcake Brownies, 553
    Wheat Germ Squares, 443
  Butter Rum Raisin Sauce, 450
  Caraway Raisin Soda Bread, 39

raisins (*continued*)
  Honey Rum Raisin Tea Cake, 556
  Meatless Mincemeat, 557
  Peanut Butter, Honey and Raisin
    Sandwiches, 87
  Peanut Butter and Apple Raisin
    Sandwiches, 98
  Peanut Butter Raisin Bran Breakfast
    Cookies, 127
  Raisin Applesauce, 407
  Raisin Bran Muffins, 545
  Raisin Chocolate Chip Peanut
    Butter, 561
  Rum Raisin Bananas, 170
  Slow-Cooked Cinnamon Raisin
    Bread Pudding, 70
  Snack Mix, Healthy, 80
  Snack Mix, Unhealthy, 80
Ranch Roast Chicken, 278
Ranch-Style Bluefish, 309
rapini. *See* broccoli rabe
raspberries
  Asparagus, Shrimp, Raspberry and
    Grapefruit Salad, 506
  Chocolate Ice Cream with
    Raspberry Swirl, 531
  drinks
    Berry Wine Punch, 459
    Raspberry Mint Seltzer, 454
    Sparkling Peach Melba, 454
  Easy Peach Melba, 419
  Gingered Berry Crisp, 421
  Honeydew Raspberry Soup, 416
  Low-Fat Peach Melba, 419
  Orange Raspberry Pancakes, 416
  pies and tarts
    Black-Bottom Raspberry Tart, 420
    Chocolate Raspberry Tart, 539
    Deep-Dish Blueberry and
      Raspberry Pot Pie, 419
    Melba Tart, 538
    Raspberry Blueberry Pie, 539
    Raspberry Nectarine Pie, 420
    Raspberry Rhubarb Pie, 539
  Prosciutto and Summer Fruit Salad,
    179
  Raspberries and Cream, 448
  Raspberry Chocolate Bombe, 495
  Raspberry Chocolate Chip Muffins,
    544
  Raspberry Lemon Laban, 419
  Raspberry Ricotta Mousse, 418
  Raspberry Soup, 416
  sauces and seasonings
    Chocolate Raspberry Sauce, 446
    Melba Sauce, 449
    Raspberry Vinaigrette, 61
    Raspberry White Chocolate Sauce,
      446
  Sugared Raspberries, 448
  Three-Berry Crisp, 421
Ratatouille, 352
Real Good French Toast, 430
Real Hot Chocolate Spiked with
  Scotch, 523

Real Mac and Cheese for the Whole Family, 236
Real Macaroni and Cheese, 236
Real Oatmeal, 426
Real Russian Dressing, 62
Real Tuna Noodle Casserole, 237
Red, Black and Green Olive Pizza, 218
Red and Yellow Tomato Salad, 400
Red Cabbage Slaw, 187
Red Caesar Dressing, 108
Red Curry Chicken, 166
Red Curry Marinade, 34
Red Curry Roast Chicken, 278
Red Onion and Herbed Cheese Pizza, 222
Red Pepper Chowder Swirled with Chili Cream, 348
Red Pepper Coulis, 53
Red Sauce, 113
red snapper
    Broiled Red Snapper with Green Chili Cream Sauce, 316
    Sweet Pepper Seared Snapper, 46
    Whole Steamed Red Snapper, 317
Red Wine Pomegranate Sauce, 52
Red Wine Whole-Grain Mustard, 561
Reduced-Calorie Meatloaf, 254
Reduced-Fat Pesto, 228
Refried Black, White or Kidney Beans, 20
Refried Pumpkin, 383
relishes, 40, 48, 559
rhubarb
    Blueberry Rhubarb Pie, 539
    Raspberry Rhubarb Pie, 539
    Strawberries with Warm Rhubarb Sauce, 417
    Strawberry Rhubarb Pie, 420
    Warm Rhubarb and Strawberry Shortcake, 422
Rib Roast of Beef with Garlic, 477
Rib Roast with Braised Wild Mushrooms, 478
Rib Roast with Creamy Horseradish Sauce, 477
Rib Roast with Garlic Jus, 477
Rib Roast with Roasted Potatoes and Capers, 477
Rib Roast with Rosemary Red Wine Glaze, 477
Rib Roast with Yorkshire Pudding, 477
rice
    basmati
        Basmati Rice, 360
        Fragrant Basmati Rice, 360
        Lemon or Lime Basmati Rice, 360
    Brown Beans and Rice, 519
    Brown Rice with Red Beans, 124
    Brown Rice with Three Cheeses, 124
    Confetti Brown Rice, 359
    fried rice
        Fried Rice from Leftovers, 114
        Fried Rice with Vegetables, 351
        Sweet Fried Rice, 171

rice (continued)
    Harvest Rice Stuffing, 384
    pilafs
        Black Pepper Pilaf, 358
        Brown Rice and Vegetable Pilaf, 359
        Brown Rice Pilaf, 359
        Brown Rice with Toasted Coconut, 359
        Brown Rice with Wheat Berries, 359
        Curried Rice Pilaf, 357
        Dirty Rice, 358
        Low-Salt, Big-Flavor Rice Pilaf, 358
        Rice and Split Pea Pilaf, 358
        Rice Pilaf with Walnuts, 358
        Sesame Brown Rice Pilaf, 519
        Simple Rice Pilaf, 357
        Spinach Pilaf, 369
        Sweet Curried Rice with Pistachios, 358
    puddings
        Apple Brandy Raisin Risotto Pudding, 361
        Brown Rice Pudding, 361
        Rice Pudding, 361
        Tofu Rice Pudding, 521
        White Chocolate Rice Pudding, 115
    risottos
        Brown Rice Risotto with Sage and Potatoes, 520
        Risotto, 360
        Risotto Milanese, 360
        Risotto with Mushrooms and Chicken Livers, 360
        Risotto with Rosemary, 360
        Spinach Risotto, 360
        Squash Stuffed with Risotto, 349
        Wild Mushroom Risotto Casserole, 245
        Wild Rice Risotto, 520
    salads
        Brown Rice and Roasted Pepper Salad, 349
        Grilled Tomatillo and Rice Salad, 384
        Rice and Bean Salad, 112
        Rice and Lentil Salad, 349
    Spiced Brown Rice, 80
    Stir-Fried Rice, 361
    Stir-Fried Rice with Spring Vegetables, 361
    Whole Wheat Brown Rice Pancakes, 512
Rich Red Tomato Salsa, 176
Ricotta and Roasted Red Pepper Pizza, 216
Ricotta and Roasted Red Pepper Sauce, 226
Ricotta Cheese Pancakes, 429
Ricotta Creamed Spinach, 369
Ricotta Rosemary Muffins, 550
risotto. See rice
Roast Beef on Rye with Horseradish Sauce, 87

Roast Beef Pita Pocket, 98
Roast Chicken Cacciatore, 274
Roast Chicken Chasseur, 280
Roast Chicken in Spicy Peanut Paste, 274
Roast Chicken Provençal, 277
Roast Chicken Véronique, 280
Roast Chicken with Apple Butter Glaze, 279
Roast Chicken with Bread, Sage and Apple Stuffing, 281
Roast Chicken with Capers and Lemon, 273
Roast Chicken with Clam and Cracker Stuffing, 281
Roast Chicken with Cranberry Cornbread Stuffing, 281
Roast Chicken with Dried Fruit Stuffing, 282
Roast Chicken with Fines Herbes, 278
Roast Chicken with Horseradish Mustard, 273
Roast Chicken with Molasses and Vinegar, 276
Roast Chicken with Orange Glaze, 277
Roast Chicken with Sherry Balsamic Glaze, 280
Roast Chicken with Tarragon and Brandy, 278
Roast Chicken with Vanilla Sauce, 280
Roast Chicken with Wild Mushroom Stuffing, 280
Roast Lamb Dijonnaise, 481
Roast Lamb Provençal, 481
Roast Lamb with Fresh Mint Sauce, 481
Roast Sirloin with Porter Barbecue Sauce, 479
Roast Sirloin with Spicy Coffee Elixir, 480
Roast Tandoori-Style Chicken, 279
Roasted Anchovy Potatoes, 490
Roasted Balsamic Tomatoes, 398
Roasted Bananas, 409
Roasted Beef Tenderloin with Caramelized Onions, 478
Roasted Beef Tenderloin with Scotch Jus, 478
Roasted Beef Tenderloin with Wasabi Steak Sauce, 478
Roasted Boneless Leg of Lamb, 481
Roasted Eggplant, 19
Roasted Eggplant and Feta Pizza, 217
Roasted Eggplant and Garlic Sauce, 227
Roasted Fish Provençal, 485
Roasted Garlic Horseradish Paste, 44
Roasted Garlic Purée, 464
Roasted Garlic Roast Chicken, 278
Roasted Onion Frittata, 126
Roasted Onions and Olives, 388
Roasted Pepper, Caper and Anchovy Pizza, 216
Roasted Pepper and Basil Meatloaf, 255

Roasted Pepper and Brown Rice Casserole, 246
Roasted Pepper and Gorgonzola Grinder, 385
Roasted Pepper and Olive Sauce, 227
Roasted Pepper and Walnut Pizza, 217
Roasted Pepper and Walnut Sauce, 227
Roasted Pepper Chili, 205
Roasted Pepper Dip, 464
Roasted Pepper Popcorn, 79
Roasted Pepper Rouille, 56
Roasted Pepper Salsa, 177
Roasted Pepper Tortellini Salad, 467
Roasted Pepper Veal Burgers, 133
Roasted Peppers with Anchovies, 380
Roasted Peppers with Black Olives and Anchovies, 183
Roasted Pineapple, 409
Roasted Pork Loin Stuffed with Apples and Prunes, 483
Roasted Potatoes with Turnips, 390
Roasted Rack of Lamb, 482
Roasted Rack of Lamb with Mustard Crumbs, 482
Roasted Rack of Lamb with Wasabi Crumbs, 482
Roasted Red Pepper Chowder, 196
Roasted Turkey Breast Studded with Hazelnuts and Garlic, 304
Roasted Turkey Breast with Mint, 501
Roasted Whole Tenderloin of Beef, 478
roasting, 476
Rolled-Up Lasagna, 120
Roquefort Buttermilk Sauce, 56
Roquefort Dressing, 64
Rosemary, Sage and Garlic Fillets, 325
Rosemary and Vermouth Sauce, 54
Rosemary-Grilled Tomato, 399
Rosemary Shrimp, Grilled, 140
roughy. *See* orange roughy
Roux, 17
rubs, 35
Ruby Salad, 368
rum
  Baba au Rhum, 557
  Butter Rum Raisin Sauce, 450
  Chocolate Rum Sauce, 446
  Hot Buttered Rum, 458
  Iced Espresso with Rum, 457
  Savarin, 557
Russian Herring Potato Salad, 185

S

Sables, 439
Saffron Buttered Popcorn, 78
Sage and Rosemary Chicken Breast Meunière, 153
Sage and Rosemary Roast Chicken, 273
Sage Glaze, 51

Sage Roast Pork with Sage Mayonnaise, 47
salad dressings. *See* dressings
Salad of Garden Lettuces and Arugula, 38
salami
  Make-Your-Own Pizza, 99
  Salami Muffaletta, 88
  Three-Meat Deli Hoagies, 93
salmon
  Brochettes of Shark, Sturgeon and Salmon, 316
  casseroles
    Herbed Salmon Casserole, 240
    Salmon Casserole, 240
    Salmon Casserole Studded with Shrimp and Herbs, 240
  Chilled Salmon Soufflé, 472
  cured
    Dill-Cured Salmon (Gravlax), 315
    Four-Color Fish Seviche, 173
    Honey-Cured Gravlax, 174
    Salmon Seviche, 315
  Flounder and Salmon Steamed in Romaine, 502
  Ginger Sesame Salmon, 161
  Grilled Salmon Chili, 208
  Grilled Salmon Steak with Lemon and Olive Oil, 138
  Grilled Salmon with Avocado Salsa, 139
  Grilled Salmon with Refried Beans, 315
  Poached Salmon and Eggs with Lemon Butter Sauce, 426
  Poached Salmon with Arugula, 516
  Poached Salmon with Lemon and Chives, 41
  Poached Salmon with Middle Eastern Cucumbers, 314
  salads
    Asparagus-Orange Salmon Salad, 188
    Dilled Salmon Salad, 501
    Grilled Salmon Potato Salad, 138
    Grilled Salmon Salad with Rosemary Vinaigrette, 188
    Pungent Tomato Salmon Salad, 188
    Summer Salmon Salad, 187
  Salmon Bisque, 198
  Salmon en Papillote with Shrimp and Asparagus, 490
  Salmon Poached in Basil Tea with Pine Nuts, 516
  Salmon Provençal, 149
  Salmon Stewed with Fennel and Mushrooms, 502
  Salmon with Molasses and Mustard, 45
  sandwiches
    Crab and Smoked Salmon Tea Sandwiches, 95
    Dilled Salmon Sandwiches, 188
    Fennel Salmon Salad Sandwiches, 88

salmon
  sandwiches (*continued*)
    Fried Salmon Sandwiches with Dill Tartar Sauce, 91
    Grilled Chèvre and Smoked Salmon on Bagels, 90
    Smoked Salmon, Feta and Tapenade Sandwiches, 88
    Smoked Salmon Salad Sandwiches, 88
    Smoked Salmon, Caviar and Cream Sauce, 233
    Smoked Salmon, Cucumber and Dill Sauce, 233
    Smoked Salmon and Onion Pizza, 221
    Smoked Salmon Coeur à la Crème, 489
    Smoked Salmon Mousse, 84
    Spiked Smoked Salmon and Gruyère Cheesecake, 472
Salsa Vinaigrette, 65
salsas, 56, 176–78, 403
Salt-Free Seasoning Mix, 109
Sauce Provençal, 53
Sauce Tonnato, 234
Sauce Véronique, 50
sauces, 11, 17. *See also* salsas
  for pasta, 69, 224–34
  savory, 42, 44, 47, 49–57, 113, 375, 385, 402
  sweet, 108, 423, 434, 444–51
  uncooked, 56–57, 108–9
Sauerkraut, Caraway, 375
Sauerkraut, Sweet Apple, 375
sausage, 129. *See also* bratwurst; frankfurters; knockwurst; salami
  Apple and Gorgonzola Sausage Patties, 252
  Apple and Sausage Pot Pie, 406
  Barley and Sausage Soup, 364
  cassoulets and stews
    Quick Cassoulet, 241
    Sausage and Bean Stew, 269
    Seafood Cassoulet, 241
    Veal and Garlic Sausage Stew, 268
  Chicken Sausages over Spinach, 136
  chilis
    All-Pork Chili, 205
    Chorizo Chicken Chili, 207
    Sausage and Quail Chili, 207
    Smoked Sausage Chili with Porter, 206
    Three-Sausage Chili, 206
  Garlic Chicken Sausage over Spinach, 156
  Grilled Maple-Glazed Breakfast Sausages, 145
  Grilled Smoked Sausages with Apple Sauerkraut, 136
  Italian Sausage with Prosciutto and Capers, 91
  pizza
    Make-Your-Own Pizza, 99
    Sausage and Mushroom Pizza, 219

sausage
  pizza (*continued*)
    Spicy Tomato and Sausage
      Meatball Pizza, 215
    Sweet Sausage, Pine Nut and
      Rosemary Pizza, 218
  Sausage and Mushroom Sauce, 230
  Sausage Meatballs and Sauce, 230
  Sausage Meatloaf, 255
  Sausage-Stuffed Cabbage, 125
  Sausage-Stuffed Mushrooms, 467
  Spicy Sausage Potato Salad, 118
  Sweet-and-Sour Hot Sausage Potato
    Salad, 118
  Turkey Sausages with Gorgonzola
    Butter, 135
  Turkey Sausages with Pesto and
    Tomato, 135
  Wild Mushroom Sausage Patties,
    252
Sautéed Apples in Applejack, 407
Sautéed Berry Syrup, 423
Sautéed Bitter Greens with Sweet
  Pepper Vinaigrette, 374
Sautéed Chicken Breasts with Apple
  Glaze, 285
Sautéed Chicken Breasts with Brandy
  Cream Reduction, 285
Sautéed Chicken Breasts with
  Vermouth and Tarragon, 287
Sautéed Fish in Lemon Butter, 324
Sautéed Fish with Lime and Olives,
  324
Sautéed Fruit Salad, 449
Sautéed Grouper Fillets with Corn-
  Pepper Relish, 311
Sautéed Potatoes, Onions and
  Smoked Salmon, 390
Sautéed Potatoes with Garden
  Vegetables, 123
Sautéed Potatoes with Garlic and
  Olives, 390
Sautéed Potatoes with Walnuts, 390
Sautéed Roughy in Anise-Parmesan
  Crust, 314
Sautéed Shrimp on Cucumber
  "Noodles," 506
Sautéed Soft-Shell Crabs with Lime
  Mayonnaise, 340
Sautéed Spring Greens, 374
Sautéed Turkey with Apple Glaze, 151
Sautéed Veal with Chardonnay and
  Basil, 158
Savarin, 557
Scalloped Potatoes with Feta, 389
Scalloped Potatoes with Onions and
  Anchovies, 389
scallops
  Brie and Scallop Pizza, 220
  Chilied Scallop Kebabs, 208
  Croissants with Scallops in Beurre
    Blanc, 488
  Dill and Fennel Scallops, 334
  Grilled Curried Scallops, 140
  Grilled Marinated Scallops, 333

scallops (*continued*)
  Grilled Scallop Kebabs in Hazelnut
    Garlic Glaze, 140
  Grilled Scallops and Shrimp
    Tabbouleh, 187
  Italian Seafood Sandwiches, 342
  Scallop and Herbed Cheese Pizza,
    220
  Scallop and Herbed Cheese Sauce,
    233
  Scallops Grilled with Horseradish
    and Prosciutto, 140
  Scallops in Wine and Lemon Sauce,
    333
  Scallops Poached with Cider and
    Cream, 333
  Scallops Vinaigrette, 333
  Scallops with Oyster and Shiitake
    Mushrooms, 162
  Seafood Mousse, 73
  Seafood Provençal, 148
  Sesame Scallop Chips, 80
  seviche
    Green Seviche, 173
    Mexican Seviche, 173
    Scallop Seviche Skewered with
      Avocado, 332
    Scallops Escabèche, 333
  soups and stews
    Mexican Bouillabaisse, 263
    Miso Soup with Scallops, 199
    Skillet Bouillabaisse, 149
  Stir-Fried Scallops with Garlic, 162
  Tempura Scallops and Shrimp, 334
Scones, Poppy Seed Buttermilk, 432
Scotch and Brown Sugar Sauce, 54
Scrambled Eggs with Cheese, 426
Scraping-the-Jar Russian Dressing,
  108
seafood. *See also specific types of
  seafood*; fish
  Asian Fried Noodles, 114
  Fried Rice from Leftovers, 114
  marinades for, 28–35
Seafood Cassoulet, 241
Seafood Mousse, 73
Seafood Pot au Feu, 506
Seafood Potato Salad, 185
Seafood Provençal, 148
Seasoned Bread Crumbs, 74
seasonings, 5, 36–48, 109
Sesame Brown Rice Pilaf, 519
Sesame Chicken Breasts, 153
Sesame Ginger Roast Chicken, 279
Sesame Porgy Fillets, 314
Sesame Scallop Chips, 80
sesame seeds
  Ginger Tahini, 561
  Sesame Tofu Vinaigrette, 62
  Sweet Sesame Marinade, 30
Sesame Tuna Sashimi, 175
Sesame Turkey, 306
Shad in Mustard Crumbs, 315
Shad Stuffed with Roe, 315
Shepherd's Pie, 254

shepherd's pie, 242, 254
sherry
  Sherried Apricot Glaze, 52
  Sherry and Balsamic Sauce, 54
  Sherry Vinaigrette, 61
Shortbread, 440
shortbread, 440–41, 554
Shortcake, 22
Shortcake Biscuits, 22
shortcakes, 22, 170, 421–22
Shredded Cheese, 74
shrimp, 332
  Balsamic Shrimp, 471
  Cajun Shrimp, 149
  Chicken and Shrimp in Garlic Black
    Bean Sauce, 150
  chilis
    Chinese Shrimp Chili, 209
    Shrimp Chili with Black Beans,
      209
    Shrimp Chili with Chickpeas, 209
  Chilied Scampi with Cannellini, 209
  Crab and Shrimp Stir-Fried with
    Lime and Grapes, 503
  Curried Tandoori-Style Shrimp, 505
  Fennel, Shrimp and Orange Sauce,
    233
  Fried Herbed Shrimp, 471
  Fried Shrimp in Beer Batter, 336
  Grilled Barbecued Shrimp, 336
  Grilled Chilied Shrimp, 139
  Grilled Rosemary Shrimp, 140
  Grilled Scallops and Shrimp
    Tabbouleh, 187
  Grilled Shrimp in Cumin Paste, 42
  Grilled Shrimp with Pesto, 335
  Japanese Grilled Shrimp, 101
  Lemon-Soy Smoked Shrimp, 472
  Make-Your-Own Pizza, 99
  Paella Casserole, 239
  Pan-Fried Shrimp in Barbecue
    Sauce, 101
  Pepper Peanut Shrimp, 472
  Quick Shrimp Étouffée, 334
  salads
    Asparagus, Shrimp, Raspberry and
      Grapefruit Salad, 506
    Avocado, Tomato and Shrimp with
      Chili Pepper Vinaigrette, 401
    Seafood Potato Salad, 185
    Shrimp and Guacamole Salad, 335
    Shrimp Salad en Brioche, 88
  sandwiches
    Italian Seafood Sandwiches, 342
    Shrimp Cake Sandwiches with
      Lemon Yogurt Sauce, 91
    Shrimp in Croissants, 488
  Sautéed Shrimp on Cucumber
    "Noodles," 506
  Seafood Cassoulet, 241
  Seafood Mousse, 73
  Seafood Provençal, 148
  Shrimp, Cucumber and Dill Sauce,
    233
  Shrimp and Oysters with Basil, 505

shrimp (*continued*)
 Shrimp Bloody Marys, 460
 Shrimp Chips, 80
 shrimp cocktail
  Deep-Fried Shrimp Cocktail, 335
  Jalapeño Shrimp Cocktail, 335
  Mustard Tarragon Shrimp
   Cocktail, 334
 Shrimp Marinated in Wine and
  Lemon, 492
 Shrimp on a Stick with Spicy
  Avocado Sauce, 490
 Shrimp Poached in Tomato
  Vinaigrette, 336
 Shrimp Provençal, 263
 Shrimp-Stuffed Shells Alfredo, 239
 Shrimp with Herbs and Pasta, 336
 Shrimp with Smoked Salmon, 472
 Shrimp with Vodka, Tomatoes and
  Cream, 149
 soups and stews
  Chili Gumbo, 210
  Hot-and-Sour Shrimp Soup, 200
  Lobster Bouillabaisse, 491
  Mexican Bouillabaisse, 263
  Seafood Pot au Feu, 506
  Shrimp Bisque, 198
  Shrimp Stew with Mint Pesto, 505
  Skillet Bouillabaisse, 149
 stir-fries
  Herbed Shrimp, 162
  Shrimp Thai Noodles, 167
  Spicy Peanut Shrimp, 166
  Stir-Fried Pork and Shrimp with
   Noodles, 168
  Stir-Fried Rice, 361
  Stir-Fried Shrimp and Tofu in
   Yogurt, 517
  Stir-Fried Shrimp with Spinach,
   371
  Stir-Fried Thai Shrimp, 150
  Sweet-and-Sour Spicy Shrimp, 162
 Tempura Scallops and Shrimp, 334
 Tuna and Shrimp Casserole with
  Herbed Cheese, 239
Sicilian Artichokes, 395
Sicilian Mint and Ricotta Burgers, 132
Sicilian Mushrooms with Savory, 47
Sicilian Oven-Braised Top Round
 Beef, 480
Sicilian Turkey Meatballs and Sauce,
 230
simmering, 11
Simple Rice Pilaf, 357
Simple Syrup, 23
Sinful Chocolate Tartlets, 495
Skillet Bouillabaisse, 149
Sliced Turkey Breast with Chutney,
 298
Sliced Turkey Breast with
 Horseradish Sauce, 304
Sliced Turkey with Lemon-Mustard
 Vinaigrette, 303
Sliced Turkey with Soy Vinaigrette,
 306

Slow-Cooked Beef Broth, 69
Slow-Cooked Chicken Broth, 69
Slow-Cooked Cinnamon Raisin
 Bread Pudding, 70
slow cookers, 67, 69–72
Slow-Roasted Shoulder of Beef with
 Chili Rub, 480
Slow-Roasted Turkey, 301
Slurry, 17
smelts
 Pan-Fried Breaded Smelts with
  Pickled Peppers, 316
 Smelt Tempura, 316
Smoked Bacon Burgers, 131
Smoked Fish Salad with Belgian
 Endive, 188
Smoked Salmon, Caviar and Cream
 Sauce, 233
Smoked Salmon, Cucumber and Dill
 Sauce, 233
Smoked Salmon, Feta and Tapenade
 Sandwiches, 88
Smoked Salmon and Onion Pizza,
 221
Smoked Salmon Coeur à la Crème,
 489
Smoked Salmon Mousse, 84
Smoked Salmon Salad Sandwiches, 88
Smoked Sausage Chili with Porter,
 206
Smoked Trout and Horseradish
 Deviled Eggs, 180
Smoked Turkey and Apple Tart, 406
Smoked Turkey and Bitter Greens,
 190
Smoked Turkey and Fontina Pizza,
 221
Smoked Turkey and Mozzarella
 Melts, 89
Smoked Turkey Chili, 209
Smoked Turkey Meatloaf, 298
Smoked Turkey Salad with Roasted
 Pepper Vinaigrette, 303
Smoked Turkey Stuffing, 297
Smoky Apple Galette, 537
Smoky Grilled Fish, 328
Smoky Lamb Stew, 269
Smoky Lentil Soup, 514
Smoky Spicy Honey Wings, 288
Smoky Tomato and Fontina Pizza,
 214
Smoky Tomato Barbecue Marinade, 31
S'mores, 532
snacks, 46, 78–84
Snapper Steamed with Green
 Peppercorns, 502
snow peas
 High-Protein Vegetarian Stir-Fried
  Noodles, 167
 Stir-Fried Sesame Vegetables, 507
 Stir-Fried Snow Peas with Minced
  Shrimp, 379
Soft- and Hard-Cooked Eggs, 19
Soft Irish Ice Cream, 494
Soft-Shell Crab Sandwiches, 341

sole
 Escabèche of Sole, 317
 Fillets of Sole Steamed with Lemon
  and Cilantro, 501
 Sole Steamed with Tangerine and
  Chives, 317
Sorbet, Quick, 74
Sorrel and Crème Fraîche, 51
Sorrel Beurre Blanc, 47
Souffléd Cottage Cheese Sandwiches,
 431
Souffléd French Toast, 488
Souffléd Sweet Potatoes, 518
soufflés, 13, 126, 355, 362, 372, 472
Sour Cherry Coulis, 447
sour cream
 Chocolate Sour Cream Frosting, 24
 Easy Sour Cream Coffee Cake, 433
 Sour Cream Coleslaw Dressing, 62
 Whole Wheat Sour Cream Biscuits,
  431
Sour Cream and Caviar Potato Salad,
 185
Sour Cream Banana Muffins, 545
Sour Cream Peach Pot Pie, 420
Sour Cream Walnut Waffles, 430
South Carolina–Style Pulled Pork,
 484
Southern Fried Chicken, 292
Southern Fried Turkey, 297
Southwest Barbecue Marinade, 32
Southwest Bread Pudding, 247
Southwest Garbanzo Turkey Salad,
 189
Soy Ginger Chicken Salad, 189
Soy Ginger Dressing, 63
Soy-Glazed Potatoes, 169
Spaghetti Squash with Artichoke and
 Mushroom Sauce, 351
Spaghetti Squash with Stir-Fried
 Vegetables, 351
Spaghetti with Fresh Tomato Sauce,
 101
Spaghetti with Stir-Fried Meat Sauce,
 167
Spaghetti with Turkey Bolognese, 500
Spanakopita Bread, 513
Spanakopita Casserole, 238
Spanish Cauliflower, 81
Sparkling Kir Punch, 459
Sparkling Peach Melba, 454
Spiced Brown Rice, 80
Spiced Cookies, 439
Spiced Fruit, 70
Spiced Gumdrop Drops, 439
Spiced Iced Tea, 456
Spiced Poached Pears, 409
Spiced Sesame Chickpeas, 519
Spiced Spinach, 370
Spiced Veal and Squash Stew, 264
spices. *See* seasonings
Spicy Anchovy Egg Salad Sandwiches,
 87
Spicy Anise Lamb, 164
Spicy Apple Butter Marinade, 33

Spicy Avocado Sauce, 57
Spicy Basil Pesto, 178
Spicy Black Bean Clams, 338
Spicy Black Bean Soup, 117
Spicy Cheese Dip, 83
Spicy Chickpea Soup, 348
Spicy Citrus Marinade, 29
Spicy Cocktail Meatballs, 251
Spicy Corn Relish, 559
Spicy Crab Popcorn, 79
Spicy Garlic Oil, 558
Spicy Ginger Vinaigrette, 64
Spicy Green Tomato Salsa, 176
Spicy Hoisin Sauce, 51
Spicy Lemonade, 454
Spicy Molasses Chicken Wings, 470
Spicy Peachy Chicken, 157
Spicy Peanut Beef, 480
Spicy Peanut Pork, 166
Spicy Peanut Sauce, 228
Spicy Peanut Shrimp, 166
Spicy Pineapple Lime Roast Chicken,
    275
Spicy Potato Chips, 391
Spicy Red Bean Peanut Soup, 199
Spicy Sausage Potato Salad, 118
Spicy Shiitake Mushrooms, 489
Spicy Soy-Ginger Roast Turkey, 305
Spicy Steak Sauce, 109
Spicy Sweet Nuts, 80
Spicy Thai Wings, 289
Spicy Tomato and Mussel Pizza, 214
Spicy Tomato and Sausage Meatball
    Pizza, 215
Spicy Tomato Juice, 459
Spicy Tomato Sauce and Red Beans,
    225
Spicy Tomato Slush, 460
Spicy Tomato Vinaigrette, 225
Spicy Tuna Sauce, 108
Spicy Turkey Meatloaf with
    Chickpeas, 256
Spicy White Cornsticks, 548
Spiked Applesauce, 407
Spiked Bananas Grilled with Vanilla
    and Candied Ginger, 146
Spiked Chocolate Mousse, 530
Spiked Fruitcake Brownies, 553
Spiked Orange Saffron Honey, 493
Spiked Smoked Salmon and Gruyère
    Cheesecake, 472
Spiked Summer Fruit Salad, 417
spinach
    Creamed Spinach with Herb
        Cheese, 369
    Creamed Spinach with Wild
        Mushrooms, 370
    Garden Pâté, 465
    Garlic Spinach, 369
    Gratin of Spinach, 374
    Lemon Anise Spinach, 38
    Out-of-Fresh-Basil Pesto, 38
    Potato and Spinach Curry, 124
    Prosciutto and Fennel Spinach, 370
    Ricotta Creamed Spinach, 369

spinach (continued)
    salads
        Ruby Salad, 368
        Spinach Salad with Blue Cheese
            Dressing, 184
        Spinach Salad with Roasted
            Peppers and Feta, 184
        Spinach Salad with Tomato
            Vinaigrette, 400
        Spinach Salad with Warm Bacon
            Dressing in Baguettes, 93
        Spinach Waldorf Salad, 367
        Tomato and Fried Spinach Salad,
            399
        Warm Orange Walnut Spinach
            Salad, 490
        Warm Spinach Salad with Chicken
            Livers, 368
        Watercress and Spinach Caesar
            Salad, 368
    soups
        Cream of Spinach Soup, 369
        Spinach and Wild Mushroom
            Soup, 368
        Spinach Orzo Soup, 368
    Spanakopita Bread, 513
    Spanakopita Casserole, 238
    Spiced Spinach, 370
    Spinach, Corn and Tomatoes, 370
    Spinach, Olive and Feta Pizza, 218
    Spinach and Blue Cheese Custard,
        372
    Spinach and Feta Soufflé, 355
    Spinach Artichoke Bread, 489
    Spinach Parmesan Soufflé, 372
    Spinach Pasta, 371
    Spinach Pesto, 178
    Spinach Pilaf, 369
    Spinach Risotto, 360
    Spinach Strudel with Tomato
        Vinaigrette, 371
    Spinach-Stuffed Mushroom Caps,
        467
    Spinach Timbales, 372
    Spinach with Capers, 369
    Spinach with Feta and Olives, 370
    Spinach with Lemon and Parsley, 369
    Spinach with Mushrooms, 369
    Spinach with Roasted Peppers and
        Green Peppercorns, 369
    Spinach with Warm Bacon
        Dressing, 369
    Stir-Fried Spinach with Hoisin
        Walnuts, 371
    Stir-Fried Spinach with Pine Nuts, 370
    Tyropites, 468
    Vegetable Pâté Niçoise, 465
Split Pea Zucchini Soup, 397
Sponge Cake (Génoise), 22
spreads, 98, 114, 466, 513
    peanut-butter, 74, 83, 561
Spring Lamb Stew, 268
squash. See also zucchini
    Acorn Squash with Gingered
        Applesauce, 383

squash (continued)
    Acorn Squash with Orange
        Molasses, 383
    Acorn Squash with Spiced Honey,
        383
    Butternut Squash Soup with Ginger
        Cream, 195
    Crookneck Squash Parmesan, 396
    Grilled Summer Squash Salad, 184
    Mixed Grilled Vegetables with
        Hummus, 125
    Ratatouille, 352
    Spaghetti Squash with Artichoke
        and Mushroom Sauce, 351
    Spaghetti Squash with Stir-Fried
        Vegetables, 351
    Spiced Veal and Squash Stew, 264
    Squash Stuffed with Risotto, 349
squid, 332
    Calamari with Potatoes and
        Tomatoes, 343
    Squid Salad, 343
Stale-Cookie Pie Crust, 115
Star-Anise Duck, 38
Steak and Onion Burger, 130
Steak Sandwich with Béarnaise, 493
Steakhouse Burgers, 130
Steamed Asparagus, 67
Steamed Clams with Garam Masala,
    43
Steamed Flounder with Yogurt Dill
    Sauce, 501
Steamed New Potatoes, 68
Steamed Paupiettes Rolled with Fresh
    Herbs, 325
Steamed Vegetable Salad with Lemon
    Dill Dressing, 184
steaming, 12, 50
Stewed Prunes, 69
Stir-Fried Apple Shortcake, 170
Stir-Fried Asparagus with Cashews,
    395
Stir-Fried Asparagus with Tofu and
    Almonds, 517
Stir-Fried Banana Split, 170
Stir-Fried Beans, 168
Stir-Fried Beef Barbecue, 165
Stir-Fried Broccoli and Apples, 517
Stir-Fried Broccoli with Hoisin
    Almonds, 168
Stir-Fried Brussels Sprouts, 375
Stir-Fried Caramel Chicken, 164
Stir-Fried Caramelized Cauliflower
    and Cashews, 378
Stir-Fried Carrots with Mint and Red
    Pepper, 168
Stir-Fried Chicken Chicory Salad, 498
Stir-Fried Chicken in Orange Black
    Bean Sauce, 500
Stir-Fried Chicken with Apples and
    Walnuts, 113
Stir-Fried Chicken with Cashews, 151
Stir-Fried Curried Vegetables, 166
Stir-Fried Curry Mixture, 166
Stir-Fried Eggs and Ham, 426

Stir-Fried Eggs with Shrimp, 426
Stir-Fried Fish and Vegetables, 161
Stir-Fried Garlic Chicken with
    Noodles, 168
Stir-Fried Garlic Green Beans, 169
Stir-Fried Herbed Mushrooms, 169
Stir-Fried Pasta Primavera, 167
Stir-Fried Poached Pears, 170
Stir-Fried Pork and Shrimp with
    Noodles, 168
Stir-Fried Quinoa, 520
Stir-Fried Rice, 361
Stir-Fried Rice with Spring
    Vegetables, 361
Stir-Fried Scallops with Garlic, 162
Stir-Fried Sesame Asparagus, 351
Stir-Fried Sesame Oysters, 505
Stir-Fried Sesame Vegetables, 507
Stir-Fried Shrimp and Tofu in Yogurt,
    517
Stir-Fried Shrimp with Spinach, 371
Stir-Fried Snow Peas with Minced
    Shrimp, 379
Stir-Fried Spinach with Hoisin
    Walnuts, 371
Stir-Fried Spinach with Pine Nuts, 370
Stir-Fried Thai Shrimp, 150
Stir-Fried Turkey and Cranberries,
    298
Stir-Fried Turkey with Ginger and
    Cashews, 306
Stir-Fried Wild Mushrooms with
    Hazelnuts, 169
Stir-Fry of Crab and Asparagus, 503
stir-frying, 159–71
stock, 6
strawberries
    Berry Wine Punch, 459
    Brandied Summer Fruit, 174
    Buttermilk Biscuits with a Heart,
        488
    Chocolate-Dipped Strawberries, 532
    Coeur à la Crème Doux, 495
    crisps
        Gingered Berry Crisp, 421
        Strawberry Lime Crisp, 421
        Three-Berry Crisp, 421
    Easy Tangy Strawberry Ice Cream,
        419
    No-Heat Strawberry Wine Soup,
        416
    pies and tarts
        Chocolate Strawberry Tartlets, 420
        Strawberry Cannoli Tart, 420
        Strawberry Meringue Pie, 420
        Strawberry Rhubarb Pie, 420
        Two-Crust Strawberry Pie, 420
    sauces
        Fresh Strawberry Sauce, 448
        Fruit and Honey Topping, 434
        Strawberry Dessert Sauce, 423
    Spiked Summer Fruit Salad, 417
    Strawberries in Grand Marnier, 417
    Strawberries with Warm Rhubarb
        Sauce, 417

strawberries (continued)
    Strawberry Lime Frappé, 455
    Strawberry Lime Preserves, 423
    Strawberry Shortcake with
        Whipped Crème Fraîche, 422
    Triple Chocolate Parfait, 531
    Triple-Dipped Strawberries, 418
    Warm Rhubarb and Strawberry
        Shortcake, 422
Streusel or Crumb Topping, 23
Stuffed Pork Loin Glazed with Cider
    Syrup, 483
Stuffed Shells, 121
stuffing, 257, 280–82, 296–98, 300,
    302, 304, 384
Stuffing-Crusted Chicken Breasts
    with Sage Butter, 152
sturgeon
    Brochettes of Shark, Sturgeon and
        Salmon, 316
    Chilied Grilled Sturgeon Fillets, 316
Succotash Salad, 364
sugar, caramelized, 12–13
Sugar Cookies, 439
Sugar Plums, 554
Sugared Raspberries, 448
Summer Antipasto, 349
Summer Bounty Vinegar, 423
Summer Fruit with Lime Crème
    Anglaise, 417
Summer Salmon Salad, 187
Sun-Brewed Iced Tea, 455
Sun-Dried Tomato and Tuna Pizza, 221
Sun-Dried Tomato and Tuna Sauce,
    234
Sun-Dried Tomato Oil, 82
Sun-Dried Tomato Rouille, 225
Sun-Dried Tomato Vinaigrette, 61
Super Hot Mustard Wings, 289
Super-Protein Health Shake, 457
Super-Rich Custard Sauce, 447
Super Smoky Burgers, 131
Super-Spicy Jerk Marinade, 30
Super Vegetable Juice Cocktail, 460
Surprise Cheeseburgers, 102
Surprise Meatloaf, 254
Suzette Sauce, 450
Sweet Almond Coffee Cake, 434
Sweet-and-Sour Apricot Chicken, 100
Sweet-and-Sour Barbecue Marinade,
    31
Sweet-and-Sour Beef Stew, 261
Sweet-and-Sour Cider Sauce, 52
Sweet-and-Sour Coleslaw, 187
Sweet-and-Sour Cranberry Fish, 328
Sweet-and-Sour Creole Vinaigrette, 63
Sweet-and-Sour Fried Chicken, 293
Sweet-and-Sour Hot Dogs, 135
Sweet-and-Sour Hot Sausage Potato
    Salad, 118
Sweet-and-Sour Lemon Pork, 165
Sweet-and-Sour Meatloaf, 255
Sweet-and-Sour Sesame Meatballs, 251
Sweet-and-Sour Smoked Turkey
    Potato Salad, 185

Sweet-and-Sour Spicy Shrimp, 162
Sweet-and-Sour Turkey Meatballs,
    121
Sweet-and-Sour Turkey Salad, 298
Sweet-and-Spicy Cornmeal Mush,
    426
Sweet-and-Spicy Stuffed Red
    Cabbage, 125
Sweet Anise Chicken, 164
Sweet Apple Sauerkraut, 375
Sweet Balsamic Dressing, 65
Sweet Chutney Mustard Dip, 104
Sweet Cream Cheese Pastry, 441
Sweet Curried Peanuts, 80
Sweet Curried Rice with Pistachios,
    358
Sweet Fried Rice, 171
Sweet Garlic Paste, 34
Sweet Mustard Dressing, 65
Sweet or Flaky Pastry Shell, 21
Sweet Pastry, 21
Sweet Pepper Seared Snapper, 46
Sweet Pepper Vinaigrette, 63
Sweet Potato Vichyssoise, 195
sweet potatoes
    Composed Salad of Grilled
        Vegetables, 184
    Fritto Misto (Fried Antipasto), 349
    pancakes
        Sweet Potato, Carrot and Apple
            Pancakes, 350
        Sweet Potato Apple Pancakes, 380
        Sweet Potato Pancakes with Ham,
            380
    Souffléd Sweet Potatoes, 518
    Sweet Potato and Apple Purée, 390
    Sweet Potato and Bacon Soup, 118
    Sweet Potato Chips, 104
    Sweet Potato Vichyssoise, 195
    Sweet Potatoes, 69
    Vitamin A Tempura, 518
    Winter Tempura, 350
Sweet Ricotta Dessert Pizza, 223
Sweet Sausage, Pine Nut and
    Rosemary Pizza, 218
Sweet Sesame Marinade, 30
Sweet Sesame Meatballs, 250
Sweet Spiked Walnuts, 559
Sweet Tomato Marinade, 31
Swiss chard. See chard
swordfish
    Broiled Swordfish Steak with
        Mignonette Sauce, 317
    Lemon Rosemary Swordfish Steak,
        317
    Mesquite-Grilled Swordfish, 139
syrups, 23, 423, 483, 558
Szechuan Ginger Dressing, 63
Szechuan Pepper Popcorn, 46

T

Tabbouleh with Lentils, 365
tacos, 95, 99, 100, 157, 345
Tamarind Eggplant with Peanuts, 47

Tandoori Curry Marinade, 34
Tangerine Seltzer, Grapefruit or, 454
Tangerine Teriyaki, 30
Tangy Fried Chicken Breasts, 288
Tapenade, 56
Tapenade Sauce, 234
Tarragon Mustard Vinaigrette, 61
Tarragon Ranch Sauce, 56
Tarragon Raspberry Sauce, 176
Tarte Lyonnaise, 355
Tarte Niçoise, 355
Tarte Tatin, 537
tarts, 13, 406, 411, 420, 495. *See also* pies
Tastes-Like-Hamburger Turkey Burgers, 132
tea (as ingredient). *See also* teas, herbal
  Double Iced Tea, 455
  Fruited Iced Tea Punch, 456
  Lemonade Iced Tea, 456
  Mint Julep Iced Tea, 456
  Spiced Iced Tea, 456
  Sun-Brewed Iced Tea, 455
  True Brewed Iced Tea, 455
  Zesty Iced Tea, 456
Tea-Smoked Mussels and Clams, 504
Tea-Steamed Black Bass, 308
teas, herbal (as ingredient)
  Fruited Iced Tea Punch, 456
  Iced Tea with Spicy Lemon Ice Cubes, 456
  Mint Julep Iced Tea, 456
  Minted Iced Tea, 455
  Minted Pears, 409
  Super Vegetable Juice Cocktail, 460
tempura, 316, 323, 334, 350, 518
Tempura Scallops and Shrimp, 334
tequila
  Jalapeño Bloody Marys, 45
  Margarita Ice, 494
  Margarita Sauce, 450
Teriyaki Grilled Fish, 329
Teriyaki London Broil, 100
Teriyaki Turkey Burgers, 132
Tex-Mex Clams, 338
Thai Chicken, 155
Thai Fried Noodles, 167
Thai Turkey Salad, 150
Three-Bean Tempura, 518
Three-Berry Crisp, 421
Three-Can Salad, 174
Three-Cheese Burgers, 131
Three-Cheese Popovers, 432
Three-Endive Slaw, 174
Three-Layer Brownies, 525
Three-Meat Deli Hoagies, 93
Three-Mushroom Pizza, 219
Three-Mushroom Sauce, 226
Three-Olive Chicken, 154
Three-Pepper Popcorn, 78
Three-Pepper Sauce, 227
Three-Sausage Chili, 206
Three-Tomato Pizza, 213

tilefish
  Mediterranean Tilefish Stew, 318
  Tortellini, Tilefish and Pesto, 318
Toasted Coconut, 68
Toasted Nuts, 23, 68
Toasted Walnut Muffins, 544
tofu
  dressings
    Asian Tofu Dressing, 513
    Egg-Free Tofu Mayonnaise, 513
    Sesame Tofu Vinaigrette, 62
  Grilled Teriyaki Tofu, 517
  Grilled Tofu Steak with Pickled Ginger, 517
  High-Protein Vegetarian Stir-Fried Noodles, 167
  Quinoa with Tofu and Mushrooms, 520
  soups
    Miso Noodle Soup, 514
    Miso Soup, 199
    Miso Soup with Brown Rice, 515
    Miso Soup with Dried Mushrooms, 514
    Miso Soup with Vegetables, 199
  Three-Bean Tempura, 518
  Tofu Braised with Wild Mushrooms, 507
  Tofu Rice Pudding, 521
  Tofu Tuna Sandwich Spread, 513
Tomatillo and Rice Salad, Grilled, 384
Tomato and Basil Potatoes, 382
Tomato Basil Consommé, 197
Tomato Butter, 16
tomato juice
  Gazpacho Cooler, 460
  Shrimp Bloody Marys, 460
  Spicy Tomato Juice, 459
  Spicy Tomato Slush, 460
Tomato Tarragon Consommé, 197
Tomato Tonnato, 400
Tomato Vinaigrette, 108
tomatoes, 11. *See also* tomato juice
  dressings
    Salsa Vinaigrette, 65
    Spicy Tomato Vinaigrette, 225
    Sun-Dried Tomato Oil, 82
    Sun-Dried Tomato Vinaigrette, 61
    Warm Sun-Dried Tomato Vinaigrette, 53
    Warm Tomato Vinaigrette, 63
  Fresh Tomatoes and Pasta, 402
  Golden Turmeric Tomato Relish, 48
  Grilled Tomatoes, 428
  High-Protein Vegetarian Tostadas, 347
  Parmesan-Crusted Baked Tomato, 398
  Pasta with Tomatoes, Basil and Feta, 402
  pizza
    Marinated Sun-Dried Tomato Pizza, 220
    Smoky Tomato and Fontina Pizza, 214

tomatoes
  pizza (*continued*)
    Spicy Tomato and Mussel Pizza, 214
    Spicy Tomato and Sausage Meatball Pizza, 215
    Sun-Dried Tomato and Tuna Pizza, 221
    Three-Tomato Pizza, 213
    Tomato, Basil and Chèvre Pizza, 214
    Tomato, Caper and Anchovy Pizza, 213
    Tomato, Fennel and Olive Pizza, 214
    Tomato and Basil Pizza, 213
    Tomato and Cheese Pizza, 213
    Tomato and Three-Onion Pizza, 213
    Tomato and Wild Mushroom Pizza, 214
Ratatouille, 352
Roasted Balsamic Tomatoes, 398
Rosemary-Grilled Tomato, 399
salads
    Cherry Tomato and Caramelized Onion Salad, 400
    Chickpea, Tomato and Onion Salad, 515
    Composed Salad of Grilled Vegetables, 184
    Corn, Black Bean and Roasted Tomato Salad, 118
    Iceberg Lettuce with Three Tomatoes, 182
    Marinated Green Tomato and White Bean Salad, 385
    Marinated Mozzarella Salad in Tomatoes, 351
    Marinated Tomato with Chèvre and Onion, 399
    Quick Tomato Salad, 399
    Red and Yellow Tomato Salad, 400
    Tomato and Crab Salad, 401
    Tomato and Fried Spinach Salad, 399
    Tomato Pesto Pasta Salad, 401
    Tomato Raita, 403
    Tomato Salad with Mozzarella and Herbs, 399
    Tomato Slaw, 400
salsas and dips
    Confetti Salsa, 177
    Gazpacho Salsa, 177
    Jalapeño Salsa, 177
    Mild Red Salsa, 403
    Rich Red Tomato Salsa, 176
    Spicy Green Tomato Salsa, 176
    Tomato and Artichoke Salsa, 56
    Tomato and Corn Salsa, 403
    Tomato Dill Salsa, 177
    Warm Basil and Tomato Dip, 84
sauces
    Capered Tomato Sauce, 109
    Easy Tomato Sauce, 109

tomatoes
  sauces (continued)
    Fresh Tomato and Cream Sauce, 402
    Fresh Tomato Sauce, 402
    Gazpacho Sauce, 57
    Ginger Tomato Sauce, 226
    Herb, Tomato and Cream Sauce, 228
    Marinated Sun-Dried Tomato Sauce, 225
    Mediterranean Tomato Sauce, 109
    Quick Fresh Tomato Sauce, 225
    Quick Meat Sauce, 229
    Sauce Provençal, 53
    Spicy Tomato Sauce and Red Beans, 225
    Sun-Dried Tomato and Tuna Sauce, 234
    Sun-Dried Tomato Rouille, 225
    Tomato, Basil and Chèvre Sauce, 226
    Tomato, Chili and Mascarpone Sauce, 53
    Tomato, Olive and Parmesan Sauce, 53
    Tomato Sauce with Fennel and Orange, 385
    Tomato Sauce with Tequila and Cream, 228
  soups
    Chilled Tomato and Roasted Pepper Soup, 174
    Gazpacho, 73
    Green Tomato Gazpacho, 385
    Leftovers Minestrone, 110
    Vegetable Broth, 19
  Tomato and Feta au Gratin, 246
  Tomato Niçoise, 401
  Tomato Sandwich, 402
  Tomato with Black Pepper and Lime, 399
  Tomato with Pesto, 401
  Tomatoes Marinated in Olive Oil, Garlic and Hot Pepper Flakes, 401
Topless Apple Pie, 536
Topless Lime Pear Pie, 537
Topless Plum Pie, 537
Tortellini, Tilefish and Pesto, 318
Tortellini with Grilled Vegetables, 120
tortillas (as ingredient)
  Chicken Fajitas, 99
  Chilied Corn Enchiladas, 346
  Corned Beef Deli Wraps, 87
  Ground Chicken Fajitas, 157
  Ham and Cheese Wraps, 87
  Health Wraps, 87
  High-Protein Vegetarian Tostadas, 347
  Hot Dog Wraps, 134
  Mexican Torta, 247
  Mixed Grilled Vegetable Tostada, 347
  Poached Egg Tostadas, 427

tortillas (continued)
  Pork Tacos, 157
  Quesadilla Casserole, 123
  Vegetarian Tacos, 157
Tossed Winter Greens with Warm Bacon Dressing, 182
Traditional Large Roast Chicken, 272
Traditional Roast Turkey, 296
Traditional Small Roast Chicken, 272
Traditional Tuna Noodle Casserole, 237
Tri-Color Roasted Pepper Pizza, 216
Tri-Colored Peppers with Herbs, 183
Triple-Cheese Potatoes au Gratin, 124
Triple Chocolate Drops, 523
Triple Chocolate Parfait, 531
Triple-Dipped Strawberries, 418
Tropical Banana Muffins, 545
Tropical Crisp, 411
Tropical Ham, 482
Tropical Sweet-and-Sour Roast Chicken, 275
trout
  Grilled Trout with Bacon and Dill, 139
  Grilled Trout with Bacon and Tarragon, 318
  Pan-Fried Trout with Tapenade Relish, 318
  Smoked Trout and Horseradish Deviled Eggs, 180
  Trout Stuffed with Pickled Ginger and Green Onions, 44
True Brewed Iced Tea, 455
tuna
  Baked Shells Stuffed with Tuna and Cheese, 239
  Carpaccio Tonnato, 176
  casseroles
    Paella Casserole, 239
    Real Tuna Noodle Casserole, 237
    Souper Tuna Noodle Casserole, 237
    Traditional Tuna Noodle Casserole, 237
    Tuna, Fontina and Ham Casserole, 237
    Tuna, Orzo and Feta Casserole, 238
    Tuna and Rice Casserole, 247
    Tuna and Shrimp Casserole with Herbed Cheese, 239
    Tuna Casserole with Just a Few Noodles, 237
    Tuna Macaroni and Cheese, 120
    Tuna Noodle Casserole Duxelles, 237
    Tuna Tortellini Casserole, 237
  Curried Tuna and Lentils, 238
  Grilled Tuna Chili on Black Beans, 209
  Grilled Tuna Steak with Warm Tomato Vinaigrette, 319
  Provençal Tuna Burgers, 134
  salads
    Grilled Tuna and Roasted Pepper Salad, 318

tuna
  salads (continued)
    Grilled Tuna Salad, 139
    Marinated Tuna and White Bean Salad, 188
    Pasta, Bean and Tuna Salad, 111
    Potato and Tuna Vinaigrette Salad, 119
  sandwiches
    Dill Tuna Melts, 89
    Dilled Tuna Sandwiches, 88
    Healthy Hoagie, 98
    Tofu Tuna Sandwich Spread, 513
    Tuna and Guacamole Pitas, 94
    Tuna Lettuce Pockets, 99
  sauces
    Sauce Tonnato, 234
    Spicy Tuna Sauce, 108
    Sun-Dried Tomato and Tuna Sauce, 234
    White Bean, Tuna and Olive Oil Sauce, 234
  Seafood Cassoulet, 241
  Sesame Tuna Sashimi, 175
  Sun-Dried Tomato and Tuna Pizza, 221
  Tomato Tonnato, 400
  Tonnato Caesar Dressing, 62
  Tuna, White Bean and Olive Pizza, 218
  Tuna Penne Primavera, 238
  Tuna Strudel, 123
  Wasabi Tuna Burgers, 134
turkey
  Buffalo Turkey, 302
  burgers
    All-American Turkey Cheeseburgers, 102
    Cranberry Turkey Burgers, 121
    Down-Home Turkey Burgers, 132
    Hoisin Burgers, 133
    Middle Eastern Turkey Burgers, 132
    Tastes-Like-Hamburger Turkey Burgers, 132
    Teriyaki Turkey Burgers, 132
  chilis
    Ground Turkey Chili, 203
    Smoked Turkey Chili, 209
    Turkey and Avocado Chili, 208
    Turkey Meatball Chili, 102
    Turkey Mole Chili, 208
  Chipotle Turkey, 150
  Cranberry Turkey Casserole, 299
  Grilled Turkey Breast with Tomato Basil Sauce, 500
  Grilled Turkey Genovese, 141
  Grilled Turkey Ham, 303
  Grilled Turkey Steaks with Steak Sauce, 304
  Healthy Hoppin' John, 519
  Inside-Out Tacos, 100
  Lemon Cilantro Turkey Breast, 501
  Lemon Mushroom Turkey, 151
  marinades for, 28–35

turkey (*continued*)

meatballs

Cranberry Turkey Meatballs, 121

Pungent Orange Turkey Meatballs, 121

Sicilian Turkey Meatballs and Sauce, 230

Sweet-and-Sour Turkey Meatballs, 121

meatloaf

Apple and Bacon Turkey Loaf, 256

Apple Turkey Meatloaf, 305

Fragrant Turkey Loaf with Pineapple, 257

Fresh and Smoked Turkey Meatloaf, 256

Layered Veal, Turkey and Prosciutto Loaf, 244

Smoked Turkey Meatloaf, 298

Spicy Turkey Meatloaf with Chickpeas, 256

Turkey and Walnut Meatloaf, 257

Turkey Cornbread Meatloaf, 256

Turkey Loaf with Ham, Lemon and Pistachios, 256

Turkey Meatloaf, 256

Turkey Meatloaf with Bread Stuffing, 257

Turkey Meatloaf with Cranberries, 256

Turkey Meatloaf with Mint and Ricotta, 256

Mustard-Glazed Smoked Turkey, 303

Orange Hoisin Turkey, 151

roast turkey

Apple Butter–Glazed Turkey with Apple-Sage Stuffing, 304

Herbed Brandy Turkey with Wild Mushroom Stuffing, 300

Lemon-Honey Turkey with Cornbread and Crab Stuffing, 302

Maple-Glazed Turkey with Smoked Turkey Stuffing, 297

Orange-Glazed Turkey Breast with Brown Rice–Dried Fruit Stuffing, 298

Pan-Roasted Turkey Legs, 122

Roasted Turkey Breast Studded with Hazelnuts and Garlic, 304

Roasted Turkey Breast with Mint, 501

Slow-Roasted Turkey, 301

Spicy Soy-Ginger Roast Turkey, 305

Traditional Roast Turkey, 296

salads

Asian Turkey Salad, 306

Classic Turkey Salad, 301

Creole Turkey Salad, 299

Green Peppercorn Turkey Salad, 301

Lemon-Walnut Turkey Salad, 302

Smoked Turkey Salad with Roasted Pepper Vinaigrette, 303

turkey

salads (*continued*)

Southwest Garbanzo Turkey Salad, 189

Stir-Fried Chicken Chicory Salad, 498

Sweet-and-Sour Smoked Turkey Potato Salad, 185

Sweet-and-Sour Turkey Salad, 298

Thai Turkey Salad, 150

Turkey Hazelnut Salad, 304

Turkey Salad Vinaigrette, 297

Turkey Tabbouleh, 301

Turkey Waldorf Salad, 305

sandwiches

Hot Turkey Sandwiches, 297

Middle Eastern Turkey Pitas, 94

Smoked Turkey and Mozzarella Melts, 89

Three-Meat Deli Hoagies, 93

Turkey Mushroom Sloppy Joes, 122

Turkey Sloppy Joes, 302

Turkey Tacos with Fresh Salsa, 99

Sautéed Turkey with Apple Glaze, 151

Sesame Turkey, 306

Sliced Turkey Breast with Chutney, 298

Sliced Turkey Breast with Horseradish Sauce, 304

Sliced Turkey with Lemon-Mustard Vinaigrette, 303

Sliced Turkey with Soy Vinaigrette, 306

Smoked Turkey and Apple Tart, 406

Smoked Turkey and Bitter Greens, 190

Smoked Turkey and Fontina Pizza, 221

soups and stews

Moroccan Turkey Stew, 264

Smoky Lentil Soup, 514

Turkey Carcass Split Pea Soup, 110

Turkey Chowder, 300

Turkey Mushroom Ragoût, 300

Turkey Noodle Soup, 296

Turkey Stew Milano, 265

Southern Fried Turkey, 297

stir-fries

Stir-Fried Turkey and Cranberries, 298

Stir-Fried Turkey with Ginger and Cashews, 306

Turkey with Garlic Black Beans, 163

Turkey Benedict, 303

Turkey Blanquette, 266

Turkey Cranberry Turnovers, 299

Turkey Cutlets in Hazelnut Crumbs, 304

Turkey Fennel Potstickers, 250

Turkey Fried Rice, 299

Turkey Kabobs Glazed with Jalapeño Jelly, 470

turkey (*continued*)

Turkey Kiev with Herbed Cheese, 300

Turkey Nuggets, 301

Turkey Sautéed with Capers, 302

turnips

Apple Turnip Soup, 513

Roasted Potatoes with Turnips, 390

turnovers, 12, 410, 469

Tuscan Chicken, 273

Tuscan Chicken Legs, 122

Twice-Baked Blue Cheese Potatoes, 393

Twice-Baked Cheddar Jalapeño Potatoes, 393

Two-Crust Strawberry Pie, 420

Two-Ton Bourbon Nut Cake, 556

Tyropites, 468

U

Ultra-Rich Spiked French Toast, 487

Unbelievably Amazing Brownies, 524

Unhealthy Snack Mix, 80

Upside-Down Maple Apple Pie, 537

V

Vanilla Popcorn, 78

veal

burgers

Herb Cheese Veal Burgers, 133

Roasted Pepper Veal Burgers, 133

Veal Oscar Burgers, 133

chops

Grilled Mustard-Glazed Veal Chops, 508

Mustard-Grilled Veal Chops, 143

Veal Chops Stuffed with Fontina and Sun-Dried Tomato, 143

Veal Chops with Rosemary, Sage and Aïoli, 46

Veal with Melted Leeks, 158

Country Pâté, 252

marinades for, 28–35

meatloaf

Herbed Veal Loaf, 257

Layered Veal, Turkey and Prosciutto Loaf, 244

Veal Loaf with Artichokes, 257

sauces for, 50–57

scallops

Grilled Veal with Peanut Sauce, 144

Marinated Veal Paillards, 143

Sautéed Veal with Chardonnay and Basil, 158

Veal Marsala, 158

Veal Scallops Sautéed with Herbes de Provence, 44

Veal Scallops with Asparagus and Capers, 508

stews

Blanquette of Veal, 266

Spiced Veal and Squash Stew, 264

veal

stews (continued)

Veal and Asparagus Stew, 265

Veal and Garlic Sausage Stew, 268

Veal Bourguignonne, 262

Veal Stew in the Style of Osso Buco, 264

Veal Stew Normandy, 266

Veal Stewed with Artichoke Hearts, 265

Veal Stewed with Chickpeas and Avocado, 265

Veal Stewed with Peppers, 267

Veal and Pork Potstickers, 250

Veal au Poivre, 508

Veal Chili with Artichokes, 205

Veal Shanks with Apples and Cream, 265

Veal Shanks with Tomato and Bay, 39

Veal with Hot and Sweet Peppers, 165

Veal with Olives, 165

Vegetable Broth, 19

Vegetable "Dogs," 98

vegetable juice

Gazpacho, 73

Jalapeño Bloody Marys, 45

Manhattan Clam Chowder, 198

Spicy Tomato Juice, 459

Spicy Tomato Slush, 460

Super Vegetable Juice Cocktail, 460

Wilted Salad Gazpacho, 110

vegetables, 9. See also specific vegetables; vegetable juice

Brown Rice and Vegetable Pilaf, 359

Harvest Rice Stuffing, 384

Harvest Vegetable Stuffing, 384

Julienned Vegetables with Lemon Honey Dip, 104

Leftovers Minestrone, 110

Leftovers Tabbouleh, 112

Miso Soup with Vegetables, 199

Puréed Vegetable Soup, 72

Vegetable Pâté Niçoise, 465

Vegetable Spread for Sandwiches, 98

Vegetable-Stuffed Deviled Eggs, 180

Vegetable Top and Chicken Carcass Soup, 110

Vegetarian Chili, 202

vegetarian dishes, 157, 167, 202, 344–55

Vegetarian Tacos, 157

Venison Chili, 204

Venison in Mustard Crust, 508

Vermouth Sauce, Rosemary and, 54

Very Nutty Brownies, 524

Vichyssoise, 72

vinegars, 423, 558

Vitamin A Tempura, 518

W

waffles, 430

Waldorf Potato Salad, 185

Waldorf Salad, Spinach, 367

Waldorf Salad, Turkey, 305

Waldorf Salad on Rye, 88

walnuts

Apple Walnut Pie, 535

Banana and Walnut Dessert Pizza, 223

bars and squares

Bourbon Walnut Fig Bars, 553

Date Nut Bars, 442

Very Nutty Brownies, 524

cakes

Apple Walnut Cake, 412

Date Nut Coffee Cake, 433

Walnut Cupcakes, 555

cookies

Walnut Brown-Edge Wafers, 440

Walnut Butter Jumbles, 437

Walnut Chocolate Chip Shortbread, 441

Walnut Fig Sinkers, 549

Walnut Oat Lace Cookies, 440

Garlic and Walnut Baguette, 489

Kasha with Walnuts and Garlic, 363

muffins

Apple Walnut Muffins, 544

Applesauce Walnut Muffins, 549

Date Nut Muffins, 545

Nutty Bran Muffins, 546

Toasted Walnut Muffins, 544

Zucchini Walnut Muffins, 548

Orange Walnut Marinade, 29

Oregano Walnut Pesto, 178

Prosciutto, Walnut and Feta Pizza, 221

Roasted Pepper and Walnut Pizza, 217

sauces and spreads

Honey Walnut Sauce, 450

Lemon Walnut Sauce, 50

Pecan or Walnut Butter, 561

Roasted Pepper and Walnut Sauce, 227

Sweet Spiked Walnuts, 559

Walnut Butter and Fig Sandwiches, 87

Walnut Garlic Baguette, 82

Walnut Popcorn, 79

Yeasted Maple Walnut Pancakes, 429

Warm Bacon Dressing, 62

Warm Basil and Tomato Dip, 84

Warm Blue Cheese Dressing, 64

Warm Buckwheat Pasta and Sesame Salad, 515

Warm Grilled Chicken Salad on Wilted Lettuce, 284

Warm Jerusalem Artichoke Salad, 183

Warm Orange Walnut Spinach Salad, 490

Warm Peaches with Sesame Praline, 496

Warm Pear Purée, 449

Warm Pink Pear Purée, 495

Warm Rhubarb and Strawberry Shortcake, 422

Warm Spinach Salad with Chicken Livers, 368

Warm Stir-Fried Grapes, 448

Warm Sun-Dried Tomato Vinaigrette, 53

Warm Tomato Vinaigrette, 63

Warm White Chocolate Egg Nog, 457

Wasabi Tuna Burgers, 134

watercress

Chilled Watercress Soup, 374

Potato Watercress Soup, 196

Watercress and Cream Sauce, 51

Watercress and Grapefruit Salad, 48

Watercress and Spinach Caesar Salad, 368

Watercress Cream Sauce, 375

Watermelon Slush, 104

Watermelon Spearmint Granita, 45

Wet Bourbon Pecans, 450

Wet Walnut Baked Apples, 409

Wheat Berries, Brown Rice with, 359

Wheat Germ Squares, 443

whisky

Orange, Scotch and Espresso Sauce, 451

Real Hot Chocolate Spiked with Scotch, 523

Scotch and Brown Sugar Sauce, 54

Whisky Pound Cakes, 555

White and Black Bean Salad, 353

White Bean, Tuna and Olive Oil Sauce, 234

White Bean and Brown Rice Soup, 514

White Cabbage Slaw, 187

White Chocolate Amaretto Pudding, 529

White Chocolate Brownies, 524

White Chocolate Brownies with Chocolate-Dipped Almonds, 525

White Chocolate Chunk Cookies, 437

White Chocolate Ice Cream, 531

White Chocolate Rice Pudding, 115

White Chocolate Sauce, 446

White Gazpacho, 175

White Wine Fines Herbes Marinade, 32

White Wine Mushrooms, 55

Whiting, Asparagus and Pine Nut Salad, 319

Whiting Baked with Apples and Thyme, 319

Whole Baked Fish, 327

Whole Fish, 68

Whole Fish Grilled in Foil with Vegetables, 138

Whole Fried Sesame Fish, 324

Whole-Grain Breakfast Cookies, 127

Whole Grilled Porgy, 313

Whole-Seed Mustard Burgers, 130

Whole Steamed Red Snapper, 317

Whole Wheat Brown Rice Pancakes, 512

Whole Wheat Buttermilk French Toast, 430

Whole Wheat Pasta Boiled with Broccoli, Ricotta and Roasted Peppers, 521
Whole Wheat Pasta with Roasted Peppers, 521
Whole Wheat Sour Cream Biscuits, 431
Whole Wheat Vanilla Yogurt French Toast, 511
Wild Mushroom, Brandy and Cream Sauce, 229
Wild Mushroom Bisque, 194
Wild Mushroom Chili, 203
Wild Mushroom Meatloaf, 255
Wild Mushroom Risotto Casserole, 245
Wild Mushroom Sausage Patties, 252
Wild Mushroom Stuffing, 384
Wild Rice Pancakes with Corn and Pepper Salsa, 512
Wild Rice Pilaf, 359
Wild Rice Risotto, 520
Wilted Chicory, 373
Wilted Salad Gazpacho, 110
wine
  Court Bouillon, 18
  drinks
    Berry Wine Punch, 459
    Flaming Warm Spiced Wine, 458
    Sparkling Kir Punch, 459
  frozen desserts
    Champagne Granita, 494
    "Champagne" with Grapefruit Ice, 459
    Mimosa Sorbet, 494
  marinades
    Easy Red Wine Marinade, 32
    Easy White Wine Marinade, 32
    Garlic and Wine Marinade, 33
    Hearty Red Wine Marinade, 33
    White Wine Fines Herbes Marinade, 32
    Wine Barbecue Marinade, 32
  No-Heat Strawberry Wine Soup, 416

wine (continued)
  sauces
    Beurre Blanc, 51
    Beurre Rouge, 54
    Bordelaise Sauce, 54
    Ginger Peach Sauce, 448
    Herbed Beurre Blanc, 51
    Red Wine Pomegranate Sauce, 52
    Wine and Mushroom Sauce, 50
Winter Tempura, 350
woks, 160
Worcestershire and Mustard Sauce, 52
Worcestershire Mustard Roast Chicken, 273

X

Xylophone Milk, 104

Y

Yeasted Maple Walnut Pancakes, 429
yogurt, 16
  Cucumber Yogurt Sauce, 144
  dressings and marinades
    Coriander Marinade, 35
    Garlic Yogurt Dressing, 108
    Lemon Yogurt Dressing, 107
    Minted Yogurt Dressing, 65
    Yogurt, Garlic and Mint Marinade, 35
    Yogurt Cilantro Dressing, 65
    Yogurt Dill Ranch Dressing, 64
  White Gazpacho, 175
  Yogurt and Herb Sauce, 51
  Yogurt Dessert Sauce, 108
  Yogurt Muffins, 549
  Yogurt Shake, 105
Yogurt Dill Chicken Salad, 284
Yorkshire Pudding, 477

Z

Zesty Iced Tea, 456
Zesty Salt Substitute, 48
zucchini
  Composed Salad of Grilled Vegetables, 184
  Garden Chili, 203
  Grilled Ratatouille, 145
  Grilled Summer Squash Salad, 184
  Harvest Quiche, 384
  Mixed Grilled Vegetable Tostada, 347
  Mixed Grilled Vegetables with Black Bean Sauce, 347
  Mixed Grilled Vegetables with Hummus, 125
  Mixed Grilled Vegetables with Peanut Sauce, 347
  muffins and breads
    Candied Ginger Zucchini Muffins, 548
    Gingered Pecan Zucchini Bread, 397
    Lemon-Lime Zucchini Muffins, 548
    Lemon Zucchini Muffins, 397
    Zucchini Apple Muffins, 549
    Zucchini Bread, 396
    Zucchini Cornbread, 397
    Zucchini Walnut Muffins, 548
  Ratatouille, 352
  soups
    Chilled Curried Zucchini Soup, 397
    Lemon Zucchini Soup, 397
    Split Pea Zucchini Soup, 397
    Zucchini Minestrone, 398
    Zucchini Soup, 397
  Stir-Fried Sesame Vegetables, 507
  Tortellini with Grilled Vegetables, 120
  Vegetarian Chili, 202
  Zucchini Sautéed with Roasted Peppers, 398